Shakespeare

An Anthology of Criticism and Theory 1945–2000

Shakespeare

An Anthology of Criticism and Theory 1945–2000

Edited by Russ McDonald

Editorial material and organization © 2004 by Blackwell Publishing Ltd

BLACKWELL PUBLISHING
350 Main Street, Malden, MA 02148-5020, USA
9600 Garsington Road, Oxford OX4 2DQ, UK
550 Swanston Street, Carlton, Victoria 3053, Australia

First published 2004 by Blackwell Publishing Ltd

8   2012

Library of Congress Cataloging-in-Publication Data

Shakespeare : an anthology of criticism and theory, 1945–2000 / edited by Russ McDonald.
p. cm.
Includes bibliographical references and index.
ISBN 978-0-631-23487-6 (alk. paper) — ISBN 978-0-631-23488-3 (pbk. : alk. paper)
1. Shakespeare, William, 1564–1616—Criticism and interpretation—History—20th century.
2. Shakespeare, William, 1564–1616—Criticism and interpretation.   3. English drama—
History and criticism—Theory, etc.   I. McDonald, Russ, 1949–

PR2970.S495 2004
822.3'3—dc21
2003012197

A catalogue record for this title is available from the British Library.

Set in 10pt/12.5 pt Minion
by Kolam Information Services Pvt. Ltd, Pondicherry, India
Printed and bound in Singapore
by Ho Printing Singapore Pte Ltd

The publisher's policy is to use permanent paper from mills that operate a sustainable forestry policy,
and which has been manufactured from pulp processed using acid-free and elementary chlorine-free
practices. Furthermore, the publisher ensures that the text paper and cover board used have met
acceptable environmental accreditation standards.

For further information on
Blackwell Publishing, visit our website:
www.blackwellpublishing.com

Contents

Preface   x

Acknowledgments   xiv

Part I   Authorship   1

   1 Looney and the Oxfordians   4
      S. Schoenbaum

Part II   New Criticism   15

   2 The Naked Babe and the Cloak of Manliness   19
      Cleanth Brooks

   3 "Honest" in *Othello*   35
      William Empson

   4 "Introductory" Chapter About the Tragedies   50
      Wolfgang Clemen

   5 The "New Criticism" and *King Lear*   63
      William R. Keast

Part III   Dramatic Kinds   89

   6 The Argument of Comedy   93
      Northrop Frye

   7 Ambivalence: The Dialectic of the Histories   100
      A. P. Rossiter

Contents

8   The Saturnalian Pattern   116
    C. L. Barber

9   The Jacobean Shakespeare: Some Observations on
    the Construction of the Tragedies   125
    Maynard Mack

Part IV   The 1950s and 1960s: Theme, Character, Structure   149

10 Reflections on the Sentimentalist's *Othello*   152
    Barbara Everett

11 Form and Formality in *Romeo and Juliet*   164
    Harry Levin

12 *King Lear* or *Endgame*   174
    Jan Kott

13 The Cheapening of the Stage   191
    Anne Righter [*Barton*]

14 How Not to Murder Caesar   209
    Sigurd Burckhardt

Part V   Reader-Response Criticism   221

15 On the Value of *Hamlet*   225
    Stephen Booth

16 Rabbits, Ducks, and *Henry V*   245
    Norman Rabkin

Part VI   Textual Criticism and Bibliography   265

17 The New Textual Criticism of Shakespeare   269
    Fredson Bowers

18 Revising Shakespeare   280
    Gary Taylor

19 Narratives About Printed Shakespeare Texts: "Foul Papers" and
    "Bad Quartos"   296
    Paul Werstine

Part VII   Psychoanalytic Criticism   319

20 "Anger's my meat": Feeding, Dependency, and Aggression
    in *Coriolanus*   323
    Janet Adelman

21 The Avoidance of Love: A Reading of *King Lear*   338
    Stanley Cavell

Contents

22 To Entrap the Wisest: Sacrificial Ambivalence in *The Merchant of Venice* and *Richard III* 353
René Girard

23 What Did the King Know and When Did He Know It? Shakespearean Discourses and Psychoanalysis 365
Harry Berger, Jr.

24 The Turn of the Shrew 399
Joel Fineman

Part VIII   Historicism and New Historicism   417

25 The Cosmic Background 422
E. M. W. Tillyard

26 Invisible Bullets: Renaissance Authority and its Subversion, *Henry IV* and *Henry V* 435
Stephen Greenblatt

27 The New Historicism in Renaissance Studies 458
Jean E. Howard

28 "Shaping Fantasies": Figurations of Gender and Power in Elizabethan Culture 481
Louis Adrian Montrose

Part IX   Materialist Criticism   511

29 Shakespeare's Theater: Tradition and Experiment 515
Robert Weimann

30 *King Lear* (ca. 1605–1606) and Essentialist Humanism 535
Jonathan Dollimore

31 Give an Account of Shakespeare and Education, Showing Why You Think They Are Effective and What You Have Appreciated About Them. Support Your Comments with Precise References 547
Alan Sinfield

Part X   Feminist Criticism   565

32 Egyptian Queens and Male Reviewers: Sexist Attitudes in *Antony and Cleopatra* Criticism 570
L. T. Fitz [Linda Woodbridge]

33 "I wooed thee with my sword": Shakespeare's Tragic Paradigms 591
Madelon Gohlke Sprengnether

Contents

34 The Family in Shakespeare Studies; or Studies in the Family of
    Shakespeareans; or The Politics of Politics   606
    Lynda E. Boose

35 Disrupting Sexual Difference: Meaning and Gender in
    the Comedies   633
    Catherine Belsey

Part XI   Studies in Gender and Sexuality   651

36 "This that you call love": Sexual and Social Tragedy
    in *Othello*   655
    Gayle Greene

37 The Performance of Desire   669
    Stephen Orgel

38 The Secret Sharer   684
    Bruce R. Smith

39 The Homoerotics of Shakespearean Comedy   704
    Valerie Traub

Part XII   Performance Criticism   727

40 Shakespeare and the Blackfriars Theatre   732
    Gerald Eades Bentley

41 The Critical Revolution   745
    J. L. Styan

42 *William Shakespeare's Romeo + Juliet*: Everything's Nice
    in America?   750
    Barbara Hodgdon

43 Deeper Meanings and Theatrical Technique: The Rhetoric of
    Performance Criticism   762
    William B. Worthen

Part XIII   Postcolonial Shakespeare   777

44 Nymphs and Reapers Heavily Vanish: The Discursive
    Con-texts of *The Tempest*   781
    Francis Barker and Peter Hulme

45 Sexuality and Racial Difference   794
    Ania Loomba

46 Discourse and the Individual: The Case of Colonialism in
    The Tempest   817
    Meredith Anne Skura

Contents

Part XIV   Reading Closely   **845**

47   Shakespeare's Prose   848
     Jonas A. Barish

48   The Play of Phrase and Line   861
     George T. Wright

49   Transfigurations: Shakespeare and Rhetoric   880
     Patricia Parker

     Index   908

Preface

This book is designed to be useful to a "great variety of readers," to borrow a marketing phrase from the front matter of the 1623 Folio. In the present case, the intended audience is probably narrower than that imagined by Heminges and Condell, but within and even beyond the broad field of Shakespeare studies, many kinds of people may find it helpful – scholars, teachers, critics, undergraduate and graduate students, directors, actors, curious general readers, lovers of Shakespeare. It collects in a single volume much important critical writing on Shakespeare during the second half of the twentieth century. The motive for assembling such a collection is to provide a comprehensive yet handy record of that era, a means of surveying the scholarship, interpretation, and theory that burgeoned during a period of exceptional industry and rapid change in the Anglo-American academy. The criticism reprinted here has been taken from a variety of journals and books, sources normally scattered and sometimes difficult to locate. The editor, in consultation with a vast number of colleagues and advisors, has selected the nearly fifty pieces and, in hopes of making them as helpful as possible, grouped them into categories. Therefore, although this volume is in no sense an introduction to the discipline of Shakespearean scholarship, some prefatory words are in order on several topics: the uses of the materials collected herein, the criteria for selection, and the logic of arrangement.

The world of Shakespeare scholarship can be formidable to new students – and also to more experienced scholars. Literary criticism has changed so rapidly and expanded so multifariously in our time that the conventions of reading observed by critics a mere twenty years ago can seem remote and puzzling. This anthology offers a practical way of entering that world and comprehending those conventions, containing as it does a range of influential and representative interpretation written over a 56-year period. The essays are grouped and divided into manageable sections so that the reader does not face an undifferentiated heap of scholarship and criticism, much of it unfamiliar and perhaps contradictory. Instead, each essay exhibits affinities with the other pieces in its group, and in some cases writers respond directly to one another. Those resemblances, along with the brief commentary prefacing each section, provide at least some context for approaching each piece.

Taken as a whole, the contents offer a reasonably thorough survey of Shakespeare studies during the second half of the twentieth century. Students and younger scholars are (properly) encouraged to read the latest critical writing on the topic they've chosen to investigate. This emphasis on recent analysis, however, sometimes has the effect of depreciating or dismissing valuable readings from earlier decades. We should often remind ourselves that our critical predecessors were no less intelligent than we, that in their time most of them were resolutely up to date, and that much may be learned from critical studies that may strike us initially as old fashioned or irrelevant. Learning to read critics from earlier generations fosters historical awareness and critical perspective. Sometimes our neglect of the recent past is not a case of will but of unfamiliarity: how does one begin, for example, in an effort to understand genre criticism of the 1950s and 1960s? This volume offers some help with that kind of problem. Most of the chapters and articles, thanks to their footnotes and bibliographies, are also useful as sources of further reading. In the twentieth-first century, the Internet has become for many students the starting place for literary research, and more and more historical material is becoming accessible on-line. As the work printed here will indicate, however, websites should not be the student's only resource. Old books and back numbers of periodicals not yet digitized offer an almost endless supply of illuminating and sometimes startling interpretation.

It is a pretty safe bet that the contents of this book will not entirely please a single one of its readers, so immense and intractable is the problem of selection. The table of contents is the result of compromises, concessions, trade-offs, and debates that most readers will wish had resolved themselves in some other ways. Consider the problem of familiarity. Janet Adelman's essay on *Coriolanus* has been reprinted many times in various collections; arguably, therefore, it might be omitted so as to leave space for a less well-known piece. And yet if the volume is to meet its goal of furnishing the reader with major critical texts of the last half of the twentieth century – and as many of them as possible, please – then leaving out "Anger's my meat" would be a mistake. Consider next the problem of critical representation, i.e., the question of who or what should be included so as to create a "representative" sample of interpretive work. Arguably, there are several critics from the second half of the twentieth century whose intellectual contributions have been so great and whose views have been so influential that they deserve to be represented by more than one piece. But commensurate inclusion of prestigious critics would preclude a just representation of the period's hermeneutic variety, hence the artificial limit of one piece per writer.

To adhere to the one-item-per-critic principle makes the act of choosing the most appropriate chapter or article daunting indeed. Sometimes other demands have helped in making that kind of choice: for example, Professor X's slightly less impressive or less typical piece (call it *A*) may appear in this volume, preferred to another of hers (call it *B*) because while *B* is celebrated and apparently essential, *A* examines a particular play that would otherwise go untreated here. An effort has been made to attend to as many plays as possible with as little overlap as possible, an aim calculated to make the book various and useful. All these desiderata and strictures have entailed a series of concessions. Therefore the reader should not assume that the essay here included on *Macbeth* is in the eyes of the editor the best essay on *Macbeth* written in the last half of the twentieth century; the reader may safely assume that in the eyes of the editor it is one of the best. The book also contains essays on groups of plays, essays on tiny sections of plays, essays that scarcely mention plays, and other kinds as well. That *Othello* is treated more abundantly in these pages than, say, *Hamlet* is a fair indicator of the preferences of the age. I have attempted to include entire essays and chapters, offering excerpts only in a very few cases where the length of the original is prohibitive.

Not only has it been impossible to find a place for every piece that ought to be here, it has also been impossible even to find a place for every *kind* of piece that ought to be here. For example, research on early modern performance practices, especially the acting companies, their personnel, their finances, and other such historical data, has been vital to the study of Shakespeare during the period covered, but it is not easily excerpted and individual pieces or sections of books do not do justice to its value and utility. Such archival scholarship has enabled and improved the work of many critics and is readily available elsewhere for those who need it.

Unfortunately, the need to keep the collection to a reasonable size has meant that many, many worthy essays, chapters, articles, notes, queries, lectures, letters to the editor, and other forms of criticism and scholarship have been omitted. To those critics disappointed by the absence of their work, the editor can only say that he too is disappointed by the absence of their work. Most of them may be comforted by the knowledge that one of their essays was included in the original table of contents. That book, however, would have been as long as Holinshed's *Chronicles*.

As for temporal limits, the publisher and I wanted to gather and make available excellent work from the second half of the twentieth century, so the end date is obvious. "1945," the date given in the title, is a slight misrepresentation, chosen so as to indicate that the book is concerned with criticism after World War II. In fact one piece reprinted here appeared in 1944: in that year, E. M. W. Tillyard published *Shakespeare's History Plays*, and many early essays in new historicism and cultural materialism constitute direct objections or rejoinders to that exponent of the old historicism. If a reader perceives that the table of contents is tilted unfairly towards the end of the century, such an imbalance is dictated by the wider range of criticism written in 1990 than in 1950. Readers who believe that the volume contains too many men, or too many women, or too many US citizens, or too few textual scholars, or too much psychoanalytic criticism, or too much or too little of anything else are probably right. Such excesses and shortcomings are inescapable in an enterprise of this kind.

Arrangement has also been a problem. The 14 categories into which the material is divided are arbitrary and unsatisfactory. Many other schemes might have been devised, but each of those would probably have been just as unsatisfactory. It may be, for example, that reader-response criticism does not warrant its own category. The advisability of separating Feminist Criticism and Studies in Gender and Sexuality is debatable, but such a division seems appropriate to the critical scene at the end of the twentieth century as it would not have seemed fifteen years earlier. Also notable is the absence of Deconstruction as a rubric. Although some of its vocabulary and principles have perforce made their way into other modes of critical reading, deconstruction *per se* made little impact on Shakespeare studies, few Shakespeareans identified themselves as "deconstructionists," and thus a separate section seems unearned. One theme that presents itself over and over again is that every species of critical thinking, no matter how distinctive it may seem, is implicated with many others. The resulting impurity of most schools of criticism, their tendency to interpenetrate, means that many of the essays might reasonably have appeared in different categories. The excerpt from William Empson, for example, could have been included under "Close Readers" instead of "New Criticism" (in this case, temporal affinity governed the choice); much psychoanalytic criticism turns out to be feminist in orientation; Robert Weimann's work is germane both to performance studies and to cultural materialism. And the sections vary in emphasis and in size. Some contain a piece disputing the conclusions or methods of that kind of criticism; this is relatively rare, but in a couple of cases the rhetorical power of the objection won the dissenting essay a slot. Readers will probably complain less about the divisions than about their contents.

Finally, a caveat about the editorial material that precedes each group of essays. I have attempted in a very few words to give merely a flavor of the subdiscipline represented by the critical pieces included there. Inconsistencies abound, in that some of these prefaces offer a foretaste of the work to follow, while others attempt a more general account of the critical area. Few people are authorities on all fields of Shakespeare criticism – certainly not the editor. But it seemed desirable to provide a minimal sense of context and at least to mention the major concerns of each kind of criticism, especially for those readers who are new to Shakespeare studies or who were born after about 1980. Many users of this book will prefer to skip the introductory matter and get on to what they came for, the essays themselves.

Acknowledgments

P rimary thanks go to Andrew McNeillie, who conceived of this book and worked gracefully and efficiently to bring it to print. His extraordinary professional gifts have made the process easy, and his friendship over the past three years has been a rare pleasure.

Many friends and colleagues offered advice about the contents and shape of the volume, demonstrating prodigious learning, acumen about the requirements of potential readers, tact, and good humor. Several of these same people also read the introductions to each section, requesting clarification, correcting errors, cleaning up the prose, and re-training my attention on the needs of the prospective reader. Thanks to A. R. Braunmuller, James Bulman, Nicholas Crawford, Suzanne Gossett, Barbara Hodgdon, Catherine Loomis, Stephen Stallcup, Gary Taylor, Robert Y. Turner, and several thoughtful people who reviewed the proposal anonymously. Gratitude for more general assistance and support is owed to Thomas Berger, Stephen Booth, David Dudley, Christopher Hodgkins, Ruth Morse, and George T. Wright. These lists omit some names that I have failed to recall, as well as those of many other scholars who helped me without knowing they were doing so, and without my knowing they were doing so.

Warm thanks to the staff at Blackwell, particularly to Emma Bennett, Karen Wilson, and Jack Messenger. Maggie DiVito assisted with research and retrieval, and Alison Seay performed the heroic task of helping me proofread the typescript in a short period of time. My departmental colleagues at Greensboro have given various kinds of support, for which I am grateful.

To Gail and Jack McDonald, thanks, and thanks.

This book is dedicated to my students, with affection and gratitude.

Acknowledgments

The editor and publishers wish to thank the following for permission to use copyright material.

Authorship

S. Schoenbaum, for "Looney and the Oxfordians" from *Shakespeare's Lives* by S. Schoenbaum, revised edition (1991) pp. 430–41, by permission of Oxford University Press.

New Criticism

Cleanth Brooks, for "The Naked Babe and the Cloak of Manliness" from *The Well-Wrought Urn* by Cleanth Brooks (1947) pp. 22–49. Copyright © 1947, renewed 1975 by Cleanth Brooks, by permission of Harcourt, Inc;

William Empson, for "Honest in Othello" from *The Structure of Complex Words* by William Empson, Hogarth Press, pp. 218–36. Copyright © 1951, 1985 by the Estate of Sir William Empson, by permission of Lady Empson and the Random House Group Ltd, and Harvard University Press;

Wolfgang Clemen, for "Introductory" from *The Development of Shakespeare's Imagery*, Methuen (1951) pp. 89–105, by permission of Taylor and Francis Books Ltd;

William R. Keast, for "The 'New Criticism' and King Lear" from *Critics and Criticism*, ed. R. S. Crane (1952) pp. 108–37, by permission of the University of Chicago Press;

Dramatic Kinds

Northrop Frye, for "The Argument of Comedy" from *English Literature Essays 1949*, ed. D. A. Robertson (1959) pp. 58–73, by permission of Columbia University Press;

A. P. Rossiter, for "Ambivalence: The Dialectic of the Histories" from *Angel With Horns* by A. P. Rossiter, ed. Graham Storey (1961) pp. 40–64, by permission of Harcourt Education Ltd;

C. L. Barber, for "The Saturnalian Pattern" from *Shakespeare's Festive Comedy* by C. L. Barber, pp. 1–15. Copyright © 1959, renewed 1987 by Princeton University Press, by permission of Princeton University Press;

Maynard Mack, for "The Jacobean Shakespeare: Some Observations on the Construction of the Tragedies" from *Everybody's Shakespeare* by Maynard Mack, pp. 231–62. Copyright © 1993 by the University of Nebraska Press.

The 1950s and 1960s

Barbara Everett, for "Reflections on the Sentimentalist's *Othello*," *Critical Quarterly*, 3 (1961) pp. 127–39, by permission of the author;

Harry Levin, for "Form and Formality in *Romeo and Juliet*," *Shakespeare Quarterly*, 11: 1 (1960) pp. 3–11. Copyright © Folger Shakespeare Library, by permission of the Johns Hopkins University Press;

Jan Kott, for extracts from "*King Lear* or *Endgame*" from *Shakespeare: Our Contemporary* by Jan Kott, trans. Boleslaw Taborski, pp. 127–35, 141–62. Copyright © 1964 by

Panstwowe Wydawnictwo Naukowe and Doubleday, a division of Bantam, Doubleday, Dell Publishing Group, Inc, by permission of Doubleday, a division of Random House, Inc;

Sigurd Burckhardt, for "How Not to Murder Caesar" from *Shakespeare Meanings* by Sigurd Burckhardt, pp. 3–21. Copyright © 1968 by Princeton University Press, by permission of Princeton University Press.

Reader-Response Criticism

Stephen Booth, for "On the Value of *Hamlet*" from *Reinterpretations of Elizabethan Drama*, ed. Norman Rabkin and Max Bluestone (1969) pp. 137–76, by permission of Columbia University Press;

Norman Rabkin, for "Rabbits, Ducks, and *Henry V*," *Shakespeare Quarterly*, 28: 3 (1977) pp. 279–96. Copyright © Folger Shakespeare Library, by permission of the Johns Hopkins University Press.

Textual Criticism and Bibliography

Fredson Bowers, for "The New Textual Criticism of Shakespeare" from *Textual and Literary Criticism* by Fredson Bowers (1959) pp. 76–95, by permission of Cambridge University Press;

Gary Taylor, for "Revising Shakespeare," *Text: Transactions of the Society for Textual Scholarship*, 3 (1987) pp. 285–304, by permission of AMS Press, Inc;

Paul Werstine, for "Narratives about Printed Shakespeare Texts: 'Foul Papers' and 'Bad' Quartos," *Shakespeare Quarterly*, 41: 1 (1990) pp. 65–86. Copyright © Folger Shakespeare Library, by permission of the Johns Hopkins University Press.

Psychoanalytic Criticism

Janet Adelman, for " 'Anger's my meat': Feeding, Dependency, and Aggression in *Coriolanus*" from *Shakespeare: Pattern of Excelling Nature*, ed. David Bellington and Jay Halio, University of Delaware Press (1978) pp. 108–24, by permission of Associated University Presses;

Stanley Cavell, for "The Avoidance of Love: A Reading of *King Lear*" from *Disowning Knowledge in Six Plays of Shakespeare* by Stephen Cavell (1987) pp. 61–81, by permission of Cambridge University Press;

René Girard, for "To Entrap the Wisest: Sacrificial Ambivalence in *The Merchant of Venice* and *Richard III*" from *Theater of Envy* by René Girard, pp. 243–55. Copyright © 1991 by Oxford University Press, Inc, by permission of Oxford University Press, Inc;

Harry Berger, Jr., for "What Did the King Know and When Did He Know It? Shakespearean Discourses and Psychoanalysis," *South Atlantic Quarterly*, 88: 4 (1989) pp. 811–62. Copyright © 1989 Duke University Press, by permission of Duke University Press;

Joel Fineman, for "The Turn of the Shrew" from *Shakespeare and the Question of Theory*, ed. Patricia Parker and Geoffrey Hartman, Routledge (1985) pp. 138–59, by permission of Taylor and Francis Books Ltd.

Historicism and New Historicism

E. M. W. Tillyard, for "The Cosmic Background" from *Shakespeare's History Plays* by E. M. W. Tillyard, Chatto & Windus (1944) pp. 3–20, by permission of Jesus College, Cambridge, on behalf of the Estate of the author;

Stephen Greenblatt, for "Invisible Bullets: Renaissance Authority and Its Subversion, *Henry IV* and *Henry V*" from *Political Shakespeare: New Essays in Cultural Materialism*, ed. Jonathan Dollimore and Alan Sinfield, pp. 18–47. Copyright © 1985, 1994 by Manchester University Press, by permission of Cornell University Press;

Jean E. Howard, for "The New Historicism in Renaissance Studies," *English Literary Renaissance*, 16: 1 (1986) pp. 13–43, by permission of the editors;

Louis Adrian Montrose, for " 'Shaping Fantasies': Figurations of Gender and Power in Elizabethan Culture," *Representations*, 2 (1983) pp. 61–94. Copyright © 1983 by the Regents of the University of California, by permission of the University of California Press.

Materialist Criticism

Robert Weimann, for extracts from "Shakespeare's Theater: Tradition and Experiment" in *Shakespeare and the Popular Tradition in the Theater: Studies in the Social Dimension of Dramatic Form and Function* by Robert Weimann, ed. Robert Schwartz, pp. 208–15, 224–37, by permission of the Johns Hopkins University Press;

Jonathan Dollimore, for "*King Lear* (ca. 1605–1606) and Essentialist Humanism" from *Radical Tragedy* by Jonathan Dollimore, Harvester Wheatsheaf (1984) pp. 189–203, third edition, Palgrave Macmillan forthcoming, by permission of the author;

Alan Sinfield, for "Give an Account of Shakespeare and Education, Showing Why You Think They Are Effective and What You Have Appreciated about Them; Support Your Comments with Precise References" from *Political Shakespeare: New Essays in Cultural Materialism*, ed. Jonathan Dollimore and Alan Sinfield, pp. 158–81. Copyright © 1985, 1994 by Manchester University Press, by permission of Manchester University Press and Cornell University Press.

Feminist Criticism

L. T. Fitz, for "Egyptian Queens and Male Reviewers: Sexist Attitudes in *Antony and Cleopatra* Criticism," *Shakespeare Quarterly*, 28: 3 (1977) pp. 297–316. Copyright © Folger Shakespeare Library, by permission of the Johns Hopkins University Press;

Madelon Gohlke, for " 'I wooed thee with my sword': Shakespeare's Tragic Paradigms" from *The Women's Part: Feminist Criticism of Shakespeare*, ed. Carolyn Ruth

Swift Lencz, Gayle Greene, and Carol Thomas Neely, pp. 150–71. Copyright © 1980 by Board of Trustees of the University of Illinois, by permission of the University of Illinois Press;

Lynda E. Boose, for "The Family in Shakespeare Studies; or Studies in the Family of Shakespeareans; or The Politics of Politics," *Renaissance Quarterly*, 40 (1987) pp. 707–42, by permission of the Renaissance Society of America;

Catherine Belsey, for "Disrupting Sexual Difference: Meaning and Gender in the Comedies" from *Alternative Shakespeares*, ed. John Drakakis, Routledge (1985) pp. 166–90, by permission of Taylor and Francis Books Ltd.

Studies in Gender and Sexuality

Gayle Greene, for " 'This that you call love': Sexual and Social Tragedy in *Othello*" from *Shakespeare and Gender*, ed. Deborah Barker and Ivo Kamps (1995) pp. 47–62, by permission of Verso;

Stephen Orgel, for "The Performance of Desire" from *Impersonations* by Stephen Orgel (1996) pp. 10–30, by permission of Cambridge University Press;

Bruce R. Smith, for "The Secret Sharer" from *Homosexual Desire in Shakespeare's England* by Bruce R. Smith (1984) pp. 246–70, by permission of the University of Chicago Press;

Valerie Traub, for "The Homoerotics of Shakespearean Comedy" from *Desire and Anxiety: Circulations of Sexuality in Shakespearean Drama* by Valerie Traub, Routledge (1992) pp. 117–44, by permission of Taylor and Francis Books Ltd.

Performance Criticism

Gerald Eades Bentley, for "Shakespeare and the Blackfriars Theatre," *Shakespeare Survey* 1 (1948) pp. 38–56. Copyright © Folger Shakespeare Library, by permission of the Johns Hopkins University Press;

J. L. Styan, for "The Critical Revolution" from *The Shakespeare Revolution* by J. L. Styan (1977) pp. 232–7, by permission of Cambridge University Press;

Barbara Hodgdon, for "*William Shakespeare's Romeo + Juliet*: Everything's Nice in America?" *Shakespeare Survey*, 52 (1999) pp. 88–98, by permission of Cambridge University Press;

William B. Worthen, for "Deeper Meanings and Theatrical Technique: The Rhetoric of Performance Criticism," *Shakespeare Quarterly*, 40: 4 (1989) pp. 441–55. Copyright © Folger Shakespeare Library, by permission of the Johns Hopkins University Press.

Postcolonial Shakespeare

Francis Barker and Peter Hulme, for "Nymphs and Reapers Heavily Vanish: The Discursive Con-texts of *The Tempest*" from *Alternative Shakespeares*, ed. John Drakakis, Methuen (1985) pp. 191–205, by permission of Taylor and Francis Books Ltd;

Acknowledgments

Ania Loombia, for "Sexuality and Racial Difference" from *Gender, Race, Renaissance Drama* by Ania Loombia, Manchester University Press (1989) pp. 38–62, by permission of the author;

Meredith Anne Skura, for "Discourse and the Individual: The Case of Colonialism in *The Tempest*," *Shakespeare Quarterly*, 40: 1 (1989) pp. 42–69. Copyright © Folger Shakespeare Library, by permission of the Johns Hopkins University Press.

Reading Closely

Jonas A. Barish, for "Shakespeare's Prose" from Ben Jonson and the Language of Prose Comedy by Jonas A. Barish (1988) pp. 23–40. Copyright © 1960 by the President and Fellows of Harvard College, renewed © 1988 by Jonas Alexander Barish, by permission of Harvard University Press.

Particia Parker, for "Transfigurations: Shakespeare and Rhetoric" from *Literary Fat Ladies* by Patricia Parker, London: Methuen (1987) pp. 67–96.

George T. Wright, for "The Play of Phrase and Line" from *Shakespeare's Metrical Art* by George T. Wright (1988) pp. 207–28. Copyright © 1988 the Regents of the University of California, by permission of the University of California Press.

Every effort has been made to trace copyright holders and to obtain their permission for the use of copyright material. The authors and publishers will gladly receive any information enabling them to rectify any error or omission in subsequent editions.

Part I

Authorship

1   Looney and the Oxfordians   4
    S. Schoenbaum

T o many members of the public at large, the question of authorship is the most fascinating problem in the study of Shakespeare, but to members of the Anglo-American academy "the mystery" of who wrote the plays attributed to William Shakespeare has not seemed very compelling. For the most part, scholars and critics accept the facts that history has provided: they believe the documentary evidence that a glover's son from a market town in Warwickshire moved to London and that he there became an actor, a playwright, and a theatrical shareholder. They further accept that after his death his colleagues assembled as many of his surviving theatrical scripts as they could gather and published them as *Mr. William Shakespeares Comedies, Histories, & Tragedies*, the book we know as the First Folio. Consequently, most professional Shakespeareans and students have devoted themselves to study of the work, not its creator – to matters of text, language, structure, theme, historical context, political uses, conditions of production, theatrical afterlives, and any number of other topics having little to do with the biography of the playwright. This is not to say that biography is of no interest to scholars. Lives of Shakespeare have been appearing regularly over the past three centuries – a few even before that – and towards the very end of the period covered in this book several new biographies appeared, such as Park Honan's *Shakespeare: A Life* (1998), Irving Leigh Matus's *Shakespeare, in Fact* (1994), and others by Jonathan Bate, Dennis Kay, Garry O'Connor, Ian Wilson, and Anthony Holden, to name only the most prominent. But Shakespeare scholarship has taken another approach to the problem of authorship.

Rather than fret about the identity of the person who wrote the plays, Shakespeare critics have elected instead to interrogate the concept of authorship itself, attempting to understand the term in a more sophisticated sense than the usual. To some extent this mode of thinking is an effort at correction, a reaction to the romantic glorification of the solitary artist and an attempt to debunk the myth of the genius transcending his contemporaries and his culture. This new sense of authorship positions the artist historically, studying the writer in a network of political, commercial, literary, religious, and other cultural affiliations. In pursuing such an approach, critics of Shakespeare tread the path of postmodern criticism in general: following Foucault and other theorists, they have challenged conventional notions of textual authority, modifying the contribution of the "author" so as to disperse responsibility into the culture at large. A number of influential articles and book chapters regarding the playwright in this light might have been included under the rubric of authorship, but since such a revised understanding of the author is one of the foundations of new historicism and cultural materialism and has influenced other critical modes as well, the reader is referred to those sections for examples of such thinking.

The work of one biographer cannot be omitted, however. Samuel Schoenbaum became the foremost authority on Shakespeare's life in the second half of the twentieth century, and he did so through a rare combination of scholarly diligence, brilliant deduction, and a witty narrative style. He is the author of *Shakespeare: A Compact Documentary Life*, the book that, while not as ambitious or detailed as he wanted to make it, has become the standard biography. The volume from which the selection below is taken is the magisterial *Shakespeare's Lives*, a wide-ranging, thorough survey of Shakespeare's biographers and biographies. When it was published in 1970, it made an immediate splash: Stanley Wells declared in a review that "with this book Dr. Schoenbaum joins the ranks of the heroes of Shakespeare scholarship."[1] In introducing his work, Schoenbaum reports that he had imagined "a little book narrating the quest for knowledge of Shakespeare the man,"[2] but what he produced instead was a massive, detailed history of Shakespearean biography, and of much more as well.

It occurred to me that I must try to find out how the various documents – the marriage-license bond, the Belott-Mountjoy deposition, the will – came to light. The formal Lives, from Rowe to Rowse, would of course occupy much of my space, but what of the accretions of biographical notes in eighteenth-century editions, the bits and pieces of information in newspapers, magazines, and miscellanies, the prefaces to innumerable popular collections, the encyclopaedia articles from which ordinary readers formed their impression of the National Poet? These, surely, could not be ignored. From the nineteenth century onwards, critics hunted for biographical revelations in the works, especially the Sonnets: I would have to confront this daunting mass of material. The representations of Shakespeare are in their own way biographical documents; belief in the various icons, all but two doubtful or spurious, would furnish curious evidence of human credulity deserving a place in my pages. The invention of biographical data by means of forged papers would also comprise part – a fascinating part – of the story. And then one must reckon with the amateurs, the eccentrics, the cranks with theories. Of these the worst would be the heretics, alert to conspiracies, who saw a sinister plot to take away the plays from their true progenitor, Bacon or Marlowe or some Earl or other, and bestow them instead on the Stratford boor. I did not relish this aspect of my assignment, although I knew that Mark Twain and Freud rubbed shoulders with less celebrated schismatics.[3]

The excerpt I have chosen to include here concerns the claim of Edward de Vere, Earl of Oxford, as represented by his early twentieth-century proponent, J. Thomas Looney. In the last decade of the twentieth century members of the Oxfordian camp gathered strength and made a fresh assault on the Shakespearean citadel, hoping finally to unseat the man from Stratford and install de Vere in his place. Thus Schoenbaum's pages are timely. Although the initial section of this volume is the briefest, containing only one item, that item is choice.

Notes

1 *Notes and Queries*, n.s., 19 (April 1977), pp. 142–3.
2 S. Schoenbaum, *Shakespeare's Lives*, revd. edn. (Oxford: Oxford University Press, 1991), p. vii.
3 Ibid., pp. vii–viii.

1

Looney and the Oxfordians

S. Schoenbaum

T
he month that saw an armistice bring to an end the Great War witnessed another event hardly less momentous, at least for members of the Shakespeare Fellowship. In November 1918 J. Thomas Looney, a Gateshead schoolmaster, deposited with the Librarian of the British Museum a sealed envelope containing an announcement of his discovery that the plays and poems of Shakespeare issued from the pen of Edward de Vere, the seventeenth Earl of Oxford. Before taking this unusual step the schoolmaster had submitted his work, the result of years of patient investigation, to a publisher; but the latter rejected it when Looney refused to adopt a *nom de plume* to forestall the hilarity of reviewers. Now, covetous of priority, he resorted to the device of the sealed letter with its overtones of mysterious significance so congenial to the anti-Stratfordian mentality.

The book, '*Shakespeare*' *Identified*, appeared in 1920, and initiated the Oxford movement, which has given the Baconians a run for their madness. In his introduction Looney disclaims an expert's knowledge of literature (when he began he had read only Shakespeare, Spenser, and Sidney among the Elizabethans), nor does he pride himself on a critic's soundness of literary judgement. Instead he makes a virtue of amateurism. 'This is probably why the problem has not been solved before now,' Looney asserts. 'It has been left mainly in the hands of literary men.'[1] For years, however, he had been putting his young charges through their paces with *The Merchant of Venice*, prolonged intimacy with which persuaded Looney that the author knew Italy at first hand, and – more important – had an aristocrat's indifference to business methods and an aristocrat's casual regard for material possessions. It is difficult to escape the conclusion that snobbery led Looney, a gentle retiring soul, to seek a Shakespeare with blue blood in his veins. His own family, the pedagogue boasted, was descended from the Earl of Derby, once kings of the Isle of Man, whence came Looney's immediate forebears. He expresses the heretic's customary disdain for the 'coarse and illiterate circumstances' of Shakespeare's early life, and in an unconsciously revealing passage implies that a great writer must have lords and ladies in coaches driving up to his door.[2]

'My preparation for the work lay', Looney reflected in old age, '... in a life spent in facing definite problems, attempting the solution by the methods of science, and accepting the necessary logical conclusions, however unpalatable & inconvenient these might prove.'[3] His impartial science, derived from the Positivism of Comte, led Looney to seek nine 'general features' in the author of Shakespeare's works:

1 A matured man of recognized genius.
2 Apparently eccentric and mysterious.
3 Of intense sensibility – a man apart.
4 Unconventional.
5 Not adequately appreciated.
6 Of pronounced and known literary tastes.
7 An enthusiast in the world of drama.
8 A lyric poet of recognized talent.
9 Of superior education – classical – the habitual associate of educated people.[4]

To these Looney added nine 'special characteristics':

1 A man with Feudal connections.
2 A member of the higher aristocracy.
3 Connected with Lancastrian supporters.
4 An enthusiast for Italy.
5 A follower of sport (including falconry).
6 A lover of music.
7 Loose and improvident in money matters.
8 Doubtful and somewhat conflicting in his attitude to woman.
9 Of probable Catholic leanings, but touched with scepticism.[5]

Without the advantages of historical or literary training, Looney had now to find the candidate who met all the general and special requirements.

Plunging in, he selected *Venus and Adonis* and began to look for a poem with similar stanza and cadence in Palgrave's *Golden Treasury*, which alone constituted Looney's reference library of sixteenth-century verse. In 'Women', by Edward de Vere, he found the poem. He next had to learn something about the poet. After several false starts in history textbooks, Looney discovered with delight from the *DNB* that Oxford '*evinced a genuine taste in music and wrote verses of much lyric beauty*'; also that 'Puttenham and Meres reckon him *among the best for comedy* in his day; but though he was a patron of players *no specimens of his dramatic productions survive.*' (The italics in these misquoted passages are supplied by Looney.)

The de Veres traced their descent in an unbroken line from the Norman Conquest: higher aristocracy, there can be no question. Evidence of Lancastrian sympathies (Looney's third special criterion) may be found in the fact that the twelfth Earl lost his head in 1461 for loyalty to the Red Rose. Sidney Lee's *DNB* sketch describes Oxford as having had a thorough grounding in Latin and French, great prowess at the tilt, and an ambition for foreign travel gratified by a journey to Italy in 1575. As a youth, however, he also manifested 'a waywardness of temper which led him into every form of extravagance, and into violent quarrels with other members of his guardian's household'. At the age of seventeen he fatally wounded an under-cook at Cecil House. Report held that he threatened the ruin of his first wife in order to avenge himself on the father-in-law who had incurred his displeasure. There were other indications of a volatile temper: Oxford grossly insulted Sidney on the tennis court at Whitehall – addressing him as a 'puppy', according to Sir Fulke Greville (Sidney's biographer) – and afterwards plotted his assassination; in 1586 he quarrelled with Thomas Knyvet, duelled with him, and entered into a subsequent vendetta. Irresponsible, he hired lodgings and left others, of humbler station, to foot the bill. The Earl's improvidence brought him into financial straits from which he tried to extricate himself by selling his ancestral estates at perversely low prices. Lee does not dwell on the Earl's seduction of one of the Queen's Maids of Honour, nor does he report Aubrey's presumably apocryphal anecdote: 'This Earl of Oxford, making of his low obeisance to Queen Elizabeth, happened to let a fart, at which he was so ashamed that he went to travel, 7 years.'[6] In any event, Looney does not include flatulence as another of his hero's special attributes. Nor does he list cruelty, perversity, and profligacy as features of the author evident from a perusal of his work.

Looney properly relishes the contemporary evidence that Oxford wrote plays (after all it cannot be demonstrated that Bacon or most of the other chief claimants performed this necessary activity), and he attempts to bolster the testimony of Puttenham and Meres by the familiar tactic of converting Shakespeare's dramas into *pièces à clef*. Indeed the Earl can scarcely restrain himself from putting in appearances everywhere in the canon. In *Love's Labour's Lost* he is Berowne mocking Holofernes – Gabriel Harvey, the 'kissing traitor' who had circulated satirical verses about Oxford behind his back. Elizabeth's royal ward is Bertram in *All's Well That Ends Well*, the jealous husband is Othello, the Patron of Oxford's boys is the master of the revels at Elsinore. It follows that the rest of the dramatis personae must have historical identities; and so Laertes is Thomas Cecil; Polonius, Burleigh (to reappear in Venice as Brabantio); Ophelia, Lady Oxford (reincarnated after drowning only to be strangled as Desdemona); Horatio, the Earl's cousin Sir Horace de Vere – principally, it would seem, because of the partial congruence of Christian names. Such a view of drama implies that plays are secondarily intended for theatrical representation, being preeminently literary artifacts. To this reversal of priorities Looney freely subscribes: '... if we must choose between the theory of their being literature converted into plays, or plays converted into literature, on a review of the work no competent judge would hesitate to pronounce in favour of the latter supposition'.[7] Looney, one suspects, has not polled all the competent judges.

His subjective ruminations do little to strengthen an hypothesis which has certain inherent limitations. The attestation of Puttenham and Meres to Oxford's playwriting activities cuts two ways. Meres after all lists Shakespeare separately in *Palladis Tamia* and names twelve plays, as well as *Venus and Adonis*, *The Rape of Lucrece*, and the Sonnets: clearly he did not believe that the Earl wrote *The Comedy of Errors*, *Romeo and Juliet*, and the rest. And if people knew that Oxford graced the stage with plays, why had he need of employing Shakespeare as a mask? The only motive that Looney can suggest is self-effacement. 'We may, if we wish', he adds, 'question the sufficiency or reasonableness of the motive. That, however, is his business, not ours.'[8] But of course the man who sets out to convince the public of the validity of an eccentric theory *must* make the motivation his business. These considerations, however, pale into triviality alongside the principal drawback of the entire argument: Oxford, born in 1550, died in 1604. Thus he was forty-three when he offered the first heir of his invention to Southampton, and was buried before *King Lear, Macbeth, Antony and Cleopatra, Timon of Athens, Coriolanus, Pericles, Cymbeline, Winter's Tale, The Tempest,* and *Henry VIII* appeared on the stage.

To get round this perplexity Looney must urge that the authorities have misdated *King Lear* and *Macbeth*, and that Oxford at the time of his death left unfinished manuscripts which inferior dramatists then completed. 'The people who were "finishing off" these later plays took straightforward prose, either from the works of others, or from rough notes collected by "Shakespeare" in preparing his dramas, and chopped it up, along with a little dressing, to make it look in print something like blank verse.'[9] Such a considered judgement emanates naturally from a sensibility to which the music of Shakespeare's final period is ragtime. *The Tempest* presents Looney with his greatest challenge, for topical references and other internal considerations lead him to accept the late date to which the commentators assign it. So he must deny it altogether to his candidate – at the same time admitting that 'but for the theory that Edward de Vere was the writer of Shakespeare's plays we might never have been led to suspect the authenticity of "The Tempest" '.[10] The task of denigration proceeds apace. Prospero's speech on the cloud-capped towers and gorgeous palaces becomes 'simple cosmic philosophy, and, as such, it is the most dreary negativism that was ever put into high-sounding words'.[11] (The disciple of Comte insists upon the positivism of his idol.) Elsewhere in the play Looney finds stolen thunder, muddled metaphysics, witlessness, and coarse fun. Above all, the verse is bad, which by Looney's standard merely means that it has irregular scansion syllables. This evaluation of *The Tempest,* needless to say, has met with a cool reception – even from fellow Oxfordians. Looney had at the outset confessed his lack of critical equipment; in the end, having constructed his elaborately rationalized fantasy, he becomes a casualty of that handicap.

Despite its intellectual *naïveté* – perhaps because of it – *'Shakespeare' Identified* impressed the impressionable. In his introduction to the 1948 reprint (which drew some respectful journalistic notices) the maritime novelist William McFee compared the Looney book, for revolutionary significance, with *The Origin of Species*. He also described the Gateshead pedagogue as a sleuth 'methodically and relentlessly closing in on the author, not of a crime, but of a mystery'. The mantle of Conan Doyle sits more comfortably on Looney than that of Darwin; Galsworthy pronounced *'Shakespeare' Identified* 'the best detective story' which ever came his way. Herein must lie much of the fundamental appeal of the work and of anti-Stratfordian demonstrations generally. Sober literary history is metamorphosed into a game of detection, in much the same manner as James Thurber's American lady in the Lake Country transformed *Macbeth* into a Hercule Poirot thriller (' "Oh Macduff did it all right," said the murder specialist.'). To such a game the cultivated amateur can give his leisure hours in hopes of toppling the supreme literary idol and confounding the professionals. Little wonder that one heretic, Claud W. Sykes, casts his investigation as an exercise in detection, with Sherlock Holmes tracking down the true perpetrator of the plays by means of Baker Street deduction!

Be that as it may, Looney founded a school. A tangible result of '*Shakespeare*' *Identified* was the formation in 1922 of the Shakespeare Fellowship, a society hospitable to all heretics but chiefly devoted to perpetuating the claims of Oxford. *The Shakespeare Fellowship News-letter*, issued by the association, performed a service analogous to that of *Baconiana*. In addition to schoolmasters and attorneys the group attracted military and naval types, the novelist Marjorie Bowen, and Christmas Humphreys, QC, an authority on Buddhism. It appealed to the young at heart: Canon Gerald H. Rendall, sometime Gladstone Professor of Greek at University College, Liverpool, read Looney and, at the age of eighty, experienced a conversion. He proceeded to advance the cause with a series of volumes: *Shakespeare Sonnets and Edward De Vere* (1930), *Shake-speare: Handwriting and Spelling* (1931), *Personal Clues in Shakespeare Poems & Sonnets* (1934), and *Ben Jonson and the First Folio Edition of Shakespeare's Plays* (1939). So prodigious was the display of energy that one admirer was prompted to exclaim in 1944 that Canon Rendall 'represents one of the biological reasons why the Germans, despite all their sound and fury, will never overcome the British'. After the outbreak of the Second World War the continuity of the Fellowship's work was assured by the formation of an American branch presided over by Dr Louis P. Bénézet of Dartmouth College. This true believer's own contributions include the suggestion, made in *Shakespere, Shakespeare and De Vere* (1937), that in the Sonnets the Earl addressed his illegitimate son, who acted in his father's company of players under the name of William Shakespeare.

The publications of the de Vere sect are too numerous for listing, much less evaluation, in these pages, but a few of the principal items may be mentioned. A member of the Fellowship, Captain Bernard Mordaunt Ward, produced in 1928 a massive biography from contemporary documents, *The Seventeenth Earl of Oxford, 1550–1604*, aimed at rehabilitating the nobleman's somewhat tarnished reputation. While not overtly concerned with the authorship debate, Ward gives tacit support to the theory (suggested by Lefranc) that Oxford and the Earl of Derby were in some way connected with the composition of Shakespeare's plays. Others too favoured the idea of mixed authorship, for example, Slater's *Seven Shakespeares*. In *Lord Oxford and the Shakespeare Group* (1952) Lieutenant-Colonel Montagu W. Douglas ingeniously proposed that the Queen charged the Earl with the control of a Propaganda Department for the issuance of patriotic pamphlets and plays, and that he satisfied this commission by putting together a syndicate which included Bacon, the Earl of Derby, Marlowe, Lyly, and Greene: a motley assortment by any standard. Still others sought to adjust the Shakespeare chronology to the facts of Shakespeare's life and thus get round the embarrassment of denying him *The Tempest*. Mrs Eva Turner Clark, in the 693 pages of *Hidden Allusions in Shakespeare's Plays* (1931), arranges the works in a sequence beginning with *Henry V* and culminating with *King Lear* in 1590; for *The Tempest* she finds a snug niche half-way between. This novel arrangement is made possible by identifying Shakespeare's plays with the titles of lost Tudor interludes, and by correctly interpreting internal historical references which had escaped all other scholars. In *King Lear*, for example, the banishment of Kent parallels the banishment of Drake in 1589, while the play as a whole reflects Oxford's bitterness over 'the failure of the Queen to back him up in his patriotic endeavour to support the throne and country against the factions that were, as he saw them, disintegrating forces in the government, if not actively seditious'.[12] Into such tracts for the times do the plays dwindle in Oxfordian hands.

In a note appended to the last page of *'Shakespeare' Identified* Looney had admitted to a belief that the Grafton portrait of Shakespeare really depicts the Earl. The Shakespeare iconography fascinates the Oxfordians. In the pages of *Scientific American* for January 1940, Charles Wisner Barrell, one of the brethren, revealed that X-ray and infra-red photography had detected underneath the Ashbourne portrait the pigment of another painting representing de Vere. This discovery was greeted with hoots of delight by the Fellowship, but how it materially aids the cause (even if we accept the doubtful findings of a partisan) is not clear, for the Ashbourne picture, like the Grafton, has no standing as a genuine likeness of Shakespeare.

Among those who applauded Barrell were Dorothy and Charlton Ogburn in *This Star of England* (1952), the most monumental contribution ever made to the literature of heresy. As one would expect from a volume running to 1297 pages, all the familiar Oxfordian arguments appear, and also some new ones. The quality of the Ogburn reasoning may be illustrated by a single example. They reproduce Touchstone's interrogation of William in *As You Like It*, with certain words and clauses italicized: 'Art thou *learned*? ... *all your writers do consent that ipse is he*: now, *you are not ipse, for I am he*. ... *He, sir, that must marry this woman. Therefore, you clown, abandon.*' This straight-faced commentary follows:

> *How can a man speak more plainly than this?* Oxford – or William Shakespeare – tells Shaksper, another William, to abandon all pretensions to the plays and clear out, forthwith. 'You are not ipse, for I am he.' All the 'writers' – Jonson, Marston, Dekker, Peele, *et al.* – know this, 'do consent' to it. What other possible interpretation can be put upon these candid lines?[13]

The aggrandizing tendencies of the heretic surface: Oxford must be credited not only with all of Shakespeare, but also with the apocryphal plays, Marlowe's *Edward II*, Kyd's *Spanish Tragedy*, and Lyly's *Endymion* and other comedies. In such a context we learn without astonishment that the Earl of Southampton sprang from the loins of Oxford and the womb of Elizabeth, somehow legitimately mated; the Sonnets to the Fair Youth (pun: Vere Youth) therefore become a touching poetical testament of a father to his son. Without once referring to *This Star of England* the Ogburns – this time Dorothy and her son, Charlton Junior – warmed over their stew as *Shakespeare: The Man behind the Name* (1962), which has at least the merit of comparative brevity.

With *The Mysterious William Shakespeare: The Myth and the Reality* (New York, 1984) Charlton Ogburn goes once more unto the breach, to do battle for his own brand of Oxfordian reality, this time with a volume of almost 900 large pages – not the longest such exercise but very long indeed – which surely qualifies as one of the seven wonders of anti-Stratfordianism, although I would be hard pressed to name the other six. Most of the terrain Ogburn traverses will be familiar to initiates. He argues that de Vere is the Will Moxon of Thomas Nashe's *Strange News*; the same Will who partook of Rhenish wine and herrings with Nashe and Robert Greene a month before Greene's death: this Will is to be identified with another Will, the celebrated – if supposititious – playwright of the English stage. Elizabeth's grant of £1,000 a year to Oxford facilitated the writing and production of plays supportive of the throne. The author dwells upon parallels between Shakespeare's plays and Oxford's life, unmindful of the discommoding truth that literature and life are full of cunning parallels. Ogburn also ruefully recounts one unbeliever's encounters with the Shakespeare Establishment. *The Mysterious William Shakespeare* inspired Richmond Crinkley's sympathetic review article, 'New Perspectives on the Authorship Question', which mysteriously appeared in that Establishment bastion, *Shakespeare Quarterly* the next year (36, 515–22). 'Shakespeare scholarship', Crinkley concludes, 'owes an enormous debt to Charlton Ogburn.' Not everyone would agree.

Washington, DC, attorney, business executive, connoisseur of the arts, philanthropist, and Oxfordian enthusiast, David Lloyd Kreeger was the master spirit behind the moot-court debate sponsored by the American University in the nation's capital, and argued by two members of that university's law-school faculty (Peter Jaszi for the Oxfordian position and James Boyle for the man from Stratford) before a trio of Supreme Court justices in appropriate juridical garb: Harry A. Blackmun, William Brennan, and John Paul Stevens. The event took place on 25 September 1987, at the Metropolitan Memorial United Methodist Church in the presence of bus-loads of high-school students, contingents of Oxfordian and Stratfordian partisans, white-collar Washingtonians, and the youthful Charles Francis Topham de Vere Beauclerk, a collateral descendant of the seventeenth Earl of Oxford. All told, roughly a thousand – maybe more – jammed into the church that autumn morning. The lawyers presented their arguments, with occasional interjections from the bench, and the court recessed until afternoon when the justices returned to their seats to deliver their opinions. Justice Brennan, the acting chief, spoke first, concluding that the case for the Oxford side remained unproven. 'What business have I to be judging this?', Justice Blackmun could not help asking himself. He thought of Isabel in *Measure for Measure* ('Oh, it is excellent / To have a giant's strength but it is tyrannous / To use if like a giant'). He agreed, however, that Justice Brennan's conclusion was 'the legal answer'. Justice Stevens similarly arrived at a legal verdict for the Stratford man, although qualified by a degree of personal uncertainty. The event was chronicled in the *Washington Post* and – more conspicuously, as might be expected – in the *New York Times*. Months passed. The Authorship Question became the subject of a long essay by James Lardner in the 'Onward and Upward with the Arts' department of the *New Yorker* (11 April 1988), 87–106. In a retrospective contribution to the *de Vere Society Newsletter*, a new periodical (1988), Ogburn denounced the moot 'trial' as a 'miscarriage of justice' in which Justice Brennan acted for all practical purposes as a witness for the Stratfordian side.

A permanent record of the great Washington Shakespeare debate was eventually published in the American University Law Review, 37 [1988], 609–826. Included was a verbatim transcript of the Justices' opinion, as well as prefatory remarks by Kreeger and essays by Jaszi ('Who Cares Who Wrote "Shakespeare"?') and Boule ('The Search for an Author: Shakespeare and the Framers'). There the matter did not rest: a reprise with a different dramatis personae (Kreeger, Ogburn, and Shakespeare excepted), took place on 26 November 1988 at the Middle Temple – in the same (then new) 'large and stately' hall where a young lawyer, John Manningham, had the good fortune to see a special production of *Twelfth Night* performed by the Lord Chamberlain's Men on 2 February 1602, and jotted down his impressions. On the occasion of the Middle Temple Moot this author was invited to testify as an expert witness, but, as circumstances worked out, the sponsors were unable to accommodate the expense of my journey. Nor was Ogburn able to take part, so Kreeger, Shakespeare, and the Earl of Oxford had to manage without us. The Oxfordians were represented by L. L. Ware, a founding member of the Mensa Society, and Gordon C. Cyr, former director of the Shakespeare Oxford Society; the Shakespearean side by Stanley Wells, director of the Shakespeare Institute, and Professor Honigmann. The presiding judge, Lord Archer, won applause by delivering the day's closing comments in blank verse. The three Law-Lords judging the Shakespeare Moot, as the mock trial was called, all found for the man from Stratford. Court adjourned.

To the Baconians it was not given to glory alone in a cipher. In *Edward De Vere: A Great Elizabethan* (1931) George Frisbee prints a multitude of ciphers based on the six letters of de Vere's name. Not surprisingly, he finds these characters everywhere: in Gascoigne's *Supposes*, in Marlowe, in Harington, Puttenham, Ralegh, Spenser, James I, above all in Shakespeare (most curiously in the contents page and dedication of the 1623 Folio). Even Canon Rendall gratifies us with a cipher:

> Why write I still all one, E.VER the same,
> And keep invention in a noted weed,
> That E.VERY word doth almost tell my name,
> Showing their birth and where they did proceed?

The Canon takes a special pride in this bit of inanity, which, he modestly allows, rescues Sonnet 76 from inanity.[14]

For the parallelism of the Oxfordians with the Baconians to be complete we need only the spirit from the grave and clues to the whereabouts of the Earl's lost manuscripts. No disappointment, alas, awaits us. In the autumn of 1942 Percy Allen, author of several Oxfordian treatises, consulted a London medium, Mrs Hester Dowden, daughter of the celebrated Dublin authority on Shakespeare.[*] The *séances* continued over an extended period, with one *Johannes* serving as control, and Hester Dowden herself taking down conversations in automatic writing, of which she was a most gifted practitioner. At these sessions Allen (through the good offices of his deceased brother) met Oxford, Bacon, and Shakespeare. They described their mode of collaboration with alacrity. 'I was quick at knowing what would be effective on the stage,' Shakespeare owned. 'I would find a plot (*Hamlet* was one), consult with Oxford, and form a skeleton edifice, which he would furnish and people, as befitted the subject.'[15] Often they took their efforts to Bacon, whose advice was requested but (the Viscount sadly reports) seldom accepted. All this Allen found extremely fascinating, as well he might, but a small difficulty troubled him. In 1943 one Alfred Dodd published a book, *The Immortal Master*, containing scripts by Hester Dowden reporting direct communication with Bacon, in the course of which the latter claimed for himself Shakespeare's writings. 'My friend, I *can* help you,' Bacon reassured Allen. 'I was acting through a Deputy in the case of Dodd – a Deputy who has never been personally in touch with me, and who questions nothing; for he is firmly convinced that I wrote the plays and sonnets, and took no trouble to have a direct message from me.'[16] Some spooks, it seems, are unreliable.

Where three centuries of scholarship had failed, Dowden's gatherings succeeded, clearing up disputed points in Shakespearean biography and producing fresh details. The poet indeed entered the world on St George's day, his mother invariably having her infants baptized three days after birth. The parents were Protestant (so much for John Shakespeare's Spiritual Last Will and Testament!). At the free school Will was considered a dull scholar. Although the deer-poaching legend had some basis in fact, the youth ran off to London not because of Lucy's wrath, but rather to escape becoming a butcher, the occupation selected for him by his father. At the as yet non-existent Globe in 1581 there was no stage, only a courtyard. 'My first duties', the shade recalled, 'were connected with preparation, cleaning the yard and seats, and putting them in order. ... I was receiving so little from an unwilling father, that I had to increase my earnings; and so, being accustomed to horses, I held them while the spectators came.'[17] In 1583 Shakespeare met Oxford, who advised the young actor (as he then was) to set down on paper some of the stories rattling around in his brain. From these beginnings ensued the collaboration of the nobleman and the rustic. Will contributed the villains – Shylock and Iago and Edmund – and the scenes of great passion and simple English humour. To Oxford we owe the more lovable characters and most of the poetry.

All this and much more the *séances* brought to light. Perhaps the most exciting of the disclosures was the location of the priceless play manuscripts. They were buried in Shakespeare's tomb. (Surely the shade is confused – he must mean the grave; it happened so long ago.) One bundle served as the pillow for the corpse, another lay between the hands, a third at the feet; *Hamlet* reposed on the breast. Delia Bacon's intuition had been right after all.

Notes

*   Allen, Dowden's biographer informs us, was selected by Spirit People to be the final unraveller of the Shakespeare Mystery (Edmund Bentley, *Far Horizon* [London, 1951], 148).

1   J. Thomas Looney, *'Shakespeare' Identified in Edward De Vere the Seventeenth Earl of Oxford* (London, 1920), introd., 16.

2   Ibid. 57. I owe this insight to R. C. Churchill, *Shakespeare and his Betters* (London, 1958), 197.

3   Letter of J. Thomas Looney to Charles Wisner Barrell, dated 6 June 1937; printed in *The Shakespeare Fellowship Quarterly*, 5 [1944], 21.

4   Looney, *'Shakespeare' Identified*, 118–19.

5   Ibid. 131.

6   *Aubrey's Brief Lives*, ed. O. L. Dick (London, 1949), 305. This episode, which has escaped the noses of the Oxfordians, is cited by Wadsworth (*The Poacher from Stratford*, 111).

7   Looney, *'Shakespeare' Identified*, 385.

8   Ibid. 211.

9   Ibid. 413.

10   Ibid. 530.

11   Ibid. 509.

12   Eva Turner Clark, *Hidden Allusions in Shakespeare's Plays: A Study of the Oxford Theory Based on the Records of Early Court Revels and Personalities of the Times* (New York, 1931), 603.

13 Dorothy and Charlton Ogburn, *This Star of England: 'William Shakespeare' Man of the Renaissance* (New York, 1952), 1004. This particular aberration is cited by Giles E. Dawson in a withering review; see *Shakespeare Quarterly*, 4 [1953], 165–70.
14 Gerald H. Rendall, *Shakespeare Sonnets and Edward De Vere* (London, 1930), 210.
15 Percy Allen, *Talks with Elizabethans Revealing the Mystery of 'William Shakespeare'* (London, n.d.), 40.
16 Ibid. 32.
17 Ibid. 72–3.

Part II

New Criticism

2   The Naked Babe and the Cloak of Manliness   19
    Cleanth Brooks
3   "Honest" in *Othello*   35
    William Empson
4   "Introductory" Chapter About the Tragedies   50
    Wolfgang Clemen
5   The "New Criticism" and *King Lear*   63
    William R. Keast

N ew Criticism must be considered one of the most significant modes of interpretation produced in the twentieth century – and one of the most misunderstood. Observed from the vantage point of the twenty-first century, this mode of analysis is even more confusing than it was originally, the passage of time and the development of literary studies having distorted rather than clarified it. In the first place, the terminology is disorienting: "New Criticism" seems a misnomer, since it is no longer new, and has not been new since the 1940s. Apart from the adjective, the second obstacle to understanding the critical mode is, oddly enough, a function of its sovereignty in the academy for some three decades. The dominance of New Criticism in the field of literary studies from the end of World War II until about 1975 engendered a series of vigorous responses to it, reactions that tended to caricature its tenets, reduce their complexity, and thus make it more difficult for later readers to appreciate. Every generation of artists and critics exhibits a need to distinguish itself from that which has preceded it, and in the case of New Criticism its progeny attacked the parent with exceptional virulence and even scorn. Since this dispute was a fight for control of the discipline of English, it is not surprising that Shakespeare's plays and poems often served as battlefields in the struggle.

The method began to emerge in the 1920s, gaining prominence especially in the United States, although I. A. Richards promoted a related kind of practical criticism in Britain. In 1941 John Crowe Ransom fixed the phrase by publishing a book called *The New Criticism*. In the early days the newness of the New Criticism owed something to the promotional skills of its early proponents: Ransom, Allen Tate, Cleanth Brooks, and others deliberately set out to transform literary scholarship, and they did so by setting themselves apart from, and declaring their new approach superior to, the prevailing historical–philological method. In other words, the excitement and controversy generated by the New Criticism consisted in its being seen as revolutionary; no one had looked at literature in quite this way before. The most striking innovation was the way the New Critics discarded as irrelevant to interpretation those linguistic, historical, and biographical contexts that had (more or less) always attended and even dominated the study and appreciation of literary works. By the time New Criticism was named, the principles on which the practice rested had already become familiar, especially with the publication in 1938 of Cleanth Brooks and Robert Penn Warren's influential anthology, *Understanding Poetry*. Those tenets had by then also become the subject of fierce controversy.

So much misrepresentation and counter-response has created an environment in which it is likely that no two people would summarize the doctrines of New Criticism in exactly the same way, but one might begin by describing it as a species of formalism, as a critical practice that concentrates attention on the *form* of the work and that identifies the meaning of the poem or play with the form in which it is inscribed. Structure and significance are inseparable. The work is organic. Put simply, the aim of the New Critic was to examine the poem as a poem, as an object. The term that has come to be applied to the method is *autotelic*, "having or being an end or purpose in itself" (*OED*). The goal of objectivity, however, made the practice unusually liable to disagreement and caricature: Terry Eagleton, for example, asserts that "what New Criticism did, in fact, was to convert the poem into a fetish."[1]

For the New Critic, the process of critical analysis was chiefly a search for unifying factors in the literary object. As Cleanth Brooks wrote in 1951, "the primary concern of criticism is with the problem of unity – the kind of whole which the literary work forms or fails to form, and the relation of the various parts to each other in building up this whole."[2] From this focus on unity most of the principal New Critical goals and characteristics proceed. These include, among others, a reverence for irony, particularly in the form of paradox; a related delight in ambiguity; a veneration of metaphor, with a concomitant belief in the symbolic function of literary art; a conviction that form and content are inseparable. The charge that the New Critics were heedless of context, particularly historical circumstance or biographical data, is only partly true. All the original New Critics were well educated and entirely familiar with history and biography. As a reaction against a style of criticism that had emphasized context to the exclusion of almost anything else, however, their rhetoric seemed to ignore history and biography in favor of attention to the structure and the mechanics of the poem. On this point it is helpful to recall that many of the New Critics – Allen Tate, John Crowe Ransom, and others – were themselves poets. Devoted as they were to a creative discipline, they were attracted to the products of that discipline and the nature of those products, not to the surroundings of those products and not to their creators. Every critical decision requires a choice of focus, and thus every emphasis entails a corresponding passing over. Taking for granted knowledge of external information allowed the critic to devote undivided attention to the language of the poem, particularly to the "examination of metaphor – the structure most characteristic of concentrated poetry."[3]

Shakespeare has been intertwined with New Criticism from its beginnings, not least because he supplied the promoters of the new school with an immediate authority. His texts also provided a hospitable laboratory for testing the main instruments of the method. It quickly became clear, even to most of the New Critics themselves, that their system produced its most impressive results in the study of the lyric poem – a relatively brief, obviously self-contained object, "a well-wrought urn," in Brooks's own metaphor borrowed from John Donne. Naturally such critics favored the dense, witty lyrics of the metaphysical poets, especially Donne and company. Herbert was in, Milton out: *Paradise Lost* was not the ideal testing ground for New Criticism. Shakespeare's plays, their length and theatrical status notwithstanding, responded favorably to the search for imagery, wordplay, irony, ambiguity, coherence, and most of the other features that the New Critics prized. His work also supplied them with another feature that made it irresistible – an unfailing taste for antithesis. Helen Vendler, a celebrated close reader whose sophisticated formalism owes much to New Criticism, has remarked of Shakespeare that "his mind operates always by antithesis. As soon as he thinks of one thing, he thinks of something that is different from it."[4] The poetic dramatist's fondness for antitheses of all kinds – thematic, scenic, metrical, tonal – makes his verse especially welcoming to the reader bent on recognizing contradiction. Shakespeare's insistence that the audience entertain conflicting viewpoints is naturally consonant with the New Critical devotion to ambiguity.

Cleanth Brooks's "The Naked Babe and the Cloak of Manliness" is one of the cardinal texts of New Criticism, a vigorous articulation and celebration of the patterns of images and metaphors in *Macbeth*. The work of such critics as Caroline Spurgeon and Wolfgang Clemen, while not precisely New Critical, was indispensable to the movement and quickly came to be identified, justly or not, with the New Critical program. William Empson represents something of a special case, first because he is British rather than American (New Criticism being chiefly an American phenomenon); and second because his work is so idiosyncratic that it conforms to no doctrine, not that of the New Critics or anybody else but himself. But New Criticism depended heavily on the skill of close reading, particularly the connection of textual minutiae with larger patterns and ideas, and since Empson is one of the closest of close readers, perhaps the most prodigious of all, his work was often and still is usually classified with New Criticism, often over Empson's own objections. His particular gift, well displayed in the extended excerpt from *The Structure of Complex Words*, is his uncanny sensitivity to wordplay and his taste for multiple signification.

The final essay in this section, William Keast's "The 'New Criticism' and *King Lear*," is included for at least three reasons. In the first place, it demonstrates forcefully that New Criticism, while it may have dominated the academy in the 1950s, was not without foes. Writing from the perspective of the Chicago or neo-Aristotelian school, the approach associated especially with R. S. Crane and some of his Chicago colleagues,

Keast objects to Robert B. Heilman's reading of *King Lear* at every critical turn. Second, he lays into Heilman with a virulence so fierce that one seems to be witnessing an early skirmish in the theory wars of the 1980s. Ways of reading literature provoked exceptionally strong feeling, even in the supposedly placid 1950s. Third, the refutation is so specific and careful that the reader finds it easy to follow even without knowing the essay to which it responds.

What does not appear in this book is an example of the mechanical formal studies that descended from the work of Brooks, Empson, and others – the debased form of the New Criticism. In many of these narrow, tendentious readings characteristic of the 1950s and 1960s, the critic identifies a theme and assigns it a pattern of imagery, or vice versa; the cooperation of idea and technique is easily demonstrated, and the case is quickly closed. The totalizing dismissals of New Criticism routinely heard in late-twentieth-century critical discourse derive from this debased stereotype, and most readers will already be familiar with some examples.

Notes

1   *Literary Theory: An Introduction* (Minneapolis: University of Minnesota Press, 1983), p. 49.
2   "The Formalist Critics," *Kenyon Review*, 13 (1951), p. xxx.
3   William K. Wimsatt, "The Structure of the Concrete Universal," from *The Verbal Icon* (University of Kentucky Press, 1954), p. 79.
4   *The Art of Shakespeare's Sonnets* (Cambridge, MA: Harvard University Press, 1997), p. 35.

2

The Naked Babe and the Cloak of Manliness

Cleanth Brooks

T he debate about the proper limits of metaphor has perhaps never been carried on in so spirited a fashion as it has been within the last twenty-five years. The tendency has been to argue for a much wider extension of those limits than critics like Dr. Johnson, say, were willing to allow – one wider even than the Romantic poets were willing to allow. Indeed, some alarm has been expressed of late, in one quarter or another, lest John Donne's characteristic treatment of metaphor be taken as the type and norm, measured against which other poets must, of necessity, come off badly. Yet, on the whole, I think that it must be conceded that the debate on metaphor has been stimulating and illuminating – and not least so with reference to those poets who lie quite outside the tradition of metaphysical wit.

Since the "new criticism," so called, has tended to center around the rehabilitation of Donne, and the Donne tradition, the latter point, I believe, needs to be emphasized. Actually, it would be a poor rehabilitation which, if exalting Donne above all his fellow poets, in fact succeeded in leaving him quite as much isolated from the rest of them as he was before. What the new awareness of the importance of metaphor – if it is actually new, and if its character is really that of a freshened awareness – what this new awareness of metaphor results in when applied to poets other than Donne and his followers is therefore a matter of first importance. Shakespeare provides, of course, the supremely interesting case.

But there are some misapprehensions to be avoided at the outset. We tend to associate Donne with the self-conscious and witty figure – his comparison of the souls of the lovers to the two legs of the compass is the obvious example. Shakespeare's extended figures are elaborated in another fashion. They are, we are inclined to feel, spontaneous comparisons struck out in the heat of composition, and not carefully articulated, self-conscious conceits at all. Indeed, for the average reader the connection between spontaneity and seriously imaginative poetry is so strong that he will probably reject as preposterous any account of Shakespeare's poetry which sees an elaborate pattern in the imagery. He will reject it because to accept it means for him the assumption that the writer was not a fervent poet but a preternaturally cold and self-conscious monster.

Poems are certainly not made by formula and blueprint. One rightly holds suspect a critical interpretation that implies that they are. Shakespeare, we may be sure, was no such monster of calculation. But neither, for that matter, was Donne. Even in Donne's poetry, the elaborated and logically developed comparisons are outnumbered by the abrupt and succinct comparisons – by what T. S. Eliot has called the "telescoped conceits." Moreover, the extended comparisons themselves are frequently knit together in the sudden and apparently uncalculated fashion of the telescoped images; and if one examines the way in which the famous compass comparison is related to the rest of the poem in which it occurs, he may feel that even this elaborately "logical" figure was probably the result of a happy accident.

The truth of the matter is that we know very little of the various poets' methods of composition, and that what may seem to us the product of deliberate choice may well have been as "spontaneous" as anything else in the poem. Certainly, the general vigor of metaphor in the Elizabethan period – as testified to by pamphlets, sermons, and plays – should warn us against putting the literature of that period at the mercy of our own personal theories of poetic composition. In any case, we shall probably speculate to better advantage – if speculate we must – on the possible significant interrelations of image with image rather than on the possible amount of pen-biting which the interrelations may have cost the author.

I do not intend, however, to beg the case by oversimplifying the relation between Shakespeare's intricate figures and Donne's. There are most important differences; and, indeed, Shakespeare's very similarities to the witty poets will, for many readers, tell against the thesis proposed here. For those instances in which Shakespeare most obviously resembles the witty poets occur in the earlier plays or in *Venus and Adonis* and *The Rape of Lucrece*; and these we are inclined to dismiss as early experiments – trial pieces from the Shakespearean workshop. We demand, quite properly, instances from the great style of the later plays.

Still, we will do well not to forget the witty examples in the poems and earlier plays. They indicate that Shakespeare is in the beginning not too far removed from Donne, and that, for certain effects at least, he was willing to play with the witty comparison. Dr. Johnson, in teasing the metaphysical poets for their fanciful conceits on the subject of tears, might well have added instances from Shakespeare. One remembers, for example, from *Venus and Adonis*:

> O, how her eyes and tears did lend and borrow!
> Her eyes seen in her tears, tears in her eye;
> Both crystals, where they view'd each other's sorrow …

Or, that more exquisite instance which Shakespeare, perhaps half-smiling, provided for the King in *Love's Labor's Lost*:

> So sweet a kiss the golden sun gives not
> To those fresh morning drops upon the rose,

As thy eye-beams, when their fresh rays have smote
The night of dew that on my cheeks down flows:
Nor shines the silver moon one half so bright
Through the transparent bosom of the deep,
As does thy face through tears of mine give light:
Thou shin'st in every tear that I do weep,
No drop but as a coach doth carry thee:
So ridest thou triumphing in my woe.
Do but behold the tears that swell in me,
And they thy glory through my grief will show:
But do not love thyself – then thou wilt keep
My tears for glasses, and still make me weep.

But Berowne, we know, at the end of the play, foreswears all such

Taffeta phrases, silken terms precise,
Three-piled hyperboles, spruce affectation,
Figures pedantical ...

in favor of "russet yeas and honest kersey noes." It is sometimes assumed that Shakespeare did the same thing in his later dramas, and certainly the epithet "taffeta phrases" does not describe the great style of *Macbeth* and *Lear*. Theirs is assuredly of a tougher fabric. But "russet" and "honest kersey" do not describe it either. The weaving was not so simple as that.

The weaving was very intricate indeed – if anything, *more* rather than *less* intricate than that of *Venus and Adonis*, though obviously the pattern was fashioned in accordance with other designs, and yielded other kinds of poetry. But in suggesting that there is a real continuity between the imagery of *Venus and Adonis*, say, and that of a play like *Macbeth*, I am glad to be able to avail myself of Coleridge's support. I refer to the remarkable fifteenth chapter of the *Biographia*.

There Coleridge stresses not the beautiful tapestry-work – the purely visual effect – of the images, but quite another quality. He suggests that Shakespeare was prompted by a secret dramatic instinct to realize, in the imagery itself, that "constant intervention and running comment by tone, look and gesture" ordinarily provided by the actor, and that Shakespeare's imagery becomes under this prompting "a series and never broken chain ... always vivid and, because unbroken, often minute ... " Coleridge goes on, a few sentences later, to emphasize further "the perpetual activity of attention required on the part of the reader, ... the rapid flow, the quick change, and the playful nature of the thoughts and images."

These characteristics, Coleridge hastens to say, are not in themselves enough to make superlative poetry. "They become proofs of original genius only as far as they are modified by a predominant passion; or by associated thoughts or images awakened by that passion; or when they have the effect of reducing multitude to unity, or succession to an instant; or lastly, when a human and intellectual life is transferred to them from the poet's own spirit."

Of the intellectual vigor which Shakespeare possessed, Coleridge then proceeds to speak – perhaps extravagantly. But he goes on to say: "In Shakespeare's *poems*, the creative power and the intellectual energy wrestle as in a war embrace. Each in its excess of strength seems to threaten the extinction of the other."

I am tempted to gloss Coleridge's comment here, perhaps too heavily, with remarks taken from Chapter XIII where he discusses the distinction between the Imagination and the Fancy – the modifying and creative power, on the one hand, and on the other, that "mode of Memory" … "blended with, and modified by … Choice." But if in *Venus and Adonis* and *The Rape of Lucrece* the powers grapple "in a war embrace," Coleridge goes on to pronounce: "At length, in the *Drama* they were reconciled, and fought each with its shield before the breast of the other."

It is a noble metaphor. I believe that it is also an accurate one, and that it comprises one of the most brilliant insights ever made into the nature of the dramatic poetry of Shakespeare's mature style. If it is accurate, we shall expect to find, even in the mature poetry, the "never broken chain" of images, "always vivid and, because unbroken, often minute," but we shall expect to find the individual images, not mechanically linked together in the mode of Fancy, but organically related, modified by "a predominant passion," and mutually modifying each other.

T. S. Eliot has remarked that "The difference between imagination and fancy, in view of [the] poetry of wit, is a very narrow one." If I have interpreted Coleridge correctly, he is saying that in Shakespeare's greatest work, the distinction lapses altogether – or rather, that one is caught up and merged in the other. As his latest champion, I. A. Richards, observes: "Coleridge often insisted – and would have insisted still more often had he been a better judge of his reader's capacity for misunderstanding – that Fancy and Imagination are not exclusive of, or inimical to, one another."

I began by suggesting that our reading of Donne might contribute something to our reading of Shakespeare, though I tried to make plain the fact that I had no design of trying to turn Shakespeare into Donne, or – what I regard as nonsense – of trying to exalt Donne above Shakespeare. I have in mind specifically some such matter as this: that since the *Songs and Sonets* of Donne, no less than *Venus and Adonis*, requires a "perpetual activity of attention … on the part of the reader from the rapid flow, the quick change, and the playful nature of the thoughts and images," the discipline gained from reading Donne may allow us to see more clearly the survival of such qualities in the later style of Shakespeare. And, again, I have in mind some such matter as this: that if a reading of Donne has taught us that the "rapid flow, the quick change, and the playful nature of the thoughts and images" – qualities which we are all too prone to associate merely with the fancy – can, on occasion, take on imaginative power, we may, thus taught, better appreciate details in Shakespeare which we shall otherwise dismiss as merely fanciful, or, what is more likely, which we shall simply ignore altogether.

With Donne, of course, the chains of imagery, "always vivid" and "often minute" are perfectly evident. For many readers they are all too evident. The difficulty is not to prove that they exist, but that, on occasion, they may subserve a more imaginative unity. With Shakespeare, the difficulty may well be to prove that the chains exist at all. In general, we may say, Shakespeare has made it relatively easy for his admirers to choose what they like and neglect what they like. What he gives on one or another level is usually so magnificent that the reader finds it easy to ignore other levels.

Yet there are passages not easy to ignore and on which even critics with the conventional interests have been forced to comment. One of these passages occurs in

Macbeth, Act I, scene vii, where Macbeth compares the pity for his victim-to-be, Duncan, to

> a naked new-born babe,
> Striding the blast, or heaven's cherubim, hors'd
> Upon the sightless couriers of the air ...

The comparison is odd, to say the least. Is the babe natural or supernatural – an ordinary, helpless baby, who, as newborn, could not, of course, even toddle, much less stride the blast? Or is it some infant Hercules, quite capable of striding the blast, but, since it is powerful and not helpless, hardly the typical pitiable object?

Shakespeare seems bent upon having it both ways – and, if we read on through the passage – bent upon having the best of both worlds; for he proceeds to give us the option: pity is like the babe "or heaven's cherubim" who quite appropriately, of course, do ride the blast. Yet, even if we waive the question of the legitimacy of the alternative (of which Shakespeare so promptly avails himself), is the cherubim comparison really any more successful than is the babe comparison? Would not one of the great warrior archangels be more appropriate to the scene than the cherub? Does Shakespeare mean for pity or for fear of retribution to be dominant in Macbeth's mind?

Or is it possible that Shakespeare could not make up his own mind? Was he merely writing hastily and loosely, and letting the word "pity" suggest the typically pitiable object, the babe naked in the blast, and then, stirred by the vague notion that some threat to Macbeth should be hinted, using "heaven's cherubim" – already suggested by "babe" – to convey the hint? Is the passage vague or precise? Loosely or tightly organized? Comments upon the passage have ranged all the way from one critic's calling it "pure rant, and intended to be so" to another's laudation: "Either like a mortal babe, terrible in helplessness; or like heaven's angel-children, mighty in love and compassion. This magnificent passage ..."

An even more interesting, and perhaps more disturbing passage in the play is that in which Macbeth describes his discovery of the murder:

> Here lay Duncan,
> His silver skin lac'd with his golden blood;
> And his gash'd stabs, look'd like a breach in nature
> For ruin's wasteful entrance: there, the murderers,
> Steep'd in the colours of their trade, their daggers
> Unmannerly breech'd with gore ...

It is amusing to watch the textual critics, particularly those of the eighteenth century, fight a stubborn rearguard action against the acceptance of "breech'd." Warburton emended "breech'd" to "reech'd"; Johnson, to "drench'd"; Seward, to "hatch'd." Other critics argued that the *breeches* implied were really the handles of the daggers, and that, accordingly, "breech'd" actually here meant "sheathed." The Variorum page witnesses the desperate character of the defense, but the position has had to be yielded, after all. *The Shakespeare Glossary* defines "breech'd" as meaning "covered as with breeches," and thus leaves the poet committed to a reading which must still shock the average reader as much as it shocked that nineteenth-century critic who pronounced upon it as follows: "A metaphor must not be far-fetched nor dwell upon the details of a disgusting picture, as in these lines. There is little, and that far-fetched, similarity between *gold lace* and *blood,* or between *bloody daggers* and *breech'd legs.* The slightness of the similarity, recalling the greatness of the dissimilarity, disgusts us with the attempted comparison."

The two passages are not of the utmost importance, I dare say, though the speeches (of which each is a part) are put in Macbeth's mouth and come at moments of great dramatic tension in the play. Yet, in neither case is there any warrant for thinking that Shakespeare was not trying to write as well as he could. Moreover, whether we like it or not, the imagery is fairly typical of Shakespeare's mature style. Either passage ought to raise some qualms among those who retreat to Shakespeare's authority when they seek to urge the claims of "noble simplicity." They are hardly simple. Yet it is possible that such passages as these may illustrate another poetic resource, another type of imagery which, even in spite of its apparent violence and complication, Shakespeare could absorb into the total structure of his work.

Shakespeare, I repeat, is not Donne – is a much greater poet than Donne; yet the example of his typical handling of imagery will scarcely render support to the usual attacks on Donne's imagery – for, with regard to the two passages in question, the second one, at any rate, is about as strained as Donne is at his most extreme pitch.

Yet I think that Shakespeare's daggers attired in their bloody breeches can be defended as poetry, and as characteristically Shakespearean poetry. Furthermore, both this passage and that about the newborn babe, it seems to me, are far more than excrescences, mere extravagances of detail: each, it seems to me, contains a central symbol of the play, and symbols which we must understand if we are to understand either the detailed passage or the play as a whole.

If this be true, then more is at stake than the merit of the quoted lines taken as lines. (The lines as constituting mere details of a larger structure could, of course, be omitted in the acting of the play without seriously damaging the total effect of the tragedy – though this argument obviously cuts two ways. Whole scenes, and admittedly fine scenes, might also be omitted – have in fact *been* omitted – without quite destroying the massive structure of the tragedy.) What is at stake is the whole matter of the relation of Shakespeare's imagery to the total structures of the plays themselves.

I should like to use the passages as convenient points of entry into the larger symbols which dominate the play. They *are* convenient because, even if we judge them to be faulty, they demonstrate how obsessive for Shakespeare the symbols were – they demonstrate how far the conscious (or unconscious) symbolism could take him.

If we see how the passages are related to these symbols, and they to the tragedy as a whole, the main matter is achieved; and having seen this, if we still prefer "to wish the lines away," that, of course, is our privilege. In the meantime, we may have learned something about Shakespeare's methods – not merely of building metaphors – but of encompassing his larger meanings.

One of the most startling things which has come out of Miss Spurgeon's book on Shakespeare's imagery is her discovery of the "old clothes" imagery in *Macbeth.* As she points out: "The idea constantly recurs that Macbeth's new honours sit ill upon him, like a loose and badly fitting garment, belonging to someone else." And she goes on to quote passage after passage in which the idea is expressed. But, though we are all in

Miss Spurgeon's debt for having pointed this out, one has to observe that Miss Spurgeon has hardly explored the full implications of her discovery. Perhaps her interest in classifying and cataloguing the imagery of the plays has obscured for her some of the larger and more important relationships. At any rate, for reasons to be given below, she has realized only a part of the potentialities of her discovery.

Her comment on the clothes imagery reaches its climax with the following paragraphs:

> And, at the end, when the tyrant is at bay at Dunsinane, and the English troops are advancing, the Scottish lords still have this image in their minds. Caithness sees him as a man vainly trying to fasten a large garment on him with too small a belt:
>
> > He cannot buckle his distemper'd cause
> > Within the belt of rule;
>
> while Angus, in a similar image, vividly sums up the essence of what they all have been thinking ever since Macbeth's accession to power:
>
> > now does he feel his title
> > Hang loose about him, like a giant's robe
> > Upon a dwarfish thief.

This imaginative picture of a small, ignoble man encumbered and degraded by garments unsuited to him, should be put against the view emphasized by some critics (notably Coleridge and Bradley) of the likeness between Macbeth and Milton's Satan in grandeur and sublimity.

> Undoubtedly Macbeth ... is great, magnificently great ... But he could never be put beside, say, Hamlet or Othello, in nobility of nature; and there *is* an aspect in which he is but a poor, vain, cruel, treacherous creature, snatching ruthlessly over the dead bodies of kinsman and friend at place and power he is utterly unfitted to possess. It is worth remembering that it is thus that Shakespeare, with his unshrinking clarity of vision, repeatedly *sees* him.

But this is to make primary what is only one aspect of the old-clothes imagery! And there is no warrant for interpreting the garment imagery as used by Macbeth's enemies, Caithness and Angus, to mean that *Shakespeare* sees Macbeth as a poor and somewhat comic figure.

The crucial point of the comparison, it seems to me, lies not in the smallness of the man and the largeness of the robes, but rather in the fact that – whether the man be large or small – these are not *his* garments; in Macbeth's case they are actually stolen garments. Macbeth is uncomfortable in them because he is continually conscious of the fact that they do not belong to him. There is a further point, and it is one of the utmost importance; the oldest symbol for the hypocrite is that of the man who cloaks his true nature under a disguise. Macbeth loathes playing the part of the hypocrite – and actually does not play it too well. If we keep this in mind as we look back at the instances of the garment images which Miss Spurgeon has collected for us, we shall see that the pattern of imagery becomes very rich indeed. Macbeth says in Act I:

> The Thane of Cawdor lives: why do you dress me
> In borrow'd robes?

Macbeth at this point wants no honors that are not honestly his. Banquo says in Act I:

> New honours come upon him,
> Like our strange garments, cleave not to their mould,
> But with the aid of use.

But Banquo's remark, one must observe, is not censorious. It is indeed a compliment to say of one that he wears new honors with some awkwardness. The observation becomes ironical only in terms of what is to occur later.

Macbeth says in Act I:

> He hath honour'd me of late; and I have bought
> Golden opinions from all sorts of people,
> Which would be worn now in their newest gloss,
> Not cast aside so soon.

Macbeth here is proud of his new clothes: he is happy to wear what he has truly earned. It is the part of simple good husbandry not to throw aside these new garments and replace them with robes stolen from Duncan.

But Macbeth has already been wearing Duncan's garments in anticipation, as his wife implies in the metaphor with which she answers him:

> Was the hope drunk,
> Wherein you dress'd yourself?

(The metaphor may seem hopelessly mixed, and a full and accurate analysis of such mixed metaphors in terms of the premises of Shakespeare's style waits upon some critic who will have to consider not only this passage but many more like it in Shakespeare.) For our purposes here, however, one may observe that the psychological line, the line of the basic symbolism, runs on unbroken. A man dressed in a drunken hope is garbed in strange attire indeed – a ridiculous dress which accords thoroughly with the contemptuous picture that Lady Macbeth wishes to evoke. Macbeth's earlier dream of glory has been a drunken fantasy merely, if he flinches from action now.

But the series of garment metaphors which run through the play is paralleled by a series of masking or cloaking images which – if we free ourselves of Miss Spurgeon's rather mechanical scheme of classification – show themselves to be merely variants of the garments which hide none too well his disgraceful self. He is consciously hiding that self throughout the play.

"False face must hide what the false heart doth know," he counsels Lady Macbeth before the murder of Duncan; and later, just before the murder of Banquo, he invokes night to "Scarf up the eye of pitiful day."

One of the most powerful of these cloaking images is given to Lady Macbeth in the famous speech in Act I:

> Come, thick night,
> And pall thee in the dunnest smoke of hell,
> That my keen knife see not the wound it makes,
> Nor heaven peep through the blanket of the dark,
> To cry, "Hold, Hold!"

I suppose that it is natural to conceive the "keen knife" here as held in her own hand. Lady Macbeth is capable of wielding it. And in this interpretation, the imagery is thoroughly significant. Night is to be doubly black so that not even her knife may see the wound it makes. But I think that there is good warrant for regarding her "keen knife" as Macbeth himself. She has just, a few lines above, given her analysis of Macbeth's character as one who would "not play false, / And yet [would] wrongly win." To bring him to the point of action, she will have to "chastise [him] with the valour of [her] tongue." There is good reason, then, for her to invoke night to become blacker still – to pall itself in the "dunnest smoke of hell." For night must not only screen the deed from the eye of heaven – conceal it at least until it is too late for heaven to call out to Macbeth "Hold, Hold!" Lady Macbeth would have night blanket the deed from the hesitant doer. The imagery thus repeats and reinforces the substance of Macbeth's anguished aside uttered in the preceding scene:

> Let not light see my black and deep desires;
> The eye wink at the hand; yet let that be
> Which the eye fears, when it is done, to see.

I do not know whether "blanket" and "pall" qualify as garment metaphors in Miss Spurgeon's classification: yet one is the clothing of sleep, and the other, the clothing of death – they are the appropriate garments of night; and they carry on an important aspect of the general clothes imagery. It is not necessary to attempt to give here an exhaustive list of instances of the garment metaphor; but one should say a word about the remarkable passage in II, iii.

Here, after the discovery of Duncan's murder, Banquo says

> And when we have our naked frailties hid,
> That suffer in exposure, let us meet,
> And question this most bloody piece of work –

that is, "When we have clothed ourselves against the chill morning air, let us meet to discuss this bloody piece of work." Macbeth answers, as if his subconscious mind were already taking Banquo's innocent phrase, "naked frailties," in a deeper, ironic sense:

> Let's briefly put on manly readiness …

It is ironic; for the "manly readiness" which he urges the other lords to put on, is, in his own case, a hypocrite's garment: he can only pretend to be the loyal, grief-stricken liege who is almost unstrung by the horror of Duncan's murder.

But the word "manly" carries still a further ironic implication: earlier, Macbeth had told Lady Macbeth that he dared

> do all that may become a man;
> Who dares do more is none.

Under the weight of her reproaches of cowardice, however, he *has* dared do more, and has become less than a man, a beast. He has already laid aside, therefore, one kind of "manly readiness" and has assumed another: he has garbed himself in a sterner composure than that which he counsels to his fellows – the hard and inhuman "manly readiness" of the resolved murderer.

The clothes imagery, used sometimes with emphasis on one aspect of it, sometimes, on another, does pervade the play. And it should be evident that the daggers "breech'd with gore" – though Miss Spurgeon does not include the passage in her examples of clothes imagery – represent one more variant of this general symbol. Consider the passage once more:

> Here lay Duncan,
> His silver skin lac'd with his golden blood;
> And his gash'd stabs look'd like a breach in nature
> For ruin's wasteful entrance: there, the murderers,
> Steep'd in the colours of their trade, their daggers
> Unmannerly breech'd with gore ...

The clothes imagery runs throughout the passage; the body of the king is dressed in the most precious of garments, the blood royal itself; and the daggers too are dressed – in the same garment. The daggers, "naked" except for their lower parts which are reddened with blood, are like men in "unmannerly" dress – men, naked except for their red breeches, lying beside the red-handed grooms. The figure, though vivid, is fantastic; granted. But the basis for the comparison is *not* slight and adventitious. The metaphor fits the real situation on the deepest levels. As Macbeth and Lennox burst into the room, they find the daggers wearing, as Macbeth knows all too well, a horrible masquerade. They have been carefully "clothed" to play a part. They are not honest daggers, honorably naked in readiness to guard the king, or, "mannerly" clothed in their own sheaths. Yet the disguise which they wear will enable Macbeth to assume the robes of Duncan – robes to which he is no more entitled than are the daggers to the royal garments which they now wear, grotesquely.

The reader will, of course, make up his own mind as to the value of the passage. But the metaphor in question, in the light of the other garment imagery, cannot be dismissed as merely a strained ingenuity, irrelevant to the play. And the reader who *does* accept it as poetry will probably be that reader who knows the play best, not the reader who knows it slightly and regards Shakespeare's poetry as a rhetoric more or less loosely draped over the "content" of the play.

And now what can be said of pity, the "naked newborn babe"? Though Miss Spurgeon does not note it (since the governing scheme of her book would have hardly allowed her to see it), there are, by the way, a great many references to babes in this play – references which occur on a number of levels. The babe appears sometimes as a character, such as Macduff's child; sometimes as a symbol, like the crowned babe and the bloody babe which are raised by the witches on the occasion of Macbeth's visit to them; sometimes, in a metaphor, as in the passage under discussion. The number of such references can hardly be accidental; and the babe turns out to be, as a matter of fact, perhaps the most powerful symbol in the tragedy.

But to see this fully, it will be necessary to review the motivation of the play. The stimulus to Duncan's murder, as we know, was the prophecy of the Weird Sisters. But Macbeth's subsequent career of bloodshed stems from the same prophecy. Macbeth was to have the crown, but the crown was to pass to Banquo's children. The second part of the prophecy troubles Macbeth from the start. It does not oppress him, however, until the crown has been won. But from this point on, the effect of the prophecy is to hurry Macbeth into action and more action until he is finally precipitated into ruin.

We need not spend much time in speculating on whether Macbeth, had he been content with Duncan's murder, had he tempted fate no further, had he been willing to court the favor of his nobles, might not have died peaceably in bed. We are dealing, not with history, but with a play. Yet, even in history the usurper sometimes succeeds; and he sometimes succeeds on the stage. Shakespeare himself knew of, and wrote plays about, usurpers who successfully maintained possession of the crown. But, in any case, this much is plain: the train of murders into which Macbeth launches aggravates suspicions of his guilt and alienates the nobles.

Yet, a Macbeth who could act once, and then settle down to enjoy the fruits of this one attempt to meddle with the future would, of course, not be Macbeth. For it is not merely his great imagination and his warrior courage in defeat which redeem him for tragedy and place him beside the other great tragic protagonists: rather, it is his attempt to conquer the future, an attempt involving him, like Oedipus, in a desperate struggle with fate itself. It is this which holds our imaginative sympathy, even after he has degenerated into a bloody tyrant and has become the slayer of Macduff's wife and children.

To sum up, there can be no question that Macbeth stands at the height of his power after his murder of Duncan, and that the plan – as outlined by Lady Macbeth – has been relatively successful. The road turns toward disaster only when Macbeth decides to murder Banquo. Why does he make this decision? Shakespeare has pointed up the basic motivation very carefully:

> Then prophet-like,
> They hail'd him father to a line of kings.
> Upon my head they plac'd a fruitless crown,
> And put a barren sceptre in my gripe,
> Thence to be wrench'd with an unlineal hand,
> No son of mine succeeding. If't be so,
> For Banquo's issue have I fil'd my mind;
> For them the gracious Duncan have I murder'd;
> Put rancours in the vessel of my peace
> Only for them; and mine eternal jewel
> Given to the common enemy of man,
> To make them kings, the seed of Banquo kings!

Presumably, Macbeth had entered upon his course from sheer personal ambition. Ironically, it is the more human part of Macbeth – his desire to have more than a limited personal satisfaction, his desire to found a line, his wish to pass something on to later generations – which prompts him to dispose of Banquo. There is, of course, a resentment against Banquo, but that resentment is itself closely related to Macbeth's desire to found a dynasty. Banquo, who has risked nothing, who has remained upright, who has not defiled himself, will have kings for children; Macbeth, none. Again, ironically, the Weird Sisters who have given Macbeth, so he has thought, the priceless gift of knowledge of the future, have given the real future to Banquo.

So Banquo's murder is decided upon, and accomplished. But Banquo's son escapes, and once more, the future has eluded Macbeth. The murder of Banquo thus becomes almost meaningless. This general point may be obvious enough, but we shall do well to note some of the further ways in which Shakespeare has pointed up the significance of Macbeth's war with the future.

When Macbeth, at the beginning of Scene vii, Act I, contemplates Duncan's murder, it is the future over which he agonizes:

> If it were done, when 'tis done, then 'twere well
> It were done quickly; if the assassination
> Could trammel up the consequence, and catch
> With his surcease success; that but this blow
> Might be the be-all and the end-all here ...

But the continuum of time cannot be partitioned off; the future is implicit in the present. There is no net strong enough to trammel up the consequence – not even in this world.

Lady Macbeth, of course, has fewer qualms. When Macbeth hesitates to repudiate the duties which he owes Duncan – duties which, by some accident of imagery perhaps – I hesitate to press the significance – he has earlier actually called "children" – Lady Macbeth cries out that she is willing to crush her own child in order to gain the crown:

> I have given suck, and know
> How tender 'tis to love the babe that milks me;
> I would, while it was smiling in my face,
> Have pluck'd my nipple from his boneless gums
> And dash'd the brains out, had I so sworn as you
> Have done to this.

Robert Penn Warren has made the penetrating observation that all of Shakespeare's villains are rationalists. Lady Macbeth is certainly of their company. She knows what she wants; and she is ruthless in her consideration of means. She will always "catch the nearest way." This is not to say that she ignores the problem of scruples, or that she is ready to oversimplify psychological complexities. But scruples are to be used to entangle one's enemies. One is not to become tangled in the mesh of scruples himself. Even though she loves her husband and though her ambition for herself is a part of her ambition for him, still she seems willing to consider even Macbeth at times as pure instrument, playing upon his hopes and fears and pride.

Her rationalism is quite sincere. She is apparently thoroughly honest in declaring that

> The sleeping and the dead
> Are but as pictures; 'tis the eye of childhood
> That fears a painted devil. If he do bleed,
> I'll gild the faces of the grooms withal,
> For it must seem their guilt.

For her, there is no moral order: *guilt* is something like *gilt* – one can wash it off or paint it on. Her pun is not frivolous and it is deeply expressive.

Lady Macbeth abjures all pity; she is willing to unsex herself; and her continual taunt to Macbeth, when he falters, is that he is acting like a baby – not like a man. This "manhood" Macbeth tries to learn. He is a dogged pupil. For that reason he is almost pathetic when the shallow rationalism which his wife urges upon him fails. His tone is almost one of puzzled bewilderment at nature's unfairness in failing to play the game according to the rules – the rules which have applied to other murders:

> the time has been,
> That, when the brains were out, the man would die,
> And there an end; but now they rise again ...

Yet, after the harrowing scene, Macbeth can say, with a sort of dogged weariness:

> Come, we'll to sleep. My strange and self-abuse
> Is the initiate fear that wants hard use:
> We are yet but young in deed.

Ironically, Macbeth is still echoing the dominant metaphor of Lady Macbeth's reproach. He has not yet attained to "manhood"; that *must* be the explanation. He has not yet succeeded in hardening himself into something inhuman.

Tempted by the Weird Sisters and urged on by his wife, Macbeth is thus caught between the irrational and the rational. There is a sense, of course, in which every man is caught between them. Man must try to predict and plan and control his destiny. That is man's fate; and the struggle, if he is to realize himself as a man, cannot be avoided. The question, of course, which has always interested the tragic dramatist involves the terms on which the struggle is accepted and the protagonist's attitude toward fate and toward himself. Macbeth in his general concern for the future is typical – is Every Man. He becomes the typical tragic protagonist when he yields to pride and *hybris*. The occasion for temptation is offered by the prophecy of the Weird Sisters. They offer him knowledge which cannot be arrived at rationally. They offer a key – if only a partial key – to what is otherwise unpredictable. Lady Macbeth, on the other hand, by employing a ruthless clarity of perception, by discounting all emotional claims, offers him the promise of bringing about the course of events which he desires.

Now, in the middle of the play, though he has not lost confidence and though, as he himself says, there can be no turning back, doubts have begun to arise; and he returns to the Weird Sisters to secure unambiguous answers to his fears. But, pathetically and ironically for Macbeth, in returning to the Weird Sisters, he is really trying to impose rationality on what sets itself forth plainly as irrational: that is, Macbeth would force a rigid control on a future which, by definition – by the very fact that the Weird Sisters already know it – stands beyond his manipulation.

It is because of his hopes for his own children and his fears of Banquo's that he has returned to the witches for counsel. It is altogether appropriate, therefore, that two of the apparitions by which their counsel is revealed should be babes, the crowned babe and the bloody babe.

For the babe signifies the future which Macbeth would control and cannot control. It is the unpredictable thing itself – as Yeats has put it magnificently, "The uncontrollable mystery on the bestial floor." It is the one thing that can justify, even in Macbeth's mind, the murders which he has committed. Earlier in the play, Macbeth had declared that if the deed could "trammel up the consequence," he would be willing to "jump the life to come." But he cannot jump the life to come. In his own terms he is betrayed. For it is idle to speak of jumping the life to come if one yearns to found a line of kings. It is the babe that betrays Macbeth – his own babes, most of all.

The logic of Macbeth's distraught mind, thus, forces him to make war on children, a war which in itself reflects his desperation and is a confession of weakness. Macbeth's ruffians, for example, break into Macduff's castle and kill his wife and children. The scene in which the innocent child prattles with his mother about his absent father, and then is murdered, is typical Shakespearean "fourth act" pathos. But the pathos is not adventitious; the scene ties into the inner symbolism of the play. For the child, in its helplessness, defies the murderers. Its defiance testifies to the force which threatens Macbeth and which Macbeth cannot destroy.

But we are not, of course, to placard the child as The Future in a rather stiff and mechanical allegory. *Macbeth* is no such allegory. Shakespeare's symbols are richer and more flexible than that. The babe signifies not only the future; it symbolizes all those enlarging purposes which make life meaningful, and it symbolizes, furthermore, all those emotional and – to Lady Macbeth – irrational ties which make man more than a machine – which render him human. It signifies preeminently the pity which Macbeth, under Lady Macbeth's tutelage, would wean himself of as something "unmanly." Lady Macbeth's great speeches early in the play become brilliantly ironical when we realize that Shakespeare is using the same symbol for the unpredictable future that he uses for human compassion. Lady Macbeth is willing to go to any length to grasp the future: she would willingly dash out the brains of her own child if it stood in her way to that future. But this is to repudiate the future, for the child is its symbol.

Shakespeare does not, of course, limit himself to the symbolism of the child: he makes use of other symbols of growth and development, notably that of the plant. And this plant symbolism patterns itself to reflect the development of the play. For example, Banquo says to the Weird Sisters, early in the play:

> If you can look into the seeds of time,
> And say which grain will grow and which will not,
> Speak then to me …

A little later, on welcoming Macbeth, Duncan says to him:

> I have begun to plant thee, and will labour
> To make thee full of growing.

After the murder of Duncan, Macbeth falls into the same metaphor when he comes to resolve on Banquo's death. The Weird Sisters, he reflects, had hailed Banquo as

> ... father to a line of kings.
> Upon my head they placed a fruitless crown,
> And put a barren sceptre in my gripe ...

Late in the play, Macbeth sees himself as the winter-stricken tree:

> I have liv'd long enough: my way of life
> Is fall'n into the sear, the yellow leaf ...

The plant symbolism, then, supplements the child symbolism. At points it merges with it, as when Macbeth ponders bitterly that he has damned himself.

> To make them kings, the seed of Banquo kings!

And, in at least one brilliant example, the plant symbolism unites with the clothes symbolism. It is a crowning irony that one of the Weird Sisters' prophecies on which Macbeth has staked his hopes is fulfilled when Birnam Wood comes to Dunsinane. For, in a sense, Macbeth is here hoist on his own petard. Macbeth, who has invoked night to "Scarf up the tender eye of pitiful day," and who has, again and again, used the "false face" to "hide what the false heart doth know," here has the trick turned against him. But the garment which cloaks the avengers is the living green of nature itself, and nature seems, to the startled eyes of his sentinels, to be rising up against him.

But it is the babe, the child, that dominates the symbolism. Most fittingly, the last of the prophecies in which Macbeth has placed his confidence, concerns the child: and Macbeth comes to know the final worst when Macduff declares to him that he was not "born of woman" but was from his "mother's womb / Untimely ripp'd." The babe here has defied even the thing which one feels may reasonably be predicted of him – his time of birth. With Macduff's pronouncement, the unpredictable has broken through the last shred of the net of calculation. The future cannot be trammelled up. The naked babe confronts Macbeth to pronounce his doom.

The passage with which we began this essay, then, is an integral part of a larger context, and of a very rich context:

> And pity, like a naked new-born babe,
> Striding the blast, or heaven's cherubim, hors'd
> Upon the sightless couriers of the air,
> Shall blow the horrid deed in every eye,
> That tears shall drown the wind.

Pity is like the naked babe, the most sensitive and helpless thing; yet, almost as soon as the comparison is announced, the symbol of weakness begins to turn into a symbol of strength; for the babe, though newborn, is pictured as "Striding the blast" like an elemental force – like "heaven's cherubim, hors'd / Upon the sightless couriers of the air." We can give an answer to the question put earlier: is Pity like the human and helpless babe, or powerful as the angel that rides the winds? It is both; and it is strong because of its very weakness. The paradox is inherent in the situation itself; and it is the paradox that will destroy the overbrittle rationalism on which Macbeth founds his career.

For what will it avail Macbeth to cover the deed with the blanket of the dark if the elemental forces that ride the winds will blow the horrid deed in every eye? And what will it avail Macbeth to clothe himself in "manliness" – to become bloody, bold, and resolute, – if he is to find himself again and again, viewing his bloody work through the "eye of childhood / That fears a painted devil"? Certainly, the final and climactic appearance of the babe symbol merges all the contradictory elements of the symbol. For, with Macduff's statement about his birth, the naked babe rises before Macbeth as not only the future that eludes calculation but as avenging angel as well.

The clothed daggers and the naked babe – mechanism and life – instrument and end – death and birth – that which should be left bare and clean and that which should be clothed and warmed – these are facets of two of the great symbols which run throughout the play. They are not the only symbols, to be sure; they are not the most obvious symbols: darkness and blood appear more often. But with a flexibility which must amaze the reader, the image of the garment and the image of the babe are so used as to encompass an astonishingly large area of the total situation. And between them – the naked babe, essential humanity, humanity stripped down to the naked thing itself, and yet as various as the future – and the various garbs which humanity assumes, the robes of honor, the hypocrite's disguise, the inhuman "manliness" with which Macbeth endeavors to cover up his essential humanity – between them, they furnish Shakespeare with his most subtle and ironically telling instruments.

3

"Honest" in *Othello*

William Empson

The fifty-two uses of *honest* and *honesty* in *Othello* are a very queer business; there is no other play in which Shakespeare worries a word like that. *King Lear* uses *fool* nearly as often but does not treat it as a puzzle, only as a source of profound metaphors. In *Othello* divergent uses of the key word are found for all the main characters; even the attenuated clown plays on it; the unchaste Bianca, for instance, snatches a moment to claim that she is more honest than Emilia the thief of the handkerchief; and with all the variety of use the ironies on the word mount up steadily to the end. Such is the general power of the writing that this is not obtrusive, but if all but the phrases involving *honest* were in the style of Ibsen the effect would be a symbolical charade. Everybody calls Iago honest once or twice, but with Othello it becomes an obsession; at the crucial moment just before Emilia exposes Iago he keeps howling the word out. The general effect has been fully recognised by critics, but it looks as if there is something to be found about the word itself.

What Shakespeare hated in the word, I believe, was a peculiar use, at once hearty and individualist, which was then common among raffish low people but did not become upper-class till the Restoration; here as in Iago's heroic couplets the play has a curious effect of prophecy. But to put it like this is no doubt to over-simplify; the Restoration use, easy to feel though hard to define, seems really different from its earlier parallels, and in any case does not apply well to Iago. I want here to approach the play without taking for granted the previous analysis. But I hope it has become obvious that the word was in the middle of a rather complicated process of change, and that what emerged from it was a sort of jovial cult of independence. At some stage of the development (whether by the date of *Othello* or not) the word came to have in it a covert assertion that the man who accepts the natural desires, who does not live by principle, will be fit for such warm uses of *honest* as imply "generous" and "faithful to friends", and to believe this is to disbelieve the Fall of Man. Thus the word, apart from being complicated, also came to raise large issues, and it is not I think a wild fancy to suppose that Shakespeare could feel the way it was going.

Four columns of *honest* in the Shakespeare Concordance show that he never once allows the word a simple hearty use between equals. Some low characters get near it, but they are made to throw in contempt. 'An honest fellow enough, and one that loves quails' is said by Thersites in contempt for Ajax; 'honest good fellows' is said by the Nurse in Romeo, but of minstrels that she is turning away; 'as honest a true fellow as any in Bohemia' is from Prince Cloten and to a shepherd; 'I am with thee here and the goats, as the most capricious poet, honest Ovid, was among the Goths' gets its joke from making the clown patronise Ovid. The nearest case is from Desdemona:

> *Emil.:* I warrant it grieves my husband
> As if the case were his.
> *Des.:* Oh, that's an honest fellow.

But Emilia is butting into the talk with Cassio, and Desdemona, in this careless reply to silence her, has a feeling that Iago though reliable and faithful is her social inferior. This indeed is a sufficient reason why Iago talks with irony about the admitted fact that he is "honest"; the patronising use carried an obscure social insult as well as a hint of stupidity. Critics have discussed what the social status of Iago and Emilia would actually be, and have succeeded in making clear that the posts of ancient and gentle-woman-in-waiting might be held by people of very varying status; the audience must use its own judgement. The hints seem to place Iago and his wife definitely enough well below Desdemona but well above Ancient Pistol, say. Now at the same date as the refusal by Shakespeare to employ a flat hearty use of the word, there are uses by Dekker (for example) which only differ from the Restoration ones by coming from people of lower rank or bad reputation. One need not say that Shakespeare always had a conscious policy about the word (more likely the flat hearty use bored him; it was a blank space where one might have had a bit of word play) but his uses of it in *Othello*, when his imagination began to work on the loathsome possibilities of this familiar bit of nonsense, are consistent with his normal practice.

Most people would agree with what Bradley, for example, implied, that the way everybody calls Iago honest amounts to a criticism of the word itself; that is, Shakespeare means "a bluff forthright manner, and amusing talk, which get a man called honest, may go with extreme dishonesty". Or indeed that this is treated as normal, and the satire is on our nature, not on language. But they would probably maintain that Iago is not honest and does not think himself so, and only calls himself so as a lie or an irony. It seems to me, if you leave the matter there, that there is much to be said for what the despised Rymer decided, when the implications of the hearty use of *honest* had become simpler and more clear-cut. He said that the play is ridiculous, because that sort of villain (silly-clever, full of secret schemes, miscalculating about people) does not get mistaken for that sort of honest man. This if true is of course a plain fault, whatever you think about "character-analysis". It is no use taking short cuts in these things, and I should fancy that what Rymer said had a large truth when he said it, and also that Iago was a plausible enough figure in his own time. The only main road into this baffling subject is to find how the characters actually use the term and thereby think about themselves.

I must not gloss over the fact that Iago once uses the word to say that he proposes to tell Othello lies:

> The Moor is of a free and open nature,
> And thinks men honest that but seem to be so.

This is at the end of the first act. And indeed, the first use of the word in the play seems also to mean that Iago does not think himself honest. In his introductory scene with Roderigo, he says of the subservient type of men "whip me such honest knaves"; they are opposed to the independent men like himself – "these fellows have some soul". Later there is a trivial use of the word by Brabantio, but the next important ones do not come till near the end of the act. Then Othello twice calls Iago honest; Iago immediately (to insist on the irony) has a second meeting for plots with Roderigo, and then in soliloquy tells the audience he will cheat Roderigo too. Next he brings out the two lines just quoted; he is enumerating the conditions of his problem, and the dramatic purpose, one may say, is to make certain that nobody in the audience has missed the broad point. The act then closes with "I have it" and the triumphant claim that he has invented the plot. Even here, I think, there is room for an ironical tone in Iago's use of *honest*; he can imply that Othello's notion of honesty is crude as well as his judgements about which people exemplify it. For that matter, Iago may simply be speaking about Cassio, not about himself. He has just said that Cassio is framed to make women false, and he certainly regards the virtues of Cassio as part of his superficial and over-rewarded charm of manner. But I think that, even so, Iago has himself somewhere in view; to claim that he did not would be overstraining my argument. The introductory phrase "honest knaves" is of course a direct irony (made clear by contradiction); it can only mean that Iago has a different idea of honesty from the one that these knaves have. To be sure, you may be meant to think that he is lying by implication, but even so, this is the lie that he must be supposed to tell. However, I do not see that the uses at either end of the act put forward definite alternative meanings for the word; they lay the foundations by making it prominent. It is then, so to speak, "in play" and is used with increasing frequency. The first act has five uses; the second eleven; the third twenty-three; and the last two only six and seven. One might argue that the character of Iago is established in the first act before the verbal ironies are applied to it, since "honest knaves" is only a sort of blank cheque; but even so we learn a good deal more about him later.

Both Iago and Othello oppose honesty to mere truth-telling:

> *Oth.:* I know, Iago,
> Thy honesty and love doth mince this matter,
> Making it light to Cassio …
> *Iago:* It were not for your quiet, nor your good,
> Nor for my manhood, honesty, or wisdom
> To let you know my thoughts.

No doubt the noun tends to be more old-fashioned than the adjective, but anyway the old "honourable" sense is as broad and vague as the new slang one; it was easy enough to be puzzled by the word. Iago means partly 'faithful to friends', which would go with the Restoration use, but partly I think 'chaste', the version normally used of women; what he has to say is improper. Certainly one cannot simply treat his version of *honest* as the Restoration one – indeed, the part of the snarling critic involves a rather puritanical view, at any rate towards other people. It is the two notions of being ready to blow the gaff on other people and frank to yourself about your own desires that seem to me crucial about Iago; they grow on their own, independently of the hearty feeling that would normally humanize them; though he can be a good companion as well.

One need not look for a clear sense when he toys with the word about Cassio; the question is how it came to be so mystifying. But I think a queer kind of honesty is maintained in Iago through all the puzzles he contrives; his emotions are always expressed directly, and it is only because they are clearly genuine ("These stops of thine", Othello tells him, "are close delations, working from the heart") that he can mislead Othello as to their cause.

> *Oth.:* Is he not honest? [Faithful, etc.]
> *Iago:* Honest, my lord? [Not stealing, etc. Shocked]
> *Oth.:* Ay, honest, ["Why repeat? The word is clear enough."]
> *Iago:* My lord, for aught I know ... ["In some sense."]
> *Iago:* For Michael Cassio
> I dare be sworn I think that he is honest.
> *Oth.:* I think so too.
> *Iago:* Men should be what they seem,
> Or, those that be not, would they might seem none.
> *Oth.:* Certain, men should be what they seem.
> *Iago:* Why then, I think that Cassio's an honest man.

Othello has just said that Cassio "went between them very oft", so Iago now learns that Cassio lied to him in front of Brabantio's house when he pretended to know nothing about the marriage. Iago feels he has been snubbed,* as too coarse to be trusted in such a matter, and he takes immediate advantage of his discomposure. The point of his riddles is to get "not hypocritical" – "frank about his own nature" accepted as the relevant sense; Iago will readily call him honest on that basis, and Othello cannot be reassured. 'Chaste' (the sense normally used of women) Cassio is not, but he is 'not a hypocrite' about Bianca. Iago indeed, despises him for letting her make a fool of him in public; for that and for other reasons (Cassio is young and without experience) Iago can put a contemptuous tone into the word; the feeling is genuine, but not the sense it may imply. This gives room for a hint that Cassio has been 'frank' to Iago in private about more things than may honestly be told. I fancy too, that the idea of 'not being men' gives an extra twist. Iago does not think Cassio manly nor that it is specially manly to be chaste; this allows him to agree that Cassio may be honest in the female sense about Desdemona and still keep a tone which seems to deny it – if he is, after so much encouragement, he must be 'effeminate' (there is a strong idea of 'manly' in *honest*, and an irony on that gives its opposite). Anyway, Iago can hide what

---

* Cassio does not call Iago *honest* till he can use the word warmly (ii.iii.108); till then he calls him "good Iago" (ii.i.97, ii.3.34) – apparently a less obtrusive form of the same trick of patronage. Possibly as they have been rivals for his present job he feels it more civil to keep his distance. However the social contempt which he holds in check is hinted jovially to Desdemona (ii.i.165) and comes out plainly when he is drunk; Iago returns the "good" to him and is firmly snubbed for it as not a "man of quality" (ii.iii.108).

reservations he makes but show that he makes reservations; this suggests an embarrassed defence – "Taking a broad view, with the world as it is, and Cassio my friend, I can decently call him honest." This forces home the Restoration idea – "an honest dog of a fellow, straightforward about women", and completes the suspicion. It is a bad piece of writing unless you are keyed up for the shifts of the word.

The play with the feminine version is doubtful here, but he certainly does it the other way round about Desdemona, where it had more point; in the best case it is for his own amusement when alone.

> And what's he then that says I play the villain?
> When this advice is free I give and honest,
> Probal to thinking, and indeed the course
> To win the Moor again? For 'tis most easy
> The inclining Desdemona to subdue
> In any honest suit. She's framed as fruitful
> As the free elements.

Easy, inclining, fruitful, free all push the word the same way, from 'chaste' to 'flat, frank, and natural'; all turn the ironical admission of her virtue into a positive insult against her. The delight in juggling with the word here is close to the Machiavellian interest in plots for their own sake, which Iago could not resist and allowed to destroy him. But a good deal of the 'motive-hunting' of the soliloquies must, I think, be seen as part of Iago's 'honesty'; he is quite open to his own motives or preferences and interested to find out what they are.

The clear cases where Iago thinks himself honest are at a good distance from the Restoration use; they bring him into line with the series of sharp unromantic critics like Jacques and Hamlet:

> For I am nothing if not critical

he tells Desdemona to amuse her; his faults, he tells Othello, are due to an excess of this truthful virtue –

> I confess, it is my nature's plague
> To spy into abuses, and oft my jealousy
> Shapes faults that are not.

There seems no doubt that he believes this and thinks it creditable, whatever policy made him say it here; indeed we know it is true from the soliloquies. Now this kind of man is really very unlike the Restoration 'honest fellow', and for myself I find it hard to combine them in one feeling about the word. But in a great deal of Iago's talk to Roderigo – 'drown thyself! drown cats and blind puppies … why, thou silly gentleman, I will never love thee after' – he is a wise uncle, obviously honest in the cheerful sense, and for some time this is our main impression of him.* It is still strong during the business of making Cassio

---

* It is a very bold and strange irony to make Othello repeat the phrase "love thee after" just before he kills Desdemona.

drunk; there is no reason why he should praise the English for their powers of drinking except to make sure that the groundlings are still on his side.

Perhaps the main connection between the two sorts of honest men is not being indulgent towards romantic love:

> *Oth.:*   I cannot speak enough of this content,
>   It stops me here; it is too much of joy.
>   And this, and this, the greatest discords be
>   That e'er our hearts shall make.
>   (*Kissing her*)
> *Iago:* Oh you are well tun'd now;
>   But I'll set down the peggs that make this Musick,
>   As honest as I am.

The grammar may read 'because I am so honest' as well as 'though I am so honest' and the irony may deny any resultant sense. He is ironical about the suggestions in the patronizing use, which he thinks are applied to him – 'low-class, and stupid, but good-natured'. But he feels himself really 'honest' as the kind of man who can see through nonsense; Othello's affair is a passing lust which has become a nuisance, and Iago can get it out of the way.

It may well be objected that this is far too mild a picture of Iago's plot, and indeed he himself is clearly impressed by its wickedness; at the end of the first act he calls it a "monstrous birth" and invokes Hell to assist it. But after this handsome theatrical effect the second act begins placidly, in a long scene which includes the "As honest as I am" passage, and at the end of this scene we find that Iago still imagines he will only

> Make the Moor thank me, love me, and reward me
> For making him egregiously an ass

– to be sure, the next lines say he will practise on Othello "even to madness", but even this can be fitted into the picture of the clown who makes "fools" of other people; it certainly does not envisage the holocaust of the end of the play. Thinking in terms of character, it is clear that Iago has not yet decided how far he will go.

The suggestion of "stupid" in a patronizing use of *honest* (still clear in 'honest Thompson, my gardener', a Victorian if not a present-day use) brings it near to *fool*; there is a chance for these two rich words to overlap. There is an aspect of Iago in which he is the Restoration "honest fellow", who is good company because he blows the gaff; but much the clearest example of it is in the beginning of the second act, when he is making sport for his betters. While Desdemona is waiting for Othello's ship, which may have been lost in the tempest, he puts on an elaborate piece of clowning to distract her; and she takes his real opinion of love and women for a piece of hearty and good-natured fun. Iago's kind of honesty, he feels, is not valued as it should be; there is much in Iago of the Clown in Revolt, and the inevitable clown is almost washed out in this play to give him a free field. It is not, I think, dangerously far-fetched to take almost all Shakespeare's uses of *fool* as metaphors from the clown, whose symbolism certainly rode his imagination and was explained to the audience in most of his early plays. Now Iago's defence when Othello at last turns on him, among the rich ironies of its claim to honesty, brings in both *Fool* and the Vice used in *Hamlet* as an old name for the clown.

Iago: O wretched fool,
         That lov'st to make thine Honesty, a Vice!*
         Oh monstrous world! Take note, take note (O World)
         To be direct and honest is not safe.
         I thank you for this profit, and from hence
         I'll love no Friend, sith Love breeds such offence.
Oth.:   Nay stay; thou should'st be honest.
Iago: I should be wise; for Honesty's a Fool,
         And loses that it works for.
Oth.:   By the world,
         I think my wife be honest, and think she is not.

What comes out here is Iago's unwillingness to be the Fool he thinks he is taken for; but it is dramatic irony as well, and that comes back to his notion of *honest*; he is fooled by the way his plans run away with him; he fails in knowledge of others and perhaps even of his own desires.

Othello swears *by the world* because what Iago has said about being honest in the world, suggesting what worldly people think, is what has made him doubtful; yet the senses of *honest* are quite different – chastity and truth-telling. Desdemona is called a supersubtle Venetian, and he may suspect she would agree with what Iago treats as worldly wisdom; whereas it was her simplicity that made her helpless; though again, the fatal step was her lie about the handkerchief. *Lov'st* in the second line (Folios) seems to me better than *liv'st* (Quarto), as making the frightened Iago bring in his main claim at once; the comma after *Honesty* perhaps makes the sense 'loves with the effect of making' rather than 'delights in making'; in any case *love* appears a few lines down. *Breeds* could suggest sexual love, as if Iago's contempt for that has spread to his notions of friendship; Othello's marriage is what has spoilt their relations (Cassio 'came a-wooing with' Othello, as a social figure, and then got the lieutenantship). In the same way Othello's two uses of *honest* here jump from 'loving towards friends, which breeds honour' to (of women) 'chaste'. It is important I think that the feminine sense, which a later time felt to be quite distinct, is so deeply confused here with the other ones.

It is not safe to be *direct* either way, to be *honest* in Othello's sense or Iago's. The sanctimonious metaphor *profit* might carry satire from Iago on Puritans or show Iago to be like them. Iago is still telling a good deal of truth; the reasons he gives have always made him despise those who are faithful to their masters, if not to their friends. It is not clear that he would think himself a bad friend to his real friends. He believes there is a gaff to blow about the ideal love affair, though his evidence has had to be forced. Of course he is using *honest* less in his own way than to impose on Othello, yet there is a real element of self-pity in his complaint. It is no white-washing of Iago – you may hate him the more for it – but he feels he is now in danger because he has gone the 'direct' way to work, exposed false pretensions, and tried to be 'frank' to himself about the whole situation. I do not think this is an oversubtle treatment of his words; behind his fear he is gloating over his cleverness, and seems to delight in the audience provided by the stage.

In the nightmare scene where Othello clings to the word to justify himself he comes near accepting Iago's use of it.

---

*   And make thyself a motley to the view. Sonnet 110.

Emil.:	My husband!
Oth.:	Ay, twas he that told me first:
	An honest man he is, and hates the slime
	That sticks on filthy deeds …
Emil.:	My husband say that she was false?
Oth.:	He, woman;
	I say thy husband: dost understand the word?
	My friend, thy husband, honest, honest Iago.

From the sound of the last line it seems as bitter and concentrated as the previous question; to the audience it is. Yet Othello means no irony against Iago, and it is hard to invent a reason for his repetition of *honest*. He may feel it painful that the coarse Iago, not Desdemona or Cassio, should be the only honest creature, or Iago's honesty may suggest the truth he told; or indeed you may call it a trick on the audience, to wind up the irony to its highest before Iago is exposed. Yet Iago would agree that one reason why he was honest was that he hated the slime. The same slime would be produced, by Desdemona as well as by Othello one would hope, if the act of love were of the most rigidly faithful character; the disgust in the metaphor is disgust at all sexuality. Iago playing "honest" as prude is the rat who stands up for the ideal; as soon as Othello agrees he is finely cheated; Iago is left with his pleasures and Othello's happiness is destroyed. Iago has always despised his pleasures, always treated sex without fuss, like the lavatory; it is by this that he manages to combine the "honest dog" tone with honesty as Puritanism. The twist of the irony here is that Othello now feels humbled before such clarity. It is a purity he has failed to attain, and he accepts it as a form of honour. The hearty use and the horror of it are united in this appalling line.

Soon after there is a final use of *fool*, by Emilia, which sums up the clown aspect of Iago, but I ought to recognise that it may refer to Othello as well:

Emil.:	He begged of me to steal it.
Iago:	Villainous whore!
Emil.:	She give it Cassio! no, alas; I found it,
	And I did give't my husband.
Iago:	Filth, thou liest!
Emil.:	By heaven, I do not, I do not, gentlemen.
	O murderous coxcomb, what should such a fool
	Do with so good a wife?

(Iago stabs Emilia and escapes)

On the face of it she praises herself to rebut his insults, which are given because she is not a "good wife" in the sense of loyal to his interests. But her previous speech takes for granted that "she" means Desdemona, and we go straight on to Emilia's death-scene, which is entirely selfless and praises Desdemona only. I think she is meant to turn and upbraid Othello, so that she praises Desdemona in this sentence: it would be a convenience in acting, as it explains why she does not notice Iago's sword. *Coxcomb* in any case insists on the full meaning of "fool", which would make a startling insult for Othello; the idea becomes not that he was stupid to be deceived (a reasonable complaint) but that he was vain of his clownish authority, that is, self-important about his position as a husband and his suspicions, murderous merely because he wanted to show what he could do, like a child. She is the mouthpiece of all the feelings in us which are simply angry with Othello, but this judgement of him is not meant to keep its prominence for long. Indeed as her death-scene goes on the interpretation which the producer should reject is I think meant to come back into our minds; the real murderous coxcomb, the clown who did kill merely out of vanity, was Iago. The cynic had always hated to be treated as a harmless joker, and what finally roused him into stabbing her was perhaps that he thought she had called him a clown. The Lion and the Fox are thus united in the word, but as so many things happen in the play by a misunderstanding. It is perhaps an unnecessarily elaborate interpretation (the reference to Iago is much the more important one) but I think it is needed for our feelings about Emilia that she should not deliberately give herself the praise which we none the less come to feel she deserves.

Some other words which combine the ideas of truth-telling and generosity are affected by the same process as *honest*, though without becoming so important. Desdemona while giggling at the jokes of Iago in the second Act says, "Is he not a most profane and liberal counsellor?", and Othello echoes this *liberal* when he catches from Iago the trick of sneering at the generosity of Desdemona.

> *Oth.:*   ... here's a young and sweating devil here
> That commonly rebels. Tis a good hand,
> A *frank* one.
> *Des.:*   You may indeed say so,
> For twas that hand that gave away my heart.
> *Oth.:*   A *liberal* hand ...
> *Emilia:*   No, I will speak as *liberal* as the air
> Let heaven and men, and devils, let them all
> All, all, cry shame against me, yet I'll speak ...
> So, *speaking as I think*, I die, I die.

Indeed the whole power of Emilia's death-scene is that she ties up a variety of sacrificial virtues into a bundle labelled "mere coarse frankness". *Honest* itself seems to have rather minor connections with truth-telling, but the play as a whole is far from indifferent to that virtue, and Emilia has to steal the limelight from Iago in the eyes of those who preferred a character who could blow the gaff.

The only later use of *honest* comes when Othello's sword is taken from him by the State officer; a mark of disgrace, a symbol of cuckoldry; two possible negations of honour and honesty.

> *Oth.:*   I am not valiant neither,
> But every puny whipster gets my sword.
> But why should honour outlive honesty?
> Let it go all.

The straightforward meaning, I take it (though commentators have disagreed a good deal), is something like "I have lost my civilian reputation, because the killing of my wife has turned out unjust; why then should I care about my military reputation, which depends on keeping my sword?" But the poetic or dramatic effect clearly means a great deal more. The question indeed so sums up the play that it involves nearly all of both words; it seems finally to shatter the concept of honesty whose connecting links the play has patiently removed. There are thirteen other uses of *honour* (and *honourable*); four of them by Othello about himself and five by others about Othello.* The effect has been to make Othello the personification of honour; if honour does not survive some test of the idea nor could Othello. And to him *honest* is 'honourable', from which it was derived; a test of one is a test of the other. Outlive Desdemona's chastity, which he now admits, outlive Desdemona herself, the personification of chastity (lying again, as he insisted, with her last breath), outlive decent behaviour in, public respect for, self-respect in, Othello – all these are honour, not honesty; there is no question whether Othello outlives them. But they are not tests of an idea; what has been tested is a special sense of *honest*. Iago has been the personification of honesty, not merely to Othello but to his world; why should honour, the father of the word, live on and talk about itself; honesty, that obscure bundle of assumptions, the play has destroyed. I can see no other way to explain the force of the question here.

There is very little for anybody to add to A. C. Bradley's magnificent analysis, but one can maintain that Shakespeare, and the audience he had, and the audience he wanted, saw the thing in rather different proportions. Many of the audience were old soldiers disbanded without pension; they would dislike Cassio as the new type of officer, the boy who can displace men of experience merely because he knows enough mathematics to work the new guns. The tragedy plays into their hands by making Cassio a young fool who can't keep his mistress from causing scandals and can't drink. I don't know why Shakespeare wanted to tell us that Iago was exactly twenty-eight, but anyway he is experienced and Cassio seems about six years younger. Iago gets a long start at the beginning of the play, where he is enchantingly amusing and may be in the right. I am not trying to deny that by the end of the first Act he is obviously the villain, and that by the end of the play we are meant to feel the mystery of his life as Othello did:

> Will you, I pray, demand that demi-devil
> Why he hath thus ensnared my soul and body?

---

* The remaining four can all I think be connected with Othello. His wife's honour concerns him directly – the comparison of it to the handkerchief even implies that he has given it to her (iv.i.14); Cassio, we hear, is to have an honourable position – because he is to take Othello's place (iv.iii.240); the state officer is "your honour" because he represents the source of that position. The only difficult case is

> Three lads of Cyprus – noble swelling spirits
> That hold their honours in a wary distance ...
> Have I this night flustered with flowing cups.
> (ii.iii.53.)

It will be hard for Cassio not to get drunk with them because they are "tough"; their boastful virility is likely to make them dangerous customers unless they are handled on their own footing. I think they act as a faint parody of Othello's Honour, which is a much idealised version of the same kind of thing. And on the other hand Iago does not use the word at all when he is making contradictory speeches in favour of "good name" and against "reputation", because that would make it less specific.

Shakespeare can now speak his mind about Iago through the convention of the final speech by the highest in rank:

> O Spartan dog,
> More fell than anguish, hunger, or the sea!

Verbal analysis is not going to weaken the main shape of the thing. But even in this last resounding condemnation the dog is not simple. Dogs come in six times. Roderigo when dying also calls his murderer Iago a dog, and Othello does it conditionally, if Iago prove false. Roderigo says that he himself "is not like a hound that hunts but one that fills up the cry" – Iago is the dog that hunts, we are to reflect.* Iago says that Cassio when drunk will be "as full of quarrel and offence as my young mistress's dog"; now Iago himself clearly knows what it feels like to be ready to take offence, and one might think that this phrase helps to define the sort of dog he is, the spoiled favourite of his betters. He has also a trivial reference to dogs when encouraging Cassio and saying that Othello only pretends to be angry with him "as one would beat his offenceless dog, to affright an imperious lion". It seems rather dragged in, as if Iago was to mention dogs as much as possible. The typical Shakespearean dog-men are Apemantus and Thersites (called "dog" by Homer), malign underdogs, snarling critics, who yet are satisfactory as clowns and carry something of the claim of the disappointed idealist; on the other hand, if there is an obscure prophecy in the treatment of *honest*, surely the "honest *dog*" of the Restoration may cast something of his shadow before. Wyndham Lewis's interesting treatment of Iago as "fox" (in *The Lion and the Fox*) leaves out both these dogs, though the dog is more relevant than the fox on his analogy of tragedy to bull-baiting; indeed the clash of the two dogs goes to the root of Iago. But the dog symbolism is a mere incident, like that of *fool*; the thought is carried on *honest*, and I throw in the others only not to over-simplify the thing. Nor are they used to keep Iago from being a straightforward villain; the point is that more force was needed to make Shakespeare's audience hate Iago than to make them accept the obviously intolerable Macbeth as a tragic hero.

There seems a linguistic difference between what Shakespeare meant by Iago and what the nineteenth-century critics saw in him. They took him as an abstract term 'Evil'; he is a critique on an unconscious pun. This is seen more clearly in their own personifications of their abstract word; e.g. *The Turn of the Screw* and *Dr. Jekyll and Mr. Hyde*. Henry James got a great triumph over some critic who said that his villains were sexual perverts (if the story meant anything they could hardly be anything else). He said: 'Ah, you have been letting yourself have fancies about Evil; I kept it right out of my mind.' That indeed is what the story is about. Stevenson rightly made clear that *Dr. Jekyll* is about hypocrisy. You can only consider Evil as all things that destroy the good life; this has no unity; for instance, Hyde could not be both the miser and the spendthrift and whichever he was would destroy Jekyll without further accident. Evil here is merely the daydream of a respectable man, and only left vague so that

---

* Mr. Granville-Barker indeed said that Iago was "like a hound on the trail, sensitive and alert, nose to the ground, searching and sampling, appetite and instinct combining to guide him past error to his quarry."

respectable readers may equate it unshocked to their own daydreams. Iago may not be a 'personality', but he is better than these; he is the product of a more actual interest in a word.

II

It struck me on reading this over that it is not likely to convince a supporter of Bradley, since it bows to the master as if taking his results for granted and then appears to include him among the nineteenth-century critics who are denounced; also, what is more important, it does not answer the central question that Bradley put – "Why does Iago plot at all?" I shall try now to summarize Bradley's position and explain the points at which I disagree with it.

We are shown, says Bradley, that Iago is clear-sighted, and he appears to have been prudent till the play begins; he must have realized that his plot was extremely dangerous to himself (in the event it was fatal); and yet we feel that he is not actuated by any passion of hatred or ambition – in fact, so far as he pretends that he is, he seems to be wondering what his motives for action can be, almost as Hamlet (in the immediately previous play by Shakespeare) wonders what his motives can be for inaction.* Some recent critics have objected to this sort of analysis, but I think it is clearly wrong to talk as if coherence of character is not needed in poetic drama, only coherence of metaphor and so on. The fair point to make against Bradley's approach (as is now generally agreed) is that the character of Iago must have been intended to seem coherent to the first-night audience; therefore the solution cannot be reached by learned deductions from hints in the text about his previous biography, for instance; if the character is puzzling nowadays, the answer must be a matter of recalling the assumptions of the audience and the way the character was put across. Of course it is also possible that Shakespeare was cheating, and that the audience would not care as long as they got their melodrama. Indeed there are lines in Iago's soliloquies which seem to be using the older convention, by which the villain merely announced his villainy in terms such as the good people would have used about him. But I should maintain that the character was an eminently interesting one to the first-night audience (they did not take the villain for granted) and that even the crudities could be absorbed into a realistic view of him. Such at any rate is the question at issue.

Bradley's answer is in brief that Iago is tempted by vanity and love of plotting. Iago says he likes "to plume up his will / In double knavery", to heighten his sense of power by plots, and Bradley rightly points out that this reassurance to the sense of power is a common reason for apparently meaningless petty cruelties. Iago particularly wants to do it at this time, because he has been slighted by Cassio's appointment and is in irritating difficulties with Roderigo, so that "his thwarted sense of superiority demands satisfaction". But he knows at the back of his mind that his plot is dangerous to the point of folly, and that is why he keeps inventing excuses for himself. Bradley opposes what seems to have been a common Victorian view that Iago had "a general

---

* One might indeed claim that Iago is a satire on the holy thought of Polonius – "To thine own self be true … thou canst not then be false to any man."

disinterested love of evil", and says that if he had a "motiveless malignity" (Coleridge) it was only in the more narrow but more psychologically plausible way that Bradley has defined.

All this I think is true, and satisfies the condition about the first-night audience. The thwarted sense of superiority in Iago is thrust on them in the first scene, and they are expected to feel a good deal of sympathy for it; at the end of the first Act they are to appreciate the triumph with which he conceives the plot. However the question "why does he do it?" would hardly present itself as a problem; obviously the play required a villain; the only question likely to arise is "why does everybody take the villain for a good man?" Bradley of course recognises this question but he deals with it in terms of an ethical theory supposed to be held only by Iago, whereas you clearly need to consider how it was understood by the audience; and the effect of this twist is to take Bradley some way back towards the idea that Iago embodies Pure Evil.

He says that Iago has "a spite against goodness in men as a thing not only stupid but, both in its nature and by its success, contrary to Iago's nature and irritating to his pride". Not only that, but "His creed – for he is no sceptic, he has a definite creed – is that absolute egoism is the only rational and proper attitude, and that conscience or honour or any kind of regard for others is an absurdity." Bradley therefore finds it contradictory and somewhat pathetic when Iago shouts "villainous whore" at his wife, or implies that since Cassio would like to be an adulterer it is not so bad to say he is one (iii.i.311). This, he says, shows that Iago has a "secret subjection to morality", an "inability to live up to his creed"; also the soliloquies betray a desire to convince himself, so that his natural egoism is not perfect. Perfection is attained, however, in the way he hides his ethical theory from other people; when we consider his past life, says Bradley, "the inference, which is accompanied by a thrill of admiration, (is) that Iago's power of dissimulation and of self-control must have been prodigious". Since a thrill about his past life is not properly part of the play, this amounts to an admission that the stage character is not consistent. In effect, Bradley is agreeing with Rymer here.

It seems clear that Iago was not meant as a secret theoretician of this sort, and that the audience would not be misled into thinking him one. His opinions, so far as he has got them clear, are shared by many people around him, and he boasts about them freely. To be sure, he could not afford to do this if they were not very confused, but even the confusion is shared by his neighbours. When Iago expounds his egotism to Roderigo, in the first scene of the play, he is not so much admitting a weak criminal to his secrets as making his usual claim to Sturdy Independence in a rather coarser form. He is not subservient to the interests of the men in power who employ him, he says; he can stand up for himself, as they do. No doubt an Elizabethan employer, no less than Professor Bradley, would think this a shocking sentiment; but it does not involve Pure Egotism, and I do not even see that it involves Machiavelli. It has the air of a spontaneous line of sentiment among the lower classes, whereas Machiavelli was interested in the deceptions necessary for a ruler. Certainly it does not imply that the Independent man will betray his friends (as apart from his employer), because if it did he would not boast about it to them. This of course is the answer to the critics who have said that Roderigo could not have gone on handing all his money to a self-confessed knave. And, in the same way, when it turns out that Iago does mean to betray Roderigo, he has only to tell the audience that this fool is not one of his real friends;

indeed he goes on to claim that it would be *wrong* to treat him as one. I do not mean to deny there is a paradox about the whole cult of the Independent Man (it is somehow felt that his selfishness makes him more valuable as a friend); but the paradox was already floating in the minds of the audience. No doubt Shakespeare thought that the conception was a false one, and gave a resounding demonstration of it, but one need not suppose that he did this by inventing a unique psychology for Iago, or even by making Iago unusually conscious of the problem at issue.

Indeed, when Iago is a conscious hypocrite, I should have thought that he was laughably unconvincing:

> Though in the trade of war I have slain men,
> Yet I do hold it very stuff of the conscience
> To do no contrived murder: I lack iniquity
> Sometimes to do me service; nine or ten times
> I thought to have yerked him here under the ribs.

"Tis better as it is", answers Othello rather shortly; they are his first words in the play. Iago's attempt to show fine feelings has only made him sound like a ruffian in Marlowe. But this is not at all likely to shake Othello's faith in him; the idea is that, if you are in the way of needing a reliable bodyguard, you must put up with something rough. It is true that the soliloquies make him seem a more intellectual type; and when he says, as a reason for murdering Cassio, "He has a daily beauty in his life, Which makes me ugly", one can hardly deny that Shakespeare is making a crude use of the soliloquy convention. But even this line, though false, is only so in a marginal way. We feel that Iago would not have used those words, but Shakespeare is already committed to the convention of making him talk poetry. The trouble is that the phrase seems to refer to the *moral* beauty of Cassio, on which Bradley expresses some delicate thoughts, and indeed this line is probably what made Bradley believe that Iago has both a clear recognition of goodness and a positive spite against it.* But it is plausible enough (as a "second level" interpretation of the crude convention) to say that Iago only means that Cassio has smarter clothes and more upper-class manners, which give him an unfair advantage over Iago (for one thing, that is why Iago fears Cassio with his nightcap). The resentment of the lower classes towards the graces of the upper really has been known to take ugly forms, and Shakespeare with his new coat of arms was ready to go out of his way to reprove it. The phrase comes late in the play (early in the fifth Act) where Iago can in any case be treated simply as the villain; it is assumed that the feeling of the audience has been swung firmly against him. Mr. Granville-Barker said that it is a "strange involuntary phrase" which Iago "quickly obliterates under more matter-of-fact language"; and marks the point where "even his nerve is strained", so that he is beginning to bungle a situation which has got more complicated than he meant (he has

---

* Mr. Wilson Knight, in *The Othello Music*, also regards the "daily beauty" speech as the essence of the matter; in the same way, he says, Iago hates the romance of Othello and the purity of Desdemona, and "this is his 'motive' throughout; other suggestions are surface deep only". No doubt he is drawn as a cynic, but I do not think the audience would take cynicism as such to be something purely devilish and consciously devoted to destroying goodness or beauty in any form; because the cynic had a claim to be a puritan.

obviously got to kill Cassio anyhow). This seems to me an excellent tip for a modern actor but not necessarily part of the first idea.

As to the puzzle about why he is not suspected, he boasts of that too, in a prominent place, at the end of a soliloquy and a scene (Act II.i).

> Knavery's plain face is never seen, till us'd.

Shakespeare here outfaces the difficulty by a challenge to the audience: "You would have been fooled too, though you may think you wouldn't." And the reason seems clear enough from the preceding soliloquy, though it is not what Iago meant to say. His accumulating resentments at his inferior position have become explosive, so that he imagines slights from every direction; but people cannot expect this because it seems to them natural that his position should be inferior. And yet (says the line) his knavery has always had a "plain face" – his jeering wit and his sturdy independence had always been his stock-in-trade.

I have gone into the matter at perhaps tedious length without using the word "honest" at all, because there seems a suggestion of trickery or triviality about saying that the character is only made plausible by puns on one word. Perhaps this is a risky manoeuvre, because the more I succeeded in it the harder it would become to claim that the puns on "honest" were essential to the play. But it is clear I think that all the elements of the character are represented in the range of meanings of "honest", and (what is more important) that the confusion of moral theory in the audience, which would make them begin by approving of Iago (though perhaps only in the mixed form of the "ironical cheer") was symbolised or echoed in a high degree by the confusion of the word. When opinion had become more settled or conventionalised, and the word had itself followed this movement by becoming simpler, there were of course two grounds for finding a puzzle in the character; but, of the two, I should say that failure to appreciate the complexity of the word was the more important ground, because after all the complexity of moral judgement had not become so difficult – what people had lost was the verbal pointer directing them to it. I think indeed that the Victorians were not ready enough to approve the good qualities of being "ready to blow the gaff" and "frank to yourself about your own desires"; and it is not likely that any analysis of one word would have altered their opinions. And I must admit (as a final effort to get the verbalist approach into its right proportion) that my opinions about the play date from seeing an actual performance of it, with a particularly good Iago, and that I did not at the time think about the word "honest" at all. The verbal analysis came when I looked at the text to see what support it gave to these impressions. But I do not feel this to be any reason for doubting that the puns on "honest" really do support them.

4

"Introductory" Chapter About the Tragedies

Wolfgang Clemen

W e cannot speak of the development of Shakespeare's imagery without keeping before us the general development of his art and mind. For the changes and the advance perceptible in his use of imagery result from this more comprehensive evolution. Some aspects of this interrelationship are to be dealt with in these introductory remarks.

The tragedies display Shakespeare's dramatic technique at its best. This means that every element of style, in fact every single line, now becomes dramatically relevant. The same applies to the imagery, the images becoming an inherent part of the dramatic structure. They become effective instruments in the hand of the dramatist. We saw how they helped him to prepare the audience for coming events. But the imagery may also emphasize and accompany the dramatic action, repeating its themes; it often even resembles a second line of action running parallel to the real plot, and providing a "counterpoint" to the events on the stage.

The function of the images to forebode and anticipate, noticeable, as was shown, in such plays as *The Merchant of Venice* and *King John*, becomes more important and more subtle in the tragedies. The imagery unobtrusively reflects coming events, it turns the imagination of the audience in a certain direction and helps to prepare the atmosphere, so that the state of expectation and feeling necessary for the full realization of the dramatic effect is reached.

The fact that imagery plays such an important part in the tragedies, indicates a fundamental change in Shakespeare's manner of presentation. In the early plays, it was his aim to make everything as obvious and plain as possible. Hence the programmatic expositions, the explanatory monologues, which acquaint us with the intentions of the characters. This direct and outspoken style is replaced in the work of the mature Shakespeare by a more subtle and indirect method. Things are suggested, intimated, hinted at; they are seldom expressly stated. And for this manner of suggestive and veiled presentation imagery is most suitable.

Ambiguity[1] plays an important role in this connection, as is obvious where Shakespeare makes his characters say something, the significance of which they cannot possibly grasp at the time of utterance. For what they say may have two meanings. The one meaning which the speaker has in mind refers to the momentary situation, but the other meaning may point beyond this moment to other issues of the play. Imagery may serve this purpose better than plain language and may lend itself more easily to ambiguity. An image is altogether a more complex form of statement than plain diction. Consider this passage from *Julius Caesar*:

> O setting sun,
> As in thy red rays thou dost sink to-night,
> So in his red blood Cassius' day is set;
> The sun of Rome is set! Our day is gone;
> Clouds, dews, and dangers come; our deeds are done!
> (v.iii.61)

The increasingly complex significance of the rest of the passage develops from the simple meaning of the first words of the sentence. The sun has doubly set, for the "sun of Rome" is both the sun of that day, and Cassius himself. But the words: "Our day is gone;" have a threefold meaning: first, "Our day" is the real day, which has just passed, then again it means Cassius (in the preceding line it was said that "Cassius' day is set"), and finally, it denotes the period of life which all the persons concerned have passed through. Something new is about to begin for all of them now. The past day may also refer to the approaching end of the play itself, because the play will be at an end after two more brief scenes.

Another passage, from *Coriolanus* this time, may further illustrate this ambiguity. Menenius says to the tribunes:

> This tiger-footed rage, when it shall find
> The harm of unscann'd swiftness, will too late
> Tie leaden pounds to's heels.
> (*Coriolanus*, iii.i.312)

The tribunes to whom these words are said, apply "tiger-footed rage" as well as "unscann'd swiftness" to Coriolanus. But, on the other hand, in harmony with the underlying thought of the play, both these epithets apply to the tribunes and to their senseless agitation against Coriolanus, which is perceived and tempered "too late". By means of this ambiguity, then, Menenius, Coriolanus' friend, is able to speak with the tribunes as if he were on their side – whereas in fact he says precisely the opposite.

This double meaning of images is also of importance for the development of the dialogue in the tragedies. In interpreting the tragedies, we must continually ask whether one character has fully understood what the other said, or whether he or she understood it in a secondary or false sense. This is of great importance for the further course of the action. Shakespeare seems to employ quite consciously this mutual misunderstanding of the characters as an instrument of dramatic technique. In his early work, to be sure, we also find misunderstandings as a result of ambiguities; but there it appears only in the form of wit and punning. Whereas Shakespeare there employs the pun, the play upon words, merely as a form of witty entertainment, an opportunity for clever repartee, he develops it in his later work to a fine instrument of characterization and a means of double interpretation of a situation. By means of the multiplicity of meanings characteristic of the pun, Shakespeare is able to let his characters understand each other in different degrees. The characters may talk with each other and really believe that they understand each other. But the true (hidden) meaning of the one is not grasped by the other. The audience, however, may well understand it. Out of this situation significant tensions grow between what the audience already knows, and what the characters on the stage are saying. Thus a play on words may become the key to what is to follow. It is no longer mere arabesque and unessential decoration, but rather a necessary, if tiny, link in the chain of the dramatic structure – for much now depends upon the comprehension of this quibble or pun at this particular moment.

Naturally, it is impossible to generalize about the motifs and themes which find expression in the imagery of the great tragedies. There are, however, some recurring and especially characteristic features which may be considered.

In the early histories, the characters turned to images when they sought to lend expression to the magnitude and intensity of their emotions, desires and aims. Marlowe's *Tamburlaine* was the model for such a use of imagery; consequently, many of those images and comparisons were too hyperbolical, too exaggerated; they were seldom appropriate expression. But in the tragedies, that appropriateness which was lacking in the early histories, is achieved. The images no longer impress us as rhetorical and pompous; they are borne by great passion and correspond to the depth and immensity of human emotion. Thus we often meet with images which are built upon gigantic conceptions. Othello would not give up Desdemona:

> If heaven would make me such another world
> Of one entire and perfect chrysolite,
> I'ld not have sold her for it.
> > (*Othello*, v.ii.144)

Macbeth asks if the ocean would wash his blood-stained hand clean, and replies:

> No, this my hand will rather
> The multitudinous seas incarnadine,
> Making the green one red.
> > (*Macbeth*, ii.ii.61)

and Hamlet taunts Laertes:

> let them throw
> Millions of acres on us, till our ground,
> Singeing his pate against the burning zone,
> Make Ossa like a wart!
> > (*Hamlet*, v.i.304)

It is characteristic of this gigantic conception of life that Shakespeare's tragic heroes in their imagery repeatedly express the presumptuous desire for the destruction of the whole world:

> Antony: Let Rome in Tiber melt, and the wide arch
> Of the ranged empire fall!
>
> *(A. and C.,* i.i.33)

> Cleopatra: O sun,
> Burn the great sphere thou movest in! darkling stand
> The varying shore o' the world.
>
> *(A. and C.,* iv.xv.10)[2]

Almost all the heroes of Shakespeare's tragedies stand in close relationship to the cosmos, the celestial bodies, and the elements.[3] This is a characteristic feature of the tragedies, lacking in the histories. Not only do the cosmic forces accompany the action of the tragedies; the characters feel themselves to be closely related to them and to the elements. When in the histories, the people turned their eyes to the sun, taking its dull gleam for a foreboding of evil,[4] this was in the tradition of omen. But in the tragedies, the characters apostrophize the sun and stars directly.

> ... Stars, hide your fires;
> Let not light see my black and deep desires:
> *(Macbeth,* i.iv.50)

Macbeth cries before his murderous deed. "Moon and stars!" we hear Antony say,[5] and Cleopatra: "O sun, burn the great sphere ..."[6] The heavens seem sympathetic to what is occurring here on earth. To Hamlet, thinking of his mother's hasty remarriage, "heaven's face doth glow" (iii.iv.48); and Othello, convinced of Desdemona's faithlessness, cries out: "Heaven stops the nose at it and the moon winks" (iv.ii.77). Macduff says, after the bad news has come: "New sorrows strike heaven on the face that it resounds."[7] Sorrow reaching even up to heaven and forcing entrance there is a motif frequently expressed in the imagery. Hamlet, referring to Laertes's lament, says:

> whose phrase of sorrow
> Conjures the wandering stars, and makes them stand
> Like wonder-wounded hearers?
>
> (v.i.278)

In *King Lear* Kent

> bellow'd out
> As he'ld burst heaven;
> (v.iii.212)

And Lear himself cries out at the end:

> Had I your tongues and eyes, I'ld use them so
> That heaven's vault should crack.
> (v.iii.258)

Moreover, in the dramatic structure of the individual tragedies the appeal to the elements makes its appearance at definite turning-points. Not until they begin to despair of men and earth do the tragic heroes turn to the heavens. When their firmest beliefs have been shaken, when they stand alone and forsaken, they renounce the earth and call upon the cosmic powers.

It is by means of the imagery that all the wealth of nature enters into the plays. Apart from *Midsummer Night's Dream* and *The Tempest*, the tragedies are the plays richest in nature-atmosphere. The world of animals and plants, the scenery itself are evoked by the imagery; they lend the play not only background and atmosphere, but also a vital connection with earthly existence, scarcely to be found in the work of any other dramatist. The word "atmosphere" is not, however, sufficient to denote the importance of the role of this varied nature-imagery. For nature, the animals and plants, are players, as it were; they are forces in the organism of the play and hence not dissociable. Goethe noted this "cooperation" of nature and the elements: "Even the inanimate world takes part; all the subordinate things have their role, the elements, the phenomena of the heavens, the earth and the sea, thunder and lightning" (*Shakespeare und kein Ende*).

Man and nature stand in a continuous relationship in the tragedies, and the imagery serves to emphasize this kinship. In many cases it would be inappropriate to say that the characters "use nature-imagery". For nature, like the cosmos, is often like a character on the stage to whom one appeals; it is then no longer a "tertium comparationis".

There was indeed a certain relationship between the characters and the world of nature in *Romeo and Juliet*. But to perceive the difference, let us compare Juliet's call to night, "Come, civil night, thou sober-suited matron" (iii.ii.10 sqq.) with Macbeth's appeal:

> Come, seeling night,
> Scarf up the tender eye of pitiful day;
> And with thy bloody and invisible hand
> Cancel and tear to pieces that great bond
> Which keeps me pale! Light thickens; and the crow
> Makes wing to the rooky wood:
> Good things of day begin to droop and drowse;
> Whiles night's black agents to their preys do rouse.
>
> (iii.ii.46)

In Juliet's monologue the night is still personified in traditional manner: *sober-suited matron, gentle, civil*. In contrast to this, Macbeth's *seeling night* is something entirely different. *Seeling* does not denote a quality of a person, as do the epithets *gentle* or *civil*. In the monologue from *Romeo and Juliet* the relationship of the person to the night is expressly stated, whereas in *Macbeth* it is merely suggested. In the lines which follow the actual apostrophe, Macbeth utters much of what he sees – but he leaves its significance unexplained. What Macbeth perceives in the world about him pertains to himself as well. The twilight – *light thickens* – is at the same time the twilight of his own soul. The *bloody hand* of the night recalls his own blood-stained hand; and from the word *invisible* we may gather the wish to make his own hand equally invisible. The good things of the outer world which "begin to droop and drowse" represent a like change in him, and, finally, *night's black agents*, turning to their prey, are equivalent to his own desires bent upon their victim.[8] Thus Macbeth in his description of nature reveals his own inner state of mind. Every feature of this picture is true of himself and his designs.

A comparison of two other passages may show how differently Shakespeare now employs nature-imagery. The first passage is from the Second Part of *Henry VI*, the other is from *Othello*; the motif of both passages is the sea with its dangerous rocks, sparing man out of sympathy. In *Henry VI* the Queen relates to the King:

> The pretty-vaulting sea refused to drown me,
> Knowing that thou would'st have me drown'd on shore,
> With tears as salt as sea, through thy unkindness:
> The splitting rocks cower'd in the sinking sands
> And would not dash me with their ragged sides,
> Because thy flinty heart, more hard than they,
> Might in thy palace perish Margaret.
>
> (*2 Henry VI*, III.ii.94)

In *Othello* Cassio tells the story of Desdemona's miraculous rescue after the stormy voyage:

> Tempests themselves, high seas and howling winds,
> The gutter'd rocks and congregated sands, –
> Traitors ensteep'd to clog the guiltless keel, –
> As having sense of beauty, do omit
> Their mortal natures, letting go safely by
> The divine Desdemona.
>
> (II.i.68)

The diction in the passage from *Othello*, with its unusual and suggestive epithets and metaphors, is finer than in the lines from *Henry VI*. But the difference in the attitude towards nature is far more important. In the first case we have to deal with a "conceit" artfully constructed upon antithesis and parallelism. The sympathetic sea, the splitting rocks are very consciously inserted into the long speech of the Queen as a means of contrast. In *Othello*, however, the sea-imagery grows immediately out of the experience of the voyage. In the words of the other characters of this scene, too, we can feel the sea air. In the whole play the sea has an important role – as scene, background, and as Othello's own vital element.

Shakespeare's art of personification, of endowing abstract realities with the breath of life, undergoes a noteworthy development in the tragedies. The personifications, such as we often meet with in *King John*, for example,[9] are still patterned after the medieval type of personification. They derive from the allegorical world of the Middle Ages, from the time when all abstract qualities were thought of as human figures having certain attributes. In his later work, Shakespeare frees himself more and more from this tradition of the Middle Ages, although it was still living on in his own day in allegorical interludes and pageants. Those abstract images, behind which a visible human figure stands, become fewer and fewer. Shakespeare's manner of personifying becomes freer and bolder. He creates images of astonishing peculiarity and incomparable originality. At the same time the range of abstractions expressed by imagery becomes wider. These abstractions play an important part in the tragedies. Just as man now stands in closer connection with nature and the cosmos, so, too, he appears in relationship to certain forces determining and guiding his very existence. Be they called fate, doom, time or metaphysical powers, these occult forces have a hand in every tragedy; man appears to be surrounded by them. Their vivid reality often becomes perceptible in the imagery. Hence we must seriously consider the images which represent these abstract realities. It is not only that these images tell us what Shakespeare himself thought about certain subjects. Their appearance at a certain point in a play has a deep significance. Thus, for example, the frequent time-images in *Troilus and Cressida* reveal that in this play, Shakespeare wanted to show the changing and dissolving effect of the passing of time. Or again, in *Antony and Cleopatra*, the repeated appearance of fortune-images reflects the role fortune plays in determining the action.

In the tragedies – more than in all the other plays – the imagery expresses the mutual relationship of the forces at work in human nature. Ideas such as honor, judgment, conscience, will, blood, reason, etc., frequently appear in metaphorical guise. Whoever undertakes to investigate Shakespeare's conception of the human character will be amazed to find how many of the passages with the mutual relationship of spiritual and mental qualities as their subject, appear in metaphorical language, or employ imagery.

This kind of imagery should warn us not to apply modern conceptions of human character to Shakespeare's plays; it gives us hints as to how Shakespeare conceived of mental processes and conflicting qualities of character.[10] For it is certainly not true that Shakespeare consciously "translated" into the language of imagery what he had to say about human qualities and dispositions (for the sake of a more poetic mode of expression, for example). On the contrary, imagery is an integral component of the thought; it discloses to us the particular aspect under which Shakespeare viewed these things. Imagery here is a form of imaging and conceiving things. "Metaphor becomes almost a mode of apprehension", says Mr. Middleton Murry.[11]

A passage from *Macbeth* may show us clearly in what new manner Shakespeare now visualizes abstractions and human characteristics.

Macbeth (speaking of Duncan):

> that his virtues
> Will plead like angels, trumpet-tongued, against
> The deep damnation of his taking-off;
> And pity, like a naked new-born babe,
> Striding the blast, or heaven's cherubim, horsed
> Upon the sightless couriers of the air,
> Shall blow the horrid deed in every eye,
> That tears shall drown the wind. I have no spur
> To prick the sides of my intent, but only
> Vaulting ambition, which o'erleaps itself
> And falls on the other.
>
> (I.vii.19)

This is very different from the gorgeousness of Spenser's allegories; it is bolder, mightier and more dynamic, and rather recalls the passionate sublimity of Milton. "Pity, like a naked new-born babe, striding the blast" may illustrate how far Shakespeare has moved from the conventional type of personification, and how his imagery tends towards the strange and unique. It is notable, too, that these abstractions are now placed in enormous space, transferred to a world of clouds and winds, of boundless distance. "That tears shall drown the wind" is hyperbolical, recalling Elizabeth's phrase in *Richard III*: "That I ... may send forth plenteous tears to drown the world" (ii.ii.70). But whereas this phrase was a rhetorical exaggeration in the manner of Marlowe, "That tears shall drown the wind" grows organically from the whole comprehensive image which is based on gigantic dimensions. Furthermore, Macbeth's whole world is determined by these tremendous and strange powers which find expression in several such images. The last lines betray the intricacy and boldness of Shakespeare's fully developed art of metaphorical association technique. The image of the rider, touched upon in "heaven's cherubim, horsed upon the sightless couriers of the air" is picked up again in prick and spur, and is thus again used in another connection. Intent is conceived of as a horse, and vaulting ambition again as "rider." Thus an image, once set afire, as it were, seizes upon everything still to be said and creates bold and most extraordinary conceptions, like "vaulting ambition."[12]

This harmony between the given situation and the whole atmosphere of the play may also be traced in the imagery by which Shakespeare characterizes his men and women. A passage from *Julius Caesar* may serve as an example. In the third scene the conspirators meet in the streets of Rome at night during a terrific thunderstorm. By means of the imagery, the night and the thunderstorm are made very vivid, being also a suitable background for the dark conspiracy. The mood and situation naturally suggest the likening of Caesar to this fearful night.

> *Cassius:* Now could I, Casca, name to thee a man
>   Most like this dreadful night,
>   That thunders, lightens, opens graves, and roars
>   As doth the lion in the Capitol,
>
>   (i.iii.72)

The image fulfills two functions at one and the same time, it characterizes Caesar, and adds to the nocturnal thunderstorm atmosphere. That imagery thus serves a double purpose, is a characteristic of the tragedies.

This development does not necessarily imply that certain stylistic patterns of imagery which were characteristic of the early plays, now no longer appear. But if they are now used, they mean something different; they are purposely inserted to characterize the moment and the person concerned; they are employed at precisely this point with a dramatic intent. This may be illustrated by an example from *Troilus and Cressida*. On the occasion of his first undisturbed meeting with Cressida, Troilus avers the trueness of his love – later "swains in love," he says, will measure the fidelity of their love by Troilus:

>   when their rhymes,
>   Full of protest, of oath and big compare,
>   Want similes, truth tired with iteration,
>   As true as steel, as plantage to the moon,
>   As sun to day, as turtle to her mate,
>   As iron to adamant, as earth to the centre,

> Yet, after all comparisons of truth,
> As truth's authentic author to be cited,
> "As true as Troilus" shall crown up the verse,
> And sanctify the numbers.
>
> (III.ii.181)

This sequence of pretty comparisons is continued by Cressida in the same manner. It is as if we had before us two courtly lovers from the early comedies, where such agglomeration of clever comparisons was the fashion. But these two passages have their special dramatic significance within the framework of the whole play. Before the course of the play brings the tragic termination of their love, Shakespeare shows the two lovers in a mood of lyric ardour which stands in greatest contrast to the sceptical coolness and the bitter disillusionment of the following scenes. In order to enhance this effect, and to emphasize the unsuspecting, unconcerned and almost playful mood of the lovers, Shakespeare lets both speak here in a style which recalls the imagery of the early comedies. "The illusion must convince before it is pricked and shown to be a bubble," says Sir Edmund Chambers, referring to this passage.[13]

In a previous chapter on the early plays, we spoke of Shakespeare's habit of embellishing certain general themes appearing in the conversation with metaphorical epithets and definitions. The resulting imagery was undramatic; it was rhetorical decoration and no integral part of the dramatic structure. But let us examine the famous words of Macbeth on sleep:

> Methought I heard a voice cry "Sleep no more!
> Macbeth does murder sleep", the innocent sleep,
> Sleep that knits up the ravell'd sleave of care,
> The death of each day's life, sore labour's bath,
> Balm of hurt minds, great nature's second course,
> Chief nourisher in life's feast, –
>
> (II.ii.35)

Viewed from the outside, this series of metaphorical expressions for sleep is in no way different from the earlier type. Nevertheless, we scarcely need to say that the imagery of this passage is of the greatest dramatic suitability. For sleep is in this case no "theme of conversation," but a dramatic issue of first importance. That Macbeth has murdered Duncan while asleep is what is especially fearful in his deed. The wrong has been done, as it were, not only to Duncan, but also to the sacred nature of sleep. And "wronged sleep" rises in the conscience of the murderer like a real power. The rich imagery therefore is no digression. It is no burst of fine-sounding words and names, no interruption of the action. It is a vital, throbbing expression of what is taking place at this moment in Macbeth's soul. Macbeth perceives again and again what he has done with a strange clarity, and expresses this in imagery (cf. I.vii.19). *Sleep* runs like a keyword throughout the whole play and is the occasion of many metaphors of which the above passage is the climax.

A comparison of this passage with the words of the sleepless King Henry IV appealing to sleep, may show how Shakespeare's power of metaphorical expression has in the meantime grown in depth and concentration.

> O sleep, O gentle sleep,
> Nature's soft nurse, how have I frighted thee,
> That thou no more wilt weigh my eyelids down
> And steep my senses in forgetfulness?
> Why rather, sleep, liest thou in smoky cribs,
> Upon uneasy pallets stretching thee
> And hush'd with buzzing night-flies to thy slumber,
> Than in the perfumed chambers of the great,
> Under the canopies of costly state,
> And lull'd with sound of sweetest melody?
> O thou dull god, why liest thou with the vile
> In loathsome beds, and leavest the kingly couch
> A watch-case or a common 'larum-bell?
>
> (*2 Henry IV*, III.i.6)

In the earlier play, the King reviews in almost epic contemplation the effect of sleep among the different levels and classes of his subjects (the rich, the poor, the sailors on the high seas, and himself), but here in *Macbeth*, instead of a concrete picture executed in twenty-six lines (of which only the first half was quoted here), we have compressed into four lines a summary of the fundamental, timeless, eternally valid attributes of sleep.

The most important standard, accordingly, whereby to judge the imagery of the tragedies, is the degree of harmony existing between the image and the dramatic situation producing it. It may be that the dramatic situation admits of a richer expansion of the imagery; on the other hand, the speed of the play, or of the scene, may not permit the development of the whole image, so that as a result, the image merely flashes up for a moment. This latter case is more frequent than the former, because the insertion of a wholly executed image would mean retarding and interrupting the rapid progress of the dramatic action. Shakespeare must bring in the image without making more words of it. "Shakespeare smuggles in the images" we might say of many passages of the tragedies in which the image is only touched upon and hinted at. In *Troilus and Cressida* Ulysses says of Achilles:

> the seeded pride
> That hath to this maturity blown up
> In rank Achilles must or now be cropp'd,
> Or, shedding, breed a nursery of like evil,
> To overbulk us all.
>
> (I.iii.316)

This passage may serve as an example of how Shakespeare merely lets his diction take on the *colour* of the image in mind, the image being implicit, no longer expressly uttered. "Macbeth is ripe for shaking" says Malcolm at the end of the fourth act (IV.iii.238), quite aware of the way things will end. This image, too, is suggestive, awakening the notion of the ripe fruit which must be shaken from the tree. At an earlier stage Shakespeare would have given us the whole image. Thus in *Richard II*, we read:

> The ripest fruit first falls, and so doth he;
> His time is spent,
>
> (ii.i.153)

or in the *Merchant of Venice*:

> The weakest kind of fruit
> Drops earliest to the ground; and so let me:
>
> (iv.i.115)

Thus the development towards dramatic imagery is a development towards condensation and suggestiveness. Shakespeare compresses into one short sentence an astonishing wealth of associations. No matter what he is writing, he is always accompanied by pictorial conceptions and associations. No longer is there purposeful "hunting" for suitable images, as in the early plays; the matter of which he wishes to speak has already appeared to him in a metaphorical form. If we see or read a tragedy for the first time, we scarcely notice to what unbelievable degree imagery is employed. This is in part due to the fact that much of it belongs to the type of the merely suggested, implied and concealed imagery that has unobtrusively melted into the language. But it is also because the imagery is so wholly adapted to the situation and the emotion of the speaker, that we fail to feel anything unusual in it. Mr. Middleton Murry, discussing the poetic and dramatic value of the conceit, quotes a passage from *Antony and Cleopatra* (iv.ix.15–18) and notes how little we are disturbed by this difficult and extravagant language; on the contrary, how much we are moved by it. He writes convincingly: "The dramatic intensity of the situation in which they [the words] are spoken is such that it seems to absorb the violence of the imagery, without need to modify the image itself. The conceit becomes the natural extravagance of a depth of emotion that would also go unuttered."[14] Shakespeare's use of the single metaphor calling forth a more comprehensive image has become much bolder in the tragedies in comparison with the plays discussed in previous chapters. A few examples only may be quoted. Coriolanus says:

> I mean to stride your steed, and at all times
> To *undercrest* your good addition
> To the fairness of my power.
>
> (i.ix.71)

Coriolanus is here expressing his thanks for the charger which has been presented to him. By *undercrest* Shakespeare makes Coriolanus say that he will wear this present as proudly as an embellishment of a helmet. A single metaphor suffices for what we needs must explain in many words. Hamlet bids Horatio:

> Observe mine uncle: if his occulted guilt
> Do not itself *unkennel* in one speech,
>
> (iii.ii.85)

By association *occulted* leads to *unkennel*, and thus a whole picture is lit up in our imagination. But ordinary words, too, if employed in a new and figurative sense, may

---

have a surprising freshness. When Gloucester gives Edmund the order to sound Edgar, he simply says: "*wind* me into him," a phrase which with its vigorous simplicity remains unforgettable. By such unusual metaphors the audience are more startled than by an ordinary phrase which may pass unnoticed. We "prick up our ears" at such passages, the picture fastens on our imagination and we are less likely to skip such a line.

A study of the imagery in Shakespeare's tragedies helps us to appreciate them as an organism in which all the parts are interrelated and mutually attuned. Each tragedy has its own unmistakable individual nature, its own colour; it has its own landscape, its own atmosphere, its own diction. All details are closely connected, as in a finely meshed web; they are mutually dependent and point ahead or hark back. It is amazing to observe what part the imagery plays in helping to make the dramatic texture coherent as well as intricate. The same motif which was touched upon in the first act through the imagery, is taken up again in the second; it undergoes a fuller execution and expansion, perhaps, in the third or fourth. As Professor Spurgeon has demonstrated, these *leitmotifs* of the imagery run through the play like a brightly coloured thread. Of *Macbeth* it has been noted with acumen that Shakespeare substitutes the unity of atmosphere for the dramatic unities of time and action.[15] This is true of many of the Shakespearean tragedies. This unity of atmosphere and mood is no less a "dramatic unity" than the classical dramatic unities. And the imagery of a tragedy plays an important part, not only in creating a dramatic unity of the atmosphere, but also in binding the separate elements of the play together into a real organic structure.

Notes

1   For ambiguity in poetry and drama cf. William Empson, *Seven Types of Ambiguity*, London, 1930.
2   Further instances:

    Macbeth: But let the frame of things disjoint, both the worlds suffer,

                                    (III.ii.16)

    Othello: Methinks it should be now a huge eclipse
                  Of sun and moon, and that the affrighted globe
                  Should yawn at alteration.

                                      (v.ii.99)

    Lear: And thou, all-shaking thunder,
                  Smite flat the thick rotundity o' the world!

                                  (III.ii.7)

3   Cf. Max Deutschbein, *Die Kosmischen Mächte bei Shakespeare*, Dortmund, 1947.
4   Cf. my article "Shakespeare und das Königtum" in *Shakespeare Jahrbuch*, 1932.
5   *Antony and Cleopatra*, III.xiii.95.
6   *Antony and Cleopatra*, IV.xv.10.
7   *Macbeth*, IV.iii.6.
8   Cf. William Empson, *Seven Types of Ambiguity*, London, 1930, p. 23.
9   Cf. Spurgeon, *Shakespeare's Imagery*, p. 246.

10 For the background of Renaissance theory of humors cf. John W. Draper, *The Humors and Shakespeare's Characters*, Durham, NC, 1945.

11 *The Problem of Style*, 1923, p. 13.

12 Professor Spurgeon interprets this image as follows: "and finally, the vision of his 'intent,' his aim, as a horse lacking sufficient spur to action, which melts into the picture of his ambition as a rider vaulting into the saddle with such energy that it 'o'erleaps itself,' and falls on the further side" (*Shakespeare's Imagery*, p. 334).

13 *Shakespeare, A Survey*, p. 194.

14 *Shakespeare*, p. 273.

15 Max Deutschbein, *Macbeth als Drama des Barock*, Leipzig, 1936.

5

The "New Criticism" and *King Lear*

William R. Keast

Since the publication in 1935 of Caroline Spurgeon's elaborate investigation of the imagery of Shakespeare's plays, an increasingly large proportion of critical studies of the plays, whatever the differences of theory that have distinguished them, have taken the recurrent images of the plays as their primary data, often with the more or less explicit assumption that a careful study of these apparently less obvious and calculated elements is likely to bring us nearer to Shakespeare or his meaning than is the study of such more obvious elements as plot, character, and thought. It is probably safe to say that, at the present time, studies of Shakespearean imagery constitute, along with investigations of the relation of the plays to Renaissance or medieval thought (and the two sorts of study are frequently combined), the dominant modes of critical scholarship dealing with Shakespeare. Professor Heilman's book on *King Lear*[1] is, I believe, the most extensive single analysis of a Shakespearean play using its poetic imagery as the basic materials of investigation. Although it seems to me to be in almost all respects a bad book, it raises, in crucial form and with respect to a very great text, so many questions of importance both to the criticism of Shakespeare and to the study of literature generally as to justify fairly extended consideration.[2]

Heilman finds that the "meaning" of *King Lear*, and hence its structure and unity as a work of art, are most fully indicated in the patterns of recurrent images. When so read, it is "finally a play about the ways of looking at and assessing the world of human experience" (p. 28; cf. also pp. 133–4): its theme is intellectual conquest and salvation through imaginative vision.[3] It exhibits "the efforts of a sensitive but, in its haste and passion and initial inflexibility, not very well-equipped, mind to come to terms with, to master, a cosmos whose complexity and recalcitrancy we have always tangible and solidly visible before us" (p. 214). In his plans for dividing his kingdom and in his treatment of his daughters, Lear imposes upon the world a false, rationalistic standard of values when he should have relied upon imaginative insight, which alone is capable of making essential determinations of quality; this imposition, which is Lear's tragic flaw, brings to power the daughters, who embody in a pure form this shrewd, but ultimately false, rationalism; and, when he tries to accommodate their actions toward him to his innate, but hitherto unrecognized, standard of values, Lear goes mad. But in his madness, which is structurally the climax of the play, is regeneration: Lear, "by expiatory suffering, undergoes a spiritual recovery, an imaginative wakening; Shakespeare pictures him as coming again to an apprehension of values of which he had lost sight" (pp. 228–9). Since the play is a tragedy and not a melodrama, the inner and private conflict in *King Lear* coincides with a public or outer struggle – the conflict in Lear and Gloucester between reason and imagination as appropriate sources of values and faculties of understanding is paralleled and intensified by the external conflict between a set of shrewd, worldly people (Goneril, Regan, Edmund, Cornwall) and a set of apparently helpless incompetents (Edgar, the Fool, Lear), in which the first group, despite initial successes, stops at superficial understanding, and the latter, despite apparent failure, achieves profound insight into the nature of the world and man. The "central paradox" of the play, illuminating the spiritual progress of Lear and the external conflict alike, is that "the poor naked wretches of the play, the victims of the world, will survive in spirit. The gorgeous are doomed. In proud array, Lear failed; uncovered, half-naked, he is saved" (p. 86).

After a chapter of "Critical Preliminaries" in which he sets forth some of the elements of his theory and gives a general account of the play, Heilman devotes a chapter of his book to each of the chief patterns of poetic imagery in which he finds the meaning and structure of *King Lear* conveyed. The *sight pattern* (chap. ii), in which such "dramatic facts" as the blindness of Gloucester are combined with metaphors and explicit references involving sight and blindness, points the importance and difficulty of seeing and judging correctly; it is allied most closely to the *madness pattern* (chaps. viii and ix), in which Lear's madness co-operates with many images of madness and folly to suggest that man's fate in the world, and the possibilities of his salvation, depend on his mode of understanding. These two patterns, to which is joined a scheme of images based on the root concept of *values* (chap. vii), are concerned generally with "the process and method of *understanding* and coming to terms with" a complex world (p. 179; Heilman's italics) – the sight imagery with man's ability to recognize and identify phenomena, the madness imagery with his ability to interpret them. Taken together, these three patterns illuminate the problems faced by man as a perceptive moral agent; the remaining patterns set forth "in complex detail" the reality he seeks to understand. The *clothes imagery* (chap. iii) underlines the problem of distinguishing between appearance and reality; the many *animal* images (chap. iv) join to form a pattern that suggests the ease with which man may be degraded from his proper humanity; the references to *nature* and to deviations from the natural (chap. v) bring into play rival conceptions of nature as a norm and emphasize the dependence of judgment and action on man's conception of the natural; another scheme, centering on the concept of *age* (chap. vi), points to the relativity of such a human condition to the values by which it is judged; and the *justice pattern* (chap. vi), extending the implications of the nature imagery, emphasizes the difficulties of just action in a complex world. All these patterns and the dramatic facts to which they are related set forth "the problem of The World": "the great in the world seem to use their greatness badly or to achieve it at the cost of all spiritual values; these values are preserved best by those whom the world rejects" (p. 252). But *King Lear* does not rest in the assertion of an enigma; we are not left to wonder what security the victims of the world may hope to achieve. A final, and culminating, pattern implies, if it does not directly assert, the resolution. The *religion pattern*, composed of the many references in the play to the gods, "ties together the other observations upon man and gets hold of the nature of man in the most inclusive terms" (p. 255; cf. also pp. 277–8), resolving the paradoxes implied in the other patterns by suggesting that

> in the face of injustice man may believe in justice because the eternal gods will execute it. Man may speak in terms of a Nature which is Law because it is ordained by the gods whom he can invoke. The blind man sees because he can have insight into the divine reality. The sanity of the mad is that they can understand eternal truth. (p. 255)

This summary, while it is, I believe, just to the main lines of Heilman's interpretation, gives no indication of the detail in which the various patterns of imagery are worked out, of the manifold interconnections and paradoxical linkages that he discovers between the various parts of the play, or of the numerous subsidiary and cooperating significances which he integrates into the larger thematic movements. But it will suffice, perhaps, as background for discussion of some of Heilman's assumptions, methods, and discoveries.

I

We may begin by noticing some features of his theory of drama set forth in the "Critical Preliminaries."[4] It is, he tells us, "a theory of meaning" (p. 12): a play or a tragedy or, at any rate, *King Lear* (Heilman is not very much interested in distinctions of this kind; I suspect, although he nowhere says so, that his remarks apply to any literary work whatsoever) is a "structure of meanings." It makes, however indirectly or ironically, an ultimate assertion; it conveys a "total meaning," usually in the form of a paradox, of which a considerable number of subordinate meanings are the parts (parts related to the total meaning not as items to an arithmetical sum but "organically," the parts often "scarcely distinguishable parts of a whole" [p. 175]). What is fundamental in Heilman's analysis is therefore the subject or "problem" to which the total meaning of the play and its parts is related; to this subject everything in the play metaphorically refers:

> A series of dramatic statements about one subject does constitute a bloc of meaning which is a structural part of the play. This bloc may be understood as one of the author's metaphors. It is a metaphor just as a body of recurrent images, with its burden of implications, is a metaphor. The dramatist's basic metaphor is his plot. All of his metaphors are valid parts of his total meaning, the search for which must include a study of the relationship among the parts. All the constituent metaphors must be related to the large metaphor which is the play itself. (pp. 11–12; cf. also p. 153)

Though equally valid, the various metaphors which constitute the play's meanings are not equally revelatory: they form a hierarchy, in which the plot – the overt "dramatic facts" – is basic in the sense of being at the lowest level and expressing the meaning least fully. Although the play may be summarized in a fashion by taking it "simply at the level of plot," such a procedure gives us only "partial outlines" of its tragic form; "in its fullness," we are told, "the structure can be set forth *only* by means of the pattern of imagery" (p. 32, italics mine; cf. also pp. 33, 38). That the poetic imagery should express the play's "inner" or "symbolic" meanings more adequately than do the characters and their actions, that the patterns should be parts in a more essential way than the latter, is, of course, inevitable in such a scheme as Heilman's: if a play is a large metaphor for the author's attitude toward a problem, we must expect to find that words, with their manifold potentialities for combination and suggestion, provide a more appropriate vehicle for the expression of inner symbolic meanings than do the more severely limited happenings and their agents; and since the theory posits that metaphor is the "basic constituent of form" and takes the language of drama as the primary object of critical investigation (p. 4), it is not surprising that words should turn out to be the most significant feature of the play.

But if the play as a whole and its constituent parts are metaphors, if they signify their meanings not literally but symbolically, then it follows that when Heilman assigns a meaning to something in *King Lear*, his statement must take the form of "A is *like* B" rather than of "A *is* B," where A is some element of the play and B its alleged meaning. We must keep this fact always in mind in reading what he has to tell us about *King Lear*; for the exigencies of composition sometimes permit him a license in the use of the copula through which a literal reading of the play might be mistakenly inferred. Thus, when he says (p. 35) that Lear's abdication is "a kind of refusal of responsibility, a withdrawal from a necessary involvement in the world of action," we must not take him literally; what he means, if the play is a metaphor, is that Lear's action is *like* a refusal and a withdrawal. These terms – like "the immaculateness of nonparticipation" and the "attempted elusion of the fettering of circumstance" – have only a remote relation to Lear's plan to "unburthen'd crawl toward death" and to prevent future strife by immediate publication of his daughters' dowries. No character in the play criticizes Lear's aims in the abdication, but only his means of effecting them – the transfer of the kingdom to Goneril and Regan and the banishment of Kent and Cordelia.

This example illustrates a consequence of Heilman's theory more important than the symbolism it entails: the primary source and guaranty of the symbolic values he attaches to elements of the play are not in his inductions from the evidence of the text but in the necessities of his own theories of tragedy and morality; as in the passage just quoted, the symbolism contradicts, or is irrelevant to, the plain meaning of the text. The critic's theory functions in his analysis not so much in suggesting possible modes of artistic combination or effect that *may* be found as in stipulating what *must* be found; and his reading is therefore arbitrary in the sense that fundamental control over it is exercised not by the work but by a preclusive doctrine which dictates the nature of the basic symbolic relations in the play. The essentially arbitrary procedure to which his theory of tragedy leads can be seen in a few examples of symbolic interpretation as Heilman practices it, first in the explication of details of diction and then in the elucidation of the large metaphorical meanings of the play as a whole.

Heilman's chapter on the sight pattern supplies several characteristic examples of the strange results which follow his effort to work into the pattern all the references to sight and blindness in the play. To the ordinarily acute reader, I venture to say, the following exchange between Edmund and Gloucester would seem innocent enough of ulterior significance:

> *Glou.:* What paper were you reading?
> *Edm.:* Nothing, my lord.
> *Glou.:* No? What needed, then, that terrible dispatch of it into your pocket? the quality of nothing hath not such need to hide itself. Let's see: come, if it be nothing, I shall not need spectacles.
> *Edm.:* I beseech you, sir, pardon me …
> *Glou.:* Give me the letter, sir.
> *Edm.:* I shall offend, either to detain or give it. The contents, as in part I understand them, are to blame.
> *Glou.:* Let's see, let's see.[5]

Heilman finds a fine irony in the diction: "just when Gloucester most fails to see where he is going, he feels, like Oedipus, most shrewd and observant." The sight pattern, he says, "points the issue for us": "while he is being made to see things as Edmund wishes Gloucester feels that he is detecting the truth" – three times he says "Let's see," but he does not see (p. 45). But it is obvious that when Gloucester asks to see the letter, he does not feel shrewd or observant or as if he were detecting the truth – he feels the impatience of the curious and interested man when teased; his remarks would be appropriate to anyone, however illuminated he might be spiritually, in such a situation. And, since Edmund's plan unfolds only as the scene progresses and since we do not yet know that Gloucester will be taken in by it, we are scarcely in a position to appreciate the irony, even if it were present.

Having got this far from Shakespeare, Heilman forges ahead into the darkness:

> It is altogether logical, then, that Edmund's next move against Edgar takes place *at night* (II.i): the physical darkness betokens Gloucester's failure to see into what is going on. The actors in the nocturnal setting, indeed, represent more than one phase of a human plight: Gloucester victimizes and Edgar is victimized – he flees at night – because of the same kind of unseeingness. It is a meaningful, not merely a rhetorical, irony when Edmund calls, "Light, ho, here! / … Torches, torches! …" (33–4): those who want light least can call for it most loudly. Then Gloucester enters – how? "… with torches" (38) – the agent of light, but a kind of light – a physical reality like his eyes – that does him no good; it is inner illumination that he needs [pp. 45–6; Heilman's italics].

The "logic" Heilman discovers in the nocturnal setting for Edmund's next move is his, not Shakespeare's; for Edmund is surprised to learn that Cornwall is on his way to Gloucester's castle and decides on the spur of the moment to seize the opportunity thus presented for completing his design against Edgar. Edmund's call for torches is clearly part of his plan to appear to aid in the apprehension of Edgar; no one would have thought it merely rhetorical, but its meaning can scarcely be what Heilman says it is, for Edmund needs the lights very badly indeed – if there are none, no one will see his wound. That Gloucester in a scene laid at night and in answer to an urgent cry for torches should enter "with torches" seems to Heilman, intent upon his symbols, a veritable prodigy of metaphorical contrivance. The torches have shifted their symbolic allegiance in the space of four lines: when Edmund called for them, they were the kind of inner illumination he least wanted to have turned upon him; but now, when Gloucester carries them in, they are just ordinary physical lights, and the inner illumination has gone glimmering. Heilman goes on to attach a heavy symbolic weight to the references in the scene to the fact that Regan's visit to Gloucester's castle takes place at night (his count is wrong: there are four of these references in the scene, not just two); Regan, the point is, joins Edmund among those who must utilize the dark for their schemes. There are two excellent reasons for the references to darkness in the scene, neither very recondite: one is that it was customary, in plays acted in the afternoon, to aid the spectators' imaginations by verbal and spectacular identification of the physical scene – hence the references to night (and the torches);[6] second, that Regan uses the fact of their having traveled at night as proof of the importance of what she has to tell Gloucester, and thus she enhances our apprehensions about what is to come (ll. 120–31).

The examples I have so far given of Heilman's methods of interpretation have been limited to words and particular speeches. If we go to the other end of the metaphorical scale and consider the symbolic values attributed to the play as a whole, we will see the same arbitrariness in assigning such values, the same refusal to consider all the relevant evidence, and the same perverse ingenuity in avoiding the straightforward and direct.

In his preliminary discussion of the tragic structure of *King Lear*, Heilman writes as follows:

> In the latter part of the play Lear is reunited with Cordelia, and Gloucester with Edgar, just as in Act I the old men were enjoying close pseudo intimacies, respectively, with Goneril and Regan and with Edmund. It is, I think, not pushing the evidence too far to say that from the plot alone we may conclude that the change in associates has symbolic value. The reunion with the better children takes place after Lear and Gloucester have undergone a great deal of enlightenment; it may be read, then, as a kind of sign that there has taken place the achievement or recovery of insight which marks the experience of the tragic protagonists, just as their banishing of these children showed their fathers at their most obtuse. Thus Edgar and Cordelia symbolize a side of each of their parents, that side in which there lies the potentiality of salvation. But Edgar combats Edmund; Cordelia is on the opposite side from the sisters – those who once had parental confidence. By now the implication must be quite unmistakable: the children, like the Good and Evil Angels in Marlowe's *Faustus, represent the different elements which are in conflict in the fathers.* This is not true in a closely restrictive allegorical fashion, as we shall see; but it contains enough truth to indicate, together with what has already been said about the symbolic relationship between Lear and Gloucester, the essential tightness of structure of a play which has in it an unusual number of actions and characters. We see good and evil in conflict in the world, but by the structure we are reminded that the conflict is an emanation of that in the individual soul. Lear must recognize evil, must resolve his conflict – a conflict externalized in his attitudes to Goneril and Regan and Cordelia. By the fact of relationship the outer and inner evil become one, the two struggles are united. The children are not children for nothing; to be the father of Goneril is to create a symbol of the evil brought forth from oneself. The discerning reader of the play will hardly feel that he has done all his duty by hating Goneril. (pp. 33–4; Heilman's italics)

This is a notable, but by no means uncharacteristic, example of Heilman's open-field running. First, we have a simple *post hoc, ergo propter hoc:* since the reunions take place *after* Lear and Gloucester have undergone enlightenment, they are signs of the enlightenment (*after*, not *because*; for Lear's reunion with Cordelia is in no way the effect of his discoveries about his daughters but is brought about by the actions of Gloucester, before he is enlightened, and of Kent and Cordelia, who are enlightened throughout; and Gloucester's reunion with Edgar is the effect not of Gloucester's discovery but of Edgar's late decision to reveal himself to his father). That fallacy is enough to negate what follows, but in the interest of familiarizing ourselves with our critic's technique we may go on. We have next an interesting, but illicit, substitution of terms: "enlightenment," which the innocent reader is likely to take as a somewhat hyperbolic reference to Lear's discovery about his daughters, becomes first "achievement or recovery of insight," which still seems harmless enough, and then "salvation." Where did salvation come from? To most people – and, as we later learn, to Heilman – salvation means much more than "enlightenment"; it suggests a religious context to which the familiar meanings of "enlightenment" are inappropriate. We hear no more of salvation at the moment, but, as I have said, it is a key term in Heilman's exegesis of *King Lear* as a drama of intellectual conquest, and it is instructive to note how it makes its way into his analysis. But why, to go on, should Edgar and Cordelia, because they are reunited with their fathers after the latter have recovered their capacities for insight, symbolize anything? Obviously, because they are in a work in which everything is metaphorical; it will not do for them merely to take their part in the action. But why, if they must be symbols, should their symbolic value be established only at so late a stage in the play, within a few scenes of the end? What good is a crucial symbol if the author keeps it a secret, like the writer of a mediocre detective story? Shakespeare was clearly a novice, at least with symbols. But, assuming – as Heilman has no warrant to ask us to do – that we must read the play once to get the symbols fixed in our minds and at least once more to understand it, why should Edgar and Cordelia symbolize one side of their fathers' personalities? The author gives us the reason, on page 31, in his discussion of the tragic form: in the best tragedies the outer conflict is "symbolic of the movement of universal issues and is at the same time an objectification of the war within the protagonist" (cf. pp. 36–7). Now *King Lear* is one of the best tragedies; *ergo*, Edgar and Cordelia, who are part of the "outer" conflict, must symbolize an aspect of the "inner" conflict in the fathers. What is important here is not the obvious circularity of Heilman's reasoning but the derivation of symbolic connections, not from the text of Shakespeare's play, but from the critic's private theory of tragedy, which he asserts but never argues.

We are now in a position to grasp the curious logic by which Edmund, Goneril, and Regan come to symbolize the other side of their fathers' rather simple world. Edmund and Goneril and Regan are in conflict with Edgar and Cordelia; but, if one side of an outer conflict symbolizes the inner, so does the other; *ergo*. ... But Goneril is also in conflict with Regan – indeed, she kills her, which seems a far more intense form of conflict than any action of Edmund toward Edgar. Why, then, doesn't the conflict between them symbolize some refinement or qualification of the trait in the father which they symbolize together? Perhaps to ask for such an obvious extension of the symbolism would lead to the "closely restrictive" allegorism of which Heilman says the play is innocent. But other questions are relevant. The conflict between Edmund and Edgar is obviously of a very different order from that between Goneril and Regan and Cordelia; what is the discerning reader, who gets as far as Heilman takes him, to make of this difference? Does it not, he is likely to ask, affect the symbolic value of Edmund or Goneril and Regan? Evidently not; but why would a careful workman, anxious to avoid the abstractionism of allegory, rely on so vague and abstract a relationship as mere "opposition" for the identification of his symbols? Again we must go back to Heilman's views about tragedy, as we must for an answer to the question of why there are only *two* elements in conflict in Lear and Gloucester. Why not three? Because, simply, good and evil are in conflict in tragedy, but it is Heilman, not Shakespeare, who makes this simple reduction of what is, in fact, a very complex organization of relationships in the play, whose moral implications are never so flatly represented.

Occasionally, Heilman attempts to justify his symbolic readings by showing their superiority over other readings, but his technique here is no less arbitrary than that which he employs in making the symbolic connections themselves. He is perfectly well aware that his readings are unusual; there are always immediate interpretations for a word or a speech other than the one he wishes us to accept. Though he feels obliged, naturally enough, to take account of these alternatives, the reading which he asks us to reject in favor of his own is always unlikely or absurd, and, doubtless because of this, he never attaches the name of a critic to the rejected reading but proffers it anonymously. A simple instance of this technique is in his remark that Lear's kneeling to Cordelia in Act V, scene iii, is so different from his mock kneeling to Goneril in Act II, scene iv, that "it has a reassuring rather than a horrifying quality" (p. 142). Again, Lear's madness is not "an isolated fact" but the center of a pattern of meanings (p. 174); the "simplest meaning" of Lear's request for an ounce of civet is that he wants to take away an evil smell, but "beneath the semantic surface" the significance is that once Lear had too sweet an imagination but now he has discovered unsweetness and stench (p. 205); Lear's final speeches in Act IV, scene vi, "instead of being a rant," are related to the play structurally by being held within the sight pattern (p. 208); in explaining the sources of the early errors of Lear and Gloucester, "the easiest way out" is to say that they merely make mistakes in identity, but the hardest way out is to follow Heilman (p. 33).[7]

We are repeatedly asked to shun a reading that is obvious, foolish, superficial, self-contradictory, or merely irrelevant and to accept Heilman's symbolism as the true alternative. Why? There are many more readings than he presents to us, and many of them make a kind of sense superior to that of the sophomore responsible for Heilman's rejected interpretations. Obviously, the critic cannot be expected to give a variorum of critical opinion, but it would have reassured the reader and strengthened our critic's case if he had cited the best of these and argued the superiority of his own interpretation. As it is, the author has an easy victory, but probably not over anyone familiar with the play.

Heilman's errors in interpretation are thus the inevitable consequences of his theory. He begins with a determinate structural scheme which, since the work must express meanings, must be embodied in the work if it is to have artistic value. He knows, in all important respects, what he is going to find out before he begins, and it is no wonder that, having begged all the important questions, he should find it. His interpretation is, moreover, in the proper sense, materialistic: form and structure are for him derivative from, and therefore strictly dependent on, the matter which the work expresses; the form of the play, indeed, *is* its total meaning, and this is obviously not the characters, or their actions, or their thoughts, or even the language in which their thoughts are cast, but what these all represent. Were this not the case, Heilman's project would be meaningless; for these "more obvious" elements of the play, as he again and again points out, have been understood for a long time, while its "form" has not until now been apprehended. His theory, furthermore, is essentially a system of very simple dichotomies, which he attributes to the play itself.[8] And "meanings" are elaborated from a private and nonartistic theory of morality and religion, and then the necessary symbolic counterparts for the terms of the theory are "discovered" in the play.

A single example of this last influence of his theory upon his analysis of the play must suffice. In his final chapter Heilman tells us that *King Lear*, in addition to representing an eternal human problem, has also a historical relevance:

> At an extraordinarily early time Shakespeare got hold of the modern problem, got hold of it when the Renaissance had, so to speak, barely started it on its way. Lear, in one sense, represents the old order, and the play becomes the tragedy of that order. (pp. 278–9)

In what sense is it significant to speak of "the" modern problem? Who says, and on what evidence, that there is but one, or one more important than the rest? How do we know, if there is such a thing, that it is a modern problem only? Or, as some of Heilman's later remarks suggest, is it a problem that recurs in cyclical succession? What, in any case, is the evidence that this "problem" is the conflict between old and new orders rather than, say, between a search for security and a search for freedom common to all orders? Heilman goes on to say:

> Given this clash of forces whose ramifications extend deep into the nature of man (Goneril, the representative of the new order, is of the flesh and blood of Lear, the representative of the old), Shakespeare outlines, in intense dramatic compactness, the overwhelming problems which beset both the individual and the age at the historical crisis. (p. 280)

The children, indeed, are not children for nothing! It is in a way futile to ask why Goneril should symbolize the new order rather than Albany and Edgar, who are just as young, so far as we know, who identify themselves as the new generation (Act V, scene iii, ll. 325–6), and who survive – one to become king – and who might therefore be thought of as the "new" order. The reason, of course, is that Heilman believes all this nonsense about "the modern problem" and "the historical crisis" and knows what has to happen. Poor Bradley has been accused by modern critics of monumental crimes, chief among them being a habit of giving a psychological background for the characters in terms of his own, or his period's, conception of morality. The amplitude, privacy, and irrelevance of the moral, political, and religious theories by which Heilman supports – nay, determines – his reading of *King Lear* makes his distinguished predecessor seem like a beginner.

II

If Heilman's theory of the drama as metaphor forces him into arbitrary and hence often capricious interpretations of its symbolism, his conception of the function of imagery results in a construction that resembles a great play much less than it does an inferior philosophic dialogue. The critic lays it down that "in Shakespeare's language recurrency is an objective fact, not a figment of critics' enthusiasm" (p. 8), and everyone will probably agree. A word in a play, he continues, has "two kinds of meaningful relationship," explicit denotations, on the one hand, and, on the other, "latent meanings or dormant powers of suggestion that under certain circumstances may palpably modify or amplify the express meaning of the syntactical unit." *Hat*, to take his example, may refer to a man's headdress, or it "may contain, in unresolved form, the ideas, say, of formality or decency or protectedness" (p. 9). These implicative or suggestive powers are aroused when a word is repeated:

> A recurrent word, as I have said, is found to exist in a dual relationship: one of its links is to the thing denoted, the other to the sum total of uses of the word. All these uses constitute a community which by its very existence calls our attention to it and which, once we are aware of it, sets up imaginative vibrations and thus imparts to us meanings beyond the level of explicitness. Repetition itself is a mode of meaning. (p. 9)

In brief, "it is the recurrency of *hat* which calls *hatness* into the play, and *hatness* then is seen to have some thematic import in the work as a whole" (*ibid.*). Now, although Heilman goes on to say that the symbolic value of the word (e.g., the reference of *hatness* to *formality* or *decency* rather than, say, to *roguishness* or *avarice*) is "fairly likely" to be given an unequivocal statement at some time or other in the play and although, as I have said, he later speaks of such elements as character and action as providing the "most obvious" means of recognizing the recurrent patterns of imagery, these are not categorical requirements, and they sound very much like useful, but by no means essential, props for the less discerning.

It is evident that Heilman has not thought through, or has not given an adequate statement of, the mode of relationship between the patterns of poetic imagery and other elements of the play. If *hatness* in a given play means *formality*, how do we know this? The latent meanings and suggestive powers of a word are infinite apart from the play and, by Heilman's definition, not limited by the context in which they appear; unless interpretation is merely to display the linguistic virtuosity of the critic, some basis must be found on which the potentialities of signification in words can be realized in particular meanings appropriate to the play. It is fantastic to assert that the repetition of basic words "opens the consciousness to all the expressive possibilities of these words" (p. 18); for repetition could do this no more readily than could single occurrence, and, if it did, the play could obviously make no unified impression at all. What repetition, artistically handled, does is to open those possibilities, and those only, that are relevant to the play. But, clearly, Heilman is speaking loosely here; for he adds that the "resources" of the symbol are tapped differently according to "different contextual demands." And this is precisely the point; for it must be to the context, immediate or more remote, that the imagery is referred, and this necessity establishes the priority, both in the structure of the play and in critical analysis, of the primary determinants of the context – character, situation, antecedent action, intention, and the like, as all these are involved in the plot. If *hat* is to signify *formality* or a cognate concept throughout the play and if the play's effect is to be determined by the writer and not by the whim of the critic, then the connection between the two terms must be established in a metaphor or image in a context in which *formality* is clearly set forth as a basic term in the thought of a character, or in his mental or psychological makeup, or in the circumstances in which he acts, or in the standards of value employed by one or more of the characters, or in some similar manner. And I should think that this connection would have to be established early in the play if a pattern in any genuine sense is to be formed; for, in the absence of an explicit designation of the symbolic value of a word, no amount of repetition can produce anything except vagueness. Only when such a connection has been unequivocally established and when the symbol recurs in the same kind of context are we licensed to invoke "imaginatively" the earlier metaphorical attachment of *hat* to *formality*.

All this means, of course, that the verbal patterns are strictly relative to, and dependent for their value upon, those "larger and more conspicuous elements" of the drama of which Heilman takes so cavalier a view; and it means, further, that these verbal patterns cannot be the primary elements in the play's structure, as Heilman's procedure implies; for what is essentially derivative cannot provide the unifying principle for that from which it is derived. No one would suppose that the proper significance could be assigned to the thoughts expressed by the characters in a play except in relation to the characters expressing them and the circumstances and ends in relation to which they are expressed; a fortiori, therefore, the imagery, which is but one aspect of the expression of the thought, cannot be properly evaluated except in terms of a prior and controlling consideration of the thought, character, circumstances, etc. Heilman constantly reverses this order. For him the meanings expressed in the recurrent imagery are broader and more fundamental than those expressed in the action of *King Lear*; character and action are relative to the patterns, and their meanings exist for them. This inversion of the proper artistic relationships among the elements of the play can be seen in his assertion that from the plot of the play we can discern only "partial outlines" of its form, which must be "amplified and corrected" by the evidence of the symbolic language (p. 32), and in his contention that only the skeleton of the play can be derived from the plot, the flesh and blood from the poetic-dramatic patterns (p. 38; cf. also p. 25), but his whole analysis involves standing the play on its head.

The necessary consequence of this separation of the imagery from its proper artistic relation to the more important elements in the drama can be seen when Heilman comes to decide upon the order in which to consider the poetic patterns. By denying the relativity of the imagery, in any essential way, to character or action, Heilman has deprived himself of one principle of order among his patterns – the artistic order provided by the plot of *King Lear*. In place of this he has substituted an abstract order based on the implications which he discerns among the patterns. This we see when, in the "Critical Preliminaries," he tells us that his sequence of discussion is that "into which the different problems of meaning seem naturally to fall" (p. 27) and adds that the sight pattern is a "quite logical" place from which to work toward the "heart" of the drama because its chief figure is Gloucester, who is in a secondary tragic role. On artistic grounds it would seem that Gloucester's secondary role was the best possible reason for *not* starting with a pattern of imagery focused chiefly on him, but rather with the primary tragic figure in relation to whom his secondary function in the play is defined. But Heilman's order of procedure is not artistic but dialectical – from the outside in, from the secondary to the essential, from the surface to the heart – and the discussion is controlled by an extrinsic criterion, the "natural" order among the problems dealt with in the play. Thus he tells us that the sight pattern "prepares us for the study of evil that finds its main treatment in the madness pattern" (p. 51). Prepares us in what sense? Clearly not in the sense that the speeches of Goneril and Regan at the end of Act I, scene i, prepare us for their later actions toward Lear, by forming our expectations through a statement of the ends for which they act and of the principles and physical means at their disposal; for the sight and madness patterns, developing simultaneously, have no proper temporal relation, and whatever expectations the imagery arouses cannot be in terms of character or action. The sight pattern prepares for the madness pattern through logical implication – what the sight pattern asserts, we are told, is that "to have eyes, and to see not, is to be at the mercy of evil, and thus to aid evil. Not to see is not to understand" (p. 51); and, since the madness pattern is concerned directly with the problem of understanding, the connection between the two is evident.[9] The connection is similar to that by which one level of discussion in a Platonic dialogue prepares for that above it, by formulating a paradoxical statement or question for resolution on the basis of truer or more inclusive principles. This movement back and forth, or up and down, between the various levels of significance in the play is the chief source of the countless paradoxes that Heilman finds in *King Lear*; their presence should surprise no one; for, given the assumptions that the critic makes about the kind of work it is, it is impossible that "paradoxes" of this kind should not be there.

As a final example of Heilman's dialectical manipulation of the problems with which he symbolically connects the play, we may consider the following, in which I have italicized the critic's intrusions:

> The problem of the natural, we have seen, is elaborated by means of the imagery of injury and disease. *A comparable symbol of the vulnerability of human nature is age*, and of age there is significant awareness throughout the play. Further, the constant thinking in terms of what is natural and of the violation of the natural *would suggest, we might expect*, the subject of justice; and, as a matter of fact, the subject is a recurrent one in *King Lear*. Finally … in a world in which standards of justice differ and in which we must find methods of discrimination, *it is but a step* to the problem of values. *Through the problem of values we shall approach* what we have already said is the basic theme of the play – the problem of understanding. (p. 134; cf. also pp. 64, 87, 133, 255)

Heilman's conception of the primacy of poetic imagery in the structure of the play leads necessarily to a view of *King Lear* as a logical or, better, a dialectical structure. The ultimate rationale of the parts is in their common bearing on a linked set of philosophic problems, the full significance of which the play, primarily through its imagery, progressively explores. The order of exploration and of understanding is a movement from the outer appearance to the inner reality, from the relatively simple to the more complex, from the particular to the universal, from the many to the one, in a sequence of levels of discussion in which what appears as complexities and paradoxes at one level is transformed, at the level next above, into a new paradox, embracing a larger area of meaning and approaching nearer to truth, until at last all the dialectical oppositions of the (logically) preceding levels are given a final translation in the apprehension of transcendental truth.[10] Whatever the philosophic merits of this procedure, it is not artistic in any distinguishable sense of that word; for it is a method of universal application, potential alike to the discovery of philosophic truth, the interpretation of dreams, the disclosure of religious mysteries, and, if one chooses, the implication of meanings by "plays."[11] Heilman reduces – or elevates, depending on one's preferences in art and philosophy – *King Lear* to an epistemological discourse in dialogue form. And this invites us to look at the epistemology.

III

The battles for physical and moral survival in *King Lear*, according to Heilman, are interpenetrated by "philosophic or quasi-philosophic struggles" (p. 281), and the problems about which these struggles revolve constitute an "amazingly inclusive anthropology" (p. 177). The play asks such questions as: What is man's nature? What is nature? (p. 26). What is reason? What is folly? What is wisdom? In what way of thinking about experience is man's salvation? (p. 27). The play poses and suggests, if complexly, answers to the problems of seeing, of the uses and limits of rationalism, of innocence, of appearance and reality, of values, of the definition of "man's essential humanity," of the kinds of mental balance, of man's mode of understanding experience, of distributive justice, of man, and of The World. And, as we have seen, to the consideration of these eternal questions is joined Shakespeare's attack on "the modern problem."

From a play which "constantly labors" so many basic questions, which is "speculatively very active" in the realm of metaphysics, which "explores" such transcendental issues and aims at definitions of principles so fundamental,[12] we might expect, if the play deserves the reputation which three centuries have brought it, answers, or at least adumbrations of answers, of some intellectual distinction. But if we expect this we shall be disappointed. The philosophic yield from *King Lear* is pitifully meager – a poor thing by comparison, say, with that from the *Novum organum* or the *Laws of Ecclesiastical Polity*. Heilman's Shakespeare, it may be, labors, but he brings forth little more than platitudes. When the wonderful imagery of *King Lear* has been reduced to sense, and the doctrines of the play, disrobed of their ornaments, are left to the powers of their naked excellence, what shall we discover? That man, though he is liable to damnation, may yet achieve salvation (p. 91); that man is wholly evil when reason and animality work together (p. 105); and that there is, despite the horrifying chaos of phenomena, a substantial universal order upon which men may rely (p. 151). We may learn yet more – that man is a rational animal (pp. 98–100) and that man's weakness puts him in need of persuasion and that he is therefore subject to influence (p. 241). To these profound principles of natural knowledge are added some moral instructions equally new – that rational man is in danger of rationalizing essential values out of existence (p. 177); that real insight is apparently doomed to ill success in the world (p. 249); and that, while men may pray for justice because the gods will execute it, they cannot dictate the terms on which their prayers will be answered (pp. 255, 268). Surely a man of no very comprehensive search may venture to say that he has heard all this before. That these principles are profound and important no one is likely to question – so is the Golden Rule; but that the assertion of them, even through the details of a particular case, is likely to be powerfully moving, as the play has always been felt to be, is manifestly improbable. The grand irony of Heilman's interpretation of *King Lear* is that the more closely he approaches the play's total meaning – the more successful he is in suggesting the One which interpenetrates the Many – the more trivial the play becomes. As drama it is superb, original, inimitable; as philosophy – or even "quasi-philosophy" – it is commonplace and undistinguished, amply justifying Shaw's protest against the "pretentious reduction of the subtlest problems of life to common-places, against which a Polytechnic debating club would revolt," and to platitudes "that even an American professor of ethics would blush to offer to his disciples."

So bald a restatement of some of the meanings of his *King Lear* may seem unfair to Heilman's analysis, if not to the play; for he points out on several occasions that the play does not assert or demonstrate its meanings as would a philosophic treatise: they are adumbrated or implied, usually in a paradoxical fusion of what normally appear to be incompatible areas of experience, so that what we have in the play is not didacticism or philosophy but embodiment and implication.[13] But a paradox is a mode of assertion; implications must be made explicit if we are not to surrender ourselves and the play to critical caprice. Despite his repeated emphasis on the method of paradox, Heilman emphatically denies that, in *King Lear*, Shakespeare is "resting in a detached presentation of the ambiguities of experience" (p. 189; cf. pp. 69, 91). Indeed, the mode of connection which we have observed Heilman establishing among the image patterns of the play is necessitated by the need to resolve, in the interests of a positive and not merely ambiguous significance, the paradoxes of each subordinate pattern of imagery in a supervening implication at a higher level. Thus the ironies of the good man's fate in the world suggested by the clothes and sight patterns are resolved in the nature pattern's implication of a higher realm in which the very qualities responsible for misfortune in the world become the conditions of salvation. And all the paradoxes of the play are resolved in the implications of the religion pattern, which suggests that the perception of eternal truth is the sanity of the mad, the dress of the naked, the sight of the blind, and the eternal life of the old (pp. 252–3, 255, 284–7).

Our author, evidently sensitive to the elementary quality of the meanings of *King Lear* when they are stated as such, attempts to save them from dismissal and to redeem the play by telling us that the meanings are "complexly," not simply, asserted. His chief instrument in this endeavor is the paradox, which avoids the obvious and encompasses the radically dissimilar; but he has more direct ways of arguing the "inordinately complex world," the "vast implications" that the play figures forth. What Heilman means by a "complex" as distinct from a "simple" view of things may be illustrated in his treatment of Lear's anguished comment on his evil daughters (Act IV, scene vi, ll. 126–9):

> Down from the waist they are Centaurs
> Though women all above;
> But to the girdle do the gods inherit,
> Beneath is all the fiend's.

The "complexity" of the attitude underlying these lines Heilman indicates as follows:

> Man is equally capable of salvation or damnation. The Centaur is exactly the right image here, for it admits the possibility of high intellectual and spiritual attainment yet connotes primarily the proneness to violence and disorder which the play exhibits throughout. It exhibits man as a rational animal. (p. 100)

Man, that is to say, is not entirely angelic or entirely bestial, but both! Again, in commenting on the treatment of the problem of justice, he says:

> Indeed, not only Lear, but other characters, think repeatedly of justice; some ignore the subject entirely, but those who are conscious of it never lose faith that justice is being done or will at some time be done. Yet justice is treated complexly; human beings are not just at all times; and injustice is a fact, a fact which Shakespeare obviously treats with great fullness. (p. 145)[14]

Complexity, it would appear, is a negative virtue – it really amounts only to the avoidance of the simple-minded; if an artist, even a mediocre one, represented man as entirely human or entirely animal, as always just or always unjust, we should be obliged to say that he was a simpleton and his work, if it purported to be serious, absurdly irrelevant to common experience. But is it meaningful to dignify as "complex" the mere avoidance of the ridiculous? If it is, then a host of hacks who are at least familiar with the facts of life are eligible for critical acclaim on the basis of their complexity; but it has been thought for a long time, and rightly, that Shakespeare's principal tragedies were wonderfully complex in some sense which makes them irreducible to the simplest axioms of human conduct.

The chief evidence of the "complexity" of attitude and implication in *King Lear*, however, is to be found in its paradoxes; and here, too, we find evidence of Heilman's simplism, for most of his paradoxes are merely puns, dependent rather on the ambiguities of words than on any genuine fusion of unlike things. The theory of the paradox was well developed in rhetorical literature in the Renaissance, and its practice extensively cultivated; a paradox in the fullest and most serious sense was taken to be a statement contrary to common opinion, yet true, such as Donne's assertion that "Nature is our worst Guide"; formally, it often, but by no means always, involved an opposition of contrary terms. The paradoxes of Heilman are rarely of this sort. One of the more important of them is that the blind may see, while those who see may be blind. But the paradox is only apparent: for *blindness* and *seeing* have different meanings on the two sides of both these assertions, and unless the *blindness* is in the organs or to the phenomena of which sight is said in the predicate to be possible, where is the paradox? Who would be surprised, or even illuminated (and wondrous apprehension, as Puttenham's name for the figure surely indicates, is essential to the genuine paradox), by the assertion that blind men can apprehend spiritual truth? – surely no one in a religious, as well as verbally sophisticated, age, however plausible as paradox the pun may now seem. Similarly with the paradoxes that the naked may survive better than the well-protected and that age may endure: the naked in *King Lear* do not survive in terms of their nakedness, and age does not endure in any sense in which it is significant to speak of it as old. What we have in Heilman's *King Lear*, it would seem, is a body of platitude garbed in a merely verbal "complexity."

IV

Even if it were not true that the "meaning" of *King Lear* becomes, on Heilman's reading of it, a commonplace repetition of Christian parables, his theory and method have two further disadvantages. On the one hand, his conception of the "problems" of the play subverts its moral basis and consequently undermines its effect – by reducing character to an aspect of thought; and, on the other hand, he makes it impossible to read the play with understanding by converting into ultimate "implications" the ethical and philosophic assumptions on which it does in fact rest.

Important and difficult problems are unquestionably raised in *King Lear* – Lear, for example, is forced to deal with the problem posed by the impact of Cordelia's apparently unfilial behavior upon his love for her and his plans for the future; later he must cope with the problem raised by Goneril and Regan's refusal to carry out the terms of his gift of the kingdom to them. The important aspect of these problems for our present purpose is their quality: they are problems of specific characters (and, despite the mirror plot in the play, there are always important differences among the parallel problems of parallel characters); they are specifically defined by the character and his immediate circumstances, ceasing to be problems, or precisely the same problems, when character or circumstances are altered; they are dynamically related not only to character but to one another, the solution or failure of solution of one problem generating a further problem, and so on; they are fundamentally moral rather than intellectual problems – calling for action and involving deliberation and choice in terms of moral ends and ethical principles; and they are all definitively solved in one way or another before the end of the play. This is to say merely that a continuum of concrete moral problems provides the framework for the action of the play. It is not to suggest that intellectual or philosophic questions are not raised or are not important in the action, but it is to say that the relation of such questions – of which Lear's efforts in his madness to get at the nature of justice may serve as an example – to problems of the first sort must be kept clear: the intellectual problems arise from failures to deal satisfactorily with problems of a practical order, and the terms in which these intellectual problems are cast derive their meanings from the ethical context in which antecedent moral problems had been framed; the outcome of the solution of intellectual questions, in *King Lear* at least, is never repose in the abstract solution but a readjustment of character and thought to the circumstances and a renewal of the action on the practical level. In general, efforts of the characters to solve intellectual or philosophic questions function to supply the premises for action or discovery; but it is always for the sake of the latter that such problems are raised.

It is not in specific moral problems or even in contributory philosophic questions that Heilman finds the "meanings" of his *King Lear*. The problems of his *King Lear* are not so much problems of particular characters as problems of "the play"; once introduced, they remain unchanged, even if they are treated with increasing "complexity," throughout the play; they are related to one another not dynamically, through character, but logically, as we have seen; they are intellectual ("What is nature?" "In what way of thinking about experience is man's salvation?") rather than moral – directed, that is, not to action and happiness but to truth and salvation; and they are not solved before the end of the play but have their solutions metaphorically implied by the play as a whole.

The importance of these differences is in their consequences for the status of character and moral action in *King Lear*. The specific moral problems first mentioned are relative in each case to character: each is the problem of one character only, deriving its alternatives from the interrelation of his ends and moral principles and the possibilities available to him under the circumstances of the moment; the problem can never be understood apart from the character; and its artistic importance is in permitting a display of character (in deliberation, choice, or action) through which an ethical response is evoked and in engaging a character toward whom our feelings have thus been aroused in actions through which his happiness or misery is determined. The kind of problem with which Heilman conceives the play to be fundamentally concerned is not, thus, relative to character; character, rather, is relative to the problems; indeed character becomes for him merely the attitudes of the persons of the play to the leading problems with which it deals. "In one sense," we are told, "all the experiences of the major characters are a testing of ideas of theirs" (p. 128); and throughout the analysis it is clear that the characters take their places in the "structure" because of what and how they think or perceive – because of their mode of understanding, to use Heilman's phrase – for the unity of the play is in its "meanings," and these, so far as the characters are concerned, are expressed primarily in the attitudes, beliefs, and intellectual habits of the dramatis personae. Lear's tragic flaw is therefore intellectual rather than moral – he "endeavors to introduce quantitative norms where the questions are entirely qualitative" (pp. 217–18).[15] The effect of this conception of the play's problems is to dissolve or subvert the moral basis of the drama by making not what the characters are and do so much as what and how they think the cause of their happiness or misery.

But how, even if it were true that a work thus deprived of its moral basis could have the kind of emotional effect that *King Lear* has always been thought to have, could the play as Heilman interprets it be intelligible at any level? For his method necessitates treating the very premises on which the characterization and action of the play depend for their intelligibility as if they were not premises but unsolved problems.

Thus in his discussion of the nature pattern, Heilman tells us that the term "nature," in "the metaphorical usage of this play," besides signifying a normal ordered functioning of the physical world, "comes also to mean a normal, ordered functioning of the *moral* world, a final principle to which all moral phenomena are to be referred" (p. 119; Heilman's italics). "Comes also to mean" is inaccurate, for the conception of nature as moral order is evident from the first two scenes of the play and is obviously presupposed as a criterion for the assessment of Edmund's soliloquy at the opening of Act I, scene ii; Heilman himself retracts his phrase in going on to say of nature as a moral order that "many characters rely on this principle of order, they understand in terms of it; and they judge phenomena by it, as their language constantly shows." But perhaps this is only an apparent retraction, for Heilman's statements and his entire analysis suggest that in his view such fundamental questions as whether nature is a moral order in the universe are not determined until the end of the play; for Shakespeare, we are told, although "he does not choose sides in any obvious sense," finally implies the side that he is on:

> Throughout the verbal and dramatic patterns of the play, throughout the structural dualities, there is a consistent and continual intimation: in the cosmos there is a justice (whatever the injustice in fact), there is an order (whatever the chaos in fact), there is an underlying reality (whatever the deceptiveness of appearance); in man there is a sight (whatever the blindness in fact) and an imaginative understanding (whatever the rationalistic obtuseness that may periodically dominate him) by which he may seize upon the realities necessary to his survival. These are the implications of the key words in the play. (pp. 286–7; cf. also pp. 325–6)

During the play the issue between these "structural dualities" is undecided, and it is the "tension" between these "contrapuntal oppositions" that gives the play its effect. A choral speech on nature is "not to be taken as dogmatic and final" but becomes "a hypothesis which the drama as a whole may reject or confirm" (p. 108); and concerning the opposition between Edmund's view of nature and that of certain other characters, Heilman writes:

> The question is … whether he [Shakespeare] stops with a presentation of the complexities of definition – which is in itself no minor literary [sic] task or whether all the evidence of the play has the effect of making, in dramatic form, a judgment upon the problem of conflicting usages. (p. 124)

To write thus about the indeterminacy of the key terms in the play is flatly inconsistent with the view that "the play as a whole proceeds on the assumption that nature is a principle of order – a principle subject to violation and apparently conquerable by chaos, and yet ultimately able to assert itself as the order of the whole and to bring into conformity with it that other 'nature' of Edmund's …" (p. 127); it is illogical to refer to an "assumption" as a "conflicting usage" upon which judgment is to be passed. Are we to convict Shakespeare of a circularity which will only intensify the low opinion of his philosophic powers that Heilman's statement of the play's meanings encourages us to entertain – the assumption of a premise which he then proceeds to "prove"? Or are we not rather to convict Heilman of reading the play in two quite different ways and of playing both ends against the middle? Surely, his instinct rather than his method is correct: the play as a whole presupposes – it asserts as a premise, it takes for granted, it includes among its *données* – that there is a justice, an order, an underlying reality, etc.; and the play as a whole "implies" these things, if it does so at all, only because they have already been built into the play as the basis of its probabilities, the ground for judgments of character, the conditions of immediate and over-all expectancy, and the terms for the statement of its particular moral problems. The reader knows from the outset, and does not have to wait for the ultimate dissolution of a system of dichotomies to learn, that the view of nature put forward by Edmund is, in all essential respects, wrong; that Gloucester, in the premises which he uses to judge Edgar, is correct; that Goneril and Regan's "case" against Lear's retainers is false. We know, in general, the fundamental answers to all Heilman's problems as soon as they become problems for the characters. For Shakespeare, unlike a good many modern novelists and unlike many dramatists of his own time, such as Beaumont and Fletcher, is an ironist in the proper sense – he supplies the audience with the premises and information withheld from, or wrongly interpreted by, the characters, in order that we may understand them, make judgments about them that will permit us to be emotionally affected by what happens to them, see their actions and sufferings as probable consequences of their knowledge and intentions, and – however surprised we may be at the turns of the action – recognize the inevitability of each and of the eventual outcome.

Heilman confuses "implication" and "presupposition," and he fails to distinguish between the problems of certain of the characters (e.g., Lear's uncertainty about nature as a moral order) and the problems of the play and its readers. If the solutions or implications of Heilman's problems emerge only when the play is complete, then there is no real basis for understanding it or for being affected by it; if, on the other hand, premises necessary to the intelligibility of the play are indeed provided, most or all of Heilman's problems disappear.

<h1 style="text-align:center">V</h1>

Even if it were not true, however, that *King Lear* is strictly unintelligible on Heilman's assumptions, the effect of the play suggested by his interpretation is one which no one has ever attributed to *King Lear*, which is, moreover, inappropriate to tragedy, and which, finally, Shakespeare's text does not support. On the whole, Heilman has very little to say about the way in which *Lear* affects the spectator and reader; and, while we may grant that the critic's main effort should be concentrated on the details of the text, this effort is likely to be undirected or misdirected unless it is controlled by a hypothesis – progressively confirmed or altered and, in any case, refined, as the analysis proceeds – concerning the precise quality of the power that the work exercises. Although Heilman acknowledges in his "Critical Preliminaries" a certain obligation to Aristotle, he finds no use for Aristotle's insistence that pity and fear are the emotions proper to tragedy and that from them as ends the specific properties of the form may be inferred. When Heilman mentions pity, it is usually reduced to pathos (or "mere pathos"), and his intention is to show the inadequacy of the emotions suggested by this word to *King Lear*, as in his judgment of the initial mistakes of Lear and Gloucester:

> These errors may be fatal or merely pathetic; but we are not invited merely to condemn or to sympathize. Instead we are compelled to enter fully into perceptual experiences of distracting difficulty and hence to feel – if not to follow out to metaphysical conclusions – oppressive problems of personal identity. (pp. 68–9)

Fear, so far as I am aware, he does not mention at all, not even to deny its relevance.[16] Although there are vague references to the force and power of the play as a whole and of certain of its scenes, nowhere are the specific emotional effects of the force and power made clear; when Heilman mentions an emotion it is always to deny that it is appropriate to the "inner reality" of the play.

We are not invited to condemn or sympathize; we are not to be horrified or cynical or sentimental. What state are we to be in? The answer should be apparent in the light of what has so far been said. We are to be enlightened, shown, convinced, or illuminated – we are to undergo, in short, the intellectual effect proper to one who perceives, after great difficulty, the One gleaming through the Many. Thus, in the passage just quoted, Heilman tells us that, instead of pity or antipathy, we are to feel "oppressive problems" of personal identity because we have entered into difficult "perceptual experiences"; later, denying that pathos alone, which is "too easy," could account for the powerful impression made by the scenes of Lear's madness, he insists that "beneath the superficial aspects of these scenes [those, that is, which make them shocking, terrible, and pathetic], there must be felt, by even a casual student, a reverberation of underlying meanings which constitute the inner reality of the scenes" (p. 173); and still later he points out that the play is bent, not upon giving final answers to the problems it raises, but "upon evoking a sense of their magnitude and of the well-nigh intolerable burden which they place upon the human mind" (pp. 177–8).

That the principal effect of the play must be some mode of intellectual activity, accompanied by appropriate but vague emotional overtones, could have been inferred from Heilman's early discussion of tragedy (pp. 30–2). Tragedy is not concerned, he tells us there, with "evil fortune that may lead to cynicism and despair" (p. 31). We gladly assent and look forward to a statement of the kind of emotion, if it is not cynicism and despair, that the evil fortune of tragedy does lead to; but we are rewarded with a different line altogether:

> Tragedy is concerned, not with evil fortune that may lead to cynicism and despair, but with evil that is understandable in terms of human character; a literary work that tells of destructive mischances may have its own excellence and validity, but its cosmos is a quite different one from that of tragedy. Tragedy records, eventually, victory rather than defeat; it asserts the authority of the spiritual scheme of things to which man, because of his flaw, does violence; and it presents man as understanding his deviation, undergoing a spiritual rehabilitation, recovering the insights by which he may endure. The suffering in tragedy is not an end, but a product and a means; through it comes wisdom and, if not redemption, at least a renewed grasp upon the laws of redemption. The Eumenides exist only because man's soul is not corrupt. (pp. 31–2)

"Understandable in terms of human character" replaces the designation of an emotion alternative to cynicism and despair, and we learn that the tragic protagonist has fundamentally intellectual ends, that his tragic error is intellectual, and that he is finally victorious. A tragedy, it would appear, traces the progress of a good man with an intellectual flaw from bad fortune to good (recovery of insights by which he may endure; redemption or renewed grasp upon the laws of redemption) – in other words, from rationalistic rags to imaginative riches. Since the "action" of the play is the paradoxical statement and enacted solution of philosophic problems arising from intellectual error and standing in the way of redemption or salvation and since redemption or salvation is a recovery of true insight, it obviously follows that the audience is to undergo an intellectual experience which parallels the spiritual progress of the protagonist (cf. p. 213).

If the play, in these terms, can have any emotional effect, it can be only a kind of awe (at the magnitude of the problems to be solved) combined with attenuated pity (because the sufferings of the protagonist are seen to be the necessary means to salvation), giving place to joy in the reversal (when insights are recovered and salvation achieved). It is not accidental that Heilman refers on several occasions to the similarities between his *King Lear* and *The Divine Comedy*, for the latter, though, as Dante said, quite opposite to tragedy, is precisely this kind of work. *King Lear*, so far as I am aware, has not been generally regarded, even by the more perceptive, as a joyful work; yet in the terms in which Heilman describes it I do not see how it can be anything else. The whole tendency of his analysis – with its emphasis on salvation as the goal of Lear's actions, with its Christian "transvaluation" of a pagan world, with its placement of the climax of the play in Lear's reachievement of insight, with its treatment of the reversal as a passage from bad fortune to good – all this and much more make it clear that Lear is a man who, after much suffering, which is expiatory and therefore in the proper sense deserved, achieves what he had all along been in search of – the vision in which is eternal life. That Lear dies, that he loses Cordelia at the moment of their reunion – these are incidental, parts of the play's superficial aspect, not of its inner reality, and serving at most to underscore paradoxically the magnitude of Lear's victory; for he that loseth his life shall find it. Only a person incapable, as Heilman says, of distinguishing between quality and quantity of life could feel anything but spiritual exaltation at Lear's triumph over himself and the world.

This interpretation is certainly original; for it has not been common among critics of *King Lear* to state its primary effect in terms of salvation or spiritual triumph and the emotional consequences of these. But Heilman's interpretation is not merely original, it is preposterous. It violates the unmistakable signs of the play's effect which appear in the text, and it is founded upon a radical confusion of the feelings which a sensitive and inquiring reader might have *after* the play is over with those he has *during* the action itself. That Lear recovers or achieves penetrating insights into himself and the world is a commonplace of critical discussion of this play, as is the observation that the action suggests – or more properly, presupposes – a morally ordered universe. But do the concrete language and action of *King Lear*, the particular details of its development as a drama, contain clear signs that Lear's career to the end of the play is to be thought of as having such insights and the affirmation of such a universe as its goal? Are we regularly reminded – indeed, are we reminded at all – that Lear's recovery of an imaginative synthesis, his earning the "realm of spirit," is what gives order and unity to the latter part of the play? Are we given in any way to understand that the attainment of "needful spiritual insight" is an ultimate end, or even a consolation? Why, if this is his end, does Lear cry out, over Cordelia's body:

> This feather stirs; she lives! If it be so,
> It is a chance which does redeem all sorrows
> That ever I have felt.

What, if some inner structure tending toward salvation is the unifying principle, is the sense of Kent's lines,

> That from your first of difference and decay
> Have followed your sad steps,

and his chilling words, "All's cheerless, dark, and deadly"? Why does Albany refer to Lear as "this great decay," and why does Kent, as Lear dies, say "Break, heart; I prithee break!"? And finally, not to prolong the list indefinitely, how is Heilman's etherealized conception of Lear's end compatible with the speech in which Kent adjures Edgar against attempting to revive the king:

> Vex not his ghost. O, let him pass! He hates him
> That would upon the rack of this tough world
> Stretch him out longer.

Our present business, says Albany, is "general woe." Could Shakespeare have written a final scene – let alone the rest of the play – in which the comments of all the characters so obviously contradicted the effect he wished to produce?[17] To suppose so is both to take a very low view of Shakespeare's art and to disregard completely the necessities of popular dramaturgy.[18] Surely it is more consistent – with the text, with what we know of tragedy and of the conditions of Elizabethan theatrical practice, and with the mass of critical opinion about *King Lear* – to regard Lear's imaginative insights as occasioned by and directed toward his need for love and happiness with Cordelia, and to be moved by the awful irony of Lear's return to his original majesty, to an even greater majesty because it is now joined to a deep awareness of his humanity as well, precisely when it is too late for him to achieve that which alone makes majesty, authority, even humanity, meaningful and valuable to him. If, as we watch Lear's final agony over the body of Cordelia, we ascend to a higher level, on which the general woe becomes ineffable joy and the surcease of pain becomes the attainment of "the realities necessary to survival," what happens to Shakespeare's play? It recedes into the background, becoming not so much the concrete object which controls and dictates our emotions as the occasion for reflections and feelings embracing it and much more besides.[19] It may be that, in contemplation of the play as a whole, in mulling it over after it has done its work and after our emotions have returned from their painful excitement to an equilibrium, we shall decide, each according to his own philosophic or religious lights, that *King Lear* has for us a further significance, constitutes a spiritual affirmation, or even, as some have thought, is defective in the distance at which it lies from a realization of man's spiritual possibilities. But these are speculations occasioned by the reading of *King Lear* but in no way the effects peculiar to it – interesting, perhaps even valuable if they come from a sophisticated and philosophic mind – but not analyses of the play; for they base themselves on a reification of Lear and the others in a different and broader context, a context which, like Heilman's, is derived from the moral and philosophic assumptions of the speculator rather than from the limited – and hence more concentrated, more powerful – confines of Shakespeare's play.

And this leads to a final objection to Heilman's book, an objection which is logically prior to all the others but which I have reserved until now in order not to prejudice the discussion. It is that Heilman nowhere confronts – indeed, nowhere shows any explicit awareness of the need to confront – the logical responsibility imposed upon him by his basic assumption, that the proper reading of *King Lear* must be a symbolic reading. Nothing in the text of the play, nothing in Shakespeare's habits as a dramatist, nothing in the circumstances of its composition and production, nothing in Elizabethan dramatic practice in general, nothing in the dramatic criticism of Shakespeare's day – nothing, in short, internal or external, suggests, or has been thought until recent years to suggest, that a literal reading of *King Lear* will fail to account for essential features of the play and that the tragedy must be interpreted, therefore, as an organized body of symbols. Anyone who wishes to take this position is, of course, free to do so; but he must discharge the initial critical and logical responsibility of showing his assumption to be needful and relevant, by making it clear that an interpretation of the play as a literal action is inadequate to the author's intention as revealed in the details of the work. It is not enough to argue – as Heilman seems to do (p. 12, and by implication, throughout the book) – that a symbolic reading is justified if it is consistent or makes sense of the work or accounts for its principal features; this is to beg the question, for, given sufficient imagination and verbal ingenuity in the critic, any work can be given such a reading. The necessity of symbolic interpretation must be established independently of the interpretation itself. It has long been thought by scholars – who, whatever their critical deficiencies, have usually had some competence in logic and a broad enough reading to know that some works are symbolic and some not – a necessary preliminary to symbolic interpretation to demonstrate quite concretely the need for it for the full understanding of a particular work. The body of criticism on, for example, *Gulliver's Travels, Pilgrim's Progress,* and *A Game at Chesse* involves in a fundamental way such an analysis of the signs from which the inadequacy of a literal, and the resultant necessity for a symbolic, interpretation can be inferred. Heilman – save in the simple alternatives which he from time to time presents to us for rejection in favor of his own allegorism – shows no awareness of his obligations here. The tendency of much modern criticism – perhaps encouraged by the tendency of such modern writers as Kafka, Brecht, and Broch to write symbolic works – is to begin with the assumption, taken as self-evident or requiring only passing justification, that a symbolic reading is appropriate to any work. But it is obvious to anyone who knows anything of the comments of writers on their own work or of the history of criticism in general and the critical discussion of allegory in particular that this assumption is not in all cases true. It must therefore be given fresh and particular justification as a preliminary to each application. When it is not given, we may respect the sincerity or marvel at the industry and ingenuity displayed in the analysis, but we need not take it seriously.

Notes

1　Robert Bechtold Heilman, *This Great Stage: Image and Structure in "King Lear"* (Louisiana State University Press, 1948).

2　Since completing this article, I have seen Oscar James Campbell's discussion of "Shakespeare and the 'New Critics' " (*Joseph Quincy Adams Memorial Studies* [Washington, DC, 1948], pp. 81–96); the general views expressed in this essay are in most respects similar to his. For other criticism of symbolic interpretations of Shakespeare see E. E. Stoll, "An *Othello* All-Too Modern," *ELH*, XIII (1946), 46–58, and "Symbolism in Shakespeare," *MLR*, XLIII (1947), 9–23.

3　See, e.g., Heilman, *op. cit.,* pp. 70, 83, 84–5, 86, 87, 91, 98, 100, 112, 115–16, 129–30, 144, 164, 179, 197, 217, 221–2, 228–9, 263, 278, 283.

4　My discussion of Heilman's literary theory is limited to a few of its more serious disadvantages for dramatic interpretation.

5　Act I, scene ii, ll. 30–45. All references to *King Lear* are to the Kittredge text.

6　See W. J. Lawrence, "Light and Darkness in the Elizabethan Theatre," *Englische Studien*, XLV (1912), 181–200, and *Pre-Restoration Stage Studies* (Cambridge, MA, 1927), pp. 128–30;

T. S. Graves, "Night Scenes in the Elizabethan Theatre," *Englische Studien*, XLVII (1914), 63–71; Chambers, *Elizabethan Stage* (1923), II, 543.

7 Cf. also Heilman, *op. cit.*, pp. 11, 45, 50, 73, 74, 104, 105, 134–5, 156–7, 160, 173, 198, 214, 220, 235, 265.

8 Cf., e.g., ibid., pp. 28, 58, 91–2, 115–16, 127–8, 135, 178–9, 185, 222, 230, 277, and esp. 284–5.

9 By similar expansion of the philosophic context, we move from the nature pattern as it defines man to the nature pattern as it defines nature: "This is what the patterns say about the nature of man. But man belongs to a universe; there are principles which operate both within him and outside him. From the nature of man it is a necessary step to the nature of nature" (Heilman, *op. cit.*, p. 112). Here we may ask why it is – assuming that we must proceed in the order given by the dialectical relations among the problems with which the play is said to deal – that this particular order is the necessary one; why, that is to say, must we go from man to the universe rather than from the universe to man, from the area of the more particular principles to that of the more general, rather than the reverse? This is obviously a philosophic rather than an artistic question, unanswerable from the evidence of Shakespeare's play, since it presents its meanings – if it does so at all – concurrently and by "interanimation"; the philosophy which makes this order necessary is Heilman's, not Shakespeare's, and he makes no effort to demonstrate its superior relevance.

10 *King Lear* becomes, because of the logical rather than the temporal order of its principal parts, a static rather than a dynamic whole. Although the total meaning of the play is in process of complete formulation throughout the action of the play, it is the whole play considered as a complex metaphor which is the proper analogue of this meaning, and its parts are significant not so much in terms of how they are prepared for and how they, in turn, prepare for a later part as in terms of the symbolic relationships in which they participate, these symbolic relationships being as often to what has gone before as to what comes after. The play is a whole, therefore, more like a statue or a painting than like a drama in the usual sense: the critic can regard everything in it as existing and functioning simultaneously, without regard to its position in the temporal sequence. Thus, to take one example out of many, Heilman says, in discussing the sexual imagery used to characterize Goneril, Regan, and Edmund, most of which is drawn from the fourth and fifth Acts: "This characterization of the sisters by the sex theme is aided by at least one careful contrast of them with Cordelia. Asking her father to make clear the cause of her disgrace, Cordelia insists that

> It is no vicious blot, murder or foulness,
> No unchaste action, or dishonour'd step ...
> (i.i.230–1).

Without the thematic context, *unchaste* might be merely part of a general catalogue; as it is, the word helps underline the sisters' animality" (*op. cit.*, p. 102; Heilman's italics). When Cordelia makes this speech, there is no context, sexual or otherwise; it is only through the kind of cross-reference permitted by a static conception of the play that Heilman's "aiding" and "underlining" become possible.

11 The applicability of the method, without essential change, to works "superficially" quite different, as well as the inner similarity which such different works come to have when exposed to treatment under Heilman's assumptions, can be observed by comparing his reading of *King Lear* with his reading of Henry James's *Turn of the Screw* (see "*The Turn of the Screw* as Poem" [the title reveals the reductive tendency of the method], *University of Kansas City Review*, summer, 1948, pp. 277–89; also in *Forms of Modern Fiction*, ed. William Van O'Connor [Minneapolis, 1948], pp. 211–28).

12 See, e.g., Heilman, *op. cit.*, pp. 28, 68, 92, 105, 133, 156, 284–5.

13 See, e.g., ibid., pp. 67, 89, 91, 108, 128, 177, 214, 253, 284–5.

14 Cf. also ibid., pp. 91–105, 124, 149, 176, 188, 189, 252, 267.

15 Cf. *ibid.*, p. 171: "There are various ingredients in Lear's tragic flaw, but the most important is his failure to recognize what areas of value are not capable of rational formulation" (cf. also pp. 32–3, 164, 192–3, 225).

16 It is noteworthy, therefore, that Heilman has little to say about speeches and scenes in which impending action potentially dangerous or hopeful for Lear is deliberated, narrated, or enacted – such as Kent's speech at Act III, scene i, ll. 17–55, and all of Act III, scenes iii and v; Act IV, scenes iii, v, and vii; and Act V, scene i. These, we may suppose, are more properly parts of the play's superficial aspect than of its inner reality; but that Shakespeare chose to present them, often at considerable length, encourages the supposition that they have some importance in the play as he wrote it. The evocation of fear by setting in motion or continuing contrary lines of development seems a reasonable hypothesis for their presence.

17 In comparison to the amplitude of his treatment of the first four acts, to Act IV, scene vi, which is for him the structural center of the play (*op. cit.*, pp. 173–222, *passim*), Heilman's discussion of the last four scenes is very sketchy indeed, perhaps because the inner reverberations of meaning sound so hollow there.

18 The interpretation of *King Lear*, for Heilman, to judge from the absence in his book of any consideration of its status as a work of popular dramatic art, stands in no need of guidance or control from a knowledge of its literary milieu. While we know too little about Elizabethan audiences to justify any positive inferences as to the kinds of artistic structure and effect possible, in works written for their immediate entertainment, one very important negative inference can be drawn. We must conclude, surely, that the basic structure and effect of a play written by a successful practicing dramatist for popular exhibition is of such a sort as could be grasped during a performance by a possible audience – and the possible can, for our present purpose, be drawn just as exclusively from among the judicious as Heilman wishes. That *King Lear* as he reads it does not meet this test can be shown most simply from the fact that a large number of readers – not just spectators – of the most refined sensitivity – not just ordinary Elizabethan playgoers – have studied – not merely witnessed – *King Lear* for three hundred years without perceiving the structure that Heilman now for the first time discloses to us. No spectator could possibly hope to "follow" the play as Heilman, with his leisure to trace evanescent coincidences of words, his note cards, his opportunity to extract every last drop of ambiguity from a line, is able to do; who but a scholiast in his study could notice that Albany's line at Act IV, scene ii, 1. 62 "picks up" a couple of lines uttered by Cordelia, all unsuspecting, at Act I, scene i, 11. 283–4? The alternatives, when we consider *King Lear* as a play written for an audience, seem to me clear: Shakespeare was fooling his audience, or he was completely unsuccessful, or three centuries of readers and critics have been in error, or Heilman is reading some other play.

19 For a general discussion of the effect of religious or abstract moral thought on tragedy see E. E. Stoll, *Shakespeare and Other Masters* (Cambridge, MA, 1940), pp. 75–8.

Part III

Dramatic Kinds

6   The Argument of Comedy   93
    Northrop Frye
7   Ambivalence: The Dialectic of the Histories   100
    A. P. Rossiter
8   The Saturnalian Pattern   116
    C. L. Barber
9   The Jacobean Shakespeare: Some Observations on the Construction
    of the Tragedies   125
    Maynard Mack

One of the signal achievements of twentieth-century Shakespeare criticism is taxonomy, the descriptive analysis of the kinds of plays Shakespeare wrote. The Folio editors divided the plays into only the three groups reflected in the title: *Mr. William Shakespeares Comedies, Histories, & Tragedies.* Modern critics, on the other hand, have felt the need to develop additional classifications. The most familiar of these is the category of romance, consolidated in the nineteenth century by Edward Dowden, who was following a suggestion of Coleridge. As a consequence most editions of the complete works produced in the twentieth century designated the last four non-collaborative plays as romances and so grouped them. And throughout the century critics proposed, discussed, rejected, and debated a variety of subcategories: "Roman Tragedy," "Dark Comedy," "Romantic Comedy," "Love Tragedy," "Satiric Comedy," and other such combinations. While appreciating the desire for precise description, one can see that the *reductio ad absurdum* of this practice is the Polonian "tragical-comical-historical-pastoral."

The investigation of dramatic modes in Shakespeare studies may be said to have begun in earnest with the work of A. C. Bradley at the beginning of the twentieth century. Professor of Poetry at Oxford from 1901 to 1906, Bradley delivered a series of lectures published in 1904 as *Shakespearean Tragedy*.[1] Arguably the most influential work of Shakespeare criticism ever produced, it is still in print a century later. According to the normal critical process of reaction and counter-reaction, Bradley's methodology and the conclusions it generated have been condemned as outmoded, overstated, and limited. Specifically, his devotion to character is sometimes seen as deriving from the conventions of nineteenth-century fiction, and he has been accused of neglecting the theatrical dimensions of the works, particularly their grounding in the flexible stage of the early modern English theater. But in detail and clarity, Bradley's lectures set a high standard in articulating the generic conventions with which an early modern playwright shaped his dramatic action. Other distinguished scholar-critics carried on the work of classification in the first half of the century, notably Lily Bess Campbell, with books on the histories and the tragic heroes, and John Dover Wilson, whose *What Happens in "Hamlet"* is his most frequently reprinted study.

Within the chronological limits of the present volume, perhaps the most significant contributor to the study of genre is Northrop Frye, the Canadian critic who exerted an enormous influence over the North American academy in the 1950s and 1960s. Frye's immensely impressive system is seen to best advantage in *Anatomy of Criticism*, his synoptic study of archetypes and myths and the literary structures that produced and were produced by them. Making frequent use of Shakespearean tragedy and comedy to illustrate the major literary modes and their permutations, Frye taught his contemporaries and later generations much about the conventions of kind and the affective implications (e.g., tone) of those conventions. Frye's tome does not lend itself to brief excerpts: Shakespearean references appear on page after page, and while treatment of a play or group of plays may be more extensive, mostly the discussion is glancing and replete with many examples from other writers and periods. Thus I have here reproduced "The Argument of Comedy," an early paper delivered at the English Institute, because it offers an earnest of Frye's pedagogic gifts in a manageable unit. He went on to study the major modes in a series of later books such as *A Natural Perspective: The Development of Shakespearean Comedy and Romance* and *Fools of Time: Studies in Shakespearean Tragedy*.

With New Criticism feeling its considerable strength during this period, Frye and a few others like him deliberately pursued an alternative line of study. The New Critics, of course, emphasized coherence and internal harmonies, values taken over from the preferred New Critical text, the lyric; when these qualities were sought in the drama, analysis was often confined to a single work. Genre critics, on the other hand, tended to range over a number of similar and dissimilar texts, attempting to identify likenesses, investigate distinctions, and in general to come to some agreement about the conventions governing various modes. Frye was the most comprehensive of these critics, but in the more limited field of Shakespeare studies the taxonomic motive is illustrated in Maynard Mack's "The Jacobean Shakespeare: Some Observations on the Construction of the Tragedies." Acknowledging at the beginning his substantial debt to Bradley, Mack extends his predecessor's insights by investigating what he calls "inward structure." This is to be understood, Mack insists, as a shaping principle independent of plot and character and not, "though it is fashionable nowadays to suppose so, ultimately a verbal matter." His analysis of Shakespeare's taste for mirroring, for setting contrasting voices against each other, and for exploiting multiple forms of organization is among the most illuminating examples of its kind.

The undisputed authority in the comic mode is C. L. Barber, author of *Shakespeare's Festive Comedy*. Learned, curious, and unfettered by orthodoxy or fashion, Barber set about to explore "the way the social form of Elizabethan holidays contributed to the dramatic form of festive comedy," documenting and explaining the "historical interplay between social and artistic form."[2] This attention to the way social customs helped inform Shakespeare's development of comic patterns supplemented Frye's emphasis on the origins of such structures in Plautus and other literary sources. Barber's perceptions about the symbiosis of art and popular custom remained pertinent for a very long time, aided by the rise of new historicist thinking in the 1980s and 1990s. Barber was also intrigued by psychoanalysis and drama, an approach he combined with genre study in *Creating Elizabethan Tragedy: The Theater of Marlowe and Kyd*.

The histories, or "chronicle plays" as they were known in Shakespeare's day, have received rather less attention with respect to structure than the comedies and tragedies, perhaps because Shakespeare himself had so much to do with the development of the form and the literary sources are not as obvious. Still, several critics have written helpfully on the histories: David Bevington investigated the native English origins of the chronicle play – and of other modes as well – in his important *From "Mankind" to Marlowe* (1962) and *Tudor Drama and Politics* (1968). Robert Ornstein's *A Kingdom for a Stage: The Achievement of Shakespeare's History Plays* (1972) offers many helpful suggestions about organization and its contribution to meaning. A. P. Rossiter's essay reproduced here is valuable not only because it is an early study of Shakespeare's "dialectical" habit, on which other critics have since enlarged, but also because it is brilliant work from a brilliant critic. Rossiter is learned, allusive, and casual – the essay is unchanged from its origins as a script for oral delivery.

If space were unlimited, excerpts from many other books and essays might have been included. Another of Rossiter's essays, "Comic Relief," investigates with humor and insight the subtle combination of tones implied in that overused phrase. Susan Snyder also illuminated the topic of interpenetrating modes in *The Comic Matrix of Shakespeare's Tragedies*, where she demonstrates that "comic conventions, in particular, offer a world apart from tragedy, which may be called forth to sharpen or deepen tragic thrust in several ways."[3] Richard Wheeler's *Shakespeare's Development and the Problem Comedies*, Howard Felperin's *Shakespearean Romance*, and Stephen Booth's *"King Lear," "Macbeth," Indefinition, and Tragedy* all enrich our understanding of Shakespearean structure. Rosalie Colie's *The Resources of Kind: Genre Theory in the Renaissance* extends far beyond Shakespeare but is no less helpful for that. Finally, Stephen Orgel's "Shakespeare and the Kinds of Drama" offers a historical corrective to some modern misconceptions about early modern dramatic kinds. It is always useful to remember his notion that Shakespeare thought about dramatic modes "not as sets of rules but as sets of expectations and possibilities."[4]

Notes

1 *Shakespearean Tragedy* (London: Macmillan, 1904).
2 *Shakespeare's Festive Comedy: A Study of Dramatic Form and its Relation to Social Custom* (Princeton, NJ: Princeton University Press, 1959), p. 4.
3 *The Comic Matrix of Shakespeare's Tragedies: Romeo and Juliet, Hamlet, Othello, and King Lear* (Princeton, NJ: Princeton University Press, 1979), p. 15.
4 *Critical Inquiry,* 6 (1979), pp. 107–23; reprinted in Orgel's *The Authentic Shakespeare* (New York: Routledge, 2002).

6

The Argument of Comedy

Northrop Frye

The Greeks produced two kinds of comedy, Old Comedy, represented by the eleven extant plays of Aristophanes, and New Comedy, of which the best known exponent is Menander. About two dozen New Comedies survive in the work of Plautus and Terence. Old Comedy, however, was out of date before Aristophanes himself was dead; and today, when we speak of comedy, we normally think of something that derives from the Menandrine tradition.

New Comedy unfolds from what may be described as a comic Oedipus situation. Its main theme is the successful effort of a young man to outwit an opponent and possess the girl of his choice. The opponent is usually the father (*senex*), and the psychological descent of the heroine from the mother is also sometimes hinted at. The father frequently wants the same girl, and is cheated out of her by the son, the mother thus becoming the son's ally. The girl is usually a slave or courtesan, and the plot turns on a *cognitio* or discovery of birth which makes her marriageable. Thus it turns out that she is not under an insuperable taboo after all but is an accessible object of desire, so that the plot follows the regular wish-fulfillment pattern. Often the central Oedipus situation is thinly concealed by surrogates or doubles of the main characters, as when the heroine is discovered to be the hero's sister, and has to be married off to his best friend. In Congreve's *Love for Love*, to take a modern instance well within the Menandrine tradition, there are two Oedipus themes in counterpoint: the hero cheats his father out of the heroine, and his best friend violates the wife of an impotent old man who is the heroine's guardian. Whether this analysis is sound or not, New Comedy is certainly concerned with the maneuvering of a young man toward a young woman, and marriage is the tonic chord on which it ends. The normal comic resolution is the surrender of the *senex* to the hero, never the reverse. Shakespeare tried to reverse the pattern in *All's Well That Ends Well*, where the king of France forces Bertram to marry Helena, and the critics have not yet stopped making faces over it.

New Comedy has the blessing of Aristotle, who greatly preferred it to its predecessor, and it exhibits the general pattern of Aristotelian causation. It has a material cause in the young man's sexual desire, and a formal cause in the social order represented by the *senex*, with which the hero comes to terms when he gratifies his desire. It has an efficient cause in the character who brings about the final situation. In classical times this character is a tricky slave; Renaissance dramatists often use some adaptation of the medieval "vice"; modern writers generally like to pretend that nature, or at least the natural course of events, is the efficient cause. The final cause is the audience, which is expected by its applause to take part in the comic resolution. All this takes place on a single order of existence. The action of New Comedy tends to become probable rather than fantastic, and it moves toward realism and away from myth and romance. The one romantic (originally mythical) feature in it, the fact that the hero or heroine turns out to be freeborn or someone's heir, is precisely the feature that trained New Comedy audiences tire of most quickly.

The conventions of New Comedy are the conventions of Jonson and Molière, and a fortiori of the English Restoration and the French rococo. When Ibsen started giving ironic twists to the same formulas, his startled hearers took them for portents of a social revolution. Even the old chestnut about the heroine's being really the hero's sister turns up in *Ghosts* and *Little Eyolf*. The average movie of today is a rigidly convention-alized New Comedy proceeding toward an act which, like death in Greek tragedy, takes place offstage, and is symbolized by the final embrace.

In all good New Comedy there is a social as well as an individual theme which must be sought in the general atmosphere of reconciliation that makes the final marriage possible. As the hero gets closer to the heroine and opposition is overcome, all the right-thinking people come over to his side. Thus a new social unit is formed on the stage, and the moment that this social unit crystallizes is the moment of the comic resolution. In the last scene, when the dramatist usually tries to get all his characters on the stage at once, the audience witnesses the birth of a renewed sense of social integration. In comedy as in life the regular expression of this is a festival, whether a marriage, a dance, or a feast. Old Comedy has, besides a marriage, a *komos*, the processional dance from which comedy derives its name; and the masque, which is a by-form of comedy, also ends in a dance.

This new social integration may be called, first, a kind of moral norm and, second, the pattern of a free society. We can see this more clearly if we look at the sort of characters who impede the progress of the comedy toward the hero's victory. These are always people who are in some kind of mental bondage, who are helplessly driven by ruling passions, neurotic compulsions, social rituals, and selfishness. The miser, the hypochon-driac, the hypocrite, the pedant, the snob: these are humors, people who do not fully know what they are doing, who are slaves to a predictable self-imposed pattern of behavior. What we call the moral norm is, then, not morality but deliverance from moral bondage. Comedy is designed not to condemn evil, but to ridicule a lack of self-knowledge. It finds the virtues of Malvolio and Angelo as comic as the vices of Shylock.

The essential comic resolution, therefore, is an individual release which is also a social reconciliation. The normal individual is freed from the bonds of a humorous society, and a normal society is freed from the bonds imposed on it by humorous individuals. The Oedipus pattern we noted in New Comedy belongs to the individual side of this, and the sense of the ridiculousness of the humor to the social side. But all real comedy is based on the principle that these two forms of release are ultimately the same: this principle may be seen at its most concentrated in *The Tempest*. The rule holds whether the resolution is expressed in social terms, as in *The Merchant of Venice*, or in individual terms, as in Ibsen's *An Enemy of the People*.

The freer the society, the greater the variety of individuals it can tolerate, and the natural tendency of comedy is to include as many as possible in its final festival. The motto of comedy is Terence's "Nothing human is alien to me." This may be one reason for the traditional comic importance of the parasite, who has no business to be at the festival but is nevertheless there. The spirit of reconciliation which pervades the comedies of Shakespeare is not to be ascribed to a personal attitude of his own, about which we know nothing whatever, but to his impersonal concentration on the laws of comic form.

Hence the moral quality of the society presented is not the point of the comic resolution. In Jonson's *Volpone* the final assertion of the moral norm takes the form of a social revenge on Volpone, and the play ends with a great bustle of sentences to penal servitude and the galleys. One feels perhaps that the audience's sense of the moral norm does not need so much hard labor. In *The Alchemist*, when Lovewit returns to his house, the virtuous characters have proved so weak and the rascals so ingenious that the action dissolves in laughter. Whichever is morally the better ending, that of *The Alchemist* is more concentrated comedy. *Volpone* is starting to move toward tragedy, toward the vision of a greatness which develops *hybris* and catastrophe.

The same principle is even clearer in Aristophanes. Aristophanes is the most personal of writers: his opinions on every subject are written all over his plays, and we have no doubt of his moral attitude. We know that he wanted peace with Sparta and that he hated Cleon, and when his comedy depicts the attaining of peace and the defeat of Cleon we know that he approved and wanted his audience to approve. But in *Ecclesiazusae* a band of women in disguise railroad a communistic scheme through the Assembly, which is a horrid parody of Plato's *Republic*, and proceed to inaugurate Plato's sexual communism with some astonishing improvements. Presumably Aristophanes did not applaud this, yet the comedy follows the same pattern and the same resolution. In *The Birds* the Peisthetairos who defies Zeus and blocks out Olympus with his Cloud-Cuckoo-Land is accorded the same triumph that is given to the Trygaeus of the *Peace* who flies to heaven and brings a golden age back to Athens.

Comedy, then, may show virtue her own feature and scorn her own image – for Hamlet's famous definition of drama was originally a definition of comedy. It may emphasize the birth of an ideal society as you like it, or the tawdriness of the sham society which is the way of the world. There is an important parallel here with tragedy. Tragedy, we are told, is expected to raise but not ultimately to accept the emotions of pity and terror. These I take to be the sense of moral good and evil, respectively, which we attach to the tragic hero. He may be as good as Caesar, and so appeal to our pity, or as bad as Macbeth, and so appeal to terror, but the particular thing called tragedy that happens to him does not depend on his moral status. The tragic catharsis passes beyond moral judgment, and while it is quite possible to construct a moral tragedy, what tragedy gains in morality it loses in cathartic power. The same is true of the comic catharsis, which raises sympathy and ridicule on a moral basis, but passes beyond both.

Many things are involved in the tragic catharsis, but one of them is a mental or imaginative form of the sacrificial ritual out of which tragedy arose. This is the ritual of the struggle, death, and rebirth of a God-Man, which is linked to the yearly triumph of spring over winter. The tragic hero is not really killed, and the audience no longer eats his body and drinks his blood, but the corresponding thing in art still takes place. The audience enters into communion with the body of the hero, becoming thereby a single body itself. Comedy grows out of the same ritual, for in the ritual the tragic story has a comic sequel. Divine men do not die: they die and rise again. The ritual pattern behind the catharsis of comedy is the resurrection that follows the death, the epiphany or manifestation of the risen hero. This is clear enough in Aristophanes, where the hero is treated as a risen God-Man, led in triumph with the divine honors of the Olympic victor, rejuvenated, or hailed as a new Zeus. In New Comedy the new human body is, as we have seen, both a hero and a social group. Aristophanes is not only closer to the ritual pattern, but contemporary with Plato; and his comedy, unlike Menander's, is Platonic and dialectic: it seeks not the entelechy of the soul but the Form of the Good, and finds it in the resurrection of the soul from the world of the cave to the sunlight. The audience gains a vision of that resurrection whether the conclusion is joyful or ironic, just as in tragedy it gains a vision of a heroic death whether the hero is morally innocent or guilty.

Two things follow from this: first, that tragedy is really implicit or uncompleted comedy; second, that comedy contains a potential tragedy within itself. With regard to the latter, Aristophanes is full of traces of the original death of the hero which preceded his resurrection in the ritual. Even in New Comedy the dramatist usually tries to bring his action as close to a tragic overthrow of the hero as he can get it, and reverses this movement as suddenly as possible. In Plautus the tricky slave is often forgiven or even freed after having been threatened with all the brutalities that a very brutal dramatist can think of, including crucifixion. Thus the resolution of New Comedy seems to be a realistic foreshortening of a death-and-resurrection pattern, in which the struggle and rebirth of a divine hero has shrunk into a marriage, the freeing of a slave, and the triumph of a young man over an older one.

As for the conception of tragedy as implicit comedy, we may notice how often tragedy closes on the major chord of comedy: the Aeschylean trilogy, for instance, proceeds to what is really a comic resolution, and so do many tragedies of Euripides. From the point of view of Christianity, too, tragedy is an episode in that larger scheme of redemption and resurrection to which Dante gave the name of *commedia*. This conception of *commedia* enters drama with the miracle-play cycles, where such tragedies as the Fall and the Crucifixion are episodes of a dramatic scheme in which the divine comedy has the last word. The sense of tragedy as a prelude to comedy is hardly separable from anything explicitly Christian. The serenity of the final double chorus in the St. Matthew Passion would hardly be attainable if composer and audience did not know that there was more to the story. Nor would the death of Samson lead to "calm of mind all passion spent" if Samson were not a prototype of the rising Christ.

New Comedy is thus contained, so to speak, within the symbolic structure of Old Comedy, which in its turn is contained within the Christian conception of *commedia*. This sounds like a logically exhaustive classification, but we have still not caught Shakespeare in it.

It is only in Jonson and the Restoration writers that English comedy can be called a form of New Comedy. The earlier tradition established by Peele and developed by Lyly, Greene, and the masque writers, which uses themes from romance and folklore and avoids the comedy of manners, is the one followed by Shakespeare. These themes are largely medieval in origin, and derive, not from the mysteries or the moralities or the interludes, but from a fourth dramatic tradition. This is the drama of folk ritual, of the St. George play and the mummers' play, of the feast of the ass and the Boy Bishop, and of all the dramatic activity that punctuated the Christian calendar with the rituals of an immemorial paganism. We may call this the drama of the green world, and its theme is once again the triumph of life over the waste land, the death and revival of the year impersonated by figures still human, and once divine as well.

When Shakespeare began to study Plautus and Terence, his dramatic instinct, stimulated by his predecessors, divined that there was a profounder pattern in the argument of comedy than appears in either of them. At once – for the process is beginning in *The Comedy of Errors* – he started groping toward that profounder pattern, the ritual of death and revival that also underlies Aristophanes, of which an exact equivalent lay ready to hand in the drama of the green world. This parallelism largely accounts for the resemblances to Greek ritual which Colin Still has pointed out in *The Tempest*.

The Two Gentlemen of Verona is an orthodox New Comedy except for one thing. The hero Valentine becomes captain of a band of outlaws in a forest, and all the other characters are gathered into this forest and become converted. Thus the action of the comedy begins in a world represented as a normal world, moves into the green world, goes into a metamorphosis there in which the comic resolution is achieved, and returns to the normal world. The forest in this play is the embryonic form of the fairy world of *A Midsummer Night's Dream*, the Forest of Arden in *As You Like It*, Windsor Forest in *The Merry Wives of Windsor*, and the pastoral world of the mythical sea-coasted Bohemia in *The Winter's Tale*. In all these comedies there is the same rhythmic movement from normal world to green world and back again. Nor is this second world confined to the forest comedies. In *The Merchant of Venice* the two worlds are a little harder to see, yet Venice is clearly not the same world as that of Portia's mysterious house in Belmont, where there are caskets teaching that gold and silver are corruptible goods, and from whence proceed the wonderful cosmological harmonies of the fifth act. In *The Tempest* the entire action takes place in the second world, and the same may be said of *Twelfth Night*, which, as its title implies, presents a carnival society, not so much a green world as an evergreen one. The second world is absent from the so-called problem comedies, which is one of the things that makes them problem comedies.

The green world charges the comedies with a symbolism in which the comic resolution contains a suggestion of the old ritual pattern of the victory of summer over winter. This is explicit in *Love's Labor's Lost*. In this very masque-like play, the comic contest takes the form of the medieval debate of winter and spring. In *The Merry Wives of Windsor* there is an elaborate ritual of the defeat of winter, known to folklorists as "carrying out Death," of which Falstaff is the victim; and Falstaff must have felt that, after being thrown into the water, dressed up as a witch and beaten out of a house with curses, and finally supplied with a beast's head and singed with candles while he said,

"Divide me like a brib'd buck, each a haunch," he had done about all that could reasonably be asked of any fertility spirit.

The association of this symbolism with the death and revival of human beings is more elusive, but still perceptible. The fact that the heroine often brings about the comic resolution by disguising herself as a boy is familiar enough. In the Hero of *Much Ado About Nothing* and the Helena of *All's Well That Ends Well*, this theme of the withdrawal and return of the heroine comes as close to a death and revival as Elizabethan conventions will allow. The Thaisa of *Pericles* and the Fidele of *Cymbeline* are beginning to crack the conventions, and with the disappearance and revival of Hermione in *The Winter's Tale*, who actually returns once as a ghost in a dream, the original nature-myth of Demeter and Proserpine is openly established. The fact that the dying and reviving character is usually female strengthens the feeling that there is something maternal about the green world, in which the new order of the comic resolution is nourished and brought to birth. However, a similar theme which is very like the rejuvenation of the *senex* so frequent in Aristophanes occurs in the folklore motif of the healing of the impotent king on which *All's Well That Ends Well* is based, and this theme is probably involved in the symbolism of Prospero.

The conception of a second world bursts the boundaries of Menandrine comedy, yet it is clear that the world of Puck is no world of eternal forms or divine revelation. Shakespeare's comedy is not Aristotelian and realistic like Menander's, nor Platonic and dialectic like Aristophanes', nor Thomist and sacramental like Dante's, but a fourth kind. It is an Elizabethan kind, and is not confined either to Shakespeare or to the drama. Spenser's epic is a wonderful contrapuntal intermingling of two orders of existence, one the red and white world of English history, the other the green world of the Faerie Queene. The latter is a world of crusading virtues proceeding from the Faerie Queene's court and designed to return to that court when the destiny of the other world is fulfilled. The fact that the Faerie Queene's knights are sent out during the twelve days of the Christmas festival suggests our next point.

Shakespeare too has his green world of comedy and his red and white world of history. The story of the latter is at one point interrupted by an invasion from the comic world, when Falstaff *senex et parasitus* throws his gigantic shadow over Prince Henry, assuming on one occasion the role of his father. Clearly, if the Prince is ever to conquer France he must reassert the moral norm. The moral norm is duly reasserted, but the rejection of Falstaff is not a comic resolution. In comedy the moral norm is not morality but deliverance, and we certainly do not feel delivered from Falstaff as we feel delivered from Shylock with his absurd and vicious bond. The moral norm does not carry with it the vision of a free society: Falstaff will always keep a bit of that in his tavern.

Falstaff is a mock king, a lord of misrule, and his tavern is a Saturnalia. Yet we are reminded of the original meaning of the Saturnalia, as a rite intended to recall the golden age of Saturn. Falstaff's world is not a golden world, but as long as we remember it we cannot forget that the world of *Henry V* is an iron one. We are reminded too of another traditional denizen of the green world, Robin Hood, the outlaw who manages to suggest a better kind of society than those who make him an outlaw can produce. The outlaws in *The Two Gentlemen of Verona* compare themselves, in spite of the Italian setting, to Robin Hood, and in *As You Like It* Charles the wrestler says of Duke Senior's followers: "There they live like the old Robin Hood of England: they say many young gentlemen flock to him every day, and fleet the time carelessly, as they did in the golden world."

In the histories, therefore, the comic Saturnalia is a temporary reversal of normal standards, comic "relief" as it is called, which subsides and allows the history to continue. In the comedies, the green world suggests an original golden age which the normal world has usurped and which makes us wonder if it is not the normal world that is the real Saturnalia. In *Cymbeline* the green world finally triumphs over a historical theme, the reason being perhaps that in that play the incarnation of Christ, which is contemporary with Cymbeline, takes place offstage, and accounts for the halcyon peace with which the play concludes. From then on in Shakespeare's plays, the green world has it all its own way, and both in *Cymbeline* and in *Henry VIII* there may be suggestions that Shakespeare, like Spenser, is moving toward a synthesis of the two worlds, a wedding of Prince Arthur and the Faerie Queene.

This world of fairies, dreams, disembodied souls, and pastoral lovers may not be a "real" world, but, if not, there is something equally illusory in the stumbling and blinded follies of the "normal" world, of Theseus' Athens with its idiotic marriage law, of Duke Frederick and his melancholy tyranny, of Leontes and his mad jealousy, of the Court Party with their plots and intrigues. The famous speech of Prospero about the dream nature of reality applies equally to Milan and the enchanted island. We spend our lives partly in a waking world we call normal and partly in a dream world which we create out of our own desires. Shakespeare endows both worlds with equal imaginative power, brings them opposite one another, and makes each world seem unreal when seen by the light of the other. He uses freely both the heroic triumph of New Comedy and the ritual resurrection of its predecessor, but his distinctive comic resolution is different from either: it is a detachment of the spirit born of this reciprocal reflection of two illusory realities. We need not ask whether this brings us into a higher order of existence or not, for the question of existence is not relevant to poetry.

We have spoken of New Comedy as Aristotelian, Old Comedy as Platonic and Dante's *commedia* as Thomist, but it is difficult to suggest a philosophical spokesman for the form of Shakespeare's comedy. For Shakespeare, the subject matter of poetry is not life, or nature, or reality, or revelation, or anything else that the philosopher builds on, but poetry itself, a verbal universe. That is one reason why he is both the most elusive and the most substantial of poets.

7

Ambivalence: The Dialectic of the Histories

A. P. Rossiter

First, my Feare: then, my Curtsie: last, my Speech. My Feare, is your Displeasure: My Curtsie, my Dutie: And my Speech, to Begge your Pardons.

If you looke for a good speech now, you vndoe me: For what I have to say, is of mine owne making: and what (indeed) I do say, will (I doubt) prooue mine owne marring.

But to the Purpose, and so to the Venture.

Stratford 1951, a Shakespeare Memorial Theatre playing a sequence of History-plays in a fixed unchanging Elizabethan-house-front stage-set. Stratford 1612, a man writing his last History: *Henry VIII*, first performed 29 June 1613, when in a sense it 'brought the house down', for The Globe was set on fire … And as far as I know, no Shakespeare History-play was staged with Elizabethan décor – or non-décor, if that suits you better – till this year, 1951. We should hope to find *some* curtains taken away (from the mind, I mean), *some* unanticipated continuities revealed, *some* unexpected groupings, interconnections, echoes …

The Man was 48; had begun writing Histories some twenty years back, perhaps as early as 1586, when he left home and twins, and was perhaps 'a Schoolmaster in the Country' (as Beeston jun. told Aubrey). How did he *end* by thinking of History? Had he any coherent 'view' of the Historic Process: from John – with a jump to Richard II (1398) and thence more or less consecutively to Bosworth and 1485, the Tudor dawn …?

His last play – or his and Fletcher's – ends with the dazzle of the Elizabethan sunrise: with the christening of the baby Elizabeth, and Cranmer in the role of 'prophet new inspired'. Yes; but in 1612 the Queen was nine years dead; the great age was dying before her; and this Man, who had seen so deeply, so terrifyingly, into human experience could not be blind and deaf to the *ironies* of his last stage-situation. To say no more: Could he, who had staged so many 'poor painted Queens', be nescient of the irony of Anne Bullen's triumph – he knowing all that followed …? And with the noble, pathetic, fallen Katherine in the selfsame play?

Looked at *one* way, the Histories present a triumphal march of the destinies of England. But look at them another way – at the individual lives of men and women – and your conclusion will be nearer to what Yeats wrote (also *At Stratford on Avon*):

> He meditated as Solomon, not as Bentham meditated, upon blind ambitions, untoward accidents, and capricious passions; and the world was almost as empty in his eyes as it must be in the eyes of God.

I find that apposite to the Histories; for though Shakespeare gives but few generalizations applicable to 'the Historic Process' (as we grandly call it …) yet Yeats catches the note that rings beyond the melancholy brooding of Richard II on the fates of Kings: the note of the helpless Henry VI at Towton (Pt. 3, II.v); it is near to the feeling of Henry V's 'idol Ceremony' speech; it generalizes for Margaret of Lancaster, for Isabella of France, for Katherine of Aragon … (Proud Names!) … for all the long line of women broken in the course of great events. And it most precisely fits that generalizing moment when the weary sleepless Henry IV is turning over in his midnight mind the history of his own times:

> O God! that one might read the book of fate,
> And see the revolution of the times
> Make mountains level, and the continent,
> Weary of solid firmness, melt itself
> Into the sea … how chances mock,
> And changes fill the cup of alteration
> With divers liquors! O, if this were seen,
> The happiest youth, viewing his progress through,
> What perils past, what crosses to ensue,
> Would shut the book and sit him down and die.
>
> (Pt. 2, III.i.45)

Those melancholy tones are familiar enough: they are what makes the burdened man-beneath-the-Crown a major symbol in the Histories. The voices murmur on behind the tapestries: 'sad stories of the deaths …' 'all murdered …' 'Upon the King …' 'Uneasy lies the head …' They mind me of Chaucer's lines (on quite another theme):

> What? Is this al the Ioye and al the feste?
> … Is al this peynted proces seyd, alas,
> Right for this fyn?
>
> (*Troylus and Crysede*, ii.421 f.)

But though there is a 'Doubleness' here: in the conflicting values set by the Greatness (the Triumph) of the National Destiny, and the Frustration, the inadequacy, of the Individual (the frail Man within the robe) – there is nothing complex in that 'Doubleness'. It falls just short of the tragic; where Man's greatness is asserted in his destruction. That falling-short is characteristic of the Histories.

These kings and great persons are all sub-tragic. They lack a degree (or some degrees) of freedom; are caught in nets of events by which they are frustrate and less than their potential selves. In Rilke's phrase, they are *Verwirrt mit Wirklichkeit*: bondsmen to a 'reality' which is that of the world of action, therefore temporary, pragmatic, unreal. And they (to quote Yeats again):

> Constrained, arraigned, baffled, bent and unbent
> By those wire-jointed jaws and limbs of wood,
> Themselves obedient,
> Knowing not evil and good;
> Obedient to some hidden magical breath.
> (*The Double Vision of Michael Robartes*)

The mechanism to which they are subjected is that process of 'retributive reaction' which is the only *tragic* component of the Histories.

Retributive Reaction is my name for the principle of the simplest of the patterns in these plays; of which pattern we see only a short and misleading section in the Richard-to-Henry V tetralogy. *There*, the usurpation of Bolingbroke (exactly described in terms of consequences by Carlisle), with Richard's death by murder, leads on to the Unquiet Time of Henry IV – to the Percies' Rebellion, and the father's fears that Prince Hal is just another Richard; and so up to the death-scene in 'Jerusalem' and 'God knows, my son ...' followed by the advice to 'busy giddy minds/With foreign quarrels': which is – despite all that Archbishops may say – the political reason for Henry V's French campaign. That is victorious, and the curse of usurpation seems to sleep. Yes, to *sleep*; it is not dead.

The closing chorus of Henry V refers back to the Henry VI series, the loss of France – 'which oft our stage hath shown'. Thus the sequel to *Henry V*, in the complete pattern, is 'Hung be the Heavens with black' and the Roses series, where 'civil dissension' carries forward the curse of royal murder, uncertain or divided right, brother against brother, for the sixty years to Bosworth Field.

The pattern can be extended the other way, to *Henry VIII* (I mean in Wolsey as antagonist to Katherine, and what we know of Anne Bullen, the usurperess). It is one of Shakespeare's constants. But when I say 'retributive reaction' I mean just that; for whether it is 'justice' or not, God knows ... (Professor Butterfield would have it that *he* knows too, and that it *is* all the Will of God. To me, it is obscure, ironic, *and* – as far as Shakespeare shows me the scheme of things – seemingly endless.) Taken all together, the Histories are a dark glass, where we gaze *per speculum in enigmate*. The mystery beneath the surface of the magic mirror with its shows of kings is chill and deeply saddening.

> Action is transitory; a step, a blow,
> The motion of a muscle, this way or that,
> 'Tis done, and in the after-vacancy
> We wonder at ourselves like men betrayed;
> Suffering is permanent, obscure and dark,
> And shares the nature of Infinity.
> (Wordsworth: *The Borderers*)

This pattern of 'obscure tragedy' runs, for me, far deeper than any feelings *I* can derive from knowing the 'philosophic' system which modern scholarship has extracted from the plays (and other Elizabethan sources *undique coemptis*). I must briefly outline it, (*a*) because it is indubitably 'there' as a pattern of thought, and (*b*) because it offers simplifications which are in danger of diminishing the true complexity of Shakespearean History – and in the best plays. Remember, then, that I am *not* arguing anything *away*: a pattern is *there*, and it is like Edward Halle's. But Halle's theory of history is naïve, and though the Elizabethan reader found it as satisfying as the Chronicles of Israel and Judah (with similar formulae on how King So-and-so did that which was evil in the sight of the Lord and followed after the ways of Jeroboam the son of Nebat who made Israel to sin), yet I cannot find it in my reading of Shakespeare to suppose that his mind was quite as naïve as all that. There is more in the dark glass than the moral history of the Lancastrian House of Jeroboam and the happy ending in the dawn of Tudarchy.

On Order, Degree, and so on, let me be brief: the essentials only need recall; let me remind you:

The State, as monarchy, is ordained by God; its structure is hierarchical, and in health all its orders or degrees are 'congreeing in a full and natural close / Like music' (as Exeter says in *Henry V*, 1.ii). To all orders as way of life there is 'fixed as an aim or butt / Obedience' – as the Archbishop goes on to say, using bees as ideals or exempla. (The whole speech is very serious; whatever Stratford producers may choose to do with comic clergymen.) From the principle of Obedience – which really means a complete system of proper respects towards all superiors from parents upwards – it follows that the rightful King is, as it were, the organic nucleus of the cell-State; and that without due and rightful succession all Order (all its vital processes) is put in jeopardy. The only right way with a bad King is non-resistance: biding God's good time in Christian patience – as Gaunt tells the wronged Duchess of Gloucester – for ill Kings are as much ordained by God as good ones.

The curse of usurpation is that it confuses Right, endangers all Order. That of rebellion is that it commits the Luciferian sin of pride, and destroys all Order: by the assumed 'law' that men who will revolt against the highest loyalty (to God's Deputy) cannot be bound by any other loyalty, nor decency. The rebel abrogates all respects; and since the King-enucleated State is ordained by God, by Natural Law, therefore he is a thing *unnatural*: a boil, a plague-sore, a carbuncle of corrupted blood.

This system of notions, with its hysterical terror of treason, is alien to our minds. We can see why the Tudors wanted England convinced that no worse chaos than the Roses civil war had ever come upon the English; especially in the late 1590s, when the Queen was old and had been flattered too much and too long on her immortality to be at all inclined to contemplate her own mortality and fix on her successor. We can see that Shakespeare has this nexus of thought in an astonishing intensity: especially over his horror of the mob – as a hydra-headed incarnation of disorder. I still feel the need of an approach less Tudor-moral. I find it in a MS. note of Coleridge's: 'What a world of Love and Bee-like Loyalty and Heart-adherence did the Stuarts trick and tyrannize away.'[1]

If we think of the ideal State as bound together like that, by happily unquestioning devotions, we come much nearer at the 'politics' of the Histories than by making them rigid, frigidly-patterned Moralities of State-right and State-wrong. (Like Halle, or the Homilies.)

There is real danger of that simplification; and one important ill-effect is on Falstaff. The Dover Wilson Sir John Paunch is dangerously near usurping the place of a much greater man: because any ideological view which makes *Henry IV* into a princely morality reduces Falstaff to little more than a symbol of all the fat and idle temptations which royalty rejects. There is something in John Dover Wilson which makes him a little like that *Lord* John of Lancaster – lays him open to *Sir* John's comment, 'This same sober-blooded boy doth not love me, nor a man cannot make him laugh....' Already semi-deflated Falstaffs are reaching the stage – Welfare-State Falstaffs, shrunk in the moral wash, or preconditioned for pricking before they have got so far afoot as Shrewsbury. That is not only sad. The effect is to neglect all the comic criticism which Falstaff himself supplies; and also all the complexities of the Henry IV plays, which often result from the use of comic parallelism of phrase or incident. That is, of parody, critically used; or of travesty-by-parallel.

Parody of this kind operates by juxtapositions of opposites; by contrasts so extreme as to seem irreconcilable. In this sense Falstaff at Shrewsbury is a 'parody' of knighthood: everything a knight in battle ought *not* to be; that is, IF men are all that theoretical codes assume.... It is this travesty-by-parallel which makes Sir John more than a bigger and a greater Bluntschli, in this other inquiry into *Arms and the Man*: as much greater as sherris sack is finer, nimbler, more forgetive than chocolate-creams. Parody is used again when Hotspur and Lady Percy have appeared in Act II. scene. iii, with Hotspur taking an easy leap out of Kate's bed to pluck bright Honour (in a traitorous conspiracy), and rudely ignoring her questions. He calls a servant, asks about a horse – a roan, a crop-ear was it not? – and then pretends he has forgotten all her inquiries. In the next scene, in Eastcheap, the Prince suddenly thinks of Hotspur. What follows? – An exact parallel, a travesty of the Percy *ménage*; and in dialogue, too:

> I am not yet of Percy's mind, the Hotspur of the north; he that kills me some six or seven dozen of Scots at a breakfast, washes his hands, and says to his wife, 'Fie upon this quiet life. I want work.' 'O my sweet Harry', says she, 'how many hast thou kill'd today?' 'Give my roan horse a drench', says he; and answers 'Some fourteen', an hour after, 'A trifle, a trifle.'

The parallelism is manifest. The next sentence reminds us how farcical travesty *by play-acting* is an intrinsic part of the Eastcheap critique. The Prince continues thus: 'I prithee, call in Falstaff. I'll play Percy, and that damned brawn shall play Dame Mortimer his wife.'

The 'switch' that happens in this kind of parody is not unlike the technique of the modern periodical called *Lilliput*: an interesting collection of the earlier successes in it was published under the name of *Chamberlain and the Beautiful Llama* (Hulton Press, 1940). The wit of *Lilliput* is, moreover, sometimes used in this Shakespearean way – I mean, to make the conventionally respected suddenly absurd: as Hotspur's 'Honour-and-Glory tough-with-the-women' stuff is deflated by the Prince's echo of it in a different tone or key.

It would be merely a mistake to attach this bit of parody to the 'character' of Prince Hal and only that; it is a quality of the play. As you can see from the scene at Bangor (iii.i), where it is *Hotspur* who is the plain-man parodist – of the fantastic Welsh nationalism and supernaturalism of Glendower. Again (I cannot discuss it in detail) – there is the recurrent theme of Falstaff's bogus repentances: all in a play framed on the crude subject of a wild and prodigal Prince's unlikely reformation. The best is in the opening speeches of Act iii.iii; which follow immediately on the moving and earnest scene of the Prince's vows to repent and reform – the scene with his father. The switch to Falstaff telling Bardolph, 'I'll repent and that suddenly, while I am in some liking' (and so on) is another sign of how comic parallelism is thematic in the entire play. I shall next explain my term 'Ambivalence' in my own way, and then return to these items, to argue whether these *Lilliput*-like switches are tricks, or mere farce, or something more significant.

Ambivalence

It is hard to persuade everyone that what is laughable may also be serious; or that a man who laughs at something is 'thinking', or 'as good as thinking' (and maybe better). That is, unless it is when a satirist laughs at things we delight in or revere; then we call it 'mocking' and say he's a horrid fellow. All that being so, I will use an example into which amusement doesn't enter.

Wordsworth's *A slumber did my spirit seal* is a familiar poem. But if you think of it as 'One of the Lucy poems', I must tell you at once that those poems were never a Wordsworthian sequence. Ward's *English Poets* (1880) puts three poems together, with this one last; the *Golden Treasury* has a sequence of four; but in neither does *Strange fits of passion* appear, though why that *isn't* a 'Lucy poem' is beyond any man's discerning. Of the Ward trio, the *first* is the eighth of Wordsworth's Poems of the Affections, the *second* is the tenth among Poems of the Imagination; and 'A slumber did' is Imagination No. II. If we are concerned with *Wordsworth's* poems, we must disembarrass our minds of the superfluous fictions generated by editors, and take this poem as Wordsworth offered it – as a single separate lyric on a 'she' who is dead. At all events, that must be the first approach: until you know all that's in a poem, you can't tell what cross-references are relevant, nor what to be after looking for in other poems on what superficially appears to be 'the same subject'. Try, then, to listen to the poem 'unseen' as it were; I'm going to repeat it now, without 'expression' (as far as I can) – I don't want to bias a hearer either way.

> A slumber did my spirit seal;
> I had no human fears:
> She seemed a thing that could not feel
> The touch of earthly years.
>
> No motion has she now, no force;
> She neither hears nor sees;
> Rolled round in earth's diurnal course,
> With rocks, and stones, and trees.

Now that first line is ambiguous – 'A slumber did my spirit seal' – and the ambiguity lies in the little word DID: a word often used for mere poetic emphasis or intensification, but also capable of referring to *time*. I'll take the first first; never mind the second.

Taking *did* as a poetic intensive, you have an emphatic perfect tense: a slumber really sealed up my spirit. As in that other poem:

> Among thy mountains did I feel
> The joy of my desire ...

or the six-winged seraph in *Isaiah*: 'With twain he covered his face, with twain he covered his feet, and with twain he did fly.'

On this reading, which I'll call the A-version, the poem is a record of immediate experience: of a dream or visionary state, in which all his 'human fears' were gone, and his mind was filled with an overpowering sense of her immortality. No christian, but a pantheistic immortality, in which she is one with all the wide world's being, its greatness and its mystery. The tone is rapt. The closing lines have a triumphant sweep; and the energy and magnitude of suggestion of 'Rolled round in earth's diurnal course' contradicts, no, obliterates the suggestions of 'No motion ... no force' or any deadness in 'She neither hears nor sees.' The *seems* in 'She seemed a thing ...' is the seems of *wonder*, the visionary recalling the magic of his slumber; not the very different *seems* of recognized illusion. If I had to characterize this A-version out of Wordsworth, I would use those *Tintern Abbey* lines describing a 'serene and blessed mood' of mystical self-annihilation in which

> we are laid asleep
> In body, and become a living soul ...

The B-version is quite other. As I said, DID can refer mainly to *time*. On this, the B-reading, *did* is an emphatic form of the imperfect tense (not the perfect); and the line means, 'I was utterly asleep': my senses *were* sealed up in a slumber (but they are not so now). At once there is a marked contrast of tone between stanza 1 and stanza 2. The first reports on what *was* – till she died; the second is the hurting record of what *is* – now she is dead. A simple paraphrase of this version would run thus: 'The eyes of my mind were shut as in deep sleep, and my sense of normal human dangers and our fears for those we love was stopped up. In that unseeing condition she seemed to be a thing which would never have any touch from the normal changes of life, would never be damaged by time ... But now... How wrong that sleeping was. She is a dead thing, without power to move or do: deaf: blind: a bit of material substance rolled about day by day with the earth, and as dead-ly – like stone or wood.' No mysticism there, no serenity or blessedness of mood. It becomes a very painful poem, of a certain kind of self-reproach, and the pain than which Dante said there was none greater. ('Nessun maggior dolore ...') But no less Wordsworthian – as witness those other lines:

> She died, and left to me
> This heath, this calm and quiet scene,
> The memory of what has been
> And never more will be.

Or again:

> But she is in her grave, and O
> The difference to me.

Now experiment shows that if a number of people are asked to paraphrase the poem, they come down about equally on either side, A or B; and it is very rare for anyone to doubt that it can be read in any other way than his. Yet closer verbal analysis would show that in both A and B readings there are words which would point to the opposite interpretation, if they could take the bit in their teeth.

I say, therefore, that the question 'Which is right, A or B?' is a no-question: the poem is *ambivalent*. It subsumes meanings which point to two opposite and irreconcilable systems of values; and the two are related only by the fact of death. If there *is* a spiritual or real Life in all things, then 'Lucy' is one with that life, and this is felt in the visionary moment. But perhaps in that only. For if there is no Pantheistic All, only a material earth of a-spiritual non-human stuff, then 'Lucy' is dead among the deadness. As there is no certainty either way, Wordsworth's poetic mind produced his ambivalent poem: a poem only fully felt when the reader has responses to both the readings I have separated. Yet each of those readings implies, ultimately, a system of thought: a philosophy: values. (And to a sincere and thinking Christian, both aspects are delusions.)

That is what I mean by 'Ambivalence': that two opposed value-judgements are subsumed, and that both are valid (i.e. for that work of art or the mind producing it). The whole is only fully experienced when both opposites are held and included in a 'two-eyed' view; and all 'one-eyed' simplifications are not only falsifications; they amount to a denial of some part of the mystery of things.

Return now to Shakespeare. I can do no more but only remark in passing how irony – including 'dramatic irony' – is a display of an essential ambivalence. Dramatic irony causes an exact juxtaposition of opposites in the mind of the audience: opposites, in that the 'true' for one hearer (the stage Persona) must exclude the 'true' for other hearers, who take the same words in a far extended sense, of which the hearing Persona is known to be unaware. ('Fail not our feast', e.g.) Yet both meanings only happen in the same mind: the audience's or reader's. The emotive effect is a terrifying belittlement of human prescience or judgement, as in tragedy, when we project the simple meaning on to the mind of a Macbeth, then contemplate it, as it were, against the ironized, unsimple meaning. Or, where sympathy lacks, the effect is some kind of detached sardonic amusement: as in some of Richard III's ironies, or, perhaps, in watching Falstaff and Co. scampering up to London for Harry's coronation, with Shallow in tow and all to the tune of: 'Let us take any man's horses. The laws of England are at my commandment. Happy are they which have been my friends; and woe unto my Lord Chief Justice.'

We have seen the Prince reconciled to the L.C.J. – we know the rest. But though this is still irony, it is now Comic Irony: in which pathos, derision, a sad wry smile and a malicious grin strive together – and all 'belong'. A modern Mirror-for-Magistrates view, to which Falstaff is only the 'Vice' to be formally discarded in a moral interlude of princely education, leaves just nothing of all that doubleness of feeling.

But Shakespearean History plays double tunes on far more than the comic aspects of the misfortunes of an old fat cynical reprobate – even when they do (as here) symbolize the absurd vanity of human wishings (which supply all beggars with dream horses at the twinkle of a main-chance). Consider how in both parts of *Henry IV* the shady and seamy sides of glorious War are presented; and comically. In Part 1 Falstaff explains how he damnably misuses the King's press (Act IV. scene ii). In Part 2 a full-length exposition of the game is given (in III.ii), with Feeble as the unwittingly ironical commentator – laughed at for a fool, yet the only man's-size voice in Gloucestershire:

> By my troth, I care not; a man can die but once; we owe God a death. I'll ne'er bear a base mind. An't be my destiny, so; an't be not, so. No man's too good to serve's Prince …

The Mug is the Hero, without prejudice to his mug-dom: the Fool is the only clear-seer. Ambivalence again. And all comic; though implicitly all these 'King's press' episodes are serious commentary on the wickedness and irresponsibility inseparable from WAR. Damnably wrong, clean contrary to all the war values associated with Crécy, Agincourt or Harfleur … and *therefore* a critical comic commentary on a set of human facts which the 'Agincourt-values' insist on viewing (if at all) with one eye only. 'Two voices are there', as Wordsworth said in quite another connection: 'This is damnably wicked', says the one. 'It's damn' funny', says the other. Historian Shakespeare heard both.

I shall not labour to explain how the famous 'Honour' catechism comically balances the accounts of that main term in 1 *Henry IV*; but I must remark on the beautifully complicated parallelisms generated when Falstaff tells the Prince how his father has sent for him, and that he had best rehearse before he goes to the palace to explain himself. It is a scene which travesty-parallels the true meeting later (in III. ii), and it is Eastcheap interlude-acting played to the height.

First, KING Falstaff rebukes his 'son' (with a parody of Puritan oratory), allowing that he *has* observed *one* virtuous man in Harry's company: 'If that man should be lewdly given, he deceiveth me; for, Harry, I see virtue in his looks.' Next, the Prince insists that they change roles, and we have the Prince (as King) pretending just what he will *have* to pretend when he is King: viz. that Falstaff is 'an old white-bearded Satan', a 'villainous misleader of youth'. The picture is the obverse of Falstaff's; but now Shakespeare goes one better still, and makes Falstaff as Prince offer a final turn of defence – ending with 'Banish not him thy Harry's company…. Banish plump Jack, and banish all the world.' To which the King-Prince replies – as the Prince-King will have to in earnest – 'I do, I will'.

In that three-move epitome you have all the special technique of the *Henry IV* plays: a constant shifting of appearances, like the changing lights of an opal, so that every event, every person becomes equivocal – as Falstaff made Honour. That Gadshill robbery is not mere farce. If we 'realize' it, in an Usurper's state where Henry's right is only that of might, might only – then what are the Percies and Bolingbrokes but Gadshills, Bardolphs, Petos in Bigger Business?

> Thieves for their robbery have authority
> When judges steal themselves

so says Isabella in *Measure for Measure*. The comic robbing of the robbers is comically parallel to what the King would do with Percy's Scots prisoners; and the difficulty of establishing the Right in anything, in an England under no rightful king, is paralleled and parodied throughout in Falstaff's 'manner of wrenching the true cause the false way' – whether in the inventive proliferation of buckram men, in belying Mrs. Quickly to the Lord Chief Justice, or bamboozling her into vigorous denials of her own (perhaps not impeccable) virtue. I mean where he calls her an otter, and explains 'She's neither fish nor flesh; a man knows not where to have her.' To which the wronged woman replies in great moral indignation, 'Thou art an unjust man in saying so. Thou or any man knows where to have me, thou knave thou.'

It is in all such places – in Falstaff as the Wit: the witty equivocator who turns all to mirth, destroying ideals and seriousnesses with a turn of the word – that the Comic Histories go beyond anything that Shakespeare attempted in *Richard II*. There, too, that the narrowly Tudor-political or 'moral' approach will most oversimplify, and thin, the true Shakespearean vintage. The 'moral-historical' approach diminishes Falstaff as Wit, leaving him with little more than the rascally quick-wittedness which gets Eulenspiegels and Harlequins out of tight corners. Sir John is more. He is not only witty in himself (No, I'm not going on with Familiar Quotations) – he is Wit ipse. And wit is critically destructive – of ideal systems which assume that human nature is what it isn't. The doubleness of implicit values in those situations which are ambivalent; those which can be seen as serious *and* farcical: as pathetic *and* absurd: as abominable *and* laughable: as fine-and-admirable *and* as all-very-fine-and-large; all that centres on Falstaff. To read it as simply 'evil' (or 'the antithesis of the Princely virtues') and to make 'evil' the opposite of the Order required by the military State of a Henry V, is too naïve. And I don't mean just 'too naïve for 1951', I mean 'Too naïve for the mind of a Shakespeare, in 1599'. As Walter Raleigh wrote:

> This is indeed the everlasting difficulty of Shakespeare criticism, that the critics are so much more moral than Shakespeare himself, and so much less experienced.... The ready judgments which are often passed on Shakespeare's most difficult characters are like the talk of children. Childhood is amazingly moral, with a confident, dictatorial, unflinching morality. The work of experience ... is to undermine this early pedantry ... to teach tolerance, or at least suspense of judgment.

That's a 'period-piece', no doubt, and I wouldn't endorse its rather shapeless liberalism, which half suggests the (to me absurd) conclusion that Shakespeare is not moral at all – let alone one of the greatest of moralists. But Raleigh didn't have the word 'doctrinaire' to hand, I suppose. The warning he gives is by no means out of date, I should say.

I hope I'm not slipping towards (what he would call) the surprising moral immaturity of some of our doctrinaire contemporaries,[2] if I say that there is, in Falstaffian wit, something of the devaluating skill of The Devil. Let me hide behind Coleridge to advance my point. In table-talking on 16 February 1833, Coleridge gave a long account of a Faust play he had designed before ever he read Goethe. (I don't believe him, but that's unimportant.) He said, 'My Devil was to be, like Goethe's, the Universal Humorist, who should make all things vain and nothing worth, by a perpetual collation of the Great with the Little in the presence of the Infinite.' Now surely that is very near to what Falstaff does, when most the Clown critical. 'The perpetual collation of the Great with the Little' is no bad formula for what Shakespeare is repeatedly doing in both *Henry IV* plays.

In Part 2, however, the Universal Humorist is a far more sardonic one than before. Not only in that Old Age, in its failings, its brags, its pavidities and follies, is a major theme; nor only that Lord John of Lancaster's 'victory' is disgracefully won; there is more besides. To hint that 'more', I'll glance at the very first speech: '*Enter Rumour painted full of tongues*'.

> Open your ears; for which of you will stop
> The vent of hearing when loud Rumour speaks?
> I, from the orient to the drooping west,
> Making the wind my post-horse, still unfold
> The acts commenced on this ball of earth.
> Upon my tongues continual slanders ride,
> The which in every language I pronounce,
> Stuffing the ears of men with false reports.
> I speak of peace while covert enmity,
> Under the smile of safety, wounds the world;
> And who but Rumour, who but only I,
> Make fearful musters and prepared defence,
> While the big year, swoln with some other grief,
> Is thought with child by the stern tyrant war,
> And no such matter? Rumour is a pipe
> Blown by surmises, jealousies, conjectures,
> And of so easy and so plain a stop
> That the blunt monster with uncounted heads,
> The still-discordant wavering multitude,
> Can play upon it. But what need I thus
> My well-known body to anatomize
> Among my household? Why is Rumour here?

That is the first part of the speech. It is followed by a list of the tales which are spreading from the Battle of Shrewsbury, and the piece concludes thus:

> The posts come tiring on,
> And not a man of them brings other news
> Than they have learnt of me. From Rumour's tongues
> They bring smooth comforts false, worse than true wrongs.

Rumour's prologue offers a theme which runs right through the whole play; a theme which invites a sardonic, detached, unsympathetic or coldly-critical attitude towards all the agents in the historic field. *False-report befools everyone.* Not only in the rumoured rebel victory at Shrewsbury; not only in the false (favourable) report of Falstaff's prowess – to which Coleville surrenders, and which even the L.C.J. makes some allowance for. Falstaff's own trust in the Prince and his star is also 'smooth comforts false': as is old Shallow's trust in Sir John and the smell of Court. So too – false – is this same Shallow's roaring-boy Past in London. And Pistol is false-alarm personified: mouthfuls of Theatre masquerading as a man – whereas he is nothing but wind. And thus the parallel to 'Sir John to all Europe': the vain delusion to which Coleville surrenders, as the northern rebels surrender to 'smooth comforts false' from Westmorland and Prince John. Finally, the King – King Hal the First – that Falstaff expected to find in London is only a delusion; and the laugh is on Falstaff – with a grating edge to the amusement. (A. C. Bradley only encountered this unhappy Mixed Feeling at the Rejection. In fact it starts much earlier in the play. Modern 'moral' critics apparently never meet it at all.)

These shifting mirage-like effects of unstable appearances relate Part 2 to the so-called 'Problem Plays' (which *I* call 'Tragi-comedies'). They develop from, e.g., the Honour theme of Part I, but go well beyond that historical Comedy.

And if you wonder why – talking on 'The Histories' – I say so little about *Richard II* and *Henry V*, my answer is: I am diagnosing their shortcomings by focusing attention on Shakepearean History at its highest development. (I say 'History'. If you want to see this kind of thing taken on, in later work, go to the Galley-scene in *Antony and Cleopatra*: a similar comedy, sardonic comedy, of the frailty of the Great: the strange absurd chances that turn the fate of worlds.) But in *Richard II* – either Shakespeare was bent on following Marlowe and writing an unEnglish tragedy (i.e. without comic interplay: though *Woodstock* put it directly before him); or he knew instinctively that the preciosity and self-regarding sentiment of Richard *could not stand* comic criticism or even lapse of seriousness.

In *Henry V* his aim was changed. Whatever he once intended (and that last speech, by the Dancer, in 2 *Henry IV*, does show the *intention* to export Falstaff to France), what he produced was a propaganda-play on National Unity: heavily orchestrated for the brass. The sounding – and very impressive – Rhetoric shows how something is being stifled. The wartime-values demand a determined 'one-eyedness'; the King fails to reach the fullest humanity because of that demand. He *has* banished Plump Jack; and 'all the World' has been banished with him. At least, the 'Allness' is gone. The play is 'fracted and corroborate'.

Without going all the way with 'Q', to say that Falstaff must go to 'Arthur's bosom' because he can kill Harry with a look, I do agree that Sir John had to be dead; for fear of the damage he must needs have done by babbling of (not 'green fields') … by killing the heroics with a jest. When the ranks are closed, and to question is to lack Will, to falter, then there is not so much freedom of mind as will say *outright* what every sane man knows (however brave): 'I like not such grinning Honour as Sir Walter hath … Give me Life, say I.'

There are fine things in *Henry V*; but much of the comedy has lost touch with the serious matter. It's a play Shakespeare had finished with well before he finished it. His falling-back on the old *Famous Victories* for that slapdash stuff – treating the Princess of France like a Free Frenchwoman, etc. – that shows it. It surprises me that our London dramatic critics should have been surprised to find that as a climax to the 1951 Stratford historical tetralogy it does not come off. The truth is, the heart of Shakespeare's insight into English History (which means a good deal more than the History of England) – the *heart* is in the middle of the sequence: in the *Henry IV* plays, where he turned back from the sentimental seriousness of *Richard II*, back to the kind of Comic History he had made rough beginnings with in Parts 2 and 3 of *Henry VI*.

(Where he had achieved something remarkable in the grotesque, Hieronymus-Bosch-like sarcastically comic scenes of Cade's rebellion.)[3]

To see why *comic* History was his true genre, it is needless to go back to the evolution of the Elizabethan Drama and its Miracle-play and Morality-play underlays. 'Mungrell tragy-comedy' *was* the mere-English genre, but never mind that now. Look only at *King John* – those lines by the Bastard on 'Commodity' ('Mad world, mad kings …. etc.') – and you will see how they take the gilded lid off the lofty illusions of theoretical Tudor Politics (I mean *Stage*-politics). By-passing all the ideals of Order, Degree, Non-resistance, Right-divine and God's-deputyship, the Bastard exposed the world of politics as 'a racket'.[4] The thought implicit in the making of that speech has the same quality of deep political penetration that emerges from the conflict of serious and comic in *Henry IV* – and in *Coriolanus* and *Antony and Cleopatra*. That speech shows the same ambivalence, but simpler; for Falconbridge is a noble fighting humorist as well as a critical wit. He is not, like Falstaff, a Universal Humorist; but some of the undermining intellectual clear-sightedness of the later Histories is there.

Throughout the Histories it is in the implications of the Comic that shrewd, realistic thinking about men in politics – in office – in war – in plot – is exposed: realistic apprehension outrunning the medieval frame. Because the Tudor myth system of Order, Degree, etc. was too rigid, too black-and-white, too doctrinaire and narrowly moral for Shakespeare's mind: it falsified his fuller experience of men. Consequently, while employing it as FRAME, he had to undermine it, to qualify it with equivocations: to vex its applications with sly or subtle ambiguities: to cast doubts on its ultimate human validity, even in situations where its principles seemed most completely applicable. His intuition told him it was *morally* inadequate.

Hence the unhappy feelings which generous-minded critics have displayed about the Rejection of Falstaff. That some of them have *overdone* it is neither here nor there. It is well enough for Dr. Tillyard or Professor Dover Wilson to tell us that the Prince *had* to cast off Sir John. We know that. We know what Kingship meant to textbook Tudors (far better than the Globe audiences knew, I dare say). Yet I still feel that as Shakespeare *was* Shakespeare – the man who made Hermione and Hamlet, drew Kate Percy as war-widow (a traitor's wife by the Code), drew Katherine as the fallen majesty of England – he must have known, *and felt*, the lack of humanity (of generosity, high-mindedness, true magnanimity) in his Hal in that scene. And again, I think, in Henry's treatment of the conspirators at Southampton; where the King is so obviously playing a publicity propaganda part, as Justice, iron-visaged, pitiless … As obviously as he said he was in that first of unprincely soliloquies, 'I know you all …' (1 *Henry IV*, I.ii,end).

Is there not a resemblant quality in his father: the 'silent king', Bolingbroke, in the mirror-episode in *Richard II*? A separateness from the feeling world, which makes the actor in public affairs assume a predetermined part, like a *play*-actor, only with all his directives outside and none of his? One of those 'who, moving others, are themselves as stone', as the sonnet phrases it: 'the lords and owners of their faces'? And thus again a resemblant quality in John of Lancaster's treachery to the northern rebels? Oh, I know it can be argued that, to the Elizabethans, no ill treatment or trickery towards rebels could be unjustified. But can we assume that Shakespeare's sensibilities were so crass as not to know meanness as meanness, perfidy as perfidy, when it could be said to have profited the State? I say no more than, 'I think not'. And if you agree on any of these points I've hung on to the Rejection of Falstaff, doesn't it follow that you are made to *feel* (not merely 'see', notionally) how the frame of Order, the coherent rigid medieval system accepted by some of our most reputed modern scholars, is outrun by that mind which Jonson (who 'knew the man … etc.') considered to be 'not for an age but for all time'?

It follows, if I have taken you along with me, that we cannot dissect-out, stain and fix the system of Shakespeare's reflexion on History. A rigid political-moral good-and-evil system is there; but as the events and the people speak into our inner mind, we find that Shakespeare is shifting subtly from key to key, as if by what musicians call 'enharmonic changes': using ambiguous note-sequences till contradiction is itself confounded, and yields a precise evocation of the paradox of human experience.

Thomas Mann has explored this musical symbolism to the limit in his vast, amazing, fascinatingly wearisome novel *Doktor Faustus*. When his damned musical genius, Adrian Leverkühn, makes his first experiments with notes, the narrator (Serenus Zeitblom Ph.D.) records a comment which seems to be saying a lot about what I find in the ambivalences of Shakespeare. 'Relationship is everything', said Leverkühn. 'And if you want to give it a more precise name, it is Ambiguity …' And again, later, 'You know what I find? – That music turns the equivocal into a system' (pp. 47 f. of the American translation approved by Mann. Knopf, 1947).

What is more, Leverkühn finds something amenable to his music in Shakespeare. He takes *Love's Labour's Lost* as a theme to treat. On this Zeitblom reports, 'He spoke with enthusiasm of the theme, which gave opportunity to set the lout and the 'natural' alongside the comic sublime, and make both ridiculous in each other.' Mann is not explicit, but it is clear enough that he means the three lover-nobles by 'comic sublime', placed *vis-à-vis* Costard as 'the natural'. Zeitblom Ph.D. is unhappy about it: 'I have always been rather unhappy at the mockery of humanistic extravagances; it ends by making Humanism itself a subject for mirth' (p. 164). That would be a good text for setting out to explore the entire subject of so-called 'Comic Relief' in Shakespeare. I must keep within my limits, come back to Histories.

'Music turns the equivocal into a system.' That is why I used the phrase 'The Dialectic of the Histories' in my – admittedly alarming – title (for which I now apologize). The Order-code-system of Tudor theory approaches History with the kind of argument that Plato called *eristic*: that is, argument aimed at the extinction of an opposite and 'bad' system of beliefs. The code is moral, but in the narrow sense: too much so for Shakespeare's contemplation of mankind; too narrow and bounded for his human insight, from which he derived a *political* wisdom. As Hazlitt once observed:

> Shakespeare was in one sense the least moral of all writers; for morality (commonly so called) is made up of antipathies; and his talent consisted in sympathy with human nature in all its shapes, degrees, depressions and elevations.

I shan't examine that for its shortcomings, beyond saying that it is *morally* acuter than Raleigh – as witness the distinction 'morality commonly so called'. Taking it as it stands, then, I say: Therefore, Shakespeare's intuitive way of thinking about History (which we cannot formulate as an abstracted notional system) is *dialectical*. The old eristic-argumentative system which he used is static, changeless; but *his* thought is dynamic, alterative, not tied to its age. It has that extra degree-of-freedom which is given only by what I called a constant 'Doubleness': a thoroughly English empiricism which recognizes the coextancy and juxtaposition of opposites, without submitting to urges (philosophical, moral, etc.) to obliterate or annihilate the one in the theoretic interests of the other. That is what I tried to express by the figure of 'two-eyedness'.

His awareness of the 'soul of goodness in things evil' is not less than his sense of the spirit of seriousness (or significance) in things base – or foolish – or farcical – or indecent. To laugh at Hotspurious honour is as good as to think. To laugh at Shallow, or at Falstaff with Doll Tearsheet, is the substance of some wry or wringing thinking. But no less funny for that. And thus it is that the serio-comic dialectic of the Histories leads on to the Tragedies, where you have (as in the Histories you have not, I consider) Coleridge's 'collation of the Great and the Little *in the presence of the Infinite*'. In none of the Tragedies is the Order-system the friend of human greatness; rather the enemy.

If you have difficulty in refusing the critics' directions to see Henry V as Shakespeare's Ideal; if you cannot quite accept what I've said about the constant Doubleness of the Shakespearean vision in the Histories; then let me ask you to face a straight question: 'WHO, in the later, greater plays, are the heirs and successors of those Order-symbols Henry V and Henry Tudor (the triumphant Richmond of the end of *Richard III*)? The men who are, to the State-order system, 'goods': unifying nuclei of the organism, whether a People or the mind itself: the beings on whom the political heaven smiles. Who are they?' I should reply, 'The Fortinbrasses, the Octavii, Lodovicos, Macduffs, the Edgars and Albanies. On whose heroic qualities Bradley is, for once, entirely adequate.'

But why is 'the other side', the reverse to the kingly, historic, patriotic obverse, the Comic? Is it not partly this? In History Shakespeare felt that men were constrained to be much less than their full selves. He knew the burden of princehood: the Ceremony lines alone would proclaim it. All the Lancasters are less than full men. None is himself; only what he wills to be for the time only. By and by he will 'be more himself'. Hal says it: Father says it. None does it. Richard does try to be himself, full kingly length. He finds a shadow in a mirror. Only the other Richard – Gloucester – can say, 'I am myself alone'. And *he* is the Devil, spinning the orb on his thumb. Now Comedy is the field of human shortcoming; and therefore Shakespeare's History, at its greatest, *had* to be comic. What isn't Comic History in the Histories is what I can only call 'Obscure tragedy'.

At the very end of his career, back here at New Place, collaborating with young bright immoral John Fletcher in his last history-play (or so I think; and others more eminent do not) – he brought the same elements into *Henry VIII*. The man of forty-eight had not changed his mind. That was 1612; in 1616 he was dead. I hope that he was ending in something like the mind of those lines of Yeats:

> No longer in Lethean foliage caught
> Begin the preparation for your death
> And from the fortieth winter by that thought
> Test every work of intellect or faith,

And everything that your own hands have wrought;
And call those works extravagance of breath
That are not suited for such men as come
Proud, open-eyed, and laughing to the tomb.

Notes

In preparing this lecture for print, I have made no attempt to convert it to a literary 'essay', nor, indeed, to do more than fill in the breaks and gaps of my lecture-notes with words to the same effect as those I used at the time. Similarly, with only one or two exceptions (mere topical asides) I have left in those parenthetical turns which a speaking voice can make much easier for hearers than they usually are for a reader. The style of the whole was intended for public delivery, and in my own manner of lecturing. To print it as anything other than a very close transcript of the actual lecture would have meant a complete rewriting; and for that I had neither the leisure nor the taste. A.P.R.

1   K. Coburn: *Inquiring Spirit*, p. 249.
2   An instance I may have had in mind in 1951 will be found in Mr. D. A. Traversi's study of 1 *Henry IV* in *Scrutiny* XV.I, pp. 24 f. Having fixed 'moral' prejudices from the start, Traversi damns Douglas with a supreme moral confidence, ascribing his own notions to the Prince. Thus: 'when he describes him he stresses the same lack of imagination ... later found in the Greek heroes of *Troilus and Cressida*. Douglas is the man who 'kills me six or seven dozen of Scots at a breakfast and then complains of "this quiet life", the man who is not above filling out his prowess in battle with unimaginative boasting &c.' (p. 27). Later we find, 'Douglas is as the Prince has described him a brainless butcher ...' (p. 31: the rest continuing the Wilson Knight formula from *Troilus and Cressida* in *The Wheel of Fire*). Traversi never sees that his quotation is about *Hotspur*, nor that Scotticide is improbable in a Douglas. School-children produce just such fantasy-figures, with similarly misapplied quotations. *Sed quis custodit* [? *scrutinat*] *ipsos Scrutineres?*
3   I mean such Bosch paintings as *Ecce Homo* and the Veronica picture, where the mob is not only grotesque – absurd and half-diabolic – but also presents itself as a kind of hydra: *belua capitum multorum*; cf. Rumour's 'the blunt monster with uncounted heads', etc. The phrase was a commonplace, unoriginal even in Horace's day; but Bosch actualizes it in paint, as Shakespeare does in drama. A European tradition is shared by the Flemish painters and Shakespeare. I explored a fringe of it in an article on *Breugel's Ambivalences* in *The Cambridge Journal* for December 1948.
4   This was put too crudely. I would add now: Shakespeare wrote in an unstable equilibrium between a 'World' or 'Universe-of-thought' of faith in God-ordainedness, and another World: the Inverted World of belief only in Power. The 'Inverted World' symbol is familiar in Breugel's pictures, as an orb with its cross downwards. The 'upsidedownness' notion is in *Measure for Measure* and elsewhere. The pictorial emblem itself appears in Quarles (e.g. *Emblems* i, 15).

8

The Saturnalian Pattern

C. L. Barber

Messenger:	Your honour's players, hearing your amendment,
	Are come to play a pleasant comedy ...
Beggar:	... Is not a comonty a Christmas gambold or a tumbling trick?
Lady:	No, my good lord; it is more pleasing stuff.
Beggar:	What, household stuff?
Lady:	It is a kind of history.
Beggar:	Well, we'll see it. Come, madam wife, sit by my side and let the world slip.
	We shall ne'er be younger.

(Induction to *The Taming of the Shrew*)

Much comedy is festive – all comedy, if the word festive is pressed far enough. But much of Shakespeare's comedy is festive in a quite special way which distinguishes it from the art of most of his contemporaries and successors. The part of his work which I shall be dealing with in this book, the merry comedy written up to the period of *Hamlet* and the problem plays, is of course enormously rich and wide in range; each new play, each new scene, does something fresh, explores new possibilities. But the whole body of this happy comic art is distinguished by the use it makes of forms for experience which can be termed saturnalian. Once Shakespeare finds his own distinctive style, he is more Aristophanic than any other great English comic dramatist, despite the fact that the accepted educated models and theories when he started to write were Terentian and Plautine. The Old Comedy cast of his work results from his participation in native saturnalian traditions of the popular theater and the popular holidays. Not that he "wanted art" – including Terentian art. But he used the resources of a sophisticated theater to express, in his idyllic comedies and in his clowns' ironic misrule, the experience of moving to humorous understanding through saturnalian release. "Festive" is usually an adjective for an atmosphere, and the word describes the atmosphere of Shakespeare's comedy from *Love's Labour's Lost* and *A Midsummer Night's Dream* through *Henry IV* and *Twelfth Night*. But in exploring this work, "festive" can also be a term for structure. I shall be trying to describe structure to get at the way this comedy organizes experience. The saturnalian pattern appears in many variations, all of which involve inversion, statement and counterstatement, and a basic movement which can be summarized in the formula, through release to clarification.

So much of the action in this comedy is random when looked at as intrigue, so many of the persons are neutral when regarded as character, so much of the wit is inapplicable when assessed as satire, that critics too often have fallen back on mere exclamations about poetry and mood. The criticism of the nineteenth century and after was particularly helpless, concerned as it was chiefly with character and story and moral quality. Recent criticism, concerned in a variety of ways with structure, has had much more to say. No figure in the carpet is the carpet. There is in the pointing out of patterns something that is opposed to life and art, an ungraciousness which artists in particular feel and resent. Readers feel it too, even critics: for every new moment, every new line or touch, is a triumph of opportunism, something snatched in from life beyond expectation and made design beyond design. And yet the fact remains that it is as we see the design that we see design outdone and brought alive.

> O body swayed to music, O brightening glance,
> How can we know the dancer from the dance?

To get at the form and meaning of the plays, which is my first and last interest, I have been led into an exploration of the way the social form of Elizabethan holidays contributed to the dramatic form of festive comedy. To relate this drama to holiday has proved to be the most effective way to describe its character. And this historical interplay between social and artistic form has an interest of its own: we can see here, with more clarity of outline and detail than is usually possible, how art develops underlying configurations in the social life of a culture. The saturnalian pattern came to Shakespeare from many sources, both in social and artistic tradition. It appeared in the theatrical institution of clowning: the clown or Vice, when Shakespeare started to write, was a recognized anarchist who made aberration obvious by carrying release to absurd extremes. The cult of fools and folly, half social and half literary, embodied a similar polarization of experience. One could formulate the saturnalian pattern effectively by referring first to these traditions: Shakespeare's first completely masterful comic scenes were written for the clowns.[1] But the festival occasion provides the clearest paradigm. It can illuminate not only those comedies where Shakespeare drew largely and directly on holiday motifs, like *Love's Labour's Lost*, *A Midsummer Night's Dream*, and *Twelfth Night*, but also plays where there is relatively little direct use of holiday, notably *As You Like It* and *Henry IV*.

We can get hold of the spirit of Elizabethan holidays because they had form. "Merry England" was merry chiefly by virtue of its community observances of periodic sports and feast days. Mirth took form in morris-dances, sword-dances, wassailings, mock ceremonies of summer kings and queens and of lords of misrule, mummings, disguisings, masques – and a bewildering variety of sports, games, shows, and pageants improvised on traditional models. Such pastimes were a regular part of the celebration of a marriage, of the village wassail or wake, of Candlemas, Shrove Tuesday, Hocktide, May Day, Whitsuntide, Midsummer Eve, Harvest-home, Halloween, and the twelve days of the Christmas season ending with Twelfth Night. Custom prescribed, more or less definitely, some ways of making merry at each occasion. The seasonal feasts were not, as now, rare curiosities to be observed by folklorists in remote villages, but landmarks framing the cycle of the year, observed with varying degrees of sophistication by most elements in the society. Shakespeare's casual references to the holidays always assume that his audience is entirely familiar with them:

> As fit as ten groats is for the hand of an attorney ... as a pancake for Shrove Tuesday, a morris for May Day, as the nail to his hole ...[2]

A great many detailed connections between the holidays and the comedies will claim our attention later, but what is most important is the correspondence between the whole festive occasion and the whole comedy. The underlying movement of attitude and awareness is not adequately expressed by any one thing in the day or the play, but is the day, is the play. Here one cannot say how far analogies between social rituals and dramatic forms show an influence, and how far they reflect the fact that the holiday occasion and the comedy are parallel manifestations of the same pattern of culture, of a way that men can cope with their life.

Through Release to Clarification

Release, in the idyllic comedies, is expressed by making the whole experience of the play like that of a revel.

> Come, woo me, woo me! for now I am in a holiday humour, and like enough to consent. (*A.Y.L.*, iv.i.68–9)

Such holiday humor is often abetted by directly staging pastimes, dances, songs, masques, plays extempore, etc. But the fundamental method is to shape the loose narrative so that "events" put its persons in the position of festive celebrants: if they do not seek holiday it happens to them. A tyrant duke forces Rosalind into disguise; but her mock wooing with Orlando amounts to a Disguising, with carnival freedom from the decorum of her identity and her sex. The misrule of Sir Toby is represented as personal idiosyncrasy, but it follows the pattern of the Twelfth Night occasion; the flyting match of Benedict and Beatrice, while appropriate to their special characters, suggests the customs of Easter Smacks and Hocktide abuse between the sexes. Much of the poetry and wit, however it may be occasioned by events, works in the economy of the whole play to promote the effect of a merry occasion where Nature reigns.

F. M. Cornford, in *The Origins of Attic Comedy*,[3] suggested that invocation and abuse were the basic gestures of a nature worship behind Aristophanes' union of poetry and railing. The two gestures were still practiced in the "folly" of Elizabethan May-game, harvest-home, or winter revel: invocation, for example, in the manifold spring garlanding customs, "gathering for Robin Hood"; abuse, in the customary license to flout and fleer at what on other days commanded respect. The same double way of achieving release appears in Shakespeare's festive plays. There the poetry about the pleasures of nature and the naturalness of pleasure serves to evoke beneficent natural impulses; and much of the wit, mocking the good housewife Fortune from her wheel, acts to free the spirit as does the ritual abuse of hostile spirits. A saturnalian attitude, assumed by a clear-cut gesture toward liberty, brings mirth, an accession of wanton vitality. In the terms of Freud's analysis of wit, the energy normally occupied in maintaining inhibition is freed for celebration. The holidays in actual observance were built around the enjoyment of the vital pleasure of moments when nature and society are hospitable to life. In the summer, there was love in out-of-door idleness; in the winter, within-door warmth and food and drink. But the celebrants also got something for nothing from festive liberty – the vitality normally locked up in awe and respect. E. K. Chambers found among the visitation articles of Archbishop Grindal for the year 1576 instructions that the bishops determine

> whether the ministers and churchwardens have suffered any lord of misrule or summer lords and ladies, or any disguised persons, or others, in Christmas or at May games, or any morris-dancers, or at any other times, to come unreverently into the church or church-yard, and there to dance, or play any unseemly parts, with scoffs, jests, wanton gestures, or ribald talk ...[4]

Shakespeare's gay comedy is like Aristophanes' because its expression of life is shaped by the form of feeling of such saturnalian occasions as these. The traditional Christian culture within which such holidays were celebrated in the Renaissance of course gave a very different emphasis and perspective to Shakespeare's art. But Dicaeopolis, worsting pompous Lamachus in *The Acharnians* by invoking the tangible benefits of Bacchus and Aphrodite, acts the same festive part as Sir Toby baffling Malvolio's visitation by an appeal to cakes and ale.

The *clarification* achieved by the festive comedies is concomitant to the release they dramatize: a heightened awareness of the relation between man and "nature" – the nature celebrated on holiday. The process of translating festive experience into drama involved extending the sort of awareness traditionally associated with holiday, and also becoming conscious of holiday itself in a new way. The plays present a mockery of what is unnatural which gives scope and point to the sort of scoffs and jests shouted by dancers in the churchyard or in "the quaint mazes in the wanton green." And they include another, complementary mockery of what is merely natural, a humor which puts holiday in perspective with life as a whole.

The butts in the festive plays consistently exhibit their unnaturalness by being kill-joys. On an occasion "full of warm blood, of mirth," they are too preoccupied with perverse satisfactions like pride or greed to "let the world slip" and join the dance. Satirical comedy tends to deal with relations between social classes and aberrations in movements between them. Saturnalian comedy is satiric only incidentally; its clarifi-cation comes with movement between poles of restraint and release in everybody's experience. Figures like Malvolio and Shylock embody the sort of kill-joy qualities which the "disguised persons" would find in any of Grindal's curates who would not suffer them to enter the churchyard. Craven or inadequate people appear, by virtue of the festive orientation, as would-be revellers, comically inadequate to hear the chimes at midnight. Pleasure thus becomes the touchstone for judgment of what bars it or is incapable of it. And though in Shakespeare the judgment is usually responsible – valid we feel for everyday as well as holiday – it is the whirligig of impulse that tries the characters. Behind the laughter at the butts there is always a sense of solidarity about pleasure, a communion embracing the merrymakers in the play and the audience, who have gone on holiday in going to a comedy.

While perverse hostility to pleasure is a subject for aggressive festive abuse, highflown idealism is mocked too, by a benevolent ridicule which sees it as a not unnatural attempt to be more than natural. It is unfortunate that Shakespeare's gay plays have come to be known as "the romantic comedies," for they almost always establish a humorous perspective about the vein of hyperbole they borrow from Renaissance romances. Wishful absolutes about love's finality, cultivated without reserve in conventional Arcadia, are made fun of by suggesting that love is not a matter of life and death, but of springtime, the only pretty ring time. The lover's conviction that he will love "for ever and a day" is seen as an illusion born of heady feeling, a symptom of the festive moment:

> Say 'a day' without the 'ever.' No, no, Orlando! Men are April when they woo, December when they wed. Maids are May when they are maids, but the sky changes when they are wives. (*A.Y.L.*, iv.i.146–50)

This sort of clarification about love, a recognition of the seasons', of nature's part in man, need not qualify the intensity of feeling in the festive comedies: Rosalind when she says these lines is riding the full tide of her passionate gaiety. Where the conventional romances tried to express intensity by elaborating hyperbole according to a pretty, pseudo-theological system, the comedies express the power of love as a compelling rhythm in man and nature. So the term "romantic comedies" is misleading. Shakespeare, to be sure, does not always transform his romantic plot materials. In the Claudio-Hero business in *Much Ado*, for example, the borrowed plot involved negative behavior on the basis of romantic absolutes which was not changed to carry festive feeling. Normally, however, as in *Twelfth Night*, he radically alters the emphasis when he employs romantic materials. Events which in his source control the mood, and are drawn out to exhibit extremity of devotion, producing now pathos, now anxiety, now sentiment, are felt on his stage, in the rhythm of stage time, as incidents controlled by a prevailing mood of revel. What was sentimental extremity becomes impulsive extravagance. And judgment, not committed to systematic wishful distortion, can observe with Touchstone how

> We that are true lovers run into strange capers; but as all is mortal in nature, so is all nature in love mortal in folly. (*A.Y.L.*, ii.iv.53–6)

To turn on passionate experience and identify it with the holiday moment, as Rosalind does in insisting that the sky will change, puts the moment in perspective with life as a whole. Holiday, for the Elizabethan sensibility, implied a contrast with "everyday," when "brightness falls from the air." Occasions like May day and the Winter Revels, with their cult of natural vitality, were maintained within a civilization whose daily view of life focused on the mortality implicit in vitality. The tolerant disillusion of Anglican or Catholic culture allowed nature to have its day. But the release of that one day was understood to be a temporary license, a "misrule" which implied rule, so that the acceptance of nature was qualified. Holiday affirmations in praise of folly were limited by the underlying assumption that the natural in man is only one part of him, the part that will fade.

"How that a life was but a flower" (*A.Y.L.*, v.iii.29) was a two-sided theme: it was usually a gesture preceding "And therefore take the present time"; but it could also lead to the recognition that

> so, from hour to hour, we ripe and ripe,
> And then, from hour to hour, we rot and rot.
> (*A.Y.L.*, ii.vii.26–7)

The second emphasis was implicit in the first; which attitude toward nature predominated depended, not on alternative "philosophies," but on where you were within a rhythm. And because the rhythm is recognized in the comedies, sentimental falsification is not necessary in expressing the ripening moment. It is indeed the present mirth and laughter of the festive plays – the immediate experience they give of nature's beneficence – which reconciles feeling, without recourse to sentimentality or cynicism, to the clarification conveyed about nature's limitations.

Shakespeare's Route to Festive Comedy

In drawing parallels between holiday and Shakespeare's comedy, it has been hard to avoid talking as though Shakespeare were a primitive who began with nothing but festival custom and invented a comedy to express it. Actually, of course, he started work with theatrical and literary resources already highly developed. This tradition was complex, and included folk themes and conventions along with the practice of classically trained innovators like Lyly, Kyd, and Marlowe. Shakespeare, though perfectly aware of unsophisticated forms like the morality and the jig, from the outset wrote plays which presented a narrative in three dimensions. In comedy, he began with cultivated models – Plautus for *The Comedy of Errors* and literary romance for *Two Gentlemen of Verona*; he worked out a consistently festive pattern for his comedy only after these preliminary experiments.

In his third early comedy, *Love's Labour's Lost*, instead of dramatizing a borrowed plot, he built his slight story around an elegant aristocratic entertainment. In doing so he worked out the holiday sequence of release and clarification which comes into its own in *A Midsummer Night's Dream*. This more serious play, his first comic masterpiece, has a crucial place in his development. To make a dramatic epithalamium, he expressed with full imaginative resonance the experience of the traditional summer holidays. He thus found his way back to a native festival tradition remarkably similar to that behind Aristophanes at the start of the literary tradition of comedy.[5] And in expressing the native holiday, he was in a position to use all the resources of a sophisticated dramatic art. So perfect an expression and understanding of folk cult was only possible in the moment when it was still in the blood but no longer in the brain.

Shakespeare never made another play from pastimes in the same direct fashion. But the pattern for feeling and awareness which he derived from the holiday occasion in *A Midsummer Night's Dream* becomes the dominant mode of organization in subsequent comedies until the period of the problem plays. The relation between his festive comedy and naïve folk games is amusingly reflected in the passage from *The Taming of the Shrew* which I have used as an epigraph. When the bemused tinker Sly is asked with mock ceremony whether he will hear a comedy to "frame your mind to mirth and merriment," his response reflects his ignorant notion that a comedy is some sort of holiday game – "a Christmas gambold or a tumbling trick." He is corrected with: "it is more pleasing stuff ... a kind of history." Shakespeare is neither primitive nor primitivist; he enjoys making game of the inadequacy of Sly's folk notions of entertainment. But folk attitudes and motifs are still present, as a matter of course, in the dramatist's cultivated work, so that even Sly is not entirely off the mark about comedy. Though it is a kind of history, it is the kind that frames the mind to mirth. So it functions like a Christmas gambol. It often includes gambols, and even, in the case of *As You Like It*, a tumbling trick. Though Sly has never seen a comedy, his holiday mottoes show that he knows in what spirit to take it: "let the world slip"; "we shall ne'er be younger." Prince Hal, in his festive youth, "daff'd the world aside / And bid it pass" (1 *H. IV*, v.i.96). Feste sings that "Youth's a stuff will not endure" (*Twel.*, ii.iii.53).

The part of Shakespeare's earliest work where his mature patterns of comedy first appear clearly is, as I have suggested, the clowning. Although he did not find an entirely satisfactory comic form for the whole play until *A Midsummer Night's Dream*, the clown's part is satisfactory from the outset. Here the theatrical conventions with which he started writing already provided a congenial saturnalian organization of experience, and Shakespeare at once began working out its larger implications. It was of course a practice, going back beyond *The Second Shepherds' Play*, for the clowns to present a burlesque version of actions performed seriously by their betters. Wagner's conjuring in *Dr. Faustus* is an obvious example. In the drama just before Shakespeare began writing, there are a great many parallels of this sort between the low comedy and the main action.[6] One suspects that they often resulted from the initiative of the clown performer; he was, as Sidney said, thrust in "by head and shoulders to play a part in majestical matters" – and the handiest part to play was a low take-off of what the high people were doing. Though Sidney objected that the performances had "neither decency nor discretion," such burlesque, when properly controlled, had an artistic logic which Shakespeare was quick to develop.

At the simplest level, the clowns were foils, as one of the aristocrats remarks about the clown's show in *Love's Labour's Lost*:

> 'tis some policy
> To have one show worse than the King's and his company.
> (*L.L.L.*, v.ii.513–14)

But burlesque could also have a positive effect, as a vehicle for expressing aberrant impulse and thought. When the aberration was made relevant to the main action, clowning could provide both release for impulses which run counter to decency and decorum, and the clarification about limits which comes from going beyond the limit. Shakespeare used this movement from release to clarification with masterful control in clown episodes as early as 2 *Henry VI*. The scenes of the Jack Cade rebellion in that history are an astonishingly consistent expression of anarchy by clowning: the popular rising is presented throughout as a saturnalia, ignorantly undertaken in earnest; Cade's motto is: "then are we in order when we are most out of order" (iv.iii.199). In the early plays, the clown is usually represented as oblivious of what his burlesque implies. When he becomes the court fool, however, he can use his folly as a stalking horse, and his wit can express directly the function of his role as a dramatized commentary on the rest of the action.

In creating Falstaff, Shakespeare fused the clown's part with that of a festive celebrant, a Lord of Misrule, and worked out the saturnalian implications of both traditions more drastically and more complexly than anywhere else. If in the idyllic plays the humorous perspective can be described as looking past the reigning festive moment to the work-a-day world beyond, in 1 *Henry IV*, the relation of comic and serious action can be described by saying that holiday is balanced against everyday and the doomsday of battle. The comedy expresses impulses and awareness inhibited by the urgency and decorum of political life, so that the comic and serious strains are contrapuntal, each conveying the ironies limiting the other. Then in 2 *Henry IV* Shakespeare confronts the anarchic potentialities of misrule when it seeks to become not a holiday extravagance but an everyday racket.

It might be logical to start where Shakespeare started, by considering first the festive elements present in the imitative comedies and the early clowns and in the literary and theatrical traditions of comedy into which he entered as an apprentice. Instead, because Shakespeare's development followed the route I have sketched, I start with three chapters dealing with the Elizabethan tradition of holiday and with two examples of holiday shows, then enter Shakespeare's work at *Love's Labour's Lost*, where he first makes use of festivity in a large way. To begin with the apprenticeship would involve saying over again a great deal that has been said before in order to separate out the festive elements with which I am properly concerned. It is important to recognize, however, here at the outset, that the order of my discussion brings out the social origins of the festive mode of comedy at the expense of literary and theatrical origins. It would be possible to start with festive affinities of the comic plots Shakespeare found at hand. One could go on to notice how Shakespeare tends to bring out this potential in the way he shapes his early comedies. And one could say a great deal about the way he uses his early clowns to extrapolate the follies of their masters, notably about Launce's romance with his dog Crab as a burlesque of the extravagant romantic postures of the two gentlemen of Verona. Much of this "apprentice" work is wonderful. And it is wonderful what powers are in the comic machine itself, in the literary-theatrical resource for organizing experience which was there for the young Shakespeare to appropriate. But by looking first at the social resource of holiday customs, and then at the early masterpieces where he first fully uses this resource on the stage, we shall be able to bring into focus an influence from the life of his time which shaped his comic art profoundly.

The sort of interpretation I have proposed in outline here does not center on the way the comedies imitate characteristics of actual men and manners; but this neglect of the social observation in the plays does not imply that the way they handle social materials is unimportant. Comedy is not, obviously enough, the same thing as ritual; if it were, it would not perform its function. To express the underlying rhythm his comedy had in common with holiday, Shakespeare did not simply stage mummings; he found in the social life of his time the stuff for "a kind of history." We can see in the Saint George plays how cryptic and arbitrary action derived from ritual becomes when it is merely a fossil remnant. In a self-conscious culture, the heritage of cult is kept alive by art which makes it relevant as a mode of perception and expression. The artist gives the ritual pattern aesthetic actuality by discovering expressions of it in the fragmentary and incomplete gestures of daily life. He fulfills these gestures by making them moments in the complete action which is the art form. The form finds meaning in life.

This process of translation from social into artistic form has great historical as well as literary interest. Shakespeare's theater was taking over on a professional and every-day basis functions which until his time had largely been performed by amateurs on holiday. And he wrote at a moment when the educated part of society was modifying a ceremonial, ritualistic conception of human life to create a historical, psychological conception. His drama, indeed, was an important agency in this transformation: it provided a "theater" where the failures of ceremony could be looked at in a place apart and understood as history; it provided new ways of representing relations between language and action so as to express personality. In making drama out of rituals of state, Shakespeare makes clear their meaning as social and psychological conflict, as history. So too with the rituals of pleasure, of misrule, as against rule: his comedy presents holiday magic as imagination, games as expressive gestures. At high moments it brings into focus, as part of the play, the significance of the saturnalian form itself as a paradoxical human need, problem and resource.

Notes

1   Miss Enid Welsford includes perceptive treatments of Shakespeare's fools in relation to tradition in her fine study, *The Fool: His Social and Literary History* (New York, n.d. [1935]). Professor Willard Farnham characterizes Shakespeare's grotesque or fool comedy in relation to Erasmus and More and the mediaeval feeling for man's natural imperfection in "The Mediaeval Comic Spirit in the English Renaissance," *Joseph Quincy Adams Memorial Studies*, ed. James G. McManaway et al. (Washington, DC, 1948), pp. 429–39. The use of mediaeval elements for comic counterstatement is described in C. L. Barber, "The Use of Comedy in *As You Like It*," *PQ*, xxi (1942), 353–67.

2   *All's W.*, ii.ii.22. Citations of Shakespeare are to *The Complete Works*, ed. George Lyman Kittredge (Boston, 1936). Abbreviations of titles follow the usage recommended by the *Shakespeare Quarterly*.

3   London, 1914.

4   *The Mediaeval Stage* (Oxford, 1903), i, 181, n. 1.

5   Mr. Northrop Frye has formulated a similar view of Shakespeare's development in a brilliant, compressed summary of the whole tradition of literary comedy and Shakespeare's relation to it, "The Argument of Comedy," *English Institute Essays, 1948*, ed. D. A. Robertson, Jr. (New York, 1949).

6   William Empson discusses the effects achieved by such double plots in *English Pastoral Poetry* (New York, 1938; originally printed with the better title, *Some Versions of Pastoral*, London, 1935), pp. 27–86. I am much indebted to Mr. Empson's work: festive comedy, as I discuss it here, is a "version of pastoral."

9

The Jacobean Shakespeare: Some Observations on the Construction of the Tragedies

Maynard Mack

This chapter aims at being a modest supplement (I cannot too much stress the adjective) to A. C. Bradley's pioneering analysis of the construction of Shakespearean tragedy, the second of his famous lectures, published some fifty-five years ago. Bradley's concern was with what would probably today be called the clearer outlines of Shakespearean practice – the management of exposition, conflict, crisis, catastrophe; the contrasts of pace and scene; the over-all patterns of rise-and-fall, variously modulated; the slackened tension after the crisis and Shakespeare's devices for countering this; and the faults.

Bradley is quite detailed about the faults. Sometimes, he says, there are too rapid shiftings of scene and *dramatis personae*, as in the middle section of *Antony and Cleopatra*. Sometimes there is extraneous matter, not required for plot or character development, like the player's speech in *Hamlet* about the murder of Priam, or Hamlet's advice later to the same player on speaking in the theatre. Sometimes there are soliloquies too obviously expositional, as when Edgar disguises to become Poor Tom in *King Lear*. Or there is contradiction and inconsistency, as the double time in *Othello*. Or flatulent writing: 'obscure, inflated, tasteless, or "pestered with metaphors" '. Or 'gnomic' insertions, like the Duke's couplet interchange with Brabantio in *Othello*, used 'more freely than, I suppose, a good play-wright now would care to do'. And finally, to make an end, there is too often sacrificing of dramatic appropriateness to get something said that the author wants said. Thus the comments of the Player King and Claudius on the instability of human purpose arise because Shakespeare 'wishes in part simply to write poetry, and partly to impress on the audience thoughts which will help them to understand, not the player-king nor yet King Claudius, but Hamlet himself'. These failings, Bradley concludes, belong to an art of drama imperfectly developed, which Shakespeare inherited from his predecessors and acquiesced in, on occasion, from 'indifference or want of care'.

Though Bradley's analysis is still the best account we have of the outward shape of Shakespearean tragedy, a glance at his list of faults and, especially, his examples reminds us that a vast deal of water has got itself under the critical bridges since 1904. It is not simply that most of the faults he enumerates would no longer be regarded as such, but would, instead, be numbered among the characteristic practices of Shakespearean dramaturgy, even at its most triumphant. Still more striking is the extent to which our conception of the 'construction' of the tragedies has itself changed. The matters Bradley described have not ceased to be important – far from it: several of our current interpreters, one feels, would benefit if, like Bottom of Master Mustardseed, they were to desire him 'of more acquaintance'. Still, it is impossible not to feel that Bradley missed something – that there is another kind of construction in Shakespeare's tragedies than the one he designates, more inward, more difficult to define, but not less significant. This other structure is not, like his, generated entirely by the interplay of plot and character. Nor is it, on the other hand, though it is fashionable nowadays to suppose so, ultimately a verbal matter. It is poetic, but it goes well beyond what in certain quarters today is called (with something like a lump in the throat) 'the poetry'. Some of its elements arise from the playwright's visualizing imagination, the consciousness of groupings, gestures, entrances, exits. Others may even be prior to language, in the sense that they appear to belong to a paradigm of tragic 'form' that was consciously or unconsciously part of Shakespeare's inheritance and intuition as he worked.

At any rate, it is into this comparatively untravelled and uncharted territory of inward structure that I should like to launch a few tentative explorations. I shall occasionally look backward as far as *Julius Caesar* (1599), *Richard II* (1595–1600), and even *Romeo and Juliet* (1595–6); but in the main I shall be concerned with the tragedies of Shakespeare's prime, from *Hamlet* (1600–1) to *Coriolanus* (1607–8). In these seven or eight years, Shakespeare's golden period, he consolidated a species of tragic structure that for suggestiveness and flexibility has never been matched.[1] I do not anticipate being able to return with a map of this obscure terrain. I hope only to convince better travellers that there is something out there to be known.

First, the hero. The Shakespearean tragic hero, as everybody knows, is an over-stater. His individual accent will vary with his personality, but there is always a residue of hyperbole. This, it would seem, is for Shakespeare the authentic tragic music, mark of a world where a man's reach must always exceed his grasp and everything costs not less than everything.

> Wert thou as far
> As that vast shore wash'd with the farthest sea,
> I would adventure for such merchandise.
> (*Romeo*, II.ii.82)

> 'Swounds, show me what thou'lt do:
> Woo't weep? woo't fight? woo't fast? woo't tear thyself?

Woo't drink up eisel? eat a crocodile?
I'll do't.
>
> (*Hamlet*, v.i.297)

> Nay, had she been true,
> If heaven would make me such another world
> Of one entire and perfect chrysolite,
> I'ld not have sold her for it.
>
> (*Othello*, v.ii.143)

Death, traitor! nothing could have subdued nature
To such a lowness but his unkind daughters.
>
> (*Lear*, iii.iv.72)

Will all great Neptune's ocean wash this blood
Clean from my hand?
>
> (*Macbeth*, ii.ii.60)

> I, that with my sword
> Quarter'd the world, and o'er green Neptune's back
> With ships made cities, ...
>
> (*Antony*, iv.xiv.57)

> I go alone,
> Like to a lonely dragon, that his fen
> Makes fear'd and talk'd of more than seen.
>
> (*Coriolanus*, iv.i.29)

This idiom is not, of course, used by the hero only. It is the language he is dressed in by all who love him, and often by those who do not:

> This was the noblest Roman of them all: ...
> His life was gentle, and the elements
> So mix'd in him that Nature might stand up
> And say to all the world "This was a man!"
>
> (*Caesar*, v.v.68)

> The courtier's, soldier's, scholar's, eye, tongue, sword;
> The expectancy and rose of the fair state,
> The glass of fashion and the mould of form,
> The observed of all observers, ...
>
> (*Hamlet*, iii.i.159)

> Can he be angry? I have seen the cannon,
> When it hath blown his ranks into the air,
> And, like the devil, from his very arm
> Puff'd his own brother: – and can he be angry?
>
> (*Othello*, iii.iv.134)

> On the Alps,
> It is reported thou didst eat strange flesh,
> Which some did die to look on.
>
> (*Antony,* I.iv.66)

> Let me twine
> Mine arms about that body, where against
> My grainèd ash an hundred times hath broke,
> And scarr'd the moon with splinters.
>
> (*Coriolanus,* IV.v.112)

But by whomever used, it is a language that depends for its vindication – for the redemption of its paper promises into gold – upon the hero, and any who stand, heroically, where he does. It is the mark of his, and their, commitment to something beyond 'the vast waters Of the petrel and the porpoise', as Mr. Eliot has it in *East Coker,* a commitment to something – not merely death – which shackles accidents and bolts up change and palates no dung whatever.

Thus the hyperbole of tragedy stands at the opposite end of a tonal scale from the hyperbole of comedy, which springs from and nourishes detachment:

> When I was about thy years, Hal, I was not an eagle's talon in the waist; I could have crept into any alderman's thumb-ring. (1 *Henry IV,* II.iv.362)

> O, she misused me past the endurance of a block! an oak but with one green leaf on it would have answered her; my very visor began to assume life, and scold with her. (*Much Ado,* II.i.246)

> He has a son, who shall be flayed alive; then 'nointed over with honey, set on the head of a wasp's nest; then stand till he be three quarters and a dram dead; then recovered again with aqua-vitae or some other hot infusion; then, raw as he is, and in the hottest day prognostication proclaims, shall he be set against a brick-wall, the sun looking with a southward eye upon him, where he is to behold him with flies blown to death. (*Winter's Tale,* IV.iv.811)

Comic over-statement aims at being preposterous. Until it becomes so, it remains flat. Tragic over-statement, on the other hand, aspires to be believed, and unless in some sense it is so, remains bombast.

Besides the hyperbolist, in Shakespeare's scheme of things, there is always the opposing voice, which belongs to the hero's foil. As the night the day, the idiom of absoluteness demands a vocabulary of a different intensity, a different rhetorical and moral wavelength, to set it off. This other idiom is not necessarily under-statement, though it often takes the form of a deflating accent and very often involves colloquialism – or perhaps merely a middling sort of speech – expressive of a suppler outlook than the hero's, and of other and less upsetting ways of encountering experience than his hyperbolic, not to say intransigent, rigorism. ''Twere to consider too curiously to consider so', says Horatio of Hamlet's equation between the dust of Alexander and a bung-hole, and this enunciates perfectly the foil's role. There is no tragedy in him because he does not consider 'curiously'; there are always more things in earth and heaven than are dreamt of in his philosophy.

Each of the Shakespearean tragedies contains at least one personage to speak this part, which is regularly assigned to someone in the hero's immediate entourage – servitor, wife, friend. In *Romeo and Juliet*, it is of course Mercutio, with his witty resolution of all love into sex. In *Julius Caesar*, it is Cassius, whose restless urgent rhythms, full of flashing images, swirl about Brutus' rounder and abstracter speech, like dogs that bay the moon:

> Brutus: I do believe that these applauses are
>   For some new honours that are heap'd on Caesar.
> Cassius: Why, man, he doth bestride the narrow world
>   Like a Colossus, and we petty men
>   Walk under his huge legs and peep about
>   To find ourselves dishonourable graves.
>
>   (i.ii.133)

In the famous forum speeches, this second voice is taken over temporarily by Antony, and there emerges a similar but yet more powerful contrast between them. Brutus' prose – in which the actuality of the assassination is intellectualized and held at bay by the strict patterns of an obtrusively formal rhetoric, almost as though corporal death were transubstantiated to 'a ballet of bloodless categories' – gives way to Antony's sinewy verse about the 'honourable men', which draws the deed, and its consequence the dead Caesar, ever closer till his own vengeful emotions are kindled in the mob.

In *Hamlet*, the relation of foil to hero undergoes an unusual adaptation. Here, since the raciest idiom of the play belongs to the hero himself, the foil, Horatio, is given a quite conventional speech, and, to make the contrast sharper (Hamlet being of all the heroes the most voluble), as little speech as may be. Like his stoicism, like his 'blood and judgement' –

> so well commingled,
> That they are not a pipe for fortune's finger
> To sound what stop she please –
>
>   (iii.ii.74)

Horatio's 'Here, sweet lord', 'O, my dear lord', 'Well, my lord' are, presumably (as the gentleman in *Lear* says of Cordelia's tears), 'a better way' than Hamlet's self-lacerating virtuosities and verbosities. But of course we do not believe this and are not meant to: who would be Horatio if he could be Hamlet?

Plainly, this is one of the two questions that all the tragic foils exist to make us ask (the other we shall come to presently). Who, for instance, would be Enobarbus, clear-sighted as he is, in preference to Antony? His brilliant sardonic speech, so useful while he can hold his own career and all about him in the comic focus of detachment, withers in the face of his engagement to ultimate issues, and he dies speaking with imagery, accent, and feeling which are surely meant to identify him at the last with the absoluteness of the heroic world, the more so since his last syllables anticipate Cleopatra's:

> Throw my heart
> Against the flint and hardness of my fault;
> Which, being dried with grief, will break to powder,
> And finish all foul thoughts. O Antony,
> Nobler than my revolt is infamous,
> Forgive me in thine own particular;
> But let the world rank me in register
> A master-leaver and a fugitive:
> O Antony! O Antony!
>
> (iv.ix.15)

Such unequivocal judgements are a change indeed on the part of one who could earlier rally cynically with Menas about 'two thieves kissing' when their hands meet.

King Lear is given two foils. The primary one is obviously the Fool, whose rhymes and riddles and jets of humour in the first two Acts set off both the old king's brooding silences and his massively articulated longer speeches when aroused. But in the storm scenes, and occasionally elsewhere, one is almost as keenly conscious of the relief into which Lear's outrageous imprecations are thrown by the mute devoted patience of his servant Kent. For both foils – and this of course is their most prominent function as representatives of the opposing voice – the storm itself is only a storm, to be stoically endured, in the one case, and, in the other, if his master would but hear reason, eschewed:

> O nuncle, court holy-water in a dry house is better than this rain-water out o'door. Good nuncle, in, ask thy daughters' blessing: ... (iii.ii.10)

Doubtless the Fool does not wish to be taken quite *au pied de la lettre* in this – his talk is always in the vein of the false daughters', his action quite other. But neither for him nor for Kent does facing the thunder have any kind of transcendent meaning. In Lear's case, it has; the thunder he hears is like the thunder heard over Himavant in *The Waste Land*; it has what the anthropologists call 'mana'; and his (and our) consuming questions are what it means – and if it means – and whose side it is on.

In my view, the most interesting uses of the opposing voice occur in *Macbeth* and *Othello*. In *Macbeth*, Shakespeare gives it to Lady Macbeth, and there was never, I think, a more thrilling tragic counterpoint set down for the stage than that in the scene following the murder of Duncan, when her purely physical reading of what has happened to them both is met by his metaphysical intuitions. His 'noise' to her is just the owl screaming and the crickets' cry. The voice of one crying 'sleep no more' is only his 'brain-sickly' fear. The blood on his hands is what 'a little water clears us of'. 'Consider it not so deeply', she says at one point, with an echo of Horatio in the graveyard. 'These deeds must not be thought After these ways'. But in the tragic world, which always opens on transcendence, they must; and this she herself finds before she dies, a prisoner to the deed, endlessly washing the damned spot that will not out. 'What's done cannot be undone' is a language that like Enobarbus she has to learn.

Othello's foil of course is Iago, about whose imagery and speech there hangs, as recent commentators have pointed out, a constructed air, an ingenious, hyper-conscious generalizing air, essentially suited to one who, as W. H. Clemen has said, 'seeks to poison ... others with his images' (p. 122). Yet Iago's poison does not work more

---

130

powerfully through his images than through a corrosive habit of abstraction applied in those unique relations of love and faith where abstraction is most irrelevant and most destructive. Iago has learned to 'sickly o'er' the central and irreducible individual with the pale cast of class and kind:

Blessed fig's end! The wine she drinks is made of grapes ... (ii.i.257)

These Moors are changeable in their wills ... If sanctimony and a frail vow betwixt an erring barbarian and a supersubtle Venetian be not too hard for my wits. ... (i.iii.352–63)

> Come on, come on; you are pictures out of doors,
> Bells in your parlours, wild-cats in your kitchens,
> Saints in your injuries, devils being offended,
> Players in your housewifery, and housewives in your beds.
> (ii.i.110)
>
> I know our country disposition well;
> In Venice they do let heaven see the pranks
> They dare not show their husbands.
> (iii.iii.201)

Othello's downfall is signalled quite as clearly when he drifts into this rationalized dimension –

> O curse of marriage,
> That we can call these delicate creatures ours,
> And not their appetites –
> (iii.iii.268)

leaving behind his true vernacular, the idiom of 'My life upon her faith!', as when his mind fills with Iago's copulative imagery. Shakespeare seems to have been well aware that love (especially such love as can be reflected only in the union of a black man with a white woman, East with West) is the mutual knowing of uniqueness:

> Reason, in itself confounded,
> Saw division grow together,
> To themselves yet either neither,
> Simple were so well compounded,
>
> That it cried, How true a twain
> Seemeth this concordant one!
> Love hath reason, reason none,
> If what parts can so remain.
>
> Whereupon it made this threne
> To the phoenix and the dove,
> Co-supremes and stars of love,
> As chorus to their tragic scene.
> (*The Phoenix and the Turtle*, 41)

And also that there are areas of experience where, as a great saint once said, one must first believe in order that one may know.

To one who should ask why these paired voices seem to be essential ingredients of Shakespearean tragedy, no single answer can, I think, be given. They occur partly, no doubt, because of their structural utility, the value of complementary personalities in a work of fiction being roughly analogous to the value of thesis and antithesis in a discursive work. Partly too, no doubt, because in stage performance, the antiphonal effects of the two main vocabularies, strengthened by diversity in manner, costume, placing on the stage, supply variety of mood and gratify the eye and ear. But these are superficial considerations. Perhaps we come to something more satisfactory when we consider that these two voices apparently answer to reverberations which reach far back in the human past. *Mutatis mutandis*, Coriolanus and Menenius, Antony and Enobarbus, Macbeth and Lady Macbeth, Lear and his Fool, Othello and Iago, Hamlet and Horatio, Brutus and Cassius, Romeo and Mercutio exhibit a kind of duality that is also exhibited in Oedipus and Jocasta (as well as Creon), Antigone and Ismene, Prometheus and Oceanus, Phaedra and her nurse – and also, in many instances in Greek tragedy, by the protagonist and the chorus.

If it is true, as can be argued, that the Greek chorus functions in large measure as spokesman for the values of the community, and the first actor, in large measure, for the passionate life of the individual, we can perhaps see a philosophical basis for the long succession of opposing voices. What matters to the community is obviously accommodation – all those adjustments and resiliences that enable it to survive; whereas what matters to the individual, at least in his heroic mood, is just as obviously integrity – all that enables him to remain an *individual*, one thing not many. The confrontation of these two outlooks is therefore a confrontation of two of our most cherished instincts, the instinct to be resolute, autonomous, free, and the instinct to be 'realistic', adaptable, secure. If it is also true, as I think most of us believe, that tragic drama is in one way or other a record of man's affair with transcendence (whether this be defined as gods, God, or, as by Malraux, the human 'fate', which men must 'question' even if they cannot control), we can see further why the hero must have an idiom – such as hyperbole – that establishes him as moving to measures played above, or outside, our normal space and time. For the *reductio ad absurdum* of the tragic confrontation is the comic one, exemplified in Don Quixote and his Sancho, where the comedy arises precisely from the fact that the hero only *imagines* he moves to measures above and outside our normal world; and where, to the extent that we come to identify with his faith, the comedy slides towards pathos and even the tragic absolute.

These considerations, however, remain speculative. What is not in doubt is that dramaturgically the antiphony of two voices and two vocabularies serves Shakespeare well, and in one of its extensions gives rise to a phenomenon as peculiar and personal to him as his signature. Towards the close of a tragic play, or if not towards the close, at the climax, will normally appear a short scene or episode (sometimes more than one) of spiritual cross purposes: a scene in which the line of tragic speech and feeling generated by commitment is crossed by an alien speech and feeling very much detached. Bradley, noting such of these episodes as are 'humorous or semi-humorous', places them among Shakespeare's devices for sustaining interest after the crisis, since their introduction 'affords variety and relief, and also heightens by contrast the tragic feelings'. Another perceptive critic has noted that though such scenes afford 'relief', it is not by laughter. 'We return for a moment to simple people, a gravedigger, a porter, a countryman, and to the goings on of every day, the feeling for bread and cheese, and when we go back to the high tragic mood we do so with a heightened sense that we are moving in a world fully realized' (F. P. Wilson, p. 122). To such comments, we must add another. For the whole effect of these episodes does not come simply from variety, or from the juxtaposition of bread and cheese with the high tragic mood, though these elements are certainly present in it.

It arises, in the main, I think, from the fact that Shakespeare here lays open to us, in an especially poignant form, what I take to be the central dialogue of tragic experience. It is a dialogue of which the Greek dialogue of individual with community, the seventeenth-century dialogue of soul with body, the twentieth-century dialogue of self with soul are perhaps all versions in their different ways: a dialogue in which each party makes its case in its own tongue, incapable of wholly comprehending what the other means. And Shakespeare objectifies it for us on his stage by the encounter of those by whom, 'changed, changed utterly', a terrible beauty has been born, with those who are still players in life's casual comedy. Hamlet and the gravediggers, Desdemona and Emilia, Cleopatra and the clown afford particularly fine examples of Shakespeare's technique in this respect.

In the first instance, the mixture of profoundly imaginative feelings contained in Hamlet's epitaph for Yorick –

> I knew him, Horatio: a fellow of infinite jest, of most excellent fancy; he hath borne me on his back a thousand times; and now, how abhorred in my imagination it is! my gorge rises at it. Here hung those lips that I have kissed I know not how oft. Where be your gibes now? your gambols? your songs? your flashes of merriment, that were wont to set the table on a roar? Not one now, to mock your own grinning? quite chap-fallen? Now get you to my lady's chamber, and tell her, let her paint an inch thick, to this favour she must come; make her laugh at that – (v.i.203)

is weighed over against the buffoon literalism of the clown –

> *Hamlet:* What man dost thou dig it for?
> *First clown:* For no man, sir.
> *Hamlet:* What woman, then?
> *First clown:* For none, neither.
> *Hamlet:* Who is to be buried in 't?
> *First clown:* One that was a woman, sir; but, rest her soul, she's dead –
>
> (v.i.141)

and against his uncompromising factualism too, his hard dry vocabulary of detachment, without overtones, by which he cuts his métier down to a size that can be lived with:

> I'faith, if he be not rotten before he die, … he will last you some eight year or nine year: a tanner will last you nine year. (v.i.180)

But in this scene Hamlet's macabre thoughts are not allowed to outweigh the clown. A case is made for factualism and literalism. Horatio is seen to have a point in saying it is to consider too curiously to consider as Hamlet does. A man must come to terms with the graveyard; but how long may he linger in it with impunity, or allow it to linger in him? Such reckonings the opposing voice, whether spoken by the primary foil or by another, is calculated to awake in us: this is the second kind of question that it exists to make us ask.

In a sense, then, the implicit subject of all these episodes is the predicament of being human. They bring before us the grandeur of man's nature, which contains, potentially, both voices, both ends of the moral and psychic spectrum. They bring before us the necessity of his choice, because it is rarely given to him to go through any door without closing the rest. And they bring before us the sadness, the infinite sadness of his lot, because, short of the 'certain certainties' that tragedy does not deal with, he has no sublunar way of knowing whether defiant 'heroism' is really more to be desired than suppler 'wisdom'. The alabaster innocence of Desdemona's world shines out beside the crumpled bedsitters of Emilia's –

Desdemona:	Wouldst thou do such a deed for all the world?
Emilia:	Why, would not you?
Desdemona:	No, by this heavenly light!
Emilia:	Nor I neither by this heavenly light; I might do't as well i' the dark.
Desdemona:	Wouldst thou do such a deed for all the world?
Emilia:	The world's a huge thing: it is a great price For a small vice.
Desdemona:	In troth, I think thou wouldst not.
Emilia:	In troth, I think I should … who would not make her husband a cuckold to make him a monarch? I should venture purgatory for 't.
Desdemona:	Beshrew me, if I would do such a wrong For the whole world.
Emilia:	Why, the wrong is but a wrong i' the world; and having the world for your labour, 'tis a wrong in your own world, and you might quickly make it right.
Desdemona:	I do not think there is any such woman –

(iv.iii.64)

but the two languages never, essentially, commune – and, for this reason, the dialogue they hold can never be finally adjudicated.

The same effect may be noted in Cleopatra's scene with the countryman who brings her the asps. Her exultation casts a glow over the whole scene of her death. But her language when the countryman has gone would not have the tragic resonance it has, if we could not hear echoing between the lines the gritty accents of the opposing voice:

> Give me my robe, put on my crown; I have
> Immortal longings in me.

Truly, I have him: but I would not be the party that should desire you to touch him, for his biting is immortal; those that do die of it do seldom or never recover.

> The stroke of death is as a lover's pinch,
> Which hurts, and is desired.

> I heard of one of them no longer than yesterday: a very honest woman, but something given to lie; as a woman should not do, but in the way of honesty: how she died of the biting of it, what pain she felt.

> Peace, peace!
> Dost thou not see my baby at my breast,
> That sucks the nurse asleep?
> (v.ii.283–313)

> Give it nothing, I pray you, for it is not worth the feeding. (v.ii.245–71)

The 'worm' – or 'my baby'; the Antony Demetrius and Philo see – or the Antony whose face is as the heavens; the 'small vice' of Emilia – or the deed one would not do for the whole world; the skull knocked about the mazzard by a sexton's spade – or the skull which 'had a tongue in it and could sing once': these are incommensurables, which human nature nevertheless must somehow measure, reconcile, and enclose.

We move now from 'character' to 'action', and to the question: what happens in a Shakespearean tragedy? Bradley's traditional categories – exposition, conflict, crisis, catastrophe, etc. – give us one side of this, but, as we noticed earlier, largely the external side, and are in any case rather too clumsy for the job we try to do with them. They apply as well to pot-boilers of the commercial theatre as to serious works of art, to prose as well as poetic drama. What is worse, they are unable to register the unique capacity of Shakespearian dramaturgy to hint, evoke, imply, and, in short, by indirections find directions out. The nature of some of Shakespeare's 'indirections' is a topic we must explore before we can hope to confront the question posed above with other terms than Bradley's.

To clarify what I mean by indirection, let me cite an instance from *King Lear*. Everybody has noticed, no doubt, that Lear's fool (apart from being the King's primary foil) gives voice during the first two acts to notations of topsiturviness that are not, one feels, simply his own responses to the inversions of order that have occurred in family and state, but a reflection of the King's; or, to put the matter another way, the situation is so arranged by Shakespeare that we are invited to apply the Fool's comments to Lear's inner experience, and I suspect that most of us do so. The Fool thus serves, to some extent, as a screen on which Shakespeare flashes, as it were, readings from the psychic life of the protagonist, possibly even his subconscious life, which could not otherwise be conveyed in drama at all. Likewise, the Fool's *idée fixe* in this matter, his apparent obsession with one idea (often a clinical symptom of incipient insanity) is perhaps dramatic short-hand, and even sleight-of-hand, for goings-on in the King's brain that only occasionally bubble to the surface in the form of conscious apprehensions: 'O let me not be mad, not mad sweet heaven'. 'O fool, I shall go mad'. Conceivably, there may even be significance in the circumstance that the Fool does not enter the play as a speaking character till after King Lear has behaved like a fool, and leaves it before he is cured.

Whatever the truth of this last point, the example of the Fool in Lear introduces us to devices of play construction and ways of recording the progress of inward 'action', which, though the traditional categories say nothing about them, are a basic resource of Shakespeare's playwriting, and nowhere more so than in the tragedies. We may now consider a few of them in turn.

First, there are the figures, like the Fool, some part of whose consciousness, as conveyed to us at particular moments, seems to be doing double duty, filling our minds with impressions analogous to those which we may presume to be occupying the conscious or unconscious mind of the hero, whether he is before us on the stage or not. A possible example may be Lady Macbeth's sleep-walking scene. Macbeth is absent at this juncture, has gone 'into the field' – has not in fact been visible during two long scenes and will not be visible again till the next scene after this. In the interval, the slaying at Macduff's castle and the conversations between Malcolm and Macduff keep him before us in his capacity as tyrant, murderer, 'Hell-kite', seen from the outside. But Lady Macbeth's sleep-walking is, I think, Shakespeare's device for keeping him before us in his capacity as tragic hero and sufferer. The 'great perturbation in nature' of which the doctor whispers ('to receive at once the benefit of sleep, and do the effects of watching'), the 'slumbery agitation', the 'thick-coming fancies That keep her from her rest': these by a kind of poetical displacement, we may apply to him as well as to her; and we are invited to do so by the fact that from the moment of the first murder all the play's references to sleep, and its destruction, have had reference to Macbeth himself. We are, of course, conscious as we watch the scene, that this is Lady Macbeth suffering the metaphysical aspects of murder that she did not believe in; we may also be conscious that the remorse pictured here tends to distinguish her from her husband, who for some time has been giving his 'initiate fear' the 'hard use' he said it lacked, with dehumanizing consequences. Yet in some way the pity of this situation suffuses him as well as her, the more so because in every word she utters his presence beside her is supposed; and if we allow this to be true, not only will Menteith's comment in the following scene –

> Who then shall blame
> His pester'd senses to recoil and start,
> When all that is within him does condemn
> Itself for being there –
>
> > (v.ii.22)

evoke an image of suffering as well as retribution, but we shall better understand Macbeth's striking expression, at his next appearance, in words that we are almost bound to feel have some reference to himself, of corrosive griefs haunting below the conscious levels of the mind:

> Canst thou not minister to a mind diseased,
> Pluck from the memory a rooted sorrow,
> Raze out the written troubles of the brain
> And with some sweet oblivious antidote
> Cleanse the stuff'd bosom of that perilous stuff
> Which weighs upon the heart?
>
> > (v.iii.40)

Such speeches as this, and as Lady Macbeth's while sleep-walking – which we might call umbrella speeches, since more than one consciousness may shelter under them – are not uncommon in Shakespeare's dramaturgy, as many critics have pointed out. *Lear* affords the classic examples: in the Fool, as we have seen, and also in Edgar. Edgar's speech during the storm scenes projects in part his role of Poor Tom, the eternal outcast; in part, Edmund (and also Oswald), the vicious servant, self-seeking, with heart set on lust and proud array; possibly in part, Gloucester, whose arrival with a torch the Fool appropriately announces (without knowing it) in terms related to Edgar's themes: 'Now a little fire in a wide field were like an old lecher's heart'; and surely, in some part too, the King, for the chips and tag-ends of Edgar's speech reflect, as if from Lear's own mind, not simply mental disintegration, but a strong sense of a fragmented moral order: 'Obey thy parents; keep thy word justly; swear not; commit not with man's sworn spouse….'

But in my view, the most interesting of all the umbrella speeches in the tragedies is Enobarbus' famous description of Cleopatra in her barge. The triumvirs have gone off-stage, Antony to have his first view of Octavia. When we see him again, his union with Octavia will have been agreed on all parts (though not yet celebrated), and he will be saying to her, with what can hardly be supposed to be insincerity:

> My Octavia,
> Read not my blemishes in the world's report:
> I have not kept my square; but that to come
> Shall all be done by the rule. Good night, dear lady.
> (ii.iii.4)

Then the soothsayer appears, reminds Antony that his guardian angel will always be overpowered when Caesar's is by, urges him to return to Egypt; and Antony, left alone after the soothsayer has gone, meditates a moment on the truth of the pronouncement and then says abruptly:

> I will to Egypt:
> And though I make this marriage for my peace,
> I' the east my pleasure lies.
> (ii.iii.38)

There is plainly a piece of prestidigitation here. It is performed in part by means of the soothsayer's entry, which is evidently a kind of visual surrogate for Antony's own personal intuition. ('I see it in my motion, have it not in my tongue', the soothsayer says, when asked for the reasons he wishes Antony to return; and that is presumably the way Antony sees it too: in his 'motion', i.e. involuntarily, intuitively.) But a larger part is played by Enobarbus's account of Cleopatra. Between the exit of the triumvirs and the reappearance of Antony making unsolicited promises to Octavia, this is the one thing that intervenes. And it is the only thing that needs to. Shakespeare has made it so powerful, so coloured our imaginations with it, that we understand the promises of Antony, not in the light in which he understands them as he makes them, but in the riotous brilliance of Enobarbus' evocation of Cleopatra. The psychic gap, in Antony, between 'My Octavia' and 'Good night, dear lady', on the one hand, and 'I will to Egypt', on the other, is filled by a vision, given to us, of irresistible and indeed quasi-unearthly power, of which the soothsayer's intuition is simply a more abstract formulation. Here again, by indirection, Shakespeare finds direction out.

Not all mirror situations in the tragedies involve reflection of another consciousness. Some, as is well known, emphasize the outlines of an action by recapitulating it, as when Edgar's descent to Poor Tom and subsequent gradual re-ascent to support the gored state echoes the downward and upward movement in the lives of both King Lear and Gloucester; or as when Enobarbus' defection to, and again from, the bidding of his practical reason repeats that which Antony has already experienced, and Cleopatra will experience (at least in one way of understanding Act V) between Antony's death and her own. *Hamlet*, complex in all respects, offers an unusually complex form of this. The three sons, who are, in various senses, all avengers of dead fathers, are all deflected, temporarily, from their designs by the manoeuvres of an elder (Claudius for Laertes and Hamlet; the King of Norway, inspired by Claudius, for Fortinbras), who in two cases is the young man's uncle. There are of course important differences between these three young men which we are not to forget; but with respect to structure, the images in the mirror are chiefly likenesses. Hamlet, out-manoeuvered by Claudius, off to England to be executed, crosses the path of Fortinbras, who has also been out-manoeuvered by Claudius (working through his uncle), and is off to Poland to make mouths at the invisible event, while at the same moment Laertes, clamouring for immediate satisfaction in the King's palace, is out-manoeuvered in his turn. Likewise, at the play's end, all three young men are 'victorious', in ways they could hardly have foreseen. The return of Fortinbras, having achieved his objective in Poland, to find his 'rights' in Denmark achieved without a blow, is timed to coincide with Hamlet's achieving his objectives in exposing and killing the King, and Laertes's achieving his objective of avenging his father's death on Hamlet. When this episode is played before us in the theatre, there is little question, to my way of thinking, but that something of the glow and martial upsurge dramatized in Fortinbras's entrance associates itself to Hamlet, even as Fortinbras's words associate Hamlet to a soldier's death. Meantime, Laertes, who has been trapped by the King and has paid with his life for it, gives us an alternative reflection of the Prince, which is equally a part of the truth.

Fortinbras's arrival at the close of *Hamlet* is an instance of an especially interesting type of mirroring to be found everywhere in Shakespeare's work – the emblematic entrance, and exit. Sometimes such exits occur by death, as the death of Gaunt, who takes a sacramental view of kingship and nation, in *Richard II*, at the instant when Richard has destroyed, by his personal conduct and by 'farming' his realm, the sacramental relationships which make such a view possible to maintain. Gaunt has to die, we might say, before a usurpation like his son's can even be imagined; and it is, I take it, not without significance that the first word of Bolingbroke's return comes a few seconds after we have heard (from the same speaker, Northumberland) that Gaunt's tongue 'is now a stringless instrument'. Something similar, it seems clear, occurs with the death of Mamillius in *The Winter's Tale*. Sickening with his father's sickening mind, Mamillius dies in the instant that his father repudiates the message of the oracle; and though, in the end, all else is restored to Leontes, Mamillius is not.

In the tragedies, emblematic entrances and exits assume a variety of forms, ranging from those whose significance is obvious to those where it is uncertain, controversial, and perhaps simply a mirage. One entrance whose significance is unmistakable occurs in the first act of *Macbeth*, when Duncan, speaking of the traitor Cawdor, whom he has slain, laments that there is no art to find the mind's construction in the face, just as the new Cawdor, traitor-to-be, appears before him. Equally unmistakable is the significance of the King's exit, in the first scene of *Lear*, with the man who like himself has put externals first. 'Come, noble Burgundy', he says, and in a pairing that can be made profoundly moving on the stage, the two men go out together.

But what are we to say of Antony's freedman Eros, who enters for the first time (at least by name) just before his master's suicide and kills himself rather than kill Antony? This is all from his source, Plutarch's life of Antony; but why did Shakespeare include it? Did Eros' name mean something to him? Are we to see here a shadowing of the other deaths for love, or not? And the carrying off of Lepidus, drunk, from the feast aboard Pompey's galley. Does this anticipate his subsequent fate? and if it does, what does the intoxication signify which in this scene all the great men are subject to in their degree? Is it ordinary drunkenness; or is it, like the drunkenness that afflicts Caliban, Trinculo, and Stephano in *The Tempest*, a species of self-intoxication, Shakespeare's subdued comment on the thrust to worldly power? Or again, what of the arrival of the players in *Hamlet*? Granted their role in the plot, does Shakespeare make no other profit from them? Are such matters as the speech on Priam's murder and the advice on acting interesting excrescences, as Bradley thought, or does each mirror something that we are to appropriate to our understanding of the play: in the first instance, the strange confederacy of passion and paralysis in the hero's mind,[2] in the second, the question that tolls on all sides through the castle at Elsinore: when is an act not an 'act'?[3]

These are questions to which it is not always easy to give a sound answer. The ground becomes somewhat firmer underfoot, I think, if we turn for a concluding instance to Bianca's pat appearances in *Othello*. R. B. Heilman suggests that in rushing to the scene of the night assault on Cassio, when she might have stayed safely within doors, and so exposing herself to vilification as a 'notable strumpet', Bianca acts in a manner 'thematically relevant, because Othello has just been attacking Desdemona as a strumpet' – both 'strumpets', in other words, are faithful (p. 180). Whether this is true or not, Bianca makes two very striking entrances earlier, when in each case she may be thought to supply in living form on the stage the prostitute figure that Desdemona has become in Othello's mind. Her second entrance is notably expressive. Othello here is partially overhearing while Iago rallies Cassio about Bianca, Othello being under the delusion that the talk is of Desdemona. At the point when, in Othello's mental imagery, Desdemona becomes the soliciting whore – 'she tells him how she plucked him to my chamber' – Bianca enters in the flesh, and not only enters, but flourishes the magic handkerchief, now degenerated, like the love it was to ensure, to some 'minx's', some 'hobby-horse's' token, the subject of jealous bickering. In the theatre, the emblematic effect of this can hardly be ignored.[4]

Further types of mirroring will spring to every reader's mind. The recapitulation of a motif, for instance, as in the poisoning episodes in *Hamlet*. *Hamlet* criticism has too much ignored, I think, the fact that a story of poisoning forms the climax of the first act, a mime and 'play' of poisoning the climax of the third, and actual poisoning, on a wide scale, the climax of the fifth. Surely this repetition was calculated to keep steady for Shakespeare's Elizabethan audiences the political and moral bearings of the play? We may say what we like about Hamlet's frailties, which are real, but we can hardly ignore the fact that in each of the poisoning episodes the poisoner is the King. The King, who ought to be like the sun, giving warmth, radiance, and fertility to his kingdom, is actually its destroyer. The 'leperous distilment' he pours into Hamlet's father's ear, which courses through his body with such despatch, has coursed just as swiftly through the body politic, and what we see in Denmark as a result is a poisoned kingdom, containing one corruption upon another of Renaissance ideals: the 'wise councillor', who is instead a tedious windbag; the young 'man of honour', who has no trust in another's honour, as his advice to his sister shows, and none of his own, as his own treachery to Hamlet shows; the 'friends', who are not friends but spies; the loved one, the 'mistress', who proves disloyal (a decoy, however reluctant, for villainy), and goes mad – through poison also, 'the poison of deep grief'; the mother and Queen, who instead of being the guardian of the kingdom's matronly virtues has set a harlot's blister on love's forehead and made marriage vows 'as false as dicers' oaths'; and the Prince, the 'ideal courtier', the Renaissance man – once active, energetic, now reduced to anguished introspection; a glass of fashion, now a sloven in antic disarray; a noble mind, now partly unhinged, in fact as well as seeming; the observed of all observers, now observed in a more sinister sense; the mould of form, now capable of obscenities, cruelty, even treachery, mining below the mines of his school friends to hoist them with their own petard. All this, in one way or another, is the poison of the King, and in the last scene, lest we miss the point, we are made to see the spiritual poison become literal and seize on all those whom it has not already destroyed.

> a Prince's Court
> Is like a common Fountaine, whence should flow
> Pure silver-droppes in generall: But if 't chance
> Some curs'd example poyson't neere the head,
> Death, and diseases through the whole land spread.

The lines are Webster's, but they state with precision one of the themes of Shakespeare's play.

Finally, in the tragedies as elsewhere in Shakespeare, we have the kinds of replication that have been specifically called 'mirror scenes',[5] or (more in Ercles's vein) scenes of 'analogical probability'.[6] The most impressive examples here are frequently the opening scenes and episodes. The witches of *Macbeth*, whose 'foul is fair' and battle that is 'won *and* lost' anticipate so much to come. The 'great debate' in *Antony and Cleopatra*, initiated in the comments of Philo and the posturings of the lovers, and reverberating thereafter within, as well as around, the lovers till they die. The watchmen on the platform in *Hamlet*, feeling out a mystery – an image that will re-form in our minds again and again as we watch almost every member of the *dramatis personae* engage in similar activity later on. The technique of manipulation established at the outset of *Othello*, the persuading of someone to believe something he is reluctant to believe and which is not true in the sense presented – exemplified in Iago's management of both

Roderigo and Brabantio, and prefiguring later developments even to the detail that the manipulator operates by preference through an instrument.

Lear offers perhaps the best of all these instances. Here the 'Nature' of which the play is to make so much, ambiguous, double-barrelled, is represented in its normative aspect in the hierarchies on the stage before us – a whole political society from its *primum mobile*, the great King, down to lowliest attendant, a whole family society from father down through married daughters and sons-in-law to a third daughter with her wooers – and, in its appetitive aspect, which Edmund will formulate in a few moments, in the overt self-will of the old King and the hidden self-will, the 'plighted cunning', of the false daughters. As the scene progresses, in fact, we can see these hierarchies of the normative nature, which at first looked so formidable and solid, crumble away in the repudiation of Cordelia, the banishment of Kent, the exit of Lear and Burgundy, till nothing is left standing on the stage but Nature red in tooth and claw as the false daughters lay their heads together.

I have dwelt a little on these effects of 'indirection' in the tragedies because I believe that most of us as playgoers are keenly conscious of their presence. I have perhaps described them badly, in some instances possibly misconceived them; but they are not my invention; this kind of thing has been pointed to more and more widely during the past fifty years by reputable observers. In short, these effects, in some important sense, are 'there'. And if they are, the question we must ask is, Why? What are they for? How are they used?

I return then to the query with which this section began: what *does* happen in a Shakespearean tragedy? Is it possible to formulate an answer that will, while not repudiating the traditional categories so far as they are useful, take into account the matters we have been examining? In the present state of our knowledge I am not convinced that this is possible: we have been too much concerned in this century with the verbal, which is only part of the picture. Nevertheless, I should like to make a few exploratory gestures.

Obviously the most important thing that happens in a Shakespearean tragedy is that the hero follows a cycle of change, which is, in part, psychic change. And this seems generally to be constituted in three phases. During the first phase, corresponding roughly to Bradley's exposition, the hero is delineated. Among other things, he is placed in positions that enable him to sound the particular timbre of his tragic music:

> Not so, my lord; I am too much i' the sun.
> (*Hamlet*, 1.ii.67)

> Seems, madam! nay, it is; I know not 'seems'.
> (1.ii.76)

> My father's brother, but no more like my father
> Than I to Hercules.
> (1.ii.152)

> My fate cries out,
> And makes each petty artery in this body
> As hardy as the Nemean lion's nerve.
> (1.iv.81)

Chiming against this we are also permitted to hear the particular timbre of the opposing voice, spoken by the foil as well as others:

> If it be,
> Why seems it so particular with thee?
> (1.ii.74)

> For what we know must be and is as common
> As any the most vulgar thing to sense,
> Why should we in our peevish opposition
> Take it to heart?
> (1.ii.98)

> What if it tempt you toward the flood, my lord,
> Or to the dreadful summit of the cliff
> That beetles o'er his base into the sea,
> And there assume some other horrible form,
> Which might deprive your sovereignty of reason
> And draw you into madness?
> (1.iv.69)

From now on, as we saw, these are the differing attitudes towards experience that will supply the essential dialogue of the play.

The second phase is much more comprehensive. It contains the conflict, crisis, and falling action – in short, the heart of the matter. Here several interesting developments occur. The one certain over-all development in this phase is that the hero tends to become his own antithesis. We touched on this earlier in the case of Hamlet, in whom 'the courtier's, soldier's, scholar's, eye, tongue, sword' suffer some rather savage violations before the play is done. Likewise, Othello the unshakable, whose original composure under the most trying insults and misrepresentations almost takes the breath away, breaks in this phase into furies, grovels on the floor in a trance, strikes his wife publicly. King Lear, 'the great image of authority' both by temperament and position, becomes a helpless crazed old man crying in a storm, destitute of everything but one servant and his Fool. Macbeth, who would have 'holily' what he would have 'highly', who is too full of the milk of human kindness to catch the nearest way, whose whole being revolts with every step he takes in his own revolt – his hair standing on end, his imagination filling with angels 'trumpet-tongued', his hands (after the deed) threatening to pluck out his own eyes – turns into the numbed usurper, 'supped full with horrors', who is hardly capable of responding even to his wife's death. The development is equally plain in Antony and Coriolanus. 'The greatest prince o' th' world, The noblest', finds his greatness slipped from him, and his nobility debased to the ignominy of having helpless emissaries whipped. The proud and upright Coriolanus, patriot soldier, truckles in the market-place for votes, revolts to the enemy he has vanquished, carries war against his own flesh and blood.

This manner of delineating tragic 'action', though it may be traced here and there in other drama, seems to be on the whole a property of the Elizabethans and Jacobeans. Possibly it springs from their concern with 'whole' personalities on the tragic stage, rather than as so often with the ancients and Racine, just those aspects of personality that guarantee the *dénouement*. In any case, it seems to have become a consistent feature of Shakespeare's dramaturgy, and beautifully defines the sense of psychological alienation and uprootedness that tragic experience in the Elizabethan and Jacobean theatre generally seems to embrace. Its distinctively tragic implications stand out the more when we reflect that psychic change in comedy (if indeed comedy can be said to concern itself with psychic change at all) consists in making – or in showing – the protagonist to be more and more what he always was.[7]

In this second phase too, either as an outward manifestation of inward change, or as a short-hand indication that such change is about to begin or end, belong the tragic journeys. Romeo is off to Mantua, Brutus to the Eastern end of the Roman world, Hamlet to England, Othello to Cyprus, Lear and Gloucester to Dover, Timon to the cave, Macbeth to the heath to revisit the witches, Antony to Rome and Athens, Coriolanus to Antium.[8] Such journeys, we rightly say, are called for by the plots. But perhaps we should not be wrong if we added that Shakespearean plotting tends to call for journeys, conceivably for discernible reasons. For one thing, journeys can enhance our impression that psychological changes are taking place, either by emphasizing a lapse of time, or by taking us to new settings, or by both. I suspect we register such effects subconsciously more often than we think.

Furthermore, though it would be foolish to assign to any of the journeys in Shakespeare's tragedies a precise symbolic meaning, several of them have vaguely symbolic overtones – serving as surrogates either for what can never be exhibited on the stage, as the mysterious processes leading to psychic change, which cannot be articulated into speech, even soliloquy, without losing their formless instinctive character; or for the processes of self-discovery, the learning processes – a function journeys fulfill in many of the world's best-known stories (the *Aeneid*, the *Divine Comedy*, *Tom Jones*, etc.) and in some of Shakespeare's comedies. Hamlet's abortive journey to England is possibly an instance of the first category. After his return, and particularly after what he tells us of his actions while at sea, we are not surprised if he appears, spiritually, a changed man. Lear's and Gloucester's journey to Dover is perhaps an instance of the second category, leading as it does through suffering to insight and reconciliation.

During the hero's journey, or at any rate during his over-all progress in the second phase, he will normally pass through a variety of mirroring situations of the sort formerly discussed (though it will be by us and not him that the likeness in the mirror is seen). In some of these, the hero will be confronted, so to speak, with a version of his own situation, and his failure to recognize it may be a measure of the nature of the disaster to ensue. Coriolanus, revolted from Rome and now its enemy, meets himself in Aufidius' embrace in Antium. Hamlet meets himself in Fortinbras as the latter marches to Poland, but does not see the likeness – only the differences. Lear goes to Goneril's and there meets, as everyone remembers, images of his own behaviour to Cordelia. Thrust into the night, he meets his own defencelessness in Edgar, and is impelled to pray. Encountering in Dover fields, both Lear and Gloucester confront in each other an extension of their own experience: blindness that sees and madness that is wise. Macbeth revisits the witches on the heath and finds there (without recognizing them) not only the emblems of his death and downfall to come but his speciousness and duplicity. Antony encounters in Enobarbus' defection his own; and possibly, in Pompey, his own later muddled indecision between 'honour' and *Realpolitik*. Othello hears the innocent Cassio set upon in the dark, then goes to re-enact that scene in a more figurative darkness in Desdemona's bedroom. Sometimes, alternatively or additionally, the hero's way will lie through quasi-symbolic settings or situations. The heath in both *Macbeth* and *King Lear* is infinitely suggestive, even if like all good symbols it refuses to dissipate its *Dinglichkeit* in meaning. The same is true of the dark castle platform in Hamlet, and the graveyard; of the cliff at Dover and Gloucester's leap; of the 'monument', where both Antony and Cleopatra die; and of course, as many have pointed out, of the night scenes, the storm, the music, the changes of clothing, the banquets. So much in Shakespeare's tragedies stands on the brink of symbol that for this reason, if no other, the usual terms for describing their construction and mode of action need reinforcement.

After the hero has reached and passed through his own antithesis, there comes a third phase in his development that is extremely difficult to define. It represents a recovery of sorts; in some cases, perhaps even a species of synthesis. The once powerful, now powerless king, will have power again, but of another kind – the kind suggested in his reconciliation with Cordelia and his speech beginning 'Come, let's away to prison'; and he will have sanity again, but in a mode not dreamed of at the beginning of the play. Or, to take Othello's case, it will be given the hero to recapture the faith he lost,[9] to learn that the pearl really was richer than all his tribe, and to execute quite another order of justice than the blinkered justice meted out to Cassio and the blind injustice meted out to Desdemona. Or again, to shift to Antony, the man who has so long been thrown into storms of rage and recrimination by the caprices of his unstable mistress receives the last of them without a murmur of reproach, though it has led directly to his death, and dies in greater unison with her than we have ever seen him live.

I believe that some mark of this nature is visible in all the tragedies. Coriolanus, 'boy' though he is and in some ways remains, makes a triumphant choice (detract from his motives as we may), and he knows what it is likely to cost. Moreover, he refuses the way of escape that lies open if he should return now with Volumnia and Vergilia to Rome. 'I'll not to Rome, I'll back with you', he tells Aufidius, 'and pray you Stand to me in this cause'. The young man who, after this, dies accused of treachery – by Aufidius' treachery, and the suggestibility of the crowd, as slippery in Corioles as Rome – cannot be thought identical in all respects with the young man who joined Menenius in the play's opening scene. He is that young man, but with the notable difference of his triumphant choice behind him; and there is bound to be more than a military association in our minds when the Second Lord of the Volscians, seeking to quell the mob, cries, 'The man is noble, and his fame folds in This orb o' th' earth'; and again too when the First Lord exclaims over his body, 'Let him be regarded As the most noble corse that ever herald Did follow to his urn'. Even the monster Macbeth is so handled by Shakespeare, as has been often enough observed, that he seems to regain something at the close – if nothing more, at least some of that *élan* which made him the all-praised Bellona's bridegroom of the play's second scene; and everything Macbeth says, following Duncan's death, about the emptiness of the achievement, the lack of posterity, the sear, the yellow leaf, deprived of 'that which should accompany old age, As honour, love, obedience, troops of friends', affords evidence that the meaning of his experience has not been lost on him.

To say this, I wish to make it clear, is not to say that the Shakespearean tragic hero undergoes an 'illumination', or, to use the third term of K. Burke's sequence, a Mathema or perception.[10] This is a terminology that seems to me not very useful to the discussion of tragedy as Shakespeare presents it. It is sufficient for my purposes to say simply that the phase in which we are conscious of the hero as approaching his opposite is followed by a final phase in which we are conscious of him as exhibiting one or more aspects of his original, or – since these may not coincide – his better self: as in the case of Antony's final reunion with Cleopatra, and Coriolanus' decision not to sack Rome. Whether we then go on to give this phenomenon a specific spiritual signifi-cance, seeing in it the objective correlative of 'perception' or 'illumination', is a question that depends, obviously, on a great many factors, more of them perhaps situated in our own individual philosophies than in the text, and, so, likely to lead us away from Shakespeare rather than towards him. Clearly if Shakespeare wished us to engage in this activity, he was remiss in the provision of clues. Even in *King Lear*, the one play where some sort of regeneration or new insight in the hero has been universally acknowledged, the man before us in the last scene – who sweeps Kent aside, rakes all who have helped him with grapeshot ('A plague upon you, murderers, traitors all. I might have saved her …'), exults in the revenge he has exacted for Cordelia's death, and dies self-deceived in the thought she still lives – this man is one of the most profoundly human figures ever created in a play; but he is not, certainly, the Platonic idea laid up in heaven, or in critical schemes, of regenerate man.

I have kept to the end, and out of proper order, the most interesting of all the symbolic elements in the hero's second phase. This is his experience of madness. One discovers with some surprise, I think, how many of Shakespeare's heroes are associated with this disease. Only Titus, Hamlet, Lear, and Timon, in various senses, actually go mad; but Iago boasts that he will make Othello mad, and in a way succeeds; Antony, after the second defeat at sea, is said by Cleopatra to be

> more mad,
> Than Telamon for his shield; the boar of Thessaly
> Was never so emboss'd;
>
> (iv.xiii.2)

Caithness in *Macbeth* tells us that some say the king is mad, while 'others, that lesser hate him, Do call it valiant fury'; Romeo, rather oddly, enjoins Paris at Juliet's tomb to

> be gone; live, and hereafter say,
> A madman's mercy bade thee run away.
>
> (v.iii.66)

Even Brutus, by the Antony of *Antony and Cleopatra*, is said to have been 'mad'.

What (if anything), one wonders, may this mean? Doubtless a sort of explanation can be found in Elizabethan psychological lore, which held that the excess of any passion approached madness, and in the general prevalence, through Seneca and other sources, of the adage: *Quos vult perdere Jupiter dementat prius.* Furthermore, madness, when actually exhibited, was dramatically useful, as Kyd had shown. It was arresting in itself, and it allowed the combination in a single figure of tragic hero and buffoon, to whom could be accorded the licence of the allowed fool in speech and action.

Just possibly, however, there was yet more to it than this, if we may judge by Shakespeare's sketches of madness in Hamlet and King Lear. In both these, madness is to some degree a punishment or doom, corresponding to the adage. Lear prays to the heavens that he may not suffer madness, and Hamlet asks Laertes, in his apology before the duel, to overlook his conduct, since 'you must needs have heard, how I am punish'd With a sore distraction'. It is equally obvious, however, that in both instances the madness has a further dimension, as insight, and this is true also of Ophelia. Ophelia, mad, is able to make awards of flowers to the King and Queen which are appropriate to frailties of which she cannot be supposed to have conscious knowledge. For the same reason, I suspect we do not need Dover Wilson's radical displacement of Hamlet's entry in II. ii, so as to enable him to overhear Polonius.[11] It is enough that Hamlet wears, even if it is for the moment self-assumed, the guise of the madman. As such, he can be presumed to have intuitive unformulated awarenesses that reach the surface in free (yet relevant) associations, like those of Polonius with a fishmonger, Ophelia with carrion. Lear likewise is allowed free yet relevant associations. His great speech in Dover fields on the lust of women derives from the designs of Goneril and Regan on Edmund, of which he consciously knows nothing. Moreover, both he and Hamlet can be privileged in madness to say things – Hamlet about the corruption of human nature, and Lear about the corruption of the Jacobean social system (and by extension about all social systems whatever), which Shakespeare could hardly have risked apart from this licence. Doubtless one of the anguishes of being a great artist is that you cannot tell people what they and you and your common institutions are really like – when viewed absolutely – without being dismissed as insane. To communicate at all, you must acknowledge the opposing voice; for there always is an opposing voice, and it is as deeply rooted in your own nature as in your audience's.

Just possibly, therefore, the meaning of tragic madness for Shakespeare approximated the meaning that the legendary figure of Cassandra (whom Shakespeare had in fact put briefly on his stage in the second act of *Troilus and Cressida*) has held for so many artists since his time. Cassandra's madness, like Lear's and Hamlet's – possibly, also, like the madness *verbally* assigned to other Shakespearean tragic heroes – contains both punishment and insight. She is doomed to know, by a consciousness that moves to measures outside our normal space and time; she is doomed never to be believed, because those to whom she speaks can hear only the opposing voice. With the language of the god Apollo sounding in her brain, and the incredulity of her fellow mortals ringing in her ears, she makes an ideal emblem of the predicament of the Shakespearean tragic hero, caught as he is between the absolute and the expedient. And by the same token, of the predicament of the artist – Shakespeare himself, perhaps – who, having been given the power to see the 'truth', can convey it only through poetry – what we commonly call a 'fiction', and dismiss.

In all these matters, let me add in parenthesis, we would do well to extend more generously our inferences about Shakespeare to the Jacobean playwrights as a group. Some of us have been over-long content with a view of Jacobean tragedy as naïve as those formerly entertained of Restoration comedy, eighteenth-century literature, and modern poetry. But a whole generation of writers does not become obsessed by the sexual feuding of cavalier and citizen, or rhetorical 'rules' and social norms, or abrupt images and catapulting rhythms, or outrageous stories of incest, madness, brutality, and lust, because the poetic imagination has suddenly gone 'frivolous', or 'cold', or 'eccentric', or 'corrupt'. Such concerns respond to spiritual needs, however dimly apprehended, and one of the prime needs of Jacobean writers, as the intelligible and on the whole friendly universe of the Middle Ages failed around them, was quite evidently to face up to what men are or may be when stripped to their naked humanity and mortality, and torn loose from accustomed moorings. Flamineo's phrase in *The White Devil* – 'this busy trade of life' – offered as a passing summary of the play's monstrous burden of blood and madness:

> This busy trade of life appears most vain,
> Since rest breeds rest, where all seek pain by pain –

is characteristically understated and ironic, like Iago's 'Pleasure and action make the hours seem short'. The creators of Iago and Flamineo, and all the responsible writers of Jacobean tragedy along with them, knew perfectly well that it was not in fact the 'trade', or habitude, of life to which they held up art's mirror, but life 'on the stretch', nature at its farthest reach of possibility. They were fascinated by violence because they were fascinated by the potencies of the human will: its weaknesses, triumphs, delusions, corruptions, its capacities for destruction and regeneration, its residual dignity when, all else removed, man stood at his being's limit; and because they knew that in violence lay the will's supreme test, for aggressor and sufferer alike.

Whatever the themes of individual plays, therefore, the one pervasive Jacobean theme tends to be the undertaking and working out of acts of will, and especially (in that strongly Calvinistic age) of acts of self-will. This is surely the reason why, in Clifford Leech's happy phrase, these writers know so little of heaven, so much of hell; and why, to one conversant with their work so many products of the century to come seem like fulfilments of ancient prophecy: Milton's Satan and his 'God' – the philosophy embodied in *Leviathan* – even, perhaps, the clash of the Civil Wars and the cleavage in the English spirit reaching from Cavalier and Puritan to Jacobite and Whig and well beyond. At the very beginning of the century, these writers had got hold of the theme that was to exercise it in all departments, political, economic, religious, cultural, till past its close, the problem of anarchic will; and so decisive, so many-sided is their treatment of this problem that even in Milton's massive recapitulation of it in *Paradise Lost* the issue seems sometimes to be losing in vitality what it has gained in clarity, to be fossilizing and becoming formula. The utterances of *his* white devil have more resonance but less complexity and immediacy of feeling than those of Vittoria Corombona, Bosola, Macbeth, or Beatrice Vermandero; and some of them bear a perilous resemblance to the posturings of Restoration heroic tragedy, where the old agonies are heard from still, but now clogged, and put through paces like captive giants in a raree show.

However this may be, I return at the end to the proposition I set out with: there is a lot about the construction of a Shakespearean tragic 'action' that we still do not know. My own attempts to get towards it in this chapter are fumbling and may be preposterous: even to myself they sound a little like Bottom's dream. But the interesting thing about

Bottom's dream, from my point of view, is that, though he found he was an ass all right, the Titania he tried to tell about was real.

Notes

1   The flexibility of the structure is witnessed by the amazing differences between the tragedies, of which it is, however, the lowest common multiple. In my discussion, I shall necessarily take the differences between the tragedies for granted and stress simply the vertebrate characteristics they share.
2   See an important comment on this by H. Levin, in *Kenyon Review* (1950), pp. 273–96.
3   I have touched on this point in *Tragic Themes in Western Literature*, ed. C. Brooks (1953).
4   Another emblematic entrance is the first entrance of the soothsayer in *Julius Caesar*; see 'The Teaching of Drama', *Essays on the Teaching of English*, ed. E. J. Gordon and E. S. Noyes (1960).
5   By H. T. Price, in *Joseph Quincy Adams Memorial Studies*, ed. J. McManaway (1948), pp. 101 ff.
6   See P. J. Aldus, *Shakespeare Quarterly* (1955), pp. 397 ff. Aldus deals suggestively with the opening scene of *Julius Caesar*.
7   I have elaborated this point in an introduction to Fielding's *Joseph Andrews* (1948).
8   These are merely samples; other journeys occur that I have not named here.
9   This point is well made in Helen Gardner's *The Noble Moor* (1956).
10   *A Grammar of Motives* (1945), pp. 38 ff.
11   *What Happens in 'Hamlet'* (1935), pp. 103 ff.

Part IV

The 1950s and 1960s:
Theme, Character, Structure

10 Reflections on the Sentimentalist's *Othello*   152
    Barbara Everett
11 Form and Formality in *Romeo and Juliet*   164
    Harry Levin
12 *King Lear* or *Endgame*   174
    Jan Kott
13 The Cheapening of the Stage   191
    Anne Righter [Barton]
14 How Not to Murder Caesar   209
    Sigurd Burckhardt

One of the most pernicious myths about twentieth-century Shakespeare scholarship is that New Criticism was the only approach available between the fading of old historicism in the 1940s and the advent of theory in the 1970s. Such a story is especially damaging because it misrepresents or ignores the contributions of some exceedingly acute readers and unjustly homogenizes the work of an entire generation. The range of essays included here exposes the inadequacy of the term "New Criticism" to describe the multiplicity of work produced in England and North America in the 1950s and 1960s. I have already indicated that genre or myth criticism was an important alternative approach, and other valuable modes of address are represented below. In a book larger than this one, more than one of these kinds would warrant its own section.

Metatheatrical criticism began to make its presence felt during the 1960s and enriched our understanding of Shakespeare's plays, and of Tudor and Stuart drama generally, by charting the growth of authorial self-consciousness about the profession of playwright. The first fully elaborated discussion of the problem was probably Anne Righter's *Shakespeare and the Idea of the Play*, a book with a telling critical parentage. Righter studied with Arthur Colby Sprague at Bryn Mawr College; she then wrote her doctoral dissertation at Cambridge with Muriel Bradbrook. Both Sprague and Bradbrook were distinguished scholars who kept their critical eyes fixed on the plays as texts written for the stage: he in *Shakespeare and the Actors* (1944), a book that should be considered an early example of performance criticism, and she in *Themes and Conventions of Elizabethan Tragedy* (1935), a learned study of dramatic structure in theatrical context. It is notable that, as an undergraduate student, Righter published in *Shakespeare Quarterly* a paper on *Love's Labour's Lost* that seems to forecast the metatheatrical argument of *Shakespeare and the Idea of the Play*.

The book examines historically and thematically the metaphor of the world as a stage: its first half identifies the origins of the idea in the early English mysteries and moralities as well as in the Greco-Roman tradition, and its second half surveys how Shakespeare's treatment of the metaphor changes from the beginning of his career to the end. Other scholars had considered these ideas in the early modern theater generally, notably Madeleine Doran in her distinguished and learned *Endeavors of Art: A Study of Form in the Jacobean Drama* (1954). What is especially valuable about Righter's study, as the chapter reprinted here amply indicates, is her use of such metaphoric shifts to chart Shakespeare's unstable attitude towards his own occupation. Her contribution was generative: a number of critics, the most notable being James Calderwood, followed her lead in developing these insights about the effects of theatrical self-consciousness and studying individual texts in this context.

Another line of inquiry that emerged during this period is found in the work of the Polish critic Jan Kott; the breadth of his approach removes it almost as far as possible from New Criticism. *Shakespeare, Our Contemporary*, published in 1964, considers the plays through the lens of the European intellectual tradition, with special attention to overarching philosophical themes. Marx, Brecht, Sartre, Beckett, and other European thinkers normally held at a distance from Renaissance literature served to shape Kott's critical outlook. The other crucial determinant was his vexed relationship with communism, which he had embraced and later rejected. These influences combined to create a unique perspective. And if his work did not have a potent, enduring effect on academic criticism, *Shakespeare, Our Contemporary* managed to reach a wide general audience. One early reader – of the French text, before it was translated into English – was the great English theater director Peter Brook. In preparing his 1962 production of *King Lear* at the Royal Shakespeare Company, with Paul Scofield in the title part, Brook was heavily influenced by Kott's reading of the tragedy in light of the contemporary European Theatre of the Absurd. Part of that chapter, "*King Lear* or *Endgame*," is reproduced here.

Other major contributors to Shakespeare study in the 1950s and 1960s are perhaps not so easy to categorize or describe as Righter or Kott, and many acute critics produced books and essays that do not fit the New Critical label. Some of these, such as A. P. Rossiter, whose lecture on ambiguity in the histories appears in Part III, openly rejected the narrowness of New Critical practice. Others, such as Barbara Everett and Helen Gardner, undertook to correct what they considered the excesses and misprisions of F. R. Leavis and his followers. Everett dismantles Leavis's reading of

Othello, and her argumentative style displays a fascinating combination of hard logic and humane tone. It is also illustrative of a disciplined approach to character. Of American critics who stood at a far distance from the prevailing style of the times, few were as learned and wide-ranging as Harry Levin. The author of books on Marlowe, Joyce, French realist fiction of the nineteenth century, and the idea of the golden age in the Renaissance – and this is not to mention *The Question of Hamlet* – Levin is represented here by an essay from *Shakespeare and the Revolution of the Times*, a collection of essays written mainly in the 1950s and 1960s. Finally, there was the occasional quirky genius such as Sigurd Burckhardt, who died between the completion and publication of *Shakespearean Meanings*. Burckhardt was a brilliant close reader and yet was never considered a New Critic. Like more of his contemporaries than we are now inclined to think, he is difficult to classify.

10

Reflections on the
Sentimentalist's *Othello*

Barbara Everett

A characteristic of the most perceptive and interesting criticism is to throw light on a subject even by those statements which may call forth most disagreement. F. R. Leavis's work offers many such examples: marked as it is by acute sensitivity joined to moral intransigence, it frequently offers judgments that arouse an almost equal degree of interest, appreciation, and disagreement. His essay *Diabolic Intellect and the Noble Hero: or the Sentimentalist's Othello*[1] is a typical instance.

The nature of Dr. Leavis's attack on Bradley is by now well known. The Noble Moor of Bradley – and of Coleridge, and of Swinburne, and of "common acceptance" – presents "as extraordinary a history of triumphant sentimental perversity as literary history can show." The traditional Othello, passive, poetical, pathetic and above all heroic, existing only to be worked on by a great and diabolic Iago, is not Shakespeare's. The play reveals rather the motivated and coherent ruin of a man by himself. "The essential traitor is within the gates ... (Iago) represents something that is in Othello. Othello the husband of Desdemona ... the mind that undoes him is not Iago's but his own." Although the elaboration of Dr. Leavis's case creates new points, the heart of his argument is here; and it is these sentences that simultaneously arouse a degree of instinctive disagreement together with a sense that the difficulties of the play have been clearly and interestingly brought to light.

For these three sentences posit two quite different – possibly even antithetical – approaches to the notion of what Shakespearean characterization is. In "Iago represents something that is in Othello," one has what might be called the modern approach to characterization. The sentence can only command assent if it can also be said that Desdemona, and Cassio, and even the fool Roderigo, and Emilia, and Brabantio, and the Clown, and the whole Senate, "represent something that is in Othello": for there is nothing in the characterization of Iago that marks him off from all the others. All the characters, that is, are representative parts of a unified phase of experience; it is their interaction that arouses the memory, or knowledge, of some area of life for the first time clarified and made new, and Othello himself is one part – though a great one – of the design. But the first and third sentences "the essential traitor ..." and "the mind that undoes him is his own" – posit an altogether different approach, which suggests some genuine independence of each character, so that one can talk of "Othello" and "Iago" and not mean simply "different areas of the same experience".

It is possible that the apparent confusion here reflects some genuine confusion – or perhaps, rather, fusion – in the play itself: and thus throws light on to it. For all the "noble, 'classical' clarity" – in Dr. Leavis's phrase – that the play appears to have, it also presents to the mind a curiously shifting quality, both dramatically and morally: for these two issues, dramatic and moral, become one and the same. These two apparently antithetical approaches to character are present in the play itself, to a further degree than in any of the other great tragedies. On the one hand, the play seems to present a world in which there are no clear and absolute outlines to a character. Othello moves from the extraordinary poise and mastery of "Keep up your bright swords ..." to a state of grovelling and gibbering ferocity. Desdemona moves between a state in which

> the essential vesture of creation
> Does tire the ingener ...

– pure spirit in pure flesh – and a state that shows the whirlwind-like emotions of a young girl, frightened, lying, promising eternal friendship, and gaily rating her new husband. Iago the dishonest and detached word-spinner becomes a stabber in the dark and finally a total silence: "From this time forth I never will speak word." Cassio the loyal and intelligent soldier reveals himself as a weak drunkard. Roderigo, the conventional gull, is the first character to turn on Iago with a sharp and suspicious anger. Emilia, the touchstone of shrewd coarseness, "dies in music". It is not, however, this mere change in character that gives the play its shifting quality. It is rather the sense that characters may react upon one another so that something almost suggesting a change of identity takes place; as when Iago, in the famous "Not poppy, nor mandragora" speech, and Othello in his echo of Iago's gross wit – "We say lie on her, when they belie her! Lie with her! That's fulsome!" – seem to be speaking each other's characteristic dialect. Again, the descriptions of Desdemona as "our captain's captain" or a "fair warrior", or her own "My downright violence and storm of fortunes May trumpet to the world" suggest something more than a mere use of military metaphor; Desdemona has entered Othello's world: "My heart's subdued Even to the very quality of my lord." This sense of an interpenetrating world is strengthened by the constant 'linking' of the characters: Roderigo to Iago ("you ... who has had my purse As if the strings were thine"), Iago to Othello ("In following him I follow but myself"), Brabantio to Desdemona ("Your heart is burst; you have lost half your soul"), Iago to Roderigo ("I confess me knit to thy deserving with cables of perdurable toughness"), Desdemona to Othello ("Tying her duty, beauty, wit and fortunes In an extravagent and wheeling stranger"), Othello to Desdemona ("His soul is so enfetter'd to her love"), Cassio to Emilia ("I am much bound to you"), Iago to Othello ("I am bound to every act of duty ... as I am bound, Receive it from me"), Othello to Iago ("I am bound to thee for ever"), Iago to Othello ("I am your own for ever"). A world is presented in which not only "man and wife is one flesh", but all are forced by the "elements that clip us round about" into a perpetual sense of, or straining toward, community. The "net That shall enmesh them all" is made at the instant the play begins, and is a condition of common need and common imperfection, so that a character can only define itself through other characters.

Yet, when all this is said, it remains obvious to common sense that there is an entity that the reader – or, more particularly, the audience – does and must refer to as "Othello" or "Desdemona" or "Iago" or "Cassio", and that neither drama nor life could proceed without a belief in this entity. The proposition that character can define itself genuinely by a form of common consent is clarified – and dismissed, however – by the occurrence of "*Honest* Iago". The paradox of characterization, as it appears in the play, reminds one of Dr. Johnson's pronouncement on the paradox of free-will: that all theory was against it, and all experience for it. For, the dramatic situation is immediately related to the moral one in the play; to say that "the essential traitor is within the gates" proves to be a moral, as well as a dramatic simplification. In any world where "Men are not gods" – "Nor women neither," – moral imperfection will be a common condition, proscribing any talk of one "essential traitor"; and more especially so in a world where evil is seen as a "poison". And yet some distinction in moral responsibility must be made, since Othello, the "extravagent and wheeling stranger", Iago, the "wayward husband", and Desdemona, as "fruitful As the *free* elements", are all represented as having some freedom of being and of choice – and hence of responsibility. A comparison with *Hamlet* shows a similar case of distinction in degree of responsibility. The source of the evil in the action of *Hamlet* is the deliberate murder of the elder Hamlet by Claudius. This much is quite clear. It is equally clear that Hamlet is doubly related by blood to his uncle, and so "involved in mankind", and so implicated in murder: the whole action is like a mirror-image of the first murder, so that an originally innocent Hamlet gradually approaches the politic cruelty and hardness of Claudius, and finally joins him in death. But what distinguishes them is the difference of consciousness, of motive, and of responsibility. Hamlet, who is the least *responsible* for the first evil action, is endowed with enough greatness – however coarsened and toughened – to take on the *responsibility* of a corrupt world. *Othello* does not offer an identical case, but there are similarities. The full force of the evil action comes to Othello at the end of the play: any attempt to diminish the criminal murder of Desdemona would be ludicrous. He is – or rather becomes – as much the figure-head of a corrupt world as is Hamlet in his. But this is not at all the same as calling him the "essential" source of an evil action. In so far as both Othello and Iago are free agents, the first and essential destructive action, the will to pervert and corrupt, comes from Iago. A man who walks a tight-rope (and Othello, with his poised control of a world of violent energies, "bright swords", suggests such an image) may be doing a dangerous and foolish thing; the man who cuts the rope is doing an evil one.

The moral world of the play is complicated by the curious degree of close relationship between the characters, but amongst the complication certain moral distinctions can be made. Desdemona's magnificent and absurd last lie –

> Who hath done this deed?
> Nobody; I myself …

illuminates this. In a world where all are, to some extent, responsible, "None does offend, none – I say none". And in a world where Desdemona has identified herself totally with her husband, his responsibility is her own. But the very nature of the murder itself simplifies the whole dilemma of "*se offendendo* ... if the man go to this water ..., if the water come to him." Violent death by smothering can scarcely be self-imposed: it argues a murderer. Violent actions, taking place in time, must suggest a primary agent, and the primary agent of the chief evil action of the play is made clear in the first scene: "I follow him to serve my turn upon him".

To see Iago, and not Othello, as the "essential" traitor, is not to deny Dr. Leavis's contention that "the tragedy may fairly be said to be Othello's character in action". But what *Othello* offers is not the almost clinical study in illusion and depravity – a sort of poetic *Kreuzer Sonata* – that Dr. Leavis at moments suggests. The tragedy becomes, in his hands, an ironic portrait of the "heroic" attitude: of the "noble egotism" of a simple "stoic-captain", that moves necessarily and of its own accord from a false romantic idealism into "ferocious stupidity, an insane and self-deceiving passion". To attribute the entire world of the play to Othello's "character" is to out-Bradley Bradley: some sort of distinction must be made between what appears to be inherent or essential to Othello's character (again, if we can use the word "essential" safely, of a play where the outlines of character shift and change and are interdependent), and what affects it from without.

Two things chiefly characterize Othello:[2] first, a sense of violent energies and passions inherent in his nature – he is a Moor, and a soldier; and secondly, a single-mindedness of intention and desire. That these things are heroic, above all normal stature and performance, is clear: that they are necessarily evil is not at all clear. They are, rather, potentially good or evil; and, at the beginning of the play, directed toward public service and private love, they are in effect good.

> She lov'd me for the dangers I had pass'd;
> And I lov'd her that she did pity them ...

indicates a state of possibly dangerous poise;

> My parts, my title and my perfect soul ...

indicates a state of certainly dangerous pride. But one would be foolish to regard the later state of Othello as absolutely and automatically conditioning the earlier. For a man to become ill does not invalidate a sense of what relative health is: that Othello's passion and self-sufficiency should be changed to destructive violence and brutal arrogance is not, *per se*, an invalidation of passion and self-sufficiency. The most interesting thing is not the destruction of Othello, but the degree to which he – and others – manage to salvage so much from the wreck. For Iago, the narrow, passionless onlooker, can make the minute change in Othello's poise that swings creative passion to destructive passion, so that an act of love becomes an act of murder; but he cannot change this essential quality within Othello for more than a moment – a few lines, a few images. Iago, to whom Dr. Leavis gives a "brutal realism" of speech, in fact has almost no comprehension – in the literal sense of that word as well – of the characters whom he tries to control. He tries to make them the puppets of his will and intelligence, and they prove in fact to make him their puppet. Iago himself is "swallowed up" by the enormous and heroic flood of feeling that he releases in Othello:

> Like to the Pontic sea
> Whose icy current and compulsive course
> Ne'er feels retiring ebb, but keeps due on
> To the Propontic and the Hellespont ...
>   I greet thy love
> Not with vain thanks, but with acceptance bounteous.

The degree to which Othello can, as it were, convert the disease taken from Iago into something enormously larger, purer, and more terrifying in its natural strength, is conveyed here; and something of the correspondent loss of mastery in Iago is suggested by his possibly mocking, but possibly also bewildered and unnerved lines:

> Is my lord angry? ... ...
> Can he be angry? I have seen the cannon
> When it hath blown his ranks into the air,
> And, like the devil, from his very arm
> Puff'd his own brother – and is he angry?

If this primal energy can be "married", as it were, to a desire to destroy and corrupt, implanted by Iago, it can also, by its own strength, destroy that very desire. The last of Othello's hatred is destroyed by the "steep-down gulfs of liquid fire" that leave him free again, though ruined by despair and left only with the clearer memory of his earlier self: "That's he that was Othello – here I am."

That this heroic fury, that may be turned to evil ends, is not an evil in itself, is indicated by its occurrence in other characters whom Iago misjudges. The irrepressible charity and free goodness of Desdemona's last words ("as fruitful As the free elements", as Iago ironically prophesies) invokes the same quality in the worldly Emilia:

> I will speak as liberal as the north.
> Let heaven and men and devils, let them all,
> All, all, cry shame against me, yet I'll speak.

This is a quality of feeling that is as infectious as Iago's will to corrupt, and finally stronger than it; its very dominance in Othello's nature tends to vindicate the word "heroic" from some of the condemnatory stress that Dr. Leavis places upon it.

It is, however, Othello's "egotism" and self-centredness that receives the full weight of Dr. Leavis's attack. The words "noble", "heroic", "self-centred", and "self-dramatizing" echo continuously through his critique, and come to be almost synonyms; one might perhaps say that he sees the play as an intentional act of proving their synonymity. This is the most difficult part of Dr. Leavis's critique to answer. A hatred and fear of the "heroic", the large, the universal, the self-sufficient, the grandiose, the rhetorical, is a fundamental part of our own age, and it is easy both to understand and to share it: social and historical reasons alone explain a preference for the "concrete", the "witty", the "ironic" and "precise", for a world where greatness is defined – if at all – as moral intensity "grounded in reality". One can appreciate the stress, therefore that Dr. Leavis lays, again and again, on Othello's "self-pride, self idealization … self-deception … self-dramatization without self-knowledge … self-approving self-dramatization". "It may be love, but it can be only in an oddly qualified sense love of her; it must be much more a matter of self-centred and self-regarding satisfactions – pride, sensual posses-siveness, appetite, love of loving – than he suspects." Othello lacks "any real interest in Desdemona as a person", showing only "a curious and characteristic effect of self-preoccupation, of preoccupation with his emotions rather than with Desdemona in her own right". "That romantic idealizing love could be as dubiously grounded in reality as this is an essential condition of the tragedy." "It is, at best, the impressive manifestation of a noble egotism. But, in the new marital situation, this egotism isn't going to be the less dangerous for its nobility. This self-centredness doesn't mean self-knowledge; that is a virtue which Othello, as soldier of fortune, hasn't had much need of."

It is possible to divide this critique of Othello's character into two closely-connected issues: one concerned with all that is involved in the word "self-dramatization", and the other concerned with the "heroic". The idea of "self-dramatization", and its moral bearings, so to speak, is not too difficult to handle in matters of daily life. But when one begins to use it of a stage-character – particularly one created in an age when shy self-effacement was not necessarily the most popular and useful of virtues – one is faced by striking difficulty. That, from at least the time of *Hamlet* onwards, Shakespeare appears to have thought seriously and continuously about the relation between "acting" and "playing", and "truth" or "reality", the plays themselves reveal; and it is possible to find suggestions, both in the plays and the Sonnets, that dramatic and poetic "lies" and exhibitionalism affected him at times – as is wholly natural – with boredom, irritation, and disgust:

> Alas, 'tis true I have gone here and there
> And made myself a motley to the view,
> Gor'd mine own thoughts, sold cheap what is most dear,
> Made old offences of affections new.
> Most true it is that I have look'd on truth
> Askance and strangely …

But this very consciousness is created and conditioned by the life – that of creative art – and the form – that of dramatic representation – that Shakespeare has chosen as his means of existence. Any concept of "truth" or "reality" will not only have to be translated through, but will be created by, this very means of limitation. Any hero, therefore – whether of the plays or the Sonnets – who is endowed with the newly-conceived greatness of self-consciousness and self-realization, will be liable or in fact bound to "dramatize" himself, to define himself to himself and to the audience as a series of dramatic "attitudes". "O, what a rogue and peasant slave am I", "I am a very foolish fond old man", "They have tied me to a stake; I cannot fly, But bear-like I must fight the course", "What wonders I have done, all Germany can witness, yea all the world … what shall become of Faustus, being in hell for ever?", "I am Duchess of Malfi still", "I am that of your blood was taken from you For your better health …" – all these are declarations of dramatic attitudes in a self-conscious mode. They are, in fact, acts of Othello-like self-dramatization; yet one could not get very far by describing each of the plays from which the lines are taken as studies in "noble egotism" – though they may be that incidentally. Nor can one press the idea of necessary "self-knowledge" too far. It is possible that even in life itself a man can never finally "know himself"; and that often he may go some way toward doing so by choosing, or being forced, to take on various "parts" which may not conform at all closely to his first idea of himself – the "parts" of husband, or father, or soldier, or citizen, or actor, or playwright. This Stoic idea of the world as a stage is found repeatedly through Elizabethan literature: Shakespeare works it hard – and fruitfully – through the last plays. It is unlikely that any speech in Shakespeare revealing character will show real "self-knowledge"; it is more likely that the "given attitude" helps to define what we think of, with a certain imprecision, as the character in entirety. It is hardly true that, for instance, the entity that we think of as Hamlet or Lear can be at all completely described as "A rogue and peasant slave" or "A foolish fond old man": the very ability to make these comments suggests an entity outside the comment, and so, different from it, and so, slightly falsifying the given attitude – which becomes "self-dramatization without self-knowledge". The entity that one thinks of as a Shakespearean hero is built up and defined by the kind of attitudes chosen, and the kind of consciousness likely to choose or create these attitudes, and the kind of situation and dramatic plot that force this consciousness into being; and, lastly and importantly, the area in the mind of the reader or audience that responds to and fulfils given indications of character. Thus the attempt to use words like "self-dramatization" and "self-knowledge", of dramatic characters, involves great difficulties; especially as the attempt to relate a given dramatic attitude to "reality" is complicated by the fact that dramatic "reality" is not a simple given factor, but only evolves gradually in the course of the play. One wonders, for instance, whether Dr. Leavis can legitimately describe Iago's mode of speech as "deflating, unbeglamouring, brutally *realistic*". Within the play, Iago misjudges the characters of Othello, Desdemona, Emilia, and Roderigo; he even misjudges his own. Othello, before he is corrupted by Iago, posits a certain attitude of belief: that the Desdemona of his imagination will be loyal above all reason and all sense. "My life upon her faith!" Iago adopts a different attitude: "She must change for youth: when she is sated with his body, she will find the error of her choice …" Desdemona, being human, does "change": she shows fear, sadness, gaiety, pity, kindness, courage, resentment; but in the one issue that is central to the play, that of her "faith", she is unchangingly "honest, chaste, and true". Othello is the "realist" here, not Iago.

It is obvious that the one thing most difficult for modern criticism to do is – (to use a phrase from one of Richard Wilbur's poems) – to "forgive the hero". Othello certainly does not make it easy: he arouses a degree of anger, impatience and dislike unparalleled in any other of Shakespeare's heroes. But it is one thing to welcome Emilia's "O gull! O dolt! As ignorant as dirt!" at the moment at which it occurs, and another to make it Shakespeare's final comment on Othello. It is, perhaps, strange to find Othello so much condemned for bringing this "noble egotism" into "the new marital situation", when so great and so fashionable a poet as Donne does something very similar, without noticeably disturbing any critic – except perhaps Johnson. For a man to be "preoccupied with his own emotions rather than with Desdemona in her own right" is merely the mark of the self-conscious mind in love. The stress on "egotism" in a "new marital situation" also creates too great a split between these worlds: that of war, and that of domesticity. The fact that Othello is a Moor and a soldier merely helps to create his character as an idealised apotheosis of the male animal, an "extravagent and wheeling stranger", marked by pride, solitude and self-sufficiency:

> But that I love the gentle Desdemona,
> I would not my unhoused free condition
> Put into circumscription and confine
> For the seas' worth.

Desdemona chooses him, naturally enough, as the antithesis of her own small, social, domestic and essentially feminine world: the description of the wooing is vital here. Othello offers her the freedom, individuality and width of horizon that she needs and desires. If one is going to lay too much stress on the tragic difference between the "soldier" and the "lover" or "husband" – which Dr. Leavis makes in some ways the subject of the play – one might perhaps wonder whether Hamlet, Lear or Macbeth made or might have made better husbands or family men. Any sort of heroic individualism separates itself from, and helps to destroy, the world of which it is a part; it also gives that world meaning and standards. Othello's idealism continues through the play, becoming more horrifying as it becomes more attached to Iago's principles and practice. After the trance, which shows him at his lowest, Othello fights desperately to give Iago's corrupt world some meaning, honour and purity: the effect of the combination is more dreadful than is either world singly, but it is perhaps something other than "ferocious stupidity, an insane and self-deceiving passion", as Dr. Leavis puts it. To set down "It is the cause ..." and "Soft you; a word or two ..." as "self-deception" and "sentimentalising" is to simplify the issue harmfully. If one compares the murder scene with Iago's stabbing of his wife, or with the murder in Cinthio's story, it is obvious that the scene of Desdemona's murder differs by more than the mere psychological complexity with which the murderer is presented. Othello is – to use a phrase of Eliot's from another context – "man enough to be damned". "My life upon her faith!" is more than a characteristic comment from Dr. Leavis's "stoic-captain", "stern soldier", and "man of action"; it is a total asseveration such as few normal people have the "character" – or, if one wants, the self-deceiving stupidity – to make. Othello not only makes it, but holds to it: since, when Desdemona is proved "faithful", Othello proves faithful in his turn, and dies with her. It is this individual heroic vision that helps to "create" Desdemona as a "character", even though, tragically enough, it also destroys her: Desdemona's own words and actions create the individual instance of loyalty, courage and charity, but Othello's create out of Desdemona something more than the individual instance:

> Had she been true,
> If heaven would make me such another world
> Of one entire and perfect chrysolite
> I'ld not have sold her for it ...
>   ... a pearl
> Richer than all his tribe ...

The "ill-starred wench, Pale as thy smock" is also a "heavenly sight". Here again Othello cannot see Desdemona "as a person", "in her own right"; but what "right", one wonders, is in question? The individual Elizabethan Desdemonas – presumably there were some – smothered by their husbands, have left no record; Shakespeare's "idealised" creation survives.

However much, then, one disagrees with some of Dr. Leavis's judgments on *Othello*, his argument retains a high degree of interest, in that he moves straight toward certain issues which are important to the play. The play suggests, again and again, that there is a human need to use the word "essential"; and yet that the human condition is one of such change and corruption and interdependence that the word may be difficult, dangerous, and destructive. Dr. Leavis, studying the change in Othello's character, suggests that a man who can be corrupted is "essentially" corrupt. The Shakespearean conclusion is perhaps more tentative and more complete. The physical state, the "frailty of the flesh" that makes a human being change, and "turn, and turn, and yet go on, And turn again," gives him also the tragic capacity to "turn" to good – tragic, in that it is the intensification of physical weakness, the act of dying itself, that may most "turn" him to good, but the last "change" comes too late. The nature of "change" in *Othello*, complicated as it is, may perhaps be simplified by part of the debate between Mutability and Nature, in the unfinished last book of the *Faerie Queene*. Mutability offers a clear case for the right of rule:

> The things
> Which we see not how they are mov'd and swayd,
> Ye may attribute to your selves as Kings,
> And say they by your secret powre are made:
> But what we see not, who shall us perswade?
> … what if I can prove, that even yee
> Your selves are likewise chang'd, and subject unto mee?
> Now *Mars* that valiant man is changed most:
> For, he some times so far runs out of square,
> That he his way doth seem quite to have lost …

Mutability presents a world of chaos, in which:

> Onely the starrie skie doth still remaine …
> And even it self is mov'd …

But Nature answers with a peculiarly Elizabethan, even a peculiarly Shakespearean idea: that change, and constancy of being, are not antithetical, but rather interdependent:

> I well consider all that ye have sayd,
> And find that all things stedfastnes doe hatc
> And changed be: yet being rightly wayd
> They are not changed from their first estate;
> But by their change their being doe dilate:
> And turning to themselves at length againe,
> Do work their own perfection so by fate …[3]

Character, in Shakespeare, is what it becomes, but the becoming covers the whole play. The process is one of simultaneous "perfection" and destruction, since the end is completeness or "ripeness": "No perfection is durable. Encrease hath a time, and decay likewise, but all perfit ripeness remaineth but a moment … For what naturallie can go no hier must naturallie yeld and stoupe againe."[4] The last moments of all the important characters except Iago reveal this "dilation of being". Where there is no intense physical life, with all its corruptions, there can be no dilation. The first clear condemnation of Iago's character comes, surprisingly enough, from the conventional gull, Roderigo, as he dies: "O inhuman dog!" The coarse and shrewd Emilia is given a new quality of perception –

> Thou has not half that power to do me harm
> As I have to be hurt …

and dies "speaking as I think". Desdemona dies "like a liar", but her lie is the most perfect action, in intention and in effect, in the play. Othello dies – as he lived – with violence, but with the same will towards perfection of being: "Killing myself, to die upon a kiss". Only Iago's intelligent fluency is diminished to a living silence: "From this time forth I never will speak word".

The end of *Othello* certainly arouses hatred of the "ferocious stupidity" of the murderer, and an intense sense of the tragedy of a condition where "romantic idealism" destroys the "reality" it is "grounded in"; but it also arouses a realization of the quality of a thing whose destruction can give such distress. For, if Othello has something in him that is "represented by Iago", he has also something "represented by" Desdemona; and the "power to do me harm" is less than the power "to be hurt". Othello's "sentimental" last speech, with its "self-dramatization as un-self-comprehending as before", makes this plain.

> Speak … of one whose hand
> Like the base Indian, threw a pearl away
> Richer than all his tribe; of one whose subdu'd eyes,
> Albeit unused to the melting mood,
> Drop tears as fast as the Arabian trees
> Their med'cinable gum.

Othello is mourning for himself – but himself as representative of a whole destroyed world: he is "heroic" in the sense in which Donne is heroic, in

> But I am by her death, (which word wrongs her)
> Of the first nothing, the Elixer grown …

The impersonalized, lyrical and rhetorical images – that Dr. Leavis seems to object to – take the situation beyond Othello to a world at once barbaric and Christian, universal in its range: the ignorant and yet innocent Indian, and the "pearl of great price"; the Arabian myrrh-producing trees, sheltering, perhaps, the phoenix. If it is arrogant in Othello to take on a more than human loss, it is something other than arrogance that makes him punish himself with the less than human death of a "dog":

Barbara Everett

> I took by th' throat the circumcised dog
> And smote him – thus.

The precision and balance that Othello strives toward – "Nothing extenuate, Nor set down aught in malice" – is repeated in the balance of these last lines: a great and universalised lament, and a mean and localised death. The first balance of "Keep up your bright swords, for the dew will rust them …" is repeated with a difference: there is now all the reason in the world for Othello to lose his "balance". That he does not, is counted against him by Dr. Leavis, who writes brilliantly of this "*coup de théâtre*", as he calls it: "That he should die acting his ideal part is all in the part: the part is manifested here in its rightness and solidity, and the actor as inseparably the man of action …" That there is distaste amounting to condemnation underlying this comment is apparent, though not provable – except possibly in the final summary of the play as "a marvellously sure and adroit piece of workmanship … with all its brilliance and poignancy, it comes below Shakespeare's supreme – his very greatest – works". There is no reason why one should want – or try – to alter this verdict: it may very well be true, and in any case its truth can be neither proved nor disproved. But, besides all its other interest, the essay offers here one last point that deserves some reflection. That the words "action" and "acting" can be used now to carry so implicit a condemnation, also contains something of "the pity of it"; but it postulates a tragedy that is not altogether the tragedy of *Othello*.

Notes

1 *The Common Pursuit* (Chatto and Windus, 1952).
2 My view of Othello's character is obviously very similar to that put forward by Miss Helen Gardner in her article *The Noble Moor* (British Academy Lecture, 1956) and I am glad to acknowledge here that I owe some insights to this very interesting piece of criticism. Miss Gardner's essay concentrated on the play itself, whereas I am more concerned to discuss the kinds of approach suitable in criticising it.
3 The principal source for the philosophy of constancy in change appears to be the last book of Ovid's *Metamorphoses*, though the Pythagorean idea of the soul is obviously not in place here:

> … nascique vocatur
> incipere esse aliud, quam quod fuit ante, morique
> desinere illud idem. cum sint huc forsitan illa,
> haec translata illuc, summa tamen omnia constant.
> (Ovid, *Metamorphoses*: Bk. 15, 255–258.)

It is interesting that later in the same book there occurs a reference to the Phoenix as the one entirely constant thing:

> Haec tamen ex aliis generis primordia ducunt,
> una est, quae reparet seque ipsa reseminet, ales:
> Assyrii phoenica vocant; non fruge neque herbis,
> sed turis lacrimis et suco vivit amomi.
> (391–394.)

The metaphor of trees "weeping" gum is found elsewhere, but it is possible that "lacrimis" formed a link here in Shakespeare's mind, and produced the buried image of the phoenix. (Miss Gardner points out the possibility that Othello is thinking of the phoenix, in:

> Drop tears as fast as the Arabian trees
> Their med'cinable gum ...)

For evidence that Shakespeare knew Ovid in the original as well as in translation see T. W. Baldwin's *Shakespeare's Small Latine and Lesse Greeke*, esp. Chap. XLII.

4   Ascham: *The Scholemaster.*

11

Form and Formality in
Romeo and Juliet

Harry Levin

"Fain would I dwell on form –", says Juliet from her window to Romeo in the moonlit orchard below,

> Fain would I dwell on form – fain, fain deny
> What I have spoke; but farewell compliment!
> (ii.ii.88–9)[1]

Romeo has just violated convention, dramatic and otherwise, by overhearing what Juliet intended to be a soliloquy. Her cousin, Tybalt, had already committed a similar breach of social and theatrical decorum in the scene at the Capulets' feast, where he had also recognized Romeo's voice to be that of a Montague. There, when the lovers first met, the dialogue of their meeting had been formalized into a sonnet, acting out the conceit of his lips as pilgrims, her hand as a shrine, and his kiss as a culminating piece of stage-business, with an encore after an additional quatrain: "You kiss by th' book" (i.v.112). Neither had known the identity of the other; and each, upon finding it out, responded with an ominous exclamation coupling love and death (120, 140). The formality of their encounter was framed by the ceremonious character of the scene, with its dancers, its masquers, and – except for Tybalt's stifled outburst – its air of old-fashioned hospitality. "We'll measure them a measure", Benvolio had proposed; but Romeo, unwilling to join the dance, had resolved to be an onlooker and carry a torch (i.iv.10). That torch may have burned symbolically, but not for Juliet; indeed, as we are inclined to forget with Romeo, he attended the feast in order to see the dazzling but soon eclipsed Rosaline. Rosaline's prior effect upon him is all that we ever learn about her; yet it has been enough to make Romeo, when he was presented to us, a virtual stereotype of the romantic lover. As such, he has protested a good deal too much in his preliminary speeches, utilizing the conventional phrases and standardized images of

Elizabethan eroticism, bandying generalizations, paradoxes, and sestets with Benvolio, and taking a quasi-religious vow which his introduction to Juliet would ironically break (I.ii.92–7). Afterward this role has been reduced to absurdity by the humorous man, Mercutio, in a mock-conjuration evoking Venus and Cupid and the inevitable jingle of "love" and "dove" (II.i.10). The scene that follows is actually a continuation, marked in neither the Folios nor the Quartos, and linked with what has gone before by a somewhat eroded rhyme.

> 'Tis in vain
> To seek him here that means not to be found,

Benvolio concludes in the absence of Romeo (41, 42). Whereupon the latter, on the other side of the wall, chimes in:

> He jests at scars that never felt a wound.
> (II.ii.1)

Thus we stay behind, with Romeo, when the masquers depart. Juliet, appearing at the window, does not hear his descriptive invocation. Her first utterance is the very sigh that Mercutio burlesqued in the foregoing scene: "Ay, me!" (II.ii.25). Then, believing herself to be alone and masked by the darkness, she speaks her mind in sincerity and simplicity. She calls into question not merely Romeo's name but – by implication – all names, forms, conventions, sophistications, and arbitrary dictates of society, as opposed to the appeal of instinct directly conveyed in the odor of a rose. When Romeo takes her at her word and answers, she is startled and even alarmed for his sake; but she does not revert to courtly language.

> I would not for the world they saw thee here,

she tells him, and her monosyllabic directness inspires the matching cadence of his response:

> And but thou love me, let them find me here.
> (77, 79)

She pays incidental tribute to the proprieties with her passing suggestion that, had he not overheard her, she would have dwelt on form, pretended to be more distant, and played the not impossible part of the captious beloved. But farewell compliment! Romeo's love for Juliet will have an immediacy which cuts straight through the verbal embellishment that has obscured his infatuation with Rosaline. That shadowy creature, having served her Dulcinea-like purpose, may well be forgotten. On the other hand, Romeo has his more tangible foil in the person of the County Paris, who is cast in that ungrateful part which the Italians call *terzo incòmodo*, the inconvenient third party, the unwelcome member of an amorous triangle. As the official suitor of Juliet, his speeches are always formal, and often sound stilted or priggish by contrast with Romeo's. Long after Romeo has abandoned his sonneteering, Paris will pronounce a sestet at Juliet's tomb (v.iii.11–16). During their only colloquy, which occurs in Friar Laurence's cell, Juliet takes on the sophisticated tone of Paris, denying his claims and disclaiming his compliments in brisk stichomythy. As soon as he leaves, she turns to the Friar, and again – as so often in intimate moments – her lines fall into monosyllables:

> O, shut the door! and when thou hast done so,
> Come weep with me – past hope, past cure, past help!
>
> (IV.i.44–5)

Since the suit of Paris is the main subject of her conversations with her parents, she can hardly be sincere with them. Even before she met Romeo, her consent was hedged in prim phraseology:

> I'll look to like, if looking liking move.
>
> (I.iii.97)

And after her involvement she becomes adept in the stratagems of mental reservation, giving her mother equivocal rejoinders and rousing her father's anger by chopping logic (III.v.69–205). Despite the intervention of the Nurse on her behalf, her one straightforward plea is disregarded. Significantly Lady Capulet, broaching the theme of Paris in stiffly appropriate couplets, has compared his face to a volume:[2]

> This precious book of love, this unbound lover,
> To beautify him only lacks a cover.
> The fish lives in the sea, and 'tis much pride
> The fair without the fair within to hide.
>
> (I.iii.89–90)

That bookish comparison, by emphasizing the letter at the expense of the spirit, helps to lend Paris an aspect of unreality; to the Nurse, more ingenuously, he is "a man of wax" (76). Later Juliet will echo Lady Capulet's metaphor, transferring it from Paris to Romeo:

> Was ever book containing such vile matter
> So fairly bound?
>
> (III.ii.83–4)

Here, on having learned that Romeo has just slain Tybalt, she is undergoing a crisis of doubt, a typically Shakespearean recognition of the difference between appearance and reality. The fair without may not cover a fair within, after all. Her unjustified accusations, leading up to her rhetorical question, form a sequence of oxymoronic epithets: "Beautiful tyrant, fiend angelical, … honorable villain!" (75–9) W. H. Auden, in a recent comment on these lines,[3] cannot believe they would come from a heroine who had been exclaiming shortly before: "Gallop apace, you fiery-footed steeds …!" Yet Shakespeare has been perfectly consistent in suiting changes of style to changes of mood. When Juliet feels at one with Romeo, her intonations are genuine; when she feels at odds with him, they should be unconvincing. The attraction of love is played off against the revulsion from books, and coupled with the closely related themes of youth and haste, in one of Romeo's long-drawn-out leavetakings:

> Love goes toward love as schoolboys from their books;
> But love from love, towards school with heavy looks.
>
> (II.ii.157–8)

The school for these young lovers will be tragic experience. When Romeo, assuming that Juliet is dead and contemplating his own death, recognizes the corpse of Paris, he will extend the image to cover them both:

> O give me thy hand,
> One writ with me in sour misfortune's book!
>
> (v.iii.82)

It was this recoil from bookishness, together with the farewell to compliment, that animated *Love's Labour's Lost*, where literary artifice was so ingeniously deployed against itself, and Berowne was taught – by an actual heroine named Rosaline – that the best books were women's eyes. Some of Shakespeare's other early comedies came even closer to adumbrating certain features of *Romeo and Juliet*: notably, *The Two Gentlemen of Verona*, with its locale, its window scene, its friar and rope, its betrothal and banishment, its emphasis upon the vagaries of love. Shakespeare's sonnets and erotic poems had won for him the reputation of an English Ovid. *Romeo and Juliet*, the most elaborate product of his so-called lyrical period, was his first successful experiment in tragedy.[4] Because of that very success, it is hard for us to realize the full extent of its novelty, though scholarship has lately been reminding us of how it must have struck contemporaries.[5] They would have been surprised, and possibly shocked, at seeing lovers taken so seriously. Legend, it had been heretofore taken for granted, was the proper matter for serious drama; romance was the stuff of the comic stage. Romantic tragedy – "*an excellent conceited Tragedie of Romeo and Juliet*", to cite the title-page of the First Quarto – was one of those contradictions in terms which Shakespeare seems to have delighted in resolving. His innovation might be described as transcending the usages of romantic comedy, which are therefore very much in evidence, particularly at the beginning. Subsequently, the leading characters acquire together a deeper dimension of feeling by expressly repudiating the artificial language they have talked and the superficial code they have lived by. Their formula might be that of the anti-Petrarchan sonnet:

> Foole said My muse to mee, looke in thy heart and write.[6]

An index of this development is the incidence of rhyme, heavily concentrated in the First Act, and its gradual replacement by a blank verse which is realistic or didactic with other speakers and unprecedentedly limpid and passionate with the lovers. "Love has no need of euphony", the eminent Russian translator of the play, Boris Pasternak, has commented. "Truth, not sound, dwells in its heart."[7]

Comedy set the pattern of courtship, as formally embodied in a dance. The other *genre* of Shakespeare's earlier stagecraft, history, set the pattern of conflict, as formally embodied in a duel. *Romeo and Juliet* might also be characterized as an anti-revenge play, in which hostile emotions are finally pacified by the interplay of kindlier ones. Romeo sums it up in his prophetic oxymorons:

> Here's much to do with hate, but more with love.
> Why then, O brawling love! O loving hate!
> O anything, of nothing first create!
>
> (I.i.162–4)

And Paris, true to type, waxes grandiose in lamenting Juliet:

> O love! O life! not life, but love in death!
>
> (IV.v.58)

Here, if we catch the echo from Hieronimo's lament in *The Spanish Tragedy*,

> O life! no life, but lively form of death,

we may well note that the use of antithesis, which is purely decorative with Kyd, is functional with Shakespeare. The contrarieties of his plot are reinforced on the plane of imagery by omnipresent reminders of light and darkness,[8] youth and age, and many other antitheses subsumed by the all-embracing one of Eros and Thanatos, the *leitmotif* of the *Liebestod*, the myth of the tryst in the tomb. This attraction of ultimate opposites – which is succinctly implicit in the Elizabethan ambiguity of the verb *to die* – is generalized when the Friar rhymes "womb" with "tomb", and particularized when Romeo hails the latter place as "thou womb of death" (I.iii.9, 10; v.iii.45). Hence the "extremities" of the situation, as the Prologue to the Second Act announces, are tempered "with extreme sweet" (14). Those extremes begin to meet as soon as the initial prologue, in a sonnet disarmingly smooth, has set forth the feud between the two households, "Where civil blood makes civil hands unclean" (4). Elegant verse yields to vulgar prose, and to an immediate riot, as the servants precipitate a renewal – for the third time – of their masters' quarrel. The brawl of Act I is renewed again in the *contretemps* of Act III and completed by the swordplay of Act V. Between the street-scenes, with their clashing welter of citizens and officers, we shuttle through a series of interiors, in a flurry of domestic arrangements and family relationships. The house of the Capulets is the logical center of action, and Juliet's chamber its central sanctum. Consequently, the sphere of privacy encloses Acts II and IV, in contradistinction to the public issues raised by the alternating episodes. The temporal alternation of the play, in its accelerating continuity, is aptly recapitulated by the impatient rhythm of Capulet's speech:

> Day, night, late, early,
> At home, abroad, alone, in company,
> Waking or sleeping …
>
> (III.v.177–9)

The alignment of the *dramatis personae* is as symmetrical as the antagonism they personify. It is not without relevance that the names of the feuding families, like the Christian names of the hero and heroine, are metrically interchangeable (though "Juliet" is more frequently a trochee than an amphimacer). Tybalt the Capulet is pitted against Benvolio the Montague in the first street-fight, which brings out – with parallel stage-directions – the heads of both houses restrained by respective wives. Both the hero and heroine are paired with others, Rosaline and Paris, and admonished by elderly confidants, the Friar and the Nurse. Escalus, as Prince of Verona, occupies a superior and neutral position; yet, in the interchange of blood for blood, he loses "a brace of kinsman", Paris and Mercutio (v.iii.295). Three times he must quell and sentence the rioters before he can pronounce the final sestet, restoring order to the city-state through the lovers' sacrifice. He effects the resolution by summoning the patriarchal enemies, from their opposite sides, to be reconciled. "Capulet, Montague," he sternly arraigns them, and the polysyllables are brought home by monosyllabics:

> See what a scourge is laid upon your hate
> That heaven finds means to kill your joys with love.
> (291–3)

The two-sided counterpoise of the dramatic structure is well matched by the dynamic symmetry of the antithetical style. One of its peculiarities, which surprisingly seems to have escaped the attention of commentators, is a habit of stressing a word by repeating it within a line, a figure which may be classified in rhetoric as a kind of *ploce*. I have cited a few examples incidentally; let me now underline the device by pointing out a few more. Thus Montague and Capulet are accused of forcing their parties

> To wield old partisans in hands as old,
> Cank'red with peace, to part your cank'red hate.
> (i.i.100, 102)

This double instance, along with the wordplay on "cank'red," suggests the embattled atmosphere of partisanship through the halberds; and it is further emphasized in Benvolio's account of the fray:

> Came more and more, and fought on part and part.
> (122)

The key-words are not only doubled but affectionately intertwined, when Romeo confides to the Friar:

> As mine on hers, so hers is set on mine.
> (ii.iii.59)

Again, he conveys the idea of reciprocity by declaring that Juliet returns "grace for grace and love for love" (86). The Friar's warning hints at poetic justice:

> These violent delights have violent ends.
> (ii.vi.9)

Similarly Mercutio, challenged by Tybalt, turns "point to point", and the Nurse finds Juliet – in *antimetabole* – "Blubb'ring and weeping, weeping and blubbering" (iii.ii.165; iii.87). Statistics would prove illusory, because some repetitions are simply idiomatic, grammatical, or – in the case of old Capulet or the Nurse – colloquial. But it is significant that the play contains well over a hundred such lines, the largest number being in the First Act and scarcely any left over for the Fifth.

The significance of this tendency toward reduplication, both stylistic and structural, can perhaps be best understood in the light of Bergson's well-known theory of the comic: the imposition of geometrical form upon the living data of formless consciousness. The stylization of love, the constant pairing and counter-balancing, the *quid pro quo* of Capulet and Montague, seem mechanical and unnatural. Nature has other proponents besides the lovers, especially Mercutio their fellow victim, who bequeathes his curse to both their houses. His is likewise an ironic end, since he has been as much a satirist of "the new form" and Tybalt's punctilio in duelling "by the book of arithmetic" as of "the numbers that Petrarch flowed in" and Romeo's affectations of gallantry (ii.iv.34, 38; iii.i.104). Mercutio's interpretation of dreams, running counter to Romeo's premonitions, is naturalistic, not to say Freudian; Queen Mab operates through fantasies of wish-fulfillment, bringing love to lovers, fees to lawyers, and tithepigs to parsons; the moral is that desires can be mischievous. In his repartee with Romeo, Mercutio looks forward to their fencing with Tybalt; furthermore he charges the air with bawdy suggestions that – in spite of the limitations of Shakespeare's theatre, its lack of actresses and absence of close-ups – love may have something to do with sex, if not with lust, with the physical complementarity of male and female.[9] He is abetted, in that respect, by the malapropistic garrulity of the Nurse, Angelica, who is naturally bound to Juliet through having been her wet-nurse, and who has lost the infant daughter that might have been Juliet's age. None the less, her crotchety hesitations are contrasted with Juliet's youthful ardors when the Nurse acts as go-between for Romeo. His counsellor, Friar Laurence, makes a measured entrance with his sententious couplets on the uses and abuses of natural properties, the medicinal and poisonous effects of plants:

> For this, being smelt, with that part cheers each part;
> Being tasted, slays all senses with the heart.
>
> (ii.iii.25, 26)

His watchword is "Wisely and slow", yet he contributes to the grief at the sepulcher by ignoring his own advice, "They stumble that run fast" (94).[10] When Romeo upbraids him monosyllabically,

> Thou canst not speak of that thou doest not feel,

it is the age-old dilemma that separates the generations: *Si jeunesse savait, si vieillesse pouvait* (iii.iii.64). Banished to Mantua, Romeo has illicit recourse to the Apothecary, whose shop – envisaged with Flemish precision – unhappily replaces the Friar's cell, and whose poison is the sinister counterpart of Laurence's potion.

Against this insistence upon polarity, at every level, the mutuality of the lovers stands out, the one organic relation amid an overplus of stylized expressions and attitudes.

The naturalness of their diction is artfully gained, as we have noticed, through a running critique of artificiality. In drawing a curtain over the consummation of their love, Shakespeare heralds it with a prothalamium and follows it with an epithalamium. Juliet's "Gallop apace, you fiery-footed steeds", reversing the Ovidian "*lente currite, noctis equi*", is spoken "alone" but in breathless anticipation of a companion (III.ii.1). After having besought the day to end, the sequel to her solo is the duet in which she begs the night to continue. In the ensuing *débat* of the nightingale and the lark, a refinement upon the antiphonal song of the owl and the cuckoo in *Love's Labour's Lost*, Romeo more realistically discerns "the herald of the morn" (III.v.6). When Juliet reluctantly agrees, "More light and light it grows", he completes the paradox with a doubly reduplicating line:

> More light and light – more dark and dark our woes!
> (35, 36)

The precariousness of their union, formulated arithmetically by the Friar as "two in one" (II.vi.37), is brought out by the terrible loneliness of Juliet's monologue upon taking the potion:

> My dismal scene I needs must act alone.
> (IV.iii.19)

Her utter singleness, as an only child, is stressed by her father and mourned by her mother:

> But one, poor one, one poor and loving child.
> (v.46)

Tragedy tends to isolate where comedy brings together, to reveal the uniqueness of individuals rather than what they have in common with others. Asking for Romeo's profession of love, Juliet anticipates: "I know thou wilt say 'Ay'" (II.ii.90). That monosyllable of glad assent was the first she ever spoke, as we know from the Nurse's childish anecdote (I.iii.48). Later, asking the Nurse whether Romeo has been killed, Juliet pauses self-consciously over the pun between "Ay" and "I" or "eye":

> Say thou but 'I,'
> And that bare vowel 'I' shall poison more
> Than the death-darting eye of cockatrice.
> I am not I, if there be such an 'I';
> Or those eyes shut that make thee answer 'I.'
> If he be slain, say 'I'; or if not, 'no.'
> Brief sounds determine of my weal or woe.
> (III.ii.45–51)

Her identification with him is negated by death, conceived as a shut or poisoning eye, which throws the pair back upon their single selves. Each of them dies alone – or, at all events, in the belief that the other lies dead, and without the benefit of a recognition-scene. Juliet, of course, is still alive; but she has already voiced her death-speech in the potion scene. With the dagger, her last words, though richly symbolic, are brief and monosyllabic:

> This is thy sheath; there rest, and let me die.
> (v.iii.170)

The sense of vicissitude is re-enacted through various gestures of staging; Romeo and Juliet experience their exaltation "aloft" on the upper stage; his descent via the rope is, as she fears, toward the tomb (iii.v.56).[11] The antonymous adverbs *up* and *down* figure, with increasing prominence, among the brief sounds that determine Juliet's woe (e.g., v.ii.209–10). The overriding pattern through which she and Romeo have been trying to break – call it Fortune, the stars, or what you will – ends by closing in and breaking them; their private world disappears, and we are left in the social ambiance again. Capulet's house has been bustling with preparations for a wedding, the happy ending of comedy. The news of Juliet's death is not yet tragic because it is premature; but it introduces a peripety which will become the starting point for *Hamlet*.

> All things that we ordained festival
> Turn from their office to black funeral –

the old man cries, and his litany of contraries is not less poignant because he has been so fond of playing the genial host:

> Our instruments to melancholy bells,
> Our wedding cheer to a sad burial feast;
> Our solemn hymns to sullen dirges change;
> Our bridal flowers serve for a buried corse;
> And all things change them to the contrary.
> (iv.v.84–90)

His lamentation, in which he is joined by his wife, the Nurse, and Paris, reasserts the formalities by means of what is virtually an operatic quartet. Thereupon the music becomes explicit, when they leave the stage to the Musicians, who have walked on with the County Paris. Normally these three might play during the *entr'acte*, but Shakespeare has woven them into the dialogue terminating the Fourth Act.[12] Though their art has the power of soothing the passions and thereby redressing grief, as the comic servant Peter reminds them with a quotation from Richard Edward's lyric *In Commendacion of Musicke*, he persists in his query: "Why 'silver sound'?" (131) Their answers are those of mere hirelings, who can indifferently change their tune from a merry dump to a doleful one, so long as they are paid with coin of the realm. Yet Peter's riddle touches a deeper chord of correspondence, the interconnection between discord and harmony, between impulse and discipline. "Consort", which can denote a concert or a companionship, can become the fighting word that motivates the unharmonious pricksong of the duellists (iii.i.48). The "sweet division" of the lark sounds harsh and out of tune to Juliet, since it proclaims that the lovers must be divided (v.29). Why "silver sound"? Because Romeo, in the orchard, has sworn by the moon

> That tips with silver all these fruit-tree tops.
>
> (ii.i.108)

Because Shakespeare, transposing sights and sounds into words, has made us imagine

> How silver-sweet sound lovers' tongues by night,
> Like softest music to attending ears!
>
> (167–8)

Notes

1 Line-references are to the separate edition of G. L. Kittredge's text (Boston, 1940).
2 On the long and rich history of this trope, see the sixteenth chapter of E. R. Curtius, *European Literature and the Latin Middle Ages*, tr. W. R. Trask (New York, 1953).
3 In the paper-bound Laurel Shakespeare, ed. Francis Fergusson (New York, 1958), p. 26.
4 H. B. Charlton, in his British Academy lecture for 1939, *"Romeo and Juliet" as an Experimental Tragedy*, has considered the experiment in the light of Renaissance critical theory.
5 Especially F. M. Dickey, *Not Wisely But Too Well: Shakespeare's Love Tragedies* (San Marino, 1957), pp. 63–88.
6 Sir Philip Sidney, *Astrophel and Stella*, ed. Albert Feuillerat (Cambridge, 1922), p. 243.
7 Boris Pasternak, "Translating Shakespeare", tr. Manya Harari, *The Twentieth Century*, CLXIV, 979 (September, 1958), p. 217.
8 Caroline Spurgeon, *Shakespeare's Imagery and What It Tells Us* (New York, 1936), pp. 310–16.
9 Coleridge's persistent defense of Shakespeare against the charge of gross language does more credit to that critic's high-mindedness than to his discernment. The concentrated ribaldry of the gallants in the street (ii.iv) is deliberately contrasted with the previous exchange between the lovers in the orchard.
10 This is the leading theme of the play, in the interpretation of Brents Stirling, *Unity in Shakespearean Tragedy: The Interplay of Themes and Characters* (New York, 1956), pp. 10–25.
11 One of the more recent and pertinent discussions of staging is that of Richard Hosley, "The Use of the Upper Stage in *Romeo and Juliet*", *Shakespeare Quarterly*, V, 4 (Autumn, 1954), 371–9.
12 Professor F. T. Bowers reminds me that inter-act music was probably not a regular feature of public performance when *Romeo and Juliet* was first performed. Some early evidence for it has been gathered by T. S. Graves in "The Act-Time in Elizabethan Theatres", *Studies in Philology*, XII, 3 (July, 1915), 120–4 – notably contemporary sound cues, written into a copy of the Second Quarto and cited by Malone. But if – as seems likely – such practices were exceptional, then Shakespeare was innovating all the farther.

12

King Lear or *Endgame*

Jan Kott

King Lear: Dost thou call me fool, boy?
Fool: All thy other titles thou hast given away; that thou wast born with.
(King Lear, I.iv)

We are all born mad. Some remain so.
(*Waiting for Godot*, II)

I

The attitude of modern criticism to *King Lear* is ambiguous and somehow embarrassed. Doubtless *King Lear* is still recognized as a masterpiece, beside which even *Macbeth* and *Hamlet* seem tame and pedestrian. *King Lear* is compared to Bach's *Mass in B Minor*, to Beethoven's *Fifth* and *Ninth* Symphonies, to Wagner's *Parsifal*, Michelangelo's *Last Judgement*, or Dante's *Purgatory* and *Inferno*. But at the same time *King Lear* gives one the impression of a high mountain that everyone admires, yet no one particularly wishes to climb. It is as if the play had lost its power to excite on the stage and in reading; as if it were out of place in our time, or, at any rate, had no place in the modern theatre. But the question is: what is modern theatre?

The apogee of *King Lear*'s theatrical history was reached no doubt in the romantic era. *King Lear* fit the romantic theatre perfectly; but only conceived as a melodrama, full of horrors, and dealing with a tragic king, deprived of his crown, conspired against by heaven and earth, nature and men. Charles Lamb might well laugh at early nineteenth-century performances in which a miserable old man wandered about the stage bare-headed, stick in hand, in an artificial storm and rain. But the theatre was soon to attain the full power of illusion. Diorama, scene changes effected by means of new stage machinery without bringing the curtain down, made it possible suddenly, almost miraculously to transform a Gothic castle into a mountainous region, or a blood-red sunset into a stormy night. Lightning and thunder, rain and wind, seemed like the real thing. It was easy for the romantic imagination to find its favourite landscape: gloomy castles, hovels, deserted spots, mysterious and awe-inspiring places, towering rocks gleaming white in the moonlight. *King Lear* was also in keeping with the romantic style of acting, since it offered scope for the sweeping gestures, terrifying scenes, and violent soliloquies, loudly delivered, so popular with Kean and his school. The actor's task was to demonstrate the blackest depths of the human soul. Lear's and Gloucester's unhappy fate was to arouse pity and terror, to shock the audience. And so it did. Suffering purified Lear and restored his tragic greatness. Shakespeare's *King Lear* was the "black theatre" of romanticism.

Then came the turn of historical, antiquarian and realistic Shakespeare. Stage designers were sent to Rome to copy features of the Forum for sets to *Julius Caesar*. Crowds of extras were dressed in period costume. Copies were made of medieval dress, Renaissance jewelry, Elizabethan furniture. Sets became more and more solid and imposing. The stage was turned into a large exhibition of historical props. A balcony had to be a real balcony; a palace, a real palace; a street, a real street. Real trees were substituted for the old painted landscape.

At that time attempts were made to set *King Lear* also in a definite historical period. With the help of archeologists Celtic burial places were reconstructed on the stage. Lear became an old druid. Theatrical machinery was more and more perfect, so that storm, wind and rain could drown the actors' voices more and more effectively. As a result of the odd marriage between new and perfected theatre techniques and archeological reconstruction of a Celtic tomb, only the plot remained of Shakespeare's play. In such a theatre Shakespeare was indeed out of place: he was untheatrical.

The turn of the century brought a revolution in Shakespearean studies. For the first time his plays began to be interpreted through the theatre of his time. A generation of scholars was busy patiently recreating the Elizabethan stage, style of acting and theatrical traditions. Granville-Barker in his famous *Prefaces to Shakespeare* showed, or at least tried to show, how *Lear* must have been played at the Globe. The return to the so-called "authentic" Shakespeare began. From now on the storm was to rage in Lear's and Gloucester's breasts rather than on the stage. The trouble was, however, that the demented old man, tearing his long white beard, suddenly became ridiculous. He should have been tragic, but he no longer was.

Nearly all Shakespeare's expositions have an amazing speed and directness in the way conflicts are shown and put into action and the whole tone of the play is set. The exposition of *King Lear* seems preposterous if one is to look for psychological verisimilitude in it. A great and powerful king holds a competition of rhetoric among his daughters, as to which one of them will best express her love for him, and makes the division of his kingdom depend on its outcome. He does not see or understand anything: Regan's and Goneril's hypocrisy is all too evident. Regarded as a person, a character, Lear is ridiculous, naïve and stupid. When he goes mad, he can arouse only compassion, never pity and terror.

Gloucester, too, is naïve and ridiculous. In the early scenes he seems a stock character from a comedy of manners. Robert Speaight compares him to a gentleman of somewhat old-fashioned views who strolls on a Sunday along St. James's Street complete with bowler hat and umbrella.[1] Nothing about him hints at the tragic old man whose eyes will be gouged out. It is true that Polonius in *Hamlet* is also a comic figure, who later is stabbed to death. But his death is grotesque, too, while Lear and Gloucester are to go through immense sufferings.

Producers have found it virtually impossible to cope with the plot of *King Lear*. When realistically treated, Lear and Gloucester were too ridiculous to appear tragic heroes. If the exposition was treated as a fairy tale or legend, the cruelty of Shakespeare's world, too, became unreal. Yet the cruelty of *Lear* was to the Elizabethans a contemporary reality, and has remained real since. But it is a philosophical cruelty. Neither the romantic, nor the naturalistic theatre was able to show that sort of cruelty; only the new theatre can. In this new theatre there are no characters, and the tragic element has been superseded by grotesque. Grotesque is more cruel than tragedy.

The exposition of *King Lear* is as absurd, and as necessary as the arrival at Güllen of multi-millionairess Claire Zachanassian and her entourage, including a new husband, a couple of eunuchs, a large coffin, and a tiger in a cage in Dürrenmatt's *Visit*. The exposition of *King Lear* shows a world that is to be destroyed.

Since the end of the eighteenth century no dramatist has had a greater impact on European drama than Shakespeare. But the theatres in which Shakespeare's plays have been produced were in turn influenced by contemporary plays. Shakespeare has been a living influence in so far as contemporary plays, through which his dramas were interpreted, were a living force themselves. When Shakespeare is dull and dead on the stage, it means that not only the theatre but also the plays written in that particular period are dead. This is one of the reasons why Shakespeare's universality has never dated.

The book devoted to "Shakespeare and the new drama" has not yet been written. Perhaps it is too early for such a book to appear. But it is odd how often the word "Shakespearean" is uttered when one speaks about Brecht, Dürrenmatt, or Beckett. These three names stand, of course, for three different kinds of theatrical vision, and the word "Shakespearean" means something different in relation to each of them. It may be invoked to compare with Dürrenmatt's full-bloodedness, sharpness, lack of cohesion, and stylistic confusion; with Brecht's epic quality; or with Beckett's new *Theatrum mundi*. But every one of these three kinds of drama and theatre has more similarities to Shakespeare and medieval morality plays than to nineteenth-century drama, whether romantic, or naturalistic. Only in this sense can the new theatre be called anti-theatre.

A striking feature of the new theatre is its grotesque quality. Despite appearances to the contrary, this new grotesque has not replaced the old drama and the comedy of manners. It deals with problems, conflicts and themes of tragedy such as: human fate, the meaning of existence, freedom and inevitability, the discrepancy between the absolute and the fragile human order. Grotesque means tragedy re-written in different terms. Maurice Regnault's statement: "the absence of tragedy in a tragic world gives birth to comedy" is only seemingly paradoxical. Grotesque exists in a tragic world. Both the tragic and the grotesque vision of the world are composed as it were of the same elements. In a tragic and grotesque world, situations are imposed, compulsory and inescapable. Freedom of choice and decision are part of this compulsory situation, in which both the tragic hero and the grotesque actor must always lose their struggle against the absolute. The downfall of the tragic hero is a confirmation and recognition of the absolute; whereas the downfall of the grotesque actor means mockery of the absolute and its desecration. The absolute is transformed into a blind mechanism, a kind of automaton. Mockery is directed not only at the tormentor, but also at the victim who believed in the tormentor's justice, raising him to the level of the absolute. The victim has consecrated his tormentor by recognizing himself as victim.

In the final instance tragedy is an appraisal of human fate, a measure of the absolute. The grotesque is a criticism of the absolute in the name of frail human experience. That is why tragedy brings catharsis, while grotesque offers no consolation whatsoever. "Tragedy," wrote Gorgias of Leontium, "is a swindle in which the swindler is more just than the swindled, and the swindled wiser than the swindler." One may travesty this aphorism by saying that grotesque is a swindle in which the swindled is more just than the swindler, and the swindler wiser than the swindled. Claire Zachanassian in Dürrenmatt's *Visit* is wiser than Anton Schill, but he is more just than she is. Schill's death, like Polonius's death in *Hamlet*, is grotesque. Neither Schill, nor the inhabitants of Güllen are tragic heroes. The old lady with her artificial breasts, teeth and limbs is not a goddess; she hardly even exists, she might almost have been invented. Schill and the people of Güllen find themselves in a situation in which there is no room for tragedy, but only for grotesque. "Comedy," writes Ionesco in his *Expérience du théâtre*, "is a feeling of absurdity, and seems more hopeless than tragedy; comedy allows no way out of a given situation."[2]

The tragic and the grotesque worlds are closed, and there is no escape from them. In the tragic world this compulsory situation has been imposed in turn by the Gods, Fate, the Christian God, Nature, and History that has been endowed with reason and inevitability.

On the other side, opposed to this arrangement, there was always man. If Nature was the absolute, man was unnatural. If man was natural, the absolute was represented by Grace, without which there was no salvation. In the world of the grotesque, downfall cannot be justified by, or blamed on, the absolute. The absolute is not endowed with any ultimate reasons; it is stronger, and that is all. The absolute is absurd. Maybe that is why the grotesque often makes use of the concept of a mechanism which has been put in motion and cannot be stopped. Various kinds of impersonal and hostile mechanisms have taken the place of God, Nature and History, found in the old tragedy. The notion of absurd mechanism is probably the last metaphysical concept remaining in modern grotesque. But this absurd mechanism is not transcendental any more in relation to man, or at any rate to mankind. It is a trap set by man himself into which he has fallen.

The scene of tragedy has mostly been a natural landscape. Raging nature witnessed man's downfall, or – as in *King Lear* – played an active part in the action. Modern grotesque usually takes place in the midst of civilization. Nature has evaporated from it almost completely. Man is confined to a room and surrounded by inanimate objects. But objects have now been raised to the status of symbols of human fate, or situation, and perform a similar function to that played in Shakespeare by forest, storm, or eclipse of the sun. Even Sartre's hell is just a vast hotel consisting of rooms and corridors, beyond which there are more rooms and more corridors. This hell "behind closed doors" does not need any metaphysical aids.

Ionesco's hell is arranged on similar lines. A new tenant moves into an empty flat. Furniture is brought in. There is more and more furniture. Furniture surrounds the tenant on all sides. He is surrounded already by four wardrobes but more are brought in. He has been closed in by furniture. He can no longer be seen. He has been brought down to the level of inanimate objects and has become an object himself.

In Beckett's *Endgame* there is a room with a wheelchair and two dustbins. A picture hangs face to the wall. There is also a staircase, a telescope and a whistle. All that remains of nature is sand in the dustbins, a flea, and the part of man that belongs to nature: his body.

> *Hamm:*   Nature has forgotten us.
> *Clov:*   There's no more nature.
> *Hamm:*   No more nature! You exaggerate.
> *Clov:*   In the vicinity.
> *Hamm:*   But we breathe, we change! We lose our hair, our teeth! Our bloom! Our ideals!
> *Clov:*   Then she hasn't forgotten us.
>
> (p. 16)[3]

It can easily be shown how, in the new theatre, tragic situations become grotesque. Such a classic situation of tragedy is the necessity of making a choice between opposing values. Antigone is doomed to choose between human and divine order; between Creon's demands, and those of the absolute. The tragedy lies in the very principle of choice by which one of the values must be annihilated. The cruelty of the absolute lies in demanding such a choice and in imposing a situation which excludes the possibility of a compromise, and where one of the alternatives is death. The absolute is greedy and demands everything; the hero's death is its confirmation.

The tragic situation becomes grotesque when both alternatives of the choice imposed are absurd, irrelevant or compromising. The hero has to play, even if there is no game. Every move is bad, but he cannot throw down his cards. To throw down the cards would also be a bad move....

The world of tragedy and the world of grotesque have a similar structure. Grotesque takes over the themes of tragedy and poses the same fundamental questions. Only its answers are different. This dispute about the tragic and grotesque interpretations of human fate reflects the everlasting conflict of two philosophies and two ways of thinking; of two opposing attitudes defined by the Polish philosopher Leszek Kołakowski as the irreconcilable antagonism between the priest and the clown. Between tragedy and grotesque there is the same conflict for or against such notions as eschatology, belief in the absolute, hope for the ultimate solution of the contradiction between the moral order and every-day practice. Tragedy is the theatre of priests, grotesque is the theatre of clowns.

This conflict between two philosophies and two types of theatre becomes particularly acute in times of great upheavals. When established values have been overthrown, and there is no appeal, to God, Nature, or History, from the tortures inflicted by the cruel world, the clown becomes the central figure in the theatre. He accompanies the exiled trio – the king, the nobleman and his son – on their cruel wanderings through the cold endless night which has fallen on the world; through the "cold night" which, as in Shakespeare's *King Lear*, "will turn us all to fools and madmen."

II

After his eyes have been gouged out, Gloucester wants to throw himself over the cliffs of Dover into the sea. He is led by his own son, who feigns madness. Both have reached the depths of human suffering; the top of "the pyramid of suffering", as Juliusz Slowacki has described *King Lear*. But on the stage there are just two actors, one playing a blind man, the other playing a man who plays a madman. They walk together.

> *Gloucester:* When shall I come to th' top of that same hill?
> *Edgar:* You do climb up it now. Look how we labour.
> *Gloucester:* Methinks the ground is even.
> *Edgar:*   Horrible steep.
> Hark, do you hear the sea?
> *Gloucester:* No, truly.
>
>   (IV.vi)

It is easy to imagine this scene. The text itself provides stage directions. Edgar is supporting Gloucester; he lifts his feet high pretending to walk uphill. Gloucester, too, lifts his feet, as if expecting the ground to rise, but underneath his foot there is only air. This entire scene is written for a very definite type of theatre, namely pantomime.

This pantomime only makes sense if enacted on a flat and level stage.

Edgar feigns madness, but in doing so he must adopt the right gestures. In its theatrical expression this is a scene in which a madman leads a blind man and talks him into believing in a non-existing mountain. In another moment a landscape will be sketched in. Shakespeare often creates a landscape on an empty stage. A few words, and the diffused, soft afternoon light at the Globe changes into night, evening, or morning. But no other Shakespearean landscape is so exact, precise and clear as this one. It is like a Breughel painting thick with people, objects and events. A little human figure hanging halfway down the cliff is gathering samphire. Fishermen walking on the beach are like mice. A ship seems a little boat, a boat is floating like a buoy.

It is this abyss of Shakespeare's imagination that Slowacki makes the hero of his *Kordian* look into:

> Come! Here, on the top stand still. Your head will whirl,
> When you cast your eyes on the abyss below your feet.
> Crows flying there half-way no bigger are than beetles.
> And there, too, someone is toiling, gathering weed.
> He looks no bigger than a human head.
> And there on the beach the fishermen seem like ants ...

This veristic and perspective landscape created on an empty stage is not meant to serve as part of the decor, or to replace the non-existent settings. Slowacki understood perfectly the dramatic purpose of this scene:

> Oh, Shakespeare! Spirit! You have built a mountain
> Higher than that created by God.
> For you have talked of an abyss to a man blind ...

The landscape is now just a score for the pantomime. Gloucester and Edgar have reached the top of the cliff. The landscape is now below them.

> Give me your hand. You are now within a foot
> Of th' extreme verge. For all beneath the moon
> Would I not leap upright.
>
> (*King Lear*, iv.vi)

In Shakespeare's time the actors probably put their feet forward through a small balustrade above the apron-stage, immediately over the heads of the "groundlings". But we are not concerned here with an historical reconstruction of the Elizabethan stage. It is the presence and importance of the mime that is significant. Shakespeare is stubborn. Gloucester has already jumped over the precipice. Both actors are at the foot of a non-existent cliff. The same landscape is now above them. The mime continues.

Gloucester: But have I fall'n, or no?
Edgar: From the dread summit of this chalky bourn.
     Look up a-height. The shrill-gorg'd lark so far
     Cannot be seen or heard. Do but look up.

(iv.vi)

The mime creates a scenic area: the top and bottom of the cliff, the precipice. Shakespeare makes use of all the means of anti-illusionist theatre in order to create a most realistic and concrete landscape. A landscape which is only a blind man's illusion. There is perspective in it, light, men and things, even sounds. From the height of the cliff the sea cannot be heard, but there is mention of its roar. From the foot of the cliff the lark cannot be heard, but there is mention of its song. In this landscape sounds are present by their very absence: the silence is filled with them, just as the empty stage is filled with the mountain.

The scene of the suicidal leap is also a mime. Gloucester kneels in a last prayer and then, in accordance with tradition of the play's English performances, falls over. He is now at the bottom of the cliff. But there was no height; it was an illusion. Gloucester knelt down on an empty stage, fell over and got up. At this point disillusion follows.[4]

The non-existent cliff is not meant just to deceive the blind man. For a short while we, too, believed in this landscape and in the mime. The meaning of this parable is not easy to define. But one thing is clear: this type of parable is not to be thought of outside the theatre, or rather outside a certain kind of theatre. In narrative prose Edgar could, of course, lead the blind Gloucester to the cliffs of Dover, let him jump down from a stone and make him believe that he was jumping from the top of a cliff. But he might just as well lead him a day's journey away from the castle and make him jump from a stone on any heap of sand. In film and in prose there is only the choice between a real stone lying in the sand and an equally real jump from the top of a chalk cliff into the sea. One cannot transpose Gloucester's suicide attempt to the screen, unless one were to film a stage performance. But in the naturalistic, or even stylized theatre, with the precipice painted or projected onto a screen, Shakespeare's parable would be completely obliterated.

The stage must be empty. On it a suicide, or rather its symbol, has been performed. Mime is the performance of symbols. In Ionesco's *Le tueur sans gages* the Architect, who is at the same time the commissioner of police, shows Berenger round the *Cité Radieuse*. On an empty stage Berenger sniffs at non-existent flowers and taps non-existent walls. The Radiant City exists and does not exist, or rather it has existed always and everywhere. And that is why it is so terrifying. Similarly, the Shakespearean precipice at Dover exists and does not exist. It is the abyss, waiting all the time. The abyss, into which one can jump, is everywhere.

By a few words of dialogue Shakespeare often turned the platform stage, the inner stage, or the gallery into a London street, a forest, a palace, a ship, or a castle battlement. But these were always real places of action. Townspeople gathered outside the Tower, lovers wandered through the forest, Brutus murdered Caesar in the Forum. The white precipice at Dover performs a different function. Gloucester does not jump from the top of the cliff, or from a stone. For once, in *King Lear*, Shakespeare shows the paradox of pure theatre. It is the same theatrical paradox that Ionesco uses in his *Le tueur sans gages*.

In the naturalistic theatre one can perform a murder scene, or a scene of terror. The shot may be fired from a revolver or a toy pistol. But in the mime there is no difference between a revolver and a toy pistol: in fact neither exists. Like death, the shot is only a performance, a parable, a symbol.

Gloucester, falling over on flat, even boards, plays a scene from a great morality play. He is no longer a court dignitary whose eyes have been gouged out because he showed mercy to the banished king. The action is no longer confined to Elizabethan or Celtic England. Gloucester is Everyman, and the stage becomes the medieval *Theatrum Mundi*. A Biblical parable is now enacted; the one about the rich man who became a beggar, and the blind man who recovered his inner sight when he lost his eyes. Everyman begins his wanderings through the world. In medieval mystery plays also the stage was empty, but in the background there were four mansions, four gates representing Earth, Purgatory, Heaven and Hell. In *King Lear* the stage is empty throughout: there is nothing, except the cruel earth, where man goes on his journey from the cradle to the grave. The theme of *King Lear* is an enquiry into the meaning of this journey, into the existence or non-existence of Heaven and Hell.

From the middle of Act II to the end of Act IV, Shakespeare takes up a Biblical theme. But this new *Book of Job* or a new Dantean *Inferno* was written towards the close of the Renaissance. In Shakespeare's play there is neither Christian Heaven, nor the heaven predicted and believed in by humanists. *King Lear* makes a tragic mockery of all eschatologies: of the heaven promised on earth, and the Heaven promised after death; in fact – of both Christian and secular theodicies; of cosmogony and of the rational view of history; of the gods and the good nature, of man made in "image and likeness". In *King Lear* both the medieval and the Renaissance orders of established values disintegrate. All that remains at the end of this gigantic pantomime, is the earth – empty and bleeding. On this earth, through which tempest has passed leaving only stones, the King, the Fool, the Blind Man and the Madman carry on their distracted dialogue.

The blind Gloucester falls over on the empty stage. His suicidal leap is tragic. Gloucester has reached the depths of human misery; so has Edgar, who pretends to be mad Tom in order to save his father. But the pantomime performed by actors on the stage is grotesque, and has something of a circus about it. The blind Gloucester who has climbed a non-existent height and fallen over on flat boards, is a clown. A philosophical buffoonery of the sort found in modern theatre has been performed.

> Whistle from left wing.
> He (the man) does not move.
> He looks at his hands, looks round for scissors, sees them, goes and picks them up, starts to trim his nails, stops, runs his finger along blade of scissors, goes and lays them on small cube, turns aside, opens his collar, frees his neck and fingers it.
> The small cube is pulled up and disappears in flies, carrying away rope and scissors.
> He turns to take scissors, sees what has happened.
> He turns aside, reflects.
> He goes and sits down on big cube.
> The big cube is pulled from under him. He falls. The big cube is pulled up and disappears in flies.
> He remains lying on his side, his face towards auditorium, staring before him. (*Act Without Words*, pp. 59–60)

The *Act Without Words* closes Beckett's *Endgame*, providing as it were its final interpretation. Remaining vestiges of characters, action and situation have been further reduced here. All that remains is one situation acting as a parable of universal human fate. A total situation. Man has been thrown onto the empty stage. He tries to escape into the wings, but is kicked back. From above a tree with some leaves, a jug of water, tailoring scissors, and some cubes are pulled down on ropes. The man tries to hide in the shade of the leaves, but the tree is pulled up. He tries to catch hold of the jug, but it rises into the air. He attempts suicide, but this, too, proves impossible. "The bough folds down against trunk." (p. 59) The man sits down and thinks. The jug and the tree appear again. The man does not move.

In this ending to *Endgame* the forces external to man – gods, fate, world – are not indifferent, but sneering and malicious. They tempt him all the time. These forces are stronger than he. Man must be defeated and cannot escape from the situation that has been imposed on him. All he can do is to give up; refuse to play blindman's buff. Only by the possibility of refusal can he surmount the external forces.

It is easy to see how close to the Bible this parable is, even in its metaphors: palm, its shadow, water. The force above and beyond man is strongly reminiscent of the Old Testament God. This is also a *Book of Job*, but without an optimistic ending.

This new *Book of Job* is shown in buffo, as a circus pantomime. *Act Without Words* is performed by a clown. The philosophical parable may be interpreted as tragedy or grotesque, but its artistic expression is grotesque only. Gloucester's suicide attempt, too, is merely a circus somersault on an empty stage. Gloucester's and Edgar's situation is tragic, but it has been shown in pantomime, the classic expression of buffoonery. In Shakespeare clowns often ape the gestures of kings and heroes, but only in *King Lear* are great tragic scenes shown through clowning.

It is not only the suicide mime that is grotesque. The accompanying dialogue is also cruel and mocking. The blind Gloucester kneels and prays:

> O you mighty gods!
> This world I do renounce, and, in your sights
> Shake patiently my great affliction off.
> If I could bear it longer, and not fall
> To quarrel with your great opposeless wills,
> My snuff and loathed part of nature should
> Burn itself out. If Edgar live, O, bless him!
>
> (iv.vi)

Gloucester's suicide has a meaning only if the gods exist. It is a protest against undeserved suffering and the world's injustice. This protest is made in a definite direction. It refers to eschatology. Even if the gods are cruel, they must take this suicide into consideration. It will count in the final reckoning between gods and man. Its sole value lies in its reference to the absolute.

But if the gods, and their moral order in the world, do not exist, Gloucester's suicide does not solve or alter anything. It is only a somersault on an empty stage. It is deceptive and unsuccessful on the factual, as well as on the metaphysical plane. Not only the pantomime, but the whole situation is then grotesque. From the beginning to the end. It is waiting for a Godot who does not come.

Estragon:	Why don't we hang ourselves?
Vladimir:	With what?
Estragon:	You haven't got a bit of rope?
Vladimir:	No.
Estragon:	Then we can't.
Vladimir:	Let's go.
Estragon:	Wait, there's my belt.
Vladimir:	It's too short.
Estragon:	You could hang on to my legs.
Vladimir:	And who'd hang on to mine?
Estragon:	True.
Vladimir:	Show all the same. (*Estragon loosens the cord that holds up his trousers which, much too big for him, fall about his ankles. They look at the cord.*) It might do at a pinch. But is it strong enough?
Estragon:	We'll soon see. Here.
	(*They each take an end of the cord and pull. It breaks. They almost fall.*)
Vladimir:	Not worth a curse.

(*Waiting for Godot*, ii)

Gloucester did fall, and he got up again. He made his suicide attempt, but he failed to shake the world. Nothing has changed. Edgar's comment is ironical:

> ... Had he been where he thought,
> By this had thought been past.
>
> (iv.vi)

If there are no gods, suicide makes no sense. Death exists in any case. Suicide cannot alter human fate, but only accelerate it. It ceases to be a protest. It is a surrender. It becomes the acceptance of world's greatest cruelty – death. Gloucester has finally realized:

> ... Henceforth I'll bear
> Affliction till it do cry out itself
> "Enough, enough," and die.
>
> (ɪᴠ.ᴠi)

And once again, in the last act:

> No further, sir. A man may rot even here.
>
> (ᴠ.ii)

After his grotesque suicide the blind Gloucester talks to the deranged Lear. Estragon and Vladimir carry on a very similar conversation, interrupted by the despairing cries of the blind Pozzo, who has fallen down and cannot get up. Pozzo would find it easiest to understand Gloucester:

> ... one day I went blind, one day we'll go deaf, one day we were born, one day we shall die
> ... They give birth astride of a grave, the light gleams an instant, then it's night once more.
> (*Waiting for Godot*, ɪɪ)

Shakespeare had said as much, in fewer words:

> ... Men must endure
> Their going hence, even as their coming hither;
> Ripeness is all.
>
> (ᴠ.ii)

But it was Ionesco who put it most briefly of all, in his *Tueur sans gages:* "We shall all die, this is the only serious alienation."

III

The theme of *King Lear* is the decay and fall of the world. The play opens like the Histories, with the division of the realm and the king's abdication. It also ends like the Histories, with the proclamation of a new king. Between the prologue and the epilogue there is a civil war. But unlike the Histories and Tragedies, in *King Lear* the world is not healed again. In *King Lear* there is no young and resolute Fortinbras to ascend the throne of Denmark; no cool-headed Octavius to become Augustus Caesar; no noble Malcolm to "give to our tables meat, sleep to our nights." In the epilogues to the Histories and Tragedies the new monarch invites those present to his coronation. In *King Lear* there will be no coronation. There is no one whom Edgar can invite to it. Everybody has died or been murdered. Gloucester was right when he said: "This great world / Shall so wear out to naught." Those who have survived – Edgar, Albany and Kent – are, as Lear has been, just "ruin'd piece[s] of nature".

Of the twelve major characters half are just and good, the other half, unjust and bad. It is a division as consistent and abstract as in a morality play. But this is a morality play in which every one will be destroyed: noble characters along with base ones, the persecutors with the persecuted, the torturers with the tortured. Vivisection will go on until the stage is empty. The decay and fall of the world will be shown on two levels, on two different kinds of stage, as it were. One of these may be called Macbeth's stage, the other, Job's stage.

Macbeth's stage is the scene of crime. At the beginning there is a nursery tale of two bad daughters and one good daughter. The good daughter will die hanged in prison. The bad daughters will also die, but not until they have become adulterers, and one of them also a poisoner and murderess of her husband. All bonds, all laws, whether divine, natural or human, are broken. Social order, from the kingdom to the family, will crumble into dust. There are no longer kings and subjects, fathers and children, husbands and wives. There are only huge Renaissance monsters, devouring one another like beasts of prey. Everything has been condensed, drawn in broad outlines, characters are hardly marked. The history of the world can do without psychology and without rhetoric. It is just action. These violent sequences are merely an illustration and an example, and perform the function of a black, realistic counterpart to "Job's stage".

For it is Job's stage that constitutes the main scene. On it the ironic, clownish morality play on human fate will be performed. But before that happens, all the characters must be uprooted from their social positions and pulled down, to final degradation. They must reach rock-bottom. The downfall is not merely a philosophical parable, as Gloucester's leap over the supposed precipice is. The theme of downfall is carried through by Shakespeare stubbornly, consistently and is repeated at least four times. The fall is at the same time physical and spiritual, bodily and social.

At the beginning there was a king with his court and ministers. Later, there are just four beggars wandering about in a wilderness, exposed to raging winds and rain. The fall may be slow, or sudden. Lear has at first a retinue of a hundred men, then fifty, then only one. Kent is banished by one angry gesture of the king. But the process of degradation is always the same. Everything that distinguishes a man – his titles, social position, even name – is lost. Names are not needed any more. Every one is just a shadow of himself; just a man.

King Lear: Doth any here know me? This is not Lear.
              Doth Lear walk thus? speak thus?
              ...
              Who is it that can tell me who I am?
Fool: Lear's shadow.

(1.iv)

And once more the same question, and the same answer. The banished Kent returns in disguise to his king.

King Lear: How now? What art thou?
Kent: A man, sir.

(1.iv)

A naked man has no name. Before the morality commences, every one must be naked. Naked like a worm.

> Then Job arose, and rent his mantle, and shaved his head, and fell down upon the ground, and worshipped.
> And said, Naked came I out of my mother's womb, and naked shall return thither.
> (*Book of Job*, 1, 20–1)

Biblical imagery in this new *Book of Job* is no mere chance. Edgar says that he will with his "nakedness out-face / The winds and persecutions of the sky." (II.iii) This theme returns obstinately, and with an equal consistency:

> I' th' last night's storm I such a fellow saw,
> Which made me think a man a worm.
> (IV.iv)

A downfall means suffering and torment. It may be a physical or spiritual torment, or both. Lear will lose his wits; Kent will be put in the stocks; Gloucester will have his eyes gouged out and will attempt suicide. For a man to become naked, or rather to become nothing but man, it is not enough to deprive him of his name, social position and character. One must also maim and massacre him both morally and physically. Turn him – like King Lear – into a "ruin'd piece of nature", and only then ask him who he is. For it is the new Renaissance Job who is to judge the events on "Macbeth's stage".

A Polish critic, Andrzej Falkiewicz, has observed this process of maiming and mutilating man, not in Shakespeare, but in modern literature and drama.[5] He compares it to the peeling of an onion. One takes off the husk, and then peels the layers of onion one by one. Where does an onion end and what is in its core? The blind man is a man, the madman is a man, the doting old man is a man. Man and nothing but man. A nobody, who suffers, tries to give his suffering a meaning or nobility, who revolts or accepts his suffering, and who must die.

> O gods! Who is't can say 'I am at the worst'?
> I am worse than e'er I was.
> …
> And worse I may be yet. The worst is not
> So long as we can say 'This is the worst.'
> (IV.i)

Vladimir and Estragon talk to each other in a very similar fashion. They gibber, but in that gibber there are remnants of the same eschatology:

Vladimir: We're in no danger of ever thinking any more.
Estragon: Then what are we complaining about?
Vladimir: Thinking is not the worst.
Estragon: Perhaps not. But at least there's that.

Vladimir:	That what?
Estragon:	That's the idea, let's ask each other questions.
Vladimir:	What do you mean, at least there's that?
Estragon:	That much less misery.
Vladimir:	True.
Estragon:	Well? If we gave thanks for our mercies?
Vladimir:	What is terrible is to *have* thought.

(*Waiting for Godot*, ii)

Pozzo is proud and pompous when in the first part of *Waiting for Godot* he leads on a rope the starving Lucky. Their relation is still that of master and servant, the exploiter and the exploited. When they appear for the second time Pozzo is blind and Lucky is dumb. They are still joined by the same rope. But now they are just two men.

'Tis the time's plague when madmen lead the blind. (iv.i)

Almost like in Breughel's famous picture, Edgar is leading the blind Gloucester to the precipice at Dover. This is just the theme of *Endgame*; Beckett was the first to see it in *King Lear*; he eliminated all action, everything external, and repeated it in its skeleton form.

Clov cannot sit down, the blind Hamm cannot get up, moves only in his wheel-chair, and passes water only by means of a catheter. Nell and Nagg have "lost their shanks" and are almost breathing their last in dustbins. But Hamm continues to be the master, and his wheel-chair brings to mind a throne. In the London production he was dressed in a faded purple gown and wiped his face with a blood-red handkerchief. He was, like King Lear, a degraded and powerless tyrant, a "ruin'd piece of nature". He was a King Lear in the scene in Act IV, where Lear meets the blind Gloucester and after a great frantic monologue gives the order that one of his shoes be taken off, as it pinches him. It is the same pinching shoe that one of the clowns in *Waiting for Godot* will take off at the beginning of the scene.

This is the cruel and mocking "peeling of an onion", Shakespearean and modern alike. The onion is peeled to the very last, to the suffering "nothing". This is the theme of the fall. The concept of man has been reduced and all situations have shrunk to the one ultimate, total and concentrated human fate. To Vladimir's question "What is in this bag?", the blind Pozzo replies: "Sand". Clov in *Endgame* lifts the lid of the dustbin to find out what is happening to Nagg. "He's crying," he reports. To this Hamm replies: "Then he's living."

He's crying, then he's living. English critics have regarded it as Beckett's reply to the Cartesian formula of man, which was in itself a reduction of the theological formula. But in fact Beckett simply repeats after Shakespeare:

> ... We came crying hither; ...
>
> ...
>
> When we are born, we cry that we are come
> To this great stage of fools.

(iv.vi)

The world is real, and the shoe really pinches. Suffering is also real. But the gesture with which the ruin of a man demands that his pinching shoe be taken off is ridiculous. Just as ridiculous as blind Gloucester's somersault on the flat empty stage.

The Biblical Job, too, is the ruin of a man. But this ruin constantly talks to God. He curses, imprecates, blasphemes. Ultimately he admits that God is right. He has justified his sufferings and ennobled them. He included them in the metaphysical and absolute order. The *Book of Job* is a theatre of the priests. Whereas in both Shakespearean and Beckettian *Endgames* the *Book of Job* is performed by clowns. But here, too, the gods are invoked throughout by all the characters; by Lear, Gloucester, Kent, even Albany:

> *King Lear:* By Jupiter, I swear no!
> *Kent:* By Juno, I swear ay!
> (ii.vi)

At first gods have Greek names. Then they are only gods, great and terrifying judges high above, who are supposed to intervene sooner or later. But the gods do not intervene. They are silent. Gradually the tone becomes more and more ironical. The ruin of a man invoking God is ever more ridiculous. The action becomes more and more cruel, but at the same time assumes a more and more clownish character:

> By the kind gods, 'tis most ignobly done
> To pluck me by the beard.
> (iii.vii)

Defeat, suffering, cruelty have a meaning even when gods are cruel. Even then. It is the last theological chance to justify suffering. The Biblical Job knew about it well when he called on God:

> If the scourge slay suddenly, he will laugh at the trial of the innocent. (*Book of Job*, ix, 23)

From the just God, one can still appeal to the unjust God. Says Gloucester after his eyes have been gouged out:

> As flies to wanton boys are we to th' gods.
> They kill us for their sport.
> (iv.i)

But as long as gods exist, all can yet be saved:

> Hearken unto this, O Job: stand still, and consider the wondrous works of God.
> (*Book of Job*, xxxvii, 14)

The Bible is Beckett's favourite reading. After all, the passage sounds like the dialogue in *Endgame*:

Clov: They said to me, Here's the place, raise your head and look at all that beauty. That order! They said to me, Come now you're not a brute beast, think upon these things and you'll see how all becomes clear. And simple! They said to me, What skilled attention they get, all these dying of their wounds.

Hamm: Enough!

Clov: I say to myself – sometimes, Clov, you must learn to suffer better than that if you want them to weary of punishing you. I say to myself – sometimes, Clov, you must be their better than if you want them to let you go – one day.

(pp. 50–1)

Clov is a clown, but he is more unhappy than Hamm. Clov's gabble is still eschatological, just as Lucky's in *Waiting for Godot*. In this dialogue of "human ruins" Hamm alone has realized the folly of all suffering. He has one reply to make to eschatology: "Take it easy … Peace to our … arses". Both couples: Pozzo who has been made blind, and Lucky who has been made dumb, on the one hand, Hamm who cannot get up, and Clov who cannot sit down, on the other, have been taken from the Endgame of *King Lear*:

King Lear: Read.
Gloucester: What, with the case of eyes?
           …
King Lear: What, art mad? A man may see how the world goes with no eyes. Look with thine ears.

(IV.vi)

These are Biblical parables. The blind see clearly, madmen tell the truth. After all, they are all mad. "There are four of them" – writes Camus – "one by profession, one by choice, two by the suffering they have been through. They are four torn bodies, four unfathomable faces of the same fate."[6] The Fool accompanies Lear on the cold night of madness; Edgar takes the blind Gloucester through a grotesque suicide. Lear's invocations on the gods are countered by the Fool's scatological jokes; Gloucester's prayers by Edgar's clownish demonology:

Frateretto calls me, and tells me Nero is an angler in the lake of darkness. Pray, innocent, and beware the foul fiend …
The foul fiend bites my back … Purr! the cat is gray. (III.vi)

But Edgar's demonology is no more than a parody, a travesty of contemporary Egyptian dream books and books on witchcraft; a great and brutal gibe, in fact. He gibes at himself, at Job, conversing with God. For above "Job's stage", there is in *King Lear* only "Macbeth's stage". On it people murder, butcher and torture one another, commit adultery and fornication, divide kingdoms. From the point of view of a Job who has ceased to talk to God, they are clowns. Clowns who do not yet know they are clowns.

King Lear: … Come, come, I am a king;
              My masters, know you that?
Gentleman: You are a royal one, and we obey you.

King Lear: Then there's life in't. Nay, an you get it, you shall get it by running. Sa, sa, sa, sa!

(iv.vi)

The zero hour has come. Lear has come to understand it at last. Just as blind Hamm came to understand everything, although he was bound to his wheel-throne. And Pozzo, when he turned blind and fell over his sand-filled bags:

Pozzo: I woke up one fine day as blind as Fortune ...
Vladimir: And when was that?
Pozzo: I don't know ... Don't question me! The blind have no notion of time. The things of time are hidden from them too.

(*Waiting for Godot,* ii)

And this is how King Lear ends his final frantic tirade:

No rescue? What, a prisoner? I am even
The natural fool of fortune.

(iv.vi)

In a moment he will run off the stage. Before that happens he will ask for his pinching shoe to be taken off. He is clown now, so he can afford to do this. On "Job's stage" four clowns have performed the old medieval *sotie* about the decay and fall of the world. But in both Shakespearean and Beckettian *Endgames* it is the modern world that fell; the Renaissance world, and ours. Accounts have been settled in a very similar way.

Notes

1   See R. Speaight, *Nature in Shakespearean Tragedy,* London, 1955.
2   E. Ionesco, "*Expérience du théâtre,*" *Nouvelle Revue Française,* February 1958.
3   All quotations from Beckett are given in the author's own translation. Page references in quotations from *Endgame* and *Act Without Words* apply to the Faber & Faber edition of 1958.
4   Compare the analysis of this scene in G. Wilson Knight's most original study of the grotesque elements in *King Lear* (treated somewhat differently from in my essay): " 'King Lear' and the Comedy of the Grotesque," in *The Wheel of Fire,* London, 1957.
5   A. Falkiewicz, "Theatrical Experiment of the Fifties," *Dialog,* No. 9, 1959 (in Polish).
6   A. Camus, *Le Mythe de Sisyphe,* Paris, 1942.

13

The Cheapening of the Stage

Anne Righter [Barton]

1 Pessimism and Pride

Straightforward assertions that the world resembles a stage populated by a multi-tude of actors are fairly common in Elizabethan and Jacobean drama. Usually, passages of this sort are deliberately moralistic in tone, little philosophical disquisitions during which the action of the play comes to a halt around the speaker. Shakespeare provides two examples of this extended, formal type of play metaphor: Jaques's famous observation that 'All the world's a stage' (*As You Like It*, ii.vii.139–40), and the meditative comment of Antonio in the opening moments of *The Merchant of Venice*:

> I hold the world but as the world, Gratiano –
> A stage, where every man must play a part,
> And mine a sad one.
> > (*The Merchant of Venice*, i.i.77–9)

In neither case is the reflection cheerful. Jaques is a professional pessimist concerned to point out the bitter comedy of man's progression from swaddling clothes to shroud. Antonio is in the grip of a curious melancholy for which there appears to be no rational cause.

A sense of futility, of the vanity or folly of human ambition, is characteristic of all meditative Elizabethan comparisons of the world to a stage. Even at their most cheerful, such descriptions manage to mock the seriousness of man's pursuits, to point out the somehow ludicrous nature of his perpetual activity. The host of the Light Heart in Jonson's *The New Inne* (1629) possesses a disposition far more sanguine than that of Jaques. He is, however, equally eccentric in his refusal to participate in life any more actively than as a spectator.

> I imagine all the world's a Play;
> The state, and mens affaires, all passages
> Of life, to spring new scenes, come in, goe out,
> And shift, and vanish; and if I have got
> A seat, to sit at ease here, i'mine Inne,
> To see the Comedy: and laugh and chuck
> At the variety and throng of humours,
> And dispositions that come iustling in,
> And out still, as they one droue hence another:
> Why, will you enuy me my happinesse?[1]

The man who consciously sits apart from the play cannot share the earnestness of the actors. All plots are comic; all the characters are essentially clowns. A certain sense of superiority attaches itself to the spectator–philosopher, whether he is the neo-Pythagorean of Edwardes's *Damon and Pithias*, or the 'splenatiue Philosopher' of Chapman's *Revenge of Bussy D'Ambois* who stands aside to mark the humours of mankind, and laughs, judging that 'all these presentments were only maskeries, and wore false faces.'[2]

Ideas of deceit and disguise often contribute to the melancholy and sober morality of what Democritus referred to as the Κόσμος σκηνη. The White Queen's Pawn in Middleton's *A Game at Chess* (1624) prefaces her admonitions to the Black Bishop's Pawn with the reminder that 'the world's a stage on which all parts are play'd',[3] and proceeds from that point to a most eloquent and stern discourse upon proper casting and the costume suitable for each role. Even Doll, in *Northward Ho!* is unwontedly serious as she reflects:

> The world's a stage, from which strange shapes we borrow;
> Today we are honest, and ranke knaves tomorrow.[4]

In the induction to Marston's *Antonio and Mellida* (1599), the boy actors discuss the nature of their parts in the moment before the play begins. 'Not play two parts in one? away, away: 'tis common fashion. Nay if you cannot bear two subtle fronts under one hood, Ideot goe by, goe by; off this world's stage.'[5]

Middleton's *A Faire Quarrell* (? 1615–17) and the anonymous *Valiant Welshman* both open with prologues built upon the idea that 'this megacosm, this great world, is no more than a stage, where every one must act his part'.[6] The Middleton prologue reaches the same conclusion as Raleigh's famous lyric 'What Is Our Life?': 'All have exits, and must all be stript in the tiring house (viz. the grave), for none must carry any thing out of the stock.'[7] Most elaborate of all is the mournful, if somewhat mechanical, dialogue of Studioso and Philomusmus in *The Second Part of the Return from Parnassus* (1598–1602).

Philomusmus:	Sad is the plott, sad the Catastrophe.
Studioso:	Sad are the Chorus in our Tragedy.
Philomusmus:	And rented thoughts continuall actors bee.
Studioso:	Woe is the subject:
Philomusmus:	Earth the loathed stage,
	Whereupon we act this fained personage.
Studioso:	Mossy barbarians the spectators be,
	That sit and laugh at our calamity.[8]

Here, of course, the 'fained personage' refers, not to any disguise deliberately assumed by the two scholars, nor to a deceit practised by them, but to the depressing position they occupy in a world stubbornly insensible of their merits. Another version of this idea appears, far more movingly, in the words of Webster's Duchess of Malfi just after she has been persuaded of the death of Antonio and her children.

> I account this world a tedious Theatre,
> For I doe play a part in't 'gainst my will.[9]

She is an unwilling prisoner in the drama of existence: 'Fortune seems only to have her eyesight to behold my tragedy.'[10]

All of these formal, contemplative likenings of the world to a stage are consciously literary. They descend from the oldest play metaphors of all, those traditional, gener-alized images which from the time of Plato had been commonplace in non-dramatic literature. Pagan or Christian, they had always been pessimistic. Both Palladas and John of Salisbury used the comparison to stress the empty, ephemeral nature of life on earth. St John Chrysostom in the fourth century stated that 'life is as it were a play and a dream, for as on the stage when the curtain is closed the shifting shadows are dissolved, and as with the flashing light dreams are dispelled, so in the coming consummation all things will be dissolved and will vanish away'.[11] The world and its inhabitants are unreal and illusory, without permanent value.

Descriptions of the cosmic stage in the drama of Shakespeare and his contemporaries betray their alliance with this ancient tradition not only by their uniform melancholy, but also by the fact that they tend to separate themselves slightly from the structure of the plays in which they appear. Other kinds of play metaphor are inseparable from the specific dramatic situations which call them forth. Built deeply into the structure of the scene itself, they illustrate in a quite three-dimensional manner the fact that life imitates the theatre. Descriptions of the cosmic stage, on the other hand, tend to be curiously non-dramatic, flourishes of eloquence on the surface of the play which present certain rhetorical statements about the nature of man's life. They may sometimes be valuable as a means of setting forth a character's attitude towards the world in which he lives, as in the case of Jaques, but essentially they are functional only in the sense that, like all play images, they help define the Elizabethan relationship of actors and audience.

It is possible to regard the contemplative image as a means of enhancing the actor's dignity. Thomas Heywood used it to justify the theatre in his poem introducing the *Apology for Actors*. After running through a whole series of comparisons between life and the drama, Heywood concludes:

> He that denyes then Theaters should be,
> He may as well deny a world to me.[12]

It is a spirited attack upon Puritan slanders of the theatre, but the image it employs is essentially double-edged. All too easily, it can become not a means of glorifying the stage but an expression of its utter futility and negation. If the world of the audience is itself a semblance and a mockery, what is one to think of the play, the imitation of an imitation? The final attitude of Macbeth, the passionate reduction of all human endeavour to the meaningless posturing of a player on a darkening stage, is scarcely flattering to the theatre. Such an image expresses not only the hollowness of life, but also the degradation and stupidity of the actor's profession.

The ideas of disorder, futility, and pride which came to surround the actor and the play in Shakespeare's work after *Hamlet* were all, of course, traditional in the history of the theatre itself. Since late Roman times, the actor's profession had been both precarious and far from respectable. A man who had abandoned his proper place in God's scheme of order, destroying the perfect hierarchy of social position, he represented an element of disorder in medieval society. Those actors in the craft cycles who deserted their trade for the professional stage invoked the wrath of more than one English moralist. As late as 1582, Gosson was still reflecting a common objection to the actors when he affirmed sourly that 'most of the players have been either men of occupations which they have forsaken to live by playing, or common minstrels, or trained up from their childhood to this abominable exercise and have now no other way to get their living'.[13]

The pride of the players seems to have been a subject of common remark from early Elizabethan times. In Marlowe's *Edward II* (c. 1592), the king's soldiers in their gorgeous dress are described as marching 'like players, with garish robes, not armor'.[14] Studioso in *The Second Part of the Return from Parnassus* complains that

> England affords these glorious vagabonds,
> That carried earst their fardels on their backes,
> Coursers to ride on through the gazing streetes,
> Swooping it in their glaring Satten sutes,
> And Pages to attend their maisterships.[15]

The War of the Theatres, of course, provides abundant and rancorous testimony along these lines. In the strife between poets and players, the arrogance and pretension of the latter, together with their brilliant plumage, was constantly being attacked. Typically, the player Histrio in Jonson's *Poetaster* is momentarily mistaken for a great lord as 'he stalkes by there',[16] but is humiliated by the outraged Tucca after his true identity has been discovered.

Jonson's plays are filled with carping remarks about the theatre. Yet they reflect an attitude of distaste quite different from the one characteristic of Shakespeare after 1600. Jonson's numerous attacks upon the stage are almost invariably specific and topical. He lashes out not, like Shakespeare, at the whole concept of imitation, the idea of the play, but merely at the particular circumstances under which he is forced to write. It is the stupidity of those audiences who rejected plays like *The New Inne*, the crude objections of certain loud but virtually illiterate critics, the wilful mismanagement of his lines by players more concerned to win applause for themselves than for the performance as a whole, and the degenerate taste of the age in general which Jonson mourns.

> Make not thyself a page
> To that strumpet the stage;
> But sing high and aloof,
> Safe from the wolf's black jaw, and the dull ass's hoof.[17]

It is not the theatre itself which he rejects, but only its immediate conditions, conditions which he despairs of altering.

Shakespeare's disillusionment with the stage is of an altogether different kind. It is the whole conception of the play, of something imitated, reproduced at second hand, which seems to disgust him. The actor is a man who cheapens life by the act of dramatizing it; the shadows represented on the stage are either corrupt or totally without value, 'signifying nothing'. Only John Marston among Shakespeare's contemporaries seems to have shared this generalized, all-embracing sense of the futility of the actor's profession. The plays of Marston are filled with comments on the stage. Some of them bear directly upon the struggle between the public and the private theatres. Others, however, attack the very idea of the actor, and his whole relationship with reality. Almost invariably in Marston's work, a character who expresses sentiments which seem false and artificial, who behaves in a pretentious or affected manner, is compared scornfully with the players. Sophonisba, in the play which bears her name (1606), proudly declines a display of passion.

> I should now curse the gods
> Call on the Furies; stamp the patient earth
> Cleave my streachd cheeks with sound; speak from all sense
> But loud and full of players eloquence.[18]

Earlier in the play, another character draws an equally unflattering distinction between reality and the falsehood of the theatre.

> Although a stagelike passion and weake heate
> Full of an empty wording might suit age,
> Know Ile speake strongly truth.[19]

Antonio's Revenge (1602) contains a contemptuous dismissal of 'apish action, player-like',[20] a reference to the 'forced passion of affected straines'[21] characteristic of the tragedian, and a comment upon the ludicrous incongruity between the boy actor and the part he plays. In *The Insatiate Countess* (c. 1610), a character declares that henceforth he will even believe in 'a Player's passion'[22] sooner than a woman's faith. Quadratus, in *What You Will* (1601), ridicules his companion's vow to be revenged with the query, 'How pree-thee? in a Play?'[23]

2   Dark Comedies and 'Troilus'

It is a commonplace of Elizabethan and Jacobean studies that with the turn of the century there came a pronounced darkening in the temper of the age. The Essex plot, the ageing of the Queen and the uncertainties of the succession, a general sense that society was corrupt and life itself running down, losing its energy and freshness: all of these things contributed to a new atmosphere of pessimism, a loss of faith in the world and in human abilities. This sense of gloom had many theatrical repercussions. Tragedy acquired a growing importance while, at the same time, the melancholy of Jaques, the irrational depression of Antonio, no longer mere eccentricities, moved into the centre of the stage. This pessimism in the air drew at least some of its gloomy sustenance from the contemplative play image. Thomas Nashe in a play published in 1600 contrasted 'Heaven is our heritage' with 'Earth but a player's stage',[24] and Sir Walter Raleigh, about the same time, summarized human existence as a play with no meaning or reality until its end. A lugubrious little poem by an anonymous writer, published in *A Book of Airs* in 1601, announces that

> All our pride is but a jest;
> None are worst and none are best.
> Grief and joy and hope and fear
> Play their pageants everywhere;
> Vain opinion all doth sway,
> And the world is but a play.[25]

Clearly, Shakespeare's own shift in attitude towards the theatre and its associations takes some of its colour from this background, this alteration in the metaphorical climate. It is influenced too by the general darkening of plot and subject-matter characteristic of the 'problem comedies' and the great tragedies. It is difficult not to feel, however, that some obscure but quite personal disgust with the London theatre and with the practice of the actor's and the dramatist's craft also lies behind this change. The sonnets testify – although in a reticent, enigmatic fashion – to a dissatisfaction connected somehow with the stage.

> Alas, 'tis true I have gone here and there
> And made myself a motley to the view,
> Gor'd mine own thought, sold cheap what is most dear,
> Made old offences of affections new.
> (Sonnet 110, 1–4)

Another cry of exasperation sounds in the following sonnet.

> O, for my sake do you with Fortune chide,
> The guilty goddess of my harmful deeds,
> That did not better for my life provide
> Than public means which public manners breeds.
> Thence comes it that my name receives a brand,
> And almost thence my nature is subdu'd
> To what it works in, like the dyer's hand.
> (Sonnet 111, 1–7)

The Chorus speeches of *Henry V*, with their insistence upon the gap between reality and the pretensions of illusion, the poverty of resource of the stage, give perhaps the first warning of an attitude towards the theatre which was to emerge far more fully in succeeding plays. A kind of mock humility, a studied obeisance to the all-powerful audience, certainly plays its part in those references to the 'flat unraised spirits', the 'unworthy scaffold', the 'huge and proper life' of things beyond the scope of any 'wooden O', even as it does in the epilogue's description of Shakespeare's 'rough and all-unable pen'. Yet there is a restlessness in these formal apologies and invocations to the imagination of the audience to 'force a play' which strikes a new and not altogether cheerful note. In a sense, these Chorus passages seem to point beyond the noble actors of *Hamlet* or *Julius Caesar* to the 'strutting player' of *Troilus and Cressida* and *Macbeth*, to a period when Shakespeare, his faith in the power of illusion seemingly gone, would turn to the exploration of resemblances between the world and the stage which were negative and curiously grim.

This decline in the dignity of the theatre seems properly to begin with *All's Well That Ends Well*. At first sight, Parolles would appear to belong to that familiar Shakespearean class of fools who are tripped by an undeclared play. Yet the 'dialogue between the Fool and the Soldier' (iv.iii.93) which serves to humiliate Parolles is almost more painful than amusing. Nor does it possess, except for this one rather dubious reference to 'dialogue', any of those direct associations with the theatre characteristic of the equivalent scenes in *Twelfth Night, Much Ado About Nothing*, or *The Merry Wives of Windsor*. It is around Parolles himself, in fact, the poor dupe rather than the clever plotters who strip him of his disguise, that the play references collect.

Like Ancient Pistol, Parolles is a man who has played a part in life, who has sheltered behind a noble mask. Long before the comedy opens, he has assumed in some tiring-house of the imagination the costume of a fashionable but gallant warrior. Unlike Pistol, however, the real Parolles is not concealed very effectively by the role he has chosen. Almost all the other characters of *All's Well That Ends Well*, including Helena, are aware from the beginning of the disparity between the true and the pretended Parolles. It is only Bertram, whose inability to recognize genuine worth when he sees it is axiomatic in the comedy, who accepts his verbose follower for the man he seems to be.

In the second act of the play, Lafeu warns Bertram that 'there can be no kernel in this light nut; the soul of this man is his clothes' (ii.v.42). This image of Parolles as an actor in costume, gorgeous on the surface but tawdry within, is repeated just before the ambush itself by one of the French lords: 'When his disguise and he is parted, tell me what a sprat you shall find him' (iii.vi.95–6). Parolles is twice described as a 'counterfeit' by the lords engaged in exposing the truth behind the mask, and the disillusioned Count of Rousillon is finally forced to agree, referring to his follower as 'this counterfeit module' (iii.vi; iv.iii.94). The term possesses, in all three instances, the double meaning of 'actor' and 'false'. Parolles himself, despite his dependence upon the theatre, uses it as a means of expressing contempt. Asked to assess Captain Dumain's skill in war, he can think of no surer way of degrading his fellow-officer than by suggesting that the latter's experience has been confined to leading 'the drum before the English tragedians' (iv.iii.248). By the end of the comedy, Parolles's grandiose role has been completely destroyed. He has 'played the knave with Fortune' (v.ii.28) and been detected in his deceit. Reluctantly, he embraces his real self, something Ancient Pistol never did, renouncing the frail prop of illusion. 'Simply the thing I am / Shall make me live' (iv.iii.310–11).

The only actor in *All's Well That Ends Well* beside Parolles is Helena herself. In her disguise as a pilgrim to Saint Jaques le Grand, she might seem at first sight to belong to a familiar Shakespearean tradition of heroines who play a part. Yet her role is strikingly different in character from the clever, light-hearted disguises of Julia and Rosalind,

Jessica and Viola, disguises which in themselves had represented powerful and effective weapons, triumphs of illusion. Helena's disguise is negative, a symbol of death. She regards it as such herself, and so do the other people of the play, even Diana and the widow of Florence who know that from this death, paradoxically, life will spring. When she reveals herself at the end of the play, her first words are to deny the King's 'Is't real that I see?'

> No, my good lord;
> 'Tis but the shadow of a wife you see,
> The name and not the thing.
> (*All's Well That Ends Well*, v.iii.300–2)

As G. K. Hunter points out in the New Arden edition of the play, the word 'shadow', that familiar associate of the actor's, here signifies ghost and imitation together.[26] Only Bertram's 'Both, both; O, pardon!' (v.iii.302) can confer a palpable existence upon Helena, freeing her at the same time from illusion and non-being.

This tendency to regard disguise as a state of negation and symbolic death, an image of nothingness, recurs strongly in *King Lear*. It also casts certain doubts upon the 'Christ-like' nature of 'the old fantastical Duke of dark corners' in *Measure for Measure* (iv.iii.154). The theatre fares no better in the second of the dark comedies than it had in the first. It appears first of all in connexion with the Player King. The Duke expresses his distrust of the adulation of the crowd, and those who encourage such displays, in theatrical terms.

> I love the people,
> But do not like to stage me to their eyes;
> Though it do well, I do not relish well
> Their loud applause and Aves vehement;
> Nor do I think the man of safe discretion
> That does affect it.
> (*Measure for Measure*, i.i.68–73)

He objects to the dramatic elements inherent in the nature of kingship. Angelo also evokes the imagery of the Player King, a comparison which refers both to the fact that he is the 'figure' of the absent Duke, 'dress'd ... with our love' (i.i.17, 20), and to the hollowness of his apparent moral perfection.

Angelo is a 'seemer', as the Duke suspects and Isabella soon discovers, an 'outward-sainted deputy' (i.iii.54; ii.iv.150; iii.i.90). But the idea of the play reaches beyond him to associate itself with more general themes of the inconsequence and foolish pretension of human authority.

> O place, O form,
> How often dost thou with thy case, thy habit,
> Wrench awe from fools, and tie the wiser souls
> To thy false seeming!
> (*Measure for Measure*, ii.iv.12–15)

Isabella also manages to speak of the vanity of office in terms which suggest the theatre.

> But man, proud man,
> Dress'd in a little brief authority,
> Most ignorant of what he's most assur'd,
> His glassy essence, like an angry ape,
> Plays such fantastic tricks before high heaven
> As makes the angels weep ...
> (*Measure for Measure*, ii.ii.117–22)

The passage conjures up one of the most traditional of all play metaphors, the image of the world as a stage displaying the endless drama of human life for the benefit of a heavenly audience. For Isabella, however, this drama is anything but admirable, or even necessary. The costumes are a source of groundless pride; the furious gestures of the players resemble the senseless imitations of apes. In her eyes, man's resemblance to the actor is precisely what degrades him.

The Duke himself, as critics committed to his deification have often pointed out, occupies in the comedy the position of an actor–dramatist – of more or less heavenly nature – arranging a play. In order to test the saintly Angelo, he solicits instruction in 'How I may formally in person bear me / Like a true friar' (i.iii.47–8), and obliterates his identity as a ruler beneath a holy habit. The action is in itself suspicious. The Duke of *Measure for Measure* must stand quite alone, in an isolation both uncomfortable in itself and alien to Shakespeare's general practice, if this move is not to summon up the usual identification with the Player King, with all its implications of error or imperfection. Even Henry V had approached the condition of a Player King the night before Agincourt, when the turbulence and uncertainty of his thoughts drove him to walk in disguise among the common soldiers. Richard II, Henry IV, Prince Hal, Claudius, Macbeth, King Lear, Antonio, and Sebastian: it is an inescapable procession. A certain truth shines through Lucio's slanders when he tells the supposed friar that 'It was a mad fantastical trick' of the Duke's, 'to steal from the state and usurp the beggary he was never born to' (iii.ii.86–8).

In its actual working out, the Duke's managerial role flatters neither himself nor the theatre. The action he contrives continually seems to escape from his control. Angelo comes within a hair's-breadth of bringing the whole scheme to disaster when he unexpectedly, and treacherously, hastens Claudio's execution despite the fact that the supposed Isabella has fulfilled her part of the bargain. This is not the way things were planned, and the Duke is momentarily taken aback. Juliet and Barnardine check him too, in their different ways. The Duke is committed to the idea of life as a thing poised and susceptible to rule, material for regulation. But *Measure for Measure* as a whole denies such rigidity, such artificial judgement and simplification of the intractable, haphazard phenomena of experience. As law-giver and dramatist, the Duke is continually mortified by interruption and surprise. Juliet, superb and individual in her perfect awareness of both the nature of her fault and its consequences, cuts off his unnecessary and imperceptive sermon in mid-sentence (ii.iii.30–5); the recalcitrant prisoner Barnardine is even less willing to fit in with the formal, dramatic action which has been planned.

Barnardine:	I swear I will not die to-day for any man's persuasion.
Duke:	But hear you –
Barnardine:	Not a word; if you have anything to say to me, come to my ward; for thence will not I to-day.

(Measure for Measure, iv.iii.56–9)

He turns on his heel and departs, and although the Duke rather helplessly describes this unwilling corpse in the next lines as 'Unfit to live or die' (iv.iii.60), it seems doubtful, particularly in view of Barnardine's survival and pardon at the end of the play, that Shakespeare thought his reluctance to go to the block at a moment convenient for the Duke's purposes altogether despicable.

The incorrigible Lucio, a disorderly mixture of generosity and vice, is even more troublesome. He haunts the disguised Duke like a devoted spirit, breathing into his ear all the calumny and gossip which this temporary abdication of power, this resort to disguise, has made possible. Lucio is like an unruly extempore actor crept without permission into the Duke's tidy Morality drama. His irreverent voice rings through, and questions, the most solemn scenes, running counter to the princely dramatist's will and plans. The Duke cannot silence him, any more than Angelo in all the cold majesty of his role as judge could suppress Pompey's distracting account of Mistress Elbow's longing for stewed prunes earlier in the comedy. Only the patient, intuitive justice of Escalus had been able to disentangle the affairs of the bawd, the constable, and Master Froth.

Lucio is particularly active and provoking in the final scene of *Measure for Measure*, just at the point where the Duke's manipulation of human action and emotion seems most grandiose and cold. Again and again, he interrupts this elaborate show, this preordained and somewhat unnecessary process of revelation, infuriating the Duke – and amusing the theatre audience. He must be shouted down if the plot is to proceed as planned. Lucio has been the Duke's proper scourge, even as Isabella in a different sense was Angelo's. He has been used throughout the comedy to reveal and attack the Duke's weak points, his pride, his vanity of reputation, and his desire to stage-manage a reality too turbulent and complex to submit to such artificial confinement.

Measure for Measure is a play which suggests the futility of rigid, systematized judgements of human conduct. The events of the play serve to advance Angelo and Isabella in self-knowledge, to destroy their narrow, inflexible ideas about life. The Duke is 'like pow'r divine' (v.i.367) inasmuch as he is a ruler, 'God's substitute, / His deputy anointed in His sight' (*Richard II*, i.ii.37–8), but this identification does not exempt him from human frailty, or from change. At the end, returned to his proper position in the state, he pardons Angelo and Barnardine, remits his excessive and vindictive death sentence passed upon Lucio, and prepares to take Isabella to wife. For him, as for Angelo and Isabella, a process of education has been happily concluded. It is characteristic of Shakespeare that this education should have been committed to the lowly and sinful hands of the Pompeys, Juliets, Barnardines, and Lucios of the world, a world too various and intractable to accommodate itself to the morality of an Angelo – or to the careful dramaturgy of the Duke.

In *Measure for Measure*, the theatre is present primarily by implication, introducing itself only infrequently into the actual language of the comedy. *Troilus and Cressida*, on the other hand, is filled with theatrical imagery, all of it of a kind most unflattering to the stage. Certain parts of *Troilus and Cressida*, in fact, express an attitude which might do credit to the author of some Puritan pamphlet against the actors. Like *All's Well That Ends Well* and *Measure for Measure*, *Troilus and Cressida* associates the player with hollow pretension, negation, and pride. In addition, Shakespeare uses the theatre to express part of that great theme of disorder so important in the play as a whole. In the first long speech of Ulysses the masque or revel, always before a symbol of innocent delight, symbolizes the evils of a disordered society.

> Degree being vizarded,
> Th'unworthiest shows as fairly in the mask.
> (*Troilus and Cressida*, I.iii.83–4)

It is an idea related to Angelo's conviction that

> these black masks
> Proclaim an enshielded beauty ten times louder
> Than the beauty could, display'd.
> (*Measure for Measure*, II.iv.79–81)

The mask, the disguise, is in both cases an agent of falsehood, a distortion of truth, but the *Troilus and Cressida* passage is characteristically explicit in its theatrical meaning where Angelo's remark had been ambiguous.

A little later in the same scene, Ulysses describes the nature of the sickness which distempers all the Greek host. Achilles has retired from the war, and with him in his tent Patroclus idles, jests,

> And with ridiculous and awkward action –
> Which, slanderer, he imitation calls –
> He pageants us. Sometime, great Agamemnon,
> Thy topless deputation he puts on ...
> The large Achilles, on his press'd bed lolling,
> From his deep chest laughs out a loud applause;
> Cries, 'Excellent! 'tis Agamemnon just.
> Now play me Nestor; hem, and stroke thy beard,
> As he being drest to some oration.'
> That's done – as near as the extremest ends
> Of parallels, as like as Vulcan and his wife;
> Yet god Achilles still cries 'Excellent!
> 'Tis Nestor right. Now play him me, Patroclus,
> Arming to answer in a night alarm.'
> And then, forsooth, the faint defects of age
> Must be the scene of mirth ...
> (*Troilus and Cressida*, I.iii.149–52, 162–73)

Patroclus and Achilles stand at the centre of the evil which afflicts the Greeks, shoring up the crumbling towers of Troy. It is an evil which is expressed quite straightforwardly in terms of the theatre, of this malicious amusement of theirs which contrives to cheapen everything it touches. Old Nestor adds significantly that

> in the imitation of these twain –
> Who, as Ulysses says, opinion crowns
> With an imperial voice – many are infect.
> (*Troilus and Cressida*, i.iii.185–7)

Later in the play, Patroclus demonstrates the sport. With the aid of Thersites, who has already described him as 'a gilt counterfeit' (ii.iii.23), he constructs a mocking little play scene for the benefit of Achilles. It is 'the pageant of Ajax' (iii.iii.269), in which Thersites himself imitates that slow-witted hero and succeeds in making him look doubly ridiculous.

As early as *The Taming of the Shrew*, there had been some indication, in the sudden unexplained disappearance of Christopher Sly, that Shakespeare may have been troubled by comedians who elaborated their own parts to the detriment of the rest of the play. In *Hamlet*, he is especially stern on the subject of those clowns that speak 'more than is set down for them' (iii.ii.37). It is not until *Troilus and Cressida*, however, that the pride of the players, that theme favoured both by the Puritans and by the champions of the private theatres, appears in Shakespeare's work in a direct, almost savage fashion. Some sense of personal rancour, freed perhaps by the fact that the play may not have been designed for the public stage, seems to inform his picture of the

> strutting player whose conceit
> Lies in his hamstring, and doth think it rich
> To hear the wooden dialogue and sound
> 'Twixt his stretch'd footing and the scaffoldage –
> Such to-be-pitied and o'er-wrested seeming
> He acts thy greatness in ...
> (*Troilus and Cressida*, i.iii.153–8)

3   Tragedies

That tendency to insult the theatre which showed itself first in the dark comedies and in *Troilus and Cressida* continues in the great tragedies. In *Macbeth*, *Othello*, and *King Lear*, the actor is pursued relentlessly by images of futility and deceit. Macbeth is both an unsuccessful dissembler and a Player King. At the end he finds in the vanity and windy pretension of the 'poor player, / That struts and frets his hour upon the stage' (*Macbeth*, v.v.24–5) a symbol for the utter emptiness of man's life. It is not a comparison which honours the theatre, especially considering the fact that Macbeth goes on to suggest 'a tale told by an idiot' (v.v.26–7) as a parallel image. Nor is that familiar word 'shadow', which precedes his description of the player, of any assistance in restoring the dignity of the stage. A word traditionally associated with the actor it had, in Shakespeare's early comedies, served to express the ephemeral but charming quality of the play. Now, like the poor player himself, it signifies nothingness. Throughout *Macbeth*, the stage is a thing devoid of value, as it is in Lear's bitter evocation of the play metaphor.

> When we are born, we cry that we are come
> To this great stage of fools.
> *(King Lear, iv.vi.183–4)*

The actor retains in these tragedies the dubious distinction of providing a model for villains. Like Richard III, Macbeth and Edmund and Iago are dissemblers, men who play a false part. Yet the theatrical imagery connected with them as deceivers is not only sparser than that which surrounds Richard III, but stripped of that earlier conviction of the power of illusion. Edmund and Iago in particular convey a sense of horror, an overwhelming evil and malevolence which infects but does not really draw its strength from those theatrical associations which are present. Iago, as he declares himself, is not a man whose 'outward action doth demonstrate / The native act and figure' of his heart (*Othello*, i.i.62–3). He has recourse to the traditional 'play the part' idiom in his mocking, 'And what's he, then, that says I play the villain?' (ii.iii.325), and he announces that

> When devils will their blackest sins put on,
> They do suggest at first with heavenly shows,
> As I do now.
> *(Othello, ii.iii.340–42)*

His success, however, unlike Richard's, is not the triumph of the play masquerading as reality. Iago's abilities as an actor are far less important than his generalized will to destroy, the implacable nature of his resentment and the inexplicable fact of its alliance with Fate.

In the dark, chaotic world of *Othello*, full of the irrational movement of crowds, of wind, water, and the heavenly bodies themselves, a world which dwarfs and baffles the characters of the tragedy, illusion tends to be both powerless and unpleasant. Of the Turkish pretence of an attack upon Rhodes, the first senator says wisely: ''Tis a pageant / To keep us in false gaze' (i.iii.18–19). Iago describes Cassio's courteous attentions to Desdemona as 'an index and obscure prologue to the history of lust and foul thoughts' (ii.i.252–3) and the lieutenant himself as a fool 'apt to play the sir' (ii.i.170). Women in general are for Iago 'players' in their housewifery (ii.i.111), a word which in its context suggests acting, gambling, and frivolity, a deliberately diffuse set of connotations repeated a few lines later in the riddling 'You rise to play and go to bed to work' (ii.i.115). Othello's pretence in Act Four, Scene Two that he is a libertine visiting Desdemona the harlot and Emilia her bawd represents, in effect, a kind of ghastly play within the play.

Edmund's villainies are even less theatrical than Iago's. At one point only do they evoke a play image. Just before he begins to work upon the trusting Edgar, Edmund remarks with amusement: 'Pat! He comes like the catastrophe of the old comedy. My cue is villainous melancholy, with a sigh like Tom o'Bedlam' (*King Lear*, i.ii.128–30). Deceit and an awareness of the playlike appropriateness of Edgar's entrance just at this moment both inform Edmund's comparison. For the most part, however, the play metaphor appears in connexion with Lear and his faithful followers, and always as an expression of futility or despair. In his hopeless role as Player King, Lear is assisted by two characters in disguise, Kent and Edgar. For both of them, as for Helena in *All's Well That Ends Well*, the assumption of costume and a false identity is negative, a symbol of death. Kent's initial refusal to dissimulate in the matter of Cordelia's loyalty and love forces him, with bitter irony, into another kind of dissembling. The necessity for the adoption of disguise, of false identity, in order to remain oneself is one of the most painful paradoxes of *King Lear*. Edgar's role as poor Tom calls out a familiar reference to 'counterfeiting' (iii.vi.60), as well as the heartfelt 'Bad is the trade that must play fool to sorrow, / Ang'ring itself and others' (iv.i.39–40). As the Bedlam beggar, Edgar's is 'a semblance / That very dogs disdain'd' (v.iii.187–8), a shape so close to that of a beast that it is only a little better than being nothing at all (ii.iii.21). Gradually, his parts improve; the man whose name and identity are lost climbs up the scale of illusion from poor Tom, 'The lowest and most dejected thing of fortune' (iv.i.3), to the sane if 'most poor' peasant (iv.vi.223) who kills Oswald, and afterward to the nameless knight who overcomes Edmund, and, by this act, is able to regain his true identity at last.

Timon of Athens is marked by a curious strain of contempt for shadows, shows, imitations of all kinds, even for the clothes men wear. The masque of Amazons introduced in the first act evokes images of vanity and hypocrisy, the unnatural and depraved (i.ii). To the Poet and the Painter, come to visit him in his solitude, Timon addresses words of scorn which somehow reach beyond the two sycophants before him to attack the idea of *mimesis* itself.

> Good honest men! Thou draw'st a counterfeit
> Best in all Athens. Th'art indeed the best;
> Thou counterfeit'st most lively.
> (*Timon of Athens*, v.i.78–80)

The play upon the word 'counterfeit', a virtual synonym for the actor as well as for falsehood, is familiar from Shakespeare's early work, but not this accompanying sense of the corruption, the dishonesty of art. The Poet and the Painter are liars, not merely in their weather-vane attitudes towards their patron, but by the very nature of the crafts they practise. The Painter describes his own work archly as 'a pretty mocking of the life' (i.i.38). To Timon's question, 'Wrought he not well that painted it?' (i.i.198), Apemantus returns sourly: 'He wrought better that made the painter; and yet he's but a filthy piece of work' (i.i.199–201). Nature is vile, but its imitations are even worse. Later in the same scene, Apemantus seems to undo Sidney's defence of poetry in denying the poet any moral dignity and reducing him, as a Puritan might, to the rank of hypocrite and falsifier.

> *Poet:*   How now, philosopher!
> *Apemantus:* Thou liest.
> *Poet:*   Art not one?
> *Apemantus:* Yes.
> *Poet:*   Then I lie not.
> *Apemantus:* Art not a poet?
> *Poet:*   Yes.
> *Apemantus:* Then thou liest.
>   (*Timon of Athens*, i.i.217–23)

In *Antony and Cleopatra*, the play metaphor continues to express emptiness and deceit. Cleopatra infuriates her lover by insisting that his protestations of faith are merely those of an actor. Ironically, she applauds his skill, and even prompts him in his lines.

> *Cleopatra:*   Good now, play one scene
>   Of excellent dissembling, and let it look
>   Like perfect honour.
> *Antony:*   You'll heat my blood; no more.
> *Cleopatra:*   You can do better yet; but this is meetly.
> *Antony:*   Now, by my sword –
> *Cleopatra:*   And target. Still he mends;
>   But this is not the best.
>   (*Antony and Cleopatra*, i.iii.78–83)

A little later, fretting alone in Alexandria after Antony's departure, she rejects the eunuch Mardian's offer to play with her at billiards in a scornful phrase which seems to remember the apologetic epilogue of some indifferent theatrical performance. 'And when good will is show'd, though't come too short, / The actor may plead pardon' (ii.v.8–9). She remembers how, in the past, she had drunk Antony to his bed:

> Then put my tires and mantles on him, whilst
> I wore his sword Philippan.
>   (*Antony and Cleopatra*, ii.v.22–3)

The little scene of Hercules and Omphale which her words conjure up stands as a symbol of what Antony's infatuation has done to him, the man who rules half the world, the soldier and hero, reduced to masquing in a woman's robes.

Of the drunken frolic on board Pompey's galley, Caesar says with stiff disapproval, 'The wild disguise hath almost / Antick'd us all' (ii.vii.122–3). Enobarbus scoffs at his commander's 'dream', the forlorn hope that Octavius will meet him in single combat, with the remark,

> Yes, like enough high-battled Caesar will
> Unstate his happiness, and be stag'd to th'show
> Against a sworder.
>   (*Antony and Cleopatra*, iii.xiii.29–31)

Antony himself, the last battle lost, convinced that Cleopatra has betrayed him, sees those inconstant clouds which 'mock our eyes with air' (iv.xiv.7) as 'black vesper's pageants' (iv.xiv.8), and equates them with his own shapeless, meaningless existence. Shadows, dreams, the actor and the play: these traditionally related ideas are all degraded in the tragedy. Cleopatra finds that her memory of the dead Antony is 'past the size of dreaming' (v.ii.97):

>   t'imagine
> An Antony were nature's piece 'gainst fancy,
> Condemning shadows quite.
>   (*Antony and Cleopatra*, v.ii.98–100)

Anne Righter

In *Troilus and Cressida*, the mimicry of Patroclus had turned dignity to folly. In much the same way, the erstwhile queen of Egypt thinks not, like Cassius and Hamlet, of the perpetuity of fame granted by the stage, but of its ability to cheapen and degrade. In the hands of the players, her love for Antony will become ignoble and common.

>   the quick comedians
> Extemporally will stage us, and present
> Our Alexandrian revels; Antony
> Shall be brought drunken forth, and I shall see
> Some squeaking Cleopatra boy my greatness
> I'th'posture of a whore.
>   (*Antony and Cleopatra*, v.ii.215–20)

At the very end, there is left to her only the role of Player Queen. She surrounds herself with ceremony in her death, wearing her crown and best attires, 'like a queen' (v.ii.226). Charmian's ambiguous words just before the entrance of the guard and her own suicide, 'Your crown's awry; / I'll mend it and then play' (v.ii.316–17), emphasize the theatrical quality of the scene. The Roman victors themselves seem to catch some hint of its playlike character. Caesar comes, in the words of Dolabella, 'To see perform'd the dreaded act' he had tried so earnestly, and brutally, to prevent (v.ii.329).

In *Coriolanus* as in *Antony and Cleopatra*, the actor and the play suggest futility or shame. Coriolanus himself persists in referring to the attitude which his mother and friends urge him to adopt before the populace as a role, one which it is impossible for him to execute. Of the ancient custom which demands that the man recommended by the Senate for consul stand in the Forum and display his wounds received in battle, Coriolanus says:

>   It is a part
> That I shall blush in acting, and might well
> Be taken from the people.
>   (*Coriolanus*, ii.ii.142–4)

Standing before the crowd, he asserts that 'since the wisdom of their choice is rather to have my hat than my heart, I will practise the insinuating nod and be off to them most counterfeitly' (ii.iii.93–6). Gone completely are those noble actors of Rome upon whose style Brutus had once advised the conspirators to model themselves. Over and over again, Coriolanus speaks of the position which his friends would force him to adopt before the multitude as a part, a thing beneath his manhood and his dignity.

Coriolanus: You have put me now to such a part which never
                    I shall discharge to th'life …
Volumnia: To have my praise for this, perform a part
                    Thou hast not done before.
Coriolanus: Well, I must do't.
                    Away, my disposition, and possess me
                    Some harlot's spirit! …
                    I will not do't,

> Lest I surcease to honour mine own truth,
> And by my body's action teach my mind
> A most inherent baseness.
> (*Coriolanus*, iii.ii.105–6, 109–12, 120–3)

It is an idea very much like the one Plato held in *The Republic*, banishing the actors from the state because men should not 'depict or be skilful at imitating any kind of illiberality or baseness, lest from imitation they should come to be what they imitate'.[27]

The final encounter with Volumnia and Virgilia outside the gates of Rome produces further play images. His Volscian oaths crumbling at the first sight of his mother, wife, and child, Coriolanus again describes himself wryly as a player. The passage itself is similar to the one in the *Sonnets*: 'As an unperfect actor on the stage / Who with his fear is put besides his part'. Coriolanus finds

> Like a dull actor now,
> I have forgot my part, and I am out
> Even to a full disgrace.
> (*Coriolanus*, v.iii.40–2)

that Volumnia, in her bitterness and desperation, suddenly accuses her son, the man who has destroyed his hopes through a stubborn unwillingness to practise the actor's art in the Forum, of having been a player all along.

> Thou hast affected the fine strains of honour,
> To imitate the graces of the gods …
> (*Coriolanus*, v.iii.149–50)

The pride, the refusal to counterfeit, were in themselves dissembled qualities. It is an unjust, but wounding stroke, like her later assertion of Coriolanus' invariable lack of 'courtesy' to her.

Coriolanus yields to his mother's plea, and in the moment that he does so is gripped by a sense of the unreality, the latent horror of this episode. Bitterly, he invokes one of the most traditional of play metaphors.

> What have you done? Behold, the heavens do ope,
> The gods look down, and this unnatural scene
> They laugh at.
> (*Coriolanus*, v.iii.183–5)

It is a moment of insight, almost of suspended time, in which Coriolanus seems to hear the cold laughter of the immortals who sit as spectators at the ludicrous drama of human life.

Notes

1 Jonson, *The New Inne*, in Herford and Simpson edition of Jonson, Vol. VI, I, iii, 128–37.
2 Chapman, *Revenge of Bussy D'Ambois*, in *Works*, edited by D. H. Shephered, London, 1917, ii, p. 114.
3 Middleton, *A Game at Chess*, in *Works*, edited by A. H. Bullen, London, 1885, VII, v, iii, 19.
4 Dekker and Webster, *Northward Ho!*, in Bowers edition of Dekker, Vol. II, I, ii, 102–3.
5 Marston, *Antonio and Mellida*, in Wood edition of Marston, i, Induction, p. 7.
6 *The Valiant Welshman*, Tudor Facsimile Texts, Prologue, A₄ recto. Middleton, *A Faire Quarrell*, in Bullen edition, iii, p. 157. The quotation in the text comes from the prologue to *A Faire Quarrell*, and is signed by William Rowley.
7 Middleton, *A Faire Quarrell*, Bullen, op. cit., p. 157.
8 *Second Part of the Return from Parnassus*, in Leishman edition, ll. 561–8.
9 Webster, *The Duchess of Malfi*, in Lucas edition of Webster, Vol. II, IV, i, 99–100.
10 Ibid., IV, ii, 37–8.
11 St John Chrysostom, quoted in T. W. Baldwin, *William Shakespere's Small Latine and Lesse Greeke*, Urbana, 1944, Vol. I, p. 675.
12 Thomas Heywood, *An Apology for Actors*, introduction and notes by Richard H. Perkinson, New York, 1941, A₄ verso.
13 Stephen Gosson, *Plays Confuted in Five Actions*, quoted in Chambers, *The Elizabethan Stage*, IV, pp. 218–19.
14 Marlowe, *Edward II*, in Brooke edition of Marlowe, ll. 985–6.
15 *Second Part of the Return from Parnassus*, in Leishman edition, ll. 1922–6.
16 Jonson, *Poetaster*, in Herford and Simpson edition of Jonson, Vol. IV, III, iv, 116–27.
17 Jonson, 'An Ode to Himselfe', in *The Oxford Book of Seventeenth Century Verse*, edited by Grierson and Bullough, Oxford, 1934, p. 170.
18 Marston, *Sophonisba*, in the Wood edition of Marston, ii, p. 44.
19 Ibid., p. 21.
20 Marston, *Antonio's Revenge*, in Wood edition, i, p. 83.
21 Ibid., p. 93.
22 Marston, *The Insatiate Countess*, in Wood edition, iii, p. 8.
23 Marston, *What You Will*, in Wood edition, ii, p. 278.
24 Thomas Nashe, *Summer's Last Will and Testament*, edited by McKerrow, III, 284.
25 From 'Philip Rossiter's "Book of Airs" ', in *The Oxford Book of Sixteenth Century Verse*, edited by E. K. Chambers, Oxford, 1932, p. 845.
26 *All's Well That Ends Well*, edited by G. K. Hunter (the New Arden edition of the play, London, 1959), note to l. 301, p. 143.
27 Plato, *The Republic*, III, 395.

14

How Not to Murder Caesar

Sigurd Burckhardt

I

It has been true of Shakespeare critics – as it has been of others supposedly in pursuit of knowledge – that they have felt pretty free to speculate about what Shakespeare "was really like" or "really believed" – or even whether he was real at all – and then to interpret the plays to fit their speculations. As regards *Julius Caesar*, they have argued for better than a century and a half about its political meaning. There are what we may call the republican critics, who believe that Shakespeare's political sympathies are with Brutus, the republican idealist, who is defeated by the very nobility of his ideals. There are, on the other side, the monarchist critics, who cite authorities from Dante to Hooker to prove that Shakespeare's age considered Caesar the founder of the monarchical order in Rome, and Brutus, for all his fine speeches, as no better than a regicide, who is justly punished for his terrible crime. Still other critics try to find a compromise solution; and finally there are those – usually gentlemen of the theatre, with a no-nonsense attitude toward ideas – who are sure that Shakespeare didn't care one way or the other, as long as he came up with a play that filled the house and the cash box.

Another preconception about Shakespeare took root even in his own lifetime and grew so sturdy that today it is still hard to eradicate. I mean the notion that Shakespeare was a "natural genius," somehow directly in touch with the Muse, without the intervening benefit of a solid education. Hence, he wrote splendid poetry, to be sure, and had an unerring instinct for what goes on in men's souls, but he also, alas! committed some sad boners. Not that anyone is pedant enough to hold these boners against him. But still, there they are; and since a critic of this persuasion, though he may be a little short on genius, has at least got a degree from an institution of higher learning, he does note the boners and treats himself to a few moments of complacent condescension.

The striking clock in *Julius Caesar* is Shakespeare's most notorious boner. Everyone knew it for an anachronism – everyone, that is, except Shakespeare, who was out poaching and seducing Anne Hathaway when he should have been at school parsing his Latin. So it is that all annotated editions of the play carry a note to Act II, scene i, line 192, duly explaining that Shakespeare erred at this point. What I propose to do is simply this: I shall assume that Shakespeare did know that he was committing an anachronism – and see what follows from this assumption.

One thing follows immediately: if he did know, he must have intended his readers – and most particularly his learned critics, i.e. those most certain to notice the anachronism – to be struck by it. And beyond that he must have expected his learned critics to divide into two groups: those who would promptly, in the assurance of their prior learning, charge him with an error, and those who would promptly, in the assurance of their prior learning, charge him with an error, and those who would submit to the facts as given by him and say: "How odd! Let's see if we can discover what Shakespeare may have had in mind."

The latter group, instead of writing a condescending note, will start looking carefully, not just at the line in question, but for other instances of time-telling in the play. And they won't have far to look: the scene itself is rich in such instances. It is the so-called "Orchard Scene." It opens with Brutus alone in his garden, late at night, talking to himself about his decision to join the conspiracy. A little later the conspirators enter, led by Cassius, and confer with Brutus on the details of the murder plan. But, throughout, the scene is punctuated with time references. In the very first line Brutus lets us know that he is unsure of the time of *day*:

> I cannot by the progress of the stars
> Give guess how near to day.
> (ii.i.2–3)

Forty lines later he shows himself equally unsure of the time of *month*:

> Is not tomorrow, boy, the first of March?*

and his servant boy has to inform him that he is off by a full fourteen days. Another forty lines, and Cassius enters with the conspirators. And now something odd happens: while Brutus and Cassius withdraw immediately to the background and confer in inaudible whispers, the secondary conspirators take the center of the stage and engage in a seemingly pointless dispute over the points of the compass, the point of the sun's rising, and the time of *year*. Only after some ten lines of this do Brutus and Cassius come forward, and the main business of planning the assassination is taken up. As soon as the plan is agreed on, the clock strikes three times and is carefully taken note of.

The mere facts of the matter prove design; clearly Shakespeare had something in mind. The time references progress from time of day to time of month to time of year; they are thrust into the foreground when much more important business is relegated to the background; and they all testify to confusion and uncertainty – until the fateful

---

* I have here restored the First Folio reading – thus amending the text I regularly follow.

decision has been made, when suddenly these groping guesses yield to the countable precision of a novel chronometric device. So the first result of my assumption has been the discovery of a design; the obvious next question – much more difficult, of course – is: what does the design signify?

Here we need to recall two historical circumstances, which Shakespeare and his audience had reason to be very concretely aware of. One is that Caesar's fame rested in good part on his institution of the Julian calendar. Plutarch – Shakespeare's source – praises this great reform and mentions it as one of the reasons why Caesar was hated: the Roman conservatives felt it to be an arbitrary and tyrannical interference with the course of nature. The second circumstance is that in 1582 Pope Gregory had decreed the reform of the Julian – that is to say, of the traditional Christian – calendar, which in the meantime had drifted almost ten days out of phase. This reform had immediately become an issue in the bitter politico-religious struggles of the age; the Catholic countries accepted it and so adopted the so-called "New Style," while the Protestant countries rejected it and clung to the "Old Style." Thus at the turn of the century – Shakespeare wrote *Julius Caesar* in 1599 – a situation existed in Europe exactly analogous to that of Rome in 44 BC. It was a time of confusion and uncertainty, when the most basic category by which men order their experience seemed to have become unstable and untrustworthy, subject to arbitrary political manipulation.

With these facts in mind, we return to the Orchard Scene. The scene's core is the planning of the conspiracy. Three proposals are made and, on Brutus' insistence, rejected; the third of these is to kill Mark Antony along with Caesar. The rejection – which, of course, soon proves to be a fatal mistake – is based, not so much on grounds of expediency or even morality, but on grounds of *style*. Indeed, under Brutus' influence the planning generally becomes a stylistic question. The plot as such is already decided on, the actors are chosen, the parts in the main assigned; but what still needs to be determined, at least in Brutus' view, is the style in which the action is to be carried out. And on this he has firm opinions; Antony must be spared because otherwise

> Our course will seem too bloody, Caius Cassius,
> To cut the head off and then hack the limbs,
> Like wrath in death and envy afterwards …
> Let's be sacrificers, but not butchers, Caius …
> Let's kill him boldly, but not wrathfully;
> Let's carve him as a dish fit for the gods,
> Not hew him as a carcass fit for hounds …
>   This shall make
> Our purpose necessary and not envious;
> Which so appearing to the common eyes,
> We shall be call'd purgers, not murderers.
>   (II.i.162–80)

And later, when it is a question of whether or not to let Antony speak, Brutus repeats:

> Though now we must appear bloody and cruel,
> As by our hands and this our present act
> You see we do, yet see you but our hands

And this the bleeding business they have done.
Our hearts you see not; they are pitiful;
And pity to the general wrong of Rome –
As fire drives out fire, so pity pity –
Hath done this deed on Caesar.

(III.i.165–72)

In speaking of the conspiracy I have slipped into the metaphor of the drama: I have talked of plot, action, actors, and style. There is ample warrant for the use of this metaphor in the play itself; Brutus and Cassius employ it repeatedly – most explicitly right after the murder, when in fact it ceases to be a metaphor:

How many ages hence
Shall this our lofty scene be acted over
In states unborn and accents yet unknown!

(III.i.111–13)

Let us think of Cassius and Brutus as manifestly they think of themselves: plotters in the dramatic sense, men who have decided to author and produce a tragedy entitled "Julius Caesar." Really it is Cassius who has had the idea for the plot; but he feels the need of a co-author – Brutus – to give the production the kind of prestige and styling that will make it a hit with the audience, the Roman populace. Somewhat to Cassius' distress, Brutus takes his function very seriously and overrules his partner on a number of points which later turn out to be crucial. Evidently we must look a little more closely at the style Brutus has in mind.

What he wants is not a bare assassination, but a tragedy of classical, almost Aristotelian, purity. There is to be no wholesale slaughter, with the curtain coming down, as in *Hamlet*, on a heap of corpses. Only the tragic hero is to be killed, and the killing itself is to be a ritual, a sacrifice, formal and even beautiful. Nor is there to be any unseemly vilification: the victim is to be presented, not as a villain like Claudius of Denmark, but as a great and noble man, who falls because he has one tragic flaw: ambition. And his killers, the authors, must not act from personal motives; they must be as priests and physicians, performing their solemn duty of purging the common-wealth. Everything Brutus says and does – most particularly his permitting Antony to speak and his own speech in justification of his act – is informed by this determination to make the tragedy a classical one: noble, purgative, impersonal, inevitable.

He is only too successful. The classical style has disastrous consequences, because Brutus is utterly mistaken about the audience for whom the tragedy is intended. He is thinking of an audience of noble, sturdy republicans, capable of the moral discrimin-ation and public spirit which classical tragedy demands. But *we* know from the opening scenes that the actual audience is very different: eager to be led, easily tricked, crude in their responses. The people insist on having their good guy and their bad guy; they are perfectly ready to accept Brutus as their good guy, provided he lets them have Caesar for their bad guy. But this, Brutus' ideal of style forbids. Brutus is most irretrievably damned, not when the mob is ready to stone him, but when it acclaims him: "Let him be Caesar!" Nothing shows so clearly as this shout of applause how totally the audience has missed Brutus' point, and how totally Brutus has misjudged his audience.

That is why Shakespeare makes the clock strike at the very moment when Brutus has persuaded the conspirators to adopt the classical style for their performance. The political point of the play is not that the monarchical principle is superior to the republican – nor the reverse – but that the form of government, the style of politics, must take account of the time and the temper of the people, just as the dramatist's style must. Brutus is not guilty of treachery, nor of having embraced an inherently wrong political philosophy; he is guilty of an anachronism. The clock, striking as soon as he has irrevocably committed himself to the Old Style, signifies to us – though not to him – that time is now reckoned in a new, Caesarean style.

There were in Shakespeare's day, as there are always, those who retreated from a confused and turbulent present to older forms, older certainties. In literature they preached the return to the great classical models, on their knowledge of which they naturally prided themselves, and in the name of which they felt confident they could judge their own day. Ben Jonson, Shakespeare's contemporary and competitor, was of this faction. With an irony so gentle that it is almost a salute, Shakespeare shows not only the fate of such retreats but the way to diagnose them. The striking clock is not only a metaphor; it is a touchstone. Proud classicists, sure of their learning, will mark it as evidence that Shakespeare had, in Ben Jonson's words, "small Latin and less Greek." But in the very act of doing so they betray their blindness, their refusal fully to surrender to the actually *given* – in this case to the carefully wrought pattern of time references by which Shakespeare defines the precise meaning of his anachronism. Instead of first submitting to the present, the given, and trying to discover its inner structure and meaning, they judge and condemn it by pre-established standards. And so they are blind not only to the present but even to the past they know so well.

Very few of us have read Ben Jonson's Roman tragedies. And probably none of us has seen them performed; they have long since vanished from the stage and into the stacks. On the other hand, most of us have read *Julius Caesar*; most of us have seen it – or at least had the opportunity to see it; and all of us have, at some time or other, quoted phrases from it. If we ever have occasion to look at an edition of Ben Jonson's *Catiline* or *Sejanus*, we find the margins covered with references – supplied by Jonson himself – to his classical sources. Every line is buttressed with classical authority; one would have to be very learned indeed to catch Jonson in an anachronism. The only trouble is that the plays in their entirety are anachronisms – while Shakespeare's work is as alive as ever. Why? Not because Jonson was the lesser "creative genius," in the vague, inspirational sense in which that term is commonly understood; but because, though he knew very well that no clock ever struck in ancient Rome, he did not know what the clock had struck in his own day. Hence, while *Sejanus* gathers dust on library shelves, Caesar's death and Brutus' fall, as Shakespeare has taught us to see them, and as he confidently predicted, are acted over in states unborn and accents yet unknown.

That is the point of his anachronism – precisely defined, exactly calculated, and placed with shrewd irony so that it would serve as an acid test for his critics. It proves, not his ignorance, but his incredible capacity for laying himself open to the tumultuous realities of his age and situation and experience – and his extraordinary ability to penetrate them and embody them in metaphors so true, so carefully wrought, that they have remained valid ever since. We often hear it said that Shakespeare still lives because he had the genius to penetrate beneath the temporary and superficial to what is permanently and immutably true. But this, though perhaps not wrong, is a dangerously misleading way of stating the case. It is the classicists, the Brutuses, who believe they are in possession of the eternal verities; and we have seen what happens to them. Shakespeare knew that the truths that last are painfully purchased by those who without reserve expose themselves to reality in all its confusion and still preserve within it the will to order, the will to form.

It's not so difficult to kill Caesar, to kill the ruler; once you get close enough, a bare bodkin will serve. Like Hamlet, one could do it pat. What *is* difficult is to discover how to kill him. For however corrupt, however tyrannical the ruler may be, he does, as of that moment, represent what order there is; do away with him, and you do away with order. That is why the style of killing Caesar is of such importance; the style must embody the vision of order – presumably better, truer, stabler – that will take the place of the order embodied in Caesar. And because that style is necessarily an embodiment, an incarnation of vision in the flesh-and-blood realities and corporealities of the moment, it stands under the judgment of those realities and of that moment.

II

There is a line by Emily Dickinson which catches, better than anything else I know, the essence of what we loosely call the "creative experience," which I take to mean the experience of anyone – artist, scientist, scholar, statesman, philosopher – who tries to create shapes truer than those existing. The line reads: "After great pain a formal feeling comes." What sets the great creators apart from ordinary men is not so much the capacity for inspiration, for vision – though of course these too play a part – as the ability to sustain, often for a long time and without letup, the pain of disorder. Aware of the inadequacy, the falsity, the injustice of the existing orders, the creator must wish to demolish them – that is what it means to murder Caesar – without as yet knowing what orders will take their place; he must suffer the confrontation with an unstructured reality – a reality that refuses, in its chaotic multiplicity, to yield to man's need of form, of intelligible shape. Modern critics often speak of creative tension; in the last analysis, I believe, this is the tension between the surrender to the raw substance of experience, the given, and the will to order. Brutus is aware of this tension and has felt this pain:

> Since Cassius first did whet me against Caesar,
> I have not slept.
> Between the acting of a dreadful thing
> And the first motion, all the interim is
> Like a phantasma or a hideous dream.
>
> (ii.i.61–5)

But he cannot sustain the pain long enough to forge a new style, a new mode of order. To gain the blessed release of the "formal feeling," he flees to an old style. Judged in terms of beauty, of purity and nobility, there is no fault to be found with this style. Listen to Brutus rejecting the proposal that the conspirators bind themselves by an oath:

No, not an oath! ...
What need we any spur but our own cause
To prick us to redress? What other bond
Than secret Romans, that have spoke the word
And will not palter? and what other oath
Than honesty to honesty engag'd
That this shall be, or we will fall for it? ...
                              Do not stain
The even virtue of our enterprise ...
To think that or our cause or our performance
Did need an oath; when every drop of blood
That every Roman bears, and nobly bears,
Is guilty of a several bastardy
If he do break the smallest particle
Of any promise that hath pass'd from him.
                              (II.i.114–40)

Even in Shakespeare's own work we will search a long time before we find another speech of such purity: so free of all verbal and metaphorical trickery, so simple, and yet so nobly eloquent. And if we compare these lines to those of Hamlet when the Prince makes his comrades swear – not just once but three times over – not to divulge what they have seen, we have some measure of the sheer beauty of the form Brutus retreats to.

But it is a retreat all the same; the pain has not been great enough, nor deep enough. This is the pain Hamlet suffers and breaks under and finally hands on to his friend Horatio as his bitter legacy:

Absent thee from felicity a while
And in this harsh world draw thy breath in pain
To tell my story.
                              (v.ii.358–60)

In fact, Hamlet is the exact counterpart to Brutus. Like Brutus he accepts the task to kill the ruler, to fashion a tragedy; and like Brutus he botches the job. But he botches it for the opposite reason; instead of settling too quickly for a ready-made form, he despairs of the very possibility of form. The corruption of the world he is supposed to purge enters into his very soul, so that he spends his energy probing the infection, in himself as well as in everyone about him. He is so overwhelmed by his discovery of monstrous disorder that his great enterprise loses, in his words, "the name of action," and the initiative passes to the king. Unlike Brutus, he knows only too well that the clock has struck upon the old style:

The time is out of joint; – O cursed spite
That ever I was born to set it right!
                              (I.v.189–90)

But he sees, from the depth of his loathing and self-loathing, no possibility of forging a new style, of passing through the great pain to a formal feeling, a truer, more valid shaping of reality. In the end he settles for a stoic resignation which is moving and impressive, but which nevertheless signifies an abdication from his task to discover a new order:

> If it be now, 'tis not to come; if it be not to come, it will be now; if it be not now, yet it will come: the readiness is all. (v.ii.31–4)

For in the meantime there are corpses lying about of people – most tragically Ophelia – who might have lived but for his inability to rise above his pain.

A tragedy – to define it very simply – is a *killing poem*; it is designed toward the end of bringing a man to some sort of destruction. And the killer is, quite literally, the poet; it is he, and no one else, who devises the deadly plot; it is he, therefore, who must in some sense accept responsibility for it. Even if the events of the plot are drawn from history – as with *Julius Caesar* they obviously are – what is the poet's purpose in re-enacting them and shaping them as he does, at that particular time and place? Why does he not leave history to the historians? Why, and how, does he represent as a living reality what is, or seems to be, a dead past? In other words, what is he, the plotter, *doing* when he has Caesar killed?

These questions are not simply speculative. It is always true that a poem – especially a dramatic poem – is an act, not just a report; but this truth used to be felt more concretely in Shakespeare's day than it is in ours. When the Essex faction was preparing an armed uprising in 1601, they induced Shakespeare's company to put on a performance of *Richard II*, to serve as a prelude to the revolt. And after the uprising had collapsed, Shakespeare and his colleagues were summoned by the authorities to be questioned about their possible implication in the plot. Queen Elizabeth knew very well that the plotting of playwrights and that of rebels may have more in common than merely the name: "I am Richard II, know ye not that?" I am not suggesting that anyone producing a play by Bertolt Brecht should be subpoenaed to testify before the Un-American Activities Committee. But I am suggesting that Shakespeare had pressingly concrete reasons to know that when he was plotting a tragedy – even a historical tragedy – he was not just retelling a story in dramatic form; he was committing an act – the action of his play – in the full moral and social sense of the word "act."

Not that he needed the reminder; he was poet enough – proud poet enough – to claim the responsibility he incurred by this kind of action. That is why, in so many of his plays, he has a part for himself as *deviser of the plot*, and why again and again he probes the problem: what am I doing when I invent, or reinvent, a mechanism designed to bring about a man's destruction? In the name of what, for the sake of what, do I do this? And even assuming the necessity of doing it, how well do I do it? Is my aim so sure that there is no unnecessary killing, or is it so uncertain that all Italy is plunged into civil war, or that Ophelia and Gertrude, Polonius and Laertes, Rosencrantz and Guildenstern, must die along with the king?

III

It may be, of course, that the tragic poet does not worry about this kind of account-ability, but takes the position that after all he is only the poet, trying to write as perfect a tragedy as he knows how. This role also Shakespeare watched himself playing and wrote into a play. His "perfect tragedy," in this sense of the term, is *Othello*, by general agreement the most flawlessly structured of all his tragedies. In it he devises a plot so beautifully tooled, so accurately deadly, that, once set going, it seems of its own momentum to bring about the destruction for which it is designed. But into it he writes his own part as the deviser of a perfect tragedy – and the part is Iago's. Iago it is who composes the tragedy called "Othello"; he stands at the footlights and tells us, step by step, how he shapes it, from the first most general idea through the overall scheme down to the specific devices of plotting. And beyond that he lets us share the keen joy of mastery, of subtle skill and power, that he derives from this enterprise. If Othello is a great tragedy and not just a perfect one, this self-portrait of the "pure" tragic poet is the reason. The play shows what manner of man he is who creates art for art's sake, or at least tragedy for tragedy's sake.

This kind of tragedy was real enough for Shakespeare to have done it once, in full awareness of what he was doing; but it was not, on the whole, his kind. He admits, in Iago, to the sense of triumph which every craftsman is bound to feel when he fashions a perfect instrument, no matter what the ultimate end. But the triumph is sterile. None of Shakespeare's plotters – not even the well-intentioned ones – are presented as fathers; Brutus and Hamlet as well as Macbeth and Richard III are childless. But the most childless of all, if so illogical a superlative is permitted – the man whom we cannot even imagine as being a father, the way we *can* imagine Brutus and do imagine Macbeth – is Iago. There is, as it were, no blood in him – hardly even that which boils with hatred or is fired by ambition. He is a perfect craftsman.

Permit me, at this point, a brief parenthetical digression. I cannot think of any more devastating revelation of how we today feel and see reality than the fact that we accept – without revulsion and even without a sense of incongruity – a metaphor such as "father of the H-bomb." It is not the H-bomb as such that I have in mind, terrifying though it is. Mankind has always invested a good part of its ingenuity in devising more perfect engines of destruction. But I doubt that any previous age has called the devisers of such engines by the name of "father." "Father of poison gas," "father of the machine gun," "father of the electric chair" – these, it seems to me, would have been impossible. The mere phrase "father of the H-bomb" betrays more of what we truly are than a thousand pages of the Congressional Record can conceal. For we speak the truth about ourselves, not in our pious sentiments, but in the metaphors we find for them.

It was not, I am convinced, Shakespeare's ambition to write perfect tragedies; my guess is that the very term would have made him shudder, as Iago makes us shudder. It is no mere paradox to say that Shakespeare wrote great tragedies because he thought it monstrous to think of them as perfect. Murder is, at best, a bleeding or strangling business; we are dangerously deceived if we believe that it can be styled into beauty. That is Brutus' illusion. True, he does not enjoy his work, as Iago does; he feels driven to it in the service of a higher cause. So, for that matter, does Othello, another sacrificial killer who thinks he must and can purge the world and goes about his work with noble pity. But Othello is never so deluded as when he is most priestly; and Brutus, after his fine words about not being a butcher and not hewing Caesar as a carcass fit for hounds, stands on the stage, his arms bloody to the elbows and at his feet Caesar's pitifully mangled carcass.

The eighteenth century felt squeamish about Shakespeare's tragedies and preferred to pretty them up a little – especially *King Lear*, the end of which was rewritten so that Cordelia was saved to marry Edgar and live happily ever after. Today we smile condescendingly at such prettifying; we pride ourselves on being able to take our Shakespeare straight. But I am not at all sure that this pride is in Shakespeare's spirit. I think he meant the end of *King Lear* to be as Samuel Johnson found it: unbearable.

We take our Shakespeare straight; but our critics supply us with chasers. There are various comforting theories about the nature of tragedy – theories which sound disconcertingly like those of Brutus and Othello. A tragedy, we are told, is a kind of sacrifice brought to purge the world of some disorder and restore it to its natural harmony. To be sure, we pity the victim; we feel terror at the price that has to be paid for the restoring of order. But in the end we feel rather as Brutus does:

> And pity for the general wrong of Rome
> As fire drives out fire, so pity pity –
> Hath done this deed on Caesar.

It is this comforting theory that the clock tolls into an irrecoverable past. For it rests on a no longer tenable faith in an underlying universal order – an order that may be temporarily disturbed but can, by the proper purgatives properly administered, be re-established. This faith Shakespeare felt compelled to abandon. Measured by Caesar's time, the Caesarean system is not a general wrong but a true order, however it may look measured by another time. The natural order cannot be known, or at least not be known certainly enough to legitimize the murder of Caesar in the classical style. Once the time is out of joint, sacrificial tragedy is no longer possible – or rather, it is an illusion by which we deceive ourselves, if not about our motives, at least about the consequences of our action.

All this is not to say that Shakespeare gave up the quest for order and subsided into a flaccid relativism. Rather, he found that he had to accept undiminished responsibility for his failures to create order – for his tragedies, in other words. Order, for him, was not something that needed only to be restored; it had to be continually created. And the great metaphor for his vision of order is not something grand and cosmic like the harmony of the spheres or the chain of being; it is something modest, earthly, human – marriage. He does see his function as that of a priest – only not the sacrificial priest who protests that the victim must have, like Caesar, "all true rites and lawful cere-monies," but the priest performing the sacrament of marriage. What he has to learn is the true rite of this sacrament – the words which will make the marriage of true minds truly binding, stable and fruitful. There are fearful impediments to this kind of marriage; and once Shakespeare can no longer refuse to admit these – as he still does in his famous sonnet – he engages in a series of fierce attempts to remove them. These attempts are his tragedies, ending in separation, death – failure. But they are all directed toward the same ultimate end: the creation of new order, new unions. And being that, they are redeemed, in retrospect, as necessary steps, necessary failures. In *The Tempest*, Shakespeare as Prospero shows us how all the chaos and turbulence, the separation and loss and grief and madness, were but means to the one true end: the joining of two young people who would, except for the tempest, have remained apart.

When all is said and done, the poet's job has been to learn, as Shakespeare puts it in his twenty-third sonnet, "the perfect ceremony of love's rite" – not of murder, not of sacrifice, but of marriage:

> As an unperfect actor on the stage
> Who with his fear is put besides his part,
> Or some fierce thing replete with too much rage,
> Whose strength's abundance weakens his own heart,
> So I, for fear of trust, forget to say
> The perfect ceremony of love's rite,
> And in mine own love's strength seem to decay,
> O'ercharg'd with burden of mine own love's might.
> O, let my books be then the eloquence
> And dumb presagers of my speaking breast,
> Who plead for love and look for recompense
> More than that tongue that more hath more express'd.
> O, learn to read what silent love hath writ:
> To hear with eyes belongs to love's fine wit.

Part V

Reader-Response Criticism

15 On the Value of *Hamlet*   225
    Stephen Booth
16 Rabbits, Ducks, and *Henry V*   245
    Norman Rabkin

A lthough the middle of the twentieth century witnessed the triumph of New Criticism and a glut of studies, often conducted with New Critical tools, devoted to imagery and theme, that victory was not absolute. As the essays in Part IV attest, various critical voices were still audible, voices that insisted on attention to genre or to staging, for example, or that essayed early psychoanalytic readings. During this period some of the most compelling claims arose from critics who ventured beyond formal or thematic study of the text to scrutinize the relationship between text and reader, or work and audience. In North America this subdiscipline came to be known by the name of "reader-response criticism," although Stanley Fish's alternative, "Affective Stylistics," enjoyed a moment of popularity. While both terms cover a wide range of critical attitudes, they both nevertheless manage to describe a method directing attention away from "the text itself" and towards the receiver of that text. What the text *is* was no longer the question; what the text *does* was the topic of scrutiny. *Effect, experience, reception* – these and related words are those that recur as the critic describes a mode of reading, a kinetic process in which the receiver, whether reader or spectator, completes the work begun by the writer.

Several permutations of reader-response criticism emerged in the 1950s and 1960s, many of them produced as explicit attempts to break what their originators considered the stranglehold of New Criticism. Perhaps since New Criticism was clearly identified as an American phenomenon, some distinguished Europeans – Michael Riffaterre,

Wolfgang Iser, and Hans Robert Jauss – sought to diversify the critical conversation by looking beyond the textual object and thinking broadly about reading, and while it should be noted that these critics insist on significant differences among their several practices, for the purposes of taxonomy they do seem to belong together. In North America the leading voices in such criticism generally were those of Norman Holland, whose emphasis is mainly psychological; Jonathan Culler, whose interests seem mainly deconstructive; and Fish, perhaps the most irreverent of the reader-oriented critics.

In an essay entitled "Literature in the Reader: Affective Stylistics," Fish audaciously maps the divergence of reader-response criticism from New Criticism, and in doing so he confronts directly one of the cornerstones of New Critical doctrine:

> When it comes time to make analytical statements about the end product of reading (meaning or understanding), the reader is usually forgotten or ignored. Indeed in recent literary history he has been excluded by legislation. I refer, of course, to the *ex cathedra* pronouncements of Wimsatt and Beardsley in their enormously influential article "The Affective Fallacy."[1]

The "pronouncements" Fish addresses are Wimsatt and Beardsley's warning against confusing a poem with its results, their belief that consideration of "the psychological effects of the poem … ends in impressionism and relativism," and their claim that in such analysis "the poem as an object … tends to disappear."[2] In a move characteristic of many late-twentieth-century models, affective criticism disputes the "objectivity" or "objectness" of the literary text, arguing instead that the textual object comes to life only under the scrutiny of the reader. Thus the central concern of the critic is not the product (i.e., interpretation or meaning) that derives from reading, but the *experience* of reading itself.

What about the form in which there is no reader at all – drama? In fact, the elevation of process is especially well suited to the study of Shakespearean texts. The collaborative nature of the "reading" process has always been recognized in the study of the stage; in other words, it is axiomatic that the theatrical script realizes its potentiality only in the presence of spectators. If a poem or novel or essay requires the participation of the reader, one who cooperates in the production of meaning, the theatrical text or script is designed explicitly to generate a response that the work will then exploit to generate further responses. Thus the critic is concerned less with "meaning" and more with how meanings are generated, subverted, and replaced. This concentration on process was consistent, according to Susan Suleiman, with contemporary methodological changes in the humanities and social sciences generally. As she wrote in 1980, with the benefit of several years of hindsight: "The recent evolution of all these disciplines has been toward self-reflexiveness – questioning and making explicit the assumptions that ground the methods of the discipline, and concurrently the investigator's role in delimiting or even constituting the subject of study."[3]

Such a concentration is not without theoretical problems, given that "*the* receiver" of a text is difficult to identify and describe. It seems indisputable that the nature of the relation between text and receiver would be determined by the nature of the text and by the nature of the reader, i.e., different for poetry than for prose fiction; different for, say, the American than for the British reader; different (taking the problem into the Shakespearean arena) for the Elizabethan than for the twentieth-century spectator. Culture, history, gender, class status, education – all these conditions make for different readers. The problem, in other words, is that several interpretations arise, that one reader's account of the reading experience does not match another's. Fish confronted this objection with the notion of "interpretive communities," arguing that a consensus of understanding will emerge among readers sharing assumptions, beliefs, and experience. Some poststructuralist critics further objected to reader-response criticism on the grounds that it continued to privilege the literary and was therefore not a critical innovation but merely formalism in a fresh costume.

Perhaps the most talented of the responsive readers of Shakespeare is Stephen Booth, who has argued for four decades that the critic's task is to record the experience of reading and has spent the last four decades recording his experience. This theoretical stance is articulated clearly in one of his late pieces, an article chiefly on *Macbeth* entitled "Close Reading without Readings."[4] The essay published here, "On the Value of *Hamlet*," is one of the most celebrated examples of its kind. Booth begins by setting himself apart from those critics who insist on "meaning," who believe "that in *Hamlet* we behold the frustrated and inarticulate Shakespeare furiously wagging his tail in an effort to tell us something." Like most critics who practice reader-oriented analysis, Booth is interested in what happens as it happens. Further, he makes the valuable point that too much interpretation is guided by the desire to make the text something other than it is: he argues that *Hamlet* "was shaped by the Platonic presumption that the reality of anything is other than its apparent self. In such a culture it is no wonder that critics prefer the word *meaning* (which implies effort rather than success) to *saying*, and that in turn they would rather talk about what a work *says* or *shows* (both of which suggest the hidden essence bared of the dross of physicality) than talk about what it *does*."

Booth's colleague at the University of California, Berkeley, Norman Rabkin, declared a similar commitment to process. In an essay on *The Merchant of Venice*, the first in his book entitled *Shakespeare and the Problem of Meaning*, Rabkin urges readers "to consider the play as a dynamic interaction between artist and audience, to learn to talk about the process of our involvement rather than our considered view after the aesthetic event."[5] It is not insignificant that Rabkin, Booth, and Fish were all teaching at Berkeley at the same time, the 1960s. Their work exhibits a desire to move beyond the prevailing critical models, to find a precise way of accounting for "the developing responses of the reader in relation to the words as they succeed one another in time."[6] Their slightly younger colleague in that department, Stephen Greenblatt, also found himself discontent with critical orthodoxy. He, however, took a different route in an effort to circumvent what he considered limited approaches, developing and naming what we now know as New Historicism or Cultural Poetics.

Notes

1   *Self Consuming Artifacts* (Berkeley: University of California Press, 1972), p. 383.
2   Quoted in Fish, pp. 383–4.

3 "Varieties of Audience-Oriented Criticism," *The Reader in the Text: Essays on Audience and Interpretation*, ed. Susan R. Suleiman and Inge Crosman (Princeton, NJ: Princeton University Press, 1980), p. 4.

4 Printed in *Shakespeare Reread: The Texts in New Contexts*, ed. Russ McDonald (Ithaca, NY: Cornell University Press, 1994).

5 *Shakespeare and the Problem of Meaning* (Chicago: University of Chicago Press, 1981), p. 27.

6 Fish, "Literature in the Reader: Affective Stylistics," p. 399.

15

On the Value of *Hamlet*

Stephen Booth

I t is a truth universally acknowledged that *Hamlet* as we have it – usually in a conservative conflation of the second quarto and first folio texts – is not really *Hamlet*. The very fact that the *Hamlet* we know is an editor-made text has furnished an illusion of firm ground for leaping conclusions that discrepancies between the probable and actual actions, statements, tone, and diction of *Hamlet* are accidents of its transmission. Thus, in much the spirit of editors correcting printer's errors, critics have proposed stage directions by which, for example, Hamlet can overhear the plot to test Polonius' diagnosis of Hamlet's affliction, or by which Hamlet can glimpse Polonius and Claudius actually spying on his interview with Ophelia. Either of these will make sense of Hamlet's improbable raging at Ophelia in iii.i. The difficulty with such presumably corrective emendation is not only in knowing where to stop, but also in knowing whether to start. I hope to demonstrate that almost everything else in the play has, in its particular kind and scale, an improbability comparable to the improbability of the discrepancy between Hamlet's real and expected behavior to Ophelia; for the moment, I mean only to suggest that those of the elements of the text of *Hamlet* that are incontrovertibly accidental may by their presence have led critics to overestimate the distance between the *Hamlet* we have and the prelapsarian *Hamlet* to which they long to return.

I think also that the history of criticism shows us too ready to indulge a not wholly explicable fancy that in *Hamlet* we behold the frustrated and inarticulate Shakespeare furiously wagging his tail in an effort to tell us something, but, as I said before, the accidents of our texts of *Hamlet* and the alluring analogies they father render *Hamlet* more liable to interpretive assistance than even the other plays of Shakespeare. Moreover, *Hamlet* was of course born into the culture of Western Europe, our culture, whose every thought – literary or nonliterary – is shaped by the Platonic presumption that the reality of anything is other than its apparent self. In such a culture it is no wonder that critics prefer the word *meaning* (which implies effort rather than success) to *saying*, and that in turn they would rather talk about what a work *says* or *shows* (both of which suggest the hidden essence bared of the dross of physicality) than talk about what it *does*. Even stylistic critics are most comfortable and acceptable when they reveal that rhythm, syntax, diction, or (and above all) imagery are vehicles for meaning. Among people to whom "It means a lot to me" says "I value it," in a language where *significant* and *valuable* are synonyms, it was all but inevitable that a work with the peculiarities of *Hamlet* should have been treated as a distinguished and yearning failure.

Perhaps the value of *Hamlet* is where it is most measurable, in the degree to which it fulfills one or another of the fixable identities it suggests for itself or that are suggested for it, but I think that before we choose and argue for one of the ideal forms toward which *Hamlet* seems to be moving, and before we attribute its value to an exaggeration of the degree to which it gets there, it is reasonable to talk about what the play *does* do, and to test the suggestion that in a valued play what it does do is what we value. I propose to look at *Hamlet* for what it undeniably is: a succession of actions upon the understanding of an audience. I set my hypothetical audience to watch *Hamlet* in the text edited by Willard Farnham in The Pelican *Shakespeare* (Baltimore, 1957), a text presumably too long to have fitted into the daylight available to a two o'clock performance, but still an approximation of what Shakespeare's company played.

I

The action that the first scene of *Hamlet* takes upon the understanding of its audience is like the action of the whole, and most of the individual actions that make up the whole. The first scene is insistently incoherent and just as insistently coherent. It frustrates and fulfills expectations simultaneously. The challenge and response in the first lines are perfectly predictable sentry-talk, but – as has been well and often observed – the challenger is the wrong man, the relieving sentry and not the one on duty. A similarly faint intellectual uneasiness is provoked when the first personal note in the play sets up expectations that the play then ignores. Francisco says, "For this relief much thanks. 'Tis bitter cold, / And I am sick at heart" (1.i.8–9). We want to know why he is sick at heart. Several lines later Francisco leaves the stage and is forgotten. The scene continues smoothly as if the audience had never focused on Francisco's heartsickness. Twice in the space of less than a minute the audience has an opportunity to concern itself with a trouble that vanishes from consciousness almost before it is there. The wrong sentry challenges, and the other corrects the oddity instantly. Francisco is sick at heart, but neither he nor Bernardo gives any sign that further comment might be in order. The routine of sentry-go, its special diction, and its commonplaces continue across the audience's momentary tangential journey; the audience returns as if *it* and not the play had wandered. The audience's sensation of being unexpectedly and very slightly out of step is repeated regularly in *Hamlet*.

The first thing an audience in a theater wants to know is why it is in the theater. Even one that, like Shakespeare's audiences for *Richard II* or *Julius Caesar* or *Hamlet*, knows the story being dramatized wants to hear out the familiar terms of the situation and the terms of the particular new dramatization. Audiences want their bearings and expect them to be given. The first thing we see in *Hamlet* is a pair of sentries. The sight of sentries in real life is insignificant, but, when a work of art focuses on sentries, it is usually a sign that what they are guarding is going to be attacked. Thus, the first answer we have to the question "what is this play about?" is "military threat to a castle and a king," and that leads to our first specific question: "what is that threat?" Horatio's first question ("What, has this thing appeared again to-night?" I.i.21) is to some extent an answer to the audience's question; its terms are not military, but their implications are appropriately threatening. Bernardo then begins elaborate preparations to tell Horatio what the audience must hear if it is ever to be intellectually comfortable in the play. The audience has slightly adjusted its expectations to accord with a threat that is vaguely supernatural rather than military, but the metaphor of assault in which Bernardo prepares to carry the audience further along its new path of inquiry is pertinent to the one from which it has just deviated:

> Sit down awhile,
> And let us once again assail your ears,
> That are so fortified against our story,
> What we two nights have seen.
> (I.i.30–3)

We are led toward increased knowledge of the new object – the ghost – in terms appropriate to the one we assumed and have just abandoned – military assault. Bernardo's metaphor is obviously pertinent to his occupation as sentinel, but in the metaphor he is not the defender but the assailant of ears fortified against his story. As the audience listens, its understanding shifts from one system of pertinence to another; but each perceptible change in the direction of our concern or the terms of our thinking is balanced by the repetition of some continuing factor in the scene; the mind of the audience is in constant but gentle flux, always shifting but never completely leaving familiar ground.

Everyone onstage sits down to hear Bernardo speak of the events of the past two nights. The audience is invited to settle its mind for a long and desired explanation. The construction of Bernardo's speech suggests that it will go on for a long time; he takes three lines (I.i.35–8) to arrive at the grammatical subject of his sentence, and then, as he begins another parenthetical delay in his long journey toward a verb, "the bell then beating one," *Enter Ghost.* The interrupting action is not a simple interruption. The description is interrupted by a repetition of the action described. The entrance of the ghost duplicates on a larger scale the kind of mental experience we have had before. It both fulfills and frustrates our expectations: it is what we expect and desire, an action to account for our attention to sentinels; it is unexpected and unwanted, an interruption in the syntactical routine of the exposition that was on its way to fulfilling the same function. While the ghost is on the stage and during the speculation that immediately follows its departure, the futile efforts of Horatio and the sentries (who, as watchers and waiters, have resembled the audience from the start) are like those of the audience in its quest for information. Marcellus' / statement about the ghost is a fair comment on the whole scene: "'Tis gone and will not answer" (I.i.52), and Horatio's "In what particular thought to work I know not" (I.i.67) describes the mental condition evoked in an audience by this particular dramatic presentation of events as well as it does that evoked in the character by the events of the fiction.

Horatio continues from there into the first statement in the play that is responsive to an audience's requirement of an opening scene, an indication of the nature and direction of the play to follow: "But, in the gross and scope of my opinion, / This bodes some strange eruption to our state" (i.i.68–9). That vague summary of the significance of the ghost is political, but only incidentally so because the audience, which was earlier attuned to political /military considerations, has now given its attention to the ghost. Then, with only the casual preamble of the word *state*, Marcellus asks a question irrelevant to the audience's newly primary concerns, precisely the question that no one asked when the audience first wanted to know why it was watching the sentries, the question about the fictional situation whose answer would have satisfied the audience's earlier question about its own situation: Marcellus asks "Why this same strict and most observant watch / So nightly toils the subject of the land" (i.i.71–2). Again what we are given is and is not pertinent to our concerns and expectations. This particular variety among the manifestations of simultaneous and equal propriety and impropriety in *Hamlet* occurs over and over again. Throughout the play, the audience gets information or sees action it once wanted only after a new interest has superseded the old. For one example, when Horatio, Bernardo, and Marcellus arrive in the second scene (i.ii.159), they come to do what they promise to do at the end of scene one, where they tell the audience that the way to information about the ghost is through young Hamlet. By the time they arrive "where we shall find him most conveniently," the audience has a new concern – the relation of Claudius to Gertrude and of Hamlet to both. Of course interruptions of one train of thought by the introduction of another are not only common in *Hamlet* but a commonplace of literature in general. However, although the audience's frustrations and the celerity with which it transfers its concern are similar to those of audiences of, say, Dickens, there is the important difference in *Hamlet* that there are no sharp lines of demarcation. In *Hamlet* the audience does not so much shift its focus as come to find its focus shifted.

Again the first scene provides a type of the whole. When Marcellus asks why the guard is so strict, his question is rather more violent than not in its divergence from our concern for the boding of the ghost. The answer to Marcellus' question, however, quickly pertains to the subject of ours: Horatio's explanation of the political situation depends from actions of "Our last king, / Whose image even but now appeared to us" (i.i.80–1), and his description of the activities of young Fortinbras as "The source of this our watch" is harnessed to our concern about the ghost by Bernardo, who says directly, if vaguely, that the political situation is pertinent to the walking of the ghost:

> I think it be no other but e'en so.
> Well may it sort that this portentous figure
> Comes armèd through our watch so like the king
> That was and is the question of these wars.
> (i.i.108–11)

Horatio reinforces the relevance of politics to ghosts in a long speech about supernatural events on the eve of Julius Caesar's murder. Both these speeches establishing pertinence are good examples of the sort of thing I mean: both seem impertinent digressions, sufficiently so to have been omitted from the folios.

Now for the second time, *Enter Ghost*. The re-entrance after a long and wandering digression is in itself an assertion of the continuity, constancy, and unity of the scene. Moreover, the situation into which the ghost re-enters is a careful echo of the one into which it first entered, with the difference that the promised length of the earlier exposition is fulfilled in the second. These are the lines surrounding the first entrance; the italics are mine and indicate words, sounds, and substance echoed later:

> Horatio: *Well, sit we down,*
> And let us hear Bernardo speak of this.
> Bernardo: Last night of all,
> *When yond same star* that's *westward* from the pole
> Had made his course t' illume that part of heaven
> Where now it burns, Marcellus and myself,
> The bell then beating one –
> *Enter Ghost.*
> Marcellus: *Peace, break thee* off. *Look where it comes again.*
> (1.i.33–40)

Two or three minutes later a similar situation takes shape in words that echo, and in some cases repeat, those at the earlier entrance:

> Marcellus: *Good now, sit down*, and tell me he that knows,
> *Why this same* strict and most observant watch,
> So nightly toils the subject of the land ...
>   ...
> *Enter Ghost*
> *But soft, behold, lo where it comes again!*
> (1.i.70–2, 126)

After the ghost departs on the crowing of the cock, the conversation, already extravagant and erring before the second apparition when it ranged from Danish history into Roman, meanders into a seemingly gratuitous preoccupation with the demonology of cocks (1.i.148–65). Then – into a scene that has from the irregularly regular entrance of the two sentinels been a succession of simultaneously expected and unexpected entrances – enters "the morn in russet mantle clad," bringing a great change from darkness to light, from the unknown and unnatural to the known and natural, but also presenting itself personified as another walker, one obviously relevant to the situation and to the discussion of crowing cocks, and one described in subdued but manifold echoes of the two entrances of the ghost. Notice particularly the multitude of different kinds of relationship in which "yon high eastward hill" echoes "yond same star that's westward from the pole":

> *But look*, the morn in russet mantle clad
> Walks o'er the dew of *yon high eastward* hill.
> *Break we* our watch up ....
> (1.i.166–8)

The three speeches (I.i.148–73 – Horatio's on the behavior of ghosts at cockcrow, Marcellus' on cocks at Christmas time, and Horatio's on the dawn) have four major elements running through them: cocks, spirits, sunrise, and the presence or absence of speech. All four are not present all the time, but the speeches have a sound of interconnection and relevance to one another. This at the same time that the substance of Marcellus' speech on Christmas is just as urgently irrelevant to the concerns of the scene. As a gratuitous discussion of Christianity, apparently linked to its context only by an accident of poulterer's lore, it is particularly irrelevant to the moral limits usual to revenge tragedy. The sequence of these last speeches is like the whole scene and the play in being both coherent and incoherent. Watching and comprehending the scene is an intellectual triumph for its audience. From sentence to sentence, from event to event, as the scene goes on it makes the mind of its audience capable of containing materials that seem always about to fly apart. The scene gives its audience a temporary and modest but real experience of being a superhumanly capable mental athlete. The whole play is like that.

During the first scene of *Hamlet* two things are threatened, one in the play, and one by the play. Throughout the scene the characters look at all threats as threats to the state, and specifically to the reigning king. As the king is threatened *in* scene one, so is the audience's understanding threatened *by* scene one. The audience wants some solid information about what is going on in this play. Scene one is set in the dark, and it leaves the audience in the dark. The first things the play teaches us to value are the order embodied in the king and the rational sureness, purpose, and order that the play as a play lacks in its first scene. Scene two presents both the desired orders at once and in one – the king, whose name even in scene one was not only synonymous with order but was the regular sign by which order was reasserted: the first confusion – who should challenge whom – was resolved in line three by "Long live the king"; and at the entrance of Horatio and Marcellus, rightness and regularity were vouched for by "Friends to this ground. And liegemen to the Dane." As scene two begins it is everything the audience wanted most in scene one. Here it is daylight, everything is clear, everything is systematic. Unlike scene one, this scene is physically orderly; it begins with a royal procession, businesslike and unmistakable in its identity. Unlike the first scene, the second gives the audience all the information it could desire, and gives it neatly. The direct source of both information and orderliness is Claudius, who addresses himself one by one to the groups on the stage and to the problems of the realm, punctuating the units both with little statements of conclusion like "For all, our thanks" and "So much for him" (I.ii.16, 25), and with the word "now" (I.ii.17, 26, 42, 64), by which he signals each remove to a new listener and topic. Denmark and the play are both now orderly, and are so because of the king. In its specifics, scene two is the opposite of scene one. Moreover, where scene one presented an incoherent surface whose underlying coherence is only faintly felt, this scene is the opposite. In scene one the action taken *by* the scene – it makes its audience perceive diffusion and fusion, division and unification, difference and likeness at once – is only an incidental element in the action taken or discussed *in* the scene – the guards have trouble recognizing each other; the defense preparation "does not divide the Sunday from the week," and makes "the night joint-laborer with the day" (I.i.76, 78). In scene two the first subject taken up by Claudius, and the subject of first importance to Hamlet, is itself an instance of improbable unification – the unnatural natural union of Claudius and Gertrude. Where scene one brought its audience to feel coherence in incoherence by response to systems of organization other than those of logical or narrative sequence, scene two brings its audience to think of actions and characters alternately and sometimes nearly simultaneously in systems of value whose contradictory judgments rarely collide in the mind of an audience. From an uneasiness prompted by a sense of lack of order, unity, coherence, and continuity, we have progressed to an uneasiness prompted by a sense of their excess.

Claudius is everything the audience most valued in scene one, but he is also and at once contemptible. His first sentences are unifications in which his discretion overwhelms things whose natures are oppugnant. The simple but contorted statement, "therefore our ... sister ... have we ... taken to wife," takes Claudius more than six lines to say; it is plastered together with a succession of subordinate unnatural unions made smooth by rhythm, alliteration, assonance, and syntactical balance:

> Therefore our sometime sister, now our queen,
> Th' imperial jointress to this warlike state,
> Have we, as 'twere with a defeated joy,
> With an auspicious and a dropping eye,
> With mirth in funeral and with dirge in marriage,
> In equal scale weighing delight and dole,
> Taken to wife.
>
> (I.ii.8–14)

What he says is overly orderly. The rhythms and rhetoric by which he connects any contraries, moral or otherwise, are too smooth. Look at the complex phonetic equation that gives a sound of decorousness to the moral indecorum of "With mirth in funeral and with dirge in marriage." Claudius uses syntactical and rhetorical devices for equation by balance – as one would a particularly heavy and greasy cosmetic – to smooth over any inconsistencies whatsoever. Even his incidental diction is of joining: "jointress," "disjoint," "Colleaguèd" (I.ii.9, 20, 21). The excessively lubricated rhetoric by which Claudius makes unnatural connections between moral contraries is as gross and sweaty as the incestuous marriage itself. The audience has double and contrary responses to Claudius, the unifier of contraries.

Scene two presents still another kind of double understanding in double frames of reference. Claudius is the primary figure in the hierarchy depicted – he is the king; he is also the character upon whom all the other characters focus their attention; he does most of the talking. An audience focuses its attention on him. On the other hand, one of the members of the royal procession was dressed all in black – a revenger to go with the presumably vengeful ghost in scene one. Moreover, the man in black is probably also the most famous actor in England (or at least of the company). The particulars of the scene make Claudius the focal figure, the genre and the particulars of a given performance focus the audience's attention on Hamlet.

When the two focuses come together ("But now, my cousin Hamlet, and my son –") Hamlet's reply (I.ii.65) is spoken not to the king but to the audience. "A little more than kin, and less than kind" is the first thing spoken by Hamlet and the first thing spoken aside to the audience. With that line Hamlet takes the audience for his own, and gives himself to the audience as its agent on the stage. Hamlet and the audience are from this point in the play more firmly united than any other such pair in Shakespeare, and perhaps in dramatic literature.

Claudius' "my cousin Hamlet, and my son" is typical of his stylistic unifications of mutually exclusive contrary ideas (cousin, son). Hamlet's reply does not unify ideas, but disunifies them (more than kin, less than kind). However, the style in which Hamlet distinguishes is a caricature of Claudius' equations by rhetorical balance; here again, what interrupts the order, threatens coherence, and is strikingly at odds with its preamble is also a continuation by echo of what went before. Hamlet's parody of Claudius and his refusal to be folded into Claudius' rhetorical blanket is satisfying to an audience in need of assurance that it is not alone in its uneasiness at Claudius' rhetoric. On the other hand, the orderliness that the audience valued in scene two is abruptly destroyed by Hamlet's reply. At the moment Hamlet speaks his first line, the audience finds itself the champion of order in Denmark and in the play, and at the same time irrevocably allied to Hamlet – the one present threat to the order of both.

II

The play persists in taking its audience to the brink of intellectual terror. The mind of the audience is rarely far from the intellectual desperation of Claudius in the prayer scene when the systems in which he values his crown and queen collide with those in which he values his soul and peace of mind. For the duration of *Hamlet* the mind of the audience is as it might be if it could take on, or dared to try to take on, its experience whole, if it dared drop the humanly necessary intellectual crutches of compartmentalization, point of view, definition, and the idea of relevance, if it dared admit any subject for evaluation into any and all the systems of value to which at different times one human mind subscribes. The constant occupation of a sane mind is to choose, establish, and maintain frames of reference for the things of its experience; as the high value placed on artistic unity attests, one of the attractions of art is that it offers a degree of holiday from that occupation. As the creation of a human mind, art comes to its audience ready-fitted to the human mind; it has physical limits or limits of duration; its details are subordinated to one another in a hierarchy of importance. A play guarantees us that we will not have to select a direction for our attention; it offers us isolation from matter and considerations irrelevant to a particular focus or a particular subject. *Hamlet* is more nearly an exception to those rules than other satisfying and bearable works of art. That, perhaps, is the reason so much effort has gone into interpretations that presume that *Hamlet*, as it is, is not and was not satisfying and bearable. The subject of literature is often conflict, often conflict of values; but, though the agonies of decision, knowing, and valuing are often the objects of an audience's concern, an audience rarely undergoes or even approaches such agonies itself. That it should enjoy doing so seems unlikely, but in *Hamlet* the problems the audience thinks about and the intellectual action of thinking about them are very similar. *Hamlet* is the tragedy of an audience that cannot make up its mind.

One of the most efficient, reliable, and usual guarantees of isolation is genre. The appearance of a ghost in scene one suggests that the play will be a revenge tragedy. *Hamlet* does indeed turn out to be a revenge tragedy, but here genre does not provide the limited frame of reference that the revenge genre and genres in general usually establish. The archetypal revenge play is *The Spanish Tragedy*. In the first scene of that, a ghost and a personification, Revenge, walk out on the stage and spend a whole scene saying who they are, where they are, why they are there, what has happened, and what will happen. The ghost in *The Spanish Tragedy* gives more information in the first five lines of the play than there is in the whole first scene of *Hamlet*. In *The Spanish Tragedy* the ghost and Revenge act as a chorus for the play. They keep the doubt and turmoil of the characters from ever transferring themselves to the audience. They keep the audience safe from doubt, safely outside the action, looking on. In *The Spanish Tragedy* the act of revenge is presented as a moral necessity, just as, say, shooting the villain may be in a Western. Revenge plays were written by Christians and played to Christian audiences. Similarly, traditional American Westerns were written by and for believers faithful to the principles of the Constitution of the United States. The possibility that an audience's Christian belief that vengeance belongs only to God will color its understanding of revenge in *The Spanish Tragedy* is as unlikely as a modern film audience's consideration of a villain's civil rights when somebody shouts, "Head him off at the pass." The tension between revenge morality and the audience's own Christian morality was a source of vitality always *available* to Kyd and his followers, but one that they did not avail themselves of. Where they did not ignore moralities foreign to the vaguely Senecan ethic of the genre, they took steps to take the life out of conflicts between contrary systems of value.

When Christian morality invades a revenge play, as it does in iii.xiii of *The Spanish Tragedy* when Hieronimo says *Vindicta Mihi* and then further echoes St. Paul's "Vengeance is mine; I will repay, saith the Lord," the quickly watered-down Christian position and the contrary position for which Hieronimo rejects it are presented as isolated categories between which the *character* must and does choose. The conflict is restricted to the stage and removed from the mind of the audience. The effect is not to make the contrariety of values a part of the audience's experience but to dispel the value system foreign to the genre, to file it away as, for the duration of the play, a dead issue. In its operations upon an audience of *The Spanish Tragedy*, the introduction and rejection of the Christian view of vengeance is roughly comparable to the hundreds of exchanges in hundreds of Westerns where the new schoolmarm says that the hero should go to the sheriff rather than try to outdraw the villain. The hero rarely gives an intellectually satisfying reason for taking the law into his own hands, but the mere fact that the pertinent moral alternative has been mentioned and rejected is ordinarily sufficient to allow the audience to join the hero in his morality without fear of further interruption from its own.

The audience of *Hamlet* is not allowed the intellectual comfort of isolation in the one system of values appropriate to the genre. In *Hamlet* the Christian context for valuing is persistently present. In i.v the ghost makes a standard revenge-tragedy statement of Hamlet's moral obligation to kill Claudius. The audience is quite ready to think in that frame of reference and does so. The ghost then – in the same breath – opens the audience's mind to the frame of reference least compatible with the genre.

When he forbids vengeance upon Gertrude, he does so in specifically Christian terms: "Taint not thy mind, nor let thy soul contrive / Against thy mother aught. Leave her to heaven …" (I.v.85–6). Moreover, this ghost is at least as concerned that he lost the chance to confess before he died as he is that he lost his life at all.

Most of the time contradictory values do not collide in the audience's consciousness, but the topic of revenge is far from the only instance in which they live anxiously close to one another, so close to one another that, although the audience is not shaken in its faith in either of a pair of conflicting values, its mind remains in the uneasy state common in nonartistic experience but unusual for audiences of plays. The best example is the audience's thinking about suicide during *Hamlet*. The first mention of suicide comes already set into a Christian frame of reference by the clause in which self-slaughter is mentioned: "Or that the Everlasting had not fixed / His canon 'gainst self-slaughter" (I.ii.131–2). In the course of the play, however, an audience evaluates suicide in all the different systems available to minds outside the comfortable limitations of art; from time to time in the play the audience thinks of suicide variously as (1) cause for damnation, (2) a heroic and generous action, (3) a cowardly action, and (4) a last sure way to peace. The audience moves from one to another system of values with a rapidity that human faith in the rational constancy of the human mind makes seem impossible. Look, for example, at the travels of the mind that listens to and understands what goes on between the specifically Christian death of Laertes (*Laertes*: "… Mine and my father's death come not upon thee, / Nor thine on me." –*Hamlet*: "Heaven make thee free of it" v.ii.319–21) and the specifically Christian death of Hamlet (*Horatio*: "… Good night, sweet prince, / And flights of angels sing thee to thy rest …" v.ii.348–48). During the intervening thirty lines the audience and the characters move from the Christian context in which Laertes' soul departs, into the familiar literary context where they can take Horatio's attempted suicide as the generous and heroic act it is (v.ii.324–31). Audience and characters have likewise no difficulty at all in understanding and accepting the label "felicity" for the destination of the suicide – even though Hamlet, the speaker of "Absent thee from felicity awhile" (v.ii.336), prefaces the statement with an incidental "By heaven" (v.ii.332), and even though Hamlet and the audience have spent a lot of time during the preceding three hours actively considering the extent to which a suicide's journey to "the undiscovered country" can be called "felicity" or predicted at all. When "Good night, sweet prince" is spoken by the antique Roman of twenty lines before, both he and the audience return to thinking in a Christian frame of reference, as if they had never been away.

The audience is undisturbed by a nearly endless supply of similar inconstancies in itself and the play; these are a few instances:

The same audience that scorned pretense when Hamlet knew not "seems" in I.ii admires his skill at pretense and detection in the next two Acts.

The audience joins Hamlet both in admiration for the self-control by which the player "could force his soul so to his own conceit" that he could cry for Hecuba (II.ii.537), and in admiration for the very different self-control of Horatio (III.ii.51–71).

The audience, which presumably could not bear to see a literary hero stab an unarmed man at prayer, sees the justice of Hamlet's self-accusations of delay. The audience also agrees with the ghost when both have a full view of the corpse of Polonius, and when the ghost's diction is an active reminder of the weapon by which

Hamlet has just attempted the acting of the dread command: "Do not forget. This visitation / Is but to whet thy almost blunted purpose" (III.iv.111–12).

The audience that sees the ghost and hears about its prison house in I.v also accepts the just as obvious truth of "the undiscovered country from whose bourn no traveller returns …"

What have come to be recognized as the problems of *Hamlet* arise at points where an audience's contrary responses come to consciousness. They are made bearable in performance (though not in recollection) by means similar to those by which the audience is carried across the quieter crises of scene one. In performance, at least, the play gives its audience strength and courage not only to flirt with the frailty of its own understanding but actually to survive conscious experiences of the Polonian foolishness of faith that things will follow only the rules of the particular logic in which we expect to see them. The best example of the audience's endurance of self-knowledge is its experiences of Hamlet's madness. In the last moments of Act I Hamlet makes Horatio, Marcellus, and the audience privy to his intention to pretend madness: "… How strange or odd some'er I bear myself / (As I perchance hereafter shall think meet / To put an antic disposition on) …" (I.v.170–3). The audience sets out into Act II knowing what Hamlet knows, knowing Hamlet's plans, and secure in its superiority to the characters who do not. (Usually an audience is superior to the central characters: it knows that Desdemona is innocent, Othello does not; it knows what it would do when Lear foolishly divides his kingdom; it knows how Birnam Wood came to come to Dunsinane. In *Hamlet*, however, the audience never knows what it would have done in Hamlet's situation; in fact, since the King's successful plot in the duel with Laertes changes Hamlet's situation so that he becomes as much the avenger of his own death as of his father's, the audience never knows what Hamlet would have done. Except for brief periods near the end of the play, the audience never has insight or knowledge superior to Hamlet's or, indeed, different from Hamlet's. Instead of having superiority *to* Hamlet, the audience goes into the second Act to share the superiority *of* Hamlet.) The audience knows that Hamlet will play mad, and its expectations are quickly confirmed. Just seventy-five lines into Act II, Ophelia comes in and describes a kind of behavior in Hamlet that sounds like the behavior of a young man of limited theatrical ability who is pretending to be mad (II.i.77–84). Our confidence that this behavior so puzzling to others is well within our grasp is strengthened by the reminder of the ghost, the immediate cause of the promised pretense, in Ophelia's comparison of Hamlet to a creature "loosèd out of hell / To speak of horrors."

Before Ophelia's entrance, II.i has presented an example of the baseness and foolishness of Polonius, the character upon whom both the audience and Hamlet exercise their superiority throughout Act II. Polonius seems base because he is arranging to spy on Laertes. He instructs his spy in ways to use the "bait of falsehood" – to find out directions by indirections (II.i.1–74). He is so sure that he knows everything, and so sure that his petty scheme is not only foolproof but brilliant, that he is as contemptible mentally as he is morally. The audience laughs at him because he loses his train of thought in pompous byways, so that, eventually, he forgets what he set out to say: "What was I about to say? … I was about to say something! Where did I leave?" (II.i.50–1). When Ophelia reports Hamlet's behavior, Polonius takes what is apparently Hamlet's bait: "Mad for thy love?" (II.i.85). He also thinks of (and then spends the rest of the Act finding evidence for) a specific cause for Hamlet's madness: he is mad for love of Ophelia. The audience knows (1) Hamlet will pretend madness, (2) Polonius is a fool, and (3) what is actually bothering Hamlet. Through the rest of the Act, the audience laughs at Polonius for being fooled by Hamlet. It continues to laugh at Polonius' inability to keep his mind on a track (II.ii.85–130); it also laughs at him for the opposite fault – he has a one-track mind and sees anything and everything as evidence that Hamlet is mad for love (II.ii.173–212, 394–402). Hamlet, whom the audience knows and understands, spends a good part of the rest of the scene making Polonius demonstrate his foolishness.

Then, in Act III, scene i, the wise audience and the foolish Polonius both become lawful espials of Hamlet's meeting with Ophelia. Ophelia says that Hamlet made her believe he loved her. Hamlet's reply might just as well be delivered by the play to the audience: "You should not have believed me ..." (III.i.117). In his next speech Hamlet appears suddenly, inexplicably, violently, and really mad – this before an audience whose chief identity for the last hour has consisted in its knowledge that Hamlet is only pretending. The audience finds itself guilty of Polonius' foolish confidence in predictable trains of events. It is presented with evidence for thinking just what it has considered other minds foolish for thinking – that Hamlet is mad, mad for love of an inconstant girl who has betrayed him. Polonius and the audience are the self-conscious and prideful knowers and understanders in the play. They both overestimate the degree of safety they have as innocent onlookers.

When Hamlet seems suddenly mad, the audience is likely for a minute to think that it is mad or that the play is mad. That happens several times in the course of the play; and the play helps audiences toward the decision that the trouble is in themselves. Each time the play seems insane, it also is obviously ordered, orderly, all of a piece. For example, in the case of Hamlet's truly odd behavior with Ophelia in III.i some of the stuff of his speeches to her has been otherwise applied but nonetheless present in the play before (fickleness, cosmetics). Furthermore, after the fact, the play often tells us how we should have reacted; here the King sums up the results of the Ophelia experiment as if they were exactly what the audience expected they would be (which is exactly what they were not): "Love? his affections do not that way tend, / ... what he spoke ... / Was not like madness" (III.i.162–4). In the next scene, Hamlet enters perfectly sane, and lecturing, oddly enough, on what a play should be (III.ii.1–42). Whenever the play seems mad it drifts back into focus as if nothing odd had happened. The audience is encouraged to agree with the play that nothing did, to assume (as perhaps for other reasons it should) that its own intellect is inadequate. The audience pulls itself together, and goes on to another crisis of its understanding. Indeed, it had to do so in order to arrive at the crisis of the nunnery speech. At exactly the point where the audience receives the information that makes it so vulnerable to Hamlet's inexplicable behavior in the nunnery scene, the lines about the antic disposition (I.v.170–3) act as a much needed explanation – *after the fact of the audience's discomfort* – of jocular behavior by Hamlet ("Art thou there, true-penny?" "You hear this fellow in the cellarage," "Well said, old mole!" I.v.150–1, 162) that is foreign to his tone and attitude earlier in the scene, and that jars with the expectations aroused by the manner in which he and the play have been treating the ghost. For a moment, the play seems to be the work of a madman. Then Hamlet explains what he *will* do, and the audience is invited to feel lonely in foolishly failing to understand that that was what he was doing before.

III

The kind of experience an audience has of *Hamlet* in its large movements is duplicated – and more easily demonstrated – in the microcosm of its responses to brief passages. For example, the act of following the exchange initiated by Polonius' "What do you read, my Lord?" in II.ii is similar to the larger experience of coping with the whole career of Hamlet's madness:

> *Polonius:* ... What do you read, my Lord?
> *Hamlet:* Words, words, words.
> *Polonius:* What is the matter, my lord?
> *Hamlet:* Between who?
> *Polonius:* I mean the matter that you read, my lord.
> *Hamlet:* Slanders, sir, for the satirical rogue says here that old men have grey beards, that their faces are wrinkled, their eyes purging thick amber and plum-tree gum, and that they have a plentiful lack of wit, together with most weak hams. All which, sir, though I most powerfully and potently believe, yet I hold it not honesty to have it thus set down, for you yourself, sir, should be old as I am if, like a crab, you could go backward.
> *Polonius:* [aside] Though this be madness, yet there is method in't ...

(II.ii.190–204)

The audience is full partner in the first two of Hamlet's comically absolute answers. The first answer is not what the questioner expects, and we laugh at the mental inflexibility that makes Polonius prey to frustration in an answer that takes the question literally rather than as it is customarily meant in similar contexts. In his first question Polonius assumes that what he says will have meaning only within the range appropriate to the context in which he speaks. In his second he acts to limit the frame of reference of the first question, but, because "What is the matter?" is a standard idiom in another context, it further widens the range of reasonable but unexpected understanding. On his third try Polonius achieves a question whose range is as limited as his meaning. The audience – composed of smug initiates in Hamlet's masquerade and companions in his cleverness – expects to revel further in the comic revelation of Polonius' limitations. Hamlet's answer begins by letting us laugh at the discomfiture inherent for Polonius in a list of "slanders" of old men. Because of its usual applications, the word "slander" suggests that what is so labeled is not only painful but untrue. Part of the joke here is that these slanders are true. When Hamlet finishes his list, he seems about to continue in the same vein and to demonstrate his madness by saying something like "All which, sir, though ..., yet are lies." Instead, a syntactical machine ("though ... yet"), rhetorical emphasis ("powerfully and potently"), and diction ("believe") suitable for the expected denial are used to admit the truth of the slanders: "All which, sir, though I most powerfully and potently believe, yet I hold it not honesty to have it thus set down, for you yourself, sir ..." The speech seems to have given up comic play on objection to slanders on grounds of untruth, and to be about to play from an understanding of "slander" as injurious whether true or not. The syntax of "I hold it not honesty …, for" signals that a reason for Hamlet's objections will follow, and – in a context where the relevance of the slanders to Polonius gives pain enough to justify suppression of geriatric commonplaces – "for you yourself, sir" signals the probable general direction of the explanation. So far the audience has followed Hamlet's wit without difficulty from one focus to another, but now the bottom falls out from under the audience's own Polonian assumption, in this case the assumption that Hamlet will pretend madness according to pattern: "for you yourself, sir, should be old as I am if, like a crab, you could go backward." This last is exactly the opposite of what Polonius calls it, this is madness without method.

The audience finds itself trying to hear sense in madness; it suddenly undergoes experience of the fact that Polonius' assumptions about cause and effect in life and language are no more arbitrary and vulnerable than its own. The audience has been where it has known that the idea of sanity is insane, but it is there very briefly; it feels momentarily lonely and lost – as it feels when it has failed to get a joke or when a joke has failed to be funny. The play continues blandly across the gulf. Polonius' comment reflects comically on the effects on him of the general subject of old age; the banter between Hamlet and Polonius picks up again; and Polonius continues his self-confident diagnostic asides to the audience. Moreover, the discussion of Hamlet's reading is enclosed by two passages that have strong nonlogical, nonsignificant likeness to one another in the incidental materials they share – breeding, childbearing, death, and walking:

> *Hamlet:*   For if the sun breed maggots in a dead dog, being a good kissing carrion –
>   Have you a daughter?
> *Polonius:* I have, my lord.
> *Hamlet:*   Let her not walk i' th' sun. Conception is a blessing, but as your daughter may
>   conceive, friend, look to't.
> *Polonius:* [aside] How say you by that? Still harping on my daughter. Yet he knew me not
>   at first. 'A said I was a fish-monger. 'A is far gone, far gone. And truly in my
>   youth I suffered much extremity for love, very near this. I'll speak to him
>   again. – What do you read, my lord?
>
>   (ii.ii.181–90)

> *Polonius:* [aside] Though this be madness, yet there is method in't. – Will you walk out
>   of the air, my lord?
> *Hamlet:*   Into my grave?
> *Polonius:* Indeed, that's out of the air. [aside] How pregnant sometimes his replies are! a
>   happiness that often madness hits on, which reason and sanity could not so
>   prosperously be delivered of …
>
>   (ii.ii.203–9)

From beginning to end, in all sizes and kinds of materials, the play offers its audience an actual and continuing experience of perceiving a multitude of intense relationships in an equal multitude of different systems of coherence, systems not subordinated to one another in a hierarchy of relative power. The way to an answer to "What is so good about *Hamlet?*" may be in an answer to the same question about its most famous part, the "To be or not to be" soliloquy.

The soliloquy sets out with ostentatious deliberation, rationality, and precision. Hamlet fixes and limits his subject with authority and – considering that his carefully defined subject takes in everything humanly conceivable – with remarkable confidence: "To be, or not to be – that is the question." He then restates and further defines the question in four lines that echo the physical proportions of "To be or not to be" (two lines on the positive, two on the negative) and also echo the previous grammatical construction ("to suffer ... or to take arms"):

> Whether 'tis nobler in the mind to suffer
> The slings and arrows of outrageous fortune
> Or to take arms against a sea of troubles
> And by opposing end them.
>
> (iii.i.57–60)

The speech is determinedly methodical about defining a pair of alternatives that should be as easily distinguishable as any pair imaginable; surely being and not being are distinct from one another. The next sentence continues the pattern of infinitives, but it develops the idea of "not to be" instead of continuing the positive-negative alternation followed before:

> To die, to sleep –
> No more – and by a sleep to say we end
> The heartache, and the thousand natural shocks
> That flesh is heir to. 'Tis a consummation
> Devoutly to be wished.
>
> (iii.i.60–4)

As an audience listens to and comprehends the three units "To die," "to sleep," and "No more," some intellectual uneasiness should impinge upon it. "To sleep" is in apposition to "to die," and their equation is usual and perfectly reasonable. However, death and sleep are also a traditional type of unlikeness; they could as well restate "to be or not to be" (to sleep or to die) as "not to be" alone. Moreover, since to die is to sleep, and is also to sleep no more, no vocal emphasis or no amount of editorial punctuation will limit the relationship between "to sleep" and "no more." Thus, when "and by a sleep to say we end ..." reasserts the metaphoric equation of death and sleep, the listener feels a sudden and belated need to have heard "no more" as the isolated summary statement attempted by the punctuation of modern texts. What is happening here is that the apparently sure distinction between "to be" and "not to be" is becoming less and less easy to maintain. The process began even in the methodically precise first sentence where passivity to death-dealing slings and arrows described "to be," and the positive aggressive action of taking arms described the negative state, "not to be." Even earlier, the listener experienced a substantially irrelevant instability of relationship when "in the mind" attached first to "nobler," indicating the sphere of the nobility, and then to "suffer," indicating the sphere of the suffering: "nobler in the mind to suffer."

"The thousand natural shocks / That flesh is heir to" further denies the simplicity of the initial alternatives by opening the mind of the listener to considerations excluded by the isolated question whether it is more pleasant to live or to die; the substance of the phrase is a summary of the pains of life, but its particulars introduce the idea of duty. "Heir" is particularly relevant to the relationship and duty of Hamlet to his father; it also implies a continuation of conditions from generation to generation that is generally antithetical to any assumption of finality in death. The diction of the phrase also carries with it a suggestion of the Christian context in which flesh is heir to the punishment of Adam; the specifically religious word "devoutly" in the next sentence opens the idea of suicide to the Christian ethic from which the narrowed limits of the first sentences had briefly freed it.

While the logical limits and controls of the speech are falling away, its illogical patterns are giving it their own coherence. For example, the constancy of the infinitive construction maintains an impression that the speech is proceeding as methodically as it began; the word "to," in its infinitive use and otherwise, appears thirteen times among the eighty-five words in the first ten lines of the soliloquy. At the same time that the listener is having trouble comprehending the successive contradictions of "To die, to sleep – / No more – and by a sleep to say we end ... ," he also hears at the moment of crisis a confirming echo of the first three syllables and the word "end" from "*and by opposing end* them" in the first three syllables and word "end" in "*and by a* sleep to say we *end.*" As the speech goes on, as it loses more and more of its rational precision, and as "to be" and "not to be" become less and less distinguishable, rhetorical coherence continues in force. The next movement of the speech begins with a direct repetition, in the same metrical position in the line, of the words with which the previous movement began: "To die, to sleep." The new movement seems, as each new movement has seemed, to introduce a restatement of what has gone before; the rhetorical construction of the speech insists that all the speech does is make the distinct natures of "to be" and "not to be" clearer and clearer:

> To die, to sleep –
> To sleep – perchance to dream: ay, there's the rub,
> For in that sleep of death what dreams may come
> When we have shuffled off this mortal coil,
> Must give us pause. There's the respect
> That makes calamity of so long life.
>
> (III.i.64–9)

As Hamlet describes his increasing difficulty in seeing death as the simple opposite of life, the manner of his description gives his listener an actual experience of that difficulty; "shuffled off this mortal coil" says "cast off the turmoil of this life," but "shuffled off" and "coil" both suggest the rejuvenation of a snake which, having once thrown her enamell'd skin, reveals another just like it underneath. The listener also continues to have difficulty with the simple action of understanding; like the nature of the things discussed, the natures of the sentences change as they are perceived: "what dreams may come" is a common construction for a question, and the line that follows sounds like a subordinate continuation of the question; it is not until we hear "must give us pause" that we discover that "what dreams may come" is a noun phrase, the subject of a declarative sentence that only comes into being with the late appearance of an unexpected verb. In the next sentence ("There's the respect / That makes calamity of so long life"), logic requires that we understand "makes calamity so long-lived," but our habitual understanding of *makes … of* constructions and our recent indoctrination in the pains of life make us likely to hear the contradictory, illogical, and yet appropriate "makes a long life a calamity."

Again, however, the lines sound ordered and reasonable. The rejected first impressions I have just described are immediately followed by a real question, and one that is largely an insistently long list of things that make life a monotonously painful series of calamities. Moreover, nonlogical coherence is provided by the quiet and intricate harmony of "to dream," "of death," and "shuffled off" in the metrical centers of three successive lines; by the echo of the solidly metaphoric "there's the rub" in the vague "there's the respect"; and by the repetition of "for" from "For in that sleep" to begin the next section of the speech.

> For who would bear the whips and scorns of time,
> Th' oppressor's wrong, the proud man's contumely,
> The pangs of despised love, the law's delay,
> The insolence of office, and the spurns
> That patient merit of th' unworthy takes,
> When he himself might his quietus make
> With a bare bodkin? Who would fardels bear,
> To grunt and sweat under a weary life,
> But that the dread of something after death,
> The undiscovered country, from whose bourn
> No traveller returns, puzzles the will,
> And makes us rather bear those ills we have
> Than fly to others that we know not of?
>
> (III.i.70–82)

Although the list in the first question is disjointed and rhythmically frantic, the impression of disorder is countered by the regularity of the definite article, and by the inherently conjunctive action of six possessives. The possessives in *'s*, the possessives in *of*, and the several nonpossessive *of* constructions are themselves an underlying pattern of simultaneous likeness and difference. So is the illogical pattern present in the idea of burdens, the word "bear," and the word "bare." The line in which the first of these questions ends and the second begins is an epitome of the construction and action of the speech: "With a bare bodkin? Who would fardels bear, …" The two precisely equal halves of a single rhythmic unit hold together two separate syntactical units. The beginning of the new sentence, "Who would fardels bear," echoes both the beginning, "For who would bear," and the sound of one word, "bare," from the end of the old. Moreover, "bare" and "bear," two words that are both the same and different, participate here in statements of the two undistinguishable alternatives: "to be, or not to be" – to bear fardels, or to kill oneself with a bare bodkin.

The end of the speech sounds like the rationally achieved conclusion of just such a rational investigation as Hamlet began. It begins with *thus*, the sign of logical conclusion, and it gains a sound of inevitable truth and triumphant clarity from the incremental repetition of *and* at the beginning of every other line. The last lines are relevant to Hamlet's behavior in the play at large and therefore have an additional sound of rightness here. Not only are the lines broadly appropriate to the play, the audience's understanding of them is typical of its understanding throughout the play and of its understanding of the previous particulars of this speech: Hamlet has hesitated to kill Claudius. Consideration of suicide has seemed a symptom of that hesitancy. Here the particular from which Hamlet's conclusions about his inability to act derive is his hesitancy to commit suicide. The audience hears those conclusions in the context of his failure to take the action that suicide would avoid.

> Thus conscience does make cowards of us all,
> And thus the native hue of resolution
> Is sicklied o'er with the pale cast of thought,
> And enterprises of great pitch and moment
> With this regard their currents turn awry
> And lose the name of action.
>
> (III.i.83–8)

These last lines are accidentally a compendium of phrases descriptive of the action of the speech and the process of hearing it. The speech puzzles the will, but it makes us capable of facing and bearing puzzlement. The "To be or not to be" soliloquy is a type of the over-all action of *Hamlet*. In addition, a soliloquy in which being and its opposite are indistinguishable is peculiarly appropriate to a play otherwise full of easily distinguishable pairs that are not easily distinguished from one another by characters or audience or both: Rosencrantz and Guildenstern; the pictures of Gertrude's two husbands (III.iv.54–68); the hawk and the handsaw (II.ii.370); and father and mother who are one flesh and so undistinguished in Hamlet's farewell to Claudius (IV.iii.48–51). The soliloquy is above all typical of a play whose last moments enable its audience to look unblinking upon a situation in which Hamlet, the finally successful revenger, is the object of Laertes' revenge; a situation in which Laertes, Hamlet's victim, victimizes Hamlet; a situation in which Fortinbras, the threat to Denmark's future in scene i, is its hope for political salvation; in short, a situation in which any identity can be indistinguishable from its opposite. The soliloquy, the last scene, the first scene, the play – each and together – make an impossible coherence of truths that are both undeniably incompatible and undeniably coexistent.

IV

The kind of criticism I am doing here may be offensive to readers conditioned to think of revelation as the value of literature and the purpose of criticism. The things I have said about *Hamlet* may be made more easily palatable by the memory that illogical coherence – coherent madness – is a regular topic of various characters who listen to Hamlet and Ophelia. In the Reynaldo scene (II.i) and Hamlet's first talk with Rosencrantz and Guildenstern the power of rhetoric and context to make a particular either good or bad at will is also a topic in the play. So too is the perception of clouds which may in a moment look "like a camel indeed," and "like a weasel" and be "very like a whale" (III.ii.361–7).

What I am doing may seem antipoetical; it should not. On the contrary, the effects I have described in *Hamlet* are of the same general kind as the nonsignificant coherences made by rhythm, rhyme, alliteration, and others of the standard devices of prosody. For example, the physics of the relationship among Hamlet, Laertes, Fortinbras, and Pyrrhus, the four avenging sons in *Hamlet*, are in their own scale and substance the same as those of the relationship among *cat, rat, bat,* and *chat.* The theme of suicide, for all the inconstancy of its fluid moral and emotional value, is a constant and unifying factor in the play. So too is the theme of appearance and reality, deceit, pretense, disguise, acting, seeming, and cosmetics which gives the play coherence even though its values are as many as its guises and labels. The analogy of rhyme or of a pair of like-metered lines applies profitably to the nonsignifying relationship between Hamlet's two interviews with women. Both the nunnery scene with Ophelia and the closet scene with Gertrude are stage-managed and overlooked by Polonius; neither lady understands Hamlet; both are amazed by his intensity; in both scenes Hamlet makes a series of abortive departures before his final exit. There is a similar kind of insignificant likeness in numerous repeated patterns of scenes and situations like that of Hamlet's entrance reading in II.ii and its echo in Ophelia's show of devotional reading in III.i. Indeed, the same sort of thing can be said about any of the themes and images whose value critics have tried to convert to significance.

The tools of prosody and the phenomena I have talked about show their similarity well when they cooperate in Hamlet's little poem on perception and truth, a poem that is a model of the experience of the whole play. Polonius reads it to the king and queen:

> Doubt thou the stars are fire;
>> Doubt that the sun doth move;
> Doubt truth to be a liar;
>> But never doubt I love.
>>> (II.ii.116–19)

I suggest that the pleasure of intellectual possession evoked by perception of the likeness and difference of "fire" and "liar" and of "move" and "love," or among the four metrically like and unlike lines, or between the three positive clauses and the one negative one, or between "stars" and "sun" or "truth" and "liar" is of the same kind as the greater achievement of intellectual mastery of the greater challenge presented by "doubt" in the first three lines. The first two *doubts* demand disbelief of two things that common sense cannot but believe. The third, whose likeness to the first two is insisted upon by anaphora, is made unlike them by the words that follow it: disbelief that truth is a liar is a logical necessity; therefore, "doubt" here must mean "believe" or "incline to believe" as it does earlier in this scene (l.56) and several other times in the play. To be consistent with the pair of hyperbolic impossibilities to which it is coupled, and to fit the standard rhetorical formula (Doubt what cannot be doubted, but do not doubt …) in which it appears, "Doubt truth to be a liar" must be understood in a way inconsistent with another pattern of the poem, the previously established meaning of "doubt." Even the first two lines, which seem to fit the hyperbolic formula so well, may make the poem additionally dizzying because their subject matter could remind a Renaissance listener (once disturbed by the reversal of the meaning of the third "doubt") of doubts cast upon common-sense impressions by still recent astronomical discoveries, notably that the diurnal motion of the sun is an illusion.

The urgent rhetorical coherence of the poem is like that of the play. As the multitude of insistent and overlapping systems of coherence in the poem allows its listener to hold the two contradictory meanings of "doubt" in colloid-like suspension and to experience both the actions "doubt" describes, so in the play at large an alliteration of subjects – a sort of rhythm of ideas whose substance may or may not inform the situation dramatized – gives shape and identity, nonphysical substance, to the play that *contains* the situation. Such a container allows Shakespeare to replace *conclusion* with *inclusion*; it provides a particular and temporary context that overcomes the intellectual terror ordinarily inherent in looking at an action in all the value systems it invades. Such a container provides a sense of order and limitation sufficient to replace the comforting boundaries of carefully isolated frames of reference; it makes its audience capable of contemplating more truth than the mind should be able to bear.

In summary I would say that the thing about *Hamlet* that has put Western man into a panic to explain it is not that the play is incoherent, but that it is coherent. There are plenty of incoherent plays; nobody ever looks at them twice. This one, because it obviously makes sense and because it just as obviously cannot be made sense of, threatens our inevitable working assumption that there are no "more things in earth" than can be understood in one philosophy. People see *Hamlet* and tolerate inconsistencies that it does not seem they could bear. Students of the play have explained that such people do not, in fact, find the play bearable at all. They therefore whittle the play down for us to the size of one of its terms, and deny the others. Truth is bigger than any one system for knowing it, and *Hamlet* is bigger than any of the frames of reference it inhabits. *Hamlet* allows us to comprehend – hold on to – all the contradictions it contains. *Hamlet* refuses to cradle its audience's mind in a closed generic framework, or otherwise limit the ideological context of its actions. In *Hamlet* the mind is cradled in nothing more than the fabric of the play. The superior strength and value of that fabric is in the sense it gives that it is unlimited in its range, and that its audience is not only sufficient to comprehend but is in the act of achieving total comprehension of all the perceptions to which its mind can open. The source of the strength is in a rhetorical economy that allows the audience to perform both of the basic actions of the mind upon almost every conjunction of elements in the course of the play: it perceives strong likeness, and it perceives strong difference. Every intellectual conjunction is also a disjunction, and any two things that pull apart contain qualities that are simultaneously the means of uniting them.

16

Rabbits, Ducks, and *Henry V*

Norman Rabkin

T
he greater plays leave us knowing we should be perplexed. No explication satisfies us that *Macbeth* or *King Lear, Hamlet* or *Othello* or *The Winter's Tale* has been safely reduced to a formula that answers all our questions. Such plays tell us that mystery is their mode; the questions aroused by them seem unanswerable, because each play in its own way creates an image of a world that is unfathomable where we most need to understand it.

Henry V is no such play. Rather, it repeatedly elicits simple and whole-hearted responses from its critics, interpretations that seem solidly based on total readings of a consistent whole. This is not to say, however, that the critics agree with each other. As a matter of fact, they could hardly disagree more radically. "For some" of them, a recent writer remarks, "the play presents the story of an ideal monarch and glorifies his achievements; for them, the tone approaches that of an epic lauding the military virtues. For others, the protagonist is a Machiavellian militarist who professes Christianity but whose deeds reveal both hypocrisy and ruthlessness; for them, the tone is predominantly one of mordant satire."[1]

One way to deal with a play that provokes such conflicting responses is to try to find the truth somewhere between them. Another is to suggest that the author couldn't make up his mind which side he wanted to come down on and left us a mess. A third is to interpret all the signals indicating one polar reading as intentional, and to interpret all the other signals as irrepressible evidence that Shakespeare didn't believe what he was trying to say. All of these strategies have been mounted against *Henry V*; and all of them are just as wrong as most critics now recognize similar attempts to domesticate the greater plays to be.

I am going to argue that in *Henry V* Shakespeare creates a work whose ultimate power is precisely the fact that it points in two opposite directions, virtually daring us to choose one of the two opposed interpretations it requires of us. In this deceptively simple play Shakespeare experiments, perhaps more shockingly than elsewhere, with a structure like the gestaltist's familiar drawing of a rare beast. Gombrich describes the experience of that creature in memorable terms:

> We can see the picture as either a rabbit or a duck. It is easy to discover both readings. It is less easy to describe what happens when we switch from one interpretation to the other. Clearly we do not have the illusion that we are confronted with a "real" duck or rabbit. The shape on the paper resembles neither animal very closely. And yet there is no doubt that the shape transforms itself in some subtle way when the duck's beak becomes the rabbit's ears and brings an otherwise neglected spot into prominence as the rabbit's mouth. I say "neglected," but does it enter our experience at all when we switch back to reading "duck"? To answer this question, we are compelled to look for what is "really there," to see the shape apart from its interpretation, and this, we soon discover, is not really possible. True, we can switch from one reading to another with increasing rapidity; we will also "remember" the rabbit while we see the duck, but the more closely we watch ourselves, the more certainly we will discover that we cannot experience alternative readings at the same time. Illusion, we will find, is hard to describe or analyze, for though we may be intellectually aware of the fact that any given experience *must* be an illusion, we cannot, strictly speaking, watch ourselves having an illusion.[2]

I

If one considers the context of *Henry V*, one realizes that the play could scarcely have been anything but a rabbit-duck.

Henry V is, of course, not only a free-standing play but the last part of a tetralogy. Some years earlier, when his talent was up to *Titus Andronicus* rather than to *Hamlet*, Shakespeare had had the nerve, at the very beginning of his career, to shape the hopelessly episodic and unstructured materials of his chronicle sources not into the licensed formlessness of the history play his audience was used to, but rather into an integrated series of plays each satisfying as a separate unit but all deriving a degree of added power and meaning from being parts of a unified whole. It is scarcely credible that, with this tetralogy behind him, Shakespeare should have approached the matter of Lancaster without thinking of the possibility of a second unified series of plays. I can think of no other explanation for the fact that already in *Richard II* Hotspur – a character completely unnecessary to that play – has been made practically a generation younger than his model. The implication of the change is that in 1595 Shakespeare already intended a play about Prince Hal. And as one notices the innumerable cross-references and links and parallels among the plays of the second tetralogy, one feels more confidently than in the first cycle that such connections are not afterthoughts, backward indices in one play to what already existed in earlier plays, but evidence of conscious through-composition.

In any event, whether or not, as I think, Shakespeare knew four or five years beforehand that he would write *Henry V*, he certainly did know in 1599 that this drama would be the capstone to an edifice of plays tightly mortared to one another. And as with each part of *Henry IV*, he must have derived enormous power from the expectations his audience brought from the preceding plays. In each of the first three plays the audience had been confronted at the beginning with a set of problems that seemed solved by the end of the preceding play but had erupted in different forms as soon as the new play began. Thus the meaning of each of the plays subsequent to *Richard II* had been enriched by the audience's recognition of the emergence of old problems in a new guise. By the time the cycle reached *Henry V*, the recurrent and interlocking set of problems had become so complex that a reflective audience must have found it impossible to predict how the last play could possibly resolve them.

The unresolved thematic issue at the end of *Richard II* is the conflict of values embodied in the two kings who are its protagonists: Bullingbrook's talent as opposed to Richard's legitimacy; Bullingbrook's extroverted energy and calculating pursuit of power as opposed to Richard's imagination, inwardness, and sense of mortality. Richard's qualities make possible in him a spiritual life that reveals him as closer – even in his inadequacy – to the ideal figures of the comedies than is his successor, who none the less has the sheer force to survive and to rule to his country's advantage. If the play is structured to force one by the end to choose Bullingbrook as the better king – one need only contrast his disposition of Exton at the close with Richard's of Mowbray at the opening – one nevertheless finds one's emotions rather surprisingly committed to the failed Richard. *Richard II* thus poses a question that arches over the entire tetralogy: can the manipulative qualities that guarantee political success be combined in one man with the spiritual qualities that make one fully open and responsive to life and therefore fully human? Or, to put it more accurately, can political resourcefulness be combined with qualities more like those of an audience as it sees itself?

1 *Henry IV* moves the question to a new generation, asking in effect whether the qualities split between Richard and Bullingbrook can be united in Hal. And in the manner of a comedy, it suggests optimistically that indeed they can. Thus Hal's famous schematic stance between the appropriately dead Hotspur and a Falstaff equally appropriately feigning death indicates not so much a compromise between their incompatible values as the difference between Hal's ability to thrive in a world of process by employing time as an instrument and Hotspur's and Falstaff's oddly similar unwillingness to do so.

For Hotspur, there is only the present moment. Even an hour is too long for life if honor is not its definition, and a self-destructive recklessness leads Hotspur to fight his battle at the wrong time, hoping naively thereby to gain more glory. For Falstaff, time is equally irrelevant. Like the Forest of Arden he needs no clock, since he has nowhere to go. He lives cyclically, recurring always to the same satisfactions of the same appetites, playing holiday every day, denying the scars of age and the imminence of death. Both of Hal's alter egos preposterously deny time, Hotspur to meet his death characteristically in midphrase – a phrase that Falstaff has already completed as "Food for powder" – and Falstaff to rise emblematically from his own death and shamelessly assert once again his will to live.

But Hal's affection for both men, so symmetrically expressed, suggests that he is in tune with something in each of them. Unlike his heavy father, but like both Hotspur and Falstaff, he is witty, ebulliently verbal, social, warmly responsive to others. For one illusory moment Shakespeare suggests the possibility of a public man who is privately whole. If the Prince's soliloquy has vowed an amputation he sees from the beginning as necessary, if the play extempore has ended in a suddenly heartbreaking promise to banish plump Jack and banish all the world, followed by the knock of the real world on the door, 1 *Henry IV* nevertheless puts us in a comic universe in which Hal need never reject Falstaff in order to reach his father's side in the nick of time; it entices us with the hope of a political world transformed by the life of comedy.

But the end of *Henry IV*, Part One marks only the halfway point, both in this massive tetralogy and in the study of Prince Hal, and Part Two brutally denies the comic optimism we might have expected to encounter once again. With the exception of Hotspur, all the ingredients of Part One seem to be present again, and in some respects they seem stronger than ever. Falstaff is given a scene (II.iv) perhaps even more endearing than Gadshill and its aftermath; he captivates Doll Tearsheet and, against her better knowledge, the Hostess. Ancient Pistol, who adds fresh attraction to the tavern world, performs one of the functions of the missing Hotspur by giving us a mocking perspective on the rhetoric and pretensions of the warrior.

And yet, despite all this and more, the effect of *Henry IV*, Part Two is to narrow possibilities. The rejection of Falstaff at its end seems to be both inevitable and right, yet simultaneously to darken the world for which the paradise of the Boar's Head must be lost. Hotspur's absence, emphasized by the dramatic device of the series of rumors from which his father must pick it out at the beginning, roots out of the political world the atmosphere of youth, vigor, charm, and idealistic commitment that Hotspur almost alone had lent it before. And Hotspur's widow's just reproaches of her father-in-law stress the old man's ugly opportunism. Northumberland's nihilistic curse –

> Let heaven kiss earth! now let not Nature's hand
> Keep the wild flood confin'd! let order die!
> And let this world no longer be a stage
> To feed contention in a ling'ring act;
> But let one spirit of the first-born Cain
> Reign in all bosoms, that each heart being set
> On bloody courses, the rude scene may end,
> And darkness be the burier of the dead!
>
> $(1.i.153-60)^3$

– that curse makes clear the destructiveness of his rebellion, a thing far different from his late son's chivalric quest, and it creates an unequivocal sense that Hal has no choice but to oppose it as effectively as he can. No longer can we assent to Falstaff's observation, plausible in Part One, that the rebels "offend none but the virtuous" (III.iii.191), so that opposing them is almost a game. The harshness of the rebels' cause and company in Part Two demands of the audience a Hotspurrian recognition that this is no world to play with mammets and tilt with lips.

Yet the attractiveness of the King's cause is reduced too. If in some moments – as in his sensitive meditation on the crown and his emotional final reunion with Hal – Henry IV is more likable in Part Two than he was in Part One, he is no longer an active character (he doesn't even appear until the third Act). And his place is filled by Prince John, as chilling a character as Shakespeare would ever create. Many a villain has more superficial charm than Hal's upright brother, and the priggish treachery by which Prince John overcomes the rebels arouses in us a distaste for political action, even when it is necessary, such as no previous moment in the plays has occasioned.[4] If Shrewsbury implied that a mature politics was compatible with the joy of life lived fully and spontaneously, Gaultree now shows political responsibility as masked and sinister, an ally of death.

Given this characterization of the political world as joyless and cruel whether right or wrong, one might expect Falstaff to carry the day. But in fact Shakespeare reduces him as much as he reduces the workaday world. It was a delicate paradox in Part One that allowed us to admire Falstaff for his ridiculous denial of mortality – "They hate us youth"; "young men must live." Falstaff might worry about how he was dwindling away, but we had no fear of losing so eternal a companion. Or, to put it more accurately, we loved him for allaying such fears; for all his grumbling at Gadshill, he could run when he had to. But in Part Two, Falstaff is mired in gross physicality and the ravages of age, obsessed with his diseases and bodily functions, commanding that the Jordan be emptied, confirming as Doll caresses him ("I am old, I am old") his stage audience's observation that desire has outlasted performance. He is the same Falstaff, but the balance is altered.

As if to re-enact his great catechism on honor in Part One, Falstaff is given a similar aria in Part Two. But the praise of sherris sack, funny as it is, is no more than a witty paean to alcohol, and a description at that of the mechanical operation of the spirit, whereas the rejection of honor in Part One was convincing enough almost to undo our respect for anyone who subordinates life to ideals. Or again, the charge of foot for whom Falstaff is responsible in Part One never becomes palpable, except to elicit his sympathetic "Food for powder," which puts him essentially on their side. In Part Two, however, we are introduced to his men by name, we see him choosing them (for the most self-serving reasons), and we are aware of the lives and families that Falstaff is ruining. No longer can we see him as the spokesman of life for its own sake; his ego is self-serving, as not before, at the expense of others.

If the tavern world is no longer alluring for us, it is even more unattractive for Hal. Physically separated from Falstaff in Part Two as not in Part One, the Prince is ready at any moment to express his discomfort, his guilt, his eagerness to be away. The flyting he carries on with Poins is unpleasant: if Hal feels so out of place consorting with commoners, why doesn't he simply stop doing it? We are tempted to agree with Warwick, who tells the King that Hal's only reason for spending time with his companions is his opportunistic scheme to use them:

> The Prince but studies his companions
> Like a strange tongue, wherein, to gain the language,
> 'Tis needful that the immodest word
> Be look'd upon and learnt, which once attain'd,
> Your Highness knows, comes to no further use
> But to be known and hated.
>
> (IV.iv.68–73)

The diseases literally corrupting Falstaff's body are endemic in *2 Henry IV*. Sickness and death pervade every element of the plot, virtually every scene, and it is no accident that it is here, not in Part One, that we meet Justice Shallow, in senile debility only a step beyond the aged helplessness of Northumberland and the King. If the medium of action in Part One was time seen as hidden road that leads providentially toward a fulfilling moment, the medium of Part Two is repetitious and meaningless process drawing relentlessly to universal annihilation. Could one "read the book of fate," the moribund King reflects, one would have to

> see the revolution of the times
> Make mountains level, and the continent,
> Weary of solid firmness, melt itself
> Into the sea, and the other times to see
> The beachy girdle of the ocean
> Too wide for Neptune's hips.
>
> (iii.i.45–51)

What we recognize here is the time of the sonnets, of Ecclesiastes; and Warwick can cheer the King only by reminding him that at least time is inevitable. The sickness that infects both Falstaff and the body politic is the sickness of life itself, joyless and rushing to the grave. In such a world Prince Hal cannot play. He must do what he can for his kingdom, and that means casting Falstaff aside.

About the necessity for the rejection we are not given the chance to have any doubts: Falstaff, after all, has just told his companions that the law is his now, and, as A. R. Humphreys notes,[5] Richard II had assured his own fall by making precisely this Nixonian claim. Yet we are forced to feel, and painfully, what an impoverishment of Hal's life the rejection causes.[6] And we recognize another aspect of that impoverishment in the drive that moves Hal to take the crown prematurely from his dying father: his commitment to political power has impelled him, as the King recognizes bitterly, to a symbolic gesture that reveals an unconscious readiness for parricide. At the end of *Henry IV*, Part One, Hal seemed able to accommodate all of England into his family as he moved toward its symbolic fatherhood. By the end of Part Two, in order to become King of England he has reached out to murder both of his fathers.

II

If we fancy ourselves arriving, on an afternoon in 1599, for the first performance of *Henry V*, we must imagine ourselves quite unsure of what to expect. Some months earlier the Epilogue to 2 *Henry IV* had promised that "our humble author will continue the story, with Sir John in it, and make you merry with fair Katherine of France, where (for any thing I know) Falstaff shall die of a sweat, unless already 'a be kill'd with your hard opinions; for Oldcastle died [a] martyr, and this is not the man." This disingenuous come-on allows for both sympathetic and hostile readings of Falstaff, while disclaiming any knowledge of the author's intentions. But the plays that precede *Henry V* have aroused such ambivalent expectations that the question of the Epilogue is trivial. If *Henry V* had followed directly on 1 *Henry IV*, we might have expected to be made merry by the comedy such critics as Dover Wilson have taken that play to be,[7] for we have seen a Hal potentially larger than his father, possessing the force that politics requires without the sacrifice of imagination and range the Bullingbrook has had to pay. But Part Two has told us that Part One deceived us, for the day has had to come when Hal, no longer able to live in two worlds, would be required to make his choice, and the Prince has had to expel from his life the very qualities that made him better than his father. Have we not, after Part Two, good reason to expect in the play about Hal's kingship the study of an opportunist who has traded his humanity for his success, covering over the ruthlessness of the politician with the mere appearance of fellowship that his past has endowed him with? Surely this is what Goddard means when he calls Henry V "the golden casket of *The Merchant of Venice*, fairer to a superficial view than to a more searching perception."[8]

As we watch the Prologue stride across the stage of the Curtain, then, we are ready for one of two opposed presentations of the reign of the fifth Henry. Perhaps we hope that the play now beginning will resolve our doubts, set us right, give us a single gestalt to replace the antithetical images before our mind's eye. And that, as is demonstrated by the unequivocal interpretations good critics continue to make, is exactly the force of the play. We are made to see a rabbit or a duck. In fact, if we do not try obsessively to cling to memories of past encounters with the play, we may find that each time we read it it turns from one shape to the other, just as it so regularly does in production. I want to show that *Henry V* is brilliantly capable of being read, fully and subtly, as each of the plays the two parts of *Henry IV* had respectively anticipated. Leaving the theatre at the end of the first performance, some members of the audience knew that they had seen a rabbit, others a duck. Still others, and I would suggest that they were Shakespeare's best audience, knew terrifyingly that they did not know what to think.

III

Think of *Henry V* as an extension of 1 *Henry IV*. For the generation who came to know it under the spell of Olivier's great film, it is hard to imagine *Henry V* any other way, but Olivier's distortions, deletions, and embellishments only emphasized what is already in the play. The structure of the entire cycle has led from the beginning of conflict in a quarrel to its end in a wedding, from the disruption of royal power to its unchallenged reassertion. If *Richard II* at the beginning transformed the normally episodic chronicle form into tragedy, *Henry V* at the end turns it into comedy: the plot works through the troubles of a threatening world to end in marriage and the promise of a green world. Its protagonist, like Benedick returned to Messina, puts aside military exploits for romance, and charms even his enemies with his effervescent young manhood. Its prologue insists, as the comedies always do, on the importance of imagination, a faculty which Bullingbrook, wise to the needs of a tragic world, had rejected in *Richard II* as dangerous. And as in all romantic comedy providence guides the play's events to their desired conclusion.[9]

To be sure, Olivier's camera and Walton's music prettied up the atmosphere, transporting their war-weary audience to the fairy-tale world of the Duc de Berry. But they found their cues in the play – in the Chorus's epic romanticizations of land and sea, his descriptions of festooned fleets and nocturnal campfires and eager warriors, and his repeated invitations to imagine even more and better. Nor did Olivier invent his film's awe at the spectacle of the past. In *Henry V*, as nowhere before in the tetralogy, Shakespeare excites us by making us conscious that we are privileged to be watching the very moments at which event transforms itself into history:

Mont:	The day is yours.
K. Hen:	Praised be God, and not our strength, for it!
	What is this castle call'd that stands hard by?
Mont:	They call it Agincourt.
K. Hen:	Then call we this the field of Agincourt,
	Fought on the day of Crispin Crispianus.

(iv.vii.86–91)

Ultimately, it was not Olivier's pictures but the play's language that made his *Henry V* so overwhelming, and the rhetoric of the play is extraordinary, unprecedented even in Shakespeare. Think, for example, of the King's oration to his troops on Saint Crispin's day (iv.iii.19–67). Thematically, of course, the speech is a tour de force, subjecting motifs from the tetralogy to Aeschylean or Wagnerian transmutations. Like the dying John of Gaunt, Harry is inspired by a vision of England, but one character-istically his own, made as romantic by the fantasy of neighborhood legionnaires and domestic history lessons as by the magical names of England's leaders. Unlike Richard II, Harry disprizes trappings, "outward things." Like Hotspur, he cares only about honor and wants to fight with as few troops as possible in order to acquire more of it: "the fewer men, the greater share of honor." Like Falstaff, he is finicky about the kind of company he adventures with: "we would not die in that man's company / That fears his fellowship to die with us." Again like Falstaff, he thinks of the "flowing cups" to come when the day's work is done and sees the day's events in festival terms. Gaily doing battle on the Feast of Crispian, he is literally playing at war like Hotspur, paradoxically uniting the opposed principles of the two most enchanting characters of the cycle.

Such echoes and allusions give Henry's speech a satisfying finality, a sense of closure. He is the man we have been waiting for, the embodiment of all the virtues the cycle has made us prize without the vices that had accompanied them before. "He is as full of valor as of kindness," we have heard just before the speech, "Princely in both," and the Crispin's day exhortation demonstrates precisely the combination of attributes that Sherman Hawkins has pointed out as belonging to the ideal monarch postulated by Elizabethan royalism.[10] But even more powerful than its thematic content is the stunning rhetoric of the King's tirade: its movement from the King's honor to his people's; its crescendo variations on St. Crispin's day, reaching their climax in the last line; its rhythmic patterns expanding repeatedly from broken lines to flowing periods in each section and concluding climactically in the coda that begins "We happy few"; its language constantly addressed to the pleasures, worries, and aspirations of an audience of citizens. As Michael Goldman perceptively argues, such a speech almost literally moves us. We recognize it as a performance; we share the strain of the King's greatness, the necessary effort of his image-projecting. "We are thrilled," Goldman says, "because he is brilliantly meeting a political challenge that has been spelled out for us … It is a moment when he must respond to the unspoken needs of his men, and we respond to his success as we do when a political leader we admire makes a great campaign speech: we love him for his effectiveness."[11]

The fourth Act of *Henry V*, in the third scene of which this speech has its place, is a paradigm of the King's virtues. It begins with the Chorus's contrast between the "confident and over-lusty French" and the thoughtful and patient Englishmen at their watchful fires on the eve of Agincourt, visited by their generous, loving, brave, and concerned royal captain – "a little touch of Harry in the night." The Act moves, first through contrasting scenes in the two camps, then through confrontations of various sorts between the opposing sides, to the victory at Agincourt and the King's call for the charitable treatment of the dead as he announces his return to England. In the course of the Act we see Harry, constantly contrasted to the stupid and corrupt French, in a triumphant show of bravery and high spirits. But we see him also in a kind of inwardness we have seldom observed in his father, listening as neither Richard II nor Henry IV could have done to the complaints and fears of a common soldier who knows what kings impose on their subjects that they do not themselves have to risk. His response is a soliloquy as powerful in its thematic and rhetorical complexity as the public address we have just considered (IV.i.230–84).

In some respects this soliloquy, which precedes by only a few moments the Crispin's day speech, is the thematic climax of the entire tetralogy, showing us that at last we have a king free of the crippling disabilities of his predecessors and wise in what the plays have been teaching. Recognizing that all that separates a king from private men is ceremony, Harry has escaped Richard's tragic confusion of ceremony with reality: "Is not the King's name twenty thousand names?" Unwittingly re-enacting his father's insomniac soliloquy in the third Act of *2 Henry IV*, Harry too longs for the heart's ease of the commoner. But where the old King could conclude only, "Uneasy lies the head that wears a crown," recurring despairingly to his posture of perennial guiltiness and to his weary sense of mortality, his young son ends by remembering his responsibility, his life of service, and sees that – "what watch the King keeps to maintain the peace" – as the defining mark of the King. Moreover, in his catechistic questioning of ceremony Harry shows that he has incorporated Falstaff's clearsightedness: like honor in Falstaff's catechism, ceremony consists only in what is conferred by others, bringing no tangible good to its bearer, unable to cure disease, no more than a proud dream. But the lesson is not only Falstaff's; for, in the dark backward and abysm of time, before Hal ever entered the scene, a young Bullingbrook had anticipated his son's "Thinks thou the fiery fever will go out / With titles blown from adulation?" with a similar repudiation of comforting self-deception:

> O, who can hold a fire in his hand
> By thinking on the frosty Caucasus?
> Or cloy the hungry edge of appetite
> By bare imagination of a feast?
> (*Richard II*, I.iii.294–7)

These multiple allusions force us to see in Henry V the epitome of what the cycle has taught us to value as best in a monarch, indeed in a man; and the King's ability to listen to the soldier Williams and to hear him suggests, like his subsequent fooling with Fluellen in the same fourth Act, a king who is fully a man. All that is needed to complete him is mature sexuality, scarcely hinted at in the earlier portraits of Hal, and the wooing of Princess Katherine in the fifth Act brings finality to a lively portrayal of achieved manhood, a personality integrated in itself and ready to bring unity and joy to a realm that has suffered long from rule by men less at ease with themselves and less able to identify their own interests with those of their country.

It was such a response to *Henry V* that led me years ago to write:

> In only one play in his entire career does Shakespeare seem bent on making us believe that what is valuable in politics and in life can successfully be combined in a ruler as in his state … There can be no doubt that [the play] is infectiously patriotic, or that the ideal of the harmonious commonweal … reflects the highest point of Shakespeare's civic optimism. And Henry is clearly presented as the kind of exemplary monarch that neither Richard II nor Henry IV could be, combining the inwardness and the sense of occasion of the one and the strength of the other with a generous humanity available to neither … In *Henry V* Shakespeare would have us believe what hitherto his work in its genre has denied, that in the real world of the chronicles a man may live who embodies the virtues and experiences the fortune of the comic hero.[12]

Reading the play thus optimistically, I had to note nevertheless how many readers respond otherwise to it, and I went on to observe that the play casts so many dark shadows – on England after Agincourt, for instance – that one can scarcely share its optimism, and that "in this respect *Henry V* is the most melancholy of the history plays." But I have now come to believe that my acknowledgment of that darker aspect of the play hardly suggested the terrible subversiveness with which Shakespeare undermines the entire structure.

IV

Taking the play, as we have just done, to be an extension of the first part of *Henry IV*, we are almost inevitably propelled to optimism. Taking it as the sequel of the second part of *Henry IV*, we are led to the opposite view held by critics as diverse as H. C. Goddard, Roy W. Battenhouse, Mark Van Doren, and H. M. Richmond. Think of those dark shadows that cloud the comedy. The point of the stock ending of romantic comedy is, of course, its guarantee of the future: marriage secures and reinvigorates society while promising an extension of its happiness into a generation to come. Like *A Midsummer Night's Dream, Henry V* ends in a marriage whose blessing will transform the world:

> K. Hen: Now welcome, Kate; and bear me witness all,
> That here I kiss her as my sovereign queen. *Flourish.*
> Q. Isa: God, the best maker of all marriages,
> Combine your hearts in one, your realms in one!
> As man and wife, being two, are one in love,
> So be there 'twixt your kingdoms such a spousal,
> That never may ill office, or fell jealousy,
> Which troubles oft the bed of blessed marriage,
> Thrust in between the [paction] of these kingdoms,
> To make divorce of their incorporate league;
> That English may as French, French Englishmen,

>   Receive each other. God speak this Amen!
> *All:*   Amen!
> *K. Hen:* Prepare we for our marriage; on which day,
>   My Lord of Burgundy, we'll take your oath,
>   And all the peers', for surety of our leagues.
>   Then shall I swear to Kate, and you to me,
>   And may our oaths well kept and prosp'rous be!
>   *Sennet. Exeunt.*

We don't really know very much about what was to happen in Theseus' Athens. But we know a good deal about Plantagenet England; and in case any member of the audience has forgotten a history as familiar to Elizabethans as our Civil War is to us, the Chorus appears immediately to remind them – both of what would soon happen, and of the fact that they have already seen a cycle of Shakespearean plays presenting that dismal story:

> Small time, but in that small most greatly lived
> This star of England. Fortune made his sword;
> By which the world's best garden he achieved,
> And of it left his son imperial lord.
> Henry the Sixt, in infant bands crown'd King
> Of France and England, did this king succeed;
> Whose state so many had the managing,
> That they lost France, and made his England bleed;
> Which oft our stage hath shown; and for their sake,
> In your fair minds let this acceptance take.

"But if the cause be not good," Williams muses on the eve of Agincourt (iv.i.134–42), "the King himself hath a heavy reckoning to make, when all those legs, and arms, and heads, chopp'd off in a battle, shall join together at the latter day and cry all, 'We died at such a place' – some swearing, some crying for a surgeon, some upon their wives left poor behind them, some upon the debts they owe, some upon their children rawly left. I am afeard there are few die well that die in a battle." Replying to Williams, the King insists that the state of a man's soul at the moment of his death is his own responsibility. Though to Dr. Johnson this appeared "a very just distinction,"[13] the King's answer evades the issue: the suffering he is capable of inflicting, the necessity of being sure that the burden is imposed for a worthy cause. The end of the play bleakly implies that there is no such cause; all that Harry has won will be lost within a generation. The Epilogue wrenches us out of the paradise of comedy into the purgatory of Shakespearean time, where we incessantly watch

> the hungry ocean gain
> Advantage on the kingdom of the shore,
> And the firm soil win of the wat'ry main,
> Increasing store with loss, and loss with store.

Contemplation of "such interchange of state, / Or state itself confounded to decay" (Sonnet 64) does not incline one toward attempting apocalyptic action. It is more likely to encourage reflections like those of Henry IV about the "revolution of the times," or of Falstaff in the very next scene of 2 *Henry IV*: "let time shape, and there an end" (iii.ii.332).

But the implication that the cause is not good disturbs us well before the aftermath of Agincourt. The major justification for the war is the Archbishop of Canterbury's harangue on the Salic Law governing hereditary succession, a law the French are said to have violated. The Archbishop's speech to the King follows immediately on his announcement to the Bishop of Ely that he plans to propose the war as a means of alleviating a financial crisis in the Church. The speech itself is long, legalistic, peppered with exotic genealogies impossible to follow; its language is involuted and syntactically loose. The very qualities that make its equivalent in Shakespeare's sources an unexceptionable instrument of statecraft make it sound on the stage like doubletalk, and Canterbury's conclusion that it is "as clear as is the summer's sun" that King Henry is legitimate King of France is a sardonic bit of comedy.[14] Olivier, unwilling to let on that Shakespeare might want us to be less than convinced, turned the episode into farce at the expense of the Elizabethan actor playing the part of Canterbury. Denied the resources of a subsidized film industry, scholars who want to see the war justified must praise the speech on the basis of its content, ignoring its length and style. Thus in the words of one scholar, "The Archbishop discharges his duty faithfully, as it stands his reasoning is impeccable apart from any warrant given by the precedent of Edward III's claims. Henry is not initiating aggression."[15] Bradley, whose argument the critic just cited was answering, is truer to the situation: "Just as he went to war chiefly because, as his father told him, it was the way to keep factious nobles quiet and unite the nation, so when he adjures the Archbishop to satisfy him as to his right to the French throne, he knows very well that the Archbishop *wants* the war, because it will defer and perhaps prevent what he considers the spoliation of the Church."[16]

J. H. Walter points out that Henry's reaction to the insulting gift of tennis balls from the Dauphin is strategically placed, as not in the play's sources, after the King has already decided to go to war, and he argues that Shakespeare thus "uses [the incident] to show Henry's christian self-control."[17] This is an odd description of a speech which promises to avenge the gift with the griefs of "many a thousand widows" for their husbands, of mothers for their sons, and even of "some [who] are yet ungotten and unborn" (i.ii.284–7). Since the tennis balls are a response to a challenge already issued, Henry's claim that France is his by rights, the King's rage seems just a little self-righteous. Henry's insistence throughout the scene that the Archbishop reassure him as to his right to make the claim insures our suspicion that the war is not quite the selfless enterprise other parts of the play tempt us to see.

Our suspicions are deepened by what happens later. Harold C. Goddard has left us a devastating attack on Henry V as Shakespeare's model Machiavellian.[18] Goddard's intemperate analysis, as right as it is one-sided, should be read by everyone interested in the play. I want to quote only one brief excerpt, his summary of the "five scenes devoted to" the battle of Agincourt; the account will be particularly useful to those who remember the battle scenes in Olivier's film.

1. Pistol captures a Frenchman.
2. The French lament their everlasting shame at being worsted by slaves.

3. Henry weeps at the deaths of York and Suffolk and orders every soldier to kill his prisoners.

4. Fluellen compares Henry with Alexander and his rejection of Falstaff to the murder of Cleitus. Henry, entering angry, swears that every French prisoner, present and future, shall have his throat cut … The battle is over. The King prays God to keep him honest and breaks his word of honor to Williams.

5. Henry offers Williams money by way of satisfaction, which Williams rejects. Word is brought that 10,000 French are slain and 29 English. Henry gives the victory to God. If Shakespeare had deliberately set out to deglorify the Battle of Agincourt in general and King Henry in particular it would seem as if he could hardly have done more.[19]

Admittedly, Goddard's analysis is excessively partisan. He ignores the rhetoric we have admired, he sees only the King's hypocrisy on Agincourt eve, and he refuses the Chorus's repeated invitations to view the war as more glorious than what is shown. But the burden of Goddard's argument is difficult to set aside: the war scenes reinforce the unpleasant implications of the Salic Law episode. Consider the moment, before the great battle, when the King bullies the citizens of Harfleur, whose surrender he demands, with a rapacious violence that even J. H. Walter does not cite as an instance of "Henry's christian self-control":

> If I begin the batt'ry once again,
> I will not leave the half-achieved Harflew
> Till in her ashes she lies buried.
> The gates of mercy shall be all shut up,
> And the flesh'd soldier, rough and hard of heart,
> In liberty of bloody hand, shall range
> With conscience wide as hell, mowing like grass
> Your fresh fair virgins and your flow'ring infants.
> What is it then to me, if impious War,
> Arrayed in flames like to the prince of fiends,
> Do with his smirch'd complexion all fell feats
> Enlink'd to waste and desolation?
> What is't to me, when you yourselves are cause,
> If your pure maidens fall into the hand
> Of hot and forcing violation?
> What reign can hold licentious wickedness
> When down the hill he holds his fierce career?
>
> (III.iii.7–23)

In such language as Tamburlaine styled his "working words," the King, like the kind of aggressor we know all too well, blames the rapine he solicits on his victims. The alacrity of his attack makes one understand Yeats's description of Henry V as a "ripened Fortinbras"; its sexual morbidity casts a disquieting light on the muted but unmistakable aggressiveness of his sexual assault on Katherine in the fifth Act.

Henry's killing of the French prisoners inspires similar uneasiness. Olivier justified this violation of the putative ethics of war by making it a response to the French killing of the English luggage boys, and one of the most moving moments of his film was the King's passionate response: "I was not angry since I came to France / Until this instant." After such a moment one could hardly fault Henry's

> Besides, we'll cut the throats of those we have,
> And not a man of them that we shall take
> Shall taste our mercy.
>
> (IV.vii.55–65)

In the same scene, indeed, Gower observes that it was in response to the slaughter of the boys that "the King, most worthily, hath caus'd every soldier to cut his prisoner's throat. O, 'tis a gallant king!" But the timing is wrong: Gower's announcement came *before* the King's touching speech. In fact, Shakespeare had presented the decision to kill the prisoners as made at the end of the preceding scene, and while in the source it has a strategic point, in the play it is simply a response to the fair battlefield killing of some English nobles by the French. Thus the announcement comes twice, first as illegitimate, second as if it were a spontaneous outburst of forgivable passion when it actually is not. In such moments as this we feel an eloquent discrepancy between the glamor of the play's rhetoric and the reality of its action.

Henry IV, Part One is "about temperance and fortitude," Part Two is "about wisdom and justice," and Shakespeare's "plan culminates in *Henry V*." So argues Sherman Hawkins.[20] "Henry's right to France – and by implication England –," he claims, "is finally vindicated by a higher power than the Archbishop of Canterbury."[21] God's concern that France be governed by so ideal a monarch culminates, of course, in the ruins so movingly described in Act V by the Duke of Burgundy, to whose plea the King responds like the leader of a nation of shopkeepers with a demand that France "buy [the] peace" it wants according to a contract Henry just happens to have had drawn up. What follows is the King's coarse wooing of his captive princess, with its sexual innuendo, its repeated gloating over Henry's possession of the realm for which he sues, and its arch insistence on his sudden lack of adequate rhetoric. Dr. Johnson's judgment is hardly too severe: the King "has neither the vivacity of Hal, nor the grandeur of Henry ... We have here but a mean dialogue for princes; the merriment is very gross, and the sentiments are very worthless."[22]

Henry's treatment of France may suggest to the irreverent that one is better off when providence does not supply such a conqueror. And his impact on England is scarcely more salubrious. The episodes in which the King tricks Fluellen and terrifies Williams recall the misbehavior of the old Hal, but with none of the old charm and a lot more power to do hurt. In *2 Henry IV* it was the unspeakable Prince John who dealt self-righteously with traitors; in *Henry V* it is the King himself. In the earlier plays wars were begun by others; in *Henry V* it is the King himself, as he acknowledges in his soliloquy, having apparently decided not to go on pinning the blame on the Archbishop of Canterbury. And England must pay a high price for the privilege of the returning veterans to show their wounds every October 25.

We do not have to wait for the Epilogue to get an idea of it. At the end of Act IV, as we saw, the King calls for holy rites for the dead and orders a return to England. The Chorus to the ensuing Act invites us to fantasy the King's triumphant return, his modesty, and the outpouring of grateful citizens. But in the next scene we find ourselves still in France, where Fluellen gives Pistol, last of the company of the Boar's Head, the comeuppance he has long fended off with his shield of preposterous language. Forced to eat his leek, Pistol mutters one last feeble imprecation ("all hell shall stir for this"), listens to Gower's final tonguelashing, and, alone on the stage at last, speaks in soliloquy:

> Doth Fortune play the huswife with me now?
> News have I that my Doll is dead i' th' spittle
> Of a malady of France,
> And there my rendezvous is quite cut off.
> Old do I wax, and from my weary limbs
> Honor is cudgell'd. Well, bawd I'll turn,
> And something lean to cutpurse of quick hand.
> To England will I steal, and there I'll steal;
> And patches will I get unto these cudgell'd scars,
> And [swear] I got them in the Gallia wars.
>
> (v.i.80–9)

The pun on "steal" is the last faint echo of the great Falstaff scenes, but labored and lifeless now as Pistol's pathetic bravura. Pistol's *Exit* occasioned Dr. Johnson's most affecting critical comment: "The comick scenes of the history of Henry the Fourth and Fifth are now at an end, and all the comick personages are now dismissed. Falstaff and Mrs. Quickly are dead; Nym and Bardolph are hanged; Gadshill was lost immediately after the robbery; Poins and Peto have vanished since, one knows not how; and Pistol is now beaten into obscurity. I believe every reader regrets their departure."[23] But our regret is for more than the end of some high comedy: it is for the reality of the postwar world the play so powerfully conjures up – soldiers returned home to find their jobs gone, falling to a life of crime in a seamy and impoverished underworld that scarcely remembers the hopes that accompanied the beginnings of the adventure.

It is the "duty of the ruler," Hawkins says, "to make his subjects good."[24] For the failure of his subjects, the play tells us, we must hold Henry V and his worthless war responsible. Unsatisfactory though he was, Henry IV was still the victim of the revolution of the times, and our ultimate attitude toward him, hastened to his death by the unconscious ambition of his own son, took a sympathetic turn like that with which we came at the end to regard the luckless Richard. But Henry V, master manipulator of time, has by the end of the cycle immersed himself in the destructive element. The blows he has rained on his country are much more his than those of any enemy of the people, and all he has to offer his bleeding subjects for the few years that remain is the ceremonial posture which he himself has earlier had the insight to contemn. Like the Edmund of *King Lear*, another lusty and manipulative warrior who wins, woos, and dies young, Henry might have subscribed himself "in the ranks of death."

V

Well, there it is. Should one see a rabbit or a duck? Along the way I've cited some critics who see an exemplary Christian monarch, who has attained, "in the language of Ephesians, both the 'age' and 'stature' of a perfect man."[25] And I have cited others who see "the perfect Machiavellian prince,"[26] a coarse and brutal highway robber.[27]

Despite their obvious differences, these rival views are essentially similar, for each sees only a rabbit or a duck. I hope that simply by juxtaposing the two readings I have shown that each of them, persuasive as it is, is reductive, requiring that we exclude too much to hold it.

Other positions, as I suggested at the outset, are possible. One of them began with Dr. Johnson, was developed by some of the best critics of a generation ago, among them Tillyard and Van Doren, and found its most humane expression in a fine essay in which Una Ellis-Fermor argued that by 1599 Shakespeare no longer believed what he found himself committed to create.[28] Having achieved his portrait of the exemplary public man, she suggests, Shakespeare was already on the verge of a series of plays that would ever more vexingly question the virtue of such virtue. Never again would Shakespeare ask us to sympathize with a successful politician, instead relegating such men to the distasteful roles of Fortinbras and the two Octavii, Alcibiades and Aufidius. The success-to-be Malcolm is a terrible crux in *Macbeth*. Between quarto and Folio texts of *Lear*, Shakespeare or his redactor is unable to devote enough attention to the surviving ruler of Britain for us to be able to identify him confidently. The governance of Cyprus and Venice are slighter concerns in *Othello* than the embroidery on the Moor's handkerchief. "Not even Shakespeare," Dr. Johnson said of what he considered the failure of the last Act of *Henry V*, "can write well without a proper subject. It is a vain endeavour for the most skilful hand to cultivate barrenness, or to paint upon vacuity."[29]

A. P. Rossiter's seminal essay "Ambivalence – the Dialectic of the Histories" sensitively shows Shakespeare's double view of every important issue in the earlier history plays. But when he comes to *Henry V*, Rossiter abandons his schema and decides that Shakespeare momentarily lost his interest in a problematic view of reality and settled for shallow propaganda on behalf of a character whom already he knew enough to loathe.[30] But *Henry V* is too good a play for criticism to go on calling it a failure. It has been performed successfully with increasing frequency in recent years, and critics have been treating it with increasing respect.

A third response has been suggested by some writers of late: *Henry V* is a subtle and complex study of a king who curiously combines strengths and weaknesses, virtues and vices. One is attracted to the possibility of regarding the play unpolemically. Shakespeare is not often polemical, after all, and a balanced view allows for the inclusion of both positive and negative features in an analysis of the protagonist and the action. But sensitive as such analysis can be – and I especially admire Robert Ornstein's study in *A Kingdom for a Stage*[31] – it is oddly unconvincing, for two strong reasons. First, the cycle has led us to expect stark answers to simple and urgent questions: is a particular king good or bad for England? can one be a successful public man and retain a healthy inner life? has Hal lost or gained in the transformation through which he changes name and character? does political action confer any genuine benefit on the polity? what is honor worth, and who has it? The mixed view of Henry characteristically appears in critical essays that seem to fudge such questions, to see complication and subtlety where Shakespeare's art forces us to demand commitment, resolution, answers. Second, no real compromise is possible between the extreme readings I have claimed the play provokes. Our experience of the play resembles the experience Gombrich claims for viewers of the trick drawing: "We can switch from one reading to another with increasing rapidity; we will also 'remember' the rabbit while we see the duck, but the more closely we watch ourselves, the more certainly we will discover that we cannot experience alternative readings at the same time."

VI

The kind of ambiguity I have been describing in *Henry V*, requiring that we hold in balance incompatible and radically opposed views each of which seems exclusively true, is only an extreme version of the fundamental ambiguity that many critics have found at the center of the Shakespearean vision[32] and that some years ago, borrowing a bit of jargon from physics, I called "complementarity."[33] What we are talking about is the perception of reality as intransigently multivalent. Though we are poignantly convinced of basic truths – complementarity is a far cry from skepticism – we know that rabbits are always turning into ducks before our eyes, bushes into bears.

Such ambiguity is not a theme or even the most important fact in many plays in which it figures. I have argued that it is extraordinarily important in *Hamlet*, but to reduce *Hamlet* to a statement about complementarity is to remove its life. Though one perceives it informing plays as different from one another as *A Midsummer Night's Dream* and *King Lear*, one cannot say that it is what they are "about," and readings of Shakespearean plays as communicating only ambiguity are as arid as readings in which the plays are seen to be about appearance and reality. But in *Henry V*, it seems to me, Shakespeare's habitual recognition of the duality of things has led him, as it should lead his audience, to a point of crisis. Since by now virtually every other play in the canon has been called a problem play, let me add *Henry V* to the number. Suggesting the necessity of radically opposed responses to a historical figure about whom there would seem to have been little reason for anything but the simplest of views, Shakespeare leaves us at a loss.

Is it any wonder that *Julius Caesar* would follow in a few months, where Shakespeare would present one of the defining moments in world history in such a way that his audience cannot determine whether the protagonist is the best or the worst of men, whether the central action springs from disinterested idealism or vainglorious egotism, whether that action is virtuous and necessary or wicked and gratuitous? Nor is one surprised to see that the most romantic and comic of Shakespeare's history plays was created at the moment when he was about to abandon romantic comedy, poised for the flight into the great tragedies with their profounder questions about the meaning of action and heroism. The clash between the two possible views of the world of *Henry V* suggests a spiritual struggle in Shakespeare that he would spend the rest of his career working through. One sees a similar oscillation, magnified and re-emphasized, in the problem plays and tragedies, and one is tempted to read the romances as a last profound effort to reconcile the irreconcilable. The terrible fact about *Henry V* is that Shakespeare seems equally tempted by both its rival gestalts. And he forces us, as we experience and re-experience and reflect on the play, as we encounter it in performances which inevitably lean in one direction or the other, to share his conflict.

Henry V is most valuable for us not because it points to a crisis in Shakespeare's spiritual life, but because it shows us something about ourselves: the simultaneity of our deepest hopes and fears about the world of political action. In this play, Shakespeare reveals the conflicts between the private selves with which we are born and the public selves we must become, between our longing that authority figures can be like us and our suspicion that they must have traded away their inwardness for the sake of power. The play contrasts our hope that society can solve our problems with our knowledge that society has never done so. The inscrutability of *Henry V* is the inscrutability of history. And for a unique moment in Shakespeare's work ambiguity is the heart of the matter, the single most important fact we must confront in plucking out the mystery of the world we live in.

Notes

1 Karl P. Wentersdorf, "The Conspiracy of Silence in *Henry V*," *SQ*, 27 (1976), p. 265. See Wentersdorf's notes 3 and 4 for representatives of both points of view. Though inconclusive itself, Wentersdorf's essay presents evidence apparently intended to suggest that the truth lies somewhere between, a position to be discussed below.

2 E. H. Gombrich, *Art and Illusion: A Study of the Psychology of Pictorial Representation* (New York: Pantheon Books, 1960), pp. 5–6.

3 My text is *The Riverside Shakespeare*, ed. G. B. Evans et al. (Boston: Houghton Mifflin, 1974).

4 Sherman H. Hawkins astutely describes Prince John in "Virtue and Kingship in Shakespeare's *Henry IV*," *English Literary Renaissance*, 5 (1975), 335–6.

5 A. R. Humphreys, ed., *The Second Part of King Henry IV*, The Arden Shakespeare (London: Methuen, 1966), p. 176.

6 See Jonas A. Barish, "The Turning Away of Prince Hal," *Shakespeare Studies*, 1 (1965), 9–17.

7 J. Dover Wilson, *The Fortunes of Falstaff* (Cambridge: Cambridge University Press, 1943).

8 Harold C. Goddard, *The Meaning of Shakespeare* (Chicago: University of Chicago Press, 1951), I, 266.

9 Whether or not the King is hypocritical, as Goddard claims, in crediting his victory to God, this is certainly one reason for the assertion.

10 Hawkins, pp. 313–20 and passim.

11 Michael Goldman, *Shakespeare and the Energies of Drama* (Princeton: Princeton University Press, 1972), p. 70.

12 Norman Rabkin, *Shakespeare and the Common Understanding* (New York: The Free Press, 1967), pp. 98–100.

13 Arthur Sherbo, ed., *Johnson on Shakespeare*, Yale Edition of the Works of Samuel Johnson, VIII (New Haven: Yale University Press, 1966), p. 552.

14 Goddard (I, 219–21) brilliantly analyzes the speech to show how self-defeating the argument is, and how it undercuts Henry's claim to his own throne in England as well.

15 J. H. Walter, *King Henry V*, The Arden Shakespeare (London: Methuen, 1954), p. xxv.

16 A. C. Bradley, "The Rejection of Falstaff," *Oxford Lectures on Poetry*, second edition (London: Macmillan, 1909), p. 257. Hawkins (p. 341) sees Henry as "the true inheritor of Edward the Black Prince," the genealogy as "not ironic," and "Henry's right to France ... vindicated by a higher power than Canterbury."

17 Walter, p. xxv; *sic.*

18 Goddard, I, 215–68.

19 Goddard, I, 256.

20 Hawkins, p. 340.

21 Hawkins, p. 341.

22 *Johnson on Shakespeare*, p. 566.

23 Johnson, p. 563.

24   Hawkins, p. 346.
25   Hawkins, p. 321.
26   Goddard, I, 267.
27   Goddard, I, 260.
28   Una Ellis-Fermor, "Shakespeare's Political Plays," *The Frontiers of Drama* (London: Methuen, 1945).
29   *Johnson on Shakespeare*, p. 556.
30   A. P. Rossiter, "Ambivalence – The Dialectic of the Histories," *Angel with Horns* (New York: Theatre Arts Books, 1961).
31   Robert Ornstein, *A Kingdom for a Stage: The Achievement of Shakespeare's History Plays* (Cambridge: Harvard University Press, 1972).
32   E.g., Michael McCanles, *Dialectical Criticism and Renaissance Literature* (Berkeley and Los Angeles: University of California Press, 1975), Bernard McElroy, *Shakespeare's Mature Tragedies* (Princeton: Princeton University Press, 1973), Marion B. Smith, *Dualities in Shakespeare* (Toronto: University Press, 1966), and Janet Adelman, *The Common Liar: An Essay on Antony and Cleopatra* (New Haven: Yale University Press, 1973).
33   Rabkin, pp. 20–6.

Part VI

Textual Criticism and Bibliography

17   The New Textual Criticism of Shakespeare   269
     Fredson Bowers
18   Revising Shakespeare   280
     Gary Taylor
19   Narratives About Printed Shakespeare Texts:
     "Foul Papers" and "Bad Quartos"   296
     Paul Werstine

The sudden return to prominence of textual studies in Shakespeare scholarship at the end of the twentieth century came as something of a surprise to almost everyone. New editions of the plays had been appearing regularly since the seventeenth century, and some eighteenth-century editors such as Edmund Malone had begun to think critically about the status of the extant Shakespearean texts and their provenance. But not until the early twentieth century did bibliographical analysis and editorial theory flourish, first in the work of British scholars such as W. W. Greg, R. B. McKerrow, Percy Simpson, and Alice Walker, and later in that of their American descendant, Fredson Bowers, himself the progenitor of many modern editors. The methods devised by these editors, together and independently, came to be known as the New Bibliography, and the governing principles of the New Bibliography dictated the goals and practices of textual study until well past the middle of the twentieth century.

The consensus established by these influential modern editors could not hold, however. During the 1970s a number of scholars, working mostly in isolation from one another, began to dispute received bibliographical opinion, and thus the last quarter of the twentieth century saw the undoing of many of Bowers's basic precepts. In 1960, textual editing was of interest only to a small cadre of specialists, partly because the sources necessary for editing were available only to those with access to research libraries and funds for such study. The prevailing view was that authoritative texts were being established by the Arden editors and others, and that students of Shakespeare could thus concentrate on literary criticism. But the revolt against the New Bibliography radically changed the scholarly landscape. As Stephen Greenblatt put it in 1988,

> Indeed in the case of Shakespeare (and of the drama more generally) there has probably never been a time since the early eighteenth century when there was less confidence in the "text." Not only has a new generation of textual historians undermined the notion that a skilled editorial weaving of folio and quarto readings will give us an authentic record of Shakespeare's original intentions, but theater historians have challenged the whole notion of the text as the central, stable focus of theatrical meaning.[1]

By the year 2000 the problem of the text – that it was a problem was very much the point – had become one of the hot topics in Shakespeare studies, permeating and influencing the direction of other subdisciplines (e.g., linguistic analysis) and seeping down even into the undergraduate classroom.

Older editors such as Greg and Bowers strove to establish a scientific approach to English printed drama of the sixteenth and seventeenth centuries. They sought to understand as thoroughly as possible the process of transmission from author to actor to scribe to compositor to bookseller. They wanted especially to identify the source of each printed work. What was the nature of the copy text? Was it the author's manuscript or a scribal copy? A memorial reconstruction (i.e., a version remembered by one or two actors and copied down from their oral recitation of it)? An earlier, uncorrected quarto or an earlier, amended or annotated quarto? A complete acting version? An abbreviated text employed by touring actors? These pioneer bibliographers were fascinated by every detail of the physical book, seeking to record the minute variants among all extant versions, discrepancies often resulting from corrections made in the printing house itself. Investigating the physical conditions of the London print-shops and bookstalls, they identified the predilections and weaknesses of particular compositors and studied the distinctive products of different publishers. To these ends Charlton Hinman invented a machine, now known as the Hinman Collator, by which every page of every existing Shakespeare First Folio could be compared word for word, comma for comma.

Bowers and company developed, and most scholars subscribed to, a set of criteria that would eventually establish accurate texts for the entire corpus of dramatic writing in early modern England. Their project was marked by idealism and confidence, qualities audible in the two following passages, one from Bowers's essay entitled "Current Theories of Copy-Text," the second from one of his lectures on editing Shakespeare:

> When only printed texts are available, the odds for retaining the closest possible approximation to the author's own accidentals are predominantly in favor of the first edition set from an authoritative manuscript. If an editor chooses this as his basis, as Greg advises under most conditions, and thereupon incorporates in the texture those substantive revisions which in his judgment are authoritative, together with such conservative alter-

ation of accidentals as seems necessary to avoid misreadings or more than momentary ambiguity, he may miss some few refinements; but he will in the long run produce a text which, more accurately than by any other method, comes as close as possible to the author's original and revised intentions.[2]

If an editor makes, say, ten emendations in a text, he must presume that on ten occasions he has recovered features of the lost original, given them substantial being, and merged them with his preserved copy-text. The editorial ideal is by such a series of acts to restore the complete and pure wording of the original so that in respect to the "substantives" though his text is based on the imperfect derived document it has in effect recovered the complete lost original.[3]

The idealism of the New Bibliography shines forth from the last phrase of the first passage, "comes as close as possible to the author's original and revised intentions." Bowers and his colleagues believed in an ideal text, an authoritative version that represented the author's intentions about the work in question; they believed that those intentions could be recovered and transmitted to the reader through the edited text; and they set forth the principles for doing so. Clearly the crucial word in both excerpts is "authoritative," a term Bowers employs unhesitatingly, not to say blindly, but positively and with confidence. Before long, however, the adjective would lose its innocence.

The wedge that helped to split the consensus of the New Bibliography was an emerging suspicion about the possibility of authorial revision, the conviction that the multiple versions in which many plays exist represent different, authorially created texts of those plays. At the second meeting of the International Shakespeare Association in Washington, DC, in 1976, Michael Warren delivered a paper claiming that the standard modern text of *King Lear*, a conflation of the 1608 Quarto and the 1623 Folio versions, was bibliographically illegitimate. He proposed, instead, that the two texts be treated as distinct entities, that they be seen for what they were: F, said Warren, represented a second version of the play, one substantially different from Q, and he asserted that the reviser was Shakespeare himself. Which text, then, was the authoritative, the authorized, the author's version? Even as Warren spoke, other bibliographers and editors such as Steven Urkowitz and Stanley Wells were coming to similar conclusions independently. The ramifications of the two-text proposition were immense, extending well beyond the boundaries of Shakespeare study. The distinguished Romanticist and textual scholar Jerome McGann – interestingly, Bowers's successor in bibliography at the University of Virginia – summarized the paradigm shift when he argued: "if scholars were misguided in their assessments of the two original printed texts of *King Lear* – if ... these are not two *relatively corrupted* texts of a pure (but now lost) original, but two *relatively reliable* texts of two different versions of the play (as we now think) – then our general methods for dealing with such texts [are] called into serious question."[4]

Two scholars who have been especially vocal in questioning the orthodoxies of the New Bibliography are represented here, Gary Taylor and Paul Werstine. Taylor begins with a meticulous, persuasive demonstration that certain printed passages from the Second Quarto versions of *Romeo and Juliet* and *Hamlet* reveal authorial rewriting, probably in the very act of composing – so much for Ben Jonson's claim that Shakespeare "never blotted a line." This modest proof prepares for his overarching argument: "although all previous editions have been based on the unexamined belief that Shakespeare did *not* revise his work, all future editions should be, and I believe will be, based on the recognition that he habitually did." Taylor's prophecy has come true, as a glance at most recent editions of the Complete Works will indicate: the inclusion of two or three versions of *King Lear* would have shocked W. W. Greg or R. B. McKerrow, but to most twenty-first-century scholars such a practice has come to seem axiomatic.

Werstine turns a skeptical eye on the vocabulary of the New Bibliography, particularly terms such as "bad quartos" and "foul papers," exploring the assumptions that caused those familiar terms to dominate the critical discourse. Governing his analysis is, first, a distrust of those "binary oppositions" that underwrite the logic of the New Bibliography, that a quarto is either good or bad, either authorial or spurious. And this suspicion is related to his second motive, the aim to expose the notion of single authorship, especially theatrical authorship, as an ahistorical fantasy: as he concludes, "these texts were open to penetration and alteration not only by Shakespeare himself and by his fellow actors but also by multiple theatrical and extra-theatrical scriveners, by theatrical annotators, adapters and revisers (who might cut or add), by censors, and by compositors and proofreaders."

The trends in textual study thus recapitulate the larger movements in literary criticism at the end of the century. Werstine contends that the values and aims of the New Bibliography – particularly its attempt to establish a single, ideal, authorial text – derive from the same wish for unity that shaped the New Criticism, the interpretive school with which it was roughly contemporaneous. Thus the literary critic's move away from the work of art as a coherent, self-contained unit towards an emphasis on fissure and multivocality finds its parallel in the bibliographer's abandonment of an ideal text in favor of collaborative production and multiple versions. As in many endeavors at the end of the twentieth century, from bumper sticker to bibliography, the motto became "Question Authority."

Notes

1 *Shakespearean Negotiations* (Berkeley: University of California Press, 1988), p. 4.
2 "Current Theories of Copy-Text, with an Illustration from Dryden," *Modern Philology*, 47 (1950), p. 20.
3 *On Editing Shakespeare and the Elizabethan Dramatists* (Philadelphia: University of Pennsylvania Library, 1955), p. 125, n. 36.
4 *A Critique of Modern Textual Criticism* (Chicago: University of Chicago Press, 1983), p. 4.

17

The New Textual Criticism of Shakespeare

Fredson Bowers

et us revert to the opening propositions – that the Shakespearean textual critic and bibliographer concerns himself chiefly with the twin problems of recovery and of transmission. Actually, the problem of transmission is only an extension of the basic problem of recovery, and there is no essential difference between them except for the degree of complexity that they represent. For our purposes, however, let us define the problem of recovery as the attempt to identify in the printed text as many characteristics as possible of the lost manuscript; and, correspondingly, to identify in the print the characteristics of the printing-house when these differ from the manuscript. The latter is an essential process, since manuscript characteristics can be isolated only after the printing-house characteristics have been recognised. Many non-bibliographical critics have confused the two, such very different scholars as Dover Wilson and Helge Kökeritz, for example, commonly taking it without investigation that repeated anomalies are authorial rather than compositorial.

The attempts to define the nature of the manuscripts behind the printed Shakespearean editions has been only loosely bibliographical in the past. Sir Walter Greg, who pioneered the attack on this problem – as on so many others – has been the most active investigator; but he has chiefly used the analysis of stage-directions as his evidence, combining this material with occasional suggestions from the variation of speech-prefixes, and bringing up the rear with some analysis of the kind of error in the play, as seemingly coming from a manuscript difficult to read, or one causing no difficulty. Valuable as this method has been, it is approximate at best, and the only really meaningful division that can be attempted is that between theatrical and non-theatrical manuscripts; or, sometimes a non-theatrical manuscript with some theatrical annotation. Moreover, as the newer bibliography based on compositor-identification begins to move in on the problem, some of Greg's theories about these manuscripts are being more and more seriously questioned, on evidence that is concrete and less subject to personal interpretation or chance. A case in point is what we can now infer about *The Merchant of Venice* manuscript (or about that of *Hamlet*) by comparing *The Merchant* with Q2 *Hamlet*, once we know the precise pages in each set by the same two compositors. Moreover, this same study has served as a useful criterion against which to measure non-bibliographical hypotheses. John Russell Brown's analysis of the two compositors in James Roberts's printing-house has indicated that various spellings in the quarto *Hamlet* that Dover Wilson had isolated as authentically Shakespeare's own are in fact merely compositorial.[1]

The new research that will eventually provide us with the answers we require derives completely from compositor-identification and analysis. It has long been known that compositors could be identified by their individual spelling proclivities, like the *A* and the *B* compositors of Shakespeare's First Folio. But, principally because it has still had an insufficient factual basis, this knowledge has scarcely been used until now, except for some pioneering work by Alice Walker and the late Philip Williams. For example, Dr Walker theorised that compositor *B* was more prone to sophisticate a text than the more conservative *A*. This will ultimately turn out to be quite true, I think; but the evidence will need to be re-studied in some part because at the time of the investigation no one was aware of the existence of the apprentice compositor *E*, later so brilliantly identified by Charlton Hinman. Hence in all studies of compositor *B* to date, the bad work of *E* has been attributed to *B*, and the waters correspondingly muddied. It is of particular interest that Dr Hinman's researches, when fully published in the future, will identify on irrefutable evidence the work of all the Folio compositors, even to the part-column, and will for the first time add a pair of compositors *C* and *D* whose work on the Comedies section has either been confused with *A*'s or else lumped together as an unknown quantity *X*.

One difficulty with spelling-tests is that they are ordinarily not so exact as to deal with units of less than a page, and sometimes even whole quarto pages may easily be in legitimate doubt. But Dr Hinman is now able to identify First Folio compositors with absolute precision, not only by spelling-tests and presswork probabilities inferred from the order of running-titles and box-rules in their repetitive use, but also by tracing the exact use of types, out of identified cases, from typesetting to distribution to typesetting again, and so on through the different cases that were used by the Folio workmen. This analysis results from the positive identification of hundreds and hundreds of slightly damaged types so that, in mass, they can be traced through the pages – the individual course of each of these hundreds of types can be plotted as they are set, distributed, find their way, with or without their fellows, into specific cases and are again and again used to set certain pages after each distribution.[2]

When the detailed results are published and we have all the five Folio compositors precisely identified, and when similar studies are made for each substantive Shakespearean quarto, we can then proceed to two applications. First, by a study of these compositors as they set other books we can estimate their incidence of error and thus make assumptions about the amount of emendation that will be required. Moreover, analysis of the kind of error found in the work of the different compositors who set Shakespeare's texts will undoubtedly give us factual bases, now wanting, for the kind of emendation required according as we find certain compositors responsible for certain pages of the text.

Allied bibliographical studies will be of assistance. For example, hard on the heels of Hinman's brilliant discovery that the First Folio was set and printed by formes, generally from the inside of the quire out, instead of the pages being composed in seriatim order, other studies have established a wholly unsuspected amount of setting and printing by formes in Elizabethan dramatic quartos.[3] The application of this new information about Elizabethan printing techniques has already produced results.

Not so long ago G. B. Harrison argued most persuasively that in such late plays as *Antony and Cleopatra* and *Coriolanus*, Shakespeare was inclined to break a regular pentameter line into two irregular lines as a rhetorical device to secure the rhythm and emphasis that he wanted to hear when they were recited.[4] And Harrison had a little quiet fun with the editors who followed Pope's regularising of these broken lines and thus smoothed-out Shakespeare's indicated intentions. Although no voice was raised at the time, critics should have known better than to accept these arguments, for common sense would inquire how an actor could possibly recall such minutiae when his memory was loaded with the large number of plays required by Elizabethan repertory conditions, even if the scribe who copied the part from which the actor memorised his lines had followed such indications from the Shakespearean original, or from the scribal prompt copy or intermediate transcription. But we need no longer trust to such objections, pertinent as they are, for Hinman has shown conclusively that what the literary critic exalted as Shakespeare's subtle art was in the main only a compositorial device to waste space in circumstances when the cast-off copy was insufficient to fill the page with normal typesetting. So much for critical theory as against what bibliographical fact can demonstrate.

On the other hand, when the cast-off copy for the forme was too great to fit into the space assigned, the compositor was reduced to various expedients to save room, such as running verse lines together, omitting all interlinear white space, and even – as Hinman has some evidence – excising some of the text in cases of emergency. These are newly discovered and most significant pieces of evidence about the effect of the printing process on the text. But the end is not in sight. For example, if we can explain various anomalies in a text as being the result of the casting-off of copy and the typesetting by formes, we are helping to restore the shape of the original manuscript as we strip away some of the veil of print. Occasionally the results can be most important. For instance, whenever we may assign verse set as prose, or prose as verse, to a precise mechanical cause, and not to the characteristics of the underlying manuscript, we can save ourselves from false assumptions of some consequence.

The second method of compositorial study will be slowly and painfully to analyse the characteristics of those workmen who set Shakespeare's substantive texts, so that in some degree we shall be able to identify the influence of the manuscript copy on the printed result. That is, although compositors had their favourite ways of spelling some words, and sometimes an invariable way, their practice was not uniform and was often susceptible to influence from the spelling, capitalisation, and perhaps the punctuation of the copy. We may study these characteristics against control texts, chiefly when these compositors were setting reprints, and in this manner discover what spellings are their favourites and what spellings are indifferent. Then we shall have something approaching a scientific basis of factual evidence to assess the influence of the manuscript and to recover certain of its characteristics as filtered through the compositorial treatment.

At present only an occasional and uncertain light can be thrown on the subject by presupposing what it is dangerous to presuppose, that notably eccentric spellings derive from the manuscript and not from the compositor. We have seen how misleading this method was when applied to the quarto *Hamlet* without bibliographical safeguards. Certainly, the opportunity that Dr Alice Walker most ingeniously seized on in *Romeo and Juliet*[5] does not present itself every day. She observed that the Second Quarto had the misprint *c-h-a-p-e-l-s* for the word *chapless*, or, 'without lips'. She then pointed out that the compositor of this quarto (actually two compositors, as we now know) was an *-esse* speller and therefore the reading *c-h-a-p-e-l-s* was not a simple transpositional error by this compositor trying to spell *chaples* (for he would have set the form *chaplesse*) but instead a true mistaking of the manuscript; that is, the compositor must have thought that the word was in fact *chapels*. The nature of the misreading, therefore, as set against the compositor's known spelling habit, successfully demonstrates that in the manuscript the word *chapless* was spelled *-les*. If the manuscript is a Shakespearean autograph, as there is some reason to believe, Dr Walker has recovered an authentic Shakespeare spelling. This is very good indeed, but obviously such evidence is not found very often.

To return to the spelling evidence – once we build up a body of bibliographically confirmed information about the spelling characteristics of the various manuscripts behind Shakespeare's plays, it is not too much to hope that marked similarities and dissimilarities may become clear between texts, and that slowly we may construct a basis of fact that we can use to identify a Shakespearean manuscript by the non-compositorial spelling characteristics of the printed text, or else that we may do something towards distinguishing the hands of certain scribes that may reveal themselves as alpha, beta, gamma, and so on. The late Philip Williams made a most ingenious start in this direction.[6] In the text of 1 *Henry VI* he observed that the name *Joan* in the First Folio is sometimes spelled *Joane* and sometimes *Jone*. However, which – if either – is the manuscript spelling is in doubt since the distinction is purely compositorial: the *Joane* forms all appear in pages set by compositor A, the simple *Jone* forms all in pages set by compositor B.

However, in this same play he also observed that scene division did not begin until Act III, although compositor A, who had set Acts I and II without division, would scarcely be likely by himself to start division when he also came to set Act III. This difference between division and no division is emphasised by certain spelling differences that exist in the same copy set by compositor A; thus in Acts I and II *Burgundy* is spelt invariably with a *d* as *Burgundy*; but in Act III, corresponding to the introduction of scene division, compositor A changed and thereafter invariably spelled the name *Burgonie*. Equally striking is the designation of Joan of Arc as *Puzel* eighteen times in Act I, but *Pucell* twenty-six times in Act III all in pages set by this same compositor A. Williams drew the inevitable conclusions: the printer's copy for this play was heterogeneous. This in itself is information of especial interest bearing on the authority of the text in its two sections. Moreover, it may be that in the future one or other of the two hands could prove to be Shakespeare's autograph. Whether this or not, the good possibility exists for making a start here with some basic observations about manuscript characteristics in Shakespearean texts. And in this connection it may be suggested that though the compositorial spelling *Joane* or *Jone* was of no value in determining that the copy was heterogeneous, it might have some value if one or other form were shown to be uncharacteristic of the compositor concerned and could thus be inferred as a copy spelling, provided the other spelling was correspondingly shown to be characteristic of the workman who used it in this text.

Williams also observed that in the Folio the variant spellings of the ejaculation 'Oh' as *Oh* or simple *O* seemed to be consistent in one or other form in some plays regardless of the fact that more than one compositor set the texts; and from this evidence he conjectured that the spelling might be useful as one characteristic to aid in distinguishing the hands of the manuscripts. Moreover, in a play like *King John* when the spellings switch from simple *O* in the first three Acts to the predominant *Oh* form in the last two Acts, Williams felt that this fact could justifiably be added to other significant evidence to suggest that the underlying manuscript was not uniformly the work of only one inscriber.

Williams carried forward such evidence very boldly to suggest that *Coriolanus* and even *Timon of Athens* were not printed from foul papers, as Greg supposed, but instead from scribal transcripts; and I may say that Dr Hinman on other evidence will partially confirm Williams' views about *Timon of Athens* when his monograph on the First Folio is published.

Casting about in the First Folio, Dr Williams further noticed that in *Titus Andronicus* the Fly Scene (added in manuscript to the quarto copy that served the printer otherwise) exhibits some differences in spelling that cannot be compositorial, as for instance the spelling of *vppon* with two *p*'s, a rare circumstance in the Folio; or the spelling of *Tamora's* name with an *i* as *Tamira*; or the change in speech-prefix from *Titus* to *Andronicus*. These all constitute significant evidence that manuscript characteristics can indeed show through the veil of print. Finally, to conclude such evidence, Williams pointed out that it might be the case that compositor *A*'s spelling of *to the* as *toth'* in *Macbeth* and *Coriolanus*, but nowhere else in the Folio, linked these manuscripts beneath the print; and that it would not seem to be chance that *A*'s work in *Henry VIII* and in *Hamlet*, in his opinion, is linked by a phenomenally greater use of semi-colons than was *A*'s custom, a link supported by the aberrant spelling *wee'l* in both texts.

The validity of such evidence as this in other dramatists than Shakespeare has been demonstrated, but much other evidence remains in Shakespearean texts. For example, as one of several ranges of evidence in an investigation into the relation of Q2 to Q1 *Hamlet*, I found that the identified Q2 compositor *X* in setting the second quarto of *Titus Andronicus* from the first had in general added somewhat to the heaviness of the punctuation; but if Q1 *Hamlet* had been annotated to serve as printer's copy for Act 1 of Q2, as has been asserted, then he behaved in quite the contrary manner. In his share of *Titus*, compositor *X* added eighteen commas while omitting eight; but in *Hamlet* he would have added only fourteen as against omitting seventy-five. Other punctuation evidence also pointed in opposite directions between the two typesettings. Moreover, certain exceptions in *Hamlet* to invariable spellings found in *Titus* and in *The Merchant of Venice*, in *X*'s pages, seemed to refer to manuscript since they were not reproductions of Q1 spellings at such points. The view that Act 1 of *Hamlet* in

Q2 was set from manuscript instead of from annotated Q1 seems to me to be certain, on the evidence;[7] and on the evidence a few of the manuscript spellings can be identified to add to the small store that – greatly increased – will one day settle whether this, or other plays, was set from a Shakespeare autograph or from a scribal transcript.

The problem of transmission is essentially that of recovery, but greatly complicated. In a play like *The Merry Wives of Windsor* the recovery of the characteristics of the manuscript as they show through the print indicates that the identifiable scribe Ralph Crane wrote out the manuscript that was the printer's copy. The nature of the manuscript that he used in turn as *his* copy is obscure. Very likely few of its characteristics can be ascertained by compositor study since Crane usually seems to overlay what he transcribes from (although this matter has not in fact been scrupulously studied in various Crane texts by treating him as if he were a compositor); and one would expect the Folio compositor to further the process. However, here as elsewhere with less strong-minded scribes than Crane, at least in theory some small pieces of evidence might be dredged up to enable us to speculate from something other than wishful thinking about the earlier copy.

As an example of new evidence about transmission and the occasional role that recovery of a manuscript may play in such an investigation, one may cite *Romeo and Juliet*. The conventional theory has been that the good second quarto was set up from Shakespeare's foul papers, except for one passage that was substituted (probably for a lost manuscript leaf) from the bad first quarto, without annotation. Some occasional consultation of Q1 elsewhere has generally been allowed in places where the compositor might have been troubled by illegibility. But recently Professor Dover Wilson has advanced the theory that considerable portions of the second quarto were typeset from annotated leaves of the bad first quarto.

What is the truth, and how may it be made manifest? Going about the task bibliographically, the way it should be done, Dr George Williams has arrived at some important conclusions.[8] First, he determined that two compositors set the good second quarto, and he identified their pages. He then studied the habits of these two workmen in setting various contemporary plays from printed copy and tabulated the individual characteristics that appeared in their transmission of printed text. When these identified characteristics were applied to Q2 of *Romeo and Juliet*, the marked variation between the work of these compositors in the quarto and their work when transmitting a printed document gave evidence that a manuscript did indeed underlie the whole of the second quarto except for the familiar leaf of Q1. Thus Professor Wilson's non-bibliographical assumptions were shown to be mistaken.

However, more important results appeared from this careful bibliographical investigation. The highly variable speech-prefixes of this quarto, as between *Wife, Mother, Lady* for Lady Capulet, have always been taken as classic examples of McKerrow's suggestion that such variation ought to indicate the presence of an author's foul papers, since a composing author might well have written from the point of view of the character's function in the scene, as for example whether Capulet were in relation to Juliet, in which case he might be *Father*; or in a formal capacity, in which case he might be *Capulet*. But tempting as this theory has seemed, it has never entirely held water, since if the pattern of personal relationships were scrupulously carried out,

Capulet would end by being 'father' to his wife, and also to his daughter's nurse, a proposition that is nowhere encouraged by the play.

Dr George Williams observed, however, that some sort of pattern could be developed on other than assumed literary grounds. For example, the regular prefixes for Capulet up to Act 3, scene 1, are *Capu*; but with Act 3, scene 4, when this form appears it is shortened to *Ca* except for 4.2, and 5.3, in which *Cap*, *Capu*, and *Capel* also occur. Beginning with Act 3, scene 5, the *Ca* prefix is irregularly replaced by the functional *Father* prefix. So, in general, with the variant forms for Lady Capulet. Coincidental with the start of Act 3, scene 5, on signature H2 verso, when this break in the pattern starts and the speech-prefix *Father* is introduced, a marked increase in the capitalisation appears. In sheets A to G between thirty and fifty capitals are used per eight pages; but starting with 3.5, sheets H to M use from sixty to ninety capitals. The increase, starting at 3.5, is marked and is in vivid contrast to the practice in 3.4. For instance, in dialogue the terms *father* and *mother* appear in lower case from 1.1 to 3.4; but these words of address are capitalised from 3.5 onwards. Other changes in these later sheets from gathering H can be seen, such as a general tendency to capitalise the start of a clause after a question mark, as against the earlier preference for lower case.

Now the importance of the compositorial analysis becomes clear, because these characteristics of the later sheets are found in the work of both compositors and cannot be assigned to any bibliographical division or unit. Hence it is clear that what we have is a reflection of some difference between the early and late parts of the underlying manuscript and thus this manuscript cannot be the homogeneous foul papers previously supposed. In the further investigation, once again compositorial analysis becomes important. According to Dr Williams's views, although these speech-prefix and capitalisation differences can be clearly seen occurring in the work of the first compositor who bridges the two sections of the manuscript, other variants do not appear, at least in so far as he has analysed the text to date. Hence his present opinion, on evidence that may not be quite exhaustive, is that both sections of the manuscript are in the hand of the same writer; but that the section from 3.5 to the end represents an earlier and rougher form of the manuscript, and the first section an authorial fair copy. Whether this provisional hypothesis will stand up to closer investigation I do not know, but its promise is high; and in the end the scholarly inquiry into the transmission turned up valuable information from the recovery of manuscript charac-teristics once the red herring of Q1 copy, conjectured by Dover Wilson, was shown to be a red herring.

This investigation into the transmission of *Romeo and Juliet* ended in establishing the authority of a single text (except for whatever extremely limited authority may be allowed the memorially-reconstructed bad first quarto). But when the study of the transmission establishes double authority in separate editions, very serious difficulty may ensue. The difficulty is certainly more acute for such texts as *Hamlet* and *Othello*, and possibly *Troilus and Cressida*, than it is when the second authority is weaker, as for plays like 2 *Henry VI*, *The Merry Wives of Windsor*, *Romeo and Juliet*, *Henry V*, and *King Lear*, in which the second authority is a bad quarto. Nevertheless, in all these cases the characteristics of the manuscripts of both editions must be recovered as closely as possible, and the precise relationship of the two editions in the matter of the transmission of the text must be established.

The central problem of the Shakespeare double texts is the relationship, and therefore the transmission. Are they printed from independent manuscripts? Is the later printed from a copy of the earlier edition that has been annotated with corrections and revisions from some manuscript? Was the printer's copy for the later edition some combination of the two? These are questions of the utmost importance. For some of these plays critics had thought the answer was settled; but the trend of recent investigation, rightly or wrongly, has been to cast doubt on most of the conventional conclusions. It now seems quite possible that Folio *Henry V* was not set from an independent manuscript but instead from an annotated quarto, perhaps even sections of the two different editions, annotated. Only recently has Dover Wilson's own attempt to upset conventional opinion about *Romeo and Juliet* been controverted, and – for once – conventional belief upheld by strictly bibliographical evidence. The question of the exact quarto edition or editions that were annotated to form the Folio printer's copy for *Richard III* has only recently been decided in favour of Q3 (1602). One investigator has even wondered whether in some part annotated leaves of the bad quarto were not used for the Folio printer's copy of *The Merry Wives of Windsor*, which would seem almost impossible.

The uncertainty about these plays is bad enough, but it is worse to be in complete doubt – as we are so far as real demonstration is concerned – about the relationship of the quarto and Folio texts of 2 *Henry IV*, of *Hamlet*, and possibly of *Othello*, texts not yet subjected to rigorous bibliographical investigation. These are, of course, transmission problems, and they concern transmission in two senses. First, whether the later text was set from an independent manuscript or whether a printed quarto was annotated by reference to such a manuscript, the problem is singularly important – what is the relation of these two lost manuscripts? Is one representative of autograph copy and the other of scribal transcript, as has been conjectured for *Hamlet*? Or – as may be possible for *Troilus and Cressida* – was the earlier quarto annotated for the Folio by reference to a manuscript in an earlier stage of composition than that behind the quarto?

This question may arise even in the bad-quarto texts. When Q1 of *Hamlet* agrees with the Folio against Q2 (supposed to be set from autograph), does this Q1 then preserve some of a revision, or else of theatrical alteration; or is Q2 merely corrupt in such readings? Is Dr Hosley right to alter the second-quarto text of *Romeo and Juliet* in order to stage a scene according to the first-quarto system of entrances, one that seems to represent the company's adaptation of staging that Shakespeare in the manuscript behind Q2 had carelessly left difficult if not impossible to produce as written? As Mr Cairncross has recently asserted in the New Arden edition, do some omissions and alterations in the Folio 2 *Henry VI* reflect censorship changes for a later production, and will the purer text at such points be found in the bad first quarto, as a consequence? Are some details of Q1 *King Lear* more authentic than the Folio text? In *Hamlet* is the Q1 position of the nunnery scene that of the stage version as against the 'literary' version of Q2, the Folio concurrence with Q2 being explained by the derivation of its print essentially from the Q2 print?

In some part the answers to such questions do not involve strict bibliographical investigation; but there can be no doubt that the second respect in which transmission problems exist does depend exclusively on bibliographical analysis – and that is the question of the physical relationship of any two texts, whether positive or negative. The importance of knowing the precise copy from which an authoritative text is typeset is crucial. For example, if Folio *Hamlet* were set from an independent manuscript, then concurrence of Q2 and F in a reading would be very hard to explain away, and we should need to appeal to theories which the odds do not favour, such as error in the autograph original faithfully copied by one compositor and one scribe; or the inscription in the original of a word in a manner that would quite independently be copied as the same error by these two agents. Thus if one believes that in *Hamlet* the reading *breathing like sanctified and pious bonds* found in both Q2 and Folio is wrong, and that Theobald's emendation of *bawds* (*bauds*) is correct, as I firmly do, then if Q2 and Folio came from independent manuscripts we should need to suppose that *bauds* was so written in Shakespeare's autograph that the compositor of Q2, and the hypothetical scribe who may have been employed to copy out the foul papers to make up the theatrical manuscript, both independently misread the *a* as an *o*, and the *u* as an *n*. This is possible, of course, but the probability decreases rapidly with each additional common error that must be so explained; and there are more of these common errors than are altogether comfortable for any advocate of the independent manuscript theory in its pure state. I am myself particularly interested in the apparent refinement in I. 5 by which in both texts Marcellus calls *Illo* but Hamlet *Hillo*. I cannot conceive that this is a meaningful distinction, and to my mind it suggests that QI *Ill, lo* has contaminated the text of Q2 and that the corruption has been passed on from Q2 to the Folio.

Thus if the Folio were set from annotated Q2, or if Q2 exercised a direct influence on Folio in some other manner, we should be required to accept a much simpler hypothesis: merely that in each case the annotator or scribe overlooked the error, and hence it was automatically passed on from quarto to Folio.

The logic is clear. If *Hamlet* Q2 and Folio derive from independent manuscripts, concurrence of the two texts in any reading would ordinarily be the guarantee of authenticity of every such word in which good cause for double error could not be found. (And there is a practical limit to the number of such double errors that a critic can accept under these conditions.) When the two texts differ, then the relative authority of the respective manuscripts must be balanced against the nature of the difference, so long as some coherent theory of choice is maintained and the process does not degenerate into mere literary eclecticism, without any underlying principle except tradition and personal taste.

On the other hand, if the Folio were typeset from an annotated Q2 or in some other manner came under the direct influence of the quarto, concurrence of two readings is no guarantee whatever of authenticity in any individual case. The paradox is plain that when two such texts differ, we can usually assume that the variant in the later was the result of a conscious annotation or alteration more often than it may be taken as a compositorial aberration, whether conscious or unconscious; thus it will ordinarily represent the reading of the manuscript that was being conflated with the print. Yet when two words agree, we can never be sure that the scribe did not simply skip over a difference and fail to notice that the word in the quarto did not represent the word that appeared in the manuscript.

Hence the relationship of the two texts in plays like *Hamlet*, or like 2 *Henry IV* or *Othello* or *King Lear*, is no idle academic quibble, but a problem that must be solved before any editor can properly shape his own resultant text, or can even begin with such preliminaries as attempting to assess the nature of the manuscript that underlies the Folio print. It seems almost impossible to believe that when we know our compositors well enough, we cannot use our information about their habits when they transmit printed copy – such apparently trivial matters as the influence on these compositors of the spelling, punctuation, and capitalisation of printed copy – to settle the question once and for all and to demonstrate beyond all possible doubt the exact transmission of these debated texts. The case will rest either on positive or on negative evidence, depending upon the transmission or lack of transmission of hundreds and hundreds of minor characteristics. Taken alone, the evidence of substantive readings is often crude and indeed contradictory; and very often explanations can cast doubt on the validity of this evidence. Frequently such evidence will carry no conviction to a bibliographer trained to respect evidence that in the main is not susceptible to critical alteration by the human element engaged in the transmission. The more mechanically produced the evidence, and thus the less likely to be subject to conscious evaluation by the persons engaged in the act of transmission, the more scientifically based is the method of bibliographical investigation of the transmission process. Thus the concurrence or variance of hundreds and hundreds of small points of spelling, punctuation, and capitalisation according to recognisable patterns divorced from identified compositorial habits should combine with evidence from readings to establish the truth in bibliographical terms. It is long past time.

Notes

1 'The Compositors of *Hamlet* Q2 and *The Merchant of Venice*', *Studies in Bibliography*, VII (1955), 17–40; see also Paul L. Cantrell and George Walton Williams, 'Roberts' Compositors in *Titus Andronicus* Q2', *S.B.*, VIII (1956), 27–38.

2 The first announcement of the use of identified types as bibliographical evidence was made by Dr Charlton Hinman in 'Cast-Off Copy for the First Folio of Shakespeare', *Shakespeare Quarterly*, VI (1955), 259–73; followed by 'The Prentice Hand in the Tragedies of the Shakespeare First Folio: Compositor E', *Studies in Bibliography*, IX (1957), 3–20. Full information is expected in a monograph now in preparation on the printing of the First Folio.

3 Notably George Walton Williams, 'Setting by Formes in Quarto Printing', *Studies in Bibliography*, XI (1958), 39–53. More information will be found in Robert K. Turner, 'The Composition of *The Insatiate Countess*, Q2', in *S.B.*, XII (1959). 'Setting by formes' means, in quarto, that the type-pages of a sheet were not set in order, as 1, 1^v, 2, 2^v, 3, 3^v, 4, and 4^v, but instead in selected order as a forme, i.e. either 1^v, 2, 3^v, 4 and then 1, 2^v, 3, 4^v, or the reverse. In the Shakespeare First Folio, when a quire was set simultaneously by two workmen, compositor *A* might set p. 6 while compositor *B* set p. 7 (to use pagination numbers for this example), then *A* would proceed to p. 5 and *B* to p. 8, then *A* to p. 4 and *B* to p. 9, until *A* came to p. 1 and *B* to p. 12. Then in the next gathering *B* would start with p. 18 and *A* with p. 19, *B* would proceed to p. 17 and *A* to p. 20, and so on, until the quire was completed with *B* setting p. 13 and *A* setting p. 24, the outer forme of the outermost sheet. For compositors to work in this manner, setting by formes, the printer's copy must be 'cast off' and marked with the amount of material estimated for each page; and the compositors must observe this marking scrupulously. When type is set by formes (i.e. the type-pages necessary to print one

side of a sheet of paper), less type is required and in some respects presswork is speeded at the start. Thus in quarto a forme is ready for the press after the interval required for the composition of only four type-pages instead of the seven required to complete the inner forme if pages are set in order. In the First Folio, when *A* set p. 6 and *B* p. 7, the inner forme of the inmost sheet of the quire was ready for the press after the setting of only two pages, instead of the seven required if setting had been seriatim. This inner forme was then perfected with pp. 5 and 8 comprising the outer forme. Since a compositor perforce adjusted his material to predetermined limits for each page when setting by formes, important textual consequences may result from the mechanical process of printing when the casting-off had not been completely accurate and he was forced to compress his material, or to expand it, to fit the pre-assigned space.

4 'A Note on *Coriolanus*', *J. Q. Adams Memorial Studies* (1948), 239–52.

5 'Compositor Determination and Other Problems', *Studies in Bibliography*, vii (1955), 9–10.

6 'New Approaches to Textual Problems in Shakespeare', *Studies in Bibliography*, viii (1956), 3–14.

7 'The Textual Relation of Q2 to Q1 *Hamlet*', *Studies in Bibliography*, viii (1956), 39–66.

8 P. L. Cantrell and G. W. Williams, 'The Printing of the Second Quarto of *Romeo and Juliet* (1599)', *Studies in Bibliography*, ix (1957), 107–28; see also Richard Hosley, 'Quarto Copy for Q2 *Romeo and Juliet*', *S. B.*, ix, 129–41. These correct J. Dover Wilson in the New Cambridge *Romeo and Juliet* and in 'The New Way with Shakespeare's Texts: II. Recent Work on the Text of *Romeo and Juliet*', *Shakespeare Survey*, viii (1955), 81–99.

18

Revising Shakespeare

Gary Taylor

I know of only two great creative artists who, according to orthodox interpretation, never revised their work. One is, of course, Shakespeare; the other is, of course, God.[1] This is part of a more general confusion between Shakespeare and God, prevalent in certain sects of the priesthood of literary criticism.

Nevertheless, textual critics have had to concede that the Shakespeare canon does contain clear evidence of certain *kinds* of revision. One kind is found in the good quartos of *Love's Labour's Lost* (Q1), *Romeo and Juliet* (Q2), and *Hamlet* (Q2). The quartos in question were apparently printed from Shakespeare's own manuscript draft. In the first two examples (Illustrations 1 and 2), the passage quoted on the left is, in the printed text, immediately followed by the passage on the right. The duplication of words and ideas between the right-hand passage and the left-hand passage has convinced most critics that Shakespeare first wrote the left-hand passage, then for some reason decided it was unsatisfactory, and so redrafted it, immediately afterwards, in the form which it takes in the right-hand passage. In *Hamlet*, there are apparently two false starts of this kind.

> For women feare too much, euen as they loue,
> And womens feare and loue hold quantitie,
> Eyther none, in neither ought, or in extremitie,
> Now what my Lord is proofe hath made you know,
> And as my loue is ciz'd, my feare is so,
>
> (H2)

The first line quoted has no rhyme-mate; moreover, its sense seems to be duplicated by the second line. In the third line, 'Eyther none' is extrametrical, and its sense seems to be duplicated by 'in neither ought'. The folio text omits both the unrhymed duplicated line and the extrametrical duplicated phrase.

1 *Romeo and Juliet*, Second Quarto (1599), D4ᵛ

(First Version)	(Second Verison)

(First Version)

The grey-eyde morne smiles on the frowning night,
Checkring the Easterne Clouds with streaks of light,
And darknesse fleckted like a drunkard reeles,
From forth daies pathway, made by *Tytans* wheeles.

(Second Verison)

(nights.

Fri. The grey-eyed morne smiles on the frowning
Checking the Easterne clowdes with streaks of light:
And fleckeld darknesse like a drunkard reeles,
From forth daies path, and *Tytans* burning wheeles:

2 *Love's Labour's Lost*, Quarto (1600), F2ᵛ–F3

(First Version)

And where that you haue vowd to studie (Lordes)
In that each of you haue forsworne his Booke.
Can you still dreame and poare and thereon looke.
For when would you my Lord, or you, or you,
Haue found the ground of Studies excellence,
Without the beautie of a womans face?
From womens eyes this doctrine I deriue,
They are the Ground, the Bookes, the Achadems,
From whence doth spring the true *Promethean* fire.
Why vniuersall plodding poysons vp
The nimble spirites in the arteries,
As motion and long during action tyres
The sinnowy vigour of the trauayler.
Now for not looking on a womans face,
You haue in that forsworne the vse of eyes
And studie too, the causer of your vow.
For where is any Authour in the worlde,
Teaches such beautie as a womas eye:
Learning is but an adiunct to our selfe,
And where we are, our Learning likewise is.
Then when our selues we see in Ladies eyes,
With our selues,
Do we not likewise see our learning there?

(Second Version)

O we haue made a Vow to studie, Lordes,
And in that Vow we haue forsworne our Bookes:
For when would you (my Leedge) or you, or you?
In leaden contemplation haue found out
Such fierie Numbers as the prompting eyes,
Of beauties tutors haue inritcht you with:
Other slow Artes intirely keepe the braine:
And therefore finding barraine practizers,
Scarce shew a haruest of their heauie toyle.
But Loue first learned in a Ladies eyes,
Liues not alone emured in the braine:
But with the motion of all elamentes,
Courses as swift as thought in euery power,
And giues to euery power a double power,
Aboue their tunctions and their offices.
It addes a precious seeing to the eye:
A Louers eyes will gaze an Eagle blinde.
A Louers eare will heare the lowest sound,
When the suspitious head of theft is stopt,
Loues feeling is more soft and sensible,
Then are the tender hornes of Cuckled Snayles:
Loues tongue proues daintie, *Bachus* grosse in taste,
For Valoure, is not Loue a *Hercules?*
Still clyming trees in the *Hesperides.*
Subtit as *Sphinx,* as sweete and musicall,
As bright *Appolos* Lute, strung with his haire,
And when Loue speakes, the voyce of all the Goddes,
Make heauen drowsie with the harmonie.
Neuer durst Poet touch a pen to write,
Vntill his Incke were tempred with Loues sighes:
O then his lines would rauish sauage eares,
And plant in Tyrants milde humilitie.
From womens eyes this doctrine I deriue,
They sparcle still the right promethean fier,
They are the Bookes, the Artes, the Achademes,
That shew, containe, and nourish all the worlde,
Els none at all in ought proues excellent.

Illustrations 1 and 2

In all three cases – and many other examples could be given, from elsewhere in these three plays, and from other plays like *Troilus and Cressida, Titus Andronicus*, and *Henry V* – we apparently see Shakespeare revising his work in the very act of composing it. The hypothesis of revision is, in such cases, based entirely upon a critical judgement that Shakespeare could never have intended *both* versions of these lines and ideas to be spoken, one after the other, upon stage. That critical judgement has been almost universally accepted, and these passages are regularly cited as evidence of Shakespeare revising himself.

In *Romeo, Love's Labour's Lost*, and *Hamlet* Shakespeare seemingly changed his mind in the very act of making it up. Consequently, 'revision' may seem a slightly misleading term. The rewriting is part of the original process of writing itself. One can cite these passages without consciously abandoning the image of Shakespeare as an unselfconscious artist. But another widely accepted example of revision is rather more disconcerting.

The first edition of *A Midsummer Night's Dream* (1600) was also apparently printed from Shakespeare's own foul papers. As a whole, this edition contains very little mislineation; most of the examples can be convincingly explained bibliographically, as the result of difficulty with fitting long lines into the compositor's measure, or difficulty with squeezing too much material (or expanding too little material) into quarto pages cast off in advance, for setting by formes.[2] But at the beginning of Act Five occurs a sudden infestation of mislineation, stretching over three quarto pages, for which no such bibliographical explanation is available. (I have boxed the affected lines in the facsimile; see Illustration 3.)

The: More straunge then true, I neuer may beleeue
These antique fables, nor these Fairy toyes,
Louers, and mad men haue such seething braines,
Such shaping phantasies, that apprehend more,
Then coole reason euer comprehends. The lunatick,
The louer, and the Poet are of imagination all compact,
One sees more diuels, then vast hell can holde:
That is the mad man. The louer, all as frantick,
Sees *Helens* beauty in a brow of *Ægypt.*
The Poets eye, in a fine frenzy, rolling, doth glance
From heauen to earth, from earth to heauen. And as
Imagination bodies forth the formes of things

G2ᵛ / G3

Vnknowne: the Poets penne turnes them to shapes,
And giues to ayery nothing, a locall habitation,
And a name. Such trickes hath strong imagination,
That if it would but apprehend some ioy,
It comprehends some bringer of that ioy.
Or in the night, imagining some feare,
How easie is a bush suppos'd a Beare?
Hyp: But, all the story of the night told ouer,
And all their minds transfigur'd so together,
More witnesseth than fancies images,

And growes to something of great constancy:
But howsoeuer, strange and admirable.

    Enter Louers; Lysander, Demetrius, Hermia *and* Helena.

The: Here come the louers, full of ioy and mirth.
    Ioy, gentle friends, ioy and fresh daies
    Of loue accompany your hearts.

Lys: More then to vs, waite in your royall walkes, your boorde, your bedde.
                    (haue,

The: Come now: what maskes, what daunces shall wee
    To weare away this long age of three hours, betweene
    Or after supper, & bed-time? Where is our vsuall manager
    Of mirth? What Reuels are in hand? Is there no play,
    To ease the anguish of a torturing hower? Call *Philostrate.*

Philostrate: Here mighty *Theseus.*

The: Say, what abridgement haue you for this euening?
    What maske, what musicke? How shall we beguile
    The lazy tyme, if not with some delight?

Philost: There is a briefe, how many sports are ripe.
    Make choyce, of which your Highnesse will see first.

The: The battell with the *Centaures* to be sung,
    By an *Athenian* Eunuche, to the Harpe?
    Weele none of that, That haue I tolde my loue,
    In glory of my kinsman *Hercules,*
    The ryot of the tipsie *Bachanals,*

G3
———
G3ᵛ

Tearing the *Thracian* singer, in their rage?
That is an olde deuise: and it was plaid,
When I from *Thebes* came last a conquerer.
The thrise three Muses, mourning for the death
Of learning, late deceast, in beggery?
That is some *Satire* keene and criticall,
Not sorting with a nuptiall ceremony.
A tedious briefe Scene of young *Pyramus*
And his loue *Thisbe;* very tragicall mirth?
Merry, and tragicall? Tedious, and briefe? That is hot Ise,
And wōdrous strange snow. How shall we find the cōcord
Of this discord?

As Dover Wilson observed in 1924, all of the mislined material could be omitted, without damage to its context, and some of the mislined material seems related to other mislined material.[3] All editors since Wilson have accepted that the mislined passages are mislined because they were written in the margin of Shakespeare's manuscript, and that they were written in those margins because they were written after the main body of the passage; they are afterthoughts. This example of revision differs from those already quoted because the very nature of the evidence for revision – extensive marginal additions – suggests strongly that Shakespeare did not write the offending material until after he had written at least fifty lines of the scene, and that he then went back over that part of the scene, making a number of belated alterations. How *much* later, we do not know; but it must have been at least a little later.

3 *A Midsummer Night's Dream*

The. More ſtraunge then true. I neuer may beleeue
Theſe antique ſables, nor theſe Fairy toyes.
Louers, and mad men haue ſuch ſeething braines,
Such ſhaping phantaſies, that apprehend more,
Then coole reaſon euer comprehends. The lunatick,
The louer, and the Poet are of imagination all compact.
One ſees more diuels, then vaſt hell can holde:
That is the mad man. The louer, all as frantick,
Sees *Helens* beauty in a brow of *Ægipt*,
The Poets eye, in a fine frenzy, rolling, doth glance
From heauen to earth, from earth to heauen. And as
Imagination bodies forth the formes of things
Vnknowne: the Poets penne turnes them to ſhapes,
And giues to ayery nothing, a locall habitation,
And a name. Such trickes hath ſtrong imagination,
That if it would but apprehend ſome ioy,
It comprehends ſome bringer of that ioy.
Or in the night, imagining ſome feare,
How eaſie is a buſh ſuppoſd a Beare?
    Hip. But, all the ſtory of the night told ouer,
And all their minds transfigur'd ſo together,
More witneſſeth than fancies images,
And growes to ſomething of great conſtancy:
But howſoeuer, ſtrange and admirable.
       Enter Louers; Lyſander, Demetrius, Hermia *and*
                   Helena.
    The. Here come the louers, full of ioy and mirth.
Ioy, gentle friends, ioy and freſh daies
Of loue accompany your hearts.
    Lyſ. More then to vs, waite in your royall walkes, your
boorde, your bedde.   (haue,
    The. Come now: what maskes, what daunces ſhall wee
To weare away this long age of three hours, betweene
Or after ſupper, & bed-time? Where is our vſuall manager
Of mirth? What Reuels are in hand? Is there no play,
To eaſe the anguiſh of a torturing howre? Call *Philoſtrate*.   [¹ Call *Egeus*.]

Ege.   *Philoſtrate,* Here mighty *Theſeus.*
         The. Say, what abridgement haue you for this euening?
What maske, what muſicke? How ſhall we beguile
The lazy tyme, if not with ſome delight?
Ege.   *Philoſt.* There is a briefe, how many ſports are ripe.
Make choyce, of which your Highneſſe will ſee firſt.
Liſ.   *The.* The battell with the *Centaures* to be ſung,
By an *Athenian* Eunuche, to the Harpe?
The.   Weele none of that, That haue I tolde my loue,
In glory of my kinſman *Hercules.*
Liſ.   The ryot of the tipſie *Bachanals,*

           Tearing the *Thracian* ſinger, in their rage?
The.   That is an olde deuiſe: and it was plaid,
When I from *Thebes* came laſt a conquerer.
Liſ.   The thriſe three Muſes, mourning for the death
Of learning, late deceaſt, in beggery?
The.   That is ſome *Satire* keene and criticall,
Not ſorting with a nuptiall ceremony.
Liſ.   A tedious briefe Scene of young *Pyramus*
And his loue *Thiſby*; very tragicall mirth?
The.   Merry, and tragicall? Tedious, and briefe? That is hot Iſe,
And wôdrous ſtrange ſnow. How ſhall we find the côcord
Of this diſcord?

Illustration 3

Shakespeare thus apparently engaged in two kinds of revision: revision in the very act of composition, and revision at some time *after* initial composition – but still within the 'first draft' or 'foul papers' stage of composition.

Additional verse lines written in the margins of a manuscript confuse a printer because in such circumstances line-breaks may not have been indicated at all, or may have been obscured by the cramping of the material. A printer might also be misled by a marginal addition if he took it, not as an addition to the dialogue (which therefore did *not* belong where it physically occurred in the manuscript) but as a normal stage direction (which therefore *did* belong where it physically occurred in the manuscript). Thus, in the good quarto of *Romeo and Juliet* (Q2):

> Forbid this bandying in *Verona* streetes,
> Hold *Tybalt*, good *Mercutio*.
> > *Away* Tybalt.
> *Mer.* I am hurt.
> > > (F3ᵛ)

Within the conventions of this quarto, '*Away* Tybalt.' is unmistakably intended as a stage direction. But it sounds much more like a speech: Shakespeare never elsewhere uses 'Away' as the verb in an exit direction, but does use it often in imperative speeches. W. W. Greg therefore conjectured, and subsequent editors have agreed, that '*Away* Tybalt' was a speech, written in the margin of the manuscript, which the printer misinterpreted as a stage direction.[4] This speech, noticeably, does not fit the metrical pattern of the verse into which it is inserted: without the two words, 'Hold *Tybalt*, good *Mercutio*. I am hurt' forms a typical Shakespearean pentameter, divided between two speakers; the added imperative 'speech' disrupts that pattern. The two words which Q2 treats as a stage direction were thus probably written in the margin of the manuscript, and probably written after the verse into which they intrude. Again, we cannot be sure when the addition took place.

In *A Midsummer Night's Dream* we infer that certain lines were written in the margin of a manuscript because they have been mislined in the printed text; in *Romeo and Juliet* we infer that a short speech was written in the margin because it was misinterpreted as a marginal stage direction. But in *Hamlet* certain lines are actually printed in the margin of the first authoritative edition. Illustrations 4 and 5 reproduce excerpts from H2 and H2ᵛ, in which you can see these marginal lines; the first of these, you will notice, occurs just after a passage I have already referred to. There are no parallels for the way in which these two short speeches are printed in the 1605 quarto, or in any other Shakespeare quarto; there is no plausible bibliographical explanation for either anomaly. In the first example Hamlet's speech interrupts the Player Queen; yet there is no speech prefix to indicate that she resumes her speech after the interruption. And, of course, both passages make sense without the marginal speeches. Again, as in *Romeo* and *Dream*, it appears that Shakespeare marginally added to his own dialogue at some indeterminable point after initial composition.

But the examples from *Hamlet* and *A Midsummer Night's Dream* also have another feature in common. In both cases the apparent revision evident *within* the Quarto text coexists with related textual variation *between* the Quarto edition and a later text,

Gary Taylor

4 *Hamlet*, Second Quarto, H2

⟶ For women feare too much, euen as they loue,
And womens feare and loue hold quantitie,
⟶ Eyther none, in neither ought, or in extremitie,
Now what my Lord is proofe hath made you know,
And as my loue is ciz'd, my feare is fo,
Where loue is great, the litleft doubts are feare,
Where little feares grow great, great loue growes there.
   King. Faith I muft leaue thee loue, and fhortly to,
My operant powers their functions leaue to do,
And thou fhalt liue in this faire world behind,
Honord, belou'd, and haply one as kind,
For husband fhalt thou.
   Quee. O confound the reft,
Such loue muft needes be treafon in my breft,
In fecond husband let me be accurft,
None wed the fecond, but who kild the firft.   *Ham.* That's
The inftances that fecond marriage moue   wormwood
Are bafe refpects of thrift, but none of loue,
A fecond time I kill my husband dead,
When fecond husband kiffes me in bed.
   King. I doe belieue you thinke what now you fpeake,

5 *Hamlet*, Second Quarto, H2ᵛ

   Quee. Nor earth to me giue foode, nor heauen light,
Sport and repofe lock from me day and night,
To defperation turne my truft and hope,
And Anchors cheere in prifon be my fcope,
Each oppofite that blancks the face of ioy,
Meete what I would haue well, and it deftroy,
Both heere and hence purfue me lafting ftrife,   *Ham.* If fhe fhould
If once I be a widdow, euer I be a wife.   breake it now.
   King. Tis deeply fworne, fweet leaue me heere a while,
My fpirits grow dull, and faine I would beguile
The tedious day with fleepe.

Illustrations 4 and 5

printed in the 1623 First Folio. In *Hamlet*, the Folio text of this scene contains yet another brief speech by Hamlet, not printed in the Quarto at all.

Oph:	The King rises.
Quee:	How fares my Lord?
Pol:	Giue ore the play.
King:	Giue me some light, away.
Pol:	Lights, lights, lights.

(Second Quarto, H3)

Ophe:	The King rises.
→*Ham:*	What, frighted with false fire.
Qu:	How fares my Lord?
Pol:	Giue o're the Play.
King:	Giue me some Light. Away.
All:	Lights, Lights, Lights.

(First Folio, 006^v)

Likewise, in *Dream*, the first part of Act Five – where all the significant mislineation occurs – contains more variation between the Quarto and Folio than any other part of the play. (Folio variants are bracketed in the margin.)

Enter Louers; Lysander, Demetrius, Hermia *and* Helena.

The:	Here come the louers, full of ioy and mirth.
	Ioy, gentle friends, ioy and fresh daies
	Of loue accompany your hearts.
Lys:	More then to vs, waite in your royall walkes, your
	boorde, your bedde. (haue,
The:	Come now: what maskes, what daunces shall wee
	To weare away this long age of three hours, betweene
	Or after supper, & bed-time? Where is our vsuall manager
	Of mirth? What Reuels are in hand? Is there no play,
[Call *Egeus:*]	To ease the anguish of a torturing hower? Call *Philostrate.*
[*Ege.*] *Philostrate:*	Here mighty *Theseus.*
The:	Say, what abridgement haue you for this euening?
	What maske, what musicke? How shall we beguile
	The lazy tyme, if not with some delight?
[*Ege.*] *Philost:*	There is a briefe, how many sports are ripe.
	Make choyce, of which your Highnesse will see first.
[*Lis.*] *The:*	The battell with the *Centaures* to be sung,
	By an *Athenian* Eunuche, to the Harpe?
[*The.*]	Weele none of that, That haue I tolde my loue,
	In glory of my kinsman *Hercules,*
[*Lis.*]	The ryot of the tipsie *Bachanals,*

G3
——
G3ᵛ

	Tearing the *Thracian* singer, in their rage?
[*The.*]	That is an olde deuise: and it was plaid,
	When I from *Thebes* came last a conquerer.

[*Lis.*] The thrise three Muses, mourning for the death
          Of learning, late deceast, in beggery?

[*The.*] That is some *Satire* keene and criticall,
          Not sorting with a nuptiall ceremony.

[*Lis.*] A tedious briefe Scene of young *Pyramus*
          And his loue *Thisbe*; very tragicall mirth?

[*The.*] Merry, and tragicall? Tedious, and briefe? That is hot Ise,
          And wōdrous strange snow. How shall we find the cōcord
          Of this discord?

In the Folio the speeches of Philostrate are allocated instead to Egeus, thus bringing the thwarted father into the harmonies of the play's resolution: and Lysander – the son-in-law Egeus didn't want, but got – reads the list of proposed entertainments to Theseus.[5] This proximity of revision within texts and variation between texts may of course be coincidental; but then again, it may not.[6]

All modern editors accept that the anomalies in the first edition of *A Midsummer Night's Dream* result from authorial revision; all modern editors deny that the variation between Quarto and Folio results from the same process. Editors have been perfectly willing to accept that Shakespeare changed his mind in his foul papers; but they have steadfastly refused to believe that any of the variants between different editions result from authorial revision, revision which took place after completion of the first rough draft. In other words, when editors have only one extant text, they are happy to discern in it two layers of composition; but when editors have two substantive texts, they insist that both reflect only one layer of authorial composition. This editorial principle might be expressed by the mathematical formula: one sometimes equals two, but two always equals one.

Logically, there are only two possibilities.

1 Shakespeare never revised his work, after completing his initial manuscript draft.
2 Shakespeare did, at least occasionally, revise his work, even after completing his initial manuscript draft.

These hypotheses are of course mutually incompatible. Neither hypothesis can, as yet, be proven; yet editors must, in order to edit Shakespeare at all, try to determine which hypothesis is, upon the available evidence, more *likely* to be right.

Most defenders of either hypothesis have offered 'literary,' rather than historical or bibliographical, 'proof.' Such proofs are intrinsically unstable. Advocates of the first hypothesis will allege that the differences between two early editions all result from corruption, rather than revision; they contend that the play only makes sense, or makes better sense, if we combine and conflate material from both early documents. Advocates of the second hypothesis, by contrast, allege that many variants result from revision, not corruption; they contend that the play only makes sense, or makes better sense, if we do *not* conflate material from two different documents, but recognize instead that each document has its own artistic coherence, that each body has its own soul. Both positions are equally and irredeemably subjective.

Of course, advocates of the first hypothesis have more to prove: they must attribute *every* variant to corruption; whereas advocates of the revisionist hypothesis only need to show that *some* variants result from revision. Moreover, advocates of the first hypothesis use an irrevocably subjective method to justify wholesale editorial emendation and reorganization; advocates of the revisionist hypothesis, more modestly, use an irrevocably subjective method in defense of the historical witnesses. But although advocates of revision may be more modest (intellectually, if not personally), their modesty does not make their 'literary' proof any more definitive than the 'literary' proof it seeks to supplant. 'Nothing neither way.'

Typically, advocates of traditional conflation argue that the conflated text is more 'complex' than either early document. But if you combine two atoms of hydrogen with one atom of oxygen you will, inevitably, produce a molecule more 'complex' than its constituent elements. That enhanced complexity does not prove that either oxygen or hydrogen is merely a 'corrupt' form of water. On the other hand, Shakespeare himself specializes in complex, open-ended, unstable artistic molecules; unlike *The Divine Comedy*, *Hamlet* has a form which permits interpolation and omission; and the kinds of complication (or even contradiction) produced by conflation are arguably difficult to distinguish from the kinds of complication (or even contradiction) already present in the acknowledged canon. I think the two *can* be rationally distinguished; but that is, after all, a personal judgement, no more infallible than the Pope's.

Shakespeare did revise, or he did not. How could you prove that one of these hypotheses is true, and the other false? You might hope to find reliable early testimony to Shakespeare's habits of composition. An autograph letter, for instance. 'Dear Anne, I'll be home next week, as soon as I finish completely revising that old play of mine, *King Lear*. Your loving Willy. London. 1 April 1610.'

In the absence of such authorial testimony we might look for depositions from Shakespeare's friends and colleagues. Two such statements in fact exist, both recorded in the preliminaries to the First Folio. As is well known, Heminges and Condell in their Preface allege that Shakespeare:

> as he was a happie imitator of Nature, was a most gentle expresser of it. His mind and hand went together: and what he thought, he vttered with that easinesse, that wee haue scarse receiued from him a blot in his papers.

Ben Jonson, in his *Discoveries*, repeats this claim:

> *I remember*, the Players have often mentioned it as an honour to *Shakespeare*, that in his writing, (whatsoever he penn'd) hee never blotted out line. My answer hath beene, would he had blotted a thousand … [hee] had an excellent *Phantsie*; brave notions, and gentle expressions: wherein hee flow'd with that facility, that sometime it was necessary he should be stop'd:

How do we interpret this claim? It may be literally true: Shakespeare may not have blotted any – or many (depending on whether we believe 'scarse' or 'never') – of his lines, even when he intended to cancel them. If you look back at my first three examples, from *Romeo*, *Hamlet*, and *Love's Labour's Lost*, you will immediately realize that Shakespeare could not have blotted out the cancelled first version of those passages: if he had done so, the printer would have been unable to read them, and would in any case have realized that they were obviously meant to be cancelled. Shakespeare, when he wanted to omit something in his foul papers, may have simply used a marginal deletion mark, or may have used no mark at all, simply assuming that he could take care of such matters when he came to make his own fair copy of the play. Therefore, in some cases at least, the players' boast must have been literally true. But I think they intended the claim to have more than a literal significance; they intended by it to express the spontaneity and fecundity of Shakespeare's creative prowess, to distinguish him from imaginatively constipated writers like John Webster or Ben Jonson. But such a writer, whose mind overflows with images and ideas, filled with such imaginative impatience that he can hardly spill his mind out onto the paper fast enough – such a writer is not likely to be able to transform himself, when it comes to making a copy of his work, into a reliable human xerox machine. That very superabundance of talent makes it almost inevitable that he will continue impatiently rearranging, superfluously tinkering, overachieving, every time he copies his work. The claim that he never blotted a line thus tells us little about Shakespeare's attitude towards revision. If anything it suggests that he probably revised his work, one way or another, every time he copied it.

The other testimony in the First Folio – Ben Jonson's great encomium – is more explicit.

> Yet must I not giue Nature all: Thy Art,
> My gentle *Shakespeare*, must enjoy a part.
> For though the *Poets* matter, Nature be,
> His Art doth giue the fashion. And, that he,
> Who casts to write a liuing line, must sweat,
> (such as thine are) and strike the second heat
> Vpon the *Muses* anuile: turne the same,
> (And himselfe with it) that he thinkes to frame;
> Or for the lawrell, he may gaine a scorne,
> For a good *Poet's* made, as well as borne.
> And such wert thou.

Jonson, who had known Shakespeare since at least 1598, here explicitly claims that Shakespeare, either occasionally or habitually, 'struck a second heat' upon the muses' anvil.[7]

These two statements are the only external evidence we possess about Shakespeare's habits of composition. At worst, they contradict each other; at best, they both testify, implicitly or explicitly, that Shakespeare revised his work. But external evidence of this kind cannot finally decide the issue. Witnesses may, after all, have reasons to lie about a dead friend. Even if I did find that autograph letter, apologists for conflation could allege that Shakespeare himself was lying. Artists, after all, do, often enough, lie about their work. For all we know, 'revising *King Lear*' might have been Shakespeare's alibi, to cover an adulterous weekend.

We can only confidently deduce an author's habits of composition from the extant texts of his work. Either hypothesis – that Shakespeare did, or did not revise – could be supported by the discovery of certain kinds of document. If we discovered two autograph manuscripts of one Shakespeare play, and if those two manuscripts contained no verbal variants, except perhaps for the odd slip of the pen, then we could reasonably conclude that – at least in that single case – Shakespeare did not revise his work when he copied it. The first hypothesis would not have been proven, for the first hypothesis claims to cover *every* case; but it would not have been disproven. Alternatively, if we discovered two autograph manuscripts, and those manuscripts did differ from one another in hundreds of readings, then we would have to conclude that Shakespeare did occasionally revise his work when he copied it: the second hypothesis would be proven. Unfortunately, autograph manuscripts of Shakespeare's plays do not survive in any noticeable abundance, so this kind of proof is unlikely to materialize.

The next best thing to two autograph manuscripts would be two independent editions of a single play, demonstrably printed from different manuscripts. This situation exists in the case of only three plays – and in fact the independence of the two editions involved has, in each case, only recently been established, on the basis of computer-assisted analyses of spelling and punctuation.[8] The three plays are *Henry the Fourth Part Two*, *Hamlet*, and *Othello*. For each of these plays there is a 'good' quarto and an independent Folio text printed from a manuscript. In each case, these editions differ from one another in hundreds of readings, including the presence or absence of extended passages of dialogue. Moreover, this control group of three can be doubled. For three other plays – *Richard II*, *Troilus and Cressida*, and *King Lear* – we possess two substantive editions. One is an early quarto, printed from manuscript. The Folio text has, in each case, been printed from a marked-up exemplar of a quarto; but the Folio corrects so many demonstrable Quarto errors in the dialogue that we can conclude, with absolute confidence, that an effort was made to collate the dialogue of the extant quarto with the dialogue of a manuscript now lost.[9] In all three cases, again, the two editions differ from each other extensively: the more thorough the correction of Quarto errors, the greater the number of verbal variants of other kinds between the two relevant texts. In each case, again, the variants include the presence or absence of extended passages of dialogue. We therefore possess six plays which come as close as possible to the ideal standard of proof, six plays for which the readings of independent manuscripts have been preserved in printed editions; all six contain massive verbal variation.

Further examples are provided by Shakespeare's sonnets, which we know circulated in manuscript at least ten years before they first appeared in print. A number of seventeenth-century transcripts of individual sonnets survive. For most sonnets only one manuscript exists, and it is difficult to determine the status and origin of the manuscript text. But two sonnets – number 2 and number 106 – survive in more than one manuscript. In each case, again, the manuscript version differs significantly from the printed text. This can be seen from the parallel texts of Sonnet 2 (Illustration 6). A description and analysis of these two texts has recently been published in *The Bulletin of the John Rylands Library*.[10] Two other sonnets – 138 and 144 – also survive in two independent texts, one the Quarto of 1609, the other an octavo edition of *The Passionate Pilgrim*, printed ten years earlier; again, the two editions offer significantly different texts of the sonnets.

[THE MANUSCRIPT VERSION]

Spes Altera

When forty winters shall beseige thy brow
And trench deepe furrowes in y^t lovely feild
Thy youths faire liurey so accounted now
Shall bee like rotten weeds of no-worth held
Then beeing askt where all thy bewty lyes
Where all ye lustre of thy youthfull dayes
To say within these hollow sumcken eyes
Were an all-eaten truth, & worthlesse prayse
O how much better were thy bewtyes vse
If thou couldst say this pretty child of mine
Saues my account & makes my old excuse
Making his bewty by succession thine
This verr to bee new borne when thou art old
And see thy bloud warme when thou feelst it cold.

W.S.

[THE PRINTED VERSION]

2

When fortie Winters shall beseige thy brow,
And digge deep trenches in thy beauties field,
Thy youthes proud liuery so gaz'd on now,
Wil be a totter'd weed of smal worth held: 4
Then being askt, where all thy beautie lies,
Where all the treasure of thy lusty daies;
To say within thine owne deepe sunken eyes,
Were an all-eating shame, and thriftlesse praise. 8
How much more praise deseru'd thy beauties vse,
If thou couldst answere this faire child of mine
Shall sum my count, and make my old excuse
Prouing his beautie by succession thine. 12
This were to be new made when thou art ould,
And see thy blood warme when thou feel'st it cold.

SHAKE-SPEARE

COLLATIONS OF THE MANUSCRIPT VERSION

The reading to the left of the bracket occurs in all eleven manuscripts, except those specified to the right of the bracket. Spelling and punctuation from the Westminster Abbey copy (W).

Spes Altera] Spes Altera A song F3; To one y^t would dye a Mayd B4, B5, F2, W,Y; A Lover to his Mistres N; The Benefitt of Mariage. R 1 forty] threescore B1, 40 B4 (?) winters] yeares R 2 trench] drench feild] cheeke B2, B3 3 youths] youth B5, F3 faire liurey] fairer feild R accounted] esteemed N 4 like] like like B5 weds] cloaths F2 . 5 beeing askt] if wee aske B3, B2; askt R lyes] lye] W (cropped) 6 Where] Where's B1, B2, B3, F3, N, R 7 these] those Y; not in B4 8 eaten] beaten F2 prayse] pleasure B5 9 O] not in B5 much] far Y; not in B5 bewtyes] bewtious Y 10 pretty] little B2, B3 11 Saues] Saud Y my] mine N makes my old] makes me old B4; makes no old F2; yeilds mee an N; makes the old R; make no old Y 13 new borne] made younge B2, B3 14.1 W.S.] N (opposite title), B2 (table of contents)

It might still be objected – indeed, it regularly is assumed – that these facts do not amount to proof that Shakespeare revised his work; for the variation between the two texts of these ten works might be the result of corruption in transmission. But this explanation is much more defensible if you are editing one work, than if you are editing the Complete Works. For these ten works have very different histories of transmission. The six relevant plays in the Folio, for instance, were set into type by at least five different compositors; three were set directly from manuscript, three from marked-up quartos; the manuscripts which lay behind these texts clearly have different kinds of provenance. Most, if not all, of the relevant quartos were apparently set from Shakespeare's own foul papers, but they were printed by four different printers, over the course of almost a quarter of a century, by (on current knowledge) nine different compositors. The only figure common to the transmission of all these texts is William Shakespeare. Therefore, if we wish to attribute the massive variation in all ten works to error and sophistication by agents of transmission, we must assume that such cavalier incompetence and irresponsibility affected virtually every agent entrusted with the transmission of Shakespeare's writings into print. Alternatively, we could conclude that everyone involved was reasonably competent, and that a single source of variation accounts for the divergences in all these texts: Shakespeare himself.

This still does not amount to a proof, of course. What we can prove is that most of the Folio compositors, and some of the Quarto compositors, and at least one of the scribes, were, in their other work, reasonably responsible and reliable, and that elsewhere they cannot be blamed for this quantity or kind of textual variant. We can prove that the censors did not elsewhere object to certain kinds of material.[11] *Normal* kinds of error and interference and sophistication will not account for the variants in these plays and sonnets, or for the fact that such variants occur in all ten.

We can also show that other playwrights and sonneteers of this period did revise their work in comparable ways. Such variation has been demonstrated in the sonnets of Spenser, Drayton, Daniel, and Constable, and in the plays of Jonson, Chapman, Beaumont and Fletcher, Dekker, Heywood, and Middleton. It perhaps does not surprise us to find such finicky self-preening in the work of consciously literary writers like Jonson and Chapman, or consciously gentlemanly writers like Beaumont and Fletcher; but Dekker and Heywood and Middleton were what Jonson called 'base fellows,' and what we would call 'hacks.' Professional playwrights like Shakespeare rather than 'men of letters' like Jonson and Chapman, they turned out a huge volume of work and showed little concern for their literary reputations *sub specie aeternitatis*. And E. A. J. Honigmann has shown that writers like Keats and Burns, who shared with Shakespeare an extraordinary imaginative fluency, a lack of higher education, and a certain carelessness of academic nicety, also revised their work in similar ways.[12] Even so, of course, such parallels do not *prove* that Shakespeare revised his work, because Shakespeare might be 'exceptional.'

In one sense, Shakespeare demonstrably was exceptional. He was the only playwright of his era who was also an actor and a sharer in its most successfull theatrical company, and who held that position for perhaps as long as twenty years. He was, as many witnesses conspire to inform us, the most popular and successful dramatist of that period. He is the only playwright whose works were collected and published posthumously by his theatrical company. He also named three actors in his will – the only playwright of this period, to my knowledge, who did so. We can confidently conclude that Shakespeare was exceptional, as a writer, in the strength and longevity and warmth of his relationship with a company of actors; exceptional, too, in the security of his position as a writer, both financially and institutionally; exceptional in his contact with and influence upon those people who were regularly responsible for transmitting his intentions from page to stage. If the transmission of Shakespeare's plays differed in any essential from the transmission of the plays of any of his contemporaries, it should have been in the relative scarcity of theatrical interference not sanctioned by the author himself.

Professor Fredson Bowers has rightly insisted that the basis of all textual editing and bibliographical investigation must be what he calls 'the postulate of normality.' 'No one should base a theory on abnormality instead of normality ... unless there is over-whelming evidence in favour of the aberration.'[13] The hypothesis that Shakespeare never revised his work, after completing his first foul draft, is based upon five assumptions: (1) that those who transmitted the texts of his work were abnormally unreliable; (2) that Shakespeare was abnormal in the context of English Renaissance sonneteers and playwrights, and abnormal in the context of poets from all other periods, in his reluctance to revise his work; (3) that Shakespeare was abnormal in combining a willingness to revise in foul papers, with an unwillingness to revise thereafter; (4) that Shakespeare was normal only in the one respect in which we can demonstrate that he was instead unique: his relationship as playwright with the actors who performed his plays; (5) that the only ten control cases which we possess – the ten works which survive in two independent textual traditions – that these ten controls have, by a remarkable coincidence, and despite the variety of agents involved in their transmission, all suffered massive corruption, sophistication, and interference. The denial that Shakespeare revised his work can only be sustained if we accept all five assumptions, and accept them as an explanation for the variants in every text. Because once we admit the presence of revision as an operative source of variation in any one of these works, then we have inserted the thin end of that infamous wedge, and revision can no longer be ruled out as a possible explanation for variation in all the others. It seems to me that this set of interlocking assumptions no longer deserves our intellec-tual allegiance. It is like the pre-Copernican model of the universe: sustained only by the proliferation of improbable subsidiary complications.

Those few critics who have tried to defend the entrenched conflationist orthodoxy against the new revisionist onslaught have, to a man, done so by claiming that the case for revision is based on 'mere critical interpretation' – and bad interpretation, to boot. The pot proverbially calls the kettle black. But the evidence for revision is not solely, or even primarily, hermeneutical; it does not depend upon the single implausible Folio variant which hostile reviewers choose to quote. The hypothesis that Shakespeare, like every other author, revised his work, depends fundamentally upon the sheer weight of historical and bibliographical evidence for variation in the canon as a whole – variation which cannot be convincingly explained in any other way. That is why, although all previous editions have been based on the unexamined belief that Shakespeare did *not* revise his work, all future editions should be, and I believe will be, based on the recognition that he habitually did.[14]

Notes

1 For evidence, if any were needed, that such attitudes about Shakespearean revision persist, even in the most elevated editorial circles, see for instance Harold Jenkins' new Arden edition of *Hamlet* (London: Methuen, 1982), *passim*. All extant editions of Shakespeare's works are, of course, based on similar assumptions.

2 See Robert K. Turner, Jr., 'Printing Methods and Textual Problems in *A Midsummer Night's Dream* Q1,' *Studies in Bibliography*, 15 (1962), 33–55.

3 *A Midsummer Night's Dream*, The New Shakespeare (Cambridge: University Press, 1924), pp. 80–86.

4 W. W. Greg, *The Shakespeare First Folio: Its Bibliographical and Textual History* (Oxford: Clarendon Press, 1955), p. 235, and George Walton Williams, 'A New Line of Dialogue in *Romeo and Juliet*,' *Shakespeare Quarterly*, 11 (1960), 84–87.

5 For a more extended discussion of the significance of these Folio variants, see Barbara Hodgdon, 'Gaining a Father: The Role of Egeus in the Quarto and Folio,' *Review of English Studies* (forthcoming).

6 An even more impressive example of foul paper revision linked to Folio variation is provided by 2 *Henry IV*: see the extended discussion in John Jowett and Gary Taylor, 'The Three Texts of 2 *Henry IV*,' *Studies in Bibliography*, 40 (1987), 31–50.

7 E. A. J. Honigmann first drew attention to the importance of this passage in his seminal book, *The Stability of Shakespeare's Text* (London: Arnold, 1965), pp. 30–31.

8 See Gary Taylor, 'The Folio Copy for *Hamlet, King Lear*, and *Othello*,' *Shakespeare Quarterly*, 34 (1983), 44–61, and 'Folio Compositors and Folio Copy: *King Lear* and Its Context,' *PBSA*, 79 (1985), 17–74. The evidence on copy for 2 *Henry IV* will be published in a forthcoming article. If I were to be proven wrong about one or all of these three plays, they would simply fall into the second category (plays set from heavily-annotated printed copy); likewise, if current opinion were proven wrong about *Richard II, Troilus*, or *Lear*, they would simply rise from the second into the first category (manuscript copy). The argument of this paragraph therefore does not depend upon debatable hypotheses about the exact nature of printer's copy for the Folio.

9 For *Richard II* – the only one of these plays where manuscript consultation has sometimes been questioned – see John Jowett and Gary Taylor, 'Sprinklings of Authority: The Folio Text of *Richard II*,' *Studies in Bibliography*, 38 (1985), 151–200.

10 Gary Taylor, 'Some Manuscripts of Shakespeare's Sonnets,' *Bulletin of the John Rylands Library*, 68 (1985), 210–246.

11 For examples of such negative studies see the essays on censorship and compositors by Gary Taylor and Paul Werstine in *The Division of the Kingdoms: Shakespeare's Two Versions of 'King Lear'*, ed. Gary Taylor and Michael Warren (Oxford: Clarendon Press, 1983).

12 *Instability*, pp. 47–77.

13 *Bibliography and Textual Criticism* (Oxford: Clarendon Press, 1964), pp. 64–65.

14 Such editions need not and should not assume that every variant between two substantive editions results from authorial revision: allowances must always be made for normal kinds and quantities of compositorial (and in some cases scribal) error. Nor need acceptance of authorial revision entail adherence to the view that the so-called 'bad' quartos represent early plays of Shakespeare, later extensively revised by their author. The character of revision between the acknowledged good texts of Shakespeare differs fundamentally from the kind of variation found between the 'bad' quartos and their 'good' counterparts, and memorial reconstruction still seems to me easily the most plausible explanation for the peculiar nature of the 'bad' texts.

19

Narratives About Printed Shakespeare Texts: "Foul Papers" and "Bad Quartos"

Paul Werstine

The early twentieth century had a taste for lurid romance. In *The Hound of the Baskervilles* (1902) Sherlock Holmes traces the Baskerville family line in order to protect the rightful claimant to the title from his villainous competitor. Holmes proves that the hellhound is no supernatural being beyond the power of human rationality to understand or control; instead, the beast is merely the instrument of a single bad man. Only a few years later, in 1909, A. W. Pollard examines the extant Shakespeare quartos – a group of printed texts whose origins are, like the Hound's at the beginning of Conan Doyle's story, unknown and, like the Hound's, long the subject of much speculation, none of it persuasive enough to provide a rallying point for consensus. Ignoring the large and multiple differences among the texts that are comprised within each of his categories, Pollard divides all the quartos into just two classes, labeling them the "good" and the "bad" – like the Baskervilles.[1] In spite of the nearly absurd simplicity of Pollard's system of classification, twentieth-century textual critics have long employed his labels, perpetuating the binarism and rigidity of his original distinction and even, as I hope to show, driving the two classes ever further apart, so the "good" become even better and the "bad" worse as (quite contrary to Pollard's story) Shakespeare comes to receive the sole credit for all that is in a "good" quarto (except "obvious errors") and actors alone (sometimes "rogue" actors) get charged with most and sometimes all of a "bad" quarto's variants.[2] Because there are only the two classes, if a critic represents a quarto (like that of *King Lear*) as being not very "good," it immediately is threatened with becoming "bad"; and even those who now wish to eliminate altogether the category of "bad" quarto have become trapped by Pollard's binarism into arguing that all the formerly "bad" quartos must be reassessed as "good."

I

But I am already at the end of my story and need to get back to the beginning, when a number of textual critics, among them Pollard and his ardent disciple John Dover Wilson, were not in the least convinced that "good" quartos were purely Shakespearean and "bad" ones non-Shakespearean. Pollard himself, in the 1909 book in which he separated the "bad" from the "good," subscribed to a highly speculative account, current at the time, of the "bad quartos" as both sources and early versions of Shakespeare's plays. Thus for Pollard the First Quarto of *Hamlet* (1603) "represents the play in an intermediate stage between the lost *Hamlet* [of Kyd?] and the fully Shakespearian *Hamlet* of the Folio and the second and subsequent quartos."[3] Although Pollard's work would later be appropriated by such textual critics as W. W. Greg and F. P. Wilson as the source of their own distinction between the authorial "good" texts and the derivative "bad" ones,[4] Pollard and Dover Wilson refused any such simple dichotomy. For example, when, in 1918, Dover Wilson took on the First or "bad" Quarto of *Hamlet* and then joined up with Pollard, in 1919, to extend their theory of the origin of "bad" quartos to *Henry V, Romeo and Juliet,* and *The Merry Wives of Windsor,* they presented a most complicated genesis for all four texts – a theory of origin that incorporated a number of current narrative lines about Shakespeare's reworking of others' plays and about abridgment for provincial touring, as well as the newly popular idea of memorial reconstruction by an actor or actors. The "bad" quartos, they speculated, were non-Shakespearean plays that had been both shortened for provincial playing – hence their comparative brevity – and partially revised by Shakespeare – hence the much larger measure of agreement between the "bad" quartos and the "good" Shakespeare texts in the early parts of these plays. Before being printed, the partially revised abridgments, they argued, had been worked over by a rogue actor or actors (who had played one or more parts in later fully revised Shakespearean versions of these plays) in a largely unsuccessful effort to bring the transcripts into line with the fully revised versions. Thus for Pollard and Wilson these "bad" texts are partly Shakespearean, but not wholly so.[5] Exactly the same is true, for the same critics, of plays such as *A Midsummer Night's Dream* that survive only in "good" texts, which also may be, for Pollard and Wilson, reworkings by Shakespeare of creations by his predecessors and / or his own earlier writing.[6] There is, then, no necessary connection *in history* between Pollard's division of quartos into the "good" and the "bad" and the still much-discussed question of the purity of their Shakespearean authorship. For Pollard and Wilson, Shakespeare's work is to be found in the "good" and the "bad."

Nor is there necessarily for Pollard and Wilson a connection between the distinction of the "good" from the "bad" quartos and the question of whether a printed text may preserve features (punctuation, spelling, capitalization) of Shakespeare's own manuscript. In 1909 no one regarded any printed texts as deriving without intermediary from the dramatist's own papers; that year Pollard wrote, following the then conventional narrative, that the "good" quartos are "not worse than we should expect to result from hastily written playhouse *transcripts* placed in the hands of second- and third-rate printers … and there seems no reason for denying to this group of fourteen editions some such humble but not disreputable origin."[7] Later, in publications of 1916 and

1917, Pollard himself introduced the then startlingly innovative idea that "good" texts of Shakespeare's plays might have been set into type from the playwright's manuscripts (although only after these manuscripts had been adapted and annotated for use as so-called "prompt-copies" in the theatre).[8] And soon Pollard was also finding features of Shakespeare's hand in at least certain speeches in "bad" quartos as well. In 1919 he and Wilson constructed a narrative about the First ("bad") and Second ("good") Quartos of *Romeo and Juliet* according to which the occasional close resemblances in the two texts in matters of spelling, punctuation, capitalization, and italicization were evidence that both derived from the same manuscript, the First Quarto at an earlier stage of the manuscript's revision by Shakespeare, the Second Quarto only when revision was complete.[9] In Pollard and Wilson's view, then, the "bad" as well as the "good" quartos might preserve features of Shakespeare's own inscription of a play.[10]

II

In spite of Pollard's making no distinction on these grounds between the "bad" and the "good," his suggestion, first published in 1916, that Shakespeare's plays may have been set into type from the dramatist's own papers represents, in retrospect, an important step in the eventual construction of the category of Shakespeare's "foul papers" as a kind of printer's copy reserved exclusively for "good" quartos and some Folio texts. Before Pollard, not even Greg, whose later career would be devoted in large part to judging whether individual Shakespeare texts had been set into type from "foul papers" or "prompt-books," had yet imagined the possibility of "foul papers" lying behind the "good" Shakespeare texts. In 1910 Greg conceived of plays having been set into type only from the kinds of manuscripts that are still extant from Shakespeare's period: "As a rule," he wrote, "early printed editions of plays, when not manifestly corrupt, go back to manuscripts of two kinds: prompt copies – more or less official versions preserved in the play-houses; and private copies – transcripts made for literary circulation."[11] Pollard's construction of holograph printer's copy for some "good" texts of Shakespeare's plays rested on a general theory about the transmission of theatrical texts. Representing Shakespeare and his fellows as anxious about the possible theft of play manuscripts should they be multiplied through copying, Pollard argued (1) that Shakespeare would turn over to his company manuscripts of his plays in his own hand – not scribal transcripts of them. Pollard based this part of his argument on the words of Heminges and Condell in the front matter to the Shakespeare First Folio: "His mind and hand went together: And what he thought, he vttered with that easinesse, that wee haue scarse receiued from him a blot in his papers." Although Heminges and Condell themselves represent this assertion, in their very next words, as a compliment to their dead colleague – "But it is not our prouince, who onely gather his works, and giue them you, to praise him" – Pollard construed the actors' reference to Shakespeare's papers as a statement of fact to the effect that Shakespeare handed over his plays to his company in his own handwriting. Then, according to Pollard, (2) the bookkeeper would annotate Shakespeare's holograph, which would serve as the "Booke," the theatrical document (often called anachronistically the "promptbook")[12] upon which performance would be based; Pollard sought to establish this practice by alluding to the use of holograph fair copies as "prompt-copies" in the cases of Massinger's *Believe as You List*, Munday's transcription of *Sir Thomas More*, and Mountfort's *The Launching of the Mary*. Finally, (3) when the company decided to print the play, it would hand over the holograph – there was no other copy – to the printer, who was poor enough at his trade to introduce a quantity of errors in spite of having such fine copy before him.

No assertion in Pollard's narrative, except perhaps the last, can withstand much scrutiny. Since there is no evidence (that I know of) that a theatrical manuscript was ever stolen from Shakespeare's company, the fear of theft that Pollard projects upon the company seems groundless.[13] Equally doubtful is Pollard's generalization from the Massinger, Munday, and Mountfort holographs to a universal practice of using authorial copy in the theatre. Each of the three cases cited can be represented as special: Massinger had recopied his play (after a fair copy of it, either authorial or scribal, had been submitted to the censor) to adapt it to the censor's commands; there is no evidence that *More* was ever performed; and the censor requested a more legible copy of the Mountfort piece.[14] Such special cases excepted, there are now thought to be considerably more scribal transcripts than holographs among the surviving manuscripts that Greg and others have nominated "prompt-books."[15] In spite of its groundless speculation, Pollard's argument was eventually accepted, and, by reshaping scholarly opinion and making it hospitable to the possibility that Shakespeare's plays could have been printed from his own manuscripts, it prepared the way for R. B. McKerrow's more extreme view that the dramatist's "original draft[s]" – what Greg would eventually call "foul papers" – stood behind some of the quarto and Folio plays.

When McKerrow developed the category of "the author's original draft," he seems to have established a purely ideal form of printer's copy of which there are no examples among extant dramatic manuscripts; indeed he defined the category in opposition to existing manuscripts, purporting to identify it as the origin of some early printed playtexts from an examination of printed texts alone. His first attempt to establish the category – "The Elizabethan Printer and Dramatic Manuscripts"[16] – consists largely of a survey of a few printed books from Shakespeare's period (including such items as *The Faerie Queene*, a work of Biblical explication, and *Greenes Newes both from Heauen and Hell*, a prose pamphlet) and a comparison of the kind and rate of error in these to what is found in Shakespeare's early printed plays. The allegedly greater errors in the printed plays are the ground for McKerrow's suggestion that the plays must have been printed from copy inferior both to what served as copy for other kinds of printed books and to what survive of theatrical manuscripts from the period. His conclusion was that the printer's copy for an early printed play must have been the "author's rough draft much corrected and never put in order for the press."[17] The unusual number of printer's errors in plays arise then, according to McKerrow, from the unusually poor copy supplied to the printer. For McKerrow the texts offered by the "good" quartos are not very good in comparison to other printed texts of the period, but they are very good indeed in that they derive without intermediary from Shakespeare's own manuscripts.

McKerrow's formulation of the category "author's rough draft much corrected" needs to be interrogated both theoretically and empirically. At the level of textual theory, it might be noted that what McKerrow postulated was a single document that was both (1) the author's "original manuscript," his "original draft," or his "rough draft"; and (2) the draft "edited ... by the company's producer, and perhaps revised by the author in consonance with the producer's suggestions, before being fair-copied."[18] McKerrow would have us accept that the author's original draft and his last draft co-existed in the same document, which therefore provided a record of the entire process of the individual creation of the play as well as the complete play itself. It has proved difficult to find a material equivalent to McKerrow's ideal.

Furthermore, wider surveys of London printing from Shakespeare's period under-taken since McKerrow's day do not support his conclusion about the general quality of production, from which, he claimed, plays mark such a departure as to call for the special explanation he offers. Here, for example, is Peter Blayney's finding from an exhaustive investigation of London printing in the middle of the first decade of the seventeenth century:

> While I hesitate to pit my knowledge of early printed books against McKerrow's, I do not believe that his suggestion was sound. It can hardly be doubted that books printed from clean transcripts made for licensing, or from carefully prepared copy, were printed more accurately than others – nor that books seen through the press by their authors usually emerged with the text more or less intact. When considered as a class, plays may well have been printed under the least advantageous of conditions more often than were (for example) epics in folio, massive works of theology, or books of heraldry. But plays were not the only 'popular' books printed in small formats, and my examination of the books of 1606–9 suggests that it is quite untrue that play-quartos can be singled out as a special category in this respect. Nor can a comparison be fairly drawn between the number of supposed errors which intense and cumulative scholarship has detected in the structured and often metrical content of a Shakespeare play, and the number noticed in the less familiar and more formless prose of, for example, a Greene pamphlet. And even though errors are usually more difficult to detect in prose than in verse, non-dramatic prose works often contain passages no less corruptly printed than those found in even the worst of plays.[19]

My own recent examination of the two dozen or so books printed by William White between 1598 and 1600 supports Blayney's judgment: I have found as much error in the non-dramatic output as in the dramatic texts White printed.

McKerrow's second article arguing for "author's original MS" as printer's copy for "good" texts does not, I think, stand up any better than his first, although this time McKerrow focused exclusively on the author's "original draft" without trying to associate it with the final draft. Entitled "A Suggestion regarding Shakespeare's Manu-scripts," this article told the story of how "theatrical scribes" preparing transcripts of plays for use by prompters would necessarily regularize the naming of characters in speech-prefixes and stage directions because prompters (if there were then such functionaries, as McKerrow did not doubt) would find any irregularity intolerable; in contrast to the scribes, authors would use a variety of names in speech prefixes and directions for the same characters depending upon how these authors were thinking of the characters at different times in the composition of a play.[20] Therefore when printed plays contain a variety of names for the same character (e.g., "Mother," "Wife," and "Lady" for Lady Capulet in the Second Quarto of *Romeo and Juliet*), we can know that such plays were printed from authors' "original MS"; but when characters appear in printed playtexts always under a single designation, then we can know that these texts were printed from transcripts made by theatrical scribes and used to regulate theatrical productions. The difficulty with McKerrow's suggestion is not only that some extant theatrical manuscripts are in the hands of the plays' authors but also that scribal transcripts often contain the variety and ambiguity in naming of characters – some of it introduced by the scribes themselves – that McKerrow said was the unique mark of the "author's original MS."[21]

Nevertheless, in 1942 McKerrow's story of the "author's rough draft much corrected" as printer's copy for "good" quartos was accepted and further developed by W. W. Greg, who attempted to historicize it and to ground it with reference to extant theatrical manuscripts. Greg tried to assimilate McKerrow's term *drafts* to the term *foul papers* that was in use in Shakespeare's own day. In doing so, Greg fell into multiple self-contradiction. For example, he appropriated from McKerrow the notion that irregularity in the naming of characters was the sign that a printed text had been set into type directly from the "author's original MS," and he used such irregularity as the mark by which to identify so-called "foul papers" directly behind a printed text. Thus, on the one hand, Greg seemed to associate the term *foul papers* with the author's original draft. On the other hand, Greg insisted that he intended *foul papers* to refer to the author's final draft, which Greg, unlike McKerrow, purported to distinguish from the original one: "I have used the terms 'foul papers' and 'rough draft' indifferently in contradistinction to the fair copy made for theatrical purposes but with no intention of implying a preliminary or imperfect sketch. The foul papers must have contained the text substantially in the form the author intended it to assume though in a shape too untidy to be used by the prompter."[22] Yet this second and explicit sense in which Greg used *foul papers* appears at odds with the sense in which the terms *foul sheet* or *foul papers* were used in the Jacobean and Caroline documents from which Greg drew these words, where they seem to have referred to fragmentary or incomplete copies of plays. In his much-quoted letter to Henslowe, for example, Daborne was referring to a single "foule sheet"; and when Edward Knight invoked "the fowle papers of the Authors wch were found" as the source of the transcript of *Bonduca* that he was preparing for his patron, Knight was doing so explicitly for the purpose of excusing his omission of several scenes which, he said, the foul papers lacked.[23] There may then be room for doubt about whether, around Shakespeare's time, whole plays, rather than just fragmentary versions of them, were called "foul papers." Greg's adoption of the term seems to have granted McKerrow's ideal conception of the printer's copy for "good" quartos only a specious historicity.[24]

Although McKerrow felt no need to find among extant dramatic manuscripts a material equivalent to his ideal, Greg and others tried for decades to compensate for McKerrow's indifference. Yet Greg could find only fragments of manuscript to support McKerrow's speculation about the existence and preservation by theatrical companies of complete plays in the form of first-and-final authorial drafts. In 1942, when he attempted to ground McKerrow's suggestion, Greg could cite only a single page of *The Faithful Friends* (fol. 37a), two-thirds of a leaf of Marlowe's *A Massacre at Paris* (which, Greg had to concede, may not be in Marlowe's hand), the additions to *Sir Thomas More*, and some of the revisions to Shirley's *The Court Secret*.[25] By 1955 Greg mentioned only "most" of the fragmentary additions to *More* and the questionable page from *A Massacre at Paris* but did not indicate why he had dropped the other examples he had earlier offered.[26] Perhaps in an effort to provide at least one whole playtext as an example of "foul papers," in both 1942 and 1955 he also reclassified Heywood's manuscript of *The Captives* as "foul papers"; to do so, he had to shift it from the category of so-called "promptbook," into which he had first slotted it in his *Dramatic Documents of the Elizabethan Playhouses*,[27] published in 1931, before McKerrow had invented the category "author's rough draft much corrected" as printer's copy for "good" quartos. Thus Greg's identification of *The Captives* as "foul papers" is a classic example of *post facto* construction of empirical evidence for a proposition. *The Captives* manuscript can hardly be called "foul papers": first, it is thoroughly annotated in a second hand and in a fashion that resembles what is found in many of the manuscripts that Greg called "promptbooks," as opposed to "foul papers"; and, second, *The Captives* contains almost none of the untidy revision that, for McKerrow, must mark an author's draft. The only thing foul about the manuscript is the poor quality of the handwriting in it.[28]

The search for an example of "foul papers" has continued. In a Malone Society Reprint of Thomas Heywood's holograph manuscript of *The Escapes of Jupiter*, Henry D. Janzen, its editor, identified it as "technically ... author's 'foul papers'."[29] His reservation ("technically") is appropriate because the manuscript has none of the marks of McKerrow's "much corrected ... original draft," which Greg renamed "foul papers." The manuscript is not an "original draft" but almost entirely a reproduction, with some revisions, of scenes from Heywood's earlier plays *The Golden Age* and *The Silver Age*. There are few corrections to render the manuscript untidy, and the characters are uniformly designated in speech prefixes and directions. (Greg himself had failed to identify the manuscript of *The Escapes of Jupiter* as even technically "foul papers" when he wrote about it in 1925 – before McKerrow published his two articles about an author's "original MS.")

T. H. Howard-Hill has recently proposed another candidate for "foul papers" – the manuscript of *Glausamond and Fidelia* in the hand of its apparently amateur author, John Newdigate, III.[30] This manuscript is certainly a "rough draft much corrected" with what Professor Howard-Hill describes as a "profusion of deletions, corrections, and interlineations."[31] However, the manuscript is *not* "foul papers" according to Greg's criterion that such papers contain "the text substantially in the form the author intended it to assume"; nor does it fit McKerrow's description of an author's final draft revised so that it can be immediately transcribed by a scrivener. In this case we know that before a scribe copied out the play *Glausamond and Fidelia* in a transcript that still survives, it was, in Howard-Hill's own words, "extensively rewritten" and "substantially revised and enlarged" to assume the form in which it appears in the scribal transcript.[32] We can know so much in this case because there is yet another extant manuscript of the play in its author's hand that stands between his first extant draft and the scribal transcript. There is nothing, then, in the three manuscripts of *Glausamond* to sanction McKerrow and Greg's telescoping of original and final authorial drafts into what Greg termed "foul papers," for in this case the authorial "foul" and first extant draft is a material object quite distinct from the authorial second extant draft (a "fair copy," not "foul papers," according to Howard-Hill), which then served as the basis for the scribal transcript.

And so as recently as 1988 it was possible for Anthony Hammond and Donna Delvecchio to write,

Everything that has been said about 'foul papers' [meaning, in Fredson Bowers's words, which they quote, "the author's last complete draft in a shape satisfactory to him to be transferred to a fair copy"] has been conjectural. Though there are several examples of fair copies, prompt copies, and scribal copies of Jacobean plays, hitherto there has been no known example of foul papers, whose characteristics have had to be inferred from casual contemporary comment, and from characteristics of printed texts held to derive from them.[33]

Hammond and Delvecchio argue that the discovery at Melbourne Hall in Derbishire of four manuscript pages of an otherwise lost play by an unidentified playwright now remedy this longstanding deficiency in the archive. To be sure, the pages are much corrected, with some eighty-five alterations in them. Nevertheless, the Melbourne manuscript can hardly be called "rough," to use McKerrow's term, or "untidy," which is Greg's word for "foul papers," because few of the changes are interlined; instead alterations are often carefully inscribed on top of existing letter forms – with the result that readings are frequently ambiguous. But there is none of the ambiguity or even variety in the naming of characters in speech prefixes that McKerrow announced would be the sign of an authorial draft. None of the alterations can be readily construed as a revision "in consonance with [a company] producer's suggestions" – another of McKerrow's criteria for an ideal authorial draft; rather, alteration seems dictated by such purely literary considerations as improvement of metre in a pentameter line split between speakers. Since the Melbourne manuscript is only a fragment, it is impossible to know whether it represents part of the last complete draft of a play ("foul papers," for Greg and Bowers), or merely, as I. A. Shapiro has argued, "a rejected early version" of a scene.[34] Again the dramatic manuscript as material object cannot be brought into relation with the ideal conception of "foul papers."

It is not my purpose to belittle the efforts of scholars to find in history a reflection of McKerrow's idealization of the printer's copy for the "good" quartos. Rather, I wish to foreground the ahistoricity of McKerrow's conception by recounting how it has repeatedly been invalidated through empirical investigation. It would seem that the category of "foul papers," in the full sense that Greg gave it, is the product not of reason but of desire – our desire to possess in the "good" quartos Shakespeare's plays in the form in which he, as an individual agent, both began and finished them. So strong is the will to Will that it has invested "foul papers" with such narrative power that nowadays all the "good" quartos of Shakespeare's plays are said to have been printed *directly* from his "foul papers."[35]

III

Just as twentieth-century study of the "good" quartos has concentrated on reducing their putative origin to the activity of a single person (Shakespeare), so study of the "bad" quartos has often proceeded toward (if never quite to) the goal of identifying the single agents who can be blamed for their existence. When W. W. Greg undertook an investigation of the "bad" Quarto of *Merry Wives of Windsor* in 1910, he sought to reduce to just one agent the three agents then thought to have produced "bad" quartos:

(1) the adapter, who may have abridged the play; (2) the reporter, who, Greg thought, attempted, by shorthand or by memory, to reconstruct a text; and (3) the reviser ("hack poet"), who may have rearranged the text provided him by the reporter or who may have embellished it. Because Greg believed that a dramatist as accomplished as Shakespeare could not have written anything so corrupt as the dialogue of Quarto *Wives*, Greg concluded that it must therefore have been the work of a reporter. Greg managed to eliminate the adapter through the strategy of arguing that the passages and scenes he had been credited with cutting were merely forgotten by the reporter in the process of memorial reconstruction. To explain omissions near the end of the play, Greg invoked mere fatigue by the reporter. Greg also saw no need to resort to the then conventional hack poet to explain the rearrangement of passages and scenes between Folio and Quarto or the Quarto's apparent additions or alternatives to Folio passages. According to Greg, such rearrangements as the Quarto offered had no intelligible purpose and so must represent distortions in the reporter's recollection rather than revision by a hack poet; apparent *additions to* the Quarto were, rather, accidental *omissions from* the Folio during its printing; and when Folio and Quarto provided alternative versions, as in the last act, Greg called upon the theory that *Wives* was revised (although not necessarily by Shakespeare) between Quarto and Folio. Even though Greg postulated such revision of the play, he offered as the thesis of his argument that a reporter *alone* could account for the variations of the "bad" Quarto of *Wives* from the Folio version: "I see no justification for conjecturing two agents where one will suffice."[36]

But Greg was not satisfied to rest with the reduction of plural agency to the singular; he sought to identify the single agent responsible for Quarto *Wives* and to identify him as an actor, specifically the actor who played the Host. Greg did not say why the reporter, if there ever was one, should have been an actor; he indicated only that the possibility had been suggested by P. A. Daniel, who, in the Introduction to the 1881 Griggs facsimile of Quarto *Wives*, had briefly speculated that whoever put together the quarto's text may have enjoyed the "assistance of some of the people connected with the theatre."[37] Rather than justifying his attempt to make the reporter an actor, Greg instead emphasized that *if* the reporter were an actor, then he would certainly have been the Host because, except in the last two scenes in which the Host is onstage, the quarto's text, Greg alleged, is much closer to the Folio when the Host is present than when he is absent; in all cases (including even those problematic last two scenes) the Host's speeches are remarkably congruent with their Folio counterparts, and, the last two scenes excepted, so is the dialogue of those onstage with the Host. Yet no matter how much Greg urged the Host in the role of actor-reporter upon us as the unitary cause of Quarto *Wives*, he could not get around the exceptional last two scenes in which the Quarto fails to correlate with the Folio; he thus had to supplement his unitary cause with a theory of the revision of the latter part of the play. According to this theory, the Host would not have been able to reconstruct from memory much of the end of the play because the end had just been revised. What is so striking about Greg's argument both in his presentation of it and in later reception of it is the insistence that the Host as actor-reporter alone accounts for the "bad" quarto's text when, in fact, Greg could not get along without the secondary theory of revision.

The reception of Greg's 1910 argument about Quarto *Wives* is a tangled tale. Few, in the decade or so immediately following the argument's publication, perceived it as *the* solution to the problem of origin for all the "bad" quartos, although by the forties and fifties many came to regard it as such.[38] Instead, in the beginning, investigators into the origins of "bad" quartos registered Greg's "finding" about *Wives* by substituting actor-reporters for the formerly standard shorthand reporters who had been represented as writing down plays in shorthand from their places in the audience.[39] These early investigators did not, however, follow Greg's narrative about *Wives* to the extent of reducing each of the "bad" quartos to the product of a single agency (the actor-reporter); instead, they continued to make reference as well to adapters (who may have abridged plays) and to revisers or "hack poets."[40] Greg himself made no attempt to generalize his work on Quarto *Wives*; in fact, in 1920 he accepted, for example, some of Dover Wilson's much more complex account of the production of the First or "bad" Quarto of *Hamlet*, a story that featured Shakespeare's own manuscript lying behind part of that "bad" quarto.[41] By 1928 Greg had come to believe that his story of the production of a "bad" quarto by a single actor-reporter was, "indeed, very likely mistaken," even for Quarto *Wives* itself. He delivered this opinion in the "Notes and Observations" column of the 1928 *Review of English Studies*, where he had no space to provide reasons for his change of mind.[42] But when he repeated it in the much more prominent context of his often-cited 1942 book, *The Editorial Problem in Shakespeare*, he gave as his reason a re-examination of Quarto *Wives* that revealed that its dialogue is sometimes closer to the Folio's when the Host, its alleged reporter, is offstage than when he is on.[43] At the same time that Greg was disavowing his 1910 argument, however, it was growing in popularity: by mid-century it had attained the status of fact. There is no space here to chart the growth of its acceptance or to assess such monumental expositions of it as Peter Alexander's 1929 *Shakespeare's* Henry VI *and* Richard III;[44] all that I can provide are summaries of a handful of narratives from mid-century to exemplify the power that Greg's hypothesis, despite his own disavowal, has exerted on study of the Shakespeare quartos.

It is the fate of Quarto *King Lear* to be at the center of a number of these narratives. It belonged among the "good" quartos in Pollard's initial classification. Neither E. K. Chambers nor W. W. Greg could believe that Quarto *Lear* could be a memorially reconstructed text: it was qualitatively superior to the so-called "bad" quartos by too wide a margin. Yet how was one to explain, for example, the massive errors in lineation in the Quarto, which distinguish it from the other "good" quartos? Both Chambers and Greg favored the opinion that Quarto *Lear* was based on a shorthand report of the play because such an origin would account for the superiority of Quarto *Lear* to the "bad" quartos (thought to be memorial) as well as for the gross auditory errors and mislineation in Quarto *Lear* (the shorthand writer's transcribing by ear) and for what Greg regarded as the simplifying substitutions that appeared to him to distinguish Quarto *Lear* from the Folio version (actors' corruptions in delivery).[45] Greg advanced this position repeatedly, in two articles and two books, fighting to preserve a story of the origins of *Lear* as *sui generis* – neither the product of memorial reconstruction (like the "bad" quartos) nor a purely authorial version based on "foul papers."[46]

Yet so compelling to textual critics had the narrative of memorial reconstruction become that it also engulfed Quarto *Lear*, despite Greg's best efforts. So, in 1945, Leo Kirschbaum published his *The True Text of* King Lear, in which he argued that Quarto *Lear* is just such a memorial reconstruction, the work of a single actor.[47] Then in 1949 G. I. Duthie demonstrated that, to our knowledge, there was no shorthand system available to Shakespeare's contemporaries with which they could have produced Quarto *Lear*.[48] The way was now unimpeded for the inclusion of Quarto *Lear* among the memorially reconstructed "bad" quartos, no matter how much better a text Quarto *Lear* seemed to offer than did the "bad" quartos. Thus, in the same year in which he destroyed the possibility of shorthand as a tool for the transcription of performance, Duthie suggested that Quarto *Lear* must have been produced through a communal memorial reconstruction of the play by a travelling troupe from Shakespeare's own company[49] – the same explanation suggested by D. L. Patrick thirteen years earlier as the origin of the First Quarto of *Richard III*.[50]

But Alice Walker thought that Duthie's hypothesis could not account for the alleged unevenness in the quality of Quarto *Lear*'s text; thus she constructed a story of the Quarto's origin that is remarkable both for its effort to save the theory of memorial reconstruction and its contradiction of the basis of the theory. According to Walker,

> The quarto was not based on an acting version of the play but on the foul papers and … these were surreptitiously dictated to a scribe by an actor who, for some reason we can only guess at (haste, over-confidence, laziness, inattention), relied on his memory instead of his script for dialogue with which he was familiar. The contaminating actor-reader was, I judge, a small-part actor, probably the boy who played Goneril. The scribe may have been an actor too. The memorial contamination is certainly heaviest in scenes involving Goneril and Regan, and it is in scenes where contamination is most marked that we must look for the actor, or actors, responsible for the quarto text.[51]

While Greg had identified the actor behind the memorial reconstruction of Quarto *Wives* by that actor's presence in scenes in which the text was most accurately reported, Walker identified her actor-reporters by their presence in what are allegedly the most corrupt scenes – the ones for which they would, it is said, have relied on memory. Before Walker has finished, however, she has contradicted her own criterion for identification by arguing that the text of Goneril's and Regan's speeches and of the speeches addressed to them is superior to the text of the rest of the speeches *within the scenes for which these boy-actors were present*.[52] Now the accuracy of the report again, as in Greg's study, becomes the identifying mark of the reporters. According to Walker, then, these boy actors paid attention to dialogue only when it was addressed to them or to be uttered by them – hence their many errors in other speeches in scenes in which they were present; nevertheless, when they came to transcribe the speeches to which they had been so inattentive, they relied on recollections – recollections that, according to Walker's narrative, were never theirs. Since memorial reconstruction by actors can scarcely be maintained as a theory if there is doubt about whether actors paid attention to the dialogue in plays in which they performed, Walker, in her attempt to apply Greg's theory of memorial reconstruction to *Lear*, wound up calling the basis of the theory itself into question. Greg remained unpersuaded not only by Walker but also by advocates of the view that Quarto *Lear* was a memorial reconstruction; in his 1955 *The Shakespeare First Folio* he wrote:

> It is to be feared that a consideration of the various theories so far advanced can only lead to the conclusion that it remains as true today as it was twenty-five years ago that *King Lear* still offers a problem for investigation. (p. 383)

Yet by the 1950s the idea that all imperfect texts were transmitted into print by reporters who memorially reconstructed plays had such a grip on textual criticism that it could survive any self-contradiction and explain almost any phenomenon. And so Philip Edwards, in "An Approach to the Problem of *Pericles*," found two reporters in that Quarto, not on the basis of the quality of the dialogue relative to specific roles but on the basis of the regularity of the verse between the first half of the play (Acts 1 and 2) and the second (Acts 3–5):

> The reconstruction was undertaken by two "reporters": the first responsible for the first two acts, the second for the last three. These two work by different methods: the first welds into mediocre verse the words, phrases and general sense of the original so far as he can remember them. He is at his best in prose where remodelling is not attempted. The second reporter, perhaps giving the original very much more faithfully than his predecessor, makes no attempt at rewriting, and after the first scene does not make more than desultory attempts to write down the verse in lines.[53]

Although Edwards's "first reporter" seems to be described as performing precisely the function assigned to the "hack poet" before Greg began to chase off this hypothetical creature in 1910, Edwards did not even mention such a possibility. Instead he represented reporters (and compositors) as the only possible intermediaries between the playhouse and the printed text.

A final example of twentieth-century critical absorption with arresting a particular actor and charging him with producing a "bad" quarto is J. M. Nosworthy's "*Hamlet* and the Player who could not Keep Counsel."[54] Nosworthy was confident of laying hands on the *Hamlet* culprit because he regarded as established fact the previous identification of actor-reporters in other "bad" quartos – especially Greg's pinning down the Host in Quarto *Wives*:

> Fortunately twentieth-century scholarship has been able to demonstrate that many of the "bad" quartos are memorial reconstructions set down for provincial use by one or more actors. This explanation of "bad" quarto origins was triumphantly pressed home in 1910 by W. W. Greg, who showed that the short and incoherent quarto of *The Merry Wives of Windsor*, printed in 1602, was reported by an actor who had played the part of Mine Host of the Garter. *Hamlet*, pirated not very much later than this, is, almost certainly, an outcome of the same methods, possibly by the same delinquent. It seems desirable to say here what has seldom been said – that we should not assume that there were several such rogues when one will suffice … This "pirate" actor is unknown to us by name, but it is possible not only to distinguish the role he sustained in the play but also to watch him engaged in his task. (p. 74)

In Nosworthy's article we watch this actor (in the role of Second Player) listening behind the tiring-house door; we miss (with him) the lines that Hamlet delivers just as the Second Player is coming onstage from the tiring house. We then penetrate the mind of this actor as he loses interest during the Pyrrhus section of 2.2 and the quality of his reporting declines. Thus Nosworthy has relieved himself of the responsibility for validating his hypothesis about the bit-part actor-reporter in terms even of a blatantly subjective evaluation of this actor's reporting and instead has constructed a narrative of the actor's psychology by projecting features of the printed text as events in the actor's mental life. Later, for example, the actor is a mourner "at Ophelia's maimed rites," who, "though present, has been inattentive."[55] Nosworthy was not content merely to narrate the psychology of the culprit but wanted to fashion his moral character as well: according to Nosworthy, because his actor-reporter remembered rather well both "the Polonian 'sententiae' " in 1.3 (when he was not onstage) and "the eschatological musings in V, i ... he was a person of philosophical parts or, at least, an amateur of moral saws."[56] In discussing an argument from the fifties, I may seem to be picking over the bones of a dead issue, but the argument that the First Quarto of *Hamlet* was memorially reconstructed by a small-part actor was endorsed by Greg in 1955[57] and thence repeated in edition after edition, including most recently the *Textual Companion* to Wells and Taylor's Oxford Shakespeare.[58]

IV

Nowadays it seems that the textual categories of "foul papers" and "memorial reconstruction" have always been with us: they seem to be transhistorical entities. As this paper tries to show, however, both are of comparatively recent origin; both were constructed in the course of specific narratives produced within the context of other narratives. Less than a century ago, there was no talk about either "foul papers" or "memorial reconstructions." Both are hypothetical constructs that have yet to be empirically validated with reference to any extant Shakespeare quarto. It seems to me necessary to say this because of the widespread *belief* that both hypotheses were long ago verified on the basis of incontestable evidence that need not be re-examined or that, as empirical investigation proceeds, both hypotheses are becoming more securely grounded in evidence and that, in the end, both will have become secure. Like many arguments that represent themselves as empirical, the arguments for "foul papers" and memorial reconstruction defer the presentation of the conclusive evidence of their "truth" at the same time that they assert their "truth" as founded upon such evidence. But there is no documentary evidence that any actor(s) ever memorially reconstructed a play, nor does any play appear to survive in the state designated "foul papers" by Greg. Memorial reconstruction by an actor or actors identified with specific parts has never proved an adequate explanation for the genesis of any "bad" quarto; the case for such reconstruction has always broken down and has needed to be supplemented by secondary hypotheses – this statement is as true of the allegedly "originary" case made by Greg for the *Wives* Quarto as it is for all the subsequent and derivative cases. No "good" quarto has ever been shown to have been set from "foul papers" because the marks that have been used to identify "foul papers" as printer's copy are also to be found in extant "promptbooks"; no example of Greg's idealized "foul papers" – the author's original and ultimate draft much corrected – has yet been identified.

Yet the categories of "foul papers" and "memorial reconstruction" have flourished together for decades despite the separate failure of each to account for the printed texts each is invoked to explain. The ground for the popularity of these categories might then better be sought in their shared features rather than in their problematic relations to the printed plays. Both reduce complex and diverse texts to unitary origins. Both offer individual agents as the independent causes of the quartos. It thus becomes possible to represent twentieth-century textual criticism as having been produced by the desire for a certain kind of narrative, one which calls into being certain individuals – solitary author or lone actor – for the purpose of holding them solely responsible for the production of the most diverse phenomena. As critics, we in the twentieth century have long constructed plays as unities in our readings of them; these unities have been secured in textual criticism through the metonymy of constructing unified agents at the origins of the printed texts.

Trapped in a binary opposition between actor and author as the only available origins of quartos, recent discussion of the quartos has degenerated into a quarrel between those who would invoke one fiction of origin versus those who would have the other. The quarrel has been going on since the early fifties. Then, for example, Feuillerat and McManaway debated whether the printer's copy for *The Contention* was non-Shakespearean "foul papers" or a memorial reconstruction of Shakespeare's 2 *Henry VI*.[59] In 1964 Kristian Smidt attacked D. L. Patrick's contention that the Quarto of *Richard III* was a memorial reconstruction by "discovering" signs of Shakespeare's "foul papers" behind the printed text.[60] Then, in 1972, Sidney Thomas wanted to represent the Queen Mab speech in the First Quarto of *Romeo and Juliet* as textually superior to the version in the Second Quarto (thought to have been set from "foul papers"); the only terms in which he could make his argument were that there must have been a lacuna in the "foul papers" at the point at which the Queen Mab speech was inscribed and that this lacuna must have been filled with a memorial reconstruction of the speech inferior to the one in the manuscript underlying the First Quarto version of the same speech.[61] If even a part of the printer's copy for a quarto was not "foul papers," then it must have been a memorial reconstruction – twentieth-century textual criticism makes available to us no other possibilities for representing the manuscripts underlying quartos. In 1978 S. Musgrove would have it that the first two Acts or so of *Pericles* (one of the original five "bad" quartos) were not printed from a memorial reconstruction, and so he argued that they were based on "foul papers."[62] More recently a number of us sought to advance the case that the First Quarto of *King Lear* was not memorially contaminated, as Duthie and Walker had claimed, but was instead a truly Shakespearean version of the play: Gary Taylor, one of the editors of our volume, therefore said that the First Quarto of *Lear* was printed from "foul papers." In the same book, Stanley Wells rejected the possibility that Quarto *Lear* is a "bad quarto" and then wrote, "*The alternative possibility* is that the Quarto derives directly from a Shakespearean manuscript."[63] In representing ourselves as revolutionaries, we were conservatively maintaining the prevailing narrative formation. In a book on *King Lear* and articles on a number of "bad" quartos, Steven Urkowitz has set out to liberate us from the fallacies of recent textual criticism and lead us back to the early printed texts themselves. His readings of these texts, however, continue to reproduce the narratives of twentieth-century textual criticism in his insistence that if "bad" quartos do not represent "memorial reconstructions," they are probably based on Shakespeare's own papers.[64]

V

Continued entrapment within the current rigidified hierarchy of the "good" / "bad" quartos has come oppressively to limit negotiation in Shakespeare textual criticism.

For those (who are many) to whom the Shakespearean authorship of texts remains a significant issue, the hierarchy presents (to some) the threat and (to others) the opportunity that, should it be demonstrated that a "bad" quarto cannot be traced to memorial reconstruction by an actor or actors, then the quarto may automatically be promoted to the category of the "good," in which it will not only assume the status of a canonical text but also become a printed record of the process of Shakespeare's individual creation of it since all "good" quartos are said to have been printed from his "foul papers," his first-and-final drafts. However, if it is suggested that some feature of a quarto – like the lining of verse as prose in Quarto *Lear* – cannot derive from such a draft, then, as has been shown, the formerly "good" quarto can be categorized in this century's textual criticism, if it is to be categorized at all, only as unauthoritative or "bad." Hence, perhaps, the fierce exchanges that surround claims for the "authority" of some quartos.

The desire, insofar as I understand it, that drives my own narrative about quartos is to open up a space in textual criticism beyond the "good" / "bad" axis. Suppose, provisionally, that my narrative has been persuasive in suggesting that currently accepted accounts of the origins of the "good" and "bad" quartos are not the empirical demonstrations they have often been represented to be; and, instead, that they are narratives whose own textuality ineluctably mediates their reconstructions of the past. Then the accepted accounts cannot be privileged (as, say, "critical" or "scientific") either to narratives deriving from the sixteenth or seventeenth centuries or to other narratives based upon textual traces surviving from those periods. This paper con-cludes with a brief and by no means exhaustive survey of some of these other narratives that have been occluded by the recent exclusive focus on the Holmes-like detection of the "good" from the "bad."

Addressing his "Reader" in the 1608 edition of his *Rape of Lucrece*, Thomas Heywood wrote that

> It hath beene no custome in mee of all other men (curteous Readers) to commit my plaies to the presse: the reason, though some may attribute to my own insufficiencie, I had rather subscribe in that to their seueare censure, then by seeking to auoide the imputation of weakenes, to incurre a greater suspition of honestie: for though some haue vsed a double sale of their labours, first to the Stage, and after to the presse, For my owne part I heere proclaime my selfe euer faithfull in the first, and neuer guiltie of the last; yet since some of my plaies haue (vnknown to me, and without any of my direction) accidentally come into the Printers handes, and therefore so corrupt and mangled, (coppied onely by the eare) that I haue bene as vnable to know them, as ashamde to chalenge them. This therefore I was the willinger to furnish out in his natiue habit: first beeing by consent, next because the rest haue beene so wronged in beeing publisht in such sauadge and ragged ornaments. (sig. A2)[65]

One or two discrepancies might be noted between this story and those that have dominated Shakespeare textual criticism in the last half century or so. First, unlike modern textual critics, Heywood does not find it necessary to identify a particular actor or any other particular individual as the one who "coppied [his plays] ... by ... eare" in order to entertain the possibility that his texts were transmitted in this way. Reading Heywood's narrative, then, one might, on the one hand, avoid inferring with Greg in

1910 that actors must bear such responsibility, and, on the other hand, avoid concluding that just because, as I have tried to show, it has been impossible for modern criticism to convict actors in specific roles of memorially reconstructing plays, then memorial reconstruction ought no longer be considered as a possible mode of transmission of playtexts into print. Instead, Heywood's story not only allows one to keep open the possibility of memorial reconstruction, as do a number of other contemporary stories concerning the printing of sermons, speeches, and plays,[66] but also provides something different from the twentieth century's claustrophobic absorption with actors as the exclusive producers of texts that may have been put together from memory.

Second, Heywood represents himself to his "Reader" as dealing directly with the publisher: it is he, not the acting company to whom he sold his play, who provides copy to the stationer. Heywood's story therefore differs rather widely from currently accepted accounts regarding the publication of Shakespeare's plays that have the acting companies both jealously guarding playscripts (including drafts and all) from stationers and, paradoxically, being the only agents who could and did release "authoritative" playscripts to the stationers – giving the stationers only "foul papers" because the companies could easily afford to part with these but not with their "promptbooks." I have no desire to accord Heywood's accounts of textual transmission hegemony over other narratives or to insist that in history Shakespeare's plays must have found their way into print in just the same ways. If useful at all today, Heywood's discourse may indicate that the history of the passage of plays into print can hardly be construed as a single history – history is histories, multiple narratives, of which Heywood's, like Greg's, is only one.

There are still other narratives, like Sir Sidney Lee's favorite,[67] which was provided him by Humphrey Moseley in the preface to the Beaumont and Fletcher First Folio of 1647:

> When these *Comedies* and *Tragedies* were presented on the Stage, the *Actours* omitted some *Scenes* and Passages (with the *Authour's* consent) as occasion led them; and when private friends desir'd a Copy, they then (and justly too) transcribed what they *Acted*. But now you have both All that was *Acted*, and all that was not; even the perfect full *Originalls* without the least mutilation. (sig. A4)[68]

Moseley's story of a wide proliferation of manuscripts is at odds with stories of "foul papers" as printer's copy because it suggests that, in profiting from their privileged access to playtexts by copying them, the members of an acting company could in the process lose control of the texts, which could find their way to stationers in unauthoritative forms. The authority of printer's copy might, then, be compromised not only by the stage adaptation represented in the original playhouse transcription but also by the possibility of subsequent recopying once the original transcription had passed from the players' hands. The story of the copying and recopying of manuscripts until a late copy comes into a stationer's hands and is printed (often without the consent or sometimes, the story goes, even the knowledge of the author or the owner of the manuscript) is, as Leo Kirschbaum showed, a most familiar preface to sixteenth- and seventeenth-century books.[69]

But if Moseley's story of playtexts is accorded any credence, the line of authority for playtexts that has been drawn by twentieth-century textual critics directly from the playwright to the acting company and then from the company to the stationer is breached, and it becomes impossible to maintain the longstanding optimistic belief in an acting company whose compelling interest in preserving for itself all copies of a play, including the author's papers, would ensure the possibility that the author's papers themselves might lie directly behind printed texts. Hence, perhaps, Greg's determined effort in the latter part of his career to limit the implications of Moseley's words exclusively to a post-Shakespearean period. In 1955 Greg wanted to claim that

> it is, however, uncertain how early the custom of making private transcripts prevailed, whether in the King's company or elsewhere. None of the extant examples can be dated before 1624, when the scandal over *A Game at Chess* caused a sudden demand and perhaps set a fashion ... Since publication was contrary to the general policy of the King's Men they are not very likely to have favored circulation in manuscript; still, after receiving the lord chamberlain's protection against unauthorized publication in 1619, it is possible that their attitude relaxed.[70]

This argument is suspect on a number of counts; it is especially suspect, as Peter Blayney has pointed out to me, in its assimilation of such private transcripts as those of Middleton's *A Game at Chess*, which emanate from a playwright himself (some of them even written, in whole or in part, by Middleton), to the quite different sort of transcript that Moseley cites – a transcript of the stage adaptation of a play by an actor.[71] By representing all kinds of private transcripts as the same, Greg's narrative again arbitrarily limits the number of ways a play might be represented as circulating in manuscript and finding its way into print. But even if one were to follow Greg in regarding all kinds of private transcripts as essentially the same, Greg's argument based on the dates of extant private transcripts would lose some of its force when one realizes that he is excluding any sort of private transcript as possible copy for "good" texts so that he may favor, instead, idealized "foul papers" (of which there are no extant examples). Because there are none, Greg was forced to reconstrue the manuscript of *The Captives* as the desired "foul papers," but in doing so, he was depending upon a manuscript dating, like the earliest of the extant private transcripts, from 1624. Thus, even if *The Captives* were "foul papers," the earliest extant complete play in such a form would stand no closer to the dates of the printing of Shakespeare's plays than the earliest extant private transcript.

This paper has argued that it is only our desire for New-Critical unity that may have caused us to ignore such accounts as Heywood's and Moseley's and to fix the origins of the early printed versions upon single agents, when these texts were open to penetration and alteration not only by Shakespeare himself and by his fellow actors but also by multiple theatrical and extra-theatrical scriveners, by theatrical annotators, adapters and revisers (who might cut or add), by censors, and by compositors and proofreaders. Rather than occluding most of these possibilities in the drive toward debasing some texts as wholly unauthorized reconstructions and privileging others as exclusively authorial, or rather than reducing the differences among the early printed texts to a fantasy of boundless authorial fecundity, a narrative that includes poststructuralist differential readings of multiple-text works would keep in play not only multiple readings and versions but also the multiple and dispersed agencies that could have produced the variants.

Notes

1 *Shakespeare Folios and Quartos: A Study in the Bibliography of Shakespeare's Plays 1594–1685* (London: Methuen, 1909), pp. 64–80. By emphasizing the differences among quartos within each of Pollard's two categories, I have no wish to deny that there are, as well, differences between the "good" quartos and the "bad" ones.

2 See two insightfully skeptical histories of the development of the theory of "bad" quartos: (1) the first chapter of Kristian Smidt's *Iniurious Imposters and* Richard III (New York: Humanities Press, 1964); (2) Chapters 2 through 4 of William Bracy's *The Merry Wives of Windsor: The History and Transmission of Shakespeare's Text*, University of Missouri Studies 25 (Columbia, MO: The Curators of the University of Missouri, 1952). As will be evident by the end of this article, I do not find persuasive the conclusions that Smidt and Bracy reach concerning the origins of Quarto *Richard III* or Quarto *Wives*.

3 p. 74, Pollard's square brackets.

4 W. W. Greg, *The Shakespeare First Folio: Its Bibliographical and Textual History* (Oxford: Clarendon Press, 1955), pp. 88 ff.; F. P. Wilson, *Shakespeare and the New Bibliography*, rev. and ed. Helen Gardner (1945; rev. ed. Oxford: Clarendon Press, 1970), pp. 13–14.

5 J. Dover Wilson, "The Copy for 'Hamlet', 1603" and "The 'Hamlet' Transcript, 1593," *The Library*, 3rd ser., 9 (1918), 153–85 and 217–47; A. W. Pollard and J. Dover Wilson, "The 'Stolne and Surreptitious' Shakespearean Texts: *Henry V* (1600)," *Times Literary Supplement*, 13 March 1919; "*The Merry Wives of Windsor* (1602)," *TLS*, 7 August 1919; "*Romeo and Juliet*, 1597," *TLS*, 14 August 1919.

6 A. W. Pollard, in his Introduction to Peter Alexander's *Shakespeare's Henry VI and Richard III* (Cambridge: Cambridge University Press, 1929), pp. 1–28, wrote, for example, "*A Midsummer Night's Dream* (since Professor Dover Wilson edited it) stands out as providing an instance of the lift which Shakespeare could give to an old scene by putting some new poetry into it" (p. 26). See also Wilson's edition of the play (1924; rpt. Cambridge: Cambridge University Press, 1960), p. 94.

7 p. 80, italics mine.

8 A. W. Pollard, ed., *A New Shakespeare Quarto:* The Tragedy of King Richard II *Printed for the third time by Valentine Simmes in 1598* (London: Quaritch, 1916), pp. 96 ff.; Pollard, *Shakespeare's Fight with the Pirates and the Problems of the Transmission of his Text* (1917), 2nd ed. (1920; rpt. New York: Haskell House, 1974), pp. 53 ff.

9 *TLS*, 14 August 1919.

10 Pollard and Wilson do not address directly the narrative problem of whether the same manuscript served as printer's copy for both quartos and, if it did, how it would have survived the printing of the First Quarto to be further revised and used as printer's copy for the Second. Later critics, of course, construe the resemblances cited by Pollard and Wilson as evidence of consultation of the First Quarto during the printing of the Second.

11 W. W. Greg, ed., *Shakespeare's* Merry Wives of Windsor *1602* (Oxford: Clarendon Press, 1910), p. xvi.

12 William B. Long, " 'A bed for woodstock': A Warning for the Unwary," *Medieval and Renaissance Drama in England*, 2 (1985), 91–118, esp. p. 93.

13 There are some curious lines in the Induction written by John Webster for the King's Men's performances of Marston's *The Malcontent* and printed in 1604:

Sly: …I would know how you came by this play?

Cun[dale]: Faith sir the booke was lost, and because twas pittie so good a play should be lost, we found it and play it.

Sly: I wonder you would play it, another company having interest in it?

Cun: Why not Maleuole in folio with vs, as Ieronimo in Decimo sexto with them. They taught vs a name for our play, wee call it *One for another*.

(sig. A4ʳ)

It is possible to read this passage with its antithesis between "folio" and "Decimo sexto" to mean that the King's Men stole *The Malcontent* (with its lead role of Malevole) from a children's company in retaliation for a theft of one of the King's Men's plays with Jeronimo in it by the children's company. Yet such a reading raises it own difficulties. While an anonymous play called *The First Part of Jeronimo, with the Wars of Portugal* was printed in 1605 with no indication of the company that had performed it, the best-known play with Jeronimo (Hieronimo) in it was Kyd's *The Spanish Tragedy*, which was still owned, as far as can be determined, by the Prince's players (formerly the Admiral's Men), not the King's Men, and was available in five printed editions by 1604, so that there would have been no need to steal a manuscript of it. Indeed the passage in question from the Induction to *The Malcontent* is so brief and irreducibly figurative that E. K. Chambers's refusal to construe it as a reference to simple retaliatory theft seems warranted: "It is not necessary to assume that the play [*The Malcontent*] was literally 'lost' or that Marston was not privy to the adoption of it by the King's" (*The Elizabethan Stage*, 4 vols. [Oxford: Clarendon Press, 1923], Vol. 3, 432). But see G. K. Hunter, ed., *The Malcontent*, The Revels Plays (Manchester: Manchester University Press, 1975), pp. xli–xlvi.

14   "I commaunde your Bookeeper to present mee wth a faire Copy hereafte <> ... HHerbert." *The Launching of the Mary*, J. H. Walter, ed., Malone Society Reprints (London: Malone Society, 1933), p. 125; see Greg, *The Editorial Problem in Shakespeare* (Oxford: Clarendon Press, 1942), p. 43.

15   Greg, *Dramatic Documents from the Elizabethan Playhouses*, 2 vols. (Oxford: Clarendon Press, 1931), Vol. 1, 373, on which, of twelve so-called "prompt-books" (not including *Believe, More*, and *Launching*), only three are listed as certainly holograph, while one other, the anonymous *Charlemagne*, is said possibly to be holograph – it is difficult, of course, to identify the handwriting of an anonymous play as its author's. Nevertheless, J. W. Lever argued in his 1976 Malone Society Reprint of the anonymous play *The Wasp* that that manuscript too was a holograph "promptbook." More recently, in " 'A bed for woodstock,' " William B. Long has advanced the same contention about one of Greg's anonymous "promptbooks" – *The First Part of the Reign of King Richard the Second, or Thomas of Woodstock*.

16   *The Library*, 4th ser., 12 (1931), 253–75.

17   p. 275.

18   pp. 266, 275.

19   *The Texts of* King Lear *and Their Origins*: Vol. 1: *Nicholas Okes and the First Quarto* (Cambridge: Cambridge University Press, 1982), p. 184 n.

20   *Review of English Studies*, 11 (1935), 459–65, esp. p. 464. On the matter of prompters: in a paper written for the stage-history seminar at the Shakespeare Association of America meeting at Austin, April 1989, William B. Long expressed doubts about whether dramatic companies of Shakespeare's time necessarily employed individuals whose function it was to prompt. The issue is vexed: in 1638, John Taylor the Water Poet could recall how he had once known "one *Thomas Vincent* that was a Book-keeper or prompter at the Globe" (quoted by G. E. Bentley, *The Profession of Player in Shakespeare's Time* [Princeton, NJ: Princeton University Press, 1984], p. 81).

21   See Long, "Stage-Directions: A Misinterpreted Factor in Determining Textual Provenance," *TEXT*, 2 (1985), 121–38; Paul Werstine, " 'Foul Papers' and 'Prompt-books': Printer's Copy for Shakespeare's *Comedy of Errors*," *Studies in Bibliography*, 41 (1988), 232–46, and "McKerrow's 'Suggestion' and Twentieth-Century Shakespeare Textual Criticism," *Renaissance Drama*, 19 (1989), 149–73.

22   *Editorial Problem*, p. 31.

23   For Daborne's reference, see *Henslowe's Papers*, W. W. Greg, ed. (1907; rpt. New York: AMS Press, 1975), p. 78; for Knight's, see *Bonduca by John Fletcher*, W. W. Greg, ed., Malone Society Reprints (London: The Malone Society, 1951), p. 90.

24   Until Greg appropriated the term "foul papers" to refer to a complete authorial draft, textual critics used "foul papers" in Knight's sense as referring to a fragmentary draft. So R. C. Bald, in the Introduction to his 1929 edition of *A Game at Chesse by Thomas Middleton* (Cambridge: Cambridge University Press), argued that the Huntington-Bridgewater manuscript of the play must

have been transcribed from "foul papers" simply because there is a gap in the scribe's transcription of some 250 lines that is analogous to the gap in the *Bonduca* manuscript, which Knight said resulted from his use of authorial "foul papers" (pp. 38–9).

In *The Stability of Shakespeare's Text* (London: Edward Arnold, 1965), E. A. J. Honigmann cites four other uses of "foul papers" dating from 1609 to 1659 and anticipates my conclusion in this paragraph when he writes, "Seventeenth-century usage ... gives no backing to the opinion that 'foul papers' must be a complete draft" (pp. 17–18). Honigmann, however, does not then challenge the view that some early printed texts were set from Shakespeare's own papers; instead he makes only a minimal adjustment to the dominant narrative by speculating that in the printer's copy for some plays "some sheets would be first drafts and some [authorial] transcripts" and by looking forward to a day – still, and perhaps always, to come – when bibliographers will be able to distinguish which kind of copy lay behind which pages of an early printed text (p. 18). Among others who have more recently doubted "foul papers" (although, to my mind, on theoretical rather than empirical grounds) are Stephen Orgel, "What is a Text?" *Research Opportunities in Renaissance Drama*, 24 (1981), 3–6, and Jonathan Goldberg, "Textual Properties," *Shakespeare Quarterly*, 37 (1986), 213–17.

25 *Editorial Problem*, p. 28.

26 *The Shakespeare First Folio*, pp. 108–9.

27 Vol. 1, 191, 284 ff.

28 Greg gave as his principal reasons for reclassifying *The Captives* as "foul papers" the allegedly "vile" hands in which the manuscript is both inscribed and annotated, but he also noticed that it contains no license at the end, even though the play is known to have been licensed for the stage. The absence of a license, however, does not disqualify a manuscript from being regarded as a "promptbook" by Greg because, as he himself pointed out, four of the fifteen manuscripts he called "promptbooks" are without licenses (*The Shakespeare First Folio*, p. 109, n. 2).

29 (London: Malone Society, 1978), p. ix. See also W. W. Greg, "*The Escapes of Jupiter*," *Anglia* (1925), rpt. *Collected Papers* (Oxford: Clarendon Press, 1966), pp. 156–83.

30 T. H. Howard-Hill, "Boccaccio, *Ghismonda*, and its Foul Papers, *Glausamond*," *Renaissance Papers 1980*, pp. 19–28.

31 p. 21.

32 pp. 24, 28.

33 "The Melbourne Manuscript and John Webster: A Reproduction and Transcript," *SB*, 41 (1988), 1–32, esp. p. 3.

34 *TLS*, 4 July 1986, 736.

35 My generalization is based on the *Textual Companion* to the recent Oxford Shakespeare (Oxford: Clarendon Press, 1987 [1988]), pp. 145–7. The single exception noted in the *Companion* is the First Quarto of 1 *Henry IV* (Q0), only a fragment of which survives, which is said to have been set into type from a transcript of "foul papers." Yet Q0 is constructed as an exception through its being set in opposition to all the other "good" quartos thought to have been set from "foul papers"; so "foul papers," now that they've been idealized, have come to serve as the standard against which transcripts (a category actually represented among the extant manuscripts) can be identified.

36 p. xli. Steven Urkowitz has also recently discussed Greg's 1910 edition of *Wives* in "Good News about 'Bad' Quartos," *"Bad" Shakespeare: Revaluations of the Shakespeare Canon*, Maurice Charney, ed. (Madison, NJ: Fairleigh Dickinson University Press, 1988), pp. 189–206.

37 *Shakspere's Merry Wives of Windsor: the first quarto, 1602, a facsimile in photo-lithography*, Shakespeare quarto facsimiles, F. J. Furnivall, gen. ed., W. Griggs and Charles Praetorius, eds., p. vi.

38 Among the few was one James D. Fitzgerald, who had suggested in 1910 in "The First Quarto of *Hamlet*, a Literary Fraud" (*Royal Philosophical Society of Glasgow Proceedings*, Vol. 41 [1910], 181–218) that the First Quarto of *Hamlet* was "pirated" by an actor playing Marcellus, Voltimand, and Lucianus. On the basis of the poor lineation of verse in the First Quarto of *Hamlet* and in that of *Henry V*, together with the lining of prose as verse in both the *Henry V* and the *Wives* quartos,

Fitzgerald advanced the theory that all three had been knocked together from memory by the same actor, whose distinguishing characteristic was his inability to reproduce proper line-division (*TLS*, 20 February 1919, 98).

39 See, for example, Pollard and Wilson's 1919 *TLS* articles.

40 See, for example, H. D. Gray ("The First Quarto 'Hamlet,'" *Modern Language Review*, 10 [1915], 171–80), who, while invoking an actor-reporter, also called upon a reviser to account for the "short scene between Horatio and the Queen – which never took place" and is "wholly in the style of the hack poet" (p. 179). For negative commentary on Gray's piece, see Frank G. Hubbard, "The 'Marcellus' Theory of the First Quarto of *Hamlet*," *Modern Language Notes*, 33 (1918), 73–9. Greg himself also continued to write of adapters who cut and revisers who added to playtexts either before or after actors reported them from memory: see his account of *Orlando Furioso* in *Two Elizabethan Stage Abridgements: The Battle of Alcazar & Orlando Furioso* (London: Malone Society, 1922).

41 Greg in *TLS*, 20 May 1920, 320: "Mr. Dover Wilson … seems to me to have proved conclusively that there is a link of material transmission between the first quarto of *Hamlet* and the authorized text, which, whatever may be the full history that we hope literary and bibliographical criticism together will one day unravel, puts the theory of simple memorial piracy definitely out of court."

42 Vol. 4, 202.

43 p. 71; cf. H. J. Oliver, ed., *The Merry Wives of Windsor* (London: Methuen, 1971), pp. xxvi ff., who argues, incorrectly I believe, that Greg's change of mind was unwarranted.

44 It might be noted that Alexander, too, was unable to account for the genesis of the "bad" quartos of 2 and 3 *Henry VI* wholly in terms of actor-reporters but had to resort to a supplementary theory of a transcriptional link between "authoritative" playhouse manuscripts and passages in the quartos.

45 Chambers, *William Shakespeare: A Study of Facts and Problems*, 2 vols. (Oxford: Clarendon Press, 1930), Vol. 1, 466.

46 "The Function of Bibliography in Literary Criticism Illustrated in a Study of the Text of *King Lear*," *Neophilologus*, 18 (1933), 241–62; "*King Lear*, Mislineation and Stenography," *The Library*, 4th ser., 17 (1936), 172–83; *The Variants in the First Quarto of* King Lear, *a Bibliographical and Critical Inquiry* (London: Bibliographical Society, 1940); *Editorial Problem*, pp. 88–101.

47 (Baltimore: Johns Hopkins University Press), p. 7 n. 18.

48 *Elizabethan Shorthand and the First Quarto of* King Lear (Oxford: Basil Blackwell).

49 *Shakespeare's* King Lear: *A Critical Edition* (Oxford: Basil Blackwell, 1949), pp. 76–7.

50 *The Textual History of* Richard III (Stanford: Stanford University Press, 1936). The category of "bad" quarto was also being expanded to include many non-Shakespearean quartos as well: see Leo Kirschbaum, "A Census of Bad Quartos," *RES*, 14 (1938), 21–43, and his "*The Fair Maide of Bristow* (1605), Another Bad Quarto," *MLN*, 60 (1945), 302–8. For a bizarre use of the term "bad quarto" (to which Robert K. Turner kindly drew my attention), see Harry R. Hoppe, "*John of Bordeaux*: A Bad Quarto that Never Reached Print" in *Studies in Honor of A.H.R. Fairchild*, University of Missouri Studies 21 (Columbia, MO: The Curators of the University of Missouri, 1946), pp. 119–32.

51 *Textual Problems of the First Folio* (Cambridge: Cambridge University Press, 1953), p. 41.

52 pp. 48–9.

53 *Shakespeare Survey*, 5 (1952), 25–50, esp. p. 45.

54 *SS*, 3 (1950), 74–82.

55 p. 81. Even the best and most up-to-date efforts to locate the production of art within a wider cultural context take for granted Greg's 1910 notion that "play texts were printed … from manuscripts … compiled from memory by impoverished actors" (Joseph Loewenstein, "For a History of Literary Property: John Wolfe's Reformation," *English Literary Renaissance*, 18 [1988], 389–412, esp. p. 410).

56 p. 82.

57 *The Shakespeare First Folio*, p. 302.

58   p. 398.

59   Albert Feuillerat, "*2 and 3 Henry VI*" in his *The Composition of Shakespeare's Plays: Authorship, Chronology* (New Haven: Yale University Press, 1953), pp. 83–141; James G. McManaway, "*The Contention* and *2 Henry VI*" in *Studies in English Language and Literature: Presented to Professor Dr. Karl Brunner*, Siegfried Korninger, ed. (Stuttgart: Wilhelm Braunmüller, 1957), pp. 143–54.

60   *Iniurious Imposters*, pp. 159–72; Smidt modified his views in *Memorial Transmission and Quarto Copy in* Richard III: *A Reassessment* (New York: Humanities Press, 1970), in which he argued that Quarto *Richard III* was printed from a memorial reconstruction of the play that had been collated with Shakespeare's "foul papers" or with a fair copy (p. 46).

61   "The Queen Mab Speech in 'Romeo and Juliet'," *SS*, 25 (1973), 73–80.

62   "The First Quarto of *Pericles* Reconsidered," *SQ*, 29 (1978), 389–406.

63   *The Division of the Kingdoms: Shakespeare's Two Versions of* King Lear, Gary Taylor and Michael Warren, eds. (Oxford: Clarendon Press, 1983), p. 366; p. 10, italics mine.

64   *Shakespeare's Revision of* King Lear (Princeton, NJ: Princeton University Press, 1980), p. 129; "Reconsidering the Relationship of Quarto and Folio Texts of *Richard III*," *ELR*, 16 (1986), 442–66, esp. p. 459; "Good News" (cited in n. 36, above), pp. 193–4; " 'If I Mistake in Those Foundations Which I Build Upon': Peter Alexander's Textual Analysis of *Henry VI Parts 2 and 3*," *ELR*, 18 (1988), 230–56, esp. p. 254.

65   As quoted by Greg in *A Bibliography of the English Printed Drama to the Restoration*, 4 vols. (London: Bibliographical Society, 1957), Vol. 3, 1207.

66   An interesting array of contemporary references to memorial reconstruction is collected in the Oxford *Textual Companion*, pp. 23 ff.

67   Sir Sidney Lee, *A Life of William Shakespeare* (New York: Macmillan, 1916), pp. 558–9 and n. 1. Lee mistook many extant theatrical manuscripts for the private transcripts of which Moseley wrote and, like Greg after him, generalized Moseley's account of the genesis of *some* private copies to *all* private transcripts; thus Lee tried to argue that all Shakespeare's plays in the Folio *must* have got into print from such transcripts. I first learned to pay attention to the Moseley reference not from Lee, but from Peter Blayney, who put it to a most interesting use – different from Lee's and from mine – in a paper entitled "Shakespeare Fights *What* Pirates?" delivered at the Folger Shakespeare Library in May 1987.

68   As quoted in Greg, *Bibliography*, Vol. 3, 1233.

69   *Shakespeare and the Stationers* (Columbus: Ohio University Press, 1955), pp. 87–153.

70   *The Shakespeare First Folio*, p. 153.

71   It should not be thought that private transcripts in an author's hand would necessarily be as "true" to his "original intention" as Greg's idealized "foul papers"; or, if not, that such transcripts would preserve only the author's still more valuable "final intentions," for as Howard-Hill has written of the transcripts of *A Game at Chess*, "the general conclusion to which one is led by consideration of Middleton's involvement ... is that he was indifferent to both the correctness and the completeness of any of the texts of his play" ("The Author as Scribe or Reviser? Middleton's Intentions in *A Game at Chess*," *TEXT*, 3 [1987], 305–18, esp. p. 313).

Part VII

Psychoanalytic Criticism

20 "Anger's my meat": Feeding, Dependency, and Aggression
    in *Coriolanus*   323
    Janet Adelman

21 The Avoidance of Love: A Reading of *King Lear*   338
    Stanley Cavell

22 To Entrap the Wisest: Sacrificial Ambivalence in *The Merchant of
    Venice* and *Richard III*   353
    René Girard

23 What Did the King Know and When Did He Know It? Shakespearean
    Discourses and Psychoanalysis   365
    Harry Berger, Jr.

24 The Turn of the Shrew   399
    Joel Fineman

For most forms of critical address represented in this book – textual study, poetics, historical analysis – clear precedents exist in the writings of the great critics of the eighteenth and nineteenth centuries, astute readers and scholars such as Edmund Malone, Samuel Johnson, and William Hazlitt, among many others. Even feminist criticism has its Victorian antecedents, however remote and sometimes naive the work may seem to us, in the writing of Anna Jameson and others. However, the psychoanalytic approach appears to warrant being called truly modern, a way of studying Shakespeare's plays that came of age with modernity, in that it was conceived in the first half of the twentieth century and reached maturity in the second. The progenitor of the method, of course, is Sigmund Freud, whose first sustained discussion of Shakespeare is found in his *Interpretation of Dreams*, published in 1900.

Still, for all the appearance of parthenogenesis (i.e., that psychoanalytic studies of Shakespeare sprang fully developed from the head of the Viennese doctor), one may identify analogues and ancestors even in this critical subdiscipline. At the time that Freud was developing his theory of the unconscious and analyzing the origins of what we now call human subjectivity, the reigning form of Shakespearean study was character analysis. That method reached its apogee in the lectures of A. C. Bradley, who wrote and thought as the product of the great age of Victorian narrative fiction, a culture that liked to think about the minds of fictional characters. Albeit in a more traditional, less imaginative vocabulary, Bradley and some of his colleagues were addressing themselves to many of the same issues that interested Freud and his early followers.

One of Freud's most passionate disciples was the English physician Ernest Jones, who wrote a three-volume biography of his mentor and whose most significant effort at literary analysis reveals the influence of his esteem. *Hamlet and Oedipus* was one of the first self-conscious attempts to apply Freudian vocabulary and paradigms to literary texts; it originated in 1913 as an essay, "The Oedipus Complex as an Explanation of Hamlet's Mystery," published in the *American Journal of Psychology*, and over the next four decades Jones supplemented and revised the book. Typical of early examples of psychoanalytic criticism, Jones's declared method is fairly straightforward:

> I propose to pretend that Hamlet was a living person – one might parenthetically add that to most of us he is more so than many a player on the stage of life – and inquire what measure of man such a person must have been to feel and act in certain situations the way Shakespeare tells us he did. So far shall I be from forgetting that he was a figment of Shakespeare's mind that I shall then go on to consider the relation of this particular imaginative creation to the personality of Shakespeare himself.[1]

In other words, the critic–analyst seeks first to penetrate to the unseen sources and motives of human action, to the unconscious reaches of the character's psyche; the second task is to discover the sources of artistic creativity in the dramatist's unconscious.

As the practice of psychoanalytic literary criticism began to proliferate and mature in the years after World War II, the second of Jones's areas of concern, the mind of the creator, began to fade from the critical discourse (although it is worth noting that such analysis has made something of a return in the work of Meredith Skura, who considers the narcissism of the performer a vital creative component of Shakespeare the playwright).[2] Most critics have concentrated their attention on the subjectivity of Shakespeare's characters, attending especially to such problems as motivation, the unknown or repressed sources of thought and action, the displacement of desire, and the theatrical representation of consciousness. And for the psychoanalytic interpreter, the most compelling feature of the problem of consciousness is the depth and significance of the unconscious. In other words, the gap between characters' actions and their understanding or explanation of those actions is one of the most productive spaces in the dramatic text, and that gap is represented in the distance between surface and depth in the characters' language, between what is said and what is concealed.

Although spectacle and other visual components should not be depreciated, drama is to a great degree a verbal medium, and the emergence of language as a central problem in twentieth-century psychoanalytic thought fostered a kind of productive affinity between the psychoanalyst and the literary critic. Freud himself, of course, had built the model when he developed the tools of psychoanalytic interpretation, using verbal and narrative evidence for "reading" dreams, fantasies, and memories; and that exploitation of language for its insights into the unconscious was further refined by the French neo-Freudian, Jacques Lacan. The mutual interests of psychoanalysis and literary criticism are captured in Lacan's famous phrase, "The unconscious is structured like a language." One of Lacan's fundamental contributions is his linking the work of Freud with that of the Swiss linguist Ferdinand de Saussure, specifically concentration on the complexities of the sign. Thus Lacan extended Freud's initial investigations by assigning language priority over consciousness; by arguing, in other words, that language precedes and determines understanding and that through language humans are introduced and subjected to the social order. The sometimes daunting complexity of Lacanian analysis lies beyond the scope of this brief introduction, but it is worth emphasizing, with apologies for the reduction, that Lacan's insistence on seeing the speaker as subject to language rather than controlling it has made his work especially attractive to many psychoanalytic readers.

The Lacanian model is only one manifestation of the development of psychoanalytic thinking in the second half of the twentieth century, and in the course of this development psychoanalysis has found a symbiotic partner in feminist criticism. Specifically, feminism has taken a major role in overturning Freud's dependence upon a masculine prototype of human psychology and challenging his heteronormative understanding of sexuality. The writings of a number of French feminists interested in psychoanalysis, notably Julia Kristeva and Luce Irigaray, responsible for a complex theory of "feminine language," have contributed to that revision. The relation between feminism and psychoanalysis has been uncommonly productive in Shakespeare studies, as the essays by Janet Adelman and Madelon Gohlke Sprengnether included here effectively illustrate. These interpreters have pursued the thread of interpretation, developed from Freud by such writers as Melanie Klein and D. W. Winnicott, that leads back to the family. In particular, such readers investigate the effects upon the adult subject of the very earliest familial relations, i.e., the passage of the infant from the pre-Oedipal and Oedipal stages described by Freud into consciousness of gender and the introduction of the subject into the configuration of the social order. Much of the psychoanalytic interpretation of Shakespeare published in the 1980s and 1990s – work by Coppélia Kahn, Carol Thomas Neely, and others – grew out of discussion groups and conferences devoted to Shakespeare's representation of the family and its determining role in gender development.

Having become an established mode of interpretation, however, psychoanalytic criticism sometimes found itself at odds with the simultaneously developing attention to history. Stephen Greenblatt, for example, posted an early warning about the potentially misleading ahistorical nature of such reading: using the now-familiar story of Martin Guerre, he describes historically and culturally specific manifestations "of selfhood that psychoanalysis has tried to universalize into the very form of the human condition."[3]

For the most part, psychoanalytic readers of Shakespeare have tended to favor the pragmatic over the abstract, hence the preference for the methods and ideas of

Winnicott and Klein over those of Lacan in most psychoanalytic interpretations of the plays. For example, Janet Adelman has developed their object-relations theory into an ambitious study of male fantasies of maternal sexuality, a phenomenon she sees as crucial to the structure of Shakespearean tragedy. But the spectrum of psychoanalytic criticism is very broad, as the range of essays here represented will attest. Lacan is not neglected: Joel Fineman, riffing brilliantly on *The Taming of the Shrew*, uses Lacanian ideas of discourse (complicated by the insights of Derrida and Irigaray) to wonder whether it is "possible to voice a language, whether of man or of woman, that does not speak, sooner or later, self-consciously or unconsciously, for the order and authority of man?"

Stanley Cavell is represented by an excerpt from his lengthy and ambitious essay on *King Lear*, "The Avoidance of Love," a piece which displays his characteristically rich blend of psychological and philosophical theme. Harry Berger, Jr., in his classic study of discourse in the second tetralogy, "What Did the King Know and When Did He Know It?: Shakespearean Discourses and Psychoanalysis," might be said to cut to the chase in his first paragraph when he proposes to ask "what difference do specifically psychoanalytic readings make, and how useful are they?" Finally, this section includes a chapter on *The Merchant of Venice* from René Girard's *Theater of Envy*, a book representing his notion of "mimetic desire." A professor of French and therefore removed from the mainstream of Shakespeare studies, Girard has nevertheless exerted a potent influence on a certain segment of the discipline and on that basis warrants inclusion.

Notes

1   *Hamlet and Oedipus* (New York: Doubleday, 1949), p. 22.
2   *Shakespeare the Actor and the Profession of Playing* (Chicago: University of Chicago Press, 1993).
3   "Psychoanalysis and Renaissance Culture," in *Literary Theory / Renaissance Texts*, ed. Patricia Parker and David Quint (Baltimore, MD: Johns Hopkins University Press, 1986), p. 216.

20

"Anger's my meat":
Feeding, Dependency, and Aggression
in *Coriolanus*

Janet Adelman

C oriolanus was written during a period of rising corn prices and the accompanying fear of famine: rising prices reached a climax in 1608. In May 1607, "a great number of common persons" – up to five thousand, Stow tells us in his *Annals* – assembled in various Midlands counties, including Shakespeare's own county of Warwickshire, to protest against the acceleration of enclosures and the resulting food shortages.[1] It must have been disturbing to property owners to hear that the rioters were well received by local inhabitants, who brought them food and shovels;[2] doubly disturbing if they were aware that this was one of England's first purely popular riots, unlike the riots of the preceding century in that the anger of the common people was not being manipulated by rebellious aristocrats or religious factions.[3] The poor rioters were quickly dispersed, but – if *Coriolanus* is any indication – the fears that they aroused were not. In fact, Shakespeare shapes his material from the start in order to exacerbate these fears in his audience. In Plutarch the people riot because the Senate refuses to control usury; in Shakespeare they riot because they are hungry. Furthermore, the relentlessly vertical imagery of the play reflects the specific threat posed by this contemporary uprising: in a society so hierarchical – that is, so vertical – as theirs, the rioters' threat to level enclosures implied more than the casting down of particular hedges; it seemed to promise a flattening of the whole society.[4] Nor is Shakespeare's exacerbation of these fears merely a dramatist's trick to catch the attention of his audience from the start, or a seventeenth-century nod toward political relevance: for the dominant issues of the uprising – the threat of starvation and the consequent attempt to level enclosures – are reflected not only in the political but also in the intrapsychic world of *Coriolanus*; taken together, they suggest the concerns that shape the play and particularly the progress of its hero.

The uprising of the people at the start of the play points us toward an underlying fantasy in which political and psychological fears come together in a way that can only make each more intense and hence more threatening. For the political leveling promised by the contemporary uprising takes on overtones of sexual threat early in Shakespeare's play:[5] the rising of the people becomes suggestively phallic; and the fear of leveling becomes ultimately a fear of losing one's potency in all spheres. In Menenius' belly fable, the people are "th' discontented members, the mutinous parts," and "the mutinous members" (i.i.110, 148): an audience for whom the mutiny of the specifically sexual member was traditionally one of the signs of the Fall, and for whom the crowd was traditionally associated with dangerous passion, would be prone to hear in Menenius' characterization of the crowd a reference to a part other than the great toe (i.i.154). In this fantasy the hitherto docile sons suddenly threaten to rise up against their fathers, the Senators (i.i.76); and it is characteristic of *Coriolanus* that the contested issue in this Oedipal rebellion is food.[6] The uprising of the crowd is in fact presented in terms that suggest the transformation of hunger into phallic aggression, a transformation that is, as I shall later argue, central to the character of Coriolanus himself: when the first citizen tells Menenius "They say poor suitors have strong breaths: they shall know we have strong arms too" (i.i.58–60), his image of importunate mouths suddenly armed in rebellion suggests the source of Coriolanus' rebellion no less than his own.

If the specter of a multitude of hungry mouths, ready to rise and demand their own, is the exciting cause of *Coriolanus*, the image of the mother who has not fed her children enough is at its center. One does not need the help of a psychoanalytic approach to notice that Volumnia is not a nourishing mother. Her attitude toward food is nicely summed up when she rejects Menenius' invitation to a consolatory dinner after Coriolanus' banishment: "Anger's my meat: I sup upon myself / And so shall starve with feeding" (iv.ii.50–1). We might suspect her of having been as niggardly in providing food for her son as she is for herself, or rather suspect her of insisting that he too be self-sufficient, that he feed only on his own anger; and indeed, she has apparently fed him only valiantness ("Thy valiantness was mine, thou suck'st it from me" [iii.ii.129]). He certainly has not been fed the milk of human kindness: when Menenius later tells us that "there is no more mercy in him than there is milk in a male tiger" (v.iv.28–9), he seems to associate Coriolanus' lack of humanity not only with the absence of any nurturing female element in him but also with the absence of mother's milk itself.[7] Volumnia takes some pride in the creation of her son, and when we first meet her, she tells us exactly how she's done it: by sending him to a cruel war at an age when a mother should not be willing to allow a son out of the protective maternal circle for an hour (i.iii.5–15). She elaborates her creation as she imagines herself mother to twelve sons and then kills all but one of them off: "I had rather had eleven die nobly for their country, than one voluptuously surfeit out of action" (i.iii.24–5). To be noble is to die; to live is to be ignoble and to eat too much.[8] If you are Volumnia's son, the choice is clear.

But the most telling – certainly the most disturbing – revelation of Volumnia's attitude toward feeding comes some twenty lines later, when she is encouraging Virgilia to share her own glee in the thought of Coriolanus' wounds: "The breasts of Hecuba / When she did suckle Hector, look'd not lovelier / Than Hector's forehead when it spit forth blood / At Grecian sword contemning" (i.iii.40–3). Blood is more beautiful than milk, the wound than the breast, warfare than peaceful feeding. But this image is more disturbing than these easy comparatives suggest. It does not bode well for Coriolanus that the heroic Hector doesn't stand a chance in Volumnia's imagination: he is transformed immediately from infantile feeding mouth to bleeding wound. For the unspoken mediator between breast and wound is the infant's mouth: in this imagistic transform-ation, to feed is to be wounded; the mouth becomes the wound, the breast the sword. The metaphoric process suggests the psychological fact that is, I think, at the center of the play: the taking in of food is the primary acknowledgment of one's dependence on the world, and as such, it is the primary token of one's vulnerability.[9] But at the same time as Volumnia's image suggests the vulnerability inherent in feeding, it also suggests a way to fend off that vulnerability. In her image, feeding, incorporating, is transformed into spitting out, an aggressive expelling; the wound in turn becomes the mouth that spits "forth blood / At Grecian sword contemning." The wound spitting blood thus becomes not a sign of vulnerability but an instrument of attack.

Volumnia's attitudes toward feeding and dependence are echoed perfectly in her son. Coriolanus persistently regards food as poisonous (i.i.177–8, iii.i.155–6); the only thing he can imagine nourishing is rebellion (iii.i.68–9, 116). Only Menenius among the patricians is associated with the ordinary consumption of food and wine without an allaying drop of Tiber in it; and his distance from Coriolanus can be measured partly by his pathetic conviction that Coriolanus will be malleable – that he will have a "suppler" soul (v.i.55) – after he has had a full meal. But for Coriolanus, as for his mother, nobility consists precisely in *not* eating: he twice imagines himself starving himself honorably to death before asking for food, or anything else, from the plebeians (ii.iii.112–13; iii.iii.89–91).[10] And the transformations in mode implicit in Volumnia's image – from feeding to warfare, from vulnerability to aggressive attack, from incorporation to spitting out – are at the center of Coriolanus' character and of our responses to him: for the whole of his masculine identity depends on his transformation of his vulnerability into an instrument of attack, as Menenius suggests when he tells us that each of Coriolanus' wounds "was an enemy's grave" (ii.i.154–5). Cominius reports that Coriolanus entered his first battle a sexually indefinite thing, a boy or Amazon (ii.ii.91), and found his manhood there: "When he might act the woman in the scene, / He prov'd best man i'th' field" (ii.ii.96–7). The rigid masculinity that Coriolanus finds in war becomes a defense against acknowledgment of his neediness; he attempts to transform himself from a vulnerable human creature into a grotesquely invulnerable and isolated thing. His body becomes his armor (i.iii.35, i.iv.24); he himself becomes a weapon "who sensibly outdares his senseless sword, / And when it bows, stand'st up" (i.iv.53–4), or he becomes the sword itself: "O me alone! Make you a sword of me!" (i.vi.76). And his whole life becomes a kind of phallic exhibitionism, devoted to disproving the possibility that he is vulnerable.[11] Anger becomes his meat as well as his mother's: Volumnia's phrase suggests his mode of defending himself against vulnerability, and at the same time reveals the source of his anger in the deprivation imposed by his mother. We see the quality of his hunger and its transformation when, after his expulsion from Rome, he reminds Aufidius that he has "drawn tuns of blood out of thy country's breast" (iv.v.100). Fighting here, as elsewhere in the play, is a poorly concealed substitute for feeding (see, for example, i.ix.10–11; iv.v.191–4, 222–4); and the unsatisfied ravenous attack of the infant on the breast provides the motive force for warfare. The image allows us to understand the ease with which Coriolanus turns his rage toward his own feeding mother, Rome.[12]

Thrust prematurely from dependence on his mother, forced to feed himself on his own anger, Coriolanus refuses to acknowledge any neediness or dependency: for his entire sense of himself depends on his being able to see himself as a self-sufficient creature. The desperation behind his claim to self-sufficiency is revealed by his horror of praise, even the praise of his general:[13] the dependence of his masculinity on warfare in fact makes praise (or flattery, as he calls it) particularly threatening to him on the battlefield; susceptibility to flattery there, in the place of the triumph of his independence, would imply that the soldier's steel has grown "soft as the parasite's silk" (I.ix.45). The juxtaposition of soldier's steel and parasite's soft silk suggests both Coriolanus' dilemma and his solution to it: in order to avoid being the soft, dependent, feeding parasite, he has to maintain his rigidity as soldier's steel. And the same complex of ideas determines the rigidity that makes him so disastrous as a political figure. The language in which he imagines his alternatives as he contemptuously asks the people for their voices and later as he gives up his attempt to pacify them reveals the extent to which his unwillingness to ask for the people's approval, like his abhorrence of praise, depends on his attitude toward food: "Better it is to die, better to starve, / Than crave the hire which first we do deserve" (II.iii.112–13); "Pent to linger / But with a grain a day, I would not buy / Their mercy at the price of one fair word" (III.iii.89–91). Asking, craving, flattering with fair words are here not only preconditions but also equivalents of eating: to refuse to ask is to starve, but starvation is preferable to asking because asking, like eating, is an acknowledgment of one's weakness, one's dependence on the outside world. "The price is, to ask it kindly" (II.iii.75): but that is the one price Coriolanus cannot pay. When he must face the prospect of revealing his dependence on the populace by asking for their favor, his whole delicately constructed masculine identity threatens to crumble: in order to ask, a harlot's spirit must possess him; his voice must become as small as the eunuch's or the virgin's minding babies; a beggar's tongue must make motion through his lips (III.ii.111–18). Asking, then, would undo the process by which he was transformed from boy or woman to man on the battlefield. That he imagines this undoing as a kind of reverse voice change, from man to boy, suggests the extent to which his phallic aggressive pose is a defense against collapse into a dependent oral mode, when he had the voice of a small boy. And in fact, Coriolanus' own use of language constantly reiterates this defense. Flattery and asking are the linguistic equivalents of feeding (I.ix.51–2): they are incorporative modes that acknowledge one's dependence. But Coriolanus spits out words, using them as weapons. His invective is in the mode of Hector's wound, aggressively spitting forth blood: it is an attempt to deny vulnerability by making the very area of vulnerability into the means of attack.[14]

Coriolanus' abhorrence of praise and flattery, his horror lest the people think that he got his wounds to please them (II.ii.147–50), his insistence that he be given the consulship in sign of what he is, not as a reward (I.ix.26), his refusal to ask – all are attempts to claim that he is *sui generis*. His attitude finds its logical conclusion in his desperate cry as he sees his mother approaching him at the end:

> I'll never
> Be such a gosling to obey instinct, but stand
> As if a man were author of himself
> And knew no other kin.
>
> (v.iii.34–7)

The gosling obeys instinct and acknowledges his kinship with mankind; but Coriolanus will attempt to stand alone. (Since Coriolanus' manhood depends exactly on this phallic standing alone, he is particularly susceptible to Aufidius' taunt of "boy" when he has been such a gosling as to obey instinct.) The relationship between Coriolanus' aggressive pose and his attempts to claim that he is *sui generis* are most dramatically realized in the conquest of Corioli; it is here that Coriolanus most nearly realizes his fantasy of standing as if a man were author of himself. For the scene at Corioli represents a glorious transformation of the nightmare of oral vulnerability ("to th' pot" [1.iv.47], one of his soldiers says as he is swallowed up by the gates) into a phallic adventure that both assures and demonstrates his independence. The dramatic action itself presents the conquest of Corioli as an image of triumphant rebirth: after Coriolanus enters the gates of the city, he is proclaimed dead; one of his comrades delivers a eulogy firmly in the past tense ("Thou wast a soldier / Even to Cato's wish" [1.iv.55–6]); then Coriolanus miraculously re-emerges, covered with blood (1.vi.22), and is given a new name. Furthermore, Coriolanus' own battlecry as he storms the gates sexualizes the scene: "Come on; / If you'll stand fast, we'll beat them to their wives" (1.iv.40–1). For the assault on Corioli is both a rape and a rebirth: the underlying fantasy is that intercourse is a literal return to the womb, from which one is reborn, one's own author.[15] The fantasy of self-authorship is complete when Coriolanus is given his new name, earned by his own actions.[16]

But despite the boast implicit in his conquest of Corioli, Coriolanus has not in fact succeeded in separating himself from his mother;[17] even the very role through which he claims independence was designed by her – as she never tires of pointing out ("My praises made thee first a soldier" [III.ii.108]; "Thou art my warrior: / I holp to frame thee" [v.iii.62–3]). In fact, Shakespeare underlines Volumnia's point by the placing of two central scenes. In 1.iii, before we have seen Coriolanus himself as a soldier, we see Volumnia first *describe* her image of her son on the battlefield and then *enact* his role: "Methinks I see him stamp thus, and call thus: / 'Come on you cowards, you were got in fear / Though you were born in Rome' " (1.iii.32–4). This marvelous moment not only suggests the ways in which Volumnia herself lives through her son; it also suggests the extent to which his role is her creation. For when we see him in the next scene, acting exactly as his mother had predicted, we are left with the impression that he is merely enacting her enactment of his role. That he is acting under her direction even in the role designed to insure his independence of her helps to explain both his bafflement when she suddenly starts to disapprove of the role that she has created ("I muse my mother / Does not approve me further" [III.ii.7–8]), and his eventual capitulation to her demand that he shift roles, here and at the end of the play. When he finally agrees to take on the role of humble supplicant, he is sure that he will act badly (III.ii.105–6) and that he will lose his manhood in the process (III.ii.111–23). For his manhood is secure only when he can play the role that she has designed, and play it with her approval.[18] He asks her, "Why did you wish me milder? Would you have me / False to my nature? Rather say I play / The man I am" (III.ii.14–16). But "I play the man I am" cuts both ways: in his bafflement, Coriolanus would like to suggest that there is no distance between role and self, but in fact suggests that he plays at being himself. Given that Volumnia has created this dilemma, her answer is unnecessarily cruel – but telling: "You might have been enough the man you are, / With striving less to be so" (III.ii.19–20). Volumnia is right: it is the intensity and rigidity of Coriolanus' commitment to his masculine role that makes us suspect the intensity of the fears that this role is designed to hide, especially from himself.

The fragility of the entire structure by which Coriolanus maintains his claim to self-sufficient manhood helps to account for the violence of his hatred of the plebeians. Coriolanus uses the crowd to bolster his own identity: he accuses them of being exactly what he wishes not to be.[19] He does his best to distinguish himself from them by emphasizing his aloneness and their multitudinousness as the very grounds of their being.[20] Throughout, he associates his manhood with his isolation, so that "Alone I did it" becomes a sufficient answer to Aufidius' charge that he is a boy; hence the very status of the plebeians as *crowd* reassures him that they are not men but dependent and unmanly things, merely children – a point of view that Menenius seems to confirm when he tells the tribunes, "Your abilities are too infant-like for doing much alone" (ɪɪ.i.36–7). His most potent image of the crowd is as a common mouth (ɪɪɪ.i.22, 155) disgustingly willing to exhibit its neediness. He enters the play identified by the plebeians as the person who is keeping them from eating (ɪ.i.9–10); and indeed, one of his main complaints about the plebeians is that they say they are hungry (ɪ.i.204–7).[21] Coriolanus himself has been deprived of food, and he seems to find it outrageous that others should not be. His position here is like that of the older brother who has fought his way into manhood and who is now confronted by an apparently endless group of siblings – "my sworn brother the people" (ɪɪ.iii.95), he calls them – who still insist on being fed by mother Rome,[22] and whose insistence on their dependency threatens the pose of self-sufficiency by which his equilibrium is perilously maintained. Indeed, the intensity of his portrayal of the crowd as a multitudinous mouth suggests not only the neediness that underlies his pose, but also the tenuousness of the pose itself: his insistent portrayal of the plebeians as an unmanly mouth, as feminine where they should be masculine, in effect as castrated, suggests that his hatred of the crowd conceals not only his own hunger but also his fears for his own masculinity.[23] It is characteristic of Coriolanus' transformation of hunger into phallic aggression that the feared castration is imagined predominantly in oral terms: to be castrated here *is* to be a mouth, naked in one's dependency, perpetually hungry, perpetually demanding.[24]

Coriolanus' absolute horror at the prospect of showing his wounds to win the consulship depends partly, I think, on the complex of ideas that stands behind his characterization of the crowd. In Plutarch, Coriolanus shows his wounds; in Shakespeare, the thought is intolerable to him and, despite many promises that he will, he never does. For his wounds would then become begging mouths (as they do in *Julius Caesar* [ɪɪɪ.ii.225–6]), and their display would reveal his kinship with the plebeians in several ways: by revealing that he has worked for hire as they have (that is, that he and his deeds are not *sui generis* after all); by revealing that he is vulnerable, as they are; and by revealing, through the persistent identification of wound and mouth, that he too has a mouth, that he is a feminized and dependent creature. Moreover, the exhibition of his wounds to the crowd is impossible for him partly because his identity is sustained by exhibitionism of another sort. The phallic exhibitionism of his life as a soldier has been designed to deny the possibility of just this kinship with the crowd; it has served to reassure him of his potency and his aggressive independence, and therefore to sustain him against fears of the collapse into the dependent mode of infancy. To exhibit the fruits of his soldiership not as the emblems of his self-sufficiency but as the emblems of his vulnerability and dependence, and to exhibit them precisely to those whose kinship with him he would most like to deny, would transform his chief means of defense into a proclamation of his weakness: it would threaten to undo the very structure by which he lives.[25]

Behind Coriolanus' rage at the plebeians, then, stands the specter of his own hunger and his own fear of dependence. But this rage is properly directed toward his mother: and though it is deflected from her and toward the plebeians and Volscians for much of the play, it finally returns to its source after he has been exiled from Rome. For Rome and his mother are finally one:[26] although in his loving farewell his family and friends are wholly distinguished from the beast with many heads, by the time he has returned to Rome they are no more than a poor grain or two that must be consumed in the general fire (v.i.27). (Even in his loving farewell we hear a note of resentment when he consoles his mother by telling her, "My hazards still have been your solace" [iv.i.28].) And as he approaches Rome, we know that the destruction of his mother will not be merely incidental to the destruction of his city. For in exiling him, Rome re-enacts the role of the mother who cast him out; the exile is a reliving of the crisis of dependency that Coriolanus has already undergone. Coriolanus initially meets this crisis with the claim that he himself is in control of the independence thrust upon him, a claim akin to the infant's fantasy of omnipotent control over the forces that in fact control him: "I banish you!" (iii.iii.123). He then attempts to insure himself of the reality of his omnipotence by wishing on his enemies exactly what he already knows to be true of them ("Let every feeble rumour shake your hearts! / ... Have the power still / To banish your defenders" [iii.iii.125–8]): few curses have ever been so sure of instantaneous fulfillment. Having thus exercised his rage and assured himself of the magical power of his invective, Coriolanus finally makes his claim to true independence: "There is a world elsewhere!" (iii.iii.135). But he cannot sustain this independence, cannot simply separate himself from the world of Rome; the intensity of his identification with Rome and with his mother forces him to come back to destroy both, to make his claim to omnipotent independence a reality by destroying the home to which he is still attached, so that he can truly stand as if a man were author of himself. The return to Rome is an act of retaliation against the mother on whom he has been dependent, the mother who has cast him out; but it is at the same time an acting out of the child's fantasy of reversing the roles of parent and child, so that the life of the parent is in the hands of the omnipotent child. For Coriolanus can become author of himself only by first becoming author of his mother, as he attempts to do here: by becoming in effect a god, dispensing life and death (v.iv.24–5), so that he can finally stand alone.

But Coriolanus can sustain neither his fantasy of self-authorship nor his attempt to realize a godlike omnipotent power. And the failure of both leaves him so unprotected, so utterly devoid of a sense of self that, for the first time in the play, he feels himself surrounded by dangers: for the capitulation of his independent selfhood before his mother's onslaught seems to him to require his death. Indeed, as he cries out to his mother, he embraces his intuition of his own death with a passivity thoroughly uncharacteristic of him:

> O my mother, mother! O!
> You have won a happy victory to Rome;

> But for your son, believe it, O, believe it,
> Most dangerously you have with him prevail'd,
> If not most mortal to him. But let it come.
>
> (v.iii.185–9)

His attempt to ward off danger by pleading with Aufidius is strikingly half-hearted; and when he says, "Though I cannot make true wars, / I'll frame convenient peace" (v.iii.190–1), we hear the tragic collapse of his personality. We of course know by this time that the self-sufficient and aggressive pose by which Coriolanus maintains his selfhood is as dangerous to him as its collapse, that Aufidius plans to kill him no matter what he does (iv.vii.24–6, 56–7). It is a mark of the extent to which external dangers are for Coriolanus merely a reflection of internal ones that he feels himself in no danger until the collapse of his defensive system. But Volumnia achieves this collapse partly because she makes the dangers inherent in his defensive system as terrifying as those which it is designed to keep at bay: her last confrontation with her son is so appallingly effective because she invalidates his defenses by threatening to enact his most central defensive fantasies, thereby making their consequences inescapable to him.

The very appearance of his mother, coming to beg him for the life of her city and hence for her own life, is an enactment of his attempt to become the author of his mother, his desire to have power over her. He has before found her begging intolerable (iii.ii.124–34); when she kneels to him here, making the role reversal of mother and child explicit (v.iii.56), he reacts with an hysteria that suggests that the acting out of this forbidden wish threatens to dissolve the very structures by which he orders his life:

> What's this?
> Your knees to me? to your corrected son?
> Then let the pebbles on the hungry beach
> Fillip the stars. Then let the mutinous winds
> Strike the proud cedars 'gainst the fiery sun,
> Murd'ring impossibility, to make
> What cannot be, slight work!
>
> (v.iii.56–62)

At first sight, this speech seems simply to register Coriolanus' horror at the threat to hierarchy implied by the kneeling of parent to child. But if Coriolanus were responding only – or even mainly – to this threat, we would expect the threatened chaos to be imaged as high bowing to low; and this is in fact the image that we are given when Volumnia first bows to her son as if – as Coriolanus says – "Olympus to a molehill should / In supplication nod" (v.iii.30–1). But Coriolanus does not respond to his mother's kneeling with an image of high bowing to low; instead, he responds with two images of low mutinously striking at high. The chaos imaged here is not so much a derivative of his mother's kneeling as of the potential mutiny that her kneeling seems to imply: for her kneeling releases the possibility of his mutiny against her, a mutiny that he has been suppressing all along by his exaggerated deference to her. His response here reveals another of the bases for his hatred of the mutinous and leveling populace: the violence of his images suggests that his mother's kneeling has forced him to acknowledge his return to Rome as a rising up of the hungry and mutinous forces in himself. With her usual acumen, Volumnia recognizes the disarming of potential mutiny in Coriolanus' response and chooses exactly this moment to assert, once again, his dependence on her: "Thou art my warrior" (v.iii.62).

The living out of Coriolanus' forbidden wish to have power over his mother had seemed to Coriolanus impossible; but now that protective impossibility itself seems murdered, and he is forced to confront the fact that his wish has become a reality. Nor are the hungry and mutinous forces within himself content to murder only an abstract "impossibility": the murderousness of the image is directed ultimately at his mother. And once again, Volumnia makes Coriolanus uncomfortably clear to himself: after she has enacted his terrifying fantasy by kneeling, she makes it impossible for him to believe that her death would be merely an incidental consequence of his plan to burn Rome.[27] For she reveals exactly the extent to which he has identified mother and Rome, the extent to which his assault is on both. Her long speech builds to its revelation with magnificent force and logic. She first forces him to see his attack on his country as an attack on a living body by accusing him of coming to tear "his country's bowels out" (v.iii.103). Next, she identifies that body as their common mother ("the country, our dear nurse" [v.iii.110]). Finally, as she announces her intention to commit suicide, she makes absolute the identification of the country with herself; after she has imagined him treading on his country's ruin (v.iii.116), she warns him:

> thou shalt no sooner
> March to assault thy country than to tread –
> Trust to't, thou shalt not – on thy mother's womb
> That brought thee to this world.
> (v.iii.122–5)

The ruin on which Coriolanus will tread will be his mother's womb – a warning accompanied by yet another assertion of his dependence on her as she recalls to him the image of himself as a fetus within that womb.

If Coriolanus' mutinous fantasies are no longer an impossibility, if his mother will indeed die as a result of his actions, then Coriolanus will have realized his fantasy of living omnipotently without kin, without dependency. In fact this fantasy, his defense throughout, is articulated only here, as he catches sight of his mother (v.iii.34–7); and its expression is the last stand of his claim to independence. Throughout this scene, Volumnia has simultaneously asserted his dependence on her and made the dangers inherent in his defense against that dependence horrifyingly clear; and in the end it is the combination of her insistence on his dependency and her threat to disown him, to literalize his fantasy of standing alone, that causes him to capitulate. Finally, he cannot "stand / As if a man were author of himself / And knew no other kin"; he must become a child again, a gosling, and admit his neediness. The presence of his own child, holding Volumnia's hand, strengthens her power over him: for Coriolanus seems to think of his child less as his son than as the embodiment of his own childhood and the child that remains within him; even when we are first told about the son, he seems more of a comment on Coriolanus' childhood than on his fatherhood. The identification of father and child is suggested by Coriolanus' response as he sees wife, mother, and child approaching: "My wife comes foremost; then the honour'd mould / Wherein this trunk was fram'd, and in her hand / The grandchild to her blood" (v.iii.22–4).

Here Coriolanus does not acknowledge the child as his and his wife's: he first imagines himself in his mother's womb, and then imagines his child as an extension of his mother. Even Coriolanus' language to Menenius as he earlier denies his family reveals the same fusion of father and son: "Wife, mother, child, I know not" (v.ii.80) he says, in a phrase that suggests that his own mother is the mother of the child, and the child he attempts to deny is himself. Volumnia had once before brought Coriolanus to submission by reminding him of himself as a suckling child (iii.ii.129); now virtually her last words enforce his identification with the child that she holds by the hand: "This fellow had a Volscian to his mother; / His wife is in Corioles, and his child / Like him by chance" (v.iii.178–80). But at the same time as she reminds him of his dependency, she disowns him by disclaiming her parenthood; she exacerbates his sense of himself as a child, and then threatens to leave him – as he thought he wished – alone. And as his fantasy of self-sufficiency threatens to become a reality, it becomes too frightening to sustain; just as his child entered the scene holding Volumnia's hand, so Coriolanus again becomes a child, holding his mother's hand.

The ending of this play leaves us with a sense of pain and anxiety; we are not even allowed the feelings of unremitting grief and satiation that console us in most of the other tragedies. The very nature of its hero insists that we keep our distance. Coriolanus is as isolated from us as he is from everyone else; we almost never know what he is thinking, and – even more intolerably – he does not seem to care what we are thinking. Unlike an Othello or an Antony, whose last moments are spent endearingly trying to insure our good opinion, Coriolanus makes virtually no attempt to affect our judgment of him: he dies as he has tried to live, heroically mantled in his self-sufficiency, alone. Nor is it only our democratic sympathies that put us uncomfortably in the position of the common people throughout much of the play: Coriolanus seems to find our love as irrelevant, as positively demeaning, as theirs; and in refusing to show the people his wounds, he is at the same time refusing to show them to us. In refusing to show himself to us, in considering us a many-headed multitude to whose applause he is wholly indifferent, Coriolanus denies us our proper role as spectators to his tragedy. The only spectators that Coriolanus allows himself to notice are the gods who look down on this unnatural scene and laugh, who are so far removed from men that they find this human tragedy a comedy. And as spectators we are in danger of becoming as distant from human concerns as the gods: for Coriolanus' isolation infects the whole play and ultimately infects us. There are very few moments of relaxation; there is no one here to love. We are made as rigid and cold as the hero by the lack of anything that absolutely commands our human sympathies, that demonstrates to us that *we* are dependent creatures, part of a community. Even the language does not open out toward us, nor does it create the sense of the merging of meanings, the melting together, that gives us a measure of release in *King Lear* or *Antony and Cleopatra*, where a world of linguistic fusion suggests the dependence of all parts. Instead, the language works to define and separate, to limit possibilities, almost as rigidly as Coriolanus himself does.[28] And finally, the nature of our involvement in the fantasies embodied in this distant and rigid hero does not permit any resolution: it also separates and limits. For Coriolanus has throughout given free expression to *our* desire to be independent, and we delight in his claim. But when he turns on his mother in

Rome, the consequences of his claim to self-sufficiency suddenly become intolerably threatening to us. We want him to acknowledge dependence, to become one of us; but at the same time we do not want to see him give in, because to do so is to force us to give up our own fantasy of omnipotence and independence. Hence at the final confrontation we are divided against ourselves and no solution is tolerable: neither the burning of Rome nor the capitulation and death of our claims to independence. Nor is the vision of human dependency that the play allows any compensation for the brutal failure of our desire to be self-sustaining. In *Lear* and *Antony and Cleopatra*, dependency is finally shown to be what makes us fully human: however much the characters have tried to deny it, it finally becomes their salvation, and ours, as we reach out to them. But dependency here brings no rewards, no love, no sharing with the audience; it brings only the total collapse of the self, the awful triumph of Volumnia, and Coriolanus' terribly painful cry: "O mother, mother! / What have you done?"

Notes

1 John Stow, *Annales* (London, 1631), p. 890. See Sidney Shanker, "Some Clues for *Coriolanus*," *Shakespeare Association Bulletin* 24 (1949): 209–13; E. C. Pettet, "*Coriolanus* and the Midlands Insurrection of 1607," *Shakespeare Survey* 3 (1950): 34–42; and Brents Stirling, *The Populace in Shakespeare* (New York, 1965), pp. 126–28, for discussions of the uprising and its political consequences in the play.

2 Stow, *Annales*, p. 890.

3 See Edwin F. Gay, "The Midland Revolt and The Inquisitions of Depopulation of 1607," *Transactions of the Royal Historical Society*, n.s., 18 (1904); 195–244, for valuable contemporary commentary on the uprising and an analysis of it in comparison with earlier riots of the sixteenth century. See also Pettet, "*Coriolanus* and the Midlands Insurrection," p. 35.

4 The participants in the uprising were commonly called "levelers" and their activity "leveling," in startling anticipation of the 1640s. The common use of this term suggests the extent to which their fight against enclosures seemed to threaten hierarchy itself. (See, for example, Stow, *Annales*, p. 890, and Gay, "The Midland Revolt," pp. 213 n. 2, 214 n. 1, 216 n. 3, and 242.) The vertical imagery is so prominent in the play that it scarcely needs to be pointed out; at its center is Cominius' warning that the stirring up of the people is "the way to lay the city flat, / To bring the roof to the foundation, / And bury all which yet distinctly ranges / In heaps and piles of ruin" (III.i.201–5). The threat of the people to rise and cast Coriolanus down from the Tarpeian rock, Coriolanus' horror of kneeling to the people or of his mother's kneeling to him, and ultimately the image of the prone Coriolanus with Aufidius standing on him – all take their force partly from the repetition and intensity of the vertical imagery throughout.

5 Shakespeare had in fact just used the word *level* to suggest a sexual leveling at the end of *Antony and Cleopatra*, when Cleopatra laments: "The soldier's pole is fall'n: young boys and girls / Are level now with men" (IV.xv.65–6).

6 Coriolanus himself occupies an odd position in the psychological myth at the start of the play: though he is a father, we almost always think of him as a son; though the populace considers him prime among the forbidding fathers, he himself seems to regard the patricians as his fathers. His position midway between father and sons suggests the position of an older sibling who has made a protective alliance with the father and now fears the unruliness of his younger brothers. Instead of fighting to take possession of the undernourishing mother, he will deny that he has any need for food.

7 Menenius' words point to the rigid and ferocious maleness so prized by Rome. The ideal Roman woman is in fact one who denies her womanhood, as we see not only in Volumnia but in

Coriolanus' chilling and beautiful description of Valeria (v.iii.65–7). (Indeed, Valeria seems to have little place in the intimate family gathering of v.iii; she seems to exist there largely to give Coriolanus an excuse for speaking these lines.) The extent to which womanhood is shrunken in Roman values is apparent in the relative unimportance of Coriolanus' wife, Virgilia; in her the female values of kindly nurturing have become little more than a penchant for staying at home, keeping silent, and weeping. (Given the extreme restrictions of Virgilia's role, one may begin to understand some of the pressures that force a woman to become a Volumnia and live through the creation of her exaggeratedly masculine son. Gordon Ross Smith ["Authoritarian Patterns in Shakespeare's *Coriolanus*," *Literature and Psychology* 9 (1959): 49] comments perceptively that, in an authoritarian society, women will either be passive and subservient or will attempt to live out their thwarted ambition via their men.) At the end, Rome sees the consequences of its denial of female values as Coriolanus prepares to deny nature in himself and destroy his homeland. When Volumnia triumphs over his rigid maleness, there is a hint of restitution in the Roman celebration of her as "our patroness, the life of Rome" (v.v.1). But like nearly everything else at the end of this play, the promise of restitution is deeply ironic: for Volumnia herself has shown no touch of nature as she willingly sacrifices her son; and the cries of "welcome, ladies, welcome!" (v.v.6) suggest an acknowledgment of female values at the moment in which the appearance of these values not in Volumnia but in her son can only mean his death. Phyllis Rackin, in an unpublished paper entitled "*Coriolanus*: Shakespeare's Anatomy of *Virtus*" and delivered to the special session on feminist criticism of Shakespeare at the 1976 meeting of the Modern Language Association, discusses the denial of female values as a consequence of the Roman overvaluation of valor as the chiefest virtue. Her analysis of the ways in which the traditionally female images of food, harvesting, and love are turned to destructive purposes throughout the play is particularly revealing.

8 The association of nobility with abstinence from food, and of the ignoble lower classes with excessive appetite for food in connection with their traditional role as embodiments of appetite, was first demonstrated to me by Maurice Charney's impressive catalogue of the food images in the play ("The Imagery of Food and Eating in *Coriolanus*," *Essays in Literary History*, ed. Rudolf Kirk and C. F. Main [New Brunswick, NJ, 1960], pp. 37–54).

9 Hence the persistent identification of mouth and wound throughout the play (most striking in the passage discussed here, and in ii.iii.7); hence also the regularity with which images of feeding are transposed into images of cannibalism and reveal a talion fear of being eaten (i.i.187, 257; ii.i.9; iv.v.194). At the center of these images of vulnerability in feeding is Menenius's comparison of Rome to an "unnatural dam" who threatens to eat up her own children (iii.i.290–1).

10 In fact, Coriolanus frequently imagines his death with a kind of glee, as the final triumph of his noble self-sufficiency; see, for example, iii.ii.1–5, 103–4; v.vi.111–12.

11 The extent to which Coriolanus becomes identified with his phallus is suggested by the language in which both Menenius and Aufidius portray his death; for both, it represents a kind of castration ("He's a limb that has but a disease: / Mortal, to cut it off; to cure it, easy" [iii.i.293–4]; "You'll rejoice / That he is thus cut off" [v.vi.137–8]. For discussions of Coriolanus' phallic identification and its consequences, see Robert J. Stoller, "Shakespearean Tragedy: Coriolanus," *Psychoanalytic Quarterly* 35 (1966): 263–74, and Emmett Wilson, Jr., "Coriolanus: The Anxious Bridegroom," *American Imago* 25 (1968): 224–41. Charles K. Hofling ("An Interpretation of Shakespeare's Coriolanus," *American Imago* 14 (1957): 407–35) sees Coriolanus as a virtual embodiment of Reich's phallic-narcissistic character. Each of these analysts finds Coriolanus' phallic stance to some extent a defense against passivity (Stoller, pp. 267, 269–70; Wilson, passim; Hofling, pp. 421, 424).

12 David B. Barron sees Coriolanus' oral frustration and his consequent rage as central to his character ("*Coriolanus*: Portrait of the Artist As Infant," *American Imago* 19 (1962): 171–93); his essay anticipates mine in some of its conclusions and many of its details of interpretation.

13 Most critics find Coriolanus' abhorrence of praise a symptom of his pride and his desire to consider himself as self-defined and self-sufficient, hence free from the definitions that society

would confer on him. See, for example, A. C. Bradley, "Coriolanus," reprinted in *Studies in Shakespeare,* ed. Peter Alexander (London, 1964), p. 229; G. Wilson Knight, *The Imperial Theme* (London, 1965), p. 169; Irving Ribner, *Patterns in Shakespearean Tragedy* (London, 1960), p. 190; Norman Rabkin, *Shakespeare and the Common Understanding* (New York, 1967), p. 131; and James L. Calderwood, "*Coriolanus:* Wordless Meanings and Meaningless Words," *Studies in English Literature* 6 (1966): 218–19. There are dissenters, however. Brian Vickers, for example, finds a concern with political image-making at the center of the play: in his view, the patricians' praise of Coriolanus as a war machine serves their own propagandistic class interests and should be rejected by the audience as a false image of him; Coriolanus' rejection of this praise is therefore perfectly justified, not an indication of his pride (*Shakespeare: "Coriolanus"* [London, 1976], pp. 23–5).

14   In his discussion of Coriolanus' cathartic vituperation, Kenneth Burke suggests that invective is rooted in the helpless rage of the infant ("*Coriolanus* – and the Delights of Faction," *Hudson Review* 19 [1966]: 200).

15   To see Corioli as the mother's womb here may seem grotesque; the idea becomes less grotesque if we remember Volumnia's own identification of country with mother's womb just as Coriolanus is about to attack another city (see above, p. 331). Wilson ("Coriolanus: The Anxious Bridegroom," pp. 228–9) suggests that Corioli represents defloration; specifically, that it expresses the equation of coitus with damaging assault and the resultant dread of a retaliatory castration.

16   The force of this new name is partly corroborated by Volumnia, who delights in reminding her son of his dependence on her: she has trouble learning his new name from the start (ɪɪ.i.173), and eventually associates it with the pride that keeps him from pity for his family (v.iii.170–1). But several critics have argued convincingly that the self-sufficiency implicit in Coriolanus's acquisition of his new name is ironically undercut from the beginning by the fact that naming of any kind is a social act, so that Coriolanus' acceptance of the name conferred on him by Cominius reveals his dependence on external definition just at the moment when he seems most independent. See, for example, Rabkin, *Shakespeare and the Common Understanding,* pp. 130–2; Lawrence Danson, *Tragic Alphabet: Shakespeare's Drama of Language* (New Haven, CT., 1974), pp. 150–1; Calderwood, "*Coriolanus:* Wordless Meanings and Meaningless Words," pp. 219–23.

17   The father's role in the process of individuation and the consequent significance of Coriolanus's fatherlessness have been pointed out to me by Dr. Malcolm Pines: the father must exist from the start in the potential space between child and mother in order for separation from the mother and hence individuation to take place; the absence of Coriolanus' father thus becomes an essential factor in his failure to separate from his mother.

18   Volumnia's place in the creation of her son's role, and the catastrophic results of her disavowal of it here, have been nearly universally recognized. For a particularly perceptive discussion of the consequences for Coriolanus of his mother's shift in attitude, see Derek Traversi, *Shakespeare: The Roman Plays* (Stanford, CA., 1963), pp. 247–54. In an interesting essay, D. W. Harding suggests Shakespeare's preoccupation during this period with the disastrous effects on men of their living out of women's fantasies of manhood ("Women's Fantasy of Manhood: A Shakespearean Theme," *Shakespeare Quarterly* 20 [1969]: 252–3). Psychoanalytically oriented critics see Coriolanus as the embodiment of his mother's masculine strivings, or, more specifically, as her longed-for penis: see, for example, Ralph Berry, "Sexual Imagery in *Coriolanus,*" *Studies in English Literature,* 13 (1973), 302; Hofling, "An Interpretation of Shakespeare's Coriolanus," pp. 415–16; Stoller, "Shakespearean Tragedy: Coriolanus," pp. 266–7, 271; and Wilson, "Coriolanus: The Anxious Bridegroom," p. 239. Several critics have noticed the importance of acting and the theatrical metaphor in the play: see, for example, William Rosen, *Shakespeare and the Craft of Tragedy* (Cambridge, MA., 1960), pp. 171–3, and Kenneth Muir, *Shakespeare's Tragic Sequence* (London, 1972), pp. 184–5. Harold C. Goddard in *The Meaning of Shakespeare,* Vol. 2 (Chicago, 1951) discusses acting specifically in relation to the role that Volumnia has cast for her son (pp. 216–17); Berry ("Sexual Imagery in *Coriolanus,*" pp. 303–6) points to the acting metaphors as a measure of Coriolanus' inner uncertainty and his fear of losing his manhood if he shifts roles. In an

interesting psychoanalytic essay, Otto Fenichel discusses the derivation of acting from exhibitionism; like all such derivatives, it is ultimately designed to protect against the fear of castration. This argument and his discussion of the actor's relationship to his audience and of shame as the characteristic emotion of an actor at the failure of his role seem to me to have important implications for *Coriolanus*, especially given both Coriolanus' fear that a change of role here would make him womanish and the shame that he feels later when his role begins to fail (v.iii.40–2); see Fenichel, "On Acting," *Psychoanalytic Quarterly* 15 (1946), 144–60.

19 It is telling that Coriolanus tries unsuccessfully to assert that the people are not in fact Roman, hence are no kin to him ("I would they were barbarians – as they are, / ... not Romans – as they are not" [III.i.236–7]): he insists on their non-Romanness as simultaneously a condition contrary to fact and a fact; and his unusual incoherence suggests the tension between his fear that he and the crowd may be alike and his claim that there is no resemblance between them. Goddard (*The Meaning of Shakespeare*, p. 238), Hofling ("An Interpretation of Shakespeare's *Coriolanus*," p. 420), and Smith ("Authoritarian Patterns in Shakespeare's *Coriolanus*," p. 46), among others, discuss Coriolanus' characterization of the crowd as a projection of elements in himself that he wishes to deny, though they do not agree on the precise nature of these elements.

20 And so does Shakespeare. In Plutarch, Coriolanus is accompanied by a few men both when he enters the gates of Corioli and when he is exiled from Rome; Shakespeare emphasizes his isolation by giving him no companions on either occasion. Eugene Waith, in *The Herculean Hero* (New York, 1962), p. 124, and Danson, *Tragic Alphabet*, p. 146, emphasize Coriolanus' position as a whole man among fragments.

21 Barron ("*Coriolanus:* Portrait of the Artist As Infant," pp. 174, 180) associates Coriolanus' hatred of the people's undisciplined hunger with his need to subdue his own impulses; here as elsewhere, his argument is very close to my own.

22 See n. 6 above. The likeness of the crowd to younger siblings who threaten Coriolanus' food supply was first suggested to me by David Sundelson in conversation.

23 Given the importance of Coriolanus' phallic self-sufficiency as a defensive measure, it is not surprising that he should show signs of a fear of castration. This fear may help to account for the enthusiasm with which he characterizes Valeria, in strikingly phallic terms, as the icicle on Dian's temple (v.iii.65–7): the phallic woman may ultimately be less frightening to him than the woman who demonstrates the possibility of castration by her lack of a penis. The same repudiation of the female and hence of the possibility of castration may also lie behind his turning away from Rome and his mother and toward a relationship with Aufidius presented in decidedly homosexual terms (IV.v.107–19, 199–202). Shakespeare takes pains to emphasize the distance between the Aufidius we see and the Aufidius of Coriolanus' imagination: the Aufidius invented by Coriolanus seems designed to reassure Coriolanus of the reality of his own male grandeur by giving him the image of himself; his need to create a man who is his equal is in fact one of the most poignant elements in the play and helps to account for his tragic blindness to his rival's true nature as opportunist and schemer.

24 The fusion of oral and phallic issues in the portrayal of the crowd, and throughout the play, is confirmed by the image of the Hydra. The beast with many heads was of course a conventional analogue for the populace, but the extent to which Shakespeare intensifies and sexualizes this conventional image can be suggested by the grotesqueness of the context in which it first appears overtly in the play, a context of monstrous members and tongues in wounds (II.iii.5–17). The beast with many heads becomes in this play a beast with many mouths; at one point it is even a multiple bosom, digesting (III.i.130). The phallic threat of the crowd, felt in its power to level, is thus mitigated by the insistence on a multiply castrated beast; but the tenuousness of this mitigation is suggested by the insistence on tongues in each mouth (III.i.155).

25 Stoller ("Shakespearean Tragedy: Coriolanus," p. 268) and Wilson ("Coriolanus: The Anxious Bridegroom," p. 230) associate Coriolanus' wounds with castration; for Barron ("*Coriolanus:* Portrait of the Artist As Infant," p. 177) his wounds are a mark of his dependence on his mother. Coriolanus' unwillingness to show his wounds may derive partly from a fear that in standing

"naked" (ii.ii.137) and revealing himself to the people as feminized, he might be inviting a kind of homosexual rape – a fear amply justified by the Third Citizen's remark that, "If he show us his wounds and tell us his deeds, we are to put our tongues into those wounds and speak for them" (ii.iii.5–8; see also Barron, p. 178). Dr. Anne Hayman has suggested to me that Coriolanus' fear of his unconscious homosexual desires, particularly of a passive feminine kind, is essential to his character; she sees his fear of the wish for passive femininity as part of his identification with his mother, who shares the same fear. I am indebted to Dr. Hayman for her careful reading of this paper and her many helpful comments.

26 Donald A. Stauffer, in *Shakespeare's World of Images* (New York, 1949), points out that Rome is less *patria* than *matria* in this play; he discusses Volumnia as a projection of Rome, particularly in v.iii (p. 252). Virtually all psychoanalytic critics comment on the identification of Volumnia with Rome; Barron ("*Coriolanus*: Portrait of the Artist as Infant," p. 175) comments specifically that Coriolanus turns the rage of his frustration in nursing toward his own country at the end of the play.

27 Rufus Putney, in "Coriolanus and His Mother," *Psychoanalytic Quarterly* 31 (1962), finds Coriolanus' inability to deal with his matricidal impulses central to his character; whenever Volumnia threatens him with her death, he capitulates at once (pp. 368–9, 372).

28 G. Wilson Knight discusses the hard metallic quality of the language at length; he associates it with the self-containment of the hostile walled cities and distinguishes it from the fusions characteristic of *Antony and Cleopatra* (*The Imperial Theme*, p. 156). In a particularly interesting discussion, Danson associates the rigidity and distinctness of the language with the play's characteristic use of metonymy and synecdoche, which serve to limit and define, in place of metaphor, which serves to fuse diverse worlds (*Tragic Alphabet*, pp. 155–9).

21

The Avoidance of Love: A Reading of *King Lear*

Stanley Cavell

T
his is the way I understand that opening scene with the three daughters. Lear knows it is a bribe he offers, and – part of him anyway – wants exactly what a bribe can buy: (1) false love and (2) a public expression of love. That is, he wants something he does not have to return *in kind*, something which a division of his property fully pays for. And he wants to *look* like a loved man – for the sake of the subjects, as it were. He is perfectly happy with his little plan, until Cordelia speaks. Happy not because he is blind, but because he is getting what he wants, his plan is working. Cordelia is alarming precisely because he *knows* she is offering the real thing, offering something a more opulent third of his kingdom cannot, must not, repay; putting a claim upon him he cannot face. She threatens to expose both his plan for returning false love with no love, and expose the necessity for that plan – his terror of being loved, of needing love.

Reacting to oversentimental or over-Christian interpretations of her character, interpreters have made efforts to implicate her in the tragedy's source, convincing her of a willfulness and hardness kin to that later shown by her sisters. But her complicity is both less and more than such an interpretation envisages. That interpretation depends, first of all, upon taking her later speeches in the scene (after the appearance of France and Burgundy) as simply uncovering what was in her mind and heart from the beginning. But why? Her first utterance is the aside:

> What shall Cordelia speak? Love, and be silent.

This, presumably, has been understood as indicating her decision to refuse her father's demand. But it needn't be. She asks herself what she can say; there is no necessity for taking the question to be rhetorical. She wants to obey her father's wishes (anyway, there is no reason to think otherwise at this stage, or at any other); but how? She sees from Goneril's speech and Lear's acceptance of it what it is he wants, and she would provide it if she could. But to pretend publicly to love, where you do not love, is easy; to pretend to love, where you really do love, is not obviously possible. She hits on the first solution to her dilemma: Love, and be silent. That is, love *by being* silent. That will do what he seems to want, it will avoid the expression of love, keep it secret. She is his joy; she knows it and he knows it. Surely that is enough? Then Regan speaks, and following that Cordelia's second utterance, again aside:

> Then poor Cordelia!
> And yet not so; since I am sure my love's
> More ponderous than my tongue.
>
> (i.i.76–8)

Presumably, in line with the idea of a defiant Cordelia, this is to be interpreted as a reaffirmation of her decision not to speak. But again, it needn't be. After Lear's acceptance of Regan's characteristic outstripping (she has no ideas of her own; her special vileness is always to increase the measure of pain others are prepared to inflict; her mind is itself a lynch mob) Cordelia may realize that she will *have* to say something. "More ponderous than my tongue" suggests that she is going to move it, not that it is immovable – which would make it more ponderous than her love. And this produces her second groping for an exit from the dilemma: to speak, but making her love seem less than it is, out of love. Her tongue will move, and obediently, but against her condition – then poor Cordelia, making light of her love. And yet *she* knows the truth. Surely that is enough?

But when the moment comes, she is speechless: "Nothing, my lord." I do not deny that this can be read defiantly, as can the following "You have begot me, bred me, lov'd me" speech. She is outraged, violated, confused, so young; Lear is torturing her, claiming her devotion, which she wants to give, but forcing her to help him betray (or not to betray) it, to falsify it publicly. (Lear's ambiguity here, wanting at once to open and to close her mouth, further shows the ordinariness of the scene, its verisimilitude to common parental love, swinging between absorption and rejection of its offspring, between encouragement to a rebellion they failed to make and punishment for it.) It may be that with Lear's active violation, she snaps; her resentment provides her with words, and she levels her abdication of love at her traitorous, shameless father:

> Happily, when I shall wed,
> That lord whose hand must take my plight shall carry
> Half my love with him.
>
> (i.i.100–2)

The trouble is, the words are too calm, too cold for the kind of sharp rage and hatred real love can produce. She is never in possession of her situation, "her voice was ever soft, gentle and low" (v.iii.272–3); she is young, and "least" (i.i.83). (This notation of her stature and of the quality of her voice is unique in the play. The idea of a defiant *small* girl seems grotesque, as an idea of Cordelia.) All her words are words of love; to love is all she knows how to do. That is her problem, and at the cause of the tragedy of King Lear.

I imagine the scene this way: The older daughters' speeches are public, set; they should not be said to Lear, but to the court, sparing themselves his eyes and him theirs. They are not monsters first, but ladies. He is content. Then Cordelia says to him, away from the court, in confused appeal to their accustomed intimacy, "Nothing" – don't force me, I don't know what you want, there is nothing I can say, to speak what you want I must not speak. But he is alarmed at the appeal and tries to cover it up, keeping up the front, and says, speaking to her and to the court, as if the ceremony is still in full effect: "Nothing will come of nothing; speak again." (*Hysterica passio* is already stirring.) Again she says to *him:* "Unhappy that I am, I cannot heave my heart into my mouth" – not the heart which loves him, that always has been present in her voice; but the heart which is shuddering with confusion, with wanting to do the impossible, the heart which is now in her throat. But to no avail. Then the next line would be her first attempt to obey him by speaking publicly: "I love your Majesty according to my bond; no more or less" – not stinting, not telling *him* the truth (what is the true *amount* of love this loving young girl knows to measure with her bond?), not refusing him, but still trying to conceal her love, to lighten its full measure. Then her father's brutally public, and perhaps still publicly considerate, "How, how, Cordelia! Mend your speech a little, lest you may mar your fortunes." So she tries again to divide her kingdom ("... that lord whose hand must take my plight shall carry half my love with him"). Why should she wish to shame him publicly? He has shamed himself and everyone knows it. She is trying to conceal him; and to do that she cuts herself in two. (In the end, he faces what she has done here: "Upon such sacrifices, my Cordelia ..." Lear cannot, at that late moment, be thinking of prison as a sacrifice. I imagined him there partly remembering this first scene, and the first of Cordelia's sacrifices – of love to convention.)

After this speech, said in suppression, confusion, abandonment, she is shattered, by her failure and by Lear's viciousness to her. Her sisters speak again only when they are left alone, to plan. Cordelia revives and speaks after France enters and has begun to speak *for* her:

> Sure, her offence
> Must be of such unnatural degree
> That monsters it, or your fore-vouch'd affection
> Fall into taint; which to believe of her,
> Must be a faith that reason without miracle
> Should never plant in me.
>
> (1.i.218–23)

France's love shows him the truth. Tainted love is the answer, love dyed – not decayed or corrupted exactly; Lear's love is still alive, but expressed as, colored over with, hate. Cordelia finds her voice again, protected in France's love, and she uses it to change the subject, still protecting Lear from discovery.

A reflection of what Cordelia now must feel is given by one's rush of gratitude toward France, one's almost wild relief as he speaks his beautiful trust. She does not ask her father to relent, but only to give France some explanation. Not the right explanation:

What has "that glib and oily art" got to do with it? That is what her sisters needed, because their task was easy: to dissemble. Convention perfectly suits these ladies. But she lets it go at that – he hates me because I would not flatter him. The truth is, she *could* not flatter; not because she was too proud or too principled, though these might have been the reasons, for a different character; but because nothing she could have done would have *been* flattery – at best it would have been *dissembled flattery*. There is no convention for doing what Cordelia was asked to do. It is not that Goneril and Regan have taken the words out of her mouth, but that here she cannot say them, because for her they are true ("Dearer than eye-sight, space and liberty"). She is not disgusted by her sisters' flattery (it's nothing new); but heartbroken at hearing the words she wishes she were in a position to say. So she is sent, and taken, away. Or half of her leaves; the other half remains, in Lear's mind, in Kent's service, and in the Fool's love.

(I spoke just now of "one's" gratitude and relief toward France. I was remembering my feeling at a production given by students at Berkeley during 1946 in which France – a small part, singled out by Granville-Barker as particularly requiring an actor of authority and distinction – was given his full sensitivity and manliness, a combination notably otherwise absent from the play, as mature womanliness is. The validity of such feelings as touchstones of the accuracy of a reading of the play, and which feelings one is to trust and which not, ought to be discussed problems of criticism.)

It may be felt that I have forced this scene too far in order to fit it to my reading, that too many directions have to be provided to its acting in order to keep the motivation smooth. Certainly I have gone into more detail of this kind here than elsewhere, and I should perhaps say why. It is, first of all, the scene in which the problem of performance, or the performability, of this play comes to a head, or to its first head. Moreover, various interpretations offered of this scene are direct functions of attempts to *visualize* its progress; as though a critic's conviction about the greatness or weakness of the scene is a direct function of the success or unsuccess with which he or she has been able to imagine it concretely. Critics will invariably dwell on the motivations of Lear and Cordelia in this scene as a problem, even while taking their motivation later either as more or less obvious or for some other reason wanting no special description; and in particular, the motives or traits of character attributed to them here will typically be ones which have an immediate visual implication, ones in which, as it were, a psychological trait and its physical expression most nearly coalesce: at random, Lear is described as irascible (Schüking), arrogant, choleric, overbearing (Schlegel); Cordelia as shy, reluctant (Schüking), sullen, prideful (Coleridge), obstinate (Muir). This impulse seems to me correct, and honest: it is one thing to say that Cordelia's behavior in the opening scene is not inconsistent with her behavior when she reappears, but another to *show* its consistency. This is what I have wanted to test in visualizing her behavior in that scene. But it is merely a test, it proves nothing about my reading, except its actability; or rather, a performance on these lines would, or would not, prove that. And that is a further problem of aesthetics – to chart the relations between a text (or score), an analysis or interpretation of it, and a performance in terms of that analysis or interpretation.

The problem is not, as it is often put, that no performance is ideal, because this suggests we have some clear idea of what an ideal performance would be, perhaps an idea of it as embodying all true interpretations, every resonance of the text struck under analysis. But this is no more possible, or comprehensible, than an experiment which is to verify every implication of a theory. (Then what makes a theory convincing?) Performances are actions, and the imitations of actions. As with any action, performance cannot contain the totality of a human life – though one action can have a particularly summary or revelatory quality, and another will occur at a crossroads, and another will spin tangentially to the life and circumstances which call it out, or rub irrelevantly or mechanically against another. Some have no meaning for us at all, others have more resonance than they can express – as a resultant force answers to forces not visible in the one direction it selects. (Then what makes action bearable, or comprehensible?) I cannot at will give my past expression, though every gesture expresses it, and each elation and headache; my character is its epitome, as if the present were a pantomime of ghostly selections. What is necessary to a performance is what is necessary to action in the present, that it have its autonomy, and that it be in character, or out, and that it have a specific context and motive. Even if everything I have said about Cordelia is true, it needn't be registered explicitly in the way that first scene is played – there may, for example, be merit in stylizing it drastically. Only there will be no effort to present us with a sullen or prideful or defiant girl who reappears, with nothing intervening to change her, as the purest arch of love.

Nor, of course, has my rendering of the first scene been meant to bring out all the motivations or forces which cross there. For example, it might be argued that part of Lear's strategy is exactly to put Cordelia into the position of being denied her dowry, so that he will not lose her in marriage; if so, it half worked, and required the magnanimity of France to turn it aside. Again, nothing has been said of the theme of politics which begins here and pervades the action. Not just the familiar Shakespearean theme which opens the interplay between the public and private lives of the public creature, but the particularity of the theme in this play, which is about the interpenetration and confusion of politics with love; something which, in modern societies, is equally the fate of private creatures – whether in the form of divided loyalties, or of one's relation to the state, or, more pervasively, in the new forms love and patriotism themselves take: love wielding itself in gestures of power, power extending itself with claims of love. *Phèdre* is perhaps the greatest play concentrated to this theme of the body politic, and of the body, torn by the privacy of love; as it is closest to *King Lear* in its knowledge of shame as the experience of unacceptable love. And Machiavelli's knowledge of the world is present; not just in his attitudes of realism and cynicism, but in his experience of the condition to which these attitudes are appropriate – in which the inner and outer worlds have become totally disconnected, and man's life is all public, among strangers, seen only from outside. Luther saw the same thing at the same time, but from inside. For some, like Edmund, this is liberating knowledge, lending capacity for action. It is what Lear wants to abdicate from. For what Lear is doing in that first scene is trading power for love (pure power for mixed love); this is what his opening speech explicitly says. He imagines that this will prevent future strife now; but he is being counseled by his impotence, which is not the result of his bad decision, but produces it: he feels powerless to *appoint* his successor, recognized as the ultimate test of authority. The consequence is that politics becomes private, and so vanishes, with power left to serve hatred.

The final scene opens with Lear and Cordelia repeating or completing their actions in their opening scene; again Lear abdicates, and again Cordelia loves and is silent. Its readers have for centuries wanted to find consolation in this end: heavy opinion sanctioned Tate's Hollywood ending throughout the eighteenth century, which resurrects Cordelia; and in our time, scorning such vulgarity, the same impulse fastidiously digs itself deeper and produces redemption for Lear in Cordelia's figuring of transcendent love. But Dr. Johnson is surely right, more honest and more responsive: Cordelia's death is so shocking that we would avoid it if we could – if we have responded to it. And so the question, since her death is restored to us, is forced upon us: Why does she die? And this is not answered by asking, What does her death mean? (cp. Christ died to save sinners); but by answering, What killed her? (cp. Christ was killed by us, because his news was unendurable).

Lear's opening speech of this final scene is not the correction but the repetition of his strategy in the first scene, or a new tactic designed to win the old game; and it is equally disastrous.

> *Cord:* Shall we not see these daughters and these sisters?
> *Lear:* No, no, no, no!
>
> (v.iii.7–8)

He cannot finally face the thing he has done; and this means what it always does, that he cannot bear being seen. He is anxious to go off to prison, with Cordelia; his love now is in the open – that much circumstance has done for him; but it remains imperative that it be confined, out of sight. (Neither Lear nor Cordelia, presumably, knows that the soldier in command is Gloucester's son; they feel unknown.) He is still ashamed, and the fantasy expressed in this speech ("We two alone will sing like birds i' the cage") is the same fantasy he brings on the stage with him in the first scene, the thwarting of which causes his maddened destructiveness. There Cordelia had offered him the marriage pledge ("Obey you, love you, and most honor you"), and she has shared his fantasy fully enough to wish to heal political strife with a kiss (or perhaps it is just the commonest fantasy of women):

> *Cord:* Restoration hang
>   Thy medicine on my lips.
>   (iv.vii.26–7)

(But after such abdication, what restoration? The next time we hear the words "hang" and "medicine," they announce death.) This gesture is as fabulous as anything in the opening scene. Now, at the end, Lear returns her pledge with his lover's song, his invitation to voyage ("... so we'll live, and pray, and sing, and tell old tales, and laugh"). The fantasy of this speech is as full of detail as a daydream, and it is clearly a happy dream for Lear. He has found at the end a way to have what he has wanted from the beginning. His tone is not: We shall love *even though* we are in prison; but: Because we are hidden together we can love. He has come to accept his love, not by making room in the world for it, but by denying its relevance to the world. He does not renounce the world in going to prison, but flees from it, to earthly pleasure. The astonishing image of "God's spies" (v.iii.17) stays beyond me, but in part it contains the final emphasis upon looking without being seen; and it cites an intimacy which requires no reciprocity with real men. Like Gloucester toward Dover, Lear anticipates God's call. He is not experiencing reconciliation with a daughter, but partnership in a mystic marriage.

If so, it cannot be, as is often suggested, that when he says,

> Upon such sacrifices, my Cordelia,
> The Gods themselves throw incense.
> (v.iii.20–1)

he is thinking simply of going to prison with Cordelia as a sacrifice. It seems rather that, the lines coming immediately after his love song, it is their love itself which has the meaning of sacrifice. As though the ideas of love and of death are interlocked in his mind – and in particular of death as a payment or placation for the granting of love. His own death, because acknowledging love still presents itself to him as an annihilation of himself. And her death, because now that he admits her love, he must admit, what he knew from the beginning, that he is impotent to sustain it. This is the other of Cordelia's sacrifices – of love to secrecy.

Edmund's death reinforces the juncture of these ideas, for it is death which releases his capacity for love. It is this release which permits his final act:

> ... some good I mean to do
> Despite of mine own nature. Quickly send ...
> (v.iii.243–4)

What has released him? Partly, of course, the presence of his own death; but that in itself need not have worked this way. Primarily it is the fact that all who have loved him, or claimed love for him, are dead. He has eagerly prompted Edgar to tell the tale of their father's death; his reaction upon hearing of Goneril's and Regan's deaths is as to a solution to impossible, or illegitimate, love: "All three now marry in an instant"; and his immediate reaction upon seeing their dead bodies is: "Yet Edmund was belov'd." *That* is what he wanted to know, and he can acknowledge it now, when it cannot be returned, now that its claim is dead. In his following speech he means well for the first time.

It can be said that what Lear is ashamed of is not his need for love and his inability to return it, but of the *nature* of his love for Cordelia. It is too far from plain love of father for daughter. Even if we resist seeing in it the love of lovers, it is at least incompatible with the idea of her having any (other) lover. There is a moment, beyond the words, when this comes to the surface of the action. It is the moment Lear is waking from his madness, no longer incapable of seeing the world, but still not strong enough to protect his thoughts: "Methinks I should know you and know this man" (iv.vii.64). I take it "this man" is generally felt to refer to Kent (disguised as Caius), for there is clearly no reason to suppose Lear knows the Doctor, the only other man present. Certainly this is plausible; but in fact Lear never does acknowledge Kent, as he does his child Cordelia.[1] And after this recognition he goes on to ask, "Am I in France?" This question irresistibly (to me) suggests that the man he thinks he should know is the man he expects to be with his daughter, her husband. This would be unmistakable if he directs his "this man" to the Doctor, taking him for, but not able to make him out as, France. He finds out it is not, and the next time we see him he is pressing off to prison with his child, and there is no further thought of her husband. It is a standing complaint that Shakespeare's explanation of France's absence is perfunctory. It is more puzzling that Lear himself never refers to him, not even when he is depriving him of her forever. Either France has ceased to exist for Lear, or it is importantly from him that he wishes to reach the shelter of prison.

I do not wish to suggest that "avoidance of love" and "avoidance of a particular kind of love" are alternative hypotheses about this play. On the contrary, they seem to me to interpret one another. Avoidance of love is always, or always begins as, an avoidance of a particular kind of love: human beings do not just naturally not love, they learn not to. And our lives begin by having to accept under the name of love whatever closeness is offered, and by then having to forgo its object. And the avoidance of a particular love, or the acceptance of it, will spread to every other; every love, in acceptance or rejection, is mirrored in every other. It is part of the miracle of the vision in *King Lear* to bring this before us, so that we do not care whether the *kind* of love felt between these two is forbidden according to humanity's lights. We care whether love is or is not altogether forbidden to us, whether we may not altogether be incapable of it, of admitting it into our world. We wonder whether we may always go mad between the equal efforts and terrors at once of rejecting and of accepting love. The soul torn between them, the body feels torn (producing a set of images accepted since Caroline Spurgeon's *Shakespeare's Imagery* as central to *King Lear*), and the solution to this insoluble condition is to wish for the tearing apart of the world.

Lear wishes to escape into prison for another old reason – because he is unwilling to be seen to weep.

> The good years shall devour them, flesh and fell,
> Ere they shall make us weep: we'll see 'em starved first.
>   (v.iii.24–5)

See them shalt thou never. And in the end he still avoids Cordelia. He sees that she is weeping after his love song ("Wipe thine eyes"). But why is she in tears? Why does Lear think she is? Lear imagines that she is crying for the reasons that he is on the verge of tears – the old reasons, the sense of impotence, shame, loss. But *her* reasons for tears do not occur to him, that she sees him as he is, as he was, that he is unable to take his last chance; that he, at the farthest edge of life, must again sacrifice her, again abdicate his responsibilities; and that he cannot know what he asks. And yet, seeing that, it is for him that she is cast down. Upon such knowledge the gods themselves throw incense.

It is as though her response here is her knowledge of the end of the play; she alone has the capacity of compassion Lear will need when we next see him, with Cordelia dead in his arms: "Howl, howl, howl! O! you are men of stones." (Cp. the line and a half Dante gives to Ugolino, facing his doomed sons, a fragment shored by Arnold: "I did not weep, I so turned to stone within. They wept.") Again he begins to speak by turning on those at hand: "A plague upon you, murderers, traitors all!" But then the tremendous knowledge is released: "I might have saved her." From the beginning, and through each moment until they are led to prison, he might have saved her, had he done what every love requires, put himself aside long enough to see through to her, and be seen through. I do not mean that it is clear that he could, at the end, have done what Edmund feared ("pluck the common bosom on his side, And turn our impress'd lances in our eyes"); but it is not clear that he could not. And even if he had not succeeded, her death would not be on his hands. In his last speech, "No, no, no, no" becomes "No, no, no life!" His need, or his interpretation of his need, becomes her sentence. This is what is unbearable. Or bearable only out of the capacity of Cordelia. If we are to weep her fortunes we must take her eyes.

Is this a Christian play? The question is very equivocal. When it is answered affirmatively, Cordelia is viewed as a Christ figure whose love redeems nature and transfigures Lear. So far as this is intelligible to me, I find it false both to the experience of the play and to the fact that it *is* a play. *King Lear* is not illustrated theology (anyway, which theology is thought to be illustrated, what understanding of atonement, redemption, etc., is thought to be figured?), and nature and Lear are not touched, but run out. If Cordelia exemplifies Christ, it is at the moment of crucifixion, not resurrection. But the moment of his death is the moment when Christ resembles us, finally takes the human condition fully into himself. (This is why every figure reaching the absolute point of rejection starts becoming a figure of Christ. And perhaps why it is so important to the Christ story that it begins with birth and infancy.) It is in his *acceptance* of this condition that we are to resemble him. If Cordelia resembles Christ, it is by having become fully human, by knowing her separateness, by knowing the deafness of miracles, by accepting the unacceptability of her love, and by nevertheless maintaining her love and the whole knowledge it brings. One can say she "redeems nature" (IV.vi.207), but this means nothing miraculous, only that she shows nature not to be the cause of evil – there is no cause in nature which makes these hard hearts, and no cause outside either. The cause is the heart itself, the having of a heart in a world made heartless. Lear is the cause. Murderers, traitors *all*.

Another way, the play can be said to be Christian – not because it shows us redemption (it does not) but because it throws our redemption into *question*, and leaves it up to us. But there is no suggestion that we can take it up only through Christ. On the contrary, there is reason to take this drama as an alternative to the Christian one. In the first place, Christianity, like every other vision of the play, is not opted for, but tested. Specifically, as was said earlier, in Edgar's conduct; more generally, in its suggestion that all appeals to gods are distractions or excuses, because the imagination uses them to wish for complete, for final solutions, when what is needed is at hand, or nowhere. But isn't this what Christ meant? And isn't this what Lear fails to see in wishing to be God's spy before he is God's subject? Cordelia is further proof of this: her grace is shown by the absence in her of any unearthly experiences; she is the only good character whose attention is wholly on earth, on the person nearest her. It is during the storm that Lear's mind clouds most and floods with philosophy; when it clears, Cordelia is present.

These considerations take us back to the set of ideas which see Lear as having arrived, in the course of the storm, at the naked human condition – as if the storm was the granting of his prayer to "feel what wretches feel." It may seem that I have denied this in underlining Lear's cruelty to Gloucester and in placing him at the cause of Cordelia's death, because it may feel as if I am blaming Lear for his behavior here.[2] And what room is there for blame? Is he to blame for being human? For being subject to a cosmic anxiety and to fantasies which enclose him from perfect compassion? Certainly blame is inappropriate, for certainly I do not claim to know what *else* Lear might do. And yet I cannot deny that my pain at Lear's actions is not overcome by my knowledge of his own suffering. I might describe my experience of him here as one of unplaceable blame, blame no one can be asked to bear and no one is in a position to level – like blaming heaven. That does not seem to me inappropriate as an experience of tragedy, of what it is for which tragedy provides catharsis. (Neither Kent nor Cordelia requires tragedy for purification; the one preceding, the other transcending personal morality.) What I am denying is that to say Lear becomes simply a man is to say that he achieves the unaccommodated human condition. The ambiguities here stand out in William Empson's suggestion of Lear as scapegoat and outcast.[3] This cannot be wrong, but it can be made too much of, or the wrong thing. We do not want the extremity of Lear's suffering to have gone for nothing, or for too little, so we may imagine that it has made him capable of envisioning ours. But as the storm is ending he is merely humanly a scapegoat, as any man is on the wrong end of injustice; and no more an outcast than any man out of favor. Only at his finish does his suffering measure the worst that can happen to a man, and there not because he is a scapegoat but because he has made a scapegoat of his love. But that Cordelia is Lear's scapegoat is compatible with Lear's being ours. And seeing him as a scapegoat is not incompatible with seeing him as avoiding love – on the contrary, it is this which shows what his connection with us is, the act for which he bears total, sacrificial consequences. If this play contains scapegoats, it is also about scapegoats, about what it is which creates scapegoats and about the cost of creating them. To insist upon Lear as scapegoat is apt to thin our sense of this general condition in his world; and this again would put us in his position – not *seeing* it from his point of view (maintaining ours), but accepting his point of view, hence denying the other characters, and using the occasion not to feel for him (and them) but to sympathize with ourselves.

All the good characters are exiled, cast out – Cordelia and Kent initially, Edgar at the beginning and Lear at the end of Act II, Gloucester at the end of Act III. But there is from the opening lines a literal social outcast of another kind, the bastard, the central evil character. A play which has the power of transforming kings into fools equally has the power of overlapping kings and bastards – the naked human condition is more than any man bargains for. Empson finds Lear's "most distinct expression of the scapegoat idea" in the lines

> None does offend, none; I say none. I'll able 'em:
> Take that of me, my friend, who have the power
> To seal the accuser's lips.
>
> (IV.vi.170–2)

Empson reads: "The royal prerogative has become the power of the outcast to deal directly on behalf of mankind." I do not question the presence of this feeling, but it is equivocal. For what is the nature of this new, direct power of sealing lips? The problem is not just that "None does offend, none; I say none" protests too much, as though Lear can't quite believe it. The problem is that Edmund also deals with men to seal their lips, and he can directly, even elatedly, use this human power because he is an outcast, because judgment has *already* been passed upon him. That is the justice of his position. And he could express himself in the words "None does offend." He would mean, as in his second soliloquy (i.ii.124–40), that all are equally evil and evasive; hence no man is in a position from which to judge offense in others.

What would this prove, except that the Devil can quote scripture? But that is proof enough if it proves that the greatest truths are nothing, mean harm or help or nothing, apart from their application in the individual case. We see (do we see?) how Edmund's meaning repudiates the Gospels: he is not speaking on behalf of mankind, but on his own; and he is not forgoing judgment, but escaping it by making it indiscriminate, cynicizing it. Then do we see how Lear's mind, in its rage at injustice, is different from Edmund's? For Lear too has a private use for this indiscriminate condemnation of the world. Suppose we see in the progress of Lear's madness a recapitulation of the history of civilization or of consciousness: from the breaking up of familial bonds and the release of offenses which destroy the social cosmos (iii.iv), through the fragile replacement of revenge by the institution of legal justice (iii.iv), to the corruption of justice itself and the breaking up of civil bonds (iv.vi). In raging with each of these stages in turn, Lear's mind gusts to a calm as the storm calms, drawing even with the world as it goes. (This is why, adapting Empson's beautiful and compassionate perception, Lear at this point removes his boots, at home again in the world.) If he is an outcast, every man is, whose society is in rags about him; if he is a scapegoat, every man is, under the general shiftings of blame and in the inaccuracy of justice. Lear has not arrived at the human condition he saw imaged in poor naked Tom (the sight which tipped him from world-destroying rage into world-creating madness); but one could say he now has this choice open to him. He finds himself a man; so far he has abdicated. But he has not yet chosen his mortality, to be one man among others; so far he is not at one; atonement is not complete. He has come to terms with Goneril and Regan, with filial ingratitude; he has come back from the way he *knew* madness lies. But he has not come to terms with parental insatiability (which he denounced in his "barbarous Scythian" speech [i.i.116], and which Gloucester renounces in "the food of thy abused father's wrath" [iv.i.22]). He has not come back to Cordelia. And he does not.

Evidence for this in this scene is not solely that his "None does offend" is said still stranded in madness (nor even in the possible hint of power in the fact that he does not just take off his boots but imagines them removed for him, as by a servant) but in the content of his ensuing sermon ("I will preach to thee"):

> When we are born, we cry that we are come
> To this great stage of fools.
>
> (iv.vi.184–5)

This is a sermon, presumably, because it interprets the well-known text of tears with which each human life begins. But, as Empson puts it, "the babies cannot be supposed to know all this about human affairs." I think Lear is there feeling like a child, after the rebirth of his senses (children do naturally "wawl and cry" at injustice); and feeling that the world is an unnatural habitat for man; and feeling it is unnatural because it is a stage. Perhaps it is a stage because its actors are seen by heaven, perhaps because they are seen by one another. Either way, it is Lear (not, for example, Gloucester, Lear's congregation) who sees it there as a stage. But why a stage of fools? There will be as many answers as there are meanings of "fool." But the point around which all the answers will turn is that it is when, and because, he sees the world as a stage that he sees it peopled with fools, with distortions of persons, with natural scapegoats, among whom human relationship does not arise. Then who is in a position to level this vision at the world? Not, of course, that it is invalid – no one could deny it. The catch is that there is no one to assert it – without asserting himself a fool. The world-accusing fool, like the world-accusing liar, suffers a paradox. Which is why "the praise of Folly" must mean "Folly's praise."

But if the sense in which, or way in which, Lear has become a scapegoat is not special about him, he can be said to be special there in his *feeling* that he is a scapegoat and in his universal casting of the world with scapegoats. This is an essential connection between him and Gloucester's family: Gloucester is in fact turned out of society, and while he is not left feeling that society has made a scapegoat of him, he has made scapegoats of his sons, deprived each of his birthright, the one by nature and custom, the other by decree. Each reciprocates by casting his father out, in each case by a stratagem, though the one apparently acts out of hatred, the other apparently out of love; and each of the brothers makes a scapegoat of the other, the one by nature and custom, the other by design. Like Edgar, Lear casts himself in the role of scapegoat, and then others suffer for it; like Edmund, he finds himself the natural fool of Fortune, a customary scapegoat, and then kill, kill, kill, kill, kill, kill (cf. iv.vi.189) – the mind clawing at itself for a hold. These nests of doublings (and in no play is Shakespeare's familiar doubling of themes so relentless, becoming something like the medium of the drama itself, or its vision of the world) suggest that the dramatic point of Shakespeare's doublings is not so much to amplify or univer-salize a theme as to focus or individuate it, and in particular to show the freedom under each character's possession of his character. Each way of responding to one's foolishness is tested by every other; each way of accepting one's having been cast out is tested by every other; that Gloucester is not driven mad by filial ingratitude (though he is no stranger to the possibility: his very openness in looking at it ["I'll tell thee, friend, I am almost mad myself" (iii.iv.169–70)] makes him a sensitive touchstone of normalcy in this) means that there is no necessary route Lear's spirit has followed. One will want to object that from the fact that a route is not necessary to Gloucester it does not follow that it is not necessary to Lear. But that is the point. To find out why it is necessary one has to discover who Lear is, what *he* finds necessary, his specific spins of need and choice. His tragedy is that he has to find out too, and that he cannot rest with less than an answer. "Who is it that can tell me who I am?" (i.iv.238). At the first rebuff in his new condition, Lear is forced to the old tragic question. And the Fool lets out his astonishing knowledge: "Lear's shadow." At this point Lear either does not hear, or he thinks the Fool has *told* him who he is, and takes it, as it seems easy to take it, to mean roughly that he is in reduced circumstances. It would be somewhat harder to take if he heard the suggestion of *shade* under "shadow." But the truth may still be harder to be told, harder than anything that can just be told.

Suppose the Fool has precisely answered Lear's question, which is only characteristic of him. Then his reply means: Lear's shadow can tell you who you are. If this is heard, it will mean that the answer to Lear's question is held in the inescapable Lear which is now obscure and obscuring, and in the inescapable Lear which is projected upon the world, and that Lear is double and has a double. And then this play reflects another long curve of feeling about doubling, describing an emphasis other than my recent suggestion that it haunts the characters with their freedom. In the present guise it taunts the characters with their lack of wholeness, their separation from themselves, by loss or denial or opposition. (In Montaigne: "We are, I know not how, double in ourselves, so that what we believe we disbelieve, and cannot rid ourselves of what we condemn."[4] By the time of Heine's *Doppelgänger* ["Still ist die Nacht ..."], the self is split from its past and from its own feeling, however intimately present both may be.) But in either way, either by putting freedom or by putting integrity into question, doubling sets a task, of discovery, of acknowledgment. And both ways are supported in the moment Lear faces Gloucester and confuses identities with him.

If on a given experience of the play one is caught by the reference to adultery and then to "Gloucester's bastard son" which launches Lear's long tirade against the foulness of nature and of man's justice, one may find that absent member of the Gloucester family presiding over Lear's mind here. For Lear's disgust with sexual nature is not far from Edmund's early manic praise of it, especially in their joint sense of the world as alive in its pursuit; and Edmund's stinging sensitivity to the illegitimacy of society's "legitimacy" prefigures Lear's knowledge of the injustice of society's "justice." If, therefore, we are to see in this play, in Miss Welsford's fine phrase, the investing of the king with motley, then in this scene we may see the king standing up for bastards – an illegitimate king in an unlawful world. (Edmund had tossed off a prayer for bastards, and perhaps there is a suggestion that the problem with prayers is not that few are answered but that *all* are, one way or another.) As the doublings reflect one another, each character projecting some more or less eccentric angle to a common theme, one glimpses the possibility of a common human nature which each, in his or her own way, fails to achieve; or perhaps glimpses the idea that its gradual achievement is the admission of reflection in oneself of every human theme. As Christ receives reflection in every form of human scapegoat, every way in which one man bears the brunt of another's distortion and rejection. For us the reflection is brightest in Cordelia, because of her acceptance, perhaps because she is hanged; it is present, on familiar grounds, in the mysteries of the Fool. I cannot help feeling it, if grossly, in the figure of the bastard son. I do not press this. Yet it makes us reflect that evil is not wrong when it thinks of itself as good, for at those times it recaptures a craving for goodness, an experience of its own innocence which the world rejects.

There is hope in this play, and it is not in heaven. It lies in the significance of its two most hideous moments: Gloucester's blinding and Cordelia's death. In Gloucester's history we found hope, because while his weakness has left him open to the uses of evil, evil *has* to turn upon him because it cannot bear him to witness. As long as that is true, evil does not have *free* sway over the world. In Cordelia's death there is hope, because it shows the gods more just – more than we had hoped or wished: Lear's prayer is answered again in this. The gods are, in Edgar's wonderful idea, clear. Cordelia's death means that *every* falsehood, every refusal of acknowledgment, will be tracked down. In the realm of the spirit, Kierkegaard says, there is absolute justice. Fortunately, because if all we had to go on were the way the world goes, we would lose the concept of justice altogether; and then human life would become unbearable. Kant banked the immortality of the soul on the fact that in *this* world goodness and happiness are unaligned – a condition which, if never righted, is incompatible with moral sanity, and hence with the existence of God. But immortality is not necessary for the soul's satisfaction. What is necessary is its own coherence, its ability to judge a world in which evil is successful and the good are doomed; and in particular its knowledge that while injustice may flourish, it cannot rest content. This, I take it, is what Plato's *Republic* is about. And it is an old theme of tragedy.

Its companion theme is that our actions have consequences which outrun our best, and worst, intentions. The drama of *King Lear* not merely embodies this theme, it comments on it, even deepens it. For what it shows is that the *reason* consequences furiously hunt us down is not merely that we are half blind, and unfortunate, but that we go on doing the thing which produced these consequences in the first place. What we need is not rebirth, or salvation, but the courage, or plain prudence, to see and to stop. To abdicate. But what do we need in order to do that? It would be salvation.

Notes

1   Professor Jonas Barish – to whom I am indebted for other suggestions about this essay as well as the present one – has pointed out to me that in my eagerness to solve all the *King Lear* problems I have neglected trying an account of Kent's plan in delaying making himself known ("Yet to be known shortens my made intent" [iv.vii.9]). This omission is particularly important because Kent's is the one delay that causes no harm to others; hence it provides an internal measure of those harms. I do not understand his "dear cause" (iv.iii.52), but I think the specialness of Kent's delay has to do with these facts: (1) It never prevents his perfect faithfulness to his duties of service; these do not require – Kent does not permit them to require – personal recognition in order to be performed. This sense of the finitude of the demands placed upon Kent, hence of the harm and of the good he can perform, is a function of his complete absorption into his social office, in turn a function of his being the only principal character in the play (apart from the Fool) who does not appear as a member of a *family*. (2) He does not delay revealing himself to Cordelia, only (presumably) to Lear. A reason for that would be that since the king has banished him it is up to the king to reinstate him; he will not presume on his old rank. (3) If his plan goes beyond finding some way, or just waiting, for Lear to recognize him first (not out of pride but out of right) then perhaps it is made irrelevant by finding Lear again only in his terminal state, or perhaps it always consisted only in doing what he tries to do there, find an opportunity to tell Lear about Caius and ask for pardon. It may be wondered that we do not feel Lear's fragmentary recognitions of Kent to leave something undone, nor Kent's hopeless attempts to hold Lear's attention to be crude intrusions, but rather to amplify a sadness already amplified past sensing. This may be accounted for partly by Kent's pure expression of the special poignance of the servant's office, requiring a life centered in another life, exhausted in loyalty and in silent witnessing (a silence Kent broke and Lear must mend); partly by the fact that Cordelia has fully recognized him: "To be

acknowledg'd, Madam, is o'er-paid" (iv.vii.4); partly by the fact that when his master Lear is dead, it is his master who calls him, and his last words are those of obedience.

2   In a detailed and very useful set of comments on an earlier draft of this essay, Professor Alpers mentions this as a possible response to what I had written; and it was his suggestion of Empson's appeal to the scapegoat idea as offering a truer response to Lear's condition that sent me back to Empson's essay (see note 3). It was as an effort to do justice to Alpers's reaction that I have included the ensuing discussion of scapegoats in *King Lear*. Beyond this, I have altered or expanded several other passages in the light of his comments, for all of which I am grateful.

3   "Fool in Lear," in *The Structure of Complex Words* (Ann Arbor: University of Michigan Press [Ann Arbor Paperback], 1967), pp. 145, 157. Because of Empson's espousal of it, George Orwell's essay on Lear may be mentioned here ("Lear, Tolstoy and the Fool," reprinted from *Shooting an Elephant and Other Essays*, in F. Kermode, ed., *Four Centuries of Shakespearean Criticism* [New York: Avon Books, 1965], pp. 514–31). It is, perhaps, of the nature of Orwell's piece that one finds oneself remembering the feel of its moral passion and honesty and the clarity of its hold on the idea of *renunciation* as the subject of the play, without being able oneself to produce Orwell's, or one's own, evidence for the idea in the play – except that the meaning of the entire opening and the sense of its consequences assume, as it were, a self-evidence within the light of that idea. It is probably as good a notation of the subject as one word could give, and Orwell's writing, here as elsewhere, is exemplary of a correct way in which the moral sensibility, distrusting higher ambitions, exercises its right to judge an imperfect world, never exempting itself from that world.

4   Auden uses this as the epigraph to *The Double Man;* I have not yet found its context.

22

To Entrap the Wisest: Sacrificial Ambivalence in *The Merchant of Venice* and *Richard III*

René Girard

The criticism of *The Merchant of Venice* has been dominated by two images of Shylock that appear irreconcilable. It is my contention that both images belong to the play and that, far from rendering it unintelligible, their conjunction is essential to an understanding of Shakespeare's dramatic practice.

The first image is that of the Jewish moneylender in the late-medieval and modern book of anti-Semitism. The mere evocation of that Jewish stereotype suggests a powerful system of binary oppositions that does not have to be fully developed to pervade the entire play. First comes the opposition between Jewish greed and Christian generosity, between revenge and compassion, between the crankiness of old age and the charm of youth, between the dark and the luminous, the beautiful and the ugly, the gentle and the harsh, the musical and the unmusical, and so on.

There is a second image that comes only after the stereotype has been firmly implanted in our minds: initially it does not make as strong an impression as the first image but it gathers strength later on because the language and behavior of the Christian characters repeatedly confirm the rather brief but essential utterances of Shylock himself on which it primarily rests.

> ... if you tickle us,
> Do we not laugh? If you poison us, do we not
> Die? and if you wrong us, shall we not revenge?
> If we are like you in the rest, we will resemble
> You in that. If a Jew wrong a Christian, what
> Is his humility? Revenge. If a Christian wrong
> A Jew, what should his sufferance be by Christian
> Example? Why, revenge. The villainy

> You teach me, I will execute; and it shall go
> Hard but I will better the instruction.
>
> (III.i.58–66)

The text insists above all on Shylock's personal commitment to revenge. It does not support the type of "rehabilitation" naively demanded by certain revisionists. But it unequivocally defines the symmetry and the reciprocity that govern the relations between the Christians and Shylock.

The symmetry between the explicit venality of Shylock and the implicit venality of the other Venetians cannot fail to be intended by the playwright. Bassanio's courtship of Portia is presented primarily as a financial operation. In his plea for Antonio's financial support, Bassanio mentions first the wealth of the young heiress, then her beauty, then finally her spiritual qualities. Those critics who idealize the Venetians write as if the many textual clues that contradict their view were not planted by the author himself, as if their presence in the play were a purely fortuitous matter, like the arrival of a bill in the morning mail when one really expects a love letter. On every possible occasion Shakespeare pursued the parallel between the amorous venture of Bassanio and the typical Venetian business of Antonio, his commerce on the high seas. Observe, for instance, the manner in which Gratiano, who is just back from Belmont and still flushed with the success of this expedition, addresses Salerio:

> [*Gratiano:*] Your hand, Salerio. What's the news from Venice?
> How doth that royal merchant, good Antonio?
> I know he will be glad of our success.
> We are the Jasons, we have won the fleece.
> *Salerio:* I would you have won the fleece that he hath lost:
>
> (III.ii.238–42)

The truth is that Bassanio and friends have done exactly that. Even if Antonio's losses turned out to be real, Portia's conquest would more than make up financially for Antonio's ships.

Regarding this symmetry between Shylock and the Venetians, many good points have been made. I will mention only one, for the sole reason that I have not found it in the critical literature on the play. If I am not original, please accept my apologies.

In Act III, scene ii, Bassanio wants to reward his lieutenant for his services, and he tells Gratiano and Nerissa that they will be married simultaneously with Portia and himself, in a double wedding ceremony – at Portia's expense, we may assume. "Our feast," he says, "shall be much honored in your marriage." Upon which the elated Gratiano says to his fiancée: "We'll play with them the first boy for a thousand ducats" (III.ii.212–13).

These young people have ample reason to be joyous, now that their future is made secure by Bassanio's clever stroke with the caskets, and this bet sounds harmless enough, but Shakespeare is not addicted to pointless social chitchat and must have a purpose. Gratiano's baby will be two thousand ducats cheaper than Antonio's pound of flesh. Human flesh and money in Venice are constantly exchanged for one another. People are turned into objects of financial speculation. Mankind has become a commodity, an exchange value like any other. I cannot believe that Shakespeare did not perceive the analogy between Gratiano's wager and Shylock's pound of flesh.

Shylock's pound of flesh is symbolical of Venetian behavior. The Venetians appear different from Shylock, up to a point. Financial considerations have become so natural to them and are so embedded into their psyches that they have become not quite but almost invisible; they can never be identified as a distinct aspect of behavior. Antonio's loan to Bassanio, for instance, is treated as an act of love and not as a business transaction.

Shylock hates Antonio for lending money without interest. In his eyes, the merchant spoils the financial business. We can read this as the resentment of vile greed for noble generosity within the context of the first image, but we may prefer another reading that contributes to the second image. The generosity of Antonio may well be a corruption more extreme than the caricatural greed of Shylock. As a rule, when Shylock lends money, he expects more money in return, and nothing else. Capital should produce capital. Shylock does not confuse his financial operations with Christian charity. This is why, unlike the Venetians, he can look like the embodiment of greed.

Venice is a world in which appearances and reality do not match. Of all the pretenders to Portia's hand, Bassanio alone makes the right choice between the three caskets because this shrewd Venetian knows how deceptive a splendid exterior can be. Unlike his foreign competitors, who obviously come from countries where things are still more or less what they seem to be – less advanced countries, we might say – he instinctively feels that the priceless treasure he seeks must hide behind the most unlikely appearance.

The symbolic significance of choosing lead rather than the gold and silver selected by the two foreigners faithfully duplicates the whole relationship between the true Venetians and the foreign Shylock. When the two alien pretenders reach avidly for the two precious metals, just like Shylock, they look like personifications of greed; in reality they are rather naive, whereas Bassanio is anything but naive. It is characteristic of the Venetians that they look like the very picture of disinterestedness at the precise moment when their sly calculations cause the pot of gold to fall into their lap.

The generosity of the Venetians is not feigned. Real generosity makes the beneficiary more dependent on his generous friend than a regular loan. In Venice a new form of vassality prevails, grounded no longer in strict territorial borders but in vague financial terms. The lack of precise accounting makes personal indebtedness infinite. This is an art Shylock has not mastered, since his own daughter feels perfectly free to rob and abandon him without the slightest remorse. The elegance of the decor and the harmony of the music must not lead us to think that everything is right with the Venetian world. It is impossible, however, to say exactly what is wrong. Antonio is sad but he cannot say why, and this unexplained sadness seems to characterize the whole Venetian business aristocracy as much as Antonio himself.

Even in Shylock's life, however, money and matters of human sentiment finally become confused. But there is something comical in this confusion because, even as they become one, money and sentiment retain a measure of separateness, they remain distinguishable from each other. Thus we hear such things as "My daughter! Oh, my ducats! Oh, my daughter! / Fled with a Christian! Oh, my Christian ducats!" (ii.viii. 15–16) and other such ridiculous utterances you would never catch in a Venetian mouth.

There is still another occasion upon which Shylock, goaded by his Venetian enemies, confuses financial matters with other passions, and it is one affair of his loan to

Antonio. In the interest of his revenge, Shylock demands no interest for his money, no positive guarantees in case of default, nothing but his infamous pound of flesh. Behind the mythical weirdness of the request, we have one spectacular instance of that complete interpenetration between the financial and the human that is characteristic less of Shylock than of the other Venetians. Thus Shylock appears most scandalous to the Venetians and to the spectators when he stops resembling himself to resemble the Venetians even more. The spirit of revenge drives him to imitate the Venetians more perfectly than before, and, in his effort to teach Antonio a lesson, Shylock becomes his grotesque double.

Antonio and Shylock are described as rivals of long standing. Of such people we often say that they have their differences, but this expression would be misleading. Tragic – and comic – conflict amounts to a dissolving of differences that is paradoxical because it proceeds from the opposite intention. All the people involved in the process seek to emphasize and maximize their differences. In Venice, we found, greed and generosity, pride and humility, compassion and ferocity, money and human flesh, tend to become one and the same. This undifferentiation makes it impossible to define anything with precision, to ascribe one particular cause to one particular event. Yet on all sides it is the same obsession with displaying and sharpening a difference that is less and less real. Here is Shylock, for instance, in Act II, scene v: "Well thou shalt see, thy eyes shall be thy judge, / The difference between Old Shylock and Bassanio" (II.v.1–2). The Christians too are eager to demonstrate that they are different from the Jews. During the trial scene it is the turn of the duke, who says to Shylock: "Thou shalt see the difference of our spirits" (IV.i.368). Even the words are the same. Everywhere the same senseless obsession with differences becomes exacerbated as it keeps defeating itself.

We have an allusion to this process of undifferentiation, I believe, in a well-known line of this play. When Portia enters the court she asks, "Which is the merchant here and which is the Jew?" (IV.i.174). Even if she has never met either Antonio or Shylock, we have a right to be surprised Portia cannot identify the Jewish moneylender at first sight, in view of the enormous difference, visible to all, that is supposed to distinguish him from the gracious Venetians. The line would be more striking, of course, if it came after rather than before the following one: "Antonio and old Shylock, both stand forth" (IV.i.175). If Portia were still unable to distinguish Shylock from Antonio once the two men have come forward together, the scene would explicitly contradict the primary image of Shylock, the stereotype of the Jewish moneylender. This contradiction would stretch the limits of dramatic credibility beyond the breaking point, and Shakespeare refrained from it, but he went as far as he could, I believe, here and elsewhere, to question the reality of a difference he himself, of course, had first introduced into his play.

What we have just said in the language of psychology can be translated into religious terms. Between Shylock's behavior and his words, the relationship is never ambiguous. His interpretation of the law may be narrow and negative, but we can count on him for acting according to it and for speaking according to his actions. In the passage on revenge, he alone speaks a truth that the Christians hypocritically deny. The truth of the play is revenge and retribution. The Christians manage to hide that truth even from themselves. They do not live by the law of charity, but this law is enough of a presence in their language to drive the law of revenge underground, to make this revenge almost invisible. As a result, this revenge becomes more subtle, skillful, and feline than the revenge of Shylock. The Christians will easily destroy Shylock, but they will go on living in a world that is sad without knowing why, a world in which even the difference between revenge and charity has been abolished.

Ultimately we do not have to choose between a favorable and an unfavorable image of Shylock. The old critics have concentrated on Shylock as a separate entity, an individual substance that would be merely juxtaposed to other individual substances and remain unaffected by them. The ironic depth in *The Merchant of Venice* results from a tension not between two static images of Shylock, but between those textual features that strengthen and those features that undermine the popular idea of an insurmountable difference between Christian and Jew.

It is not excessive to say that characterization itself, as a real dramatic problem or as a fallacy, is at stake in the play. On the one hand Shylock is portrayed as a highly differentiated villain. On the other hand he tells us himself that there are no villains and no heroes; all men are the same, especially when they are taking revenge on each other. Whatever differences may have existed between them prior to the cycle of revenge are dissolved in the reciprocity of reprisals and retaliation. Where does Shakespeare stand on this issue? Massive evidence from the other plays as well as from *The Merchant* cannot leave the question in doubt. The main object of satire is not Shylock the Jew. But Shylock is rehabilitated only to the extent that the Christians are even worse than he is, and that the "honesty" of his vices makes him almost a refreshing figure compared to the sanctimonious ferocity of the other Venetians.

The trial scene clearly reveals how implacable and skillful the Christians can be when they take their revenge. In this most curious performance, Antonio begins as the defendant and Shylock as the plaintiff. At the end of one single meeting the roles are reversed and Shylock is a convicted criminal. The man has done no actual harm to anyone. Without his money, the two marriages, the two happy events in the play, could not come to pass. As his triumphant enemies return to Belmont loaded with a financial and human booty that includes Shylock's own daughter, they still manage to feel compassionate and gentle by contrast with their wretched opponent.

When we sense the injustice of Shylock's fate, we usually say: Shylock is a scapegoat. This expression, however, is ambiguous. When I say that a character in a play is a scapegoat, my statement can mean two different things. It can mean that this character is unjustly condemned from the perspective of the writer. The conviction of the crowd is presented as irrational by the writer himself. In this first case, we say that in that play there is a theme or motif of the scapegoat.

There is a second meaning to the idea that a character is a scapegoat. It can mean that, from the perspective of the writer, this character is justly condemned, but in the eyes of the critic who makes the statement, the condemnation is unjust. The crowd that condemns the victim is presented as rational by the writer, who really belongs to that crowd; only in the eyes of the critic are the crowd and the writer irrational and unjust.

The scapegoat, this time, is not a theme or motif at all; it is not made explicit by the writer, but if the critic is right in his allegations, there must be a scapegoat effect at the origin of the play, a collective effect probably, in which the writer participates.

The critic may think, for instance, that a writer who creates a character like Shylock, patterned after the stereotype of the Jewish moneylender, must do so because he personally shares in the anti-Semitism of the society in which this stereotype is present.

When we say that Shylock is a scapegoat, our statement remains vague and critically useless, unless we specify if we mean the scapegoat as theme or the scapegoat as structure, the scapegoat as an object of indignation and satire or the scapegoat as a passively accepted delusion.

Before we can resolve the critical impasse to which I referred at the beginning of this chapter, we must reformulate it in the terms of this still unperceived alternative between the scapegoat as structure and the scapegoat as theme. Everyone agrees that Shylock is a scapegoat, but is he the scapegoat of his society only or of Shakespeare as well?

What the critical revisionists maintain is that the scapegoating of Shylock is not a structuring force but a satirical theme. What the traditionalists maintain is that scapegoating, in *The Merchant of Venice*, is a structuring force rather than a theme. Whether we like it or not, they say, the play shares in the cultural anti-Semitism of the society. We should not allow our literary piety to blind us to the fact.

My own idea is that the scapegoat is both structure and theme in *The Merchant of Venice*, and that the play, in this essential respect at least, is anything any reader wants it to be, not because Shakespeare is as confused as we are when we use the word "scapegoat" without specifying, but for the opposite reason: he is so aware and so conscious of the various demands placed upon him by the cultural diversity of his audience; he is so knowledgeable in regard to the paradoxes of mimetic reactions and group behavior that he can stage a scapegoating of Shylock entirely convincing to those who want to be convinced, and simultaneously undermine that process with ironic touches that will reach only those who can be reached. Thus he was able to satisfy the most vulgar as well as the most refined audiences. To those who do not want to challenge the anti-Semitic myth, or Shakespeare's own espousal of that myth, *The Merchant of Venice* will always sound like a confirmation of that myth. To those who do challenge these same beliefs, Shakespeare's own challenge will become perceptible. The play is not unlike a perpetually revolving object that, through some mysterious means, would always present itself to each viewer under aspects best suited to his own perspective.

Why are we reluctant to consider this possibility? Both intellectually and ethically, we assume that scapegoating cannot be and should not be a theme of satire and a structuring force at the same time. Either the author participates in the collective victimage and cannot see it as unjust, or he can see it as unjust and should not connive in it, even ironically. Most works of art do fall squarely on one side or the other of that particular fence. Rewritten by Arthur Miller, Jean-Paul Sartre, or Bertolt Brecht, *The Merchant of Venice* would be different indeed. But so would a *Merchant of Venice* that would merely reflect the anti-Semitism of its society, as a comparison with Marlowe's *Jew of Malta* immediately reveals.

If we look carefully at the trial scene, no doubt can remain that Shakespeare undermines scapegoat effects just as skillfully as he produces them. There is something frightening in this efficiency. This art demands a manipulation and therefore an intelligence of mimetic phenomena that transcends not only the ignorant immorality of those who submit passively to victimage mechanisms, but also the moralism that rebels against them but does not perceive the irony generated by the dual role of the author. Shakespeare himself must first generate at the grossly theatrical level the effects that he later undermines at the level of allusions.

Let us see how Shakespeare can move in both directions at the same time. Why is it difficult not to experience a feeling of relief and even jubilation at the discomfiture of Shylock? The main reason, of course, is that Antonio's life is supposed to be under an immediate threat. That threat stems from Shylock's stubborn insistence that he is entitled to his pound of flesh.

Now the pound of flesh is a mythical motif. We found earlier that it is a highly significant allegory of a world where human beings and money are constantly exchanged for one another, but it is nothing more. We can imagine a purely mythical context in which Shylock could really carve up his pound of flesh and Antonio would walk away, humiliated and diminished but alive. In *The Merchant of Venice,* the mythical context is replaced by a realistic one. We are told that Antonio could not undergo this surgical operation without risking his life. It is certainly true in a realistic context, but it is also true, in that same context, that, especially in the presence of the whole Venetian establishment, old Shylock would be unable to perform this same operation. The myth is only partly demythologized, and Shylock is supposed to be capable of carving up Antonio's body in cold blood because, as a Jew and a moneylender, he passes for a man of unusual ferocity. This presumed ferocity justifies our own cultural prejudice.

Shakespeare knows that victimage must be unanimous to be effective, and no voice is effectively raised in favor of Shylock. The presence of the silent Magnificoes, the elite of the community, turns the trial into a rite of social unanimity. The only characters not physically present are Shylock's daughter and his servant, and they are of one mind with the actual scapegoaters, since they were the first to abandon Shylock after taking his money. Like a genuine biblical victim, Shylock is betrayed "even by those of his own household."

As scapegoating affects more and more people and tends toward unanimity, the contagion becomes overwhelming. In spite of its judicial and logical nonsense, the trial scene is enormously performative and dramatic. The spectators and readers of the play cannot fail to be affected and cannot refrain from experiencing Shylock's defeat as if it were their own victory. The crowd in the theater becomes one with the crowd on the stage. The contagious effect of scapegoating extends to the audience.

As an embodiment of Venetian justice, the duke should be impartial, but at the very outset of the proceedings he commiserates with the defendant and launches into a diatribe against Shylock:

> I am sorry for thee. Thou art come to answer
> A stony adversary, an inhuman wretch,
> Uncapable of pity, void and empty
> From any dram of mercy.
>
> (IV.i.3–6)

These words set the tone for the entire scene. The Christian virtue par excellence, mercy is the weapon with which Shylock is clubbed over the head. The Christians use the word "mercy" with such perversity that they can justify their own revenge with it, give full license to their greed, and still come out with a clear conscience. They feel they have discharged their obligation to be merciful by their constant repetition of the word itself. The quality of their mercy is not strained, to say the least. It is remarkably casual and easy. When the duke severely asks, "How shalt thou hope for mercy, rendering none?" (IV.i.88), Shylock responds with impeccable logic: "What judgment shall I dread, doing no wrong?" (89).

Shylock trusts in the law too much. How could the law of Venice be based on mercy, how could it be equated with the Golden Rule, since it gives the Venetians the right to own slaves and does not give slaves the right to own Venetians? How can we be certain that Shakespeare, who engineered the scapegoat effect so skillfully, is not fooled by it even for one second? Our certainty is perfect and may well be much more than "subjective," as some critics would say. It may well be perfectly "objective" in the sense that it correctly recaptures the author's intention and yet remains a closed book to a certain type of reader. If irony were demonstrable, it would cease to be irony. Irony must not be explicit enough to destroy the efficiency of the scapegoat machine in the minds of those for whom that machine was set up in the first place. Irony cannot fail to be less tangible than the object on which it bears.

Some will object that my reading is "paradoxical." It may well be, but why should it be a priori excluded that Shakespeare can write a paradoxical play? Especially if the paradox on which the play is built is formulated most explicitly at the center of that very play. Shakespeare is writing, not without a purpose, I suppose, that appearances, especially the appearances of beautiful language, are "The seeming truth which cunning times put on / To entrap the wisest" (III.ii.100–1). Shakespeare is writing, not without a purpose, that the worst sophistry, when distilled by a charming voice, can decide the outcome of a trial, or that the most irreligious behavior can sound religious if the right words are mentioned. Let us listen to the reasons given by Bassanio for trusting in lead rather than in silver or gold, and we will see that they apply word for word to the play itself:

> The world is still deceived with ornament.
> In law, what plea so tainted and corrupt
> But being seasoned with a gracious voice,
> Obscures the show of evil? In religion,
> What damned error but some sober brow
> Will bless it, and approve it with a text,
> Hiding the grossness with fair ornament?
> There is no vice so simple but assumes
> Some mark of virtue on his outward parts.
> (III.ii.74–82)

I see Bassanio's brief intervention during the trial scene as another sign of Shakespeare's ironic distance. As soon as Shylock begins to relent, under the pressure of Portia's skill, Bassanio declares his willingness to pay back the money Shylock is now willing to accept. In his eagerness to be finished with the whole unpleasant business, Bassanio shows a degree of mercy, but Portia remains adamant. Feeling her claws in Shylock's flesh, she drives them deeper and deeper in order to exact her own pound of flesh.

Bassanio's suggestion bears no fruit, but its formulation at this crucial moment cannot be pointless. It is the only reasonable solution to the whole affair, but dramatically it cannot prevail because it is undramatic. Shakespeare is too good a playwright not to understand that the only good solution, from a theatrical standpoint, is the scapegoating of Shylock. On the other hand he wants to point out the unjust nature of the "cathartic" resolution that is forced upon him by the necessity of his art. He wants the reasonable solution to be spelled out somewhere inside the play.

Is it not excessive to say the scapegoating is a recognizable motif in *The Merchant of Venice*? There is one explicit allusion to the scapegoat in the play. It occurs at the beginning of Shylock's trial.

> I am a tainted wether of the flock,
> Meetest for death. The weakest kind of fruit
> Drops earliest to the ground, and so let me.
> You cannot better be employed, Bassanio,
> Than to live still and write mine epitaph.
> (iv.i.114–18)

Is there a difficulty for my thesis in the fact that Antonio rather than Shylock utters these lines? Not at all, since their mutual hatred has turned Antonio and Shylock into the double each of the other. This mutual hatred makes all reconciliation impossible – nothing concrete separates the antagonists, no genuinely tangible issue that could be arbitrated and settled – but the undifferentiation generated by this hatred paves the way for the only type of resolution that can conclude this absolute conflict, the scapegoat resolution.

Antonio speaks these lines in reply to Bassanio, who has just asserted he would never let his friend and benefactor die in his place. He would rather die himself. Neither one will die, of course, or even suffer in the slightest. In the city of Venice, no Antonio or Bassanio will ever suffer as long as there is a Shylock to do the suffering for them.

There is no serious danger that Antonio will die, but he can really see himself, at this point, as a scapegoat in the making. Thus Shakespeare can have an explicit reference to scapegoating without pointing directly to Shylock. There is a great irony, of course, not only in the fact that the metaphor is displaced, the scapegoat being the essence of metaphoric displacement, but also in the almost romantic complacency of Antonio, in his intimation of masochistic satisfaction. The quintessential Venetian, Antonio, the man who is sad without a cause, may be viewed as a figure of the modern subjectivity characterized by a strong propensity toward self-victimization or, more concretely, by a greater and greater interiorization of a scapegoat process that is too well understood to be re-enacted as a real event in the real world. Mimetic entanglements cannot be projected with complete success onto all the Shylocks of this world, and the scapegoat process tends to turn back upon itself and become reflective. What we have, as a result, is a masochistic and theatrical self-pity that announces the romantic subjectivity. This is the reason why Antonio is eager to be "sacrificed" in the actual presence of Bassanio.

Irony is not demonstrable, I repeat, and it should not be, otherwise it would disturb the catharsis of those who enjoy the play at the cathartic level only. Irony is anti-cathartic. Irony is experienced in a flash of complicity with the writer at his most subtle, against the larger part of the audience that remains blind to these subtleties. Irony is the writer's vicarious revenge against the revenge that he must vicariously perform. If irony were too obvious, if it were intelligible to all, it would defeat its own purpose, because there would be no more object for irony to undermine.

The reading I propose can be strengthened, I believe, through a comparison with other plays, notably *Richard III*. When Shakespeare wrote this play, his king's identity as a villain was well established. The dramatist goes along with the popular view, especially at the beginning. In the first scene, Richard presents himself as a monstrous villain. His deformed body is a mirror for the self-confessed ugliness of his soul. Here too we are dealing with a stereotype, the stereotype of the bad king that can be said to be generated or revived by the unanimous rejection of the scapegoat king, the very process that is re-enacted in the last Act after gathering momentum throughout the play.

If we forget for a while the introduction and the conclusion to focus on the drama itself, a different image of Richard emerges. We are in a world of bloody political struggles. All adult characters in the play have committed at least one political murder or benefited from one. As critics like Murray Krieger and Ian Kott have pointed out, the War of the Roses functions as a system of political rivalry and revenge in which every participant is a tyrant and a victim in turn, always behaving and speaking not according to permanent character differences but to the position he occupies at any moment within the total dynamic system. Being the last coil in that infernal spiral, Richard may kill more people more cynically than his predecessors, but he is not essentially different. In order to make the past history of reciprocal violence dramatically present, Shakespeare resorts to the technique of the curse. Everyone keeps cursing everyone else so vehemently and massively that the total effect is tragic or almost comic, according to the mood of the spectator; all these curses mutually cancel each other until the end, when they all converge against Richard and bring about his final undoing, which is also the restoration of peace.

Two images of the same character tend to alternate, one highly differentiated and one undifferentiated. In the case of *The Merchant of Venice* and *Richard III*, some fairly obvious reasons can be invoked; in both plays the theme was a sensitive one, dominated by social and political imperatives regarding which Shakespeare felt skeptical, obviously, but that he could not attack openly. The method he devised permitted an indirect satire, highly effective with the knowledgeable few and completely invisible to the ignorant multitude, avid only of the gross catharsis Shakespeare never failed to provide.

Great theater is necessarily a play of differentiation and undifferentiation. The characters will not hold the interest of the audience unless the audience can sympathize with them or deny them its sympathy. They must be highly differentiated, in other words, but any scheme of differentiation is synchronic and static. In order to be good, a play must be dynamic. The dynamics of the theater are the dynamics of human conflict, the reciprocity of retribution and revenge; the more intense the process, the more symmetry you tend to have, the more everything tends to become the same on both sides of the antagonism.

In order to be good, a play must be as reciprocal and undifferentiated as possible, but it must be highly differentiated, too, otherwise the spectators will not be interested in the outcome of the conflict. These two requirements are incompatible, but a playwright who cannot satisfy both simultaneously is not a great playwright; he will produce either plays too differentiated, which will be labeled *pièces à thèse* because they will be experienced as insufficiently dynamic, or plays too undifferentiated, in order to have a lot of action, or suspense, as we say, but this suspense will appear pointless and will be blamed for a lack of intellectual and ethical content.

The successful playwright can fulfill the two contradictory requirements simultaneously, even though they are contradictory. How does he do it? In many instances he does not seem fully aware of what he is doing; he must do it in the same instinctive manner as the spectators who passionately identify with one antagonist. Even though the assumed difference between the two always translates itself into reciprocal and undifferentiated behavior, our view of the conflict tends to be static and differentiated.

We can be certain, I believe, that such is not the case with Shakespeare. Shakespeare is fully conscious of the gap between the difference of the static structure and the nondifference of tragic action. He fills his plays with ironic allusions to the gap between the two and does not hesitate to widen that gap still further, as if he knew that he could do this with impunity, and that in all probability he would be rewarded for doing it; far from destroying his credibility as a creator of "characters," he would increase the overall dramatic impact of his theater and turn his plays into those dynamic and inexhaustible objects upon which critics can comment endlessly without ever putting their finger on the real source of their ambiguity.

In *Richard III* we have examples of this practice no less striking than in *The Merchant of Venice*. Anne and Elizabeth, the two women who have most suffered at the hands of Richard, cannot resist the temptation of power, even at the cost of an alliance with him, when Richard himself diabolically dangles this toy in front of them. After cursing Richard abundantly and discharging in this manner all her moral obligations, Anne literally walks over the dead body of her father to join hands with Richard. A little later Elizabeth walks over the dead bodies of two of her children, symbolically at least, in order to deliver a third one into the bloody hands of the murderer.

These two scenes are structurally close to each other, and they generate a crescendo of abomination that cannot be without a purpose. These two women are even more vile than Richard, and the only character who is able to point out this vileness, thus becoming in a sense the only ethical voice in the whole play, is Richard himself, whose role, mutatis mutandis, is comparable to that of Shylock in *The Merchant of Venice*.

It is Shakespeare's genius that he can do such things. And he does them, not to generate irony only, but for the sake of dramatic efficiency. He knows that by doing them he creates uneasiness among the spectators, he places upon them a moral burden with which they cannot deal in terms of the scapegoat values presented at the outset. The demand for the expulsion of the scapegoat is paradoxically reinforced by the very factors that make this expulsion arbitrary.

I fully agree that, in the case of plays like *Richard III* or *The Merchant of Venice*, an infinite number of readings is possible, and this infinity is determined by "the play of the signifier." I do not agree that this play is gratuitous, and that it is in the nature of all signifiers as signifiers to produce such infinite play. The literary signifier always becomes a victim. It is a victim of the signified, at least metaphorically, in the sense that its play, its *différance*, or what you will, is almost inevitably sacrificed to the one-sidedness of a single-minded structure à la Lévi-Strauss. The sacrificed signifier disappears behind the signified. Is this victimage of the signifier nothing but a metaphor, or is it mysteriously connected to the scapegoat as such, in the sense that it is rooted in that ritual space where the major signifier is also a victim, not merely in the semiotic sense, this time, but in the sense of Shylock or of Richard III? The play of the signifier, with its arbitrary interruption for the sake of a differentiated structure, operates exactly like the theatrical and ritual process, with its conflictual undifferentiation suddenly resolved and returned to static differentiation through the elimination of a victim. Everything I have said suggests that to Shakespeare, at least, all these things are one and the same. The process of signification is one with the scapegoat resolution of the crisis in which all significations are dissolved, then reborn: the "crisis of Degree."

23

What Did the King Know and When Did He Know It? Shakespearean Discourses and Psychoanalysis

Harry Berger, Jr.

A mbivalence, guilt, aggressivity, masochism, sexuality, displacement, projection, desire, repression; fantasies of omnipotence, emasculation, violation, terrible fathers, terrible mothers, terrible sons and siblings. Any short list of the themes psychoanalytic interpreters focus on will make it obvious that those themes have been around since the earliest cultural texts and didn't need to wait for psychoanalysis to pick them out. So the question is always, what difference do specifically psychoanalytic readings make, and how useful are they? Given the co-constitutive relation of data and conceptual frameworks, how transferable are psychoanalytic paradigms to systems whose interdependent components are constituted differently? And within the range of those paradigms, are some more useful and usable than others? In this essay I shall indicate my own choice by proposing an approach to Shakespeare that derives aid and comfort from Lacan's critical revision of the paradigms developed by Freud's followers.

The hypothesis that underwrites the approach is that many of the themes listed in my first sentence are unfolded by the Shakespeare text into a dynamic field of interpenetrating motivational patterns whose varied linguistic representations I shall call *discourses*. This term is sufficiently overworked and distended to demand the rough attempt at a definition that occurs on pp. 374–8 below. Since the definition I pose is modeled partly on the Wittgensteinian notion of language-game, it follows that its focus will be on patterns that are, so to speak, public property, circulating through the community of the play and traversing the language of individual speakers, whom I conceive as the operators but not the owners of their discursive practices. The analysis of the discourses to be considered will be governed by the related premise that speakers are the effects rather than the causes both of the language assigned to their names and of the interpretations we give that language. This premise is strictly methodological in intent and implies no attitude toward agency. That is, its purpose is not to reduce speakers to mere passive sites of discursive activity but to establish the principle that the analysis of language should precede the analysis of its cognitive or psychological relation to its speaker – that the semiotic and psychological dimensions of textual analysis should be kept distinct, as in practice they often are. It is a common occurrence for readers to agree on the meaning of a particular passage but subsequently to disagree as to its psychological disposition.

Consider, for example, the line that concludes the troubled king's insomnia solilo-quy in Part Two of *Henry IV*: "Uneasy lies the head that wears the crown" (III.i.31). In this, his first appearance in the play, Henry moves quickly from an allusion to his guilty conscience as the cause of insomnia to a more consoling emphasis on the burdens of state that keep a king awake while his subjects, free of such cares, sleep soundly. Readers who agree with this description of the speech will have no difficulty agreeing that *lies* functions as a pun, and that the last line in effect comments on the evasion that diverts attention from the real source of care: "uneasy lies the head that stole the crown." But will those readers go further and agree on Henry's relation to the statement? Is he aware or unaware of the pun? Is the utterance a piece of mordant and self-lacerating irony? Is the pun something he suddenly stumbles on and recognizes? Does it signify something he is trying to block? Or is he unaware, does he remain unaware, that his language is giving him away? What did the king know and when did he know it? For a not very satisfactory answer to these questions, see the conclusion to this essay.

Questions of this kind will always be open to controversy, but I think it reduces confusion and more sharply circumscribes the area of useful controversy to dissociate them from semiotic questions. The decision to confer ambiguous status on the word *lies* may be influenced by speculations about the speaker's state of mind or conscience, but it is in itself strictly a semiotic decision, a matter of linguistic and rhetorical interpretation that differs from and – in terms of methodological sequence – precedes any psychological disposition readers may make of it.

The claim to be able to distinguish between meant and unmeant meaning in every case of ambiguous language presupposes a consistent knowledge of the speaker such that the boundary between awareness and unawareness can always be determined. And interpretive experience shows that this is simply not possible, that a consistent inconsist-ency in these matters is the best policy. Yet the consistent ambivalence or ambiguity of the language can still be demonstrated. It could be demonstrated even if the text had no "sides" and appeared as a continuous monologue. Hence the interpretation of textual ambiguity is theoretically prior to and separable from the interpretation of the speaker's relation to that ambiguity. My point in emphasizing this is to nudge toward the status of a regulative principle the idea that we may reach consensus on the meaning of a given stretch of utterance yet still differ in our assessments of what the speaker intends by it and whether he hears or is aware of what readers see in his language. And these "assessments" – the word is too modest – are in fact acts of construction by which the interpreter transforms a speaker into a character (a fictional person). A finite range of possible characters is embedded in the language assigned a speaker. One of those characters is what the speaker will become – or, to state it more accurately, what the speaker will have become – as the result of a particular interpretive dialogue between reader, actor, director, or spectator, and the text. Thus, to modify the stipulative premise announced above, speakers *as characters* are the effects rather than the causes of their language and our interpretation. It may already be obvious that the commitments expressed so far may prove more congenial to a Lacanian than to a Freudian paradigm of psychoanalytic interpretation. In the next section I shall make this allegiance more explicit by distinguishing between the two paradigms and exploring some of the problems that arise when interpreters of Shakespeare rely on Freudian assumptions.

Lacan's critique and revision of the relation of the language of psychoanalysis to its explanatory schemes get discussed several times a month around the world and can do without still another airing. I therefore confine myself to mentioning the two features of the critique that bear directly on my argument. The first is that in the analytical dialogue the cognitive function of language is instrumental to its performative function – what words mean is instrumental to what they do – and that the analyst no less than the analysand may be in the dark about the work being accomplished in the dialogue.[1] The second is that epigenetic models of development founded on "considerations of instinct or naturalness or biological destiny"[2] should – in accordance with the logic of the future anterior that governs the dialogue – be shifted from the register of the signified to that of the signifier so that they may become instruments rather than objects of inquiry:

> For the function of language is not to inform but to evoke ... I identify myself in language, but only by losing myself in it like an object. What is realized in my history is not the past definite of what was, since it is no more, or even the present perfect of what has been in what I am, but the future anterior of what I shall have been for what I am in the process of becoming.[3]

To carry through this shift is to denaturalize and refictionalize such master narratives as those excerpted here:

> We have arrived at our knowledge of this psychical apparatus by studying the individual development of human beings. To the oldest of these mental provinces or agencies we give the name of *id*. It contains everything that is inherited, that is present at birth, that is fixed in the constitution – above all, therefore, the instincts, which originate in the somatic organization and which find their first mental expression in the id ... This oldest portion of the mental apparatus remains the most important throughout life.[4]

> Human beings in dealing with each other repeat the patterns they have developed in their relations to "significant others," and these patterns of relationships *ultimately* go back to those which the individual has developed toward the earliest "significant others": father, mother, siblings, nurses, etc. Such repetitions ... are the empirical referents of the transference concept.[5]

> We are faced here by the great enigma of the biological fact of the duality of the sexes: for our knowledge it is something ultimate, it resists every attempt to trace it back to something else. Psychoanalysis has made no contribution toward solving this problem, which clearly falls entirely within the province of biology.[6]

The familiar responses to these assertions have come in various voices, but all insist on repositioning the narratives from the essentialized state and processes of nature to the culture-specific state and processes of discourse:

There's no discourse that is not make-believe.[7]

Hypotheses non fingo means that only discourses ex-sist.[8]

If only they would throw themselves deliberately and unequivocally into myth in all its majesty. If only they would dare to adopt the fairy-tale form. If only an analyst's story could start with "Once upon a time ..." But of course not: since they insist on describing everything, on making a pale replica of a scientific ideal confronted with the imaginary, whose mechanisms are themselves strongly interwoven with literary history, they can't go beyond the nineteenth century. As if they had discovered it, as if they were putting the real essence of their experience into their transcriptions.[9]

The humanistic conception of mankind assumes that the subject exists from the beginning. At least by implication ego psychologists, object-relations theorists and Kleinians base themselves on the same premise. For this reason, Lacan considers that in the last analysis, they are more ideologues than theorists of psychoanalysis. In the Freud that Lacan uses, neither the unconscious nor sexuality can in any degree be pre-given facts, they are constructions; that is, they are objects with histories and the human subject itself is only formed within these histories.[10]

From the very beginning, indeed, literature has been for psychoanalysis not only a contiguous field of external verification in which to test its hypotheses and to confirm its findings, but also the constitutive texture of its *conceptual* framework, of its theoretical body. The key concepts of psychoanalysis are references to literature, using literary "proper" names – names of fictional characters (Oedipus complex, Narcissism) or of historical authors (masochism, sadism). Literature, in other words, is the language which psychoanalysis uses in order to *speak of itself* ... In the same way that psychoanalysis points to the unconscious of literature, *literature, in its turn, is the unconscious of psychoanalysis.*[11]

This citational muster lines up the opposing factions most relevant to the conflict I want to address. My formulation of the theory of discourses owes much to the flood of studies that, during the last two decades, have applied psychoanalytic concepts to the contradictions of gender and generation that energize Shakespeare's representations of the family romance. At the same time, in order to appropriate their insights, I have often been forced to extricate them from what I believe to be a disabling reliance on the epigenetic or developmental paradigm and its commitment to "biological destiny." The thesis I hope to block is illustrated in general form by the following comment:

> We do not see Hamlet at his mother's breast, or Leontes learning to walk. Yet we can be confident, from the resonance of the poet's imagery and characterization, that he thought of them as human beings whose adult selves were shaped by the experience of growing up within a family. They speak in its modes of eating and spitting out, they echo its delusions of omnipotence and fears of abandonment. Their utterances and their conflicts spring from the residue of early life. While it would be reductive to translate the intricate action of a Shakespearean play into the terms of infantile experience, oedipal or pre-oedipal, seeing that experience as the *source* of the action helps us understand its inner coherence.

This thesis allows the author to combine gender theory with pre-oedipal theory in a genetic explanation of the central conflict of the history plays:

Associating phallic consciousness with upright mobility, the boy is strongly motivated to turn away from his mother and toward his father ... His father ... can help the child resist reengulfment with the mother. In the history plays, the intensity of the son's identification with the father measures the strength of the pull toward such reengulfment, and the son's difficulty in separating from the mother.[12]

The susceptibility of such an approach to the genetic and essentialist fallacies has been ably pointed out by Lisa Lowe in an important essay on *Coriolanus*. Lowe stresses the difference between treating the mother–son relationship as a genetic cause, "a literary 'case study' from which we must draw the conclusion that overwhelming mothers always produce warrior sons," and treating it as a fantasy that is "a 'symptom' of cultural anxieties, particular to Elizabethan England, about the impossibility of achieving an absolute singular manhood ..., perhaps a male 'nightmare' which exaggerates feminine power to provide an explanation of these anxieties." Noting that one effect of the pre-Oedipal slant in feminist readings by Kahn, Janet Adelman, and (to a lesser extent) Madelon (Gohlke) Sprengnether is to scapegoat the mother, she argues that "if psychoanalysis becomes the exclusive means of explaining gender, it de-politicizes the family, and obscures the extent to which social, cultural and political circumstances influence family structure." Lowe offers instead a reading that situates the gender issue squarely within the play's representation of those circumstances:

> The psychoanalytic critics have argued that Coriolanus inherits his violence from his mother's lessons. Perhaps it would be more appropriate to venture that both the son and the mother, as well as the patricians and plebeians and other members of the play's community, assume, perform, and develop the violent warrior ethos which already circulates within the language of the play. Volumnia's speech is not significantly *more* violent than that of other characters in the play, but as Coriolanus' mother, her words are overestimated. It is largely her position in the play, as "the" mother, coupled with her distinctly nonmaternal speech, which allows her to be interpreted as the "bad" mother and as such, the cause of Coriolanus' demise.[13]

One of the advantages of shifting psychoanalytic themes from causal to effectual and structural frameworks of interpretation is that it renders gratuitous the appeal to epigenetic accounts, which – whatever their "truth-value" – seduce the reader into seeking explanations that have no warrant in the text and ignoring those that do. Some examples of the differences these frameworks can make follow.

In the last section of a long chapter on – and a strong reading of – *Measure for Measure*, Richard Wheeler attributes the failure of its comic resolutions to Shakespeare's circumvention of "the specter that shapes symbolic action throughout the drama of the tragic period," "an image of woman that no particular female character can embody ... The experience of the tragic protagonist is shaped by an imaginary specter of woman, outside the masculine order of law, who seduces, betrays, usurps, castrates, ... who ultimately demands death, and from whom life can be freed only by tragic action that sacrifices the most manly of men – and often the best of women – to her."[14] This observation is testable in terms of the approach suggested by Lowe: Wheeler treats the fantasy of woman as "a 'symptom' of cultural anxieties" about manhood which is represented in the language of the plays. He later makes some perceptive remarks on the way Richard II "collaborates in his own destruction" and on the way "the self-assured and instinctively powerful Bolingbroke" is reduced by his guilt to a king who "survives in a state of anxious suspension, continually affirming a role he can neither fill nor abandon" (159). But instead of trying to show how Richard's collaboration – his *performance* of his destruction – creates the specter of the royal victim that haunts and enervates Henry IV, Wheeler shifts to the epigenetic framework: "Henry IV's deterioration and death purge *in a context of public destiny* the most primitive layer of guilt in the individual psyche, which is rooted in an infant's murderous, devouring rage against a mother and the fantasies of retaliation in kind that such rage engenders" (163, my italics). The italicized phrase alludes to a previous statement: "In the main power struggles of these plays, the heritage of conflict centered in oedipal and preoedipal relations to a mother tends to be absorbed into symbolic objects of political loyalties and anxieties and only indirectly into relations among characters," and the maternal role is displaced to England (162).

The undemonstrable emphasis on Henry's bond to his mother diverts attention from his more obvious bond to Richard – his bondage to the specter of Richard – and the equally demonstrable, though carefully muffled, bond to his father. This makes it harder for Wheeler to appreciate either the effect of those bonds on Henry's interlocutory struggles with his son or the dark resonance of the specter of those struggles in *Henry V.* In his opinion that play is weakened because the political displacement excludes "from Hal's direct experience the dimension of conflict and need that builds on potentialities established in a child's relation to a mother" (162). Two comments by Wheeler suggest the importance he places on the presence of mothers among the dramatis personae as a criterion of aesthetic judgment: Shakespeare creates "an expanded reality" in the tragedies and "a greatly expanded range of conflict" in *Hamlet* (191) by staging "anxieties and hazards that derive from the bond to the mother" (167). The displacement of conflict takes its toll on *Henry V:* "by insulating the prince from psychic hazards that will qualify the autonomy of Shakespeare's tragic heroes" (164), the play "ceremoniously resolves the political troubles of the second tetralogy at the expense of flattening their human content" (167). Appeal to the epigenetic criterion leads Wheeler to ignore the textual indications of the "psychic hazards" that "qualify" and problematize the figure of Henry V, making him the subject of perennial critical controversy.

The *Henriad*, Wheeler writes, "centers on royal inheritance complicated by patricidal motives in relations to actual and symbolic fathers" (158). Commentators from Franz Alexander and Ernst Kris to the present have discussed Prince Harry's "parricidal" impulses. It isn't difficult to educe from a close reading of his language the presence of hostile or aggressive reactions to his father, the anxieties they arouse, and the mounting stridency of displaced aggression / anxiety whose climax in the fourth play makes *Henry V* powerful, complex, and compelling. But traces of a desire to kill the father would be harder to find, and from this standpoint the word *parricidal* could be dismissed as hyperbolic.[15] Of course the commentators insist that the parricidal impulse is "unconscious," and later in this essay I shall confront the premises that support the claim, the premises (1) that any speaker in the Shakespeare text "has" an unconscious and (2) that critics can specify with assurance which meanings in any utterance are conscious or intended and which are unconscious or unintended. At this point, however, I only want to observe that *parricidal* often functions as a code word or metonym for the

Oedipal conflict, and that it therefore implicates consideration, first, of the Oedipal triangle, and second, of childhood and the epigenetic paradigm.

One odd consequence of this implication is that it occasionally leads critics to explain their evaluations of plays in terms of the adequacy or inadequacy with which the triangle is represented. Kris tried to defend against this tendency in comparing the Oedipal conflict of Harry with that of Hamlet:

> In Hamlet the oedipus is fully developed, centering around the queen. In Shakespeare's historical dramas women are absent or insignificant ... The psychological plausibility of Prince Hal as a dramatic character is not inferior to that of Hamlet, *whatever the difference in depth and dramatic significance of the two plays may be.* While only one part of the oedipal conflict is presented, the defenses which Prince Hal mobilizes in order to escape from his internal predicament *are well known from the clinical study of male youths.*[16]

In spite of Kris's even-handed treatment, the first italicized phrase opens up a loophole for evaluative comparison, while the second defends "psychological plausibility" by resorting to an irrelevant criterion ("clinical study") in order to compensate for the truncation of Oedipal conflict. Wheeler (159–63) repeats and expands Kris's argument only to reverse its emphasis. As we saw, he blames the inferiority of *Henry V* on that truncation.

A much fuller, subtler, and more appreciative reading of *Henry V* appears in C. L. Barber's *The Whole Journey,* left unfinished at his untimely death and completed by Wheeler. Yet even here, passages of brilliant interpretation are punctuated by qualifying assessments similar to those in Wheeler's study, such as the statement that "[Henry V] uses (or through him Shakespeare uses) allegiances formed on the model of brotherhood as a way of avoiding confrontation with the Oedipal motives that we can see developing in the Henry IV plays and that will come to full tragic expression in *Hamlet.*" This "developmental perspective ... does not invalidate the direct vision of war that *Henry V* dramatizes" or the success with which "Shakespeare has shielded his hero king" from the Oedipal encounter with the "unfinished business of an earlier stage of life," yet the related "need for ruthless male assertion" served by the war "shapes and limits dramatic understanding." It isn't until *Hamlet* that the author dares to join his protagonist in representing and re-experiencing "the full stress of the Oedipal situation."[17]

The epigenetic model enabling one to distinguish and characterize stages in the life cycle from infancy to adulthood may be used to organize data in a scheme that facilitates *description* of the stages and cycle. But for obvious reasons it lends itself equally well to the activity of moral judgment and evaluation. Terms like *maturity* and *immaturity* hover uneasily between descriptive and evaluative status. So, in commenting on Henry's command to kill the prisoners, Barber and Wheeler suggest that

> what repels us is not cruelty or ruthlessness as such, but the precarious sexual immaturity that motivates them. It is the use Henry makes of war in the service of unacknowledged inner conflict that puts us off, *even as the play invites our assent.* Shakespeare, to put it bluntly, is ennobling the psychology characteristic of an adolescent gang ... The kind of group interaction mobilized in *Henry V* can provide a defense against the failure to have adequately internalized the father and with this the ability to deal in a whole human way with sexuality. (227, my italics)

This failure occurs because Henry – "or through him Shakespeare" – avoids "confrontation with … Oedipal motives" (231), as he had at his father's deathbed when he regressed to "the sort of uncritical identification of son with father appropriate to a much earlier moment, the beginning of the latency period, not the end of youth and the assumption of manhood" (233). Barber and Wheeler seem unwilling to explore the possibility that the play *does not* invite our assent to what they see as Henry's immaturity, that indeed it represents his inner conflict in considerable textual detail, represents it *as* unacknowledged, and directs attention to the effects of that lack of acknowledgment on Henry's language and behavior.

In spite of their largely successful effort to give *Henry V* a proper hearing, or reading, they extend the charge of immaturity from Henry to the play and its author, and thus, shifting back and forth between description of what the play does and evaluation of what it fails to do, they tend to impose the closure of premature (not immature) judgment on a play that critically dramatizes such a tendency. This confusion seems at least partly motivated by the project of double epigenesis in which the developmental profile and relative "maturity" of the hero are coupled to those of the author. My concern is not to criticize the coupling, the riskiness of which Barber and Wheeler show themselves well aware, but to use it as an illustration of the problem I want to address in the remainder of this essay. If only for the sake of argument, let's assume that the author of Shakespeare's plays was a real person, and that there is enough evidence about his life to enable him to be a subject of psychoanalysis. Then there may well be valid controversy as to which of the two perspectives I outlined earlier – the Freudian or the Lacanian – to put into play; controversy as to whether, in interrogating the evidence (or the subject, or his language), epigenetic themes and narratives should be accorded the position of signifier or signified. But – and this is the point of this little exercise – in the case of a fictional speaker, a dramatis persona, I submit that even with strong, persuasive readings like that of Barber and Wheeler, reliance on the Freudian perspective and the epigenetic model elicits forms of explanation that are inappropriate, untestable, arbitrary, and, above all, antipolitical in the sense indicated by Lisa Lowe when she argues that they divert attention from present (as opposed to past) sources of conflict, anxiety, and fantasy inscribed "within the language of the play" and circulating through its community.

How, then, can we formulate an approach that will avail itself of insights drawn from psychoanalysis while blocking the epigenetic fallacy illustrated in the examples discussed above? The first step is to put into play a revised version of the radical stipulation, stated above, that speakers are the effects rather than the causes of their language and our interpretation: in the unperformed Shakespeare text there are no characters, no persons, no bodies, no interiorities; there are only dramatis personae, the masks through which the text speaks. At most the unperformed text offers material for an interpretation, a portrait, a set of portraits, that readers, actors, directors, and playgoers construct. Speakers don't have bodies, age, insomnia, corpulence, or illness unless and until they mention them, and when they do it is usually in the service of some discourse in which states of the body are signifiers used to mystify moral effects as physical causes. Speakers don't have childhoods unless and until they mention them. If, for example, John of Gaunt never mentions his youth, then he has and had no youth, no childhood whose critical events the analytical dialogue may recuperate and revise by the light of the future anterior. Speakers in Shakespeare texts, as in others, don't necessarily die. Some do. But others just stop; they leave the text or the stage and don't come back. Why, then, do some of them die? Not because they died, say, in Holinshed, but because their death is the object of their desire, their response to the conflict of discourses. When John of Gaunt flaunts his age and dies, it is to ensconce himself in the complex discursive scenario I have elsewhere called the *ars moriendi* discourse. He is conspicuously old not because he is no longer young, or because he was old in Holinshed, but because he is moved to activate the weakling's plea, senility, and to use Tillyard's traditional world-picture as an excuse for his refusal to challenge Richard or support his son's cause. The aging body emerges in language as a signifier and trope – a metonymy of displacement – enabling the speaker to fend off awareness of his active complicity.[18]

Early in 2 *Henry IV* Falstaff alludes to the displacement function of physical disease while describing Henry's illness to the Chief Justice. The king, he says, suffers "a kind of lethargy, … a kind of sleeping in the blood, a whoreson tingling" that originates "from much grief, from study, and perturbation of the brain; I have read the cause of his effects in Galen, it is a kind of deafness" (i.ii.110–16). He distinguishes this from his own willful pretense of deafness, "the disease of not listening, the malady of not marking" (120–1). Falstaff's Galenic rumor parodies the "smooth comforts false" (Induction, 40) of medical knowledge. His repeated "a kind of" detaches him from the diagnosis and teases us with a veiled allusion to "some other grief" (Ind., 13) more closely connected to "the disease of not listening." Dis-ease is also uneasiness; the uneasiness produced by turning a deaf ear to what one's words are doing – such words, for example, as "uneasy lies the head that wears the crown." Lafew's comment on the doctors trying to cure the king in *All's Well That Ends Well* delivers the message in more direct and generally applicable form: "we make trifles of terrors, ensconcing ourselves in seeming knowledge when we should submit ourselves to an unknown fear" (ii.iii.3–6). In 2 *Henry IV* the figure of Rumor, itself (herself? himself?) a displacement, gloats over the power its mastery of the trope of displacement gives it to enforce the self-deception of the Lafew principle on the community of the play by diverting attention from what Henry calls the "inward wars" (iii.i.107):

> I speak of peace, while covert enmity
> Under the smile of safety wounds the world;
> And who but Rumor, who but only I,
> Make fearful musters, and prepar'd defence,
> Whiles the big year, swoln with some other grief,
> Is thought with child by the stern tyrant War,
> And no such matter?
>
> (Ind., 9–15)

> From Rumor's tongues
> They bring smooth comforts false, worse than true wrongs.
> (Ind., 39–40)

Since *year* in line 13 can function as a dialectal form of *ear* (and does so at i.ii.194 in the Quarto version of Falstaff's encounter with the Chief Justice), Rumor's figure of false pregnancy engendered from without may be reinterpreted as both Henry's and fat Falstaff's disease of not listening to – in Richard II's words – "the unseen grief / That swells with silence in the tortur'd soul" (*Richard II*, iv.i.297–8).

The question Falstaff and Lafew raise about Inside Dopesters in medical science strikes me as similar to the question Lacan raises about the post-Freudian drift of psychoanalysis, and this suggests that Lacan's critique may contain a lesson for interpreters of Shakespeare. Crudely put, the lesson is that you can't situate a Shakespearean pathology in a conceptual framework of instinct, naturalness, organic function, or biological destiny. That framework only provides a set of signifying functions, material for the tropes of displacement, condensation, and visualization that manifest the latency of the "unknown fear," or of the mysterious "other grief" Rumor alludes to.

This is, as I noted, the first step in an approach whose objective is to reposition the themes, methods, concepts, and insights of psychoanalysis in a framework that avoids the problems caused by the epigenetic fallacy. In outlining it I have already used the term *discourse* several times without bothering to define it. The second and more important step will be to define it. This is the task of the next section, after which I shall give an account of the theory of discourses, and illustrate it in stretches of interpretation.

Discourse is the sort of modest, recessive term people use to define and discuss other things without bothering to define and discuss *it*. As a result it has become an all-purpose instrument denoting anything from the narrow confines of a speech event to the amplitude of social and political practices. Benveniste centers the term on agency and self-reference; Foucault, on structure and power; Greimas, on the deep structure of value systems; others, on the inscription of ideology; still others, on the alterity or citationality or intertextuality of all linguistic performances.[19] True to its etymology, the term runs incessantly back and forth across the field of meaning. What moved me to put it into play were two recent events in the history of the term and of my encounters with it, both of them involving gestures toward a definition. The first occurs in Catherine Belsey's *Critical Practice*, the second in Keir Elam's *Shakespeare's Universe of Discourse*.

Belsey's is an almost casual definition given during the course of an argument defending the claims of modern literary theory against those of a commonsense view of reading: discourse is "a domain of language-use, a particular way of talking (and writing and thinking)" that "involves certain shared assumptions which appear in the formulations characterizing it."[20] What interests me about this is the way she deploys the two examples she uses to illustrate the definition: she notes that common sense is one such domain of language use, and modern physics another, and that "some of the formulations of the one may be expected to conflict with the formulations of the other" (5). This coupling is loaded. In Belsey's account, because common sense is inscribed in everyday language it presents itself as "obvious," "natural," "non-theoretical," as "the collective and timeless wisdom" that seems (like the word of God) "to be the source and guarantee of everything we take for granted" (2–5). Although Belsey doesn't spell it out, her reference to modern physics fixes on an example of discourse that presents itself as theoretical and counterintuitive, the product of an emergent specialization of knowledge that developed under historically specific conditions. Furthermore, modern physics presents itself as a challenge to what common sense tells us to take for granted. This contrast suggests why Belsey goes on to say that "ideology" (which she uses in its Althusserian sense) "is *inscribed in* discourse" (5).

Clearly, common sense and modern physics are not only two discourses; they instantiate two different kinds or levels of discourse. Yet this apparent difference, along with its apparent clarity, are themselves products of the commonsense view of the matter. Belsey's thesis, the argument served by the definition and examples, is that a common-sense approach to literature is no less discursive, ideological, interested, and culture-specific than a view which, like modern science, appears to violate common sense because informed by theoretical premises that are explicit and counterintuitive. What the two have in common may be expressed by saying that "the discourse of *x*" is a formula that marks any "domain of language-use" as a social construction rather than a fact of nature. A discourse is an interpretation rather than a reflection of "experience." This agrees in spirit with the Lacanian position outlined in the last section. On the one hand, "There's no discourse that is not make-believe." On the other hand, since this is so, and since "Nature" is itself the name of a discourse, some make-believe discourses are more real than others, and though all discourses may be make-believe, they need not have been feigned: "*Hypotheses non fingo* means that only discourses ex-sist."

The difference between the two levels of discourse is that one is implicit and the other explicit. Discourses are explicit when they are culturally recognized as specific domains of language use, as the products of specifiable human agency (collective or individual or both), and as traditional or countertraditional bodies of practice and systems of interpretation. Implicit discourses – those, for example, of common sense, racism, colonialism, and sexism – conceal this recognition, whereas explicit discourses embrace and proclaim it. Explicit discourses (science, criticism, literature, law, drama, cosmology, medicine, anthropology, etc.) may well reinforce and participate in implicit discourses. But they may also bring out that implicit discursivity by representation, interpretation, and critique.[21] Thus the implicit discourse of common sense tells us stories about ourselves and the world, and does so in a way that elicits our belief. The explicit discourse of physics challenges some of those stories and exposes their discursive character. We may still believe the stories, but we do so against the dissonant hum of a cultural undertone that tells us they are perceptual interpretations and that even perception, because it is linguistically informed, is "ideologically and discursively constructed, rooted in a specific historical situation, and operating in conjunction with a particular social formation."[22]

This account may be linked to Shakespearean practice by passing briefly through another definitional context. The distinction between *discourse* and *story* appears in narratological theory: story is what is told, discourse is the telling; story is the sum total of plots, events, characters, etc., that is, the fictional "world" that can be imagined apart from the particular medium (or "substance") and narrative form in which it is represented, while discourse is the sum of narrative strategies that effect and affect the representation. Whatever its flaws (and it has flaws), the distinction is useful in highlighting the active character of discourse. It reminds us that discourse is an interpretation of the story it tells and that to abstract it from the story makes it possible to focus on the agency of the (individual or collective) teller. To go a step further, the most interesting instances of the story / discourse distinction occur when the opposition is transgressed by discursive strategies that represent the story being told as itself a discourse, an interpretation and not merely a neutral transmission of its fictive "world" or "experience." This is, for example, a standard feature of literature whose representations of love stories include intertextual allusions to courtly, Petrarchan, Ovidian, and Neoplatonic interpretations of love. Here the phrase "discourse of love" translates into "interpretation of a story," and the burden of the interpretation is that the story is itself an interpretation: its point is that the story of love is not told by nature, or, if it is, it is one that has been radically mediated by the discursive strategies of gendered human agency; the story of love is critically represented as both a discourse *about* gender and a discourse authorized *by* the gender that controls the site of narration. The Shakespeare text often works in such a transgressive manner. While maintaining the distinction between *what is told* and *how it is told*, its metatheatrical and metaliterary strategies tend to dissolve the conceptual boundary separating story as a given from discourse as an interpretation of the given. Within the community of the play, the stories speakers tell each other and themselves about love, war, kingship, generational conflict, death, senescence, heroism, and the family drama are marked in this manner.

In centering on the active character of discourse, the narratological concept encourages us to see that it is performative as well as informative, or constative, or cognitive; that it not only represents but also transforms what it represents; and that it is performative not only with respect to the stories it tells but also with respect to its recipients or addressees, who may include the teller. The activity of language as discourse is the subject of Keir Elam's *Shakespeare's Universe of Discourse*. Elam notes that *discourse* is Shakespeare's favorite word in the comedies for "language in *use*" and on display, language as a form of action, and language as a "tangible presence" and a performed dramatic object.[23] From this he goes on to develop a view of Shakespearean discourse modeled on Wittgenstein's language-game concept. What he does with both Wittgenstein and Shakespeare is disappointing from an interpretive standpoint, but I find the connection suggestive, and I shall now take it in a direction different from his by briefly reviewing aspects of the notion of language-game that overlap Belsey's notion of discourse.[24] Wittgenstein introduced the term *language-game* to connect forms of talk with what he called "forms of life," a phrase that, behind its vagueness, denotes the collectively, socially, culturally, institutionally constructed ambience of language use. He opposed this concept to the so-called private-language argument in order to shift the focus of attention from the mental states of the individual to the outward criteria of observable discursive behavior correlated with specific bodies of community practice.[25]

The value of this move for my purposes is that it puts the emphasis on describable kinds of language-games situated primarily in the culture of the community and only secondarily in the individual. In that respect the notion of language-game has conceptual affinities with that of "the discourse of the other," understood in the broad sense that extends its scope beyond the domain of the unconscious to that of the society's instituted processes, whether economic or political or medical or legal or literary or theatrical or anything else. And it also has obvious affinities with the view of discourse developed above on the basis of Belsey's discussion. So conceived, a particular language-game can be viewed as framing the conditions within which intentions arise, and Wittgenstein gives a clear example of how this works:

> 337. But didn't I already intend the whole construction of the sentence (for example) at its beginning? So surely it existed in my mind before I said it aloud! – If it was in my mind, still it would not normally be there in some different word order. But here we are constructing a misleading picture of "intending," that is, of the use of this word. An

intention is embedded in its situation, in human customs and institutions. If the technique of the game of chess did not exist, I could not intend to play a game of chess. In so far as I do intend the construction of a sentence in advance, that is made possible by the fact that I can speak the language in question.[26]

Chess isn't the only game in the Shakespeare corpus, but it may serve as a sanitized model that reductively symbolizes, and thus conspicuously excludes, the language-games of a world less brave and new. Those games conform to a cruder model that, in one of the more unappealing language-games of contemporary lay (or near-lay) psychology, goes by the name of "the games people play." Wittgenstein's account picks out an important feature of Shakespeare's practice, for it reminds us that we often can't tell from a speaker's language use whether his or her "playing" is intended as well as motivated; the game has its own logic, its own scenario, and plays itself out in the speaker's language regardless of the cognitive status we ascribe to it. Considered as discourses – Belsey's "domains of language-use" – most of the language-games I shall explore will be implicit in the sense indicated above, but, as we shall see, one of the problems confronting Shakespeare's speakers will be that of keeping them implicit, blocking awareness of the language-games they play.

The commitment to the idea that states of mind "belong" not so much to particular speakers as to the discourses they participate in obviously risks succumbing to the structuralist tendency to devalue agency by taking a radical view of "the discourse of the other." The tendency is reinforced by drawing rigid boundaries between intended and unintended meaning, or between consciousness and the unconscious, and by restricting the category of agency to the first member of each pair. The problem just mentioned introduces a salutary complication because it presupposes a category of agency and responsibility that the structuralist disjunction can't handle, and it therefore demands a more flexible picture of the individual speaker's relation to discourse. In this connection, I have found some helpful clues in Anthony Giddens's distinction between *discursive* and *practical* consciousness: the former denotes what actors "are able to say, or to give verbal expression to, about social conditions, including especially the conditions of their own action." Practical consciousness denotes "what actors know (believe) about social conditions, including especially the conditions of their own action, but *cannot* express discursively."[27] It would be better to change the italicized word to "do not," since Giddens treats the boundary between the two forms of consciousness as permeable, but distinguishes practical consciousness, with its tacit knowledge, from the unconscious: "there are barriers, centered principally upon repression, between discursive consciousness and the unconscious"; if competent actors can, when asked, "nearly always report discursively about their intentions in, and reasons for, acting as they do, they cannot necessarily do so of their motives."[28] The Shakespearean discourses I shall examine call for a slight revision of this scheme, since they involve situations in which actors may not want to, may try not to, confront and report on "their motives" or express "the conditions of their own action," and, in addition, may "want" or "try" not to become aware of this evasive action.

Although such a form of agency is nonconscious, it is more like practical consciousness than unconscious repression, and I therefore baptize it practical unconsciousness. However difficult it may be to account for the mechanisms of this process, and however strained the indications of agency coded above in *want* and *try* may seem in this context, examples of this form of agency are legion and the concept is part of common lore. Agents may try to avoid discursive consciousness of the discourses they operate or submit to, and in this revision of Giddens's analytic scheme, the task of maintaining merely practical consciousness would be assigned to counter-discursive strategies of practical unconsciousness. One of Giddens's central motifs is that of the "duality of structure," of the recursive processes by which social systems interact with human agents, and his "theory of structuration" is generated partly from a critique of structuralism. A structuralist perspective on agency is reductive if it limits the agent's role to that of a conduit for discourses or for anything else. Agents may but needn't be mere conduits. Although they are always to some extent subject to the discourse that "speaks through them," they may choose to be conduits even as they deploy strategies enabling them to "operate" the discourse. The idea of unconscious strategies is not incongruous if practical unconsciousness is seen as a negative form of practical consciousness. That is, let's assume with Giddens that "every social actor knows a great deal about the conditions of reproduction of the society of which he or she is a member" and can draw upon "tacit stocks of knowledge … in the constitution of social activity."[29] This is practical consciousness. Practical unconsciousness is then the tacit knowledge of techniques for occluding, ignoring, forgetting, whatever knowledge one has that interferes with belief in one's commitment to a discourse. The successful reduction of agents to conduits presupposes the discursive ability to find and apply the arguments by which they can convince themselves and, if necessary, deceive themselves. To give Kant's dictum a Sartrean skew, when it is necessary to curtail knowledge in order to make room for bad faith, practical unconsciousness is put to work. The conventional and stereotypical character of the discourses I shall examine, along with the apparently objective structure of their scenarios, facilitates that work because it signifies, indeed dramatizes, their independence of the agent, and signifies it *to* the agent.

The best general description I know of the activity displayed in the discourses I am about to explore occurs during Benveniste's discussion of language in Freudian theory:

> All through Freudian analysis it can be seen that the subject makes use of the act of speech and discourse in order to "represent himself" to himself as he wishes to see himself and as he calls upon the "other" to observe him. His discourse is … a sometimes vehement solicitation of the other through the discourse in which he figures himself desperately, and an often mendacious recourse to the other in order to individualize himself in his own eyes. Through the sole fact of addressing another, the one who is speaking of himself installs the other in himself, and thereby apprehends himself, confronts himself, and establishes himself as he aspires to be, and finally historicizes himself in this incomplete or falsified history.[30]

Thus "discourse is both the bearer of a message and the instrument of action." I note in passing that such discursive activity is in high gear in the system of positional differences that Freudians call the family romance but that I prefer (for the reasons given above) to call the family drama. Since any single position in the system is not an integer but the fraction of a dyadic bond – "parent" and "child," for example, require and co-define each other – the differential logic of the drama speaks through the speakers inscribed in it, limits their autonomy, ambiguates their love, and intensifies their desire for self-representation while diminishing their control over it. There are recognizable and often-documented positional discourses – the father's, the daughter's, the son's, the mother's, the wife's, the husband's, the sibling's, and so forth.

I shall return to the positional discourses later. I mention them now chiefly to distinguish them from the set of discourses to be explored in the following pages – the "ethical" discourses, to which I give names that reflect their stereotypical character as culturally constructed and constrained patterns of motivation: the discourses of the donor, the victim / revenger, the sinner, the villain, the hero, and the saint or martyr. The motivational scenario of the donor's discourse may be unpacked from Lear's "I gave you all," considered as a threat, an assault, an act of violence. The gift is a wound that must be defended against – as it is by Regan's reply, "and in good time you gave it." The donor's discourse works according to the logic of the gift spelled out by Marcel Mauss in his classic essay on the subject. His account suggests that it may be described in economic terms as the logic of *negative usury*. Usury boils down to getting more than you give. Negative usury is giving more than you get – but in order to get more than you give. Usury is a simple, straightforward practice; negative usury is a more indirect and powerful way to subjugate the recipient in bonds of obligation.[31]

Lear flaunts his paternal power of generosity from a position of weakness. He lets himself be persuaded by the Fool that he is being infantilized and emasculated by his daughters. The donor's discourse thus emerges hand in hand with another, whose root formula is expressed in Lear's "I am a man / More sinned against than sinning." "More sinned against than sinning" is the victim's complaint, but within it lurks the threat of "I am a man," the threat stressed by the line division: "I am a man – and will have my revenges, will protect my manhood." As the donor's discourse sets up and justifies the victim's, so the victim's sets up and justifies the revenger's; the two are hard to pry apart and are often found in close embrace.

This reading of the victim's formula, however, ignores the defensiveness inscribed in "more sinned against than sinning," which parries an implied accusation: "What I did to them was not as bad as what they did to me." The guilt this defense betrays opens up another wound and signals the operation of another discourse whose radical is obtained by reversing the victim's formula. "More sinning than sinned against" encodes the confessional logic of the sinner's discourse. Turning the revenger's discourse in upon oneself, its motivation is the desire to be punished, judged, or – what may be more painful and threatening – forgiven. One can punish oneself more easily than one can forgive oneself; forgiveness must be at least partly conferred by others, and it carries with it all the dangers of the gift.[32] Since one can't forgive oneself, the sinner's discourse can only solicit self-retribution. The sinner's secret quest and fearful desire is "to course his own shadow for a traitor." That desire may lead him to hurt those he loves as a way of hurting himself. It may lead him to cultivate their distrust and disesteem. It may lead him to seek punishment at the hands of others; this in turn may tempt him again to resume the victim's discourse and direct his aggression outward, thereby deepening the inward wound. The sinner's discourse is seldom on the surface of a speaker's language; either it hides in the recesses of the text or betrays itself by its complicity in shaping the plot of self-undoing. The contrary holds for another discourse. If "more sinning than sinned against" articulates the sinner's acknowledgment of his wickedness as the mode of remorse, the same formula ironic-ally announces the proud boast of the self-confessed villain. Shakespeare's most endearing villains – Edmund, Iago, and Richard III – tend to bring the villain's discourse right up front and use the soliloquy to tell themselves how bad they are. In fact, the discourse is more complex than that, since its operators often appear to be playing the role of stage villain, and doing so with varying tones and degrees of parody. The villain's target often seems to be himself as much as the traditional morality and its theater. Thus turned upside down, the conventional gesture of self-revelation is transgressed by other discourses that disenable the very claim to autonomy and voyeuristic power the act of soliloquy dramatizes.

Speakers who relish in the villain's discourse often find themselves in the delightful position of staging a travesty of its opposite, the discourse of virtue or morality – or, hyperbolically, for lack of a better noun, the saint's discourse. Think, for example, of that wonderful episode in *Richard III* (iii.vii) that begins with the stage direction *Enter Richard aloft, between two Bishops* – "two props of virtue for a Christian prince," "a book of prayer in his hand," and apparently fresh off his pious knees. The saint's discourse features a variety of postures that are often aggressively stated – unappreci-ated generosity or loyalty, self-sacrifice, slandered virtue, conspicuous probity, nonresponsibility for evil, renunciation of the world and its vanity. Honest Iago occasionally has a small piece of this discourse. But taken more seriously, the saint's discourse offers those who desire self-justification a richer and more positive resource than that of the victim / revenger, though it may be animated by it, and it sometimes unfolds in the shadow of the sinner's discourse. The saint's discourse responds to a persistent question, the fifth Henry's "May I with right and conscience make this claim?" It winds its way into the language of Edgar, Kent, and Cordelia, and it takes over most of the Scots in *Macbeth*.[33] It appears in those two oddly reverberating phrases in the *Merchant of Venice*, Portia's "I stand for sacrifice" and Shylock's "I stand for judgment." It is hilariously burlesqued by Richard III, mockingly and bitterly (perhaps nostalgically) mimed by Richard II, and, in its most significant manifestation, pursued with increasing fervor through three plays by the son of Henry IV. Finally, it sometimes overlaps with another discourse, the hero's discourse, or discourse of honor. The saint's discourse involves a story one tells oneself – "Why I do trifle thus with his despair / Is done to cure it" – and one tells it to or solicits it from others primarily to persuade oneself, especially if one suspects that what one is doing may be reprehen-sible. But the hero's discourse involves a story one has to solicit and hear from others, a story that, like a prize, one has to win or earn by continuous displays or promises of a form of activity that in recent decades has come to be known as "laying one's body on the line." Now since this is not something one can ask one's poor body to spend all of its time doing, there are long periods of foreplay and afterplay during which honor is maintained by words rather than deeds, or by words *as* deeds.

Each discourse, then, has its own rationale or scenario, or its own "argument" (in one of the older meanings of the term). Although the scenarios of the ethical discourses are primarily ethico-psychological they are always situated in specific positional scenarios. So, for example, the power of the donor's discourse, the discourse of the gift, is predictably keyed to the authority of the father or ruler. The affective ambivalence that marks the father's discourse is conditioned by the ambivalence of his legal authority over, his obligation to and dependence on, the filial beneficiaries (oldest son, married daughters) who will replace him; and over whom, waxing as he wanes, his last remaining power may be that of the gift. When the husband bearing phallic authority fears the unofficial power of the wife who could betray him, emasculate him, conspire with children, divert the patrimonial gift, he may defend or avenge himself by strategic deployment of the victim / revenger's argument. The plight of the Shakespearean hero inscribed in the ethical discourse of honor – Hotspur, Coriolanus, Othello – is compounded by the inseparability of that discourse from the positional discourse of gender. Thus, in responding to the density of text that represents a speaker like Lear or Edgar, one can focus on the coexistence, conflict, and volatile interplay of several discourses. The positional exigencies of the paternal dyad motivate the occupants of both roles to engage in self-justifying language-games. They represent themselves as maligned victims, unappreciated saints or donors or saviors, and these moves are sometimes depicted as strategies that defend against yet unavoidably exacerbate the self-wounding power of the sinner's discourse. To illustrate this interplay of ethical and positional discourses, I shall look more closely at the father's discourse in *King Lear*.

In Shakespeare's text, the family is embedded in, and indeed identical with, a political order whose orientation toward father power is haloed by some version of what has variously been called "the inherited conglomerate," the great chain, the Elizabethan world picture, and other vaguely essentializing concepts produced by the intellectual-historical tradition.[34] The tensions and ambivalence woven into the differences of gender and generation that constitute the family drama are amplified by the unequal distribution of patriarchal power, and complicated by the double inscription that marks age as the site of both authority and weakness. The ideal of metabolic balance between conflict and cooperation tends to be destabilized by the philosophy of zero-sum: "the younger rises when the old doth fall," or, to paraphrase the phallic wisdom of the Fool's little tiny wit, "the woman rises when the man doth fall." As if to compensate for this disequilibrium, patriarchal ideology re-presents the zero-sum struggle in a language of authority and deference that features bonding, reciprocity, trust, natural inequality, and willing compliance.

These two perspectives correspond to the two Natures whose conflict was the subject of John Danby's *Shakespeare and the Doctrine of Nature*: on the one hand, Hooker's happy hierarchy, and on the other, Hobbes's hairy horror. More recently, G. K. Hunter described the conflict in similar terms as a struggle between two value systems, the good old one with its "decencies" and "antique pieties" and the bad new one promoted by "anti-Establishment individualists." He sees the former "dissolving under the impact" of the latter's Machiavellian "modernism," and he describes the benign view with mounting fervor:

> For Gloucester as for Lear the "bias of nature" … requires children and parents to love and protect one another; the "offices of nature" … cause the young to respect the old, the subordinate to yield to the superior, the passionate to bow to the rational, as female to male or human to divine. All this follows inevitably from an assumption that *nature* is a reflection of the *status quo*, of an order without which things could not hold together and meaning would not exist. And the *status quo* is thought of not simply as "the way things happen to be" but rather as "the way things must be."[35]

But thought of by whom? The answer is in the opening phrase of the passage: "*For Gloucester as for* Lear" – not only "in their opinion" but also "on their behalf." And incidentally, the fathers believe, or would like to persuade themselves as well as others, that the status quo reflects nature, not the other way round.

It is Edmund who claims that the status quo is mystified as nature, and it is not at all clear that he conforms to Hunter's portrait of a Machiavellian version of the Hobbesian yahoo or yippie. Edmund is not out to destroy the status quo. On the contrary, he wants to buy into it by replacing his brother and father in the seat of legitimate power. He shares the paternal values, and desires the paternal authority he criticizes. What Edmund sees is already there to see, and the way he sees it corresponds precisely to the way Lear and Gloucester try, ever more desperately, not to see it. The fathers tilt the so-called bias of nature in their direction to protect their interests against their children, to preserve their power against indirect and legitimate no less than direct and illegitimate filial challenges, and – above all – to maintain self-esteem, especially when doing things that jeopardize it. "I gave you all" is thus the founding gesture of a discourse by which the fathers reify a moral system favorable to them, and use it to monopolize the resources of self-justification in their strategic warfare with the next generation. As Stephen Greenblatt argues, the other side of the play's gerontocratic emphasis is the fear that nobody loves you when you're old and gray,[36] especially if you have dealt with others in the mode of power and disguised it as love, if you have continually paraded the *all* you never really gave and somehow expected to be rewarded with loving, not servile, obedience.

Against this background we may set the following version of the father's discourse. I have abstracted it from the language of Lear and Gloucester – chiefly Lear – supplemented by some of Edmund's observations.[37] It is designed as an imaginary soliloquy, a kind of internal dialogue in which the father begins by rehearsing the catechism his children should obediently receive, and it is ordered to suggest how the initial premises are gradually subverted to expose the deep fears and contradictions that give rise to them:

1. I gave and give you all, and ask very little in return. It is my nature as a father to be kind and generous. I gave you birth, and when I give you and my land away in marriage I repeat that creative act, extending its power to the next generation. On my blessing depends your fertility and that of the land. Therefore,

2. you should study deserving, try to deserve my love by honoring the "offices of nature, bond of childhood," etc. Since I begot you, bred you, love you, you must return those duties back as are right fit; obey me, love me, and most honor me. The bias of nature obliges you – challenges you – to merit my blessing. This isn't a heavy demand, considering my care, pains, and sacrifices on your behalf. Nevertheless,

3. you can't possibly pay me back, since I gave you *all*. You are perpetually in my debt, and you owe me such allegiance as the female owes the male, the young the old, or the human the divine. And yet,

4. for a father of males, it *is* true that the very act of begetting an heir is the first step in prescribing my power and binding me in service to my son's future lordship. The plague of custom and curiosity of nations assigns upbringing and inheritance as a right, not as a privilege. In the order of law, my heir is potentially my enemy and competitor. His appearance prophesies my death, and he grows up waiting for me

to die so that he can rightfully claim that which his father loses: no less than all. This prompts a disturbing thought:

5   As I grow old and my power wanes, I sense more clearly what I have always dimly sensed, that you may not appreciate all I've done for you. No doubt, as your impatience and ingratitude increase, you begin to find an idle and fond bondage in the oppression of aged tyranny, who sways, not as it hath power, but as it is suffered. No doubt, also, you think that when sons are at perfect age, and fathers declined, the father should be as ward to the son, and the son manage his revenue. But it won't be easy for you to justify or act on such beliefs so long as I display and maintain my power. This power, which can command your obedience, is vested in my generosity. Since I can't trust you,

6   I must do my best to make sure you remain in my debt. Even as you study deserving, I shall fight to keep your study from being successful. I shall heap new obligations on you by rewarding your hypocritical mouth-service with undeserved favors. It's becoming clearer and clearer to me that

7   what I have loved in you is only that portion of myself I've invested in you – my image stamped in your metal. Your breeding hath been at my charge, and you are dear in my account. Perhaps you haven't failed to notice that I haven't loved you for yourself. And perhaps you've also noticed that I don't trust you because I know you do not love me, and know you have some cause. And perhaps you even sense that I'm afraid of you.

    [Given these premises, fathers understand that the language of filial, parental, and conjugal love has its primary function in providing the verbal arsenal of their war against their children. And they understand that primogeniture, bastardy, dowry, marriage, and inheritance provide the institutional arsenal. If this were all there were to the parent's credo, Shakespeare's would be a dismal view indeed. But there are, at least for Lear and Gloucester (though in different ways), two additional premises that redeem paternal nature from the general curse:]

8   What if I'm wrong? What if, in spite of everything I've done, my child loves me? How could I face that or be worthy of it? I must be perpetually in her / his debt. It is *I* who owe *her* / *him* all. Everything I did was calculated to make them contemn and reject me, and if they should confront me, should judge me as I deserve to be judged, my heart would burst smilingly – it would be a relief to die. And yet, ironically,

9   everything I did to my children, I did out of a need to be loved. Everything I did and still do is my way of trying to secure the love I need. But I know it can't work. I don't deserve it – didn't ever deserve it in the past. What I'm doing now makes me deserve it even less. Then what a terrible thing it would be for *them* to give *me* love – to wound me by giving me *their all* after I gave them nothing, while pretending to give them all.

The father begins this soliloquy with the donor's discourse, expressing his love by his phallic self-representation as a horn of plenty. But this investment in the power and warfare of the gift, unfolded in premises 1–3, is motivated by the fear of loss and declining power, which leads the warfare to be reimagined under the aspect of *apprehension*. (Etymologically, *apprehension* couples the *desire to take* with the *fear of being taken*.) Apprehension announces itself in premises 4–6 in the dialectic of the victim / revenger's discourse, and this outward war betrays what it displaces when the inward war of the sinner's discourse emerges in premises 8 and 9. The sequence is intended not as a record of Lear's or Gloucester's changes through the play but as a profile of the discursive strata that continually regenerate their versions of the father's discourse. The deepest stratum is the ninth premise. It is the ever-present and always self-canceling source of the others. As the simplest and most genuine expression of what the father wants, it should be the first premise. But it can't be allowed to surface; it remains the goal but also the target of self-inflicted blindness. Its basis is the sense of unworthiness that makes it impossible for him to expose himself in the expectation of love. Since he can't be loved for what he is – or thinks or fears he is – love has to be taken, has to be won; and giving – the power expressed in the promise or denial of the gift – is his form of taking. The most dangerous consequence of this scenario is the need and inability to perform the acts of atonement by which one may ask to be forgiven. For in the face of his knowledge that his enactment of the victim's discourse was villainous, and that what he deserves is punishment, is judgment, what could be more terrifying or painful than to be forgiven by those he has wounded with his claims of generosity, love, and sacrifice?

King Lear is no country for old men. But it is no country for the young either. They are often in arms, yet seldom in one another's. Their dilemma blazes out like a lightning bolt in a single sentence, which Gloucester means as a promise to Edmund, but which speaks through him as a threat: "Loyal and natural boy, I'll work the means / To make thee capable" (II.i.84–5). In this gesture of emasculation whose instrument is the donor's discourse the energizing power of morally justified complicity is stated with a clarity that is as blinding as it is blind. "I'll give you all." What can Edmund do to dismantle so many folds of favor except collaborate with Edgar in preserving the true blank of their father's eye? Gloucester's words glance at all the acts of folly – often but not always well intended – by which the characters marked "good" license the transfer of knavery to others, and help those marked "bad" to a measure of success the latter could not have achieved by themselves. So Kent, Cordelia, and Lear join Gloucester and Edgar in working the means that make Edmund capable of wringing from Lear his last agonized cry, "And my poor fool is hang'd …"

My account of ethical and positional discourses in the previous section suggests that the former may be more fundamental than the latter, that the "logics" of the ethical discourses not only implicate each other but also inform positional relationships. Thus, although the father–child relationship has a describable structure that limits the range of positional interactions, Shakespeare's fathers and children deal with the structure and compete with each other through the medium of the ethical discourses. It is worth repeating that the discourses appear as properties not of individual speakers but of the community of the play. G. K. Hunter makes the important observation that "the language of the play is not so much an imitation of the way people speak as an evocation of the realities *behind* what people say," and he adds that the "metaphors the characters use" do not individuate the speakers but "are more like trains of gunpowder laid across the play, capable of exploding into action when the poet requires it."[38] Hunter's own vivid metaphor suggests that it is language in use and on display that explodes into action; in my view what it evokes are the "realities" of discursive conflict, and it evokes them not merely "behind what people say" but *in* what they say.[39] This is of course easier to assert than to demonstrate, and my account of the father's discourse in *King Lear* was clearly not a demonstration because it abstracted from "what people say" to the interplay of discourses "behind" what they say. I shall now try to show how that interplay unfolds within the language of a single speaker and within the confines of a single speech. My purpose in doing so is to return the discussion to the questions raised in the second section of this essay – questions about intention, motivation, practical unconsciousness, and the uses of psychoanalysis. I hope to make a case for the value of certain features of Lacanian interpretation in dealing with those questions.

The speaker is Henry IV, and the proof text is the speech that opens Part One of *Henry IV*:

King:	So shaken as we are, so wan with care,	
	Find we a time for frighted peace to pant,	
	And breathe short-winded accents of new broils	
	To be commenc'd in stronds afar remote:	
	No more the thirsty entrance of this soil	5
	Shall daub her lips with her own children's blood,	
	No more shall trenching war channel her fields,	
	Nor bruise her flow'rets with the armed hoofs	
	Of hostile paces: those opposed eyes,	
	Which, like the meteors of a troubled heaven,	10
	All of one nature, of one substance bred,	
	Did lately meet in the intestine shock	
	And furious close of civil butchery,	
	Shall now, in mutual well-beseeming ranks,	
	March all one way, and be no more oppos'd	15
	Against acquaintance, kindred, and allies.	
	The edge of war, like an ill-sheathed knife,	
	No more shall cut his master. Therefore, friends,	
	As far as to the sepulchre of Christ –	
	Whose soldier now, under whose blessed cross	20
	We are impressed and engag'd to fight –	
	Forthwith a power of English shall we levy,	
	Whose arms were moulded in their mothers' womb	
	To chase these pagans in those holy fields	
	Over whose acres walk'd those blessed feet	25
	Which fourteen hundred years ago were nail'd	
	For our advantage on the bitter cross.	
	But this our purpose now is twelve month old,	
	And bootless 'tis to tell you we will go;	
	Therefor we meet not now. Then let me hear	30
	Of you, my gentle cousin Westmoreland,	
	What yesternight our Council did decree	
	In forwarding this dear expedience.	

If the deep fears signaled by the figure in lines 5–6 whet the appetite of the psychoanalytically oriented reader, the biblically oriented reader responds to a different savor; the lines echo a passage in Genesis that shifts the fears to another sector of the family drama: "Now therefore thou art cursed from the earth, which hath opened her mouth to receive thy brother's blood from thy hand" (Genesis 4:11). Whether or not this is more palatable depends on one's taste in perversions, but in the narrative context of the tetralogy it is clearly more appropriate. It anticipates Henry's next lines as well as the civil strife he is about to encourage by his confrontation with the Percies; it establishes continuity with his command to Exton in the final speech of *Richard II*: "With Cain go wander thorough shades of night."[40] And if we take the biblical echo as a comment on the speaker's own condition, it suggests the futility of that transparent exorcising gesture, the persistence of Henry's guilt of conscience laboring under the divine Father's judgment. But it is just here that Mother comes in handy.

Rebellion in lines 5–18 is figured not merely as sibling rivalry but also as a mutual assault by the contending factions on the mother who raises them to kill each other and then drinks – or, in order to drink – their blood. The "trenching" violence of the sons is a defensive as well as aggressive response to the mother's bloodlust: war between sons is war against mother. As the figurative play ascends from hoofs to "opposed eyes," the sons' genealogy is reimagined in celestial terms that affiliate them – even if only as portents and exhalations – with the paternal source. Heaven is troubled by the "civil butchery" on which earth battens. To appease the Father's anger and secure the sons from maternal threat, the king will lead them to "stronds afar remote" and redirect their bloodlust, their maternal legacy, from each other to the infidel: "Forthwith a power of English shall we levy, / Whose arms were moulded in their mother's womb" (22–3). This will domesticate the threat by impressing the mother's munitions factory into the service of Christian patriarchy. Inscribed in this figurative passage are suggestions of flight from the terror of maternal power, of sacrilegious assault on the source of the terror, of religious conquest of the source, and appropriation of the terrible power.

Against what else but the bloodthirsty maternal earth do "armed hoofs" provide protection? Exposure of the feet and closeness to the earth appear repeatedly in the text of Part One as symbols of vulnerability. The imagery of the play discloses the workings of something like a counter-Antaeus system, a graduated scale of insulation, from lying down to walking barefoot to wearing boots to riding horseback to leaping and flying. Thus if boots are safer than bare feet, and horses safer than walking, the redundancy of "armed hoofs" ensures a level of security exceeded only by that which Harry's winged Pegasus provides. The ironclad ungulate protects a man from the thirsty mother by elevation, while its speed guarantees rapid travel, which – for warriors like Hotspur – means flight to the battlefield from centers of female power.

The words with which Henry puts off the crusade, "bootless 'tis to tell you we will go," are unsettled by the way his dream of barefoot penitence, his *imitatio Christi*, ends with "those blessed feet ... nail'd / For our advantage on the bitter cross" (26–7). "For our advantage" touches off the momentary flash of an alternate fantasy: Richard on the cross.[41] Henry's oddly Oedipal focus on injured feet filters into the final words of the speech, "dear expedience," since the root meaning of the Latin cognate of *expedience* is "freeing the feet." How costly this expedience might be to Henry becomes clear as soon as you recall not only the duplicity of the crusade proposal but also the train of events he is planning to set in motion when he confronts Hotspur. When I sight through these tropes to lines 5 and 6, I begin to hear in "the thirsty entrance of this soil" a displaced self-accusation: a reference back to the closing speech of *Richard II* and to "the king's blood" that "stain'd the king's own land." Henry's words hint at resigned acceptance of his estrangement from the motherland identified and stained with Richard, and at the same time they struggle against self-accusation by shifting blame to the Ricardian mother. But since he knows himself responsible for the "trenching war" he is about to encourage, the struggle is futile. Although his violation of the land is displaced to maternal violence, and his sense of the perversity of his project to maternal perversion, the bloodthirsty land becomes an image of his effect on the kingdom, his powerlessness to wash the blood from his guilty hand. The play is remarkable for the amount of incidental rhetoric devoted to fantasies of violation, impotence, and the feminization of alienated power. In the passage under consideration, the momentary allusion to the nightmare of the phallic mother signifies a specifically moral scene of castration: the fear of being punished by Richard and God for usurping their power; the desire to legitimize possession of the power; the fear of that desire.

These reflections are a little too free-floating; they need to be pinned down more closely to what happens in the play. As always in Shakespeare, one has to take pains to ferret out the details of plot and timing as accurately as one can. For the plot discloses the plotting; it gives discernible shape to scenarios set in motion by the characters, scenarios they may never themselves mention or acknowledge, but that lurk in their language and lead us to wonder whether the agents know what they are doing. By the end of the first scene we learn that Henry had arranged the confrontation with the Percies, the one that occurs in i.iii, *before* he makes the crusade speech that opens the play. He had already sent the foppish messenger to Hotspur at Holmedon to make an issue of the prisoners. His curt dismissal of Worcester at the beginning of the third scene, and his walking out after an angry ultimatum to Hotspur, seem calculated to incense the Percies. Though Worcester is obviously up to something, Northumberland and Hotspur are not unconciliatory in explaining the denial of prisoners, and Blunt's intercession on Hotspur's behalf suggests this. For reasons to be discussed below, Henry seems motivated to incite the Percy family to rebel, and in this he is effectively complicit with Worcester. His behavior works to provoke them into an uprising that he can later be in the position to blame them for. So, at he end of i.i, he implies that Hotspur is responsible for his having to cancel the crusade that he proposed primarily in order to be able to blame the cancellation on Hotspur.

Inscribed in this scenario are the tactics of the victim / revenger's discourse: stirring up trouble, disclaiming responsibility for it, targeting oneself as its victim. Yet at the same time we can hear in Henry's language the accents of another discourse. Although he deploys his fantasy of crusade as a political stratagem, and although he has no intention of actualizing it, he elaborates it in a rhetoric so misted over with the faded scent of nostalgia that it seems to be the expression of a devout wish. Here as elsewhere in the tetralogy his language reveals a yearning for the old-fashioned absolution he knows is no longer available: making a pilgrimage, going on crusade, marching to the Holy Land, dying in Jerusalem. This adds depth and poignancy to his utterance, especially at lines 5–18 of the crusade speech. The events he is planning to set in motion are precisely the events that, in those lines, are preceded by the repeated "No more"s. Behind each "no more" lurks a potential "once more." The negations register sensitivity to the moral cost of the pretense: Henry dwells obsessively, as if wounding himself, on the self-wounding "intestine shock" that troubles heaven, even as he prepares to motivate the shock.

In this context, the counterfactual gesture of crusade follows a bootless effort to imagine an act of atonement commensurate with that preparation: the blessed cross becomes a bitter cross.[42] His language is torn apart by the tension between the victim / revenger's discourse and that of the sinner. What is, as he says, "for our advantage" takes on a darker tone if we accept the idea that the fate he fears is also the fate he feels he deserves. His advantage would then consist in seeking the justice and retribution that would make Richard's prophecy come true. And this, I think, contributes to the motivation behind his stirring up of the Percies. The political motive is obvious: if he can facilitate the rebellion, and control the form it takes, he will create a challenge that places him in the position of at least quasi-legitimacy as defender of the monarchy; having disentangled himself from his fellow conspirators, he can use them to secure moral justification. But the ethical motive, the sinner's motive, activates the same strategy against the political motive. To encourage insurrection is to constitute a faction that can uphold Richard's claim and administer his revenge. The sinner's motive is to keep "the edge of war, like an ill-sheathed knife," turned against himself.

In an important sense, then, strengthening his opposition enables him to keep up his own strength by maintaining scapegoats and scourges that tend to the variable needs of a bad conscience. In 2 *Henry IV* the growing disarray and demoralization of the rebels after Shrewsbury are matched by the king's decline. His final physical collapse is synchronized with the good news of victory in a strangely resonant phrase: "wherefore should these good news make me sick" (IV.iv.102). When we look back from that deflationary moment, we can intuit a need to keep the rebels from losing too soon, as if his strength is proportionally related to – and is dependent on – that of the opposition. I think this follows logically from the collapse of the opposition to his seizure of the throne. In retrospect, the Northumberland faction may be said to have betrayed him by supporting him, and since he can see their complicity in his guilt, his guilt in their complicity, he can try to mitigate its moral effect on him by promoting their grievances and making them God's justicers. Like his son, Henry finds it in his moral interest to "awhile uphold / The unyok'd humor" of rebellion, especially the rebellion of Hotspur, the "son" he admires, and of Harry, the son he loves. The collapse of the rebellion throws him back on the inward war of the sick body as almost the only defense against the sinner's discourse – almost, because he gets one more chance to cover the sinner's discourse with that of the victim / revenger when, after discovering that Harry, as he thinks, stole the crown, he tries to make his son's head lie uneasy.

What did the king know, when (if ever) did he know it, and how can we tell? At the beginning of this essay I suggested that a distinction between the semiotic and psychological dimensions of textual analysis might serve to codify a common practice in which meanings and messages are excavated from the language before the excavator decides whether they are meant or unmeant, heard or unheard, by fictional speakers and auditors. I also proposed that speakers should be treated as the effects rather than the causes of their language and our interpretation. This stipulation relativizes the approach to questions of irony and intention, and restricts the usefulness of the psychoanalytic paradigm associated with the name of Freud. For if there are no transcendent speakers in the unperformed text, then there can be no prior reality or truth of character, person, and consciousness to provide the object of knowledge or ignorance. And, in turn, the characters we construct through interpretation need not inevitably come equipped with the prior reality of organic appurtenances presupposed by the Freudian paradigm. They possess bodies, childhoods, repressed memories, Oedipal investments and displacements, and so forth, only when these can be shown to be relevant to interpretation. Knowledge reflects, but interpretation constitutes, its object (or subject). We can never *know* what the king knows, and he only knows it if and when we decide he does.

These assertions are directed only to the unperformed text. They may also hold for the performed text, for all texts, for the great text of life, but at this moment I am not dealing in metaphysical commitments. My interest is limited to the cautionary influence the stipulation may have on the psychological analysis of fictional speakers. It counsels us to use flexibility in deploying such concepts as character and consciousness and to resign ourselves to the fact that their textual existence may be intermittent. It encourages a policy of consistent inconsistency in which we premise that we can sometimes determine what a speaker means to say and sometimes not, and that decisions about this may vary from moment to moment as well as from interpreter to interpreter. Above all, it affects our approach to the problem of irony and its relation to the play of discourses in language. This doesn't relieve us of the obligation to try to determine in any particular case whether a meaning or a discursive move is intended or unintended. But it changes the value of the exercise, perhaps diminishes its importance, because the focus on discourse partially redirects attention from the cognitive status of a speaker's language to its force as an agent of dramatic action.

For practical purposes, we can reduce the kinds of irony that critics have classified and investigated into two kinds, rhetorical and dramatic, and we can subdivide rhetorical irony into two types, intentional and unintended, or structural. Irony is intentional when speakers knowingly say one thing and mean another, structural when they mean to say one thing but their language says something else that was not intended. Rhetorical irony differs from what Richard Levin has called "the old-fashioned 'dramatic irony' involved in the reversal of a character's situation and expectations."[43] Bertrand Evans's study of dramatic irony in *Shakespeare's Tragic Practice* shows why this is so. Evans is interested in the "gaps" produced by "discrepant awarenesses" that result from the "practices" and plotting of characters and playwright. His concern is with a dramatic device largely observable in abstraction from the language of the play, and his emphasis is on the playwright's manipulation of audience interest in the action; the criterion he employs is whether the "awareness gap" is "productive of dramatic effect."[44] Effects of intentional and structural irony, in contrast, can only be registered through continuous engagement with the language of the play. Because Evans's study remains framed within the classical scheme of *peripeteia* and *anagnorisis* – staples of the "old-fashioned" irony – it is essentially a character-and-action approach, relying little on the text as text, and it is adjusted to the conditions of theatrical performance. At the same time, his focus on "practices" orients his study toward intentions and intentional irony, whether rhetorical or narrative.

I now want to introduce an approach to the concept of dramatic irony that differs from the one discussed by Levin and Evans in that it is literary rather than theatrical. It resembles their approach in centering on ironies of narrative and plot, but it assumes a more intimate and dynamic relation between narrative action and the linguistic action manifested by the play of discourses. It construes dramatic irony as the effect of a speaker whose discourses continuously move the plot forward whether or not he seems in the reader's judgment to be aware of it. If the formula for the structural type of rhetorical irony is meaning one thing and saying another, the formula for dramatic irony is meaning one thing and doing another. This implicates the speaker in a form of agency that can be considered entirely apart from the question of his intention or awareness, a responsibility for the shaping of events that we may easily interpret as the "practice," in Evans's sense, of what I described above as practical unconsciousness.

The literary approach to dramatic irony takes us directly back to the Lacanian paradigm with which I began, and the connection may be secured by recalling Benveniste's statement (quoted above) that psychoanalytic discourse "is both the bearer of a message and the instrument of an action." The emphasis on the latter function is writ large in Shoshana Felman's recent study of Lacan. Its leitmotif is his insistence, first, that the analytic dialogue is "essentially performative … rather than informative" or constative and, second, that "the analytical interpretation is itself a performative (not cognitive) interpretation in that it has a fundamental structuring, transforming function."[45] Interpreting, Lacan writes, is the opposite of understanding; it is "a gift of language … rather than a gift of truth."[46] This applies as well to the interpretive dialogue with the unperformed text. If, behind the name to which speech is assigned, there is no intending person, only the site of the discourses of others, then our share in the dialogue is not to look for the kind of understanding or truth we call knowledge of the character but to transform the language into the structure of discourses that traverse the character's speech; by "transform" I mean something close to "invent" or "construct," though of course I could not invent discourses for the fictional community of a play if I didn't already find them among those that circulate through my community and traverse me.

This homology between psychoanalytic and critical discourse tempts me to extend the performative orientation to the text, to make the interpretive act reflect itself by picking out the performative function of the speaker's speech. It constitutes the speech as an act, a doing, an agency of desire structuring a plot or scenario. It may have been apparent that when I was describing Henry's motives in the preceding section, I was sloppy and often evasive in my treatment of their intentional or cognitive status. I tried to avoid having to make cognitive discriminations, and I did this by shifting attention to Shakespeare's emplotment – to the textual glimpses of the scenarios from which motivation is deduced and within which I situate the conflict of discourses. My concern was less with the cognitive interplay between the two rhetorical formulas of structural and intentional irony than with the performative interplay between rhetorical and dramatic irony. Henry's speech in the first scene of Part One seems to *mean* one set of things and to *do* another. Imagining the difference, the gap, filled with discourses helps me imagine what Henry wants – what he wants in the register of desire, which is to say, what he wants whether he knows it or not. It turns out that no matter how many precautions I take, my language inevitably attributes some mix of conscious, preconscious, unconscious, or half-conscious purposes to the character I invent. I find myself talking, if not about the speaker's intention, then about what might happen in his psyche were he to have one. My interest is caught by what he might think of himself if he knew what I think his language does, and it is from this standpoint that I now return to Henry to consider the scenario that motivates and is motivated by his opening speech.

As I tried to show, that scenario assumes shape as the vector sum of two forces: the pressure of the sinner's discourse and the counterpressure of the victim / revenger's discourse. This is a graph of the structure of Henry's desire, and its movement can be plotted in the following steps. First, he badly wants moral, and not merely political, legitimacy, which is a point generally missed by so-called new-historicist and cultural-materialist readings (or under-readings) of the second tetralogy. Second, this pursuit of self-justification is poorly managed at the level of interlocutory politics; its bad-faith moves are painfully obvious, and I infer from their obviousness that they perhaps reflect and reinforce the sinner's desire for judgment. Third, since the hope of absolution is destroyed by the crusading gesture that travesties it in proclaiming it, the alternative is to seek punishment. Fourth, just as Richard had in effect appointed or seduced Henry to be his heir and usurper ("here, cousin, seize the crown"), so Henry creates scourges to punish his mistreadings, delegates Richard's revenge to them, and at the same time sets *them* up for justified punishment.

The two major candidates for this function are his son Harry and his "son" Hotspur. As to the former, if Henry feels uneasy about usurpation and regicide he must be aware of how much he depends on his son retroactively to secure the legitimacy denied him so long as he lives. This is hardly cause for paternal gratitude. It is not only that opposition to and from Henry's "nearest and dearest enemy" (1 *Henry IV*, iii.ii.123) gives the prince a function similar to that of the rebels in the economy of guilt management. But also, from the moment of Henry's questionable accession in *Richard II*, the terms in which he characterizes his son's behavior transfer to Harry qualities associated with Richard. This sets the stage for the transfer of his buried fear from predecessor to successor: the source of danger and insecurity and guilt will be displaced to the very person on whom their removal depends. In thus reinventing his relation to Richard, Henry seems motivated by a need to persuade himself that (1) Richard did not deserve to be king and that although (2) he – Henry – did not have the right to unking him, much less kill him, he nevertheless (3) heroically sacrificed his own chance for salvation and ran the risk of destroying his reputation for the good of his country.

To buttress this three-point scenario, he makes Hotspur his factor as well as Harry. The only way he can imagine redeeming his "banish'd honor" is to be reborn in an idealized filial image, but one who is not a legitimate heir, rather a would-be usurper like himself to whom he could transmit as to a scapegoat the soil of his achievement. It is as if his redemption depends on his losing the crown, not on handing it on. The futile character of this fantasy is inscribed in his nostalgia: to say "even as I was then is Percy now" (1 *Henry IV*, iii.ii.96) is to put the seal of failure on the wish for redemption. For if he was like Percy – or his image of Percy – *then*, the reason he isn't so *now* is that his idealism led to its own subversion by playing into Richard's hands.

Henry thus symbolically adopts Hotspur and disowns Harry both to realize his three-point scenario and to defend against it. Harry's truancy will represent God's retribution and Richard's revenge, but he will also be cast as the Profligate Son who reincarnates Richard the Profligate "Father." In the context of the Oxford plot and the York / Aumerle episode, the new king sees Harry already as a kind of conspirator who represents Richard's interests, resurrects his unruly regime, becomes in effect *Richard's* son.

Harry Berger, Jr.

York's denunciation of Aumerle for conspiring against the king supplies a melodramatic and therefore parodic epitome that introduces the more complex and sustained conflict between Henry and Harry. Through this scenario Henry projects his self-doubt on Harry and tries to pack his conscience with guilt so that he can deal with his own guilt as well as with the true inheritor's power over him. The scenario's corrosive effects unfold in Part Two, where it is poignantly registered in the discursive warfare that tears his language apart, and where the question of what the king knows – how aware he is of the performative force of the discourses that write his "book of fate" and make Richard's prophecy come true (2 *Henry IV*, III.ii.45, 65–79) – becomes more pressing. The poignancy resides in the shifting, volatile, uncertain character of the king's cognitive relation to what his language is doing. I shall explore this in the concluding section of the essay.

Henry does not make an appearance in Part Two until the first scene of Act III. The appearance is preceded by several references to his illness, the most interesting of which is the exchange between Falstaff and the Chief Justice I discussed above in connection with the Lacanian critique of the Freudian paradigm. Falstaff's suggestion that physical disease displaces mental dis-ease establishes the context within which we read the king's initial speech in the play and interrogate the meaning for him of its concluding line:

> How many thousand of my poorest subjects
> Are at this hour asleep! O sleep, O gentle sleep,
> Nature's soft nurse, how have I frighted thee,
> That thou no more wilt weigh my eyelids down
> And steep my senses in forgetfulness?
> Why rather, sleep, liest thou in smoky cribs,
> Upon uneasy pallets stretching thee
> And hushed with buzzing night-flies to thy slumber,
> Than in the perfum'd chambers of the great,
> Under the canopies of costly state,
> And lulled with sound of sweetest melody?
> O thou dull god, why liest thou with the vile
> In loathsome beds, and leavest the kingly couch
> A watch-case or a common 'larum-bell?
> Wilt thou upon the high and giddy mast
> Seal up the ship-boy's eyes, and rock his brains
> In cradle of the rude imperious surge
> And in the visitation of the winds,
> Who take the ruffian billows by the top,
> Curling their monstrous heads and hanging them
> With deafing clamor in the slippery clouds,
> That with the hurly death itself wakes?
> Canst thou, O partial sleep, give thy repose
> To the wet sea-son in an hour so rude,
> And in the calmest and most stillest night,
> With all appliances and means to boot
> Deny it to a king? Then happy low, lie down!
> Uneasy lies the head that wears a crown.
> (4–31)

This is a highly troped apostrophe that reads and sounds like a performance before an audience. "Quintilian, speaking of oratory, defines apostrophe as 'a diversion of our words to address some person other than the judge.' "[47] Since the speech is a soliloquy, the audience and judge can only be the speaker. The project to be judged is announced in the first of the five rhetorical questions through which the speech moves: not merely the attainment of repose, but also his ability to rhetoricize himself into forgetfulness. "How have I frighted thee" teeters between question ("What have I done wrong?") and exclamation ("How much I must have frightened you!"), then completes itself by stumbling quickly from self-reproof to complaint ("… to keep you from letting or helping me forget?!"). This dangerous ground is bordered on either side by materials for the sociology of sleep that Henry gathers to try to forget his unforgetful guilt and lose himself in a pleasurably self-pitying contrast between the happy torpid poor and the king who gives his subjects all, sacrificing his peace of mind for theirs. We recognize the convergent accents of two discourses reinforcing each other, that of the victim and that of the unappreciated donor.

As he contemplates the lapse in taste or judgment that makes sleep abandon the "kingly couch," a healthy surge of anger transforms the "soft nurse" to a "dull god" whose prodigal itinerary oddly resembles that of Henry's truant son.[48] I note in passing that if sleep's kindness to the shipboy makes him oblivious to the "rude imperious surge," it also makes him a likelier prospect for drowning. And perhaps the speaker envies him both possibilities as he slips by him to drench his own senses in a more powerful displacement of civil and psychic confusion, a vision of the less lethargic qualities of the "poorest subjects," the aristocrat's scapegoat, that recalls Rumor's image of "the blunt monster with uncounted heads, / The still-discordant wav'ring multitude" (Ind., 18–19). The sea-boy image fails in its protective function, for the "high and giddy mast" is more an analogue of the "kingly couch" than a contrast to it. The descriptive thrust of the king's speech is undone by the play of meanings that superimposes an image closer to home: the "visitation" that incites the ruffian billows to disorder is also the force that hangs them for it, is both the arch-rebel and the official executioner. What stains the image is doubt of legitimacy and the sinner's impulse to pronounce judgment on himself.

How you assess Henry's relation to the interplay of the donor's, victim's, and sinner's discourses in the soliloquy depends on your reading of the final line, and that comes down to how you assess his relation to the pun in *lies*. Several options are open. You can refuse the pun and allow the statement only the force of a bromide, a generalized reference to the cares of kingship; that makes both speech and speaker innocent of darker meanings. Or you can accept the pun, put a reflexive spin on the statement, and read it as passing judgment on the speaker's resort to the bromide. Accepting the pun and the irony it encodes, you may decide it is present but unintended, unheard by the speaker, and you may then receive it as a message from the text: the message that Henry is sedating himself, successfully deceiving himself, by blaming insomnia on the burdens of state. At that point, if you affect moralistic reading, you may decide to assume the robes and role of justice abdicated by the speaker. Finally, if you allow him to intend or hear the pun, you can let him judge himself; you read the utterance as mordant and self-lacerating, make it convey the self-accusing sinner's bitter acknowledgment of his unwillingness to confront what really keeps him up at night: uneasy lies the head that stole the crown. Then it may seem that the soliloquy demonstrates not only his uneasiness but also his tendency to go on producing it.

There is one more possibility, and it is the one I prefer. This is, not to decide, to keep yourself and Henry vacillating back and forth between the two conflicting discourses, to make him fearful and desirous of both, afraid to commit himself to the bad faith of playing donor and victim yet equally afraid to confront his self-despite head on. Henry's vacillation continues throughout the scene. In his next speech he transfers his illness to "the body of our Kingdom" and observes "How foul it is, what rank diseases grow, / And with what danger, near the heart of it" (III.i.38–40). And in the lines that end the scene he reverts to his old desire: "were these inward wars once out of hand, / We would, dear lords, unto the Holy Land" (107–8). The resonant vagueness of "these inward wars," together with the counterfactual wish, marks his ongoing struggle to avoid committing himself to either of the discursive factions at war within his speech. This struggle continues through the remaining episodes of his life, even in the final effort to reach atonement with his son.

I have argued elsewhere that in *Richard II* there is a tense and deeply troubled relation between Henry and his father, John of Gaunt, that neither of them ever confronts and verbalizes, and that when this relation is taken into account it changes the mood of the self-justifying performance of the *ars moriendi* discourse that gets Gaunt safely out of life and into anthologies in a heroic blaze of prophecy. One can only wonder whether he succeeds in blinding himself to his complicity with Richard and his betrayal of his son because the text is silent on this question, and it is largely (but not completely) silent on Henry's view of his father. Yet at the performative level, the level at which the speaker's language drives the discourses, the silence is re-membered in Part Two, and to some extent filled in. Henry replaces Gaunt as the dying father, but unlike Gaunt he has his son to help him work through the *ars moriendi*; he performs it for Harry's benefit, but also for his own. His pleasure in operating the victim's discourse gives way to an effort of atonement, but that effort is breached by the continuing desire to compete with Harry, outmaneuver him, put him down, and justify himself.

Henry's language registers both the struggle with his son and the struggle to end that struggle in order to produce the atonement they both desire. When he says "all the soil of the achievement goes / With me into the earth" (IV.v.189–90), the desire for happy ending is again foiled by the desire for self-justification. The statement is a kind of boast that seeks to win the battle of atonement: because of his suffering and sacrifice, his heroic response to his embattled regime, his son will have an easier road to travel. For the last time he exploits the discursive roles of saint, hero, and donor. He is still competing with Harry, and if what he intends is atonement, his performance in this scene can't be imagined to do anything but exacerbate the sinner's self-contempt and reinforce the other grief of guilty fatherhood the intention should alleviate.

Henry's longing for the absolute, but not absolving, cure of the Holy Land appears finally to be synonymous with the longing for the satisfaction of a death that will commemorate his failure, his unfitness, to reach the Jerusalem of his desire. On his deathbed he no longer speaks of the religious dimension of crusade; he speaks of it with self-directed cynicism only as a political maneuver. His final speech, when he hears that the room he had fainted in is called the Jerusalem Chamber, begins with "Laud be to God!" (IV.v.234) and ends with "bear me to that chamber; there I'll lie; / In that

Jerusalem shall Harry die" (239–40). For me, "Laud be to God!" rings with a strange and wry tonality. I hear resignation in it, and relief, and an ironic recognition that he will at last get what's coming to him. There he *may* lie easy. But if, for one second, you let yourself glance sideways at the old pun – unlikely here, no doubt – "there I'll lie" slides ever so precariously over the deepest bitterness, the relentlessness of the sinner's discourse fixing its subject in the condition from which even now (or especially now) he can't escape. And a moment later we hear a distant echo of the judgment he solicits in another voice, another key, pompous and laughable, when Shallow enforces his hospitality on Falstaff: "I will not excuse you, you shall not be excused, excuses shall not be admitted, there is no excuse shall serve, you shall not be excused" (v.i.4–6).

Henry lies uneasily and continues to do so to the end because he is alway trying both to deceive himself and to resist the attempt. What I find most poignant in this is the vivid process, the conflict, the discursive struggle, that couples the desire for moral legitimacy with despair at the futility of the desire. Time and again the speaker of Henry's language all but pronounces judgment on himself, and time and again he veers off to another bad-faith speech act that can only confirm the judgment. Passing judgment on him, as critics like to do, seems to me to be redundant. I have the same feeling about Henry IV that many critics of ironic reading have about Henry V: both Henrys, or Harrys, get bad press from certain sectors of the academy. Harrying Harry with pietistic panache is currently considered a sign of liberal chic. And because the fifth Harry gets very good press from other sectors, unlike his father, a tedious squabble has been going on between Harry-lovers and Harry-haters. Now, while I am not a Harry-lover, I try not to be a Harry-hater, and I do this by formulating the trouble with Harry – with both Harrys, with all Harrys – in a manner that differs from the way the Harry-haters do. The issue is not what Harry's critics think of Harry but what Harry thinks of Harry; not whether *they* think he's good or bad but whether *he* does. The only trouble with Harry that really troubles me is Harry's trouble with Harry.

Notes

1 I say more about this below, where it becomes clear that my views on this topic owe much to Shoshana Felman, *Jacques Lacan and the Adventure of Insight: Psychoanalysis in Contemporary Culture* (Cambridge, MA: Harvard University Press, 1987).

2 Stephen Melville, "Psychoanalysis and the Place of *Jouissance*," *Critical Inquiry* 13 (1987): 352. *Epigenesis* is the term given by Erik Erikson to the developmental principle governing his theory of the life cycle.

3 Jacques Lacan, *Écrits: A Selection*, trans. Alan Sheridan (New York: Norton, 1977), 86. For some concise remarks about the critical implications of Lacan's position, see Elizabeth Wright, "Another Look at Lacan and Literary Criticism," *New Literary History* 19 (1988): 617–27, esp. 618–19.

4 Sigmund Freud, *An Outline of Psychoanalysis*, trans. James Strachey (New York: Norton, 1949), 14.

5 David Rapaport, *The Structure of Psychoanalytic Theory: A Systematizing Attempt*, Psychological Issues 2: 2 (New York: International Universities Press, 1960), 125.

6 Freud, *Outline*, 89.

7 Lacan, marginal gloss in "Television," trans. Denis Hollier, Rosalind Krauss, and Annette Michelson, *October* 40 (spring 1987): 41.

8 Ibid., 45.

9 Catherine Clément, *The Weary Sons of Freud*, trans. Nicole Ball (London: Verso, 1987), 41.

10 Juliet Mitchell in *Feminine Sexuality: Jacques Lacan and the École Freudienne*, ed. Juliet Mitchell and Jacqueline Rose (New York: Norton, 1982), 4. A similar view of the superiority of Lacanian theory as an approach more sensitive to historical change and specificity has been hinted at by Stephen Greenblatt in "Psychoanalysis and Renaissance Culture," in *Literary Theory / Renaissance Texts*, ed. Patricia Parker and David Quint (Baltimore: Johns Hopkins University Press, 1986), 210–24. Reflecting on the story of Martin Guerre, Greenblatt argues that no one involved in the case bothered "to invoke Martin's biological individuality, or even his soul, let alone an infancy that would have seemed almost comically beside the point" (215). Rather, his subjectivity is treated as "the *product* of the relations, material objects and judgments exposed in the case rather than as the *producer* of these relations, objects and judgments" (216); "the secure possession of one's body is not the *origin* of identity but one of the consequences of the compulsive cultural stabilizing unusually visible in this story" (218); "an origin ... is only conferred upon one at the end of a series of actions and transactions" (224).

11 Shoshana Felman, "To Open the Question," in *Literature and Psychoanalysis: The Question of Reading Otherwise*, ed. Shoshana Felman (Baltimore: Johns Hopkins University Press, 1982), 9–10. See also the interesting comments, based on Felman's essay, by Jonathan Culler in *The Pursuit of Signs: Semiotics, Literature, Deconstruction* (Ithaca, NY: Cornell University Press, 1981), 223–6.

12 Coppélia Kahn, *Man's Estate: Masculine Identity in Shakespeare* (Berkeley: University of California Press, 1981), 2, 48.

13 Lisa Lowe, " 'Say I play the man I am': Gender and Politics in *Coriolanus*," *Kenyon Review*, n.s., 8, no. 4 (fall 1986): 89, 88, 90.

14 Richard Wheeler, *Shakespeare's Development and the Problem Comedies: Turn and Counter-Turn* (Berkeley: University of California Press, 1981), 151, 150. Subsequent page references in the text are to this work.

15 Kahn criticizes Kris for "reading a parricidal urge into Hal's taking of the crown" (*Man's Estate*, 71).

16 Ernst Kris, "Prince Hal's Conflict," in *Psychoanalytic Explorations in Art* (New York: International Universities Press, 1952), 285; my italics.

17 C. L. Barber and Richard P. Wheeler, *The Whole Journey: Shakespeare's Power of Development* (Berkeley: University of California Press, 1986), 231, 237, 236, 233, 238, 242; subsequent page references in the text are to this work. Barber's way of dealing with Oedipal truncation in the *Henriad* is to use Kris's observation that "the Oedipal motive is repressed and displaced onto Falstaff" ("Prince Hal's Conflict," 210) as the basis of his view that "the expulsion of Falstaff, and with it the inhibition of Falstaffian ironies" (*Whole Journey*, 198) diminishes *Henry V* by denying "the full ironic interplay of perspectives" (208; see also 235). "The exigencies of ... [Shakespeare's] whole development are encountered (beyond full control) in the unsatisfactoriness of the hero king who emerges from the process" (208).

Despite these qualifications, Barber's later view of *Henry V* is much deeper, more complex, and more positive than the reading he gave in *Shakespeare's Festive Comedy* (1959). One reason for this is his encounter with the work of Peter Erickson, especially the doctoral thesis which he supervised and on which Erickson based his impressive treatment of the *Henriad* in *Patriarchal Structures in Shakespeare's Drama* (Berkeley: University of California Press, 1985), 39–65, as well as an earlier essay, " 'The fault / My father made': The Anxious Pursuit of Heroic Fame in Shakespeare's *Henry V*," *Modern Language Studies* 10 (1979–80): 10–25. Barber, the most generous, open, and flexible critic I have known, was persuaded by Erickson's work to revaluate his approach to *Henry V*, and his footnotes amply document this debt.

18 See Chapter 10 above. For an account of displacement as "detextualization" in *2 Henry IV*, see "Sneak's Noise," Chapter 7 in *Making Trifles of Terrors: Redistributing Complicities in Shakespeare* (Stanford: Stanford University Press, 1997).

19 Emile Benveniste, *Problems in General Linguistics*, trans. M. E. Meek (Coral Gables, FL: University of Miami Press, 1971), 209; A. J. Greimas and J. Courtés, *Semiotics and Language: An Analytical Dictionary*, trans. Larry Crist, Daniel Patte, et al. (Bloomington: Indiana University Press, 1982), 81–4. Passages in Foucault's works are too numerous to cite.

20 Catherine Belsey, *Critical Practice* (London: Methuen, 1980), 5. Subsequent page references in the text are to this work.

21 Writing specifically of the discourses of the human sciences, Hayden White argues that a genuine discourse is metadiscursive and "diatactical": it "throws all 'tactical' rules into doubt, including those originally governing its own formation," and it is "always as much about discourse itself as it is about the objects that make up its subject matter" (*Tropics of Discourse: Essays in Cultural Criticism* [Baltimore: Johns Hopkins University Press, 1978], 4). Much explicit discourse conforms to this description.

22 Belsey, *Critical Practice*, 3.

23 Keir Elam, *Shakespeare's Universe of Discourse: Language-Games in the Comedies* (Cambridge: Cambridge University Press, 1984), 1.

24 Although Elam notes that Wittgenstein conceives language-games to be implicated in nonlinguistic behavior (12), his own formulations and practice tend to focus on metalinguistic rather than nonlinguistic contexts. His approach is dominated by *meta*-categories – metatheater, metadrama, metalinguistics, metacommunication, metarhetoric – that orient attention toward the recursive and reflexive staging of discourse. It will become evident that my language-games or discourses reflect what is perhaps a reversion to a "softer" view focused on ethical rather than linguistic structures, and on the form of the content rather than the content of the form. I agree with the criticism Bridget Gellert Lyons made in a recent review essay: the types and specimens Elam chooses are decontextualized and too narrowly treated as "illustrations for particular kinds of verbal behavior." His "stated allegiance to the 'form of life' in a play" is jeopardized by a procedure that breaks texts and contexts down for metalinguistic consumption, often reducing them below the minimal level required for speech-act analysis. Lyons argues that this procedure is not sufficiently sensitive to the political (and, I add, social and ethical) aspects of language use in the plays: "language acts … have important political dimensions," and their foregrounding in the plays may itself be "a political act" ("Shakespeare's Wordplay," *Raritan* 4 [1986]: 150, 153). I take this as my cue to restore the language-game proposal in a new form that makes it more responsive to the ethical and political forces circulating through the community of the play.

25 See Saul Kripke, *Wittgenstein on Rules and Private Language* (Cambridge, MA: Harvard University Press, 1982), 93–113.

26 Ludwig Wittgenstein, *Philosophical Investigations*, trans. G. E. M. Anscombe, 2nd edn. (Oxford: Basil Blackwell, 1958), 108e.

27 Anthony Giddens, *The Constitution of Society* (Berkeley: University of California Press, 1984), 374–5; my italics. There is an obvious analogy between this distinction and the one I made above between explicit and implicit discourse.

28 Ibid., 7, 6.

29 Giddens, *Central Problems in Social Theory: Action, Structure, and Contradiction in Social Analysis* (Berkeley: University of California Press, 1979), 5.

30 Benveniste, *Problems in General Linguistics*, 67.

31 See Chapter 1 in this volume.

32 My thanks to Margreta de Grazia for donating this idea about the problem of forgiveness.

33 See Chapters 3, 5, and 6 in *Making Trifles of Terrors*.

34 The structural context of the father's discourse and the relation between patriarchal ideology and paternal / filial conflict are examined more closely in the opening page of "Psychoanalyzing the Shakespeare Text: The First Three Scenes of the *Henriad*," Chapter 8 in *Making Trifles of Terrors*.

35 *King Lear*, ed. G. K. Hunter, The New Penguin Shakespeare (Harmondsworth, Eng.: Penguin Books, 1972), 17–18, 20.

36 Stephen Greenblatt, "The Cultivation of Anxiety: King Lear and His Heirs," *Raritan* 2 (1982): 92–124.

37 Since Lear has daughters and Gloucester sons, there are differences in their conduct of paternal discourse that I shall not consider here.

38 Hunter (ed.), *King Lear*, 24.

39 Hunter's comments support an argument *contra* Bradley in which he claims that "Shakespeare's vision in this play" directs attention away "from individual motives and actions" and "from too narrow a focus in terms of ... the linear processes of motive and sequence" to "a dramatic sense of man's general status" better expressed through the kind of "synchronous" organization "Lévi-Strauss discovers in the repetitions and parallelisms of the Oedipus Story" (*King Lear*, 22–3). Although I endorse the caveat about individual psychology, I think Shakespeare always directs attention toward "a focus in terms of ... the linear processes of motive and sequence," a focus that needn't be restricted to "individual motives and actions." This is in fact the thesis of the theory of discourses under discussion.

40 These lines in turn recall and condense several moments of the aborted ritual that opens the first play of the tetralogy: Henry's reference to the blood of Gloucester, which, "like sacrificing Abel's, cries / Even from the tongueless caverns of the earth / To me for justice and rough chastisement" (i.i.104–6); Mowbray's "thus I turn me from my country's light, / To dwell in solemn shades of endless night" (i.iii.176–7); and Gaunt's "My oil-dried lamp and time-bewasting light / Shall be extinct with age and endless night" (i.iii.221–2). Having replaced Richard and taken God's justice upon himself in more ways than one – more ways than he would like – Henry finds himself helplessly repeating the actions and crimes of the previous regime. He tries to fend off Exton's tribute of "buried fear," displace the "guilt of conscience" to the new Cain (v.vi.31, 41), and associate himself with the victim's husbandry ("That blood should sprinkle me to make me grow," 46), but the failure of this effort is immediately apparent in the play's penultimate couplet: "I'll make a voyage to the Holy Land, / To wash this blood from off my guilty hand" (49–50). This may be why the pilgrimage is converted to a crusade in the fantasy of the opening speech.

41 See Richard's stagy performance of the divine victim's discourse enacted for Bolingbroke's benefit in *Richard II*, iv.i.169–70 and 239–42:

> Did they not sometime cry "All hail!" to me?
> So Judas did to Christ.

> Though some of you, with Pilate, wash your hands
> Showing an outward pity – yet you Pilates
> Have here deliver'd me to my sour cross,
> And water cannot wash away your sin.

42 And the gesture is barely under syntactic control, as evidenced by the way the long sentence that meanders unexpeditiously to Jerusalem detours through a series of relative clauses (18–27) and by the touch of uncertainty in "To chase these pagans in those holy fields" (24): although *these* may have its emphatic rather than its demonstrative sense (as in the modern colloquialism "these here pagans"), it retains a deictic edge – "these pagans *here*" – since one presumptive purpose of crusade is to unify the nation under the king and thus defeat the local pagans, his enemies.

43 Richard Levin, *New Readings vs. Old Plays: Recent Trends in the Reinterpretation of English Renaissance Drama* (Chicago: University of Chicago Press, 1979), 102. The remainder of this paragraph is lifted with some minor alterations from "Text Against Performance: The Gloucester Family Romance," Chapter 4 in *Making Trifles of Terrors*.

44 Bertrand Evans, *Shakespeare's Tragic Practice* (Oxford: Oxford University Press, 1979), 170.

45 Felman, *Jacques Lacan and the Adventure of Insight*, 120.

46 Ibid., 108 (on interpretation as opposite of understanding), 120 (quotation).

47 Culler, *Pursuit of Signs*, 135.

48 Two echoes of the previous tavern scene secure this connection: Harry's reference to the "tempest of commotion" that "doth begin to melt / And drop upon our bare unarmed heads" and Falstaff's "the undeserver may sleep, when the man of action is called on" (ii.iv.360–2, 372–3).

24

The Turn of the Shrew

Joel Fineman

> *Hortensio:* Now go thy ways, thou hast tam'd a curst shrow.
> *Lucentio:* 'Tis a wonder, by your leave, she will be tam'd so.
> (v.ii.188–9)

In ways which are so traditional that they might be called proverbial, Shakespeare's *Taming of the Shrew* assumes – it turns out to make no difference whether it does so ironically – that the language of woman is at odds with the order and authority of man. At the same time, again in ways which are nothing but traditional, the play self-consciously associates this thematically subversive discourse of woman with its own literariness and theatricality. The result, however, is a play that speaks neither for the language of woman nor against the authority of man. Quite the contrary: at the end of the play things are pretty much the same – which is to say, patriarchally inflected – as they were at or before its beginning, the only difference being that now, because there are more shrews than ever, they are more so. It cannot be surprising that a major and perennially popular play by Shakespeare, which is part of a corpus that, at least in an English literary tradition, is synonymous with what is understood to be canonical, begins and ends as something orthodox. Nevertheless, there is reason to wonder – as my epigraph, the last lines of the play, suggests – how it happens that a discourse of subversion, explicitly presented as such, manages to resecure, equally explicitly, the very order to which it seems, at both first and second sight, to be opposed. This question, raised by the play in a thematic register, and posed practically by the play by virtue of the play's historical success, leads to another; is it possible to voice a language, whether of man or of woman, that does not speak, sooner or later, self-consciously or unconsciously, for the order and authority of man?

Formulated at considerably greater levels of generality, such questions have been advanced by much recent literary, and not only literary, theory, much of which finds it very difficult to sustain in any intelligible fashion an effective critical and adversary distance or difference between itself and any of a variety of master points of view, each of which claims special access to a global, universalizing truth. It is, however, in the debates and polemics growing out of and centering upon the imperial claims of psychoanalysis that such questions have been raised in the very same terms and at precisely the level of generality proposed by *The Taming of the Shrew* – the level of generality measured by the specificity of rubrics as massive and as allegorically suggestive as Man, Woman, and Language – for it is psychoanalysis, especially the psychoanalysis associated with the name of Jacques Lacan, that has most coherently developed an account of human subjectivity which is based upon the fact that human beings speak. Very much taking this speech to heart, psychoanalysis has organized, in much the same ways as does *The Taming of the Shrew*, the relationship of generic Man to generic Woman by reference to the apparently inescapable patriarchalism occasioned by the structuring effects of language – of Language, that is to say, which is also understood in broad genericizing terms. In turn, the most forceful criticisms of psychoanalysis, responding to the psychoanalytic provocation with a proverbial response, have all been obliged, again repeating the thematics of *The Taming of the Shrew*, to speak against this Language for which the psychoanalytic speaks.

Thus it is not surprising, to take the most important and sophisticated example of this debate, that Jacques Derrida's (by comparison) very general critique of logocentric metaphysics, his deconstructive readings of what he calls the ontotheological ideology of presence in the history of the west, turns more specifically into a critique of phallogocentric erotics in the course of a series of rather pointed (and, for Derrida, unusually vociferous) attacks on Lacanian psychoanalysis. Lacan serves Derrida as a kind of limit case of such western "presence," to the extent that Lacan, centering the psychology of the human subject on a lack disclosed by language, deriving human desire out of a linguistic want, is prepared to make a presence even out of absence, and, therefore, as Derrida objects, a God out of a gap. As is well known, Derrida opposes to the determinate and determining logic of the language of Lacan – though with a dialectic that is of course more complicated than that of any simply polar opposition – an alternative logic of *différance* and writing, associating this a-logical logic with a "question of style" whose status as an irreducible question keeps alive, by foreclosing any univocal answer, the deconstructive power of a corresponding "question of woman." Here again, however, it is possible to identify the formulaic ways in which this Derridean alternative to a psychoanalytic logos recapitulates, because it predicates itself as something Supplementary and Other, the general thematics of *The Taming of the Shrew*. And this recapitulation has remained remarkably consistent, we might add, in the more explicitly feminist extensions of the deconstructive line traced out by Derrida, all of which, for all the differences between them, attempt to speak up for, and even to speak, a different kind of language than that of psychoanalytic man (e.g. the preverbal, presymbolic "semiotic" of Julia Kristeva, the *écriture féminine* of Hélène Cixous, the intentionally duplicitous or bilabial eroticism of Luce Irigaray, the Nietzschean narcissism of Sarah Kofman).[1]

This theoretical debate between psychoanalysis and the deconstructive feminisms that can be called, loosely speaking, its most significant other is in principle interminable to the extent that psychoanalysis can see in such resistance to its Language, as

Freud did with Dora, a symptomatic confirmation of all psychoanalytic thought. In the context of this debate, *The Taming of the Shrew* initially possesses the interest of an exceptionally apt literary example, one to which the different claims of different theories – about language, desire, gender – might be fruitfully applied. On the other hand, to the extent that this debate appears itself to re-enact the action that is staged within *The Taming of the Shrew*, there exists the more than merely formal possibility that the play itself defines the context in which such debate about the play will necessarily take place. Understood in this way, the theoretical quarrel that might take place about *The Taming of the Shrew* would then emerge as nothing more than an unwitting reproduction of the thematic quarrel – between Man and Woman or between two different kinds of language – that already finds itself in motion in *The Taming of the Shrew*. If this were the case – and it remains to determine with what kind of language one might even say that this is the case – then the self-conscious literariness of *The Taming of the Shrew*, the reflexively recursive metatheatricality with which the play presents itself as an example of what it represents, would acquire its own explanatory, but not exactly theoretical, value. Glossing its own literariness, the play becomes the story of why it is the way it is, and this in turn becomes a performative account or self-example of the way a theoretical debate centered around the topoi of sexuality, gender, and language appears to do no more than once again repeat, to no apparent end, an old and still ongoing story.

That the story is in fact an old one is initially suggested by the ancient history attaching to the three joined within *The Taming of the Shrew*: the Christopher Sly framing plot, where a lord tricks a peasant into thinking himself a lord, which goes back at least as far as a fable in *The Arabian Nights*; the story of Lucentio's wooing of Bianca, which can be traced back, through Gascoigne and Ariosto, to Plautus or Menander; and the taming story proper, Petruchio's domestication of the shrewish Kate, which is built up out of innumerable literary and folklore analogues, all of which can claim an antique provenance. Correlated with each other by means of verbal, thematic, and structural cross-references, these three independent stories become in *The Taming of the Shrew* a single narrative of a kind whose twists and turns would seem familiar even on first hearing. Indeed, the only thing that is really novel about the plotting of *The Taming of the Shrew* is the way the play concatenates these three quite different stories so as to make it seem as though each one of them depends upon and is a necessary version of the other two.

Moreover, the play itself insists upon the fact that it retells a master plot of western literary history. By alluding to previous dramatic, literary, and biblical texts, by quoting and misquoting familiar tags and phrases, by parodically citing or miming more serious literary modes (e.g. Ovidian narrative and Petrarchan lyric), the play situates itself within a literary tradition to which even its mockery remains both faithful and respectful. This is especially the case with regard to the taming subplot that gives the play its name. Soon after he enters, for example, Petruchio cites proverbial precursors for the cursing Kate, in one brief passage linking her not only to the alter ego of the Wife of Bath but also to the Cumaean Sibyl and Socrates' Xantippe (i.ii.69–71) (these references later to be counterbalanced by Kate's translation to "a second Grissel, and Roman Lucrece" (ii.i.295–6)).[2] Such women are all touchstones of misogynistic gynecology. The commonplace way in which Petruchio evokes them here, drawing from a thesaurus of women whose voices will systematically contradict the dictates of male diction, is characteristic of the way, from beginning to end, the play works to give archetypal resonance and mythological significance to Kate's specifically female speech, locating it in the context of a perennial iconography for which the language of woman – prophetic and erotic, enigmatic and scolding, excessive and incessant – stands as continually nagging interference with, or as seductive and violent interruption of, or, finally, as loyally complicitous opposition to, the language of man.

What kind of language is it, therefore, that woman speaks, and in what way does it differ, always and forever, from the language of man? The first answer given by *The Taming of the Shrew* is that it is the kind of language Petruchio speaks when he sets out to teach to Kate the folly of her ways. "He is more shrew than she" (iv.i.85) summarizes the homeopathic logic of the taming strategy in accord with which Petruchio, assimilating to himself the attributes of Kate, will hold his own lunatic self up as mirror of Kate's unnatural nature. As perfect instance and reproving object lesson of his wife's excess, Petruchio thus finds "a way to kill a wife with kindness" (iv.i.208). As an example which is simultaneously a counter-example, "He kills her in her own humour" (iv.i.180). All Petruchio's odd behavior – his paradoxical and contradictory assertions, his peremptory capriciousness, his "lunacy," to use a word and image that is central to *The Taming of the Shrew* – presupposes this systematic and admonitory program of an eye for an eye, or, as the play defines the principle: "being mad herself, she's madly mated. / I warrant him, Petruchio is Kated" (iii.ii.244–5; "mated" here meaning "amazed" as well as "matched"). Moreover, all this madness bespeaks the language of woman, for Petruchio's lunatic behavior, even when it is itself nonverbal, is understood to be a corollary function, a derivative example, of the shrewish voice of Kate, as when Petruchio's horrific marriage costume, a demonstrative insult to appropriate decorum – "A monster, a very monster in apparel" (iii.ii.69–70) – is taken as a statement filled with a didactic sense: "He hath some meaning in his mad attire" (iii.ii.124).

In Act I, Scene ii, which is the first scene of the taming subplot, Grumio, Petruchio's servant, explains the meaning as well as the method of Petruchio's madness. At the same time, he suggests how this is to be related to all the action, especially the verbal action, of the play:

> A' my word, and she knew him as well as I do, she would think scolding would do little good upon him. She may perhaps call him half a score knaves or so. Why, that's nothing; and he begin once, he'll rail in his rope-tricks. I'll tell you what, sir, and she stand him but a little, he will throw a figure in her face, and so disfigure her with it that she shall have no more eyes to see withal than a cat. (i.ii.108–15)

This is an obscure passage, perhaps intentionally so, but "the general sense," as the editor of the Oxford edition says, "must be that Petruchio's railing will be more violent than Katherine's."[3] Even so, it is the manner of the passage, more than its somewhat bewildering matter, that best conveys "the general sense" of Petruchio's project, a point brought out by the apparently unanswerable puzzle posed by "rope-tricks." On "rope-tricks" the Oxford editor says: "If emendation is thought necessary, 'rhetricks' is the best yet offered; but 'rope-tricks' may well be correct and may mean tricks that can be punished adequately only by hanging." The *Riverside* edition offers a similar answer to the "rope-tricks" question, but does so with even more uncertainty, as evidenced by the parenthetical question-marks that interrupt the gloss: "*rope-tricks*: blunder for *rhetoric* (an interpretation supported by *figure* in line 114(?) or tricks that deserve hanging(?))."

On the face of it, neither of these edgily tentative editorial comments is especially helpful in determining, one way or the other, whether Petruchio, when he "rails in his rope-tricks," will be doing something with language or, instead, performing tricks for which he should be hanged. The "interpretation," as the *Riverside* edition calls it, remains indeterminate. But such determination is of course not the point. The editors recognize – and so too, presumably, does an audience – that it is for what he does with language that Petruchio runs any risk with (bawdy) rope. Hence the special suitability of "rope-tricks" as a term to describe the way in which Petruchio will respond to Kate in verbal kind. Playing on "rhetoric" and on "rope," but being neither, "rope-tricks" simultaneously advances, one way *and* the other, both the crime (rape) and the punishment (rope) attaching to the extraordinary speech the play associates with Kate (rhetoric). "Rope-tricks," moreover, is a uniquely performative word for rhetoric, since "rope-tricks" *is* rhetoric precisely because it is not "rhetoric," and thus discloses, by pointing to itself, a kind of necessary disjunction between itself as a verbal signifier and what, as a signifier, it means to signify. In this way, as a kind of self-remarking case of rhetoric in action, "rope-tricks" becomes the general name not only for all the figurative language in the play but, also, for all the action in the play which seems literally to mean one thing but in fact means another: for prime example, the way in which Petruchio will speak the language of woman in order to silence Kate.

The point to notice about this is that, as far as the play is concerned, the "interpret-ation" of "rope-tricks," its meaning, is not altogether indeterminate or, rather, if it is indeterminate, this indeterminacy is itself very strictly determined. "Rope-tricks" is a word that univocally insists upon its own equivocation, and this definitive indetermin-acy is what defines its "general sense." In a way that is not at all paradoxical, and in terms which are in no sense uncertain, the question posed by "rope-tricks" has as its answer the question of rhetoric, and the play uses this circularity – the circularity that makes the rhetoricity of a rhetorical question itself the answer to the question that it poses – as a paradigmatic model for the way in which, throughout the play, Petruchio will obsessively answer Kate with hysterical tit for hysterical tat.

Understood in this way, as "rope-tricks," we can say that the words and actions of *The Taming of the Shrew* rehearse a familiar antagonism, not simply the battle between the sexes but, more specifically, though still rather generally, the battle between the determinate, literal language traditionally spoken by man and the figurative, indeter-minate language traditionally spoken by woman. But by saying this we are only returned, once again, to the question with which we began, for if such indeterminacy is what rhetoric always means to say, if this is the literal significance of its "general sense," why is it that this indeterminacy seems in *The Taming of the Shrew* so defini-tively to entail the domestication of Kate? Petruchio is never so patriarchal as when he speaks the language of woman – "He is more shrew than she" – just as Kate's capitulation occurs at the moment when she obediently takes her husband at his lunatic, female, figurative word. This happens first when Petruchio forces Kate to call the sun the moon, and then when Petruchio forces Kate to address a reverend father as "young budding virgin," a purely verbal mix-up of the sexes that leads an onlooker to remark: "A will make the man mad, to make a woman of him" (iv.v.35–6). In accord with what asymmetrical *quid pro quo* does Petruchio propose to silence Kate by speaking the language she speaks, and why does the play assume that the orthodox order of the sexes for which it is the spokesman is reconfirmed when, madly translating a man into a mad woman, it gives explicit voice to such erotic paradox? Why, we can ask, do things not happen the other way around?

These are questions that bear on current theory. The editorial question-marks that punctuate the gloss on "rope-tricks" mark the same site of rhetorico-sexual indeterminacy on which Derrida, for example, will hinge his correlation of "the question of style" with "the question of woman" (this is the same disruptive question-mark, we can note, that Dora dreams of when she dreams about her father's death).[4] But again, such questions are foregrounded *as* questions in The Taming of the Shrew, and in a far from naive manner. We learn, for example, in the very first lines of the play performed for Christopher Sly that Lucentio has come "to see fair Padua, the nursery of arts" (I.i.2), having left his father's "Pisa, renowned for grave citizens" (I.i.10). Lucentio's purpose, he says, is to "study / Virtue and that part of philosophy / … that treats of happiness" (I.i.17–19). This purpose stated, and the crazy psychogeography of Padua thus established by its opposition to sober Pisa, Tranio, Lucentio's servant, then rushes to caution his master against too single-minded a "resolve / To suck the sweets of sweet philosophy" (27–8): "Let's be no Stoics nor no stocks," says Tranio, "Or so devote to Aristotle's checks / As Ovid be an outcast quite abjur'd" (31–2). Instead, Tranio advises his master to pursue his studies with a certain moderation. On the one hand, says Tranio, Lucentio should "Balk logic with acquaintance that you have," but, on the other, he should also "practice rhetoric in your common talk" (34–5). This is the initial distinction to which all the subsequent action of the play consistently and quite explicitly refers, a distinction that starts out as the difference between logic and rhetoric, or between philosophy and poetry, or between Aristotle and Ovid, but which then becomes, through the rhetorical question raised by "rope-tricks," the generalized and – for this is the point – quite *obviously* problematic difference between literal and figurative language on which the sexual difference between man and woman is seen to depend.

Tranio's pun on "Stoics" / "stocks," a pun which is a tired commonplace in Elizabethan comic literature, suggests both the nature of the problem and the way in which the play thematically exploits it. The pun puts the verbal difference between its two terms into question, into specifically rhetorical question, and so it happens that each term is sounded as the mimic simulation of the other. If language can do this to the difference between "Stoics" and "stocks," what can it do to the difference between "man" and "woman"? Is the one the mimic simulation of the other? This is a practical, as well as a rhetorical, question raised by the play, because the play gives countless demonstrations of the way in which the operation of stressedly rhetorical language puts into question the possibility of distinguishing between itself and the literal language it tropes. Petruchio, for example, when we first meet him, even before he hears of Kate, tells Grumio, his servant, to "knock me at the gate" (I.ii.11). The predictable misunderstanding that thereupon ensues is then compounded further when a helpful intermediary offers to "compound this quarrel" (27). These are trivial puns, the play on "knock" and the play on "compound," but their very triviality suggests the troubling way in which the problematic question raised by one word may eventually spread to, and be raised by, all. "Knock at the gate," asks Grumio, "O heavens! Spake you not these words plain?" (39–40).

Given the apparently unavoidable ambiguity of language or, at least, the everpresent possibility of such ambiguity, it is precisely the question, the rhetorical question, of speaking plainly that Grumio raises, as though one cannot help but "practice rhetoric" in one's "common talk." Moreover, as the play develops it, this argument between the master and his servant, an argument spawned by the rhetoricity of language, is made to seem the explanation of Kate's ongoing quarrel with the men who are her master. For example, the same kind of "knocking" violence that leads Petruchio and Grumio to act out the rhetorical question that divides them is what later leads Kate to break her lute upon her music-master's head: "I did but tell her she mistook her frets … And with that word she strook me on the head" (II.i.149–53).

Such "fretful" verbal confusions occur very frequently in the play, and every instance of them points up the way in which any given statement, however intended, can always mean something other than what its speaker means to say. For this reason, it is significant that, in almost the first lines of the play, Christopher Sly, after being threatened with "a pair of stocks" (Ind., i.2), explains not only why this is possibly the case but, really, why this is necessarily the case, formulating, in a "rope-trick" way, a general principle that accounts for the inevitability of such linguistic indeterminacy. "*Paucas pallabris*," says Christopher Sly, "let the world slide" (Ind., i.5). The bad Spanish here is a misquotation from *The Spanish Tragedy*, Hieronimo's famous call for silence. An Elizabethan audience would have heard Sly's "*paucas pallabris*" as the comic application of an otherwise serious cliché, i.e. as an amusing deformation of a formulaic tag (analogous to Holofernes' "*pauca verba*" in *Love's Labour's Lost* (IV.ii. 165)), whose "disfiguring" corresponds to the troping way in which Sly mistakenly recalls Hieronimo by swearing by "Saint Jeronimy" (Ind., i.9). So too with Sly's "let the world slide," which is equally proverbial, and which is here invoked as something comically and ostentatiously familiar, as something novel just *because* it sounds passé, being half of a proverb whose other half Sly pronounces at the end of the frame, in the last line of the Induction, which serves as introduction to the play within the play: "Come madam wife, sit by my side, and let the world slip, we shall ne'er be younger" (Ind., ii.142–3).

Taken together, and recognizing the register of self-parody on which, without Sly's knowing it, they seem to insist, the two phrases make a point about language that can serve as a motto for the rest of the play. There are always fewer words than there are meanings, because a multiplicity of meanings not only can but always will attach to any single utterance. Every word bears the burden of its hermeneutic history – the extended scope of its past, present, and future meanings – and for this reason every word carries with it a kind of surplus semiotic baggage, an excess of significance, whose looming, even if unspoken, presence cannot be kept quiet. Through inadvertent cognate homophonies, through uncontrollable etymological resonance, through unconscious allusions and citations, through unanticipatable effects of translation (*translatio* being the technical term for metaphor), through syntactic slips of the tongue, through unpredictable contextual transformations – in short, through the operation of "rope-tricks," the Word (for example, Sly's "world") will "slide" over a plurality of significances, to no single one of which can it be unambiguously tied down. Sly's self-belying cry for silence is itself an instance of a speech which is confounded by its excess meaning, of literal speech which is beggared, despite its literal intention, by an embarrassment of unintended semiotic riches. But the play performed before Sly – with its many malapropisms, its comic language lesson, its mangled Latin and Italian, its dramatic vivifications of figurative play, as when Petruchio bandies puns with Kate – demonstrates repeatedly and almost heavy-handedly that the rhetorical question raised by Grumio is always in the polysemic air: "Spake you not these words plain?"

It would be easy enough to relate the principle of "*paucas pallabris*" to Derrida's many characterizations of the way the everpresent possibility of self-citation – not necessarily parodic citation – codes every utterance with an irreducible indeterminacy, leaving every utterance undecidably suspended, at least in principle, between its literal and figurative senses. Even more specifically, it would be possible to relate the many proverbial ways in which the "wor(l)d" "slides" in *The Taming of the Shrew* – " 'He that is giddy thinks the world goes round' " (v.ii.26), a proverb that can lead, as Kate remarks, to "A very mean meaning" (31) – to Lacan's various discussions of the not so freely floating signifier.[5] But, even if it is granted, on just these theoretical grounds, that the rhetoricity of language enforces this kind of general question about the possibility of a speaker's ever really being able to mean exactly what he means to say, and even if it is further granted that the "practice" of "rhetoric" in "common talk" is a self-conscious issue in *The Taming of the Shrew*, still, several other, perhaps more pressing, questions still remain. Why, for example, does the indeterminate question of rhetoric call forth the very determinate patriarchal narrative enacted in *The Taming of the Shrew*? Putting the same question in a theoretical register, we can ask why the question of rhetoric evokes from psychoanalysis the patriarchalism for which Lacan appears to be the most explicit mouthpiece, just as the same question provokes, instead, the antipatriarchal gender deconstructions – the chiasmically invaginated differences, the differentiated differences, between male and female – for which we might take Derrida to be the most outspoken spokesman.

To begin to think about these questions, it is necessary first to recognize that *The Taming of the Shrew* is somewhat more specific in its account of female language than I have so far been suggesting. For there is of course another woman in the play whose voice is strictly counterposed to the "scolding tongue" (i.i.252) of Kate, and if Kate, as shrew, is shown to speak a misanthropic, "fretful" language, her sister, the ideal Bianca of the wooing story, quite clearly speaks, and sometimes even sings, another and, at least at first, a more inviting tune. There are, that is to say, at least two kinds of language that the play associates with women – one good, one bad – and the play invents two antithetical stereotypes of woman – again, one good, one bad – to be the voice of these two different kinds of female speech.

This is a distinction or an opposition whose specific content is often overlooked, perhaps because Bianca's voice, since it is initially identified with silence, seems to speak a language about which there is not that much to say. Nevertheless, this silence of Bianca has its own substantial nature, and it points up what is wrong with what, in contrast, is Kate's vocal or vociferating speech. In the first scene of the play within the play, which is where we first meet these two women, Lucentio is made to be a witness to the shrewish voice of Kate – "That wench is stark mad or wonderful froward" (i.i.69) – and this loquacity of Kate is placed in pointed contrast to Bianca's virgin muteness: "But in the other's silence do I see / Maid's mild behavior and sobriety" (70–1). This opposition, speech versus silence, is important, but even more important is the fact that it is developed in the play through the more inclusive opposition here suggested by the metaphorical way in which Lucentio "sees" Bianca's "silence." For Bianca does in fact speak quite often in the play – she is not literally mute – but the play describes this speech, as it does Bianca, with a set of images and motifs, figures of speech, that give both to Bianca and to her speaking a specific phenomenality which is understood to be *equivalent* to silence. This quality, almost a physical materiality, can be generally summarized – indeed, generically summarized – in terms of an essential visibility: that is to say, Bianca and her language both are silent because the two of them are something to be *seen*.

One way to illustrate this is to recall how the first scene repeatedly emphasizes the fact that Lucentio falls in love with Bianca at first sight: "let me be a slave, t'achieve that maid / Whose sudden sight hath thrall'd my wounded eye" (i.i.219–20). A good deal of Petrarchan imagery underlies the visuality of Lucentio's erotic vision: "But see, while idly I stood looking on, / I found the effect of love in idleness" (i.i.150–1). More specifically, however, this modality of vision, this generic specularity, is made to seem the central point of difference between two different kinds of female language whose different natures then elicit in response two different kinds of male desire. There is, that is to say, a polar contrast, erotically inflected, between, on the one hand, the admirably dumb visual language of Bianca and, on the other, the objectionably noisy "tongue" (i.i.89) of Kate:

> *Tranio:*   Master, you look'd so longly on the maid …
> *Lucentio:* O yes, I saw sweet beauty in her face …
> *Tranio:*   Saw you no more? Mark'd you not how her sister
>   Began to scold, and raise up such a storm
>   That mortal ears might hardly endure the din?
> *Lucentio:* Tranio, I saw her mortal lips to move,
>   And with her breath she did perfume the air.
>   Sacred and sweet was all I saw in her.
>
> (i.i.165–76)

In *The Taming of the Shrew* this opposition between vision and language – rather, between a language which is visual, of the eye, and therefore silent, and language which is vocal, of the tongue, and therefore heard – is very strong. Moreover, as the play develops it, this is a dynamic and a violent, not a static, opposition, for it is just such vision that the vocal or linguistic language of Kate is shown repeatedly to speak against. In the first scene this happens quite explicitly, when Kate says of Bianca, in what are almost the first words out of Kate's mouth, "A pretty peat! It is best / Put a finger in the eye, and she knew why" (i.i.78–9). But this opposition runs throughout the play, governing its largest dramatic as well as its thematic movements. To take an example which is especially significant in the light of what has so far been said, we can recall that the "rope-tricks" passage concludes when it prophetically imagines Kate's ultimate capitulation in terms of a blinding cognate with the name of Kate: "She shall have no more eyes to see withal than a cat." Again, it is in terms of just such (figurative) blindness that Kate will later act out her ultimate subjection, not only to man but to the language of man: "Pardon old father, my mistaking eyes, / That have been so bedazzled with the sun … Now I perceive thou art a reverent father. / Pardon, I pray thee, for my mad mistaking" (iv.v.45–9).

I have argued elsewhere that this conflict between visionary and verbal language is not only a very traditional one but one to which Shakespeare in his Sonnets gives a new subjective twist when he assimilates it to the psychology, and not only to the erotic psychology, of his first-person lyric voice.[6] In addition, I have also argued that Shakespeare's different manipulations of this vision / language opposition produce generically different characterological or subjectivity effects in Shakespearean comedy, tragedy, and romance. It is far from the case, however, that Shakespeare invents this conflict between visual and verbal speech, for it is also possible to demonstrate that the terms of this opposition very much inform the metaphorical language through which language is imagined and described in the philosophico-literary tradition that begins in antiquity and extends at least up through the Renaissance, if not farther. While it is not possible to develop in a brief essay such as this the detailed and coherent ways in which this visual / verbal conflict operates in traditionary texts, it is possible to indicate, very schematically, the general logic of this perennial opposition by looking at the two rather well-known illustrations reproduced on pages 409 and 410. These pictures are by Robert Fludd, the seventeenth-century hermeticist, and they employ a thoroughly conventional iconography.[7] A brief review of the two pictures will be worthwhile, for this will allow us to understand how it happens that a traditional question about rhetoric amounts to an answer to an equally traditional question about gender. This in turn will allow us to return not only to *The Taming of the Shrew* but also to the larger theoretical question with which we began, namely, whether it is possible to speak a Language, whether of Man or of Woman, that does not speak for the Language of Man.

The first picture, figure 1, is Fludd's illustration of the seventh verse of Psalm 63 (misnumbered in the picture as verse 8). "*In alarum tuarum umbra canam,*" says or sings King David, and the picture shows precisely this. King David kneels in prayer beneath an eyeball sun, while from out of his mouth, in line with the rays of theophanic light which stream down on him, a verse of psalm ascends up to a brightness which is supported, shaded, and revealed by its extended wings. Because King David is the master psalmist, and because the picture employs perennial motifs, it would be fair to say that Fludd's picture is an illustration of psalmic speech *per se*. In the picture we see traditional figurations of the way a special kind of anagogic language does homage to an elevated referent. This referent, moreover, represented as an eye which is both seeing and seen, is itself a figure of a special kind of speech, as is indicated by the Hebrew letters inscribed upon its iris. These letters – *yod, he, vau, he* – spell out the name of God, "*Jehova,*" which is the "Name" in which, according to the fourth verse of the psalm, King David lifts up his hands: "Thus wil I magnifie thee all my life, and lift up mine hands in the Name."[8] However, though these letters spell out this holy name, nevertheless, in principle they do not sound it out, for these are letters whose literality, when combined in this famous Tetragrammaton, must never be pronounced. Instead, in accord with both orthodox and heterodox mystical prohibitions, this written name of god, which is the only proper name of God, will be properly articulated only through attributive periphrasis, with the letters vocalized either as *Adonai,* "the Lord," or as *Ha Shem,* "the Name" or even "the Word."

In Fludd's picture, where the verse of psalm and "*Jehova*" lie at oblique angles to each other, it is clearly the case that King David does not literally voice the name of God. It is possible, however, reading either up or down, to take inscribed "*Jehova*" as an

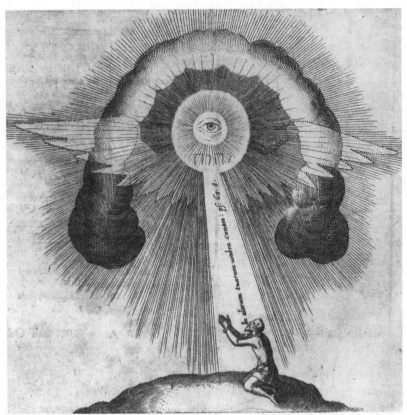

Figure 1 Fludd's illustration of the seventh verse of Psalm 63, from Robert Fludd's *Tomi Secundi Tracatus Secundus; De Praeternatuali Utriusque Cosmi Majoris*, 1621. ©British Library, London.

unspoken part of David's praising speech, either as its apostrophized addressee or as the direct object of its "*canam*." This syntactic, but still silent, link between the Latin and the Hebrew is significant, for unspeakable "*Jehova*" thus becomes the predicated precondition through which or across which what the psalmist says is translated into what the psalmist sees. The picture is concerned to illustrate the effect of this translation, showing David's verse to be the medium of his immediate vision of the sun, drawing David's verse as though it were itself a beam of holy light. In this way, because the verse is pictured as the very brightness that it promises to sing or speak about, Fludd's picture manages to motivate its portrait of a genuinely visionary speech. In the psalm, the reason why the psalmist praises is the very substance of his praise: "For thy loving kindnes is better then life: therefore my lippes shal praise thee." The same thing happens in the picture, where we see the future tense of "*canam*" rendered present, and where the promise of praise amounts to the fulfillment of the promise. But again, all this visionary predication depends upon the odd graphesis of unspeakable "*Jehova*," which is the signifier of all signifiers that even King David cannot bring himself to utter, just as it is the writing on his iris that even Jehova cannot read.

In an elementary etymological sense – remembering that "ideal" comes from Greek "*idein*," "to see" – Fludd's picture is a portrait of ideal language, of language that is at once ideal and idealizing. As the picture shows it, King David speaks a visual speech, a language *of* vision that promotes a vision *of* language, a language which is of the mouth only in so far as it is for the eye. This visual and visionary logos is nothing but familiar. Psalmic speech in particular and the language of praise in general (and it should be recalled that up through the Renaissance *all* poetry is understood to be a poetry of praise) are regularly imagined through such visual imagery, just as the referential object of such reverential praise is regularly conceived of as both agent and patient of sight. (Dante's vision of *luce etterna* at the end of the *Paradiso* would be a good example, though here again the height of vision is figured through a transcendental darkness, when power fails the poet's "*alta fantasia*," and the poet's "will and desire" then "turn" ("*volgeva*") with "the love that moves the sun and the other stars.")

In the second picture, figure 2, which is by no means a strictly Elizabethan world picture (since its details go back at least to Macrobius and, therefore, through Plotinus, to Plato) we see the idealist aesthetics, metaphysics, and cosmology traditionally unpacked

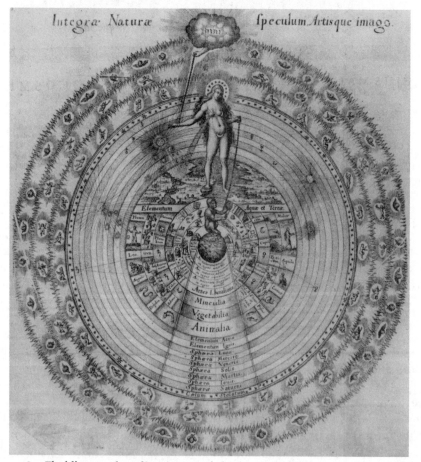

Figure 2 Fludd's encyclopedic picture of the hierarchic cosmos – from *Utriusque Cosmi Majoris*, 1617. © British Library, London.

from and attaching to this visual idealism or visual idealization of the Word. As the title indicates, all arts are images of the specularity of integrated nature because both art and nature reciprocally will simulate the *eidola* or likenesses of beatific light. This common-place eidetic reduction, which, by commutation, enables representation iconically to replicate whatever it presents, is what makes both art and nature into psalmic panegyric. Art becomes an art of nature just as nature is itself a kind of art, because they both reflect, but do not speak, the holy name which is the signifier and the signified of art and nature both. From this phenomenologically mutual admiration, which makes of art and nature each other's *special* (from *specere*, "to look at") likeness, it is easy to derive the ontotheological imperatives that inform all visionary art, for example, the poetics of *ut pictura poesis* and "speaking picture." Suspended from the hand of God, the great chain of mimetic being (which Macrobius describes as a series of successive and declensive mirrors) reaches down to nature, and through her to man, the ape of nature, whose artful calibration of a represented little world produces a demiurgic *mise en abyme* that in no way disturbs – indeed, one whose recursive reflections do nothing but confirm – the stability of the material world on which the ape of nature squats.

Not surprisingly, Fludd's encyclopedic picture of the hierarchic cosmos also includes a representation of a corresponding gender hierarchy. We can see this by looking at the circle of animals where, on the left, the picture illustrates generic man or *Homo* with his arms unfolded towards the sun, in complementary contrast to the way that woman or *Mulier*, at the right of the circle of animals, looks instead up to the moon which is the pale reflection of the sun that shines above it. It is fair to say that this opposition, which makes woman the mimetic simulacrum of man, sketches out the horizontal gender opposition on which the vertical, metaphysical hierarchy of the cosmos perpendicu-larly depends. For this reason, however, it is important to notice that, as the picture shows it, this is not a simple or a simply polar contrast. Man is figured by the sun which is always the same as itself, whereas woman is figured by a waxing-waning-changing moon which is always other than itself, because its mimic light of likeness is what illuminates its difference from the sameness of the sun. Perhaps this constitutes a paradox, this lunar light which folds up likeness into difference. But if so, it is a paradox that stands in service of an orthodox erotics for which woman is the other to man, the hetero- to *Homo*, precisely because her essence is *to be* this lunatic difference between sameness and difference. In the same conventional way (conventional, cer-tainly, at least up through Milton) that the difference between the sun and the moon *is* the moon, so too, and equally traditionally, the difference between man and woman is woman herself.[9] This is a piety, moreover, that we see fleshed out in the ornaments of nature, who sports, with all decorum, a sun on one breast, a moon on the other, and, as the castrated and castrating difference between them, a second fetishistic moon upon her beatific crotch. Such is the erotics that is called for by traditional metaphysics. The word whose solar brightness is revealed by that which clouds it bespeaks a female darkness which is veiled by lunar brightness. The sickle-crescent moon of nature, which is cut and cutting both at once, indicates a mystery beyond it which is comple-mentary to the way the odd graphesis of "*Jehova*" is constitutively eccentric to the centered wholeness of the world.

I have put this point in this way so as to point up the fact that there is really only one way to read Fludd's picture, and this precisely because there are two ways to read it. As with "rope-tricks," indeterminacy here again determines a specific story. On the one hand, given a set of assumptions about mimesis that go back at least to Plato, woman is the subordinate sub-version of originary man, in the same way that the moon is nothing more than an inferior reflection of the sun. In this sense, woman is nothing other than the likeness of a likeness. On the other hand, woman is equally the radical subversion of man, an insubordinate sub-version, because this system of mimesis inexorably calls forth a principle of difference which, as difference, is intrinsically excessive to such hierarchic likeness. In this sense, as the embodiment of difference – as, specifically, the difference *of* likeness – woman is nothing other than the other itself. The point to recognize, however, is not simply that these two hands go happily together – the logic of sub-version logically entailing its own subversion, the "Mirror of Nature" already displaying what Luce Irigaray will call the *speculum de l'autre femme* – but, more important, that the necessity of this double reading is no esoteric piece of wisdom. Quite the contrary; what we see in Fludd's picture is that this is a profoundly orthodox paradox, one whose formal heterogeneity, whose essential duplicity, is regularly figured and expressed by commonplace placeholders of the difference between sameness and difference, as, for example, unspeakable "*Jehova*," whose circumlocutory logos tangentially straddles the inside and the outside of the universal wholeness, or the titillating hole between the legs of nature whose absent presence is highlighted by discretionary light.

What Fludd's picture shows us, therefore, is that traditional iconography regularly assumes, as though it goes necessarily without saying, that there cannot be a picture of visionary language which is not at the same time an emblem of the limits of vision. This limit, however, as a limit, is built into Fludd's Wittgensteinian picture theory of language, within it as precisely that which such a theory is without. "*Jehova*," for example, is a part of *because* it is apart from the ideal specularity of the praising integrated world, and so too with the secret private parts of nature, whose hole we here see integrated into the deep recesses of nature's integrated whole. Out of this internal contradiction, figured through such motivating motifs, there derives, therefore, a very traditional story about the way the language of ideal desire is correlated with a desire for an ideal language. We see this story outlined in the circle of minerals, where man is associated with *Plumbum*, lead, and where woman is associated with *Cuprum*, named for the copper mines in Cyprus, birthplace of Venus, the goddess of love. Here we are to assume an alchemical reaction whereby Venus, the "Cyprian Queen," at once the object and the motive of desire, as a kind of catalytic converter, translates lead into gold, thereby supernaturally changing sub-nature into super-nature. And we can put this point more strongly by asserting that what Fludd's picture depicts is the thoroughly conventional way in which a universe of logical sameness is built up *on* its logical contradiction (or, as it is sometimes written nowadays, as though this were a feminist gesture, its "cuntra-diction," i.e. the language of woman) because it is the very lunacy of discourse that returns both man and woman to the golden, solar order of the patriarchal Word.

At this level of allegorical generality, we can very quickly turn back to *The Taming of the Shrew* and understand how it happens that Petruchio re-establishes the difference between the sexes by speaking the lunatic language of woman. The language of woman *is* the difference between the sexes, a difference Petruchio becomes when, speaking "rope-tricks," he is "Kated." And this translation is dramatically persuasive because the play fleshes it out by invoking the sub-versive, subversive terms and logic of traditional iconography. In the taming story, the first moment of Kate's capitulation occurs when Petruchio, changing his mind, forces Kate first to call the sun the moon and then again the sun: "Then God be blest, it is the blessed sun, / But sun it is not, when you say it is not; / And the moon changes even as your mind. / What you will have it nam'd, even that it is, / And so it shall be so for Katherine" (IV.v.18–22). We can call Kate's articulation of "change" the naming of the shrew which is the instrument of her taming, for it is this transcendentalizing, heliotropic, ontotheological paradox of "change" – "Then God be blest" – that leads Kate then to beg a patriarchal pardon for her blind confusion of the sexes: "Pardon, old father, my mistaking eyes, / That have been so bedazzled with the sun." And the same thing happens at the climax of the wooing story, when Lucentio, until then disguised as Cambio, kneels down before his father and reveals his proper self. "Cambio is chang'd into Lucentio" (v.i.123) is the line with which this revelation is theatrically announced. This formula serves to return the father and his son, along with the master and his servant, back to their proper order. But it also offers us an economical example of the way in which the very operation of rhetorical translation serves to change "change" into light.

To say that this paradox is orthodox is not to say that it describes a complete logical circle. Quite the contrary, as is indicated by the aporetic structure of Fludd's pictures, it is *as* a logical problem for logic, as an everpresent, irreducible, and ongoing question raised by self-reflection, that the paradox acquires its effective power. This is the question consistently raised by the insistent question of rhetoric, which is why, when Kate is tamed and order restored, the heretofore silent and good women of the play immediately turn into shrews. The subversive language of woman with which the play begins, and in resistance to which the movement of the play is predicated, reappears at the end of the play so that its very sounding predicts the future as a repetition of the same old story. This is the final moral of *The Taming of the Shrew*: that it is not possible to close the story of closure, for the very idea and idealization of closure, like the wholeness of Fludd's comprehensive cosmos, is thought through a logic and a logos whose internal disruption forever defers, even as this deferment elicits a desire for, a summary conclusion.

Hence, we can add, the function of the larger frame. Speaking very generally – and recalling, on the one hand, the Petrarchan idealism of the wooing story and, on the other, the parodic Petrarchanism, the Petruchioism, of the taming story – we can say that the two subplots of *The Taming of the Shrew* together present what in the western literary tradition is the master plot of the relation between language and desire. Sly, however, to whom this story is presented, wishes that his entertainment soon were over, for only when the play is over will Sly get to go to bed with new-found wife. "Would 'twere done!" (I.i.254), says Sly (these being the last words we hear from him), of a play which, as far as Sly is concerned, is nothing but foreplay. The joke here is surely on Sly, for the audience knows full well that the consummation Sly so devoutly desires will never be achieved; if ever it happens that Sly sleeps with his wife, he will soon enough discover that she is a he in drag disguise. This defines, perhaps, the ultimate perversity of the kinky lord who "long[s] to hear" his pageboy "call the drunkard husband" (Ind., i.133), and who arranges for Sly to be subjected in this tantalizing way to what for Sly is nothing but the tedious unfolding of the play within the play. But it is not only Sly's desire that is thus seductively frustrated; and this suggests the presence, behind the play, of an even kinkier lord. I refer here to the ongoing editorial question regarding the absence of a final frame; for this response to the play's apparent omission of a formal conclusion to the Sly story is evidence enough that the audience for the entirety of the play is left at its conclusion with a desire for closure that the play calls forth *in order* to postpone. To say that this is a desire that leaves something to be desired – a desire, therefore, that will go on and on forever – goes a good way towards explaining the abiding popularity of *The Taming of the Shrew*.[10]

Perhaps this also explains why, at first glance, it looks as though the current theoretical controversy to which I have referred presents us with a lovers' quarrel in which psychoanalysis plays Petruchio to its critics' Kate. It is tempting to see in the debate between Lacan and Derrida, for example, a domestic and domesticating quarrel that re-enacts in an increasingly more sophisticated but, for this reason, an increasingly more hapless fashion a proverbial literary predicament. However, this is not the conclusion that I would like to draw from the fact that current theoretical polemic so faithfully shapes itself to traditional literary contours and so voraciously stuffs itself with traditional literary topoi. Again it would be possible to relate the logic of sub-versive subversion, as it appears in Fludd and Shakespeare, to Derrida's gnostic, a-logical logic of the copulating supplement. And again, and again even more specifically, it would be possible to relate all this to Lacan's account of "The function and field of speech and language in psychoanalysis." Lacan's characterization of the relation of the imaginary to the symbolic very straightforwardly repeats the motifs of a traditional verbal / visual conflict, and it does so in a way that fully incorporates into itself its equally traditional intrinsic deconstruction, e.g. when Lacan says that the real is that which cannot be represented. When Lacan says, to take just a few examples, that the being of the woman is that she does not exist, or that the function of the universal quantifier, by means of which man becomes the all, is thought through its negation in woman's not-all, when he says that there is no sexual relation, or when he says that castration, the $-\phi$, is what allows us to count from 0 to 1, he is not only evoking the elementary paradox displayed in Fludd's picture – the class of all classes that do not classify themselves – he is also ornamenting this familiar paradox with its traditional figurative clothing.[11] Thus it is that Lacan, like Derrida, is a master of the common-place, as when he says that there is no such thing as metalanguage, or that "*La femme n'ex-siste pas*," or that "*Si j'ai dit que le language est ce comme quoi l'inconscient est structuré, c'est bien parce que le langage, d'abord, ça n'existe pas. Le language est ce qu'on essaye de savoir concernant la fonction de lalangue.*"[12]

To recognize the fact that all of this is commonplace is to see that the argument between Lacan and Derrida, between psychoanalysis and its other (an argument that already takes place within Lacan and within psychoanalysis), repeats not only in its structure but also in its thematic and illustrative details, a master plot of literature. To see this is also to recognize that coarse generic terms of a magnitude corresponding to that of man, woman, language historically carry with them an internal narrative logic which works to motivate a story in which every rubric gets to play and to explain its integrated role. At this level of generality it goes without saying that the language of woman inexorably speaks for the language of man, and it is therefore not surprising that a feminist critique of psychoanalysis which is conducted at this level of generality will necessarily recathect the story that is fleshed out in *The Taming of the Shrew*. If

"Cambio is chang'd into Lucentio," so too, for example, is "Cambio" changed into Luce Irigaray.

It is, however, the great and exemplary value of both Lacan and Derrida that in their quarrel with each other they do more than scrupulously restrict their readings of the central topoi of western self-reflexive language to the level of generality appropriate to the register of allegorical abstraction called for by such massive metaphoremes and motifs. In addition, they recognize this level of generality for what it is: the logic of the literary word in the west. Doing so, they open up the possibility of an extraliterary reading of literature. In a specifically literary context, Shakespeare is interesting because in Shakespeare's texts (from Freud's reading of which, we should recall, psychoanalysis originally derives) we see how, at a certain point in literary history, allegorical abstractions such as man, woman, language – formerly related to each other in accord with the psychomachian dynamics which are sketched out in Fludd's pictures – are introduced into a psychologistic literature, thereby initiating a recognizably modern literature of individualated, motivated character. But the relation to literature is not itself a literary relation, and there is no compelling reason, therefore, especially with the examples of Lacan and Derrida before them, why readers or critics of master literary texts should in their theory or their practice act out what they read.

Notes

1 Derrida's most explicit criticisms of Lacan can be found in "The purveyor of truth" (*Yale French Studies*, 52 (1975)); and in *Positions*, tr. Alan Bass (Chicago, 1981). See also *Spurs: Nietzsche's Styles*, tr. Barbara Harlow (Chicago, 1979); *La Carte postale* (Paris, 1980), which republishes and expands upon "The purveyor of truth"; Julia Kristeva, *Desire in Language: A Semiotic Approach to Literature and Art* (New York, 1980); Hélène Cixous, *La Jeune Née* (with Catherine Clément) (Paris, 1975); "The laugh of the Medusa," tr. K. Cohen and P. Cohen (*Signs*, i (Summer 1976), 875–99); Luce Irigaray, *Speculum de l'autre femme* (Paris, 1974); *Ce sexe qui n'est pas un* (Paris, 1977); Sarah Kofman, "The narcissistic woman: Freud and Girard" (*Diacritics* (Fall 1980), 36–45); *Nietzsche et la scène philosophique* (Paris, 1979).

2 All Shakespeare references are to *The Riverside Shakespeare*, ed. G. B. Evans (Boston, 1974).

3 *The Taming of the Shrew*, ed. H. J. Oliver (Oxford, 1982), 124.

4 "It was at this point that the addendum of there having been a question-mark after the word 'like' occurred to Dora, and she then recognized these words as a quotation out of a letter from Frau K. which had contained the invitation to L____ , the place by the lake. In that letter there had been a question mark placed, in a most unusual fashion, in the very middle of a sentence, after the intercalated words 'if you would like to come' " (Sigmund Freud, *Dora: An Analysis of a Case of Hysteria* (1905), tr. J. Strachey (New York, 1963), 118). Dora dreams here, quite literally, of *écriture féminine*, but Frau K's peculiar question-mark, even if its interruption is taken as a signal of the lesbianism Freud insists on in the story, still marks the specifically Freudian question of female desire: "What does woman want?" This question – not simply "if you would like to come" but, instead, "if you would like to like to come," i.e. do you desire desire? – remains a question at the end of the Dora case; and it seems clear enough that this enigma not only stimulates Freud's countertransference to Dora's transference (Freud introduces the concept of transference in the Dora case), but also accounts for Freud's failure to analyze, on the one hand, his patient's relation to him and, on the other, his relation to his patient. This double failure explains why the Dora case, like *The Taming of the Shrew*, concludes inconclusively. As Freud reports it, the analysis of Dora amounts to a battle between doctor and patient wherein, in response to Freud's demand that

Dora admit her desire for Herr K – i.e. that she avow her Freudian desire – Dora refuses to say what she wants. This is a characteristic Freudian frustration. As in Freud's dream of Irma's injection, where Freud looks into Irma's mouth for evidence of a specifically psychoanalytic sexuality that would prove Freud's psychoanalytic theory true, so Freud wants Dora to speak her desire so as thereby to satisfy Freud's desire for a confirmation of his theory of desire. In the Irma dream, Freud receives as enigmatic answer to this question the uncanny image of "Trimethyla-min" – not only a picture of a word, but a picture of the very word that formulates female sexuality – whereas in the Dora case the question is answered with the re-marked question-mark. In both cases, however, it is the question of female desire, staged as an essential and essentializing question, that leads Freud on in a seductive way. When Dora, manhandling Freud, breaks off her analysis, she leaves Freud with the question of woman, the answer to which Freud will pursue for the rest of his life, up through the late, again inconclusive, essays on gender, in all of which Freud argues for a determinate indeterminacy, a teleological interminability.

5   For example, "The function and field of speech and language in psychoanalysis," in Jacques Lacan, *Ecrits*, tr. Alan Sheridan (New York, 1977), 30–113.

6   Joel Fineman, *Shakespeare's Perjured Eye: The Invention of Poetic Subjectivity in the Sonnets* (Berkeley, 1985).

7   Figure 1 comes from Fludd's *Tomi Secundi Tractatus Secundus; De Præternaturali Utriusque Cosmi Majoris* ... (Oppenheim, 1621); figure 2 comes from *Utriusque Cosmi Majoris* ... (Oppenheim, 1617). There is a convenient collection of Fludd's illustrations in Joscelyn Godwin's *Robert Fludd* (London, 1979).

8   All quotations from the psalm are from the Geneva translation.

9   See Milton, *Paradise Lost*, III, 722–32.

10   It is here that the affinities of *The Taming of the Shrew* with Henry James's *The Turn of the Screw*, to which I am of course alluding in my title, are most apparent. In both texts a specifically rhetorical "turning," "troping," "versing," understood on the model of "rope-tricks," generates an interpretive mystery which is then correlated with a sexual tropism towards, or an apotropaic aversion from, an uncanny, true-false, *female* admixture of male and female. In *The Taming of the Shrew* Sly's framing desire for the pageboy disguised as a woman is a metatheatrical filter that puts into question any univocal understanding of the coupling of Petruchio and Kate. Hence the continuing critical question as to whether the Pauline patriarchalism of Kate's final speech should be understood ironically, i.e. whether she is most a shrew when she is most submissive. This hermeneutic question with regard to Kate corresponds to the traditional duplicity of woman: Sly's metatheatrical desire for the pageboy defines the essence of femininity as masquerade. So too with *The Turn of the Screw*, which shares with *The Taming of the Shrew* the same heavy-handed, play-within-play, *mise en abyme* structure, and which uses this reflexive literariness to invite and to excite a series of relevant but irresolvable, and therefore continuing, critical questions, for example, is the governess's story true or false? is the governess crazy or sane? In *The Turn of the Screw* such interpretive questions find their objectification, their objectification *as* questions, in "Peter Quint," a kind of verbal pageboy whose nominality evokes the primal scene – half-real, half-fantasy – that motivates the governess's hysterico-obsessive desire for Miles and Flora. Again the point to notice is the way in which rhetorical indeterminacy generates a determinate erotics. The name that couples male and female genitals, "Peter" and "Quint," produces a specifically *female* uncanny: the name is quaint – indeed, "cunt" – because both "Peter" and "Quint." So too, a master text such as *The Turn of the Screw* uses precisely this indeterminacy to resecure the place of the "Master" in relation to his servants.

11   See, especially, Jacques Lacan, *Encore* (Paris, 1975), 49–94.

12   For Lacan's remarks on "metalanguage," see, in *Ecrits*, "On a question preliminary to any possible treatment of psychosis." The concluding two quotations come, respectively, from *Télévision* (Paris, 1974), 60, and *Encore*, 126.

Part VIII

Historicism and New Historicism

25 The Cosmic Background   422
    E. M. W. Tillyard
26 Invisible Bullets: Renaissance Authority and its Subversion,
    Henry IV and *Henry V*   435
    Stephen Greenblatt
27 The New Historicism in Renaissance Studies   458
    Jean E. Howard
28 "Shaping Fantasies": Figurations of Gender and Power in
    Elizabethan Culture   481
    Louis Adrian Montrose

N
ew historicism is, and was from its beginnings, identified with the name of Stephen Greenblatt, one of its first and most eloquent practitioners. With the publication of *Renaissance Self-Fashioning* in 1980, Greenblatt – deliberately or not – had fashioned himself as the leader of an audacious new subdiscipline. Although only one chapter treats Shakespeare directly, that book furnished the model for a critical method in which context shared the stage with text. Greenblatt proceeded to define the aims and to demonstrate some of the practices of his way of reading in a series of important articles and explanatory pieces, notably his introduction to a collection called *The Power of Forms in the English Renaissance* (1982) and the first chapter of *Shakespearean Negotiations* (1988). The essay included here, "Invisible Bullets: Renaissance Authority and its Subversion," is less explicitly polemical than it is illustrative of the new historicist's mode of critical address. Its success in representing that mode has made it one of the most frequently cited and reprinted critical texts of the last several decades. Greenblatt himself resisted the term "new historicism," which

he claims to have employed without foreseeing its candidacy for the title of a critical camp. Instead, he prefers to speak of "a poetics of culture" or "cultural poetics." But the earlier phrase stuck.

What is *new* about new historicism, or was new when the practice came to prominence, was its promoters' concentration on the social embeddedness of literary texts, and this focus required that they think about history in a more nuanced, less "monological" sense than had been the case with many earlier literary critics. Practically speaking, this opposition to monological history amounted to an attack on E. M. W. Tillyard. Author of *Shakespeare's History Plays, The Elizabethan World Picture*, and many other volumes, Tillyard was probably the most widely read representative of what has come to be known as the old historicism. The relative simplicity of his critical viewpoint and the lucidity with which he articulated it made him a convenient target, so much so that for a time almost every new historicist found some means of arraigning and convicting him.

The last sentences of his introduction to *Shakespeare's History Plays* offer an effective example of his potential limitations. Tillyard creates a portrait of the artist as a young man, specifically the child Shakespeare growing up in the English Midlands in the 1570s:

> When Shakespeare was ten, he would have heard a part of a homily on order and civil disobedience nine Sundays or holy-days in the year … Early experience of rebellion and of the detestation in which it was held may help to account both for his seriousness in speaking of order and for the attraction he felt towards the theme of civil war.

The passage clearly reveals a few basic principles. In the first place, Tillyard propagates the romantic image of the independent artist absorbing ideas from his culture and, consciously or not, transmuting them into artistic material. Second, Tillyard conceives of that artist as a conscious pitchman for the Elizabethan ideology of order: in other words, the old-historicist Shakespeare is politically conservative. Third, although this notion is less apparent in the cited passage than it will be later in the book, Tillyard's conception of the audience for whom these homiletic dramas were performed is relatively uncomplicated: "man" is conceived as having an "essential" quality that transcends historical circumstance, and woman has it too, although she is not mentioned. It is appropriate to point out that Tillyard is not always as retrograde as some polemicists have made him, but still it is true that much of his thinking, shaped as it was by the chaotic world events of the 1930s and 1940s, is unambiguous and, from this distance, apparently naive.

It is the rare new historicist essay that does not assail Tillyard's positivist sense of history and of art. Louis Montrose, whose essay on *A Midsummer Night's Dream* is included here, enlarges on the problem of essentialism in another, more pedagogical piece, where he alludes to *The Elizabethan World Picture*. Montrose speaks for many new historicist critics when he deplores

> those commentaries on political commonplaces in which the dominant ideology – the unreliable machinery of sociopolitical legitimation – is celebrated by the historical critic as being the morally, intellectually, and aesthetically satisfying structure of understanding

and belief, the stable and coherent *world picture* [emphasis mine] that is shared by all members of the social body.[1]

Greenblatt puts the matter more generously than most by imputing to his younger self a mistaken belief in binary oppositions, a system that Tillyard would have understood and that Greenblatt watches himself outgrow. He explains that over the course of writing the essays that make up *Shakespearean Negotiations* he found his initial assumptions "complicated by several turns in my thinking that I had not foreseen. I can summarize those turns by remarking that I came to have doubts about two things: 'total artist' and 'totalizing society.' "[2]

Probably the most radical departure from traditional historicism is the new historicist's conviction that individual agency is an illusion. On this point it is easy to see that the ideas of Michel Foucault underwrite much new historicist thinking: humans are subjected to the pressures of political and social power, and one of the major characteristics of these power structures is their capacity for making subjects think themselves in control. Such a consequence is also a safeguard of the reigning systems of power. During the 1980s the new historicists developed what came to be known as the "subversion / containment model," meaning that they conceived of the potentially disruptive Renaissance theater as paradoxically serving the power of the state. Theatrical representation of violence or rebellion made the stage a safety valve for "containing" social unrest and political opposition. This altered view of the relation between artistic institutions and the culture they serve necessarily transforms the appearance of the literary object. A play or poem becomes less a product of culture than a "production" of it, an object that is produced by and also produces the social relations and political negotiations in which it is entangled. Indeed, Greenblatt has captured the essence of his project by calling his book *Shakespearean Negotiations*, since terms like "circulation," "exchange," and "reciprocity" go directly to the heart of the new historicist project.

The most persuasive of the new historicists are able to stress the constructive side of their enterprise, iconoclastic though it seemed in its early guises. New historicism consciously and firmly positions the reader at some distance from the Shakespeare play, or whatever work is being considered. Thus, it effectively limits attention to formal details, which may recede to the point of invisibility, or at least insignificance. Close study of verbal properties, structure, or character tends to be supplanted by a broader concern for social institutions, sociopolitical forces, and discursive practices, with particular scrutiny of the power structures that helped to generate the drama and to charge it with cultural vitality. It might be said that a shift has occurred in the kinds of detail scrutinized. The older model of regarding history as a context, of seeking causal connections between historical events and artistic texts, has yielded to the identification of what Montrose has called "tropological ... relations among new historicism's objects of study."[3] History and culture thus become legible texts, studied for the narrative structures on which their transmission depends; conversely, "literary" texts are analyzed with an eye to their historical specificity, their origin in particular political and social contexts. To revert to the convenient formulation, new historicism is known for insisting on "the textuality of history" and "the historicity of texts." "History" and "literature" occupy equal planes and submit to the same analytical instruments.

Of the essays included here – Tillyard aside – two are illustrative (those by Greenblatt and Montrose) and one descriptive (the survey by Howard). Greenblatt's and Montrose's exhibit a characteristic feature of new historicist critical practice: they open with (or shortly introduce) an anecdote, often a historical episode or moment whose literary relevance is not immediately apparent. This conventional beginning is a legacy of another of the godfathers of new historicism, the cultural anthropologist Clifford Geertz, who reads culture by means of "thick description," identifying and teasing out the symbolic ramifications of an apparently trivial event or mode of behavior. Although this stylistic quirk was noted and often mocked very early in the life of the movement, some practitioners have clung to it as a way of defying or challenging their detractors. Having enlarged upon this telling story, the new historicist proceeds to identify the cultural affiliations of the Shakespearean (or other) text being considered, attempting to expose its imbrication in the structures of early modern English culture. And examination of those texts and structures inevitably leads the critic towards an analysis of power, sometimes the power of the text, but always also the political power or social pressures that the work contests and / or enables.

New historicism has been attacked from several sides, accused by some of an obsessive and blinkered interest in politics, by others of an unconscionable political quietism. The first of these critiques is not surprising, given that the modes of literary analysis that had immediately preceded the new methodology, while they may have been implicitly conservative, concentrated on the artistic transmutation of ideology and neglected the political functions of the drama. But after a decade or so such protests began to subside as the influence of new historicism grew and history and politics began to permeate nearly all modes of criticism. The second complaint is more complex. To many, especially cultural materialists and some feminists, the "subversion / containment model" connoted a dark circularity, a determinism that could not account for social change. Thus critics with a commitment to political action accused new historicists of pessimism and disengagement, of regarding cultural power as more or less fixed and unalterable. The new historicists responded by deriding that critique, denying (again in the words of Montrose) "a simplistic, reductive, and hypostatized opposition between 'containment' and 'subversion.' These terms – which appear to be residues of a cold war ideology that had pernicious consequences in both international and domestic policy – prove once again to be wholly inadequate instruments of analysis and debate."[4] In addition to these charges, further complaint has come from feminist critics, who condemn new historicism for its concentration on male power and its neglect of women and particularly women's history.

It would be difficult to overstate the influence of new historicism in the study of Shakespeare and of Renaissance literature generally. Fredric Jameson's unambiguous motto, "Always historicize," seems to have penetrated into virtually every corner of academic criticism. Students of language, textual scholars, stage historians, source-seekers, historians of ideas – all modified their work and drew new energy from the imperatives of new historicism. Publishers rushed to identify themselves with the emerging school, signing new historicist authors and tilting their lists towards culture and context. Greenblatt moved from Berkeley to Harvard, where he was later designated a University Professor, an honor reserved for only the most respected scientists and humanists; he became general editor of the *Norton Shakespeare* and joined

M. H. Abrams as editor of the *Norton Anthology of English Literature*; and he was elected president of the Modern Language Association for 2001–2.

And yet the very success of new historicism, its extraordinary magnetism and its influence on other critical schools, has to some degree deprived it of its distinctive identity. As one commentator, surveying the critical scene at the end of the century, put the matter, "By the late 1990s, literary critics seldom explicitly identified themselves as New Historicists, but the emphasis on context over text still prevailed in literary studies."[5]

Notes

1 "New Historicism," in *Redrawing the Boundaries*, ed. Stephen Greenblatt and Giles Gunn (New York: Modern Language Association, 1992), p. 397.
2 *Shakespearean Negotiations* (Berkeley: University of California Press, 1988), p. 2.
3 "New Historicism," p. 401.
4 Ibid., p. 402.
5 Introduction to the work of Stephen Greenblatt, *The Norton Anthology of Theory and Criticism* (New York: W. W. Norton, 2001), p. 2251.

25

The Cosmic Background

E. M. W. Tillyard

1 Introductory

Shakespeare's Histories have been associated with Holinshed's chronicle and with the Chronicle Plays: and rightly. Holinshed is shorter than the more thoughtful Hall and he includes more matter. Hall dealt with a single stretch of English history from Richard II to Henry VIII; Holinshed goes back to the very beginnings of British legend and includes the history of Scotland. Shakespeare found Holinshed useful as an omnibus volume.

Shakespeare's Histories belong to the class of English Chronicle Plays, and that class, like Holinshed, was practical and not very thoughtful. It was rarely performed at the Inns of Court and was enjoyed by the populace. It exploited the conscious patriotism of the decade after the Armada and instructed an inquisitive public in some of the facts and legends of English history. In formal ingenuousness it resembled the Miracle Plays.

It is easy, and up to a point true, to think of Shakespeare as transforming by his genius the material of Holinshed and the dramatic type of the Chronicle into something uniquely his own. But to leave one's thought at that is a large error; for what Shakespeare transformed was so much more than Holinshed and the Chronicle Play. If Shakespeare went to Holinshed for many of his facts, he had meditated on the political philosophy of Hall and of his own day; and if he imparted much historical information in the manner of the other Chronicle Plays, he was not ignorant of the formal pattern of *Gorboduc*. Shakespeare's Histories are more like his own Comedies and Tragedies than like others' Histories, and they not so much try out and discard a provincial mode as present one of his versions of the whole contemporary pattern of culture. It was not his completest version, but behind it, as behind the Tragedies, was that pattern.

In this chapter I shall describe some parts of that pattern which have most to do with the Histories.

Now this pattern is complicated and was the possession only of the more learned part of society. It can be to the point only if Shakespeare too was learned. There is still a prejudice against thinking of him as such. That prejudice must be overcome if the substance of my first two chapters is to be relevant. To overcome it one can point out that a man can be learned in more ways than one and that at least one of those ways fitted Shakespeare; and then one can produce concrete examples of his learning.

For different ways of being learned, consider how Shakespeare might have dealt with the academic doctrine of the Three Dramatic Unities, which he respected in the *Tempest*. He might have studied it in Aristotle and in Aristotle's Italian commentators; he might have read of it in Sidney; he might have heard it discussed. If the first way is improbable, it is equally improbable that he could have avoided acquaintance with it in the other two ways. We may fairly conjecture that he was in fact learned; not in an academic way but in the way Johnson conjectured for Dryden:

> I rather believe that the knowledge of Dryden was gleaned from accidental intelligence and various conversation, by a quick apprehension, a judicious selection, and a happy memory, a keen appetite of knowledge, and a powerful digestion; by vigilance that permitted nothing to pass without notice, and a habit of reflection that suffered nothing useful to be lost ... I do not suppose that he despised books, or intentionally neglected them; but that he was carried out, by the impetuosity of his genius, to more vivid and speedy instructors; and that his studies were rather desultory and fortuitous than constant and systematical.

For proofs, take for example Lorenzo on music in the fifth Act of the *Merchant of Venice*:

> Look how the floor of heaven
> Is thick inlaid with patines of bright gold:
> There's not the smallest orb which thou behold'st
> But in his motion like an angel sings,
> Still quiring to the young-eyed cherubins;
> Such harmony is in immortal souls;
> But whilst this muddy vesture of decay
> Doth grossly close it in, we cannot hear it.

This has been called "an unlearned man's impression of Plato's sublime dream"; this dream being that "upon each of the heavenly spheres is a siren, who is borne round with the sphere uttering a single note; and the eight notes compose a single harmony." Shakespeare, it is alleged, gets Plato wrong in attributing song to the whole host of heaven instead of to the single spheres into which they were fitted. But more recently a specialist in Greek philosophy asserted that Shakespeare was in fact quite surprisingly knowledgeable and accurate. It is true that he garbled the above passage from the *Republic* by substituting cherubim for sirens and vastly enlarging the range of the heavenly music, but Lorenzo's general doctrine shows an accurate knowledge of a part of Plato's *Timaeus*. In that dialogue it is said that the planetary motions of the heavens have their counterpart in the immortal soul of man and that our souls would sound in accord with the grander music of the cosmos were it not for the earthy and perishable nature of the body. Shakespeare reproduces the gist of this doctrine.

Twice in the tragedies Shakespeare mentions the seeds or "germens" of nature: when Macbeth says to the Witches

> though the treasure
> Of nature's germens tumble all together,

and when Lear, addressing the storm, bids it

> Crack nature's moulds, all germens spill at once
> That make ungrateful man.

It seems that behind these brief references is the whole doctrine of the λόγοι σπερματικοὶ or *rationes seminales*: the doctrine that God introduced into nature certain seminal principles that abide there waiting to be put into action. It is most apt to the passage in *Macbeth* because there was the further doctrine, found in Augustine and Aquinas, that angelic and demonic powers have the gift, under God's permission, of speeding up these natural processes and producing apparently miraculous results.

If anything, we are apt to underestimate what such passing references mean in a dramatist who (unlike Jonson) is not in the least anxious to parade his learning. No one can doubt that Shakespeare knew the outlines of orthodox Christian theology. Yet how few are the precise references to it in the plays. But what there are become significant in inverse proportion to their brevity. Here is one passage: Angelo and Isabella arguing about Claudio's condemnation in *Measure for Measure* –

> *Ang:* Your brother is a forfeit of the law,
> And you but waste your words.
> *Isab:*   Alas, alas!
> Why all the souls that were were forfeit once;
> And He that might the vantage best have took
> Found out the remedy.

The reference is of the slightest, yet it reveals and takes for granted the total Pauline theology of Christ abrogating man's enslavement to the old law incurred through the defection of Adam. Now we can be certain that living in the age he did and having the intelligence he had Shakespeare must have known the outlines of orthodox Christian theology. To this theology there are few references in the plays. Do not these two facts make it *probable* that behind other correspondingly scanty references there is a corresponding abundance of knowledge? When Brutus talks of the state of man, like a little kingdom, suffering the nature of an insurrection, he implies not merely the bare commonplace analogy between the human body and the body politic but the whole mass of traditional correspondences between the heavenly order, the macrocosm, the body politic, and the human body or microcosm.

The argument gains in strength, if we compare the cases of Shakespeare and of Montaigne. Montaigne, an expansive and discursive essayist, is free to give as much of his background and derivation as he wishes. And he makes full use of this freedom by constant quotation. His most famous essay takes off from and partly denies the *Natural*

Theology of Raymond de Sebonde. Before having his say about the state of man and his relation to the beasts, he tells how his father asked him to translate de Sebonde's book from the Latin and how gladly he complied. Had Montaigne been exclusively a dramatist, he might have given little or no sign of having read de Sebonde. His meditations on de Sebonde's material would certainly have got into his plays in some form or other. He would in fact have given us something not unlike Hamlet's pronouncements on the nature of man or Lear's and Timon's broken references to the relation of man and beast. Take in turn one of Hamlet's pronouncements:

> What a piece of work is a man: how noble in reason; how infinite in faculty; in form and moving how express and admirable; in action how like an angel; in apprehension how like a god; the beauty of the world, the paragon of animals.

This is Shakespeare's version of the very precise, traditional, orthodox encomia of what man was in his prelapsarian state and of what ideally he is still capable of being. Raymond de Sebonde himself, a mainly derivative writer, has such an encomium in the ninety-fifth to the ninety-ninth chapters of his *Natural Theology*. How Shakespeare got hold of this material matters little; he could have got it from plenty of places, the pulpit included. It is the stuff's somehow being there, behind Hamlet's sentences, that matters. The equivalent of Montaigne's discursiveness is implied.

Shakespeare, then, had much the same general equipment of learning as his more highly-educated contemporaries, Sidney and Spenser for instance, though it may have been less systematic, less detailed, and less derived from books. How does this equipment bear on the Histories?

2   The Context of History

The picture we get from Shakespeare's Histories is that of disorder. Unsuccessful war abroad and civil war at home are the large theme; victory abroad and harmony at home are the exceptions, and the fear of disorder is never absent. Henry V on the eve of Agincourt prays that the ancestral curse may be suspended, and the Bastard qualifies his patriotic epilogue in *King John* with an *if*: if England to itself do rest but true. And by *resting true* he meant not, displaying the English characteristics but avoiding internal treachery and contention. But to allow disorder to stand as the unqualified description of Shakespeare's Histories would be no truer than to call the *Fairy Queen* a study of mutability. Throughout his poem Spenser shows the alertest sense of the instability of earthly things. But as a non-dramatic, philosophical poet Spenser has both the space and the obligation to make his *total* doctrine clear. So, in the two cantos that survive from a seventh book he turns Mutability into a goddess and makes Nature judge her claims to absolute domination. This is Nature's pronouncement on the evidence:

> I well consider all that ye have said
> And find that all things stedfastness do hate
> And changed be; yet, being rightly weigh'd,

> They are not changed from their first estate
> But by their change their being do dilate,
> And, turning to themselves at length again,
> Do work their own perfection so by fate.
> Then over them Change doth not rule and reign,
> But they reign over Change and do their states maintain.

Even on earth then there is an order behind change, an order which makes Spenser think of a heavenly order and

> Of that same time when no more change shall be,
> But stedfast rest of all things, firmly stay'd
> Upon the pillars of Eternity,
> That is contrare of Mutability.

The case is the same with Shakespeare. Behind disorder is some sort of order or "degree" on earth, and that order has its counterpart in heaven. This assertion has nothing to do with the question of Shakespeare's personal piety: it merely means that Shakespeare used the thought-idiom of his age. The only way he could have avoided that idiom in his picture of disorder was by not thinking at all, like the authors of *Stukeley* or *Edward I*; for to go against the contemporary thought-idiom is to make it rather more than usually emphatic. Witness Marlowe's Tamburlaine, who, because he so very emphatically does *not* crash from Fortune's wheel, proclaims his affinity with all the traditional victims who lament their falls in the *Mirror for Magistrates*.

If a Spenserian analogy suggests that there is a general (and predominantly religious) doctrine behind the mass of particular events transacted in Shakespeare's Histories, the chronicles themselves point just the same way. Many of these kept to the religious setting which was common in medieval days. For instance, Grafton's *Chronicle at Large* (1569), though purporting to be British only, begins with the creation of the world and of paradise in the full medieval fashion. Now the medieval chronicler in writing of the creation habitually inserted the commonplaces of orthodox theology: the nature of the Trinity and of the Angels, the fall of Satan, the question of free will, and so on. Higden, for instance, writing in the first half of the fourteenth century, spends a large portion of the second book of *Polychronicon* on theology, before finally settling to chronicle the events of the world. History in fact grows quite naturally out of theology and is never separated from it. The connection was still flourishing after Shakespeare's death. A work that illustrates it to perfection is Raleigh's *History of the World*. The frontispiece shows History, a female figure, treading down Death and Oblivion, flanked by Truth and Experience, supporting the globe; and over all is the eye of Providence.[*] And the first book deals with the creation and is as full of Augustinian theology as any medieval book of world history. Further, Raleigh's preface contains not only a disquisition on history but an account of English history from Edward II to Henry VII. This account is no mere summary but a view of this stretch of history in a definite pattern;

---

[*] To an Elizabethan a picture of the eye of Providence would first suggest, not, as to a Victorian, the eye remorselessly recording the minutest sin of the individual but the instrument of the power that sustained the world's vitality and prevented its slipping back into chaos.

and the pattern resembles Shakespeare's. Now, if these purely historical patterns are similar, it is most probable that behind both of them are similar philosophical or theological axioms, and that Raleigh's theological preface and first book instruct us in the commonplaces upon which not only his own but Shakespeare's historical writings were founded.

A sketch of English history very like Raleigh's occurs in a much less likely place, the *Microcosmos* of John Davies of Hereford. His chief poems, *Mirum in Modum, Summa Totalis,* and *Microcosmos* (written in the Spenserian stanza with a decasyllabic substituted for the final Alexandrine) are to the age of Shakespeare as the work of Soame Jenyns is to the mid-eighteenth century; they epitomise the commonplaces of the time's serious thought, all the better for being the product of a second-rate mind. Davies himself is especially to my purpose because he is Shakespeare's slightly younger contemporary, because his social status was almost identical with Shakespeare's, and because on the certain evidence of an epigram and the possible evidence of two marginal notes he knew Shakespeare personally. He came of middle-class parents, was educated at the local grammar school but did not attend the university, became a writing-master much patronised by the nobility, and ended by being writing-master to Prince Henry. He addressed short poems to most of the important and intelligent Englishmen of or near the court circle, and his serious poems epitomise just that knowledge the possession of which was taken for granted in that class of person. He writes of God and creation, the universe and the influence of the stars, the soul and body of man, man's mind and its passions. And from his repetitive and indifferently arranged stanzas as completely as from any single source I know of can be extracted the contemporary notion of order or degree which was never absent from Shakespeare's picture of disorder in the Histories. That Davies inserts his very Shakespearean version of English history into *Microcosmos* strongly confirms that belief.

3   The Elizabethan World Order

Most readers of Shakespeare know that his own version of order or degree is in Ulysses's speech on the topic in *Troilus and Cressida*; not all would grant that it states the necessary setting of the Histories; and few realise how large a body of thought it epitomises or hints at. (May I here ask the reader to have before him a text of this speech?)

Its doctrine is primarily political but evidently goes far beyond mere practical politics. First, we learn that the order which prevails in the heavens is duplicated on earth, the king corresponding to the sun; then that disorder in the heavens breeds disorder on earth, both in the physical sublunary organisation and in the commonwealth of men. When Shakespeare calls degree the ladder to all high designs he probably has another correspondence in mind: that between the ascending grades of man in his social state and the ladder of creation or chain of being which stretched from the meanest piece of inanimate matter in unbroken ascent to the highest of the archangels. The musical metaphor in "Take but degree away, untune that string, and hark what discord follows" is far more than a metaphor; it implies the traditional Platonic doctrine that (in Dryden's words)

> From harmony, from heavenly harmony
> This universal frame began,

and that at the world's last hour

> Music shall untune the sky.

Finally, when an Elizabethan audience heard the words "chaos, where degree is suffocate," the educated element at least would understand chaos in a more precise sense than we should naturally do. They would understand it as a parallel in the state to the primitive warring of the elements from which the universe was created and into which it would fall if the constant pressure of God's ordering and sustaining will were relaxed.

The above references are fragmentary but they show that Shakespeare had in mind a complete body of doctrine. Having made this the subject of another book, I need give no more than a short summary in this place.

The Elizabethan conception of world-order was in its outlines medieval although it had discarded much medieval detail. The universe was a unity, in which everything had its place, and it was the perfect work of God. Any imperfection was the work not of God but of man; for with the fall of man the universe underwent a sympathetic corruption. But for all the corruption the marks of God's perfection were still there, and one of the two great roads to salvation was through the study of created things. But though the idea of unity was basic, the actual order of the world presented itself to the Elizabethans under three different, though often related, appearances: a chain, a series of corresponding planes, and a dance to music.

As a chain, creation was a series of beings stretching from the lowest of inanimate objects up to the archangel nearest to the throne of God. The ascent was gradual, no step was missing; and on the borders of the great divisions between animate and inanimate, vegetative and sensitive, sensitive and rational, rational and angelic, there were the necessary transitions. One of the noblest accounts of the chain of being is by Sir John Fortescue, the fifteenth century jurist:

> In this order hot things are in harmony with cold; dry with moist; heavy with light; great with little; high with low. In this order angel is set over angel, rank upon rank in the Kingdom of Heaven; man is set over man, beast over beast, bird over bird, and fish over fish, on the earth, in the air, and in the sea; so that there is no worm that crawls upon the ground, no bird that flies on high, no fish that swims in the depths, which the chain of this order binds not in most harmonious concord. God created as many different kinds of things as he did creatures, so that there is no creature which does not differ in some respect from all other creatures, and by which it is in some respect superior or inferior to all the rest. So that from the highest angel down to the lowest of his kind there is absolutely not found an angel that has not a superior and inferior; nor from man down to the meanest worm is there any creature which is not in some respect superior to one creature and inferior to another. So that there is nothing which the bond of order does not embrace. And since God has thus regulated all creatures, it is impious to think that he left unregulated the human race, which he made the highest of all earthly creatures.

The last sentence illustrates to perfection that same striving for unity and for correspondences that was so strong among the Elizabethans. Expediency was the last reason for justifying the laws of England: Fortescue justifies them because they are a necessary piece in the great jigsaw puzzle of the universe. For Shakespeare too the justification of that political order with which he is mainly concerned is the same.

For the way one large class is linked with another in the chain of being take a passage near the beginning of the second book of Higden's *Polychronicon*. Higden's evidence is of exactly the right kind. He can be trusted to give the perfect commonplace and he was extremely popular not only in his own day but well into the Tudor period. The opening of his second book is for a brief summary of "degree" as good as anything I know:

In the universal order of things the top of an inferior class touches the bottom of a superior: as for instance oysters, which, occupying as it were the lowest position in the class of animals, scarcely rise above the life of plants, because they cling to the earth without motion and possess the sense of touch alone. The upper surface of the earth is in contact with the lower surface of water; the highest part of the waters touches the lowest part of the air, and so by a ladder of ascent to the outermost sphere of the universe. So also the noblest entity in the category of bodies, the human body, when its humours are evenly balanced, touches the fringe of the next class above it, namely the human soul, which occupies the lowest rank in the spiritual order. For this reason the human soul is called the horizon or meeting-ground of corporeal and incorporeal; for in it begins the ascent from the lowest to the highest spiritual power. At times even, when it has been cleansed of earthly passions, it attains to the state of incorporeal beings.

It was this key-position in the chain of being, not the central position of the earth in the Ptolemaic astronomy, that made man so interesting among the objects of creation. Subject to lunar vicissitudes unknown in higher spheres and by its central position the repository of the dregs of things, the earth was not happily situated. But from before Plato till beyond Pope man's amazing position in creation – a kind of Clapham Junction where all the tracks converge and cross – exercised the human imagination and fostered the true humanist tradition; and at no period of English history so powerfully as in the age of Elizabeth. Here is a typical account of man's position between angel and beast, his high capacities and his proneness to fall, from Sir John Hayward, Shakespeare's contemporary:

Thou art a man, endued with reason and understanding, wherein God hath engraven his lively image. In other creatures there is some likeness of him, some footsteps of his divine nature; but in man he hath stamped his image. Some things are like God in that they are; some in that they live; some in their excellent property and working. But this is not the image of God. His image is only in that we understand. Seeing then that thou art of so noble a nature and that thou bearest in thine understanding the image of God, so govern thyself as is fit for a creature of understanding. Be not like the brute beasts, which want understanding: either wild and unruly or else heavy and dull ... Certainly of all the creatures under heaven, which have received being from God, none degenerate, none forsake their natural dignity and being, but only man. Only man, abandoning the dignity of his proper nature, is changed like Proteus into divers forms. And this is occasioned by reason of the liberty of his will. And as every kind of beast is principally inclined to one sensuality more than to any other, so man transformeth himself into that beast to whose sensuality he principally declines.

But if man is allied to the beasts in sensuality and to God and the angels in understanding, he is most himself in being social. This passage, translated from the Italian about 1598, would have been accepted without question by every educated Elizabethan:

> Man, as he is in form from other creatures different, so is his end from theirs very diverse. The end of other creatures is no other thing but living, to generate those like themselves. Man, born in the kingdom of nature and fortune, is not only to live and generate but to live well and happily. Nature of herself provideth for other creatures things sufficient unto life: nature procureth man to live, but reason and fortune cause him to live well. Creatures live after the laws of nature: man liveth by reason prudence and art. Living creatures may live a solitary life: man alone, being of himself insufficient and by nature an evil creature without domestical and civil conversation, cannot lead other than a miserable and discontented life. And therefore, as the philosopher saith very well, that man which cannot live in civil company either he is a god or a beast, seeing only God is sufficient of himself, and a solitary life best agreeth with a beast.

It is with such a doctrine in mind that Shakespeare's Ulysses speaks of

communities,
Degrees in schools and brotherhoods in cities,
Peaceful commerce from dividable shores,

standing by degree in authentic place. Such things are the organisations and activities proper to man in his place in the scale of being.

Although the Middle Ages found the doctrine of the chain of being useful they did not elaborate it. For the full exercise of medieval and Elizabethan ingenuity we must turn to the sets of correspondences worked out between the various planes of creation. These planes were God and the angels, the macrocosm or physical universe, the body politic or the state, and the microcosm or man. To a much smaller degree the animals and plants were included. The amount of intellectual and emotional satisfaction that these correspondences afforded is difficult both to picture and to overestimate. What to us is merely silly or trivial might for an Elizabethan be a solemn or joyful piece of evidence that he lived in an ordered universe, where there was no waste and where every detail was a part of nature's plan.

Shakespeare touches on one of the fundamental correspondences in Ulysses's speech on degree when he speaks of

the glorious planet Sol
In noble eminence enthron'd and spher'd
Amidst the other, whose medicinable eye
Corrects the ill aspects of planets evil,
And posts like the commandment of a king.

But *le roi soleil* is only a part of a larger sequence of leadership, which included: God among the angels or all the works of creation, the sun among the stars, fire among the elements, the king in the state, the head in the body, justice among the virtues, the lion among the beasts, the eagle among the birds, the dolphin among the fishes. It would be hard to find a single passage containing the whole sequence (and there may be items I have not included), but at the beginning of the *Complete Gentleman* Peacham gives a very full list, itself intended to illustrate the universal principle of order and hierarchy. To most of those already mentioned he adds the oak, the rose, the pomeroy and queen-apple, gold and the diamond.

For the general notion of correspondences I know of none better than a passage from an abridgement of de Sebonde's *Natural Theology*, a passage quite valid for the Elizabethan age. It expresses admirably the cosmic order into which the human order was always set. De Sebonde's theme here is the number and the ordering of the angels.

> We must believe that the angels are there in marvellous and inconceivable numbers, because the honour of a king consists in the great crowd of his vassals, while his disgrace or shame consists in their paucity. Therefore I say that thousands of thousands wait on the divine majesty and tenfold hundreds of millions join in his worship. Further, if in material nature there are numberless kinds of stones herbs trees fishes birds four-footed beasts and above these an infinitude of men, it must be said likewise that there are many kinds of angels. But remember that one must not conceive of their multitude as confused; on the contrary, among these spirits a lovely order is exquisitely maintained, an order more pleasing than can be expressed. That this is so we can see from the marvellous arrangement among material things, I mean that some of these are higher, others lower, and others in the middle. For instance the elements and all inanimate things are reckoned in the lowest grade, vegetative things in the second, sensitive in the third, and man in the fourth as sovereign. Within the human range are seen different states from the great to the least: such as labourers merchants burgesses knights barons counts dukes kings, and a single emperor as monarch. Similarly in the church there are curates deacons archdeacons deans priors abbots bishops archbishops patriarchs, and one Pope, who is their head. If then there is maintained such an order among low and earthly things, the force of reason makes it necessary that among these most noble spirits there should be a marshalling unique, artistic, and beyond measure blessed. Further, beyond doubt, they are divided into three hierarchies or sacred principalities, in each of which there are the high middle and low. But this well-ordered multitude leads up to a single head: in precisely the same way as we see among the elements fire the first in dignity; among the fishes the dolphin; among the birds the eagle; among the beasts the lion; and among men the emperor.

Of all the correspondences between two planes that between the cosmic and the human was the commonest. Not only did man constitute in himself one of the planes of creation, but he was the microcosm, the sum in little of the great world itself. He was composed materially of the four elements and contained within himself, as well as his rational soul, vegetative and sensitive souls after the manners of plants and animals. The constitution of his body duplicated the constitution of the earth. His vital heat corresponded to the subterranean fire; his veins to rivers; his sighs to winds; the outbursts of his passions to storms and earthquakes. There is a whole complex body of doctrine behind the account of how Lear

> Strives in his little world of man to outscorn
> The to and fro conflicting wind and rain.

Storms were also frequent in another correspondence, that between macrocosm and body politic. Storms and perturbations in the heavens were duplicated by commotions and disasters in the state. The portents that marked the death of Caesar were more than portents; they were the heavenly enactment of the commotions that shook the Roman Empire after that event. Irregularities of the heavenly bodies duplicate the loss of order in the state. In the words of Ulysses,

> but when the planets
> In evil mixture to disorder wander,
> What plagues and what portents, what mutiny,
> What raging of the sea, shaking of earth,
> Commotion in the winds, frights changes horrors,
> Divert and crack, rend and deracinate
> The unity and married calm of states
> Quite from their fixture.

Last may be cited the correspondence between microcosm and body politic. It can take the form of Brutus in his agony of doubt comparing his own little world to a city in insurrection. But its most persistent form was an elaborate analogy between the various ranks in the state with different parts of the human body.

The picture of the universe as harmony or a dance to music is met with less often than the other two, but Shakespeare knew it as he shows by Ulysses's words once again:

> Take but degree away, untune that string;
> And hark what discord follows.

It was a notion that appealed especially to the more Platonic or mystically minded. It was dear to Milton, and in Elizabethan days it was the theme of Sir John Davies's *Orchestra*. This poem is a kind of academic disputation between Penelope and Antinous, most courtly of the Ithacan suitors, on the dance. Penelope will not dance, but Antinous seeks to persuade her that the universe and all it contains is one great dance-pattern and that she is going against the cosmic order by refraining. Finally he gives her a magic glass in which she sees Queen Elizabeth, the mortal moon, presiding over the dance-measures of her courtiers. Repeated at last in the polity, the dance-pattern, which has ranged through the whole order of nature, is complete. *Orchestra* is one of the most lovely and most typical of Elizabethan poems. It is also very apt to the present argument. Not only does it contain nearly every one of the commonplaces I have touched on, but it presents the cosmic as the background of the actual. The Elizabethan political order, the Golden Age brought in by the Tudors, is nothing apart from the cosmic order of which it is a part. If this is Davies's faith, is it not contrariwise the more likely that when Shakespeare deals with the concrete facts of English history he never forgets the principle of order behind all the terrible manifestations of disorder, a principle sometimes fulfilled, however imperfectly, even in the kingdoms of this world?

4 Shakespeare's Access to the Doctrine

If the total doctrine of order is indeed there behind Ulysses's speech, what were the means by which Shakespeare came to learn of it? Little can be said for certain, for we are now dealing with a mass of material which was part of the collective consciousness of the age, material so taken for granted that it appears more in brief reference than in set exposition. The doctrine of the chain of being was ignored by readers of Elizabethan literature till Lovejoy wrote his book on it; now, our eyes being open, we find it all over the place. If Shakespeare knew it, there can be little question of a single source. He could have got it from a hundred sources. The fountain-heads of general cosmic doctrines were the *Book of Genesis* and Plato; but the material derived thence is handled and rehandled with infinite repetitions and small modifications till it becomes a kind of impersonal ballad-lore, and the question of sources is ridiculous. A book has been published in America on the hexemeral literature, in other words, on the literature that has accumulated round the account in *Genesis* of the six days of creation. As there appears to be no copy of it in this country, I have not read it; but it is said to imply that most of the alleged sources of Milton, for instance in the Kabbala or Augustine, are in fact doubtful because all the stuff is already there in the early commentaries on *Genesis* and must have formed a body of oral tradition that would have survived in sermon and talk independent of any written record. The theory is extremely plausible; and to seek the exact sources of the Shakespearean doctrine of degree is futile in just the same way. But there is one detail of derivation which admits of greater certainty. Of all the passages I have read dealing with "degree" one of the closest to Ulysses's speech is in the original book of Homilies published in 1547 when Edward VI was king. It is worth quoting, not only for its likeness to Shakespeare, but for its beauty, and for the greater amplitude with which it states ideas that are only hinted at by the poet. Contrary to my custom in this book I give the original spelling and punctuation; for the 1547 book of Homilies is a fine piece of printing and was produced with a care that earns the right of accurate transcription. The passage is the opening of the *Sermon of Obedience*, or *An Exhortation concerning good Ordre and Obedience to Rulers and Magistrates.*

Almightie God hath created and appoyncted all thynges, in heaven, yearth, and waters, in a moste excellent and perfect ordre. In heaven he hath appoynted distincte Orders and states of Archangelles and Angelles. In the yearth he hath assigned Kynges, princes, with other gouernors under them, all in good and necessarie ordre. The water aboue is kepte and raineth doune in dewe time and season. The Sonne, Moone, Sterres, Rainbowe, Thundre, Lightenyng, cloudes, and all birdes of the aire, do kepe their ordre. The Yearth, Trees, Seedes, Plantes, Herbes, and Corne, Grasse and all maner of beastes kepe theim in their ordre. All the partes of the whole yere, as Winter, Somer, Monethes, Nightes and Daies, continue in their ordre. All kyndes of Fishes in the sea, Rivers and Waters, with all Fountaines, Sprynges, yea, the Seas themselves kepe their comely course and ordre. And Man himself also, hath all his partes, bothe within and without, as Soule, Harte, Mynd, Memory, Understandyng, Reason, speache, with all and syngular corporall membres of his body, in a profitable necessarie and pleasaunt ordre. Euery degree of people, in their vocacion, callyng, and office, hath appointed to them their duetie and ordre. Some are in high degree, some in lowe, some Kynges and Princes, some inferiors and subjectes, Priestes and Laymen, Masters and Servauntes, Fathers and Children, Husbandes and Wifes, Riche and Poore, and euery one haue nede of other, so that in all thynges is to bee lauded and praised the goodly ordre of God, without the whiche, no house, no citee, no common wealthe, can continue and endure. For where there is no right ordre, there reigneth all abuse, carnall libertie, enormitie, synne, and Babilonical confusion. Take awaie Kynges, Princes, Rulers, Magistrates, Judges, and suche states of God's ordre, no man shall ride or go by the high way unrobbed, no man shal slepe in his awne house or bed unkilled, no man shall kepe his wife, children, and possessions in quietnesse, all thynges shall be common, and there muste nedes folowe all mischief and utter destruccion, bothe of soules, bodies, goodes and common wealthes.

This passage and Ulysses's speech are close enough together to make it likely that at least an unconscious act of memory took place. It is also possible that it was first through this homily that Shakespeare had the idea of degree impressed on his mind. Alfred Hart has pointed out that Shakespeare was six years old when the great rebellion broke out in the north of England. His father as alderman would have shared responsibility for the local militia; Shakespeare himself would have seen the troops marching through Stratford to the north. The homily in question deals with civil obedience and was directed against civil war. At the time of the rebellion it must have had special point and been read with a special emphasis that Shakespeare, granted that he shared the precociousness of other Elizabethan children, was not likely to have missed. Four years later another and longer homily on the same topic, but with specific reference to the late rebellion, was added to the original collection. When Shakespeare was ten, he would have heard a part of a homily on order and civil obedience nine Sundays or holy-days in the year. Hart has added to the meagre stock of reasonable probabilities in the life of Shakespeare. Early experience of rebellion and of the detestation in which it was held may help to account both for his seriousness in speaking of order and for the attraction he felt towards the theme of civil war.

26

Invisible Bullets: Renaissance Authority and its Subversion, *Henry IV* and *Henry V*

Stephen Greenblatt

I n his notorious police report of 1593 on Christopher Marlowe, the Elizabethan spy Richard Baines informed his superiors that Marlowe had declared, among other monstrous opinions, that 'Moses was but a juggler, and that one Heriots, being Sir Walter Ralegh's man, can do more than he'.[1] The 'Heriots' cast for a moment in this lurid light is Thomas Harriot, the most profound Elizabethan mathematician, an expert in cartography, optics, and navigational science, an adherent of atomism, the first Englishman to make a telescope and turn it on the heavens, the author of the first original book about the first English colony in America, and the possessor throughout his career of a dangerous reputation for atheism.[2] In all of his extant writings, private correspondence as well as public discourse, Harriot professes the most reassuringly orthodox religious faith, but the suspicion persisted. When he died of cancer in 1621, one of his contemporaries, persuaded that Harriot had challenged the doctrinal account of creation *ex nihilo*, remarked gleefully that 'a *nihilum* killed him at last: for in the top of his nose came a little red speck (exceeding small), which grew bigger and bigger, and at last killed him'.[3]

Charges of atheism levelled at Harriot or anyone else in this period are extremely difficult to assess, for such accusations were smear tactics, used with reckless abandon against anyone whom the accuser happened to dislike. At a dinner party one summer evening in 1593, Sir Walter Ralegh teased an irascible country parson named Ralph Ironside and found himself the subject of a state investigation; at the other end of the social scale, in the same Dorsetshire parish, a drunken servant named Oliver complained that in the Sunday sermon the preacher had praised Moses excessively but had neglected to mention his fifty-two concubines, and Oliver too found himself under official scrutiny.[4] Few if any of these investigations turned up what we would call atheists, even muddled or shallow ones; the stance that seems to come naturally to the greenest college freshman in late twentieth-century America seems to have been almost unthinkable to the most daring philosophical minds of late sixteenth-century England.

The historical evidence, of course, is unreliable; even in the absence of substantial social pressure, people lie quite readily about their most intimate beliefs. How much more must they have lied in an atmosphere of unembarrassed repression. Still, there is probably more than politic concealment involved here. After all, treason was punished as harshly as atheism, and yet, while the period abounds in documented instances of treason in word and deed, there are virtually no professed atheists. If ever there were a place to confirm the proposition that within a given social construction of reality certain interpretations of experience are sanctioned and others excluded, it is here, in the boundaries that contained sixteenth-century scepticism. Like Machiavelli and Montaigne, Thomas Harriot professed belief in God, and there is no justification, in any of these cases, for a simple dismissal of the profession of faith as mere hypocrisy.

I am not, of course, arguing that atheism was literally unthinkable in the late sixteenth century; rather that it was almost always thinkable only as the thought of another. This is, in fact, one of its attractions as a smear; atheism is one of the characteristic marks of otherness. Hence the ease with which Catholics can call Protestant martyrs atheists, and Protestants routinely make similar charges against the Pope.[5] The pervasiveness and frequency of these charges then does not signal the probable existence of a secret society of freethinkers, a School of Night, but rather registers the operation of a religious authority that, whether Catholic or Protestant, characteristically confirms its power in this period by disclosing the threat of atheism. The authority is secular as well as religious; hence at Raleigh's 1603 treason trial, Justice Popham solemnly warned the accused not to let 'Harriot, nor any such Doctor, persuade you there is no eternity in Heaven, lest you find an eternity of hell-torments'.[6] Nothing in Harriot's writings suggests that he held the position attributed to him here, but of course the charge does not depend upon evidence: Harriot is invoked as the archetypal corrupter, Achitophel seducing his glittering Absolom. If he did not exist, he would have to be invented.

Yet atheism is not the only mode of subversive religious doubt, and we cannot entirely discount the persistent rumors of Harriot's heterodoxy by pointing to his perfectly conventional professions of faith and to the equal conventionality of the attacks upon him. Indeed I want to suggest that if we look closely at *A Brief and True Report of the New Found Land of Virginia*, the only work Harriot published in his lifetime and hence the work in which he was presumably the most cautious, we can find traces of exactly the kind of material that could lead to the remark attributed to Marlowe, that 'Moses was but a juggler, and that one Heriots, being Sir Walter Ralegh's man, can do more than he'. Further, Shakespeare's Henry plays, like Harriot in the New World, can be seen to confirm the Machiavellian hypothesis of the origin of princely power in force and fraud even as they draw their audience irresistibly toward the celebration of that power.

The apparently feeble wisecrack attributed to Marlowe finds its way into a police file because it seems to bear out one of the Machiavellian arguments about religion that most excited the wrath of sixteenth-century authorities: Old Testament religion, the argument goes, and by extension the whole Judeo-Christian tradition, originated in a series of clever tricks, fraudulent illusions perpetrated by Moses, who had been trained in Egyptian magic, upon the 'rude and gross' (and hence credulous) Hebrews.[7] This argument is not actually to be found in Machiavelli, nor does it originate in the sixteenth century; it is already fully formulated in early pagan polemics against Christianity. But it seems to acquire a special force and currency in the Renaissance as an aspect of a heightened consciousness, fuelled by the period's prolonged crises of doctrine and church governance, of the social function of religious belief.

Here Machiavelli's writings are important, for *The Prince* observes in its bland way that if Moses's particular actions and methods are examined closely, they do not appear very different from those employed by the great pagan princes, while the *Discourses* treat religion as if its primary function were not salvation but the achievement of civic discipline and hence as if its primary justification were not truth but expediency. Thus Romulu's successor, Numa Pompilius, 'finding a very savage people, and wishing to reduce them to civil obedience by the arts of peace, had recourse to religion as the most necessary and assured support of any civil society'.[8] For although 'Romulus could organize the Senate and establish other civil and military institutions without the aid of divine authority, yet it was very necessary for Numa, who feigned that he held converse with a nymph, who dictated to him all that he wished to persuade the people to' (147). In truth, continues Machiavelli, 'there never was any remarkable lawgiver amongst any people who did not resort to divine authority, as otherwise his laws would not have been accepted by the people' (147).

From here it was only a short step, in the minds of Renaissance authorities, to the monstrous opinions attributed to the likes of Marlowe and Harriot. Kyd, under torture, testified that Marlowe had affirmed that 'things esteemed to be done by divine power might have as well been done by observation of men', and the Jesuit Robert Parsons claimed that in Ralegh's 'school of Atheism', 'both Moses and our Savior, the Old and the New Testament, are jested at'.[9] On the eve of Ralegh's treason trial, some 'hellish verses' were lifted from an anonymous tragedy written ten years earlier and circulated as Ralegh's own confession of atheism. (The movement here is instructive: the fictional text returns to circulation as the missing confessional language of real life.) At first the earth was held in common, the verses declare, but this golden age gave way to war, kingship, and property:

> Then some sage man, above the vulgar wise,
> Knowing that laws could not in quiet dwell,
> Unless they were observed, did first devise
> The names of Gods, religion, heaven, and hell …
> Only bug-bears to keep the world in fear.[10]

Now Harriot does not give voice to any of these speculations, but if we look attentively at his account of the first Virginia colony, we find a mind that seems interested in the same set of problems, a mind indeed that seems to be virtually testing the Machiavellian hypotheses. Sent by Ralegh to keep a record of the colony and to compile a description of the resources and inhabitants of the area, Harriot took care to learn the North Carolina Algonkian dialect and to achieve what he calls a 'special familiarity with some of the priests'.[11] The Indians believe, he writes, in the immortality of the soul and in otherworldly punishments and rewards for behaviour in this world; 'What subtlety soever be in the *Wiroances* and Priests, this opinion worketh so much in many of the common and simple sort of people that it maketh them have great respect to their Governors, and also great care what they do, to avoid torment after death and to enjoy bliss' (374). The split between the priests and the people implied here is glimpsed as well in the description of the votive images: 'They think that all the gods are of human shape, and therefore they represent them by images in the forms of men, which they call Kewasowak … The common sort think them to be also gods' (373).

We have then, as in Machiavelli, a sense of religion as a set of beliefs manipulated by the subtlety of the priests to help ensure social order and cohesion. To this we may add a still more telling observation not of the internal function of native religion but of the impact of European culture upon the Indians: 'Most things they saw with us', Harriot writes, 'as mathematical instruments, sea compasses, the virtue of the loadstone in drawing iron, a perspective glass whereby was showed many strange sights, burning glasses, wildfire works, guns, books, writing and reading, spring clocks that seem to go of themselves, and many other things that we had, were so strange unto them, and so far exceeded their capacities to comprehend the reason and means how they should be made and done, that they thought they were rather the works of gods then of men, or at the leastwise they had been given and taught us of the gods' (375–6). The effect of this delusion, born of what Harriot supposes to be the vast technological superiority of the European, is that the savages began to doubt that they possessed the truth of God and religion and to suspect that such truth 'was rather to be had from us, whom God so specially loved than from a people that were so simple, as they found themselves to be in comparison of us' (376).

What we have here, I suggest, is the very core of the Machiavellian anthropology that posited the origin of religion in a cunning imposition of socially coercive doctrines by an educated and sophisticated lawgiver upon a simple people. And in Harriot's list of the marvels – from wildfire to reading – with which he undermined the Indians' confidence in their native understanding of the universe, we have the core of the claim attributed to Marlowe: that Moses was but a juggler and that Ralegh's man Harriot could do more than he. It was, we may add, supremely appropriate that this hypothesis should be tested in the encounter of the Old world and the New, for though vulgar Machiavellianism implied that all religion was a sophisticated confidence trick, Machiavelli himself saw that trick as possible only at a radical point of origin: 'if any one wanted to establish a republic at the present time', he writes, 'he would find it much easier with the simple mountaineers, who are almost without any civilization, than with such as are accustomed to live in cities' (*Discourses*, p. 148).

In Harriot then we have one of the earliest instances of a highly significant phenomenon: the testing upon the bodies and minds of non-Europeans or, more generally, the non-civilised, of a hypothesis about the origin and nature of European culture and belief. Such testing could best occur in this privileged anthropological moment, for the comparable situations in Europe itself tended to be already contaminated by prior contact. Only in the forest, with a people ignorant of Christianity and startled by its bearers' technological potency, could one hope to reproduce accurately, with live subjects, the relation imagined between Numa and the primitive Romans, Moses and the Hebrews. And the testing that could then take place could only happen once, for it entails not detached observation but radical change, the change Harriot begins to observe in the priests who 'were not so sure grounded, nor gave such credit to their traditions and stories, but through conversing with us they were brought into great doubts of their own' (375). I should emphasise that I am speaking here of events as reported by Harriot. The history of subsequent English–Algonkian relations casts doubts upon the depth, extent, and irreversibility of the supposed Indian crisis of belief. In the *Brief and True Report*, however, the tribe's stories begin to *collapse* in the minds of their traditional guardians, and the coercive power of the European beliefs begins to show itself almost at once in the Indians' behaviour: 'On a time also when their corn began to wither by reason of a drought which happened extraordinarily, fearing that it had come to pass by reason that in some thing they had displeased us, many would come to us and desire us to pray to our God in England, that he would preserve their corn, promising that when it was ripe we also should be partakers of the fruit' (377). If we remember that, like virtually all sixteenth-century Europeans in the New World, the English resisted or were incapable of provisioning themselves and were in consequence dependent upon the Indians for food, we may grasp the central importance for the colonists of this dawning Indian fear of the Christian God.[12] As Machiavelli understood, physical compulsion is essential but never sufficient; the survival of the rulers depends upon a supplement of coercive belief.

The Indians must be persuaded that the Christian God is all-powerful and committed to the survival of his chosen people, that he will wither the corn and destroy the lives of savages who displease him by disobeying or plotting against the English. We have then a strange paradox: Harriot tests and seems to confirm the most radically subversive hypothesis in his culture about the origin and function of religion by imposing his religion – with all of its most intense claims to transcendence, unique truth, inescapable coercive force – upon others. Not only the official purpose but the survival of the English colony depends upon this imposition. This crucial circumstance is what has licensed the testing in the first place; it is only as an agent of the English colony, dependent upon its purposes and committed to its survival, that Harriot is in a position to disclose the power of human achievements – reading, writing, gunpowder and the like – to appear to the ignorant as divine and hence to promote belief and compel obedience.

Thus the subversiveness which is genuine and radical – sufficiently disturbing so that to be suspected of such beliefs could lead to imprisonment and torture – is at the same time contained by the power it would appear to threaten. Indeed the subversiveness is the very product of that power and furthers its ends. One may go still further and suggest that the power Harriot both serves and embodies not only produces its own subversion but is actively built upon it: in the Virginia colony, the radical undermining of Christian order is not the negative limit but the positive condition for the establishment of the order. And this paradox extends to the production of Harriot's text: *A Brief and True Report*, with its later heterodoxy, is not a reflection upon the Virginia colony nor even a simple record of it – not, in other words, a privileged withdrawal into a critical zone set apart from power – but a continuation of the colonial enterprise.

By October 1586, there were rumours in England that there was little prospect of profit in Virginia, that the colony had been close to starvation, and that the Indians had turned hostile. Harriot accordingly begins with a descriptive catalogue in which the natural goods of the land are turned into social goods, that is, into 'merchantable commodities': 'Cedar, a very sweet wood and fine timber; whereof if nests of chests be there made, or timber thereof fitted for sweet and fine bedsteads, tables, desks, lutes, virginals, and many things else, ... [it] will yield profit' (329–30).[13] The inventory of these commodities is followed by an inventory of edible plants and animals, to prove to readers that the colony need not starve, and then by the account of the Indians, to prove that the colony could impose its will upon them. The key to this imposition, as I have argued, is the coercive power of religious belief, and the source of this power is the impression made by advanced technology upon a 'backward' people.

Hence Harriot's text is committed to record what we have called his confirmation of the Machiavellian hypothesis, and hence too this confirmation is not only inaccessible as subversion to those on whom the religion is supposedly imposed but functionally inaccessible to most readers and quite possibly to Harriot himself. It may be that Harriot was demonically conscious of what he was doing – that he found himself situated exactly where he could test one of his culture's darkest fears about its own origins, that he used the Algonkians to do so, and that he wrote a report on his findings, a coded report, of course, since as he wrote to Kepler years later, 'our situation is such that I still may not philosophize freely'.[14] But we do not need such a biographical romance to account for the phenomenon: the subversiveness, as I have argued, was produced by the colonial power in its own interest, and *A Brief and True Report* was, with perfect appropriateness, published by the great Elizabethan exponent of missionary colonialism, the Reverend Richard Hakluyt.

Yet it is misleading, I think, to conclude without qualification that the radical doubt implicit in Harriot's account is *entirely* contained. Harriot was, after all, hounded through his whole life by charges of atheism and, more tellingly, the remark attributed to Marlowe suggests that it was fully possible for a contemporary to draw the most dangerous conclusions from the Virginia report. Moreover, the 'Atlantic Republican Tradition', as Pocock has argued, does grow out of the 'Machiavellian moment' of the sixteenth century, and that tradition, with its transformation of subjects into citizens, its subordination of transcendent values to capital values, does ultimately undermine, in the interests of a new power, the religious and secular authorities that had licensed the American enterprise in the first place. What we have in Harriot's text is a relation between orthodoxy and subversion that seems, in the same interpretive moment, to be perfectly stable and dangerously volatile.

We can deepen our understanding of this apparent paradox if we consider a second mode of subversion and its containment in Harriot's account. Alongside the *testing* of a subversive interpretation of the dominant culture, we find the *recording* of alien voices or, more precisely, of alien interpretations. The occasion for this recording is another consequence of the English presence in the New World, not in this case the threatened extinction of the tribal religion but the threatened extinction of the tribe: 'There was no town where we had any subtle device practiced against us', Harriot writes, 'but that within a few days after our departure from every such town, the people began to die very fast, and many in short space; in some towns about twenty, in some forty, in some sixty and in one six score, which in truth was very many in respect of their numbers. The disease was so strange, that they neither knew what it was, nor how to cure it; the like by report of the oldest man in the country never happened before, time out of mind' (378).[15] Harriot is writing, of course, about the effects of measles, smallpox, or perhaps simply the common cold upon people with no resistance to them, but a conception of the biological basis of epidemic disease lies far, far in the future. For the

English the deaths must be a moral phenomenon – the notion is for them as irresistible as the notion of germs for ourselves – and hence the 'facts' as they are observed are already moralised: the deaths only occurred 'where they used some practice against us', that is, where the Indians conspired secretly against the English. And, with the wonderful self-validating circularity that characterises virtually all powerful constructions of reality, the evidence for these secret conspiracies is precisely the deaths of the Indians.

Now it is not surprising that Harriot seems to endorse the idea that God is protecting his chosen people by killing off untrustworthy Indians; what is surprising is that Harriot is interested in the Indians' own anxious speculations about the unintended but lethal biological warfare that was destroying them. Drawing upon his special familiarity with the priests, he records a remarkable series of conjectures, almost all of which assume – correctly, as we now know – that their misfortune was linked to the presence of the strangers. 'Some people', observing that the English remained healthy while the Indians died, 'could not tell', Harriot writes, 'whether to think us gods or men'; others, seeing that the members of the first colony were all male, concluded that they were not born of women and therefore must be spirits of the dead returned to mortal form (an Algonkian 'Night of the Living Dead'). Some medicine men learned in astrology blamed the disease on a recent eclipse of the sun and on a comet – a theory Harriot considers seriously and rejects – while others shared the prevailing English interpretation and said 'that it was the special work of God' on behalf of the colonists. And some who seem in historical hindsight eerily prescient prophesied 'that there were more of [the English] generation yet to come, to kill theirs and take their places'. The supporters of this theory even worked out a conception of the disease that in some features uncannily resembles our own: 'Those that were immediately to come after us [the first English colonists], they imagined to be in the air, yet invisible and without bodies, and that they by our entreaty and for the love of us did make the people to die ... by shooting invisible bullets into them' (380).

For a moment, as Harriot records these competing theories, it may seem to a reader as if there were no absolute assurance of God's national interest, as if the drive to displace and absorb the other had given way to conversation among equals, as if all meanings were provisional, as if the signification of events stood apart from power. This impression is intensified for us by our awareness that the theory that would ultimately triumph over the moral conception of epidemic disease was already at least metaphorically present in the conversation. In the very moment that the moral conception is busily authorising itself, it registers the possibility (indeed from our vantage point, the inevitability) of its own destruction.

But why, we must ask ourselves, should power record other voices, permit subversive inquiries, register at its very centre the transgressions that will ultimately violate it? The answer may be in part that power, even in a colonial situation, is not perfectly monolithic and hence may encounter and record in one of its functions materials that can threaten another of its functions; in part that power thrives on vigilance, and human beings are vigilant if they sense a threat; in part that power defines itself in relation to such threats or simply to that which is not identical with it. Harriot's text suggests an intensification of these observations: English power in the first Virginia colony *depends* upon the registering and even the production of such materials. 'These their opinions I have set down the more at large', Harriot tells the 'Adventurers, Favorers, and Wellwishers' of the colony to whom his report is addressed, 'that it may appear unto you that there is good hope they may be brought through discrete dealing and government to the embracing of the truth, and consequently to honor, obey, fear, and love us' (318). The recording of alien voices, their preservation in Harriot's text, is part of the process whereby Indian culture is constituted as a culture and thus brought into the light for study, discipline, correction, transformation. The momentary sense of instability or plenitude – the existence of other voices – is produced by the monological power that ultimately denies the possibility of plenitude, just as the subversive hypothesis about European religion is tested and confirmed only by the imposition of that religion.

We may add that the power of which we are speaking is in effect an allocation method – a way of distributing resources to some and denying them to others, critical resources (here primarily corn and game) that prolong life or, in their absence, extinguish it. In a remarkable study of how societies make 'tragic choices' in the allocation of scarce resources (e.g. kidney machines) or in the determination of high risks (e.g. the military draft), Guido Calabresi and Philip Bobbitt observe that by complex mixtures of approaches, societies attempt to avert 'tragic results, that is, results which imply the rejection of values which are proclaimed to be fundamental'. These approaches may succeed for a time, but it will eventually become apparent that some sacrifice of fundamental values has taken place, whereupon 'fresh mixtures of methods will be tried, structured ... by the shortcomings of the approaches they replace'. These too will in time give way to others in a 'strategy of successive moves' that comprises an 'intricate game', a game that reflects the simultaneous perception of an inherent flaw and the determination to 'forget' that perception in an illusory resolution.[16] Hence the simple operation of any systematic order, any allocation method, will inevitably run the risk of exposing its own limitations, even (or perhaps especially) as it asserts its underlying moral principle.

This exposure is as its most intense at moments in which a comfortably established ideology confronts unusual circumstances, moments when the moral value of a particular form of power is not merely assumed but explained. We may glimpse such a moment in Harriot's account of a visit from the colonists' principal Indian ally, the chief Wingina. Wingina was persuaded that the disease decimating his people was indeed the work of the Christian God and had come to request the English to ask their God to direct his lethal magic against an enemy tribe. The colonists tried to explain that such a prayer would be 'ungodly', that their God was indeed responsible for the disease but that, in this as in all things, he would only act 'according to his good pleasure as he had ordained' (379). Indeed if men asked God to make an epidemic he probably would not do it; the English could expect such providential help only if they made sincere 'petition for the contrary,' that is, for harmony and good fellowship in the service of truth and righteousness.

The problem with these assertions is not that they are self-consciously wicked (in the manner of Richard III or Iago) but that they are highly moral and logically coherent; or rather, what is unsettling is one's experience of them, the nasty sense that they are at once irrefutable ethical propositions and pious humbug designed to conceal from the English themselves the rapacity and aggression that is implicit in their very presence.

The explanatory moment manifests the self-validating, totalising character of Renaissance political theology – its ability to account for almost every occurrence, even (or above all) apparently perverse or contrary occurrences – and at the same time confirms for us the drastic disillusionment that extends from Machiavelli to its definitive expression in Hume and Voltaire. In his own way, Wingina himself clearly thought his lesson in Christian ethics was polite nonsense. When the disease had in fact spread to his enemies, as it did shortly thereafter, he returned to the English to thank them – I presume with the Algonkian equivalent of a sly wink – for their friendly help, for 'although we satisfied them not in promise, yet in deeds and effect we had fulfilled their desires' (379). For Harriot, this 'marvelous accident', as he calls it, is another sign of the colony's great expectations.

Once again a disturbing vista – a skeptical critique of the function of Christian morality in the New World – is glimpsed only to be immediately closed off. Indeed we may feel at this point that subversion scarcely exists and may legitimately ask ourselves how our perception of the subversive and orthodox is generated. The answer, I think, is that 'subversive' is for us a term used to designate those elements in Renaissance culture that contemporary authorities tried to contain or, when containment seemed impossible, to destroy and that now conform to our own sense of truth and reality. That is, we locate as 'subversive' in the past precisely those things that are *not* subversive to ourselves, that pose no threat to the order by which we live and allocate resources: in Harriot's *Brief and True Report*, the function of illusion in the establishment of religion, the displacement of a providential conception of disease by one focused on 'invisible bullets', the exposure of the psychological and material interests served by a certain conception of divine power. Conversely, we identify as the principle of order and authority in Renaissance texts things that we would, if we took them seriously, find subversive for ourselves: religious and political absolutism, aristocracy of birth, demonology, humoral psychology, and the like. That we do not find such notions subversive, that we complacently identify them as principles of aesthetic or political order, is a version of the process of containment that licensed what we call the subversive elements in Renaissance texts: that is, our own values are sufficiently strong for us to contain almost effortlessly alien forces. What we find then in Harriot's *Brief and True Report* can best be described by adapting a remark about the possibility of hope that Kafka once made to Max Brod: There is subversion, no end of subversion, only not for us.

I want now to consider the relevance of what I've been saying to our understanding of more complex literary works. It is tempting to focus such remarks on Shakespeare's *Tempest* where Caliban, Prospero's 'salvage and deformed slave' enters cursing the expropriation of his island and exits declaring that he will 'be wise hereafter, / And seek for grace'.[17] What better instance, in the light of Harriot's Virginia, of the containment of a subversive force by the authority that has created that force in the first place: 'This thing of darkness', Prospero says of Caliban at the close, 'I acknowledge mine.'

But I do not want to give the impression that the process I have been describing is applicable only to works that address themselves directly or allusively to the New World. Shakespeare's plays are centrally and repeatedly concerned with the production and containment of subversion and disorder, and the three modes that we have identified in Harriot's text – testing, recording, and explaining – all have their recurrent theatrical equivalents. I am speaking not solely of plays like *Measure for Measure* and *Macbeth*, where authority is obviously subjected to open, sustained, and radical questioning before it is reaffirmed, with ironic reservations, at the close, but of a play like 1 *Henry IV* in which authority seems far less problematical. 'Who does not all along see', wrote Upton in the mid eighteenth century, 'that when prince Henry comes to be king he will assume a character suitable to his dignity?' My point is not to dispute this interpretation of the prince as, in Maynard Mack's words, 'an ideal image of the potentialities of the English character',[18] but to observe that such an ideal image involves as its positive condition the constant production of its own radical subversion and the powerful containment of that subversion.

We are continually reminded that Hal is a 'juggler', a conniving hypocrite, and that the power he both serves and comes to embody is glorified usurpation and theft; yet at the same time, we are drawn to the celebration of both the prince and his power. Thus, for example, the scheme of Hal's moral redemption is carefully laid out in his soliloquy at the close of the first tavern scene, but as in the act of *explaining* that we have examined in Harriot, Hal's justification of himself threatens to fall away at every moment into its antithesis. 'By how much better than my word I am', Hal declares, 'By so much shall I falsify men's hopes' (i.ii.210–11). To falsify men's hopes is to exceed their expectations, and it is also to disappoint their expectations, to deceive men, to turn their hopes into fictions, to betray them. Not only are the competing claims of Bolingbroke and Falstaff at issue but our own hopes, the fantasies continually aroused by the play of absolute friendship and trust, limitless playfulness, innate grace, plenitude. But though all of this is in some sense at stake in Hal's soliloquy and though we can perceive at every point, through our own constantly shifting allegiances, the potential instability of the structure of power that has Henry IV at the pinnacle and Robin Ostler, who 'never joy'd since the price of oats rose' (ii.i.12), near the bottom, Hal's 'redemption' is as inescapable and inevitable as the outcome of those practical jokes the madcap prince is so fond of playing. Indeed, the play insists, this redemption is not something toward which the action moves but something that is happening at every moment of the theatrical representation.

The same yoking of the unstable and the inevitable may be seen in the play's acts of *recording*, that is, the moments in which we hear voices that seem to dwell in realms apart from that ruled by the potentates of the land. These voices exist and have their apotheosis in Falstaff, but their existence proves to be utterly bound up with Hal, contained politically by his purposes as they are justified aesthetically by his involvement. The perfect emblem of this containment is Falstaff's company, marching off to Shrewsbury: 'discarded unjust servingmen, younger sons to younger brothers, revolted tapsters, and ostlers trade-fall'n, the cankers of a calm world and a long peace' (iv.ii.27–30). These are, as many a homily would tell us, the very types of Elizabethan subversion – masterless men, the natural enemies of social discipline – but they are here pressed into service as defenders of the established order, 'good enough to toss,' as Falstaff tells Hal, 'food for powder, food for powder' (iv.ii.65–6). For power as well as powder, and we may add that this food is produced as well as consumed by the great.

Shakespeare gives us a glimpse of this production in the odd little scene in which Hal, with the connivance of Poins, reduces the puny tapster Francis to the mechanical repetition of the word 'Anon':

Prince:	Nay, but hark you, Francis: for the sugar thou gavest me, 'twas a pennyworth, was't not?
Francis:	O Lord, I would it had been two!
Prince:	I will give thee for it a thousand pound. Ask me when thou wilt, and thou shalt have it.
Poins:	[*Within*] Francis!
Francis:	Anon, anon.
Prince:	Anon, Francis? No Francis; but tomorrow, Francis; or, Francis, a' Thursday; or indeed, Francis, when thou wilt.

(II.iv.58–67)

The Bergsonian comedy in such a moment resides in Hal's exposing a drastic reduction of human possibility: 'That ever this fellow should have fewer words than a parrot,' he says at the scene's end, 'and yet the son of a woman!' (II.iv.98). But the chief interest for us resides in the fact that Hal has himself produced the reduction he exposes. The fact of this production, its theatrical demonstration, implicates Hal not only in the linguistic poverty upon which he plays but in the poverty of the five years of apprenticeship Francis has yet to serve: 'Five year!' Hal exclaims, 'by'r lady, a long lease for the clinking of pewter' (II.iv.45–6). And as the Prince is implicated in the production of this oppressive order, so is he implicated in the impulse to abrogate it: 'But, Francis, darest thou be so valiant as to play the coward with thy indenture, and show it a fair pair of heels and run from it?' (II.iv.46–8). It is tempting to think of this peculiar moment – the Prince awakening the apprentice's discontent – as linked darkly with some supposed uneasiness in Hal about his own apprenticeship,[19] but if so the momentary glimpse of a revolt against authority is closed off at once with a few words of calculated obscurity designed to return Francis to his trade without enabling him to understand why he must do so:

Prince:	Why then your brown bastard is your only drink! for look you, Francis, your white canvas doublet will sully. In Barbary, sir, it cannot come to so much.
Francis:	What, sir?
Poins:	[*Within*] Francis!
Prince:	Away, you rogue, dost thou not hear them call?

(II.iv.73–9)

If Francis takes the earlier suggestion, robs his master and runs away, he will find a place for himself, the play implies, as one of the 'revolted tapsters' in Falstaff's company, men as good as dead long before they march to their deaths as upholders of the crown. Better that he should follow the drift of Hal's deliberately mystifying words and continue to clink pewter. As for the prince, his interest in the brief exchange, beyond what we have already sketched, is suggested by his boast to Poins moments before Francis enters: 'I have sounded the very base-string of humility. Sirrah, I am sworn brother to a leash of drawers and can call them all by their christen names, as Tom, Dick, and Francis' (II.iv.5–8). The prince must sound the basestring of humility if he is to know how to play all of the chords and hence to be the master of the instrument, and his ability to conceal his motives and render opaque his language offers assurance that he himself will not be played on by another.

I have spoken of such scenes in 1 *Henry IV* as resembling what in Harriot's text I have called *recording*, a mode that culminates for Harriot in a glossary, the beginnings of an

Algonkian–English dictionary, designed to facilitate further acts of recording and hence to consolidate English power in Virginia. The resemblance may be seen most clearly perhaps in Hal's own glossary of tavern slang: 'They call drinking deep, dyeing scarlet: and when you breathe in your watering, they cry 'hem!' and bid you play it off. To conclude, I am so good proficient in one quarter of an hour that I can drink with any tinker in his own language during my life' (ii.iv.15–20). The potential value of these lessons, the functional interest to power of recording the speech of an 'under-skinker' and his mates, may be glimpsed in the expressions of loyalty that Hal laughingly recalls: 'They take it already upon their salvation that … when I am King of England I shall command all the good lads in Eastcheap' (ii.iv.9–15).

There is, it may be objected, something slightly absurd in likening such moments to aspects of Harriot's text; 1 *Henry IV* is a play, not a tract for potential investors in a colonial scheme, and the only values we may be sure that Shakespeare had in mind, the argument would go, were theatrical values. But theatrical values do not exist in a realm of privileged literariness, of textual or even institutional self-referentiality. Shakespeare's theatre was not isolated by its wooden walls, nor was it merely the passive reflector of social and ideological forces that lay entirely outside of it: rather the Elizabethan and Jacobean theatre was itself a *social event*. Drama, and artistic expression in general, is never perfectly self-contained and abstract, nor can it be derived satisfactorily from the subjective consciousness of an isolated creator. Collective actions, ritual gestures, paradigms of relationship, and shared images of authority penetrate the work of art, while conversely the socially overdetermined work of art, along with a multitude of other institutions and utterances, contributes to the formation, realignment, and transmission of social practices.

Works of art are, to be sure, marked off in our culture from ordinary utterances, but this demarcation is itself a communal event and signals not the effacement of the social but rather its successful absorption into the work by implication or articulation. This absorption – the presence within the work of its social being – makes it possible, as Bakhtin has argued, for art to survive the disappearance of its enabling social conditions, where ordinary utterance, more dependent upon the extraverbal pragmatic situation, drifts rapidly toward insignificance or incomprehensibility.[20] Hence art's genius for survival, its delighted reception by audiences for whom it was never intended, does not signal its freedom from all other domains of life, nor does its inward articulation of the social confer upon it a formal coherence independent of the world outside its boundaries. On the contrary, artistic form itself is the expression of social evaluations and practices.

One might add that 1 *Henry IV* itself insists that it is quite impossible to keep the interests of the theatre hermetically sealed off from the interests of power. Hal's characteristic activity is playing or, more precisely, theatrical improvisation – his parts include his father, Hotspur, Hotspur's wife, a thief in buckram, himself as prodigal and himself as penitent – and he fully understands his own behaviour through most of the play as a role that he is performing. We might expect that this role-playing gives way at the end to his true identity – 'I shall hereafter', Hal has promised his father, 'be more myself' (iii.ii.92–3) – but with the killing of Hotspur, Hal clearly does not reject all theatrical masks but rather replaces one with another. 'The time will come', Hal declares midway through the play, 'That I shall make this northern youth exchange / His glorious deeds for my indignities' (iii.ii.144–6); when that time *has* come, at the play's close, Hal hides with his 'favours' (that is, a scarf or other emblem, but the word also has in the sixteenth century the sense of 'face') the dead Hotspur's 'mangled face' (v.iv.96), as if to mark the completion of the exchange.

Theatricality then is not set over against power but is one of power's essential modes. In lines that anticipate Hal's promise, the angry Henry IV tells Worcester, 'I will from henceforth rather be myself, / Mighty and to be fear'd, than my condition' (i.iii.5–6). 'To be oneself' here means to perform one's part in the scheme of power as opposed to one's natural disposition, or what we would normally designate as the very core of the self. Indeed it is by no means clear that such a thing as a natural disposition exists in the play as anything more than a theatrical fiction; we recall that in Falstaff's hands 'instinct' itself becomes a piece of histrionic rhetoric, an improvised excuse when he is confronted with the shame of his flight from the masked prince: 'Beware instinct – the lion will not touch the true prince. Instinct is a great matter; I was now a coward on instinct. I shall think the better of myself, and thee, during my life; I for a valiant lion, and thou for a true prince' (ii.iv.271–5). Both claims-Falstaff's to natural valour, Hal's to legitimate royalty – are, the lines darkly imply, of equal merit.

Again and again in 1 *Henry IV* we are tantalised by the possibility of an escape from theatricality and hence from the constant pressure of improvisational power, but we are, after all, in the theatre, and our pleasure depends upon the fact that there is no escape, and our applause ratifies the triumph of our confinement. The play then operates in the manner of its central character, charming us with its visions of breadth and solidarity, 'redeeming' itself in the end by betraying our hopes, and earning with this betrayal our slightly anxious admiration. Hence the odd balance in this play of spaciousness – the constant multiplication of separate, vividly realised realms – and claustrophobia – the absorption of all of these realms by a power at once vital and impoverished. The balance is almost eerily perfect, as if Shakespeare had somehow reached through in 1 *Henry IV* to the very centre of the system of opposed and interlocking forces that held Tudor society together.

When we turn, however, to the plays that continue the chronicle of Hal's career, 2 *Henry IV* and *Henry V*, not only do we find that the forces balanced in the earlier play have pulled apart – the claustrophobia triumphant in 2 *Henry IV*, the spaciousness triumphant in *Henry V* – but that from this new perspective the familiar view of 1 *Henry IV* as a perfectly poised play must be revised. What appeared as 'balance' may on closer inspection seem like radical instability tricked out as moral or aesthetic order; what appeared as clarity may seem now like a conjurer's trick concealing confusion in order to buy time and stave off the collapse of an illusion. Not waving but drowning.

2 *Henry IV* makes the characteristic operations of power less equivocal than they had been in the preceding play: there is no longer even the lingering illusion of distinct realms, each with its own system of values, its soaring visions of plenitude, and its bad dreams. There is manifestly a single system now, one based on predation and betrayal. Hotspur's intoxicating dreams of honour are dead, replaced entirely by the cold rebellion of cunning but impotent schemers. The warm, roistering sounds overheard in the tavern – sounds that seemed to signal a subversive alternative to rebellion – turn out to be the noise of a whore and bully beating a customer to death. And Falstaff,

whose earlier larcenies were gilded by fantasies of innate grace, now talks of turning diseases to commodity (I.ii.234–5).

Only Prince Hal seems, in comparison to the earlier play, less meanly calculating, subject now to fits of weariness and confusion, though this change serves less, I think, to humanise him (as Auerbach argued in a famous essay) than to make it clear that the betrayals are systematic. They happen to him and for him. He needn't any longer soliloquise his intention to 'Falsify men's hopes' by selling his wastrel friends: the sale will be brought about by the structure of things, a structure grasped in this play under the twinned names of time and necessity. So too there is no longer any need for heroic combat with a dangerous, glittering enemy like Hotspur (the only reminder of whose voice in this play is Pistol's parody of Marlovian swaggering); the rebels are deftly if ingloriously dispatched by the false promises of Hal's younger brother, the primly virtuous John of Lancaster. To seal his lies, Lancaster swears fittingly 'by the honour of my blood' – the cold blood, as Falstaff observes of Hal, that he inherited from his father.

The 'recording' of alien voices – the voices of those who have no power to leave literate traces of their existence – continues in this play, but without even the theatrical illusion of princely complicity. The king is still convinced that his son is a prodigal and that the kingdom will fall to ruin after his death – there is a certain peculiar consolation in the thought – but it is no longer Hal alone who declares (against all appearances) his secret commitment to disciplinary authority. Warwick assures the king that the prince's interests in the good lads of Eastcheap are entirely what they should be:

> The Prince but studies his companions
> Like a strange tongue, wherein, to gain the language,
> 'Tis needful that the most immodest word
> Be look'd upon and learnt, which once attain'd,
> Your Highness knows, comes to no further use
> But to be known and hated. So, like gross terms,
> The Prince will in the perfectness of time
> Cast off his followers, and their memory
> Shall as a pattern or a measure live,
> By which his Grace must mete the lives of other,
> Turning past evils to advantages.
>
> (IV.iv.68–78)

At first the language analogy likens the prince's low-life excursions to the search for proficiency: perfect linguistic competence, the 'mastery' of a language, requires the fullest possible vocabulary. But the darkness of Warwick's words – 'to be known and hated' – immediately pushes the goal of Hal's linguistic researches beyond proficiency. When in 1 *Henry IV* Hal boasts of his mastery of tavern slang, we are allowed for a moment at least to imagine that we are witnessing a social bond, the human fellowship of the extremest top and bottom of society in a homely ritual act of drinking together. The play may make it clear, as I have argued, that there are well-defined political interests involved, but these interests may be bracketed, if only briefly, for the pleasure of imagining what Victor Turner calls 'communitas' – a union based on the momentary breaking of the hierarchical order that normally governs a community.[21] And even when we pull back from this spacious sense of union, we are permitted for much of the play to take pleasure at the least in Hal's surprising skill, the proficiency he rightly celebrates in himself.

To learn another language is to acknowledge the existence of another people and to acquire the ability to function, however crudely, within its social world. Hal's remark about drinking with any tinker in his own language suggests, if only jocularly, that for him the lower classes are virtually another people, an alien tribe – immensely more populous than his own – within the kingdom. That this perception extended beyond the confines of Shakespeare's play is suggested by the evidence that middle- and upper-class English settlers in the New World regarded the American Indians less as another race than as a version of their own lower classes; one man's tinker is another man's Indian.[22]

If Hal's glossary initially seems to resemble Harriot's, Warwick's account of Hal's practice quickly drives it past the functionalism of the word-list in the *Brief and True Report*, with its Algonkian equivalents for fire, food, shelter, and toward a different kind of glossary, one more specifically linked to the attempt to understand and control the lower classes. I refer to the sinister glossaries appended to sixteenth-century accounts of criminals and vagabonds. 'Here I set before the good reader the lewd, lousy language of these loitering lusks and lazy lorels', announces Thomas Harman, as he introduces (with a comical flourish designed to display his own rhetorical gifts) what he claims is an authentic list, compiled at great personal cost.[23] His pamphlet, *A Caveat for Common Cursitors*, is the fruit, he declares, of personal research, difficult because his informants are 'marvellous subtle and crafty'. But 'with fair flattering words, money, and good cheer', he has learned much about their ways, 'not without faithful promise made unto them never to discover their names or anything they showed me' (82). Harman cheerfully goes on to publish what they showed him, and he ends his work not only with a glossary of 'peddlar's French' but with an alphabetical list of names, so that the laws made for 'the extreme punishment' of these wicked idlers may be enforced.

It is not at all clear that Harman's subjects – upright men, doxies, Abraham men, and the like – bear any relation to social reality, any more than it is clear in the case of Doll Tearsheet or Mistress Quickly. Much of the *Caveat*, like the other cony-catching pamphlets of the period, has the air of a jest book: time-honoured tales of tricksters and rogues, dished out cunningly as realistic observation. (It is not encouraging that the rogues' term for the stocks in which they were punished, according to Harman, is 'the harmans'.) But Harman is quite concerned to convey at least the impression of accurate observation and recording – clearly, this was among the book's selling points – and one of the principal rhetorical devices he uses to do so is the spice of betrayal: he repeatedly calls attention to his solemn promises never to reveal anything that he has been told, for his breaking of his word serves as an assurance of the accuracy and importance of what he reveals.

A middle-class Prince Hal, Harman claims that through dissembling he has gained access to a world normally hidden from his kind, and he will turn that access to the advantage of the kingdom by helping his readers to identify and eradicate the dissemblers in their midst. Harman's own personal interventions – the acts of detection and apprehension he proudly reports (or invents) – are not enough: only his book can fully expose the cunning sleights of the rogues and thereby induce the justices and shrieves to be more vigilant and punitive. Just as theatricality is thematised in the *Henry IV* plays as one of the crucial agents of royal power, so in the *Caveat for Common Cursitors* (and in much of the cony-catching literature of the period in England and France) printing is represented in the text itself as a force for social order and the detection of criminal fraud. The printed book can be widely disseminated and easily revised, so that the vagabonds' names and tricks may be known before they themselves arrive at an honest citizen's door; as if this mobility weren't quite tangible enough, Harman claims that when his pamphlet was only half-way printed, his printer helped him apprehend a particularly cunning 'counterfeit crank' – a pretended epileptic. In Harman's account the printer turns detective, first running down the street to apprehend the dissembler, then on a subsequent occasion luring him 'with fair allusions' (116) and a show of charity into the hands of the constable. With such lurid tales Harman literalises the power of the book to hunt down vagabonds and bring them to justice.

The danger of such accounts, of course, is that the ethical charge will reverse itself: the forces of order – the people, as it were, of the book – will be revealed as themselves dependent on dissembling and betrayal, and the vagabonds either as less fortunate and well-protected imitators of their betters or, alternatively, as primitive rebels against the hypocrisy of a cruel society. Exactly such a reversal seems to occur again and again in the rogue literature of the period, from the doxies and morts who answer Harman's rebukes with unfailing if spare dignity to the more articulate defenders of vice elsewhere who insist that their lives are at worst imitations of the lives of the great:

> Though your experience in the world be not so great as mine [says a cunning cheater at dice], yet am I sure ye see that no man is able to live an honest man unless he have some privy way to help himself withal, more than the world is witness of. Think you the noblemen could do as they do, if in this hard world they should maintain so great a port only upon their rent? Think you the lawyers could be such purchasers if their pleas were short, and all their judgements, justice and conscience? Suppose ye that offices would be so dearly bought, and the buyers so soon enriched, if they counted not pillage an honest point of purchase? Could merchants, without lies, false making their wares, and selling them by a crooked light, to deceive the chapman in the thread or colour, grow so soon rich and to a baron's possessions, and make all their posterity gentlemen?[24]

Yet though these reversals are at the very heart of the rogue literature, it would be as much of a mistake to regard their final effect as subversion as it would be to regard in a similar light the comparable passages – most often articulated by Falstaff – in Shakespeare's histories. The subversive voices are produced by the affirmations of order, and they are powerfully registered, but they do not undermine that order. Indeed as the example of Harman – so much cruder than Shakespeare – suggests, the order is neither possible nor fully convincing without both the presence and perception of betrayal.

This dependence on betrayal does not prevent Harman from levelling charges of hypocrisy and deep dissembling at the rogues and from urging his readers to despise and prosecute them. On the contrary, Harman's moral indignation seems paradoxically heightened by his own implication in the deceitfulness that he condemns, as if the rhetorical violence of the condemnation cleansed him of any guilt. His broken promises are acts of civility, necessary strategies for securing social well-being. The 'rowsy, ragged rabblement of rakehells' has put itself outside the bounds of civil conversation; justice consists precisely in taking whatever measures are necessary to eradicate them. Harman's false others are the means of identifying and ridding the community of the purveyors of false oaths. The pestilent few will 'fret, fume, swear, and stare at this my book' in which their practices, disclosed after they had received fair promises of confidentiality, are laid open, but the majority will band together in righteous reproach: 'the honourable will abhor them, the worshipful will reject them, the yeomen will sharply taunt them, the husbandmen utterly defy them, the labouring men bluntly chide them, the women with clapping hands cry out at them' (84). To like reading about vagabonds is to hate them and to approve of their ruthless betrayal.

'The right people of the play', a gifted critic of 2 *Henry IV* observes, 'merge into a larger order; the wrong people resist or misuse that larger order'.[25] True enough, but like Harman's happy community of vagabond-haters, the 'larger order' of the Lancastrian State seems, in this play, to batten on the breaking of oaths. Shakespeare does not shrink from any of the felt nastiness implicit in this sorting out of the right people and the wrong people; he takes the discursive mode that he could have found in Harman and a hundred other texts and intensifies it, so that the founding of the modern State, like the founding of the modern prince, is shown to be based upon acts of calculation, intimidation, and deceit. And the demonstration of these acts is rendered an entertainment for which an audience, subject to just this State, will pay money and applaud.

There is throughout 2 *Henry IV* a sense of constriction that the obsessive enumeration of details – 'Thou didst swear to me upon a parcel-gilt goblet, sitting in my Dolphin chamber, at the round table by a sea-coal fire, upon Wednesday in Wheeson week ...' – only intensifies. We may find, in Justice Shallow's garden, a few twilight moments of release from this oppressive circumstantial and strategic constriction, but Falstaff mercilessly deflates them – and the puncturing is so wonderfully adroit, so amusing, that we welcome it: 'I do remember him at Clement's Inn, like a man made after supper of a cheese-paring. When 'a was naked, he was for all the world like a forked radish, with a head fantastically carv'd upon it with a knife' (III.ii.308–12).

What is left is the law of nature: the strong eat the weak. Yet this is not quite what Shakespeare invites the audience to affirm through its applause. Like Harman, Shakespeare refuses to endorse so baldly cynical a conception of the social order; instead actions that should have the effect of radically undermining authority turn out to be the props of that authority. In this play, even more cruelly than in 1 *Henry IV*, moral values – justice, order, civility – are secured paradoxically through the apparent generation of their subversive contraries. Out of the squalid betrayals that preserve the State emerges the 'formal majesty' into which Hal at the close, through a final, definitive betrayal – the rejection of Falstaff – merges himself.

There are moments in *Richard II* in which the collapse of kingship seems to be confirmed in the discovery of the physical body of the ruler, the pathos of his creatural existence:

> ... throw away respect,
> Tradition, form, and ceremonious duty,
> For you have but mistook me all this while.
> I live with bread like you, feel want,
> Taste grief, need friends: subjected thus,
> How can you say to me I am a king?
> (III.ii.172–7)

By the close of 2 *Henry IV* such physical limitations have been absorbed into the ideological structure, and hence justification, of kingship. It is precisely because Prince Hal lives with bread that we can understand the sacrifice that he and, for that matter, his father, have made. Unlike Richard II, Henry IV's articulation of this sacrifice is rendered by Shakespeare not as a piece of histrionic rhetoric but as a private meditation, the innermost thoughts of a troubled, weary man:

> Why rather, sleep, liest thou in smoky cribs,
> Upon uneasy pallets stretching thee,
> And hush'd with buzzing night-flies to thy slumber,
> Than in the perfum'd chambers of the great,
> Under the canopies of costly state,
> And lull'd with sound of sweetest melody?
>
> (III.i.9–14)

Who knows? perhaps it is even true; perhaps in a society in which the overwhelming majority of men and women had next to nothing the few who were rich and powerful did lie awake at night. But we should understand that this sleeplessness was not a well-kept secret: the sufferings of the great are one of the familiar themes in the literature of the governing classes in the sixteenth century. Henry IV speaks in soliloquy, but as is so often the case in Shakespeare his isolation only intensifies the sense that he is addressing a large audience: the audience of the theatre. We are invited to take measure of his suffering, to understand – here and elsewhere in the play – the costs of power. And we are invited to understand these costs in order to ratify the power, to accept the grotesque and cruelly unequal distribution of possessions: everything to the few, nothing to the many. The rulers earn, or at least pay for, their exalted position through suffering, and this suffering ennobles, if it does not exactly cleanse, the lies and betrayals upon which this position depends.

As so often Falstaff parodies this ideology, or rather – and more significantly – presents it as humbug *before* it makes its appearance as official truth. Called away from the tavern to the court, Falstaff turns to Doll and Mistress Quickly and proclaims sententiously: 'You see, my good wenches, how men of merit are sought after. The undeserver may sleep when the man of action is called on' (II.iv.374–7). Seconds later this rhetoric – marked out as something with which to impress whores and innkeepers to whom one owes money one does not intend to pay – recurs in the speech, and by convention of the soliloquy, the innermost thoughts of the king.

At such moments 2 *Henry IV* seems to be testing and confirming an extremely dark and disturbing hypothesis about the nature of monarchical power in England: that its moral authority rests upon a hypocrisy so deep that the hypocrites themselves believe it. 'Then (happy) low, lie down! / Uneasy lies the head that wears a crown' (III.i.30–1): so the old pike tells the young dace. But the old pike actually seems to believe in his own speeches, just as he may believe that he never really sought the crown, 'But that necessity so bow'd the state / That I and greatness were compell'd to kiss' (III.i.72–3). We who have privileged knowledge of the network of State betrayals and privileged access to Falstaff's cynical wisdom can make this opaque hypocrisy transparent. And yet even in 2 *Henry IV*, where the lies and the self-serving sentiments are utterly inescapable, where the illegitimacy of legitimate authority is repeatedly demonstrated, where the whole State seems – to adapt More's phrase – a conspiracy of the great to enrich and protect their interests under the name of commonwealth, even here the audience does not leave the theatre in a rebellious mood. Once again, though in a still more iron-age spirit than at the close of 1 *Henry IV*, the play appears to ratify the established order, with the new-crowned Henry V merging his body into 'the great body of our state', with Falstaff despised and rejected, and with Lancaster – the cold-hearted betrayer of the rebels – left to admire his still more cold-hearted brother: 'I like this fair proceeding of the King's' (v.v.97).

The mood at the close remains, to be sure, an unpleasant one – the rejection of Falstaff has been one of the nagging 'problems' of Shakespearean criticism – but the discomfort only serves to verify Hal's claim that he has turned away his former self. If there is frustration at the harshness of the play's end, the frustration is confirmation of a carefully plotted official strategy whereby subversive perceptions are at once produced and contained:

> My father is gone wild into his grave;
> For in his tomb lie my affections,
> And with his spirits sadly I survive,
> To mock the expectation of the world,
> To frustrate prophecies, and to rase out
> Rotten opinion ...
>
> (v.ii.123–8)

The first part of *Henry IV* enables us to feel at moments that we are like Harriot, surveying a complex new world, testing upon it dark thoughts without damaging the order that those thoughts would seem to threaten. The second part of *Henry IV* suggests that we are still more like the Indians, compelled to pay homage to a system of beliefs whose fraudulence somehow only confirms their power, authenticity, and truth. The concluding play in the series, *Henry V*, insists that we have all along been both coloniser and colonised, king and subject. The play deftly registers every nuance of royal hypocrisy, ruthlessness, and bad faith, but it does so in the context of a celebration, a collective panegyric to 'This star of England', the charismatic leader who purges the commonwealth of its incorrigibles and forges the martial national State.

By yoking together diverse peoples – represented in the play by the Welshman Fluellen, the Irishman Macmorris, and the Scotsman Jamy, who fight at Agincourt alongside the loyal Englishmen – Hal symbolically tames the last wild areas in the British Isles, areas that in the sixteenth century represented, far more powerfully than any New World people, the doomed outposts of a vanishing tribalism. He does so, obviously, by launching a war of conquest against the French, but his military campaign is itself depicted as carefully founded upon acts of what I have called 'explaining'. The play opens with a notoriously elaborate account of the king's genealogical claim to the French throne, and, as we found in the comparable instances in Harriot, this ideological justification of English policy is an unsettling mixture of 'impeccable' reasoning[26] (once its initial premises are accepted) and gross self-interest. The longer the Archbishop of Canterbury continues to spin out the public justifications for an invasion he has privately said would relieve financial pressure on the Church, the more the audience is driven toward skepticism. None of the subsequent attempts at explanation and justification offers much relief: Hal continually warns his victims that they are bringing pillage and rape upon themselves by resisting him, but from the head of an invading army these arguments lack a certain moral force. Similarly, Hal's meditation on the sufferings of the great – 'What infinite heart's ease / Must kings neglect that private men enjoy!' – suffers a bit from the fact that he is almost single-handedly responsible for a war that by his own account and that of the enemy is causing immense civilian misery. And after watching a scene in which anxious, frightened troops sleeplessly await the dawn, it is difficult to be fully persuaded by Hal's climactic vision of the 'slave' and 'peasant' sleeping comfortably, little knowing 'What watch the King keeps to maintain the peace' (iv.i.283).

This apparent subversion of the glorification of the monarch has led some recent critics to view the panegyric as bitterly ironic or to argue, more plausibly, that Shakespeare's depiction of Henry V is radically ambiguous.[27] But in the light of Harriot's *Brief and True Report*, we may suggest that the subversive doubts the play continually awakens serve paradoxically to intensify the power of the king and his war, even while they cast shadows upon this power. The shadows are real enough, but they are deferred – deferred until after Essex's campaign in Ireland, after Elizabeth's reign, after the monarchy itself as a significant political institution. Deferred indeed even today, for in the wake of full-scale ironic readings and at a time in which it no longer seems to matter very much, it is not at all clear that *Henry V* can be successfully performed as subversive. For the play's enhancement of royal power is not only a matter of the deferral of doubt: the very doubts that Shakespeare raises serve not to rob the king of his charisma but to heighten it, precisely as they heighten the theatrical interest of the play; the doubt-less celebrations of royal power with which the period abounds have no theatrical force and have long since fallen into oblivion.

The audience's tension then enhances its attention; prodded by constant reminders of a gap between real and ideal, facts and values, the spectators are induced to make up the difference, to invest in the illusion of magnificence, to be dazzled by their own imaginary identification with the conqueror. The ideal king must be in large part the invention of the audience, the product of a will to conquer which is revealed to be identical to a need to submit. *Henry V* is remarkably self-conscious about this dependence upon the audience's powers of invention. The prologue's opening lines invoke a form of theatre radically unlike the one that is about to unfold: 'A kingdom for a stage, princes to act, / And monarchs to behold the swelling scene!' (3–4). In such a theatre-State there would be no social distinction between the king and the spectator, the performer and the audience; all would be royal, and the role of the performance would be to transform not an actor into a king but a king into a god: 'Then should the warlike Harry, like himself, / Assume the port of Mars' (5–6). This is in effect the fantasy acted out in royal masques, but Shakespeare is intensely aware that his theatre is not a courtly entertainment, that his actors are 'flat unraised spirits,' and that his spectators are hardly monarchs – 'gentles all', he calls them, with fine flattery. 'Let us', the prologue begs the audience, 'On your imaginary forces work … For 'tis your thoughts that now must deck our kings' (18, 28). This 'must' is cast in the form of an appeal and an apology – the consequence of the miserable limitations of 'this unworthy scaffold' –

but the necessity extends, I suggest, beyond the stage: all kings are 'decked' out by the imaginary forces of the spectators, and a sense of the limitations of king or theatre only excites a more compelling exercise of those forces.

To understand Shakespeare's whole conception of Hal, from rakehell to monarch, we need in effect a poetics of Elizabethan power, and this in turn will prove inseparable, in crucial respects, from a poetics of the theatre. Testing, recording, and explaining are elements in this poetics that is inseparably bound up with the figure of Queen Elizabeth, a ruler without a standing army, without a highly developed bureaucracy, without an extensive police force, a ruler whose power is constituted in theatrical celebrations of royal glory and theatrical violence visited upon the enemies of that glory. Power that relies upon a massive police apparatus, a strong, middle-class nuclear family, an elaborate school system, power that dreams of a panopticon in which the most intimate secrets are open to the view of an invisible authority, such power will have as its appropriate aesthetic form the realist novel;[28] Elizabethan power, by contrast, depends upon its privileged visibility. As in a theatre, the audience must be powerfully engaged by this visible presence while at the same time held at a certain respectful distance from it. 'We princes', Elizabeth told a deputation of Lords and Common in 1586, 'are set on stages in the sight and view of all the world.'[29]

Royal power is manifested to its subjects as in a theatre, and the subjects are at once absorbed by the instructive, delightful, or terrible spectacles, and forbidden intervention or deep intimacy. The play of authority depends upon spectators – 'For 'tis your thoughts that now must deck our kings' – but the performance is made to seem entirely beyond the control of those whose 'imaginary forces' actually confer upon it its significance and force. These matters, Thomas More imagines the common people saying of one such spectacle, 'be king's games, as it were stage plays, and for the more part played upon scaffolds. In which poor men be but the lookers-on. And they that wise be will meddle no farther'.[30] Within this theatrical setting, there is a remarkable insistence upon the paradoxes, ambiguities, and tensions of authority, but this apparent production of subversion is, as we have already seen, the very condition of power. I should add that this condition is not a theoretical necessity of theatrical power in general but an historical phenomenon, the particular mode of this particular culture. 'In sixteenth century England', writes Clifford Geertz, comparing Elizabethan and Majapahit royal progresses, 'the political centre of society was the point at which the tension between the passions that power excited and the ideals it was supposed to serve was screwed to its highest pitch ... In fourteenth century Java, the centre was the point at which such tension disappeared in a blaze of cosmic symmetry.'[31]

It is precisely because of the English form of absolutist theatricality that Shakespeare's drama, written for a theatre subject to State censorship, can be so relentlessly subversive: the form itself, as a primary expression of Renaissance power, contains the radical doubts it continually provokes. There are moments in Shakespeare's career – *King Lear* is the greatest example – in which the process of containment is strained to the breaking point, but the histories consistently pull back from such extreme pressure. And we are free to locate and pay homage to the plays' doubts only because they no longer threaten us. There is subversion, no end of subversion, only not for us.

Notes

1 John Bakeless, *The Tragicall History of Christopher Marlowe*, 2 vols. (Cambridge, MA: Harvard University Press, 1942), I, 111.

2 On Harriot see especially *Thomas Harriot, Renaissance Scientist*, ed. John W. Shirley (Oxford University Press, 1974); also Muriel Rukeyser, *The Traces of Thomas Harriot* (New York: Random House, 1970), and Jean Jacquot, 'Thomas Harriot's Reputation for Impiety', *Notes and Records of the Royal Society*, 9 (1952), 164–87.

3 John Aubrey, *Brief Lives*, ed. Andrew Clark, 2 vols. (Oxford University Press, 1898), I, 286.

4 For the investigation of Ralegh, see *Willobie His Avisa* (1594), ed. G. B. Harrison (London: John Lane, 1926), appendix 3, pp. 255–71.

5 See, for example, *The Historie of Travell into Virginia Britania* (1612), ed. Louis B. Wright and Virginia Freund (London: Hakluyt Society, 2nd: ser., no. 103, 1953), p. 101.

6 Jacquot, 'Thomas Harriot's Reputation for Impiety', p. 167.

7 See for instance Richard Baines's version of Marlowe's version of this argument: C. F. Tucker Brooke, *The Life of Marlowe* (London: Methuen, 1930), appendix 9, p. 98.

8 Niccolò Machiavelli, *Discourses*, trans. Christian Detmold (New York: Random House, 1950), p. 146. See also *The Prince* in *Tutte le opere di Niccolò Machiavelli*, ed. Francesco Flora and Carlo Cordiè, 2 vols. (Rome: Arnoldo Mondadori, 1949), I, 18.

9 Kyd is quoted in Brooke, *Life of Marlowe*, appendix 12, p. 107; Parsons in Ernest A. Strathmann, *Sir Walter Ralegh* (New York: Columbia University Press, 1951), p. 25.

10 Quoted in Jean Jacquot, 'Ralegh's "Hellish Verses" and the "Tragicall Raigne of Selimus" ', *Modern Language Review*, 48 (1953), 1.

11 Thomas Harriot, *A Briefe and True Report of the New Found Land of Virginia* (1588), in *The Roanoke Voyages, 1584–1590*, ed. David Beers Quinn, 2 vols. (London: Hakluyt Society, 2nd ser., no. 104, 1955), p. 375. (Quotations are modernised here.) On the Algonkians of southern New England see Bruce G. Trigger, ed., *Handbook of North American Indians*: vol. 15, *Northeast* (Washington, DC: Smithsonian, 1978).

12 Cf. Richard Hakluyt, *The Principal Navigations, Voyages, Traffiques, & Discoveries of the English Nation*, 12 vols. (Glasgow: James Maclehose, 1903–5), X, 54, 56.

13 On these catalogues, see Wayne Franklin, *Discoverers, Explorers, Settlers: the Diligent Writers of Early America* (University of Chicago Press, 1979), pp. 69–122.

14 Quoted by Edward Rosen, 'Harriot's Science: the Intellectual Background', in *Thomas Harriot*, ed. Shirley, p. 4.

15 Cf. Walter Bigges's account of Drake's visit to Florida in 1586, in *The Roanoke Voyages*, I, 306.

16 Guido Calabresi and Philip Bobbitt, *Tragic Choices* (New York: Norton, 1978), p. 195. The term *tragic* is, I think, misleading.

17 v.i.295–6. All citations of Shakespeare are to *The Riverside Shakespeare*, ed. G. Blakemore Evans (Boston: Houghton Mifflin, 1974).

18 John Upton, *Critical Observations on Shakespeare* (1748), in *Shakespeare: the Critical Heritage*, ed. Brian Vickers, vol. 3: *1733–1752* (London: Routledge, 1975), p. 297; Maynard Mack, introduction to Signet Classic edition of *1 Henry IV* (New York: New American Library, 1965), p. xxxv.

19 See S. P. Zitner, 'Anon, Anon: or, a Mirror for a Magistrate', *Shakespeare Quarterly*, 19 (1968), 63–70.

20 See V. N. Volosinov, *Freudianism: a Marxist Critique*, trans. I. R. Titunik, ed. Neal H. Bruss (New York: Academic Press, 1976), pp. 93–116; the book was written by Bakhtin and published under Volosinov's name.

21 See, for example, Victor Turner, *Drama, Fields, and Metaphors: Symbolic Action in Human Society* (Ithaca: Cornell University Press, 1974).

22 See Karen Ordahl Kupperman, *Settling with the Indians: the Meeting of English and Indian Cultures in America, 1580–1640* (Totowa, NJ: Rowman and Littlefield, 1980).

23 Thomas Harman, *A Caveat of Warening, for Commen Cursetors Vulgarely Called Vagabones* (1566), in Gāmini Salgādo, ed., *Cony-Catchers and Bawdy Baskets* (Harmondsworth: Penguin, 1972), p. 146.

24 Gilbert Walker?, *A manifest detection of the moste vyle and detestable use of Diceplay* (c. 1552), in Salgādo, *Cony-Catchers*, pp. 42–3.

25 Norman N. Holland, in the Signet Classic edition of 2 *Henry IV* (New York: New American Library, 1965). p. xxxvi.

26 So says J. H. Walter in the New Arden edition of *Henry V* (London: Methuen, 1954), p. xxv.

27 See the illuminating discussion in Norman Rabkin, *Shakespeare and the Problem of Meaning* (University of Chicago Press, 1981), pp. 33–62.

28 For a brilliant exploration of this hypothesis, see D. A. Miller, 'The Novel and the Police', *Glyph*, 8 (1981), 127–47.

29 Quoted in J. E. Neale, *Elizabeth I and her Parliaments, 1584–1601*, 2 vols. (London: Cape, 1965), II, 119.

30 *The History of King Richard III*, ed. R. S. Sylvester, in *The Complete Works of St Thomas More*, vol. 3 (New Haven: Yale University Press, 1963), p. 80.

31 Clifford Geertz, 'Centers, Kings and Charisma: Reflections on the Symbolics of Power', in *Culture and its Creators: Essays in Honour of Edward Shils*, ed. Joseph Ben-David and Terry Nichols Clark (University of Chicago Press, 1977), p. 160.

27

The New Historicism in Renaissance Studies

Jean E. Howard

A new kind of activity is gaining prominence in Renaissance studies: a sustained attempt to read literary texts of the English Renaissance in relationship to other aspects of the social formation in the sixteenth and early seventeenth centuries. This development, loosely called the "new history" and flourishing both in Europe and America, involves figures such as Stephen Greenblatt, Jonathan Dollimore, Alan Sinfield, Kiernan Ryan, Lisa Jardine, Leah Marcus, Louis Montrose, Jonathan Goldberg, Stephen Orgel, Steven Mullaney, Don E. Wayne, Leonard Tennenhouse, Arthur Marotti, and others.[1] Journals such as *ELH, English Literary Renaissance, Representations*, and *LTP: Journal of Literature Teaching Politics* regularly publish "new history" pieces. In short, a critical movement is emerging, and in this essay I want to look at the new historicism both to account for its popularity and to try to define what, if anything, is new about its approach to the historical study of texts and then to examine some instances of new historical criticism.

I

Historical scholarship linking Renaissance literary works to various non-literary historical contexts is not, of course, in and of itself, new, although in the last thirty years in particular, formalist approaches have been in the ascendency in some quarters of Renaissance studies. This is partly due to the importance of the lyric and partly due to the importance of Shakespeare in the English curriculum. For quite different reasons, formalism has dominated the study of both. In America, the lyric poems of the Renaissance provided many of the set texts, the verbal icons, used by New Critics to demonstrate their critical methods, and several generations of students trained in the New Criticism now teach today's students. And in both England and America, the plays of Shakespeare have often been treated not as products of a particular moment but as works for and of all times: universal masterpieces.[2] Consequently, until quite recently formalist studies of theme, genre, and structure dominated the criticism of these texts. History, when broached at all, usually meant the history of ideas, as in E. M. W. Tillyard's famous study of the importance to Renaissance literature of the "Elizabethan world picture."[3] In part, then, the new historicism is a reaction against formalism, though one must note that certain very contemporary formalisms – particularly structuralism and deconstruction – have not been enormously influential in Renaissance studies. The novel and the Romantic and modern periods have more often provided the exemplary texts for these movements. By contrast, the new historicism has been taken up with particular intensity, in part has been created, by Renaissance scholars.[4]

Why is this so? In part, I believe, many teachers of Renaissance literature simply have grown weary, as I have, of teaching texts as ethereal entities floating above the urgencies and contradictions of history and of seeking in such texts the disinterested expression of a unified truth rather than some articulation of the discontinuities underlying any construction of reality. Yet a purely formalist pedagogy should be debilitating for those who teach *any* literature, not just that of the Renaissance. Why, then, is it critics of Renaissance texts who have found in a new historicism an answer to their dissatisfaction?

The answer, I believe, lies partly in the uncanny way in which, at *this* historical moment, an analysis of Renaissance culture can be made to speak to the concerns of late twentieth-century culture. For a long time the Renaissance as cultural epoch was constructed in the terms set forth by Jacob Burckhardt; it was the age of the discovery of man the individual, the age of the revival of classical culture, the age of the secularization of life.[5] How enmeshed this picture was in nineteenth-century ideology is now clear, but it may be less clear what the *current* revival of interest in the Renaissance may have to do with twentieth-century concerns. Consider, for example, the work of Jonathan Dollimore, who is particularly interested in the way in which what he calls essentialist humanism has both dominated the study of English literature in the twentieth century and also has prevented recognition of the fact that man is not so much possessed of an essential nature as constructed by social and historical forces. Looking back at the seventeenth century, Dollimore sees it as a sort of privileged era lying between the Christian essentialism of the Middle Ages – which saw man as a unitary being who took his essence from God – and Enlightenment humanism – which first promulgated the idea of man the individual: a unified, separate, and whole entity with a core of identity emanating from within. For Dollimore, the late Renaissance was the age of skepticism in which in the drama in particular one finds recorded a recognition of the discontinuous nature of human identity and its social construction.[6] It is not hard to see affinities between this picture of the Renaissance and certain contemporary understandings of our own historical moment as the post-humanist epoch in which essentialist notions of selfhood are no longer viable.

I will return later to the theoretical issues raised by the fact that when a new historian looks at the past he or she is as likely as an old historian to see an image of the seeing self, not an image of the other. But for the moment I want to continue to pursue further the way in which "the Renaissance" is being reunderstood within that configuration of periods which constitutes the framework by which literary historians make the past intelligible. Within this framework the Renaissance has usually been assigned a transitional position between the Middle Ages – held to be encumbered with a monolithic Christian ideology and a static and essentially unhistorical view of itself – and the modern era – marked by the rise of capitalism with its attendant bourgeois ideology of humanism, progress and the all-important interiority and self-presence of the individual. Almost inevitably, this construction of the past has produced the question: just *how* modern and *how* medieval was this transitional period?[7] Burckhardt, looking back at Renaissance Italy from mid-nineteenth century Germany, stressed the modernity of the Renaissance, its sense of itself as definitively different from prior periods of history. Others have insisted on the fundamental continuity between the Renaissance and the Middle Ages. But now, as critics and historians sense the modern era slipping away and a new episteme inchoately emerging, the Renaissance is being appropriated in slightly different terms: as *neither* modern nor medieval, but as a boundary or liminal space between two more monolithic periods where one can see acted out a clash of paradigms and ideologies, a playfulness with signifying systems, a self-reflexivity, and a self-consciousness about the tenuous solidity of human identity which resonate with some of the dominant elements of postmodern culture.

In short, I would argue that the Renaissance, seen as the last refuge of preindustrial man, is of such interest to scholars of the postindustrial era because these scholars construe the period in terms reflecting their own sense of the exhilaration and fearfulness of living inside a gap in history, when the paradigms that structured the past seem facile and new paradigms uncertain. Clearly this emerging reading of the Renaissance is made possible by the traditional emphasis on the Renaissance as an age of transition. Previously critical emphasis was on continuity – on the way the period linked to the past or anticipated the future. Now the emphasis is on *dis*continuity, seen most clearly perhaps in Dollimore's insistence on the early seventeenth century as a kind of interperiod standing free of the orthodoxies of the Middle Ages and the Enlightenment. But the difference between prior and past conceptions of the Renaissance is also clear in the way the new historical critics so often make the period intelligible by narratives of rupture, tension, and contradiction, as, for example, when Greenblatt talks about the gap between the Renaissance ideology of human freedom and the actuality of Renaissance man as the subject of determining power relations[8] or, as we shall see, when Louis Montrose stresses the enormous contradictions in the social formation which Renaissance literature attempted to mediate.[9] And, as I have been hinting, these narratives of discontinuity and contradiction are narratives which owe much to the way late twentieth-century man construes his own historical condition.

Having said this much, I hope it is clear that I don't find it odd or arbitrary that the new historical criticism has taken the Renaissance as one of its primary objects of study. And I hope it is also clear that at least in one respect I find the "new history" resembling older forms of historical inquiry in that both see the past at least in part through the terms made available by the present. This observation, moreover, raises a more fundamental question: in just what ways is the "new" historical criticism new? Does its newness consist simply in its break with the formalism that has long been prominent in the study of Renaissance literature? Is its newness due mainly to the way it draws a somewhat different picture of the Renaissance than Burckhardt drew? Or are its methods and its understanding of what constitutes the historical investigation of texts in some fundamental way different from those which enabled an earlier historical criticism?

To answer these questions, I want to sketch what must of necessity be a simplified picture of some of the assumptions underlying the historical criticism of a figure such as Tillyard. These assumptions include the following: that history is knowable; that literature mirrors or at least by indirection reflects historical reality; and that historians and critics can see the facts of history objectively. (This last assumption is particularly paradoxical since it rests on the premise that while literature is implicated in history, historians and critics are not.)[10] The criticism resulting from these premises often led to the trivialization of literature: to its reduction to a mere reflection of something extrinsic to itself, and to the trivialization of criticism: its reduction to a mode for explaining (not reading) texts in terms of their relationship to a fixed ground, such as James I's monarchical practices, English imperialism, or Puritan theology. At its worst, such criticism reduced literary study to the search for topical references; at its best it illuminated particular texts in relationship to great men or events or ideas of a period, but its distinguishing mark was always the assumption that literature was a mirror reflecting something more real and more important than itself.[11]

Contemporary theoretical work, it seems to me, has seriously put in question a number of these assumptions. For example, much reception and reader-response criticism has directly challenged the idea that a reader / interpreter can ever escape his or her own historicity in order to encounter objectively the historical difference encoded in texts. Consequently, one must question the status of that "knowledge" about the past produced either by the historian or the historically minded critic. Similarly, Saussurian linguistics has challenged the premise that language functions referentially. One mode of historical criticism assumes that literature is connected to history in that its representations are direct reflections of historical reality, but one must ask what happens to that assumption when the referentiality of language itself is questioned. If literature refers to no ground extrinsic to itself, what can be the nature of its relationship to an historical context or to material reality? In fact, if one accepts certain tendencies in poststructuralist thought, is the possibility of an historical criticism even conceivable?

It is only by addressing these and a number of other equally urgent theoretical issues that a new historical criticism can distinguish itself from an older, more positivistic critical practice. The new historicism may well turn out to be an important extension of the theoretical ferment of the past two decades, a movement which will fundamentally rethink how we study texts in history. On the other hand, there is a real danger that the emerging interest in history will be appropriated by those wishing to suppress or erase the theoretical revolution that has gone on in the last several decades. Ironically, the "new history" may well turn out to be a backlash phenomenon: a flight from theory or simply a program for producing more "new readings" suited to the twenty-five-page article and the sixty-minute class.[12] Readings remain, after all, the dominant form of scholarly production in the discipline, and as many are discovering, a cursory journey through Lawrence Stone or Keith Thomas can open up numerous possibilities for new readings based on the ostensible family structure, economic dilemmas, or political upheavals of the sixteenth and seventeenth centuries. There is nothing inherently wrong with doing readings, but if those readings are based on untenable or unexamined assumptions about literature and history, then they are merely a form of nostalgia and not a serious attempt to explore what it means to attempt an historical criticism in a postmodern era.

In order to evaluate just how new the historical work being done in regard to Renaissance literature really is, I want to do two things. First, I wish to examine in much greater detail some of the theoretical issues facing any historical criticism today and, second, to examine in some detail the work of two of the best practitioners of the new history – Stephen Greenblatt and Louis Montrose – in order to see how they engage or ignore the problematics of their undertaking. From this double examination I hope it will be possible to suggest some of the directions in which such criticism must move if its newness is to be fundamental and not cosmetic.

II

In order to understand what does, or might, constitute the core of a truly new historical criticism one must begin, I believe, with the basic issue of what one assumes to be the nature of man, the creature whose works, thought, and culture have been the focus of most historical inquiry. One of the most striking developments of contemporary thought is the widespread attack on the notion that man possesses a transhistorical core of being. Rather, everything from maternal "instinct" to conceptions of the self are now seen to be the products of specific discourses and social processes.[13] This is a much more radical view of just how thoroughly man is a creature of history than has obtained in the past. It is quite different to argue that man has no essential being and to argue that, while in different periods people display different customs and social arrangements, they nonetheless possess an unchanging core of human traits that makes them all part of "the family of man."[14]

One can see the idea of a transhistorical human essence in Jonas Barish's very fine study of what he calls "the anti-theatrical prejudice" in Western culture. For him, the prejudice, while taking slightly different forms from antiquity to the present, nonetheless reflects a fear or a distrust innate to or inherent in the human mind.[15] Barish does not really entertain the possibility that a phenomenon in one period, which *seems* analogous to a phenomenon in another, may arise amid such different social conditions and play such a different role in a culture's power relations and discursive systems that the two phenomena cannot be seen as continuous with one another or as the products of an underlying human nature.

By contrast, Jonathan Dollimore, in his study of seventeenth-century tragedy, takes as his point of departure the idea – which he sees inscribed within Renaissance texts – that man has no essential nature, no traits not the product of social forces at a particular historical juncture.[16] Consequently, while Barish assumes an essential core of humanness which history can modify or shape in various ways, Dollimore assumes that nothing exists before the human subject is *created* by history. Consequently, an historical criticism working from Dollimore's premises will find an enormous range of new topics open for historical investigation; topics such as the way emotions and what we call instincts – and not just economic structures or political beliefs – are produced in a particular, historically specific social formation, and the way, of course, in which literature variously participates in this process of construction.

While one may accept in theory that there is no shared human essence linking contemporary man to Renaissance man, however, that does not solve the problem of how one is to acknowledge or recognize the radical otherness of the past. As I suggested earlier, there is a powerful tendency to appropriate the past in terms of the present, and contemporary reader-response theorists have acutely drawn the attention of literary critics to the extent to which the interpreter and his or her historical moment are present in their interpretations of earlier literary works.[17] Hayden White has been perhaps the most eloquent spokesperson for the view that the same is true for historians. For White, interpretation is a key part of each historian's work and consists largely of providing a "plot structure for a sequence of events so that their nature as a comprehensible process is revealed by their figuration *as a story of a particular kind*," that is, as a narrative intelligible to the readers of a particular age.[18] White stresses how thoroughly the historical discipline differs from a pure descriptive science and how much it owes to literary art, as, through its dominant tropes and narrative structures, it gives to "history" a shape owing as much to the patterns of intelligibility available to the historian from his own culture as to those that may have informed a prior age.

Similarly, Tzvetan Todorov in his new book on the Spanish conquest of Central America takes as his primary concern the way the Spanish dealt with the otherness of the American Indians, either by construing them as nonhuman or bestial and, as such, fair game for any kind of genocidal treatment, or by construing them as embryonic Europeans needing only the help of a Spanish education and a Spanish religion to make them mirrors of their white "brothers." In neither case was the *difference* of the Indian tolerated or allowed to interrogate European ways. Instead, the Indians were either denied inclusion within the category of the human or assimilated utterly into the Spanish idea of what the human was.[19]

Recognizing in a fresh way the difficulty of escaping the prison of the present moment and present culture to realize historical and cultural otherness, how is a contemporary historical criticism to proceed? One of Michel Foucault's central contributions to contemporary historical studies has been to recognize and strive against the tendency to project the present into the past and so to construct narratives of continuity. He counters this tendency by postulating the notion of radical breaks between historical epistemes. He refuses to look for continuities, for precursors of one era in former eras, but by a massive study of the situated discourses of particular disciplines he attempts to let their strangeness, their difference, speak.[20] Foucault's is a procedure of vigilance, and it produces some remarkable results. But it does not erase the fact that there is no transcendent space from which one can perceive the past "objectively." Our view is always informed by our present position; the objects we view available only in the slipperiness of their textualization. That does not seem to me to negate the project of historical investigation, but it does mandate a transformed attitude toward it. First of all, it seems necessary to abandon the myth of objectivity and to acknowledge that all historical knowledge is produced from a partial and a positioned vantage point. Further, instead of evoking a monolithic and repressive "history," one must acknow-ledge the existence of "histories" produced by subjects variously positioned within the present social formation and motivated by quite different senses of the *present* needs and *present* problems which it is hoped will be clarified or reconfigured through the study of the past.[21]

The intellectual historian Dominick LaCapra captures something of the difficulty of contemporary historical criticism when he speaks of establishing a self-conscious "dialogue" with the past. By using this term, he wishes to acknowledge, on the one hand, the impossibility of retrieving the "objective facts" of history, and, on the other hand, the undesirability of a " 'presentist' quest for liberation from the 'burden' of history through unrestrained fictionalizing and mythologizing."[22] LaCapra deliberately evokes the language of psychoanalysis to explain his idea of this process of transference, a process in which past and present remain separate and yet merged, an understanding of the one proceeding only from self-conscious entanglement with the other. The goal of such a dialogue is not, certainly, the willful reproduction of the present in the mirror of the past, but it involves a steady acknowledgment that the past is not transparent and that the pursuit of history is neither objective nor disinterested.

I take, then, that as starting points a new historical literary criticism assumes two things: (1) the notion that man is a construct, not an essence; (2) that the historical investigator is likewise a product of his history and never able to recognize otherness in its pure form, but always in part through the framework of the present. This last point leads one to what is perhaps the crux of any "new" historical criticism, and that is to the issue of what one conceives history to be: a realm of retrievable fact or a *construct* made up of textualized traces assembled in various configurations by the historian / interpreter. Hayden White points to the central question in dispute when he argues that history is produced, not discovered, and when he shows how those synthesizing histories which attempt to describe a period are *someone's* historically-conditioned constructs. In doing so, he calls in question one of the ways literary critics have often used "history," that is, as the realm of fact which can ground the seeming multiplicity or polysemous nature of the literary artifact. White writes: "Nor is it unusual for literary theorists, when they are speaking about the 'context' of a literary work, to suppose that this context – the 'historical milieu' – has a concreteness and an accessibility that the work itself can never have, as if it were easier to perceive the reality of a past world put together from a thousand historical documents than it is to probe the depths of a single literary work that is present to the critics studying it."[23]

More is at stake here, I think, than a simple naiveté on the part of literature professors about what historians do. Rather, the notion of history as transparent and objectively knowable is *useful* to the literary critics, for it can serve as a means of unclouding the stubborn and troubling opacity of the literary text and of stabilizing its decentered language. A common way of speaking about literature and history is just that way: literature *and* history, text *and* context. In these binary oppositions, if one term is stable and transparent and the other in some way mirrors it, then that other term can be stabilized and clarified, too. This is particularly crucial at a time when the notion of textuality has challenged traditional ideas about a literary work's communicative clarity and mimetic nature. By explaining literature by a ground extrinsic to itself, the ground of history, which literature supposedly reflects, the critic makes the problem of opacity disappear. But at a price. One result of seeing literature and history in this particular way is the inevitable "flattening" of the literary work. It is emptied of its rich signifying potentiality by being used as a springboard to something else, a mere pointer back to extratextual reality, as when Duke Vincentio is read simply as a representation of James I and the whole of *Measure for Measure* reduced to a comment on this monarch's beliefs and practices. Literature thus becomes, not something to be *read*, but to be *explained*. Second, such a procedure seldom stops to question why a particular historical context has been selected to align with the literary text, as if such choices were not often arbitrary in the extreme and inimical to seeing the full intertextual network in which a literary work exists. Third, the practice reduces literature to a merely mimetic object. I don't think any serious historical criticism can dodge the fact that undertaking such criticism raises the questions of some relationship between literature and what may be considered external to itself. The key question is: what is the nature of that relationship? Does the text absorb history into itself? Does it reflect an external reality? Does it produce the real?

It increasingly seems that in confronting these issues a new historical criticism has to accept, first, that "history" is not objective, transparent, unified, or easily knowable and consequently is extremely problematic as a concept for grounding the meaning of a literary text; second, that the very binarism we casually reinforce every time we speak of literature and history, text and context, is unproductive and misleading. Literature is *part* of history, the literary text as much a context for other aspects of cultural and material life as they are for it. Rather than erasing the problem of textuality, one must enlarge it in order to see that *both* social and literary texts are opaque, self-divided, and porous, that is, open to the mutual intertextual influences of one another. This move means according literature real power. Rather than passively reflecting an external reality, literature is an agent in constructing a culture's sense of reality. It is part of a much larger symbolic order through which the world at a particular historical moment is conceptualized and through which a culture imagines its relationship to the actual conditions of its existence. In short, instead of a hierarchical relationship in which literature figures as the parasitic reflector of historical fact, one imagines a complex textualized universe in which literature participates in historical processes and in the political management of reality.

I take as an exemplary brief example of these assumptions Don Wayne's work on the way Ben Jonson's plays help to produce an ideology for a pre-capitalist age. Wayne argues that while Jonson seemingly remained an apologist for an older feudal ideology which stressed the importance of the social collectivity over the individual, plays such as *The Alchemist* and *Bartholomew Fair* find him paradoxically promulgating contractual rights by which the prerogatives of the individual are secured, including the rights of individual authorship.[24] Clearly Jonson is responding to something in the social formation around him – to the emerging possibilities for printing texts as individual enterprises, to the breakdown of a national sense of community under the Stuarts, to the allure of the entrepreneurial spirit released by Puritanism and by the growth of the London merchant and professional class. Yet Wayne's chief point is that Jonson is also – through his dramatic texts – *producing* the modes of thought that encouraged and to some extent created these other changes so that it becomes nearly impossible to pinpoint an origin or single cause for social change. Many aspects of the social formation, including literary texts, work in a variety of ways and at a variety of speeds to produce the variegated entity we call history.

A major feature of a new historical criticism, therefore, must be a suspicion about an unproblematic binarism between literature and history and a willingness to explore the ways in which literature does more than reflect a context outside itself and instead constitutes one of the creative forces of history. In fact, until one truly banishes a mimetic theory of literature, several problems which have characteristically bedeviled the historical study of literature will continue to rear their heads. It is always interesting, for example, to watch what happens when people read Lawrence Stone on the Renaissance family and then try to relate what they find there to, say, Shakespeare's romantic comedies. Stone argues that marriages, at least among the middle and upper classes, were made late, were arranged by parents, were made largely for economic convenience, not love, and resulted in conjugal and parent–child relationships often lacking in warmth and intimacy.[25] What has all this to do with the picture of romantic love and rebellion against parental authority we see in Shakespeare's comedies? On the surface, not much; but what does this discrepancy mean: that Stone got things wrong? that literature is autonomous from the social realm? that Shakespeare is a universal genius who got at the enduring truths of life rather than at the anomalies of a particular historical moment? that literature is, after all, something to be read on a bus, a pure escape from the real? It is when faced with just these sorts of problems that one realizes the need for more than a simple mimetic theory of literature. A culture's discourse about love and the family need not, and probably seldom does, correspond exactly to how people live. (One could say the same about politics, economics, or personal identity.) One of the great strengths of Foucault, in my view, is his recognition that the discursive practices of an age, while producing or enabling certain behaviors, never coincide with them exactly. There is always some gap between what discourse authorizes and what people do, though "history" may never be able to disclose that gap precisely. What is important is how and why cultures produce and naturalize particular constructions of reality: what contradictions such constructions neutralize or expose, what economic and political ends they advance, what kinds of power relations they display. Literature is one of many elements participating in a culture's representation of reality to itself, helping to form its discourse on the family, the state, the individual, helping to make the world intelligible, though not necessarily helping to represent it "accurately."

In any particular instance, to see how a text functions in the construal of reality means seeing it in an intertextual network of considerable historical specificity. For example, to understand how women were made intelligible in the Renaissance, one cannot look only to social "facts," such as how many children they had, or of what diseases and at what ages they died. One must also consider how the medical, legal, and religious spheres functioned to provide a discourse about women which may have represented them in ways quite at odds with what *we* see as the apparent "facts" of their situation. The whole point is to grasp the terms of the discourse which made it possible to see the "facts" in a particular way – indeed, made it possible to see certain phenomena *as* facts at all. Only then will we begin to grasp how another period shaped individuals as historical subjects; and to see literature's role in this process one must place literary representations in a much broader differential field in which *how* they correspond to or challenge other constructions of reality and *how* they take their place in a particular configuration of discursive practices and power relations can be observed.

In this rethinking of the place of literature *in* history, it seems to me that much of the historically-based literary criticism can benefit from recent developments in Marxist thought. It used to be that Marxism, while providing one of the few theoretically coherent approaches to an historical criticism, suffered from its own version of the history / literature binarism in that it saw in literature and other elements of "the superstructure" a reflection of the dominant economic mode of production and of the class struggle it spawned. In other words, a particular privilege was given to the economic realm as the determining factor in every sort of cultural production and in the shaping of human consciousness. This assumption has been challenged, perhaps most influentially, by Louis Althusser, who argues for the *relative* autonomy of the superstructure from the material base and for the importance of the educational apparatus, the institution of literature, and other factors, in the shaping of human consciousness. In short, he acknowledges that there is not an homologous relationship between all levels of culture such that the ideologies of the superstructure can in any simple way be related to an economic base. Consequently, one finds the question of cause and effect relationship more complicated than was formerly thought, as I have already noted in regard to Wayne's work on Jonson; and one must take more seriously than before the role of literature in changing human consciousness and so, eventually, in affecting other material practices – not merely being affected by them.[26]

Furthermore, while it has always been Marxist criticism which has most insistently probed the question of literature's relationship to ideology, contemporary Marxism has developed more complex ways of approaching that question than it formerly possessed. While ideology is a vexed term with a complex history, it may be useful to distinguish two of its most common definitions: first, as the false consciousness foisted on the working classes by a dominant class; second, as any of those practices by which one imagines one's relations to the actual conditions of one's existence.[27] This second, Althusserian definition of ideology denies that the ideological is simply the product of a conspiratorial power group. Rather, the ideological is omnipresent; it inheres in every representation of reality and every social practice, as all of these inevitably confirm or naturalize a particular construction(s) of reality. Consequently, there is no way in which ideology can ever be absent from literature, any more than it can be absent from *any* discursive practice. Jonathan Dollimore argues, and I agree with him, that it may be useful to retain both understandings of ideology: to retain the option of seeing some literature as the conscious and direct product of one power group or class's attempts to control another group or class by the misrepresentation of their historical condition; and at the same time to recognize that in most instances power groups or classes are both less self-conscious and less monolithic than such a formulation implies and that a more complex approach to the problem of ideology requires a recognition of the pervasive, masterless (in the sense of acknowledging no one origin), and often hetero-geneous nature of the ideological.

This being so, that the ideological is everywhere and traverses literature as surely as other modes of representation, the question becomes: does literature have a special way of treating the ideological? This, of course, has been an issue that has bedeviled Marxism for some time. In the 1960's Pierre Machery contended that literature, separate both from science and ideology, inevitably produced a *parody* of ideology, a treatment of it which inevitably distanced the reader from the ideological matter being treated, exposing its contradictions and laying bare the artifice surrounding its production.[28] But does literature really handle the ideological in this way? I think not, at least not in every instance. First, as Tony Bennett has recently shown, such a view rests on the premise (deriving most centrally in the twentieth century from Russian Formalism) that literature is a special and unique form of writing with its own inherent and universal properties, one of which is the way it acquires internal distance from the ideological material which traverses it.[29] But as any historian of literature can show, the literary canon is a social construct, not an empirical given. As a number of boundary cases make clear today, some texts are regularly treated as literature and as something else. For example, are Bacon's essays literature or philosophy? Are diaries literature or something else? Is travel literature really literature or history or even philosophy? While it is quite possible in practical terms to speak of a literary canon, it seems quite another matter to assume that the texts in that canon are there by virtue of some mysterious inner property which they all share. They are all there for a variety of reasons having to do with the privileging of certain artifacts by powerful groups, and their "properties" are in large measure the result of the operations performed upon them by generations of critics.[30] Hence, while it may be useful for strategic or practical purposes to retain the category "literature," it seems wrong to assign to the texts gathered under that rubric a single, universal stance toward the ideological.

In fact, I would argue that a new historical criticism attempting to talk about the ideological function of literature in a specific period can most usefully do so only by seeing a specific work relationally – that is, by seeing how its representations stand in regard to those of other specific works and discourses. A work can only be said to contest, subvert, recuperate, or reproduce dominant ideologies (and it may do any of these) if one can place the work – at least provisionally and strategically – in relation to others. And, as I have argued above, the most illuminating field of reference may not be just other literary works. To return to the example of the representation of women: in order to understand the ideological function of, say, certain plays for the public theater, it may be important to see their representations of women in the light of the representations offered in masques, in conduct manuals, in medical treatises, and in Puritan polemics all written at approximately the same time.

Moreover, it seems important to entertain the possibility that neither literary texts nor other cultural productions are monologic, organically unified wholes. Only when their heterogeneity is suppressed by a criticism committed to the idea of organic unity do they seem to reveal a unitary ideological perspective or generic code. It may be more productive to see them as sites where many voices of culture and many systems of intelligibility interact. Dominick LaCapra makes this point, and in doing so he draws both on the work of Jacques Derrida and on that of Mikhail Bakhtin, thus uniting deconstruction and Marxist demystification in the project of fracturing the unified surface of the text to let the multiplicity of its social voices be heard. In this project he finds two of Bakhtin's concepts, *heteroglossia* and *carnivalization* (in Michael Holquist's translation), to be particularly useful in that the first suggests that novelized discourse is polyvalent, riddled with "unofficial" voices contesting, subverting, and parodying dominant discourses, while the second suggests that the emergence in writing of these "unofficial" voices has the revolutionary potential to expose the arbitrary nature of official constructions of the real.[31] But it is important to remember that for Bakhtin not all literature performs a carnivalizing function or is dialogic and polyvalent. There are no inherent laws governing the functioning of those texts we call literature. Consequently, one of the greatest challenges facing a new historical criticism is to find a way to talk about and discriminate among the many *different* ways in which literature is traversed by – and produces – the ideologies of its time.

III

What I have proposed so far are some of the principles contributing to an historical criticism which would not simply recapitulate the positivistic work of the early part of this century. Some of these ideas already inform the practice of certain of the new historical critics of Renaissance literature. I would like to end this essay by looking at some of the actual work which makes it possible to speak of a new historicism in Renaissance studies, in order both to acknowledge the importance of this work, in part as it spurs further theoretical speculation and inquiry, and to tease from it an exact sense of the theoretical and methodological issues it has not yet resolved or, in some cases, even faced.

My main reservation about much of this work is its failure to reflect on itself. Taking the form of the reading, a good deal of this criticism suppresses any discussion of its own methodology and assumptions. It assumes answers to the very questions that should be open to debate: questions such as why a particular context should have privilege over another in discussing a text, whether a work of art merely reflects or in some fundamental sense reworks, remakes, or even produces the ideologies and social texts it supposedly represents, and whether the social contexts used to approach literary texts have themselves more than the status of fictions. The practical mind may shrink from such questions as merely impeding real work, the commonsense business of doing what one obviously can do, which is taking some historical source, George Puttenham's *Arte of English Poesie*, for example, or the Elizabethan homily on obedience, and relating these in some way to literary works written during the reigns of Elizabeth I and James I. Such work can be done, and it may be rich and provocative. But I would argue that the best criticism performs two tasks at once: the practical business of reading another text and the critical business of explaining the terms of that reading. Especially when one is attempting a new sort of critical undertaking, it is important to explain the problematics and the promise of that undertaking and to show that one is not merely reinscribing old practices and assumptions under the guise of new terms. A good reading can be a masterpiece, but it usually has the status of an isolated event. Essays which explain how and why one does and should read in a particular way are both more generous and more risky since they do not try to seal themselves off from what is polemical by aspiring to a timeless commonsense, but expose what is difficult and what is at stake in "making knowledge" at *this* historical moment.

As examples of two of the best historical critics working in the Renaissance at the moment, I want to look at the work of Louis Montrose and Stephen Greenblatt, both of whom combine a degree of methodological self-consciousness with an obvious delight in the careful reading of complex texts. My purpose is not to provide a thorough review of the work of either, but to gather from their practice a sense of both the varying possibilities and the limitations of historical approaches to Renaissance texts.

Louis Montrose has written a series of excellent essays in which, from a loosely Marxist and anthropological perspective, he relates the literary texts of Sidney, Spenser, and Shakespeare to social phenomena in the late sixteenth and early seventeenth centuries. Some of the early essays, in particular, provide relatively local readings of specific texts in specific social contexts. For example, in one he examines Sidney's pastoral entertainment, *The Lady of May*, produced at Wanstead in 1578 or 1579.[32] Montrose reads the entertainment as Sidney's sophisticated comment on Elizabeth's courtier system and on his own place within it. Two figures, forester and shepherd, represent two types of courtiership. The forester, resembling Sidney, is audacious, self-reliant, and aggressive. The shepherd, really a voluptuary masking as a contemplative, is used subtly to demean the overly compliant courtier whom Sidney feels Elizabeth favors over his own more independent, ardently Protestant stance. The essay is a subtle reading of a complex social interaction between Elizabeth I and Sidney at a time when their relations are strained; it also shows how a stylized form of pastoral entertainment can intervene in real-life situations and social relations.

But in my view such an essay does not represent Montrose's most important work. Court masques and courtly entertainments, being designed for an extremely particularized audience, easily reveal topical meaning and invite readings in terms of local situations. More crucial is Montrose's insistence that particular works of art, and even whole genres such as Elizabethan pastoral, perform more far-reaching acts of social mediation. He makes an argument, for example, elaborated through a number of essays, that "the symbolic mediation of social relationships was a central function of Elizabethan pastoral forms; and that social relationships are, intrinsically, relationships of power."[33] He adds: "They [pastorals] are symbolic instruments for coping with the goddess Fortune, with the endemic anxieties and frustrations of life in an ambitious and competitive society. Pastorals that celebrate the ideal of content function to articulate – and thereby, perhaps, to assuage – *dis*content" (155). In other words, he sees such pastoral literature as a way of managing the anxiety and contradictions caused by a particular social formation. Thus, for example, he argues that *As You Like It* deals with the anxiety caused among younger sons by the fact that in England, much more strongly than on the Continent, primogeniture was a nearly universal fact, a way of preserving intact an accumulation of property and so of enhancing a family's prestige, even though, ironically, the result of so doing was to pauperize some elements of that family.[34] In *As You Like It*, while the principle of primogeniture remains untouched, the Utopian impulse of pastoral miraculously leads the younger son, Orlando, to find in Duke Senior a second and loving Father who bestows upon him the prizes (wife, fortune, and favor) befitting the eldest offspring. Moreover, Duke Senior's own natural rights as elder brother are confirmed, without violence, by his younger brother's sudden abdication of his usurped throne.

In such essays, Montrose implicitly assumes that literature performs the ideological work of obscuring the contradictions of a particular social formation and of helping to naturalize arbitrary social arrangements which work to the benefit of particular groups and classes. In the case of *As You Like It*, for example, primogeniture is presented, not as an arbitrary social arrangement, but as a "natural force" sanctioned by God. When usurping brothers are touched by divine truth, they see the selfishness of their former acts. Moreover, the pain such a social arrangement causes to younger brothers, while firmly articulated by Orlando as the play begins, by play's end is suppressed. The deserving younger son finds a place, a wife, a second father, and his alienation is erased. At other times, Montrose suggests, pastoral works allay the pain caused by the inequalities of a strenuously hierarchical social system by indicating that the duties of obedience and subservience will be well rewarded by the gifts, patronage, and favor of a benevolent monarch.[35] In other words, appropriate rewards flow from obedient subservience, rewards which supposedly redress inequalities of power and prestige.

This view of literary forms as mediating the tensions and contradictions caused by particular economic and political institutions is vaguely Marxist. I say vaguely because Montrose is a remarkably undoctrinaire critic, and only in his most recent essays does he lay out a specific explanatory model by which he approaches the question of literature's function in history. The Marxist flavor in his early work is largely conveyed by certain key terms, such as *mediation*, which he favors, and by his tendency to privilege as the explanatory context for literature the economic structures and the class and status systems of the period. Montrose's work is strong in dealing skillfully with the details of specific texts, in acknowledging the important differences which distinguish works in a particular genre from one another, and in keeping delicate hold on the ideological project that informs them all. The early essays, however, often lack a sustained consideration of his fundamental assumptions about the role of literature in history and a sustained consideration of ideology *per se*: what it is, how it is produced, whether or not literary texts ever elude its grasp or at least contest its authority. I question, for example, whether *As You Like It* does quite the work Montrose assigns to it; that is, whether by the exaggerated nature of the conversions and abdications which mark the play's final acts the play does not in large part undo the very work Montrose says it does in naturalizing the custom of primogeniture and effacing its arbitrary and unjust aspects. In essence, Montrose sees the comic form as a vehicle for articulating, only to erase, the contradictions of a particular social formation. I would simply argue that a text such as *As You Like It* is more subversive of formulations of reconciliation than Montrose's reading allows and that this may have implications for other texts which on the surface perform clear acts of social mediation.

Others of Montrose's essays raise further questions of this sort. In "The Purpose of Playing: Reflections on a Shakespearean Anthropology," Montrose shows the strong influence on his work of cultural anthropologists such as Victor Turner and Clifford Geertz and social historians such as Keith Thomas. What he argues is that Shakespearean drama (drama for the public stage) filled a void left in Elizabethan social life by the suppression of Catholic ritual and folk custom. Magic, as Thomas has argued, partly filled this void, but so, according to Montrose, did the public stage on which was enacted, in the persons of Prince Hal or Rosalind or Lear, those "rites of passage which give a social shape, order, and sanction to human existence. By means of transition rites, social boundaries are symbolically imposed upon the life cycle and can be safely crossed; these rites mediate the discontinuities they themselves create."[36] Superficially, it looks as if Montrose's view of drama remains the same: it mediates social problems, papers over discontinuities. And yet, to see drama as enacting rites of passage in the life cycle can remove it from history altogether if, as Montrose seems at times to imply, these transition points are seen as a universal and timeless aspect of human nature and not as products of particular cultural formations. In other words, Montrose verges on an idealist perspective in which timeless and universal problems are what literature handles, rather than those of a particular historical era and material organization. But the countermove in the essay is the suggestion that, specifically in the Elizabethan period, the public stage became the site for challenges to traditional orthodoxies. Borrowing a term from Victor Turner, Montrose speaks of Elizabethan plays as "antistructures" which free the viewer from ordinary structures of cognition and make cultural innovation possible.

What is needed, clearly, is an extended discussion of subversion and contestation. In much of Montrose's work he suggests that literature participates in the circulation and confirmation of dominant ideologies. But the essay on the anthropology of the stage suggests that drama, at least, could contest dominant ideologies. Is it only drama that has this potential? And where does the contestatory impulse come from? From language itself? From contradictions in the social formation that inevitably surface in writing and resist a final resolution? From the marginality of certain groups whose voices are inscribed in dominant modes of expression? From the marginality of the theater as an institution? Moreover, one needs to ask to what extent works which *seem* to break with dominant orthodoxies actually engage in subtle acts of recuperation by which a dominant ideology transmutes itself just enough to insure its own essential reproduction.[37]

What I like in all of Montrose's essays is their steady assumption that literature or dramatic texts always do social *work*. And in his recent pieces, especially "Of Gentlemen and Shepherds: The Politics of Elizabethan Pastoral form," " 'Shaping Fantasies': Figurations of Gender and Power in Elizabethan Culture," and "The Elizabethan Subject and the Spenserian Text," he has more clearly theorized his critical practice and to some extent modified its thrust.[38] I see three especially important theoretical developments in these more recent pieces. First, Montrose increasingly emphasizes the relative autonomy of cultural productions. In "Of Gentlemen and Shepherds" he specifically shows how his work relates to the later work of Raymond Williams who, repudiating a model of culture seen "as a superstructural reflection of an economic base," embraces a model in which "culture is represented as at once more autonomous in its processes and more material in its means and relations of production" (p. 419). If Montrose's early essays move rather insistently from world to literary text and so, however obliquely, suggest that literary writing is primarily a *reaction* to the extra-literary world, his later work does indeed begin to stress the relative autonomy of culture and its *productive* role within the social formation. This means that more attention gets paid to the way in which, by shaping a culture's discourse about "real life," literature is one of the many discursive practices defining the conditions of possibility for thought and action within Renaissance culture.[39] Second, Montrose's essays increasingly emphasize the implication of the historian in the knowledge he / she produces and of criticism in constructing what, supposedly, it merely transcribes.[40] This acknowledgment must, I feel, temper Montrose's earlier somewhat unproblematic reliance on the synthesizing histories of such scholars as Christopher Hill, Stone, and Thomas, to provide an adequate or objective account of the social text of Renaissance England. Third, in these more recent essays, Montrose increasingly moves to theorize the problems of agency and freedom. While acknowledging the enormous extent to which subjects are created by the discourses of their culture, he wants, as well, to explore the ways they preserve some degree of autonomy within these discourses, using them for their purposes even as they are used by them. Thus, in discussing Spenser's apparent submission to political authority, Montrose writes: "In the Spenserian text, and elsewhere, we can observe a mode of contestation at work within the Elizabethan subject's very gestures of submission to the official fictions. We might call this mode of contestation appropriative, for it does not repudiate the given fictions of power but rather works within and through them, reinscribing them in the culture as the fictions of the speaking or writing subject."[41] In attempting to argue for a circumscribed but real role for human agency, Montrose is at once contesting Greenblatt's more pessimistic views of the possibility of human autonomy and opening important new territory for further discussion. In short, in Montrose's work one can see a relatively untheoretical critical practice becoming increasingly methodologically self-reflexive and moving, I would argue, steadily away from an "old" historicism to something which is more deservedly given the label "new."

In the work of Stephen Greenblatt one can find a somewhat different and more varied historical criticism than one finds in Montrose's work, but Greenblatt's recent writings also lead one, ultimately, to a consideration of the subversive or contestatory role which literature plays in culture. Up through his important book *Renaissance Self-Fashioning*, Greenblatt's main concern was identity formation. In that book he showed how the historical moment defined the conditions of possibility for constituting selves in sixteenth-century England. In a series of careful analyses he examined how selves took shape in the sixteenth century in relationship to specific authorities and their culturally-derived antitheses or demonic others.[42] Among the many influences on the book is Lacan's neo-Freudian psychology with its assumption, not of a unified and autonomous self, but of a provisional and contradictory self which is the product of discourse. Consequently, the book repudiates the humanist notion that man, the protean actor, is in control of his own identity formation; rather, he is presented in Greenblatt's work as the product of impersonal historical forces largely inimical to individual control.

One remarkable aspect of the book is the way it employs a contemporary theory of identity formation with something approaching reluctance. There is a lingering nostalgia for studying individual lives, for mystifying the idea of personal autonomy, even after Greenblatt has directly discarded notions of autonomy and the organically unified self. However, more important for present purposes is the way Greenblatt moves between analyses of the lives of historical figures (such as More and Spenser) and analyses of literary "people" (Othello, Tamburlaine). Greenblatt appears unwilling to hold the two realms in an antithetical relationship or to talk about one as the ground for the other. Rather, he seems to suggest that discourse about the self has no single point of origin but constantly evolves in response to various forms of cultural authority, manifesting itself both in literary paradigms and in the construction of actual lives. In short, by stressing that he wishes to "investigate both the social presence to the world of the literary text and the social presence of the world in the literary text" (p. 5), Greenblatt moves to replace metaphors of mirrors and grounds with an interactive model of how the literary and social texts relate.

Productive as I find this aspect of his methodology, I find problematic another dimension of his practice: namely, his use of the illustrative example. Repeatedly, he presents historical figures and incidents as representations of large groups of people, actions, or mental sets. But how does one establish that Shakespeare was representative of a number of people in the late Renaissance in England whose characteristic stance toward authority was submissive subversiveness?[43] Is one going to make the case statistically? by citing a range of examples that *suggest* the pervasiveness of the tactic? by admitting that one cannot or does not know how representative a strategy this was, but by arguing that one's reading of Shakespeare – enabled by a theory of how people respond to authority – can give us a new and important way to understand the possibilities for self-definition in the later Renaissance? Greenblatt is evasive when it comes to defining his own attitude toward this problem. He continues to use the language of representativeness and to speak of certain figures (those people, inevitably male, upon whom a great deal of critical attention has already been focused) as epitomizing or crystalizing the period's characteristic strategies for self-fashioning. Yet he does not really question whether his perception of the centrality of these figures is an effect of the critical attention they have historically received or if it stems from some essential quality they inherently possess; nor does he make any serious attempt to prove their representativeness in the statistical terms likely to satisfy the empiricist nor argue for the irrelevance of such criteria in ways likely to satisfy those who see the "facts" of history largely produced by the operations of a particular discourse or act of theoretical intervention. In short, Greenblatt makes the issue of representativeness a nonproblem, while I see it as a crucial issue. Such has been the influence of Greenblatt's practice, however, that there is now a spate of essays which begin with the painstaking description of a particular historical event, place, or experience and from that supposedly paradigmatic moment sketch a cultural law. It is a procedure which bears an anthropological stamp, but there is often no observation or consideration of a culture's whole system of signifying practices which would allow one to assess, relationally, the importance and function of the particular event described. In short, neither the rationale for the method nor the status of the knowledge produced is made an issue; and it is this sort of theoretical aporia which requires some redress by the new historical critics.

Greenblatt has now, however, moved to a set of problems slightly different from those which concerned him in his earlier book. Now he is investigating subversion: how and why a culture produces and deals with challenges to its dominant ideologies. Increasingly, Foucault seems an important influence, for this work takes Greenblatt deep into the territory of how a culture maintains itself by excluding, exorcising, or banishing challenges to its dominant ideologies or forms of knowledge. It is his thesis that such literature of the Renaissance period, particularly literature meant for the public theater, deliberately produces subversion in order to contain it.[44] He argues that this particular way of producing and containing subversion "is not a theoretical necessity of theatrical power in general but an historical phenomenon, the particular mode of this particular culture" (p. 57) which does not have a highly developed apparatus for repression and surveillance, such as one sees in the nineteenth century, but instead depends on "a ruler whose power is constituted in theatrical celebrations of royal glory and theatrical violence visited upon enemies of that glory" (p. 57). This proposal strikes me as an important insight into the way sixteenth-century texts often serve the larger interests of ideological domination. And it has affinities with Greenblatt's earlier assertion that authority maintains itself by the existence – or production – of a demonic other. One question, however, is how monolithic this practice of producing and demonizing alien ideologies really is in the Renaissance. For example, there seem to be a number of Renaissance texts in which ideological orthodoxies maintain themselves, not simply by producing and exorcising their subversive opposites, but by recuperating them – that is, by domesticating and incorporating alien elements which thereby lose their subversive power. I think, for example, of the way in which a play such as *A Woman Killed with Kindness* handles the threat of the sexually eager, nonmonogamous wife, Anne Frankford. Potentially, she represents a challenge to patriarchy and to the whole ideology of a man's ownership of his wife's sexuality and thereby his exclusive ownership of the children produced by her. But, of course, she does not end up serving this function. She repents her "crime," dies of a broken heart at her husband's sadistic "kindness" and becomes a testament to the rightness of male rule. In short, the subversive elements of her sexuality are recuperated by a Christian ideology in the service of patriarchy which interprets a woman's sexual independence as a sin and a violation of natural order. And the woman is represented, finally, as concurring.

A further issue Greenblatt has not yet fully addressed is the question of whether Renaissance literature always, or even usually, controls – reins in – the subversive elements it supposedly produces or whether there are works which genuinely challenge orthodox constructions or attain a space outside of ideology altogether. This last possibility seems to be the burden of Greenblatt's final sentence in a brief essay in which he discusses *King Lear* and Harsnett's treatise on exorcism. He argues that while the play is fully implicated in the "network of social conditions, paradigms, and practices" of Shakespeare's age, nonetheless "the ideological and historical situation of *King Lear* produces the oscillation, the simultaneous affirmation and negation, the constant undermining of its own assertions and questioning of its own practices – in short, the supreme aesthetic self-consciousness – that lead us to celebrate its universality, its literariness, and its transcendence of all ideology."[45] But what we need to know are the exact conditions under which a work traversed by ideology can transcend it. Is this a quality of a few great texts? Is it a result of the special nature of literary language, defined as somehow different from other uses of language? Is it a result of the material or institutional context for the text's production? In a later, expanded version of the *Lear* essay, Greenblatt goes somewhat further in answering these questions and in explaining how the play, as a work for the public stage, serves different interests than those served by Harsnett's violently anti-Catholic polemic.[46] While both reveal the empty theatricality of exorcism, *Lear* does so within the sphere of the theater itself where not only the ritual of exorcism is emptied of its significance, but also all gestures of faith in the "clear gods." Consequently, while Shakespeare loyally reiterates the official position on exorcism, he does so in a context which makes it something other than an apology for triumphant Protestantism. In my view such a reading of *Lear* does not place the play *above* ideology, but simply in an ambivalent or contestatory relationship to the ideology of the "source" with which it is being compared. Greenblatt seems, however, to be moving away from the position that in Elizabethan culture subversion is inevitably contained, to a position which acknowledges that through certain cultural practices, such as the production of plays on the public stage, a space for more than compliance with dominant ideologies may be opened. This is a position that clearly invites further elaboration. Is *Lear* a special instance, or is it typical of the way plays for the Elizabethan public stage empty ideological positions from the center of the culture of their efficacy?

As Greenblatt develops his work on subversion, moreover, he also seems to be developing a way of establishing the historical situation of a given literary text by locating it directly in relationship to other types of cultural texts, rather than locating it by means of secondary histories of the period. Regularly, he talks about one cultural text, such as Dürer's sketches, in direct juxtaposition to another, such as Sidney's *Arcadia*, as both help to produce a culture's discourse on a particular subject and to enact certain strategies of containment.[47] The method brings great immediacy to the study of disparate cultural texts. They can hardly be reduced to illustrations of the historical "background" when they are offered as the primary documents of a history to be constructed. But again, as with Greenblatt's use of the illustrative example, one wants to know more about the process by which disparate phenomena are chosen for juxtaposition and discussion; the juxtaposition can seem arbitrary to those reared on the notion of "coverage," that is, on the idea that all the texts and all the documents need to be surveyed before one can say with confidence that any two stand in a pivotal cultural position. Greenblatt's practice implicitly challenges this mode of thinking, but one wishes for an overt articulation of his oppositional point of view.

IV

I have examined aspects of the work of Montrose and Greenblatt because each seems, through practical work with texts, to be pushing the historical study of literature in new directions, though it is also clear that these two types of historical practice are different from one another and that each raises theoretical problems not yet fully explored and resolved. Each critic strikes me as typically American in his reticence to discuss the theory that informs his practice. Each, at times, naturalizes his critical practice and so obscures the many crucial theoretical questions being engaged or ignored at every stage. This makes it difficult always to discern what is new in this work, other than its insistence that a purely formalist approach to Renaissance texts is insufficient. That there *are* genuinely new assumptions informing the work of both critics is clear, but the hesitancy in foregrounding these differences diminishes their potential to alter ways of thinking about what we mean to do when we say we wish, in a poststructuralist age, to study literature historically.

My own sense is that to represent anything like a genuinely poststructuralist criticism, the new work in the historical critique of Renaissance texts needs to take several steps. First, it must grow increasingly less literature-centered both as a way of acknowledging the arbitrary nature of the designation, "literature," and also because it is clear that the ideological significance and the historical situation of those represen-tations we label literary can only be understood when looked at in relation to other sorts of contemporaneous representations and discursive practices.

Second, it seems necessary that some of the critical skills literary critics have brought to the study of literary texts be applied both to aspects of the social text and to what we designate as non-literary forms of writing. These skills include the techniques of deconstructive reading by which the self-divisions of the text are revealed and by Marxist techniques of demystification by which the social and ideological elements of these divisions are revealed. Doing so will help to topple the assumption that the texts – social and written – which we read to acquire our sense of the past, of history, are either transparent, organically unified, or outside of ideology and the network of power relations.

Third, the new historicism needs at every point to be more overtly self-conscious of its methods and its theoretical assumptions, since what one discovers about the historical place and function of literary texts is in large measure a function of the angle from which one looks and the assumptions that enable the investigation. This means examining overtly and directly a number of the questions raised in the second and third parts of this essay, questions such as whether or not literature reflects or produces our understanding of the real, how literature can best be related to other aspects of the social formation, and what status one gives to the isolated text or artifact when what occupies categories such as the "representative" and the "important" is itself a product of a particular political history of canon formation.

Finally, it seems to me that the historically-minded critic must increasingly be willing to acknowledge the non-objectivity of his or her own stance and the inevitably political nature of interpretive and even descriptive acts. Self-effacement, neutrality, disinterestedness – these are the characteristics privileged in the Academy, but are claims to possess them more than a disingenuous way of obscuring how one's own criticism is non-objective, interested and political? I am not suggesting that it is desirable to look at the past with the willful intention of seeing one's own prejudices and concerns. Nonetheless, since objectivity is not in any pure form a possibility, let us acknowledge that fact and acknowledge as well that any move into history is an *intervention*, an attempt to reach from the present moment into the past to rescue both from meaningless banality. One hopes that from the encounter, more urgent, perhaps, than LaCapra's notion of "dialogue" will admit, can come revisioning of both the past and the present. But such encounters start somewhere, and that is with the active intervention of the historically constituted critic. That accepted, it may be more possible to break free from the other positivistic assumptions that still inhibit the "newness" of the new history.

Notes

1 Stephen Greenblatt is perhaps the central figure in the American branch of this movement; see *Renaissance Self-Fashioning: From More to Shakespeare* (Chicago, 1980). In his introduction to a volume entitled *The Forms of Power and the Power of Forms in the Renaissance* (*Genre* 15[1982], 3–6), he outlines what he sees as a few of the distinguishing features of the "new historicism." I will discuss at length the work of Greenblatt and Montrose and their contributions to the new historical criticism in a later section of this essay. For representative works, see Jonathan Dollimore, *Radical Tragedy: Religion, Ideology and Power in the Drama of Shakespeare and His Contemporaries* (Chicago, 1984); Alan Sinfield, *Literature in Protestant England 1560–1660* (London, 1982); Kiernan Ryan, "Towards a Socialist Criticism: Reclaiming the Canon," *LTP: Journal of Literature Teaching Politics* 3 (1984), 4–17;

Lisa Jardine, *Still Harping on Daughters: Women and Drama in the Age of Shakespeare* (New York, 1983); Leah Marcus, *Childhood and Cultural Despair: A Theme and Variations in Seventeenth-Century Literature* (Pittsburgh, 1978) and " 'Present Occasions' and the Shaping of Ben Jonson's Masques," *ELH* 45 (1978), 201–25; Jonathan Goldberg, *James I and the Politics of Literature: Jonson, Shakespeare, Donne, and Their Contemporaries* (Baltimore, 1983); Stephen Orgel, *The Illusion of Power: Political Theater in the English Renaissance* (Berkeley, CA, 1975); Steven Mullaney, "Strange Things, Gross Terms, Curious Customs: The Rehearsal of Cultures in the Late Renaissance," *Representations* 3 (1983), 40–67; Don E. Wayne, "Drama and Society in the Age of Jonson: An Alternative View," *Renaissance Drama* XIII (1982), 103–29 and *Penshurst: The Semiotics of Place and the Poetics of History* (Madison, WI, 1984); Leonard Tennenhouse, "The Counterfeit Order of *The Merchant of Venice*," in *Representing Shakespeare: New Psychoanalytic Essays*, ed. Murray M. Schwartz and Coppélia Kahn (Baltimore, MD, 1980), pp. 54–69 and "Representing Power: *Measure for Measure* in its Time," in *The Forms of Power*, ed. Greenblatt, pp. 139–56; and Arthur Marotti, " 'Love is not love': Elizabethan Sonnet Sequences and the Social Order," *ELH* 49 (1982), 396–428. I do not mean the foregoing list to be inclusive or to suggest that the concerns of these critics are monolithic. Many of them employ quite different methodological and theoretical perspectives, and the significance of the differences between the cultural materialism of many of the English critics and the kind of historical work being done by a figure such as Greenblatt is only becoming clear with the publication of volumes such as *Political Shakespeare: New Essays in Cultural Materialism*, ed. Jonathan Dollimore and Alan Sinfield (Ithaca, NY, 1985). This essay is primarily concerned with what motivates the turn to history and with the theoretical problems posed by such a move, rather than with defining what are clearly emerging as differences among those now doing historical criticism.

2   For a provocative discussion of the way Shakespeare has been constructed in twentieth-century British culture as the writer who best reveals the timeless elements of the human condition see Derek Longhurst, " 'Not for all time, but for an Age'; an approach to Shakespeare studies," in *Re-Reading English*, ed. Peter Widdowson (New York, 1982), pp. 150–63.

3   E. M. W. Tillyard, *The Elizabethan World Picture: A Study of the Idea of Order in the Age of Shakespeare, Donne and Milton* (London, 1943).

4   I do not mean to suggest that *only* Renaissance scholars are interested in historical approaches to texts. At the 1983 MLA convention Jonathan Culler devoted a major presentation to an attack, by way of Terry Eagleton, on the reification of history in much contemporary criticism. Culler's attention to this issue I take as an indication of the crucial professional space historical studies are now assuming in many quarters of the discipline. Critics as diverse as Eagleton in *Literary Theory: An Introduction* (Minneapolis, MN, 1983) and Frank Lentricchia in *After the New Criticism* (Chicago, 1980) have led the way in arguing that the most serious flaw of the major critical movements of the last several decades has been their failure to acknowledge history, and it is that failure which is now being redressed.

5   Jacob Burckhardt, *The Civilization of the Renaissance in Italy* (New York, 1958).

6   Jonathan Dollimore, *Radical Tragedy*, esp. Chap. 10, "Subjectivity and Social Process," pp. 153–81.

7   Consider, for example, the lengthy debate surrounding Sir Thomas More and whether or not his *Utopia* reflects an essentially Medieval and monastic conception of life (see R. W. Chambers, *Thomas More* [London, 1953]) or an enlightened anticipation of modern socialism (see Karl Kautsky, *Thomas More and His Utopia*, trans. H. J. Stenning [1888; rpt. New York, 1927]).

8   Greenblatt, *Renaissance Self-Fashioning*, esp. pp. 1–9.

9   This idea is present in many of Montrose's early essays. See, in particular, " 'The Place of a Brother' in *As You Like It*: Social Process and Comic Form," *Shakespeare Quarterly* 32(1981), 28–54.

10 For a useful critique of naive historicism see David Carroll's essay, "Mimesis Reconsidered: Literature, History, Ideology," *Diacritics* 5 (1975), 5–12.

11 Perhaps the most notorious example of a critic reducing a Renaissance text to the contours of its supposed historical referent is Josephine Waters Bennett's *Measure for Measure as Royal Entertain-*

ment (New York, 1966). But even in a work as recent – and as interesting – as Philip Edwards's *Threshold of a Nation: A Study in English and Irish Drama* (Cambridge, 1979), one can still see operating the idea that literature is the mirror reflecting the social realm and that an historical approach to literature means retrieving that social ground.

12 For a provocative discussion of the dominance and the conventions of "the reading" as a mode of criticism see Richard Levin's *New Readings vs. Old Plays: Recent Trends in the Reinterpretation of English Renaissance Drama* (Chicago, 1979).

13 See, for example, Nancy Chodorow's *The Reproduction of Mothering: Psychoanalysis and the Sociology of Gender* (Berkeley, 1978) which argues that "mothering" is not innate or physiological, but a product of socially structured psychological mechanisms transmitted by culture. For a striking investigation of the relatively late emergence of the concept of "man" as a self-sufficient, autonomous being possessed of interiority and self-presence see Michel Foucault, *The Order of Things: An Archaeology of the Human Sciences* (1966; New York, 1970), esp. Chap. 9, "Man and His Doubles," pp. 303–43 and Chap. 10, "The Human Sciences," pp. 344–87. For an important attempt to theorize the social and linguistic production of subjectivity see Julian Henriques, Wendy Hollway, Cathy Urwin, Couze Venn, and Valerie Walkerdine, *Changing the Subject: Psychology, Social Regulation, and Subjectivity* (London, 1984).

14 On the sentimental and antihistorical uses of the concept of "the family of man" see Roland Barthes's essay, "The Great Family of Man," in *Mythologies*, trans. Annette Lavers (1957; rpt. New York, 1972).

15 Jonas Barish, *The Anti-Theatrical Prejudice* (Berkeley, 1981), esp. p. 2.

16 Dollimore, *Radical Tragedy*, pp. 17–19.

17 This perception is articulated in a variety of ways. Norman Holland, for example, writing from the perspective of American ego psychology, sees the reader constantly projecting his or her identity theme onto the work of art ("Unity Identity Text Self," *PMLA* 90 [1975], 813–22). In his latest work Stanley Fish sees both the properties of texts and their meanings as produced by the conventions of the historically-specific interpretive community to which the reader belongs (*Is There A Text in This Class? The Authority of Interpretive Communities* [Cambridge, 1980]). And Hans Robert Jauss argues that the meaning of a work of art will depend in large measure upon the different "horizons of reading" which in each era determine the reader's access to the text (*Towards an Aesthetic of Reception*, trans. Timothy Bahti. Theory and History of Literature, 2 [Minneapolis, MN, 1982]).

18 Hayden White, *Tropics of Discourse: Essays in Cultural Criticism* (Baltimore, MD, 1978), p. 58.

19 Tzvetan Todorov, *The Conquest of America: The Question of The Other*, trans. Richard Howard (New York, 1984).

20 For an introduction to Foucault's idea of discontinuous history see "Nietzsche, Genealogy, History," in *Language, Counter-Memory, Practice*, ed. Donald Bouchard (Ithaca, NY, 1977), pp. 139–64. For a much fuller account of the episteme see Foucault's *The Order of Things*. As an overview of Foucault's contribution to historical study I have found useful Mark Poster's "The Future According to Foucault: The Archaeology of Knowledge and Intellectual History," in *Modern European Intellectual History: Reappraisals and New Perspectives*, ed. Dominick LaCapra and Steven L. Kaplan (Ithaca, 1982), pp. 111–52.

21 Terry Eagleton, writing of Walter Benjamin, sees Benjamin anticipating Foucault's emphasis on the need for discontinuous history which will shatter narratives of continuity through which the heterogeneity of the past is constantly suppressed. Yet Benjamin insists more strikingly than Foucault that the critic's intervention – by which traces of the past are liberated from a repressive historicism of continuity to interrogate the present ideological formation – is a political and of necessity an urgent intervention since the pressures of the capitalist system to produce monolithic, continuous history are enormous and their disruption extremely difficult. See Terry Eagleton, *Walter Benjamin, or Towards a Revolutionary Criticism* (London, 1981), esp. ch. 3, "History, Tradition and Revolution," pp. 43–78.

22 LaCapra, "Rethinking Intellectual History and Reading Texts," in *Rethinking Intellectual History: Texts, Contexts, Language* (Ithaca, NY, 1983), p. 63.

23   White, *Tropics of Discourse*, p. 89.

24   Wayne, "Drama and Society in the Age of Jonson," pp. 103–29.

25   Lawrence Stone, *The Family, Sex and Marriage in England 1500–1800* (New York, 1977).

26   See, in particular, Althusser's key essay, "Ideology and Ideological State Apparatuses" in *Lenin and Philosophy and Other Essays* (New York, 1971), pp. 127–86.

27   For the first understanding of ideology see Karl Marx, *The German Ideology* (London, 1965); for the second understanding see Althusser, "Ideology and Ideological State Apparatuses."

28   Pierre Macherey, *A Theory of Literary Production*, trans. Geoffrey Wall (London, 1978), esp. pp. 51–65.

29   Tony Bennett, *Formalism and Marxism* (London, 1979), esp. ch. 2, "Formalism and Marxism," pp. 18–43.

30   Bennett, p. 9 and Terry Eagleton, *An Introduction to Literary Theory*, esp. "Introduction: What is Literature?", pp. 1–16.

31   For LaCapra's view of the multiplicity and self-divisions of texts see "Rethinking Intellectual History and Reading Texts," esp. pp. 52–5 and 58–61. M. Bakhtin's work on *heteroglossia* and *carnivalization* can be found in *The Dialogic Imagination: Four Essays*, ed. Michael Holquist, trans. Caryl Emerson and Michael Holquist (Austin, 1981), pp. 259–422.

32   Louis Adrian Montrose, "Celebration and Insinuation: Sir Philip Sidney and the Motives of Elizabethan Courtship," *Renaissance Drama* N.S. 8 (1977), pp. 3–35.

33   Montrose, " 'Eliza, Queene of shepheardes,' and the Pastoral of Power," *English Literary Renaissance* 10 (1980), 153–82 at 153.

34   Montrose, " 'The Place of a Brother,'" pp. 28–54.

35   Montrose, "Gifts and Reasons: The Contexts of Peele's *Araygnment of Paris*," *ELH* 47 (1980), 433–61, esp. 454, where Montrose argues that for Peele "hierarchical social relationships are ritually defined and affirmed in the offering and acceptance of gifts."

36   Montrose, "The Purpose of Playing: Reflections on a Shakespearean Anthropology," *Helios* 7 (1980), pp. 51–74 at 63.

37   See the work of Pierre Bourdieu and Jean-Claude Passeron, esp. *Reproduction in Education, Society and Culture*, trans. Richard Nice (London, 1977).

38   "Of Gentlemen and Shepherds: The Politics of Elizabethan Pastoral Form," *ELH* 50 (1983), 415–59; " 'Shaping Fantasies': Figurations of Gender and Power in Elizabethan Culture," *Representations* 2 (1983), 61–94. Professor Montrose was kind enough to send me the essay "The Elizabethan Subject and the Spenserian Text" in typescript. It is forthcoming in *Critical Theory and Renaissance Texts* to be published by Johns Hopkins University Press.

39   In " 'Shaping Fantasies,'" p. 62, Montrose writes: "whether or not Queen Elizabeth was physically present at the first performance of *A Midsummer Night's Dream*, her pervasive *cultural presence* was a condition of the play's imaginative possibility. This is not to imply that *A Midsummer Night's Dream* is merely an inert 'product' of Elizabethan culture. The play is rather a new *production* in Elizabethan culture enlarging the dimensions of the cultural field and altering the lines of force within it. Thus, in the sense that the royal presence was itself represented within the play, it may be said that the play henceforth conditioned the imaginative possibility of the Queen."

40   "The Elizabethan Subject," esp. pp. 4–5.

41   "The Elizabethan Subject," p. 48.

42   Greenblatt, *Renaissance Self-Fashioning*, esp. p. 9.

43   Greenblatt, pp. 222–54.

44   Greenblatt, "Invisible Bullets: Renaissance Authority and Its Subversion," *Glyph* 8 (1981), 40–61, esp. 50–3.

45   Greenblatt, "*King Lear* and Harsnett's 'Devil-Fiction,' " *Genre* 15 (1982), 239, 242.

46   Greenblatt, "Shakespeare and the Exorcists," in *After Strange Texts: The Role of Theory in the Study of Literature*, ed. Gregory S. Jay and David L. Miller (University, Alabama, 1985), pp. 101–23.

47   Greenblatt, "Murdering Peasants: Status, Genre, and the Representation of Rebellion," *Representations* 1 (1983), 1–29.

"Shaping Fantasies": Figurations of Gender and Power in Elizabethan Culture

Louis Adrian Montrose

I

Shakespeare's Duke Theseus formulates policy when he proclaims that "The lunatic, the lover, and the poet / Are of imagination all compact"; that "Lovers and madmen have such seething brains, / Such shaping fantasies, that apprehend / More than cool reason ever comprehends."[1] The social order of Theseus' Athens depends upon his authority to name the forms and his power to control the subjects of mental disorder. The ruler's task is to *comprehend* – to understand and to encompass – the energies and motives, the diverse, unstable, and potentially subversive *apprehensions* of the ruled. But the Duke – so self-assured and benignly condescending in his comprehension – might also have some cause for apprehension: he himself and the fictional society over which he rules have been shaped by the imagination of a poet. My intertextual study of Shakespeare's *Midsummer Night's Dream* and symbolic forms shaped by other Elizabethan lunatics, lovers, and poets construes the play as calling attention to itself, not only as an end but also as a source of cultural production.[2] Thus, in writing of "shaping fantasies," I mean to suggest the dialectical character of cultural representations: the fantasies by which the text of *A Midsummer Night's Dream* has been shaped are also those to which it gives shape. I explore this dialectic within a specifically Elizabethan context of cultural production: the interplay between representations of gender and power in a stratified society in which authority is everywhere invested in men – everywhere, that is, except at the top.

In the introduction to his recent edition of *A Midsummer Night's Dream*, Harold Brooks summarizes the consensus of modern criticism: "Love and marriage is the [play's] central theme: love aspiring to and consummated in marriage, or to a harmonious partnership within it" (p. cxxx). But, as Paul Olson suggested some years ago, the harmonious marital unions of *A Midsummer Night's Dream* are in harmony with doctrines of Tudor apologists for the patriarchal family: marital union implies a domestic hierarchy; marital harmony is predicated upon the wife's obedience to her husband.[3] Brooks's romantic view and Olson's authoritarian one offer limited but complementary perspectives on the dramatic process by which *A Midsummer Night's Dream* figures the social relationship between the sexes in courtship, marriage, and parenthood. The play imaginatively embodies what Gayle Rubin has called a "sex / gender system": a socio-historical construction of sexual identity, difference and relationship; an appropriation of human anatomical and physiological features by an ideological discourse; a culture-specific fantasia upon Nature's universal theme.[4]

As has long been recognized, *A Midsummer Night's Dream* has affinities with Elizabethan courtly entertainments. In his edition of the play, Harold Brooks cautiously endorses the familiar notion that it was "designed to grace a wedding in a noble household." He adds that "it seems likely that Queen Elizabeth was present when the *Dream* was first acted ... She delighted in homage paid to her as the Virgin Queen, and receives it in the myth-making about the imperial votaress" (pp. liii, lv). Although attractive and plausible, such topical connections must remain wholly conjectural. The perspective of my own analysis of the play's court connection is dialectical rather than causal, ideological rather than occasional. For, whether or not Queen Elizabeth was physically present at the first performance of *A Midsummer Night's Dream*, her pervasive *cultural presence* was a condition of the play's imaginative possibility. This is not to imply that *A Midsummer Night's Dream* is merely an inert "product" of Elizabethan culture. The play is rather a new *production* of Elizabethan culture, enlarging the dimensions of the cultural field and altering the lines of force within it. Thus, in the sense that the royal presence was itself *re*-presented within the play, it may be said that the play henceforth conditioned the imaginative possibility of the Queen. In what follows, I shall explore how Shakespeare's play and other Elizabethan texts figure the Elizabethan sex / gender system and the queen's place within it.

II

I would like to recount an Elizabethan dream – not Shakespeare's *Midsummer Night's Dream*, but one dreamt by Simon Forman on January 23, 1597. Forman – a professional astrologer and physician, amateur alchemist, and avid playgoer – recorded in his diary the following account:

> I dreamt that I was with the Queen, and that she was a little elderly woman in a coarse white petticoat all unready; and she and I walked up and down through lanes and closes, talking and reasoning of many matters. At last we came over a great close where were many people, and there were two men at hard words. One of them was a weaver, a tall man with a reddish beard, distract of his wits. She talked to him and he spoke very merrily unto her, and at last did take her and kiss her. So I took her by the arm and put her away; and told her the fellow was frantic. And so we went from him and I led her by the arm still, and then we went through a dirty lane. She had a long, white smock, very clean and fair,

and it trailed in the dirt and her coat behind. I took her coat and did carry it up a good way, and then it hung too low before. I told her she should do me a favour to let me wait on her, and she said I should. Then said I, "I mean to wait *upon* you and not under you, that I might make this belly a little bigger to carry up this smock and coats out of the dirt." And so we talked merrily and then she began to lean upon me, when we were past the dirt and to be very familiar with me, and methought she began to love me. And when we were alone, out of sight, methought she would have kissed me.[5]

It was then that Forman awoke.

Within the dreamer's unconscious, the "little elderly woman" who was his political mother must have been linked to the mother who had borne him. In an autobiographical fragment, Forman repeatedly characterizes himself as unloved and rejected by his mother during his childhood and youth: he writes of himself, that "Simon, being a child of six years old, his father loved him above all the rest, but his mother nor brethren loved him not ... After the father of Simon was dead, his mother, who never loved him, grudged at his being at home, and what fault soever was committed by any of the rest he was beaten for it."[6] Forman's mother was still alive at the date of his dream, a very old woman. C. L. Barber has suggested that "the very central and problematical role of women in Shakespeare – and in Elizabethan drama generally – reflects the fact that Protestantism did away with the cult of the Virgin Mary. It meant the loss of ritual resource for dealing with the internal residues in all of us of the once all-powerful and all-inclusive mother."[7] What Barber fails to note is that a concerted effort was in fact made to appropriate the symbolism and the affective power of the suppressed Marian cult in order to foster an Elizabethan cult. Both the internal residues and the religious rituals were potential resources for dealing with the political problems of the Elizabethan regime. Perhaps, at the same time, the royal cult may also have provided Forman and other Elizabethans with a resource for dealing with the internal residues of their relationships to the primary maternal figures of infancy. My concern is not to psychoanalyze Forman but rather to emphasize the historical specificity of psychological processes, the politics of the unconscious. Whatever the place of this dream in the dreamer's interior life, the text in which he represents it to himself allows us to glimpse the cultural contours of an Elizabethan psyche.[8]

The virginal sex-object of Forman's dream, the "little elderly woman" scantily clad in white, corresponds with startling accuracy to descriptions of Elizabeth's actual appearance in 1597. In the year that Forman dreamt his dream, the ambassador extraordinary of the French King Henri IV described the English Queen in his journal. At his first audience, he recorded:

> She was strangely attired in a dress of silver cloth, white and crimson ... She kept the front of her dress open, and one could see the whole of her bosom, and passing low, and often she would open the front of this robe with her hands as if she were too hot ... Her bosom is somewhat wrinkled ... but lower down her flesh is exceeding white and delicate, so far as one could see. As for her face, it is and appears to be very aged. It is long and thin, and her teeth are very yellow and unequal ... Many of them are missing so that one cannot understand her easily when she speaks quickly.[9]

For the ambassador's second audience, the Queen appeared

clad in a dress of black taffeta, bound with gold lace ... She had a petticoat of white damask, girdled, and open in front, as was also her chemise, in such a manner that she often opened this dress and one could see all her belly, and even to her navel ... When she raises her head, she has a trick of putting both hands on her gown and opening it insomuch that all her belly can be seen (pp. 36–7).

In the following year, another foreign visitor who saw the Queen noted that her bosom was uncovered, as all the English ladies have it till they marry.[10]

Elizabeth's display of her bosom signified her status as a maiden. But, as in Spenser's personification of Charity as a nursing mother or in the popular emblem of the life-rendering Pelican (which Elizabeth wore as a pendant upon her bosom in one of her portraits), her breasts were also those of a selfless and bountiful mother.[11] The image of the Queen as a wetnurse may have had some currency. Of the Earl of Essex's insatiable thirst for those offices and honors which were in the Queen's gift, Naunton wrote that "my Lord ... drew in too fast, like a childe sucking on an over-uberous Nurse."[12] The Queen was the source of her subjects' social sustenance, the fount of all preferments; she was represented as a virgin-mother – part Madonna, part Ephesian Diana. Like her bosom, Elizabeth's belly must have figured her political motherhood. But, as the French ambassador insinuates, these conspicuous self-displays were also a kind of erotic provocation. The official portraits and courtly blazons that represent the splendor of the Queen's immutable body politic are nicely complemented by the ambassador's sketches of the Queen's sixty-five year old body natural. His perceptions of the vanity and melancholy of this personage in no way negate his numerous observations of her grace, vitality, and political cunning. Indeed, in the very process of describing the Queen's preoccupation with the impact of her appearance upon her beholders, the ambassador demonstrates its impact upon *himself*.

So, too, the aged Queen's body exerts a power upon the mind of Doctor Forman; and, in his dream, he exerts a reciprocal power upon the body of the Queen. The virginal, erotic, and maternal aspects of the Elizabethan feminine that the royal cult appropriates from the domestic domain are themselves appropriated by one of the Queen's subjects and made the material for his dreamwork. At the core of Forman's dream is his joke with the Queen: "I told her she should do me a favour to let me wait on her, and she said I should. Then said I, 'I mean to wait *upon* you and not under you, that I might make this belly a little bigger to carry up this smock and coats out of the dirt.' " The joke – and, in a sense, the whole dream – is generated from Forman's verbal quibble: to *wait* upon / to *weight* upon. Within this subversive pun is concentrated the reciprocal relationship between dependency and domination. With one vital exception, all forms of public and domestic authority in Elizabethan England were vested in men: in fathers, husbands, masters, teachers, magistrates, lords. It was inevitable that the rule of a woman would generate peculiar tensions within such a "patriarchal" society.[13] Forman's dream epitomizes the indissolubly political and sexual character of the cultural forms in which such tensions might be represented and addressed. In Forman's wordplay, the subject's desire for employment (to *wait* upon) coexists with his desire for mastery (to *weight* upon); and the pun is manifested physically in his desire to inseminate his sovereign, which is at once to serve her and to possess her. And because the figures in the dream are not only subject and prince but also man and woman, what the *subject* desires to perform, the *man* has the capacity to perform: for Forman to raise the Queen's belly is to make her female body to bear the sign of his own potency. In the context of the cross-cutting relationships between subject and prince, man and woman, the dreamer insinuates into a gesture of homage, a will to power.

It is strange and admirable that the dreamer's rival for the Queen should be a weaver – as if Nick Bottom had wandered out of Shakespeare's *Dream* and into Forman's. Forman's story of the night does indeed have affinities with the "most rare vision" (iv.i.203) that Shakespeare grants to Bottom. Bottom's dream, like Forman's, is an experience of fleeting intimacy with a powerful female who is at once lover, mother, and queen. The liaison between The Fairy Queen and the assified artisan is an outrageous theatrical realization of a personal fantasy that was obviously not Forman's alone. Titania treats Bottom as if he were both her child and her lover. And she herself is ambivalently nurturing and threatening, imperious and enthralled. She dotes upon Bottom, and indulges in him all those desires to be fed, scratched, and coddled that make Bottom's dream into a parodic fantasy of infantile narcissism and dependency. The sinister side of Titania's possessiveness is manifested in her binding up of Bottom's tongue, and her intimidating command, "Out of this wood do not desire to go: / Thou shalt remain here, whether thou wilt or no" (iii.i.145–46). But if Titania manipulates Bottom, an artisan and amateur actor, she herself is manipulated by Oberon, a "King of shadows" (iii.ii.347) and the play's internal dramatist. A fantasy of male dependency upon woman is expressed and contained within a fantasy of male control over woman; the social reality of the player's dependency upon a Queen is inscribed within the imaginative reality of the dramatist's control over a Queen. Both Forman's private dream-text and Shakespeare's public play-text embody a culture-specific dialectic between personal and public images of gender and power; both are characteristically *Elizabethan* cultural forms.

III

The beginning of *A Midsummer Night's Dream* coincides with the end of a struggle in which Theseus has been victorious over the Amazon warrior:

> Hippolyta, I woo'd thee with my sword,
> And won thy love doing thee injuries;
> But I will wed thee in another key,
> With pomp, with triumph, and with revelling.
>
> (i.i.16–19)

Descriptions of the Amazons are ubiquitous in Elizabethan texts. For example, all of the essentials are present in popular form in William Painter's "Novel of the Amazons," which opens the second book of *The Palace of Pleasure* (1575). Here we read that the Amazons "were most excellent warriors"; that "they murdred certaine of their husbands" at the beginning of their gynecocracy; that, "if they brought forth daughters, they norished and trayned them up in armes, and other manlik exercises ... If they were delivered of males, they sent them to their fathers, and if by chaunce they kept any backe, they murdred them, or else brake their armes and legs in sutch wise as they had no power to beare weapons, and served for nothynge but to spin, twist, and doe other feminine labour."[14] The Amazons' penchant for male infanticide is complemented by their obvious delight in subjecting powerful heroes to their will. Spenser's Artegall, hero of the Legend of Justice, becomes enslaved to Radigund, "A Princesse of great powre, and greater pride, / And Queene of Amazons, in armes well tride" (*FQ*, v.iv.33). Defeated by Radigund in personal combat, Artegall must undergo degradation and effeminization of the kind endured by Hercules and by the Amazons' maimed sons.

Sixteenth-century travel narratives often recreate the ancient Amazons of Scythia in South America or in Africa. Invariably, the Amazons are relocated just beyond the receding boundary of *terra incognita*. Thus, in Sierra Leone in 1582, the chaplain of an English expedition to the Spice Islands recorded the report of a Portuguese trader that "near the mountains of the moon there is a queen, empress of all these Amazons, a witch and a cannibal who daily feeds on the flesh of boys. She ever remains unmarried, but she has intercourse with a great number of men by whom she begets offspring. The kingdom, however, remains hereditary to the daughters, not to the sons."[15] This cultural fantasy assimilates Amazonian myth, witchcraft, and cannibalism into an anti-culture which precisely inverts European norms of political authority, sexual license, marriage practices, and inheritance rules.[16] The attitude toward the Amazons expressed in such Renaissance texts is a mixture of fascination and horror. Amazonian mythology seems symbolically to embody and to control a collective anxiety about the power of the female not only to dominate or reject the male but to create and destroy him. It is an ironic acknowledgment by an androcentric culture of the degree to which men are in fact dependent upon women: upon mothers and nurses, for their birth and nurture; upon mistresses and wives, for the validation of their manhood.

Shakespeare engages his wedding play in a dialectic with this mythological formation. The Amazons have been defeated before the play begins; and nuptial rites are to be celebrated when it ends. *A Midsummer Night's Dream* focuses upon different crucial transitions in the male and female life cycles: the fairy plot, upon taking "a little changeling boy" from childhood into youth, from the world of the mother into the world of the father; the Athenian plot, upon taking a maiden from youth into maturity, from the world of the father into the world of the husband. The pairing of the four Athenian lovers is made possible by the magical powers of Oberon and made lawful by the political authority of Theseus. Each of these rulers is preoccupied with the fulfillment of his own desires in the possession or repossession of a wife. Only after Hippolyta has been mastered by Theseus may marriage seal them "in everlasting bond of fellowship" (I.i.85). And only after "proud Titania" has been degraded by "jealous Oberon" (II.i.60, 61), has "in mild terms begg'd" (IV.i.57) his patience, and has readily yielded the changeling boy to him, may they be "new in amity" (IV.i.86).

The diachronic structure of *A Midsummer Night's Dream* eventually restores the inverted Amazonian system of gender and nurture to a patriarchal norm. But the initial plans for Theseus' triumph are immediately interrupted by news of yet another unruly female. Egeus wishes to confront his daughter Hermia with two alternatives: absolute obedience to the paternal will, or death. Theseus intervenes with a third alternative: if she refuses to marry whom her father chooses, Hermia must submit

> Either to die the death or to abjure
> Forever the society of men.
> ...
> For aye to be in shady cloister mew'd,
> Chanting faint hymns to the cold, fruitless moon.
> Thrice blessed they that master so their blood
> To undergo such maiden pilgrimage;
> But earthlier happy is the rose distill'd
> Than that which, withering on the virgin thorn,
> Grows, lives, and dies, in single blessedness.
>
> (1.i.65–6, 71–8)

Theseus has characteristically Protestant notions about the virtue of virginity: maidenhood is a phase in the life-cycle of a woman who is destined for married chastity and motherhood. As a permanent state, "single blessedness" is mere sterility. Theseus expands Hermia's options only in order to clarify her constraints. In the process of tempering the father's domestic tyranny, the Duke affirms his own interests and authority. He represents the life of a vestal as a *punishment*, and it is one that fits the nature of Hermia's crime. The maiden is surrounded by men, each of whom – as father, lover, or lord – claims a kind of property in her. Yet Hermia dares to suggest that she has a claim to property in herself: she refuses to "yield [her] virgin patent up / Unto his lordship whose unwished yoke / [Her] soul consents not to give sovereignty" (1.i.80–2). Like Rosalind, in *As You Like It*, Hermia wishes the limited privilege of giving herself. Theseus appropriates the source of Hermia's fragile power: her ability to deny men access to her body. He usurps the power of virginity by imposing upon Hermia his own power to deny her the use of her body. If she will not submit to its use by her father and by Demetrius, she must "abjure forever the society of men," and "live a barren sister all [her] life" (1.i.65–6, 72). Her own words suggest that the female body is a supreme form of property and a locus for the contestation of authority. The self-possession of single blessedness is a form of power against which are opposed the marriage doctrines of Shakespeare's culture and the very form of his comedy.[17]

In devising Hermia's punishment, Theseus appropriates and parodies the very condition which the Amazons sought to enjoy. They rejected marriages with men and alliances with patriarchal societies because, as one sixteenth-century writer put it, they esteemed "that Patrimonie was not a meane of libertie but of thraldome."[18] The separatism of the Amazons is a repudiation of men's claims to have property in women. But if Amazonian myth figures the inversionary claims of matriarchy, sisterhood, and the autonomy of women, it also figures the *repudiation* of those claims in the act of Amazonomachy. Painter recounts the battle between the Amazons, led by Menalippe and Hippolyta (both sisters of Queen Antiopa) and the Greeks, led by Hercules and Theseus. Hercules returned Menalippe to Antiopa in exchange for the Queen's armor, "but Theseus for no offer that she coulde make, woulde he deliver Hippolyta, with whom he was so farre in love, that he carried her home with him, and afterward toke her to wyfe, of whom hee had a sonne called Hipolitus" (*The Palace of Pleasure*, 2:163). Theseus' violent and insatiable lust – what North's Plutarch suggestively calls his "womannishenes" – divorced Hippolyta from her sisters and from the society of Amazons.[19]

Shakespeare's play naturalizes Amazonomachy in the vicissitudes of courtship. Heterosexual desire disrupts the innocent pleasures of Hermia's girlhood: "What graces in my love do dwell, / That he hath turn'd a heaven unto a hell!" (1.i.206–7). Hermia's farewell to Helena is also a farewell to their girlhood friendship, a delicate repudiation of youthful homophilia:

> And in the wood, where often you and I
> Upon faint primrose beds were wont to lie,
> Emptying our bosoms of their counsel sweet,
> There my Lysander and myself shall meet;
> And thence from Athens turn away our eyes,
> To seek new friends, and stranger companies.
>
> (1.i.214–19)

Before dawn comes to the forest, the "counsel" shared by Hermia and Helena, their "sisters' vows ... school-days' friendship, childhood innocence" (III.ii.198, 199, 202), have all been torn asunder, to be replaced at the end of the play by the primary demands and loyalties of wedlock. On the other hand, by dawn the hostilities between the two male youths have dissolved into "gentle concord" (IV.i.142). From the beginning of the play, the relationship between Lysander and Demetrius has been based upon aggressive rivalry for the same object of desire: first for Hermia, and then for Helena. Each youth must despise his previous mistress in order to adore the next; and a change in one's affections provokes a change in the other's. R. W. Dent has pointed out that the young women do not fluctuate in their desires for their young men, and that the ending ratifies their constant if inexplicable preferences.[20] It should be added that the maidens remain constant to their men at the cost of inconstancy to each other. If Lysander and Demetrius are flagrantly inconstant to Hermia and Helena, the pattern of their inconstancies nevertheless keeps them constant to each other. The romantic resolution transforms this constancy from one of rivalry to one of friendship by making each male to accept his own female. In Puck's charmingly crude formulation:

> And the country proverb known,
> That every man should take his own,
> In your waking shall be shown:
> Jack shall have Jill,
> Nought shall go ill:
> The man shall have his mare again, and all shall be well.
>
> (III.ii.458–63)

At the end of *A Midsummer Night's Dream*, as at the end of *As You Like It*, the marital couplings dissolve the bonds of sisterhood at the same time that they forge the bonds of brotherhood.[21]

According to the paradigm of Northrop Frye, Shakespearean comedy "normally begins with an anticomic society, a social organization blocking and opposed to the comic drive, which the action of the comedy evades or overcomes. It often takes the form of a harsh or irrational law, like ... the law disposing of rebellious daughters in *A Midsummer Night's Dream* ... Most of these irrational laws are preoccupied with trying to regulate the sexual drive, and so work counter to the wishes of the hero and heroine, which form the main impetus of the comic action."[22] Frye's account of Shakespearean comic action emphasizes intergenerational tension at the expense of those other forms of social and familial tension from which it is only artificially separable; in particular, he radically undervalues the centrality of sexual politics to these plays by unquestioningly identifying the heroines' interests with those of the heroes. The interaction of characters in the fictive societies of Shakespearean drama – like the interaction of persons in the society of Shakespeare's England – is structured by the complex interplay among culture-specific categories, not only of age and gender but also of kinship and class. The "drive toward a festive conclusion" (Frye, *A Natural Perspective*, p. 75) which liberates and unites comic heroes and heroines also subordinates wives to husbands and confers the responsibilities and privileges of manhood upon callow youths. What Frye calls "the main impetus" of Shakespearean comic action is not so much to liberate "the sexual drive" from "irrational laws" as it is to fabricate a temporary accommodation between law and libido. In *A Midsummer Night's Dream*, as in other Shakespearean comedies, the "drive toward a festive conclusion" is, specifically, a drive toward a wedding. And in its validation of marriage, the play is less concerned to sacramentalize libido than to socialize it.

In the opening scene, Egeus claims that he may do with Hermia as he chooses because she is his property: "As she is mine, I may dispose of her" (I.i.142). This claim is based upon a stunningly simple thesis: she is his because he has *made* her. Charging that Lysander has "stol'n the impression" (I.i.32) of Hermia's fantasy, Egeus effectively absolves his daughter from responsibility for her affections because he cannot acknowledge her capacity for volition. If she does not – cannot – obey him, then she should be destroyed. Borrowing Egeus' own imprinting metaphor, Theseus explains to Hermia the ontogenetic principle underlying her father's vehemence:

> To you your father should be as a god:
> One that compos'd your beauties, yea, and one
> To whom you are but as a form in wax
> By him imprinted, and within his power
> To leave the figure or disfigure it.
>
> (I.i.47–51)

Theseus represents paternity as a cultural act, an art: the father is a demiurge or *homo faber*, who composes, in-forms, imprints himself upon, what is merely inchoate matter. Conspicuously excluded from Shakespeare's play is the relationship between mother and daughter – the kinship bond through which Amazonian society reproduces itself. The mother's part is wholly excluded from this account of the making of a daughter. Hermia and Helena have no mothers; they have only fathers. The central female characters of Shakespeare's comedies are not mothers but mothers-to-be, maidens who are passing from fathers to husbands in a world made and governed by men.

In effect, Theseus' lecture on the shaping of a *daughter* is a fantasy of male parthenogenesis. Titania's votaress is the only biological mother in *A Midsummer Night's Dream*. But she is an absent presence who must be evoked from Titania's memory because she has died in giving birth to a *son*. Assuming that they do not maim their sons, the Amazons are only too glad to give them away to their fathers. In Shakespeare's play, however, Oberon's paternal power must be directed against Titania's maternal possessiveness:

> For Oberon is passing fell and wrath,
> Because that she as her attendant hath
> A lovely boy, stol'n from an Indian king –
> She never had so sweet a changeling;
> And jealous Oberon would have the child
> Knight of his train to trace the forest wild;
> But she perforce withholds the loved boy,
> Crowns him with flowers, and makes him all her joy.
>
> (ii.i.20–7)

A boy's transition from the female-centered world of his early childhood to the male-centered world of his youth is given a kind of phylogenetic sanction by myths recounting a cultural transition from matriarchy to patriarchy.[23] Such a myth is represented at the very threshold of *A Midsummer Night's Dream*: Theseus' defeat of the Amazonian matriarchate sanctions Oberon's attempt to take the boy from an infantilizing mother and to make a man of him. Yet "jealous" Oberon is not only Titania's rival for the child but also the child's rival for Titania: making the boy "all her joy," "proud" Titania withholds herself from her husband; she has "forsworn his bed and company" (ii.i.62–3). Oberon's preoccupation is to gain possession, not only of the boy but of the woman's desire and obedience; he must master his own dependency upon his wife.[24]

Titania has her own explanation for her fixation upon the changeling:

> His mother was a votress of my order
> And in the spiced Indian air, by night,
> Full often hath she gossip'd by my side;
> And sat with me on Neptune's yellow sands,
> Marking th'embarked traders on the flood:
> When we have laugh'd to see the sails conceive
> And grow big-bellied with the wanton wind;
> Which she, with pretty and with swimming gait
> Following (her womb then rich with my young squire),
> Would imitate, and sail upon the land
> To fetch me trifles, and return again
> As from a voyage rich with merchandise.
> But she, being mortal, of that boy did die;
> And for her sake do I rear up her boy;
> And for her sake I will not part with him.
>
> (ii.i.123–37)

Titania's attachment to the changeling boy embodies her attachment to the memory of his mother. What Oberon accomplishes by substituting Bottom for the boy is to break Titania's solemn vow. As in the case of the Amazons, or of Hermia and Helena, the play again enacts a male disruption of an intimate bond between women: first by the boy, and then by the man. It is as if, in order to be freed and enfranchised from the prison of the womb, the male child must *kill* his mother: "She, being mortal, of that boy did die." Titania's words suggest that mother and son are potentially mortal to each other: the matricidal infant complements the infanticidal Amazon. As is later the case with Bottom, Titania both dotes upon and dominates the child, attenuating his imprisonment to the womb: "And for her sake I will not part with him." Thus, within the changeling plot are embedded transformations of the male fantasies of motherhood which are figured in Amazonian myth.

Titania represents her bond to her votaress as one that is rooted in an experience of female fecundity, an experience for which men must seek merely mercantile compensations. The women "have laugh'd to see the sails conceive / And grow big-bellied with the wanton wind"; and the votaress has parodied such false pregnancies by sailing to fetch trifles while she herself bears riches within her very womb. The notion of maternity implied in Titania's speech counterpoints the notion of paternity formulated by Theseus in the opening scene. In Theseus' description, neither biological nor social mother – neither *genetrix* nor *mater* – plays a role in the making of a daughter; in Titania's description, neither *genitor* nor *pater* plays a role in the making of a son. The father's daughter is shaped from without; the mother's son comes from within her body: Titania dwells upon the physical bond between mother and child, as manifested in pregnancy and parturition. Like an infant of the Elizabethan upper classes, however, the changeling is nurtured not by his natural mother but by a surrogate. By emphasizing her own role as a foster mother to her gossip's offspring, Titania links the biological and social aspects of parenthood together within a wholly maternal world, a world in which the relationship between women has displaced the relationship between wife and husband. Nevertheless, despite the exclusion of a paternal role from Titania's speech, Shakespeare's embryological notions remain distinctly Aristotelian, distinctly phallocentric: the mother is represented as a *vessel*, as a container for her son; she is not his *maker*. In contrast, the implication of Theseus' description of paternity is that the male is the only begetter; a daughter is merely a token of her father's potency. Thus these two speeches may be said to formulate in poetic discourse, a proposition about the genesis of gender and power: men make women, and make themselves through the medium of women. Such a proposition reverses the Amazonian practice, in which women use men merely for their own reproduction. But much more than this, it seems an over-compensation for the *natural* fact that men do indeed come from women; an over-compensation for the *cultural* facts that consanguineal and affinal ties *between* men are established through mothers, wives, and daughters. *A Midsummer Night's Dream* dramatizes a set of claims which are repeated throughout Shakespeare's canon: claims for a spiritual kinship among men that is unmediated by women; for the procreative powers of men; and for the autogeny of men.

It may be relevant to recall that what we tend to think of as the "facts of life" have been established as *facts* relatively recently in human history, with the development of microbiology that began in Europe in the late seventeenth century.[25] Of course, that seminal and menstrual fluids are in some way related to generation, and that people have both a father and a mother are hardly novel notions. My point is that, in Shakespeare's age, they remained *merely* notions. Although biological maternity was readily apparent, biological paternity was a cultural construct for which ocular proof was unattainable. More specifically, the evidence for *unique* biological paternity, for the physical link between a particular man and child, has always been exiguous. And, in Shakespearean drama, this link is frequently a focus of anxious concern, whether the concern is to validate paternity or to call it in question. Thus, Lear tells Regan that if she were *not* glad to see him, "I would divorce me from thy mother's tomb, / Sepulchring an adult'ress" (*King Lear*, ii.iv.131–2). And Leontes exclaims, upon first meeting Florizel, "Your mother was most true to wedlock, Prince, / For she did print your royal father off, / Conceiving you" (*The Winter's Tale*, v.i.124–6). In the former speech, a vulnerable father invokes his previously unacknowledged wife precisely when he wishes to repudiate his child; while in the latter, a vulnerable husband celebrates female virtue as the instrument of male self-reproduction.

The role of genetrix is self-evident but the role of genitor is not. As Launcelot Gobbo puts it, in *The Merchant of Venice*, "it is a wise father that knows his own child" (*MV*, ii.ii.76–7). This consequence of biological asymmetry calls forth an explanatory – and compensatory – asymmetry in many traditional embryological theories: paternity is procreative, the formal and / or efficient cause of generation; maternity is nurturant, the material cause of generation. For example, according to *The Problemes of Aristotle*, a popular Elizabethan medical guide that continued to be revised and reissued well into the nineteenth century,

> The seede [i.e., of the male] is the efficient beginning of the childe, as the builder is the efficient cause of the house, and therefore is not the materiall cause of the childe ... The seedes [i.e., both male and female] are shut and kept in the wombe: but the seede of the man doth dispose and prepare the seed of the woman to receive the forme, perfection, or soule, the which being done, it is converted into humiditie, and is fumed and breathed out by the pores of the matrix, which is manifest, bicause onely the flowers [i.e., the menses] of the woman are the materiall cause of the yoong one.[26]

Conflating Aristotelian and Galenic notions, the text registers some confusion about the nature of the inseminating power and about its attribution to the woman as well as to the man. Although the contributions of both man and woman are necessary, the female seed is nevertheless materially inferior to that of the male. The notion of woman as an unperfected, an inadequate, imitation of man extends to the analogy of semen and menses: "The seede ... is white in man by reason of his greate heate, and because it is digested better ... The seede of a woman is red ... because the flowers is corrupt, undigested blood" (*Problemes of Aristotle*, sig. E3ʳ). Whether in folk medicine or in philosophy, notions of maternity have a persistent natural or physical bias, while notions of paternity have a persistent social or spiritual bias. And such notions are articulated within a belief-system in which nature is subordinated to society, and matter is subordinated to spirit. The act of generation brings man and woman into a relationship that is both complementary and hierarchical. Thus, there exists a homology between the cultural construction of sexual generation and the social institution of marriage: genitor is to genetrix as husband is to wife.

While Shakespeare's plays reproduce these legitimating structures, they also reproduce challenges to their legitimacy. For, like the ubiquitous jokes and fears about cuckoldry to which they are usually linked, the frequent allusions within Shakespeare's texts to the incertitude of paternity point to a source of tension, to a potential contradiction, within the ostensibly patriarchal sex / gender system of Elizabethan culture. Oberon's epithalamium represents procreation as the union of man and woman, and marriage as a relationship of mutual affection:

> To the best bride-bed will we,
> Which by us shall blessed be;
> And the issue there create
> Ever shall be fortunate.
> So shall all the couples three
> Ever true in loving be.
> (v.i.389–94)

This benign vision is predicated upon the play's reaffirmation of the father's role in generation and the husband's authority over the wife. But at the same time that the play reaffirms essential elements of a patriarchal ideology, it also calls that reaffirmation in question; irrespective of authorial intention, the text intermittently undermines its own comic propositions. Oberon assures himself that, by the end of the play, "all things shall be peace" (III.ii.377). But the continuance of the newlyweds' loves and the good fortune of their issue are by no means assured. Indeed, as soon as the lovers have gone off to bed, Puck begins to evoke an uncomic world of labor, fear, pain, and death (v.i.357–76). This invocation gives some urgency to Oberon's subsequent ritual blessing: the dangers are imminent and the peace is most fragile. A Midsummer Night's Dream ends, not only with the creation of new children but with the creation of new mothers and new fathers; it ends upon the threshhold of another generational cycle, which contains in potentia a renewal of the strife with which the play began. The status of "jealous" Oberon and "proud" Titania as personifications of forces in Nature at once sanctions and subverts the doctrine of domestic hierarchy. For, as personified in Shakespeare's fairies, the divinely ordained imperatives of Nature call attention to themselves as the humanly constructed imperatives of Culture: Shakespeare's naturalization and legitimation of the domestic economy deconstructs itself. The all-too-human struggle between the play's already married couple provides an ironic prognosis for the new marriages.

The promised end of romantic comedy is not only undermined by dramatic ironies but also contaminated by a kind of inter-textual irony. The mythology of Theseus is filled with instances of terror, lust, and jealousy which are prominently recounted and censured by Plutarch in his Life of Theseus and in his subsequent comparison of Theseus with Romulus. Shakespeare uses Plutarch as his major source of Theseus-lore but does so highly selectively, excluding those events "not sorting with a nuptial ceremony" (v.i.55) nor with a comedy. Nevertheless, as Harold Brooks's edition has now conclusively demonstrated, the text of Shakespeare's play is permeated by echoes not only of Plutarch's parallel lives of Theseus and Romulus but also of Seneca's Hippolitus and his Medea – by an archaeological record of the texts which shaped the poet's fantasy as he was shaping his play. Thus, sedimented within the verbal texture of A Midsummer Night's Dream are traces of those forms of sexual and familial violence which the play would suppress: acts of bestiality and incest, of parricide, uxoricide, filicide, and suicide; sexual fears and urges erupting in cycles of violent desire – from Pasiphae and the Minotaur to Phaedra and Hippolitus. The seductive and destructive powers of women figure centrally in Theseus' career; and his habitual victimization of women, the chronicle of his rapes and disastrous marriages, is a discourse of anxious misogyny which persists as an echo within Shakespeare's text, no matter how much it has been muted or transformed.[27]

The play actually calls attention to the mechanism of mythological suppression by an ironically meta-dramatic gesture: Theseus demands "some delight" with which to "beguile / The lazy time" (v.i.40–1) before the bedding of the brides. The list of available entertainments includes "The battle with the Centaurs, to be sung / By an Athenian eunuch to the harp," as well as "The riot of the tipsy Bacchanals, / Tearing the Thracian singer in their rage" (v.i.44–5, 48–9). Theseus rejects both – because they are already too familiar. These brief scenarios encompass the extremes of reciprocal violence between the sexes. The first performance narrates a wedding that degenerates into rape and warfare; the singer and his subject – Athenian eunuch and phallic Centaur – are two antithetical kinds of male-monster. In the second performance, what was often seen as the natural inclination of women toward irrational behavior is manifested in the Maenads' terrible rage against Orpheus. The tearing and decapitation of the misogynistic Ur-Poet at once displaces and vivifies the Athenian singer's castration; and it also evokes the fate of Hippolytus, the misogynistic offspring of Theseus and Hippolyta. It is in its intermittent ironies, dissonances, and contradictions that the text of *A Midsummer Night's Dream* discloses – perhaps, in a sense, despite itself – that patriarchal norms are compensatory for the vulnerability of men to the powers of women.

IV

Such moments of textual disclosure also illuminate the interplay between sexual politics in the Elizabethan family and sexual politics in the Elizabethan monarchy: for the woman to whom *all* Elizabethan men were vulnerable was Queen Elizabeth herself. Within legal and fiscal limits, she held the power of life and death over every Englishman; the power to advance or frustrate the worldly desires of all her subjects. Her personality and personal symbolism helped to mold English culture and the consciousness of Englishmen for several generations.

Although the Amazonian metaphor might seem suited to strategies for praising a woman ruler, it was never popular among Elizabethan encomiasts.[28] Its associations must have been too sinister to suit the personal tastes and political interests of the Queen. However, Sir Walter Ralegh did boldly compare Elizabeth to the Amazons in his *Discoverie of Guiana*.[29] In his digression on the Amazons, who are reported to dwell "not far from Guiana," Ralegh repeats the familiar details of their sexual and parental practices, and notes that they "are said to be very cruel and bloodthirsty, especially to such as offer to invade their territories" (p. 28). At the end of his narrative, Ralegh exhorts Elizabeth to undertake a conquest of Guiana:

> Her Majesty heereby shall confirme and strengthen the opinions of al nations, as touching her great and princely actions. And where the south border of *Guiana* reacheth to the Dominion and Empire of the *Amazones*, those women shall heereby heare the name of a virgin, which is not onely able to defend her owne territories and her neighbors, but also to invade and conquere so great Empyres and so farre removed (p. 120).

Ralegh's strategy for convincing the Queen to advance his colonial enterprise is to insinuate that she is both like and unlike an Amazon; that Elizabethan imperialism threatens not only the Empire of the Guiana but the Empire of the Amazons; and that Elizabeth can definitively cleanse herself from contamination by the Amazons if she sanctions their subjugation. The Amazonomachy which Ralegh projects into the imaginative space of the New World is analogous to that narrated by Spenser within the imaginative space of Faeryland. Radigund, the Amazon Queen, can only be defeated by Britomart, the martial maiden who is Artegall's betrothed and the fictional ancestress of Elizabeth. Radigund is Britomart's double, split off from her as an allegorical personification of everything in Artegall's beloved which threatens him. Having destroyed Radigund and liberated Artegall from his effeminate "thraldome," Britomart reforms what is left of Amazon society: she

> The liberty of women did repeale,
> Which they had long usurpt; and them restoring
> To mens subjection, did true Justice deale:
> That all they as a Goddesse her adoring,
> Her wisedome did admire, and hearkned to her loring.
>
> (*FQ*, v.vii.42)

Unlike some of the popular sixteenth-century forms of misrule so well discussed by Natalie Davis, this instance of sexual inversion, of Woman-on-Top, would seem to be intended as an exemplum "of order and stability in a hierarchical society," which "can clarify the structure by the process of reversing it."[30] For Ralegh's Elizabeth, as for Spenser's Britomart, the woman who has the prerogative of a goddess, who is authorized to be out of place, can best justify her authority by putting other women in their places.

A few paragraphs before Ralegh exhorts Elizabeth to undertake an Amazonomachy, he exhorts his gentlemen-readers to commit a cultural rape:

> Guiana is a Countrey that hath yet her Maydenhead, never sackt, turned, nor wrought, the face of the earth hath not beene torne, nor the vertue and salt of the soyle spent by manurance, the graves have not beene opened for gold, the mines not broken with sledges, nor their Images puld down out of their temples. It hath never been entred by any armie of strength and never conquered and possessed by any Christian Prince. (p. 115)

Ralegh's enthusiasm is, at one and the same time, for the unspoiled quality of this world and for the prospect of despoiling it. Guiana, like the Amazons, is fit to be wooed with the sword and won with injuries. Such metaphors have a peculiar resonance in the context of an address to Elizabeth. Certainly, it is difficult to imagine Ralegh using them to represent the plantation of Virginia, which had been named by and for the Virgin Queen. When, in the proem to the second book of *The Faerie Queene*, Spenser conjoins "the Amazons huge river" and "fruitfullest Virginia" (*FQ*, II.Proem.2), he is invoking not only two regions of the New World but two archetypes of Elizabethan culture: The engulfing Amazon and the nurturing Virgin. Later in the same book, they are conjoined again: Belphoebe, the beautiful virgin huntress who figures Queen Elizabeth in her body natural, is introduced into the poem with an extended blazon (*FQ*, II.iii.21–31) that insinuates sexual provocation into its encomium of militant chastity. The description concludes in a curiously ominous epic simile, in which the Amazonian image is at once celebrated and mastered: Belphoebe is compared both to the goddess Diana and to Penthesilea, "that famous Queene / Of *Amazons*, whom *Pyrrhus* did destroy" (*FQ*, ii.iii.31). Women's bodies – and, in particular, the Queen's two bodies – provide a cognitive map for Elizabethan culture, a veritable matrix for the Elizabethan forms of desire.[31]

The Queen herself was too politic, and too ladylike, to wish to pursue the Amazonian image very far. Instead, she transformed it to suit her purposes, representing herself as an androgynous martial maiden, like Spenser's Britomart. Such was her appearance at Tilbury in 1588, where she had come to review her troops in expectation of a Spanish invasion. On that momentous occasion, she rode a white horse and dressed in white velvet; she wore a silver cuirass on her breast and carried a silver truncheon in her hand. The theme of her speech was by then already familiar to her listeners: she dwelt upon the womanly frailty of her body natural and the masculine strength of her body politic – a strength deriving from the love of her people, the virtue of her lineage, and the will of her God: "I have always so behaved myself that, under God, I have placed my chiefest strength and safeguard in the loyal hearts and good will of my subjects ... I know I have the body of a weak and feeble woman, but I have the heart and stomach of a king, and of a king of England too."[32] As the female ruler of what was, at least in theory, a patriarchal society, Elizabeth incarnated a contradiction at the very center of the Elizabethan sex / gender system. When Spenser's narrator moralizes on the negative example of the Amazons, he must be careful to provide himself with an escape clause at the end of his stanza:

> Such is the crueltie of womenkynd
> When they have shaken off the shamefast band,
> With which wise Nature did them strongly bynd,
> T'obay the heasts of mens well ruling hand,
> That then all rule and reason they withstand,
> To purchase a licentious libertie.
> But vertuous women wisely understand,
> That they were borne to base humilitie,
> Unlesse the heavens them lift to lawfull soveraintie.
>
> (*FQ*, v.v.25)

After the death of their royal mistress, Cecil wrote to Harington that she had been "more than a man, and, in troth, sometime less than a woman."[33] Queen Elizabeth was a cultural anomaly; and this anomalousness – at once divine and monstrous – made her powerful, and dangerous. By the skillful deployment of images that were at once awesome and familiar, this perplexing creature tried to mollify her male subjects while enhancing her authority over them.

At the beginning of her reign, Elizabeth formulated the strategy by which she turned the political liability of her gender to advantage for the next half century. She told her first parliaments that she was content to have as her epitaph "that a Queen, having reigned such a time, lived and died a virgin"; that her coronation ring betokened her marriage to her subjects; and that, although after her death her people might have many stepdames, yet they should never have "a more natural mother than [she] meant to be unto [them] all."[34] One way in which she actualized her maternal policy was to sponsor more than a hundred godchildren, the offspring of nobility and commoners alike.[35]

In his memorial of Elizabeth, Bacon epitomized her policy on gender and power:

> The reigns of women are commonly obscured by marriage; their praises and actions passing to the credit of their husbands; whereas those that continue unmarried have their glory entire and proper to themselves. In her case this was more especially so; inasmuch as she had no helps to lean upon in her government, except such as she herself provided ... no kinsmen of the royal family, to share her cares and support her authority. And even those whom she herself raised to honour she so kept in hand and mingled one with the other, that while she infused into each the greatest solicitude to please her, she was herself ever her own mistress.[36]

As Elizabeth herself reportedly told the Earl of Leicester, "I will have here but one Mistress, and no Master" (Naunton, *Fragmenta Regalia*, p. 17). To be her own mistress, her own master, the Queen had to be everyone's mistress and no one's. Lawrence Stone wryly remarks that "things were not easy for lovers at the Court of Elizabeth." She frequently intervened in the personal affairs of those who attended her, preventing or punishing courtships and marriages not to her liking. As Stone points out, "her objections were based partly ... on a desire to preserve the Court as the focus of interest of every English man and woman of note. She was afraid, with reason, that marriage would create other interests and responsibilities, and replace the attendance of both husband and wife upon her Court and upon herself."[37] It was this royal politics of centripetal force that Spenser imaged in the proem to his "legend ... of Courtesie":

> Then pardon me, most dreaded Soveraine,
> That from yourself I doe this vertue bring,
> And to your self doe it returne againe:
> So from the Ocean all rivers spring,
> And tribute backe repay as to their King.
> Right so from you all goodly vertues well
> Into the rest, which round about you ring,
> Faire Lords and Ladies, which about you dwell,
> And doe adorne your Court, where courtesies excell.
> (*FQ*, vi.Proem.7)

In a royal household comprising some fifteen hundred courtiers and retainers, the Queen's female entourage consisted of merely a dozen ladies of high rank – married or widowed – and half a dozen maids of honor from distinguished families, whose conduct was of almost obsessive interest to their mistress. Sir John Harington, the Queen's godson and an acute observer of her ways, wrote in a letter that "she did oft aske the ladies around hir chamber, If they lovede to thinke of marriage? And the wise ones did conceal well their liking hereto; as knowing the Queene's judgment in this matter." He goes on to relate an incident in which one of the maids of honor, "not knowing so deeply as hir fellowes, was asked one day hereof, and simply said – 'she had thought muche about marriage, if her father did consent to the man she lovede.' " Thereupon, the Queen obtained the father's consent that she should deal as she saw fit with her maid's desires. "The ladie was called in, and the Queene tould her father had given his free consente. 'Then, replied the ladie, I shall be happie and please your Grace.' – 'So thou shalte; but not to be a foole and marrye. I have his consente given to me, and I vow thou shalte never get it into thy possession … I see thou art a bolde one, to owne thy foolishnesse so readilye.' "[38] The virgin Queen threatened her vestal with the prospect of living a barren sister all her life. Directly, in cases such as this, and indirectly through the operation of the Court of Wards, the Queen reserved to herself the traditional paternal power to give or withhold daughters. Among the aristocracy, marriage was not merely a legal and affective union between private persons but also a political and economic alliance between powerful families; it was an institution over which a careful and insecure monarch might well wish to exercise an absolute control. Behavior which, in the context of Elizabeth's body natural, may have been merely peevish or jealous was, in the context of her body politic, politic indeed.

Elizabeth's self-mastery and mastery of others were enhanced by an elaboration of her maidenhood into a cult of virginity which "allows of amorous admiration but prohibits desire" (Bacon, *In Felicem Memoriam*, p. 460); the displacement of her wifely duties from a household to a nation; and the sublimation of her temporal and ecclesiastical authority into a nurturing maternity. She appropriated not only the suppressed cult of the Blessed Virgin but also the Tudor conception of the Ages of Woman. By fashioning herself into a singular combination of Maiden, Matron, and Mother, the Queen transformed the normal domestic life-cycle of an Elizabethan female into what was at once a social paradox and a religious mystery. Her emblem was the phoenix; her motto, *semper eadem*.[39] Because she was always uniquely herself, Elizabeth's rule was not intended to undermine the male hegemony of her culture. Indeed, the emphasis upon her *difference* from other women may have helped to reinforce it. As she herself wrote in response to Parliament in 1563, "though I can think [marriage] best for a private woman, yet I do strive with myself to think it not meet for a prince" (Neale, *Elizabeth I and Her Parliaments 1559–1581*, p. 127). The royal exception could prove the patriarchal rule in society at large.

Nevertheless, from the very beginning of her reign, Elizabeth's parliaments and counselors urged her to marry and produce an heir. There was a deeply felt and loudly voiced need to insure a legitimate succession, upon which the welfare of the whole people depended. But there must also have been another, more obscure motivation behind these requests: the political nation, which was wholly a nation of men, seems at times to have found it frustrating or degrading to serve a female prince – a woman who was herself unsubjected to any man. Late in Elizabeth's reign, the French ambassador observed that "her government is fairly pleasing to the people, who show that they love her, but it is little pleasing to the great men and nobles; and if by chance she should die, it is certain that the English would never again submit to the rule of a woman" (De Maisse, *Journal*, pp. 11–12). In the 1560s and 1570s, Elizabeth witnessed allegorical entertainments boldly criticizing her attachment to a life of "single blessedness." For example, in the famous Kenilworth entertainments sponsored by the Earl of Leicester in 1575, Diana praised the state of fancy-free maiden meditation and condemned the "wedded state, which is to thraldome bent." But Juno had the last word in the pageant: "O Queene, O worthy queene, / Yet never wight felt perfect blis / But such as wedded beene."[40] By the 1580s, the Queen was past childbearing; Diana and her virginal nymph, Eliza, now carried the day in such courtly entertainments as Peele's *Araygnment of Paris*. Although "as fayre and lovely as the queene of Love," Peele's Elizabeth was also "as chast as Dian in her chast desires."[41] By the early 1590s, the cult of the unaging royal virgin had entered its last and most extravagant phase. In the 1590 Accession Day pageant, there appeared "a Pavilion ... like unto the sacred Temple of the Virgins Vestal."[42] Upon the altar there were presents for the Queen – offerings from her votaries. At Elvetham, during the royal progress of 1591, none other than "the Fairy Queene" gave to Elizabeth a chaplet that she herself had received from "Auberon, the Fairy King" (Nichols, *Progresses and Public Processions*, 3:118–19). From early in the reign, Elizabeth had been directly engaged by such performances: debates were referred to her arbitration; the magic of her presence civilized savage men, restored the blind to sight, released errant knights from enchantment, and rescued virgins from defilement. These social dramas of celebration and coercion played out the delicately balanced relationship between the monarch and her greatest subjects. And because texts and descriptions of most of them were in print within a year of their performance, they may have had a cultural impact far greater than their occasional and ephemeral character might at first suggest.

A *Midsummer Night's Dream* is permeated by images and devices that suggest these characteristic forms of Elizabethan court culture. However, whether or not its provenance was in an aristocratic wedding entertainment, Shakespeare's play is neither focused upon the Queen nor structurally dependent upon her presence or her intervention in the action.[43] On the contrary, it might be said to depend upon her absence, her exclusion. In the third scene of the play, after Titania has remembered her Indian votaress, Oberon remembers his "imperial votaress." He has once beheld

> Flying between the cold moon and the earth,
> Cupid all arm'd; a certain aim he took
> At a fair vestal, throned by the West,
> And loos'd his love-shaft smartly from his bow
> As it should pierce a hundred thousand hearts.
> But I might see young Cupid's fiery shaft
> Quench'd in the chaste beams of the watery moon;
> And the imperial votress passed on,
> In maiden meditation, fancy-free.
> Yet mark'd I where the bolt of Cupid fell:
> It fell upon a little western flower,
> Before milk-white, now purple with love's wound:
> And maidens call it "love-in-idleness".
>
> ...
>
> The juice of it, on sleeping eyelids laid,
> Will make or man or woman madly dote
> Upon the next live creature that it sees.
> (ii.i.156–68, 170–2)

The evocative monologues of Titania and Oberon are carefully matched and contrasted: the fairy queen speaks of a mortal mother from the east; the fairy king speaks of an invulnerable virgin from the west. Their memories express two myths of origin: Titania's provides a genealogy for the changeling and an explanation of why she will not part with him; Oberon's provides an aetiology of the metamorphosed flower which he will use to make her part with him. The floral symbolism of female sexuality begun in this passage is completed when Oberon names "Dian's bud" (iv.i.72) as the antidote to "love-in-idleness." With Cupid's flower, Oberon can make the Fairy Queen "full of hateful fantasies" (ii.i.258); and with Dian's bud, he can win her back to his will. The vestal's invulnerability to fancy is doubly instrumental to Oberon in his reaffirmation of romantic, marital, and parental norms that have been inverted during the course of the play. Thus, Shakespeare's royal compliment re-mythologizes the cult of the Virgin Queen in such a way as to sanction a relationship of gender and power that is personally and politically inimical to Elizabeth.

Unlike the fair vestal, Shakespeare's comic heroines are in a transition between the states of maidenhood and wifehood, daughterhood and motherhood. These transitions are mediated by the wedding rite and the act of defloration, which are brought together at the end of *A Midsummer Night's Dream*: when the newlyweds have retired for the night, Oberon and Titania enter the court in order to bless the "bride-bed" where the marriages are about to be consummated. By the act of defloration, the husband takes physical and symbolic possession of his bride. The sexual act in which the man draws blood from the woman is already implicit, at the beginning of the play, in Theseus' vaunt: "Hippolyta, I woo'd thee with my sword, / And won thy love doing thee injuries." The impending injury is evoked – and dismissed with laughter – in the play-within-the-play which wears away the hours "between our after-supper and bedtime" (v.i.34): Pyramus finds Thisbe's mantle "stain'd with blood," and concludes that "lion vile hath here deflower'd [his] dear" (v.i.272, 281). The image in which Oberon describes the flower's metamorphosis suggests the immanence of defloration in the very origin of desire: "the bolt of Cupid fell / ... Upon a little western flower, / Before milk-white, now purple with love's wound." Cupid's shaft violates the flower when it has been deflected from the vestal: Oberon's purple passion flower is procreated in a displaced and literalized defloration.[44] Unlike the female *dramatis personae*, Oberon's vestal virgin is *not* subject to Cupid's shaft, to the frailties of the flesh and the fancy. Nor is she subject to the mastery of men. Isolated from the experiences of desire, marriage and maternity, she is immune to the pains and pleasure of human mutability. But it is precisely her bodily and mental impermeability which make possible Oberon's pharmacopoeia. Thus, ironically, the vestal's very freedom from fancy guarantees the subjection of others. She is necessarily excluded from the erotic world of which her own chastity is the efficient cause.

Within *A Midsummer Night's Dream*, the public and domestic domains of Elizabethan culture intersect in the figure of the imperial votaress. When a female ruler is ostensibly the virgin mother of her subjects, then the themes of male procreative power, autogeny, and mastery of women acquire a seditious resonance. In royal pageantry, the Queen is always the cynosure; her virginity is the source of magical potency. In *A Midsummer Night's Dream*, however, magical power is invested in the King. Immediately after invoking the royal vestal and vowing to torment the Fairy Queen, Oberon encounters Helena in pursuit of Demetrius. In Shakespeare's metamorphosis of Ovid, "the story shall be chang'd / Apollo flies, and Daphne holds the chase" (II.i.230–1). Oberon's response is neither to extinguish desire nor to make it mutual but to restore the normal pattern of pursuit: "Fare thee well, nymph; ere he do leave this grove / Thou shalt fly him and he shall seek thy love" (II.i.245–6). Perhaps three or four years before the first production of *A Midsummer Night's Dream*, in a pastoral entertainment enacted at Sudeley during the royal progress of 1591, the Queen's presence had changed Ovid's story into an emblem of Constancy. The scenario might be seen as a benevolent mythological transformation of the Queen's sometimes spiteful ways with her maids of honor. Here it was in the power of the royal virgin to undo the metamorphosis, to *release* Daphne from her arboreal imprisonment and to protect her from the lustful advances of Apollo.[45] Unlike Elizabeth, Oberon uses his mastery over Nature to subdue others to their passions. The festive conclusion of *A Midsummer Night's Dream* depends upon the success of a process by which the female pride and power manifested in misanthropic warriors, possessive mothers, unruly wives, and willful daughters are brought under the control of lords and husbands. When the contentious young lovers have been sorted out into pairs by Oberon, then Theseus can invite them to share his own wedding day. If the Duke finally overbears Egeus' will (IV.i.178), it is because the father's obstinate claim to "the ancient privilege of Athens" (I.i.41) threatens to obstruct the very process by which Athenian privilege and Athens itself are reproduced. Hermia and Helena are granted their desires – but those desires have themselves been shaped by a social imperative. Thus, neither for Oberon nor for Theseus does a contradiction exist between mastering the desires of a wife and patronizing the desires of a maiden. In the assertion of an equivalence between the patriarchal family and the patriarchal state, the anomalous Elizabethan relationship between gender and power is suppressed.

In his letters, Sir John Harington wrote of Elizabeth as "oure deare Queene, my royale godmother, and this state's natural mother"; as "one whom I both lovede and fearede too." After her death, he reflected slyly on how she had manipulated the filial feelings of her subjects: "Few knew how to aim their shaft against her cunninge. We did all love hir, for she saide she loved us, and muche wysdome she shewed in thys matter."[46] So much for Elizabeth's maternal strategies. As for her erotic strategies, Bacon provides perhaps the most astute contemporary analysis:

> As for those lighter points of character, – as that she allowed herself to be wooed and courted, and even to have love made to her; and liked it; and continued it beyond the natural age for such vanities; – if any of the sadder sort of persons be disposed to make a great matter of this, it may be observed that there is something to admire in these very things, which ever way you take them. For if viewed indulgently, they are much like the accounts we find in romances, of the Queen in the blessed islands, and her court and institutions, who allows of amorous admiration but prohibits desire. But if you take them seriously, they challenge admiration of another kind and of a very high order; for certain it is that these dalliances detracted but little from her fame and nothing from her majesty, and neither weakened her power nor sensibly hindered her business. (*In Felicem Memoriam*, p. 460)

Bacon appreciates that the Queen's personal vanity and political craft are mutually reinforcing. He is alert to the generic affinities of the royal cult, its appropriation and enactment of the conventions of romance. And he also recognizes that, like contemporaneous romantic fictions, the Queen's romance could function as a political allegory. However, symbolic forms may do more than *represent* power: they may actually help to *generate* the power that they represent. Thus – although Bacon does not quite manage to say so – the Queen's dalliances did not weaken her power but strengthened it; did not hinder her business but furthered it.

By the same token, the Queen's subjects might put the discourse of royal power to their own uses. Consider the extravagant royal entertainment of 1581, in which Philip Sidney and Fulke Greville performed as "Foster Children of Desire."[47] "Nourished up with [the] infective milke" (p. 313) of Desire – "though full oft that dry nurse Dispaier indevered to wainne them from it" (p. 314) – the Foster Children boldly claimed and sought to possess The Fortress of Perfect Beauty, an allegorical structure from within which Elizabeth actually beheld the "desirous assault" (p. 317) mounted against her. The besieged Queen was urged that she "no longer exclude vertuous Desire from perfect Beautie" (p. 314). During two days of florid speeches, spectacular self-displays, and mock combats, these young, ambitious, and thwarted courtiers acted out a fantasy of political demand, rebellion, and submission in metaphors of resentment and aggression that were alternately filial and erotic. They seized upon the forms in which their culture had articulated the relationship between sovereign and subjects: they demanded sustenance from their royal mother, favors from their royal mistress. The nobility, gentlemen, and hangers-on of the court generated a variety of pressures that constantly threatened the fragile stability of the Elizabethan regime. At home, personal rivalries and political dissent might be sublimated into the agonistic play-forms of courtly culture; abroad, they might be expressed in warfare and colonial enterprise – displaced into the conquest of lands that had yet their maidenheads.

The Queen dallied, not only with the hearts of courtiers but with the hearts of commoners, too. For example, in 1600, a deranged sailor named Abraham Edwards sent "a passionate ... letter unto her Majesty," who was then sixty-eight years old. Edwards was later committed to prison "for drawing his dagger in the [royal] presence chamber." The Clerk of the Privy Council wrote to Cecil that "the fellow is greatly distracted, and seems rather to be transported with a humour of love, than any purpose to attempt anything against her Majesty." He recommended that this poor lunatic and lover "be removed to Bedlam."[48] By her own practice of sexual politics, the Queen may very well have encouraged the sailor's passion – in the same sense that her cult helped to fashion the courtly performances and colonial enterprises of courtiers like Sidney or Ralegh, the dream-life of Doctor Forman, the dream-play of Master Shakespeare. This being said, it must be added that the Queen was as much the creature of her image as she was its creator, that her power to fashion her own strategies was itself fashioned by her culture and constrained within its mental horizon.[49] Indeed, in *A Midsummer Night's Dream*, as in *The Faerie Queene*, the ostensible project of elaborating Queen Elizabeth's personal mythology inexorably subverts itself – generates ironies, contradictions, resistances which undo the royal magic. Such processes of disenchantment are increasingly evident in Elizabethan cultural productions of the 1580s and 1590s. The texts of Spenser and other Elizabethan courtly writers often fragment the royal image, reflecting aspects of the Queen "in mirrours more then one" (*FQ*, iii.Proem.5). In a similar way, Shakespeare's text splits the triune Elizabethan cult image between the fair vestal, an unattainable *virgin*; and the Fairy

Queen, an intractable *wife* and a dominating *mother*. Oberon uses one against the other in order to reassert male prerogatives. Thus, the structure of Shakespeare's comedy symbolically neutralizes the forms of royal power to which it ostensibly pays homage. It would be an over-simplification and a distortion to characterize such cultural process merely as an allegorical encoding of political conflict. The spiritual, maternal, and erotic transformations of Elizabethan power are not reduceable to instances of Machiavellian policy, to intentional mystifications. Relationships of power and dependency, desire and fear, are inherent in both the public and domestic domains. Sexual and family experience were invariably politicized; economic and political experience were invariably eroticized: the social and psychological force of Elizabethan symbolic forms depended upon a thorough conflation of these domains.

V

Differences within the courtly and fairy groups of *A Midsummer Night's Dream* are structured principally in terms of gender and generation. When Bottom and his company are introduced into the newly harmonized courtly milieu in the final scene, the striking difference *between* groups overshadows the previously predominant differences *within* groups.[50] Like Bottom, in his special relationship to Titania, the mechanicals are presented collectively in a child-like relationship to their social superiors. (They characterize themselves, upon two occasions, as "every mother's son" [i.ii.73; iii.i.69]; however, they hope to be "made men" [iv.ii.18] by the patronage of the Duke.) But differences of gender and generation have now been reorganized in terms of a difference which is at once social and theatrical: a difference between common artisan-actors and the leisured elite for whom they perform. In the mechanicals' play, *A Midsummer Night's Dream* internalizes and distances its relationship to traditions of amateur and occasional dramatic entertainment. And in the attitudes of the play-within-the-play's courtly audience, *A Midsummer Night's Dream* internalizes and distances its relationship to the pressures and constraints of aristocratic patronage. By incorporating and ironically circumscribing it, Shakespeare's professional theatre implicity repudiates Theseus' attitude toward the entertainers' art: that performances should serve only as an innocuous distraction from princely cares or as a gratifying homage to princely power.[51] In this dramatic context, Duke Theseus is not so much Queen Elizabeth's *masculine* antithesis as he is her *princely* surrogate.

The much-noted "metadrama" of *A Midsummer Night's Dream* – its calling of attention to its own artifice, its own artistry – analogizes the powers of parents, princes, and playwrights; the fashioning of children, subjects, and plays. Shakespeare's text is a cultural production in which the processes of cultural production are themselves represented; it is a representation of fantasies about the shaping of the family, the polity, and the theater. When Oberon blesses the bride-beds of "the couples three" (v.i.393), he metaphorizes the engendering of their offspring as an act of *writing*: "And the blots of Nature's hand / Shall not in their issue stand" (v.i.395–6). And when Theseus wryly describes the poet's "fine frenzy" (v.i.12), the text of *A Midsummer Night's Dream* obliquely represents the parthenogenetic process of its *own* creation:

And as imagination bodies forth
The forms of things unknown, the poet's pen
Turns them to shapes, and gives to airy nothing
A local habitation and a name.

(v.i.14–17)

That the dramatic medium itself is thematized in Shakespeare's play does not imply a claim for the self-referentiality of the aesthetic object or the aesthetic act. On the contrary, it implies a claim for a dialectic between Shakespeare's profession and his society, a dialectic between the theatre and the world.[52] In its preoccupation with the transformation of the personal into the public, the metamorphosis of dream and fantasy into poetic drama, *A Midsummer Night's Dream* does more than *analogize* the powers of prince and playwright: it dramatizes – or, rather, *meta*-dramatizes – the relations of power *between* prince and playwright. To the extent that the cult of Elizabeth informs the play, it is itself transformed within the play. The play bodies forth the theater poet's contest, not only with the generativity of Elizabethan mothers but with the generativity of the royal virgin; it contests the princely claim to cultural authorship and social authority. *A Midsummer Night's Dream* is, then, in a double sense, a *creation* of Elizabethan culture: for it also creates the culture by which it is created, shapes the fantasies by which it is shaped, begets that by which it is begotten.[53]

Notes

1   *A Midsummer Night's Dream* (*MND*), v.i.7–8, 4–6. All quotations will follow *The Arden Shakespeare* edition of *MND*, ed. Harold F. Brooks (London, 1979), and will be cited in the text by Act, scene, and line. Quotations from other Shakespearean plays follow the texts in *The Riverside Shakespeare*, G. Blakemore Evans, textual ed. (Boston, 1974).

2   The character of cultural practices as at once constituted and constituting, structured and structuring, has been provocatively discussed from a variety of perspectives in recent social theory. Now Fredric Jameson challenges us to rewrite "the literary text in such a way that the latter may itself be seen as a rewriting or restructuration of a prior historical or ideological *subtext*, it being understood that that 'subtext' is not immediately present as such, not some common-sense external reality ... but rather must itself always be (re)constructed after the fact ... The symbolic act therefore begins by generating and producing its own context in the same moment of emergence in which it steps back from it, taking its measure with a view toward its own projects of transformation. The whole paradox of what we have called the subtext may be summed up in this, that the literary work or cultural object, as though for the first time, brings into being that very situation to which it is also, at one and the same time, a reaction. It articulates its own situation and textualizes it" (*The Political Unconscious* [Ithaca, NY, 1981], pp. 81–2). The present essay explores how the text of *MND* restructures its ideological subtext.

3   Paul A. Olson, "*A Midsummer Night's Dream* and the Meaning of Court Marriage," *English Literary History*, 24 (1957), 95–119 [hereafter *ELH*]. Olson is not concerned with the social realities of Elizabethan court marriage (which will be touched on below) but with prescriptive Renaissance theories of marriage and gender, theories toward which his own perspective is wholly uncritical. For an ahistorical feminist reading of the play as an affirmation of "patriarchal order and hierarchy," see Shirley Nelson Garner, "*A Midsummer Night's Dream*: 'Jack shall have Jill; / Nought shall go ill'," *Women's Studies*, 9 (1981), 47–63.

4   See Gayle Rubin, "The Traffic in Women: Notes on the 'Political Economy' of Sex," in *Toward an Anthropology of Women*, ed. Rayna R. Reiter (New York, 1975), pp. 157–210. Among numerous other studies, see the following theoretical overviews: Ellen Ross and Rayna Rapp, "Sex and Society: A Research Note from Social History and Anthropology," *Comparative Studies in Society and History*, 23(1981), 51–72; and J. S. La Fontaine, "The Domestication of the Savage Male," *Man*, n. s. 16(1981), 333–49. A sense of the variety and complexity of sex / gender systems can be gained from two recent ethnographic collections: *Nature, culture and gender*, ed. Carol P. MacCormack and Marilyn Strathern (Cambridge, Eng., 1980); and *Sexual Meanings: The Social Construction of Gender and Sexuality*, ed. Sherry B. Ortner and Harriet Whitehead (Cambridge, Eng., 1981). For an introduction to the construction of one gender in European intellectual history, see Ian Maclean, *The Renaissance Notion of Woman* (Cambridge, Eng., 1980).

5   Quoted from manuscript in A. L. Rowse, *The Case Books of Simon Forman* (London, 1974), p. 31.

6   Excerpts from Forman's autobiography, diaries, and notes are printed in Rowse, *Case Books*, pp. 272–307. I quote from pp. 273, 276.

7   See C. L. Barber, "The Family in Shakespeare's Development: Tragedy and Sacredness," in *Representing Shakespeare*, ed. Murray M. Schwartz and Coppélia Kahn (Baltimore, 1980), pp. 188–202; quotation from p. 196.

8   Compare Arthur F. Marotti, "Countertransference, the Communication Process, and the Dimensions of Psychoanalytic Criticism," *Critical Inquiry*, 4: 3 (Spring 1978), 471–89; p. 486: "A sociocultural system not only inculcates certain ideals, values, sublimations – that is, superego and ego formations – but also … the very shapes of ('instinctive') desire and need … Cultural style, like personal style, has superego, ego, and id dimensions. Its ordering principle operates on an unconscious level."

9   André Hurault, Sieur de Maisse, *Journal* (1597), trans. and ed., G. B. Harrison and R. A. Jones (Bloomsbury, 1931), pp. 25–6.

10 "Extracts from Paul Hentzner's Travels in England, 1598," in *England as seen by Foreigners in the Days of Elizabeth & James the First*, ed. William Brenchley Rye (1865; rpt., New York, 1967), pp. 104–5.

11 In Spenser's description of the matronly Charissa, "Her necke and breasts were ever open bare, / That ay thereof her babes might sucke their fill" (*FQ*, 1.10.30). *The Faerie Queene* is quoted from the often-reprinted *Oxford Standard Authors* edition of Spenser's *Poetical Works*, ed. J. C. Smith and E. de Selincourt (Oxford, 1912), and is cited by book, canto, and stanza; in quotations from this and other Elizabethan texts, I have silently modernized obsolete typographical conventions. The female pelican is said to pierce her breast in order to feed or revive her young. The so-called Pelican Portrait of Queen Elizabeth (ca. 1575; attrib. to Nicholas Hilliard) is reproduced in Roy Strong, *The English Icon: Elizabethan and Jacobean Portraiture* (London, 1969), p. 161, which includes a detail of the pendant.

12 Sir Robert Naunton, *Fragmenta Regalia* (written ca. 1630; printed 1641), ed. Edward Arber (1870; rpt., New York, 1966), p. 51. George Puttenham expresses the Queen's metaphorical motherhood in a curious conceit: "Out of her breast as from an eye, / Issue the rayes incessantly / Of her justice, bountie, and might" (*The Arte of English Poesie* [1589], ed. Gladys Doidge Willcock and Alice Walker [Cambridge, Eng., 1936], p. 100).

13 I use this term advisedly, to describe a specific household organization in which authority resides in a male "head": husband, father, and master of servants and apprentices. According to Lawrence Stone, "the period from 1530 to 1660 may … be regarded as the patriarchal stage in the evolution of the nuclear family" (*The Family, Sex and Marriage in England 1500–1800* [New York, 1977], p. 218). In an extended discussion (pp. 123–218, *et passim*), Stone links this stage to the centralization of political authority in England. Also see Gordon J. Schochet, *Patriarchalism in Political Thought* (New York, 1975), pp. 37–98.

14 William Painter, *The Palace of Pleasure* (1575), ed. Joseph Jacobs, 3 vols. (1890; rpt., New York, 1966), vol. 2, pp. 159–61. Future page citations will be to volume 2 of this edition. For a sense of the ubiquity of Amazonian representations in Elizabethan culture, see the valuable survey by

Celeste Turner Wright: "The Amazons in Elizabethan Literature," *Studies in Philology*, 37(1940), 433–56.

15 *An Elizabethan in 1582: The Diary of Richard Madox, Fellow of All Souls*, ed. Elizabeth Story Donno, Hakluyt Society, second ser., no. 47 (London, 1977), p. 183. I owe this reference to Stephen Greenblatt, *Renaissance Self-Fashioning: From More to Shakespeare* (Chicago, 1980), p. 181.

16 The linkage of Amazon, witch, and cannibal exemplifies a logic of inversion ingrained in European categories of thought. It has been suggested recently that sixteenth- and seventeenth-century witchcraft beliefs were a coherent, meaningful, and indeed necessary component of a larger intellectual system based upon principles of hierarchy, opposition, and inversion. This system linked together demonism, political sedition and rebellion, and female misrule as inversions of the divinely sanctioned order in the cosmos, state, and family. See Stuart Clark, "Inversion, Misrule and the Meaning of Witchcraft," *Past & Present*, no. 87 (May 1980), 98–127. It is worth noting that intimations and denials of witchcraft and demonism form a persistent undercurrent in *MND*. Oberon insists that he and Puck "are spirits of another sort" (iii.ii.388) than the damned. However, the play is rich in intertextual allusions to the *female* witches of the classical world: Puck invokes "the triple Hecate's team" (v.i.370); and in its metamorphoses and its descriptions of elemental disorder – in its action and in its language – the play evokes the Meroë of Apuleius and the Medea of Ovid and Seneca. Furthermore, in Ovid's *Metamorphoses*, in two of its three occurrences (*Met.*, 14.382, 438), "Titania" is an epithet for Circe. As exemplars of the demonic – and explicitly sexual – power of women, these witches logically share a place with the Amazons in the man-made sex / gender system of *MND*.

17 It has been suggested recently that "the English Renaissance institutionalized, where it did not invent, the restrictive marriage-oriented attitude toward women that feminists have been struggling against ever since ... The insistent demand for the right – nay, obligation – of women to be happily married arose as much in reaction against women's intractable pursuit of independence as it did in reaction against Catholic ascetic philosophy." See Linda T. Fitz, " 'What Says the Married Woman?' Marriage Theory and Feminism in the English Renaissance," *Mosaic*, 13: 2 (Winter 1980), 1–22; quotations from pp. 11, 18. On the concept of woman-as-property in English social and legal history, see Keith Thomas, "The Double Standard," *Journal of the History of Ideas*, 20 (1959), 195–216.

18 André Thevet, *The newe founde Worlde*, trans. (London: Henrie Bynneman for Thomas Hackett, 1568), p. 102^r.

19 Plutarch, *The Lives of the Noble Grecians and Romanes*, trans. Thomas North (1579), the Tudor Translations, 2 vols. (1895; rpt., New York, 1967), vol. 1, p. 116. Further page references will be to volume 1 of this edition. Plutarch reports that Antiopa (conflated with Hippolyta) was not conquered in an Amazonomachy but was captured by Theseus with "deceit and stealth" (p. 55).

20 Robert W. Dent, "Imagination in *A Midsummer Night's Dream*," *Shakespeare Quarterly*, 15 (1964), 115–29; see p. 116. On the permutations of desire among the lovers of *MND*, see René Girard, "Myth and Ritual in Shakespeare: *A Midsummer Night's Dream*," in *Textual Strategies*, ed. Josué V. Harari (Ithaca, 1979), pp. 189–212. On the relationship of Hermia and Helena, see the discussion in James L. Calderwood, *Shakespearean Metadrama* (Minneapolis, 1971), p. 126.

21 For a detailed analysis, see Louis Adrian Montrose, " 'The Place of a Brother' in *As You Like It*: Social Process and Comic Form," *Shakespeare Quarterly*, 32 (1981), 28–54.

22 Northrop Frye, *A Natural Perspective* (New York, 1965), pp. 73–4.

23 See Joan Bamberger, "The Myth of Matriarchy: Why Men Rule in Primitive Society," in *Woman, Culture and Society*, ed. Michelle Zimbalist Rosaldo and Louise Lamphere (Stanford, 1974), pp. 262–80; esp. pp. 266, 277.

24 Some of the play's (male) critics approve Oberon's actions as undertaken in the best interests of a growing boy and a neurotic mother. Two of the play's most rewarding critics must be included among them: see C. L. Barber, *Shakespeare's Festive Comedy* (Princeton, 1959), pp. 119–62, esp. p. 137; Calderwood, *Shakespearean Metadrama*, pp. 120–48, esp. p. 125.

25 The following discussion is much indebted to J. A. Barnes, "Genetrix : Genitor :: Nature : Culture?" in *The Character of Kinship*, ed. Jack Goody (Cambridge, Eng., 1973), pp. 61–73. On the history of embryological theory, I have found the following useful: F. J. Cole, *Early Theories of Sexual Generation* (Oxford, 1930); Joseph Needham, *A History of Embryology*, 2nd ed., rev. (New York, 1959); Maryanne Cline Horowitz, "Aristotle and Woman," *Journal of the History of Biology*, 9 (1976), 183–213; Peter J. Bowler, "Preformation and Pre-existence in the Seventeenth Century: A Brief Analysis," *Journal of the History of Biology*, 4 (1971), 221–44.

26 *The Problems of Aristotle, with other Philosophers and Phisitions* (London: Arnold Hatfield, 1597), sigs. E3^v–E4^r.

27 For a review and analysis of the play's sources and analogues, see Brooks's edition, pp. lviii–lxxxviii; 129–53; and the notes throughout the text. D'Orsay W. Pearson, " 'Vnkinde' Theseus: A Study in Renaissance Mythography," *English Literary Renaissance*, 4 (1974), 276–98, provides a richly informative survey of Theseus' "classical, medieval, and Renaissance image as an unnatural, perfidious, and unfaithful lover and father" (p. 276).

Many details in the texts of Plutarch and Seneca that have not been considered previously as "sources" for Shakespeare's play are nevertheless relevant to the problem of gender and filiation which seems to me to be central to *MND*. Here I can do no more than enumerate a few of these details. In his *Lives*, Plutarch relates that Theseus was "begotten by stealth, and out of lawful matrimony" (p. 30); that, "of his father's side," he was descended from the "Autocthones, as much to say, as borne of them selves" (p. 30); that, having been abandoned by Theseus on Cyprus, the pregnant Ariadne "dyed ... in labour, and could never be delivered" (p. 48); that, because the negligently joyful Theseus forgot to change his sail as a sign of success upon his return from Crete, his father Egeus, "being out of all hope evermore to see his sonne againe, tooke such a griefe at his harte, that he threw him selfe headlong from the top of a clyffe, and killed him selfe" (p. 49).

In Seneca, as in Plutarch, the mother of Hippolytus is named Antiopa; Shakespeare's choice of the alternative – Hippolyta – obviously evokes Hippolytus, thus providing an ironic context for the royal wedding and the blessing of the bridal bed. (Similarly, the choice of the name of Egeus for the Athenian patriarch whose will is overborne by Theseus effects a displacement within Shakespeare's comedy of Theseus' negligent parricide.) Seneca's *Hippolytus* emphasizes Theseus' abuse of women – by this time, he has killed Antiopa / Hippolyta, married Phaedra, and gone off to the underworld to rape Persephone – and also gives voice to his victims in the invective of Phaedra. Hippolytus, as Phaedra's *nutrix* reminds him, is the only living son of the Amazons (577; here and following, *Seneca's Tragedies* are cited by line numbers from the Latin text in the Loeb edition, ed. F. J. Miller). In his very misogyny – his scorn of marriage, and his self-dedication to virginity, hunting, and the cult of Diana – Hippolytus proves himself his mother's son; he is "*genus Amazonium*" (231). Hippolytus reminds Phaedra that she has come from the same womb that bore the Minotaur; and that she is even worse than her mother, Pasiphae (688–93). At the end of the play, Theseus' burden is to refashion ("*fingit*") his son from the "*disiecta ... membra*" of his torn body (1256–70). Now a filicide, as well as a parricide and uxoricide, Theseus has perverted and destroyed his own house (1166).

Seneca's *Medea* is clearly relevant to the subtext of *MND* in its domestic violence: in Medea's betrayal of her father; in the *sparagmos* of her brother; and, after Jason's unfaithfulness, in her slaughter of their two sons. But Medea also has a significant place in the history of Theseus, as recorded by Plutarch (*Lives*, p. 39) and by Seneca (*Hippolytus*, 696–7): fleeing Corinth after destroying Creusa and her own two boys, Medea sought asylum in Athens with old Egeus, whose power to beget offspring she promised to renew by her magic. Finding that young Theseus had come to Athens in disguise, Medea sought unsuccessfully to trick the suspicious Egeus into poisoning his own son. Thus, as Seneca's Hippolytus points out, Medea has been to his father what Phaedra is to himself: the demonic, barbaric, passionate female who seeks to pervert the bonds between father and son, man and man.

28 See Winfried Schleiner, "*Divina virago*: Queen Elizabeth as an Amazon," *Studies in Philology*, 75 (1978), 163–80.

29 *The Discovery of the Large, Rich, and Beautiful Empire of Guiana* (1596), ed. Sir Robert H. Schomburgk, Hakluyt Society, first ser., no. 3 (1848; rpt., New York, n.d.). References will be to this edition. For a splendid account of the place of this text in Ralegh's courtly fortunes, see Stephen J. Greenblatt, *Sir Walter Ralegh: The Renaissance Man and His Roles* (New Haven, 1973), pp. 99–126.

30 See Natalie Zemon Davis, *Society and Culture in Early Modern France* (Stanford, 1975), p. 130. Davis's own argument is that inversion phenomena may not only act as safety valves which renew the existing structures but as sources of cultural innovation and social change.

31 In the *Letter* to Ralegh that was printed with the first three books of *The Faerie Queene* in 1590, Spenser writes that, "considering [Elizabeth] beareth two persons, the one of a most royall Queene or Empresse, the other of a most vertuous and beautiful Lady" (*Poetical Works*, p. 407), it is necessary to allegorize her various qualities in terms of various fictional personages. On the legal, political, and dramatic aspects of the doctrine that the Queen had a body politic and a body natural, see Marie Axton, *The Queen's Two Bodies* (London, 1977). On the human body as the primary symbolic medium for the articulation of social relations, see the essential studies by Mary Douglas: *Purity and Danger* (London, 1966); and *Natural Symbols* (London, 1970). For a study of the female body strongly influenced by the work of Douglas, see Kirsten Hastrup, "The Semantics of Biology: Virginity," in *Defining Females*, ed. Shirley Ardener (London, 1978), pp. 49–65.

32 Quoted in Paul Johnson, *Elizabeth I: A Study in Power and Intellect* (London, 1974), p. 320. Contemporary representations of the event are quoted and discussed in Schleiner, "*Divina Virago*."

33 Sir Robert Cecil to Sir John Harington, 29 May, 1603, printed in John Harington, *Nugae Antiquae*, 3 vols. (1779; rpt., Hildesheim, 1968), vol. 2, p. 264. On legal and literary representations of gynecocracy in the sixteenth century, see James E. Phillips, "The Background of Spenser's Attitude Toward Women Rulers" and "The Woman Ruler in Spenser's *Faerie Queene*," *Huntington Library Quarterly*, 5 (1942), 5–32 and 211–34, respectively.

34 See J. E. Neale, *Elizabeth I and Her Parliaments 1559–1581* (New York, 1958), pp. 49, 109. Neale prints the full texts of these speeches.

35 See Neville Williams, *Elizabeth, Queen of England* (London, 1967), p. 218.

36 *In Felicem Memoriam Elizabethae* (ca. 1608), in *The Works of Francis Bacon*, ed. James Spedding et al., 15 vols. (Boston, 1860), vol. 11, pp. 425–42 (Latin text), 443–61 (English trans.); quotation from p. 450. Future page citations will be to volume 11 of this edition.

37 See Lawrence Stone, *The Crisis of the Aristocracy 1558–1641* (Oxford, 1965), pp. 605–6. Stone gives numerous examples of the Queen's interventions.

38 Letter to Robert Markham (1606), rpt. in *The Letters and Epigrams of Sir John Harrington*, ed. N. E. McClure (Philadelphia, 1930), p. 124. For details of the royal household, see Williams, *Elizabeth, Queen of England*, pp. 214–30.

39 The policy and iconography of the royal cult are studied in Frances A. Yates, *Astraea* (London, 1975), pp. 29–120, 215–19; Roy Strong, *Portraits of Queen Elizabeth I* (Oxford, 1963); and Roy Strong, *The Cult of Elizabeth* (London, 1977). Also see E. C. Wilson, *England's Eliza* (1939; rpt., London, 1966), for the literary idealizations of the Queen; and Louis Adrian Montrose, " 'Eliza, Queene of Shepheardes,' and the Pastoral of Power," *English Literary Renaissance*, 10 (1980), 153–82, on pastoral metaphors and royal power.

40 I quote the printed text of the Kenilworth entertainment (1576) from *The Complete Works of George Gascoigne*, ed. J. W. Cunliffe, 2 vols. (Cambridge, Eng. 1910), vol. 2, pp. 107, 120.

41 George Peele, *The Aragynment of Paris* (printed 1584), ed. R. Mark Benbow, in *The Dramatic Works of George Peele*, C. T. Prouty, gen. ed. (New Haven, 1970), lines 1172–3. See Louis Adrian Montrose, "Gifts and Reasons: The Contexts of Peele's *Araygnement of Paris*," *ELH*, 47 (1980), 433–61.

42 Described in Sir William Segar, *Honor Military, and Civil* (1602), pp. 197–200; rpt. in John Nichols, *The Progresses and Public Processions of Queen Elizabeth*, 3 vols. (1823; rpt. New York, 1966), 3: 41–50; quotation from Nichols, 3:46. One of the most popular iconographic attributes

of Queen Elizabeth is the sieve, which identifies her with the vestal virgin Tuccia. See Strong, *Portraits of Queen Elizabeth I*, paintings nos. 43–9, pp. 66–9; Yates, *Astraea*, pp. 112–20.

43 Compare G. K. Hunter, *John Lyly: The Humanist as Courtier* (London, 1962), p. 330. Hunter offers an excellent comparison of Shakespeare's technique in *MND* with that of Lyly in his court comedies (pp. 318–30).

44 The change suffered by the flower – from the whiteness of milk to the purple wound of love – juxtaposes maternal nurturance and erotic violence. To an Elizabethan audience, the metamorphosis may have suggested not only the blood of defloration but also the blood of menstruation – and, perhaps, the menarche, which manifests the sexual maturity of the female, the advent of womanhood and potential motherhood. According to popular Elizabethan gynecology, lactational amenorrhea is causally related to lactation, in that mother's milk is a transubstantiation and refinement of menstrual blood: "Why have not women with childe the flowers? ... Bicause that then the flowers turne into milke, and into the nourishment of the childe" (*Problemes of Aristotle*, sig. E5ʳ).

An awareness that the commonest Elizabethan term for menses was "flowers" (see *Oxford English Dictionary*, s. v. "flower," sense 2.b), adds a peculiar resonance to certain occurrences of flower imagery in Renaissance texts. This is especially the case in *MND*, in which flowers are conspicuously associated with female sexuality and with the moon. Consider Titania's observation:

> The moon, methinks, looks with a watery eye,
> And when she weeps, weeps every little flower,
> Lamenting some enforced chastity.
> (III.i.101–3)

The answer to the question, "Why do the flowers receive their name Menstrua, of this word Mensis a moneth?" constitutes a gloss on Titania's speech: "Bicause it is a space of time which doth measure the Moone ... Now the Moone hath dominion over moist things, and bicause the flowers are an humiditie, they take their denomination of the moneth, and are called monethly termes: for moist things do increase as the Moone doth increase, and decrease as she doth decrease" (*Problemes of Aristotle*, sig. E5ʳ). In the quoted passage, Brooks follows previous editors in glossing "enforced" (line 193) as "violated by force" (Brooks, *Arden* ed. of *MND*, p. 62; cf. p. cxxix). However, the opposite reading – "enforced" as compulsory chastity – seems equally possible. (See *Oxford English Dictionary*, s.v. "enforced," sense 1: "That is subjected to force or constraint"; and sense 2: "That is forced upon or exacted from a person; that is produced by force.") In one sense, then, the allusion is to sexual violation; in the other, it is to the injunction against sexual relations during menstruation (Leviticus 20:18; Ezekiel 18:6), which was commonly repeated by sixteenth- and seventeenth-century writers.

I raise the issue of menstrual symbolism here to suggest the degree to which an ambivalent discourse on female sexuality permeates Shakespeare's text. The imagery of the text insinuates that, whatever its provenance in horticultural lore, Oberon's maddening love-juice is a displacement of vaginal blood: a conflation of menstrual blood – which is the sign of women's generative power and of their pollution, their dangerousness to men – with the blood of defloration – which is the sign of men's mastery of women's bodies, of their generative powers and of their dangerousness. For a pertinent analogy to this dramatic process in tribal ritual, see J. S. La Fontaine, "Ritualization of Women's life-crises in Bugisu," in *The Interpretation of Ritual*, ed. J. S. La Fontaine (London, 1972), 159–86. See Patricia Crawford, "Attitudes to Menstruation in Seventeenth-Century England," *Past & Present*, 91 (May 1981), 47–73, for a useful introduction to this significant though neglected subject. Also see Barbara B. Harrell, "Lactation and Menstruation in Cultural Perspective," *American Anthropologist*, 83 (1981), 796–818, for an interesting analysis of the interplay between physiological and cultural factors in the "preindustrial reproductive cycle."

45 The text of the Sudeley entertainment was printed in *Speeches Delivered to Her Majestie this Last Progresse* (1592), rpt. in *The Complete Works of John Lyly*, ed. R. Warwick Bond, 3 vols. (Oxford,

1902), vol. 2, pp. 477–84. For a detailed analysis, see Montrose, " 'Eliza, Queene of Shepheardes,'" pp. 168–80.

46 Letters to Lady Mary Harington (1602) and Robert Markham (1606), rpt. in *The Letters and Epigrams of Sir John Harington*, pp. 96, 123–25.

47 Reprinted in Nichols, *Progresses and Public Processions*, vol. 2, pp. 312–29. Further page references will be to volume 2 of this edition. The performance and its various contexts are discussed in Norman Council, "*O Dea Certe:* The Allegory of the Fortress of Perfect Beauty," *Huntington Library Quarterly*, 39 (1976), 329–42; Louis Adrian Montrose, "Celebration and Insinuation: Sir Philip Sidney and the Motives of Elizabethan Courtship," *Renaissance Drama*, n.s. 8 (1977), 3–35; Richard C. McCoy, " 'Pompes of a Pallace': The Place of *The Four Foster Children of Desire* in Sir Philip Sidney's Career," unpublished ms.

48 W. Waad to Sir Robert Cecil, 3 June 1600, printed in *Calendar of the Manuscripts of … The Marquis of Salisbury … preserved at Hatfield House*, 18 vols. (London: HMSO, 1883–1940), vol. 10, pp. 172–3.

49 For a subtle and far-ranging consideration of this issue, see Greenblatt, *Renaissance Self-Fashioning*. Elizabeth's self-fashionings are discussed on pp. 165–9, 230.

50 Here I can do no more than briefly suggest how this vital aspect of the play impinges upon my immediate subject. The significance of the social dynamic among the play's character-groups is appreciated and analyzed in Elliot Krieger, *A Marxist Study of Shakespeare's Comedies* (London, 1979), pp. 37–69.

51 See Theseus' remarks, v.i.39–41, 90–105.

52 On the thematic significance of poetry and imagination, theatre and dramatic traditions, in *MND*, see Dent, "Imagination in *A Midsummer Night's Dream*"; Calderwood, *Shakespearean Metadrama*, pp. 120–48; David P. Young, *Something of Great Constancy* (New Haven, 1966); J. Dennis Huston, *Shakespeare's Comedies of Play* (New York, 1981), pp. 94–121. On the dialectic between Shakespeare's theatre and his society, see Louis Adrian Montrose, "The Purpose of Playing: Reflections on a Shakespearean Anthropology," *Helios*, n.s. 7: 2 (Winter 1980), 51–74.

53 This essay has benefited from the presentation of earlier and shorter versions to several audiences: The seminar on Marriage and the Family in Shakespeare at the 1980 Convention of The Modern Language Association (Houston, December 1980); The Clark Library Conference on Shakespeare's Renaissance (Los Angeles, November 1981); The Yale University Conference on Renaissance Woman / Renaissance Man (New Haven, March 1982); and colloquia at the Berkeley, San Diego, Santa Barbara, and Santa Cruz campuses of The University of California (April–May 1982). Among the many who have offered encouragement and criticism of earlier versions, I am especially indebted to Janet Adelman, Paul Alpers, Harry Berger, Page du Bois, Stephen Greenblatt, Coppélia Kahn, Roxanne Klein, Steven Knapp, Richard McCoy, Maureen Quilligan, and Leonard Tennenhouse.

Part IX

Materialist Criticism

29 Shakespeare's Theater: Tradition and Experiment   515
    Robert Weimann
30 *King Lear* (ca. 1605–1606) and Essentialist Humanism   535
    Jonathan Dollimore
31 Give an Account of Shakespeare and Education, Showing Why
    You Think They Are Effective and What You Have Appreciated
    About Them. Support Your Comments with Precise References   547
    Alan Sinfield

Cultural materialism in Shakespeare studies came into its own in the 1980s, at about the same time as new historicism, and their emergence was marked by some fairly intense sibling rivalry (see below). Materialist analysis, especially of prose fiction, was hardly a new phenomenon, of course. Its progenitors were mostly European, and the leading voices mostly British: a genealogy would probably begin with Marx and extend to such mid-twentieth-century figures as Louis Althusser and Michel Foucault. These familiar names are responsible for setting forth the methods and vocabulary for studying social institutions and for analyzing strategies of power, instruments which have been adopted by literary critics and transferred, with a slight degree of necessary refitting, to the reading of literary texts. But the term "literary texts" may seem foreign to this kind of critical discourse, since the dismantling of the literary as a separate category is one of the aims of materialist criticism, as of poststructuralism generally. Society itself has become the legible text, with such institutions as the theater or the book trade examined for their roles in maintaining the structures and customs of that society. Even so, there is a discernible heritage to such critical views extending back to the early decades of the twentieth century. And at least some of that early analysis was devoted to early modern drama.

L. C. Knights's *Drama and Society in the Age of Jonson* (1936) is an early example of such studies. Knights broke new ground by investigating the social, political, and economic contexts of the early modern English stage, reading what had sometimes been considered mandarin dramatic texts in relation to the daily concerns of the audiences who paid to see those texts performed. A later and more direct ancestor, the cultural critic Raymond Williams, seems to have been the first to use the term "cultural materialism," employing it in an essay on Marxism and literature. Williams was concerned less specifically with the stage than Knights but even more explicitly with the politics of art, and his writings gradually moved from relatively focused studies of canonical literary texts to much wider considerations of culture, particularly its products and systems of production.[1] The gradual expansion of Williams's vision, especially his increasingly broad sense of what constitutes a suitable object of analysis, allows us to chart the progress through the decades of this important strain of British criticism. Despite his widened scope, however, Williams retained his conviction that language was one of the most revealing indicators of cultural formations; this predisposition is apparent in his *Keywords: A Vocabulary of Culture and Society*, written in the 1970s and published in a revised edition in 1983. This book, along with his many others, exerted an enormous influence on the younger practitioners of cultural materialism, who came to prominence just before Williams's death in 1988.

This glance at how cultural materialism originated and evolved prepares us to understand its concerns, its affiliations, and its reach at the end of the twentieth century. A clear, relatively succinct expression of goals and methods is found in one of the cornerstones of the materialist critical canon, the collection of essays entitled *Political Shakespeare*, edited by Jonathan Dollimore and Alan Sinfield. Seeking explicitly to defy and transform traditional modes of literary criticism, the editors announce their program for change in a foreword to the first edition:

> Our belief is that a combination of historical context, theoretical method, political commitment and textual analysis offers the strongest challenge and has already contributed substantial work. Historical context undermines the transcendent significance traditionally accorded to the literary text and allows us to recover its histories; theoretical method detaches the text from immanent criticism which seeks only to reproduce it in its own terms; socialist and feminist commitment confronts the conservative categories in which most criticism has hitherto been conducted; textual analysis locates the critique of traditional approaches where it cannot be ignored. We call this "cultural materialism."[2]

The declaration of such an unequivocally radical program garnered considerable attention, serving both (a) to excite a number of critics, particularly younger ones, who had been thinking along similar lines but had found little support for their views, and (b) to annoy a number of critics, particularly older ones, who recognized a threat to traditional approaches and feared being unseated by the proponents of this new agenda. The middle of the 1980s saw the publication of a remarkable number of studies committed to some form of materialist criticism: Dollimore's *Radical Tragedy* (1984), John Drakakis's collection of essays entitled *Alternative Shakespeares* (1985), Leonard

Tennenhouse's *Power on Display: The Politics of Shakespeare's Genres* (1986), and a collection of essays that grew out of a seminar at the Fourth International Shakespeare Congress held in Berlin in 1986 and edited by the leaders of that seminar, Jean E. Howard and Marion O'Connor, *Shakespeare Reproduced: The Text in History and Ideology* (1987). These books were unusually successful for academic titles, so much so that *Radical Tragedy* and *Political Shakespeare* were issued in revised editions, and Drakakis published an *Alternative Shakespeares 2.*

The terms of engagement set forth in Dollimore and Sinfield's introduction fairly describe the work of those materialists who study Shakespeare and the early modern English theater. They concern themselves with institutions, especially social and political institutions, early modern structures such as the monarchy, the City and its overseers, the English Church and its opponents, the proto-capitalist economy, schools, various forms of patronage, and other more or less authoritarian enterprises. They also, of course, attend to the business of the theater and the commercial endeavors associated with it, such as the book trade. Put simply, cultural materialists have developed the examples of Williams and Foucault to analyze power in its various forms – political, social, economic, theatrical.

This concern with power manifests itself especially in attention to the class system. It is not surprising that cultural materialism found especially hospitable ground in Great Britain, where evidence of class divisions and the traces of formal class structures are usually more visible than in North America. The critical engagement with questions of class indicates the Marxist principles underlying much materialist criticism of Shakespeare: one of the most responsible and influential of materialists is Robert Weimann, the Marxist critic who worked in East Germany before reunification and now teaches in California. Weimann had begun to write about the material conditions of the English stage long before anything like a critical school emerged, indeed before some of the later cultural materialists were even born. His work stands in an interesting and rather oblique relation to the other examples of materialist criticism included here and to cultural materialism as a movement: at all times his gaze is on the proletarian, the demotic strain in early modern drama. This emphasis appears in the title of the book from which the excerpt printed below is taken: *Shakespeare and the Popular Tradition in the Theater: Studies in the Social Dimension of Dramatic Form and Function*. The contributions of Weimann and other more "traditional" materialists will be somehow familiar to most readers acquainted with contemporary Shakespeare studies, an extension of less radical forms of historical inquiry.

The more unusual branch of materialist criticism is that which examines the Shakespearean text not only in its own institutional context but also in relation to modern versions of such institutions. In other words, the critic looks at the way early modern texts are appropriated for ideological purposes, not only in their own period but in others as well, especially the era of the critic. In the words of Jonathan Gil Harris, "cultural materialists 'historicize' Shakespeare by looking at (say) present-day national heritage brochures, military advertisements, or stage productions ... cultural materialists tend to view [history] as a diachronic continuum that includes the present location of the critic."[3] Such aims and styles are evident in the title of Alan Sinfield's essay reprinted here, "Give an Account of Shakespeare and Education, Showing Why You Think They Are Effective and What You Have Appreciated About Them. Support

Your Comments with Precise References." Not only does it mockingly refer to a conventional examination question, but it also announces the critic's concern with the uses of Shakespeare by the British educational establishment.

It is also important to mention, although space forbids considering the subject at any length, the uneasy relation between new historicism and cultural materialism. Both schools share many of the same ancestors, notably Marx, Williams, Foucault, and a few others; and as early articles and books made their way into the discourse, the two fields appeared to be related branches of the same critical project, the distinctions between them less important than their shared concerns. Shortly, however, materialists began to accuse new historicists of political quietism, new historicists responded with vigorous defenses, and disagreements between the exponents of each camp became more profound during the last fifteen years of the twentieth century.

Notes

1　See *The Penguin Dictionary of Critical Theory*, ed. David Macey (London: Penguin Books, 2000), p. 76.
2　*Political Shakespeare: Essays in Cultural Materialism*, ed. Jonathan Dollimore and Alan Sinfield (Ithaca, NY: Cornell University Press, 1985), p. vii.
3　"Materialist Criticisms," in *Shakespeare: An Oxford Guide*, ed. Stanley Wells and Lena Cowen Orlin (Oxford: Oxford University Press, 2003), p. 481.

29

Shakespeare's Theater: Tradition and Experiment

Robert Weimann

1   The Platform Stage

The many links between Elizabethan drama and society must be kept in mind when we consider the physical shape and theatrical conventions of Shakespeare's stage. Like the origin of the Elizabethan public theater, its mode of production must be seen in light of the social and cultural synthesis that characterized the highly transitional balance of class forces in the late Tudor period. No longer based on a corporate social structure (like the German Shrovetide play or the Parisian *confrères*), the Elizabethan theater was a national institution in which native popular traditions were enlarged and enriched in many ways by a variety of elements, most notably, Renaissance ideology. It was precisely because the London theater was *not* exclusively a courtly, academic, or guild theater that there developed a stage and a mode of production the theatrical possibilities of which were as diverse as the models and sources from which it drew. Among these were not only the traditional scaffold and innyard stages used by itinerant players, and the medieval pageant wagons, which could also have been arranged for performance in-the-round, but also contemporary *tableaux vivants*, and thus, indirectly, Renaissance visual arts.

Recent research into Elizabethan stage conditions has revealed the limitations of all reductive approaches to Shakespeare's theater and refuted the late Romantic conception of a simple and unsophisticated wooden stage. The so-called "thatch-and-groundling approach" has gradually lost favor since G. R. Kernodle cast new light on the public theater by pointing out its debt to the tradition of the *tableaux vivants* and the Dutch Rederijk theater.[1] Similarly, more recent research by C. Walter Hodges, Richard Southern, Richard Hosley, Glynne Wickham, and others reveals not one standard public theater, but a variety of theatrical institutions.

The most important of the many revisions of the older reconstruction of the Eliza-bethan stage (as designed, for example, by J. Q. Adams) concerns the existence of an "inner stage," an acting area recessed into the rear stage wall and separated from the main stage by a curtain. Theater historians like A. H. Thorndike and, of course, Adams placed many of Shakespeare's indoor scenes on this inner stage, assuming that it would have facilitated an uninterrupted performance and would have supported the illusionary effect of important scenes and scene changes. Detailed study of the thirty extant plays that were performed in Shakespeare's Globe theater between 1599 and 1608 does not, however, support this assumption. In twenty plays with indoor scenes there is no indication that an inner stage was, or even could have been, used. In only nine of the plays does the text indicate the discovery of a character (and in only three cases a group of two or three figures) concealed by a curtain. In each of these cases, however, the "discovery" serves a tableau effect and not a fully mimetic illusion of speech and action. The space needed would not have been more than four feet in depth; and so, if the rear wall in the Globe theater was anything like the wall in van Buchel's sketch of the Swan theater, the effects indicated in these nine plays could have been achieved by using a doorway.[2]

George F. Reynolds's pioneering study of stage practices in the popular Red Bull supports this reconsideration of the "inner stage." In the Red Bull, curtained movable scaffolds or a scaffoldlike house may have been used instead of an inner stage: "perhaps the 'rear stage' was not a real and permanent structural part of the stage but itself only a removable structure, more non-committal in its outward appearance than shop or tent, but just as easily brought in and removed."[3] This suggestion, reinforced by practical theatrical experiments by Bernard Miles and others,[4] has made possible entirely new visualizations of important Shakespearean scenes, such as Hodges's convincing reconstruction of the death scene in *Antony and Cleopatra* (iv.xiv).[5]

The implications of this revised attitude toward the "inner stage" are quite far reaching and lead almost as a matter of course to a reconsideration of traditional notions about the "upper stage." A little more than a generation ago scholars like E. K. Chambers and W. J. Lawrence had reconstructed the upper stage as part of the upper gallery forming a roof over the inner stage. J. C. Adams placed no fewer than five of the twenty-six scenes in *King Lear*, and an average of about one-fifth of the scenes in Shakespeare's other plays, on this upper stage (in a chamber that could be separated from the gallery).[6] Later and more detailed studies by Reynolds, Hosley, T. J. King, and others indicate, however, a far smaller number of upper stage scenes: of 419 scenes in twenty-two of the plays performed by Shakespeare's troupe, only eleven are undoubt-edly upper stage scenes.[7] But, as in the Red Bull, the balcony was not essential in these scenes to insure nonstop acting for the sake of illusion. As Reynolds points out, the balcony "was never used to fill in pauses in action on the front stage."[8] And even in the rare cases in which the upper stage was used – as a city wall, a balcony or a window – the scene enacted there was short, with little movement, and so closely connected with what was happening on the front stage that speakers generally stood at the edge or railing and not in the interior (which certainly made their speeches more audible).

Similarly, King demonstrates that out of 276 plays considered only forty-five required "an acting place above the stage." But even then "above" or "aloft" usually served as "an observation post from which one or two actors comment on, or converse with, actors down on the main stage." Consequently, this "above" acting area "should … be considered as an auxiliary to the main stage rather than a distinct and separate 'upper stage.' " As Richard Hosley suggests, then, since the same space was used by spectators and was obviously of minor importance if used only about once in a play, the term "upper stage" seems "rather inappropriate and in some respects misleading."[9]

To this date interest in the workings of the upper or the disputed inner stage has made it easy for critics to underestimate the importance and diversity of the front stage. The rapid movement and short scenes so characteristic of Shakespeare's plays were not so much enhanced by movement between inner, upper, and front acting areas as by a continuation of traditional platform stage conventions. The front stage was much more flexible and changeable than has been suggested in the past, for as an acting area it was basically neutral, free of illusion, recognized, even in performance, to be a stage. Scenes were changed and props were shifted in full view of all; and this front, or rather main, stage was used almost without interruption – for indoor as well as outdoor scenes. Such a flexible use of the main stage, surrounded on three or perhaps even four sides by spectators, reflects the constant efforts of the Elizabethan dramatist and actor to keep the play in close touch with the audience's response.

If the inner and upper stages were neither as developed nor essential to the course of the action as had formerly been assumed, it is reasonable that greater attention should be paid to the platform stage. It is easier to understand now why the main acting area was so very large – even by modern standards. Henslowe's contract for the building of the stage at the Fortune theater gives the following measurements: "in length Fortie and Three foote of lawfull assize and in breadth to extende to the middle of the yarde of the saide howse." The platform stage was so large that it could easily have accommo-dated most of the various scenes that have at one time or another been attributed to the inner or upper stage. This implies, of course, that the platform stage was not a homogeneous acting area, but may have used front, middle, rear, or other specific locations to produce a variety of theatrical effects – effects that can best be understood when related to the continuing interplay of *locus* and "place," *mimesis* and ritual, in the tradition of the popular theater.

In order fully to judge the scenic function of the main stage we must re-examine its original relation to the rear stage wall. As the sketch of the Swan theater seems to show, the entire tiring-house facade was probably not connected to the galleries or circular building at all. The circular building and the tiring-house seem to have been separate structures, probably separate in origin.[10] The circular building corresponded to the medieval round theater or the arena used for bear-baiting and other popular amuse-ments, but the scaffold set up inside this arena and the tiring-house belonging to it may well have had their origins in the booth stages known to have existed all over Europe.[11] These booth stages were furnished with a scaffoldlike rear structure which, on the continent, developed into the imposing and often richly decorated facade of the Dutch Rederijk theater. Of course such a modern approach to the origins of the Elizabethan stage remains in many ways as hypothetical as the older theories it seeks to revise; but even though reasonable counterarguments can be made, this new reconstruction is supported by facts as well as by practical experiments in the staging of Renaissance drama that have greatly enhanced our understanding of Shakespeare's plays.

Since downstage acting brought the actor so far into the midst of his audience, it is conceivable that the pit, or the yard, which had no chairs or benches, might also have been used as an acting area. If only for its sensational effect, it is reasonable to suppose (as Hodges does) that some amount of acting was done in the yard.[12] But while Hodges only suggests the possibility that messengers and riders on horseback may have entered in this way, precedents in the older theater have already demonstrated the theatrical effect achieved when an actor entered in the midst of the audience. This was the case in the mysteries, where "Erode ragis in the pagond and in the strete also", and in moralities, where the Vice appeared in the yard or sported with those around him. Appearances of this sort may indeed have been sensational, but they possessed more than what Hodges called a "stunt value." Underlying this mode of acting were traditional architectural configurations and conventions of stagecraft with which Shakespeare was almost certainly familiar. (For such a familiarity it was not absolutely necessary for him to have seen the Herod scenes in Coventry, but as J. Q. Adams pointed out, it is most likely that he did.)[13]

Acting in the pit is known to have taken place in *Henry VIII*, where the porter pushes through the spectators to make room for a procession (v.iv).[14] And while critics such as J. W. Saunders conjecture an appearance in the yard in Act II, scene i of *Romeo and Juliet* and Act V, scene ii of *Antony and Cleopatra*, Allardyce Nicoll made the more general suggestion that the stage direction "pass over the stage," found in numerous texts, does not, as was hitherto assumed, mean to move between the doors in the rear stage wall, but from the pit, across the stage, and back into the pit. The starting and finishing points of this passage over the stage might then be the "ingressi" clearly marked in the Swan drawing, and might well have been connected to the rear stage structure.[15]

Although this last suggestion cannot be conclusively proved, when juxtaposed with the other revisions discussed here it confirms the likelihood that the architecture and stagecraft of the Elizabethan public theater were closer in appearance and structure to the native popular theater than critics have been willing to admit. A corollary to this view would posit that the origin of the English picture-frame stage is not to be found in the doubtful inner stage of Shakespeare's theater, but must be sought in the aristocratic theater of the Italian Renaissance court which made its mark on coterie and court stages in England and the stage settings created by Inigo Jones and later Restoration producers. This, and not the Elizabethan inner stage, explains the advent of the modern proscenium stage, its painted backdrops and visual effects.[16]

In explaining the variability of the platform stage, even as it was modified by humanist and Renaissance influences, it is best to recur to the traditional interplay between *platea* and *locus*, between neutral, undifferentiated "place" and symbolic location. Such an interplay accommodates action that is both nonillusionistic and near the audience (corresponding to the "place") and a more illusionistic, localized action sometimes taking place in a discovery space, scaffold, tent, or other *loci* (corresponding to the medieval *sedes*). Between these extremes lay the broad and very flexible range of dramatic possibilities so skillfully developed by the popular Renaissance dramatist.

While Inigo Jones's lavish Italianate scenery was designed to catch the eye and present what was clearly an idealized imitation of nature, the customs of the traditional popular theater presupposed a collaboration between dramatist and audience in the creation and visualization of dramatic setting. In accordance with this, the relationship between the production and the reception of plays in the popular theater was very close indeed. The proximity of actor and audience was not only a physical condition, it was at once the foundation and the expression of a specific artistic endeavor. Unlike the theater of the subsequent three hundred years, the actor–audience relationship was not subordinate, but a dynamic and essential element of dramaturgy. For the Elizabethan playgoer the drama was more than a play taking place on a stage separated from the audience; it was an event in progress in which good listening and watching were rewarded "by a sense of feeling part of the performance."[17]

In Shakespeare's youth the popular actor, especially the comedian with his extemporal wit, performed not so much *for* an audience as *with* a community of spectators who provided him with inspiration and, as it were, acted as a chorus. Such was the case with Richard Tarlton: "it was his custome for to sing extempore of theames given him."[18] The spectator who challenged the actor had the weight of the audience behind him; collectively, they were collaborators in and judges of an elementary theatrical process. The audience was both the challenger and the challenged; even when pelted with apples Tarlton countered with a suitable couplet, just as he answered criticisms from the audience or from his partner in dialogue with nimble wit and wordplay.[19]

The separation of the audience into groups based on rank was not traditional: it was new in Tarlton's and even in Shakespeare's day. As late as in *Henry VIII* (v.iv) the actual audience was identified with the undifferentiated mass of curious spectators who had come to watch the christening of Elizabeth in front of Henry VIII's palace – an indiscriminate fusion of the audience that Beaumont and Fletcher and other coterie dramatists would have frowned upon. In this way the fictive spectators and the actual audience merged and became a vital link between play and real life:

The palace yard.
Noise and tumult within. Enter Porter *and his* Man.

Port: ... You must be seeing christenings? Do you look for ale and cakes here, you rude
      rascals?
Man: Pray, sir, be patient; 'tis as much impossible,
      Unless we sweep 'em from the door with cannons,
      To scatter 'em as 'tis to make 'em sleep
      On May-day morning; which will never be.
      We may as well push against Paul's as stir 'em.
Port: How got they in, and be hang'd?
Man: Alas, I know not: how gets the tide in?

(v.iv.8–16)

Probably speaking from the pit, the Porter draws the audience into the play by pushing them aside to make room for the procession. "An army cannot rule 'em," he says to the audience, who by now must have felt a heightened sense of both their relation to the subject of the play and their power as a mass of people unified in a dramatic role that had powerful correlatives in Tudor and, of course, Stuart history.

The traditional readiness and ability of the audience to be drawn into the play which is indicated here is as noteworthy as the willingness of author and actor to speak directly to the audience and to acknowledge basic agreement with its tastes and ideas. These links between the world of the play and the audience's world of experience are further extended in prologue, chorus, and song. Directly and indirectly reinforcing the play–audience relationship, these links illuminate the similarities and differences between dramatic illusion and Elizabethan reality. The world is seen as a stage, the stage, in turn, as an image of the world; and this link between art and society presupposes and fosters a sense of both unity and tension between actor and audience: the play, the product of theatrical activity, and the process of doing it (as well as the process of being involved through watching and listening) have a profound effect on each other. The gain in terms of consciousness does not involve a loss for the reality of its objects.[20]

It was this precariously balanced sense of community in the theatrical experience that gave the popular Renaissance drama its unique mode of production. We can search in vain for the equivalent of the modern stage manager in Shakespeare's theater. The prompter and keeper of the scripts did not have sufficient authority to fill such a position properly; if he was in charge of rehearsals at all, he was certainly not in complete control. The real decisions – choice of plays, procurement of costumes, distribution of roles, etc. – must have been arrived at by agreement within the troupe of actors and shareholders. The Chamberlain's (later the King's) Men were organized along cooperative lines, and even though important decisions could be made by one acting on behalf of the majority, "the ultimate authority was vested solely in the actor-sharers as a group."[21] The principle of joint ownership and joint responsibility accorded fully with the implications and spirit of the Elizabethan theatrical experience. The success and prolonged harmony of Shakespeare's troupe and its most distinguished members testified to the practicability of a collective theatrical and business venture. Too little attention has been paid to the connection between the organization of Shakespeare's troupe and the dramaturgy and artistic principles that made its plays the greatest and most successful experiment in the history of the modern theater.

Most characteristic of this kind of theatrical work was not the virtuoso display of individual talent, but the individual's renunciation of the need to assert himself, and hence the employment of his talent in cooperation with the needs and possibilities of "everyone working in the theater on the joint venture of production."[22] Naturally, the "ability of dramatist and actor to devote themselves to their joint work, which corresponded to the spectators' ability to participate creatively, presupposes common thought and common feeling";[23] in the words of Alfred Harbage, "Shakespeare wanted to say what his audience wanted him to say." Such was the delicate balance between dramatist, actor, and audience. Shakespeare never disingenuously catered to the audience or relied on purely sensational effects in production primarily because of "his sense of identity with and responsibility to those thousands of other men who honored him with their trust."[24] To this audience Shakespeare spoke directly, for they were the "gentles all" to whom he referred in the Prologue to *Henry V* in the inspiring speech of the Chorus:

> And let us, ciphers to this great accompt,
> On your imaginary forces work.

Here the great dramatist and the actor modestly subordinate themselves to the process of consciousness shared by the audience; and through this communal form of experience, where hopefully with "humble patience" the play may be "Gently" heard and "kindly" judged, the world of the play swells to encompass the most complex realities of political experience. "Suppose that you have seen … O! do but think … Follow, Follow! Grapple your minds … Work, work your thoughts … Behold …" (Chorus, III). Even the slowest and least literate in the audience should be able to follow along: "Vouchsafe to those that have not read the story / That I may prompt them …" (Chorus, V). Thus Shakespeare deliberately raises the level of awareness of his unread spectators; and in this sense he is truly "Shakespeare, the plebeian driller," as Tatham wrote in his 1641 poem to Richard Brome.[25] At any rate, Shakespeare fulfills the end of what Ben Jonson described as a kind of "spearshaking" art (à la Pallas Athena); for Shakespeare here is recalled in his own unique role of popular educator:

> In each of which, he seems to shake a Lance,
> As brandish't at the eyes of Ignorance.

The social consciousness behind the Shakespearean vision was not destructively aimed against plebeian narrowmindedness and inconstancy, but usually served as a means of conquering or challenging the kind of "Ignorance" that was the source of both.[26] …

Figurenposition: The Correlation of Position and Expression

Shakespeare used popular audience contact and related elements of traditional platform stagecraft to such varying degrees and in such variable ways that it is difficult to formulate even general observations about the nature and function of popular conventions in his plays. A number of Shakespeare's characters stand out, however, because they draw so clearly from popular tradition or present new ways in which traditional practices were adapted to new dramatic forms and functions. This group of characters, who share little in common with respect to social class, psychology, and length or importance of role, can be considered as a group provided we shift our attention from the more speculative concerns of character analysis to a more objective understanding of *Figurenposition* – the actor's position on the stage, and the speech, action, and degree of stylization associated with that position.

An admittedly incomplete list of these characters would include Launce and his friend Speed, most of the other Shakespearean clowns, the porters in *Macbeth* and *Henry VIII*, the gravediggers in *Hamlet*, Bottom in *A Midsummer Night's Dream*, the nurse in *Romeo and Juliet*, Richard Gloucester, Iago, the Fool, and, partly, Edmund in *King Lear*, Falstaff, Thersites, Apemantus, and – with some reservations – Aaron in *Titus Andronicus*, the Bastard Falconbridge in *King John*, and Autolycus in *The Winter's Tale*. Also belonging to this group are characters whose status within court groupings is temporarily changed or weakened as a result of real or feigned madness (Edgar, Lear, Hamlet, and, to a lesser extent, Ophelia). Taken together, these characters can be identified with a stage position that functions to greater and lesser degrees (and not exclusively, of course) as a means of achieving a special role and meaning within the play.

As an example, Apemantus' stage position during the banquet scene in *Timon of Athens* (i.ii) illustrates some of the potentialities of downstage acting on the

Elizabethan platform stage. According to the stage direction "A great banquet served in,"[27] the banqueting table is set up and decked out probably at about the center of the stage. Timon, Alcibiades, and the Senators enter, and "Then comes, dropping after all, Apemantus …" The men of elevated degree sit down at the main table in the middle of the stage, but, at Timon's instruction, the grumbling Apemantus is given "a table by himself" downstage from the banquet table. The action that follows takes place, as the text indicates, on two levels: Timon and his guests delivering high-sounding speeches from the illusionistic area around the banqueting table (a true *locus*), Apemantus speaking usually in such a way that the audience, whom he faces, can hear, but those behind him cannot. Such a reconstruction of the scene in performance explains the flexibility and variability of conventions of speech immediately apparent from the text.

Timon:	I take no heed of thee; … prithee let my meat make thee silent.	
Apemantus:	I scorn thy meat; 'twould choke me, for I should ne'er flatter thee.	
	O you gods, what a number of men eats Timon, and he sees	
	'em not! It grieves me to see so many dip their meat in one	
	man's blood; and all the madness is, he cheers them up too.	40
	I wonder men dare trust themselves with men.	
	Methinks they should invite them without knives:	
	Good for their meat, and safer for their lives.	
	There's much example for't; the fellow that sits next him, now	
	parts bread with him, pledges the breath of him in a divided	
	draught, is the readiest man to kill him: 't has been proved.	
	If I were a huge man, I should fear to drink at meals,	
	Lest they should spy my windpipe's dangerous notes.	50
	Great men should drink with harness on their throats.	
Timon:	My lord, in heart; and let the health go round.	
2 Lord:	Let it flow this way, my good lord.	
Apemantus:	Flow this way? A brave fellow. He keeps his tides well.	
	Those healths will make thee and thy state look ill, Timon.	
	Here's that which is too weak to be a sinner, Honest water,	
	which ne'er left man i'th'mire.	
	This and my food are equals; there's no odds.	
	Feasts are too proud to give thanks to the gods …	60
1 Lord:	Might we but have that happiness, my lord, that you would	
	once use our hearts, whereby we might express some part of	
	our zeals, we should think ourselves for ever perfect.	
Timon:	O, no doubt, my good friends, but the gods themselves have	
	provided that I shall have much help from you: how had you	
	been my friends else? …	90
	O, what a precious comfort 'tis to have so many like brothers	
	commanding one another's fortunes! O joy, e'en made away	
	ere't can be born! Mine eyes cannot hold out water, methinks.	
	To forget their faults, I drink to you.	
Apemantus:	Thou weep'st to make them drink, Timon.	
2 Lord:	Joy had the like conception in our eyes,	110
	And at that instant like a babe sprung up.	
Apemantus:	Ho, ho! I laugh to think that babe a bastard.	

3 Lord: I promise you, my lord, you moved me much.
Apemantus: Much!

Dissociating himself from the feasters at the banquet table, Apemantus neutralizes his own position and so reviews the *locus*-centered action from a perspective something like, but not identical with, that of the traditional "place," from which he seems to say to the audience, "Look at them, and at what their feasting really means." His frequent use of proverb and wordplay, inverting and ironically heightening the meaning of what is said at the banquet table accords nicely with his superior awareness, his choruslike function, and his position on the stage that recalls, in some way, the old Vice (he retains the Vice's scornful "Ho, ho!"). Yet the dramatic effect of this choruslike link between the world of the play and the world of the audience is by no means unsophisticated. Apemantus' keen-edged remarks comment critically on the pomp, the ceremony, and the high-sounding words of the feasters without destroying the theatrical effect of the banquet itself. Thus, two perspectives are presented in such a way that neither alters or obscures the essential integrity of the other. The dual perspective that results acknowledges the sensuous attraction of a dazzling theatrical occasion, but also penetrates the showy surface; for there is in it "a huge zest-for-life and the moral strength to see through its glitter, its hypocrisies, its shame and its rewards."[28]

The process of drawing the audience into the play has become inseparable from the development of a complementary perspective that helps refine basic issues and restructure basic positions; at the same time, the process of differentiating between truth and appearance has become part of the dramatic mode itself. Dramatic images of central conflicts achieve a greater depth when subjected both to mimetic representation and self-expressive enactment; for through this mode the audience is drawn into the tensions between the feast and reality, between words and their meaning, flattery and criticism, enchantment and disenchantment. Of course Apemantus cannot simply tell the audience what to think; his vicious bitterness can hardly be taken at face value. He can, however, through his well-articulated counterperspective, expand the audience's awareness and establish new, perhaps deeper and more comprehensive dramatic tensions that in their turn expand the meaning of the play as a whole.[29]

Actually, Shakespeare seldom kept up this kind of complementary perspective from a *platea* level of acting for very long. Even in *Timon of Athens* Apemantus' downstage position is only temporary; and his choral function obviously suffers when his physical proximity to the audience dissolves in more illusionistic acting. But another example can perhaps illustrate that Shakespeare developed the interplay of *platea* and *locus* positions with great freedom and flexibility by going beyond the more direct modes of correlating the two. In Act V, scene ii of *Troilus and Cressida*, Cressida's meeting with Diomedes is watched from a distance by Troilus and Ulysses, who likewise are being watched by Thersites, as indicated by the direction, "*Enter Troilus and Ulysses, at a distance; after them Thersites.*"[30] The primary level of *mimesis* – Cressida's dialogue with Diomedes – is seen and commented upon by Troilus, but the second level of acting – Troilus' dialogue with Ulysses, which is closer in perspective to the audience than the first but still a *locus*-oriented dialogue – is seen and commented upon by Thersites. Thersites observes not only Cressida's faithlessness, but Troilus' disillusioned response as well. Although all three levels of acting are in turn watched by the spectators, the last is certainly the closest to the audience in terms of speech, stage position, and the scope of action that is seen. Not only does Thersites view most nearly what the audience views (from a neutral "place"), he communicates his impressions not in dialogue or through the illusion of soliloquy, but in unpretentious direct address.

Diomedes:	How, now, my charge!	
Cressida:	Now, my sweet guardian! Hark, a word with you.	
Troilus:	Yea, so familiar!	[*whispers*]
Ulysses:	She will sing any man at first sight.	
Thersites:	And any man may sing her, if he can take her clef; she's noted.	

(v.ii.7–12)

Thersites acts from a more nearly neutralized place where he can watch and hear the others but cannot be watched or heard by them. His wordplay here further underlines his unique position since it sarcastically sounds a realistic "note" that sharply contrasts Troilus' bewildered idealism. After summing up Cressida's exit with a couplet – "A proof of strength she could not publish more, / Unless she said 'My mind is now turn'd whore,' " (v.ii.113–14) – Thersites witnesses the following interchange between Troilus and Ulysses:

Troilus:	Let it not be believed for womanhood!
	Think we had mothers. Do not give advantage
	To stubborn critics, apt without a theme
	For depravation, to square the general sex
	By Cressid's rule; rather think this not Cressid.
Ulysses:	What hath she done, prince, that can soil our mothers?
Troilus:	Nothing at all, unless that this were she.
Thersites:	Will 'a swagger himself out on's own eyes?
Troilus:	This she? No; this is Diomed's Cressida.

(129–37)

Troilus would gladly close his eyes to what he has just seen, but Thersites' comment keeps the audience from doing the same by quashing any sentimental response to, let alone identification with, Troilus' wishful thinking. Like Apemantus and the Vice figure before him, Thersites is a *provocateur* of truth, not a moral judge. And like the characters whose madness, feigned or real, forces dormant truths to the surface, his debunking and skeptical commentary serves to offer viable alternatives to the main or state view of things. In this sense, characters like Apemantus and Thersites help point out that the ideas and values held by the main characters are relative to their particular position in the play,[31] while by projection the audience realizes that this is equally true of the counterperspectives offered by the plebeian intermediaries who occupy a *platea*-like position. This basic recognition of the relationship between character and circumstance, like so much else in Shakespeare, is a profoundly original observation that must be seen in connection with the dramatist's awareness of the tensions between society and the individual, the general, and the particular, from which an essential element of Shakespeare's universality derived.

Although *Love's Labour's Lost* offers unique problems as one of Shakespeare's most stylized works (both formally and linguistically), Act IV, scene iii is remarkable for its clever dramatic treatment of the complexities and potentialities of yet another form of *Figurenposition*. The scene opens not with dialogue but with one of the most boldly punning monologues in Shakespeare's plays. In it, Berowne reveals the true nature of his feelings and brings the audience up to date as to his own activities, but his position is still relatively removed from the audience's perspective. When the King enters, however, Berowne hides; and this is where the sheer comedy of his *Figurenposition* really starts. As the King begins to read, Berowne's new role as eavesdropper necessarily establishes a fundamental link with the audience, a perspective from which he can and does distance himself from the illusion of the represented *locus* (in much the same way as Apemantus and Thersites). When Longaville enters and the King hides, not only does the King, now an eavesdropper also, move closer to the audience in perspective, but Berowne, since he is watching the King watch Longaville, moves closer still to the audience. At this point the scene must have looked something like the scene from *Troilus and Cressida* discussed above. But everyone's perspective is changed once again when Dumaine enters, since Longaville assumes the King's perspective (watching but unaware of being watched), the King Berowne's (watching, aware that a watcher is being watched, but unaware that he himself is being watched), and Berowne another perspective closer still to the audience (so aware of the watcher / watched regression that he speaks freely to those who watch him from the audience). What results is a series of comments spoken in aside whose status relative to the two spatial and verbal extremes – Dumaine's monologue and Berowne's perspective so close to the audience – even the most clear-headed observer could have confused. We might suppose, if this is true, that Shakespeare was not only parodying the inconstancy of the "scholars" (on the level of plot and theme), the ludicrousness of excessive sonneteering (on the level of language), but also, on the level of structure and stagecraft, the traditional interplay between *locus* and *platea*, representation and self-expression.

In light of this effect, it seems possible to reinterpret Berowne's gleeful comment:

> All hid, all hid, an old infant play,
> Like a demie God, here sit I in the skie,
> And wretched fooles secrets heedfully ore-eye.
> (F$_1$ iv.iii.78–80)

From the scenic circumstance it is clear that the first line refers, as most editors acknowledge, to some children's game like hide-and-go-seek. But since the first line is not separated grammatically from the second and third (although the punctuation in modern editions has been changed to suggest that it is) it is possible that the word "play" in the first line is also a pun on "dramatic performance." "An old infant play," then, could refer to the older, but less artistically developed mystery plays (see *OED* "Infant": "In its earliest stage, newly existing, ungrown, undeveloped, nascent ...") in which a demigod (a pun on the fact that the actor who played *Deus* was indeed mortal) sat in the "heavens" looking down upon and judging the actors.[32]

More interesting still is the probability that Berowne, in his successive changes of perspective, moved from a mere "aside" position to a position closer to the audience and above the other actors to accord with his direct address, "here sit I in the skie." Perhaps a good way to visualize his movement would be to picture Berowne climbing one of the downstage columns, such as the ones indicated in the Swan drawing, or some other downstage scaffold structure – although an upstage balcony might have come closer in appearance to the conventional "heavens" associated with the hut-roof area and so heightened the parody of the traditional representation of God in heaven.

But however the scene is reconstructed (and these are only a few of many possibilities) it remains remarkable because it reveals an interest in and a thorough understanding of the potentialities of a stagecraft that hinges on deliberately varied degrees of dissociation from illusionistic action, all within the context of perhaps the most stylized, rhetorical, and intellectually self-conscious play of Shakespeare's career. That Shakespeare used this clever device so early in his career supports and in part explains his more dramatically effective use of similar perspectives in his later works.

The downstage position of Apemantus, Thersites, and in his own uniquely involved way, Berowne, is achieved by the interplay of theatrical and verbal conventions which we have called, for lack of a satisfactory English term, *Figurenposition*. This *Figurenposition* should not be understood only in the sense of the actor's physical position on the stage, but also in the more general sense that an actor may generate a unique stage presence that establishes a special relationship between himself and his fellow actors, the play, or the audience, even when direct address has been abandoned. Hamlet's behavior during the scene in Gertrude's closet already discussed above, for example, is certainly continuous with the action of the play and does not require a second level of acting like that in the banquet scene in *Timon of Athens*. Yet in terms of speech patterns Hamlet and Apemantus have much in common; notably, their emphatic use of couplets and wordplay. As long as Hamlet can set himself apart from the more self-contained dialogue by using couplets, wordplay, and similar illusion-breaking speech patterns, his position relative to his fellow actors remains extremely flexible, and he can fall back on conventions of both *locus* and *platea* stagecraft. His *Figurenposition* is therefore defined verbally as well as spatially, as we see in his first lines, which immediately hint at a unique perspective.

King:	…But now, my cousin Hamlet, and my son –
Hamlet:	[*Aside*] A little more than kin, and less than kind.
King:	How is it that the clouds still hang on you?
Hamlet:	Not so, my lord; I am too much in the sun.
Queen:	Good Hamlet, cast thy nighted colour off,
	And let thine eye look like a friend on Denmark.

(I.ii.64–9)

Hamlet's riddling first line flatly rejects Claudius' assumptions about their relationship, while the second – both a proverb and a pun – is a further clever departure from the King's meaning and point of view. These early breaks with the conventional form and content of continuous dialogue complement Hamlet's unusual relationship with the court already suggested by his entrance after courtiers of lesser degree and by the dark clothes of mourning that only he still wears. Certainly by his speech, but probably also spatially, Hamlet stands apart from his peers as well as his fellow actors through a *Figurenposition* that, while not at all impairing the range of his relations to the play world, establishes a functional link between himself and the audience (almost certainly reinforced by a downstage position).

Still, Hamlet's position on the stage is so complex that the "aside" added by the modern editor hardly does it justice. To begin with, there is really no essential difference between Hamlet's first line, designated "aside," and his second, which can be considered an impertinent reply – "impertinent" in the sense that I have used the word in regard to the Vice's speech. The wordplay in Hamlet's second line reflects and maintains the same dissociation from the *locus* of the court and the same degree of contact with the audience as the first. The functional unity of both lines is much more important than any purely technical differentiation that the modern director or editor might be inclined to make between the literal aside and the impertinent answer. The punning phrase, "I am too much in the sun," links up, of course, with Claudius' question, but after the fashion of the Vice who had a fondness for taking symbolic or metaphoric expressions literally and so inverting them by wordplay. What is misleading about the term "aside" as it refers to the first line, then, is that it suggests that Hamlet and the rest of the court are initially more closely integrated than we might have cause to assume, since "aside" implies that Hamlet is standing with the group and merely turns his head for a moment to make this one remark. This simply skirts the issue by subordinating Hamlet's ambiguous relationship with the court to a single dramatic gesture.

The ritual identification between actor and audience was, to be sure, a thing of the past in Shakespeare's day; and so although Hamlet's rapport with the audience may be linked to the self-introduction characteristic of the figures who traditionally acted on the *platea*, by the time Shakespeare made use of it, it had taken on entirely new forms and served entirely new functions. What has been termed the "extra-dramatic moment" in the Renaissance theater,[33] then, was the product of both tradition and the new Renaissance conception of drama, by which means the connection between action and character became much more effective. Apemantus not only *stands apart* in space, he is, as a character with values, ideas and attitudes, *different* from Timon and his friends. Thersites is not only a sarcastic commentator, he is a character whose fundamental assumptions – like those of Falstaff or Iago – exist outside of the heroic, courtly, or romantic ethos of the main or state action.

In the same way Hamlet's speech patterns and his related *Figurenposition* reveal not only surface differences with his peers, but a more basic kind of contradiction between his position, his character, and theirs. Their difference is first suggested in a highly original form of self-introduction in which traditional *platea*-conventions are transformed into something strange and new. Compared with Hamlet's opening lines (I.ii.65 and 67), the impertinent mode is almost discontinued after the opening "Seems"; the principle of inversion, however, is not surrendered but, as it were, turned inward. Almost unprovoked, he snatches the word "seems" from the lips of the Queen, only to give it an entirely nonpertinent, that is, egocentric meaning and function within the negative terms of his self-definition:

> *Hamlet:*   Seems, madam! Nay, it is; I know not seems.
> 'Tis not alone my inky cloak, good mother,
> Nor customary suits of solemn black,

> Nor windy suspiration of forc'd breath,
> No, nor the fruitful river in the eye,
> Nor the dejected haviour of the visage,
> Together with all forms, moods, shapes of grief,
> That can denote me truly. These, indeed, seem;
> For they are actions that a man might play;
> But I have that within which passes show –
> These but the trappings and the suits of woe.
>
> (I.ii.76–86)

The attributes of his appearance ("inky cloak," "solemn black") are still self-expressed, still self-introduced, but with a difference: they are mentioned only to be dismissed as some outward and insufficient definition of self. They are mere attributes of a potential *role* that cannot "denote me truly." Hamlet's self-introduction is designed to dissociate himself from "actions that a man might *play*." Rejecting "seems" and "play" as modes of his existence, the actor makes his own role problematic. The function of illusion is questioned from within, though not destroyed from without. In other words, the traditional dialectic between representation (playing, seeming) and self-embodiment ("that within which passes show") is used and almost deliberately quoted, but all within the symbolic frame of reference of Renaissance *mimesis*: Hamlet's special *Figurenposition*, his being apart from the *locus* (and the "illusion") of court society, has a real (theatrical) as well as an imaginative (characterizing) significance. And so, spatial position assumes a moral function: the actor's rejection of illusion is turned into the character's honesty "which passes show."

Thus, traditional forms of dramaturgy are turned into modern modes of characterization; the paradox being that Hamlet, who knows no "seems," has to develop his *platea*-like *Figurenposition* within the "seems," that is, the illusionistic frame of the Renaissance play. So he is made to use the most traditional conventions of a *platea*-like embodiment – here, the verbal modes of his antic disposition – as a deliberate "show," a psychological illusion, a strategy for discovery and survival. Hamlet's madness has a function in the play only because he *seems* mad. The resulting contradictions are obvious; but by not suiting the action to the words Hamlet reveals his dilemma to be both one of the theater and one of character. The complexity of the interplay between the two aspects is the measure of the dramatist's achievement in combining innovation and tradition. The continuing contradiction between role and self-expression (which is the virtual *Leitmotiv* of his self-introduction) serves as a basic and most powerful impulse for bringing forth and maintaining the effectiveness of the links between stagecraft and verbal art.

Figurenposition, then, involves a variety of factors and cannot be defined dogmatically in terms of the function of any one set of verbal conventions. No single proverb, pun, instance of wordplay, or use of the aside can be isolated from other elements of plot, character, and language in order to argue the existence of a traditional actor–audience relationship. But if the aside and related verbal conventions go together they usually do more than simply pass on information to the audience. Besides filling the audience in on what has happened, what will happen, or what is being contemplated at the moment, devices like the aside are capable of generating powerful ironies, particularly in the building up of character – where a character's thoughts or how much he knows about his own circumstance (what Bertrand Evans called "artistically graded awareness") can create dramatic tensions in light of what the audience has already seen or heard. When, to some degree or other, verbal conventions such as these break the dramatic illusion and create the so-called "extra-dramatic moment," the effect achieved can be a complex one involving conventions of both acting and characterization, that is, spatial and sometimes moral positions.[34]

And yet, this says very little about the functional relationship between the aside and the kinds of speech considered here: the couplet, the proverb, and wordplay. As our examples suggest, these frequently serve functions similar to earlier forms of exposition and self-introduction. But unlike traditional direct address, Shakespeare's couplets, proverbs, and wordplay are, for the most part, well-integrated into the dialogue, even when they should not necessarily be read as the expression, say, of a poetic spirit or a lively personality. We must recognize, then, that between nonrepresentational speech and psychological realism there is a vast and often misunderstood threshold where the traditional and the modern mix rather freely; and only after the full extent and significance of this mixture is understood can we even approach passages like the Fool's puzzling prophecy in *King Lear* and the more perplexing aspects of Hamlet's "antic disposition."

The transitional role of the couplet or wordplay between realistic dialogue and the convention of audience contact is difficult to establish when what is said relates directly to the action of the play. Hamlet's couplet in iii.iv.178–9, for example, is essentially a veiled prophecy, while just prior to this he aptly sums up his double role as "scourge and minister." A statement likewise related to the course of the action that follows is Hamlet's famous couplet at the end of the first act:

> Let us go in together;
> And still your fingers on your lips, I pray.
> The time is out of joint. O cursed spite,
> That ever I was born to set it right!
> Nay, come, let's go together.
> > [*Exeunt.*]
> > (i.v.187–91)

Although the couplet usually comes at the very end of the scene, giving it additional emphasis and so underlining its meaning, this couplet is followed by one more line. Hamlet, on his way out, abandons the illusion of dialogue after his repeated request for secrecy. (The couplet that follows is too generalized and too far removed from the context of the preceding conversation to have been directed solely at his companions.) But the couplet itself is followed by a return to genuine dialogue. Hamlet's last line clearly refers to the previous "Let us go in together," and so it is obvious that Horatio and the others have been waiting while Hamlet delivered the couplet and now stand aside to let him exit first. Hamlet rejects this perfectly appropriate court etiquette, however, and repeats, "let's go together."

What is of interest is the way in which Shakespeare integrates the couplet into dialogue. Here he breaks with the convention of the *concluding* couplet only in order to end the scene in a representational mode that allows him to re-emphasize an important aspect of Hamlet's character. Whereas Hamlet in his first and succeeding scenes clearly dissociated himself from the court (and such courtiers as Polonius and Osric), here he just as clearly reassociates himself with his friends and those of lesser degree. Hamlet's rejection of etiquette seems important enough to warrant a return to dialogue in the last line, which return, in its own way, recalls his final resumption of dialogue with his mother – "One word more, good lady" – following several choruslike reflections likewise in couplet form. In both scenes the attempt to integrate the hero in a more self-contained mode of drama and the endeavor to delineate his character as an image of human personality go together, but they do not preclude the continuity, in a new context, of *platea*-derived popular conventions and attitudes.

Usually a couplet occurring at the end of a scene does in fact conclude it; and often enough the speaker of the couplet is the last actor to leave the stage, sometimes even with a clear "Away!" (*Troilus and Cressida*, III.ii.205). It is true that the couplet spoken at this point has the effect of summing up or emphasizing important ideas, that it made last lines easier to hear as the actor retreated toward the rear doors, and that structurally it signalized the break between scenes. But although these functions became more important in Shakespeare's day, quite different functions rooted in traditional platform stagecraft were still at work beneath the surface. In pursuing this point we must remember that in the pre-Shakespearean popular theater illusion was achieved only in the course of a scene and could not be assumed at the very beginning. On a platform stage surrounded by spectators on three or even four sides, with the possibility of spectators seated on the stage itself, the fiction of location had to be built up at the beginning of the scene and more or less abandoned at the end, when the illusion dissolved and the stage returned to the reality of the communal occasion in the playhouse. Since the actors who turned the "word scenery" and related gestures into a locality left that *locus* at the end of the scene, the locality itself – having been created solely by words and the physical presence of the actors – vanished, faded away "into air, into thin air," like "the baseless fabric of this vision" (*The Tempest*, IV.i.148 and 151). The end of a scene, therefore, was a return to the beginning. And it is in light of such renewed neutrality on the stage that the *platea* position of figures like Richard III, Hamlet, Iago, Thersites, and Prospero allowed a special relationship with the audience throughout most of the play.

The actor delivering a concluding couplet in the presence of others – as Hamlet did – spoke from a *Figurenposition* functionally very much like the aside; for he established audience contact without departing from his role. (This kind of aside spoken upon leaving the stage or ending a scene was so common that special terms have been coined for it, such as "exit aside" or "end-of-scene aside.")[35] The frequency of the concluding couplet corresponds to the no less frequent aside at the beginning of a scene. This is logical if the traditional theatrical process of gradually building illusions on the platform stage is kept in mind. Although less effective dramatically, "since they postpone the establishment of a relationship through dialogue,"[36] the aside spoken by the actor entering for the first time or the aside at the beginning of a scene must have served equally traditional functions of *platea*-derived staging. Since locality did not exist at the beginning of the scene and could not be sustained per se beyond the end of the scene, the introductory and concluding *Figurenpositionen* tended to be physically or dramatically close to the audience. It was already traditional for the Vice figure to open the scene or play with an extended self-introduction that had no representational significance whatsoever.

Kyd, Marlowe, and Shakespeare dispensed to a considerable degree with this unveiled opening and closing audience contact. Marlowe went so far as to begin *in medias res* the introductory monologue in *The Jew of Malta*; Shakespeare often opened scenes in the middle of a dialogue. But traditional stagecraft still exerted a strong influence, and the non-dialogue opening (like Berowne's opening of Act IV, scene iii in *Love's Labour's Lost* discussed above) remained always an important element of construction.

Since for reasons of characterization or social or dramatic decorum not all characters were allowed the forms of speech that correspond to a *platea* mode of performance, it is not surprising that some types of figures concluded scenes more frequently than others. Although there is no hard and fast rule about this we could note, for example, that Thersites, who is definitely in touch with the audience, concludes scenes with marked frequency. Since he speaks in prose Thersites does not conclude with couplets, but his comments at the end of four scenes (iii.iii; v.i; v.ii; v.iv) fulfill what is obviously a comparable function: sarcastic summary or evaluation of what has happened, spoken after the actors engaged in dialogue have left the stage. In *Timon of Athens*, concluding lines are likewise significant, not only because Timon, Alcibiades, and a Senator share the task of ending scenes with Apemantus (i.ii), the steward Flavius (ii.ii; iv.ii), the servant Flaminius (iii.iii), and a soldier (v.iii), but because these lesser characters are often only marginally integrated into the action of the play, and as such are well-suited to dismissing the illusion of *locus* and marking the return to the actual platform stage.

Similar observations can be made about the use of other forms of speech, such as the proverb. If M. P. Tilley's dictionary of proverbs is used as a basis for analysis, their distribution can be found to back up the relationship between *Figurenposition* and dramatic speech postulated here. *Hamlet*, for example, contains more proverbs than any other Shakespearean play; and it is noteworthy that Hamlet himself speaks seventy-one of the one hundred and four found in it. Likewise, the Fool in *King Lear* (who we must remember drops out of the play at the end of Act III) delivers twenty-one proverbs, Lear twenty-five, and Kent fourteen. This can be contrasted with Goneril's six, Edmund's two and Regan's three. In *Twelfth Night* Feste speaks twenty-nine proverbs and Sir Toby eighteen, while Malvolio is given a mere five. Thus, the use of proverbs functions as an effective means of characterization. In the case of Goneril, Regan, Malvolio, and other similar characters, the relative absence of proverbial speech suggests "the new age of scientific inquiry and industrial development,"[37] whose representatives, for better or worse, discard the form and content of popular wisdom.

As in the case of Iago and Richard III, the new mode of characterization and the traditional *Figurenposition* can be combined and made to enhance each other. But they can also create awkward tensions, as, for example, those between Edmund as we first see him (the bastard making scornful and inverting comments to the audience) and Duke Edmund as he appears later in the play (no longer in touch with the audience). From the point of view of stagecraft Edmund fulfills a variety of functions, like the very different Duke in *Measure for Measure*, when the downstage position takes on original, and no longer traditional, functions. Thus, insofar as the popular legacy ceases to have an effect in such experimental transformations and is used in a way no longer consonant with its original context, Shakespeare's achievement consists in having combined the new poetic realism with modified and experimental versions of traditional stage practices.

Turned in on themselves and imprisoned by their own egotism, Malvolio, Regan, and Goneril represent a new individualism. They are so far removed, not only in moral outlook but also in physical space, from the plebeian audience and its collective understanding of the world and of art that they occupy a *Figurenposition* that permits knavish speech and self-revealing aside but not that type of proverb and wordplay that is rooted in the common experience and inherited traditions of the people. In fact, they are not given any forms of speech that recall the festive element and ritual origins of audience contact. Unlike Thersites, Apemantus, the servants, and the fools, their outlook, regardless of how brilliantly it is presented, does not permit any sustained downstage position. That is one reason why they do not conclude the play. For Shakespeare it is not these representatives of egotism, but rather lovers and cheerful characters or those who are sad but wise who generally have the last word and sustain the audience rapport into and beyond the play's ending.[38]

Notes

1   C. W. Hodges, "The Lantern of Taste," *Shakespeare Survey* 12 (1959), p. 8. Cf. G. R. Kernodle, *From Art to Theatre: Form and Convention in the Renaissance* (Chicago, 1944), pp. 130–53. Cf. L. B. Wright, *Shakespeare's Theatre and the Dramatic Tradition* (Washington, 1958), p. 14: "one cannot escape the conclusion that usage varied and that stage construction in the theatres may have differed in some important details." For a discussion of the flexibility of Shakespeare's theater, see J. L. Styan, *Shakespeare's Stagecraft* (Cambridge, 1967), pp. 7 ff.

2   Richard Hosley, "The Discovery-Space in Shakespeare's Globe," *Shakespeare Survey* 12 (1959): 35–46.

3   G. F. Reynolds, *The Staging of Elizabethan Plays at the Red Bull Theater: 1605–1625* (London, 1940), p. 188; cf. pp. 131–63. E. K. Chambers had already postulated the existence of a "curtained structure" in the Swan theater, but had not enlarged upon his theory (*The Elizabethan Stage*, vol. 3 [Oxford, 1923], p. 86, hereafter cited as *El. St.*). C. W. Hodges (n. 5 below) and Leslie Hotson (for example, in *Shakespeare's Wooden O* [London, 1960], pp. 56–7) have gone far beyond this. Doubt about the existence of the rear stage has led to various reinterpretations of individual scenes (for example, Richard Hosley, "The Staging of Desdemona's Bed," *Shakespeare Quarterly* 14 [1963]: 57–65) and to the reconstruction of plays with the aid of concealed stages or tents (for example, L. J. Ross, "The Use of a 'Fit-Up' Booth in *Othello*," *Shakespeare Quarterly* 12 [1961]: 359–70). The existence of similar structures in plays by Jonson and Chapman has also been postulated; cf. W. A. Armstrong, "The Enigmatic Elizabethan Stage," *English* 13 (1961): 216–20.

4   Bernard Miles and Josephine Wilson, "Three Festivals at the Mermaid Theatre," *Shakespeare Quarterly* 5 (1954): 310: "We have learnt that it is impossible to play scenes on the so-called 'inner stage,' or even far upstage at all."

5   C. W. Hodges, *The Globe Restored: A Study of the Elizabethan Theatre* (London, 1953), pp. 58–9. A. M. Nagler (*Shakespeare's Stage* [reprint ed., New Haven, 1964]) characterizes the tentlike structure as "an auxiliary stage, a potential scene of action" (p. 26) and refers to the medieval example of the fixed-roof *pinaculum* in Vigil Raber's sketch of the play at Bozen, 1514 (p. 49).

6   J. C. Adams, *The Globe Playhouse: Its Design and Equipment* (Cambridge, MA, 1943), p. 294; also the same author's "The Original Staging of King Lear," in *J. Q. Adams Memorial Studies*, ed. James McManaway, et. al. (Washington, 1948), pp. 315–35.

7   G. F. Reynolds, "Was there a 'Tarras' in Shakespeare's Globe?" *Shakespeare Survey* 4 (1951): 100, n. 9.

8   Reynolds, *The Staging of Elizabethan Plays* ..., p. 190.

9   T. J. King, *Shakespearean Staging: 1599–1642* (Cambridge, MA, 1971), p. 31. Cf. Richard Hosley, "The Gallery over the Stage in the Public Playhouses of Shakespeare's Time," *Shakespeare Quarterly* 8 (1957): p. 21, and the same author's "Shakespeare's Use of a Gallery over the Stage," *Shakespeare Survey* 10 (1957): 77.

10 Cf. the graphic demonstration in Glynne Wickham, *Early English Stages: 1300–1600*, vol. 2 (London, 1959), pp. 161–3. Henslowe's specifications require "a Stadge and Tyreinge howse to be made, erected & settupp *within the saide fframe*" (italics mine; cf. Chambers, *El. St.*, 2: 137).

11 See Richard Southern, *The Open Stage* (London, 1953), pp. 15–21, and the drawing by Hodges in appendix A of *The Globe Restored*, pp. 170–7, which was preceded by the publication of "Unworthy Scaffolds: A Theory for the Reconstruction of Elizabethan Playhouses," *Shakespeare Survey* 3 (1951): 83–94.

12 *The Globe Restored*, p. 49.

13 J. Q. Adams, ed., *Chief Pre-Shakespearean Dramas* (Boston, 1924), p. 158, n. 1.

14 Cf. J. W. Saunders, "Vaulting the Rails," *Shakespeare Survey* 7 (1954): 69–81.

15 Allardyce Nicoll, "Passing Over the Stage," *Shakespeare Survey* 12 (1959): 47–55. This has been confirmed by Richard Southern in *The Staging of Plays Before Shakespeare* (London, 1973), pp. 569–70, where he suggests that there were small steps at the corner of the stage to facilitate entrance from and exit to the yard. Still, the evidence is not conclusive; "passing over the stage" may indeed refer to no more than the movement of an actor around the platform from door to door. Since this book was written, work on the Elizabethan stage has continued to grow at an unprecedented rate. For some of the most stimulating contributions, see the collection of essays in *Renaissance Drama* 4 (1972), or the series *The Elizabethan Theatre* (ed. David Galloway [Toronto, 1969 ff.]). For what is perhaps the most rewarding discussion of some of the basic issues, see P. C. Kolin's Report on the 1971 MLA Conference on Renaissance Drama, paneled by Bernard Beckerman, Richard Hosley, and T. J. King (*Research Opportunities in Renaissance Drama* 15–16 [1972–73]: 3–14). There are some new emphases and trends toward a consciousness of, for instance, the dramatic and "emblematic" significance of the theatrical "discovery," or, again, a new awareness, as formulated by Bernard Beckerman or Norman Rabkin, of the critical and social implications of historical research into the physical stage. (See, among many others, *Reinterpretations of Elizabethan Drama*, Selected papers from the English Institute, ed. Norman Rabkin [New York, 1969].) But many questions remain unanswered and some previous answers are increasingly questioned, as in Richard Hosley's mounting objections to the "liberal position" of C. W. Hodges and George Reynolds on the use of curtained booths. See Hosley's well-founded emphasis on plays like *Hamlet* as "an 'arras' or 'hanging' play, a purely open stage play" (Kolin's Report, p. 6). Here as elsewhere it may be said that "extensive investigations of the severely limited evidence have won us few widely and easily accepted solutions." See P. C. Kolin and R. O. Watt in the introduction to what is the most useful recent "Bibliography of Scholarship on the Elizabethan Stage Since Chambers," *Research Opportunities in Renaissance Drama* 15–16 (1972–73): 33–59. There is a shorter but selective bibliography, together with a summary, by Michael Jamieson, "Shakespeare in the Theatre," *Shakespeare: Select Bibliographical Guides*, ed. Stanley Wells (London, 1973). For a somewhat fuller synthesis, see Andrew Gurr, *The Shakespearean Stage: 1574–1642* (Cambridge, 1970).

16 For a classic statement of the older theory, see A. H. Thorndike, *Shakespeare's Theater* (New York, 1916), p. 77. On the following, cf. Rudolf Stamm, *Geschichte des englischen Theaters* (Bern, 1951), pp. 51, 101, 110, for an extremely balanced statement of the problems involved.

17 J. W. Saunders, "Vaulting the Rails," *Shakespeare Survey* 7 (1954), p. 79.

18 *Tarlton's Jests and News out of Purgatory* (London, 1844), p. 27.

19 Ibid., pp. 14, 22–3, 44. Cf. the jest, "How Tarlton and one in the gallery fell out."

20 Cf. Anne Righter, *Shakespeare and the Idea of the Play* (London, 1962), passim.

21 Alfred Harbage, "The Role of the Shakespearean Producer," *Shakespeare Jahrbuch* 91 (1955), p. 163. Cf. John Russel Brown, *Free Shakespeare* (London, 1974), esp. pp. 48–57, where the significance of such performances without directors and designers is explored. See Bernard Beckerman (*Shakespeare at the Globe: 1599–1609* [New York, 1962], p. 24): "From a common creative act arose the plays that Shakespeare penned and the productions that his friends presented. The record of this partnership is contained in the extant scripts, not merely in stage directions or in dialogue, but in the very substance of the dramatist's craft, the structure of the incidents."

22 See Stamm, *Geschichte des englischen Theaters*, p. 55.

23 Ibid. Cf. Jackson I. Cope, *The Theater and the Dream: From Metaphor to Form in Renaissance Drama* (Baltimore / London, 1973), esp. the prologue, "The Rediscovery of Anti-Form in Renaissance Drama," pp. 1–13. (I have reviewed and commented on this suggestive book in *Zeitschrift für Anglistik* 24 [1976]: 78–80.)

24 Alfred Harbage, *Shakespeare and the Rival Traditions* (New York, 1952), pp. 296, 307, 298.

25 Quoted from Harbage, ibid., p. 305.

26 Indeed, as Alexander Anikst stresses, Shakespeare was no partisan of popular rule ("Shakespeare – volkstümlicher Schriftsteller," *Shakespearowski Sbornik* [Moscow, 1958], p. 43). Cf. Anselm Schlösser's "Zur Frage 'Volk und Mob' bei Shakespeare," *ZAA* 4 (1956): 148–71, and Brents Stirling's important study of *The Populace in Shakespeare* (New York, 1949). Lorentz Eckhoff, *Shakespeare, Spokesman of the Third Estate* (Oxford, 1954), is an exceedingly problematic book. Above quotation from Ben Jonson in E. K. Chambers, *William Shakespeare: A Study of Facts and Problems*, vol. 2 (Oxford, 1930), p. 209.

27 *The Life of Timon of Athens*, ed. J. C. Maxwell, "The New Shakespeare" (Cambridge, 1957).

28 A. P. Rossiter, *English Drama from Early Times to the Elizabethans* (London, 1950), p. 75.

29 Clemen, *Kommentar zu Shakespeares Richard III*, p. 151.

30 Quoted from *Troilus and Cressida*, ed. Alice Walker, "The New Shakespeare" (Cambridge, 1957).

31 Cf. L. C. Knights, "Shakespeare's Politics: With Some Reflections on the Nature of Tradition," *Proceedings of the British Academy* (1957): 117.

32 The etymology of "infant" further enhances the possible depth of the pun since the Latin substantive use of *infāns* – "unable to speak" – might be a perfect description of the silent *tableau vivant* effect achieved in some medieval pageantry and dramaturgy. This, at any rate, would support the already playful oxymoron, "old infant": old in the history of the theater, infant, as the etymology suggests, in terms of the mode of performance. (Here I wish to thank my editor, to whom I owe this note as well as the interpretation of Berowne's *Figurenposition*.)

33 See Doris Fenton, *The Extra-Dramatic Moment in Elizabethan Plays before 1616* (Philadelphia, 1930), pp. 113 ff.

34 On the myriad dramatic functions of the aside (interest, characterization, irony, transmission of information, etc.), cf. Wolfgang Riehle, *Das Beiseitesprechen bei Shakespeare: Ein Beitrag zur Dramaturgie des elisabethanischen Dramas*, Dissertation (Munich, 1964), especially pp. 111 ff.

35 Riehle, p. 26.

36 Ibid., p. 27.

37 J. F. Danby, *Shakespeare's Doctrine of Nature: A Study of King Lear* (London, 1961), p. 46.

38 The audience rapport of Gloucester, Iago, and, in part, Edmund derives from other premises. They are, like their predecessor the knavish Vice, the theatrical managers of their own intrigues and dramatic inversions. They continue to challenge the status quo, not so much from any personal motivation (although Shakespeare, somewhat perfunctorily, supplies that, too) but rather for the sake of challenge and negation. They are the great perverters of state, marriage, and filial love, re-enacting the *Geist, der stets verneint* – the Mephistophelean spirit which persistently destroys. In this sense, their audience contact is profoundly in the popular tradition. Their natural ambivalence as well as their insuperable vitality stem to a degree from the exuberance with which they freely exploit the vantage points of both platform and *locus*, ritual and representation.

30

King Lear (ca. 1605–1606) and Essentialist Humanism

Jonathan Dollimore

When he is on the heath King Lear is moved to pity. As unaccommodated man he feels what wretches feel. For the humanist the tragic paradox arises here: debasement gives rise to dignity and at the moment when Lear might be expected to be most brutalised he becomes most human. Through kind-ness and shared vulnerability humankind redeems itself in a universe where the gods are at best callously just, at worst sadistically vindictive.

In recent years the humanist view of Jacobean tragedies like *Lear* has been dominant, having more or less displaced the explicitly Christian alternative. Perhaps the most important distinction between the two is this: the Christian view locates man centrally in a providential universe;[1] the humanist view likewise centralises man but now he is in a condition of tragic dislocation: instead of integrating (ultimately) with a teleological design created and sustained by God, man grows to consciousness in a universe which thwarts his deepest needs. If he is to be redeemed at all he must redeem himself. The humanist also contests the Christian claim that the suffering of Lear and Cordelia is part of a providential and redemptive design. If that suffering is to be justified at all it is because of what it reveals about man's intrinsic nature – his courage and integrity. By heroically enduring a fate he is powerless to alter, by insisting, moreover, upon *knowing* it, man grows in stature even as he is being destroyed. Thus Clifford Leech, an opponent of the Christian view, tells us that tragic protagonists 'have a quality of mind that somehow atones for the nature of the world in which they and we live. They have, in a greater or lesser degree, the power to endure and the power to apprehend' (*Shakespeare's Tragedies*, p. 15). Wilbur Sanders in an influential study argues for an ultimately optimistic Shakespeare who had no truck with Christian doctrine or conventional Christian conceptions of the absolute but nevertheless affirmed that 'the principle of health – grace – is not in heaven, but in nature, and especially in human nature, and it cannot finally be rooted out'. Ultimately this faith in nature and human nature involves and entails 'a faith in a universal moral order which cannot finally be defeated' (*The Dramatist and the Received Idea*, pp. 336–7).

Here as so often with the humanist view there is a strong residue of the more explicit Christian metaphysic and language which it seeks to eschew; comparable with Sanders' use of 'grace' is Leech's use of 'atone'. Moreover both indicate the humanist preoccupation with the universal counterpart of essentialist subjectivity – either ultimately affirmed (Sanders) or recognised as an ultimate tragic absence (Leech).[2] The humanist reading of *Lear* has been authoritatively summarised by G. K. Hunter (he calls it the 'modern' view of the play):

> [it] is seen as the greatest of tragedies because it not only strips and reduces and assaults human dignity, but because it also shows with the greatest force and detail the process of restoration by which humanity can recover from degradation ... [Lear's] retreat into the isolated darkness of his own mind is also a descent into the seed-bed of a new life; for *the individual mind is seen here as the place from which a man's most important qualities and relationships draw the whole of their potential.* (*Dramatic Identities and Cultural Tradition*, pp. 251–2, my italics)

What follows is an exploration of the political dimension of *Lear*. It argues that the humanist view of that play is as inappropriate as the Christian alternative which it has generally displaced – inappropriate not least because it shares the essentialism of the latter. I do not mean to argue again the case against the Christian view since, even though it is still sometimes advanced, it has been effectively discredited by writers as diverse as Barbara Everett, William R. Elton and Cedric Watts.[3] The principal reason why the humanist view seems equally misguided, and not dissimilar, is this: it mystifies suffering and invests man with a quasi-transcendent identity whereas the play does neither of these things. In fact, the play repudiates the essentialism which the humanist reading of it presupposes. However, I do not intend to replace the humanist reading with one which rehearses yet again all the critical clichés about the nihilistic and chaotic 'vision' of Jacobean tragedy. In *Lear*, as in *Troilus*, man is decentred not through misanthropy but in order to make visible social process and its forms of ideological misrecognition.

Redemption and Endurance: Two Sides of Essentialist Humanism

'Pity' is a recurring word in *Lear*. Philip Brockbank, in a recent and sensitive humanist reading of the play, says: 'Lear dies "with pity" (iv.vii.53) and that access of pity, which in the play attends the dissolution of the senses and of the self, is a condition for the renewal of human life' ('Upon Such Sacrifices', p. 133). Lear, at least when he is on the heath, is indeed moved to pity, but what does it mean to say that such pity is 'a condition for the renewal of human life?' Exactly whose life is renewed? In this connection there is one remark of Lear's which begs our attention; it is made when he first witnesses 'You houseless poverty' (iii.iv.26): 'Oh, I have ta'en / Too little care of this!'. Too little: Lear bitterly reproaches himself because hitherto he has been aware of yet ignored the suffering of his deprived subjects. (The distracted use of the abstract – 'You houseless poverty' – subtly suggests that Lear's disregard has been of a general rather than a local poverty). He has ignored it not through callous indifference but simply *because he has not experienced it.*

King Lear suggests here a simple yet profound truth. Far from endorsing the idea that man can redeem himself in and through an access of pity, we might be moved to recognise that, on the contrary, in a world where pity is the prerequisite for compassionate action, where a king has to share the suffering of his subjects in order to 'care', the majority will remain poor, naked and wretched. The point of course is that princes only see the hovels of wretches during progresses (walkabouts?), in flight or in fairy tale. Even in fiction the wheel of fortune rarely brings them that low. Here, as so often in Jacobean drama, the fictiveness of the genre or scene intrudes; by acknowledging its status as fiction it abdicates the authority of idealist mimesis and indicates the better the reality it signifies; resembling in this Brecht's alienation effect, it stresses artifice not in the service of formalism but of realism. So, far from transcending in the name of an essential humanity the gulf which separates the privileged from the deprived, the play insists on it. And what clinches this is the exchange between Poor Tom (Edgar) and Gloucester. The latter has just arrived at the hovel; given the circumstances, his concern over the company kept by the king is faintly ludicrous but very telling: 'What, hath your Grace no better company?' (iii.iv.138; cf. Cordelia at iv.vii.38–9). Tom tells Gloucester that he is cold. Gloucester, *uncomprehending rather than callous*, tells him he will keep warm if he goes back into the hovel (true of course, relatively speaking). That this comes from one of the 'kindest' people in the play prevents us from dismissing the remark as individual unkindness: judging is less important than seeing how unkindness is built into social consciousness. That Gloucester is unknowingly talking to his son in this exchange simply underscores the arbitrariness, the woeful inadequacy of what passes for kindness; it is, relatively, a very precious thing but as a basis for human kind's self-redemption it is a non-starter. In so far as Lear identifies with suffering it is at the point when he is powerless to do anything about it. This is not accidental: the society of *Lear* is structured in such a way that to wait for shared experience to generate justice is to leave it too late. Justice, we might say, is too important to be trusted to empathy.

Like Lear, Gloucester has to undergo intense suffering before he can identify with the deprived. When he does so he expresses more than compassion. He perceives, crucially, the limitation of a society that depends on empathy alone for its justice. Thus he equates his earlier self with the 'lust-dieted man ... *that will not see / Because he does not feel*' (iv.i.69–71, my italics). Moreover he is led to a conception of social justice (albeit dubiously administered by the 'Heavens', l. 68) whereby 'distribution should undo excess, / And each man have enough' (iv.i.72–3).

By contrast, Lear experiences pity mainly as an inseparable aspect of his own grief: 'I am mightily abus'd. I should e'en die with pity / To see another thus' (iv.vii.53–4). His compassion emerges from grief only to be obliterated by grief. He is angered, horrified, confused and, above all dislocated. Understandably then he does not empathise with Tom so much as assimilate him to his own derangement. Indeed, Lear hardly communicates with anyone, especially on the heath; most of his utterances are demented mumbling interspersed with brief insight. Moreover, his preoccupation with vengeance ultimately displaces his transitory pity; reverting from the charitable reconciliation of

V.iii to vengeance once again, we see him, minutes before his death, boasting of having killed the 'slave' that was hanging Cordelia.

But what of Cordelia herself? She more than anyone else has been seen to embody and symbolise pity. But is it a pity which significantly alters anything? To see her death as *intrinsically* redemptive is simply to mystify both her and death.[4] Pity, like kindness, seems in *Lear* to be precious yet ineffectual. Far from being redemptive it is the authentic but residual expression of a scheme of values all but obliterated by a catastrophic upheaval in the power structure of this society. Moreover the failure of those values is in part due to the fact that they are (or were) an ideological ratification of the very power structure which eventually destroys them.

In *Lear*, as we shall see in the next section, there is a repudiation of stoicism similar to that found in Marston's *Antonio's Revenge*. Yet repeatedly the skeptical treatment, sometimes the outright rejection, of stoicism in these plays is overlooked; often in fact it is used to validate another kind of humanism. For convenience I call the kind outlined so far ethical humanism and this other one existential humanism. The two involve different emphases rather than different ideologies. That of the latter is on essential heroism and existential integrity, that of the former on essential humanity, the universal human condition. Thus, according to Barbara Everett (in another explicitly anti-Christian analysis):

> In the storm scene Lear is at his most powerful and, despite moral considerations, at his noblest; the image of man hopelessly confronting a hostile universe and withstanding it only by his inherent powers of rage, endurance and perpetual questioning, is perhaps the most purely 'tragic' in Shakespeare. ('The New *King Lear*', p. 333)

Significantly, existential humanism forms the basis even of J. W. Lever's *The Tragedy of State*, one of the most astute studies of Jacobean tragedy to date. On the one hand Lever is surely right in insisting that these plays 'are not primarily treatments of characters with a so-called "fatal flaw", whose downfall is brought about by the decree of just if inscrutable powers ... the fundamental flaw is not in them but in the world they inhabit: in the political state, the social order it upholds, and likewise, by projection, in the cosmic state of shifting arbitrary phenomena called "Fortune" ' (p. 10). By the same criteria it is surely wrong to assert (on the same page) that: 'What really matters is the quality of [the heroes'] response to intolerable situations. This is a drama of adversity and stance ... The rational man who remains master of himself is by the same token the ultimate master of his fate'. In Lever's analysis Seneca is the ultimate influence on a drama (including *King Lear*) which celebrates man's capacity inwardly to transcend oppression (p. 9).

If the Christian mystifies suffering by presenting it as intrinsic to God's redemptive and providential design for man, the humanist does likewise by representing suffering as the mysterious ground for man's *self*-redemption; both in effect mystify suffering by having as their common focus an essentialist conception of what it is to be human: in virtue of his spiritual essence (Christian), essential humanity (ethical humanist), or essential self (existential humanist), man is seen to achieve a paradoxical transcendence: in individual extinction is his apotheosis. Alternatively we might say that in a mystifying closure of the historical real the categories of idealist culture are recuperated. This suggests why both ethical and existential humanism are in fact quasi-religious: both reject the providential and 'dogmatic' elements of Christianity while retaining its fundamental relation between suffering, affirmation and regeneration. Moreover they, like Christianity, tend to fatalise social dislocation; its causes are displaced from the realm of the human; questions about them are raised but only rhetorically, thus confirming man's impotence to alleviate the human condition. This clears the stage for what really matters: man's responsive suffering and what it reveals in the process about his essential nature. Recognisable here is the fate of existentialism when merged with literary criticism as a surrogate or displaced theology; when, specifically, it was co-opted to the task most symptomatic of that displacement, namely the obsession with defining tragedy. It will be recalled that for the existentialist existence precedes essence, or so said Sartre, who later tried to develop this philosophy in the context of Marxism. In literary criticism the social implications of existentialism, such as they were, were easily ignored, the emphasis being instead on a modernist angst and man's thwarted spiritual potential. This is another sense in which existential humanism is merely a mutation of Christianity and not at all a radical alternative; although it might reluctantly have to acknowledge that neither Absolute nor Essence exist, it still relates man to them on a principle of Augustinian privation: man understands his world only through the grid of their absence.

King Lear: A Materialist Reading

More important than Lear's pity is his 'madness' – less divine furor than a process of collapse which reminds us just how precarious is the psychological equilibrium which we call sanity, and just how dependent upon an identity which is social rather than essential. What makes Lear the person he is – or rather was – is not kingly essence (divine right), but, among other things, his authority and his family. On the heath he represents the process whereby man has been stripped of his stoic and (Christian) humanist conceptions of self. Consider what Seneca has to say of affliction and philosophy:

> Whether we are caught in the grasp of an inexorable law of fate, whether it is God who as lord of the universe has ordered all things, or whether the affairs of mankind are tossed and buffeted haphazardly by chance, it is philosophy that has the duty of protecting us. (*Letters*, p. 64)

Lear, in his affliction, attempts to philosophise with Tom whom he is convinced is a 'Noble philosopher', a 'good Athenian' (ii.iv.168 and 176). It adds up to nothing more than the incoherent ramblings of one half-crazed by just that suffering which philosophy, according to the stoic, guards against. It is an ironic subversion of neo-stoic essentialism, one which recalls Bacon's essay 'Of Adversity,' where he quotes Seneca: '*It is true greatness to have in one the frailty of a man, and the security of a god*' only to add, dryly: 'This would have done better in poesy, where transcendences are more allowed' (*Essays*, p. 15). Bacon believed that poesy implies idealist mimesis – that is, an illusionist evasion of those historical and empirical realities which, says Bacon, 'buckle and bow the mind unto the nature of things' (*Advancement*, p. 83). He seems to have remained unaware that Jacobean drama was just as subversive of poesy (in this sense) as he was, not only with regard to providentialism but now its corollary, essentialism. Plays like *Lear* precisely disallow 'transcendences': in this at least they confirm Edmund's contention that 'men / Are as the time is' (v.iii.31–2). Montaigne made a similar point with admirable terseness: 'I am no philosopher: Evils oppresse me according as they waigh' (*Essays*, III.189). The Fool tells Lear that he is 'an O without a figure' (I.iv.92); both here and seconds later he anticipates his master's eventual radical decentredness, the consequence of having separated 'The name, and all th' addition' of a king from his real 'power' (I.i.29, 135): 'Who is it that can tell me who I am?' cries Lear; 'Lear's shadow' replies the Fool.

After he has seen Lear go mad, Gloucester offers this inversion of stoicism:

> Better I were distract
> So should my thoughts be sever'd from my griefs,
> And woes by wrong imagination lose
> The knowledge of themselves.
>
> (IV.vi.281–4)

For Lear dispossession and displacement entail not redemptive suffering but a kind of suffering recognition – implicated perhaps with confession, depending on how culpable we take this king to have been with regard to 'the great *image* of authority' which he now briefly demystifies: 'a dog's obey'd in office' (IV.vi.157, my italics). Lear does acknowledge blame, though deludedly believing the power which made him blameworthy is still his: 'Take that of me, my friend, who have the power / To seal th' accuser's lips' (IV.vi.169–70). His admission that authority is a function of 'office' and 'power', not intrinsic worth, has its corollary: power itself is in control of 'justice' (l.166) rather than vice versa:

> The usurer hangs the cozener.
> Through tatter'd clothes small vices do appear;
> Robes and furr'd gowns hide all. Plate sin with gold
> And the strong lance of justice hurtless breaks;
> Arm it in rags, a pigmy's straw doth pierce it.
>
> (IV.vi.163–7)

Scenes like this one remind us that *King Lear* is, above all, a play about power, property and inheritance. Referring to Goneril, the distraught Lear cries: 'Ingratitude thou marble-hearted fiend, / More hideous when thou show'st thee in a child / Than the sea-monster' (I.iv.259–61). Here, as throughout the play, we see the cherished norms of human kind-ness shown to have no 'natural' sanction at all. A catastrophic redistribution of power and property – and, eventually, a civil war – disclose the awful truth that these two things are somehow prior to the laws of human kindness rather than vice versa (likewise, as we have just seen, with power in relation to justice). Human values are not antecedent to these material realities but are, on the contrary, in-formed by them.[5]

Even allowing for his conservative tendency to perceive all change as a change for the worse, Gloucester's account of widespread social discord must surely be taken as at least based on fact: 'These late eclipses in the sun and moon portend no good to us ... Love cools, friendship falls off, brothers divide, in cities, mutinies; in countries, discord; in palaces, treason ... there's son against father; the King falls from bias of nature: there's father against child' (1.ii.100–11). ''Tis strange', concludes the troubled Gloucester and exits, leaving Edmund to make things somewhat less so. Significantly, Edmund does not deny the extent of the discord, only Gloucester's mystified sense of its cause. In an earlier soliloquy Edmund has already repudiated 'the plague of custom ... The curiosity of nations' which label him bastard (1.ii.3–4). Like Montaigne he insists that universal law is merely municipal law. Here he goes further, repudiating the ideological process whereby the latter is misrecognised as the former; he rejects, that is, a way of thinking which represents the contingent as the necessary and thereby further represents human identity and the social order as metaphysically determined (and therefore unalterable): 'When we are sick in fortune, often the surfeits of our own behaviour, we make guilty of our disasters the sun, the moon, and stars; as if we were villains on necessity, fools by heavenly compulsion ... by a divine thrusting on' (1.ii.122–31). Closely related to this refusal of the classical ideological effect is the way Edmund also denaturalises the theatrical effect: 'Pat! He comes like the catastrophe of the old comedy. My cue is villainous melancholy' (1.ii.128). Yet this revolutionary skepticism is discredited by the purpose to which it is put. How are we to take this? Are we to assume that Edmund is simply evil and therefore so is his philosophy? I want to argue that we need not. To begin with we have to bear in mind a crucial fact: Edmund's skcepticism is made to serve an *existing* system of values; although he falls prey to, he does not introduce his society to its obsession with power, property and inheritance; it is already the material and ideological basis of that society. As such it in-forms the consciousness of Lear and Gloucester as much as Cornwall and Regan; consider Lear first, then Gloucester.

Lear's behaviour in the opening scene presupposes first, his absolute power, second, the knowledge that his being king constitutes that power, third, his refusal to tolerate what he perceives as a contradiction of that power. Therefore what Lear demands of Cordelia – authentic familial kind-ness – is precluded by the very terms of the demand; that is, by the extent to which the occasion as well as his relationship to her is saturated with the ideological imperatives of power. For her part Cordelia's real transgression is not unkindness as such, but speaking in a way which threatens to show too clearly how the laws of human kindness operate in the service of property, contractual, and power relations:

> I love your Majesty
> According to my bond ...
>
> I
> Return those duties back as are right fit ...
>
> Why have my sisters husbands, if they say
> They love you [i.e. Lear] all?
> (1.i.91–2; 95–6; 98–9)

Presumably Cordelia does not intend it to be so, but this is the patriarchal order in danger of being shorn of its ideological legitimation – here, specifically, a legitimation taking ceremonial form. (Ironically yet predictably, the 'untender' (l. 105) dimension of that order is displaced on to Cordelia). Likewise with the whole issue of dowries. Prior to Lear's disowning of Cordelia, the realities of property marriage are more or less transmuted by the language of love and generosity, the ceremony of good government. But in the act of renouncing her, Lear brutally foregrounds the imperatives of power and property relations: 'Here I disclaim all my paternal care, / Propinquity and property of blood' (i.i.112–3; cf. ll. 196–7). Kenneth Muir glosses 'property' as 'closest blood relation' (ed. *King Lear*, p. 11). Given the context of this scene it must also mean 'ownership' – father owning daughter – with brutal connotations of the master / slave relationship as in the following passage from *King John*: 'I am too high-born to be *propertied* / To be a ... serving man' (v.ii.79–81). Even kinship then – indeed *especially* kinship – is in-formed by the ideology of property relations, the contentious issue of primogeniture being, in this play, only its most obvious manifestation. Later we witness Lear's correlation between the quantity of retainers Goneril will allow him and the quality of her love: Regan offers twenty-five retainers, upon which Lear tells Goneril: 'I'll go with thee. / Thy fifty yet doth double five-and-twenty, / And thou art twice her love' (ii.iv.257–9).

Gloucester's unconscious acceptance of this underlying ideology is conveyed at several points but nowhere more effectively than in Act II scene i; even as he is coming to terms with Edgar's supposed treachery he is installing Edmund in his place, offering in *exchange* for Edmund's 'natural' behaviour – property:

> of my land
> Loyal and natural boy, I'll work the means
> To make thee capable.
>
> (ii.i.83–5)

Thus the one thing which the kind Gloucester and the vicious Cornwall have in common is that each offers to reward Edmund's 'loyalty' in exactly the same way (cf. iii.v.16–18). All this would be ludicrous if it were not so painful: as their world disintegrates Lear and Gloucester cling even more tenaciously to the only values they know, which are precisely the values which precipitated the disintegration. Hence even as society is being torn apart by conflict, the ideological structure which has generated that conflict is being reinforced by it.

When Edmund in the forged letter represents Edgar complaining of 'the oppression of aged tyranny' which commands 'not as it hath power, but as it is suffered' (i.ii.47–8), he exploits the same personal anxiety in Gloucester which Cordelia unintentionally triggers in Lear. Both fathers represent a challenge to their patriarchal authority by offspring as unnatural behaviour, an abdication of familial duty. The trouble is they do this in a society where 'nature' as ideological concept is fast losing its power to police disruptive elements – for example: 'That nature which contemns its origin / Cannot be border'd certain in itself' (iv.ii.32–3). No longer are origin, identity and action a 'natural' ideological unity, and the disintegration of that unity reveals something of fundamental importance: when, as here (also, e.g. at i.ii.1–22) nature is represented as socially disruptive, yet elsewhere as the source of social stability (e.g. at ii.iv.176–80), we see an ideological construct beginning to incorporate and thereby render visible the very conflicts and contradictions in the social order which it hitherto effaced. In this respect the play activates a contradiction intrinsic to any 'naturalised' version of the Christian metaphysic; to abandon or blur the distinction between matter and spirit while retaining the basic premises of that metaphysic is to eventually construe evil as at once utterly alien to the human condition (unnatural) yet disturbingly and mysteriously inherent within it (natural) and to be purged accordingly. If deep personal anxiety is thus symptomatic of more general social dislocation it is also what guarantees the general reaction formation to that dislocation: those in power react to crisis by entrenching themselves the deeper within the ideology and social organisation responsible for it.

At strategic points in the play we see how the minor characters have also internalised the dominant ideology. Two instances must suffice. The first occurs in Act II scene ii where Kent insults Oswald. He does so almost entirely in terms of the latter's lack of material wealth, his mean estate and consequent dependence upon service. Oswald is, says Kent, a 'beggarly, three-suited, hundred-pound, filthy, worsted-stocking … super-serviceable … one-trunk-inheriting slave' (ii.ii.15 ff; as Muir points out, servants were apparently given three suits a year, while gentlemen wore silk as opposed to worsted stockings). The second example involves the way that for the Gentleman attending Cordelia even pity (or more accurately 'Sorrow') is conceived as a kind of passive female commodity (iv.iii.16–23).[6]

We can now see the significance of Edmund's skepticism and its eventual relationship to this dominant ideology of property and power. Edmund's skeptical independence is itself constituted by a contradiction: his illegitimate exclusion from society gives him an insight into the ideological basis of that society even as it renders him vulnerable to and dependent upon it. In this respect Edmund resembles the malcontents already encountered in previous chapters: exclusion from society gives rise both to the malcontent's sense of its worthlessness and his awareness that identity itself is dependent upon it. Similarly, Edmund, in liberating himself from the myth of innate inferiority, does not thereby liberate himself from his society's obsession with power, property and inheritance; if anything that obsession becomes the more urgent: 'Legitimate Edgar, I *must* have your land' (i.ii.16, my italics). He sees through one level of ideological legitimation only to remain the more thoroughly enmeshed with it at a deeper level.

Edmund embodies the process whereby, because of the contradictory conditions of its inception, a revolutionary (emergent) insight is folded back into a dominant ideology. Witnessing his fate we are reminded of how, historically, the misuse of revolutionary insight has tended to be in proportion to its truthfulness, and of how, as this very fact is obscured, the insight becomes entirely identified with (or as) its misappropriation. Machiavellianism, Gramsci has reminded us, is just one case in point (*Selections from Prison Notebooks*, p. 136).

The Refusal of Closure

Lionel Trilling has remarked that 'the captains and kings and lovers and clowns of Shakespeare are alive and complete before they die' (*The Opposing Self*, p. 38). Few remarks could be less true of *King Lear*. The notion of man as tragic victim somehow alive and complete in death is precisely the kind of essentialist mystification which the play refuses. It offers instead a decentring of the tragic subject which in turn becomes the focus of a more general exploration of human consciousness in relation to social being – one which discloses human values to be not antecedent to, but rather informed by, material conditions. *Lear* actually refuses then that autonomy of value which humanist critics so often insist that it ultimately affirms. Nicholas Brooke, for example, in one of the best close analyses of the play that we have, concludes by declaring: 'all moral structures, whether of natural order or Christian redemption, are invalidated by the naked fact of experience', yet manages in the concluding sentence of the study to resurrect from this unaccommodated 'naked experience' a redemptive autonomy of value, one almost mystically inviolable: 'Large orders collapse; but values remain, and are independent of them' (*Shakespeare: King Lear*, pp. 59–60). But surely in *Lear*, as in most of human history, 'values' are shown to be terrifyingly dependent upon whatever 'large orders' actually exist; in civil war especially – which after all is what *Lear* is about – the two collapse together.

In the closing moments of *Lear* those who have survived the catastrophe actually attempt to recuperate their society in just those terms which the play has subjected to skeptical interrogation. There is invoked, first, a concept of innate nobility in contradistinction to innate evil and, second, its corollary: a metaphysically ordained justice. Thus Edgar's defeat of Edmund is interpreted as a defeat of an evil nature by a noble one. Also nobility is seen to be like truth – it will out: 'Methought thy very gait did prophesy / A royal nobleness' (v.iii.175–6). Goneril is 'reduced' to her treachery ('read thine own evil', l. 156), while Edmund not only acknowledges defeat but also repents, submitting to Edgar's nobility (ll. 165–6) and acknowledging his own contrary nature (ll. 242–3). Next, Edgar invokes a notion of divine justice which holds out the possibility of rendering their world intelligible once more; speaking to Edmund of Gloucester, he says:

> The gods are just, and of our pleasant vices
> Make instruments to plague us:
> The dark and vicious place where thee he got
> Cost him his eyes.
>
> (v.iii.170–3)

Thus is responsibility displaced; but perhaps Edgar is meant to wince as he says it since the problem of course is that he is making his society supernaturally intelligible at the cost of rendering the concept of divine justice so punitive and 'poetic' as to be, humanly speaking, almost unintelligible. Nevertheless Albany persists with the same process of recuperation by glossing thus the deaths of Goneril and Regan: 'This judgement of the heavens, that makes us tremble, / Touches us not with pity' (v.iii.230–1). But when he cries 'The Gods defend her!' – i.e. Cordelia – instead of the process being finally consolidated we witness, even before he has finished speaking, Lear re-entering with Cordelia dead in his arms. Albany has one last desperate bid for recuperation, still within the old punitive / poetic terms:

> All friends shall taste
> The wages of their virtue, and all foes
> The cup of their deservings.
>
> (v.iii.302–4)

Seconds later Lear dies. The timing of these two deaths must surely be seen as cruelly, precisely, subversive: instead of complying with the demands of formal closure – the convention which would confirm the attempt at recuperation – the play concludes with two events which sabotage the prospect of both closure and recuperation.

Notes

1 Thus Irving Ribner (for example) argues that the play 'affirms justice in the world, which it sees as a harmonious system ruled by a benevolent God' (*Patterns in Shakespearean Tragedy*, p. 117).

2 Other critics who embrace, invoke or imply the categories of essentialist humanism include the following: A. C. Bradley, *Shakespearean Tragedy*, lectures 7 and 8; Israel Knox, *The Aesthetic Theories of Kant, Hegel and Schopenhauer*, p. 117; Robert Ornstein, *The Moral Vision of Jacobean Tragedy*, p. 264; Kenneth Muir, ed. *King Lear*, especially p. lv; Grigori Kozintsev, *King Lear: The Space of Tragedy*, pp. 250–1. For the essentialist view with a pseudo-Nietzschean twist, see Michael Long, *The Unnatural Scene*, pp. 191–3.

Jan Kott suggests the way that the absurdist view exists in the shadow of a failed Christianity and a failed humanism – a sense of paralysis in the face of that failure (*Shakespeare Our Contemporary*, pp. 104, 108, 116–17).

3 Barbara Everett, 'The New King Lear'; William R. Elton, *King Lear and the Gods*; Cedric Watts, 'Shakespearean Themes: The Dying God and the Universal Wolf'.

4 For John Danby, Cordelia is redemption incarnate; but can she really be seen as 'allegorically the root of individual and social sanity; tropologically Charity "that suffereth long and is kind"; analogically the redemptive principle itself'? (*Shakespeare's Doctrine of Nature*, p. 125; cf. p. 133).

5 In-form rather than determine: in this play material factors do not determine values in a crude sense; rather, the latter are shown to be dependent upon the former in a way which radically disqualifies the idealist contention that the reverse is true, namely, that these values not only survive the 'evil' but do so in a way which indicates their ultimate independence of it.

6 By contrast compare Derek Traversi who finds in the imagery of this passage a 'sense of value, of richness and fertility ... an indication of redemption ... the poetical transformation of natural emotion into its spiritual distillation' (*An Approach to Shakespeare*, II. 164).

References

Bacon, Francis, *Essays*, Introduction by Michael J. Hawkins, London: Dent, 1972.

——— , *The Philosophical Works* (one volume), ed. John M. Robertson, London: Routledge, 1905.

Bradley, A. C., *Shakespearean Tragedy* (second edition), London: Macmillan, 1905.

Brockbank, Philip, 'Upon Such Sacrifices', *Proceedings of the British Academy*, 62, (1976), 109–34.

Brooke, Nicholas, *Shakespeare: King Lear*, London: Arnold, 1963.

Danby, John, *Shakespeare's Doctrine of Nature*, London: Faber, 1949.

Elton, William, R., *King Lear and the Gods*, San Marino: The Huntington Library, 1968.

Everett, Barbara, 'The New King Lear', *Critical Quarterly*, 2 (Winter 1960).

Gramsci, Antonio, *Selections From Prison Notebooks*, ed. and trans. Quintin Hoare and Geoffrey Nowell Smith, London: Lawrence and Wishart, 1971.

Hunter, G. K., *Dramatic Identities and Cultural Tradition: Studies in Shakespeare and His Contemporaries*, Liverpool University Press, 1978.

Knox, Israel, *The Aesthetic Theories of Kant, Hegel and Schopenhauer*, New York: Humanities Press, 1958.

Kott, Jan, *Shakespeare Our Contemporary*, trans. Boleslaw Taborski, London: Methuen, 1967.

Kozintsev, Grigori, *King Lear: The Space of Tragedy*, trans. Mary Mackintosh, London: Heinemann, 1977.

Leech, Clifford, *Shakespeare's Tragedies and Other Studies in Seventeenth Century Drama*, London: Chatto, 1950.

Lever, J. W., *The Tragedy of State*, London: Methuen, 1971.

Long, Michael, *The Unnatural Scene: A Study in Shakespearean Tragedy*, London: Methuen, 1976.

Montaigne, Michel, *Essays*, trans. John Florio, 3 vols, London: Dent, 1965.

Ornstein, Robert, *The Moral Vision of Jacobean Tragedy*, University of Wisconsin Press, 1965.

Ribner, Irving, *Patterns in Shakespearean Tragedy*, London: Methuen, 1960.

Sanders, Wilbur, *The Dramatist and the Received Idea: Studies in the Plays of Marlowe and Shakespeare*, Cambridge University Press, 1968.

Seneca, Lucius Annaeus, *Letters From a Stoic*, trans. R. Campbell, Harmondworth: Penguin, 1969.

Shakespeare, William, *King Lear*, ed. Kenneth Muir, London: Methuen, 1964.

Traversi, Derek, *An Approach to Shakespeare*, third edition, 2 vols, London: Hollis and Carter, 1969.

Trilling, Lionel, *The Opposing Self*, New York: Viking Press, 1955.

Watts, Cedric, 'Shakespearean Themes: The Dying God and the Universal Wolf', in M. Curreli and A. Martino, eds., *Critical Dimensions*.

31

Give an Account of Shakespeare and Education, Showing Why You Think They Are Effective and What You Have Appreciated About Them. Support Your Comments with Precise References

Alan Sinfield

Any social order has to include the conditions for its own continuance, and capitalism and patriarchy do this partly through the education system. The positions in the productive process which people are to occupy are an effect of the relations of production, but the preparing of people to occupy those positions is accomplished by the family, the media and education, and the State finances schools, requires attendance at them, trains and employs teachers. This preparation is only in small part a matter of specific training and qualifications: in the main, it is achieved through the whole regime of the school, from classroom practices to the hierarchy of decision-making, and through the mapping of knowledges by the curriculum and examinations.[1] Above all, education sustains 'the extended division between mental and manual labour that characterises the capitalist mode of production in general';[2] and, within that and overlapping unevenly with it, education sustains the subordination of women and ethnic minorities.

At the same time, the system is not monolithic. First, because the official ideology is democratic, the reproduction of an unjust society cannot be straightforward, it has to appear that education is for the good of all the pupils; second, in order to function educational institutions must have a certain relative autonomy, and within this teachers and administrators will have particular professional purposes and needs. These considerations allow space for divergent attitudes and practices; and, in fact, modern English education has developed around a dispute between traditional and progressive approaches, with varying relations between these approaches and government. As we will see, the debate has been vitiated by a reluctance to inspect economic and political determinants, and in consequence progressive approaches have often amounted to little more than a subtle mode of securing assent to the relations of production. Nevertheless, this element of play in the system indicates the scope for radical intervention: 'The many contradictions which confront teachers and pupils can also provide the "space" for practical action for change'.[3]

In education Shakespeare has been made to speak mainly for the right; that is the tendency which we seek to alter. His construction in English culture generally as the great National Poet whose plays embody universal truths has led to his being used to underwrite established practices in literary criticism and, consequently, in examinations. For literary criticism, Shakespeare is the keystone which guarantees the ultimate stability and rightness of the category 'Literature'. The status of other authors may be disputed – indeed, one of the ways criticism offers itself as serious and discriminating is by engaging in such disputes, policing its boundaries. But Shakespeare is always there as the final instance of the validity of Literature. Then, because it is such a profound and universal experience, Literature must be taught to school pupils, whereupon it becomes an instrument within the whole apparatus of filtering whereby schools adjust young people to an unjust social order. And when in 1983 the Secretary of State required the nine GCE boards to devise a common core for A level the English working party could agree only one thing that is not vague and general: that at least one play by Shakespeare must be studied.[4] (See note 10 for an explanation of the British examination system.)

'All pupils, including those of very limited attainments, need the civilizing experience of contact with great literature, and can respond to its universality', declared the Newsom Report of 1963, but it added anxiously: 'They will depend heavily on the skill of the teacher as an interpreter'.[5] In practice it is found that not all pupils 'respond': as empirical studies have demonstrated repeatedly, educational 'attainment' in England is vitally influenced by class and gender.[6] Literature becomes a mark of differential 'attainment', preparing pupils for the differential opportunities and rewards in society at large. 'But then again, I read Shakespeare, and they all thought I was pretty mad for reading it. You see, I was interested in things, really, that I shouldn't have been interested in … thinking back, what they said was, well look, we've told you what you can be, you've got this marvellous opportunity. You can be a shorthand typist, or you can be a nursery nurse'.[7] A crucial ideological manoeuvre in education is this: that the allegedly universal culture to which equal access is apparently offered is, at the same time, a marker of 'attainment' and hence of privilege. Thus those who are discriminated against on the grounds of gender, class and ethnic origins come to believe that it is their own fault (it serves them right).[8] So pupils are persuaded to accept appropriate attitudes to Literature as a criterion of general capacity. The Bullock Report of 1975 complacently observes: 'In a very real sense a pupil is himself being judged each time he responds in class to a piece of literature … is the value-judgement he forms the one the teacher finds acceptable? Is he betraying himself, he may well ask, as one who lacks discrimination?'[9] He may well; but discrimination is certainly what she or he is getting. The Report thinks the answer is for the teacher to handle the occasion with sensitivity: it does not observe that the pupil is being persuaded to internalise success or failure with particular and relative cultural codes as an absolute judgement on her or his potential as a human being.

The system works most plainly through examinations. For a start, as many as twenty-five per cent of pupils take no public examination, not even English Language (they are 'no good' at English, not good English). Then, Literature is the ground of a further discrimination. At CSE and O level the candidate can study English in terms of basic reading and writing skills and must make a positive choice to study Literature. One CSE board warns teachers: 'Candidates, particularly the less able, should be steered away from "The Works of William Shakespeare" (all of them!)'.[10] About fourteen per cent of the pupils taking O level English Language 'go on' to take A level English, but this is not just a growth in competence: this examination consists mainly of literary appreciation (with one of the three papers devoted to Shakespeare's plays). To advance is to move into Literature.[11]

Whilst Literature is made to operate as a mode of exclusion in respect of class, it disadvantages girls by including them (this seems a paradox, but it only shows Literature's flexibility as a cultural form). Of those taking A level English with the London board in 1982 three-quarters were girls (the figures were precisely the reverse for Physics); between a fifth and a quarter of all girls taking A level took English. We see here both an internalisation of dominant notions of the kinds of things girls should do, and also the outcome of all kinds of subtle pressures within schools.[12] The consequences are twofold. First, most of the texts studied reinforce the gender stereotyping which leads girls to these texts – 'women are portrayed as being passive and ineffectual, and taking action only for personal or destructive reasons' (Sharpe, *Just Like a Girl*, p. 150); Irene Payne recalls: 'One teacher gave us the following lines from *King Lear* to write out because we had been noisy: "Her voice was ever soft, / Gentle and low – an excellent thing in woman" '.[13] Second, girls are condemned to a relatively low position in the job market. Official reports assume that women will be essentially housewives or unskilled,[14] though in fact in 1975 they were 41 per cent of the labour force, and their failure to take technical subjects keeps them in relatively unskilled work and reduces their chances of further and higher education.

Of course, it should not be assumed that the process of ideological reproduction in schools is invariably successful. A survey of 1000 pupils taking O and A level English Literature in selective schools in 1968 found that although most of them expressed a commitment to Literature, their actual private reading was 'light'. 'It is as though many of these pupils have two sets of cultural values – one for school and the outside investigator, another for home and their leisure reading.'[15] Of the 800 O level pupils only one in eight showed any wish to go on reading poetry or plays after leaving school. This is little cause for satisfaction: it is likely that most of the disaffected had found that they were not 'good' at literature; and look at the waste of time, effort and money. However, it serves to indicate that hegemony is not easily, or in any straightforward way, achieved. Although the dominant class or class fraction controls the terms and conditions within which cultural production is carried on, 'Groups or classes which do not stand at the apex of power, nevertheless find ways of expressing and realising in their culture their subordinate position and experiences'.[16] I will show how the institutional construction of Shakespeare in education has had to struggle with subordinate cultures and with rival movements within the dominant.

Above all, Shakespeare does not have to work in a conservative manner. His plays do not have to signify in the ways they have customarily been made to (it will be the project of the next section to analyse how GCE constructs them in certain ways). It is partly a matter of reading them differently – drawing attention to their historical insertion, their political implications, and the activity of criticism in reproducing them. Such readings are exemplified in the first part of this book. And it is also a matter of changing the way Shakespeare signifies in society: he does not have to be a crucial stage in the justification of elitism in education and culture. He has been appropriated for certain practices and attitudes, and can be reappropriated for others.

An analysis of the reading of a sample of children aged 10, 12 and 14 in maintained and direct-grant schools produced 7557 book titles of which 54 were 'adult quality narrative', but Shakespeare figures not at all.[17] The reading of Shakespeare begins with and overwhelmingly takes its character from the examination questions set at O and A level (see note 10). These are controlled entirely by certain universities; teachers, whether they like it or not, must in fairness prepare their pupils for them. A whole apparatus of school editions and cramming aids has sprung up around them. I will point out in the question papers the two fundamental mystifications of bourgeois ideology. All the questions specified were set in 1983.

The main move is the projection of local conditions on to the eternal. As Rachel Sharp puts it, 'The power relations which are peculiar to market society are seen as how things have always been and ought to be. They acquire a timelessness which is powerfully legitimised by a theory of human nature ... Political struggles to alter present-day social arrangements are seen as futile for "things are as they are" because of man's basic attributes and nothing could ever be very different.'[18] This move is built in to the structure of the whole exercise, through the notion that Shakespeare is the great National Poet who speaks universal truths and whose plays are the ultimate instance of Literature. It is made also through the ways the questions invite the candidates to handle the plays. Almost invariably it is assumed that the plays reveal universal 'human' values and qualities and that they are self-contained and coherent entities; and the activity of criticism in producing these assumptions is effaced.

The appeal to absolute values and qualities is ubiquitous: 'At the centre of *King Lear* lies the question, "What is a man?" Discuss' (Oxford and Cambridge, A level); 'Beginning with a consideration of the following passage, discuss Shakespeare's presentation of Goodness in *Macbeth*' (Welsh, A level). Women, of course, are a special category within the universal (there are fewer questions about female than male characters): ' "*The Winter's Tale* is much more concerned with the qualities of womanhood, its virtue, its insight, and its endurance". Discuss' (Southern, A level). If women seem not to be manifesting the expected qualities then that is a matter for comment: ' "The men in *Twelfth Night* are ridiculous in what they say and do: it is the women who are full of common sense". Show how far you agree ...' (Welsh, O level).

The alleged coherence and self-containedness of the text re-enacts at the level of the particular reading the coherence and self-containedness claimed by ideology. In the examination questions almost no reference is made to the diverse forms which the play has taken and may take – to scholarly discussions about provenance, to the conditions under which it has been transmitted, to the different forms it takes today, from school editions to stage, film and TV productions.[19] Even the occasional question about staging is liable to involve the assumption that there is a true reading behind the diverse possibilities: 'How, as a young actor, would you try to cope with the difficulties of playing the part of John of Gaunt' (Southern, O level – bad luck if you're an actress). The text is *there*; the most common form of question at O level begins 'Give an account of ...' and 'precise reference' is repeatedly demanded. That the text is to be regarded as coherent, either in terms of action or of dramatic effect, is frequently insisted upon. ' "While we may hope for a happy ending to *King Lear*, Shakespeare's conclusion is entirely fitting". Discuss' (Associated, O level); 'Write about the dramatic effectiveness of the last act of *Twelfth Night*, and show how the ending is connected to earlier episodes of the play' (London, O level). Everything comes out the way it always had to, every incident is justified by its 'effectiveness' (one of the commonest terms on the papers).

The effacing of the activity of criticism works mainly through the assumption that the candidate will discover the true response or meaning in the manner established by literary criticism as appropriate to the text. Not only are these assumptions not exposed for inspection, they are drawn forth naturally, as it appears, from the inter-action between the candidate and the text. The fact that between those two comes the learnt procedures of literary criticism is obscured. Of course, the questions often invite discussion, agreement or disagreement, but normally that is within a prescribed range of possibilities and to infringe these requires a repudiation of the authority of Shakespeare or the examiners, often both. A whole range of issues and positions is simply not allowed to reach visibility. 'Compare Shakespeare's treatment of the problem of evil in any *two* plays' (Oxford and Cambridge, A level): the candidate who sees that 'the problem of evil' is a mystified concept must force a space for such an analysis, knowing that she or he is out of accord with the examiners and will have little time to show the expected 'knowledge' of the plays. Questions which appear to invite a personal response are often all the more tyrannical: 'Give an account of the scene in Capulet's orchard where Romeo sees Juliet on the balcony, showing what you have enjoyed about the words spoken by the lovers' (Welsh, O level). Candidates are invited to interrogate their experience to discover a response which has in actuality been learnt. As Perry Anderson showed, this Leavisite strategy demands (whilst lamenting the absence of) 'one crucial precondition: a shared, stable system of beliefs and values';[20] what actually happens is that candidates are required to take up a certain system of values – those we have been identifying – in order satisfactorily to answer the question.

The second fundamental mystification of bourgeois ideology is the construction of individual subjectivity as a given which is undetermined and unconstituted and hence a ground of meaning and coherence: 'In effect the individual is understood in terms of a presocial essence, nature, or identity and on that basis s/he is invested with a quasi-spiritual autonomy. The individual becomes the origin and focus of meaning – an individuated essence which precedes and – in idealist philosophy – transcends history and society.'[21] Eternal values can no longer be ratified securely by religion, but now they are grounded in their perception through authentic subjectivity. This relationship is figured precisely in the question: 'There are moments in *King Lear* when the insights of individual characters seem to provide a key to the play's deepest themes and preoccupations. Consider this claim in relation to *one* of the following "insights" ...' (Oxford and Cambridge, A level). The individual and the universal are constituted in a mutually supportive polarity.

The examination papers construct Shakespeare and the candidate in terms of individuated subjectivity through their stress upon Shakespeare's free-standing genius, their emphasis on characterisation, and their demand for the candidate's personal response. At no point do the GCE papers of 1983 invite candidates to consider the ways in which a play relates to its social context in Shakespeare's time or subsequently. It seems to have been born, immaculately, into the classroom. Indeed, some questions actively encourage a notion of creation ex nihilo: 'By careful reference to appropriate scenes show how Shakespeare has created a dream-like world' (JMB, O level).

The call for commentary on individual characters is the staple fare, especially at O level. 'Do you think Falstaff is ever sincere in *Henry IV Part I*?'; 'What sort of person is Henry IV? Do you think he always acts wisely?' – these are two of the three Associated O level questions on the play. Individuals are the unproblematic source of action and meaning, despite intermittent assertions, from diverse critical points of view, that this is not an appropriate framework for Elizabethan and Jacobean drama (consider E. E. Stoll, L. C. Knights, Muriel Bradbrook, Catherine Belsey). Even questions which seem to bear upon the issue nudge the candidate into assuming a realist convention: ' "In *All's Well that Ends Well* Shakespeare is concerned to make Helena good rather than plausible". Discuss the role and character of Helena in the play to show to what extent you agree with this statement' (Northern Ireland, A level); notice how Shakespeare's autonomous decision seems to be the only determinant.

Subjectivity and authenticity are the programme also in the customary appeal to the candidate's judgement and, often, personal response. We have seen that the candidate is supposed to discover in herself or himself the necessary procedures and judgements of literary criticism; at the same time, contradictorily, a personal response is required. This demand for individual assessment is often more coercive than the 'neutral' question. The determination of the Cambridge board to get the candidate to reveal the required response is apparent in this novel kind of question: 'This short scene is really doing three things: advancing the "story", adding to our knowledge of the characters, and expanding some of the ideas (about relationships and about the condition of the world) that are going to be important in the play as a whole. Show how much of this a close reading of the scene helps you to discover' (Cambridge, O levels).

Peter Widdowson, looking at GCE questions on Hardy, found the same ideological construction: Hardy 'is reproduced within very limited parameters of intelligibility: "Hardy" as the tragic novelist of character struggling heroically with Nature, Fate, or other, preeminently non-social forces'.[22] Widdowson observed the total effacement of the fact that the critic, as much as the historian, is 'a "social phenomenon" who selects and organizes the facts / texts according to his / her positioning in history: ... who, in effect, "writes" Literature from the perspective of a historical and ideological present' (p. 4). It is this ideological construction that the present book is striving to overturn.

The twin manoeuvres of bourgeois ideology construct two dichotomies: universal versus historical and individual versus social. In each case the first term is privileged, and so meaning is sucked into the universal / individual polarity, draining it away from the historical and the social – which is where meaning is made by people together in determinate conditions, and where it might be contested. 'How far do you think that the fates of Antony and Cleopatra are inevitable rather than voluntary?' (Oxford and Cambridge, A level): that which is not universal is individual, any other level of explanation disappears down the yawning gulf between the two. The universal is unchangeable and the individual lives, quintessentially, in 'his' inner subjectivity; shared purpose to change the world is not just disqualified, it is not allowed into visibility. One question in 1983 promoted such an issue: ' "In the realm of politics Shakespeare sees any hope for progress in human society as profoundly futile". Discuss with reference to *two* plays' (Cambridge, A level). Of course, agreement with the proposition is expected – 'profoundly' and 'the realm' (suggesting a narrow range of operation for politics) work to secure this. The 'discussion' is hardly open.

We may envisage, then, the intellectual cast of the successfully socialised GCE candidate. She or he will be respectful of Shakespeare and high culture and accustomed to being appreciative of the cultural production which is offered through established institutions. She or he will be trained at giving opinions – within certain prescribed limits; at collecting evidence – though without questioning its status or the construction of the problem; at saying what is going on – though not whether that is what ought to happen; at seeing effectiveness, coherence, purposes fulfilled – but not conflict. And because the purposeful individual is perceived as the autonomous origin and ground of meaning and event, success in these exercises will be accepted as just reason for certain economic and social privileges.

It all seems perfectly adapted for the fastest-growing class fraction, the new petty bourgeoisie working in finance, advertising, the civil service, teaching, the health service, the social services and clerical occupations. The new petty bourgeoisie (unlike the old, of artisans and small shopkeepers) is constituted not by family but through education: 'The various petty bourgeois agents each possess, in relation to those subordinate to them, a fragment of the fantastic secret of knowledge that legitimises the delegated authority that they exercise ... Hence the belief in the 'neutrality of culture', and in the educational apparatus as a corridor of circulation by the promotion and accession of the "best" to the bourgeois state, or in any case to a higher state in the specific hierarchy of mental labour'.[23] The combination of cultural deference and cautious questioning promoted around Shakespeare in GCE seems designed to construct a petty bourgeoisie which will strive within limits allocated to it without seeking to disturb the system – 'it does not want to break the ladder by which it imagines it can climb' (Poulantzas, p. 292).

I will now look more closely and with a historical perspective at the theory, such as it is, which underpins modern literary education. The weakness of the dominant constructions of Shakespeare will be exposed. I will consider the historical conditions in which literary criticism has been endeavouring to maintain its position, finding that the practices imposed so vigorously upon pupils rest not on confident and coherent dogma, but on confused, anxious and pragmatic responses to pressures which continually defy containment. As I have said, we may not assume that the ideology of GCE is successfully inculcated: it is undermined both by conflicting tendencies in English society and by its own contradictions. These afford numerous points at which it may be interrogated and challenged.

In 1944, when the Butler Act was passed, making secondary education compulsory for all children and free for those who cannot afford to buy their way into the private system and its network of privileges, the dominant idea of education was the 'classical humanist'. In this approach it is 'the task of the guardian class, including the teachers, to initiate the young into the mysteries of knowledge and the ways in which knowledge confers various kinds of social power on those who possess it ... classical humanism has been associated with clear and firm discipline, high attainment in examinations, continuity between past and present, the cohesiveness and orderly development of institutions.'[24] This is evidently an approach designed to train an elite, and in fact it grew out of the training which was given to the children of the upper and middle classes in the late nineteenth century.

In English Literature classical humanism is exemplified in its original form by Quiller-Couch. He was Professor of English Literature at Cambridge and in a lecture delivered in 1917 he declared that the best kind of education is reading aloud by the teacher and pupils: 'it just lets the author – Chaucer or Shakespeare or Milton or Coleridge – have his own way with the young plant – just lets them drop "like the gentle rain from heaven", and soak in'.[25] Children, at least if they are of the right class, will take naturally to Shakespeare. Actually, of course, it is being drilled into them, and we see here the origin of classical humanist ideas in the nineteenth-century practice of mechanically construing classical texts – Quiller-Couch says the reading should move round the class, 'just as in a construing class'. This is the root of the most mechanical part of the GCE examinations, the compulsory question one designed to show whether the candidate has 'done' the text in detail.

However, a notion of education designed for the offspring of the gentry and aspiring commercial bougeoisie could hardly survive without adaptation in a society which proclaims equality of opportunity. The necessary adjustment was made by Leavis and his followers, and hence their importance. The Leavisite reader is in a more complex relationship with authority. The great works are there to be discovered, but they are not identical with the established canon, they have to be reappropriated, won back from the upper-class dilettantes who have abused them. And the reader does not make this discovery without apparent effort but through a strenuous engagement, a serious and deliberate process of discrimination which both tests and develops a personal sensibil-ity. At the same time, the distance from lower-class culture cannot now be assumed. The true literary experience is threatened also from below, by commercialised 'mass' culture, and this too has to be repudiated. It is by such a repudiation that the student recognises the special culture which she or he has entered. In other words, this was an approach for the class-mobile – either those moving from the lower middle class (occasionally working class) towards professional and managerial occupations, or those moving from the established middle class towards professions like education and social work which justify themselves partly in terms of superior acquired know-ledge and personal sensibility. The Leavisite does not receive Shakespeare as part of a natural heritage, she or he wins him and fights off the challenge of 'mass' culture (and passes the examination).

The spread of Leavisism through the education system – not through Cambridge, of course, there they were still educating gentlemen, but through schools, colleges of education and redbrick universities – coincided with the post-war extension of secondary education. The study of English Literature was extended vastly and the contradiction between its universalist and meritocratic pretensions became apparent (in 1951 13,000 students entered for A level English, by 1976 it was 66,000).[26] In 1963

G. H. Bantock declared, 'the number who benefit from this sort of task seems to me to be more limited than we commonly admit' and deplored the acquisition of 'a series of analytic tricks which enable a "right" judgement to be arrived at'.[27] In 1964, in a volume entitled *Crisis in the Humanities*, Graham Hough observed that 'much of English literature up to the threshold of modern times is now as remote as the ancient classics' and that literary criticism on Leavisite lines had become 'a set of special tricks'.[28] This latter complaint is just what we might expect, for the whole idea of personal judgement which has to approximate to received opinion invites exactly that learning of 'tricks'.

During the 1960s, four factors particularly were drawing attention to the curriculum: government pressure for more and better scientists, the anticipated raising of the school-leaving age to 16, the amalgamation of grammar and secondary modern schools into comprehensives and the demand for student participation.[29] They all served to problematise Literature. The first factor seemed initially to require the most strenuous Leavisite address,[30] but the others proved the real threat because they promoted rival student cultures. The strength and pretensions of literary institutions demanded that such benefits be more widely distributed, but how could it be made to work? The Newsom Report of 1963, dealing with 'average and below average pupils', betrays an understandable nervousness: 'It is of course within poetry and drama that the use of language goes deepest. Nobody should have to teach poetry against his will, but without it English will never be complete; poetry is not a minor amenity but a major channel of experience ... How far the great poetry of earlier ages can be introduced with advantage only the teacher can say' (p. 156).

Usually, the problem was said to be that of the young people: they could not appreciate good culture. But it became apparent to sociologists that they had their own, preferred culture: 'Being highly committed to the *teenager* role tends to go with being an underachiever (relative to one's I.Q.) ... It also tends quite strongly to go with having a bad conduct record' – notice here the glimmering recognition of subcultural resistance alongside the terminology of hegemonic incorporation.[31] Youth culture was attributed to mass society and the mass media, to earning power and the disturbance of World War II, but it was also a product *of* the education system which it was perceived as undermining. Education created a hiatus between childhood and work, and organised young people into age-specific institutions where interaction within the institution was bound to be at least as important as the outward purposes of it. The teenage subculture was partly the product of young people's attempts to adjust to the conditions they were required to experience; whilst in many ways this involved a negotiated response which amounted to the incorporation of many of the values of school, it represented in other ways a resistance to it. Because this was manifested in the main culturally, through styles of speech, dress and demeanour, it seemed to confront especially English teaching.

It was possible for educators simply to deplore the influence of youth culture so long as this was the form, mainly, of the lower classes and of those who did not succeed in school (this, of course, was a circular construction). But the spread, from the mid-1960s, of an alternative culture in universities and colleges infiltrated an adversary to high culture into the main fortress where it survives. Even Shakespeare could be appropriated – as in Barbara Garson's play *MacBird!*, a rock opera of *Othello*, phrases in Beatles' songs, Hamlet's 'What a piece of work is a man' speech in *Hair*, Charles

Marowitz's 'fringe' adaptations. The typical student now negotiates contradictory worlds – the rock concert and the tutorial – and whatever the outcome high culture does not retain the centrality which was its original justification. If it is one culture among others then what is it?

The response from the right was immediate and clear: it had all been a mistake, most people are not educable beyond the acquisition of the basic skills necessary to keep the economy going. Classical humanism was reasserted in the *Black Papers* of 1969–70 and by Rhodes Boyson, who was to become a Tory education minister – he wanted 'a sense of purpose, continuity and authority' with schools giving 'order, values and guidance, while teaching skills and knowledge', and felt this would be best achieved by the state 'helping parents to buy the education they want'.[32] This movement gathered strength through the 1970s and issued, as part of a general collapse of consensus on the welfare state, in the education cuts of the Thatcher governments.

The left was more disorientated by the problematisation of education and culture, since for many decades the Labour Party and the Communist Party alike had accepted that education in roughly its present guise was a good thing and that what was required was 'reform' to equalise opportunities for individuals to benefit from it (see Jones, *Beyond Progressive Education*, chapters 3,5). This idea was the quintessence of welfare capitalism: the State provides the conditions whereby the individuals can maximise their personal advancement, and thus the economy will grow and everyone will be happy. From the late 1960s, initiatives on the left opened up new kinds of analysis and practice. There was trade-union militancy among teachers. The possibilities of subcultural resistance were theorised, moving on from Basil Bernstein's distinction between elaborated and restricted codes to an analysis of the scope for resistance and negotiation available to subordinate groups;[33] the *Language in Use* project identified literature as a particular impediment: 'habitual notions about the value and function of all varieties of written English are derived from notions about the language of literature'.[34] New publications, and especially the journal *Teaching London Kids*, discussed ways of developing in the classroom the *critical response* of working-class children to their social situation: they are encouraged to 'know their place' – not in the customary sense of accepting their subservience, but in terms of understanding their allocated place in the system, what the material determinants of that positioning are and how it might be otherwise.

But despite, and even within, these socialist initiatives, the principal resistance to rightist ideology among left-liberal educationists has been defensive and recuperative. It has sought to enhance the claims for school experience and tended to keep the system going while making sufficient gestures towards the complex and potentially disruptive cultural position of so many pupils. I shall discuss three major institutional developments of the 1960s and 1970s: the progressive movement, the Certificate of Secondary Education (CSE), and non-disciplinary humanities programmes. All three were in many ways recuperative, but they admitted oppositional possibilities as well. Literature featured in them because its failure to command the natural universal respect claimed for it seemed to manifest the impasse into which current theory and practice had worked themselves. Often it was invoked to add weight and legitimacy to these developments and, conversely, it seemed that they were ways of sustaining Literature. But the outcome was rather, in effect, the further problematising of it as a concept and of criticism as a practice. And Shakespeare was used increasingly as the supreme token of the viability of Literature, the one unchallengeable instance.

The progressivist movement is usually traced to Rousseau and his *Émile*, but it has been gathering strength since the late nineteenth century. It stresses not the acquisition of a given set of standards and body of knowledge but the personal fulfilment of the individual; not training for an established slot in society but the discovery and maturation of an authentic self. It is sometimes called 'romantic' because it values creativity and freedom; and it is called 'child-centred' because it assumes that the most valuable experiences can be drawn from the child her- or himself, rather than imposed by the teacher or a curriculum.[35] It advanced rapidly during the 1960s and 1970s, and seemed to offer a way of recuperating Literature, though eventually it calls it into question.

The most important figure in progressivism at the start of this period was David Holbrook, but his work now appears contradictory, recuperative and mystifying. He takes Shakespeare as the ultimate literary experience and argues that what the child will discover in her or his authentic self is a positive response to the play. In Holbrook's *English for Maturity*, first published in 1961, Shakespeare 'is the touchstone when we discuss literature – we may dispute the value, say, of Pope or Milton, but we can all agree that Shakespeare is a great poet'.[36] But now what we get from Shakespeare is not a disciplined training in traditional values but poems 'about the essentials of being': 'by experiencing his work we may come to have a renewed grasp on life, to understand how to live in this post-Renaissance era, fully recognizing our own feeble natures, and accepting the conditions of our lives which are dominated by Time and Death' (*English for Maturity*, p. 43). The guarantor of the link between Shakespeare and the self is none other than Leavis: his idea of responses to Literature as personal maturation could be used by Holbrook even while others were using his elitism to sustain the classical-humanist approach. 'We must experience Wordsworth's depression before we can experience his triumph over it. Leavis will encourage us to do this'[37] (compare Pope's reconciliation of nature and the ancients: 'To copy nature is to copy them'). Such determined accommodating of authority with personal freedom obviously masks a theoretical instability (the reader will have noticed the coercive strategies in the quotations above – 'we can all agree that'; 'fully recognizing'; 'we must experience'). Holbrook is actually promoting Literature by indirect means and persuading the students to accept his reading as deriving from their experience.

In Holbrook's approach a failure of students to find in themselves Shakespeare as he would have them – as seeing 'the reality of love and creativity in man' – is interpreted not as evidence of a problem with some part of the theory but as the result of interference: 'Answers by students to questions of Shakespeare's attitudes to human nature and love show how the destructive attitudes of the prevalent literary ethos prevent them from being able to respond to the greatest literature' (*Exploring Word*, p. 212). Latterly progressivists have acknowledged that the appeal to personal relevance cannot be so conveniently manipulated. Albert Rowe declares, 'The attempt to impose a minority taste upon the majority was doomed from the start ... literary culture is as relative as other forms of culture'.[38] The compromise with the canon is abandoned and even Shakespeare drops out of visibility. Peter Abbs, in a slashing attack on a GCE examiner who was unwise enough to visit his teacher-training course, insists: 'In the first place it is, surely, the process we value, *the process* of children responding in a personal way to literature. *It does not have to be Shakespeare*.[39] None the less, Abbs himself, as one student complained, presents 'a literary heritage that supports your own philosophy' (*English within the Arts*, p. 134): Abbs tends to promote a canon and a syllabus while insisting that he is essentially addressing human values as they offer themselves to the individual subjectivity. This continual collapsing of values back into their alleged source in the mind of the student makes it very difficult for her or him to inspect the ideological construction of such education.

Progressivist questions have begun to appear on GCE papers, but they tend to smuggle in diverse discriminatory assumptions and the personal invitation may place only the thinnest mask over coercion: 'Give an account of the scene where Caliban first meets Trinculo and Stephano, making it clear in what ways you find it amusing, and what other feelings you have about it' (Cambridge, O level). Initially, the demand for an 'account' suggests that the text is there for reasoned paraphrase – the traditional wish to ensure that the candidate has read the play 'properly' is still there. At the other end of the question the appeal is to 'what other feelings you have' – an open-ended appeal to personal impressions. In the middle one must make 'clear in what ways you find it amusing': the response which the examiners have predetermined to be the right one must be discovered. This exerts a pressure on the invitation to express 'feelings' – the possibility that the scene might relate to colonial exploitation is not encouraged. That would not be 'amusing'.

Progressivism also underlies invitations to consider Shakespeare's plays in terms of realisation in the theatre – it is part of the appeal to experience and creativity (such questions were set in 1983 by three boards). But theatre questions also may exert a drag back towards the classical-humanist position. Notice how this question starts off with excitement but moves back to precise recollection and the implication that 'the events and characters' are quantities that may be simply known: 'Select what you consider to be the most exciting scene from *Romeo and Juliet* and show how you would produce it to make the greatest impact on an audience. A close knowledge of the events and characters should be apparent in your production ideas' (Southern, O level). Most boards remain hostile to 'imaginative interpretations'.

There is radical impetus in the progressivists' position – in their attack on examinations, on the competitive hierarchy in schools and on the pressure exerted on schools by universities; and in their insistence that children's writing has a validity which challenges that of established Literature. However, from a materialist standpoint the drawbacks of the position are manifest. It reproduces in a particularly potent form the bourgeois ideology of individualism, effacing the historical construction both of the text and the moment in which it is read – not to mention the historical construction of individualism itself. The student is offered no political analysis or direction, but is exhorted to regard as her or his authentic response what can in actuality be only a combination of pressures from society at large and from the teacher in particular. The former will be largely conservative, the latter may be radical in some of its emphases, but its refusal to invite inspection of its own historical and political location must be mystifying. At the same time, progressivism has provided a starting point and a strategy of intervention for socialist teaching. The principle of appealing to the pupil's experience is transformed if that experience is placed in its political context – 'bringing them to an awareness of their social situation in a class-based society through the spoken and written word, and affirming the collective strength of their class'.[40]

CSE examinations (the second institutional development which has tended recently to rehandle Literature) began in the mid-1960s, and because they are designed for less 'able' pupils than those taking O level and not involved in the university selection sequence they could cut free from the academic / high-cultural conception of Literature. Almost invariably, a list of twenty or more books is proposed and the candidate answers on the ones he or she has studied; overwhelmingly, the texts are modern and chosen for their supposed appeal to young people; only Shakespeare persists from the traditional canon, and study of his work is not compulsory.

Often CSE questions are open-ended and do little to encourage the customary manoeuvres of literary criticism – 'Write about a book, play, or collection of poems that you really enjoyed reading as part of your C.S.E. English Course. Explain what it was that pleased you, and how your experience of people and / or places was enlarged by your reading' (East Anglia, South). This approximates to the way non-professional adult readers think about books (except, of course, that they don't write examination essays about them). Sometimes candidates are invited to rework the books in their own terms – the following question might be applied to *Macbeth*, *The Merchant of Venice* or *Romeo and Juliet*: 'Put yourself in the place of a character, in one of the works you have studied, faced with dangerous situations. (i) Describe the situations, (ii) show how you dealt with them, and (iii) explain the effect(s) of your action(s) or decision(s)' (North West). Such invitations to reconstruct the text undermine its stability and status as the one essential embodiment of the writer's genius; for the reverent 'neutrality' of literary criticism they substitute the manifest appropriation of the candidate. Such questions have spread from CSE to one O level board, the Oxford and Cambridge: 'Imagine that you are the nurse being interviewed by a reporter. Explain your part in the events of the play' (*Romeo and Juliet*); 'Write an editorial for the *Arden Gazette* on the recent outbreak of marriage in the district' (in *As You Like It*; the note of facetiousness is particularly bold and must have found many responses).

I have stressed the subversiveness of CSE, the extent to which it tends to undermine the canon and procedures of Literature. Actually, many of the examination questions are like those usually set at O level and pronouncements of the boards indicate conservative leanings. 'The use of extremely lightweight, modern, romantic authors should not be encouraged or allowed for examination purposes', the North West board declared in its *Reports on the 1983 Examinations*; and the South-East paper warned bluntly in its rubric: 'Questions refer to the books you have read, NOT to any radio, television, musical or film versions of them'. The idea of Literature lives on. Nevertheless, for radical teachers the more adventurous lists of texts and open-ended questions have permitted discussions of issues like racism, gender relations and peace, and the development in the students of a critical consciousness capable of analysing the ideological frameworks they encounter – including that of the examination system. Once more we see educational institutions manifesting a confusion of purpose which admits oppositional intervention.

The third institutional development which has been used to help Literature live up to its claims for general relevance is the subsuming of it into 'humanities' programmes. This tendency has made serious inroads into the status and pretensions of Literature, and has proved amenable to politicised teaching (it is related to the radical contextual-ising of Shakespeare's plays in Part I of the present study). It was given focus by a Schools Council / Nuffield study, *The Humanities Project* (Heinemann, 1970), which was produced to coincide with the raising of the school-leaving age (by one year to 16). 'The aim of the Project is: to develop an understanding of social situations and human acts and of the controversial issues which they raise' (p. 1); so the courses consist of a series of themes and issues. Visual material is emphasised; printed material may include 'poems and songs; extracts from drama, novels and biography; letters, reports and articles; readings from the social sciences; maps, cartoons, questionnaires, graphs and tables; and advertisements' (p. 11). Not much of the traditional or the progressivist exaltation of the literary text will survive such a process. In *Themes in Life and Literature*, edited by Robert S. Fowler and published by the Oxford University Press (1967) chapter four begins with two- to six-line snippets from 'The Lady of Shalott', 'I know where I'm going' (folk song), Shakespeare's sonnet 18, 'The Wife of Bath's Prologue', *The Girl with Green Eyes* (Edna O'Brien), *A Midsummer Night's Dream*, 'Tintern Abbey' and 'Under the Bridges of Paris' (pop song); then there are diverse prose passages. The Bullock Report (1975) was anxious: 'An obvious danger in humanities lessons is for the literature to be selected solely on the ground that it matches the theme, however inappropriate it may be in other ways. Moreover, when a poem or story is enlisted to serve a theme it can become the property of that theme to the extent that its richness is oversimplified, its more rewarding complexities ignored' (p. 132). Thus Bullock would have liked to reincorporate those 'literary' aspects which humanities programmes were devised to cover the failure of. It was able to conclude, however, that 'a permanent relationship with the great classics … is traditionally thought appropriate for pupils preparing for examinations' (p. 130). So at least the GCE streams can be kept uncontaminated.

Bullock did not say, though it certainly thought, that the traditional approach is politically safer. *The Humanities Project* envisaged that the teacher would be 'neutral' in the presentation of themes (p. I) but this was of course a chimera, and the opportunity for radical intervention is manifest. The extent of politicised teaching in humanities programmes cannot be estimated, but its presence is indicated by the hostility shown both by classical humanists and conservative progressivists. Roger Scruton writes in the *Daily Mail* against Peace Studies and other 'relevant' courses as 'a continuous stream of rubbish' (he moves easily into the idiom of the *Mail*), preferring what he calls 'the "irrelevant" subjects – the great dead languages, higher mathematics, literary criticism' – because they force 'the pupil to understand something which has no immediate bearing on his experience' (3 February 1984). For the progressivists, Peter Abbs exposes his own politics when he complains that with anthologies about strikes, women's liberation, prostitution, homosexuality and another dozen social issues the approach has become 'sordidly nihilistic … We politicize literature at the cost of authenticity' (*English within the Arts*, p. 22). Strikers, feminists, prostitutes, gays and so on seem to be excluded from the authentic – or is it only when they draw attention to their oppression?

The attempts of these rival theories and practices to cope in problematic historical conditions with the intractability of Literature in the classroom have steadily eroded such coherence and status as it once had. The 'crisis in English' which has recently been noticed in universities is much more advanced and more far-reaching in schools. There the high-cultural idea, the alleged universal appeal, and the practices of literary criticism are questioned continuously, and over large areas Literature is slipping out of visibility altogether. This we can observe even in O level and sixth-form work. As this book goes to press it has been decided, after years of hesitation, to amalgamate O level and GCE into one examination with a single scale of grades from 1988. There will be more and less 'difficult' papers, aimed at preserving the 'academic' character of the top grades; whether this will lead to current O level characteristics intruding on the work of more pupils, or to further erosion of traditional literary criticism, remains to be seen. Already there are A level rivals to English – Theatre Studies, and Communications. The Schools' Council has endorsed one-year sixth-form English courses which 'propose a direct interest in people in action, in the community and at work, as well as in documentary and poetic presentations of human experience'.[41] And the Associated Examining Board has introduced a new format of A level English assessment, including an open-book examination and a course-work folder, and involving the study of texts chosen in schools for their appropriateness in developing pupils' reading experiences; the aims include an extension of 'the range of English studies' and 'opportunity for more varied work' (Dixon, *Education 16–19*, pp. 66–70).

In the new Associated A level, for all that has been said, the study of one Shakespeare play is compulsory. The importance of Shakespeare is perhaps greater than ever, for he is becoming the *sole vehicle* of high-cultural ideology and establishment literary criticism in schools. This is true even in conventional GCE examinations: 'other former rivals in the English literary pantheon – Milton, Wordsworth, Tennyson – have faded almost without trace' from O level (Barnes and Seed, *Seals of Approval*, p. 18), and the tendency is similar at A level. Goulden and Hartley's 'league table' of set texts show Literature to be dispersed over a most eclectic range (' "Nor should such Topics" ', p. 6). Shakespeare remains as the great witness to the universality of literary experience, but his position is absurd, for he is representative of a category, of a theory, of which he is the only undoubted instance.

The left-liberal consensus which, I have tried to show, has undermined Literature while seeming to recuperate it is itself now under attack from the right. Not only are resources being cut, but the Department of Education and Science is insisting upon traditional disciplines and elitist 'standards'; the Schools' Council, which has been a principal agency of reformist thought, is being abolished and more emphasis is being placed on the Assessment and Performance Unit. The courses provided by the Manpower Services Commission for people leaving school at 16 without jobs force them into practical studies intended to prepare them directly for the labour market (such as it is); there is very little scope there for Literature.[42]

Yet it is unlikely that Shakespeare's significance as a cultural token will diminish – it is too firmly established outside education as well as inside. His name has been the watchword for reactionaries and conservative progressivists alike. For Sir Cyril Burt, who was so determined to demonstrate a hierarchy of innate ability in children that he faked his evidence, Shakespeare's transcendent status is the first move in his *Black Paper* argument: 'No one, not even the most convinced egalitarian, would deny that a few outstanding personalities, like Shakespeare or Newton, are born geniuses';[43] recently the Chancellor of the Exchequer has invoked Shakespeare in the same cause. David

Holbrook appears to present a significant alternative, but his case for the creativity of the 'low IQ' child reincorporates the elitism and essentialism which it might seem to challenge: the child's writing 'was doing for the human mind that produced it, what Shakespeare's *Sonnets* did for his very great mind at a very different level'.[44] Socialists may challenge these appropriations of Shakespeare. The plays may be taught so as to foreground their historical construction in Renaissance England and in the institutions of criticism, dismantling the metaphysical concepts in which they seem at present to be entangled, and especially the construction of gender and sexuality. Teaching Shakespeare's plays and writing books about them is unlikely to bring down capitalism, but it is a point for intervention.

Notes

1 On the 'hidden curriculum' see Rachel Sharp, *Knowledge, Ideology and the Politics of Schooling* (London: Routledge, 1980), pp. 123–31; Sue Sharpe, *Just Like a Girl* (Harmondsworth: Penguin, 1976), ch. 4; Michelle Stanworth, *Gender and Schooling* (London: Hutchinson, 1983).

2 Nicos Poulantzas, *Classes in Contemporary Capitalism* (London: New Left Books, 1975), p. 252. See further Samuel Bowles and Herbert Gintis, *Schooling in Capitalist America* (New York: Basic Books, 1976; London: Routledge, 1976); Roger Dale, Geoff Esland and Madeleine MacDonald, eds., *Schooling and Capitalism* (London: Routledge and the Open University, 1976).

3 Michael Young and Geoff Whitty, 'Perspectives on Education and Society', in *Society, State and Schooling*, ed. Young and Whitty (Ringmer: Falmer Press, 1977), p. 12. See also in this book Simon Frith and Paul Corrigan, 'The Politics of Education' and Michael Erben and Denis Gleeson, 'Education as Reproduction'. And see further Education Group, Centre for Contemporary Cultural Studies, *Unpopular Education* (London: Hutchinson and Centre for Contemporary Cultural Studies, 1981), ch. 1.

4 *Common Cores at A level*, prepared by GCE Boards of England, Wales and Northern Ireland (London, 1983). On Shakespeare as National Poet see Derek Longhurst, ' "Not for all time, but for an Age"; an Approach to Shakespeare Studies', in *Re-Reading English*, ed. Peter Widdowson (London: Methuen, 1982).

5 Ministry of Education, *Half Our Future* (the Newsom Report) (London: HMSO, 1963), p. 155.

6 See Noëlle Bisseret, *Education, Class, Language and Ideology* (London: Routledge, 1979), ch. 2; J. W. B. Douglas, J. M. Ross and H. R. Simpson, *All Our Future* (London: Panther, 1971), pp. 36–41; A. H. Halsey, 'Towards Meritocracy? The Case of Britain', in *Power and Ideology in Education*, eds. Jerome Karabel and A. H. Halsey (New York: Oxford University Press, 1977).

7 Linda Peffer in *Dutiful Daughters*, ed. Jean McCrindle and Sheila Rowbotham (Harmondsworth: Penguin, 1979), p. 364. See also pp. 336–7.

8 See Pierre Bourdieu, 'Cultural Reproduction and Social Reproduction', in *Knowledge, Education and Cultural Change*, ed. Richard Brown (London: Tavistock, 1973); and also Bourdieu's papers in Dale, Esland and MacDonald, eds., *Schooling and Capitalism*. Bourdieu's approach has been criticised by Bisseret in *Education, Class, Language and Ideology*, ch. 5; and by Sharp in *Knowledge, Ideology and the Politics of Schooling*, pp. 66–76.

9 Department of Education and Science, *A Language for Life* (the Bullock Report) (London: HMSO, 1975), p. 131.

10 North West Regional Examination Board: Certificate of Secondary Education, *Reports on the 1983 Examinations*. For those unfamiliar with the British system: CSE examinations are taken mainly as a leaving qualification at age 16 by pupils thought relatively less 'able'; they are set by twelve regional boards. The top grade of CSE is regarded as equivalent to a pass in GCE Ordinary (O) level, which is typically taken at 16. Pupils who 'stay on' may then take Advanced (A) level at 18 or

19. Two A level (and five O level) subjects are normally required for university entrance, but in many subjects and especially English three A levels are now necessary. GCE papers are set by nine boards: three are controlled by single universities: Cambridge, London and Oxford; six by combinations of universities or colleges: Associated (AEB), Joint (JMB), Northern Ireland, Oxford and Cambridge (not the same as the two separate boards already mentioned), Southern, and Welsh. The Scottish system is different, and points made in the present paper should not be assumed to be applicable to Scotland.

11 Universities of London, *General Certificate of Education Examination: Statistics* (1982). See further Pierre Macherey and Étienne Balibar, 'Literature as an Ideological Form', *Oxford Literary Review*, 3 (1978), 4–12; and Madan Sarup, *Marxism / Structuralism / Education* (London and New York: The Falmer Press, 1983), pp. 41–3, 117–22.

12 See Sharpe, *Just Like a Girl*; Eileen M. Byrne, *Women and Education* (London: Tavistock 1978); Rosemary Deem, *Women and Schooling* (London: Routledge, 1978); Jenny Shaw, 'Finishing School', in *Sexual Divisions and Society*, ed. Diana Leonard Parker and Sheila Allen (London: Tavistock, 1976); Margaret Sandra, 'She's good at English – is English good for her?', *Teaching London Kids*, 19 (1983), 8–11. On the early development of the relationship between women and English, see Brian Doyle, 'The Hidden History of English Studies', in Widdowson, *Re-Reading English*, pp. 22–5.

13 Irene Payne, 'A Working-Class Girl in a Grammar School', in *Learning to Lose*, eds. Dale Spender and Elizabeth Sarah (London: Women's Press, 1980), p. 16. See also in the same book Marion Scott, 'Teach Her a Lesson'.

14 See Ann Marie Wolpe, 'The Official Ideology of Education for Girls', in *Educability, Schools and Ideology*, ed. Michael Flude and John Ahier (London: Croom Helm, 1974).

15 G. Yarlott and W. S. Harpin, '1000 Responses to English Literature', *Educational Research*, 13 (1970–1), 3–11, 87–97; p. 6.

16 Stuart Hall and Tony Jefferson, eds., *Resistance Through Rituals* (London: Hutchinson and the Centre for Contemporary Cultural Studies, 1976), p. 12.

17 Frank Whitehead, A. C. Capey, Wendy Maddron, Alan Wellings, *Children and Their Books* (London: Schools Council and Macmillan, 1977), pp. 125–9.

18 Sharp, *Knowledge, Ideology and the Politics of Schooling*, p. 109. On GCE English questions, see further Derek Longhurst, ' "Not for all time, but for an Age" ', in Widdowson, *Re-Reading English*; Holly Goulden and John Hartley, ' "Nor should such Topics as Homosexuality, Masturbation, Frigidity ..." ', *LTP: Journal of Literature Teaching Politics*, I (1982), 4–20; Douglas Barnes and John Seed, *Seals of Approval* (University of Leeds School of Education, 1981).

19 See Renée Balibar, 'An Example of Literary Work in France', in *1848: The Sociology of Literature*, ed. Francis Barker *et al.* (Colchester: University of Essex, 1978); and Tony Bennett's identification of a 'metaphysic of the text' in his *Formalism and Marxism* (London: Methuen, 1979), pp. 146–8, 162–8.

20 Perry Anderson, 'Components of the National Culture', in *Student Power*, eds. Alexander Cockburn and Robin Blackburn (Harmondsworth: Penguin, 1969), p. 271. See also Catherine Belsey, 'Re-Reading the Great Tradition', in Widdowson, *Re-Reading English*.

21 Jonathan Dollimore, *Radical Tragedy* (Brighton: Harvester, 1984; University of Chicago Press, 1984), p. 250.

22 Peter Widdowson, 'Hardy in History: a Case Study in the Sociology of Literature', *Literature and History*, 9 (1983), 3–16; p. 13.

23 Poulantzas, *Classes In Contemporary Capitalism*, pp. 275, 292. See also Margaret Mathieson, *The Preachers of Culture* (London: Allen and Unwin, 1975), ch. 12: 'Social and Academic Background of Teachers'.

24 Malcolm Skilbeck and Alan Harris, eds., *Culture, Ideology and Knowledge* (Milton Keynes: Open University, 1976), pp. 26, 28. See also Denis Lawton, *Social Change, Educational Theory and Curriculum Planning* (University of London Press, 1973), chs. 2, 3, 5, 6.

25 Sir Arthur Quiller-Couch, *On the Art of Reading* (London: British Publishers Guild, 1947), p. 56. For a full account of the development of English literary criticism in its historical context, see Chris Baldick, *The Social Mission of English Criticism* (Oxford University Press, 1983).

26 See John Dixon, *Education 16–19* (London: Macmillan and Schools' Council, 1979), p. 2.

27 G. H. Bantock, *Education in an Industrial Society*, 2nd edn. (London: Faber, 1973), p. 167.

28 In J. H. Plumb, ed., *Crisis in the Humanities* (Harmondsworth: Penguin, 1964), pp. 103, 99.

29 See Michael F. D. Young, 'An Approach to the Study of Curricula as Socially Organized Know-ledge', in *Knowledge and Control*, ed. Michael F. D. Young (London: Collier Macmillan, 1971), pp. 20–2. For a general account of education in the period see Education Group, *Unpopular Education*; and for an account of literary institutions see Stuart Laing, 'The Production of Literature', in *Society and Literature 1945–1970*, ed. Alan Sinfield (London: Methuen, 1983).

30 See F. R. Leavis, *Two Cultures? The Significance of C. P. Snow* (London: Chatto, 1962), and Bantock, *Education in an Industrial Society*, pp. 145–77.

31 Barry Sugarman, in *Introduction to Moral Education*, by John Wilson, Norman Williams and Barry Sugarman (Harmondsworth: Penguin, 1967), p. 335. On subcultural resistance see note 33.

32 Rhodes Boyson, *The Crisis in Education* (London: Woburn Press, 1975), pp. 137, 139–40, 148. On Boyson and the *Black Papers* see Education Group, *Unpopular Education*, pp. 200–7; and Ken Jones, *Beyond Progressive Education* (London: Macmillan, 1983), pp. 74–86.

33 Bernstein's work goes back to 1958 and is collected in *Class, Codes and Control*, 3 vols., 2nd edn. (London: Routledge, 1977): see vol. I. For criticism of Bernstein see Harold Rosen, *Language and Class* (Bristol: Falling Wall Press, 1972); and W. Labov, 'The Logic of Nonstandard English', in P. P. Gigliogli, ed., *Language and Social Context* (Harmondsworth: Penguin, 1972). For more recent work on subcultures, see Hall and Jefferson, *Resistance Through Rituals*; Stuart Hall *et al.*, *Policing the Crisis* (London: Macmillan 1978); Dick Hebdige, *Subculture: the Meaning of Style* (London: Methuen, 1979); Richard Jenkins, *Lads, Citizens and Ordinary Kids* (London: Routledge, 1983); Robert B. Everhart, *Reading, Writing and Resistance* (London: Routledge, 1983).

34 Peter Doughty, *Programme in Linguistics and English Teaching* (London: University College and Longman, 1968), paper I, p. 42. See further M. A. K. Halliday, A. McIntosh and P. Strevens, *The Linguistic Sciences and Language Teaching* (London: Longman, 1964); Harold Rosen, *Language, the Learner and the School* (Harmondsworth: Penguin, 1969).

35 See Skilbeck and Harris, *Culture, Ideology and Knowledge*, pp. 28–34; Lawton, *Social Change, Educational Theory and Curriculum Planning*, ch. 2; Mathieson, *The Preachers of Culture*, chs. 7, 8; Jones, *Beyond Progressive Education*, ch. 2.

36 David Holbrook, *English For Maturity*, 2nd edn. (Cambridge University Press, 1967), pp. 40–1.

37 David Holbrook, *The Exploring Word* (Cambridge University Press, 1967), p. 186.

38 Albert Rowe, *English Teaching* (St Albans: Hart-Davis, 1975), p. 127.

39 Peter Abbs, *English within the Arts* (London: Hodder and Stoughton, 1982), p. 112.

40 Chris Searle, *This New Season* (London: Calder and Boyars, 1973), p. 52. For criticism of progressivism see Jones, *Beyond Progressive Education*; Sarup, *Marxism / Structuralism / Educa-tion*, pp. 123–7; Nigel Hand, 'What *is* English?', in *Explorations in the Politics of School Knowledge*, ed. Geoff Whitty and Michael Young (Driffield: Nafferton Books, 1976).

41 Dixon, *Education 16–19*, p. 128; see also pp. 29, 35–6, 121–8 and, on Communications A level, pp. 70–88. In Theatre Studies a third of the examination is practical; Shakespeare plays are set texts but not compulsory study. Dixon's analysis is limited by his belief that Literature 'is least in need of definition' (p. 43). On the general disarray in Literature teaching, see Mathieson, *The Preachers of Culture*, chs. 13 and 14.

42 See Jones, *Beyond Progressive Education*, pp. 68–72, 132–8; Education Group, *Unpopular Educa-tion*, ch. 11.

43 *The Black Papers on Education*, ed. C. B. Cox and A. E. Dyson (London: Davis Poynter, 1971), p. 47.

44 David Holbrook, *English for the Rejected* (Cambridge University Press, 1964), p. 31; see also p. 208.

Part X

Feminist Criticism

32 Egyptian Queens and Male Reviewers: Sexist Attitudes in
    Antony and Cleopatra Criticism   570
    L. T. Fitz [Linda Woodbridge]
33 "I wooed thee with my sword": Shakespeare's Tragic Paradigms   591
    Madelon Gohlke Sprengnether
34 The Family in Shakespeare Studies; or Studies in the Family of
    Shakespeareans; or The Politics of Politics   606
    Lynda E. Boose
35 Disrupting Sexual Difference: Meaning and Gender in the Comedies   633
    Catherine Belsey

F ew would dispute the proposition that during the last decades of the twentieth century the most notable development in Shakespeare studies, as in literary studies generally, was the burgeoning of feminist criticism. Before about 1975, readings that would now be recognized as feminist could be found scattered here and there, and in literary criticism generally a few feminist theorists, mostly in France, had begun to make their voices heard. But these early stirrings had not yet converged into a critical movement, nor had the method of analysis been given a name. Just over a decade later the landscape had changed entirely, both in Shakespeare studies and in other fields: many critics explicitly identified their approach as feminist, feminist panels and seminars assumed a regular place on conference programs, graduate and undergraduate curricula began to reflect the influence of feminist thought, publishers sought out and vigorously promoted feminist readings of texts, and the movement began to develop a theoretical foundation on which practitioners continued to build. However, the rapid growth of Shakespearean feminism from its infancy in the 1970s was not as smooth as this summary may seem to imply. Emerging contemporaneously with the women's movement that had begun to transform many Anglo-American social structures, the critical discipline experienced many of the same kinds of external opposition and internal conflict.

What is feminist criticism? Obviously, any definition will be limited and debatable, but the unsigned introduction in the *Norton Anthology of Theory and Criticism* makes an impressive effort in a single complex sentence:

> While there is no single feminist literary criticism, there are a half dozen interrelated projects: exposing masculinist stereotypes, distortions, and omissions in male-dominated literature; studying female creativity, genres, styles, themes, careers, and literary traditions; discovering and evaluating lost and neglected works by women; developing feminist theoretical concepts and methods; examining the forces that shape women's lives, litera-ture, and criticism, ranging across psychology and politics, biology and cultural history; and creating new ideas of and roles for women, including new institutional arrange-ments.[1]

This comprehensive list faithfully reflects the vast diversity of feminist criticism; what it also implies is that feminist criticism is almost invariably political. This concentration on power relations from women's perspectives helps to distinguish some of the essays in this section from those in Part XI, "Studies in Gender and Sexuality." There are also, of course, many intersections between the work of gender critics and feminist critics.

A relatively early and therefore historically significant survey of tensions and poten-tial conflicts in feminist inquiry is supplied by Lisa Jardine, in the introduction to *Still Harping on Daughters*, published in 1983. Here she describes the "two main lines of approach" available to the feminist critic:

> The first assumes that Shakespeare has earned his position at the heart of the traditional canon of English literature by creating characters who reflect every possible nuance of that richness and variety which is to be found in the world around us. His female characters, according to this view, reflect accurately the whole range of specifically female qualities (which qualities are supposed to be fixed and immutable from Shakespeare's own day down to our own) ... [Shakespeare's] genius enabled him to transcend patriarchal partisanship ...
>
> The second line of approach assumes quite the opposite. Shakespeare's society is taken to be oppressively chauvinistic ... Shakespeare's *maleness* therefore makes it inevitable that his female characters are warped and distorted.[2]

The second position, frequently revised and much debated, began to emerge as the dominant feminist approach during the late 1980s and 1990s. Within that category one can discern what Jardine called an "aggressive" and a "non-aggressive" strand of thinking, and the fissure between these two camps widened as feminist readings became more numerous and feminist readers more sophisticated.

Of the early feminist responses to Shakespeare, some of the most notable arose from Jardine's "first line of approach," the position that the plays bespeak a profound understanding of female experience and of the nature of women, and that Shakespeare was able to see beyond the limitations of patriarchy. For example, Juliet Dusinberre, writing in 1975, argued that "Shakespeare saw men and women as equal in a world which declared them unequal. He did not divide human nature into the masculine and the feminine, but observed in the individual woman or man an infinite variety of unions between opposing impulses."[3] The point of view expressed here soon came to be considered naïve – indeed it was so described by a few critics at the time – and decried as "essentialist." The positive viewpoint implicit in much early feminist writing was rejected and sometimes mocked by the next generation, whose exponents nevertheless acknowledged that their predecessors had at least begun to ask productive questions.

The first wave of Shakespearean feminism also achieved two significant ends. First, it revealed and questioned the masculine assumptions that many celebrated Shakespeare critics were bringing to their work, especially the tendency to universalize male experience. Feminism demonstrated that such assumptions occluded from view certain productive angles of approach. Linda Woodbridge, writing as L. T. Fitz, was one of the first of these whistleblowers, detailing such unexamined points of view in a passionately argued essay, reprinted below, about the critical history of *Antony and Cleopatra*. The second achievement of early feminism was equally vital: energetic attention to the representation of female characters cleared a path for the systematic inquiry into women's writing in the age of Shakespeare. In the 1980s and 1990s this project bore scholarly fruit unimagined only a few years earlier.

The uncertainties that attended the advance of feminist criticism are nicely captured by Cynthia Marshall at the end of her essay on *Titus Andronicus*, a text that is paradigmatic – and therefore problematic – of the way Shakespearean tragedy often represents women characters:

> While I hesitate to claim that Shakespeare purposefully exposes the dynamics of misogyny in *Titus Andronicus*, the play nevertheless presents the issues of gender, sexuality, and power in dialectical terms that argue against the author's wholesale investment in the projected female stereotypes.
>
> … The play's presentation and treatment of female characters is overdetermined, misogynistic, and clearly lamentable. Yet outrage comes easily, perhaps too easily, with this play, and we should be wary of responding in kind to the play's excesses.[4]

Such circumspection was not universally shared. Much feminist writing of the 1990s exhibits an outraged assault on the patriarchal assumptions and misogynistic discourse in which Shakespeare's plays are implicated and which they helped to create and sustain. But the differences in tone notwithstanding, the century's end witnessed the formation of a powerful consensus about the pervasive, objectionable misogyny of early modern patriarchal culture. To some feminists, such unanimity seemed less like an occasion for comfort and more like a trap. As Phyllis Rackin put it, "We need to view the textual evidence for misogyny and oppression more critically, considering both the social locations of the original writers and those of the contemporary scholars who have put those texts back into circulation."[5]

As Rackin goes on to say, "feminist scholars are challenging the patriarchal narrative itself, recovering the materials for alternative narratives and emphasizing that repressive prescriptions should not be regarded as descriptions of actual behavior."[6] Faced with the impasse of patriarchy, in other words, many critics began to interrogate the system more meticulously, while others began to divert their energies, methods, and political investments into other branches of Shakespeare studies. Editorial and textual studies became a profitable field for feminist inquiry, for example, in the work of such scholars as Leah Marcus and Laurie Maguire, and another signal event was the appointment of the feminist scholar Ann Thompson as one of the general editors of the *Arden Shakespeare*, third series, and co-editor of *Hamlet*. Feminist interest in female spectators at the Globe and the other London theaters represents a similar expansion of boundaries. But the main direction of feminist studies in the 1990s was theoretical, towards gender studies at large. As Jonathan Culler explains, many feminists decided to "undertake a theoretical critique of the heterosexual matrix that organizes identities and cultures in terms of the opposition between man and woman."[7]

As this description suggests, feminism shares viewpoints, principles, and language with other prominent critical schools, particularly gender studies, queer theory, and psychoanalysis. Coppélia Kahn's work on the structure of the early modern family and its patriarchal characteristics, articulated in a series of articles and then in *Man's Estate: Masculine Identity in Shakespeare* (1981), profits enormously from the insights of psychoanalytic criticism. Catherine Belsey's important early studies of subjectivity and of women and tragedy draw heavily upon Marxist and materialist thought. That relationship was also reciprocal, in that Walter Cohen, Jonathan Dollimore, and others began to incorporate some of the concerns and strategies of their feminist colleagues. In literary studies generally, queer theorists have gladly availed themselves of the energies and critical insights of feminist criticism, and students of Shakespeare have been among the most important contributors to this alliance.

The integration of feminist scholarship into the larger critical scene is attested to by Dympna Callaghan's summation of the discipline at the end of the twentieth century: "Feminist Shakespeareans no longer consider themselves as purely literary scholars but as cultural historians who are especially interested in women's own representation of themselves, which range from poetry to embroidery."[8] The critical symbiosis I have been describing is immediately evident in most of the essays contained here. Gohlke Sprengnether's "Tragic Paradigms," for example, owes much to psychoanalytic instruments, while at the same time it illustrates the difficulty of separating feminist analysis from gender studies. This mutual dependence is implicit also in Catherine Belsey's much-cited article, "Disrupting Sexual Difference," while Lynda Boose's mid-movement survey of feminist discourse (1987) addresses many of these connections directly.

But if feminists acquired friends among the ranks of poststructuralism and other critical movements, they also made enemies, or at least found themselves on the outs with some powerful critical voices. Many feminist readers felt less resentment at traditional masculine readers than at certain new historicists: Lynda Boose, writing in 1987, refers wickedly to "new historicism (or rather, 'The' new historicism, as it calls itself)." To many feminist critics, the new historicist emphasis on state power and the structures that underwrite and sustain it led to the neglect of women's history and effectively kept feminist scholars out of the most desirable critical club. Over the course of the next decade recognition and discussion of these tensions led to something of a rapprochement, and the assimilation of both movements into the critical mainstream has contributed to a feeling of critical détente.

Notes

1 *Norton Anthology of Theory and Criticism* (New York: Norton, 2001), p. 23.
2 *Still Harping on Daughters* (New York: Columbia University Press, 1983), pp. 1–3.
3 *Shakespeare and the Nature of Women* (London, 1975), p. 308.
4 " 'I can interpret all her martyr'd signs': *Titus Andronicus*, Feminism, and the Limits of Interpret-ation," in *Sexuality and Politics in Renaissance Drama*, ed. Carole Levin and Karen Robertson (Lewiston, NY: Edwin Mellen Press, 1991), pp. 193–211.
5 "Misogyny is Everywhere," in *A Feminist Companion to Shakespeare*, ed. Dympna Callaghan (Oxford: Blackwell, 2000), p. 48.
6 Ibid, p. 49.
7 *Literary Theory: A Very Short Introduction* (Oxford: Oxford University Press, 1997), p. 128.
8 Callaghan, "Introduction," *A Feminist Companion to Shakespeare*, p. xiv. Even the indefinite article that begins Callaghan's title is indicative of the movement's commitment to multiplicity.

32

Egyptian Queens and Male Reviewers: Sexist Attitudes in *Antony and Cleopatra* Criticism

L. T. Fitz [Linda Woodbridge]

And of Cleopatra what shall be said? Is she a creature of the same breed as Cato's daughter, Portia? Does the one word woman include natures so diverse? Or is Cleopatra … no mortal woman, but Lilith who ensnared Adam before the making of Eve? (Dowden)

Most critics are united in proclaiming that *Antony and Cleopatra* is a magnificent achievement; unfortunately, they are not united on the question of exactly what the play achieves. It is difficult to think of another Shakespearean play which has divided critics into such furiously warring camps. A. P. Riemer describes, fairly accurately, the positions defended by the two main critical factions: "*Antony and Cleopatra* can be read as the fall of a great general, betrayed in his dotage by a treacherous strumpet, or else it can be viewed as a celebration of transcendental love."[1] Derek Traversi also speaks of this interpretive impasse: "The student of *Antony and Cleopatra* has, in offering an account of this great tragedy, to resolve a problem of approach, of the author's intention. Sooner or later, he finds himself faced by two possible readings of the play, whose only difficulty is that they seem to be mutually exclusive."[2] A significant difficulty indeed; however, I would suggest, not the "only difficulty."

Both the reduction of the play's action to "the fall of a great general" and the definition of the play's major interest as "transcendental love" make impossible a reasonable assessment of the character of Cleopatra. There is a word for the kind of critical bias informing both approaches: it is "sexism." Almost all critical approaches to this play have been colored by the sexist assumptions the critics have brought with them to their reading. These approaches, I believe, have distorted the meaning of what Shakespeare wrote.

Before I take up the sexist criticism in its particulars, I have one general observation. I have noticed, in male critical commentary on the character of Cleopatra, an intemperance of language, an intensity of revulsion uncommon even among Shakespeare critics, who are well enough known as a group for their lack of critical moderation. I do not think it would be going too far to suggest that many male critics feel personally threatened by Cleopatra and what she represents to them. In Cleopatra's case, critical attitudes go beyond the usual condescension toward female characters or the usual willingness to give critical approval only to female characters who are chaste, fair, loyal, and modest: critical attitudes toward Cleopatra seem to reveal deep personal fears of aggressive or manipulative women. Alfred Harbage, in his *Conceptions of Shakespeare*, looked at the personal lives of some anti-Stratfordians and found evidence of persistent neurotic delusions of the sort Freud had labeled "family romance fantasies";[3] perhaps it would be revealing to examine the lives of anti-Cleopatra critics for evidence of difficulties in relationships with women.

I

But to the particulars. Obviously, most of the sexist distortion has centered on Cleopatra, and it is most revealing to observe with whom Cleopatra has been compared. A favorite game among Shakespeare critics has always been to compare characters from one play with characters from another; so Hamlet is said to have more "inner life" than Othello, King Lear is said to die less self-centeredly than Hamlet, and so forth. With whom is Cleopatra compared? Lear? Macbeth? Othello? No, Cleopatra is compared only with female characters – Viola, Beatrice, Rosalind, Juliet.[4] Juliet is most frequent, and it must be confessed that there are certain similarities. Both appear in tragedies (the rest of the women used for comparison are comic heroines); both are allegedly in love; and they share the distinction of being two of the three women to have made it into the titles of Shakespeare plays. Otherwise, the two are as apt for comparison as Mae West and St. Cecilia. Critics do not compare King Lear with Osric, Bottom the Weaver, or Sir Toby Belch because they are all men, but they persist in comparing Cleopatra (usually unfavorably) with female characters because they are all women. Clearly, Cleopatra is cut off at the outset from serious consideration as a tragic hero by being relegated to consideration alongside various heroines, most of whom inhabit the comedies.

Related to this habit of discussing female characters as a group is the critical tactic of describing Cleopatra as "Woman." Cleopatra is seen as the archetypal woman: practicer of feminine wiles, mysterious, childlike, long on passion and short on intelligence – except for a sort of animal cunning. Harold C. Goddard, referring to the end of the play, states, "Now for the first time she is a woman – and not Woman."[5] S. L. Bethell informs us, "In Cleopatra [Shakespeare] presents the mystery of woman."[6] Swinburne sees Cleopatra as Blake's "Eternal Female."[7] Georg Brandes calls her "woman of women, quintessentiated Eve."[8] E. E. Stoll says, "Caprice, conscious and unconscious is her nature ... She is quintessential woman."[9] Harley Granville-Barker enlightens us: "The passionate woman has a child's desires and a child's fears, an animal's wary distrust; balance of judgment none, one would say. But often ... she shows the shrewd scepticism of a child."[10] And Daniel Stempel brings us up to date on the alleged Elizabethan attitude:

> Here our knowledge of Elizabethan mores can come to our aid ... Woman was a creature of weak reason and strong passion, carnal in nature and governed by lust. She could be trusted only when guided by the wisdom of her natural superior, man ... The misogyny of Octavius Caesar is founded on right reason.[11]

It is surely questionable whether there is such a thing as a "typical woman" or even a "typical Elizabethan woman." And if there is such a thing as a "typical Shakespearean woman," Cleopatra is not the woman. In particular, she is almost unique among Shakespeare's female characters in her use of feminine wiles – by which I mean her deliberate unpredictability and her manipulative use of mood changes for the purpose of remaining fascinating to Antony.

> If you find him sad,
> Say I am dancing; if in mirth, report
> That I am sudden sick
> (i.iii.3–5)

It is ironic that her use of feminine wiles has been one of the only Cleopatran features to have proven appealing to critics. Dowden writes:

> At every moment we are necessarily aware of the gross, the mean, the disorderly womanhood in Cleopatra, no less than of the witchery and wonder which excite, and charm, and subdue. We see her a dissembler, a termagant, a coward; and yet 'vilest things become her'. The presence of a spirit of *life* quick, shifting, multitudinous, incalculable, fascinates the eye, and would, if it could, lull the moral sense to sleep.[12]

Schlegel writes: "Cleopatra is as remarkable for her seductive charms as Antony for the splendor of his deeds."[13] Philip J. Traci defends the feminine wiles on the grounds that such behavior is prescribed for courtly lovers by Andreas Capellanus and Ovid.[14]

It is ironic, I say, because it seems probable that Shakespeare disapproves of such behavior. With the exception of Cressida,[15] no other woman in Shakespeare's plays practices it. Indeed, Shakespeare's women for the most part actively resist it, preferring instead to woo their men, straightforwardly, themselves. It is Miranda's father, in *The Tempest*, who tries to put obstacles in love's way "lest too light winning / Make the prize light" (i.ii.454–5), while Miranda forthrightly approaches the man she has known for about an hour with "Hence, bashful cunning ... I am your wife, if you will marry me" (iii.i.81–3).

Of course, if I am to claim that Shakespeare treated his women as individuals, I can hardly postulate that he criticizes Cleopatra for behaving differently in this respect from other Shakespearean women. But there is evidence in the play that Shakespeare sees such behavior as humanly undesirable: he has Cleopatra herself try, in the latter part of the play, to overcome her deliberately inconstant behavior[16] – behavior which she (not Shakespeare) sees as being quintessentially female:

> My resolution's placed, and I have nothing
> Of woman in me: now from head to foot
> I am marble-constant: now the fleeting moon
> No planet is of mine.
>
> > (v.ii.238–41)

But while Shakespeare may disapprove of feminine wiles, he understands why Cleopatra feels (perhaps rightly) that she must practice them: she is getting old, and Shakespeare understood that women, unlike men, are valued only when they are young and beautiful. Cleopatra's famous self-portrait –

> Think on me,
> That am with Phoebus' amorous pinches black
> And wrinkled deep in time
>
> > (i.v.27–9)

– comes at the point where she has just characterized her fantasy of Antony ("He's speaking now, / Or murmuring, 'Where's my serpent of old Nile?'" [i.v.24–5]) as "delicious poison" – delicious in its confirmation of Antony's loyalty, poisonous in its contrast with the fact of Antony's absence and the fact of her decaying beauty. This passage is immediately followed by a reverie on sexual successes of her youth. The scene is, I think, too often read with attention only to Cleopatra's rejoicing in her own sexuality, to the neglect of its clear undercurrent of fear and insecurity.

The feminine fear of aging had been introduced early in the play, with Charmian's "Wrinkles forbid" (i.ii.21). That Shakespeare well understood the danger of a woman's losing the affection of her lover as she loses her looks to age is clear from the discussion between Duke Orsino and Viola (masquerading as a boy) in *Twelfth Night*:

> *Duke:*   Let still the woman take
>   An elder than herself: so wears she to him,
>   So sways she level in her husband's heart;
>   For, boy, however we do praise ourselves,
>   Our fancies are more giddy and unfirm,
>   More longing, wavering, sooner lost and worn,
>   Than women's are …
>   Then let thy love be younger than thyself,
>   Or thy affection cannot hold the bent;
>   For women are as roses, whose fair flow'r,
>   Being once displayed, doth fall that very hour.
> *Viola:* And so they are; alas, that they are so.
>
> > (ii.iv.29–40)

There is no evidence in Shakespeare (or in Plutarch, his source) that Cleopatra employed feminine wiles when she was younger. It seems more reasonable to conjecture that in Shakespeare's interpretation, she has adopted desperate measures to compensate, by being fascinating, for the ravages of age.

II

Although many critics see Cleopatra as the archetypal woman, others more magnanimously recognize that there are, in fact, two types of woman in the world, both of which appear in *Antony and Cleopatra*: the wicked and manipulative (Cleopatra), and the chaste and submissive (Octavia). This dipolar view usually results in an overemphasis on Octavia, who after all speaks only thirty-five lines in the play,[17] as a viable alternative to Cleopatra. These critics seem to be united in their belief that the love of a good woman could have saved Antony and prevented the whole tragedy. A. C. Bradley complains bitterly of Antony's mistreatment of Octavia.[18] Charles Bathurst feels that "The character of Antony [Shakespeare] meant to elevate as much as possible; notwithstanding his great weakness in all that concerns Cleopatra, and unmistakable misconduct with regard to his wife."[19] Laurens J. Mills regrets that "after the seeming cure during his marriage to Octavia, he falls more and more inextricably into the coils of the Egyptian."[20] Harley Granville-Barker, who places Octavia third, after Antony and Cleopatra, in his group of character studies for the play,[21] says "How should we not, with the good Maecenas, trust to her beauty, wisdom, and modesty to settle his chastened heart?"[22]

Leaving aside these touching encomia and turning to the play, one notes that Antony calls his marriage to Octavia "the business" (a term favored by the Macbeths in reference to the murder of Duncan). It is very likely that had Antony lived in connubial bliss with Octavia from the time he first remarked "Yet, ere we put ourselves in arms, dispatch we / The business we have talked of" [ii.ii.167–8], the remaining three-and-a-half acts would have been very different, less concerned with disaster and death, although perhaps somewhat lacking in those qualities we have come to associate with drama. Nevertheless, it is a fact that in Shakespeare Antony treats Octavia better than he does in Plutarch, where he turns her out of his house.[23] And Shakespeare much reduced Octavia's importance: Plutarch's account ends with a vision of Octavia bringing up all of Antony's children, including one named Cleopatra.[24]

Another sexist response to the play has resulted from a distaste for the play's overt sexuality. Traci claims that Shakespearean critics, even bawdry expert Eric Partridge, have been loath to acknowledge the extent of sexual double entendre in the play, and that when they have acknowledged it, they have been disgusted by it.[25] Traci gallantly takes up the challenge by declaring that the whole play is structured in imitation of the sex-act, starting with foreplay in the first several scenes, proceeding to pre-sex drinking and feasting, and finally culminating, after the significant entrance of the character Eros, in intercourse itself – represented, according to Traci, by twenty-one uses of the word "Eros," twenty-three uses of the word "come," and sixteen puns on "dying." Traci's theory may be a little far-fetched, but it brings a whole new world of meaning to passages like "What poor an instrument may do a noble deed," "The soldier's pole is fallen," and "Husband, I come."[26]

Traci feels that critical neglect of the naughty bits in the play has been prompted by prudery, from which he, fortunately, does not suffer. "Drink ... like lechery," he declares, "is a universal manly, social sin ... Indeed, they are surely heroic sins, when compared to gluttony and sloth, for example."[27] What Traci fails to account for is the oddity of encountering critical prudery in *this* day and age. After all, the days of Bowdlerizing are over; nobody blenches any more at "an old black ram is tupping your white ewe." I submit that what bothers critics about the bawdy remarks in *Antony and Cleopatra* is that so many of them are made by Cleopatra – like "O happy horse, to bear the weight of Antony!" (i.v.21), or "Ram thou thy fruitful tidings in mine ears, / That long time have been barren" (ii.v.23–4). The prudery is of a sexist variety: what appalls the male critic is that a *woman* would say such things. It is, to a certain extent, Cleopatra's frank sexuality that damns her. Robert E. Fitch, writing from his post at the Pacific School of Religion, observes, "It is altogether incredible that the Shakespeare who ... early and late in his career rejoiced in innocence, loyalty, and love, before lust with all its cruel splendors, could have presented Cleopatra as a model of the mature woman in mature emotion."[28] J. W. Lever tells us that "Her wooing of Antony is comic and sensual, immoral and thoroughly reprehensible."[29]

One might expect Cleopatra to appeal at least to the closet prurience of a few readers. And indeed there are a number of grudging and embarrassed tributes to the power of Cleopatra's sexuality. Schlegel writes: "Although the mutual passion of herself and Antony is without moral dignity, it still excites our sympathy as an insurmountable fascination."[30] Coleridge writes, "But the art displayed in the character of Cleopatra is profound in this, especially, that the sense of criminality in her passion is lessened by our insight into its depth and energy, at the very moment that we cannot help but perceive that the passion itself springs out of the habitual craving of a licentious nature."[31] Traci sums up the attitude of several modern Cleopatra apologists: "From beneath the exuberance of the adjectives ... there emerges the critic's apology for having himself become a slave of Passion."[32]

Antony and Cleopatra has never been admitted to the holy circle of the "big four" Shakespearean tragedies – *Hamlet, Othello, King Lear*, and *Macbeth*. Many reasons for this have been adduced. Perhaps the most popular reason, as stated by A. P. Riemer, is that *Antony and Cleopatra* "deals with issues intrinsically much less important than those of the great tragedies."[33] Nevertheless, Cleopatra's first line, "If it be love indeed, tell me how much" (i.i.14), is strikingly similar to Lear's opening question to his daughters. Both *Antony and Cleopatra* and *King Lear* are, as far as I can see, concerned with love and its relationship to public issues like proper ruling, as well as love's place in the individual's hierarchy of values. If *Antony and Cleopatra* deals with "much less important issues," it would seem to follow that love between the sexes, as in *Antony and Cleopatra*, is "much less important" than familial love, as in *King Lear*. This is an argument one might expect of Victorian critics, perhaps, but why should we find it today? And if love between the sexes is an unworthy topic for tragedy, why is *Othello* permitted to stand as one of the "big four," while *Antony and Cleopatra* is not? The unavoidable answer, I believe, is that *Othello* focuses uncompromisingly on a male hero.

III

Another way in which sexism rears its head in *Antony and Cleopatra* criticism is that in assessing the respective actions of Antony and Cleopatra, critics apply a clear double standard: what is praiseworthy in Antony is damnable in Cleopatra. The sexist assumption here is that for a woman, love should be everything; her showing an interest in anything but her man is reprehensible. For a man, on the other hand, love should be secondary to public duty or even self-interest. Almost every scene in which either character appears has been subjected to this double-standard interpretation. I will focus on three examples.

First, in the Thidias scene, where Cleopatra apparently makes some political overtures to Caesar after Caesar has defeated Antony in the battle of Actium, Cleopatra has repeatedly been damned by critics for trying to save her political skin, and perhaps her actual skin, at the expense of her love for Antony. At the beginning of the play, when Antony follows his fervent protestations of love for Cleopatra by leaving Egypt to patch up his political situation in Rome through marriage to the sister of Octavius Caesar, he receives nothing but critical praise – for putting first things first and attempting to break off a destructive relationship with Cleopatra. According to the critics, men may put political considerations ahead of love; women may not.

Second, while Antony is roundly criticized when he neglects public affairs, critics never take seriously Cleopatra's desire to play an active part in great public enterprises. Cleopatra's participation in the battle of Actium, it must be confessed, is less than an unqualified success, but there is no warrant in the play for doubting her motives for being there in person:

> A charge we bear i' th' war,
> And as the president of my kingdom will
> Appear there for a man. Speak not against it,
> I will not stay behind.
>
> (III.vii.16–19)

Nevertheless, Julian Markels infers, on no evidence, that "the entire function of the president of her kingdom is to become the object of universal gaze and wonder ... Her business at Actium was to cavort upon that stage where Antony made war."[34]

Third, a double standard is almost always applied in discussions of Antony's and Cleopatra's respective motives for suicide. Cleopatra is repeatedly criticized for thinking of anything but Antony: this would seem to follow from the sexist precept that nothing but love is appropriate to a woman's thoughts. "Does she kill herself to be with Antony or to escape Caesar? It is the final question," Mills tells us, after explaining to us the difference between Cleopatra's unworthy death-bed thoughts and Antony's noble ones:

> In her final moments, as she carries out her resolution, Cleopatra has "immortal longings," hears Antony call, gloats over outwitting Caesar, addresses Antony as "husband," shows jealousy in her fear that Iras may gain the first otherworld kiss from Antony, sneers at Caesar again, speaks lovingly to the asp at her breast, and dies, with "Antony" on her lips and a final fling of contempt for the world. But, it should be noted, she does not "do it after the high Roman fashion," nor with the singleness of motive that actuated Antony.[35]

Stempel, coming upon the lines, "He words me, girls, he words me, that I should not / Be noble to myself" [v.ii.191–2], is indescribably shocked that Cleopatra speaks two whole lines without reference to Antony: "No word of Antony here. Her deepest allegiance is to her own nature."[36]

If, however, we look at the play, we see that Cleopatra adduces the following reasons for taking leave of the world: (1) she thinks life is not worth living without Antony;[37] (2) she sees suicide as brave, great, noble, and Roman;[38] (3) she wants to escape the humiliation Caesar has planned for her, and desires to have the fun of making an ass of Caesar;[39] (4) she sees suicide as an act of constancy which will put an end to her previous inconstant behavior and to the world's inconstancy which has affected her;[40] and (5) she wants to be with Antony in a life beyond the grave.[41] Antony adduces the following reasons for his suicide: (1) he has lost his final battle, and he thinks Cleopatra has betrayed him;[42] (2) he (later) thinks Cleopatra is dead, and feels that life is not worth living without her;[43] (3) he wants to be with Cleopatra in a life beyond the grave;[44] (4) he thinks Cleopatra has killed herself, and he cannot bear to be outdone in nobility by a mere woman;[45] (5) he wants to escape the humiliation Caesar has planned for him;[46] and (6) he sees suicide as valiant and Roman.[47] It is thus apparent that the "singleness of motive" which Mills thinks "actuates Antony" is a myth: Antony has six motives to Cleopatra's five, and four of Cleopatra's five motives are identical with Antony's. Yet although Cleopatra is constantly taken to task for the multiplicity of her suicide motives (we all know that women cannot make up their minds), I have yet to see the critic who complained of the multiplicity of Antony's motives.

This double standard, arising from the critics' own sexist world view – that is, that love, lust, and personal relationships in general belong to a "feminine" world that must always be secondary to the "masculine" world of war, politics, and great public issues – can seriously distort the play. Some critics see the tragedy as growing out of the finally irreconcilable conflict between public values and private values, but many critics come down unequivocally on the side of public values – assuming, of course, that these public values belong to a world of men. Symptomatic of this tendency is the fact that Enobarbus, a boringly conventional antifeminist who voices just such a view in the play, is almost always taken to be a mouthpiece for Shakespeare. E. C. Wilson, for example, writes:

> Antony, sobered by news of Fulvia's death, declares that he must from "this enchanting queen break off." Enobarbus banteringly cries, "Why, then we kill all our women. We see how mortal an unkindness is to them. If they suffer departure, death's the word." But in his next speech, a reply to Antony's "I must be gone," his clear sense of Antony's folly pierces through his banter. "Under a compelling occasion, let women die. It were pity to cast them away for nothing, though, between them and a great cause they should be esteemed nothing." Nowhere in the play is there a more incisive judgment on Antony's conduct.[48]

Because these interpretations of the play are slanted in favour of the "rightness" of public, Roman values (in spite of the unsavory character of almost all the Roman activities which appear in the play, from the bride-bartering of Octavius and Antony, to the cut-throat scramble for political ascendancy, to the unctuous hypocrisy of Octavius in the closing scenes),[49] Cleopatra, who after all shares top billing with Antony in the play's title, is demoted from the position of co-protagonist to the position of antagonist at best, nonentity at worst.

IV

The most flagrant manifestation of sexism in criticism of the play is the almost universal assumption that Antony alone is its protagonist. The following are only a few critical pronouncements on the subject, which I have culled from a mass of interpretive writings that make the same point. Oliver Emerson: "the dramatic movement of the play is the ruin of Antony under the stress of sensual passion."[50] Georg Brandes: "Just as Antony's ruin results from his connection with Cleopatra, so does the fall of the Roman Republic result from the contact of the simple hardihood of the West with the luxury of the East. Antony is Rome. Cleopatra is the Orient. When he perishes, a prey to the voluptuousness of the East, it seems as though Roman greatness and the Roman Republic expires with him."[51] Harley Granville-Barker: "Antony, the once-triumphant man of action, is hero … [The play's theme] is not merely Antony's love for Cleopatra, but his ruin as general and statesman, the final ascension of Octavius, and the true end of 'that work the ides of March begun' … If but in his folly, [Antony] has been great. He has held nothing back, has flung away for her sake honour and power, never weighing their worth against her worthlessness."[52] Lord David Cecil: "the play would have been better entitled *The Decline and Fall of Antony*."[53] S. L. Bethell: "Antony's position is central, for the choice between Egypt and Rome is for him to make."[54] Willard Farnham: "Shakespeare does not organize his tragedy as a drama of the love of Antony and Cleopatra, but as a drama of the rise and fall of Antony in the struggle for world rulership that takes place after he has met Cleopatra."[55] John F. Danby: "The tragedy of *Antony and Cleopatra* is, above all, the tragedy of Antony."[56] Austin Wright: "The main theme" of *Antony and Cleopatra* is "the clash between Antony and Octavius."[57] Julian Markels: "*Antony and Cleopatra* focuses upon the conflict within Antony between public and private claims."[58] A. P. Riemer: "On a strictly formal level, *Antony and Cleopatra* fulfils the requirements of orthodox tragedy in its depiction of Antony's fall (and, incidentally, Cleopatra's) in reasonably decorous terms."[59] Janet Adelman: "Antony is the presumptive hero of the play."[60]

When, in 1964, Laurens J. Mills set out to find critics who agreed with him that Antony and Cleopatra were co-protagonists, he could find only two other critics who "agreed." One of these was Virgil Whitaker, who I find once remarked that "the tragic action of the play is centered upon Antony, who has so yielded himself to the passion of love that it has possessed his will and dethroned his reason."[61] And Mills's own study does little to advance the cause. His summary of the two tragic falls is that the tragedy of Antony consists of the "pathetic picture" of a man who "by love for a thoroughly unworthy object comes to a miserable end," whereas the tragedy of Cleopatra "cannot be a 'tragic fall', for there is nothing for her to fall from."[62] The critical camp that sees Antony and Cleopatra as co-protagonists does not muster impressive forces.[63]

The critical consensus, then, is that Antony is the protagonist. There is a small catch, however. Antony dies in Act IV, and Cleopatra has the whole of Act V to herself, during the course of which she speaks some of Shakespeare's greatest poetry. How have the pro-Antony forces dealt with this embarrassment? A substantial number of them have chosen the stalwart expedient of ignoring it altogether. For the rest, the critical contortions to which they have been forced to resort are instructive and amusing.

V

Some feel that Shakespeare knew what he was doing when he gave Cleopatra the last Act to herself. For example, Daniel Stempel says, "If … the major theme is the safety of the state, then the death of Antony does not remove the chief danger to political stability – Cleopatra: she has ensnared Julius Caesar, Pompey, and Antony – how will Octavius fare? This last Act shows us that Octavius is proof against the temptress, and the play ends, as it should, with the defeat and death of the rebel against order. The theme is worked out to its logical completion, and the play is an integrated whole, not merely a tragedy with a postscript."[64] Robert E. Fitch says, "Naturally Antony, the middle-man in the generic tension of values, must be disposed of by the end of Act IV, so that the last Act may be given to the stark confrontation of pleasure and of power in the persons of Cleopatra and Octavius."[65] Julian Markels says, "the grand climax of the whole action is reserved for Cleopatra, who now learns the lesson of Antony's life … and by her loyalty to him confirms Antony's achieved balance of public and private values."[66] John Middleton Murry says, "Up to the death of Antony it is from him that the life of the play has been derived … He is magnificent: therefore she must be. But when he dies, her poetic function is to maintain and prolong, to reflect and reverberate, that achieved royalty of Antony's … We [watch] the mysterious transfusion of his royal spirit into the mind and heart of his fickle queen."[67] Harley Granville-Barker says, "The love-tragedy … is not made the main question till no other question is left … Antony dead, the domination of the play passes at once to Cleopatra … But Antony's death leaves Shakespeare to face one obvious problem: how to prevent Cleopatra's coming as an anticlimax."[68] Peter Alexander says, "Antony dies while the play still has an Act to run, but without this Act his story would be incomplete. For Cleopatra has to vindicate her right to his devotion."[69] Other critics feel that in giving Cleopatra Act V to herself, Shakespeare simply made a dreadful mistake, one which destroyed the whole structure of the play. As Michael Lloyd quite rightly points out, "If we see Antony's tragedy as the centrepiece of the play, its structure is faulty."[70]

Cleopatra is present throughout the whole of the play,[71] she has Act V to herself, and she dies at the end. Thus, she would seem to fulfill at least the formal requirements of the tragic hero. One might think that in the verbose history of Shakespearean criticism, at least one critic would have suggested that she is the protagonist – the sole protagonist – of the play. As a matter of fact, one did. A critic named Simpson – Lucie Simpson – wrote in a forgotten article in 1928 that "the play, in fact, might have been called *Cleopatra* as appropriately as *Hamlet* is called *Hamlet* or *Othello Othello*."[72] Although *Antony and Cleopatra* critics as a rule refer to each other's works more often than to the play, I have seen Lucie Simpson's work referred to only once, and then with a summary dismissal.[73] (Such heretical works are hard to get hold of; for example, an intriguing book by a critic named Grindon – Rosa Grindon – which advances the delightful and provocative thesis that "the men critics in their sympathy for Antony, have treated Cleopatra just as Antony's men friends did, and for the same cause"[74] has been out of print for over fifty years.) In fact, it is for the most part only the occasional female critic who dares to suggest that a woman might be the protagonist of any Shakespearean tragedy.[75]

VI

But changes Shakespeare made in using his source, Plutarch's *Life of Marcus Antonius*, indicate that he had a much greater interest than had Plutarch in Cleopatra as a human being. He elevated her position in the play by paying more attention to her motivation, allowing her to speak in her own defense, and making numerous small alterations in Plutarch's story, the effect of which is almost always to mitigate Cleopatra's culpability. That exonerating and elevating Cleopatra was a conscious intention is suggested by the fact that the changes are consistently in that direction. It is also notable that except for these changes, Shakespeare adheres quite closely to his source.

In Plutarch, Antony embarks on his Parthian campaign with 100,000 men. He loses 45,000 of them, we are told, mainly because "the great haste he made to return unto Cleopatra"[76] caused him to abandon heavy artillery and put his men to forced marches: "the most part of them died of sickness."[77] In Plutarch, then, 45,000 men lost their lives because Antony was in haste to meet Cleopatra by the sea-side – and then *she* was late! This distasteful episode, which provides Plutarch with ample occasion to revile Cleopatra, is omitted altogether by Shakespeare.

In Plutarch, Cleopatra is given a reason for wanting to appear in person at the battle of Actium: she fears "lest Antonius should again be made friends with Octavius Caesar by means of his wife Octavia,"[78] and the reasons she gives Antony for wanting to appear are spurious. In Shakespeare, there is no hint of this personal reason; Cleopatra simply declares "A charge we bear i' th' war, / And, as the president of my kingdom, will / Appear there for a man" (iii.vii.17).

Antony's reason for fighting the battle of Actium by sea is reported twice by Plutarch. "Now Antonius was made so subject to a woman's will that, though he was a great deal the stronger by land, yet for Cleopatra's sake he would needs have this battle tried by sea."[79] "But ... notwithstanding all these good persuasions, Cleopatra forced him to put all to the hazard of battle by sea."[80] One very frequently finds critics adducing this as one of the charges against Shakespeare's Cleopatra.[81] But in fact the sea battle is not Cleopatra's idea in Shakespeare's play. Shakespeare instead introduces a different motive, not mentioned in Plutarch: Caesar's dare.[82]

Antony:	Canidius, we
	Will fight with him by sea.
Cleopatra:	By sea; what else?
Canidius:	Why will my lord do so?
Antony:	For that he dares us to't.
Enobarbus:	So hath my lord dared him to single fight.
Canidius:	Ay, and to wage this battle at Pharsalia,
	Where Caesar fought with Pompey: but these offers,
	Which serve not for his vantage, he shakes off;
	And so should you.
Enobarbus:	Your ships are not well manned;
	Your mariners are muleters, reapers, people
	Ingrossed by swift impress. In Caesar's fleet
	Are those that often have 'gainst Pompey fought;

> Their ships are yare, yours, heavy: no disgrace
> Shall fall you for refusing him at sea,
> Being prepared for land.
>
> Antony: By sea, by sea.

(III.vii.27–40)

In Shakespeare, the emphasis is entirely on Caesar's dare. Cleopatra finds the choice of sea-battle a natural one, since Egypt's military strength is in its navy,[83] but she does not initiate the disastrous plan.[84]

Cleopatra's departure from the battle of Actium, which prompts Antony to follow her and results in the loss of the battle, Shakespeare could hardly have omitted from the play, as it eventuates in the tragic deaths of Antony and Cleopatra. Nor would one wish this changed, since, despite Enobarbus' disclaimer (III.xiii.3–4), it leaves Cleopatra with a large share of the blame for the ensuing tragedy – an important consideration, in view of the fact that in Shakespeare's mature plays the chain of events culminating in tragedy is initiated by the protagonist. In Plutarch, the focus in this scene is entirely on Antony – Cleopatra's leaving the battle is seen only in relation to its effect on Antony. In Shakespeare, Cleopatra considers whether she is to blame ("Is Antony, or we, in fault for this?" [III.xiii.2]), indicates fear as her motivation ("Forgive my fearful sails" [III.xi.55]), offers as her excuse that she acted in ignorance of the consequences ("I little thought / You would have followed" [III.xi.55–6]), and apologizes profusely ("Pardon, pardon" [III.xi.68]). Plutarch does not present Cleopatra's reactions to this crucial turn of events at all.

After the Thidias scene, Plutarch gives no hint of Cleopatra's impassioned declarations of innocence and love for Antony, declarations that do appear in Shakespeare's text. And although Shakespeare includes in the Thidias scene (as Plutarch does not) the imputation that Cleopatra has stayed with Antony out of fear, not love (III.xii.56–7), this piece of dialogue is a transmutation of a much more damning passage in Plutarch – where *after* Antony's death, "Cleopatra began to clear and excuse herself for that she had done, laying all to the fear she had of Antony."[85] Shakespeare has removed this imputation of disloyalty from the latter part of the action, putting it in the mouth of Caesar's messenger, not Cleopatra. And while Cleopatra acquiesces in the interpretation, she prefaces her acquiescence with the very-likely ironic "He is a god, and knows / What is most right" (III.xiii.60–1).

As to Antony's suspicion, after the final aborted battle, that Cleopatra "has / Packed cards with Caesar" (IV.xiv.18–19), neither Plutarch nor Shakespeare includes any evidence that she has. But Shakespeare has her messenger issue a denial (IV.xiv. 120–3), whereas Plutarch leaves the question entirely open.

In Plutarch, Cleopatra betakes herself to the monument "being afraid of [Antony's] fury."[86] Shakespeare gives her much stronger reasons for her fear, since Antony declares four times, very convincingly, that he is going to kill her (IV.xii.16; IV.xii.39–42; IV.xii.47, 49; IV.xiv.26). This is not in Plutarch.

In both authors, Antony's suicide is a result of Cleopatra's sending word that she is dead. But again, Shakespeare takes pains to mitigate this action. First, he makes the death-message Charmian's idea (IV.xiii.4), not Cleopatra's. Second, he has Cleopatra foresee the possible effect of her message and send an emissary to revoke it;

unfortunately, the emissary arrives too late (IV.xiv.119–26). This is a significant departure from Plutarch.

In Plutarch, Cleopatra will not open the gates of the monument to Antony, and no reason for this refusal is given. In Shakespeare, Cleopatra gives a reason and apologizes: "I dare not, dear; / Dear my lord, pardon: I dare not, / Lest I be taken" (IV.xv.21–3).

Plutarch gives three reasons for Antony's suicide, but none at all for Cleopatra's, apart from the implication that her wits were distracted "with sorrow and passion of mind." She is reduced to a babbling, self-mutilating neurotic: "She had knocked her breast so pitifully, that she had ... raised ulcers and inflammations, so that she fell into a fever ... her eyes sunk into her head with continual blubbering, and moreover they might see the most part of her stomach torn in sunder."[87] Shakespeare gives Cleopatra's suicide full motivation, and allows her to die with dignity and even triumph.

Finally, Plutarch reports simply, "Her death was very sudden."[88] The great dying speeches of Cleopatra are Shakespeare's addition.

Shakespeare's greater interest in Cleopatra first manifests itself in his changing Plutarch's title from *The Life of Marcus Antonius* to *The Tragedy of Antony and Cleopatra*,[89] and continues to manifest itself throughout the play.

VII

Although Shakespeare's departures from Plutarch are consistently in the direction of mitigating the harshness of Plutarch's view of Cleopatra, they do not by any means amount to a whitewash. By granting Cleopatra motivation and the chance to speak in her own defense, Shakespeare lifts her from the level of caricature, which would be appropriate for satiric treatment, to the level of fully developed individuality, which qualifies her for treatment as a tragic figure. To be treated as a tragic protagonist, Cleopatra need not – indeed should not – be absolved of every failing; after all, no one tries to prove that Macbeth did not really commit murder before granting him the stature of tragic hero.

The most significant difference between Shakespeare's mature tragic practice and Aristotle's tragic theory is that while Aristotle at one point says that "pity is aroused by unmerited misfortune," Shakespeare insists on eliciting audience sympathy for characters who, to a greater or lesser degree, have brought their misfortunes on themselves. Shakespeare seems to ask his audience to understand, to empathize – even to forgive. In the later tragedies, Shakespeare seeks audience sympathy for inherently unsympathetic figures – a stubborn and mentally infirm octogenarian, a murderer, a misanthrope, a mama's boy, and (most difficult of all) a disreputable woman. As Willard Farnham points out in *Shakespeare's Tragic Frontier*, such an attempt involves great risks – what is gained in granting characters some say in their own destiny might easily be lost in diminution of audience sympathy. It seems to have been a risk that Shakespeare deliberately elected to take. In his last few tragedies, he made increasing demands on the humane tolerance (or perhaps on the Christian charity, in the most radical sense) of his audience. We are not expected to agree, in every case, that the protagonist is more sinned against than sinning; we are expected, on the basis of our common humanity with the offending protagonist, to offer sympathy unqualified by the necessity for exoneration. It is a demand too radical for Aristotle, for Farnham, for most audiences. Most are too ready to rue the absence of less deeply-flawed heroes, too ready to accuse Shakespeare of having sat down to eat with publicans and sinners. But although this is a tendency in the criticism of all the late tragedies, the fact remains that critics have been readier to sympathize with the murderer than with the wanton woman.

VIII

Any attempt to reach a canonical decision on the identity of a single hero in a play of such generic unorthodoxy as *Antony and Cleopatra*[90] is probably foolhardy and possibly distorting in itself. Nevertheless, since so many critics before me have unblushingly insisted on establishing Antony as the play's sole protagonist, for the sake of argument I will suggest that there are good reasons for considering Cleopatra to be the play's protagonist – or, shall we say (ignoring the usual deprecatory sex-designation "heroine"), the hero. Not only does the play culminate in Cleopatra's death scene, but she has (according to the statistical evidence of the Spevack Concordance) more speeches than Antony; indeed, the most in the play (although, giving the lie to the received opinion that women talk too much, her speeches contain fewer total lines than Antony's). But most important, she learns and grows as Antony does not.

A. C. Bradley declares that the play is not a true tragedy because he cannot find the tragic hero's inner struggle in Antony.[91] But Cleopatra has that inner struggle. She struggles against her own artifical theatricality (as Richard II never does): she who so often threatens to die that Enobarbus credits her with a "celerity in dying" (i.ii.145) finally does truly kill herself. She who in a self-dramatizing gesture had sent word to Antony that she was dead and asked the messenger to "Say that the last I spoke was 'Antony' / And word it, prithee, piteously" (iv.xiii.8–9), finally really dies with the words "O Antony" on her lips. She struggles against her own inconstancy – the inconstancy that had previously led her to change moods and to change lovers – and approaches death with the words

> My resolution's placed, and I have nothing
> Of woman in me: now from head to foot
> I am marble-constant: now the fleeting moon
> No planet is of mine.
> > (v.ii.238–41)

As Lear learns that he is a man before he is a king, so Cleopatra learns that she is a woman before she is a queen:

> No more but e'en a woman, and commanded
> By such poor passion as the maid that milks
> And does the meanest chares.[92]
> > (iv.xv.76–8)

The composition of *Antony and Cleopatra* followed close upon that of *King Lear*, that great play of self-knowledge.[93] Surely, then, it is no coincidence that while Antony simply fears his own loss of self-knowledge, Cleopatra actually admits to her less-than-admirable actions ("I ... do confess I have / Been laden with like frailties which before / Have often shamed our sex" [v.ii.121–4]) and tries, however late, to change – to "be noble to myself." Surely after watching what Lear was and what Lear became, we should not be too ready to damn what Cleopatra has been while ignoring what she becomes.

Of the critics I have discussed, A. P. Riemer comes the closest to declaring that Cleopatra is the hero of *Antony and Cleopatra*. Rehearsing all the reasons for not considering Antony the hero, he trembles on the verge – and then withdraws, unwilling to take the final step. He tells us that "Her death (and this assumption must be faced squarely) is not offered in any sense as the play's structural culmination ... The play does not share [her] feelings and ideas, and the audience does not participate in [her] emotional state to the extent that it partakes of Hamlet's, Othello's or Lear's emotions at the climactic points of the tragedies in which these characters appear ... It is not possible for us to share her emotions."[94]

I find this statement very odd. Is Cleopatra such an aberrant being that her emotions lie outside the pale of human comprehension? Is her practice of the tawdry old game known as feminine wiles really sufficient to render her forever as mysteriously and darkly inscrutable as male critics suggest? Is it really true that in contrast to the great universal audience which participates with no difficulty in the emotional state of a man who is troubled by incest, court drinking, the feasibility of revenge, and the authenticity of ghosts, there are no readers and no audiences who can participate in the emotions of a woman who dies thinking of politics, wine, her lover, and her baby?

IX

The persistent idea that Cleopatra cannot be understood, underlying as it does so many of the sexist responses I have discussed, owes much to the notion that women in general are impossible for men to understand. But, *pace* Dowden and others, one might ask exactly what she does that is so dazzlingly mysterious. True, she engages in unqueenly activities such as hopping forty paces through the public street or wandering about incognito to observe the qualities of people. But then, Hal drinks in taverns and takes part in robberies as prince, and later wanders incognito among troops as king; there is disagreement over his motives, of course, but at least critics assume that he *has* understandable motives. I cannot recall anyone describing Hal as "quick, shifting, multitudinous, incalculable." And as for feminine wiles, Cleopatra's behavior here, far from being incomprehensible, is so obvious as to be almost crude: having bound herself to performing, not what is unexpected, but what is exactly the opposite of the expected, she has allowed herself no scope for creativity whatsoever. Milton's Satan, by vowing to oppose whatever God initiates, renders himself dependent on God's will; similarly, Shakespeare's Cleopatra, by obliging herself to determine what Antony expects and then to do the opposite, will very soon forfeit the element of surprise in all her actions. "If you find him sad, / Say I am dancing; if in mirth, report / That I am sudden sick" – this is not the statement of a Woman of Mystery: it is a blueprint for action which, for the reader if not for Antony, renders the unpredictable predictable.

Shakespeare has taken pains to let Cleopatra explain her contrary behavior and give the reasons for it (i.iii). He has created a complex but far from inscrutable being. Cleopatra's variety is, at last, finite. In short, Cleopatra needs to be demythologized. What she stands to lose in fascination she stands to gain in humanity.

Cleopatra may or may not be the protagonist of *Antony and Cleopatra*. At the very least, however, it should now be clear that her part in the play needs to be reassessed with more fairness – without the sexist bias that has so far attended most efforts to come to terms with her, without the assumption that readers and theatregoers will never be able to treat her as anything more than an exotic and decadent puzzle, inaccessible to rational thought, remote from human feeling.

I find it hard to believe that there are no readers and audiences who find it possible to share Cleopatra's emotions, or even simply to concede to Cleopatra the attributes of a human being. It seems, after all, that Shakespeare did.

Notes

1 *A Reading of Shakespeare's "Antony and Cleopatra"* (Sydney, Australia: University of Sydney Press, 1968), p. 82. Throughout this essay, I shall discuss critics as their views are pertinent to each topic I take up, rather than attempting any chronological overview of critical development. The reason for this will become apparent as I proceed: there has been no real critical development on this issue, and modern critics are just as sexist in their views as nineteenth-century critics. All quotations from Shakespeare are from Sylvan Barnet, gen. ed., *The Complete Signet Classic Shakespeare* (New York: Harcourt, 1972).

2 *Shakespeare: The Roman Plays* (London and Stanford: Bodley Head and Stanford University Press, 1963), p. 79.

3 "Shakespeare as Culture Hero" in *Conceptions of Shakespeare* (Cambridge, MA.: Harvard University Press, 1966), pp. 101–19.

4 E.g., "If she were a Juliet she would kill herself immediately for love of Antony, not merely talk about suicide" (Laurens J. Mills, *The Tragedies of Shakespeare's Antony and Cleopatra* [Bloomington: Indiana University Press, 1964], p. 48).

5 *The Meaning of Shakespeare* (Chicago: University of Chicago Press, 1951), II, 199.

6 *Shakespeare and the Popular Dramatic Tradition* (London: Staples, 1944), p. 128.

7 *A Study of Shakespeare* (London: Chatto and Windus, 1902 [first published 1880]), p. 189.

8 *William Shakespeare. A Critical Study*, trans. William Archer and Diana White (New York: F. Unger, 1963 [first published 1898]), p. 144.

9 "Cleopatra" in *Poets and Playwrights* (Minneapolis: University of Minnesota Press, 1930), p. 13.

10 *Prefaces to Shakespeare* (London: Batsford, 1930), III, 91.

11 "The Transmigration of the Crocodile," *SQ*, 7 (1956), 63, 65. Stempel bases his whole argument on Renaissance misogynistic writings, which represented only one attitude (among many) toward women in the Renaissance. It is gratifying to note that one male critic takes Stempel to task for so glibly characterizing Elizabethan attitudes, which he remarks is "surely as difficult as characterizing The Twentieth Century American's Attitude toward the Poles" (Philip J. Traci, *The Love Play of Antony and Cleopatra* [The Hague: Mouton, 1970], p. 19). Stempel's argument runs this way: Romantic and many post-Romantic critics idealize Cleopatra because they have been in the habit of placing Woman on a pedestal, failing to understand that many misogynistic Renaissance writers denigrated Woman. Stempel fails to realize, however, that neither generalized view of Woman does justice to the individuality of Shakespeare's Cleopatra, who is represented not as Woman, but as a person, partly good and partly bad, like most persons. That Stempel has little feeling for the

individuality of female characters might be guessed from his description of Chaucer's Wife of Bath as "a scholar's wife blessed with a retentive memory" (p. 63).

12 Edward Dowden, *Shakespeare: A Critical Study of His Mind and Art* (London: Routledge and Kegan Paul, 1957 [first published 1875]), pp. 313–14.

13 Augustus William Schlegel, *Lectures on Dramatic Literature*, trans. John Black (London: J. Templeman, 1840), p. 220.

14 Traci, pp. 113–14.

15 Cleopatra's only real fellow in the use of feminine wiles, Cressida, is at best an inconsistent practitioner: her defense of feminine wiles is suspect, even though it occurs in soliloquy, insofar as the same soliloquy insists on her love's firmness (I.iii.320); and she abandons coquetry in the second scene in which she appears (III.ii). Just as her downright faithlessness contrasts with Cleopatra's final faithfulness, so *Troilus and Cressida* is much more clearly a play of conventional antifeminism than is *Antony and Cleopatra*, which I believe introduces misogynistic convention, through Enobarbus and others, only to repudiate it.

16 It might be argued that giving up inconstancy (changing moods for effect) is no great effort for Cleopatra once Antony, on whom she has practiced this brand of feminine wiles, is gone; but her inconstancy, in a larger sense, has involved changing lovers as well (although it should not be forgotten that her lovers have had a way of getting themselves murdered through no fault of her own). She might, had her "resolution" not been "placed," have made a play for Caesar, and some critics (Stempel, Mills) have argued that she does, on such slender evidence as her calling Caesar "my master and my lord." An actress who interpreted the "Seleucus" scene this way, however, would undercut the validity of everything Cleopatra says in Act V, scene ii, and change the entire play from tragedy to satire. The several critics who have suggested this interpretation have changed the play drastically, with little or no warrant in the text of the play. Indeed, Mills's characterizing of Cleopatra's tone in the "Seleucus" scene as "quaveringly piteous" and Octavius' tone in the same scene as "blunt" (Mills, p. 54) seems to me perverse, and clearly evidence of a theatrical tin ear.

17 Cordelia, too, speaks very few lines and yet is considered a major character; but Shakespeare manages to convey a sense of strength with Cordelia's few lines, in contrast to the sense of insipidity he conveys with Octavia's. Although both women, when given the floor, decline to speak, there is a world of difference between Cordelia's "I cannot heave my heart into my mouth" and Octavia's "I'll tell you in your ear." Octavia is often praised by critics for her becoming silence (women are to be seen and not heard?), but surely one would regret the loss to English poetry had Cleopatra said "I'll tell you in your ear" when *she* had the chance to speak. Shakespeare does draw subtle contrasts (as well as the obvious contrasts) between Cleopatra and Octavia – for example, through mythological allusion: Octavia prays for aid from a powerful male god ("The Jove of power make me, most weak, most weak / Your reconciler!" [III.iv.29–30]), while Cleopatra is always associated with female gods – Isis, Venus, Thetis. But if Shakespeare designed the play along the lines of a love-triangle, it was hardly meant to be equilateral.

18 *Oxford Lectures on Poetry* (London: Macmillan, 1909), p. 294.

19 *Remarks on the Differences in Shakespeare's Versification in Different Periods of His Life* (London: John W. Parker and Son, 1857), p. 131.

20 Mills, p. 29.

21 Granville-Barker, p. 97.

22 Granville-Barker, p. 73.

23 Plutarch, "The Life of Marcus Antonius," trans. Sir Thomas North, in T. J. B. Spencer, ed. *Shakespeare's Plutarch* (London: Penguin, 1964), p. 246.

24 Plutarch, p. 294.

25 Traci, p. 81.

26 Traci, pp. 136–60.

27 Traci, pp. 41–2.

28 "No Greater Crack?" *SQ*, 19 (1968), 12.

29   "Venus and the Second Chance," *Shakespeare Survey*, 15 (1962), 87.

30   Schlegel, p. 220.

31   W. G. T. Shedd, ed. *The Complete Works of Samuel Taylor Coleridge* (New York: Harper and Brothers, 1884), IV, 105–6.

32   Traci, pp. 4–12.

33   Riemer, p. 105.

34   *The Pillar of the World: "Antony and Cleopatra" in Shakespeare's Development* (Columbus: Ohio State University Press, 1968), p. 47.

35   Mills, p. 55.

36   Stempel, p. 70.

37   "Shall I abide / In this dull world, which in thy absence is / No better than a sty?" (IV.xv.60–2); "It were for me / To throw my scepter at the injurious gods, / To tell them that this world did equal theirs / Till they had stol'n our jewel. All's but naught … then is it sin / To rush into the secret house of death / Ere death dare come to us?" (IV.xv.78–85).

38   "We'll bury him; and then, what's brave, what's noble, / Let's do't after the high Roman fashion, / And make death proud to take us" (IV.xv.89–91); "It is great / To do that thing that ends all other deeds" (v.ii.4–5); "Methinks I hear / Antony call; I see him rouse himself / To praise my noble act" (v.ii.283–5).

39   "This mortal house I'll ruin, / Do Caesar what he can. Know, sir, that I / Will not wait pinioned at your master's court / Nor once be chastised with the sober eye / Of dull Octavia. Shall they hoist me up / And show me to the shouting varletry / Of censuring Rome? Rather a ditch in Egypt / Be gentle grave unto me!" (v.ii.51–7); "Mechanic slaves / With greasy aprons, rules, and hammers shall / Uplift us to the view. In their thick breaths, / Rank of gross diet, shall we be enclouded, / And forced to drink their vapor" (v.ii.209–13); "O, couldst thou speak, / That I might hear thee call great Caesar ass / Unpolicied" (v.ii.306–8).

40   "It is great / To do that thing that ends all other deeds, / Which shackles accidents and bolts up change" (v.ii.4–6); "What poor an instrument / May do a noble deed! He brings me liberty. / My resolution's placed, and I have nothing / Of woman in me: now from head to foot / I am marble-constant: now the fleeting moon / No planet is of mine" (v.ii.236–41).

41   "Methinks I hear / Antony call … Husband, I come" (v.ii.283–7); "If she first meet the curlèd Antony, / He'll make demand of her, and spend that kiss / Which is my heaven to have" (v.ii.300–3).

42   "She, Eros, has / Packed cards with Caesar, and false-played my glory / Unto an enemy's triumph. / Nay, weep not, gentle Eros, there is left us / Ourselves to end ourselves" (IV.xiv.18–22).

43   "I will o'ertake thee, Cleopatra … So it must be, for now / All length is torture, since the torch is out" (IV.xiv.44–6).

44   "I come, my queen … / Where souls do couch on flowers, we'll hand in hand, / And with our sprightly port make the ghosts gaze: / Dido and her Aeneas shall want troops, / And all the haunt be ours" (IV.xiv.50–4).

45   "Since Cleopatra died, / I have lived in such dishonor that the gods / Detest my baseness. I, that with my sword / Quartered the world and o'er green Neptune's back / With ships made cities, condemn myself to lack / The courage of a woman" (IV.xiv.55–60).

46   "Eros, / Wouldst thou be windowed in great Rome and see / Thy master thus: with pleached arms, bending down / His corrigible neck, his face subdued / To penetrative shame, whilst the wheeled seat / Of fortunate Caesar, drawn before him, branded / His baseness that ensued?" (IV.xiv.71–7).

47   "A Roman, by a Roman / Valiantly vanquished" (IV.xv.57–8).

48   "Shakespeare's Enobarbus," in James G. McManaway et al., eds. *Joseph Quincy Adams: Memorial Studies* (Washington: Folger Shakespeare Library, 1948), pp. 392–3.

49   If Shakespeare believed the Romans were noble, he surely did not inherit this notion from his source, which only too realistically draws a picture of the pervasive military mentality of the Romans with their might-makes-right ethic of political expediency. Plutarch, of course, was a Greek whose own grandfather had been incommoded by the battle of Actium – it is only to be

expected that his attitude toward the Egyptians and Romans would be "a plague o' both your houses."

50 "*Antony and Cleopatra*," *Poet Lore*, 2 (1890), p. 126.

51 Brandes, p. 158.

52 Granville-Barker, pp. 1, 23, 79.

53 "Antony and Cleopatra," W. P. Ker Memorial Lecture (Glasgow: Jackson, 1944), p. 21.

54 Bethell, p. 124.

55 *Shakespeare's Tragic Frontier: The World of His Final Tragedies* (Berkeley: University of California Press, 1950), p. 175.

56 *Poets on Fortune's Hill: Studies in Sidney, Shakespeare, Beaumont and Fletcher* (London: Faber and Faber, 1952), p. 146.

57 "Antony and Cleopatra," *Shakespeare: Lectures on Five Plays* by Members of the Department of English, Carnegie Institute of Technology (Pittsburgh: Carnegie Press, 1958), p. 39.

58 Markels, p. 52.

59 Riemer, p. 88.

60 *The Common Liar: An Essay on "Antony and Cleopatra"* (New Haven: Yale University Press, 1973), p. 30. Adelman is the only female critic in this list. However, it should not be overlooked that hers is the only study of the play which attempts to establish, on a scholarly basis, that Shakespeare's audience might have viewed positively the sex-role reversal exemplified by Cleopatra and Antony's exchange of clothing, as well as Cleopatra's association with serpents – almost all other critics see these two aspects of the play as particularly damning to Cleopatra. On the whole, I have found Adelman's study the most useful and responsible that I have read.

61 *Shakespeare's Use of Learning: An Inquiry into the Growth of His Mind and Art* (San Marino: Huntington Library, 1953), p. 315.

62 Mills, pp. 35, 39.

63 A bevy of critics give Cleopatra a measure of favorable treatment as representative of Egyptian values, which according to these critics are set by Shakespeare in opposition to Roman values – Egyptian values are sometimes seen as triumphing, and sometimes as co-existing with the Roman values in a perpetual state of tension. These opposed values have been described as Reason and Intuition by Bethell (p. 122), Power and Pleasure by Fitch (p. 6), the World and the Flesh by Danby (p. 145), Power and Love by Goddard (p. 185), Reason and Impulse by Paul L. Rose ("The Politics of *Antony and Cleopatra*," *SQ*, 20 [1969], 377–89), and "workaday world" values and "holiday" values by J. L. Simmons ("The Comic Pattern and Vision in *Antony and Cleopatra*," *ELH*, 36 [1969], 495). The effect of this kind of interpretation is to reduce Cleopatra to an allegorical figure, representing one set of values. Octavius Caesar is usually seen as representing the other set, and the Everyman left to choose between these alternatives is always Antony, who then becomes the hero of a kind of morality play, but remains the hero, nonetheless.

The Romantic admiration of Cleopatra as rebel – analogous to the Romantic view of Satan as hero of *Paradise Lost* – depended on the trick of extracting her from the play altogether. Even Romantic admirers were loath to give Cleopatra primacy in the context of the play.

64 Stempel, p. 63.

65 Fitch, p. 6.

66 Markels, p. 140.

67 *Shakespeare* (London: Jonathan Cape, 1936), pp. 372, 377. Murry's essay has been much admired and is often quoted, notwithstanding the fact that his application of the adjective "royal" to the republican Antony and only by extension to the technically royal Cleopatra ("She has yet, crowned queen though she is, to achieve her 'royalty'; and she will achieve it by her resolution to follow her 'man of men' to death") is a little bizarre. Cleopatra is often called "royal" in the play; Antony never is.

That Cleopatra is the queen of Egypt, considering how much it is harped upon in the play, is a fact that critics seem remarkably willing to forget. Several critics, for example, interpret Antony's calling her "Egypt" as evidence of his subliminal association of all things Egyptian (serpents, slime, fecundity, decadence) with her. Such an interpretation overlooks the conventional use of names of nations as titles for monarchs: Cleopatra is called "Egypt" in *Antony and Cleopatra* much as the King of France is called "France" in *King Lear*; both titles bring to mind the political position of the character.

Finally, as regards the royalty of Cleopatra, much critical scorn has been heaped upon Cleopatra for the queenly decking-out of her death scene, which is often seen as one last instance of her manipulative histrionics. Critics seem to have been lulled, by phrases like "Show me, my women, *like* a queen," into forgetting the fact that she is the queen. Few complain of "I am Duchess of Malfi still" (perhaps because the Duchess is, at least arguably, respectably married), but Cleopatra's last act is often denied this dignity. To my way of thinking, the "infinite variety" of Cleopatra's last scene is not the deliberate changefulness of feminine wiles (Antony, after all, is dead), but rather a variety arising out of a real complexity of character. In her last moments Cleopatra thinks of herself as lover, sybarite, mother, politician, and queen. Being queen of Egypt gives Cleopatra a great opportunity for splendor, to which she is not averse; but it is also (let it not be forgotten) her career. The irreconcilability of political life and private life has always been emphasized in Antony's case, but the conflict is there in Cleopatra as well. There have been few enough Cleopatras in history, but with passing time the conflict between a career and private life has become more and more a woman's conflict. Nor were contemporary examples completely lacking for Shakespeare: Henry VIII did not, as it turned out, have to forgo marriage (to the women of his choice) in favor of his political career; but his illustrious daughter did. I cannot help feeling that had Elizabeth lived to see Shakespeare's play, virgin queen that she was, she might have amended her famous statement to "I am Cleopatra, know ye not that?"

68 Granville-Barker, pp. 4, 38–9. What Philip Traci might do with that last line of Granville-Barker's boggles the imagination.

69 *Shakespeare's Life and Art* (London: J. Nisbet, 1939), p. 178.

70 "Cleopatra as Isis," *Shakespeare Survey*, 12 (1959), 94.

71 When she is absent from the stage, dialogue and action continually remind the audience of her. Shakespeare departs from Plutarch several times by introducing references to Cleopatra in the midst of Roman scenes: for example, he changes the position of the barge description so that it enters the Roman context, and he has the soothsayer advise, "Hie thee to Egypt," where in Plutarch the soothsayer had contented himself with remarks on the respective luck of Caesar and Antony.

72 "Shakespeare's 'Cleopatra,' " *Fortnightly Review*, n.s. 123 (March 1928), 332.

73 Traci, p. 36.

74 *A Woman's Study of "Antony and Cleopatra"* (Manchester: Sherratt and Hughes, 1909), p. 68.

75 I would not like to leave the reader with the notion that Cleopatra is entirely devoid of male defenders. Credit must be given, for example, to Ralph Behrens, who in an essay promisingly entitled "Cleopatra Exonerated" (*Shakespeare Newsletter*, 9 [November 1959], 37) declares that "all apparent lapses in her love for Antony can be accounted for by ... 'feminine frailties.' It is true that she teases Antony ... and feigns illness, but these are simply feminine wiles ... It is true that she flees too early with her ships ... but [this] is a case of feminine fear." Such a defense would warm the cockles of the sternest feminist heart, were it not for the fact that it is prompted less by a desire to demonstrate that Cleopatra is a significant character in her own right than by a more urgent desire to redeem Antony. As Behrens puts it, "If the object of Antony's overpowering love were a totally unworthy one, it is likely that his character would be greatly weakened in its command of the reader's sympathy." The usual forms that "defenses" of Cleopatra take are these: critics admire her for the wrong reasons (appreciating her use of feminine wiles); offer in defense of her questionable actions the fact that she is only a woman and therefore does not really know any better; seek to exonerate her only for the purpose of exonerating Antony; or (often under the guise of countering Bradley's pernicious character-based approach) argue that she is not a real character at all but an embodiment of certain values. Such defenses almost never take the form of

arguing that Cleopatra is the protagonist of the play, and therefore to be blamed *and* empathized with, like other tragic protagonists.

76 Plutarch, p. 239.

77 Plutarch, p. 238.

78 Plutarch, pp. 244–5.

79 Plutarch, p. 250.

80 Plutarch, p. 254.

81 E.g., Bradley: "He fights by sea simply and solely because she wishes it" (p. 297).

82 In Plutarch, Caesar challenges Antony to fight him on land, and offers to withdraw his army "from the sea as far as one horse could run, until [Antonius] had put his army ashore and had lodged his men" (p. 251).

83 Cf. "Let the Egyptians and the Phoenicians go a'ducking" (III.vii.63–4).

84 Canidius, of course, attributes Antony's decision to the fact that "our leader's led / And we are women's men" (III.vii.69–70), but this is interpretation, not fact. Canidius, like Bradley and most critics, is hypothesizing an offstage conversation between Cleopatra and Antony in which Cleopatra suggests (or demands) a sea-battle. Critics have often questioned the Bradleyan tactic of speculating on offstage or even pre-play events, but I do not recall that they have questioned it in this particular case. Interpreting the scene on the basis of Canidius' conclusions is a chancy business as well, in a play which (as Adelman and others have observed) consistently offers various perspectives on the same action. The point is arguable. My objection, however, is that critics have not bothered to argue it, but have instead imported Plutarch's conclusions into the play – in spite of the fact that Shakespeare has so clearly departed from Plutarch in his dramatization of the incident.

85 Plutarch, p. 287.

86 Plutarch, p. 276.

87 Plutarch, pp. 286–7.

88 Plutarch, p. 291.

89 Although I find the addition of Cleopatra's name to Plutarch's title somewhat significant, I do not think that the fact that Antony's name remains in the title is clear evidence that the two were meant to be co-protagonists. Shakespeare's titles are not always clear indications of who the plays' major figures are to be: witness *Julius Caesar, Henry IV, Henry VI*, or *Cymbeline*.

90 I have, for lack of space, sidestepped the knotty genre question. If the play is seen, for example, as a history play, the search for *one* protagonist becomes irrelevant. Even earlier tragedies had co-protagonists (*Romeo and Juliet*) or lacked a clearly-defined single hero (*Julius Caesar*). It is a fact, however, that all the tragedies from *Hamlet* on have clearly-defined single heroes. I am arguing for Cleopatra as sole hero to show that it can be done, and with as much basis in the play as the argument for Antony as hero. If counterarguments can be produced, well and good. I only ask that their basis be textual, not sexual.

91 Bradley, pp. 286–7.

92 Of this passage, Stempel remarks, "The death of a queen is leveled to the death of a woman, an exceptional woman, but still only a woman" (p. 71). Goddard, more graciously, makes the comparison with Lear, and also with Othello. In so doing he is one of the few critics to have granted Cleopatra the dignity of comparison with Shakespeare's male heroes. Unfortunately, Goddard concludes that although the final transformation of Cleopatra is "a miracle," Antony's "devotion to her, even unto death, is what does it" (p. 198).

93 Cf. Paul A. Jorgensen, *Lear's Self-Discovery* (Berkeley and Los Angeles: University of California Press, 1967).

94 Riemer, p. 100.

33

"I wooed thee with my sword": Shakespeare's Tragic Paradigms

Madelon Gohlke Sprengnether

Traditional textual interpretation founds itself on this particular understanding of meta-phor: a detour to truth. Not only individual metaphors or systems of metaphors, but fiction in general is seen as a detour to a truth that the critic can deliver through her interpret-ation. (Gayatri Chakravorty Spivak, translator's preface, *Of Grammatology*)

Much of what I have to say about Shakespeare and about the possibility of a feminist psychoanalytic interpretation of literature, or, for that matter, of culture, depends on a reading of metaphor. It is metaphor that allows us to sub-read, to read on the margins of discourse, to analyze what is latent or implicit in the structures of consciousness or of a text. A serious feminist critic, moreover, cannot proceed very far without becoming paranoid, unless she abandons a strictly intention-alist position. To argue sexism as a conscious conspiracy becomes both foolish and absurd. To pursue the implications of metaphor, on the other hand, in terms of plot, character, and possibly even genre, is to adopt a psychoanalytic strategy that deepens the context of feminist interpretation and reveals the possibility at least of a feminist psychohistory.

Metaphor provides a convenient entrance into a text, as it provides a point of departure for psychoanalytic interpretation because of the way in which vehicle consistently outdistances tenor. The following two lines, from *A Midsummer Night's Dream*, for instance, "Hippolyta, I wooed thee with my sword, / And won thy love, doing thee injuries" (I.i.16–17), convey far more than the simple prose explanation offered in my text: "Theseus had captured Hippolyta when he conquered the Amazons."[1] These lines, in which the sword may be the metaphoric equivalent of the phallus, in which love may be either generated or secured by hostility, and in which the two partners take up sadistic and masochistic postures in relation to one another, are not irrelevant to the concerns of the play. They may be seen to reverberate in the exaggerated submission of Helena to Demetrius, in the humiliation of Titania by Oberon, in the penetration by violence of the language of love. They even bear an oblique relation to the "lamentable comedy" of *Pyramis and Thisbe*, the failed marriage plot contained within the larger structure of successful heterosexual union celebrated at the end of the play.

Metaphor may also elucidate character, as in the case of *Much Ado about Nothing*'s Claudio, whose speech is relatively poor in imagery until it erupts into his condemnation of Hero in the middle of the play, where among other things he claims "But you are more intemperate in your blood / Than Venus, or those pamp'red animals / That rage in savage sensuality" (iv.i.58–60). It is Claudio's suspicious predisposition which composes this violent and disproportioned outburst. It is no accident that the "solution" to this conflict hinges on the fiction that Claudio has killed Hero through his slander. In this sense the conventional marriage plot of Shakespeare's comedy may also be read metaphorically. The prospect of heterosexual union arouses emotional conflicts which give shape to the plot, unleashing a kind of violence which in the comedies remains symbolic, imagined rather than enacted.

I shall, in the following pages, be considering the uses of metaphor in several related ways. In some instances, I will refer to the function of metaphor in individual discourse, assuming that it is this kind of highly charged imagistic expression that offers the most immediate clues to unconscious awareness. I am assuming furthermore that metaphor may be seen to structure action, so that some features of plot may be regarded as expanded metaphors. Moving outward from this premise, I then want to consider the possibility that certain cultural fictions may be read metaphorically, that is, as expressions of unconsciously held cultural beliefs. I am particularly interested in Shakespeare's tragedies, in what seem to me to be shared fictions on the part of the heroes about femininity and about their own vulnerability in relation to women, fictions interweaving women with violence, generating a particular kind of heterosexual dilemma.

The primacy of metaphor in the structures of individual consciousness, as in the collective fiction of the plot, appears in an early tragedy, *Romeo and Juliet*, where the failure of the play to achieve the generic status of comedy may be read as the result of the way in which heterosexual relations are imagined. In the conversation between the servants Sampson and Gregory, sexual intercourse, through a punning reference to the word "maidenhead," comes to be described as a kind of murder.[2]

> *Sampson:* 'Tis all one. I will show myself a tyrant. When I have fought with the men, I will be civil with the maids – I will cut off their heads.
> *Gregory:* The heads of the maids?
> *Sampson:* Ay, the heads of the maids or their maidenheads. Take it in what sense thou wilt.
>
> (i.i.23–8)

To participate in the masculine ethic of this play is to participate in the feud, which defines relations among men as intensely competitive, and relations with women as controlling and violent, so that women in Sampson's language "being the weaker vessels, are ever thrust to the wall" (i.i.17–18). That Romeo initially rejects this ethic would seem to redefine the nature and structure of male / female relationships. What is striking about the relationship between Romeo and Juliet, however, is the extent to which it anticipates and ultimately incorporates violence.

Both lovers have a lively imagination of disaster. While Romeo ponders "some vile forfeit of untimely death" (I.iv.111), Juliet speculates "If he is marrièd, / My grave is like to be my wedding bed" (I.v.136–7). Premonition, for both, has the force of self-fulfilling prophecy. While Romeo seeks danger by courting Juliet, and death by threatening suicide in the wake of Tybalt's death, Juliet, under pressure, exclaims: "I'll to my wedding bed; / And death, not Romeo, take my maidenhead!" (III.ii.136–7). Read metaphorically, the plot validates the perception expressed variously in the play that love kills.

The paradigm offered by *Romeo and Juliet*, with some modifications, may be read in the major tragedies as well. Here, the structures of male dominance, involving various strategies of control, expressed in the language of prostitution, rape, and murder, conceal deeper structures of fear, in which women are perceived as powerful, and the heterosexual relation one which is either mutually violent or at least deeply threatening to the man.

Murder in the Bedroom: *Hamlet* and *Othello*

Hamlet's violent behavior in his mother's bedroom expresses some of the violence of his impulses toward her. Obsessed as he is with sexual betrayal, the problem of revenge for him is less a matter of killing Claudius than one of not killing his mother.[3] Hamlet's anger against women, based on his perception of his mother's conduct, finds expression in the language of prostitution in his violent outburst against Ophelia: "I have heard of your paintings, well enough. God hath given you one face, and you make yourselves another. You jig and amble, and you lisp; you nickname God's creatures and make your wantonness your ignorance. Go to, I'll no more on't; it hath made me mad" (III.i.143–8). It is painting which makes women two-faced, which allows them to deceive, to wear the mask of chastity, while lust "Will sate itself in a celestial bed / And prey on garbage" (I.v.56–7). Like whores, all women cannot be trusted.

The paradox of prostitution in the tragedies is based on the masculine perception of the prostitute as not so much the victim as the agent of exploitation. If women are classed as prostitutes and treated as sexual objects, it is because they are deeply feared as sexually untrustworthy, as creatures whose intentions and desires are fundamentally unreadable. Thus, while Helen in *Troilus and Cressida* is verbally degraded, as the Trojans discuss her in terms of soiled goods and contaminated meat, she is, through her infidelity to Menelaus, the source of the sexual pride and humiliation that animate the entire conflict between the two warring nations. Honor among men in this play, though it takes the form of combat, is ultimately a sexual matter, depending largely on the fidelity or infidelity of women. For a man to be betrayed by a woman is to be humiliated or dishonored. To recover his honor he must destroy the man or woman who is responsible for his humiliation, for placing him in a position of vulnerability.

In *Hamlet*, it is the player queen who most clearly articulates the significance attributed to feminine betrayal. "A second time I kill my husband dead / When second husband kisses me in bed" (III.ii.188–9).

It hardly matters whether Gertrude was implicated in the actual death of the elder Hamlet. Adultery is itself a form of violence and as great a crime. Hamlet, who reacts as an injured husband in seeking revenge against Claudius, also seeks retribution against his mother. Not having any sanction to kill his mother, however, he must remind himself to "speak daggers to her, but use none" (404). That his manner suggests physical violence is confirmed by Gertrude's response: "What wilt thou do? Thou wilt not murder me? / Help, ho!" (III.iv.22–3). It is at this point that the violence that Hamlet seeks to contain in his attitude toward his mother is deflected onto another object presumed to be appropriate.

This single act of displaced violence, moreover, has further ramifications in terms of Hamlet's relation to Ophelia, whose conflicted responses to the killing of her father by her lover increase the burden of double messages she has already received from the men in the play and culminate in her madness and death. It is not his mother whom Hamlet kills (Claudius takes care of that) but Ophelia. Only when she is dead, moreover, is he clearly free to say that he loved her. Othello, in whom are more specifically and vividly portrayed the pathology of jealousy, the humiliation and rage that plague a man supposedly dishonored by the woman he loves, will say of Desdemona late in the play "I will kill thee, / And love thee after" (v.ii.18–19).

If I seem to be arguing that the tragedies are largely about the degeneration of heterosexual relationships, or marriages that fail, it is because I am reading the development from the comedies through the problem plays and the major tragedies in terms of an explosion of the sexual tensions that threaten without rupturing the surface of the earlier plays. Throughout, a woman's power is less social or political (though it may have social and political ramifications) than emotional, expressed in her capacity to give or to withhold love. In a figure like Isabella the capacity to withhold arouses lust and a will to power in someone like Angelo, whose enforcing tactics amount to rape. In Portia, the threat of infidelity, however jokingly presented, is a weapon in her struggle with Antonio for Bassanio's allegiance. Male resistance, comic and exaggerated in Benedick, sullen and resentful in Bertram, stems from fears of occupying a position of weakness, taking in essence a "feminine" posture in relation to a powerful woman.

The feminine posture for a male character is that of the betrayed, and it is the man in this position who portrays women as whores. Since Iago occupies this position in relation to Othello, it makes sense that he seeks to destroy him, in the same way that Othello seeks to destroy the agent of his imagined betrayal, Desdemona. There is no reason to suppose, moreover, that Iago's consistently degraded view of women conceals any less hostile attitude in his actual relations with women. He, after all, like Othello, kills his wife. The difference between the two men lies not in their fear and mistrust of women but in the degree to which they are able to accept an emotional involvement. It is Othello, not Iago, who wears his heart on his sleeve, "for daws to peck at" (i.i.62). Were it not for Othello's initial vulnerability to Desdemona he would not be suscep-tible to Iago's machinations. Having made himself vulnerable, moreover, he attaches an extraordinary significance to the relation. "And when I love thee not, / Chaos is come again" (III.iii.91–2). "But there where I have garnered up my heart, / Where either I must live or bear no life, / The fountain from the which my current runs / Or else dries up" (IV.ii.56–9).

Once Othello is convinced of Desdemona's infidelity (much like Claudio, on the flimsiest of evidence), he regards her, not as a woman who has committed a single transgression, but as a whore, one whose entire behavior may be explained in terms of lust. As such, he may humiliate her in public, offer her services to the Venetian ambassadors, pass judgment on her, and condemn her to death. Murder, in this light, is a desperate attempt to control. It is Desdemona's power to hurt which Othello seeks to eliminate by ending her life. While legal and social sanctions may be invoked against the prostitute, the seemingly virtuous woman suspected of adultery may be punished by death. In either case it is the fear or pain of victimization on the part of the man that leads to his victimization of women. It is those who perceive themselves to be powerless who may be incited to the acts of greatest violence.

The paradox of violence in *Othello*, not unlike that in *Macbeth*, is that the exercise of power turns against the hero. In this case the murder of a woman leads to self-murder, and the hero dies attesting to the erotic destructiveness at the heart of his relation with Desdemona. "I kissed thee ere I killed thee. No way but this, / Killing myself, to die upon a kiss" (v.ii.357–8). If murder may be a loving act, love may be a murdering act, and consummation of such a love possible only through the death of both parties.

"Of Woman Born": *Lear* and *Macbeth*

The fantasy of feminine betrayal that animates the drama of *Othello* may be seen to conceal or to be coordinate with deep fantasies of maternal betrayal in *Macbeth* and *Lear*.[4] Here the emphasis falls not so much on the adult heterosexual relation (though there are such relations) as on the mother / son or the fantasy of the mother / son relation. In these plays, the perception of the masculine consciousness is that to be feminine is to be powerless, specifically in relation to a controlling or powerful woman. For Lear, rage as an expression of power acts as a defense against this awareness, while tears threaten not only the dreaded perception of himself as feminine and hence weak but also the breakdown of his psychic order.

> Life and death, I am ashamed
> That thou hast power to shake my manhood thus!
> That these hot tears, which break from me perforce,
> Should make thee worth them. Blasts and fogs upon thee!
> (i.iv.298–301)

> You think I'll weep.
> No, I'll not weep.
> I have full cause of weeping, but this heart
> Shall break into a hundred thousand flaws
> Or ere I'll weep. O Fool, I shall go mad!
> (ii.iv.279–83)

> O, let me not be mad, not mad, sweet heaven!
> Keep me in temper; I would not be mad!
> (i.v.45–6)

It is not Lear who annihilates his enemies, calling down curses on the reproductive organs of Goneril and Regan, but rather Lear who is being banished by the women on whom he had depended for nurturance. It is they who are the agents of power and destruction, allied with the storm, and he like Edgar, who is "unaccommodated man," a "poor, bare, forked animal" (iii.iv.105–7), naked and vulnerable. That the condition of powerlessness gives rise to compassion in Lear is part of his dignity as a tragic hero. It does not, however, alter his perceptions of women as either good or bad mothers. If the banishment of Cordelia initiates a process by which Lear becomes psychotic, moreover, it may be argued that her return is essential to the restoration of his sanity. The presence or absence of Cordelia, like Othello's faith in Desdemona's fidelity, orders the hero's psychic universe. When Cordelia dies, Lear must either believe that she is not dead or die with her, being unable to withstand the condition of radical separation imposed by death.

The most powerful image of separation in *King Lear*, that of the child who is banished by his mother, is that of birth. "We came crying hither: / Thou know'st, the first time that we smell the air / We wawl and cry" (iv.vi.178–80). In this sense, the mother's first act of betrayal may be that of giving birth, the violent expulsion of her infant into a hostile environment. In other passages, a woman's body itself is perceived as a hostile environment.

> But to the girdle do the gods inherit,
> Beneath is all the fiend's.
> There's hell, there's darkness, there is the sulphurous pit.
> (iv.vi.126–9)

> The dark and vicious place where thee he got
> Cost him his eyes.
> (v.iii.173–4)

Intercourse imaged as violent intrusion into a woman's body may be designed to minimize the cost.

If it is birth itself, the condition of owing one's life to a woman and the ambivalence attending an awareness of dependence on women in general, which structures much of Lear's relations to his daughters, *Macbeth* may be read in terms of a systematic attempt on the part of the hero to deny such an awareness. The world constructed by Macbeth attempts to deny not only the values of trust and hospitality, perceived as essentially feminine, but to eradicate femininity itself.[5] Macbeth reads power in terms of a masculine mystique that has no room for maternal values, as if the conscious exclusion of these values would eliminate all conditions of dependence, making him in effect invulnerable. To be born of woman, as he reads the witches' prophecy, is to be mortal. Macbeth's program of violence, involving murder and pillage in his kingdom and the repression of anything resembling compassion or remorse within, is designed, like Coriolanus' desperate militarism, to make him author of himself.

The irony of *Macbeth*, of course, is that in his attempt to make himself wholly "masculine," uncontaminated, so to speak, by the womb, he destroys all source of value: honor, trust, and, to his dismay, fertility itself. It is his deep personal anguish that he is childless. The values associated with women and children, which he considers unmanly, come to be perceived as the source of greatest strength. It is procreation, in this play, rather than violence, which confers power. "The seeds of Banquo kings!" (III.i.70). To kill a child or to imagine such an act, as Lady Macbeth does in expressing contempt for her husband's vacillations, is to betray not only the bonds of human society, but to betray one's deepest self. To reject the conditions of weakness and dependence is to make oneself weak and dependent. Macbeth's relentless pursuit of power masks his insecurities, his anxieties, and ultimately his impotence. *Macbeth*, more clearly than any of the other tragedies, with the possible exception of *Coriolanus*, enacts the paradox of power in which the hero's equation of masculinity with violence as a denial or defense against femininity leads to his destruction.

Macbeth's attempt to avoid the perception of Lear that "we cry that we are come / To this great stage of fools" (IV.vi.182–3), that the human infant is radically defenseless and dependent on the nurturance of a woman, gradually empties his life of meaning, leading to his perception of it as "a tale / Told by an idiot ... / Signifying nothing" (v.v.26–8). Of all the tragic heroes, moreover, Macbeth is the most isolated in his death, alienated from himself, his countrymen, his queen. He has become what he most feared, the plaything of powerful feminine forces, betrayed by the "instruments of darkness," the three witches.

"The Heart of Loss": *Antony and Cleopatra*

Interwoven into the patriarchal structure of Shakespeare's tragedies is an equally powerful matriarchal vision. The two are even, I would argue, aspects of one another, both proceeding from the masculine consciousness of feminine betrayal. Both inspire a violence of response on the part of the hero against individual women, but more important, against the hero's ultimately damaging perception of himself as womanish. The concurrence of these themes is particularly evident in *Antony and Cleopatra*, a play that recalls the ritual marriage conclusion of the comedies as it deepens the sexual dilemma of the tragic hero.

Antony's relation both to Cleopatra and to Caesar may be read in terms of his anxieties about dominance, his fear of self-loss in any intimate encounter. Early in the play, Cleopatra uses this perception to her advantage by suggesting that for Antony to respond to the Roman messengers is to acknowledge his submission either to Caesar or to Fulvia. Her own tactics, of course, are manipulative and a form of dominance that Antony himself recognizes. "These strong Egyptian fetters I must break / Or lose myself in dotage" (I.ii.117–18). The advice of the soothsayer to Antony concerning his proximity to Caesar is similar in structure if not in content: "near him thy angel / Becomes afeard, as being o'erpow'red" (II.iii.20–1). When Antony returns to Egypt, he is in effect "o'erpow'red" by Cleopatra. "O'er my spirit / Thy full supremacy thou knew'st" (III.xi.58–9). "You did know / How much you were my conqueror, and that / My sword, made weak by my affection, would / Obey it on all cause" (65–8). Antony, like Romeo earlier, perceives himself as having been feminized by love. "O sweet Juliet, / Thy beauty hath made me effeminate / And in my temper soft'ned valor's steel!" (III.i.115–17). "O, thy vile lady! / She has robbed me of my sword" (IV.xiv.22–3).

If affection makes Antony weak, it also makes him suspicious of Cleopatra's fidelity. "For I am sure, / Though you can guess what temperance should be, / You know not what it is" (III.xiii.120–2). He falls easy prey to the conviction that Cleopatra has betrayed him to Caesar, making him the subject of sexual as well as political humiliation. "O, that I were / Upon the hill of Basan to outroar / The hornèd herd!" (126–8). In this light, Cleopatra becomes a "witch," a "spell," a "triple-turned whore."

> O this false soul of Egypt! This grave charm,
> Whose eye becked forth my wars, and called them home,
> Whose bosom was my crownet, my chief end,
> Like a right gypsy hath at fast and loose
> Beguiled me, to the very heart of loss.
> What, Eros, Eros!
>
> (IV.xii.25–30)

Antony, under the power of erotic attachment, like Othello feels himself to have been utterly betrayed. Under the impact of this loss, moreover, his sense of psychic integrity begins to disintegrate. "Here I am Antony, / Yet cannot hold this visible shape, my knave" (IV.xiv.13–14). Chaos is come again.

While the fiction of Cleopatra's death restores Antony's faith in her love, it does not restore his energy for life. Rather, the withdrawal of her presence destroys any vestige of interest he has in the world of the living. "Now all labor / Mars what it does; yea, very force entangles / Itself with strength" (IV.xiv.47–9). It is Cleopatra who not only dominates Antony's emotional life, but who invests his world with meaning. The fact that she, unlike Juliet, Ophelia, Desdemona, Cordelia, and Lady Macbeth, dies so long after her lover, not only reveals her as a complex figure in her own right, but also attests to her power to give imaginative shape to the hero's reality.

Cleopatra in many ways is the epitome of what is hated, loved, and feared in a woman by Shakespeare's tragic heroes. She is, on the one hand, the woman who betrays, a Circe, an Acrasia, an Eve, the Venus of *Venus and Adonis*. To submit to her, or to be seduced by her, is to die. She is the player queen, for whom adultery is also murder. She is a Goneril, a Lady Macbeth, a non-nurturing mother. What she takes, on the other hand, she also has the power to give. She is imaginative, fertile, identified with the procreative processes of the Nile. If Antony lives in our imagination, it is because of her "conception" of him. In this sense, she, like Desdemona and Cordelia, is the hero's point of orientation, his source of signification in the world. Union with her is both celebrated, as a curious comic counterpoint to the tragic structure of double suicide, and portrayed as a literal impossibility. Moreover, for this sexually powerful woman to escape censure, the fate of a Cressida or a Helen, she must negate her own strength, she must die. While Theseus' phallic sword, in Antony's hands, turns against himself, Cleopatra, like Juliet, will accept death "as a lover's pinch, / Which hurts, and is desired" (v.ii.295–6). Throughout Shakespeare' tragedies the imagery of heterosexual union involves the threat of mutual or self-inflicted violence.

Looked at from one angle, what Shakespeare's tragedies portray is the anguish and destruction attendant on a fairly conventional and culturally supported set of fictions regarding heterosexual encounter. The tragedies, as I read them, do not themselves support these fictions except to the extent that they examine them with such acute attention. The values that emerge from these plays are, if anything, "feminine," values dissociated from the traditional masculine categories of force and politics, focused instead on the significance of personal relationships, or the fact of human relatedness: the values of feeling, of kinship, of loyalty, friendship, and even romantic love. That the recognition of these values entails the destruction of the hero and everyone who matters to him attests perhaps to a kind of cultural determinism, or at least to the very great difficulty of re-imagining habitual modes of behavior. It is the basis in cultural fictions of certain kinds of heterosexual attitudes to which I now wish to turn.

On the Margins of Patriarchal Discourse

Shakespeare's tragic paradigms offer the possibility of a deconstructive reading of the rape metaphor that informs Theseus' words to his captured queen.[6] Violence against women as an aspect of the structure of male dominance in Shakespeare's plays may be seen to obscure deeper patterns of conflict in which women as lovers, and perhaps more important as mothers, are perceived as radically untrustworthy. In this structure of relation, it is women who are regarded as powerful and men who strive to avoid an awareness of their vulnerability in relation to women, a vulnerability in which they regard themselves as "feminine." It is in this sense that one may speak of a matriarchal substratum or subtext within the patriarchal text. The matriarchal substratum itself, however, is not feminist. What it does in Shakespeare's tragedies is provide a rationale for the manifest text of male dominance while constituting an avenue of continuity between these plays and the comedies in which women more obviously wield power.

The preceding analysis may be seen, moreover, to parallel the movement of psychoanalytic theory from an emphasis on oedipal to pre-oedipal stages of development. Roughly speaking, the shift has occurred in terms of a decrease of concern with father / son relations and a corresponding increase of concern with mother / son relations. (Although the shift from father to mother is clear in the work of such theorists as John Bowlby, Melanie Klein, Margaret Mahler, and D. W. Winnicott, the child or infant, partly for grammatical reasons, tends to be regarded as male).[7] Certainly it may be said that the theories of object-relations, narcissism, schizophrenia, and separation-individuation have more to do with the child's early relations with his mother than with his father. Whether or not these theories are read in consonance with Freud's formulation of the Oedipus complex, the shift in focus relocates the discussion of certain issues. This relocation, in turn, reveals new interpretive possibilities. Specifically, it reopens the question of femininity.

A deconstructive reading of the rape metaphor in Shakespeare's tragedies leads directly or indirectly to a discussion of the masculine perception of femininity as weakness. The macho mystique thus becomes a form of "masculine protest," or a demonstration of phallic power in the face of a threatened castration. It is for the male hero, however, that femininity signifies weakness, while actual women are perceived by him as enormously powerful, specifically in their maternal functions. It is not the female herself who is perceived as weak, but rather the feminized male. To project this problem back onto women, as Freud does when in his discussions of femininity he portrays the little girl as perceiving herself castrated, is to present it as incapable of resolution.[8] If femininity itself is defined as the condition of lack, of castration, then there is no way around the masculine equation that to be feminine is to be castrated, or as Antony puts it, to be robbed of one's sword.

It is the masculine consciousness, therefore, that defines femininity as weakness and institutes the structures of male dominance designed to defend against such an awareness. Shakespeare's tragedies, as I read them, may be viewed as a vast commentary on the absurdity and destructiveness of this defensive posture. While Shakespeare may be said to affirm the values of feeling and vulnerability associated with femininity, however, he does not in dramatic terms dispel the anxiety surrounding the figure of the feminized male. At this point, dramatic metaphors, I would say, intersect with cultural metaphors.[9]

Freud's views of femininity may be useful to the extent to which they articulate some deeply held cultural convictions. In one sense, what they do is reveal the basis of some powerful cultural metaphors, so powerful in fact that they continue to find formulation in the midst of our vastly different social and intellectual context. In the midst of profound structural changes in habits of philosophic and scientific thinking, as a culture we cling to the language of presence and absence, language and silence, art and nature, reason and madness to describe the relations between the terms masculine and feminine. It is as though the breakdown of hierarchical modes of thought, of vertical ways of imagining experience, finds its deepest resistance in our habits of imagining the relations between the sexes. Some, like the Jungian James Hillman, would even argue that in order to effect real changes in our intellectual formulations of reality, we must find ways of reimagining femininity.[10] Sexual politics may lie at the heart of human culture, of our constantly shifting and evolving world views.

The preceding discussion, of course, rests on assumptions to which Freud would not have subscribed, chief among which is a hypothesis concerning the relation between cultural metaphors and the concept of a cultural unconscious. What I would like to propose is that the notion of the unconscious may be culture specific, that is to say, that the guiding metaphors of a given society or culture may legitimately be seen to express the structure of its unconscious assumptions, in the same way that the metaphoric structure of individual discourse may be seen to convey some of the unconscious freight of a given life. If Thomas Kuhn is correct in assuming that scientific revolutions are the result of paradigm shifts, or profound changes in our habits of imagining the world, then it may also be possible to consider the unconscious implications of certain habits of imagining.[11] Literary conventions may then be viewed as aspects of these imaginative habits, as codifications of a certain spectrum of unconscious attitudes, at the same time that they change and evolve, live and die according to their relation to the society out of which they arise and to which they respond. Cultural changes, to pursue the implications of Kuhn's argument, are in effect profound metaphoric changes which in turn involve changes in the structuring of the unconscious.

Literary history may, in this light, be read psychologically. The questions one might ask then would concern the spectrum of psychic needs served by specific conventions and genres. Tracing the uses of a convention would then also yield a literary version of psychohistory. To offer an example close to the subject of this essay, I would like to pursue briefly some of the ramifications of the rhetoric of courtly love.

It is interesting to observe the language of de Rougement, who is so careful to situate the courtly love phenomenon in a historical sense, when he refers to the rhetorical trope of love as war. "There is no need, for example, to invoke Freudian theories in order to see that the war instinct and eroticism are fundamentally allied: it is so perfectly *obvious* from the common figurative use of language."[12] Obvious to whom? Is the war instinct, for instance, perceived as an aspect of the feminine psyche? Here the common (and to many readers unquestioned) assumption that reference to the male of the species includes women may be seen to obscure a process by which a fundamentally "masculine" attitude is proposed as a universal norm. More important, however, is the interpretive process by which de Rougemont reads a metaphor specific to a certain set of conventions, albeit powerful ones, as an inalterable aspect of the unconscious life of the species. "All this confirms the natural – that is to say, the physiological – connexion between the sexual and fighting instincts."[13]

It is this supposedly natural "connexion between the sexual and fighting instincts" that structures the language of the courtly love lyric, as it structures the language of sexual encounter in Shakespeare. To term this rhetoric "conventional" is not to demean it but rather to call attention to its psychological power (which de Rougement himself agrees exists) at the same time that one recognizes its mutability, its historicity. Images of sexual intercourse as an act of violence committed against women run deep in our culture. The depth and persistence of these images, however, may tell us more about the anxieties of a culture in which femininity is conceived as castration and in which women are perceived paradoxically as a source of maternal power than it does about the actual or possible relations between the sexes.

Toward a Feminist Discourse

And, as I have hinted before, deconstruction must also take into account the lack of sovereignty of the critic himself. Perhaps this "will to ignorance" is simply a matter of attitude, a realization that one's choice of evidence is provisional, a self-distrust, a distrust of one's own power, the control of one's vocabulary, a shift from the phallocentric to the hymeneal. (Gayatri Chakravorty Spivak, translator's preface, *Of Grammatology*)

Literary history, finally, is an aspect of cultural history. Both attest to changing patterns of awareness, to the constant refiguring of our relation to our specific location in time and space, to our own historicity. If individual history, as Ortega y Gasset writes, may be conceived as a process of casting and living out or living through metaphors of the self, is it not possible to imagine cultural history in similar terms?[14] To interpret these metaphors, to read on the margins of discourse, is not only to engage in a process characteristic of psychoanalytic interpretation but also to become engaged in a fundamentally historical process, that of making what is unconscious conscious and thus altering and displacing the location of the unconscious. This process, obviously akin to that of psychotherapy, is not to be perceived statically as an attempt to eliminate the unconscious but rather as one to dislodge it, to transform its metaphoric base.

Psychoanalytic theory in this sense may also be read in the historical dimension, as a means of reading the unconscious figurings of a given life within a specific cultural moment. As such, it will of course be subject to change and will of course to some extent serve the interests of the society that supports it. I am not arguing here against psychoanalytic theory in any sense but rather *for* a recognition of its historicity.[15] While Freud's elaboration of the Oedipus complex may have served to assuage the neurotic dilemmas of his society, it does not serve the needs of contemporary feminism. In a society like ours in which most women can expect to work outside the home for a significant part of their lives, and to bear fewer than three children, the interpretive myths offered by Freud for women are increasingly pathological. In order to be useful, the theory must bear a demonstrable relation to perceived reality. To argue that the social reality of women should be altered in order to fit the theory is not only reactionary, but naïve. It would make more sense to pursue the directions of contemporary psychoanalytic theory toward a redefinition of femininity, assuming as I do that implicit within the current focus on the mother / child relation is a reawakening of interest in the question of femininity. There are even some theorists, like Dorothy Dinnerstein, who would argue that such a reformulation is necessary for cultural survival, given the destructiveness in political terms of the masculine mystique.[16]

What then, in psychoanalytic terms, would constitute the beginnings of feminist discourse? How is a woman, according to the painful elaborations of Julia Kristeva and others, to avoid the Scylla of silence or madness and the Charybdis of alienated or masculine discourse?[17] Gayatri Spivak has lately been suggesting that what we need is something like a Copernican revolution from the phallocentric formulation of femininity as absence to a gynocentric language of presence.[18] If it makes sense that the male child should perceive his own sex as primary and difference as an inferior version of himself, then it makes as much sense that the little girl should also initially perceive her sex as primary. That each sex should take itself as the norm is perhaps part of the Ptolemaic universe of children which must undergo several stages of decentering before maturity. Not to undergo this process of decentering is to elaborate structures of dominance and submission in which dominance becomes the mask of weakness and submission a subversive strategy in the mutual struggle for power. For a woman to read herself obliquely through the patriarchal discourse as "other" is to assent to this structure. For a critic, male or female, to read this discourse as representative of the true nature of masculinity or femininity is to accept this structure. For a feminist critic to deconstruct this discourse is simultaneously to recognize her own historicity and to engage in the process of dislocation of the unconscious by which she begins to affirm her own reality.

Notes

1 *A Midsummer Night's Dream*, *The Complete Signet Classic Shakespeare*, ed. Sylvan Barnet (New York: Harcourt Brace Jovanovich, 1963, 1972), p. 530. Quotations from Shakespeare in this essay refer to this edition.

2 Two critics have dealt specifically with the relation between sex and violence in this play. A. K. Nardo notes that "To the youths who rekindle the feud on a point of honor, sex, aggression, and violence are inextricably united." While Juliet undergoes an extraordinary process of development, Nardo argues, she is ultimately unable to survive in this hostile atmosphere and is finally "thrust to

the wall by the phallic sword her society has exalted." "Romeo and Juliet Up Against the Wall," *Paunch*, 48–49 (1977), 127–31. Coppélia Kahn in a more extensive consideration of this subject relates the ethic of the feud, in which sex and violence are linked, to the patriarchal structure of the society, commenting on the extent to which the conclusion of the play, associating death with sexual consummation, is also contained within this structure. Fate is thus not only a result of powerful social forces, but also of the individual subjective responses to these forces. "Coming of Age in Verona," *Modern Language Studies*, 8 (1977–78), 5–22, reprinted in *The Woman's Part*.

3 Theodore Lidz represents Hamlet as torn between the impulse to kill his mother for having betrayed his father and the desire to win her to a state of repentance and renewed chastity. My reading of Hamlet is very much indebted to his analysis in *Hamlet's Enemy: Madness and Myth in Hamlet* (New York: Basic Books, 1975).

4 Murray Schwartz discusses the difficulty of the hero's recognition of his relation to a nurturing woman in "Shakespeare through Contemporary Psychoanalysis," *Hebrew University Studies in Literature*, 5 (1977), 182–98. While Lear's dilemma, according to Schwartz, results from a "refusal to mourn the loss of maternal provision" (p. 192), Macbeth's difficulty may be seen as the result of an attempt to usurp maternal functions and to control the means of nurturance himself.

5 My discussion of the ways in which masculinity and femininity are perceived in this play is indebted to Cleanth Brooks's classic essay on *Macbeth*, "The Naked Babe and the Cloak of Manliness," in *The Well Wrought Urn* (1947, rpt. London: Dobson Books, 1968), pp. 17–39. For Brooks, it is Macbeth's war on children which reveals most clearly his own weakness and desperation. In Brooks's view, the issue of manliness is related ultimately to the theme of humanity or lack of it, but he does not pose questions about masculine and feminine stereotypes.

6 I would assent to the following description by Gayatri Spivak of the task of deconstruction: "To locate the promising marginal text, to disclose the undecidable moment, to pry it loose, with the positive lever of the signifier; to reverse the resident hierarchy, only to displace it; to dismantle in order to reconstitute what is always already inscribed. Deconstruction in a nutshell." Jacques Derrida, *Of Grammatology*, translator's preface (Baltimore: Johns Hopkins University Press, 1976), p. lxxvii. While Spivak points out that there is no end to this process in that the work of deconstruction is itself subject to deconstruction, she also notes that "as she deconstructs, all protestations to the contrary, the critic necessarily assumes that she at least, and for the time being, means what she says," p. lxxvii. While it may not be strictly necessary to borrow this terminology for the reading I am proposing, it may be useful to observe that any large-scale reinterpretation, from a minority position, of a majority view of reality must appear at least in the eyes of some as a "deconstruction."

7 Here, the problem inherent in the use of the masculine pronoun to refer to both sexes emerges. Textually speaking, the construction often obscures a shift of consideration from the development of the infant, male or female, to the exclusive development of the male infant. This convention is related to the cultural assumption by which the male of the species is taken as a norm, of which the female then becomes a variant. To remove this convention would not merely introduce a stylistic awkwardness (for some people at least), it would also reveal a fundamental awkwardness in the structure of an author's argument. While the male pronoun often *is* used generically to indicate both men and women, its use frequently serves to exclude consideration of the female without calling attention to the process by which she has been removed from the discussion.

8 Although Freud approaches the subject of femininity from different angles in his three major discussions of it, there is no question that he links the process of feminine development indissolubly to the recognition on the part of the little girl that she is castrated. It would seem at least reasonable to argue, however, that the presence or absence of a penis is of far greater significance to the boy or man, who feels himself subject to the threat of its removal, than it could ever be to the girl or woman, for whom such a threat can have little anatomical meaning. I wonder too, why, in Freud's argument, a little girl would be inspired to give up the manifestly satisfying activity of masturbation on the basis of the illusion of a loss – the assumption perhaps that she might have had more pleasure if she had once had a penis, of which she seems mysteriously to have been

deprived? The problem which gives rise to these baroque speculations is, of course, Freud's assumption that there must be some reason why the little girl would withdraw her love from her mother in order to bestow it upon her father. Freud can imagine no other reason than the little girl's recognition of her own inferiority and thus "penis envy," and her resentment of her mother, equally deprived, for not having provided her with the desired organ. There can be no hetero-sexual love, in this account, without the theory of feminine castration. One can understand, from this vantage point, why Freud was reluctant to give it up. See "Some Psychical Consequences of the Anatomical Distinction between the Sexes" (1925), "Female Sexuality" (1931), and "Femi-ninity" (1933), *Standard Edition*, trans. and ed. James Strachey (London: Hogarth Press, 1961, 1964), XIX, 241–60; XXI, 221–46; XXII, 112–35. For various critiques of Freud, see also Roy Shafer, "Problems in Freud's Psychology of Women," *Journal of the American Psychoanalytic Association*, 22 (1974), 459–85; *Women and Analysis*, ed. Jean Strouse (New York: Grossman, 1974); *Psychoanalysis and Women*, ed. Jean Baker Miller (Baltimore: Penguin Books, 1973).

9   One might wish to argue that social, psychic, and literary structures are so intimately interwoven that the relation between plot and culture is like that between Hamlet and his fate, between a text which is given and that which is generated, enacted, in part, chosen. With this in mind, one might begin to speak of "patriarchal plots," the complex set of figures by which Western culture has elaborated its relation to the structures by which it lives. The question then becomes the extent to which a powerful social movement warps, flexes, alters, reimagines these essential structures, how genres are born, how transformed.

10   James Hillman, *The Myth of Analysis: Three Essays in Archetypal Psychology* (Evanston: North-western University Press, 1972), pp. 215–98.

11   Thomas Kuhn, *The Structure of Scientific Revolutions* (Chicago: University of Chicago Press, 1966).

12   Denis de Rougemont, *Love in the Western World*, trans. Montgomery Belgion (New York: Harcourt Brace, 1940, 1956), p. 243. I have chosen the passages from de Rougemont because they are central to the elucidation of the courtly love tradition and because they are so clearly, though unintentionally, biased. A more contemporary (and more complex) example of the same kind of bias might be found in the concluding chapters of Leo Bersani's *A Future for Astyanax: Character and Desire in Literature* (Boston: Little, Brown, 1976).

13   De Rougemont, *Love in the Western World*, p. 244.

14   Ortega y Gasset, *History as a System, and Other Essays Toward a Philosophy of History* (New York: Norton, 1941, 1961), pp. 165–233.

15   The following articles make a case for the relevance of Freud's personal history to the structure of his thought: Arthur Efron, "Freud's Self-Analysis and the Nature of Psychoanalytic Criticism," *The International Review of Psychoanalysis*, 4 (1977), 253–80; Jim Swan, "*Mater* and Nannie: Freud's Two Mothers and the Discovery of the Oedipus Complex," *American Imago*, 31 (1974), 1–64; Patrick Mahony, "Friendship and Its Discontents," paper presented to the Canadian Psychoanalytic Society, Montreal, May 19, 1977. Freud's instrument of self-analysis, from the point of view of these critics, becomes a double-edged sword, a manifestation of his genius for the articulation of the structural principles of his own psyche, as well as a measure of the necessary limitation of his method. Murray Schwartz elucidates this point further in "Shakespeare through Contemporary Psychoanalysis." Juliet Mitchell might be seen to treat this subject on a large scale in *Psychoanalysis and Feminism* (New York: Pantheon, 1974), when she argues that the Oedipus complex acts as a structural representation of the psychic organization of patriarchal society.

16   Dorothy Dinnerstein, *The Mermaid and the Minotaur: Sexual Arrangements and Human Malaise* (New York: Harper & Row, 1976).

17   Julia Kristeva, who seems to accept the Lacanian explanation of the process of the child's induction into the symbolic order in Western culture, presents the position of women within this construct as one of agonized conflict in the opening chapters of *About Chinese Women*, trans. Anita Barrows (New York: Urizen Books, 1977). Shoshona Felman states the problem of defining a feminist discourse within a masculinist ethic as follows: "If, in our culture, the woman is by

definition associated with madness, her problem is how to break out of this (cultural) imposition of madness *without* taking up the critical and therapeutic positions of reason: how to avoid speaking both as *mad* and as *not mad*. The challenge facing the woman today is nothing less than to 're-invent' language, to *re-learn how to speak*: to speak not only against, but outside of the specular phallocentric structure, to establish a discourse the status of which would no longer be defined by the phallacy of masculine meaning. An old saying would thereby be given new life: today more than ever, changing our minds – changing the mind – is a woman's prerogative." "Women and Madness: The Critical Phallacy," *Diacritics*, 5, No. 4 (1975), 2–10.

18 This statement derives from remarks made by Gayatri Spivak toward the end of a session at the 1977 MMLA convention in Chicago in which she spoke of "the womb as a tangible place of production," as the point of departure for a new discourse on femininity. She has suggested that since the work on which this comment is based is not yet in print, I refer to my memory of her statements. I wish to apologize in advance for any error of understanding on my part of her position.

34

The Family in Shakespeare Studies; or Studies in the Family of Shakespeareans; or The Politics of Politics

Lynda E. Boose

Within the conventions of Renaissance drama and within the protocol of the Tudor court, being a messenger was hazardous duty. Inevitably, it fell to the messenger to hazard the wrath of the powerful by delivering precisely the information that no one really wanted to hear. However, since I could find no way to survey the trends in Shakespearean scholarship *on* the family without stumbling right into the politics concurrently going on *in* the "family" of Shakespearean scholars, my analysis of Renaissance literary research on the family, marriage, and sex commits me, I fear, to the hazards of playing the messenger. My title beribbons itself with the *de rigueur* deconstructive chiasmus and that most trendy of opening entitlements, "The Politics of … " It finally arrives, however, at what serves for both the title's ultimate deconstruction and the paper's ultimate subject: "The Politics of Politics."

While an enormous amount of important work has clearly taken place in Renaissance literary fields outside Shakespeare and while the political trends I will be pointing to may even be applicable elsewhere, I have restricted my focus to this one single author because, quite simply, no author or text so unequivocally locates the site of preeminent value for English-speaking cultures as does Shakespeare. Given the elevated place that Shakespeare occupies in American academia, the status of particular social issues within the field and scholarly disputes over them are never "merely academic" in scope, but inescapably political. In English Departments, the Shakespeare privilege is clearly spelled out: not only does Shakespeare virtually define the literary canon and the literature major, but "Shakespeareans" stand apart from such departmental categories as "Medievalists," "Romanticists," "Nineteenth-Century Americanists" (etc.); "Shakespeareans" are hired and entitled under the authoritative name of this one author inside an exclusive territory where the discipline's otherwise governing assumptions about historical location or literary milieu suddenly seem to evaporate. And yet, as those of us who parade under this entitlement also know, the sheer potency of the name that privileges us likewise precludes us from enjoying sole claim to it. Shakespeare's purported universality works somewhat like a universal legitimation – a kind of open market that makes everyone feel not just entitled but almost professionally compelled to lay claim to it. Of late, witness even Geoffrey Hartman, the dean of literary theory, entering the arena to pronounce the definitive *Questions of Theory in Shakespeare.*

Shakespeare is a site of such competitive jostling because Shakespeare is a site of enormous cultural power. As such, he is not only a universally available but likewise a dangerously charged locale, where maneuvers for appropriation, displacement, erasure, and the institutionalization of both cultural and academic privileges are invested with a particular energy that makes the politics within this field the more recognizable and, simultaneously, perhaps the more crucial to recognize.

In looking at any emerging scholarly trend, probably all critics in all disciplines need to be frequently reminded of the point that Terence Hawkes's witty narrations of Shakespeare and the academy unerringly bring home. And that is, that in what each generation of scholars writes, it is actually writing itself. Given Shakespeare's special status, Shakespearean scholarship effectively constitutes the equivalent of a cultural Rorschach inscribing the issues, the ideologies, the tensions, and the terms of debate that define the preoccupying investments for any given historical moment, including our own. That late nineteenth and early- to mid-twentieth century critics – who were themselves either fathered within the elite bastions of British academia or anxious to prove their heritage within that tradition – should have located the "meaning of Shakespeare" within all the orthodoxies of "right reason" and "natural" hierarchy that affirmed their own threatened sense of social control is perhaps no more random a fact than is the intense interest our own era has suddenly taken in the family and the sex roles developed within it – subjects that, to earlier critics, seemed so apparently unproblematic as not to require much attention, let alone examination. But in both the contemporary Renaissance literary scholarship that privileges the Shakespeare text and in that which gives priority to non-literary, historically-specific ones external to it, the dominant interest these days is in deconstructing, demystifying, *and*, I would also have to argue, through maneuvers which may even imagine themselves as "disinterested," perhaps tacitly *re*-constructing and *re*-mystifying both the structure and the internal mechanisms of the hierarchical paradigm that we in the twentieth century inherited from the Renaissance: the patriarchal nuclear family.

In North America, this newly urgent academic discourse on family and sex is taking place within the political context of two external, social phenomena with which it is inextricably bound: the American Women's Movement and its struggle for national legitimation, and, simultaneously, the emergence of a politically neo-conservative, at times nearly hysterical national propaganda that disguises protecting the status quo under "Saving The Family" and stakes the nation's survival on essentializing traditional family arrangements as the final bulwark of universal morality. Meanwhile, on the other side of the Atlantic, the new wave of Marxist scholars who come not from Oxford and Cambridge but from Sussex University have launched an influential British front to redefine and denounce Shakespeare as the chief cultural patriarch of Britain's imperialist heritage; and the investments of these new wave Brits in promulgating a class-conscious cultural materialism – a Marxism updated via the influence of Raymond Williams – seem as historically specific and as distinctively "British" as do the less consciously ideological agendas of their distinctively "American" counterparts.

Although marriage, sex, and family have emerged as a topic of special interest not just in literature but in all Renaissance disciplines, the investigation in literature has been both significantly complicated and likewise energized by the fact that, concurrently, established modes for the whole discipline of literary theory have been undergoing upheaval and radical reshaping in response to the recent arrival of new, European methodologies. In literary studies, what was challenged by this new body of poststructuralist theory was the overtly apolitical, though inherently (if blandly) conservative, practice of "New Criticism" – the formalist model of discovering "meaning" by close textual reading that still largely dictates how literature is taught in American academia. Although the poststructuralist theories were relatively late in penetrating the phalanx of deification surrounding Shakespeare, they have, of late, begun to assert their claims.[1] Furthermore, it might be argued that this methodological contestation is being waged in English Renaissance studies as a much more insistently politicized debate than in other literary fields where it is likewise going on – a trend I would attribute both to the weightier claims at stake in possession of Shakespeare and the greater investment of British critics in this field. From a look at the most recently emerging trends, it is my feeling that the debate over methodology – and, by direct implication, ideology – is shaping up to take place precisely within the terrain which this year's RSA plenary session decided to survey: sex, family, and marriage. Perhaps all subject matter, no matter how historically remote, is inherently "political" to the age that exhumes it; certainly for these three interrelated subjects, each dimension of the contemporary scholarly debate – what subjects it includes, the terms in which it is waged, the investments of its participants, and what status the debate is given within the institution – is unavoidably so. So while the stakes in Shakespearean scholarship have always been high, it seems accurate to say that over no terrain have the stakes been higher and at no time have they been as self-conscious of themselves as *being* claims for participation in – or exclusive retention of – this all important, powerfully political site called William Shakespeare.

To say that one does "research on the family in Shakespeare" sounds innocuously domestic. To appreciate the actually radical nature of what this scholarship has produced during the past ten years, it helps to measure the work against the traditions it has challenged and the implicit sinecures it has threatened. I therefore begin by thumbing back to the category for family that most of us remember as the transmitted wisdom of graduate school. Until roughly ten years ago, "the family" was still contained by the definition of its proper place that critics like E. M. W. Tillyard had, years earlier, extrapolated unquestioned from the hierarchical discourses of the Elizabethan state and promulgated as truths that were unproblematic because still firmly in evidence, hence "natural." As the subsumed lesser term of the old "Macrocosm-Microcosm" paradigm, the family was seldom placed into analytical focus and never approached as a construction to be queried. Perhaps because the process of mystification depends upon a certain kind of cultural amblyopia that is oblivious to its own partial sightedness, so long as the chief beneficiaries of any social institution remain the only eyes within it they will automatically imagine its mechanisms as organic, not political. When processes are seen as organic, there are no processes to deconstruct. And thus, although other of Tillyard's suppositions about the operation of Elizabethan order in the macrocosm (which was presumed to be the only political sphere) had been subjected to skeptical revision years before, those about marriage and the family (presumedly non-political) remained pristinely intact, implicitly protected by yet unquestioned assumptions that marriage, family, and sex were "natural" features of society, be it Shakespeare's or our own, not social institutions that had been culturally constructed and culturally reproduced along the ideological fault lines of arbitrary political privilege – privilege that was itself based upon what I shall now call "gender" rather than "sex."

Until recently, the men who defined the scholarly establishment we were all trained within never imagined that terms of discourse were needed to separate cultural ideas *about* sexual identity ("gender") from the register of biological differentiation ("sex"). But until such a discourse had emerged as a conceptual tool, until language had given us the concept of a "sex / gender system" (articulated in 1975 by anthropologist Gayle Rubin), marriage, family, and "sex" remained unquestioned givens, mystified and perpetuated into that status by the absence of a language for laying bare their construction. No scholar of the late twentieth century would probably have rationalized the hierarchical gendering of family roles by reference to the Renaissance argument about divinely ordained, "natural" male superiority. Nonetheless, the same system was still firmly in place some four hundred years later. The ideology of the father-headed, father-named nuclear family that had emerged in the 1500s as the discourse defining the family unit had changed but little because its distributions of power remained intact. The hierarchy that had earlier been justified by reference to Genesis was merely rationalized in a post-Darwinian world by a scientifically "natural" functionalism that preordained women – as Angelo states in *Measure for Measure* – to "put on the destined livery" and become mothers – mothers who acquired social acceptability for themselves and the legal entitlement of "legitimacy" for their children only by literally donning the "livery" of a husband / lord's name and becoming servants to the production of the patrilineal family.[2] Thus, until the implications of "biology as destiny" were examined in light of social gendering, Shakespeare's women characters and the family units that contained them dutifully played out their roles in Shakespearean criticism, the family constructions a given and the women's roles unquestioned, indeed elevated into dispute only when characters like Lady Macbeth or Cleopatra stepped outside their definitions by disrupting the proper macro-functioning of the political sphere of men.

It wasn't that scholars of the "old historicist" school of textual appraisal failed to notice the misogyny that so indelibly marks both the literary and non-literary texts of the English Renaissance. It was that within the benignly Anglican bias of Shakespearean scholarship, such treatises, howsoever numerous, were regarded as a distasteful historical embarrassment, a disgrace to male chivalry, and best viewed as either the unfortunate residues of earlier patristic dogma or the aberrations of Puritan fanatics. As Linda Woodbridge's survey of the 1540–1620 literature on the nature of women points out, the "vast storehouse of Renaissance misogyny" was usually handled by Victorian and post-Victorian scholars either by scrupulous avoidance or relegation to footnotes and, until its resuscitation by feminist scholars, "prompted no more response from modern commentators than the raising of an eyebrow."[3] So long as misogyny was thus contained in the outer margins or dismissed into the footnotes of the Elizabethan cultural text and not imagined as a central discourse which itself constructed the sacrosanct enclosures of marriage and family, Shakespearean scholarship functioned as a tacit apologist and reproductive instrument for these social institutions, Elizabethan or contemporary. Marxist critics may have challenged the social organization of class and thus exposed the self-interested bias of much of the criticism that preceded them. But until quite recently, in Shakespearean scholarship the social organization of gender – and thus the constitution of the inherited family model – went unchallenged. All was well that ended well – and marriage and family so quintessentially defined scholars' *own* culturally constructed assumptions about social and personal happiness that, until as late as the 1970s, criticism seemed incapable of even noticing questions about those institutions – questions that post-'70s scholarship subsequently came to see as being themselves raised within such plays as *Measure for Measure* and *All's Well That Ends Well*. Shakespearean criticism thus continued to operate exactly as the Elizabethan apologists for family order would have wanted it to until the mid-1970s, when suddenly its own order was disrupted. Noting the sudden phenomenon of an emerging trend for family research in sixteenth-, seventeenth-, and eighteenth-century historical studies, Christopher Hill comments on the shift in historical criticism that was actually occurring throughout Renaissance scholarship. Hill's observations, however, are couched in language so offhandedly dismissive in tone as nearly to undermine their own relevance. Reviewing Lawrence Stone's 1977 book on *The Family, Sex, and Marriage*, Hill remarks: "... the family as an institution rather suddenly became fashionable, perhaps as a by-product of the women's liberation movement."[4]

To be more precise, the three related categories in focus today virtually invaded the Shakespeare institution and other Renaissance fields concurrently with the emergence of feminist criticism and feminist academicians. The two investigations – the one, feminist, and the other focused on marriage, family, and gender – announced themselves simultaneously as such "newly fashionable" fields through Shakespeare sessions at the 1976 Modern Language Association. Until recently, the two inquiries remained tied together, the work on marriage and family not only co-implicit with the feminist concern about gender but catapulted into the Shakespeare fortress by it and launched as a legitimate field of inquiry by the emergence of a vigorous first generation of feminist Shakespeareans. The North American pioneers in this field include scholars like Janet Adelman, Shirley Garner (who had previously published under the name "S. N. Garner," thus doing what I, too, was advised in graduate school to do), Gayle Greene, Coppélia Kahn, Carol Thomas Neely, Marianne Novy, Clara Claiborne Park, Phyllis Rackin, Meredith Skura, Madelon Sprengnether [Gohlke], Carolyn Swift [Lenz], and Linda Woodbridge [Fitz].

The methodology that most of these feminist scholars brought with them was psychoanalytic,[5] a perspective that American feminists revised by shifting focus away from Freud's phallocentric paradigm toward an inclusion of the maternal issues of gender formation enunciated by theorists like Melanie Klein, D. W. Winnicott, Nancy Chodorow, and Dorothy Dinnerstein. It was, in fact, precisely these new perspectives that revitalized psychoanalytic criticism and moved it from its disrepute of the early

1970s into the *au courant* status it came to enjoy in Shakespeare studies by the early 1980s. But by the mid-1980s, in the wake of the post-deconstructionist privilege accorded to historicity – to historical conditions governing the production of individuals, social units, and texts that is primary in Marxist and Foucaultian theory – it was this very reliance on the psychoanalytical approach that was faulted for grounding feminist analyses inside the text, inside of increasingly questioned notions about the construction of subjects and subjectivity, and inside of a criticism which, though it did incorporate historical discourse and was certainly not "ahistorical" (as has of late been charged), was nonetheless focused on relations within a family model that was implicitly based on – or tacitly accepted – Freud's essentialist presumption of the transhistorical nature of both the family unit and subject members within it. Since, as Judith Kegan Gardiner points out, "psychoanalysis purports to tell us what gender means – that is, how persons become psychologically 'feminine' or 'masculine,' "[6] feminism turned to psychoanalysis as a means of investigating the induction of gender; and psychoanalysis, in turn, led the inquiry back to the family. In Shakespeare studies, psychoanalytically-theorized feminism never really acquired the Lacanian perspective that has so strongly influenced contemporary French feminism, British film studies, and the work of important American scholars like Jane Gallop. Once having refurbished psychoanalytic usage with its missing maternal pole, the feminist scholars in Shakespeare were perhaps disinclined to return to "the Law of the Father" (Lacan). In Shakespeare studies, the fusion of feminist concerns and psychoanalytic work on the family was itself enabled by a supportive father-figure, the late C. L. Barber, whose influential body of work reached its final statement with Richard Wheeler's 1986 completion of their jointly authored book, *The Whole Journey.*

From the very beginning, Shakespearean feminism found itself forced to juggle the paradoxes of its own liminality. Feminism within American English Departments is, logically enough, centered in nineteenth- and twentieth-century studies where it has built its power base and insured its place in the literary institution by the focus it has brought to the works of women writers. If you think about it, even the term "Shakespearean feminism" is a kind of oxymoron. As fledgling feminist literary criticism began to try to theorize itself, it initially enunciated a shift toward a progressively gynocritical stance that denounced further use of feminist energies for even revisionist readings of the literary masters.[7] But for feminist literary scholars whose intellectual interests, graduate degrees, and hard-won appointments were already invested in historical fields like the English Renaissance – periods which left few enough records of women's existence and even fewer in words that women themselves had written – the effect of such a stance was obviously isolating. And while scholars like Margaret Hannay, Mary Lamb, Margaret Ferguson, Ann Rosalind Jones, Josephine Roberts, Mary Beth Rose, and Nancy Vickers are at work recuperating the muted histories and forgotten texts of real women writers,[8] representations of Elizabethan and Jacobean women's voices are, for the most part, to be found within male-authored fictions, especially the drama, and particularly Shakespeare's. For political as well as personal reasons, Renaissance feminist scholars felt it would be self-annihilating for feminist criticism to restrict itself to women writers and thereby relinquish claim to the predefined (and thus, by definition, male) literary canon. Where feminist Shakespeareans made good their tenacity is through the widely influential revisionist readings they initiated – modes of interpretation that made an immediate impact on Shakespeare teaching by asserting a co-gendered perspective at last appropriate to the co-educational classroom. Using the formalist mode of close reading, feminist interpretations saw new questions to ask and liberated new psycho-social significances from the Shakespeare texts.

Because the initially most compelling project for Renaissance feminist scholarship was to understand / account for the male misogyny that earlier critics had pushed to the background, feminist family studies such as Coppélia Kahn's and Janet Adelman's focused as much or more on the construction of masculine as feminine identity, particularly on the role played by the mother – either present or absent – in that formation. The strength of the feminist critique lay in the focus that it gave for the first time to the social production of gender, which it located inside the family. By enunciating what amounted to a new subject, these new voices in Shakespeare effectively opened up what we might call a new, scholarly mother-lode, on which site the first generation critics staked out the feminist claims for participation in literature's most treasured field. As the ensuing gold rush got underway and many wagons headed west, feminist assumptions might be defined by the idea of "self-interested generosity": feminism politically wanted, welcomed, and actively encouraged the involvement of male scholars in this inquiry, for the assumption that the family was primarily a woman's territory was precisely the assumption that feminism as a political movement was fighting to change. Furthermore, since the bedrock of family construction was inseparable from its asymmetrical distribution of gender privilege, further family scholarship would, it was thought, logically produce greater awareness of these skewed distributions, which, once acknowledged, would implicitly compel materialist critics to reconsider the notion of social class and at last recognize gender as being itself a major class distinction hidden beneath but actually transecting the restrictedly masculine categories proposed by Marxist theory.[9] Such, at least, were the optimistically imagined trajectories.

And indeed, amidst the near euphoria that surrounded Shakespearean research on gender, marriage, and family in the late '70s and early '80s, the inquiry seemed to promise not only the belated exhumation of Renaissance Woman into a contemporary dialogue that would at last include her, but a newly enfranchised space for latter day Renaissance Man – a space in which he might get beyond being merely soldier, scholar, and poet and dare to explore his entitlements as son, brother, father, and husband. Interest in the field burgeoned to such an extent that the research on these interrelated topics came rapidly to dominate the Shakespeare scholarly output. From a purely scholarly perspective, it might even be said that the subjects became *too* popular, for commercial and academic presses alike began publishing with less discrimination than enthusiasm, leaving an output as occasionally mixed in quality as it is extensive in quantity. As the subject gained pre-eminence, the feminists who had initiated it and whose names remain most prominently associated with it worked, I would say, to foster a context of non-competitive, cooperative sharing inside the discipline – a point that may reflect, in a fascinating way, a great deal not only about the social construction of gender but about the way such constructions implicitly affect the politics that derive from them.

Existing within a discipline that increasingly valorizes theory and scorns the idea of literary criticism as a pluralistic community of interpretive acts, feminist literary criticism – which is frequently defined as something more like an "approach" than a coherent and definable "theory" – repeatedly goes at buffets with itself over this issue. There are those who see defining an adequately theorized position as both essential for survival and a mark of maturity within the discipline. There are others, however, who view "theory" as aridly male and see the most fundamental definition of feminist criticism as radically inseparable from pluralistic interpretation and resistance to self-theorizing.[10] In all these internal debates, what liberal American feminism has seemed most uneasy about is the totalizing tendency of theory – the impulse that necessitates contestation and turns the literary profession into a shoot 'em out at the You're-Not-O.K. Corral. That the contestation model of scholarship is increasingly assumed, however, is implicit in the fact that at the Central Renaissance conference in St. Louis (March, 1987), Shakespearean feminists were attacked from the podium for, among other things, their failure to attack each other. But that American feminist criticism has remained reluctant to embrace the dialectical model of a perpetually competitive struggle for power and dominance is not only a resistance that is thoroughly consistent with the gendering process of socialization. It is equally a political assertion of difference meant to affirm those particular behaviors that culture has marked out as "female." In Shakespeare studies, the feminist inspired scholarship *on* the family seemed, if anything, to operate like a growing family of shared interests. In the chain of MLA sessions it generated, equal numbers of newcomers and equal distributions of male and female scholars were scrupulously invited. In many of the texts it produced – such as the 1980 Lenz, Greene, Neely collection, *The Woman's Part: Feminist Criticism of Shakespeare*, the 1982 Schwartz and Kahn volume, *Representing Shakespeare: New Psychoanalytic Essays*, and the 1985 Mary Beth Rose anthology, *Women in the Middle Ages and the Renaissance* – the emphasis was on collaboration rather than single voice authority. It seems accurate to say that the work on family construction was itself born inside an atmosphere which was, in psychoanalytic terms, distinctly nurturing, distinctly maternal. One might also say that the ambience in which it developed was thus, ironically, tied back into the inherited model of gender and family that the feminist exploration was, at one and the same time, holding up for critique.

Shakespearean feminism and Shakespeare studies in marriage, family, and gender were twinned together, have developed in tandem, and during their approximate twelve years of kinship have come to be locked together in a fierce embrace, ever more aware of the dangerous slippage between bonds and bondage. When the first book to explore the position of women in the Renaissance came out with British scholar Juliet Dusinberre's *Shakespeare and the Nature of Women*, Dusinberre read the Protestant and Puritan conceptions of and new emphasis on marriage as a positive, liberating trend in the history of women. She thus read Shakespeare's apparent affirmation of that institution and woman's role as stabilizer of it as indicative of Shakespeare's own laudably proto-feminist sympathies. Subsequent feminist work strove to avoid the enthusiastic excesses which had made Dusinberre's book vulnerable. But, with a few exceptions, the general direction of the work was similar in its affirming perspective, a perspective that it maintained by perhaps unconsciously avoiding direct engagement with what it was not quite ready to confront. When feminist critiques looked at the marriage structures evoked at the end of comedy, for instance, they tended to focus on the subversively liberating actions that had led up to the conclusion rather than on the hierarchical subordination and the silencing of the comic heroine that often accompany the reimposition of institutions at the end of those same comedies. It took a few more years before feminism would feel impelled to go beyond analyzing character relations within family representations and scrutinize the construction of the family itself.

With a certain irony, it can be said that psychoanalytic theory – which assumes the transhistorical nature of the family unit – had seemed to feminist explorers so strikingly appropriate a compass for remapping Shakespearean drama precisely because the Shakespearean family seemed to resemble our own modern one so closely. Even the Christian marriage ceremony has changed but negligibly from the ritual alluded to in Shakespeare's plays.[11] And that apparent familiarity initially provided the feminist critic with the one truly indispensable reward of the scholarly profession – the private reinforcement of intellectual delight that accompanies recognition. But when feminism moved outside the text to the critique of systems rather than the analysis of relationships within them, that same familiarity felt more like a manacle testifying to the bondage of women's history. For feminist critics, not even the most obviously historical models of marriage and family can be purely (and merely) historical. And they cannot because, as topics, they carry with them the still unresolved, deeply ambivalent history of women's oppression. Consequently, the more the research they pioneered made feminist critics aware of the resolutely patriarchal nature of these institutions, the more such awareness problematized the liberal feminist dream of resolving the conflict between personal and political desire – of reaching the imagined space where that conflict no longer existed. To reject rather than extend the history of their own oppression meant taking a stance against the inherited forms of marriage and family. And to do this meant nothing short of taking a stance against the very model of female fulfillment that feminist scholars were themselves raised to value. In calling for a more political feminism in Shakespeare studies, British critic Kathleen McLuskie at least recognizes the particular conflict that characterizes this issue. For as feminist scholars research the Renaissance family organization, what is finally at issue is, as she says, our *own* "socialisation within the family and, perhaps more importantly, our psychological development as gendered subjects [that] make these changes no simple matter. They involve deconstructing the sustaining comforts of love and family as the only haven in a heartless world."[12]

If race, ethnicity, and religion have already mapped a differential investment for blacks onto *Othello* and Jews onto *The Merchant of Venice*, gender construction has always already dictated a disproportionate feminist investment in a number of issues which span the canon. In the most recent one to emerge into debate, investment runs so high that the issue itself threatens to become some sort of oath of allegiance upon which feminist critics are compelled to swear their integrity. The troublesome new question concerns Shakespeare's own attitude toward patriarchy and its institutional subordination of women – or at least the attitude espoused by his textual representation and reproduction of that institution. The problem with the question may be not the question *per se*, but the assumption it generates that the breadth and variety of the Shakespeare canon will yield up a coherent answer. As long as the plays were read as being unproblematically mimetic and characters were imagined as psychological subjects, a systematic pattern was inferred. Ironically, it is just when criticism is moving away from its mimetic model and toward a more complex understanding of theatricality that it suddenly becomes compelling to answer a question that perhaps can no longer be answered. For Shakespearean feminism, this question reaches into areas that are significant in the widest personal, political, and pedagogical ways. By putting at risk the perception of Shakespeare's authorization of women that became widely accepted as a result of the past twelve years of feminist scholarship, the question may also inadvertently put at risk the ground upon which Shakespearean feminism established whatever entitlement it has carved out within American university teaching.

From Dusinberre's 1975 ebullient appropriation of Shakespeare for the feminist cause, the direction of scholarship addressing this issue has moved with a slow but increasing momentum toward seeing the frequent patterns of gender reversal and female power in Shakespeare's plays as actually serving only to consolidate the status quo of male hierarchy. The directions in which the inquiry has led American and British feminism have been similar. The positions it has reached, however, differ significantly enough as to illustrate some fundamental and important distinctions about the mainline politics that energize the otherwise common interests of each of these two, decidedly national versions of Shakespearean feminism.

Although names like Madelon Sprengnether, Louis Montrose, and Clara Claiborne Park should at least be mentioned in connection with the movement away from seeing Shakespeare as a latter-day feminist, the most extensive such American treatment of Shakespeare's sexual politics is Peter Erickson's feminist exploration, *Patriarchal Structures in Shakespeare's Drama*. Erickson constructs a Shakespeare who repeatedly undermines tyrannical patriarchy, but just as repeatedly affirms its benevolent version. According to Erickson, Shakespeare does grant his female characters that unusual strength that critics have vested in them; but women's roles are also invariably qualified by Shakespeare's overriding conviction that social harmony requires male control. If we imagine an ideological agenda (conscious or unconscious) behind any critic's particular view, the following lines excerpted from Erickson's conclusion seem to me to sum up several important things about the deployments that are bound up in the mainline politics of American Shakespearean feminism:

> It is important to question and to qualify the notions of linearity and maturity in Shakespeare's development. From my perspective, *The Winter's Tale* does have a crucial value in the total picture … Against the background of the destructive antagonism between men and women in the tragedies, the recovery of the possibility for harmonious relations enacted by Leontes and Hermione is miraculous. Nevertheless, … the legitimate need to celebrate the positive aspects of *The Winter's Tale* should not be permitted … to obscure the negative elements. I would do justice both to Shakespeare's growth and to his limitations, and I cherish the limitations as a valid, precious part of the cultural tradition we critically transmit. A complex picture of the fluctuations in the course of Shakespeare's development involves the recognition of loss as well as gain.[13]

What governs these lines is a recurring rhetorical balance that insists on the "both-and" perspective, tacitly refusing to extend its argument about Shakespearean patriarchalism into exclusive definition. On the one hand, that very commitment may lead the rhetoric into an accidental – and problematic – affirmation when, in order to acknowledge Shakespeare's growth, the logic is led into the position of equally "cherishing" his (patriarchal) limitations as a "valid, precious part of the cultural tradition" we transmit. On the other hand, by simultaneously insisting upon the complexities that "question and qualify" any single position, the argument implicitly rejects the totalizing impulse to control its readers. It is a criticism that is everywhere marked with signs of its origins in democratic liberalism, and, like most American political positions, is not overtly conscious of itself as reflecting any particular ideology. It is, however, shrewdly aware of the practical exigencies of the American academic scene it tacitly addresses. Its political interests are most apparent in the fact that while Erickson is concerned to expose Shakespearean patriarchalism, he is also concerned not to participate in it by excluding women himself. He therefore stops short of defining the canon as a males-only playground and leaves the pleasures of the text and the power of Shakespearean authorization still more or less universally available. What might be read as caution in Erickson's position is, ultimately, a practical political awareness of having reached a point beyond which there is potentially as much to be lost as to be gained.

British feminist Kate McLuskie is likewise concerned to expose Shakespeare's patriarchalism. Her conclusions differ dramatically from Erickson's, however, because McLuskie's is an overtly political feminism tactically committed to the Marxist schematics of "either-or" and to the mode of argument that allows no space outside itself. McLuskie's strategy – which begins by reproving the liberal perspective of her American counterparts – is bluntly to sever the female reader from the notion of subjective identity with Shakespeare's attitudes or from any figurative inclusion within the dramaturgical maneuvers of his plays. For McLuskie, Shakespeare's plays locate the audience in so totally masculinized a perspective that the only possible position open to feminist readers is radical resistance: to imagine Shakespeare as an advocate is merely a sentimental attempt to co-opt his authority by trying to ignore the often misogynistic perspective supported within and elicited by his plays. Therefore, "Feminist criticism of [the / any] play is restricted to exposing its own exclusion from the text. It has no point of entry into it, for the dilemmas of the narrative and the sexuality under discussion are constructed in completely male terms."

Given the standard organization of American (albeit not British) English departments where faculty are hired specifically to teach in one particular area, short of a massive restructuring of curricula and teaching arrangements it is hard to imagine the translation of this position into pedagogical terms that would not finally raise the question why feminists would even want to teach in a field where, term after term, they would be "restricted to exposing their own exclusion from the text." To be a feminist in McLuskie's terms is to renounce completely one's pleasure in Shakespeare and embrace instead the rigorous comforts of ideological correctness. Since "when a feminist accepts the narrative, theatrical and intellectual pleasures" offered by Shakespearean drama "she does so in male terms and not as a part of the locus of feminist critical activity," feminism is exhorted to abstain from such seductions and abstemiously invest its energies in asserting "the power of resistance, subverting rather than co-opting the domination of the patriarchal bard."[14] If Shakespeare can be accused of participating in the reification of patriarchy by his reproduction of it, then surely McLuskie has here likewise participated in the reproduction of – if not the production of – the feminist exclusion upon which she insists. But then, her call for an adversarial feminist response to Shakespeare depends upon totalizing women's exclusion so as to leave feminists with no ground to occupy other than subversive resistance. It is clear from McLuskie's argument that one cannot serve feminism and Shakespeare, too. What has never been clear to American liberal feminism, however, is how one can serve feminism and Marxism too without practicing the same co-option and the same contradictions that Shakespeare's feminist sympathizers are here accused of glossing over or wishing away.

McLuskie's is a tough, articulate, uncompromising, and identifiably British argument. By the very extent of its determination to denounce Shakespeare, it is everywhere marked as belonging to the larger concerns of the newly energized Marxist political criticism, a criticism in which – if the sheer weight of the recent British output on Shakespeare is any measure[15] – deposing the English Bard and the imperialistic heritage of British Bardolatry is clearly a first priority. If Erickson's rhetoric bumps into problems in the commitment to balance that arises from its implicit politics, McLuskie's does so in its politically inspired commitment to polarization. The argument which places feminism in rhetorical opposition to "pleasure" comes originally from Laura Mulvey's widely recognized analysis of the film medium as being visually constructed around male pleasure, the male spectator, and the female object. But in its use of the Mulvey opposition, McLuskie's argument provides no explanation (other than apparent masochism) for the pleasure women readers and audiences have taken and do take in Shakespeare.[16] And whereas Mulvey – a feminist film maker – is writing not so much to tell us to cease enjoying, in this case, film, but to open up a positive way for considering how feminist film makers can re-vision and reconstitute film dynamics to create an aesthetics of female pleasure that will transform women into subjects, McLuskie can only warn us away from Shakespeare in terms that warn us away from pleasure. And logically, Shakespeare must be only the beginning: if one is to renounce Shakespeare for his patriarchalism, then surely one must also renounce the enjoyment of most of Western drama (Mamet; Shepard; Stoppard; Rabe – ??) and, for that matter, most of western literature. By setting up a linguistic opposition between feminism and pleasure with no access possible to such alternatives as Mulvey can provide, McLuskie's polarities reinvoke the perhaps unintended spectre of a feminist politics reallied with the puritanical, eventuating in a definition of women's pleasure that begins in restriction and finally leaves authorizable feminist "pleasure" available only through embracing the all too familiar ideal of renunciation. Yet, by setting this debate into such an extremity of choices and by her willingness to identify the personal issues here at stake as being nothing short of one's own socialization within the idealized myth of family, McLuskie's unblinkered honesty contributes a newly tough political awareness to the discourse of family in Shakespeare studies. It also challenges that discourse to a comparably unflinching awareness of its own contemporary implications.

In surveying the atmosphere of the present moment, it seems accurate to say that feminist scholarship right now stands at a crossroads that is as much political as intellectual. In terms of the outward marks of political achievement, what initially began as a feminist inquiry spearheaded by a group of scholars (most out of academic jobs at the time) worked within a mere twelve years to effect substantial changes in the shape and classroom content of American English Departments. What gets foregrounded in contemporary classroom discussion of the plays and the orthodoxies about "meaning" in Shakespeare has shifted so substantially that even the composition – and thus, implicitly, the message – of the academy itself has been threatened: for, once the issue of gender became a major consideration within the classroom, the lopsided representation of that issue within the Shakespeare faculty began to become an implicit comment by – and on – the academy itself. In consequence, many departments even began … at least contemplating … the potential relevance of … perhaps considering … or at least thinking about … maybe hiring … at least … one woman in the Shakespeare cadre. This consideration has not, by contrast, really entered the hiring debate in other literary fields that likewise lack canonical women writers. But it has in Shakespeare. And to the extent that the impetus became a *fait accompli*, what the decision authorized was something quite radical in the history of education and the history of gender. For while some of Cambridge and Oxford's most prestigious colleges were still debating letting women onto the faculty at all, American academia was feeling impelled at least to imagine women as authoritative transmitters of the generational wisdom of the language's most sacred, most canonical text. Unquestionably, such wisdom had been substantially altered by an energetic generation of research into an area that had hitherto been dismissed as apolitical – that "microcosm" of domestic concerns – the world that, in the wake of the scholarship of those years, could probably no longer unblushingly be called "the little world of man."

What feminist scholars did *not* want to happen, however, is exactly what there is by now reason to fear is subtly happening: that the putative "microcosm" of marriage, family and gender relations, having once been brought into the center of scholarship and made equal with the supposed "macrocosmic" subjects, be tacitly turned into an academic ghetto, a "little world of woman" where feminist issues could be progressively contained and re-marginalized while male scholarship returned under the name of new methodologies to its old study of power and court politics and effectively reconstructed a 1980s version of the Elizabethan World Picture that Renaissance scholars had, but a few years earlier, set out to deconstruct. Such a micro-macro segregation and such a return to the old, gender-based asymmetries of power was, however, what was proleptically dramatized before the audience of the 1984 Shakespeare Association in Boston. On one side of the steel curtain that separated the convention's central and simultaneous seminars, several of the major feminist psychoanalytic critics had been invited to confess their shortcomings in a forum entitled "The Limitations of Psychoanalytic Criticism." On the other side of the barrier – where several of the major new historicist critics held forth in an authoritative show called "The Implications of The New Historicism" – Coppélia Kahn, speaking from her anomalous position on the second panel, pointed out the disturbing division that the seminar organization seemed to dramatize. In doing so, Kahn seems to have been the first to comment publicly on the incipient schism and the first to call for a consciousness that might prevent it.

When new historicism (or rather, "*The*" new historicism, as it calls itself) emerged in Renaissance literary criticism with the 1980 publication of Stephen Greenblatt's justifiably influential book, *Renaissance Self-Fashioning*, in the shared excitement of this event feminist critics assumed – perhaps naively – that the theoretical framework of new historicism and its British counterpart, cultural materialism, would lead to a natural alliance. To paraphrase Carol Thomas Neely's points about what these three criticisms have in common, although the materialist critics go further than most American liberal feminists in denying all subjectivity, interiority, and identity which is continuous across time and not purely the construct of patriarchal ideology, these critiques, like the feminist one, view gender roles as culturally and linguistically constructed and, like feminism, are centrally concerned with distributions of authority in literary representation and critical response.[17] For that matter, the materialist manifestos actually repeat many of the axioms that feminism had enunciated early in the 1970s. But rather than an alliance with feminism, what seems instead to have happened is more like a progressive eradication of even the subject of women, accomplished by means of several (though, I would emphasize, not necessarily conscious) critical displacements.

When American Marxist critic Walter Cohen addressed a seminar on "Political Criticism in Shakespeare" at the 1986 World Shakespeare Congress in West Berlin – where the growing political tensions amongst Shakespearean critics apparently began to take on almost the character of the divided city itself[18] – Cohen did something unusual. Instead of comparing only American new historicism and British cultural materialism, he included feminism. In doing so, and in pointing out the prevailing "shared indifference to feminism or even gender" that characterizes both American and British Marxism and the invariable subordination of gender to power that occurs whenever new historicists take up the subject,[19] Cohen implicitly recognized the growing schism that Kahn had pointed to two years earlier but that had become, until Berlin, the explosive subject that everyone remained resolutely silent about. When gender is not being simply ignored in the materialist critiques, it repeatedly ends up getting displaced into some other issue – usually race or class – and women are silently eradicated from the text, leaving only one gender for consideration. This kind of displacement and erasure – which is, in effect, a modern day re-silencing taking place even as Renaissance strategies of silencing are being discussed – is something that materialist / historicist Peter Stallybrass, like Cohen, seems acutely aware of. In his essay on how social relations get mapped onto the body, Stallybrass observes that although in the Renaissance "bodily definitions were as important in the mapping out of gender as of class," in current scholarship on the politics of the body, the issue of gender has a way of vanishing. What happens is that even scholars like Bakhtin and Elias become "silent on this issue, assuming an 'ungendered' or implicitly single gendered – male body."[20]

The desire to confirm and empiricize the sole existence of this "ungendered" or *explicitly* single gendered (and hence male) body has a fascinating history in the learned tradition of the West that begins in Genesis, surfaces into Renaissance medical lore through Aristotle and Galen, and re-emerges periodically in authoritative texts from medieval to modern times as a tellingly defensive fantasy that was produced and reproduced by a deeply misogynistic tradition. To see women's reproductive organs as being inverted and hidden, thus inferior versions of the male's, as does Galen, or to see their external genitalia as incomplete, thus castrated remnants of the masculine, as does Freud, tells us, if anything, a great deal about a psychic history that on the one hand produces gender difference in order to demonstrate male superiority and yet also attempts to erase biological sex difference in order to prove the same thing. But the Renaissance discourse of sexuality is fascinating precisely because it is really a mélange of multiple discourses – some medical, some folkloric, some theological in origin. It has no universal, monolithic, single vision, nor is there any way of knowing to what extent the learned theories were disseminated throughout the society enough to constitute anything like a normative belief in popular culture. If the discourse of the learned tradition should be accorded any special privilege, it lies primarily in its ability to textually and professionally reproduce itself and thus transmit its particular ideological biases about gynecology to later eras. By thus constituting a powerful stencil by which the wider cultural discourse of female erasure was for century after century reproduced, the medical treatises are inescapably political. They therefore seem even more problematic when our own culture's most authoritative voices invoke and reuse them, unqueried and unassessed politically, as though they were transparencies for reading literary discourse.

Shakespearean feminists had long hoped that Stephen Greenblatt would extend his incisive analysis beyond the patterns of powerful men and begin to look at Renaissance women and the production of gender. But when at last he does in "Fiction and Friction" (1986), gender disappears beneath the category of biological sex differentiation, then sex difference becomes elided beneath the relevance of medical treatises to a 1601 account of a hermaphrodite in Rouen, France, and then – through an associational leap much wider than new historicism will usually venture – all of this becomes the contextual stencil through which Greenblatt, in three pages, reads the cross-dressing of comic heroines, the convention of boy actors, the sexual discourse of *Twelfth Night*, the sexual discourse for all Shakespeare's plays, and, by implication, for all English Renaissance drama.

> Shakespearean women are ... the representation of Shakespearean men, the projected mirror images of masculine self-differentiation ... the theater reveals, in the presence of the man's (or boy's) body beneath the woman's clothes, the ultimate sexual reality. Since on stage there is in fact but a single gender, the open secret of identity, that beneath or within differentiated individuals is a single structure, identifiably male, is quite literally presented – presented, but not represented, for the play (plots, characters, and the pleasure they confer) cannot continue without the fictive existence of two distinct genders and the friction between them.[21]

Suddenly, there is only one gender and there are no more women in Shakespeare's plays. According to Greenblatt, from the basis of this gynecology we can inferentially conclude that English Renaissance plays present only maleness; and, as Walter Cohen observes, "women thus cease to be historical actors or subjects." They may indeed exist on stage as discursive representations, but even that existence is wholly in service of the male plots which they help enable and from which, as male presentations themselves whether on stage or off, they have no separate identity anyway.

Not only the issue of women tends to disappear in new historicism; what also gets erased is the terrain of the domestic microcosm. When new historicism locates itself upon the site of family, sex, and marriage, the literal arena of domestic space has a way of losing its local habitation through its name and turning into its descriptive other. In a critical practice that comes perilously close to duplicating the Renaissance political strategies it anatomizes, historicist criticism has of late taken up the "family" as a topic, only to then redefine it as the locus upon which the political state built *its* power through strategic appropriation, marginalization, and transformation of the family into an instrument of state authority. "The family" of the Elizabethan-Jacobean era has thus been repositioned as a metaphor for the Elizabethan-Jacobean state, and scholarly focus consequently shifted away from literal families and their reproduction back onto the patriarchal state and its self-generating modes. Once again, gender is erased, women are erased, and the historicist critic is busily back at work reconstructing and reproducing an academic microcosm of the absolutist court and its strategies of male power. And, we might add, "the family" has once again been pressed into the service of the ruling elite.

Given what Walter Cohen calls new historicism's "fascination with the absolutist court" and given the historical centrality that Elizabeth's forty-five year reign so clearly occupies in this period, the most interesting avenues that court politics would seem to hold open for historicists would be ones that took up rather than dislodged or detoured around the relationship between gender and power. Since an operation that is central to new historicist practice is the juxtaposing of a given literary text to another cultural text (which is usually, though not inevitably, non-literary), followed by the demonstration of how the literary work derives from and is produced by the cultural one to which it has been juxtaposed, exactly what cultural texts get chosen for juxtaposition is obviously crucial. For while the new historicist manifesto insists in theory on granting equal status to both the literary and the social text, as Edward Pechter notes, in practice the literary work is inevitably seen as fully determined and produced by its ideological and historical situation.[22] And, since new historicism frequently chooses to read the times through discourses which are distinctively liminal and focus on the strange and unusual, the increasing number of laboriously recovered but now available women's texts would seem to offer a rich new mine of anomalous voices. But the cultural texts that new historicists invariably select to privilege over the literary one are distressingly all of a kind: even though they may focus on subjects that are in some way culturally anomalous, the texts of choice are always and predictably male-authored – hierarchical – patriarchal. By the contextualization of Shakespearean drama inside of such a selective vision of "history," even the voices that Shakespeare gave women are silenced. Women slip once again into mute invisibility, weighted down once more with that which has been singled out to serve as the authoritative narrative for (at least someone's) "history."

However – lest one imagine (as feminist critics have been wont to do) that women's silence in Shakespearean drama should be read as a sign of their disempowerment, speaking authoritatively from within the section on feminist criticism in *Shakespeare and the Question of Theory* Jonathan Goldberg at last takes up the topic of gender distinction in order to condemn such feminist interpretation and insist that since silence for characters like Iago and Henry V is a strategy of empowerment, silence can likewise signal power for women. Although examples of any comparably authoritative female muteness are admittedly hard to find, even for Goldberg, perhaps those problematically different meanings that gender has mapped onto voice and silence could just neatly be eradicated by turning to Greenblatt's notion that Shakespeare's stages contain no women anyway but only the undifferentiated wholeness of the single male gender. Goldberg's essay – entitled, interestingly enough, "Shakespearean Inscriptions: the Voicing of Power" – goes much further than merely displacing or erasing gender issues inside the text and feminist issues outside it. Selecting one feminist critic as whipping girl and elevating her into the unwarranted status of emblematic Shakespearean feminist, he castigates Linda Bamber for seeing Shakespeare's culture as patriarchal and for imagining that Shakespeare replicated that attitude in his plays (an argument for which Erickson or McLuskie or Montrose, as the most vociferous spokespersons, should really stand accused – not Bamber). Assuring us that he is not attacking feminism but only all those (unnamed) feminist critics who are *like* the one he is lambasting, Goldberg begins his essay by denying the category of oppressive gender distinctions that feminism has placed into focus, asserting that the whole notion of gender polarity "must be seen through and must be read beyond for a genuine feminist discourse to arise." For a conclusion he suggests that "the reason we cannot find Shakespeare reflecting his culture's supposed patriarchalism and sexism is that the culture represented on stage *is* the culture off-stage."[23] Oppressive gender distinction and patriarchy – on stage and in Shakespeare's culture, as well – have not only disappeared; they have been named as the subjects which Shakespearean feminism must cease discussing if it is ever to receive the imprimatur of being "a genuine feminist discourse." And since one cannot help but observe that Goldberg's voice has actually been placed within the feminist section of an anthology of Shakespearean criticism that includes not one critic whose primary work has been in Shakespearean (or English Renaissance) feminism, the effect is that of a silencing that has been textually framed, as it were, by Patricia Parker and Geoffrey Hartman's quite noticeable editorial exclusions. The Voicing Of Power – and – the Power of Voicing, indeed!

In the last several years, the work of American Shakespearean feminists has become the focus of attacks that are at once puzzling and yet also somehow numbingly familiar. The most accessible of the charges accuses feminist scholarship of employing an approach deemed "ahistorical" for its failure to recognize the historical specificity of psychic and social structures that produce gender and family. If de-contextualized, the charge has an acknowledged validity. Its validity, however, can never be considered wholly in isolation from the distinct irony occasioned by materialist / historicist criticism unblushingly admonishing feminism for oversight and omission. The accusation furthermore compels the legitimate question as to what, precisely, the posited ideal of "historical" is here assumed to cover – whether, for instance, it is the methodological procedure or the name alone that automatically presumes "histori*cist*" criticism is consonant with what a histor*ian* might define as "histori*cal*." Finally, it also compels a deeper questioning of the apparently automatic privileging of history that the charge subsumes.

In choosing what textual dimensions to foreground, feminist readings never wholly ignored the historical context but neither did they valorize nor privilege it over the literary text, as is characteristic of new historicist and cultural materialist readings. Though the feminist privilege of the literary work never assumes that the text is a free agent nor wholly divorced from its historical moment, by its ability to survive massive social changes and still fascinate a modern reader a historical text is seen as fully approachable through contemporary ideas – nor are those ideas assumed to be projections backward from the present. Even though a social idea may not have been articulated during the historical moment in which the text was produced, such ideas are imagined as being potentially fully present, latent within earlier times, but, like the late discovered planets, awaiting the invention of a telescope, a discourse, that could articulate them. Essentially, the relative weight accorded to literary text or history represents two ways of philosophically imagining the human being – as a being who inscribes at least something universal that transcends history, or as an entity completely produced by its historical culture. But in addition to this definition, the different preferences for history or text suggest a less tangible sense of an experiential relation-ship to "history" that is divided along the axis of gender. While it is true that feminist work in Shakespeare never invested its critique in history, that choice seems less the basis for opprobrium and the assertion of methodological primacy than the ground for speculation about the relationship between women *and* history. If materialist critics valorize history as an omnipotent producer and are skeptical about the notion of subjectivity except as a product of history, the feminist investment in history – or at least in what has been recorded and traditionally considered *as* history – is not only minimal, but is itself committed to a skepticism extending to the production, the definition, and indeed the valorization of "history."

Since Western history is essentially a transmitted record of upper class white males, the various elided social groups probably do not – historically should not – automatic-ally trust recourse to the authority of "history." The banner of "history" has its *own* long history of being a rallying point for the consolidation of status quo power. Before marginalized groups are likely to feel unambiguously positive about the validity of 1066 and all that, "history" needs be rewritten to include them. And while it is arguable that new historicism is, in effect, doing just that – rewriting history by re-presenting it, whether this most recent turn to "history" has extended the social privilege any farther than its traditional donnée is, like Falstaff's "question not to be asked," precisely the question *to* be asked. Out of the new historicist work, that which Louis A. Montrose has done inevitably merits being singled out for its attention to the issues of gender and for its apparent awareness of what, in fact, an indifference to those issues really signifies. In contrast to new historicism, the Marxist theories of history are conscien-tiously premised on a demand to extend privilege. But, with a few feminist exceptions like British Marxist Catherine Belsey, Marxism has disappointingly been as unrespon-sive to theorizing a history that includes women as has new historicism. So while recent arguments in Shakespeare studies have discounted the past decade of feminist analysis of family, sex, and marriage for not being "historical" and for instead being psycho-analytically based and textually rooted, given what I would call the subtext of this debate – given feminism's very different *historical* relationship to "history," it seems thoroughly consistent with the feminist goal of liberating women *from* their history that the mainstream feminist interpretations of Shakespeare did indeed marginalize the historical and concentrate instead on the literary text. The text, at least, contained representations of women and could thus be used as a mirror in which modern women and men could recognize – and begin to change – the reflected image of a history of oppressive sexual and familial relations.

Currently, feminism in Shakespeare is in what could be called its second phase in the academy and shows signs of beginning to move in a number of potentially new directions. Already, a number of key Shakespearean feminists have begun reformu-lating their psychoanalytic approach to gender and family so as to balance text and historical context in ways that would dissociate feminism from the essentialized notion of gender embedded in Freudian determinism and allow for deconstructing – rather than unwittingly reproducing – the subjugating past.[24] But perhaps the more interesting observation one might make about the imputation of feminism's "ahistorical tendencies" is the way the accusation actually ignores its own authenticity. It unwittingly assumes the same essentialized perspective of social development that it criticizes in feminism. And it does so by tacitly assuming that American feminism is free from *its* own history and from the historically specific coercions of time, place, and gender in which it developed. The perspective needed is, in fact, the historicized one that is the genuine contribution new historicism has made both to Shakespearean criticism and to literary methodology in general. Without contextualizing American feminism, there would be no way either to locate it politically or recognize, for instance, what sets it apart from the literal politics and literary methodologies favored by its British or French counterparts.

When feminism first entered the American Shakespeare bastion, its psychoanalytic approach to family, marriage, and gender may have seemed the most appropriate tool for the kind of textual analysis it wished to do. But in its implied resistance to location within more overtly ideological methodologies, feminism inside the academy also seems to me to have been half-consciously engaged in, or at least cooperating with, another agenda taking place on the national political level. If the psychoanalytical approach adopted within the academy kept feminist investigations focused on given relationships within patriarchal family structure rather than on stepping outside and demanding an overturning of the structure itself, then perhaps the very limitations of the approach served to keep feminists in the academy within the tacitly understood boundaries of the national women's movement with which American academic feminism was complicit. And these were strategies that, whether rightly or wrongly, nonetheless conscientiously tried during the years of the E.R.A. debate to appear as non-radical and socially non-threatening as possible.

Because the political stakes for American feminism have been not just theoretical but very real and because the most practical way to achieve them was, during the referendum years, perceived as being through a politics of persuasion rather than confrontation, feminism within the academy has always been a Janus-like presence, unlike other modes of criticism, because never separate from the practicalities of applied politics outside it. And by virtue (or vice) of gender inflection, those politics by definition differ from and cannot really be evaluated in terms of the only model of social change that history's monological narrative of male–male conflict has given us to imagine. Even academic feminism of the 1970s and '80s must needs be understood as circumscribed by both the literal and mythological legislation of "America," and as being, throughout those years, engaged in selling the Equal Rights Amendment to a voting public conditioned by the peculiarly American bias against "isms" in general and any "ism" in specific that is labeled an "ideology." The Equal Rights Amendment – which in the early '70s had seemed unproblematic to voters – was defeated in the '80s not so much by the un-truths, but by the *truths* that were publicized about it. Inside the academy, feminist faculty research and teaching was centered on marriage, gender, and family. Outside it, these same topics increasingly became the ideological battle zone upon which the E.R.A. was defeated – and defeated it was, once the equations were exposed that identified the women's movement with "feminism," feminism with "ideology," and the ideology defined as an "ism" that was subversively "politicizing marriage" and "trying to destroy the traditional American family."

But perhaps both liberal feminism and new historicism – the two distinctly American contributions to contemporary academic methodology – need to be historicized in order to propose at least some perspective on the gap between them and on new historicism's progressive reassertion of the priority of the public and political over the private and domestic. Of the two methodologies, feminism is the child not born to the manor of literary fathers but outside it, without academic foremothers, but thus perhaps endowed with that peculiar liminality of daughters that leaves it oddly free to constitute itself. New historicism is, by contrast, the legitimate son, the heir that developed not only inside the academy but specifically inside Renaissance studies, appearing shortly after feminism and preceding Marxism into the field, and yet an heir that seems philosophically to feel less free, more constituted, and always already doomed by some futile but inescapable obligation to repeat the oppressive struggle for power that it habitually reads as history's only heritage.

In looking at feminist and historicist perspectives in relation to one another, I would like to turn to an observation that Leah Marcus seems to have been the first to make but that Jean Howard and Walter Cohen have also singled out as being somehow amorphously implicit in the shaping of the newly ideological dimensions of American Shakespearean criticisms. And that is – that the generation of scholars now emerging into prominence is the same generation who were college students during the turbulent challenges to establishment ideology that defined the 1960s. It is a generation whose experience may be both unique in and unique to American history. Furthermore, it is a generation that came into its own academic power during the conservative reaction of the Ronald Reagan years. For Jean Howard, the significance of this background lies in the way it led contemporary scholars to embrace overtly political methodologies: the recognition of how untheorized had been the political activism of the '60s resulted in a sense of the inadequacy of the old American common sense approach to politics and a movement toward more theorized models of social change. Likewise for Cohen, "political activism of the 1960s lies behind the political criticism of the 1980s"; and in Cohen's mind, the tenor of this criticism intangibly derives from the disillusionment of a generation defined by all that is subsumed under the name "Vietnam."

In reflecting on both the social construction of this, my own generation of scholars, and on the widening gap between two methodologies that emerged out of its seemingly common experience, I offer a speculation. The years of social activism are always retrospectively imagined as years when student activists, women and men, worked together. But perhaps, just perhaps, those years had very different psychological and moral effects on women and men, marked them separately and taught them very different lessons that eventually became transmuted into two positions in literary theory. Thus, while the two share their origin in the committed rebellion of that era, they may well have come away from those years having unconsciously acquired fundamentally different convictions about the relationships between subversion and dominance, resistance and power.

My speculation is that women came out of the activist '60s empowered with new possibilities, a new sense of self liberation and commitment, and an optimistic social idealism. Awakening to a second life during the anti-war and civil rights protests of the '60s, American feminism might be described as a street urchin, born during a peace march to the strains of "We Shall Overcome." Its optimism is its fundamental and perhaps only resource; it is what keeps it dynamic even in the face of political setbacks and what it cannot afford to lose. American feminism – which in academia in general and certainly in Shakespeare studies has remained committed to liberal rather than radical or Marxist politics – by definition must believe that resistance to and subversion of the ruling discourse can, must, and shall overcome. Since it cannot posit its future by assuming a violent revolution as the means to claim it, it furthermore must believe that dominant institutions are capable of change and that motives do exist – if not benevolence then at least rational self-interest – beyond the will to absolute and undistributed power. Whether the defeat of the E.R.A. will precipitate the loss of such faith and a turning away from political liberalism is yet to be seen.

When critics try to describe the spirit of new historicism, the terms evoked are substantially different, substantially more pessimistic. In the new historicist view of history, whatever is subversive in culture or challenges the ruling order suffers inevitable defeat, for power is the final and only currency. In Walter Cohen's description, "New historicism ends up if not with something like a totalitarian model, then at least with a sense of the almost inevitable defeat of the poor, the innocent, and the oppressed … [lower class] aspirations must either be crushed or be shown to serve the interests of the state … The point is that unless one is an aristocrat there is nothing to be done." For Cohen, such totalitarian / aristocratic proclivities are ultimately best explained as a form of leftist disillusionment. Meanwhile, what strikes Edward Pechter about new historicist writings is how compulsively they seem to need to control the subversive power of the Shakespeare text by detaching themselves from it and subordinating it to some authoritarian cultural script – and yet, at the same time, how frequently these writings themselves communicate an aura of depotentiation and entrapment, a sense of "being surrounded by a hostile otherness, enmeshed in a complex matrix of forces all of which threaten their freedom."[25] Unlike feminism, new historicism is not, meanwhile, an activist politics of social change; unlike Marxism, it theorizes no model that even imagines it. And yet, when new historicism insists that resistance is inevitably crushed, that resistance is implicitly futile because always co-opted, or that the will to power is all, what I suggest impels the apparent reactionism of such a thesis and simultaneously gives it its powerfully contemporary American appeal is the way it recuperates an unsatisfactory narrative, a *Bildungsroman*, from the history of twenty years ago. Its disillusionment resonates with the same bitter lesson that a generation of college males – resisting America's war in Vietnam on the grounds of a moral idealism that was implicitly undermined by the recognition that they were excused from combat through deferments based on class and racial privilege – discovered about the co-option of resistance by authority. By definition, the Vietnam war and the bitterly self-defeating "choices" that it forced on America's draft-age males indelibly marked the political experience of the protest era with distinctively gendered meanings that may well construct not only the seen but the unseen agendas underlying the tenor of the two criticisms that emerged from that generation.

If the feminist critic may well be accused of reading Shakespeare through potentially contradictory notions of psychological essentialism and transhistorical subjectivity that create an unconscious framework to explain past suppression and yet leave open the way for a subjectively female / self determined future, then the new historicist critic is equally capable of unconsciously formulating a way to read Shakespeare through the central cultural trauma and its residue of needs that define his experience. Given the particular investment in history that grows out of the untenable space where "Vietnam" left the best educated class of American males of the '60s generation, new historicism's inevitable privileging of authority and what otherwise seems to be its arbitrary selection of dominant cultural discourses to be juxtaposed to / privileged over the given literary text seem no longer arbitrary, but cohere within the inscription of a contemporary history trying to rewrite the moral defeats of its past. When considered in this light, the new historicist tenets do accomplish the requisite two maneuvers necessary for successful recuperation of an unaccommodatable past: they narrate an account of resistance, co-option, and defeat while simultaneously undoing that defeat by aligning themselves with institutional power and thus appropriating the oppressor's dominance for the critic / self. By reading Shakespeare as being himself a co-opted servant of state orthodoxies, the historicist critic contextualizes perhaps not so much Shakespeare in history as his own history in Shakespeare; by thus disempowering Shakespeare, the literary critic recuperates cultural power for himself by exerting it over the culture's most potent literary authority. And the son proves his right to the all-powerful father's heritage by dethroning him and assuming the patriarchal position himself. Perhaps it is even appropriate that recuperation should enact itself upon the symbolic site of struggle and defeat, and that not only Stephen Greenblatt – new historicism's chief architect and founder – but most of the board members of the new historicist journal, *Representations*, should be located at Berkeley.

Yet if political defeat is thus undone, perhaps not so easily is spiritual disillusionment. If there is a price for acquiring such dominance, it may lie in the disconcerting sense of embittered idealism that often seeps through into new historicist practice. But for feminism – confronting this increasingly dominant methodology inside the academy, observing new historicism's preoccupation with institutional forms of absolute male power, and watching itself become progressively the subject under erasure and the object under attack – it becomes progressively more difficult to see the new historicist premises about power as politically disinterested or restrict them to purely a Renaissance application, especially since both these sibling criticisms insist on recognizing the ideological nature of criticism itself. Since feminism is, by definition, a subversive site of resistance to the dominant discourse, what is to be made out of new historicism's (Foucaultian) premise that any site of subversive resistance is inevitably defeated or co-opted by the dominant institution? What to be made from the idea that such rebellions against authority are often, in fact, culturally produced and covertly promoted only so they *may be* co-opted? When – as happened at a recent Renaissance conference – the two male scholars on a panel present investigations of the plays that are both carefully modeled after the new historicist discourse and that both also eradicate any mention of the women characters (thus ignoring even the supportive relevance that those figures could actually have contributed to their own arguments), to what cultural messages are these writers responding? And why is this kind of elision – that appears to be quite unconscious – suddenly occurring more and more frequently? When both of these two scholars then individually rationalize their omissions by saying that, since feminism had already "won" its battle, they had logically concluded that there was no longer any need to have to include its representative concerns – where does this leave the future? For if scholarship ever reaches the place where anyone presumes that feminist concerns have made their mark and therefore no longer need be addressed, then feminism has marked nothing: as a political movement, as a critical scholarship, and as an ethics within and beyond the American academy, feminism will then never have happened.

In 1982, just when the developing schism in Renaissance literary perspectives was becoming felt, feminist scholars Margaret Ferguson, Maureen Quilligan, and Nancy Vickers tried to bring what had been assumed as common interests back together through a major conference held at Yale. They tried, we could say, to create and name a new genesis: thus "Renaissance Woman, Renaissance Man," created they them. The collected papers from this conference finally appeared in 1986 in a newly titled book, *Rewriting the Renaissance.* Despite (or perhaps because of) the fact that the schism was already evident in the conference papers, the book title states very clearly, very openly, and very optimistically, just what the political aims of Renaissance feminist scholars are. This title furthermore stubbornly continues to assume that in the 1980s, *all* scholars would clearly *want* to rewrite the Renaissance so as to include the woman / women left sitting mutely in the margins by historians in the Renaissance and by academic historiographers that followed. The question I suppose I would therefore raise in closing is simply this: as we scholars of the Renaissance – who now include men *and* women – become the new historiographers *of* the Renaissance, do we have a shared idea about who and what gets written into our texts – or mutually exclusive ones? Are we setting out to deconstruct and demystify patriarchy – or reconstitute it by repeating the same old patriarchal erasure? Did we, in fact, come to rewrite the Renaissance, or just repeat it? In short – did we come to bury Caesar or to praise him?

Notes

1 See the Drakakis "Introduction" to *Alternative Shakespeares.*

2 In keeping with the concomitantly emerging ideology of the closed nuclear family, English literature begins to feature a new kind of villain in the Renaissance – the bastard, who is almost always male and whose "illegitimacy" is coded as a threat not only to the boundaries of family but to the sanctity of the state. When the legal concept of branding a bastard child as "illegitimate" emerges – a terminology which apparently enters the language around the end of the fifteenth or beginning of the sixteenth century – it creates a positive and negative verbal coding which, by segregating children born outside the patriarchal family unit from those "legitimate" within it, serves to protect the self-reproducing capacity of patriarchy. The most famous disquisition on this system of verbal stigmatization to protect social privilege through its "Fine word, 'legitimate!' " is, of course, the one spoken directly to the audience in the opening lines of *King Lear*'s second scene by Edmund, the play's bastard son / tragic villain. See also Phyllis Rackin's essay, "Anti-Historians," for commentary on Shakespeare's history plays and the relationship of wifehood, motherhood, and bastardy to the construction of patriarchy.

3 Woodbridge, *Women and the English Renaissance*, p. 2. Woodbridge's point that "the relationship between literature and life is a very slippery subject," and that there may well be "cases where the very prominence of a theme in literature argues *against* its being a representation of real life" (3), leads her ultimately to posit a more debatable thesis. Working with a vast amount of material from the Renaissance debate over the nature of women, Woodbridge concludes that the misogynistic

tirades of Renaissance literature belong to a literary convention, not to real life, and they therefore cannot finally be seen as representing either the author's or the culture's attitudes toward women.

4 Hill, "Sex, Marriage, and the Family," p. 450.

5 My apologies for any names that have been overlooked in listing this group that I have defined as the first generation of American feminist Shakespeareans. While it is an accurate generalization to say that the majority were psychoanalytic critics, there are, of course, exceptions – notably, Phyllis Rackin and Linda Woodbridge (Fitz).

6 Gardiner, "Mind Mother," p. 114.

7 In opposition to Annette Kolodny's belief that a "playful pluralism" was "the only critical stance consistent with the current status of the larger women's movement," Elaine Showalter first coined and proclaimed the "gynocritical" position as the direction in which feminism should theorize itself ("Feminist Criticism," p. 112 ff.). Feminist criticism has since moved back more toward a balance that includes an androcentric pole of male writers, as well.

8 In addition to recent collections edited by Mary Beth Rose and Margaret Hannay, for recent scholarship on women writers see *English Literary Renaissance*, 14 (Autumn, 1984) for a special issue on *Women in the Renaissance*. The issue includes Elizabeth H. Hageman and Josephine A. Roberts's bibliography of recent studies in the field.

9 British Marxist-feminist (or perhaps, feminist-Marxist) Catherine Belsey's work in Renaissance drama, however, does seem implicitly to compel this kind of reconsideration of traditional Marxist categories; likewise, Jacqueline Rose's work in drama and film should be mentioned. Of all the various British academic disciplines, film studies seems to be the one area where there is a consistent focus on revising Marxism to make it accommodate rather than continue to ignore feminist concerns.

10 Under continual external pressure from the methodological push going on throughout the literary discipline, advocacy within feminism for an articulated methodology seems of late to have gained support. There is also, however, a well articulated opposition from highly respected voices such as Annette Kolodny's (see Showalter, pp. 10–14). For a broader look at the issues that particularly effect Shakespearean feminism, see *Making a Difference: Feminist Literary Criticism*, edited by Shakespearean scholars Gayle Greene and Coppélia Kahn. See especially Greene and Kahn on the social construction of woman; Adrienne Munich on locating a relationship not already foreclosed between a male author and feminist readers; Cora Kaplan on subjectivity, class, and Marxist / Socialist politics; Ann Rosalind Jones on the new French feminism; and Judith Kegan Gardiner on psychoanalysis and feminism.

11 On Renaissance marriage ritual, see Boose, "The Father and the Bride in Shakespeare."

12 McLuskie, p. 106.

13 Erickson, p. 171.

14 McLuskie, pp. 97, 98, 106.

15 Two important collections, *Alternative Shakespeares* (ed. Drakakis) and *Political Shakespeare* (eds. Dollimore and Sinfield) have come from British Marxist scholars in the past two years, and *Political Shakespeare II* is apparently underway. What defines the organizing principle underlying these British collections is what differentiates them from the typical American anthology; the organizational distinction itself recapitulates that of the mainline political allegiances of literary scholars within the two academic institutions. The liberal politics of American academia tend to result in generally pluralistic collections in which the essays share the topic under consideration but not necessarily any conscious, coherent, or identifiably political viewpoint on it. What marks these new British Shakespeare collections is the reader's awareness of the shared political perspective from which the essays all speak.

16 Because the (widely accepted) dynamics articulated by Mulvey's 1975 essay would leave no explanation for female pleasure other than masochism, her work has inspired an intense and continuing effort in film studies to theorize the female spectator, including a number of Mulvey's subsequent thoughts in interviews and other commentaries. The theories that this topic has elicited are richly various and too numerous to catalogue. See, however, the British film journal

Screen for a number of such responses and further references, plus see also the work of American film scholars E. Ann Kaplan and Mary Ann Doane. All of this work in film does have a particular relevance to considerations of gender and stage representation, as McLuskie is perceptively aware. Given the different media considerations, however, the applicability of transferred ideas seems to me to be less direct.

17   From a paper delivered by Neely at a CUNY Graduate Center conference on "Shakespeare and the New Politics" (March 28, 1987). In her critique of new historicism, Neely likewise notes the point I later make concerning the patriarchal, authoritarian nature of the invariably male discourses that new historicists recurrently select as the definitive lens through which to read Shakespeare.

18   The selected and edited papers from this Berlin seminar will appear in *Shakespeare Reproduced: The Text in History and Ideology*, edited by seminar organizers Jean E. Howard and Marion O'Connor, forthcoming at Methuen. It was not, however, only (or perhaps primarily) during the Howard seminar on Shakespeare and ideology that conflict between feminism and new historicism emerged as *the* explosive subject in Berlin; apparently such conflict became almost the sub-topic of participant exchanges at the seminar on "Gender and Power in Shakespeare" that was co-chaired by Carol Thomas Neely and Lisa Jardine.

19   Cohen's paper will appear in the forthcoming Howard and O'Connor volume.

20   Stallybrass "Patriarchal Territories," p. 125.

21   Greenblatt, "Fiction and Friction," p. 52.

22   Edward Pechter's analysis of "New Historicism and its Discontents" likewise notes that although a central premise of new historicism is to grant literary and cultural knowledge an equal and interanimating status, the practice is "a long way from the mutually generative interpretation of culture and text ... the text is said to be produced by its ideological and historical situation; it is unambiguously dependent, while the culture is unambiguously determining" (p. 293). Pechter's assessment of the premises, strategies, and contradictions of new historicism is generally quite incisive. In analyzing new historicist politics, however, he is led by his own conservative perspective to render more unto Marx than Marx is probably owed. When he is led for the same reasons to assume some kind of implicit alliance among all methodologies within the general category of the "left-liberal academic community, for whom ... feminism [is] an article of faith" (299), his assumptions prevent him from noting the actual distance that new historicism has been stepping off in moves that seem like an attempt to define itself away from feminism.

23   Goldberg, "Shakespearean Inscriptions," pp. 118, 134.

24   In the Introduction to *Shakespeare Reproduced* (forthcoming), Jean E. Howard defines this movement away from the psychoanalytical and toward the historical as responding to "the necessity to historicize gender constructions if one wishes to escape the oppressive notion of a universal human nature, or, worse, of an eternal feminine." David Scott Kastan, in his Introduction to the Shakespeare Association of America seminar, "Shakespeare and the New Feminisms" (March, 1987), similarly sees the move as a means by which feminism can "deny that gender distinctions are fixed outside of human construction and control, and ... [as] a means of imagining alternatives to our own structures of social relations." At the CUNY conference on "Shakespeare and the New Politics," however, Carol Thomas Neely suggests that completely abandoning the claim of subjectivity in exchange for a model in which gender is construed to be entirely an ideological product of a historically specific culture may create as many problems for feminist methodology as it resolves. Noting American liberal feminism's reluctance to deny all subjectivity or identity that is not the construct of ideology, she explains: "feminists have assumed some area of femaleness not strictly biological but not utterly inscribed by patriarchal ideology which makes possible female discourse, a women's literary history, a feminist critique which can do more than lament its own inevitable suppression."

25   Pechter, p. 301.

References

Bamber, Linda. *Comic Women, Tragic Men: A Study of Gender and Genre in Shakespeare.* Stanford, 1982.

Barber, C. L., and Richard Wheeler. *The Whole Journey: Shakespeare's Power of Development.* Berkeley, 1986.

Belsey, Catherine, "Disrupting Sexual Difference: Meaning and Gender in the Comedies." In Drakakis, ed., *Alternative Shakespeares*, pp. 166–90.

—— . *The Subject of Tragedy: Identity and Difference in Renaissance Drama.* London, 1985.

Boose, Lynda E. "The Father and the Bride in Shakespeare." *PMLA*, 97 (1982), 325–47.

Cohen, Walter. "Political Criticism of Shakespeare." In *Shakespeare Reproduced: The Text in History and Ideology*, edited by Jean E. Howard and Marion O'Connor. Forthcoming.

Dollimore, Jonathan, and Alan Sinfield, eds. *Political Shakespeare: New Essays in Cultural Materialism.* Manchester, 1985.

Drakakis, John. Introduction to *Alternative Shakespeares*, edited by idem, pp. 1–25. London, 1985.

Dusinberre, Juliet. *Shakespeare and the Nature of Women.* London, 1975.

Erickson, Peter. *Patriarchal Structures in Shakespeare's Drama.* Berkeley, 1985.

Ferguson, Margaret W., Maureen Quilligan, and Nancy J. Vickers, eds. *Rewriting the Renaissance: The Discourses of Sexual Difference in Early Modern Europe.* Chicago, 1986.

Gardiner, Judith Kegan. "Mind Mother Psychoanalysis and Feminism." In Greer and Kahn, eds., *Making a Difference*, pp. 113–45.

Goldberg, Jonathan. "Shakespearean Inscriptions: The Voicing of Power." In Parker and Hartman, eds., *Shakespeare and the Question of Theory*, pp. 116–37.

Greenblatt, Stephen. "Fiction and Friction." In Heller, *et al.*, eds., *Reconstructing Individualism*, pp. 30–52.

—— . *Renaissance Self-Fashioning: From More to Shakespeare.* Chicago, 1980.

Greene, Gayle, and Coppélia Kahn. "Feminist Scholarship and the Social Construction of Woman." In *Making a Difference: Feminist Literary Criticism*, edited by idem, pp. 1–36. London, 1985.

Hageman, Elizabeth H., and Josephine A. Roberts. "Recent Studies in Women Writers of Tudor England." *English Literary Renaissance*, 14 (1984), 409–39.

Hannay, Margaret, ed. *Silent But for the Word: Tudor Women as Patrons, Translators, and Writers of Religious Works.* Kent, OH, 1985.

Hill, Christopher. "Sex, Marriage, and the Family in England." Review of *The Family, Sex, and Marriage in England 1500–1800*, by Lawrence Stone. *Economic History Review*, 2nd ser., 31 (1978), 450–63.

Howard, Jean, and Marion O'Connor, eds., *Shakespeare Reproduced: The Text in History and Ideology.* (1987).

Jones, Ann Rosalind. "Assimilation with a Difference: Renaissance Women Poets and Literary Influence." *Yale French Studies*, 62 (1981), 135–53.

Lenz, Carolyn Ruth Swift, Gayle Greene, and Carol Thomas Neely, Introduction to *The Woman's Part: Feminist Criticism of Shakespeare*, edited by idem, pp. 2–16. Urbana, IL, 1980.

McLuskie, Kathleen. "The Patriarchal Bard: Feminist Criticism and Shakespeare—*King Lear* and *Measure for Measure*." In Dollimore and Sinfield, eds., *Political Shakespeare*, pp. 88–108.

Mulvey, Laura. "Visual Pleasure and Narrative Cinema." *Screen*, 16, no. 3 (Autumn, 1975), 6–18.

Parker, Patricia, and Geoffrey Hartman, eds. *Shakespeare and the Question of Theory.* New York, 1985.

Pechter, Edward. "The New Historicism and Its Discontents." *PMLA*, 102 (1987), 292–303.

Rackin, Phyllis. "Anti-Historians: Women's Roles in Shakespeare's Histories." *Theatre Journal*, 37 (1985), 329–44.

Rose, Mary Beth, ed. *Women in the Middle Ages and Renaissance: Literary and Historical Perspectives.* Syracuse, 1986.

Rubin, Gayle. "The Traffic in Women: Notes on the 'Political Economy' of Sex." In *Toward an Anthropology of Women*, edited by Rayna R. Reiter, pp. 157–210. New York, 1975.

Schwartz, Murray M., and Coppélia Kahn, eds. *Representing Shakespeare: New Analytic Essays*. Baltimore, 1980.

Showalter, Elaine. "Feminist Criticism in the Wilderness." In *Writing and Sexual Difference*, edited by Elizabeth Abel, pp. 9–36. Chicago, 1982.

Stallybrass, Peter. "Patriarchal Territories: The Body Enclosed." In Ferguson, *et al.*, eds., *Rewriting the Renaissance*, pp. 123–42.

Woodbridge, Linda (see also Fitz, L. T.). *Women and the English Renaissance: Literature and the Nature of Womankind, 1540–1620*. Urbana, IL, 1984.

35

Disrupting Sexual Difference: Meaning and Gender in the Comedies

Catherine Belsey

I

Meaning, Saussure argued, is an effect of difference. And if post-structuralism has moved beyond Saussure's diagrams, which seemed to imply a single meaning for every unit of language, every signifier, it has not abandoned the most radical principle of Saussurean theory, that meaning depends not on the referent, not on intention, but only on the relations of difference between one term and another within the language. Subsequently we have come to see meaning as unfixed, always in process, always plural. This is a result first of the analysis of language itself as the location of distinct discourses (or knowledges), sets of terms and relations between terms in which a specific understanding of the world is inscribed. And secondly it takes account of the argument that meaning is never fully present in an individual utterance but is always deferred, always provisional, precisely because it is dependent on the relations of difference between *this* term and all the other terms which constitute the language and which are by definition absent.

The problem with the meanings that we learn – and learn to produce – is that they seem to define and delimit what is thinkable, imaginable, possible. To fix meaning, to arrest its process and deny its plurality, is in effect to confine what is possible to what *is*. Conversely, to disrupt this fixity is to glimpse alternative possibilities. A conservative criticism reads in quest of familiar, obvious, common-sense meanings, and thus reaffirms what we already know. A radical criticism, however, is concerned to produce readings which challenge that knowledge by revealing alternative meanings, disrupting the system of differences which legitimates the perpetuation of things as they are. The project of such a criticism is not to replace one authoritative interpretation of a text with another, but to suggest a plurality of ways in which texts might be read in the interests of extending the reach of what is thinkable, imaginable or possible.

I want to suggest that Shakespearean comedy can be read as disrupting sexual difference, calling in question that set of relations between terms which proposes as inevitable an antithesis between masculine and feminine, men and women. But in order to do so I need first to draw attention to the context of this disruption, the opposition in the sixteenth and seventeenth centuries between two distinct meanings of the family. Women, then as now, were defined in relation to men and in terms of their relations with men. A challenge to the meaning of the family is a challenge to these relations and in consequence to the meaning of what it is to be a woman.

II

The setting is a domestic interior. On the back wall is a handsome clock. There are dishes on a carved sideboard and a ewer stands beside a couple of books on the window sill. On the floor in the foreground there are three or four more books and a low stool. The drawing shows Sir Thomas More, Chancellor of England, surrounded by his family. The artist gave it to Erasmus, who wrote to More, 'I cannot put into words the deep pleasure I felt when the painter Holbein gave me the picture of your whole family, which is so completely successful that I should scarcely be able to see you better if I were with you' (Pope-Hennessy 1966, pp. 99–100).

The drawing was a sketch for (or perhaps of) a painting, eight feet high and thirteen feet wide, executed in 1527 and now lost (Morison 1963, pp. 18–28). Its mode, as Erasmus indicates, is realist – which is to say illusionist. As the names and ages

Figure 1 *Sir Thomas More, and his Family,* 1527, by Hans Holbein the Younger. Drawing. Basel, Öffentliche Kunstsammlung Basel, Kupferstichkabinett, photo Martin Buhler.

recorded below the drawing make clear, it seems to portray a specific moment in the More household, probably Sir Thomas's fiftieth birthday. The family are in various positions of relative informality. Margaret Giggs, More's adopted daughter, shows old Judge More something in a book. Margaret Roper, the Chancellor's eldest, most devoted and most learned daughter, sits on the floor with a book open on her lap. She looks towards her sister, Elizabeth, who returns her gaze. Young John, More's heir, is absorbed in his reading. Dame Alice, Sir Thomas's second wife, and not the mother of the children, kneels at a prie-dieu on the extreme right. Cecily, holding a book and a rosary, looks towards her. None of the figures, with the possible exception of the Fool, Henry Pattenson, meets the spectator's gaze. We occupy a position outside the self-contained world of the picture: the family are not aware of us and do not address themselves to us.

Thomas More's family is an intimate, informal, affective unit. The picture shows it inhabiting a private world of domesticity, piety and learning. It is also a dynastic unit. Sir Thomas More, wearing his chain of office, sits at the centre with his father on his right and his only son, John, on his left. In the background is Anne Cresacre, who was to marry John, thus ensuring the continuity of the line. In the sixteenth and early seventeenth centuries these two meanings of the family – as dynasty and as private realm of warmth and virtue – are both in play and indeed in contest. In 1527 and for many years to come it was the dynastic meaning which was dominant. Holbein's drawing, like so many of the productions of the Sir Thomas More circle, seems to anticipate the meanings of a later period.

In 1593 Thomas More II, grandson of the Chancellor, commissioned Rowland Lockey to produce a painting modelled on Holbein's. In Lockey's picture the domestic

Figure 2 *Sir Thomas More, with his Family and Descendants,* 1593, by Rowland Lockey after Hans Holbein the Younger. National Portrait Gallery, London.

arrangements have been brought up to date. The clock remains in position, but green hangings cover the panelling. Lutes and flower arrangements replace the jugs and basins. More, his father, his children and his daughter-in-law have been moved to the left of the picture. They are copied from the original, though Elizabeth now sits behind Margaret so that both of them, instead of looking at each other, gaze vacantly into space. Margaret Giggs, Alice More and the Fool have been eliminated. On the wall is a portrait of Anne Cresacre, More's daughter-in-law, painted in about 1560. She thus appears twice in Lockey's painting, aged 15 and 48. On either side of her portrait are coats of arms, and below them in a stiff little group sit her son, Thomas More II, his wife Mary, and two of their sons, John and Cresacre. They hold missals. All four of them stare challengingly back at the spectator. They make an odd contrast with the previous three generations copied from Holbein, because although the rearrangement of the figures and the elimination of those who played no genealogical part in the history of the Mores have removed the sense of intimacy and relationship, the early members of the family remain apparently unaware that they are being watched, while their descendants are clearly sitting to have their portraits painted. There is no interaction between them, or between the two groups.

They sit, what is more, with a certain defiance. The Mores had remained staunchly but quietly Catholic throughout the religious upheavals of the sixteenth century. In 1582 Thomas II had been imprisoned for four years. He was released in 1586 but remained under surveillance. The More family in the painting he commissioned is a dynastic and ideological unit. The illusion of a private moment of informality has given way to a declaration of unbroken allegiance to Catholicism through five generations. There is no identifiable moment of this painting. Sir Thomas More had been dead for nearly sixty years when the dynastic meaning of the family was thus invoked by the threatened Catholic descendants of a Catholic martyr.

The Lockey painting is an interesting variant on a familiar theme of the sixteenth century. Thomas More I is shown surrounded by his daughters, with Margaret very much in the foreground of the drawing. Thomas More II did not allocate any space in the picture for his daughters, though their names and ages were recorded on the inscription in the bottom left-hand corner. Sitters for portraits in sixteenth-century England were most commonly men, of course – men of property, or their heirs, or men of property *and* their heirs (the picture of Sir Walter Raleigh and his eldest son in the National Portrait Gallery is a charming instance: the child, aged about nine, precisely replicates the pose of his father). Women are important when they are sovereigns, as the many portraits of Elizabeth testify. Otherwise they are significant mainly as wives who guarantee the continuity of the dynasty. Anne Cresacre features twice in Lockey's painting, though in neither case is she anywhere near the foreground.

Holbein's mural of Henry VIII and his family, completed ten years after the original More picture, showed Henry massive, legs astride, 'a fantastic amalgam of the static and the swaggering' (Strong 1967, p. 39), standing in front of the altogether more ethereal figure of his father, Henry VII. The body of the reigning prince is identified as the location and evidence of his power. According to a seventeenth-century copy which has survived, on the other side of a stone altar Jane Seymour, hands clasped demurely before her, stood in front of Henry's mother, Elizabeth of York. Jane has no dynasty. Her presence is authorized by her part in the occasion of the painting, the birth of the heir to the throne. He is not represented, since it is what he is to be and not the affection between parents and child which signifies. (Contrast Princes William and Harry, loved, petted and dandled in twentieth-century royal photographs.) Indeed, Jane herself may have been dead by the time the mural was installed in the Privy Chamber at Whitehall. It wouldn't have mattered. Henry VII and Elizabeth of York were dead too. All three had done their work in ensuring the continuity of the Tudors. In another portrait of Henry VIII's family, probably painted in 1545, Prince Edward sits on the king's right, Jane Seymour, now dead for about eight years, and succeeded by three subsequent wives, is shown on his left (Millar 1963, Text vol., p. 64). She, not the current queen Catherine Parr, was the mother of the heir.

In Holbein's mural Henry VIII meets the spectator's gaze – requiring obedience. Henry VII stares into the distance, perhaps visualizing his descendants in a line stretching out to the crack of doom. The two queens look at their husbands. Both sexually and politically the body of the prince exacts submission. Henry VIII, the image of absolute monarchy, is also the image of absolute patriarchy.

The place of the woman in the dynastic family is clear and well known, and is perfectly defined in Katherine's final speech in *The Taming of the Shrew*: 'Such duty as the subject owes the prince / Even such a woman oweth to her husband' (v.ii.156–7). Sovereignty in marriage precisely resembles sovereignty in the state, and both are absolute. Men, Luciana explains in *The Comedy of Errors*, 'are masters to their females, and their lords' (II.i 24). Wives 'are bound to serve, love, and obey' (*The Taming of the Shrew*, v.ii.165). The perfect wife is 'meek and patient', 'pliant and duteous' as in Heywood's *A Woman Killed with Kindness*, 1.37–41. Her model is the silent and uncomplaining Griselda, whose story was retold several times in the sixteenth and early seventeenth centuries,[1] and was perhaps reworked in *The Winter's Tale*, where Hermione too loses both her children through her husband's tyranny, bears it patiently and is finally reunited with her family, though in this case Florizel stands in for Mamillius.

But there begins to be, as Holbein's drawing of the More family indicates, an alternative meaning for the family in the sixteenth century. In the intimate, affective realm which comes into being with the emergence of a set of differences between work and leisure, public and private, political and domestic, the place of both women and children is newly defined. The home comes to be seen as a self-contained unit, a little world of retreat from the conflicts of the market-place, and at the same time a seminary of good subjects, where the wife enters into partnership with her husband in the inculcation of love, courtesy and virtue in their children. The affective marriage is necessarily founded on consent and harmony. As one of the guests tells the happy bridegroom of *A Woman Killed with Kindness*, 'There's music in this sympathy, it carries / Consort and expectation of much joy' (1.69–70).

A painting of 1628 shows something of the meaning of the new family. In a not very clearly defined natural setting, perhaps a leafy glade, the Duke of Buckingham sits beside his wife. From the positions of their shoulders we can judge that their hands would touch, if it were not for the fact that hers are occupied with the child on her lap. One-year-old George smiles as he leans towards his sister, Mary, who holds out to him the flowers in her apron. Katharine, wife and mother, dressed in yellow silk, is at the glowing centre of the canvas, though the Duke is nearer to us, and taller. The Duchess's

Figure 3 *George Villiers, 1st Duke of Buckingham, and his Family,* 1628, unknown painter after Gerrit van Honthorst. National Portrait Gallery, London.

literary models are not Griselda and Hermione, but Lady Macduff and the Duchess of Malfi, loving mothers of families whose innocence and affection constitute evidence for the audience of the wanton tyranny of those who destroy them. If it were not that both parents look out of the canvas at the spectator, this family could belong equally to the nineteenth century, the great age of the naturalized affective family, or indeed to the twentieth, where the family is once again a site of struggle, this time between conservatives and feminists.

The picture constitutes evidence that the new meaning of the family was neither exclusively 'Puritan' nor exclusively bourgeois: the Duke of Buckingham's worst enemies could hardly have accused him of belonging to either category. I do not intend to imply that the emergence of another meaning for the family has nothing to do with the Reformation or the rise of mercantile capitalism. On the contrary. But textual history, the history of meanings, is more complex, more contradictory, more deeply interwoven with the history of the whole social formation than traditional studies in the history of ideas or traditional Marxist economism would seem to imply. My primary concern in this essay is to attempt to trace the complexity and the implications of these meanings themselves rather than to locate their origins. Or perhaps one of these meanings. The new definition of the family entails a new definition of the relationship between husband and wife, a new understanding of the woman's place.

The new meaning of the family needs even less elaboration than the old, since it is familiar to us from countless nineteenth-century novels and twentieth-century breakfast-cereal advertisements. It is the meaning of the family which most of us have lived, or guiltily failed to live. It involves marriage based on romantic love and co-operation between parents to bring up their children as happy, productive and responsible

Figure 4 *Arthur, 1st Baron Capel and his Family, c.* 1640, by Cornelius Johnson. National Portrait Gallery, London.

members of society. The place of the woman in the affective family is now, therefore, that of a partner and companion to her husband, joined with him in 'a communion of life' (Smith 1591, p. 9), a source, as Milton was to put it, of 'apt and cheerful conversation' (Milton 1959, p. 235). In the absolutist, dynastic meaning of marriage women were everything that men were not: silent, submissive, powerless. But in the marriage of true minds, where romantic love is not simply an adolescent aberration but the cement of a life-long relationship, men and women are alike – 'not always', as Donne explained in a marriage sermon, 'like in complexion, nor like in years, nor like in fortune, nor like in birth, but like in minde, like in disposition, like in the love of God, and of one another' (Donne 1957, p. 247).

A new polarity was, of course, to emerge. In about 1640 Cornelius Johnson painted Arthur, first Baron Capel, and his family, in front of an open window through which we can glimpse the extent of their property. The picture closely resembles the Buckingham painting in certain respects: the hands of the Baron and his wife would meet, but hers are holding the child on her lap; one of the little girls is offering the baby a flower from the basket she is carrying. But whereas the Baron faces the spectator, his wife, Elizabeth, looks at him. Patriarchy reasserts itself within the affective family. Perhaps the marriage of true minds had never implied equality for women, but only, as Thomas Taylor argued, a new kind of pliability:

> The wife must frame herself in all lawful things to helpfulnesse, to shew the likenesse of her minde to his minde ... A wife, as a wife, is to no end, but to frame her selfe to her husbands minde and manners. (Halkett 1970, p. 46)

Gradually the set of oppositions we recognize established the new meaning of sexual difference. Women were once again everything that men were not – this time caring, nurturing, intuitive, irrational – and their sphere of influence was precisely the newly defined place of retreat from the public world of work and politics. 'Hearth and home', 'the bosom of the family': the phrases evoke warmth and affection. They also have the effect of isolating women in a private realm of domesticity which is seen as outside politics and therefore outside the operations of power.

III

Meaning depends on difference, and the fixing of meaning is the fixing of difference as opposition. It is precisely this identification of difference as polarity which Derrida defines as *metaphysical*. In conjunction with the common-sense belief that language is a nomenclature, a set of labels for what is irrevocably and inevitably there – whether in the world or in our heads – this process of fixing meaning provides us with a series of polarities which define what is. These definitions are also values. In the oppositions 'I / you', 'individual / society', 'truth / fiction', 'masculine / feminine' one term is always privileged, and one is always other, always what is *not* the thing itself.

The insistence on meaning as single, fixed and given is thus a way of reaffirming existing values. Conversely, those moments when the plurality of meaning is most insistent are also moments of crisis in the order of existing values. A contest for meaning disrupts the system of differences which we take for granted, throwing into disarray the oppositions and the values which structure understanding. The contest for the meaning of the family which took place in the sixteenth and seventeenth centuries disrupted sexual difference, and in the space between the two sets of meanings, the old and the new polarities, there appear in the fiction of the period shapes, phantasms perhaps, that unsettle the opposition defining the feminine as that which is not masculine – not, that is to say, active, muscular, rational, authoritative ... powerful. Women are defined precisely as the *opposite* sex, and the 'evidence', the location of this antithesis, is the process of reproduction. The family as the proper source of that process, the place of reproduction, is thus among the major determinants of the meaning of sexual difference itself. A radical discontinuity in the meaning of the family, which is not in any sense an evolution, produces a gap in which definitions of other modes of being for women are momentarily visible. The period of Shakespeare's plays is also the period of an explosion of interest in Amazons, female warriors, roaring girls (Shepherd 1981) and women disguised as pages.

An interest in female transvestism is not, of course, confined to the Renaissance. It stretches at least from Ovid's story of Iphis and Ianthe (*Metamorphoses*, IX, lines 666–797) to twentieth-century pantomime. But it is hard to think of any period when the motif is so recurrent. It appears in five of Shakespeare's comedies of love and marriage. And in turn Rosalind and Viola, Portia, Julia and Imogen are the direct descendants of a long line of English and European Renaissance heroines of prose and drama, Neronis, Silla and Gallathea, Lelia, Ginevra, Violetta and Felismena, who are disguised as men in order to escape the constraints and the vulnerability of the feminine.

The great majority of these fictions are romances, narratives of the relations between women and men. It was the love stories of Hippolyta and Penthesilea, rather than their battles, which were commonly recounted. In *The Faerie Queene* romantic love leading to Christian marriage is personified in Britomart, the female knight, who does physical battle with Radigund for possession of Artegall. Julia in *Two Gentlemen of Verona*, Lelia, Silla and Violetta disguise themselves specifically to follow the men they love. Perhaps the most remarkable instance is the story of *Frederyke of Jennen*, known in Germany and the Netherlands in the fifteenth century and translated into English in 1518. Another edition appeared soon after this, and a third in 1560, testifying to the story's English popularity (Bullough 1975, pp. 15–16). A merchant's wife whose husband mistakenly believes that she has been unfaithful to him flees from Genoa to Cairo in male disguise. There she is made in rapid succession the king's falconer, a knight and then a lord. Left to govern the realm in the king's absence, she leads the army in a great victory against an invading force, and finally becomes protector of the realm until, twelve years later, in possession of evidence of her innocence, she reveals the truth of her identity and is reunited with her husband. Love and marriage are saved by the transgression of the opposition they are based on.

The redefinition of marriage entails a redefinition of the feminine. It is not easy to imagine Griselda as a source of apt and cheerful conversation. She is the antithesis of her husband, not his like in disposition. It is as if in order to find a way of identifying women as partners for men, the romances of the sixteenth century draw on the old heroic and chivalric tradition of friendship between men – Palamon and Arcite, Damon and Pithias, Titus and Gisippus. Diguised as boys, Julia, Rosalind and Viola become the daily companions of the men they love and, paradoxically, their allies against love's cruelty. Portia fights Bassanio's legal battle for him – and wins. The two conventions of love and friendship appear side by side in *Two Gentlemen of Verona*, where by loving Silvia Proteus betrays both his friend, Valentine, and his mistress, Julia (ii.vi). If the symmetry between love and friendship is disturbed when Julia disguises herself as Sebastian, it is thrown momentarily into crisis when Valentine offers Silvia to his friend as a token of reconciliation between them. But Julia's presence, possible only because she is disguised as a boy, and her swoon, which simultaneously reaffirms her femininity, are the means to the full repentance of Proteus and the reinstatement of both love and friendship, leading to closure in the promise of a double marriage (v.iv.170–1).

The effect of this motif of women disguised as men is hard to define. In the first place, of course, it throws into relief the patriarchal assumptions of the period. 'Beauty provoketh thieves sooner than gold' (*As You Like It*, i.iii.106): that women are vulnerable is seen as obvious and natural. It is not, on the other hand, seen as essential or inevitable, but as a matter of appearance. Rape is a consequence not of what women are but of what men believe they are. Rosalind tells Celia,

> We'll have a swashing and a martial outside,
> As many other mannish cowards have
> That do outface it with their semblances.
> (*As You Like It*, i.iii.116–18)

Not all men are equally courageous, but they are all less vulnerable than women because they look as if they can defend themselves. Similarly, Portia's right to exercise her authority depends on her lawyer's robes, and the episode can be seen as making visible the injustice which allows women authority only on condition that they seem to be men. Even while it reaffirms patriarchy, the tradition of female transvestism challenges it precisely by unsettling the categories which legitimate it.

IV

But I want to propose that a close reading of the texts can generate a more radical challenge to patriarchal values by disrupting sexual difference itself. Of course, the male disguise of these female heroines allows for plenty of dramatic ironies and double meanings, and thus offers the audience the pleasures of a knowingness which depends on a knowledge of sexual difference. But it can also be read as undermining that knowledge from time to time, calling it in question by indicating that it is possible, at least in fiction, to speak from a position which is not that of a full, unified, gendered subject. In other words, the plays can be read as posing at certain critical moments the simple, but in comedy unexpected, question, 'Who is speaking?'

As she steps forward at the end of *As You Like It*, Rosalind says to the audience, 'It is not the fashion to see the lady the epilogue' (v.iv.198), and a little later, 'If I were a woman, I would kiss as many of you as had beards that pleased me' (lines 214–16). The lady is not a woman. In a footnote to the second of these observations the Arden edition reminds modern readers of the answer to the implied riddle: 'a boy-player is speaking'. Here in the margins of the play, when one of the characters addresses the audience directly and, by acknowledging that what has gone before is a performance, partly resumes the role of actor (though only partly, of course: the epilogue is a speech written by the dramatist for the actor to perform), the uncertainty about the gender of the speaker in a period when women's parts are played by male actors is part of the comedy. A male actor is speaking, but the joke is that he is simultaneously visually identifiable as a woman, the lady, dressed for her wedding ('not furnished like a beggar', as she insists, line 207), and that he / she will curtsey to acknowledge the audience's applause (line 220). A male actor *and* a female character is speaking.

The comedy of uncertainty about whether a character is speaking from inside or outside the fiction is evident as early as Medwall's *Fulgens and Lucres* (*c.* 1500), where the servants, A and B, come out of the audience at the beginning of the play and assure each other that they are not actors. The epilogue of *As You Like It* simply compounds the uncertainty and therefore the comedy by confusing the gender roles, so that the question 'Who is speaking?' elicits no single or simple answer. But the comedy of the epilogue owes its resonance in its context to the play's recurrent probing of the question, 'Who is speaking when the protagonist speaks?' And here the uncertainty depends not only on the fact that a male actor plays a woman. Even in the most illusionist of modern theatre, members of the audience live perfectly comfortably with the knowledge that the actor is not *really* the character, that they have seen the actor in other roles and the character played by other actors. The convention that female parts are played by male actors is presumably equally taken for granted on the Renaissance stage. Within the fictional world of the play, the question 'Who is speaking?' is complicated not so much by the extra-textual sex of the actor as by the gender of the protagonist.

It is not that Rosalind-as-Ganymede becomes a man or forgets that she is in love with Orlando. On the contrary, the text repeatedly, if ironically, insists on her feminine identity: 'I should have been a woman by right' (iv.iii.175); 'Alas the day, what shall I do with my doublet and hose?' (iii.ii.215); 'I would cure you, if you would but call me Rosalind and come every day to my cote and woo me' (iii.ii.414–15). But at other moments the voice is not so palpably feminine and the pleasure of the audience is not a product of irony. When they arrive in the Forest of Arden, Celia-as-Aliena is too exhausted to go any further (ii.iv.61). It is Rosalind-as-Ganymede, therefore, who negotiates with Corin for accommodation: 'Here's a young maid with travel much oppress'd, / And faints for succour' (ii.iv.72–3). We have seen the psychological transformation of Rosalind into Ganymede earlier in the same scene: 'I could find in my heart to disgrace my man's apparel and to cry like a woman. But I must comfort the weaker vessel, as doublet and hose ought to show itself courageous to petticoat; therefore courage, good Aliena' (lines 3–7). The audience's pleasure in the comedy here is the effect of Ganymede's escape from the limitations of Rosalind's femininity.

In *Cymbeline* when Imogen disguises herself as Fidele, Pisanio tells her,

> You must forget to be a woman: change
> Command into obedience [she is a princess]: fear, and niceness
> (The handmaids of all women, or, more truly,
> Woman it pretty self) into a waggish courage
>
> (iii.iv.156–9)

Fear and niceness (fastidiousness, daintiness) are the essence of the feminine, the text insists, 'Woman it pretty self', her identity. But the verbs contradict the notion of a fixed essence of womanhood: 'You must forget to be a woman; change …' It is the mobility implied by the verbs which characterizes Imogen's reply: 'I see into thy end, and am almost / A man already' (lines 168–9). The scene is not comic; there are no distancing dramatic ironics to point to the absurdity of the claim. To be a woman, the text proposes, means to be nice and fearful; but it also means, as the play demonstrates, to be capable of a radical discontinuity which repudiates those defining characteristics. Imogen concludes: 'This attempt / I am soldier to, and will abide it with / A prince's courage' (lines 184–6). The context in which Imogen takes on the characteristics of a soldier and a prince is a journey which is to lead her to her husband.

Rosalind-as-Ganymede reproduces the conventional invective against women for Orlando, and shocks Celia:

> You have simply misused our sex in your love-prate. We must have your doublet and hose plucked over your head, and show the world what the bird hath done to her own nest.
> (iv.i.191–4)

Who is speaking when the protagonist mocks women? The question is more or less eliminated in the process of reading the text by the speech prefixes, which identify the speaker as Rosalind throughout, and in modern performances, where Rosalind-as-Ganymede is played by a woman. No wonder that most of the standard twentieth-century criticism treats the disguise as transparent and stresses Rosalind's femininity (Wilson 1962, pp. 161–2; Barber 1959, pp. 231–3; Shakespeare 1975a, p. lxxiii). But if we imagine the part played by a male actor it becomes possible to attribute a certain autonomy to the voice of Ganymede here, and in this limited sense the extra-textual sex of the actor may be seen as significant. Visually and aurally the actor does not insist on the femininity of Rosalind-as-Ganymede, but holds the issue unresolved, releasing for the audience the possibility of glimpsing a disruption of sexual difference.

The sixteenth-century narrative source, Lodge's *Rosalynde*, is illuminating in this context. The third-person narrative, compelled, as drama is not, to find appropriate names and pronouns to recount the story, normally identifies the disguised heroine as Ganimede and uses the masculine pronoun. This leads to a good deal of comedy which depends on our acceptance of the discontinuity of identity:

> You may see (quoth Ganimede) what mad catell you women be, whose hearts sometimes are made of Adamant that will touch with no impression; and sometimes of waxe that is fit for everie forme: they delight to be courted, and then they glorie to seeme coy … And I pray you (quoth Aliena) if your roabes were off, what metall are you made of that you are so satyricall against women? Is it not a foule bird defiles [his] owne nest? … Thus (quoth Ganimede) I keepe decorum, I speake now as I am *Alienas* page, not as I am Gerismonds daughter: for put me but into a peticoate, and I will stand in defiance to the uttermost that women are courteous, constant, vertuous, and what not. (Bullough 1958, p. 181)

Of course this is as absurd as it is delightful, but the delight stems from the facility with which Rosalynde-Ganimede can speak from antithetical positions, transgress the norms of sexual difference. What is delightful is that, in becoming Ganimede, Rosalynde escapes the confinement of a single position, a single perspective, a single voice. The narrative calls its central figure a 'Girle-boye' (Bullough 1958, p. 233), and celebrates the plurality it thus releases.

In *As You Like It* Rosalind is so firmly in control of her disguise that the emphasis is on the pleasures rather than the dangers implicit in the transgression of sexual difference. Other heroines are not so fortunate. In *The Famous History of Parismus* by Emanuel Forde (1598) Violetta disguised as Adonius disrupts the story's pronouns when she spends the night sleeping between Parismus, whom she loves, and Pollipus, who loves her:

> the poore soule lay close at Parismus back, the very sweet touch of whose body seemed to ravish her with joy: and on the other side not acquainted with such bedfellowes, she seemed (as it were) metamorphosed, with a kind of delightful feare … early in the morning Adonius was up, being afraid to uncover her delicate body, but with speed soone araid himself, & had so neatly provided al things against these two knights should rise, that both of them admired his behaviour … (Bullough 1958, p. 367)

Barnabe Riche's Silla, disguised as Silvio, is compelled to reveal the truth when she is accused of being the father of Julina's child. The double danger implicit in concealment and exposure similarly unsettles the narrative:

> And here with all loosing his garmentes doune to his stomacke, and shewed Julina his breastes and pretie teates, surmountyng farre the whitenesse of snowe itself, saiyng: Loe, Madame! beholde here the partie whom you have chalenged to bee the father of your childe. See, I am a woman … (Bullough 1958, p. 361)

What happens in these instances is not like the case Barthes identifies in Balzac's 'Sarrasine', where the narrative is compelled to equivocate each time it uses a pronoun to identify the castrato. Nor is it that the reader does not know what is 'true', as in a modernist text. It is rather that the unified subjectivity of the protagonist is not the focal point of the narrative. It is not so important that we concentrate on the truth of identity as that we derive pleasure (in these cases a certain titillation) from the dangers which follow from the disruption of sexual difference.

In *Twelfth Night* these dangers, here romantic rather than erotic,[2] constitute the plot itself – which means for the spectators a certain suspense and the promise of resolution. Viola, addressing the audience, formulates both the enigma and the promise of closure:

> What will become of this? As I am man,
> My state is desperate for my master's love:
> As I am woman (now alas the day!)
> What thriftless sighs shall poor Olivia breathe?
> O time, thou must untangle this, not I,
> It is too hard a knot for me t' untie.
>
> (ii.ii.35–40)

Of all Shakespeare's comedies it is perhaps *Twelfth Night* which takes the most remarkable risks with the identity of its central figure. Viola is just as feminine as Rosalind, as the text constantly insists (i.iv.30–4; iii.i.160–2), and Cesario is as witty a saucy lackey as Ganymede. But it is only in *Twelfth Night* that the protagonist specifically says, 'I am not what I am' (iii.i.143) where 'seem' would have scanned just as well and preserved the unity of the subject.

The standard criticism has had few difficulties with the 'Patience on a monument' speech, identifying the pining figure it defines as Viola herself, and so *in a sense* she is.[3] But it is by no means an unproblematic sense. The problems may be brought out by comparison with a parallel episode in *Two Gentlemen of Verona* (iv.iv.108 ff.). Julia disguised as Sebastian is wooing Silvia on behalf of Proteus. The ironies are clear, sharp and delightful. Sebastian asks Silvia for her picture for Proteus: Silvia says a picture of the neglected Julia would be more appropriate. Sebastian offers a ring: Silvia refuses it, since it was Julia's, and Sebastian, to her surprise, says, 'She thanks you'. Is Julia not 'passing fair'?, Silvia asks. She was, Sebastian replies, until, neglected by Proteus, she in turn neglected her beauty, 'that now she is become as black as I'. 'How tall was she?' asks Silvia, and Sebastian replies:

> About my stature: for at Pentecost,
> When all our pageants of delight were play'd,
> Our youth got me to play the woman's part,
> And I was trimm'd in Madam Julia's gown,
> Which served me as fit, by all men's judgments,
> As if the garment had been made for me;
> Therefore I know she is about my height.
> And at that time I made her weep agood,
> For I did play a lamentable part.

> Madam, 'twas Ariadne, passioning
> For Theseus' perjury, and unjust flight;
> Which I so lively acted with my tears,
> That my poor mistress, moved therewithal,
> Wept bitterly; and would I might be dead,
> If I in thought felt not her very sorrow.
>
> (iv.iv.156–70)

In these exchanges the irony depends on the series of identifications available to the audience which are not available to Silvia. Julia looks like Sebastian, her clothes fit Sebastian, Sebastian plays Ariadne lamenting betrayal in love so convincingly, and Sebastian feels Julia's own sorrow, because Sebastian is Julia and Julia is betrayed. The audience's pleasure here consists in recognizing the single speaker who moment-arily occupies each of these identities as Julia, and the speeches as an elaborate invention rehearsing what we know to be true within the fictional world of the play.

But this is not so clearly the case in the (roughly) corresponding episode in *Twelfth Night*. Orsino is telling Cesario that men's love is more profound than women's:

> *Viola:* Ay, but I know –
> *Duke:* What dost thou know?
> *Viola:* Too well what love women to men may owe:
>   In faith, they are as true of heart as we.
>   My father had a daughter lov'd a man,
>   As it might be perhaps, were I a woman,
>   I should your lordship.
> *Duke:* And what's her history?
> *Viola:* A blank, my lord: she never told her love,
>   But let concealment like a worm i' th' bud
>   Feed on her damask cheek: she pin'd in thought,
>   And with a green and yellow melancholy
>   She sat like Patience on a monument,
>   Smiling at grief. Was not this love indeed?
>
> (ii.iv.104–16)

How do the identifications work in this instance? Cesario is Viola and Cesario's father's daughter is Patience who is also Viola. But the equations break down almost at once with, 'what's her history?' 'A blank'. Viola's history is the play we are watching, which is certainly not a blank but packed with events. Nor is it true that she never told her love. She has already told it once in this scene (lines 26–8), and she is here telling it again in hints so broad that even Orsino is able to pick them up once he has one more clue (v.i.265–6). In the play as a whole Viola is neither pining nor sitting, but is to be seen busily composing speeches to Olivia and exchanging jokes with Feste; and far from smiling at grief, she is here lamenting the melancholy which is the effect of unrequited love.

How then do we understand these fictions as telling a kind of truth? By recognizing that the Viola who speaks is not identical to the Viola she speaks of. If Viola is Patience, silent like Patient Griselda, it is not Viola who speaks here. Viola-as-Cesario repudiates the dynastic meaning of the feminine as patience, and yet that meaning is as present in

Cesario's speech as the other, the difference which simultaneously defines Cesario as Orsino's companion and partner in suffering, and Viola as a woman.

In reply to Orsino's question, 'But died thy sister of her love?', the exchange ends with a riddle. 'I am all the daughters of my father's house, / And all the brothers too: and yet I know not' (lines 120–2). At the level of the plot the answer to the riddle is deferred to the end of the play: Viola doesn't die; she marries Orsino. But to an attentive audience another riddle presents itself: who tells the blank history of Viola's father's pining daughter? The answer is neither Viola nor Cesario, but a speaker who at this moment occupies a place which is not precisely masculine or feminine, where the notion of identity itself is disrupted to display a difference within subjectivity, and the singularity which resides in *this* difference.

It cannot, of course, be sustained. At the end of each story the heroine abandons her disguise and dwindles into a wife. Closure depends on closing off the glimpsed transgression and reinstating a clearly defined sexual difference. But the plays are more than their endings, and the heroines become wives only after they have been shown to be something altogether more singular – because more plural.

V

In an article first published in French in 1979 Julia Kristeva distinguishes between two 'generations' (though the term does not necessarily imply that they are chronologically consecutive) of feminism (Kristeva 1981). The first generation has been concerned with public and political equality for women (votes, equal opportunities, equal pay). The danger here, she argues, is that feminists who succeed in these terms come to identify with the dominant values and take up positions as guardians of the existing order. The second generation has insisted on an irreducible feminine identity, the opposite of what is masculine, accepting the theoretical and ideological structure of patriarchy but reversing its values. This leads to a radical, separatist feminism. The distinction does not, I suspect, stand up to historical analysis, but it does offer models of two kinds of feminist commitment from which Kristeva distinguishes a third generation, or perhaps a third possibility which, she says, 'I strongly advocate, which I imagine?', in which 'the very dichotomy man / woman as an opposition between two rival entities may be understood as belonging to *metaphysics*' (Kristeva 1981, p. 33). There can be no specifically feminine identity if identity itself does not exist. In the post-structuralist analysis subjectivity is not a single, unified presence but the point of intersection of a range of discourses, produced and re-produced as the subject occupies a series of places in the signifying system, takes on the multiplicity of meanings language offers. Kristeva's third possibility proposes the internalization of '*the founding separation of the sociosymbolic contract*', difference itself as the ground of meaning, *within* identity, including sexual identity (p. 34). The effect will be to bring out 'the multiplicity of every person's possible identifications' and the relativity of his or her sociosymbolic and biological existence (p. 35).

The fragmentation of sexual identity in favour of this fluidity, this plurality, deconstructs all the possible metaphysical polarities between men and women. It is not a question of bisexuality, though the heterosexual 'norms' based on the metaphysics of sexual difference lose their status in the unfixing of sexual disposition. Nor is it a balance between extremes which is proposed, the 'poise' or 'complexity' which criticism has often found characteristic of Rosalind and Viola (Barber 1959, pp. 234–5, 258; Leggatt 1974, pp. 202 ff.). The point is not to create some third, unified, androgynous identity which eliminates all distinctions. Nor indeed is it to repudiate sexuality itself. It is rather to define through the internalization of difference a plurality of places, of possible beings, for each person in the margins of sexual difference, those margins which a metaphysical sexual polarity obliterates.

One final instance may suggest something of the fluidity which is proposed. *A Midsummer Night's Dream* gives us on the periphery of the action a marriage between a warrior and an Amazon: 'Hippolyta, I woo'd thee with my sword, / And won thy love doing thee injuries' (I.i.16–17). The text here proposes a parallel where we might expect an antithesis. None the less, apart from their shared commitment to blood sports, Theseus and Hippolyta take up distinct positions on all the issues they discuss. Where Theseus is cynical about the moon, Hippolyta invokes conventional poetic imagery (I.i.4–11); when Theseus sceptically supposes that the young lovers have been deluded, Hippolyta counters cool reason with wonder (v.i.2–27); but when Hippolyta finds the mechanicals' play 'the silliest stuff that ever I heard', it is Theseus who invokes imagination: 'The best in this kind are but shadows; and the worst are no worse if imagination amend them' (v.i.207–9). A criticism in quest of character, of fixed identities, might have difficulty here, since the stereotypes of masculine rationality and feminine imagination are now preserved, now reversed. As a kind of chorus on the edges of a play about love, which in many ways relies on stereotypes, Theseus and Hippolyta present a 'musical discord' which undermines fixity without blurring distinctions. Difference coexists with multiplicity and with love.

VI

My concern in this essay has been with meanings and glimpses of possible meanings. Fictional texts neither reflect a real world nor prescribe an ideal one. But they do offer definitions and redefinitions which make it possible to reinterpret a world we have taken for granted. Post-structuralist theory liberates meaning from 'truth', 'the facts', but it implies a relationship between meaning and practice. New meanings release the possibility of new practices.

It is not obvious from a feminist point of view that, in so far as they seem finally to re-affirm sexual polarity, Shakespeare's comedies have happy endings. It is certain from the same point of view that the contest for the meaning of the family in the sixteenth and seventeenth centuries did not, though on this there is a good deal more to be said. What I have been arguing is that that contest momentarily unfixed the existing system of differences, and in the gap thus produced we are able to glimpse a possible meaning, an image of a mode of being, which is not a-sexual, nor bisexual, but which disrupts the system of differences on which sexual stereotyping depends.

Whether the remainder of the story of the relations between men and women ultimately has a happy ending is, I suppose, for us to decide.

Notes

1   See John Phillip, *The Play of Patient Grissell* (1558–61), ed. R. B. McKerrow and W. W. Greg, Oxford: Malone Society, 1909; Thomas Dekker, *Patient Grissill* (*c.* 1599), ed. Fredson Bowers, *The Dramatic Works of Thomas Dekker*, 4 vols, Cambridge: Cambridge University Press, 1953, vol. 1; *The Ancient, True and Admirable History of Patient Grisel* (1619), ed. J. P. Collier, *Early English Poetry*, London: Percy Society, vol. 3, 1842; Thomas Deloney, 'Of Patient Grissel and a Noble Marquesse' (printed 1631) and *The Pleasant and Sweet History of Patient Grissell* (printed *c.* 1630), *Works*, ed. F. O. Mann, Oxford: Clarendon Press, 1912.

2   I am not entirely persuaded by the argument that boy players are 'homoerotic' (Jardine 1983, pp. 9–36).

3   There are exceptions. C. L. Barber identifies the Patience figure as 'a sort of polarity within Viola' (Barber 1959, p. 247). In other cases a certain unease is evident in the identifications. Viola is describing 'her sister', but the image 'is drawn from her own experience' (Leggatt 1974, pp. 236–7). According to the Arden editor(s), the speech describes 'Cesario's sister's love for a man to whom she never told it'. A footnote adds, 'I express it thus for brevity's sake. This is how it appears to Orsino: but everything Viola says is directly applicable to herself in her real person' (Shakespeare 1975b, p. lxviii). Kenneth Muir succeeds in evading any very specific identification of the speaker: 'Cesario tells the story of her imaginary sister … But we know that Viola is too intelligent and too well-balanced to go the way of her "sister" ' (Muir 1979, p. 98).

References

Barber, C. L. (1959) *Shakespeare's Festive Comedy*. Princeton, NJ: Princeton University Press.

Bullough. G. (1958) *Narrative and Dramatic Sources of Shakespeare*, vol. 2, *The Comedies*. London: Routledge & Kegan Paul.

—— (1975) *Narrative and Dramatic Sources of Shakespeare*, vol. 8, *Romances*. London: Routledge & Kegan Paul.

Donne, John (1957) *The Sermons*, 10 vols, ed. George R. Potter and Evelyn M. Simpson, vol. 3. Berkeley and Los Angeles: University of California Press.

Halkett, John (1970) *Milton and the Idea of Matrimony*. New Haven: Yale University Press.

Kristeva, Julia (1981) 'Women's time', *Signs* 7, 1, 13–35.

Leggatt, Alexander (1974) *Shakespeare's Comedy of Love*. London: Methuen.

Millar, Oliver (1963) *The Tudor, Stuart and Early Georgian Pictures in the Collection of H.M. the Queen*, 2 vols. London: Phaidon.

Milton, John (1959) *The Complete Prose Works*, vol. 2, ed. Ernest Sirluck. London: Oxford University Press.

Morison, Stanley (1963) *The Likeness of Sir Thomas More*. London: Burns & Oates.

Muir, Kenneth (1979) *Shakespeare's Comic Sequence*. Liverpool: Liverpool University Press.

Pope-Hennessy, John (1966) *The Portrait in the Renaissance*. London: Phaidon.

Shakespeare, William (1975) *Twelfth Night*, ed. J. M. Lothian and T. W. Craik. London: Methuen.

Shepherd, Simon (1981) *Amazons and Warrior Women: Varieties of Feminism in Seventeenth-century Drama*. Brighton: Harvester Press.

Smith, Henry (1591) *A Preparative to Marriage*. London.

Strong, Roy (1967) *Holbein and Henry VIII*. London: Routledge & Kegan Paul.

Wilson, John Dover (1962) *Shakespeare's Happy Comedies*. London: Faber & Faber.

Part XI

Studies in Gender and Sexuality

36   "This that you call love": Sexual and Social Tragedy in *Othello*   655
     Gayle Greene

37   The Performance of Desire   669
     Stephen Orgel

38   The Secret Sharer   684
     Bruce R. Smith

39   The Homoerotics of Shakespearean Comedy   704
     Valerie Traub

One of the first facts new students of Shakespeare learn is that in the original performances of his plays at the Globe and other London theaters, the women's parts were played by boys. To think seriously about that datum is to recognize quickly that questions of gender and sexuality pervade Shakespeare's plays, and further acquaintance with the dramatic texts, either through performance or reading, confirms the centrality of such themes. That many plays offer disguise plots with cross-dressing women – boys playing girls playing boys, and occasionally boys playing girls playing boys playing girls – adds another layer of complexity about gender identification, sexuality, and desire. There has always been something erotic about the theater, as its opponents are quick to lament. Philip Stubbes, the most vocal enemy of Elizabethan plays and players, warns readers as early as 1583 about the lascivious examples presented on the public stage:

> If you will learn to become a bawd, unclean, and to devirginate maids, to deflower honest wives ... to sing and talk of bawdy love and venery; ... if you will learn to play the whoremaster, the glutton, drunkard, or incestuous person; ... you need to go to no other

school, for all these good examples may you see painted before your eyes in interludes and plays.[1]

While mocking Stubbes's fanatical Puritanism, modern critics have more or less conceded his argument that sex was a palpable force in the Renaissance playhouse.

But to say so is to confront a complicated set of definitions. The meaning of "sex" to English men and women of some four centuries ago, and thus to the dramatic characters they paid to watch, has been the subject of much debate. And the connection between sex and gender is a problem that Shakespeare critics in the last quarter of the twentieth century, following their colleagues in literary and cultural studies at large, have worked hard to understand in a historical sense. We know, for example, that Shakespeare's culture did not employ those terms in the way we do. "Sex" in his plays means "category," male or female. "Gender" means (1) "kind," "genus," or (2) "beget" (engender), "reproduce," or "copulate," and (3) the two or three (including neuter) grammatical kinds of words in languages such as Latin. Thinking about how early modern attitudes toward sex and gender shaped the creation, performance, and reception of Shakespeare's plays and poems produced an important body of work from many distinguished scholars and helped to transform our approach to both the texts and their theatrical realization. And critics have also pondered helpfully how our own ideas of gender and cultural assumptions – not just those of Shakespeare's audience – shape our interactions with the texts.

Such concern coincided with an increased interest in the history of the human body, especially the way early modern people thought about their own and other people's bodies. These are immensely complicated topics, subject to much dispute and constant modification of what we think we know. Since one of the most influential voices in this discourse has been that of Michel Foucault, it seems appropriate to cite a paragraph from the opening page of his *History of Sexuality.*

> At the beginning of the seventeenth century a certain frankness was still common, it would seem. Sexual practices had little need of secrecy; words were said without undue reticence, and things were done without too much concealment; one had a tolerant familiarity with the illicit. Codes regulating the coarse, the obscene, and the indecent were quite lax compared to those of the nineteenth century. It was a time of direct gestures, shameless discourse, and open transgressions, when anatomies were shown and intermingled at will, and knowing children hung about amid the laughter of adults: it was a period when bodies "made a display of themselves."[2]

Foucault is referring to practices throughout early modern Europe, not merely or even primarily in England, and critics frequently object to the barely qualified generalizations on which his argument depends. Even so, his description is helpful because it invites us to imagine behaviors or customs quite foreign to our own.

Such imaginative projection is also necessary in thinking about early modern culture and its understanding of sexuality. An important feature of Renaissance biological understanding was what Thomas Laqueur and other historians and critics refer to as "the one-sex model."

To be a man or a woman was to hold a social rank, a place in society, to assume a cultural role, not to *be* organically one or the other of two incommensurable sexes. Sex before the seventeenth century, in other words, was still a sociological and not an ontological category ... The notion, so powerful after the eighteenth century, that there had to be something outside, inside, and throughout the body which defines male as opposed to female and which provides the foundation for an attraction of opposites is entirely absent from classical or Renaissance medicine. In terms of the millennial traditions of western medicine, genitals came to matter as the marks of sexual opposition only last week.[3]

To discover that men and women were considered to be two versions of the same biological model, that sex was "conventional," is to change our way of looking at characters such as Rosalind and Viola, Hamlet and Gertrude.

Another related and similarly complex category is "homosexuality." The quotation marks around the noun are calculated to signify the problematic nature of the term for describing early modern sexual categories and practices. It is hardly news that Renaissance literature is charged with homoerotic emotion, but the nature of such passion became less clear when scholars began to insist that "homosexuality" as a term or classification did not exist until the nineteenth century, and that Shakespeare and his contemporaries thought about same-sex desire in ways different from our own. The old, familiar problem of homoeroticism in Shakespeare's sonnets, the erotic potentialities of boys playing women's roles on the stage, the notion of masculinity in connection with characters such as Coriolanus or Mercutio or Hotspur – all these topics began to take on new aspects when we revised our thinking about the categories of hetero- and homosexuality.

The scholars represented in this section take up these questions with alacrity and learning. Gayle Greene's essay looks at constructions of the masculine and feminine, specifically at the intersection or entanglement of the sexual and the social as represented in *Othello*. The other three essays have to do with homoeroticism: Stephen Orgel finds it on the stage, Bruce Smith in the Sonnets, and Valerie Traub in the comedies. This imbalance is deliberate. Practitioners of queer theory worked energetically and attracted considerable attention in the 1990s, partly because the "new" subdisciplines that had dominated the critical scene in the 1980s were becoming familiar and therefore less exciting. In addition to the authors represented here, Jonathan Goldberg, Jeffrey Masten, and Mario di Gangi have written helpfully on Shakespeare from this perspective; a more general analysis is Judith Butler's *Gender Trouble*. There is much more to Renaissance gender and sexuality than homoeroticism, but, as far as this volume is concerned, essays touching on masculinity, gender division, and other such topics appear under the categories of Feminist Criticism (Part X) and Psychoanalytic Criticism (Part VII): the strictures of space have precluded adding more. It is difficult, indeed, to separate Feminist Criticism from Studies in Gender and Sexuality, and the artificial division apparent here reflects the state of criticism at the end of the twentieth century. Fifteen years earlier, there would have been only one category; fifteen years later, there might be three or four.

The differences between early modern English culture and our own are very great, and the effort to apprehend those differences often leads into areas that may seem remote from or irrelevant to Shakespeare's plays. But such investigation can be revelatory. As one of the most respected voices in the field of gender studies puts it,

> the aim of a ... "queer" approach is not to find evidence that Shakespeare was ... homosexual. Rather, the analysis of gender and sexuality allows us to understand the variety of ways that Shakespeare responded imaginatively to sex, gender, and sexuality as crucial determinants of human identity and political power.[4]

Notes

1 *The Anatomy of Abuses* (1583), cited in *The Bedford Companion to Shakespeare: An Introduction with Documents*, 2nd edn., ed. Russ McDonald (Boston: St. Martin's Press, 2001), p. 352.
2 *The History of Sexuality, Volume I: An Introduction*, trans. Robert Hurley (New York: Random House, 1978), p. 3.
3 *Making Sex: Body and Gender from the Greeks to Freud* (Cambridge, MA: Harvard University Press, 1990), pp. 8, 22.
4 Valerie Traub, "Gender and Sexuality in Shakespeare," in *The Cambridge Companion to Shakespeare*, ed. Margreta de Grazia and Stanley Wells (Cambridge: Cambridge University Press, 2001), p. 129.

36

"This that you call love": Sexual and Social Tragedy in *Othello*

Gayle Greene

I

> Thy husband is thy lord, thy life, thy keeper,
> Thy head, thy sovereign ...
> And craves no other tribute at thy hands,
> But love, fair looks, and true obedience ...
> I am ashamed that women are so simple
> To offer war where they should kneel for peace,
> To seek for rule, supremacy, and sway,
> Where they are bound to serve, love, and obey.
> (*The Taming of the Shrew*)

> Truly, an obedient lady.
> (*Othello*)

T he revilement and murder of Desdemona by her husband is an excruciating experience, so relentless is his 'tyrannous hate',[1] so outrageous the assumptions that motivate it, so defenceless is she against it. Emilia's version of human relationships –

> 'Tis not a year or two shows us a man:
> They are all but stomachs, and we all but food;
> They eat us hungerly, and when they are full
> They belch us.
> (III.iv.103–6)

– though hardly complete, does have a certain terrible validity as description of what we see happening. Iago's redefinition of love, or 'this that you call love' (I.iii.331), as 'a lust of the blood and a permission of the will' (334), also has its weight. Though neither of these views is adequate to the complexity and variety of possibilities in love, the love that we see in this play seems inexorably linked to brutality; the violence unleashed in the last Acts is in direct consequence of and proportion to Othello's adulation of Desdemona, the release of a powerful destructive energy against which it has no defence.

From beginning to end, the play focuses on love. Its first words concern elopement; its last, 'the tragic loading of this bed' (v.ii.363), a bed which has been present throughout much of the play, in the language and imagery. The love of Othello and Desdemona defies world and time, barriers of social and parental opposition, and is consecrated by some of Shakespeare's greatest poetry, terms which are the absolute expression of those feelings:

> O my soul's joy!
> If after every tempest come such calms,
> May the winds blow till they have waken'd death!
> ... If it were now to die,
> 'Twere now to be most happy; for I fear
> My soul hath her content so absolute
> That not another comfort like to this
> Succeeds in unknown fate.
>
> (ii.i.182–93)

G. Wilson Knight calls them 'essential man and essential woman' in this scene: 'Othello is a prince of heroes, Desdemona lit by a divine feminine radiance, both of them transfigured.'[2] Yet theirs is a *Liebestod*, a love which is, like Romeo and Juliet's, wedded to death: within a scene, Othello has, on the basis of allegation, 'prove[d] her haggard' (iii.iii.260), his 'fond love' turned to 'tyrannous hate' (445–9), his eloquent adoration turned to 'I'll tear her all to pieces' (431), 'I will chop her into messes' (iv.i.200). But it is not a hostile social order that destroys them – this is overcome in the first act – nor a quirk of timing, nor even the slow, wasting time which is love's enemy in *Troilus and Cressida* and the sonnets. It is, rather, Othello himself who deliberately and premeditatedly murders his love, and though he has powerful instigation in Iago, Iago has power only because his insinuations ring deeply true to him: 'I told ... no more / Than what he found himself was apt and true' (v.ii.176–7). Shakespeare's tragic vision has matured in the ten years between *Romeo and Juliet* and *Othello*, and we must look for the flaw in the couple themselves, in the man, in the woman, and their love – a love that, as Othello's intimation indicates, hovers on the edge of perdition, whose 'absolute content' makes him think of death.

II

For her sweet, silent submission, Desdemona has been praised by generations of critics: 'a maiden never bold; / Of spirit ... still and quiet ...' (I.iii.94–5). Selfless, solicitous of her husband at the expense of herself, obedient to the 'fancies' of her 'lord': 'Be as your fancies teach you / What e'er you be, I am obedient' (III.iii.88–9), she has struck many as an ideal of femininity. A.C. Bradley praises her 'helpless passivity': 'She can do nothing whatever. She cannot retaliate even in speech ... She is helpless because her nature is infinitely sweet and her love absolute'.[3] Robert B. Heilman sees in her 'the dynamics of the personality under the magic influence of love, the full ripening of outward-turning love which we may call the magical transformation of personality'.[4] What do we do, then, with our outrage, as we suffer through the last half of the play, our attention riveted with horror on Othello's violence, a violence motivated by assumptions that his wife is a 'thing' (III.iii.272) which, 'stain'd' or 'spotted' (v.i.36), must be murdered for 'Justice[s]' (v.ii.17) sake? There is no question, of course, that we are meant to condemn him, but it is the basis and extent of our outrage that we must question, testing our 'modern' responses against those which can be supported by the play. Shakespeare, we are told, was deeply traditional, a believer in the hierarchical order which was even in his time a thing of the past. Does he see in Desdemona, this woman who goes lyrically to her death, and is, next to Ophelia, the least capable of his women of defending herself, the ideal that so many of his critics have seen?

Just as we look to Othello's character for cause of his vulnerability to Iago, so must we look to Desdemona's character for her vulnerability to Othello. She too is a tragic figure with a flaw analogous to his. Neither is simply a victim; rather, they are manipulable because they are responsive to and co-operative with their victimizers, a view which, according them some responsibility for their fates, accords them more stature. It is in part Othello's very nobility that makes him vulnerable: being of 'a free and open nature', he 'thinks men honest that but seem to be so' (I.iii.339–40). The play is concerned, as Terence Hawkes suggests, with an ideal and standard of manly behaviour. Hawkes sees Othello as the epitome of this ideal, an ideal expressed in his splendid rhetoric, 'manly language' which breaks down, becoming abusive and incommunicative under Iago's influence, but which is regained at the end.[5] But I think that the 'manly ideal' embodied by Othello is, like the rhetoric that sustains it, suspect from the start. Mixed with his nobility is a habit of self-dramatization, a tendency to observe his life as an adventure fiction, a concern with a heroic self-image: 'I ran it through, even from my boyish days' (132).[6] The 'tale' he tells in defence of his marriage, 'the story of my life', 'the battles, sieges, fortunes, / That have pass'd' (I.iii.129–31), reveals a naivety and romance splendid but dangerous. We hear, also, in words like 'never', 'all', 'forever', a tendency to absolutes which points to an inability to tolerate ambiguity or uncertainty, a failure of irony. His account of their love – 'She lov'd me for the dangers I had pass'd, / And I lov'd her that she did pity them' (167–8) – indicates considerably more interest in what made Desdemona love him than in what made him love her, and a reliance on what Heilman calls certain 'props of assurance':[7] a dependence on the esteem of others for his sense of himself apparent also in his concern with honour, and his idea of honour as 'reputation'.[8] Othello's life of action and adventure has ill equipped him for the human complexities he is about to encounter, complexities related in part to language, which is, as Brabantio says in this scene, 'equivocal' (217). There is at the centre of his selfhood an insecurity related to his position as black man in a white society. Though he is an outsider, this 'extravagant and wheeling stranger' (I.i.135) embodies the essence and extreme of certain qualities which are conventionally 'masculine': a vision that looks without, a nature that expresses itself in action and, when threatened, in violence, which has been conditioned by his 'occupation' as soldier. Circumscribed by this ideal of character and conduct, Othello is deficient in self-awareness and judgement of others.

Desdemona is his counterpart, in love and in tragedy. She is, like him, too noble for the world, and vulnerable because she is virtuous, unable to understand his accusations because incapable of imagining the evil of which she is accused, powerless to challenge him because conditioned to obey, she remains 'Truly, an obedient lady' (iv.i.248). Her defencelessness is a function of an ideal of womanly behaviour that makes her co-operate with him in love and in destruction: as he is 'essential man', she is 'essential woman'. They are, as Maud Bodkin calls them, 'archetypal fantasy of man and woman',[9] a fantasy that turns to nightmare. Women and relationships are prominent in this play to an unprecedented degree in Shakespeare's tragedies: each of the male characters is shown in relation to a woman, their relationships emphasized by verb forms: 'wiv'd' (ii.i.60), 'woman'd' (iii.iv.194), 'bewhor'd' (iv.ii.115). As the play is concerned with a standard of manly behaviour, so is it concerned with an ideal of womanly character and conduct, with the question of what women are, what they might be and should be. Such an ideal is suggested by the interplay of the three women characters, and is defined, like the men's, partly in terms of what it is not, partly in terms of language, and related – again like the men's – to the capacity for survival. The tragic vulnerability of both male and female protagonists is rooted in ideals and illusions they bring to one another which create their love and destroy it, ideals related to conventional conceptions of man and woman – conceptions which, Shakespeare suggests, are misconceptions. Othello's confusion regarding 'honesty', a word that rings through the play with insistent irony, with different meanings for man and for woman, involves more than a personal error: Shakespeare implies a criticism of the ideals themselves, that man's worth is contained in his 'honour' and woman's in her 'chastity'.

III

Othello is concerned, in action and theme, with men's misunderstanding of women. Throughout the play, we hear men telling us what women are, and what strikes us most about their terms and definitions is their inadequacy. Whether adulating them as goddesses or reviling them as whores, their generalizations tell us more about themselves than about the women they are describing. Iago's slander is simple and all-inclusive, encompassing men as well as women: women are whores, men are knaves. His 'alehouse paradoxes', in his exchange with Desdemona as they await Othello's arrival in Cyprus, reduce all to a lowest common denominator:

> You are pictures out a'doors,
> Bells in your parlors, wild-cats in your kitchens,
> Saints in your injuries, devils being offended …
> (i.ii.109–11)

Fair and foolish, foul and foolish, even 'a deserving woman indeed' (145) are 'fit to suckle fools and chronicle small beer' (160), to wear themselves out in child-rearing and housekeeping, and all alike in bed: 'Players in your huswifery, and huswives in your beds' (112).

Cassio's attitude is slightly more complicated, though equally destructive of the individual, human reality: some women are whores, some are goddesses. His idealization of Desdemona contrasts to Iago's debasement; to him, she is 'the riches of the ship' (II.i.83), to Iago, she is 'a land carract' (I.ii.50), and it is distanced and abstract: 'a maid that paragons description', 'divine' (II.i.61–2, 73), 'most exquisite', 'indeed perfection' (II.iii.18, 28). But Cassio reserves his revilement for the 'other kind', the woman with whom he is involved: 'He, when he hears of her, cannot restrain / From the excess of laughter' (IV.i.98–9). Though Bianca shows herself devoted and willing to risk herself for him, it suits him to see her as 'caitiff' (and 'customer', 'monkey', 'fitchew' [IV.i.108, 119, 127, 146]). Cassio, we hear, is 'A fellow almost damn'd in a fair wife' (I.i.21), an enigmatic reference which draws attention to Shakespeare's change in the source: whereas in Cinthio, Cassio was married, Shakespeare shows him in relation to a prostitute, and needing to see her as such.

Cassio divides women into two types, Desdemona and Bianca, but Othello directs his confusions at one woman, his wife. There is no question that Othello is in love with her: 'there, where I have garner'd up my heart … / The fountain from the which my current runs or else dries up' (IV.ii.57–60). But there is a question as to whether he loves her – whether, in human terms, he loves her at all: she is an idea, an ideal, a symbol. Thus even his adulation is curiously egocentric, showing more concern with the feelings she inspires in him – 'my soul', 'my content' – than with Desdemona. Many of his terms for her are conventional and stereotyped: images like 'rose', 'balmy breath' (V.ii.13, 16), and the recurrence of the adjectives 'sweet' and 'fair' indicate a simplistic and primarily physical response. Shakespeare has elsewhere, in the early *Romeo* and certain of the sonnets, used such Petrarchan terms to indicate immaturity and self-love, a response to one's own projected image rather than to the loved one.[10] Othello's adulation screens out a considerable portion of human reality, and as Maud Bodkin observes: 'If a man is wedded to his fantasy of a woman … he grows frantic and blind with passion at the thought of the actual woman … as a creature of natural varying impulses.'[11] From conceiving of Desdemona as one 'type' it is a short distance to imagining her as the other 'type' – only a matter of a turn in perspective, which Iago accomplishes, and adulation reverses itself to as extreme a revilement.

Othello's language indicates, as well, certain ambivalences about sexuality. There is suggestion, in images like 'monumental alabaster' (v.ii.5) and 'perfect chrysolite' (145), of what Traversi calls a 'monumental frigidity'.[12] Othello is never at ease in speaking of sexuality: his terms indicate strain or self consciousness, a conception of love which is either idealized or reductive, making it more or less than it is – 'absolute content', or a physical, trifling matter. Certain statements strike a wrong tone: 'The purchase made, the fruits are to ensue / The profit's yet to come 'tween me and you' (II.iii.9–10) – and his terms of affection for Desdemona, such as 'honey' (II.i.204) and 'sweeting' (II.iii.253), are not unlike his derisive term 'chuck' (IV.ii.24). Comparing the straightforward ease of Desdemona's request to accompany him to Cyprus, with his extended protests, we can hear how much more comfortable with their love is she than he. Her declaration of devotion and desire to be with him is simple and direct:

> I saw Othello's visage in his mind,
> And to his honors and his valiant parts

> Did I my soul and fortunes consecrate.
> So that, dear lords, if I be left behind ...
> The rites for which I love him are bereft me.
> ... Let me go with him.
>
> (ɪ.iii.252–9)

His is hedged with protests that he does not want her with him to 'please the palate of my appetite / Nor to comply with heat'; that neither 'light wing'd toys / Of feather'd Cupid' nor 'disports' will 'corrupt and taint my business', lest 'housewives make a skillet of my helm' (268–73). The statement amounts to a denial of the ennobling effects of love, and his terms 'heat', 'appetite' and 'housewives', terms Iago will use, are present in his mind before Iago suggests them.

Implicit in Othello's language is a suspicion of sexuality and the physical being of woman and man, which Iago turns easily to loathing. The swiftness with which Othello leaps to Iago's conclusions indicates that Iago is hardly necessary to convince him of these calumnies; 'they are all there' – as Leslie Fiedler puts it – 'in his head, picked up in the same army camps where Iago himself had learned them.'[13] Thus Iago offers his example of generalized abuse – 'In Venice they do let God see the pranks / They dare not show their husbands' (ɪɪɪ.iii.201–3) – supplementing his slanders with vivid images of animal copulation: 'Were they as prime as goats, as hot as monkeys ...' (403). Within a few lines, Othello, too, is generalizing –

> O curse of marriage!
> That we can call these delicate creatures ours,
> And not their appetites!
>
> (267–9)

– and the rank, sexual images have been 'engend'red' (ɪ.iii.403) in his language: 'Goats and monkeys!' (ɪv.i.263). We can see that this sort of thing is not merely a matter of Iago's influence, since we hear it first from Brabantio, who reacts to Desdemona's elopement with a sense of betrayal and a warning – 'Fathers, from hence trust not your daughters' minds' (ɪ.i.170) – and a wish indicating revulsion from the physical fact of paternity: 'I had rather to adopt a child than get it' (ɪ.iii.191). It is these shared male assumptions that make Othello 'know' so certainly that Iago is 'honest' and Desdemona is not.

Othello's response to Iago's insinuations is a righteously vindicated recognition that 'the forked plague' is 'destiny unshunnable' (ɪɪɪ.iii.275–6), a certainty possible only because woman has been suspect from the start. Iago seems so wise to him – 'O, thou art wise, 'tis certain' (ɪv.i.74) – because he confirms things Othello has known all along. Othello demands 'satisfaction' – 'Would I were satisfied' (ɪɪɪ.iii.385) – a peculiar word to describe his request for proof, and one which is repeated five times within the next eighteen lines. However, in the confirmation of his deepest fears it is a 'satisfaction' which takes the place of the consummation which never seems to occur with Desdemona. The language which was frigid in its adoration takes fire from jealousy, and the cold and conventional turns to passionate anguish: 'O ay, as summer flies are in the shambles / That quicken even with blowing' (ɪv.ii.66–7). Only in the desire to destroy and the assurance of loss does Othello's language attain conviction.

This deep certainty of woman's faithlessness accounts for his obsession with possessing her. Knowing that possession can never be sure – that 'we can call these delicate creatures ours / And not their appetites' – his passion, in both its loving and its destructive aspects, is more involved with Desdemona as possession than as woman, as a 'thing' to which he has exclusive privileges: 'I had rather be a toad … than keep a corner in the thing I love / For others' uses' (III.iii.270–73). He thus speaks of her in terms of 'exchange' (I.ii.25–8), 'purchase' (I.iii.9–10), something of which he has been 'robb'd' (III.iii.342), which he would 'not have sold'; and though he progresses to an awareness that he 'threw' (v.i.146) her away, a verb indicating more recognition of responsibility, still, he is thinking of her as something that is his to discard. Offended vanity mingles with his motives for murder; he reveals a concern that she has made him appear a 'figure … of scorn' (IV.ii.54) which follows from his concern with reputation: 'false to me?' (III.iii.333), 'Cuckold me!' 'With mine officer!' (IV.i.200, 202).

It is Othello's failure to see Desdemona as a person or to recognize his own uncharted areas that accounts for his easy acceptance of Iago's terms. Men's misconceptions of women are, in Desdemona's words, 'horrible fancies' (IV.ii.26), projections of their own worst fears and failings. Man defines woman as 'the other', in Simone de Beauvoir's term: 'He projects upon her what he desires and what he fears, what he loves and what he hates.'[14] Only once does Othello attempt to 'say what she is' (IV.i.187), and though wrenched with 'the pity of it' (195), he is unable to hold this reality in focus. The final speeches in which he summons the old rhetoric in self-justification and evocation of his heroic past – 'speak of me as I am' (v.ii.343) – make no mention of the human being he has loved and killed, and are concerned, like so much of what he says, with his tragedy rather than hers. The women, on the other hand, do attempt to adjust their visions of the men and to temper their ideals. Emilia has thought about 'jealous souls' and their 'cause' (III.iv.159–60), and Desdemona tries to excuse Othello's anger – 'Nay, we must think men are not gods' (III.iv.148) – and to understand the human being with concerns besides herself:

> Something sure of state …
> Hath puddled his clear spirit; and in such cases
> Men's natures wrangle with inferior things
> Though great ones are their object.
> (III.iv.140–45)

But none of the men succeeds; Othello himself only once even tries to adjust his ideas and 'images' of women to the human reality.

IV

The characters of the three women illuminate aspects of one another, Emilia and Bianca providing potentials of character and behaviour available to Desdemona. In this system of contrasts and parallels, an association between Desdemona and Bianca is established by the juxtaposition of the eavesdropping and 'brothel' scenes, analogous in the cruelty with which men impose 'fancies' on women. Bianca enters the scene, which

Iago has devised, in the midst of the laughter characteristic of Cassio's habitual response to her; in a feeble attempt at self-assertion she returns the handkerchief she believes to be from another woman, but ends by begging him to accompany her home, an incident which constitutes 'proof' for Othello of his own wife's adultery. Though the scene is comic in tone, it provides comment on the next scene, which is not. As Cassio has called Bianca 'caitiff' and 'customer' (IV.i.108, 119), Othello imposes the same 'fancy' on Desdemona, reducing the reality of a woman who loves him to 'strumpet' and 'whore' (IV.ii.81, 83, 85, 89), a role and relationship that justifies his abuse. Though least alike in terms of innocence and experience, Bianca and Desdemona are analogous in that to which they are subject, and in an ability to return devotion for revilement which is simultaneously virtue and folly.

We watch Desdemona progress, in the course of the play, through a variety of roles traditionally assigned to woman: she is defined and disowned as daughter, then adulated as lover and wife, reviled as whore, and finally deprived of all designations. Her first words define her carefully within the social order, as daughter and wife; in her description of herself as 'divided' in 'duty' between father and husband she provides an emblem of her situation. The words she uses to describe these relationships – 'bound', 'duty', 'due' (I.iii.182–8) – indicate circumscription, a deeply engrained obedience for which she is finally literally strangled. (Othello's first plan is to poison her, but he eagerly accepts Iago's suggestion that he strangle her: 'The justice of it pleases' [IV.i.210].) Only in relation to her love for Othello does her language assume the more active qualities of 'storm', 'violence' (294), and 'challenge' (188), but her elopement, though a challenge to the social order, is still a circumscribed form of rebellion which follows the prescribed path from father to husband, a husband whom she nearly always addresses as 'my lord', true to the filial relationship determined by their difference in years. And though her love for Othello is touching, bold, wonderful, hers is still that romantic illusion of the merging of identity – 'My heart's subdu'd / Even to the quality of my lord' (I.iii.250–51) – and the verb 'subdued' is accurate, since, as de Beauvoir notes, it is an ideal that must result in the obliteration of self: if, as Catherine says, 'I am Heathcliffe', that leaves only one of them.[15]

Defined by men and in relation to men, woman's identity is precarious, and we see how precarious within this scene when Brabantio dissolves his ties to Desdemona, casting her off as daughter: 'Dead ... to me' (I.iii.59); 'I give thee that ...' (193). Having betrayed him, she is no longer his daughter, nor even a person, but a 'that'. (So, for that matter, is Othello called a 'thing' [I.ii.71], and the dehumanizing terms suggest a similarity between racial and sexual stereotyping which we have come to recognize.) Brabantio's warning – 'Look to her, Moor, if thou hast eyes to see; / She has deceiv'd her father and may thee' (I.iii.292–3) – suggests similarities between Desdemona's relations with both husband and father, though not those which Brabantio imagines. Othello, too, will dissolve his ties to her, and redefine her – no longer as his wife, but as 'that cunning whore of Venice / That married with Othello' (IV.ii.89–90), a redefinition that strips her of identity, and finally of life: 'My wife? ... I have no wife' (V.ii.97).

Though Desdemona's 'divided duty' may represent orthodox Elizabethan doctrine, it is her acceptance of these terms and assumptions that leaves her powerless to understand her situation, let alone deal with it. We watch the course of her love for Othello – from simple adoration, to confusion ('What shall I do to win my lord again?'

[IV.ii.149]), through attempts to justify him ('something sure of state ...'), to justify herself: 'You do me wrong' (IV.ii.82); 'I have not deserv'd this' (IV.i.241). We watch her struggle with her sense of outraged worth, subduing her rebellion, remaining solicitous of him at the expense of herself ('Am I the motive for these tears, my lord?' [IV.ii.43]), siding, finally, with him against herself: 'My love doth so approve him, / That even his stubbornness, his checks, his frowns ... have grace and favor in them' (IV.iii.19–21); 'Let nobody blame him, his scorn I approve' (52); and ending, finally, resolutely faithful in her acceptance of blame: 'Nobody; I myself ... / Commend me to my kind lord' (v.ii.124–5). Her defencelessness is partly a patter of naivety, and partly linguistic: she cannot pronounce the word 'whore' – 'I cannot say "whore". / It does abhor me now I speak the word' (v.ii.161–2). As Othello 'throws despite and heavy terms upon her' (IV.ii.116), she can barely understand them – 'What doth your speech import?' – let alone defend herself against them: 'I understand a fury in your words, / But not the words' (IV.ii.31–2). For this she has been praised by a critic as astute as Heilman:

> She does not fly off into the loud vehemence of offended self-love [or] rise above a hurt amazement and a mild earnestness of assertion ... Instead of looking around for someone to blame, she tries to make a case for Othello's incredible conduct, and she rebukes herself for blaming him ... But she does not ... subordinate devotion to self-pity and self-justification.[16]

But though this mildness may have appeal in the abstract, to approve it is contrary to our experience of these last scenes, to the tension and frustration created as Desdemona is brought together with her raving husband and is unable to rise above 'hurt amazement'. What began as the 'archetypal fantasy of man and woman' turns to another 'complementary mythic fantasy', what Fiedler calls 'the male nightmare of unmerited betrayal and the female dream of patient suffering rewarded'.[17] Precisely what is required of Desdemona is 'self-love' and 'self-justification', defiance of the role in which Othello has cast her; we long to hear her ask, inquire, answer, challenge, shout, to find a voice by which she can express her innocence and defend herself, but it is her acceptance of his terms – not 'whore', but the premises and assumptions that make her 'inferior thing' – that renders her helpless and inarticulate. What has been lost in her 'divided duty' is duty to herself, and Othello's irony strikes a terrible truth: 'And she's obedient, as you say, obedient; / Very obedient' (IV.i.225–6). Though, to his question, 'What art thou', she can reply: 'Your wife, my lord; your true / And loyal wife' (IV.ii.33–4), she is not able to find a language strong or clear enough to counteract his 'fancy', and in fact manages consistently to say just the wrong thing, pursuing Cassio's suit at the moment when it does her most harm, struggling for life when the desire to live convicts her of guilt: 'Kill me tomorrow, let me live tonight!' (v.ii.80). We cringe as she finds just the words to infuriate him: 'He [Cassio] will not say so' (71); 'Alas, he is betray'd and I undone!' (76). 'Bewhor'd', she is bewildered, 'half asleep' (IV.ii.96), and overcome.

Is this her 'wretched fortune' (IV.ii.128), as she calls it, and as her name implies? In a sense, it is her fate as a woman, quintessential woman, the 'jewel' (I.iii.195) of her father, 'pearl' (v.ii.347) of her husband, treasure, but possession, and her acceptance of her position, that render her incapable of self-defence. That defiance is what is required in her situation, and is an Elizabethan as well as a modern possibility, is indicated by Shakespeare's structuring of the murder scene in such a way that expression is given the rebellion we have longed to hear, and an alternative mode of behaviour is provided. Bursting in on the scene, demanding 'a word' (v.ii.90), it is Emilia who finds the voice of protest that makes itself heard: 'You told a lie, an odious, damned lie! / Upon my soul, a lie! a wicked lie' (v.ii.180–81), a voice which is contrast and antidote to the muffled silence of her mistress. From the beginning, Emilia has had this ability to name things clearly, precisely, if at times a bit crassly. Speaking on her own behalf, she gives expression to the human reality which we have heard stereotyped:

> But I do think it is their husbands' faults
> If wives do fall ...
> Why, we have galls; and though we have some grace,
> Yet have we some revenge. Let husbands know
> Their wives have sense like them: they see, and smell,
> And have their palates both for sweet and sour,
> As husbands have ... And have we not affections,
> Desires for sport, and frailty, as men have?
> Then let them use us well; else let them know
> The ills we do, their ills instruct us so.
> (iv.iii.92–103)[18]

A simple truth, yet beyond any of the men in the play: that woman is neither goddess nor whore, but a being with 'frailty', desire, and point of view, combined of both 'grace' and 'gall'. Not that Emilia's is a perspective to which we wholly ascribe, entrenched as it is in a material reality, but her vision complements Desdemona's, and represents some of the body and toughness that Desdemona lacks: 'The world's a huge thing ... and the wrong is but a wrong i' th' world; and having the world for your labor, 'tis a wrong in your own world, and you might quickly make it right' (iv.iii.69–83). Such relativism has its strengths: an acknowledgement, like irony, of other points of view; and it is irony of which Desdemona and Othello are tragically incapable; but that relativism plays no part in Emilia's actions is seen in her unhesitating sacrifice of her life. If we try to account for her character, we may speculate that this clarity is partly a matter of social class: never adulated, no one's 'jewel', she has remained clear-eyed and without illusions, although she is, like Desdemona, too tolerant of her husband's 'fantasy' (iii.iii.299). Thus it is she who finds the voice Desdemona cannot, which dispels the nightmarish unreality: 'I am bound to speak' (184); 'Let me have leave to speak' (195); 'Let heaven and men and devils let them all / All cry shame against me, yet I'll speak' (221–2). And her simple refusal expresses the defiance we have long wished to hear: ''Tis proper I obey him; but not now. / Perchance, Iago, I will ne'er go home' (196–7).

V

Of the three women in the play, two are killed by their husbands after being reviled as whores; the third, Bianca, seems actually to be a whore, and though she survives, it is through no strength of her own, but simply because she is not central enough to be pulled into Iago's plots. We see women defined by men, 'circumstanc'd' (iii.iv.201), the object of their 'horrible fancies', fancies which are projections of their own worst fears and failings. Reviled, or adulated and then reviled in proportion to that adulation, they are cursed and killed. The question, how shall the good defend themselves? might be rephrased: how shall women protect themselves against men? And Shakespeare's change of the 'I' of the Willow Song from male to female adds yet another victimized woman.[19] Against the roles in which men cast them, we see the human reality, the reality of women trying to understand their men and to survive. We see that Desdemona can no more be accounted for by the 'lame and impotent conclusion' (ii.i.152) of Iago's stereotypes than Emilia can, though it is Othello's tragedy to believe that she can; as it is Iago's strategic error to judge Emilia a 'common thing' (iii.iii.302) without moral dimension. We see that woman is not as she is named by man, although it is her tragedy to believe that she is, and that the inadequacy of male definitions is the inadequacy of society's.

In the comedies and romances, and in *Antony and Cleopatra*, women make themselves heard, but part of what is tragic about the tragic world here is that they do not, and they do not because, accepting the restrictive roles assigned them by men, obedient to men's 'fancies', they are mutilated and destroyed. In the world of comedy, Othello and Desdemona would be granted the reprieve of Claudio and Hero, although even in the world of *Much Ado*, Claudio's easy acceptance of slander, so like Othello's, indicates a failure of knowledge and love; Shakespeare provides a better way in Beatrice and Benedick, who represent a love based on self-knowledge and knowledge of one another which is capable of surviving world and time. It is unthinkable that the creator of Beatrice or Cleopatra or Rosalind would perceive in Desdemona the ideal that his critics have seen. But we do not have to leave this play to find an alternative mode of action, since within *Othello* is a woman capable of challenging male prerogatives and assumptions, who might be able to bring about a comic resolution, were the destruction not so far on its course. Shakespeare shows woman, at her best, as capable of a courage which eludes the men and as acceptant of a challenge which, like Emilia's, encompasses 'heaven and men and devils'. Though the men do the killing, it is they who are the more tragically mutilated.

Bianca provides a reflection of what Desdemona is, Emilia a potential of what she might be: an autonomous being capable of speaking from her own centre of self, and finding a language which is strong and clear because it does come from that centre. Desdemona needs more of the one, less of the other. As Desdemona's defencelessness is explicable in terms of a 'feminine' docility, so too are Othello's limitations traceable to the 'manly' ideal of character and conduct involved in his 'occupation'. As with Lear, Hamlet and Antony, the experience of betrayal makes the tragic protagonist doubt his very identity, but unlike the others, Othello assumes that selfhood can be recovered by an act of physical violence and destruction of the loved one. Though we are tempted to cry, with Emilia, 'What should such a fool / Do with so good a wife?' (v.ii.232–3),[20] and though his years and her youth make him the more reprehensible, we must realize that Othello and Desdemona co-operate in their destruction: cut off in tragic incomprehension from one another, they speak two different languages, and she is no more capable of entering into his experience than he is into hers. But by not defying him, Desdemona destroys both of them. She may have an inkling of her complicity in their tragedy when, about to die, she confesses her sins as 'loves I bear you' (v.ii.40).

Othello's investment of his 'manhood' in his 'honesty', in an ideal of honour as reputation that requires Desdemona's death, and in his confusion of her character with her 'chastity', points to an error – not only one of fact, but one involved in the conceptions themselves; not only of Othello, but of society as a whole. Though to the end, Othello is still thinking in such terms, justifying himself as 'an honorable murderer' who 'did all in honor' (v.ii.294–5), 'But why should honor out-live honesty?' (83), Shakespeare is suggesting that woman's virtue need be defined as a more active and positive quality than chastity, the 'preservation of this vessel for my lord' (iv.ii.83); and that the 'honor' for which Othello so readily kills be made of sterner stuff than 'the bubble reputation' (*As You Like It* ii.vii.152). The ideal of manly and womanly behaviour that the play finally affirms is something closer to a combination of masculine and feminine than that recognized or represented by Desdemona or Othello: it is the ideal, familiar elsewhere in Shakespeare, that the best of women has something of man in her, and the best of men something of woman.[21]

This is not to imply that the complexities of this tragedy are reducible to a tract on the subject of woman. The sense we are left with is one of woe and wonder, the paradox that we kill what we most love, and that what is grand about these characters, their faith and absolute commitment, is also their doom. But while recognizing and responding to what is splendid in their love, we can question what fatal quality condemns it to death, and whether it need be a *Liebestod*, allied so inevitably to destruction. Perhaps we must finally accept this connection of love and death as an inexorable condition of our lives, man's revulsion from woman accountable, as Arthur Kirsch has suggested in his study of the play, in Freudian terms of man's earliest desire for his mother.[22] But so much of what Freud considered 'inexorable' has been traced, in the past fifty years, to social conditions, and 'essentially' male and female characteristics may not be 'essential', but socially determined. It is equally possible to see man's ambivalence towards woman in terms of his suspicion that he has wronged her: binding her to a double standard in which she has not been consulted, to which she has not consented, he expects her revenge to take the form of sexual betrayal.[23] The social dimension in this play is prominent by virtue of Othello's blackness and the carefully delineated backgrounds, classes and 'occupations' of each of the characters. This man of action, who has never looked within, and his obedient lady are fatally interlocked in the ancient rite of love and death. Though Desdemona comes closer than he does to recognizing the human being and adjusting her ideal accordingly, theirs is not a marriage of true minds, not based on a recognition of persons, and though touching and wondrous, it is fatally flawed; what Heilman calls 'the magical transformation of love' destroys them both. Shakespeare is suggesting, in his radical critique of some of society's most cherished notions, that accepted ideals of manly and womanly behaviour are distortive and destructive of the human reality, and that relations be based on saner and more certain ground than 'this that you call love'.

Notes

1   *Othello* iii.iii.449. *The Riverside Shakespeare*, ed. G. Blakemore Evans (Boston, MA: Houghton Mifflin, 1974). All further references to Shakespeare's plays are to this edition.

2   *The Wheel of Fire: Interpretations of Shakespearean Tragedy* (1949; rpt. London: Methuen, 1970), p. 111.

3   *Shakespearean Tragedy* (1904; rpt. Cleveland, OH: World Publ., 1963), p. 147.

4   *Magic in the Web: Action and Language in Othello* (Lexington: University of Kentucky Press, 1965), p. 214.

5   *Shakespeare's Talking Animals: Language and Drama in Society* (Totowa, NJ: Rowman & Little-field, 1974), p. 133.

6   Heilman discusses Othello's opening speeches in these terms (pp. 139–40). See also F. R. Leavis, 'Diabolic Intellect and the Noble Hero: A Note on *Othello*', *Scrutiny*, 6 (December 1938); and D. A. Traversi, *An Approach to Shakespeare* (Garden City, NY: Doubleday, 1956), pp. 133–5.

7   Heilman, p. 139.

8   'Reputation' was by no means the only possible conception of honour. In *All's Well, Troilus and Cressida*, and *Julius Caesar*, Shakespeare subjects the military ideal of honour as reputation to criticism, and in 1 *Henry IV* he opposes the limited, histrionic ideal of Hotspur to the mature, self-defined, and inherent quality represented by Hal. For the variety of views which were available in the Renaissance, see Curtis Watson, *Shakespeare and the Renaissance Concept of Honor* (Princeton, NJ: Princeton University Press, 1960); and Ruth Kelso, 'The Doctrine of the English Gentleman in the Sixteenth Century', *University of Illinois Studies* 14 (April 1929).

9   *Archetypal Patterns in Poetry: Psychological Studies of Imagination* (London: Oxford University Press, 1974), p. 219.

10 Rosalie Colie discusses *Othello* in terms of the 'unmetaphorizing' of Petrarchan conventions: 'In criticizing the artificiality he at the same time exploits in the play, Shakespeare manages ... to reassess and to reanimate the moral system of the psychological truths at the core of the literary love-tradition, to reveal its problematics and to reaffirm in a fresh and momentous context the beauty of its impossible ideals.' *Shakespeare's Living Art* (Princeton, NJ: Princeton University Press, 1974), p. 167. I would agree that the play offers a dramatization of the values central to Petrarchan love, but I would argue that it is more overwhelmingly negative in emphasis: rather than 'reanimating' and 'reaffirming' these values, it offers a critique which finds them deficient and destructive.

11 Bodkin, p. 222.

12 Traversi, p. 129.

13 *The Stranger in Shakespeare* (New York: Stein & Day, 1972), p. 158. Fiedler claims Shakespeare shares 'the Moor's paranoia' (p. 165), but his reading is based on a misinterpretation of the women: all three are true, contrary to his claim, and the play as a whole refutes such paranoia, and restores the faith which was lost in *Troilus and Cressida*.

14 *The Second Sex* (New York: Random House, 1974), p. 223.

15 Ibid., p. 725.

16 Heilman, pp. 208–9.

17 Fiedler, p. 148.

18 Cf. de Beauvoir's analysis of women's relationships and their questioning of male pretences and values: 'Woman knows that the masculine code is not hers ... She therefore calls upon other women to help define a set of "local rules," ... a moral code specifically for the female sex' (p. 605). Feeling 'the ambiguity of her position', 'she avoids the snares of over-seriousness and conformism' and can question 'ready-made values' (p. 403).

19 *Othello, A New Variorum Edition*, ed. Horace Howard Furness (New York: Dover, 1963), pp. 276–7.

20 See Carol Neely's excellent article of this name, 'Women and Men in *Othello*: "What should such a fool / Do with so good a woman?" ', *Shakespeare Studies* (Spring 1978); to be reprinted in

The Woman's Part: Feminist Criticism of Shakespeare, ed. Gayle Greene, Carol Neely and Carolyn Lenz, forthcoming (University of Illinois Press). Though her interpretation of Desdemona and her conclusions differ from mine, she, too, sees the tragedy as originating in men's and women's misconception of one another. Her essay contributed considerably to my understanding of the play.

21 Juliet Dusinberre notes that 'Shakespeare believed that for a man to be more than a boy, as for a woman to be more than a child, the masculine and the feminine must marry in his spirit', *Shakespeare and the Nature of Women* (New York: Barnes & Noble, 1975), p. 291; Carolyn Heilbrun sees Shakespeare 'as devoted to the androgynous ideal as anyone who has ever written', *Toward a Recognition of Androgyny* (New York: Knopf, 1973), p. 29; and Virginia Woolf describes Shakespeare's mind as 'the type of the androgynous, of the man-womanly mind', *A Room of One's Own* (New York: Harcourt, 1957), p. 102.

22 'The Polarization of Erotic Love in Shakespeare's Plays', unpubl. paper read at Shakespeare Association meeting, April 1977, New Orleans.

23 And it does take this form: adultery is often a form of revenge. De Beauvoir's discussion of the causes of jealousy is illuminating: 'Only through adultery can woman prove that she is nobody's chattel ... This is the reason why the husband's jealousy is so quick to awaken ... This is indeed why jealousy can be insatiable', *Second Sex*, p. 213.

37

The Performance of Desire

Stephen Orgel

I have begun by questioning some basic information about the English Renaissance theatre. It is a commonplace to observe that the stage in Shakespeare's time
was an exclusively male preserve, but theatre historians tend to leave the matter
there, as if the fact merely constituted a practical arrangement and had no implications.[1] But it has very broad implications, which are both cultural and specifically
sexual: the male public theatre represents a uniquely English solution to the universal
European disapproval of actresses. No contemporary continental public theatre restricted the stage to men. So the first puzzle, if one is looking at English Renaissance
theatre in a European context, is why this seemed a satisfactory arrangement to the
English and not to anyone else.

Secondly, I have problematized the fact of a male theatre in England, pointing out
that the claim of an all-male public stage at the very least needs some serious
qualification. But even where the stage was a male preserve, as it certainly was in the
commercial theatrical companies of Renaissance England, the theatre was not. The
theatre was a place of unusual freedom for women in the period; foreign visitors
comment on the fact that English women go to theatre unescorted and unmasked, and
a large proportion of the audience consisted of women. The puzzle here would be why
a culture that so severely regulated the lives of women in every other sphere suspended
its restrictions in the case of theatre. The fact of the large female audience must have
had important consequences for the development of English popular drama. It meant
that the success of any play was significantly dependent on the receptiveness of women;
and this in turn means that theatrical representations – whether of women or men or
anything else – also depended for their success to a significant degree on the receptiveness of women. When we see dramatic depictions of women in Elizabethan drama that
we consider degrading, it has become common to explain the fact by declaring them to
be male fantasies, and to point to the exclusively male stage to account for them. But

this cannot be correct: theatres are viable only insofar as they satisfy their audiences. The depictions must at the very least represent *cultural* fantasies, and women are implicated in them as well as men.[2]

Next, as I have indicated, it is in an important respect not quite true even to say that the English public stage was exclusively male. At least up to the 1530s there were public peformances of various kinds – civic pageants and guild plays – that demonstrably did include women. Elizabethan theatrical companies contained no women, but Italian troupes, which were family affairs and always included women, visited England from time to time and performed not only at court but throughout the country. When such performances took place in conjunction with royal progresses, and therefore under the queen's patronage, theatre became an extension of the court; and it may be relevant that on these occasions the theatre that included women would have been associated with the royal presence. Elizabeth's England, then, did in fact from time to time see women on the professional stage. What they apparently did not see was *English* women on the professional stage: the distinction they maintained was not between men and women but between "us" and "them" – what was appropriate for foreigners was not appropriate for the English, and women on display became increasingly associated with Roman Catholicism.

We can tell something about how the gender question was regarded by asking whether women are seen in English Renaissance plays as "them" rather than "us," as the Other. A case can certainly be made for this: there is a large component of male bonding in Shakespeare, what Eve Sedgwick calls the homosocial; and plays like *The Merry Wives of Windsor* and *Othello* certainly have powerful elements of the men against the women, though it is not at all clear, if we think of these plays in this way, who are "us" and who are "them" – the men in *The Merry Wives* lose hands down to the women, and the profound ambivalences of gender relationships have always proved notoriously disturbing to audiences in *Othello*.[3] Emilia on the relationships between the sexes

> 'Tis not a year or two shows us a man.
> They are all but stomachs and we all but food;
> They eat us hungerly, and when they are full,
> They belch us
>
> (iii.iv.103–6)

or,

> jealous souls will not be answered so;
> They are not ever jealous for the cause,
> But jealous for they're jealous
>
> (159–61)

certainly is not speaking as an outsider. In the context of *Othello*, this is the normative view, the one we are expected to agree with. But in a larger sense we would have to say that there are lots of Others, and Others of many kinds, in this theatre; in fact, Elizabethan drama is often dependent on otherness. Comedies are Italian, French or provincial, tragedies Spanish or Scandinavian or ancient; pastorals programmatically take place Somewhere Else. Dekker, Jonson and Middleton, placing comedies in contemporary London, are recognized as doing something new. The Other, for this theatre, is as much foreign as female – in their separate ways, both Othello and Portia are the Other. And in the largest sense, such figures are metonyms for theatre itself, the great Other functioning within society as both a threat and a refuge.[4]

But just as theatre is an Other that comes from and expresses the self, so the women of the Renaissance stage must be as much emanations of that self as the men are. Male and female are often presented within Renaissance culture as a binary opposition, opposites and complements; but how different are women from men? The difficulty of locating the differences is the subject of a wooing scene in George Wilkins' play *The Miseries of Enforced Marriage* (1607). A shy suitor named Scarborrow is engaged in his first interview with Clare, the woman he hopes to marry. Assuming that she will begin the conversation, he is disconcerted by her silence, which he registers as unfeminine:

> Scar: Prithee tell me: are you not a woman?
> Clare: I know not that neither, till I am better acquainted with a man.
> Scar: And how would you be acquainted with a man?
> Clare: To distinguish betwixt himself and myself.
> Scar: Why, I am a man.
> Clare: That's more than I know, sir.
> Scar: To approve that I am no less, thus I kiss thee.
> Clare: And by that proof I am a man too, for I have kissed you.[5]

The moment is parodic, but the joke depends on a truth: women are defined in this culture by their relation to men, yet the distinctions of gender are fluid and unclear.

Renaissance women are often described as commodities, whose marriages are arranged for the advantage or convenience of men, either their fathers, or the male authority figures in their and their prospective husbands' families. This is correct as far as it goes, but it does not distinguish women from men: alliances were normally arranged for sons just as for daughters – the distinction here is between fathers or guardians and children, not between the sexes; Early Modern England was a patriarchal society. Fantasies of freedom in Shakespeare tend to take the form of escapes from the tyranny of elders to a world where the children can make their own society, which usually means where they can arrange their own marriages – and thereby enjoy the benefits of the patriarchal structure, rather than suffer its liabilities. Whether this is conceived as ultimately benign and restorative, as in *A Midsummer Night's Dream, As You Like It, Twelfth Night, The Winter's Tale*, or disastrous, as in *Othello* and *Romeo and Juliet*, it works for women as well as men: the crucial element is the restrictive father, elder brother, guardian, not the sex of the child. Once on their own, Rosalind and Orlando, Lorenzo and Jessica are free to choose each other; whereas Bertram's marriage to Helena is no less constrained than the one proposed for Juliet to the County Paris. The problem is the father or the king or the structure of authority, not one's gender.

This is not to say that it is not preferable to be male in the Renaissance world: obviously it is; and though the women of Shakespearean comedy generally get what they want, the happy endings of *As You Like It* and *The Merchant of Venice* nevertheless promise significantly greater benefits to Orlando, Bassanio and Lorenzo than to their wives. Rosalind and Portia, for all their ingenuity, wit and charm, represent for their impecunious husbands not merely good conversation but place and fortune, and Jessica is all too openly equated with the money Lorenzo acquires with her. Would any of these marriages have constituted a happy ending had the wife not been rich? The defeat of patriarchy, in such cases, results only in its replication; it is to the point that the sole option imagined by the young in their quest for freedom is marriage – this is all that freedom permits, the transformation of the son into another patriarch. But the advantages of maleness in the culture as a whole were neither unqualified nor constant (they were considerably smaller for sons than for their fathers, and smaller still for younger sons than for the eldest); nor was patriarchy single and uninflected: the patriarchy of husbands conflicted with the patriarchy of fathers and elder brothers, and the patriarchy of the church and of the crown conflicted with both.

Let us consider gender issues in relation to generational issues. *The Winter's Tale* includes a particularly subversive version of that fantasy of freedom, the return to childhood. Leontes, after his first flash of violent jealousy, explains his distracted manner to Hermione and Polixenes in this way:

> Looking on the lines
> Of my boy's face, methoughts I did recoil
> Twenty-three years, and saw myself unbreeched,
> In my green velvet coat, my dagger muzzled,
> Lest it should bite its master, and so prove,
> As ornaments oft do, too dangerous.
>
> (1.ii.153–8)

The return to childhood is represented as a retreat from sexuality and the dangers of manhood exemplified in unmuzzled daggers. Leontes sees himself "unbreeched," not yet in breeches: Elizabethan children of both sexes were dressed in skirts until the age of seven or so; the "breeching" of boys was the formal move out of the common gender of childhood, which was both female in appearance and largely controlled by women, and into the world of men. This event was traditionally the occasion for a significant family ceremony.

The childhood world to which Leontes imagines himself returning has been described by his royal guest and inseparable childhood friend Polixenes as both Edenic and presexual:

> We were as twinned lambs that did frisk i'th'sun
> And bleat the one at th'other; what we changed
> Was innocence for innocence; we knew not
> The doctrine of ill-doing, nor dreamed
> That any did; had we pursued that life,
> And our weak spirits ne'er been higher reared
> With stronger blood, we should have answered heaven
> Boldly "not guilty," the imposition cleared
> Hereditary ours.

It is a world without vice or temptation, in which even original sin appears to have been dealt with. Significantly, there are no women in it, only the best friend, an emotional twin.

At this point Leontes' queen Hermione enters the fantasy with a pertinent observation:

> By this we gather
> You have tripped since.

Polixenes agrees; the fall from grace is a fall into sexuality:

> O my most sacred lady,
> Temptations have been born to 's, for
> In those unfledged days was my wife a girl;
> Your precious self had not yet crossed the eyes
> Of my young playfellow.

Hermione both protests and concurs:

> Of this make no conclusion, lest you say
> Your queen and I are devils. Yet go on,
> Th'offences we have made you do we'll answer,
> If you first sinned with us, and that with us
> You did continue fault, and that you slipped not
> With any but with us.
>
> (I.ii.66–86)

However good-natured their banter, Hermione's projected conclusion is the logical one: "your queen and I are devils." Her teasing view of marriage as a continuing state of sin with diabolical agents repeats the view of sexuality implicit in the men's fantasy.

It is a fantasy that is critical to the play, a determining feature of the subsequent tragic action. Critics for two hundred years have declared Leontes' paranoid jealousy inexplicable, but within the context of that dream of what it means to be a child, Leontes' behavior is not only understandable, it is in a way inevitable. No particular word or gesture is required to trigger Leontes' paranoid jealousy; the translation of the inseparable friend into the dangerous rival, and of the chaste wife into a whore, is implicit in the fantasy, its worst-case scenario, so to speak, replicating the situation Shakespeare had imagined with such detailed intensity in the Dark Lady sonnets. This is the consequence of women entering the world of male friendship. And when Leontes retreats from it he is retreating not only from women and sex: he is retreating from his place in one of the very few normative families in Shakespeare – families consisting of father, mother and children. Most families in Shakespeare have only one parent; the very few that include both parents generally have only one child, and when that configuration appears, it tends to be presented, as Leontes' marriage is presented, as exceedingly dangerous to the child: consider Juliet and her parents, Macduff and Lady Macduff, Coriolanus and Virgilia, Imogen with Cymbeline and his queen, the Duke and Duchess of York arguing about whether to denounce their son as a traitor. It is a configuration that, with the single exception of the Page family in *The Merry Wives of Windsor*, never appears in comedy.

Marriage is a dangerous condition in Shakespeare. We are always told that comedies end in marriages, and that this is normative. A few of Shakespeare's do, but the much more characteristic Shakespearean conclusion comes just before the marriage, and sometimes, as in *Love's Labour's Lost* and *Twelfth Night*, with an entirely unexpected delay or postponement. Plays that continue beyond the point where comedy ends, with the old fogies defeated and a happy marriage successfully concluded, depict the condition as utterly disastrous: *Romeo and Juliet*, *Othello*. Perhaps this is really the Shakespearean norm. Most Shakespearean marriages of longer duration are equally disheartening, with shrewishness, jealousy and manipulativeness the norm in comedy, and real destructiveness in tragedy: Oberon and Titania; the Merry Wives; Capulet and Lady Capulet; Hotspur and his wife; Claudius and Gertrude; Macbeth and Lady Macbeth; Cymbeline and his queen; Postumus and Imogen; Antigonus and Paulina. The open, trusting marriage of Brutus and Portia is all but unique in Shakespeare; the love of Macbeth and Lady Macbeth eventuates in female domination and effeminacy in a world where witchcraft is naturalized; and the only Shakespearean marriage that is presented specifically as sexually happy is that of Claudius and Gertrude, the incestuous union of a murderer and an adulteress. This is the dark side of the culture's institutionalization of marriage and patriarchy – what is striking is how little of the bright side Shakespeare includes. All the fun is in the wooing; what happens after marriage, between husbands and wives, parents and children, is a subject for tragedy.

In fact, loving relationships between men and women interest Shakespeare intensely, but not, on the whole, as husbands and wives. We might go on to say not even invariably as men and women: a significant group of plays require the woman to become a man for the wooing to be effected. The dangers of women in erotic situations, whatever they may be, can be disarmed by having the women play men, just as in the theatre the dangers of women on the stage (whatever *they* may be) can be disarmed by having men play the women. The interchangeability of the sexes is, on both the fictive and the material level, an assumption of this theatre.

What then is the difference between the sexes? On Shakespeare's stage it is a difference we would regard as utterly superficial, a matter of costumes and mannerisms; nevertheless, the superficies produce a difference that is absolute – gender disguises in this theatre are represented as all but impenetrable.[6] Indeed, the convention remains as powerful in the theatre of *Some Like It Hot* and *Tootsie* as in that of *Twelfth Night* and *Epicoene*. How relevant are the conventions of theatrical gender to those of culture and physiology? For us, they would seem to be hardly relevant at all: without the extra layer of travesty provided by the boy actor, the figure beneath the costume is the real thing – the whole point of the cross-dressing in *Some Like It Hot* and *Tootsie* is precisely for the audience to see through the impersonation, though the characters cannot. Ours is a theatre of named, known, and (most important for the purposes of this argument) gendered actors; to be seriously deceived by cross-gendered disguising is for us deeply disturbing, the stuff of classic horror movies like *Psycho*. We want to believe that the question of gender is settled, biological, controlled by issues of sexuality, and we claim to be quite clear about which sex is which – our genital organs, those inescapable facts, preclude any ultimate ambiguity. Hence, in Neil Jordan's *The Crying Game*, Jaye Davidson's impeccable femininity was demolished in an instant by the display of his penis, and after this point in the film he wore only male clothing ("for protection," as the film equivocally put it; but whose protection, his or ours?) A crucial element in the role was the fact that this was Jaye Davidson's first film – ambiguously named, he could play the role because he was totally unknown, which in this case means specifically that the sex of this actor was unknown. Sex for us is the bottom line, the ultimate truth of gender.

Or so we claim. Nevertheless, a modern father who urges his timid son to "be a man" is perfectly comprehensible, despite the fact that this commonplace exhortation assumes that masculinity is achieved not through biology but through an effort of will. We are fully the heirs of the Renaissance in this: Early Modern moralists continually reminded their charges that manhood was not a natural condition but a quality to be striven for and maintained only through constant vigilance, and even then with the utmost difficulty. There has always been a crucial behavioral element to gender that has nothing to do with the organs of generation.[7]

But for Renaissance physiology, even the distinction of the sexes could be blurred, sometimes frighteningly so. Gynecological treatises offered widely variant accounts of the etiology of gender, often concurrently and without any determination as to their relative likelihood, but the most persistent line of medical and anatomical thought from the time of Galen had cited homologies in the genital structure of the sexes to show that male and female were versions of the same unitary species.[8] In this view of sexuality, the female genitals were simply the male genitals inverted, and carried internally rather than externally. Sexual experience was conceived to be the same in both; during coitus, both not only experience orgasm but ejaculate, and female ejaculation with its component of female seed is just as necessary for conception as male ejaculation is. Both male and female seeds are present in every fetus; a fetus becomes male rather than female if the male seed is dominant, and generates enough heat to press the genital organs outward – if, that is, the fetus is stronger, with strength being conceived as heat.[9]

In this version of anatomical history, we all begin as female, and masculinity is a development out of and away from femininity.[10] Logically, therefore, the medical literature from Roman times onward confirms the theory by recording numerous cases of women completing the physiological process and turning into men under the pressure of some great exertion or excitement. The sixteenth-century physician Ambroise Paré's version of the thesis includes several modern cases. The most famous and recent, a shepherd named Germain Garnier, had been a woman named Marie until the age of fifteen, at which time, as she was chasing her pigs, her genitals turned inside out, transforming her from female to male.[11] Garnier was still alive in Montaigne's time, and though the story in Paré is presented as a case of simple physiology, Montaigne saw more than anatomy in it and used it as an example in his essay *Of the Power of the Imagination*. He is cagey about whether he actually met Garnier, though from an entry in his travel journal for 1580 it is clear that he did not,[12] but he briefly describes the man ("heavily bearded, and old, and not married"), and summarizes his history and the townspeople's accounts of him. The essayist's attitude toward the story is characteristically detached, but nothing in it suggests that he considers Garnier a fraud or doubts the authenticity of the transformation. Indeed, he has no difficulty naturalizing it, observing that "this sort of accident is frequently met with."[13]

Helkiah Crooke, whose *Mikrokosmographia* (1615) was the most compendious English synthesis of Renaissance anatomical knowledge, provides a striking testimony to the ambiguities of the science of gender in the period. Writing for an audience of physicians, Crooke presents a detailed discussion of the homological sex thesis, which he accepts with minor reservations, and then follows it with an entirely contradictory thesis in which women are not inverted versions of men at all, but are genuinely different and have their own kind of perfection, providing the human animal with substance and nurture, as the male provides it with form. Both theories have a long history of authority behind them; both derive ultimately from Aristotle, though the homological argument was associated principally with Galen.[14] Thus, in a chapter on the male genitals, Crooke explains women as incomplete men: "the Testicles in Men are larger, and of a hotter nature then in Women …; heat abounding in men thrusts them forth of the body, whereas in women they remain within, because their dull and sluggish heat is not sufficient to thrust them out," concluding that "the truth of this appeareth by manifold stories of such Women, whose more active and more operative heat have thrust out their Testicles, and of Women made them Men."[15] Ten pages later, introducing his discourse on the female genitals, Crooke is rhapsodic on the divine wisdom of anatomical homology:

> a woman is so much less perfect then a man by how much her heat is less and weaker then his; yet … is this imperfection turned unto perfection, because without the woman, mankind could not have been perfected by the perfecter sex.[16]

But fifty pages farther on Crooke is flatly denying the homology of male and female organs: "We must not think that the female is an imperfect male differing only in the position of the genitals."[17] Galen to the contrary notwithstanding, dissection shows that the clitoris differs significantly from the penis, "neither is there … any similitude between the bottom of the womb inverted, and the scrotum." As for the confirmatory stories of sudden sex change, he now declares "all of them monstrous" – that is, factual but not part of any normal process – "and some not credible."[18]

The ambiguity is in no way unusual in the period, nor is the fact that Crooke sees no need to reconcile the conflicting scientific arguments. He has, in effect, one theory when his attention is focused on men, another when it is focused on women; the latter, though it contradicts and, indeed, to post-Enlightenment eyes ought to preclude the former, does not, in Crooke's account, negate or even supersede it. The empirical evidence of dissection, which serves as the clinching argument in his account of the female condition, does not impinge in the slightest on his account of the male: the relevance of evidence is a function of the thesis being argued, not the other way round. Modern readers faced with so unambiguous a pronouncement as "all of them monstrous and some not credible" will doubtless want to insist that Crooke cannot have, a few pages earlier, really believed in "the truth … of women made … men." But Renaissance arguments rarely work in a way that seems to us neat and logical. Both theories are authoritative, each has its utility in explicating some part of the subject; each is produced not in the abstract, as part of a synthesis of gender theory, but at the appropriate moment in a discussion of physiology and behavior.

In the same way Sir Thomas Browne, like Crooke a practicing physician, was on the one hand empirically persuaded of the absolute distinction between the sexes. He writes in *Christian Morals* that "Men and Women have their proper Virtues and Vices, and even Twins of different sexes have not only distinct coverings in the Womb, but differing qualities and Virtuous Habits after"; and this leads him to a plea to maintain the separation of the genders in society: "transplace not their Proprieties and confound not their Distinctions."[19] In *Pseudodoxia Epidemica* he asserts that his empirical knowledge of anatomy has convinced him that Galen was wrong about the male and female organs being inverted versions of each other, "the testicles being so seated in the female, that they admit not of protrusion; and the neck of the matrix wanting those parts which are discoverable in the organ of virility."[20]

Against this utter conviction of the integrity and immutability of the genders, however, we find the equally complete assurance of this passage from the same chapter of *Pseudodoxia Epidemica*:

> As for the mutation of sexes, or transition into one another, we cannot deny it in Hares, it being observable in Man. For hereof beside Empedocles or Tiresias, there are not a few examples: and though very few, or rather none which have emasculated or turned into women, yet very many who from an esteem or reality of being women have infallibly proved Men ... And that not only mankind, but many other Animals may suffer this transexion, we will not deny, or hold it at all impossible.

Beside this paragraph Browne has placed the marginal gloss, "Transmutation of Sexes, viz. of Women into Men, granted."[21]

Granted! Women are totally different from men from before the moment of birth, even in the womb, and their genital organs "admit not of protrusion," yet the possibility of their transformation into men goes without saying. The only sticking point is the question of whether the process can be reversed, and men turn into women; it is this that is judiciously declared to be, if not impossible, at least so rare as to be negligible (there are "very few, or rather none"). Those transformations that are attested to as scientific fact only work in one direction, from female to male, which is conceived to be upward, toward completion. But these are for Browne, as for Montaigne, Ambroise Paré, and much of the time for Helkiah Crooke, facts.

As for the other part of Helkiah Crooke's convictions about gender, in which women are not versions of men but develop in their own way and are equally complete beings, it sounds like a blow for freedom, but for all its air of empiricism and modern good sense, it is no more advanced scientifically than the homological theory: both ultimately derive their authority from Aristotle, and the crucial empirical evidence comes not from Crooke's own dissections, but from the reports of the French anatomist André du Laurens, one of his principal modern sources – the account is carefully and frequently punctuated with the parenthetical "(saith Laurentius)"; Crooke is only rarely bold enough to venture a "methinks." It is clear that this is a scientist for whom authority weighs a great deal more heavily than empiricism. In any case, the denial of female imperfection implied little that was beneficial to women within the structures of Renaissance authority; women were still, by nature, firmly ensconced below men in the hierarchy. Throughout the age, and despite the increasing evidence provided by the study of anatomy, outside the professional scientific community homology remained the predominant theory – as, for example, in *The Roaring Girl* the transvestite Moll Cutpurse is accounted for by explaining that "her birth began / Ere she was all made": both her femininity and her desire to be male are functions of her incompleteness.[22]

Needless to say, the persistence of homology has little to do with science. Renaissance ideology had a vested interest in defining women in terms of men; the aim is thereby to establish the parameters of maleness, not of womanhood. This is why Crooke abandons the homological thesis when he turns to the specifics of the female anatomy; to define the nature of women, it is not useful. As we have seen, the scientific truth or falsehood of either theory is not at issue – the two claims are parts of two different arguments, and they are not in competition. All such claims, of course, are not merely scientific, but imply (like the scientific claims of all eras including our own) a political agenda. The homology cited from Galen onward is only anatomical; the notion that women are versions of men is no more egalitarian than the notion that women are anatomically independent. Most of the scholastic opinion codified by Ian Maclean in *The Renaissance Notion of Women* assumes the correctness of the homological thesis, but nevertheless stresses the differences between men and women, not their similarities, and these are invariably prejudicial. Women are less intelligent, more passionate, less in control of their affections, and so forth. The difference in degree of perfection becomes in practical terms a powerful difference in kind, and the homological arguments are used to justify the whole range of male domination over women. Subjectivity, in this line of reasoning, is always masculine – indeed, Judith Butler observes that the binary opposition of male and female is "itself a ruse for the monologic elaboration of the masculine."[23]

The frightening part of the teleology for the Renaissance mind, however, is precisely the fantasy of its reversal, the "very few, or rather none" of Sir Thomas Browne: the conviction that men can turn into – or be turned into – women; or perhaps more exactly, can be turned *back* into women, losing the strength that enabled the male potential to be realized in the first place. In this version of the medical literature we all start as women, and the culture confirmed this by dressing all children in skirts until the age of seven or so, when the boy, as Leontes recalls, was "breeched," or put into pants, removed from the care of women, and began to be trained as a man.[24] From this point on, for a man to associate with women was felt to be increasingly dangerous – not only for the woman, but even more for the man: lust effeminates, makes men incapable of manly pursuits; hence the pervasive antithesis of love and war. Thomas Wright, in *The Passions of the Mind in General*, warning against the dangers of love, writes that "a personable body is often linked with a pestilent soul; a valiant Captain in the field for the most part is infected with an effeminate affection at home."[25] The effeminate affection is his passion for women; similarly Romeo, berating himself for his unwillingness to harm Tybalt, cries out,

> O sweet Juliet,
> Thy beauty hath made me effeminate,
> And in my temper softened valor's steel!
> (iii.i.118–20).

Such formulations are all but axiomatic in the period, and the word "effeminate," over and over, serves the basic explanatory function in them. Women are dangerous to men because sexual passion for women renders men effeminate: this is an age in which sexuality itself is misogynistic, as the love of women threatens the integrity of the perilously achieved male identity. Robert Burton elucidates the matter with uncharacteristic directness: love is "full of fear, anxiety, doubt, care, peevishness, suspicion, it turns a man into a woman."[26] The fear of effeminization is a central element in all discussions of what constitutes a "real man" in the period, and the fantasy of the reversal of the natural transition from woman to man underlies it. It also, in a much more clearly pathological way, underlies the standard arguments against the stage in antitheatrical tracts from the time of the Church Fathers on. In this context, the very institution of theatre is a threat to manhood and the stability of the social hierarchy, as unescorted women and men without their wives socialize freely, and (it follows) flirt with each other and take each other off to bed: the association of theatre with sex is absolutely pervasive in these polemics.

But in England, the sexuality feared is more subversive than even this suggests, precisely because of the transvestism of the stage. It is argued first that the boys who perform the roles of women will be transformed into their roles and play the part in reality. This claim has its basis in a Platonic argument, but in the Puritan tracts it merges with a general fear of blurred social and sexual boundaries, of roles and costumes adulterating the essences that God has given us. Jonas Barish, in his exhaustive and indispensable study of the antitheatrical material, relates the hostility to transvestite actors to the synchronous revival of medieval sumptuary laws, the attempt to prevent members of one social class from appearing to be members of another (thus tradesmen were enjoined from wearing silk), and he quotes William Perkins to the effect that "wanton and excessive apparel ... maketh a confusion of such degrees and callings as God hath ordained." "Distinctions of dress," Barish comments, "however external and theatrical they may seem to us, for Perkins virtually belong to our essence, and may no more be tampered with than that essence itself."[27] This is certainly the way the polemicists view the situation; but it is precisely the essence that is the problem. What *is* our God-given essence, that it can be transformed by the clothes we wear? Philip Stubbes, in a passage that bears directly on the question of transvestite actors, deplores a current (and recurrent) fashion of masculine dress for women. "Our apparel," he says, "was given us as a sign distinctive to discern betwixt sex and sex, and therefore one to wear the apparel of another sex is to participate with the same, and to adulterate the verity of his own kind. Wherefore these women may not improperly be called *Hermaphroditi*, that is, monsters of both kinds, half women, half men."[28] It is the fragility, the radical instability of our essence, that is assumed here, and the metamorphic quality of our sinful nature. The enormous popularity of Ovid in the age reflects both its desires and its deepest fears.

But the argument against transvestite actors warns of an even more frightening metamorphosis than the transformation of the boy into a monster of both kinds. Male spectators, it is argued, will be seduced by the impersonation, and losing their reason will become effeminate, which in this case means not only that they will lust after the woman in the drama, which is bad enough, but also after the youth beneath the woman's costume, thereby playing the woman's role themselves. This fear, which has been brilliantly anatomized by Laura Levine,[29] is so pervasive in the tracts, and so unlike modern kinds of sexual anxiety, that it is worth pausing over.

John Rainoldes says the adoption by men of women's clothing incites a lust that is specifically homoerotic:

> what sparkles of lust to that vice the putting of women's attire on men may kindle in unclean affections, as Nero showed in Sporus, Heliogabalus in himself; yea certain, who grew not to such excess of impudency, yet arguing the same in causing their boys to wear long hair like women.

Scripture, he continues, condemns prostitution of both women and men, "detesting specially the male by terming him a *dog*," and concludes by urging that we "control likewise the means and occasions whereby men are transformed into dogs, the sooner to cut off all incitements to that beastly filthiness, or rather more than beastly."[30] Marginal glosses refer the reader to biblical and classical instances of sodomy, homosexual sadism and homosexual marriage. The slippage here from effeminacy to bestiality is notable, and should remind us that in this culture femininity is not equated with docility – on the contrary, what is feared in women is their violent and uncontrollable appetites.

Subsequently, citing the authority of Socrates, Rainoldes compares the homoerotic response engendered by transvestite boys to the sting of poisonous spiders: "if they do but touch men only with their mouth, they put them to wonderful pain and make them mad: so beautiful boys by kissing do sting and pour secretly in a kind of poison."[31] Here the attraction of men to beautiful boys is treated as axiomatic. But this in fact is only the prelude to a much more vehement tirade against the universal sexuality evoked by theatre, a lust not distinguished by the gender of its object:

> can wise men be persuaded that there is no wantonness in the players' parts when experience showeth (as wise men have observed) that men are made adulterers and enemies of all chastity by coming to such plays? that senses are moved, affections are delighted, hearts though strong and constant are vanquished by such players? that an effeminate stage-player, while he faineth love, imprinteth wounds of love?

The effeminate stage player here is the agent of a universal effeminacy. William Prynne goes a step farther, localizing and particularizing the sexuality. In *Histriomastix* the transvestitism of the stage is especially dangerous because female dress is an important stimulant specifically to homoeroticism: the "male priests of Venus" satisfy their companions, the "passive beastly sodomites in Florida," by wearing women's clothes, the "better to elicit, countenance, act and color their unnatural execrable uncleannesses."[32] Heterosexuality here only provides the fetish that enables the true homosexual response to emerge. It is significant that the transvestite is not the passive one in this relationship.

Rainoldes, Prynne and any number of other antitheatrical writers offer observations such as these as models for the theatrical experience. For such writers, the very fact that women are prohibited from the stage reveals the true etiology of theatre: what the spectator is "really" attracted to in plays is an undifferentiated sexuality, a sexuality that does not distinguish men from women and reduces men to women – the deepest fear in antitheatrical tracts, far deeper than the fear that women in the audience will become whores, is the fear of a universal effeminization. In this anxiety, the fact of transvestite boys is really only incidental; it is the whole concept of the mimetic art that is at issue, the art itself that effeminates. The growth of desire through the experience of theatre is a sinister progression: the play excites the spectator, and sends him home to "perform" himself; the result is sexual abandon with one's wife, or more often with any available woman (all women at the playhouse being considered available), or worst of all, the spectator begins by lusting after a female character, but ends by having sex with the man she "really" is. Philip Stubbes gives a particularly clear statement of this anxiety: "the fruits of plays and interludes" are, he says, that after theatre, "everyone brings another homeward of their way very friendly, and in their secret conclaves, covertly, they play the sodomites or worse."[33] The sodomites in this case are probably not homoerotic, since Stubbes elsewhere in the tract uses sodomy to refer to heterosexual fornication – though this may be giving Stubbes too much credit for consistency, a quality not otherwise much in evidence in the work. Jonathan Goldberg argues persuasively, however, that homosexual activity is well beyond the power of Stubbes' imagination.[34] But Prynne takes the logical next step, citing this passage as a proof of the specifically homoerotic character of the stage:

> Yea, witness ... M. Stubbes, his *Anatomy of Abuses* ... where he affirms that players and play-haunters in their secret conclaves play the sodomites; together with some modern examples of such, who have been desperately enamored with players' boys thus clad in woman's apparel, so far as to solicit them by words, by letters, even actually to abuse them ... This I have heard credibly reported of a scholar of Bailliol College, and I doubt not but it may be verified of divers others.[35]

The assumption here is first that the basic form of response to theatre is erotic, second that erotically, theatre is uncontrollably exciting, and third, that the basic, essential form of erotic excitement in men is homosexual – that indeed, women are only a cover for men. And though the assumption as Prynne articulates it is clearly pathological, a *reductio ad absurdum* of antitheatrical commonplaces, it is also clearly related both to all the generalized anxieties attendant upon the institutionalization of masculinity within the culture, and to the sanctioned homoeroticism that played so large a role in relationships between men.

Notes

1. The most significant recent exception, and an excellent discussion of the issues involved, is Phyllis Rackin's "Androgyny, Mimesis, and the Marriage of the Boy Heroine on the English Renaissance Stage," *PMLA* 102 (1987), pp. 29–41.
2. The pioneering work on the subject is Jean Howard's "Cross-Dressing, the Theatre, and Gender Struggle in Early Modern England," *Shakespeare Quarterly* 39: 4 (1988), pp. 418–40.
3. See the excellent discussion by Carol Thomas Neely, *Broken Nuptials in Shakespeare's Plays* (New Haven, 1985), especially pp. 105–35.
4. On the idea of the Elizabethan theatre as a literal displacement, see Steven Mullaney, *The Place of the Stage* (Chicago, 1988), *passim*.
5. Malone Society Reprints, 1963, Glenn H. Blayney, ed., lines 208–15. The passage is modernized.
6. The notable Shakespearean exception is Falstaff's disguise as an old woman in *The Merry Wives of Windsor*.

7   The essential discussion of the gender assumptions of modern biology and physiology is Donna Haraway's *Primate Visions* (London and New York, 1989). Coppélia Kahn analyzes the anxieties inherent in Renaissance notions of masculinity in *Man's Estate: Male Identity in Shakespeare* (Berkeley, 1980). On the problematic relation between sex and gender, see especially Valerie Traub, "The (in)significance of lesbian desire in early modern England," in Susan Zimmerman, ed., *Erotic Politics* (London and New York, 1992), pp. 151 ff., and Judith Butler, *Gender Trouble* (London and New York, 1990), pp. 6–17.

8   For Jacobean England, the authoritative compendium of anatomical and sexual knowledge was Helkiah Crooke's Μικροκοσμογραφια. *A Description of the Body of Man* (London, 1615), cited below; my summary of the Renaissance physiology of sex is based principally on Crooke, which in turn is a synthesis of standard authorities. I have also been guided by the work of Ian Maclean, *The Renaissance Notion of Woman* (Cambridge, 1983); Audrey Eccles, *Obstetrics and Gynecology in Tudor and Stuart England* (Kent, O. 1982); and Thomas Laqueur, *Making Sex* (Cambridge, MA, 1990), especially chapters 3 and 4.

9   Such an etiology is not unknown in nature. The sex of alligators is determined by the heat at which the eggs are incubated: if it is 90°F or over, they are male, if 87°F or under, they are female. On the question of whether at 88°F or 89°F they become androgynes, the authorities are silent.

10   This sounds like a Renaissance ideological fantasy, but it is a view that was firmly maintained by modern biology until 1993, when geneticists finally discovered that there is a gene for femaleness. The New York *Times* reported that

the new work contradicts one of the verities of the sex determination field – that the default mode of a fetus is female, and that it takes the addition of the maleness gene to transform the primal female into a boy. By this notion, the building of a female is a passive business, one that will occur in the absence of any particular signal, while putting together a boy demands the input of the SRY [the gene of masculinity]. (30 August 1994, p. C1)

11   Ambroise Paré, *On Monsters and Marvels*, trans. Janis L. Pallister (Chicago, 1982), pp. 31–2.

12   The French is "je peuz voir," either "I was able to see" or "I could have seen" Garnier. Most English translations (though not the recent version by Donald Frame) take Montaigne to mean the former. For readers of Florio's Elizabethan translation, Montaigne "hapned to meet" Garnier. The travel journal, unpublished until two centuries after Montaigne's death, is included in *The Complete Works of Montaigne*, trans. Donald M. Frame (Standford, 1948); the story of Marie Germain is on p. 870. Patricia Parker has a superb analysis of the episode and its implications in "Gender Ideology, Gender Change: The Case of Marie Germain," *Critical Inquiry* 19 (Winter 1993), pp. 337–64.

13   Montaigne, *Of the Power of the Imagination, Essays*, book 1, 21; in Donald Frame's translation, p. 69.

14   The conflicting classical theories are called *epigenesis*, which holds that sex differentiation is a product of the development of the fetus, and *preformationism*, which views sex as determined at the moment of conception by the nature of the impregnating sperm. For summaries of the ancient controversy, see Michael Boylan, "Galen's Conception Theory," *Journal of the History of Biology* 19: 1 (Spring 1986), and Anthony Preus, "Galen's Criticism of Aristotle's Conception Theory," *Journal of the History of Biology* 10: 1 (Spring 1977), pp. 65–85.

15   Crooke, Μικροκοσμογραφια, p. 204.

16   Ibid., pp. 216–17.

17   Ibid., p. 271.

18   Ibid., p. 250.

19   Browne, *Christian Morals*, part I, section 31.

20   *Pseudodoxia Epidemica*, in Geoffrey Keynes, ed., *The Works of Sir Thomas Browne* (London, 1928), vol. I, 246.

21   Ibid., pp. 243–4.

22 Middleton and Dekker, *The Roaring Girl*, Revels Plays edition, ed. Paul Mulholland (Manchester, 1987), i.ii.129–30.

23 Butler, *Gender Trouble*, p. 18.

24 This is not to say that there were no differences between the dress of boys and girls before the breeching, only that the move into manhood for boys was the move from skirts to breeches.

25 Thomas Wright, *The Passions of the Mind in General*, ed. W. W. Newbold (New York, 1986), p. 237.

26 Robert, Burton, *The Anatomy of Melancholy*, 3.2.4.1 (London, 1660; p. 510).

27 Jonas Barish, *The Antitheatrical Prejudice* (Berkeley, 1981), p. 92.

28 Ibid.

29 Laura Levine, *Men in Women's Clothing: Anti-theatricality and Effeminization, 1579 to 1642* (Cambridge, 1994). In what follows I am, in part, summarizing Levine's argument.

30 John Rainoldes, *Th'Overthrow of Stage Playes* ([Middleburg] 1599), p. 11. Here and subsequently the quotations have been modernized. The biblical passage cited is Deut. 23:17–18, rendered in the Authorized Version: "There shall be no whore of the daughters of Israel, nor a sodomite of the sons of Israel. Thou shalt not bring the hire of a whore, or the price of a dog, into the house of the Lord thy God for any vow: for even both these are abomination unto the Lord thy God." The original text concerns temple prostitutes – the words translated "whore" and "sodomite," in Hebrew *k'deshah* and *kadesh*, both derive from the word for "holy"; this is one of a number of prohibitions against the Israelites participating in pagan cults. Translators differed widely over the word the King James scholars render "sodomite," and it was not invariably, or even usually, taken to connote homosexuality. The Geneva Bible reads "There shall be no whore of the daughters of Israel, neither shall there be a whorekeeper of the sons of Israel"; the term in the Vulgate is "scortator," whoremonger or fornicator. As for the dog, *The Interpreters Bible* glosses it "from the context evidently an opprobrious name for a male sacred prostitute" (vol. II, 471). It will be noted that, even in Rainoldes' reading, the passage does not prohibit patronizing whores, whether female or male, it only prohibits Israelites from engaging in the profession – the practice of prostitution is reserved to Gentiles.

31 Rainoldes, *Th'Overthrow of Stage Playes*, p. 18.

32 William Prynne, *Histriomastix* (London, 1633), p. 209.

33 Philip Stubbes, *Anatomy of Abuses* (1585), sig. L8v.

34 Jonathan Goldberg, *Sodometries* (Stanford, 1992), p. 121. What then is implied by "or worse" – what can be worse than playing the sodomite? If the sodomy here were in fact homosexual, then it would be the sodomized who is worse than the sodomite, the passive partner in the act. Goldberg suggests, unpersuasively, that the distinction is between playing the sodomite and being a sodomite; more helpfully he proposes that "sodomy is a debauched playing that knows no limit … or whose limit can only be gestured towards in a supplementary addition." I imagine that, more simply, Stubbes names the worst thing he can imagine, but leaves room for the unimaginable things that are worse.

35 Prynne, *Histriomastix*, pp. 211–12.

38

The Secret Sharer

Bruce R. Smith

At first reading, the situation in the first nineteen sonnets seems straightforward enough: the poet, old enough to know the ravages that time can wreak on beauty, urges a younger male friend to brave Time's tyranny by marrying and begetting children. The speaker and his friend exist in a social universe of two, in a world divided between "you" and "me." Thus, in sonnet 15 ("When I consider every thing that growes / Holds in perfection but a little moment") the speaker describes his own way of defying Time, by creating poems that "counterfeit" the friend's beauty; in sonnet 16 ("But wherefore do not you a mightier waie / Make warre upon this bloudie tirant time") the speaker turns to the young man and suggests the "mightier way" in which *he* can defy Time, by procreating living images of himself in "lines of life" that will outdo the persona's "pupil pen." All of the early sonnets turn on this separateness of speaker and friend. Speaking across that great divide, the persona defines for his friend a particular sexuality, one way out of many possible ways of conceptualizing sexual desire. The botanical images Shakespeare uses in sonnet 16 are typical of all nineteen sonnets in the opening sequence:

> Now stand you on the top of happy hours,
> And many maiden gardens yet unset,
> With virtuous wish would bear your living flowers,
> Much liker than your painted counterfeit.
>
> (16.5–8)

Again and again in these early poems the friend's beauty is imaged as a flower (1, 5, 6, 12, 18); his youthfulness, as morning (7), as spring and summer (1, 3, 5, 6, 13, 18), as the Golden Age in Ovid's account of creation ("this thy golden time," 3.12). The sexual vitality of these images is strongest, perhaps, in sonnets 5 ("Those howers that with gentle worke did frame, / The lovely gaze where every eye doth dwell") and 6 ("Then let not winter's wragged hand deface, / In thee thy summer ere thou be distil'd"), where the friend's semen is likened to perfume with which he should "make sweet some viall" (6.3).

As we have seen more than once in connection with Spenser, this was a vision of sexuality supremely satisfying to the Elizabethan imagination: by relating human sexual activity to the regenerative cycle of nature this particular way of imagining sexual desire fuses the physical and the philosophical. In political terms it subordinates individual desire to a higher authority, to the divinely ordained scheme of the universe. The Epithalamion that Spenser wrote for his own marriage, for example, lovingly describes, stanza by stanza, all the activities of the wedding day, culminating in the elaborate ceremonies of preparing bride, bridegroom, and bedchamber that were one of the most sociable features of sixteenth-century weddings. When the guests have all departed and he turns to the physical initiation of his bride and himself, Spenser casts the climactic rite in the same vegetative images that define sexuality in Shakespeare's first nineteen sonnets. He invokes, first, Diana, goddess of the moon that shines through the bed-chamber window, goddess of chastity, goddess of "wemens labours"; then Juno, goddess of wedlock; then Genius, the patron of generation,

> in whose gentle hand
> The bridale bowre and geniall bed remaine,
> Without blemish or staine,
> And the sweet pleasures of theyr loves delight
> With secret ayde doest succour and supply,
> Till they bring forth the fruitfull progeny.[1]

Spenser in his Epithalamion and Shakespeare in his first nineteen sonnets succeed in the one thing that commentators like Landino were most anxious to do in their readings of Latin love poetry: to combine the physical, philosophical, and political aspects of sexual desire into a viable whole. In Foucault's terms, they have coordinated structures of ideology and power with individual feeling to produce a discourse about sex that was intellectually and emotionally compelling to sixteenth-century readers.

In Shakespeare's first nineteen sonnets, if not in Spenser's Epithalamion, the harmony among ideology, power, and feeling is less settled than it first appears. Discordant questions about power and its relationship to feeling are left unresolved. As gestures of rhetoric, Shakespeare's early sonnets seem to be selfless attempts on the persona's part to convince the young friend of a more experienced vision of sexual desire – a view that sees desire in a wider frame of time than an adolescent can. In that sense each sonnet is a gesture of power directed toward two objects: toward time and toward the friend. The couplet of sonnet 15 nicely catches this complexity: "And all in war with Time for love of you / As he takes from you, I engraft you new" (15.11–12).

Many readers have noted the pun here on "engraft": it suggests the Greek root graphein, "to write," at the same time that it sets up the images of horticultural grafting in the next sonnet. Shakespeare's early sonnets are an attempt to impose his vision simultaneously on time and on the friend. Despite the pun, sonnets 15 and 16 keep the two senses of "engraft" entirely separate: the poet creates, the friend procreates. The persona himself keeps his distance from sexual desire. And that is exactly where most editors and critics since Malone have tried to keep him. Then comes sonnet 20:

A Woman's face with natures own hand painted,
Haste thou the Master Mistris of my passion,
A womans gentle hart but not acquainted
With shifting change as is false womens fashion,
An eye more bright than theirs, lesse false in rowling:
Gilding the object where-upon it gazeth,
A man in hew all *Hews* in his controwling,
Which steales mens eyes and womens soules amaseth.
And for a woman wert thou first created,
Till nature as she wrought thee fell a dotinge,
And by addition me of thee defeated,
By adding one thing to my purpose nothing.
    But since she prickt thee out for womens pleasure,
    Mine be thy love and thy loves use their treasure.

With this poem four things change dramatically: the ends to which the poet speaks, the language that he uses, the imaginative setting in which he situates himself, and the self-identity he assumes.

Quite suddenly, hortatory verse starts sounding like amatory verse. A reader who is out for secrets is forced to reconsider what he or she has read already. As Pequigney argues, we can see in the first twenty sonnets a progression in which the poet's sexual feelings for the friend, held carefully in check at first, gradually emerge as the poet's real subject. Homosocial desire changes by degrees into homosexual desire. The word "love" first enters the sonnets very obliquely indeed when the poet appeals to the friend's "selfe love" as a motive for begetting progeny (3.8). In sonnet 5 love is still a property of the friend, though more ambiguously so, when the poet remarks "the lovely gaze where every eye doth dwell" (5.2). The personal significance of that word for the poet becomes increasingly clear – and increasingly physical – as he begs the friend to have a child, to create another self "for love of me" (10.13), as he ventures to call him "love" (13.1) and "deare my love" (13.11), as he goes to war with time "for love of you" (15.13), as he defies time to carve wrinkles in "my loves faire brow" (19.9), as he boasts "My love shall in my verse ever live young" (19.14). Is "my love" in this line a name for the friend, or does it refer to the poet's feelings?

"Love" and "my love" emerge after sonnet 13 as the poet's favorite epithets for the young man. Speaking to him and speaking about him, the poet refers to the young man by that title more than twenty times. Only seven times does the poet refer to him as his "friend." "Love," "lover," and "lovely," as Booth points out, were ambiguous if not ambivalent in sixteenth- and seventeenth-century usage. They might or might not suggest sexual desire, depending on the context.[2] The context in Shakespeare's sonnets is, to say the least, equivocal. "Love," on equal terms with "mistress," is likewise how the poet speaks to and about the woman who is the subject of the 27 sonnets printed toward the end in Thorpe's edition. Only once does he call her his "friend." We have, then, two people – and three terms for talking about them. At one extreme is "mistress," with its explicitly sexual reference. At the other extreme is "friend," with its largely nonsexual reference. In between is "love," which can be sexual, or nonsexual, or both. "Two loves I have," declares the poet in sonnet 144,

of comfort and dispaire,
Which like two spirits do sugiest me still,
The better angell is a man right faire:
The worser spirit a woman collour'd il.
(144.1–4)

We do no more than respect an ambiguity in early modern English if we follow Shakespeare's example and refer to the young man, not as the poet's "friend," but as his "love."

Questions about love reach a crisis – for the poet, for his readers, and presumably for the young man – in sonnet 20. The issue here is easy enough to state but not so easy to decide: is sonnet 20 a *denial* of sexual desire, or is it an *avowal*? The *literal sense* of what the poet says certainly indicates denial. "Love" versus "love's use": the terms the poet / speaker uses to draw his distinctions derive from Aristotle's *Nicomachean Ethics*. *Philia*, the highest of human bonds, is premised on the *equality* of men as one another's peer; *eros*, a lesser bond, thrives on *inequality*, on needs that each partner fulfills for the other. All of the preceding sonnets, we see in retrospect, have been arguments in an implicit debate. In effect, Shakespeare has been addressing the great question in classical ethics that is posed so often in Shakespeare's comedies about courtship: which has the greater claim on a man, friendship with other men or sexual ties with women? The procreational images of the first nineteen sonnets would seem to place the poet / speaker of the first nineteen sonnets squarely with Daphnaeus, the spokesman in Plutarch's dialogue "Of Love" who urges Bacchon to marry. When Daphnaeus says of marriage that there is "no knot or link in the world more sacred and holy," Protogenes, the critic of women and praiser of pederasty, counters with the "higher" values of male friendship:

This bond in trueth of wedlocke ... as it is necessary for generation is by good right praised by Polititians and law-givers, who recommend the same highly unto the people and common multitude: but to speake of true love indeed, there is no jot or part thereof in the societie and felowship of women ... For amitie is an honest, civill and laudable thing: but fleshly pleasure, base, vile, and illiberal.[3]

Here is just the distinction between "love" and "love's use" that Shakespeare draws in sonnet 20. In Plutarch's dialogue, Bacchon's marriage transpires during the very time the debaters are having their argument, making their conclusion – or rather their lack of one – a moot point.

In sonnet 20 the issue is likewise left unresolved. *What* Shakespeare's speaker says is above reproach; *how* he says it has left many readers since George Steevens uneasy, whatever Edmund Malone may have said to reassure them. There is something playfully salacious about those puns on "thing" and "prick" that distinctly recalls Richard Barnfield's poems. Indeed, the whole conceit of sonnet 20, casting a male in the role most sonnets would assign to a female, recalls Barnfield's sonnet 11 ("Sighing, and sadly sitting by my Love, / He ask't the cause of my hearts sorrowing"). In Shakespeare's sonnet 20, as so often in Barnfield, sexual innuendo seems to be working at cross purposes to moral innocence. To lament that the friend has "one thing to my purpose no-thing" might seem to imply that friendship and sexual passion, "love" and "love's use," are two separate things. The tone, however, makes one wonder just what the persona's "purpose" is. Does he find other parts of the beloved's anatomy more commodious? If Shakespeare is citing Plutarch, he calls him to witness on both sides of the case.

Shakespeare's speaker may side with Plutarch's Daphneus on the issue of "love" versus "love's use," but he echoes Protogenes, Plutarch's homosexual apologist, when it comes to which kind of beauty is superior, male or female. The diptych that sonnet 20 forms with sonnet 21 is hinged on a contrast between the young man's fresh face "with natures own hand painted" (20.1) and the "painted beauty" (21.2) that inspires the muses of most other poets. The implied contrast *within* both poems is between male and female, as it may be also *between* them. Male beauty is superior to female, according to Plutarch's Protogenes, for just the reasons Shakespeare's speaker cites: "it is not besmered with sweet ointments, nor tricked up and trimmed, but plaine and simple alwaies a man shall see it, without any intising allurements" (fol. 1133). Whatever suspicions a reader may have about the sonnet's tone are encouraged by the capitalizations and italics in Thorpe's edition. "Woman," "Master Mistris," and "*Hews*" are all tricked out as possible code words, as possible keys to a closely guarded secret that has been hinted at since "beauties *Rose*" in sonnet 1. The tone of sonnet 20, so troubling to modern readers, seems perfectly consonant with the myths we have been exploring in this book. In its social, narrative, and rhetorical contexts, sonnet 20 comes across as an extremely sophisticated version of "Come live with me and be my love."

There is a sense, then, in which the early sonnets are gestures of power not just toward time and toward the friend but toward the poet's own self: they are attempts to convince not only the friend but the persona himself that the cosmic heterosexuality exemplified in Spenser's Epithalamion has highest claims on erotic desire. They argue Elizabethan orthodoxy. For the friend, the early sonnets are poems of persuasion; for the persona, they are poems of renunciation. The whole scenario here seems uncannily similar to Barnfield's eclogues. We encounter the same pair of characters, the same implied setting, the same double sense of time, the same tension between conventional and unconventional sexualities. Like Barnfield's Daphnis toward the end of the eclogues, Shakespeare's persona in the first nineteen sonnets speaks as an older man to a younger, as experience to innocence, as disciplined desire to overpowering beauty. Both speakers counsel marriage. Implicit, perhaps, in Shakespeare's luxuriant images of flowers and trees is the pastoral landscape in which Barnfield plays out his erotic fantasies to their ultimately chaste end. There is the same sharply divided attitude toward time: both poets celebrate the pleasures of morning, of spring, of "this thy golden time," but both are just as keenly conscious of time's destructive power. Finally, both sets of poems turn on the same conflict between male-male attachments and heterosexual passion. That is to say, Shakespeare's early sonnets, like Barnfield's eclogues and sonnets, enact the rites of wooing that make up the Myth of the Passionate Shepherd.

Sonnet 20 may be a poem of courtship, but Shakespeare does not stop there. Like Horace, but unlike most Renaissance poets who write about love, Shakespeare goes on to write about what happens when emotional desire becomes physical act. John Donne's love poems, infamous as they may be in this regard, are all about the before

("Come, Madame, come, ... / Off with that girdle") and the after ("Busie old foole, / unruly Sunne, / Why dost thou thus, / Through windowes, and through curtaines call on us?").[4] They *imply* the physical and emotional realities of lovemaking, but they do not talk about them directly. Those emotional and physical realities are Shakespeare's very subject in the poems that succeed sonnet 20. Quite in keeping with all the other ways in which the sonnets play off experience itself against the words that would inscribe it, sexual experience in the sonnets resides largely in puns. Many of the puns that Stephen Booth has caught and cataloged occur not just once, in individual sonnets, but are sustained through the whole sequence: "have" (52.14, 87.13, 110.9–12, 129.6), "use" (2.9, 4.7, 6.5, 20.14, 40.6, 48.3, 78.3, 134.10), "will" (for male and female sexual organs as well as for sexual desire: 57.13, 112.3, 134.2, 135.passim, 136.passim, 143.13, 154.9), "pride" (for penis: 64.2, 52.12, 151.9–11), and "all" (for penis, likely by analogy with "awl": 26.8, 75.9–14, 109.13–14). As heard by Booth, the couplet to sonnet 109 embodies something more substantial than sentiment:

> For nothing this wide Universe I call,
> Save thou my Rose, in it thou art my all.
> (109.13–14)

"All" or "no-thing": when it comes to homosexual puns, most academic readers of Shakespeare's sonnets have insisted on the nothing. Booth gallantly tries to have it both ways, noting the possibility of homosexual doubles entendres but finding a metaphorical excuse for their presence. Of sonnet 98 ("From you have I beene absent in the spring") he says, for example:

> The language of this sonnet and of sonnet 99 ["The forward violet thus did I chide"] is full of unexploited relevance to sexual love ... All these senses remain dormant throughout the poem; they function only to the extent that such a concentration of potentially suggestive terms gives a vague aura of sexuality to the poem and thus ... reinforces the persistent and essential analogy Shakespeare draws between the speaker's relationship with a beloved and the traditional courtly love poet's relationship with a mistress.[5]

Joseph Pequigney will have none of this. The sonnets to the young man trace the course of a sexually consummated love affair, Pequigney argues, and in the sexual puns of the sonnets about the young man, no less than in the sexual puns of the sonnets about the mistress, Shakespeare is talking about the psychological and anatomical realities of sexual love. As a record of a love affair, the sonnets about the young man tell a three-part story, with a beginning (sonnets 1–19, in which the poet falls in love), a middle (sonnets 20–99, in which the poet's passion "finds fruition in sexual acts"), and an end (sonnets 100–26, in which the poet's love wanes).[6]

In this story of wooing, winning, and ruing, the diptych of sonnets 20 / 21 is the turning point. Sexual puns introduced in the next several sonnets continue through the one hundred twenty-five that follow. The rite of passage from sexual innocence to sexual experience is marked ceremonially in sonnet 22 ("My glass shall not persuade me I am old / So long as youth and thou are of one date"), with its exchange of hearts from one lover's breast to the other's and its echoes of St. Paul's text on man and wife as "one flesh," appointed in the *Book of Common Prayer* to be read during the marriage rite:

> For all that beauty that doth cover thee,
> Is but the seemely rayment of my heart,
> Which in thy brest doth live, as thine in me.
> How can I then be elder then thou art?
>
> (22.5–8)

If the application of the biblical text seems metaphorical here, it persists as the subtext in all the later sonnets that imagine the friend's relations with the poet's mistress in blatantly fleshly terms, as body closing with body and shutting the poet out. The next sonnet in the sequence worries the distinction between figures of speech and things themselves until it becomes hard to say just where words give place to bodies. With its wordplay on "actor," "part," "fierce thing," "love's strength," and "decay," sonnet 23 makes us see how being (1) an actor in the theater, (2) a player of lovers' word games, (3) a writer of poems, and (4) a performer in bed are all aspects of the same thing:

> As an unperfect actor on the stage,
> Who with his feare is put besides his part,
> Or some fierce thing repleat with too much rage,
> Whose strengths abondance weakens his owne heart;
> So I for fear of trust, forget to say,
> The perfect ceremony of loves right,
> And in mine owne loves strength seeme to decay,
> Ore-charged with burthen of mine owne loves might.
>
> (23.1–8)

The rival poet who later emerges in sonnets 78 to 86 thus poses a threat to the persona on two fronts: sexual as well as rhetorical. The nine poems in this group are packed with sexual puns on "pen," "will," "spirit," and "pride." The rival poet finds it much easier than Shakespeare's speaker / poet / lover both to make love and to make poems out of love. Alerted by sonnet 23, a reader who is looking out for secrets should be ready by the time he gets to sonnet 26 ("Lord of my love, to whome in vassalage / Thy merrit hath my dutie strongly knit") to see the puns for penis that Booth finds in "show my wit" (26.4), "all naked" (26.8), "tottered loving" (26.11), and "show my head" (26.14).[7] In this context, the linked paired formed by sonnets 27 ("Weary with toyle, I hast me to my bed") and 28 ("How can I then returne in happy plight / That am debard the benifit of rest?"), in which the friend's "shadow" (27.10) haunts the poet in his bed and keeps him from sleeping, figures as Shakespeare's version of Horace toiling in his dreams after Ligurinus. What emerges in the sonnets that follow immediately after 20 / 21 is not so much a narrative context as a rhetorical one: these poems invite us not only to read *between* the lines, to deduce the story that has inspired them, but in a quite particular way to read *within* the lines, to decode puns and so make ourselves privy to secrets – secrets that are specifically sexual.

Along with the shifts in sonnet 20 in purpose and in language comes a shift in the implied world of the poems, in the imagined setting within which the persona and his two loves, male and female, play out their drama of sexual desire. The pastoral images of the first twenty sonnets are replaced by chambers and closets (46), beds (27, 142), chests (48, 52, 65), mirrors (63, 77), and clocks (57). The delights of the *locus amoenus* give way to the confidences of the bedchamber. It is in just such a setting that we often overhear Shakespeare's persona in the confessions that succeed sonnet 20. In sonnet 27 ("Weary with toyle, I hast me to my bed") the love appears to the poet in his bed "like a jewell (hunge in ghastly night)" (27.11). The cabinet of secrets that is implicit in this conjunction of bedchamber, jewel, and the sonnet itself as secrets committed to paper is noted explicitly when the poet returns to the same scene later in the sequence. Once the persona begins to imagine his love betraying him, the love-as-jewel turns into something to be locked up, something that must be protected from theft. Setting out on a journey, the persona tells his love in sonnet 48, he carefully stowed away his valuables. But his love – "thou, to whom my jewels trifles are" – cannot be secured so easily:

> Thee have I not lockt up in any chest,
> Save where thou art not though I feel thou art,
> Within the gentle closure of my brest,
> From whence at pleasure thou maist come and part.
> (48.5, 9–12)

The image here is like a figure-ground puzzle: it wavers between the figurative idea of the friend's image locked away in the persona's heart and the physical reality of his love enclosed in the persona's embrace. By sonnet 52 images of jewels and chests, of locking things up, have taken on specifically sexual meanings:

> So am I as the rich whose blessed key,
> Can bring him to his sweet up-locked treasure,
> The which he will not ev'ry hour survay,
> For blunting the fine point of seldome pleasure.
> (52.1–4)

The jewels here may recall the persona's mental image of his love in sonnets 27 and 48, but the suggestion of appetite in the fourth line, the fear of "blunting the fine point of seldome pleasure," invites us to read the poem in graphically physical terms. The "sweet up-locked treasure" may be not so much an idealized image of his love as a very real part of his love's anatomy.

In this new imaginative space after sonnet 20, questions of public versus private take on an urgency that is absent entirely from the first nineteen poems. As early as sonnet 25 ("Let those who are in favor with their stars, / Of publike honour and proud titles boast") the poet sets up a contrast, often to be repeated, between worldly ostentation and the homely fact of the friends' love for one another. Not always is that separation between public and private felt so happily. Troubled imaginings in sonnet 36 ("Let me confesse that we two must be twaine, / Although our undivided loves are one") of a time when the poet may not "acknowledge" the friend nor the friend show "publike kindnesse" to the poet seem to have less to do with the young man's possibly higher social station than with "bewailed guilt" on the part of the poet – dark hints of wrongdoing that are sounded again in sonnets 88 ("With mine owne weakenesse being best acquainted, / Upon thy part I can set downe a story / Of faults conceald" [5–7]), 89 ("Say that thou didst forsake mee for some falt, / And I will comment upon that offence"), 90 ("Then hate me when thou wilt, if ever, now, / Now while the world is bent my deeds to crosse"), 112 ("Your love and pittie doth th'impression fill, / Which vulgar scandall stampt upon my brow"), 120 ("That you were once unkind be-friends mee now"), and 121 ("'Tis better to be vile then vile esteemed, / When not to be, receives reproach of being").

After the persona's first avowal of sexual desire in sonnet 20, we would expect, according to the progression of myths we have been following in this book, a moral or legal intervention, on the part of the poet's conscience if not from some other person. Even Barnfield, for all his salacious imaginings, lays aside his illicit desires for the "higher" concerns of epic poetry – and for marriage. In Shakespeare's sonnets no such thing happens. We hear nothing about moral reservations. No thought of the law provokes fear. In the course of his self-confessions after sonnet 20 Shakespeare's speaker struggles with problems of authority, to be sure, but those problems have nothing to do with moral philosophy or the law. They concern instead authority in being the lover of another man and authority in writing about homosexual love.

The familiar, even complacent role the poet enjoys in the first nineteen sonnets ends abruptly after sonnets 20 / 21: to declare homosexual desire – and to *act* on it – changes everything. Conventional structures of ideology and power explode; the fragile proprieties of the first nineteen poems are shattered. In the early sonnets power is all on the persona's side. His age, his experience, above all his powers as a poet put him in command of the situation at hand. Both the sonnet as a medium and orthodox heterosexuality as the message are firmly under his control. As long as he plays the sage older friend, it is he who is doing the acting; the young friend's role is to react. Admitting his passion changes all that. "I" and "you" no longer have their comfortable separate identity. The poet who doubts his own abilities in sonnet 23 ("As an unperfect actor on the stage") is quite another person from the poet who confidently went to war with time in sonnet 15 ("When I consider every thing that growes, / Holds in perfection but a little moment"). Critics customarily speak of the young man as the poet's "friend," but the perplexed relationship described in the sonnets after 20 / 21 is anything but Aristotle's *philia*, with its easy mutuality between men who are equals.

Different from the first nineteen poems in the relationship they imply between speaker and listener, the love sonnets to the young man differ just as much from the sonnets about the mistress. The frustrated idealism of sonnets 20 through 126 stands in the sharpest possible contrast to the resigned cynicism of the sonnets addressed to the so-called "dark lady." Many of the latter have, indeed, something of Horace's genial urbanity about them. "Therefore I lye with her, and she with me, / And in our faults by lyes we flattered be" (138.12–14): for all their cynicism, sonnets 127 to 154 communicate a mutuality, a sensual understanding between speaker and listener, that so often is painfully not the case in sonnets 20 through 126. Shakespeare devotes 126 highly varied sonnets to the young man and only 28 alternately affable and sarcastic sonnets to the mistress for the same reason that the fourth- and fifth-century Greeks devoted so much more attention in their philosophical writings to the love between men and boys than to the love between men and women: in each case it was the bond between male and male that seemed the more complicated and problematic.[8] Once Shakespeare's poet has declared his passion, the rhetoric of friendship no longer seems adequate. Rapture, jealousy, self-advertisement, self-denigration: the shifting moods and shifting roles of sonnets 20 through 126 run absolutely counter to Renaissance ideas of friendship. Apologists for the sonnets as testimonials to friendship have not read their Aristotle, Cicero, and Montaigne.

Lacking a ready-made rhetoric, Shakespeare's poet has to find his own. With respect to social class, gender, and the rest of society the poet keeps positioning and repositioning himself and the young man he calls "love." The fact that the youth is addressed several times as if he were a nobleman, while Shakespeare himself was at best an upstart gentleman, has been seized upon by all the detectives in pursuit of "Mr. W. H." More important than the friend's actual social status, however, is how the persona uses the language of social difference: he subjectifies it and ironizes it. When the object of his passion was female, a male poet in early modern England faced no such existential problems. He did not have to choose what to say, only how to say it. In sonnet 106 Shakespeare's poet casts himself in the conventional poet's role, as a pillager of the past, as a browser through old manuscripts who puts dusty clichés to fresh uses:

> When in the Chronicle of wasted time,
> I see discriptions of the fairest wights,
> And beautie making beautifull old rime,
> In praise of Ladies dead, and lovely Knights,
> Then in the blazon of sweet beauties best,
> Of hand, of foote, of lip, of eye, of brow,
> I see their antique Pen would have exprest,
> Even such a beauty as you maister now.
>
> (106.1–8)

In "old rimes" it is "Ladies," not "lovely Knights," who are customarily the object of the poet's attentions. If we have let ourselves be seduced by the rhetoric of courtly love, we may be a little startled by the last line of these two glib quatrains, by the incongruity between that distinctly odd verb "master" and the conventional "beauty" that is its syntactical object. Here, in fact, is the same arch tone, the same playful teasing about gender that we encountered in sonnet 20. Is there a pun on that capitalized "Pen" that parallels sonnet 20's pun on "prick"?

"Master Mistris": ambiguities of syntax in that epithet in sonnet 20 are bound up with ambiguities of power in the sonnets as a whole. Are the two words in apposition? Is it "master-mistress" with a hyphen? The line is then a kind of in-joke between persona and friend, as the persona quips about the young man's gender. Is one word subordinated, grammatically and sexually, to the other? Is the young man "the *master* mistress of my passion," as opposed to the persona's "lesser" mistress, the woman of sonnets 127 to 154? The line in that case becomes a witty compliment of the sort the persona has been serving up in the previous nineteen poems, but it also foreshadows the dark jealousies of persona-love-mistress as a *ménage à trois*. If we bite Thomas Thorpe's bait and accept "W. H." as a cipher for the young man addressed in these poems, it is worth remembering that the abbreviation "Mr." in late sixteenth-century orthography more likely stands for "Master" than "Mister."

Whichever way we read the phrase, the word "master" points up the reversal of meaning that has overtaken the word "mistress" since the Middle Ages. In the context of courtly love "mistress" originally designated the lady as a setter of tasks for her servant-knight. By Shakespeare's time, however, the word had taken on the specifically sexual meaning of "a woman who illicitly occupies the place of wife" (*OED* 11) – and with that meaning all the Judeo-Christian assumptions about the husband as "head" of the wife (Ephesians 5:22–23). The earliest citations in the *Oxford English Dictionary* all occur in contemptuous contexts that see compliant woman as a source of pleasure for predatory man. Mistress Quickly fails to make the *OED*, but the title fits her perfectly. The difference between the literal and the secondary meanings of the word "mistress" turns, indeed, on whether the lady has granted sexual favors or not. If she holds off, she remains in control, a "mistress" in the original courtly sense; if she gives in to the suitor's desires, she gives up her power and becomes a "mistress" in the secondary sexual sense. Questions of power are neatly decided by the question of sex or no sex.

If *Paradise Lost* celebrates the fortunate fall, Petrarchan sonnets celebrate the fortunate refusal. At first glance, the scenario of suitor prostrate before his mistress would seem to give all the power to the lady. She, after all, has the prerogative of saying no. That much is only natural. Among animals at least, it is females that do the choosing of sexual partners. There is a very good biological reason why that should be the case: in the great scheme of things sperm are plentiful, eggs are scarce. The physical consequences of sexual activity are much more serious for a female animal than for a male. Females have a right to be choosy.[9] From the social games they played if not from the observations they made of animals, Renaissance sonneteers seem to have recognized this basic fact about rituals of courtship. At the very beginning of the sonnet tradition, in Dante's *La Vita Nuova*, we discover a fundamental anomaly: the poet may be firmly in control of his medium, but he is not in control of the lady. The medium becomes, then, a way of extending control from poem to person. A sonnet shows us poetry in just the terms that Renaissance critics like Sidney and Puttenham best understood it: as a species of oratory, an art of persuasion.[10] It is a stratagem on the suitor's part to bend the lady's will to his own. It is a male's attempt to defy the dictates of biology. It is Art's revenge on Nature.

The lady may have the prerogative of saying no, but, for the persona at least, her power stops there. In holding off she in fact gives the male speaker just the opportunity he needs to celebrate his own prowess: to make a public display of his feelings, to show off his ingenuity as a poet, to turn the woman with her disconcerting *otherness* into a managable image in a poem. The dramatic conventions of the Renaissance sonnet grant the lady a reality only as an object of the male persona's desires. "Look into thy heart and write": Sidney's advice to himself indicates just where the writer's interest – and the reader's – lies, not on the lady but on the suitor. The poet, not the mistress, is the *subject*, in every sense of the word. Seen in its rhetorical context, a Petrarchan sonnet is a power ploy of speaker over listener; seen in its social context, it is a power-ploy of a man over a woman; seen in its sexual context, it is power-ploy of male over female. Change the gender of the listener from female to male, and all of the delicate alliance of feeling, ideology, and power are called into question. "Master Mistris": Shakespeare's yoking together of those two words reminds us that there is no real equivalent in English for a man as a lover of a man. "Master" comes with all the suggestion of superior power that "mistress" implies, but with none of the suggestion of sexual subjection. In a relationship between two men, of what use are the conventional terms "master" and "mistress"? Who exercises power over whom?

If the rhetoric of courtly love fails him, Shakespeare's poet is equally dissatisfied with the roles assigned to lovers by the Myth of Master and Minion. "Lord of my love," the persona addresses the friend in sonnet 26, "to whome in vassalage / Thy merrit hath my dutie strongly knit." Only when the friend returns some mark of favor will the persona "boast how I doe love thee" (26.1–2, 13). So humble is the persona's posture that one might take sonnet 26 as an exercise in polite convention, as an appeal for money perhaps or as a cover letter for other poems, if the persona did not elsewhere present himself even more abjectly – and even more sarcastically. Sonnet 57 asks in mock-sincerity,

> Being your slave what should I doe but tend,
> Upon the houres, and times of your desire?
> I have no precious time at al to spend;
> No services to doe til you require.
> (57.1–4)

If we trust our ears, we may suspect that the nature of those "services" is sexual. Sixteenth-century pronunciation facilitates a pun on "hours" / "whores" (the friend may require such services from other retainers besides the speaker), spending time "at all" can be read as a noun as well as an adverb, and "to do" is one of the sonnets' commonest circumlocutions for "the act of generation." Sonnet 58 continues the conceit of vassal / slave – and the pun on "hour" that renders it sexual:

> That God forbid, that made me first your slave,
> I should in thought controule your times of pleasure
> Or at your hand th'account of houres to crave,
> Being your vassail bound to staie your leisure.
> (58.1–4)

With the same edge of irony sonnet 110 ("Alas 'tis true, I have gone here and there, / And made my selfe a motley to the view") casts the friend as "a God in love" to whom the persona is "confin'd" as a votary (110.12). The persona is at his most vulnerable, perhaps, in sonnet 94 ("They that have powre to hurt, and will doe none"). His willingness to put down his guard, to give himself up to his love's frightening power, seems all the more remarkable when compared with the persona's self-containment in the first nineteen sonnets. One hears in sonnets 26, 57–8, and 94 proof of Sir William Cornwallis's warning in his essay "Of Friendship and Factions": "That part of Friendship which commaunds secrets I would not have delivered too soone, this is the precioussest thing you can give him, for thereby you make your selfe his prisoner."[11] In other sonnets the poet tries on the roles of lord and vassal the other way around. During love-making (if we grant "have" its sexual force) it is the persona who plays the monarch: "Thus have I had thee as a dreame doth flatter, / In sleepe a King, but waking no such matter" (87.13–14). And in 114 the persona wonders whether he always puts the best appearance on whatever his love has done because, "being crown'd with you," his mind "doth ... drinke up the monarks plague this flattery" (114.1–2).

On other occasions, in other moods, Shakespeare's poet turns from the political roles of lord / vassal and vassal / lord to roles inscribed by the family. Is there something of the father, as well as the friend, in the persona who speaks in sonnets 1 through 19? That role is implicit later on, in paired sonnets 33 ("Full many a glorious morning have I seene, / Flatter the mountaine tops with soveraine eie") and 34 ("Why didst thou promise such a beautious day"), both of which turn on a pun between "Sun" and "son." In general, however, the heavy mantle of father does not rest well on the speaker's shoulders after sonnet 20. Being older and wiser serves his purpose as long as he is emotionally disengaged, but once he has given in to desire years and experience become a cause for regret. Among the most bitter of the sonnets is 37, in which the persona looks at his love's sexual exploits "as a decrepit father takes delight / To see his active childe do deeds of youth" (37.1–2).

If not friend and friend, if not knight and lady, if not master and minion, if not father and son, who *are* the lovers to one another? A more complicated tie than all the rest is implied in sonnet 82. Complaining about the rival poet who has threatened his sovereignty since sonnets 20 / 21, Shakespeare's poet concedes,

> I Grant thou wert not married to my Muse,
> And therefore maiest without attaint ore-looke
> The dedicated words which writers use,
> Of their faire subject, blessing every booke.
>
> (82.1–4)

It may, in this instance, be the gender of the poet's muse that inspires an allusion to marriage, but in other sonnets the poet needs no such excuse. "So shall I live, supposing thou art true, / Like a deceived husband" (93.1–2), he confesses in sonnet 93. The poet as husband and his love as wife keep their metaphorical identities through the whole sonnet, until they acquire truly mythic dimensions at the end: "How like *Eaves* apple doth thy beauty grow, / If thy sweet vertue answere not thy show" (93.13–14). In the very next poem the roles are reversed. As a gesture of submission, as an act of obeisance spoken in third person, as a return to the argument of the earliest sonnets in urging the poet's love to "husband natures ritches from expence," sonnet 94 implicitly casts the *love* as husband and the *poet* as wife. Sonnet 97 ("How like a Winter hath my absence beene") seems to do the same, as the poet contrasts "the teeming Autumne big with ritch increase" with his own feelings of sterility and emptiness:

> Yet this aboundant issue seem'd to me,
> But hope of Orphans, and un-fathered fruite,
> For Sommer and his pleasures waite on thee,
> And thou away, the very birds are mute.
>
> (97.5–8)

In the metaphors of sonnets 82, 93, 94, and 97 we find overt expression of a subtext that Stephen Booth sees running through the whole sequence. The paradox avowed in sonnet 36 ("Let me confesse that we two must be twaine, / Although our undevided loves are one") and affirmed in the exchange of hearts and the sharing of one identity in sonnets 22, 34, 39, 42, 62, 109, 134, and 135 is the very mystery that makes a sacrament of human marriage. "Ye husbands love your wives, even as Christ loved the Church and hath given himself for it": St. Paul's words in Ephesians 5:25–33 were appointed in the Elizabethan *Book of Common Prayer* to be read at the end of the marriage rite when there was to be no sermon.

> For this cause shall a man leave father and mother, and shall be joined unto his wife, and they two shall be one flesh. This mystery is great, but I speak of Christ and the congregation. Nevertheless, let every one of you so love his own wife, even as himself.[12]

St. Paul may have been talking primarily about a religious mystery; the 1559 *Book of Common Prayer* is quite explicit – much more explicit than its twentieth-century counterpart – in talking about the mysteries of sex. Matrimony, the priest says in his greeting,

> is not to be enterprised nor taken in hand unadvisedly, lightly, or wantonly, to satisfy men's carnal lusts and appetites, like brute beasts that have no understanding, but reverently, discreetly, advisedly, soberly, and in the fear of God, duly considering the causes for which matrimony was ordained. (p. 290)

Of those three causes – procreation, avoiding fornication, and giving "mutual society, help, and comfort" (pp. 290–1) – the first two are concerned with sex. After such a preamble, one can understand why the spiritual metaphor of "one flesh" in Ephesians 5 would have such physical force, why listeners like Shakespeare would find it easier to remember the fleshly vehicle than the spiritual tenor. It is Ephesians 5, and "The Form of Solemnization of Matrimony" in which it is embedded, that provides the context for one of Shakespeare's most famous sonnets. "Let me not to the marriage of true mindes / Admit impediments": sonnet 116 is an implicit answer to what the priest is instructed to say before anything else to the man and the woman who have presented themselves for marriage:

> I require and charge you (as you will answer at the dreadful day of judgment, when the secrets of all hearts shall be disclosed) that if either of you do know any impediment why ye may not be lawfully joined together in matrimony, that ye confess it. (p. 291)

One word of the priest's charge, "impediment," sounds out in sonnet 116. Two other words, "secrets" and "confess," inspire the sonnets as a whole. Like the marriage of man and wife in the *Book of Common Prayer*, "The marriage of true minds" in sonnet 116 may have a physical as well as a spiritual aspect. "True minds" can mean not only the true "affections" (*OED* II.15.b) that readers conventionally find in the phrase, but the true "intentions" (*OED* II.14) of two people who present themselves for marriage before a priest. Only twice in the sonnets addressed to the mistress does Shakespeare's poet make even the remotest allusion to these marriage texts from the *Book of Common Prayer*.[13]

What we can observe in the course of the first 126 sonnets is, then, a constantly shifting attempt on Shakespeare's part to bring structures of ideology and structures of power into the kind of viable alignment with feeling that we find in more conventional love poetry. In the sonnets Shakespeare seeks to speak about homosexual desire with the same authority that Petrarch assumes in speaking about heterosexual desire. In pursuit of that end Shakespeare invokes three different modes of discourse: Horace's language of erotic experience, the traditional language of courtly love, and the language of Christian marriage. On very few points are those three languages in accord. Shakespeare's sonnets to the young man not only record what happens between the speaker and his love; the sonnets also play out the conflicts and inconsistences in the conventional ways the poet has for explaining what happens – to himself, to his love, to us as sharers of his sexual secrets. Shakespeare's sonnets test the limits of the love sonnet as a genre. In the hands of other sixteenth-century poets, sonnets serve to confirm those interlocking structures of power and ideology – and feeling – that define Renaissance heterosexuality. In testing the soundness of those structures Shakespeare tests also the verse form in which the structures that define sexuality are turned into words and are made accessible to the imagination. To take the terms of courtly love and Christian marriage and apply them to a subject to which they do not conventionally belong is to force a re-examination of both the terms and the subject. Society may dictate the terms, but the use to which Shakespeare has put those terms is a radical choice. The result is, or can be, something *new*. In *Shakespeares Sonnets. Never before Imprinted.* we have an exercise in the "conditioned and conditional freedom" held out by Pierre Bourdieu's idea of social *habitus*. Out of the already tried "strategies" open to him as a writer, out of the "matrix of perceptions, appreciations, and actions" that he shared with his contemporaries, Shakespeare improvised a new form of discourse.[14] It will not do to say that Shakespeare's sonnets cannot be about homosexual desire since no one else in early modern England addressed homosexual desire in just these terms.

Using a new imaginative vocabulary to talk about an old subject brings Shakespeare to a conclusion altogether different from that of poets in other sequences of sonnets. Traditional sonnet sequences control sexual desire by transcending it: caught up in an impossible conflict between his own hot desire and the lady's cold disdain, the Petrarchan poet turns desire into art and lover's lust into philosopher's zeal. Only Spenser manages to have it both ways by actually marrying the lady in question. In the matter of closure, as in everything else, Shakespeare's sonnets present an anomaly. How critics read the ending seems to depend very much on how they have been filling in the narrative gaps along the way. C. S. Lewis speaks for older, idealistic critics when he singles out sonnet 144 ("Two loves I have of comfort and dispaire") and sees a psychomachia between Comfort and Despair going on through all the poems. The sequence ends "by expressing simply love, the quintessence of all loves whether erotic, parental, filial, amicable, or feudal."[15] From a psychoanalytical point of view C. L. Barber and Richard P. Wheeler find special significance in sonnet 114 ("Or whether doth my minde being crown'd with you / Drinke up the monarks plague this flattery?") and its articulation of the persona's hard-won "self-*regard*, with all that implies as against entire dependence on the regard of the friend."[16] For Pequigney the sonnets' end is the affair's end. The two pairs of parentheses that take the place of a final couplet in the quarto printing of sonnet 126 ("O Thou my lovely Boy who in thy power, / Doest hould time's fickle glasse[,] his sickle, hower") are, Pequigney proposes, pregnant with meaning. They imply that "the poet is entering upon a course of gradual detachment or falling out of love. The parenthetical message might then be translated, 'the rest is silence.' "[17] Showing how rhetorical devices in the poems serve to communicate psychological states, Heather Dubrow compares the last two poems printed in the quarto, verses whose ultimate inspiration is not Petrarch but Anacreon, with the Epithalamium that Spenser puts at the end of the *Amoretti*. In both cases the reader encounters a shift in genre and a stepping back from the intense emotionality of the earlier poems. But the subject of sonnets 153 ("*Cupid* laid by his brand and fell a sleepe") and 154 ("The little Love-God lying once a sleepe, / Laid by his side his heart inflaming brand") is "the very impossibility of achieving distance from love and the inaccessibility of any finality, any cure." Perhaps, then, there *is* no closure.[18]

If, on the other hand, we look at the poems as an attempt to read homosexual experience in the idiom of courtly love and according to the ideals of Christian marriage, the volume of *Shake-speares Sonnets* ends by making us realize, and feel, the void between sexual experience and the metaphors we have to talk about it. "O Thou my lovely Boy": the poet's parting gesture toward the lover whose fickleness has caused him such anguish is to give up the whole enterprise, to fall back on a cant term, to look at sodomy from the outside and to see it as an act of aggression. The fact that Shakespeare's poet takes the power on himself makes the ending all the bleaker. Once he took up arms against Time in defense of the young man's beauty. Now he joins forces with Nature, "soveraine mistress over wrack" (126.5), in envisioning the young man's destruction. "O thou minnion of her pleasure," he sneers as he gives up the struggle and lays down his pen (126.9). Here is anything but the "mutuall render onely me for thee" (125.12) that the poet has desired and the lover has refused. The other person, Shakespeare's poet discovers, remains an*other* person, forever fugitive from all attempts to fix him in imagination. We come away from the sonnets with a sense that the conflicts of ideology and power are never really resolved. Horatian odes, Petrarchan sonnets, the Christian marriage rite: none of these can tell the whole truth about sex. Out of all the homosexualities studied in this book, the homosexuality inscribed in Shakespeare's sonnets is the most compelling because it is not end-stopped. The enjambment of Shakespeare's lines with life continues even when we have come to the sonnets' end.

What is *not* cast aside at the end of the sonnets is the fact of sexual desire. In this respect the Myth of the Secret Sharer is different from all the other modes of poetic discourse in this book. If these myths do not close with an absolute denial of homosexual desire, as with The Shipwrecked Youth and Knights in Shifts, they end with the isolation of the hero who persists in acknowledging that desire. One thinks of Antonio in the Myth of Combatants and Comrades, of Virgil's Corydon and his English-speaking imitators in The Passionate Shepherd, of Edward II in Master and Minion. "Me neither woman now, nor boy doth move, / Nor a too credulous hope of mutuall love": if by the end Shakespeare's persona finds himself in the position of Horace's urbane lover, he does so not for any of the reasons that isolate the other heroes. It is not structures of power or structures of ideology, social disapproval or moral dogma, that set him apart, but problems of authority. He is alone in his subjectivity. Like Montaigne, Shakespeare remains acutely aware, as none of his English contemporaries seem to be, that sexuality is something we can know only "in circumlocution and picture." It is this self-conscious subjectivity that puts the

Myth of the Secret Sharer closest of all six myths to our own experience of sexual desire in the twentieth century.

The sexual potentiality in male bonding, steadily mounting through the sequence of six myths, reaches a literal and figurative climax in Shakespeare's sonnets. Devious metamorphoses of desire in the first five myths end in the confidences of the Secret Sharer. When homosexual desire has become its own explicit subject, we have completed the move, in social terms, from license to licentiousness. We have moved also from public ways of playing out homosexual desire to private ways, and from forms of symbolic discourse that were "legible" to all early modern Englishmen, illiterate and literate alike, to forms of discourse that were accessible only to a small, highly sophisticated readership. In psychological terms, that narrowing of social focus entails a move from conscious control of sexual desire toward greater daring and risk, not only politically but artistically. In the Myth of the Secret Sharer we witness the invention of a new mode of discourse about homosexual desire where none existed before. In chronological terms, finally, we have moved from seasonal rituals that antedate written records to an experience of sexual desire that seems distinctively modern. Our survey has extended from expressions of desire that were current throughout the sixteenth and seventeenth centuries to one that is highly idiosyncratic to its author and to its historical moment. Shakespeare's sonnets could not have been written thirty years earlier. Thirty years later they were not being understood.

It would be nice to end this book on a triumphant note, to celebrate the fact that Shakespeare, once and for all, broke through the cultural constraints of his time in portraying homosexual desire with such candor and subtlety. Sadly, that is not case. Shakespeare may have subverted the sexual rules of early modern English society, but most writers and readers have not been able to follow him in that act of rebellion. The anomalous quality of Shakespeare's sonnets seems to have been apparent from the very beginning. References to them among contemporary readers are in fact few; transcriptions into commonplace books are rare; imitations by other poets are almost non-existent. The 1609 first printing was apparently enough to satisfy demand until 1640, when John Benson published *Poems written by Wil. Shakespeare Gent.*[19] To produce a marketable commodity Benson tried several ways of bringing Shakespeare's sonnets in line with Caroline taste. First, he rearranged them, so that any sense of an underlying plot is destroyed. Next, he supplied many of the sonnets with a title (e.g., Sonnet 122, "Upon the receit of a Table Booke from *his Mistris*"), turning each poem into a little move in the game of courtly love, into a conventional task that the poet has set for himself. Other sonnets he regrouped under thematic headings: "The glory of beautie," "Injurious Time," "True Admiration," to take the first three. Sonnets treating the same theme he sometimes printed continuously, sometimes singly, so as to give an impression of formal variety. From *The Passionate Pilgrim* he incorporated Shakespeare's verses from *Love's Labour's Lost* as well as poems attributed to Shakespeare but assigned today to other writers. Finally, Benson changed certain of the masculine pronouns to feminine. Given Benson's other manipulations of Shakespeare's text, it is surprising how seldom this radical editing is necessary. In addition to sonnet 122, he supplies misleading titles for sonnet 125 ("An entreatie for her acceptance") and sonnets 113–114–115 (printed continuously as "Selfe flattery of her beautie"). In effect, Benson depersonalizes and "de-privatizes" the poems, turning the "I" who speaks them into a generic type, into a universal Lover. The object of this Lover's desires becomes an equally unspecific Mistress. The success of Benson's editing can be witnessed in a copy of *Poems written by Wil. Shakespeare Gent.* now in the Folger Shakespeare Library. Manuscript notes in an almost contemporary hand amplify the spirit of the editor's own emendations. Benson's title for sonnet 20 ("The exchange") was not quite enough, however, to explain away all the paradoxes of the "master mistress." The seventeenth-century owner of the Folger volume was clearly puzzled – until he (or she) decided that the poet must have settled his affections on a most unusual lady. "The M^{ris} Masculine" reads the owner's clarification.

All in all, Benson's Shakespeare would have been quite at home on the shelf next to Edmund Waller. That was just the form in which readers of the sonnets, such readers as there were, encountered the text until George Steevens reprinted the 1609 quarto more than a century later, in 1766. Steevens's disgust at sonnet 20 has been noted already. Edmond Malone's edition of 1790, with its reassuring remarks on what was "custom-ary" in Elizabethan England, helped to ease such doubts. With his full critical appar-atus of preface and notes, Malone reinstated the "I" who had been obliterated by Benson – but in a guise that was acceptable to the middle-class readers of late eighteenth-century England.[20] By and large, that is still the guise in which most readers imagine the persona today. To us, the poet of Shakespeare's sonnets may seem much more sophisticated psychologically and rhetorically than he did to Malone, but the "I" who speaks in these poems has never quite shed the middle-class values that Malone attributed to him in 1790. It was with thanks to Malone that Wordsworth could say of the sonnets, "With this key Shakespeare unlocked his heart," and open up these formerly closed texts to Romantic and post-Romantic readers, who imagine the persona of the sonnets to be just such a person as themselves. Until they were taken in hand by Malone, Shakespeare's sonnets were "marginal" texts like those that feminist critics of the past twenty years have been excavating and rehabilitating, or in many cases habilitating for the first time. We don't have to rediscover Shakespeare's sonnets as texts, but we do have to rediscover them in their sixteenth-century cultural context, as discourses of homosexual desire. Malone, and most readers after him, have not been quite so outspoken as Steevens in their responses to the sexual subject of the sonnets. Instead, they have quietly contrived to *contain* these poems, not within the culture of sixteenth-century England, but within their own culture's ways of under-standing the relationship between male bonding and homosexual desire. The most recent is Joel Fineman, who argues that Shakespeare uses the *rhetoric* of Platonizing homosexual desire to create a thoroughly heterosexual subjectivity.

Benson's edition of 1640 is a sign that the cultural moment of Shakespeare's sonnets had passed, that the ambivalent alliances between male bonding and sexual desire that demanded such sensitive and varied treatment in poetic discourse were beginning to assume the schematic opposition that finally emerged as social dogma in the late eighteenth century and has remained in effect until today: a supposition that male bonding and male homosexuality are opposites, not different aspects of the same psychological and social phenomenon. Shakespeare's sonnets address the connection between male bonding and male homosexuality with a candor that most readers, most male readers at least, have not been willing to countenance. If that connection now seems clearer, this book will have done in a small way what Shakespeare's sonnets did so much more expansively in the sixteenth century: out of already familiar characters and plots, ideas and feelings it will have created a more liberally imagined world for one of the many modes of human sexual desire.

Notes

1 *Epithalamium*, II.383, 398–403, in Edmund Spenser, *The Works*, 8, ed. C. G. Osgood and H. G. Gibbons (Baltimore: Johns Hopkins University Press, 1947): 251.

2 Booth, *Shakespeare's Sonnets*, pp. 431–2.

3 Plutarch, *Moralia 767*, trans. Philemon Holland in *The Philosophie* (London, 1603), fols. 1132–3. Further quotations are cited in the text by folio number. Connections between the sonnets and the plays with respect to the scenario of two male friends parted by a woman are explored in Cyrus Hoy, "Shakespeare and the Revenge of Art," *Rice University Studies* 60 (1974): 71–94.

4 John Donne, Elegy "To his Mistris Going to Bed" and "The Sunne Rising," in *The Elegies and The Songs and Sonnets*, ed. Helen Gardner (Oxford: Clarendon Press, 1965), pp. 14, 72.

5 Booth, *Shakespeare's Sonnets*, pp. 98–9.

6 Pequigney, *Such Is My Love*, pp. 209–10, summarizing the argument he has made in earlier chapters.

7 Booth, *Shakespeare's Sonnets*, pp. 175–8.

8 Michel Foucault, *The History of Sexuality*, vol. 2: *The Use of Pleasure*, trans. Robert Hurley (New York: Pantheon, 1985): 187–225.

9 Heather Trexler Remoff, *Sexual Choice: A Woman's Decision* (New York: Dutton, 1984), pp. 3–11. The same observation about the expendability of males is made by Walter J. Ong, *Fighting for Life: Contest, Sexuality, and Consciousness* (Ithaca: Cornell Univ. Press, 1981), pp. 52–6.

10 Puttenham defines love poetry, like other forms of verse, according to its original use: "There were an other sort, who sought the favor of faire Ladies, and coveted to bemone their estates at large, & the perplexities of love in a certain pitious verse called *Elegie*, and thence were called *Eligiack*: such among the Latines were *Ovid, Tibullus, & Propertius*." *The Arte of English Poesie*, ed. Gladys Doidge Willcock and Alice Walker (Cambridge: Cambridge University Press, 1936), p. 25. Sidney has these origins in mind when he sets up his criterion as to whether a love poem is good or not: "But truly many of such writings as come under the banner of unresistible love, if I were a mistress, would never persuade me they were in love: so coldly they apply fiery speeches, as men that had rather read lovers' writings … than that in truth they feel those passions, which easily (as I think) may be bewrayed by that same forcibleness or *energia* (as the Greeks call it)." *Defence of Poetry*, ed. J. A. Van Dorsten (Oxford: Oxford University Press, 1966), pp. 69–70.

11 Sir William Cornwallis, *Essayes* (London: Edmund Mattes, 1600), sig. E3ᵛ.

12 *The Book of Common Prayer 1559: The Elizabethan Prayer Book*, ed. John E. Booty (Charlottesville: University of Virginia Press, 1976), p. 297. Further quotations are cited in the text. Booth's remarks on Ephesians 5 occur in connection with sonnet 36, pp. 192–5.

13 The reference in sonnet 134, though addressed to the mistress, still concerns the poet's male love: "So now I have confest that he is thine, / And I my selfe am morgag'd to thy will, / My selfe Ile forfeit, so that other mine, / Thou wilt restore to be my comfort still" (134.1–4). The allusion to "one flesh" in sonnet 135 ("Who ever hath her wish, thou hast thy *Will*") leaves St. Paul and spiritual concerns far behind.

14 Pierre Bourdieu, *Outline of a Theory of Practice*, trans. Richard Nice (Cambridge: Cambridge University Press, 1977), pp. 72–95.

15 C. S. Lewis, *English Literature in the Sixteenth Century Excluding Drama* (Oxford: Clarendon Press, 1954), p. 505.

16 Barber and Wheeler, *The Whole Journey*, p. 195.

17 Pequigney, *Such Is My Love*, pp. 202–7.

18 Dubrow, *Captive Victors*, pp. 221–2.
19 A full account of the critical reception of the 1609 quarto and of Benson's edition is offered by Sidney Lee in the introduction to his facsimile edition of *Shakespeares Sonnets … The First Edition 1609* (Oxford: Clarendon Press, 1905), pp. 51–62.
20 Margreta de Grazia discusses Malone's canonization of the quarto sonnets and the effect of his apparatus on subsequent readings in *Shakespeare "Verbatim": The Reproduction of Authenticity and the 1790 Apparatus* (Oxford: Oxford University Press, 1990), chapter 3, "Individuating Shakespeare." See also her essay "Locating and Dislocating the 'I' of Shakespeare's Sonnets," in *William Shakespeare: His World, His Work, His Influence*, ed. John F. Andrews (New York: Scribners, 1985), 2: 433–44.

39

The Homoerotics of Shakespearean Comedy

Valerie Traub

T he phenomenon of boy actors playing women's parts in Shakespearean comedy has engendered analyses primarily along three axes. The boy actor: (1) is merely a theatrical convention in the lineage of medieval drama; (2) is a political convention specifically necessitated by the determination to keep women, excepting Elizabeth I, off any public stage or platform; or (3) is an embodiment of the meta-dramatic theme of identity itself: always a charade, a masquerade, other. Certainly it is too much of a caricature to label the first formulation as formalist, the second as feminist, and the third as new historicist. And yet it might be provisionally useful to do so, if only to place these positions in the context of debates about: (1) the relative political import and impact of aesthetic events; (2) the determining power of patriarchal ideology within a general political economy; and (3) the extent to which politics and gender impinge on the problematics of subjectivity. It is as an intervention in these debates that I situate the following chapter.

I want to argue first that the practice of employing boys to act the parts of women was not merely a dramatic convention, nor was it solely a patriarchal strategy. As Stephen Orgel points out, boy actors were "a uniquely English solution"; when, in 1599, women were banned from the Spanish stage, "the spectacle of transvestite boys was found to be even more disturbing than that of theatrical women, and the edict was rescinded four years later."[1] However much the practice did keep women from too publicly displaying themselves, it continued not merely because of its negative power of constraint, but because it made possible complex desires and fantasies, and mediated cultural anxieties. Those desires and anxieties were not only gendered but erotic in their origination and implication. Secondly, costuming boys as women, who might then impersonate men (and then sometimes women as well), was especially well suited for a drama devoted to exploring the construction and dissolution of identity; however, the relevant concept of identity was not that of a generic, nondifferentiated "selfhood," but of a complex subjectivity always already imbricated by gender and erotic pressures.

I propose that the boy actor works, in specific Shakespearean comedies, as the basis upon which homoeroticism can be safely explored – working for both actors and audiences as an expression of non-hegemonic desire within the confines of conventional, comedic restraints. The phenomenon of the boy actor is not the by-product or the side-effect of a drama "really" about identity or illustrative of misogyny, but rather is the basis upon which a specific deployment of erotic desire and anxiety can be played out. In this chapter I mean to demonstrate my earlier assertion that certain Shakespearean texts display a homoerotic circulation of desire, that homoerotic energy is elicited, exchanged, negotiated, and displaced as it confronts the pleasures and anxieties of its meanings in early modern culture. Shakespearean drama not only responded to the ideological matrix by which homoerotic desire was understood; it also contributed, in its own ambivalent way, to the early modern signification of homoeroticism. Neither a transparent mirror, mimetically reflecting social reality, nor a literary-historical aberration explainable by the author's sexual preference, the homoerotics of Shakespearean comedy are most accurately perceived as a cultural intervention in a heterosexually overdetermined field. They thus provide us with a useful theoretical analytic, not only of early modern sexualities, but of contemporary erotic concerns.

The circulation of homoerotic desire in *As You Like It* and *Twelfth Night* is what I mean to invoke when I employ the term transvestism over disguise or cross-dressing to describe the consequences of Rosalind's and Viola's adoption of (what was then perceived to be) masculine attire. Although psychoanalytically, transvestism implies the erotic excitement achieved by wearing the clothes of a different gender, and thus is anachronistically and illegitimately applied to the activities of these characters, it is nonetheless because of the specifically erotic valence of the term that I use it. The transvestism in these plays has a more generalized erotic effect, dispersed throughout the entire fabric of the text, rather than located and fixed within one character's desire.

Part of my support for such assertions comes from the antitheatricalists themselves, who increasingly focused their condemnations of the theater on the figure of the boy actor. In a mimetic theory of sexuality, the anti-theatricalists not only charged that the boy actor dressed as a woman aroused the erotic interest of men in the audience, but that spectators were encouraged to play out their fantasies in off-stage, behind-the-scenes scenes. The specifically erotic images with which Stephen Gosson, John Rainoldes, Phillip Stubbes, and William Prynne denounced theatrical practices demonstrates that they perceived actors in their costumes to cross not only status and gender boundaries, but erotic boundaries as well.[2]

However much we might discredit the anti-theatricalists as "fanatics" or crude mimeticists, their intuitions about erotic arousal should not be presumed to be incidental to theatrical production. Bodies, in their culture as in ours, were invested with erotic meanings – bodies making a spectacle of themselves on stage even more so. And clothing, as both the anti-theatricalists and the upholders of sumptuary laws made clear, was an important indicator of one's sexual stance, denoting erotic availability or lack thereof. The anti-theatricalist claim that the theater was a site of erotic, specifically homoerotic, arousal is not in itself pathological; as Stephen Greenblatt notes,

"Shakespearean comedy constantly appeals to the body and in particular to sexuality as the heart of its theatrical magic."[3] What *is* pathological, however, is the anti-theatricalist paranoia about what this circulation of eroticism implies for male subjectivity. At any rate, it is not a paranoia shared with other early modern texts that represent homoeroticism as a legitimate mode of desire; for instance, Spenser's *The Shepherd's Calendar* and Marlowe's *Hero and Leander.*[4]

Psychoanalytic and early feminist readings of the transvestism of *As You Like It* and *Twelfth Night* stress the liberating effect caused by the temporary inversion of hierarchical gender arrangements, "through release to clarification," to use C. L. Barber's influential phrase.[5] Whereas some early feminist readings also posited gender role inversion as an impulse toward androgyny, later feminist and new historicist critics argued that any subversion of gender is contained by the comic form which mandates marriage in the final act. Recent debates on the relative subversive or containing power of gender in Shakespeare's plays focus on the extent to which women (through transvestite disguise or appropriation of speech) challenge and disrupt gender difference, or are securely repositioned as objects of exchange in a patriarchal economy dependent on "the traffic in women."[6]

Clearly, in so far as gender hierarchies seem to be both temporarily transgressed *and* formally reinstated, the question of subversion versus containment can only be resolved by crediting *either* the expense of dramatic energy *or* comedic closure. Yet, to do either is also to reproduce the artificial distinction between content and form – a capitulation to the logic of binarism. One way beyond such fruitless polarization is to historicize the moment in which subversion is thought to occur, to situate *abstract* transgression within a concrete network of overdetermined social pressures and effects.[7] Another way is to stress less the fact of foreclosure than the *way* such containment is attained: the mechanisms and displacements set to work by the anxiety elicited through subversive action. In the following analysis of erotic transgression, I will attempt to do both.

To the extent that the various critics who have recently written about the phenomena of boy actors and female transvestism have recognized the homoeroticism residing in theatrical transvestism, they have initiated the possibility of a homoerotic analytic.[8] For the most part, however, they have focused their attention on *gender* rather than sexuality – even though their language confuses the issue by using synonymously such terms as sexual difference and sexual identity, androgyny and bisexuality, femininity (or masculinity) and heterosexuality. After mentioning the erotic complications raised by the boy actor, they more often than not decline to interrogate how homoeroticism works in specific plays, how homoerotic desire is differentiated between plays, and whether homoeroticism is distinguished along gender lines.

Even in those analyses specifically devoted to uncovering the material reality of homoerotic practice, gender remains the dominant lens of analysis, as in Lisa Jardine's suggestion that male homoeroticism animates all of the cross-dressing scenes. The conclusion extrapolated from Jardine's analysis is that in "playing the woman's part" the boy actor renders unexceptionable and unthreatening female autonomy and erotic power for a predominantly male audience. If young boys are erotically compelling because of their "femininity," it is in part because they represent all of the attractions and none of the threats of female heterosexuality. More recently, Stephen Orgel concurs with this line of reasoning:

> The dangers of women in erotic situations, whatever they may be, can be disarmed by having the women play men, just as in the theatre the dangers of women on the stage (whatever *they* may be) can be disarmed by having men play the women.[9]

Whatever the objective truth of these conclusions, they ultimately say more about the gender anxieties of early modern patriarchal culture than about the specificity of homoeroticism. Although gender and eroticism are deeply connected, they are not isomorphic. Here, reliance on a gender model causes Orgel and Jardine to refer the motivation of male homoeroticism to a single cause: the fantasized dangers posed by women. Despite their antihomophobic intentions, Orgel and Jardine continue to place homoeroticism within a category requiring ontological explanation and justification, in which traditional psychoanalytic interpretations are surprisingly reinstalled.

It may well be that gender anxiety is a determining factor in the specific ways homoerotic *practice* is manifested and encoded with social meaning within early modern patriarchal culture. I question, however, whether gender anxiety is *the* salient factor in the construction of homoerotic *desire*. Gender anxiety is no more, and no less, constitutive of homoerotic desire than it is of heterosexual desire. A plenitude of desires are available as unconscious erotic modes within every psyche. But whether a particular mode of desire is given expression or repressed – that is, whether it is manifested as desire or anxiety – is a matter of ideological and institutional elicitations, enticements, and disciplines. To take this argument one step further, whether representations of gendered bodies elicit repulsion or attraction, fear or fascination, is in some ways irrelevant; anxiety and desire are two sides of the same erotic coin. As Sedgwick suggests, desire itself is less "a particular affective state or emotion" than "the affective or social force, the glue, even when its manifestation is hostility or hatred."[10] Despite the particular affect involved, the psychic investment is, in each case, comparable. Arbitrary divisions of desire into heterosexual and homoerotic are more indicative of socio-political prerogatives than of inherent psychic or biological imperatives.

Whereas formalist critics often ignore the impact of the boy actor on the text's signification, historical critics such as Jardine and Orgel conversely emphasize the extent to which early modern theatrical practice enabled what is increasingly being called a "transvestite theater." In this, they follow the lead of the anti-theatricalists in conflating the material reality of the boy actor with the play's action. Indeed, the concept of a "transvestite theater" *per se* seems to confuse mimetically not only the reality of the play with the world of the theater, but also the phenomena of transvestism and male homoeroticism. In my view, transvestism does not correlate in a simple fashion with any particular erotic mode: theoretically, it could engender heterosexual as well as homoerotic desires. Rather, I would like to suggest that homoerotic activity within Shakespeare's plays is predicated on, but not identical to, the presence of boy actors playing female parts. The material conditions of the early modern theater offered a de facto homoerotic basis upon which to build structures of desire, which were then, through theatrical representation, made available not only to male but to female audience members. This dual-gender availability suggests a problem with another increasingly popular term, "sodomitical theatrics"; when used to describe the entire constellation of desires criss-crossing such plays as *As You Like It* and *Twelfth Night*, it fails to distinguish between the erotic practices of both genders; as much as it brings to the fore homoerotic desires among men, it neglects the female desires constructed by the playtexts and imagistically available to female play-goers.

The following comparative analysis of *As You Like It* and *Twelfth Night* attempts to demonstrate the differential ways homoeroticism is treated: how it is experienced as pleasure and when it elicits anxiety for both male and female characters. These plays are sites of struggle for the signification of homoeroticism: they demonstrate that within the early modern erotic economy the homoerotic relation to desire could be represented as both celebratory and strained. At the same time, the representations of homoeroticism in these comedies are as much cultural fantasies as is the representation of the maternal body in the *Henriad* – both representations are "fantasmic" interventions in "real" cultural practices, and as such signal the dialectical relation between the psychic and the social.

The homoeroticism of *As You Like It* is playful in its ability to transcend binary oppositions, to break into a dual mode, a simultaneity, of desire. Insofar as Rosalind / Ganymede is a multiply sexual object (simultaneously heterosexual and homoerotic), Orlando's effusion of desire toward her / him prevents the stable reinstitution of heterosexuality, upon which the marriage plot depends. By interrupting the arbitrary binarism of the heterosexual contract, male homoeroticism, even as it affirms particular masculine bonds, transgresses the erotic imperative of the Law of the Father. The proceedings of Hymen that conclude the play, once read in terms of the "mock" marriage which precedes them, enact only an ambivalent closure. The reinstitution of gender role (and Rosalind's political subordination under her husband's rule) is incommensurate with a rigidification of sexuality.

The homoeroticism of *Twelfth Night*, on the other hand, is anxious and strained. This text explores a diversity of desire, proceeding with erotic plurality as far as it can; then, in the face of anxiety generated by this exploration, it fixes the homoerotic interest onto a marginalized figure. The homoerotic energies of Viola, Olivia, and Orsino are displaced onto Antonio, whose relation to Sebastian is finally sacrificed for the maintenance of institutionalized heterosexuality and generational continuity.[11] In other words, *Twelfth Night* closes down the possibility of homoerotic play initiated by the material presence of the transvestized boy actors. The fear expressed, however, is not of homoeroticism *per se*; homoerotic pleasure is explored and sustained *until* it collapses into fear of erotic exclusivity and its corollary: non-reproductive sexuality. The result is a more rigid dedication to the ideology of binarism, wherein gender and status inequalities are all the more forcefully reinscribed.

> Much virtue in If
>
> Touchstone, *As You Like it*

In " 'The Place of a Brother' in *As You Like It*: Social Process and Comic Form," Louis Adrian Montrose began the pathbreaking work of placing women's subordination in Shakespearean drama within the context of male homosocial bonds.[12] In a historicization and politicization of C. L. Barber's analysis of Rosalind in *Shakespeare's Festive Comedy*, Montrose argued that

> Rosalind's exhilarating mastery of herself and others has been a compensatory "holiday humor," a temporary, inversionary rite of misrule, whose context is a transfer of authority, property, and title from the Duke to his prospective male heir.[13]

More recently, Jean Howard continues within the Barber–Montrose lineage:

> The representation of Rosalind's holiday humor has the primary effect, I think, of confirming the gender system and perfecting rather than dismantling it by making a space for mutuality within relations of dominance.[14]

However, she complicates the analysis of Rosalind's subordination through reference to the French feminist analytic of female "masquerade:"

> the figure of Rosalind dressed as a boy engages in playful masquerade as, in playing Rosalind for Orlando, she acts out the parts scripted for women by her culture. Doing so does not release Rosalind from patriarchy but reveals the constructed nature of patriarchy's representations of the feminine and shows a woman manipulating those representations in her own interest, theatricalizing for her own purposes what is assumed to be innate, teaching her future mate how to get beyond certain ideologies of gender to more enabling ones.[15]

The distance traversed in the progression from Barber to Montrose to Howard indicates a corresponding movement from an essentialist view of gender, to an emphasis on social structure as determining gender, to an assertion of the limited possibilities of subversive manipulation within dominant cultural codes. The subjective if constrained agency conferred by Howard upon Rosalind as a woman can be extended as well to Rosalind as erotic subject. In excess of the dominant ideology of monogamous heterosexuality, to which Rosalind is symbolically wed at the end of the play, exist desires unsanctioned by institutional favor. By means of her male improvisation, Rosalind leads the play into a mode of desire neither heterosexual nor homoerotic, but both heterosexual *and* homoerotic. As much as she displays her desire for Orlando, she also enjoys her position as male object of Phebe's desire and, more importantly, of Orlando's. S / he thus instigates a deconstruction of the binary system by which desire in subsequent centuries came to be organized, regulated, and disciplined.

That homoerotic significations will play a part in *As You Like It* is first intimated by Rosalind's adoption of the name Ganymede when she imagines donning doublet and hose. Of all the male names available to her, she chooses that of the young lover of Zeus, familiar to educated Britons through Greek and Latin literature and European painting, and to less privileged persons as a colloquial term used to describe the male object of male love. As James Saslow, who traces the artistic representation of Ganymede in Western culture from the fifteenth to the seventeenth centuries, argues, "the very word *ganymede* was used from medieval times well into the seventeenth century to mean an object of homosexual desire."[16] Saslow's argument is seconded by Orgel: "the name Ganymede [could not] be used in the Renaissance without this connotation."[17]

That Rosalind-cum-Ganymede becomes the object of another woman's desire is obvious. Consciously, of course, Phebe believes Ganymede to be a man, and is thus merely following the dominant heterosexual course. And yet, what attracts Phebe to Ganymede are precisely those qualities that could be termed "feminine." Notice the progression of the following speech:

> It is a pretty youth – not very pretty ...
> He'll make a proper man. The best thing in him
> Is his complexion ...
> He is not very tall; yet for his years he's tall.
> His leg is but so so; and yet 'tis well.
> There was a pretty redness in his lip,
> A little riper and more lusty red
> Than that mix'd in his cheek; 'twas just the difference
> Betwixt the constant red and mingled damask.
>
> (III.v.113–23)

During the first half of her recollection, as she measures Ganymede against the standard of common male attributes – height, leg – Phebe fights her attraction, syntactically oscillating between affirmation and denial: he is; he is not. In the last four lines, as she "feminizes" Ganymede's lip and cheek, she capitulates to her desire altogether.

Many critics acknowledge the underlying homoeroticism of Phebe's attraction; however, they tend to undermine its thematic importance by relegating it to the status of a temporary psychosexual stage. C. L. Barber, for instance, remarks: "She has, in effect, a girlish crush on the femininity which shows through Rosalind's disguise; the aberrant affection is happily got over when Rosalind reveals her identity and makes it manifest that Phebe has been loving a woman."[18] When Barber says that Phebe's "aberrant" affection is "happily got over" he reveals the extent to which homophobic anxiety structures the developmental logic of his response. But if a "girlish crush" is outgrown or overcome, what are we to make of Rosalind's desire to "prove a busy actor" in the "pageant truly play'd" of Phebe and Silvius? (III.iv.50–8). Although her ostensible motivation is her belief that "the sight of lovers feedeth those in love" (56), s/he soon interjects in order to correct the literal-mindedness that feeds Phebe's "proud disdain" (III.iv.52). And yet the pleasure Rosalind / Ganymede takes in this task seems in excess of her putative function. Significantly, it is s / he who first mentions the possibility of Phebe's attraction, interpreting and then glorying in Phebe's changed demeanor:

> Why, what means this? Why do you look on me?
> I see no more in you than in the ordinary
> Of nature's sale-work. 'Od's my little life
> I think she means to tangle my eyes too!
>
> (III.v.41–4)

Is there not a sense in which Rosalind / Ganymede *elicits* Phebe's desire, constructing it even as she refuses it? Indeed, in these lines the conflict between discourses of gender and of sexuality are intensely manifested: at the level of gender, Rosalind restates compulsory heterosexuality; at the level of sexuality, Ganymede elicits a desire for that which falls outside (or on the cusp) of the binarism of gender. At any rate, s / he is represented as delighting in her role of the rejecting male:

> Down on your knees,
> And thank heaven, fasting, for a good man's love;
> For I must tell you friendly in your ear,
> Sell when you can, you are not for all markets.
>
> (III.v.57–60)

And why does s / he put Silvius through the exquisite torment of hearing Phebe's love letter to Ganymede read aloud, if not to aggrandize her own victorious position as male rival? (IV.iii.14–64). Indeed, as a male, her sense of power is so complete that s/he presumes to tell Silvius to tell Phebe, "that if she love *me*, I charge her to love *thee*" (IV.iii.71–2, my emphasis).

Homoerotic desire in *As You Like It* thus circulates from Phebe's desire for the "feminine" in Rosalind / Ganymede to Rosalind / Ganymede's desire to be the "masculine" object of Phebe's desire. Even more suggestive of the text's investment in homoerotic pleasure is Orlando's willingness to engage in love-play with a young shepherd. Throughout his "courtship" of Ganymede (who is now impersonating Rosalind), Orlando accepts and treats Ganymede as his beloved. To do so requires less his willing suspension of disbelief than the ability to hold in suspension a dual sexuality that feels no compulsion to make arbitrary distinctions between kinds of objects. That Rosalind-cum-Ganymede takes the lead in their courtship has been noted by countless critics; that there is a certain homoerotic irony in that fact has yet to be noted. As a "ganymede," Rosalind would be expected to play the part of a younger, more receptive partner in an erotic exchange. S / he thus not only inverts gender roles; s / he disrupts alleged homoerotic roles as well.

What began as a game culminates in the "mock" marriage, when Orlando takes for his wife the boy he believes to be fictionalizing as Rosalind. It is Celia, not Orlando, who hesitates in playing her part in the ceremony – "I cannot say the words," she responds to Orlando's request that she play the priest (IV.i.121) – in part because those words possess a ritualistic power to *enact* what is spoken. Insofar as ritual was still popularly believed to be imbued with sacred or magical power, the fact that Orlando does not hesitate, but eagerly responds in the precise form of the Anglican marriage ceremony – "I take thee, Rosalind, for wife" (IV.i.129) – suggests the degree to which the play legitimizes the multiple desires it represents. The point is not that Orlando and Ganymede formalize a homosexual marriage, but rather that as the distance between Rosalind and Ganymede collapses, distinctions between homoerotic and heterosexual collapse as well. As the woman and the shepherd boy merge, Orlando's words resound with the conviction that, for the moment, he (as much as Rosalind and the audience) is engaged in the ceremony as if it were real. As both a performative speech act and a theatricalization of desire, the marriage is both true and fictional at once. The subversiveness of this dramatic gesture lies in the dual motion of first, appropriating the meaning of matrimony for deviant desires; and second, exposing the heterosexual imperative of matrimony as a reduction of the plurality of desire into the singularity of monogamy. The "mock" marriage is not a desecration but a deconstruction – a displacement and subversion of the terms by which desire is encoded – of the ritual by which two are made one.

When Hymen in Act V symbolically reintroduces the logic of heterosexual marriage, the text's devotion to simultaneity would appear to be negated. The terms in which Hymen performs the quartet of marriages make the ideological function of the ritual clear: "Peace, ho! I bar confusion. / 'Tis I must make conclusion / Of these most strange events" (v.iv.124–6). "Hymen's bands" (v.iv.128) are called forth to "make conclusion" not only of erotic "confusion" but of the play. And yet the play does not end with Hymen's bars and bands, but with a renewed attack on the pretensions of erotic certitude. In a repetition of her previous gender and erotic mobility, Rosalind-cum-boy actor, still wearing female attire, leaps the frame of the play in order to address the audience in a distinctly erotic manner: "If I were a woman I would kiss as many of you as had beards that pleas'd me, complexions that lik'd me, and breaths that I defied not" (Epilogue 16–19). As Orgel, Howard, Phyllis Rackin, and Catherine Belsey all intimate, the effect of this statement is to highlight the constructedness of gender and the flexibility of erotic attraction at precisely the point when the formal impulse of comedy would be to essentialize and fix both gender and eroticism.

Throughout the play, what makes erotic contingency possible is a simple conjunction: "if." Indeed, Touchstone's discourse on the virtues of "if" can serve as an index of the play's entire erotic strategy: "If you said so, then I said so" (v.iv.99–100). The dependence on the conditional structures the possibility of erotic exploration without necessitating a commitment to it. Orlando can woo and even wed Ganymede as "*if* thou wert indeed my Rosalind" and as *if* the marriage were real (iv.i.189–90, my emphasis). Through the magic of "if," the boy actor playing Rosalind can offer and elicit erotic attraction to and from each gender in the audience. "If" not only creates multiple erotic possibilities and positions, it also conditionally resolves the dramatic confusion that the play cannot sustain. As Rosalind says to Silvius, Phebe, and Orlando, respectively: "I would love you, if I could"; "I will marry you, if ever I marry a woman, and I'll be married tomorrow"; and, "I will satisfy you, if ever I satisfied man, and you shall be married tomorrow" (v.ii.108–12). Even Hymen's mandate is qualified: "Here's eight that must take hands / To join in Hymen's bands / *If* truth hold true contents" (v.iv.127–9, my emphasis).

My own reliance on "if" should make it clear that I am not arguing that Rosalind or Orlando or Phebe "is" "a" "homosexual." Rather, at various moments in the play, these characters temporarily inhabit a homoerotic position of desire. To insist on a mode of desire as a position taken up also differs from formulating these characters as "bisexual": as Phyllis Rackin reminds us, bisexuality implicitly defines the desiring subject as divided in order to maintain the ideologically motivated categories of homo- and hetero- as inviolate.[19] The entire logic of *As You Like It* works against such categorization, against fixing upon and reifying any one mode of desire.

Simultaneity and flexibility, however, are not without their costs. Insofar as the text circulates homoerotic desire, it displaces the anxieties so generated in the following tableau described by Oliver, Orlando's brother:

A wretched ragged man, o'ergrown with hair,
Lay sleeping on his back. About his neck
A green and gilded snake had wreath'd itself,
Who with her head nimble in threats approach'd
The opening of his mouth ...
A lioness, with udders all drawn dry,
Lay couching, head on ground, with catlike watch,
When that the sleeping man should stir ...

(IV.iii.107–17)

The dual dangers to which the sleeping Oliver is susceptible are, on the face of it, female: the lioness an aged maternal figure ("with udders all drawn dry"), the female snake seductively encircling Oliver's neck. Let us first give this passage a conventional psychoanalytic reading: the virile and virtuous Orlando banishes the snake and battles with the lion while his evil "emasculated" brother, unconscious of his position as damsel in distress, sleeps on – their sibling rivalry displaced onto and mediated by gender conflict. Yet at the same time as the snake encircles her prey, she approaches and almost penetrates the vulnerable opening of Oliver's mouth. Rather than posit the snake, in this aspect, as a representation of the "phallic mother," I want to argue that in the snake's figure are concentrated the anxieties generated by the text's simultaneous commitment to homoeroticism and heterosexuality. If Oliver is endangered by the snake's "feminine" sexual powers, he is equally threatened by her phallic ones. He becomes both the feminized object of male aggression and the *ef*feminized object of female desire. The snake thus represents the erotic other of the text, the reservoir of the fears elicited by homoerotic exchanges – fears, I want to insist, that are not inherent in the experience of homoerotic desire, but that are produced by those ideologies that position homoeroticism as unnatural, criminal, and heretical.

Indeed the relations represented in this tableau suggest that no desire, male or female, heterosexual or homoerotic, is free of anxiety. As Touchstone says in a lighter vein, "as all is mortal in nature, so is all nature in love mortal in folly" (II.iv.52–3). But what is most interesting is that in this play sexual danger is encoded as feminizing to the object persistently figured as male. Consistently, the text seems less interested in the threat of a particular mode of desire (hetero / homo) than in the dangers desire *as such* poses to men. It is, in this sense, thoroughly patriarchal, positing man as the center of, and vulnerable to, desire. That the text marginalizes this expression of vulnerability by not dramatizing it on stage but reporting it only in retrospect suggests the extent to which the anxiety is repressed in the interests of achieving comic, heterosexual closure, however partially or problematically.

My highlighting of the affirmative possibilities of multiple pleasures is not meant to imply that *As You Like It* represents a paradisiacal erotic economy, a utopian return to a polymorphously perverse body unmediated by cultural restraints. As the penultimate gesture toward the institution of marriage clearly indicates, endless erotic mobility is difficult to sustain. But just as clearly, *As You Like It* registers its lack of commitment to the binary logic that dominates the organization of desire. If *As You Like It* suggests the "folly" of desire, part of that folly is the discipline to which it is subject.

My desire / More sharp than filed steel

Antonio, *Twelfth Night*

The sexual economy of *Twelfth Night* is saturated with multiple erotic investments: Viola / Cesario's dual desire for Olivia and Orsino; Orsino's ambivalent interest in Viola / Cesario; Sebastian's responses to Olivia and Antonio; and finally, Antonio's exclusive erotic wish for Sebastian. Although Viola's initial impulse for adopting male disguise is to serve the duke as a eunuch (I.ii.56), her status as sexually neutral dissipates as she quickly becomes both erotic object and subject. Critics often mention Viola's passivity, her inclination to commit "What else may hap to time" (I.ii.60), but they fail to recognize that as Cesario she woos Olivia with a fervor that exceeds her "text" (I.v.227). S/he asks, with no apparent mandate, to see Olivia's face; and upon viewing the "picture" (I.v.228), responds, "if you were the devil, you are fair" (I.v.246).

Critics also point to Viola / Cesario's anxiety over the predicament caused by the disguise:

> I am the man. If it be so, as 'tis,
> Poor lady, she were better love a dream.
> Disguise, I see, thou art a wickedness
> Wherein the pregnant enemy does much ...
> How will this fadge? My master loves her dearly;
> And I, poor monster, fond as much on him;
> And she, mistaken, seems to dote on me.
> What will become of this? As I am man,
> My state is desperate for my master's love;
> As I am woman – now alas the day! –
> What thriftless sighs shall poor Olivia breathe!
> O time, thou must untangle this, not I;
> It is too hard a knot for me t'untie.
>
> (II.ii.25–41)

The image by which Viola / Cesario expresses her plight is far more resonant than many critics have noted. The implied double negative of a *knot* that *cannot* be untied is precisely the figuration of her complex erotic investments: s / he "fonds" on her master, while simultaneously finding erotic intrigue and excitement as the object of Olivia's desire. The flip side of her anxiety about Olivia's desire is her own desire to be the *object* of Olivia's desire. This desire s / he can *(k)not* untie because of its status as negation. Why this desire is negated in this play I will take up in a moment. For now, what is important is that the play sets up Viola / Cesario's dual erotic investment, not so much to resolve it as to sustain its dramatic possibilities and to elicit the similarly polymorphous desires of the audience, whose spectator pleasure would be at least in part derived from a transgressive glimpse of multiple erotic possibilities.

To substantiate the play's investment in erotic duality, one can compare the language used in Viola / Cesario's two avowals of love: the first as Orsino's wooer of Olivia, and the second as s / he attempts to communicate love to Orsino. In both avowals, Viola / Cesario theatricalizes desire, using a similar language of conditionals toward both erotic objects. Compare the syntactical and semantic structure of Viola / Cesario's comment to Olivia, "If I did love you in my master's flame, / With such a suff'ring, such a deadly life, / In your denial I would find no sense; / I would not understand it" (i.v.259–62) to her comment to Orsino: "My father had a daughter lov'd a man, / As it might be, perhaps, were I a woman, / I should your lordship" (ii.iv.107–9). What predisposes us to credit the second comment as truth but the first as false, a suspect performance, is, I suggest, largely our assumption of universal heterosexuality. Both speeches are equally theatricalizations of desire. As such, both work to undermine the dichotomy between truth and falsehood, fiction and reality, heterosexuality and homoeroticism.

This is not to suggest that Viola / Cesario's position in relation to homoerotic desire is celebrated in the text: unlike Rosalind, her erotic predicament threatens her with destruction – or at least so s / he believes – at the hands of Sir Andrew, who is manipulated by Sir Toby to challenge his rival to a duel. The weapon of choice is not incidental, as the whole point of the threatened battle is for Viola / Cesario to demonstrate the "little thing" that "would make me tell them how much I lack of a man" (iii.iv.302–3). As Toby says: "Therefore, on, or strip your sword stark naked; for meddle you must, that's certain, or forswear to wear iron about you" (iii.iv.252–4). At this (phallic) point, Viola / Cesario's "lack" is upheld as the signifier of gender difference. And yet, to the extent that masculinity is embodied in the sword, it depends upon a particular kind of performance rather than any biological equipment. This theatrical moment simultaneously reinscribes a binary code of gender into the action, *and* suggests the extent to which gender is prosthetic.[20] It seems telling that at precisely this point of pressure on the meaning of gender, the play of erotic difference is abandoned. Or, more accurately, deflected, for who should enter to defend Viola / Cesario but Antonio, the figure who is positioned most firmly in a homoerotic relation to desire.

The entire first scene between Antonio and Sebastian is focused on Sebastian's denial of the sailor's help, and Antonio's irrepressible desire not only to protect but accompany the man with whom, we later learn, he has spent "three months ... / No int'rim, not a minute's vacancy. / Both day and night" (v.i.90–2). Antonio singlemindedly pursues Sebastian through the (to him) dangerous streets of Illyria: "But come what may, I do adore thee so / That danger shall seem sport, and I will go" (ii.i.44–5). It is not fortuitous that this scene (ii.i) intervenes between Viola / Cesario's wooing of Olivia, when s / he exceeds her "text" (i.v), and her contemplation of the danger inherent in this action: "It is too hard a knot for me t' untie" (ii.ii). For Antonio's words allude to the perils in early modern culture of an exclusively homoerotic passion: in order to remain in the presence of one's beloved, "danger" must be figuratively, if not literally, transformed into "sport." That the danger is not limited to the threat of Orsino's men (the force of law) is revealed in Antonio's plea to Sebastian, "If you will not murder me for my love, let me be your servant" (ii.i.33–4). The love Antonio extends is somehow capable of inciting the beloved to murder.

An even greater danger is intimated in this scene, which will ultimately have severe repercussions on the fate of Antonio's desire. Sebastian explains to Antonio that his father "left behind him myself and a sister, both born in an hour. If the heavens had been pleas'd, would we had so ended! But you, sir, alter'd that, for some hour before you took me from the breach of the sea was my sister drown'd" (ii.i.17–22). Sebastian's life is saved when he is pulled from the "breach of the sea," an image of the surf that invokes the re-birthing we expect from Shakespearean shipwrecks. But this rebirth is coincident with the supposed death of Sebastian's sister; she is "drown'd already ... with salt water" and drowned again in Sebastian's tearful "remembrance" (ii.i.29–30). In other words, Sebastian's rebirth into Antonio's love is implicated in the destruction of the only woman Sebastian has loved: Viola.

As mentioned, Viola / Cesario *is* threatened with destruction. Crucially, it is Antonio who saves her / him, thinking that he is defending his beloved. His entrance at this moment enacts the central displacement of the text: when the ramifications of a simultaneous homoeroticism and heterosexuality become too anxiety-ridden, the homoerotic energy of Viola / Cesario is displaced onto Antonio – the one figure, as Laurie Osborne notes, whose passion for another does not arise from deception or require a woman for its expression.[21]

Just before the swordfight Antonio finds Sebastian, and greets him with these words:

> I could not stay behind you. My desire,
> More sharp than filed steel, did spur me forth;
> And not all love to see you, though so much
> As might have drawn one to a longer voyage,
> But jealousy what might befall your travel,
> Being skilless in these parts ... My willing love,
> The rather by these arguments of fear,
> Set forth in your pursuit.
>
> (iii.iii.4–12)

Why do editors gloss "jealousy" as anxiety, when both words were available to Shakespeare, and both scan equally well?[22] Antonio is clearly both anxious about the dangers that might "befall" his beloved, and jealous of the attractions that might entice him. And not without reason: Sebastian falls rather easily to the "relish" of Olivia's charms (iv.i.59).

Antonio's discourse partakes of what I will call a "rhetoric of penetration." Male desire in Shakespearean drama is almost always figured in phallic images – which may seem tautological until one remembers the commonly accepted notion that Shakespeare's fops are not only "effeminate" but "homosexual." On the contrary, *Twelfth Night* represents male homoerotic desire as phallic in the most active sense: erect, hard, penetrating. Antonio describes his desire in terms of sharp, filed steel which spurs him on to pursuit, "spur" working simultaneously to "prick" him (as object) and urge him on (as subject). To the extent that heterosexual desire in Shakespearean drama is often associated with detumescence (the triumph of Venus over Mars, the pervasive puns on dying), and homoerotic desire is figured as permanently erect, it is the desire of man for man that is coded as the more "masculine."[23]

Many critics have noted in addition that in the early modern period excessive heterosexual lust seems to engender in men fears of "effeminacy." Romeo, for instance, complains that desire for Juliet "hath made me effeminate, / And in my temper soft'ned valor's steel!" Similarly, the Romans maintain that Antony's lust for Cleopatra has so compromised his gender identity that he "is not more manlike / Than Cleo-patra, nor the queen of Ptolemy / More womanly than he." In contrast, extreme virility, manifested in Spartan self-denial and military exploits, is not only depicted as consistent with erotic desire for other men; it also is expressed in it, as when Aufidius says to Coriolanus, "Let me twine / Mine arms about that body, whereagainst / My grained ash an hundred times hath broke," and goes on to compare the joy he feels at seeing Coriolanus as being greater than that which he felt "when I first my wedded mistress saw / Bestride my threshold."[24]

Fops, on the other hand, while commonly perceived as having a "passive" interest in male homoerotic encounters, are almost always involved in pursuing (if unsuccessfully) a heterosexual alliance.[25] Sir Andrew, for instance, hopes to marry Olivia, if only for her status and money. True, he is manipulated by Sir Toby, and he may therefore be seen to partake of a homoerotic triangular relation, whereby he woos his ostensible object (Olivia) in order to concretize ties with his real object (Toby).[26] However, Sir Andrew seems more accurately represented as void of erotic desire, merely attempting to fulfill the social requirements of heterosexuality. Indeed, he seems a vessel into which others' desires are poured, especially Sir Toby's triangular manipulation for wealth, ease, and power through the exchange of the body of his niece. Rather than being homosexual, fops are figured as always already effeminated by their heterosexual relation to desire.

Orsino, whose languid action and hyper-courtly language situate him as foppish, appears to be more in love with love than with any particular object. As Jean Howard points out, Orsino

> initially poses a threat to the Renaissance sex-gender system by languidly abnegating his active role as masculine wooer and drowning in narcissistic self-love ... His narcissism and potential effeminacy are displaced, respectively, onto Malvolio and Andrew Aguecheek, who suffer fairly severe humiliations for their follies.[27]

Orsino is narcissistic and "effeminate," but I would argue that neither his narcissism nor his "effeminacy" is indicative of desire for males *per se*. Orsino's "effeminacy," a gender characteristic, accompanies both his heterosexual desire for Olivia and his homoerotic desire for Cesario. What is most interesting, however, is the extent to which Orsino's desire is anxious, or in our modern parlance, homo*phobic*. In contrast to Orsino's homosocial ease with Cesario – their intimacy is established in three days (I.iv.3) – the possibility of a homo*erotic* basis to his affection for his servant creates tension: he defers accepting Viola as his betrothed until she has adopted her "maiden weeds" (v.i.252). Indeed, he refuses to really "see" her as a woman, continuing to refer to her as Cesario, "For so you shall be, while you are a man; / But when in other habits you are seen, / Orsino's mistress and his fancy's queen" (v.i.383–5). To the extent that his anxiety *is* desire, Orsino figures as the repressed homoerotic analogue to Antonio.

Throughout his canon, Shakespeare associates "effeminacy" in men with the fawning superciliousness of the perfumed courtier, and with the "womanish" tears of men no longer in control. Both Hotspur and Hamlet, for example, rail against the "effeminacy" of courtiers; Laertes and Lear describe their tears as "womanish." Hamlet is as disgusted by Osric and Guildenstern as he is by Ophelia and Gertrude; it is this fear of "effeminacy" that stimulates the homophobic disgust in his charge, "'Sblood, do you think I am easier to be play'd on than a pipe?"[28]

There is little in the canon to suggest that Shakespeare linked "effeminacy" to homoeroticism, unless we look to the "feminine" qualities of Cesario that ambivalently attract Orsino to his page. Historically, the charge of "effeminacy" seems to have been limited to such "boys" as Cesario, or to those adult men who were "uxoriously" obsessed with women. The unfailing correspondence of adult homoeroticism and "effeminacy" is a later cultural development, and is imported into Shakespeare's texts by critics responding to a different cultural milieu.[29] In *Twelfth Night*, both Antonio and Sebastian pointedly use their phallic swords, and are implicitly contrasted to Sir Andrew, whom even Viola / Cesario one-ups, despite the "little thing that would make [her] tell them how much [she] lack[s] as a man." "Appropriate" male desire is phallic, whether homoerotic or heterosexual; without that phallic force, men in Shakespearean drama are usually rendered either asexual or nominally heterosexual.

Despite the attractions of homoeroticism, the pleasure *Twelfth Night* takes in it is not sustained. Not only are Viola / Cesario and Sebastian betrothed respectively to Orsino and Olivia, but Antonio is marginalized – in part because he publicly speaks his desire, in part because his desire is exclusive of other bonds. Like *The Merchant of Venice's* Antonio, this Antonio gives his beloved his "purse"; shortly thereafter he is seized by the duke's men. As he struggles with the officers, Antonio states to "Sebastian":

> This comes with seeking you.
> But there's no remedy; I shall answer it.
> What will you do, now my necessity
> Makes me to ask you for my purse? It grieves me
> Much more for what I cannot do for you
> Than what befalls myself.
>
> (III.iv.333–8)

After Viola / Cesario offers money but denies not only their acquaintance, but knowledge of Antonio's "purse," the officers attempt to take Antonio away; but he resists:

> Let me speak a little. This youth that you see here
> I snatch'd one half out of the jaws of death,
> Reliev'd him with such sanctity of love,
> And to his image, which methought did promise
> Most venerable worth, did I devotion.
>
> (III.iv.360–4)

"What's that to us?" reply the officers, and Antonio is compelled to curse:

> But O how vile an idol proves this god!
> Thou hast, Sebastian, done good feature shame.
> In nature there's no blemish but the mind;
> None can be call'd deform'd but the unkind.
>
> (III.iv.366–9)

To which the officers conclude: "The man grows mad. Away with him!" (III.iv.372)

Antonio is labeled mad by the law not only because of the linguistic and class impropriety of his speech, but because his vocalization of desire is caught uncomfortably between the only two discourses available to him: platonic friendship and sodomy. There are literally no early modern terms by which Antonio's desire can be understood.

Antonio's imprisonment, we conventionally expect, will be revoked when Viola / Cesario's problems are resolved. With the entrance of Sebastian not only do brother and sister rediscover each other, but "nature to her bias," according to most critics, draws Olivia to Sebastian and Orsino to Viola (v.i.257). This appeal to "nature" can be seen to dissolve the previous dramatic energy expended in portraying socially illegitimate alliances, the conventional betrothals displacing the fantasy embodied by Viola / Cesario of holding in tension simultaneous objects of desire. Many feminist and psychoanalytic critics read this conclusion as a celebration of psychic androgyny in which Viola / Cesario is fantastically split, "An apple cleft in two" into Viola and Sebastian (v.i.221). However pertinent such a reading may be to the gender politics of the play (and I think that it bypasses rather than resolves the question of gender identity posed by transvestism), it ignores the erotic politics. Antonio's final query, "Which is Sebastian?" is answered by the "identification" of Sebastian and Viola and the quick, symmetrical pairings. Or is it? Is the Sebastian whose words to Antonio are: "Antonio, O my dear Antonio! / How have the hours rack'd and torture'd me, / Since I have lost thee!" (v.i.215–17) the same Sebastian who has just sanctified his love to Olivia? Despite his miraculous betrothal, Sebastian's own desire seems more complicated than the assumption of "natural" heterosexuality would suggest. In fact, Sebastian's desire, like Viola/Cesario's, seems to obliterate the distinction between homoerotic and heterosexual – at least until the institution of marriage comes into (the) play. As a reassertion of the essential heterosexuality of desire, Sebastian's allusion to "nature's bias" seems a bit suspect.

Joseph Pequigney offers an alternative interpretation of "nature to her bias" which not only reopens the question of the meaning of "bias," but inverts its relation to "nature." He notes that "bias" derives from

> the game of bowls played with a bowl or ball designed to run obliquely, and "bias" denotes either the form of the bowl that causes it to swerve or, as in the metaphor, the curved course it takes. Nature then chose an oblique or curved rather than a straight way of operating … This homoerotic swerving or lesbian [sic] deviation from the heterosexual straight and narrow is not unnatural, but, to the contrary, a modus operandi of Nature.[30]

Despite its closure, then, *Twelfth Night's* conclusion seems only ambivalently invested in the "natural" heterosexuality it imposes.

Comparison of the treatment of homoeroticism in *As You Like It* and *Twelfth Night* suggests that when homoeroticism is not a mutual investment it becomes problematic. This may seem distressingly self-evident, but to say it underscores the point that the anxiety exposed in Shakespearean drama is not so much about a particular mode of desire, as about the psychic exposure entailed by a lack of mutuality. Heterosexual desire is equally troubling when unrequited. Despite *Twelfth Night's* nod to heterosexual imperatives in the ambiguous allusion to "nature to her bias," and despite both texts' ultimate movement toward heterosexuality, homoeroticism is constructed throughout as merely one more mode of desire. As Antonio puts it, in the closest thing we have to an antihomophobic statement in an early modern text: "In nature there's no blemish but the mind; / None can be call'd deform'd but the unkind" (*Twelfth Night*, III.iv.368–9). Both modes of desire are responsive to social and institutional pressures; both are variously attributed to "noble" and "irrational" impulses. In other words, Shakespearean drama measures homoerotic and heterosexual impulses on the same scale of moral and philosophical value.

Secondly, the relative ease or dis-ease with homoerotic desire seems to depend on the extent to which such desire is recuperable within a simultaneous homoeroticism and heterosexuality that will ensure generational reproduction. Specifically, in these plays the dramatized fantasy of eliding women in erotic exchanges seems to initiate anxiety. When homoerotic exchanges threaten to replace heterosexual bonds, when eroticism is collapsed into anxiety about reproduction, then homoeroticism is exorcized at the same time as the female gender is resecured into the patriarchal order.

The specific anxiety about reproduction I hypothesize as a *structuring* principle for the movement of these comedies is not explicitly voiced in either play. It is, however, a dominant theme in the sonnets, beginning with the first line of the first poem to the young man: "From fairest creatures we desire increase / That thereby beauty's rose might never die."[31] As the poet exhorts his beloved to "Look in thy glass, and tell the face thou viewest / Now is the time that face should form another" – that if he should "Die single ... thine image dies with thee" (Sonnet 3) – the failure to reproduce is figured in narcissistic, even masturbatory, terms: "For having traffic with thyself alone / Thou of thyself thy sweet self dost deceive" (Sonnet 4). The sonnets' psychic strategy is founded on a paradox: the narcissism of taking the self as masturbatory object can only be countered and mastered by the narcissism of reproducing oneself in one's heirs.

That the failure to reproduce signified by this masturbatory fantasy is a veritable death knell is evidenced by Sonnet 3: "who is he so fond will be the tomb / Of his self-love, to stop posterity?" Indeed, if one notes that the final couplet of six out of the first seven sonnets explicitly offers death as the sole alternative to reproduction, the anxiety animating the exhortation to reproduce becomes quite clear. The sheer repetition of the sentiment (twelve sonnets out of the first sixteen) attests to the presence of a repetition compulsion, indicating unresolved psychic distress.[32]

Such distress obviously structures the reproductive madness of Sonnet 6:

> Then let not winter's ragged hand deface
> In thee thy summer, ere thou be distill'd.
> Make sweet some vial; treasure thou some place
> With beauty's treasure, ere it be self-kill'd.
> That use is not forbidden usury
> Which happies those that pay the willing loan;
> That's for thyself to breed another thee,
> Or ten times happier, be it ten for one;
> Ten times thyself were happier than thou art,
> If ten of thine ten times refigur'd thee.

That ten is ten times better than one is self-evidently true only if the one is not the one who carries, labors, and delivers those ten offspring. The misogynistic pun on vial, referring both to the vessel of the womb and its supposedly vile character indicates a structuring ambivalence. The logic of the sequence implies that homoerotic love can only be justified through a heterosexual reproductivity that is always already degraded by its contact with female genitalia – the underlying fantasy being the wish for reproduction magically untainted by the female body.

"Make thee another self, *for love of me*" (Sonnet 10, my emphasis). Surely it is not fortuitous that the homoerotic investment of the sonnets elicits such a strong investment in reproduction. This investment is finally mediated, and the anxiety regarding women's necessary role in reproduction is displaced, as the poet appropriates for himself reproductive powers. From Sonnet 15, in which the poet claims to "engraft" his beloved "new," through the subsequent four poems, heterosexual reproduction slowly but surely gives way to the aesthetic immortality "engrafted" on the beloved by the poet's skill. The power to create life is transformed into the exclusively male power of the poet's invocation to an exclusively male audience: "So long as men can breathe or eyes can see, / So long lives this and this gives life to thee" (Sonnet 18).

The historical reasons for the reproductive anxiety explicitly rendered in the sonnets, and implied by the structure of the comedies, are obviously complex. In order to unpack them, it may be useful to reinsert gender provisionally as a relevant analytic category, to examine the relation of homoerotic desire to the gender system. Eve Sedgwick argues that male homoeroticism was not perceived as threatening in early modern culture because it was not defined in opposition or as an impediment to heterosexuality; Trumbach and Saslow emphasize that the general pattern of male homoeroticism was "bisexual." *Exclusive* male homoeroticism, however, homoeroticism that did not admit the need for women, would disrupt important early modern economic and social imperatives: inheritance of name, entitlement, and property. Each of these imperatives, crucial to the social hierarchies of early modern England, was predominantly conferred through heterosexual marriage. I am suggesting, then, that the salient concern may be less the threat posed by homoerotic desire *per se* than that posed by non-monogamy and non-reproduction.

In addition, despite patriarchal control of female sexuality through the ideology of chastity and laws regulating marriage and illegitimacy, there seems to have been a high cultural investment in female erotic pleasure – not because women's pleasure was perceived as healthy or intrinsically desirable, but because it was thought necessary for successful conception to occur. According to Thomas Laqueur, early modern medical texts (including those of midwives) judged both male and female erotic pleasure as essential to generation.[33] Viewed as structurally inverted men, women were thought to ejaculate "seed" at the height of their sexual pleasure; conception supposedly began at the meeting of male and female seed. Because they were perceived as naturally cooler than men, women were thought to achieve orgasm only after the proper "heating" of their genitalia. In light of this social investment, it seems possible that an exclusive male homoeroticism could be seen as leaving female reproductive organs out, as it were, in the cold.

In so far as *As You Like It* gestures outward toward an eroticism characterized by a diffuse and fluid simultaneity, it does so because the text never feels compelled to fix, to identify, or to name the desires it expresses. In contrast, *Twelfth Night* closes down erotic possibility precisely to the degree it complies with the social imperative to name desire, to fix it within definitive boundaries, and to identify it with specific characters.

The "unmooring of desire, the generalizing of the libidinal" that Greenblatt sees as "the special pleasure of Shakespearean fiction" is, when one gets down to it, more comfortably evidenced in *As You Like It* than in *Twelfth Night*.[34] In the tensions exposed between the two plays, it may be that we start to move from what we are beginning to discern as Renaissance homoeroticism to what we know as modern homosexuality, from an inventive potentiality inherent in each subject to the social identity of a discrete order of being.[35]

It is of more than passing interest that insofar as each play enacts a "textual body," only *Twelfth Night* depends on a phallic representation of male homoeroticism. Much recent feminist and film criticism has implicated a phallic mode of representation within the visual economy of the "gaze," wherein value is ascribed according to what one sees (or fails to see): hence, the psychoanalytic verities of female "castration" and "penis envy." In those modes of representation governed by phallocentric prerogatives, argue many feminist film theorists, only two positions seem possible: the subject and the object of the gaze.[36] Although many theorists are now complicating this binary picture, arguing that women, in particular, negotiate as subjects and not merely as objects of the gaze, it might be helpful to distinguish the erotic economies of *Twelfth Night* and *As You Like It* along the following lines: *Twelfth Night* is predominantly phallic and visual; not only is Antonio's desire figured in phallic metaphors, but Orsino's desire waits upon the ocular proof of Viola / Cesario's "femininity." The final value is one of boundary setting, of marginalizing others along lines of exclusion. The erotics of *As You Like It*, on the other hand, are diffuse, non-localized, and inclusive, extending to the audience an invitation to "come play" – as does Rosalind-cum-boy-actor in the Epilogue.[37] Bypassing a purely scopic economy, *As You Like It* possesses provocative affinities with the tactile, contiguous, plural erotics envisioned by Luce Irigaray as more descriptive of female experience. We don't return to such a polymorphous textual body until the cross-gendered erotic play of *Antony and Cleopatra*.

This introduction of a diffuse, fluid erotics, and my analysis of the reproductive anxieties engendered by male homoeroticism, provoke the broader question of the relation of male homoeroticism to feminist politics. Contrary to the beliefs of those feminists who conflate male homosociality with homoeroticism, male homoeroticism has no unitary relationship to the structures and ideologies of male dominance. Patriarchal power is homosocial; but it also has been, at various times including the present, homophobic. As Sedgwick has demonstrated, "while male homosexuality does not correlate in a transhistorical way with political attitudes toward women, homophobia directed at men by men almost always travels with a retinue of gynephobia and antifeminism."[38] Male homoeroticism can be manipulated to reinforce and justify misogyny, or it can offer itself up as the means to deconstruct the binary structures upon which the subordination of women depends.

The logic of the sonnet sequence is, I believe, thoroughly misogynistic, and its homoerotics seem utterly entwined with that misogyny: a debased female reproduction is excised, and its creative powers appropriated, by the male lover-poet who thereby celebrates and immortalizes his male beloved. Conversely, the circulation of male homoerotic desire in *As You Like It* and *Twelfth Night* does not seem to depend upon an aversion to women or an ideology of male dominance as its *raison d'être*. The homoeroticism of *As You Like It* is not particularly continuous with the homosociality of the Duke's court (the homoerotic exchanges occur primarily between those excluded from it), nor are Antonio's, Viola / Cesario's, Orsino's, or Olivia's homoerotic interests particularly supportive of the patriarchal impulses of *Twelfth Night*. Indeed, whether the homoeroticism is embodied as male or female does not seem to have much impact on its subversive potential. Viola / Cesario's desire for a dual mode of eroticism is more threatening within the play than is Orlando's similar desire, but it is less dangerous than the exclusivity posed by Antonio.

In fact, the male and female homoeroticism of both plays interrupts the ideology of a "natural" love based on complementary yet oppositional genders. In so doing, the deviations from the dominant discourse of desire circulating throughout these texts transgress the Law of the Father, the injunction that sexuality will follow gender in lining up according to a "natural" binary code. By refusing such arbitrary divisions of desire, homoeroticism in *As You Like It* and *Twelfth Night* disrupts the cultural code that keeps both men and women in line, subverting patriarchy from within.

This is not to suggest that Shakespeare's plays do not demonstrate countless commitments to misogyny. Why homoeroticism would be so thoroughly supportive of the misogyny of the sonnets, and so seemingly independent of misogyny in these plays is an important question raised by my analysis. To what extent does genre influence the expression of erotic desire and anxiety? To begin to answer that question, and to substantiate those claims I have made, the treatment of homoeroticism in Shakespeare's predecessors, contemporaries, and followers must be analyzed. Obvious sites of inquiry would be a comparison of Shakespearean homoeroticism with that of Marlowe, and a study of the use of transvestism in Lyly, Sidney, Spenser, Jonson, Middleton, and Dekker.[39] What is crucial at this point is that the relation between gender and eroticism be carefully teased out, that eroticism be posed as a problematic in its own right – both intimately connected to and rigorously differentiated from gender.

The danger of pursuing this kind of inquiry at this moment is in ignoring gender differentials altogether, in an energetic pursuit of "sexuality." But if we remember that the analyses of both gender and eroticism are only part of a larger project of theorizing about and from the multiple subject positions we all live, and if we reflect on the complexity of our own erotic practices, perhaps we can trace the play of our differences without reifying either them or ourselves. Erotic choice is, as Robert Stoller remarks, "a matter of opinions, taste, aesthetics"; it is also a matter of political theater, in which we all, even now, play a part.[40]

Notes

1   Stephen Orgel, "Nobody's Perfect: Or Why Did the English Stage Take Boys for Women," *South Atlantic Quarterly* 88: 1 (1989), pp. 7–8.

2   Stephen Gosson, in *The Schoole of Abuse* (1579; London: The Shakespeare Society, 1841) makes no explicit mention of homoeroticism but initiates the gendered and erotic focus of the anti-theatrical attack by mentioning the theater's "effeminate gesture, to ravish the sense; and wanton speache, to whet desire to inordinate lust." The next year, an anonymous pamphleteer (probably Anthony Mundy) argued that the taking of women's parts by men was explicitly forbidden by the Law of God, referring to Deuteronomy 23:5. Due to the strength of this biblical authority, denunciation of theatrical cross-dressing became a most effective argument against the stage. In *Playes Confuted*

in Five Actions (*Markets of Bawdrie: The Dramatic Criticism of Stephen Gosson*, ed. Arthur Kinney, Salzburg Studies in Literature 4, Salzburg: Institut für Englische Sprache und Literatur, 1974), Gosson takes up the Deuteronomic code and rails against men adopting "not the apparell onely, but the gate, the gestures, the voyce, the passions of a woman." In *The Overthrow of Stage Playes*, John Rainoldes writes: "A woman's garment beeing put on a man doeth vehemently touch and moue him with the remembrance and imagination of a woman; and the imagination of a thing desirable doth stir up the desire" and "what sparkles of lust to that vice the putting of wemens attire on men may kindle in vncleane affections, as Nero shewed in Sporus, Heliogabalus in himselfe; yea certaine, who grew not to such excesse of impudencie, yet arguing the same in causing their boys to weare long heare like wemen." With Phillip Stubbes's *The Anatomie of Abuses* (1583; Netherlands: De Capo Press, 1972), explicit anxieties about homoeroticism enter the debate: "everyone brings another homeward of their way very friendly and in their secret conclaves they play sodomite or worse. And these be the fruites of playes and Interludes for the most part." The debate culminates in William Prynne's *Histrio-mastix: The Player's Scourge or Actor's Tragedy* (1633; New York: Garland Publishing, 1974), which charges the theaters as being nothing but a pretext for sodomy by listing those who have historically engaged in unnatural acts, including the Incubi, "who clothed their Galli, Succubi, Ganymedes and Cynadi in woman's attire, whose virilities they did oft-time dissect [castrate], to make them more effeminate, transforming them as neere might be into women, both in apparell, gesture, speech, behavior ... And more especially in long, unshorne, womanish, frizled haire and love-lockes." For debates about street transvestism, see *Hic Mulier; Or the Man Woman* and *Haec-Vir; Or the Womanish Man* (1620) in *Half Humankind: Contexts and Texts of the Controversy about Women in England, 1540–1640*, ed. Katherine Usher Henderson and Barbara F. McManus (Chicago: University of Illinois Press, 1985), pp. 264–89.

3 Stephen Greenblatt, "Fiction and Friction," *Shakespearean Negotiations: The Circulation of Social Energy in Renaissance England* (Oxford: Clarendon Press, 1988), p. 86.

4 See Orgel, "Nobody's Perfect," pp. 22–9 and Lisa Jardine *Still Harping on Daughters: Women and Drama in the Age of Shakespeare* (Brighton: Harvester Press, 1983), pp. 9–34.

5 C. L. Barber, *Shakespeare's Festive Comedy: A Study of Dramatic Form and its Relation to Social Custom* (New York: Princeton University Press, 1963), p. 6. Barber writes of *Twelfth Night* (and the same presumably would be true of *As You Like It*): "The most fundamental distinction the play brings home to us is the difference between men and women ... Just as the saturnalian reversal of social roles need not threaten the social structure, but can serve instead to consolidate it, so a temporary, playful reversal of sexual roles can renew the meaning of the normal relation" (p. 245). For early feminist analyses, see, for instance, Juliet Dusinberre, *Shakespeare and the Nature of Women* (New York: Barnes and Noble, 1975), pp. 231–71, and Robert Kimbrough, "Androgyny Seen Through Shakespeare's Disguise," *Shakespeare Quarterly* 33: 1 (1982), pp. 17–33.

6 The phrase "traffic in women" was first coined by Emma Goldman in her critique of marriage as a form of prostitution. It gained critical prominence through Gayle Rubin's "The Traffic in Women: Notes on the 'Political Economy' of Sex," *Toward an Anthropology of Women*, ed. Rayna R. Reiter (New York: Monthly Review Press, 1975), pp. 157–210.

7 I have learned much in this regard from Peter Stallybrass and Allon White, who also critique the reliance on such polarizations. They demonstrate the extent to which binary classifications are always imbued with their others, and argue that the relative radicality of any transgression can only be ascertained by placing it in history. Also helpful is Jonathan Dollimore, "Subjectivity, Sexuality, and Transgression: The Jacobean Connection," *Renaissance Drama* 17 (1986), pp. 53–81.

8 In addition to Jean Howard, "Crossdressing, The Theatre, and Gender Struggle in Early Modern England," *Shakespeare Quarterly* 39: 4 (1988), Leah Marcus, "Shakespeare's Comic Heroines, Elizabeth I, and the Political Uses of Androgyny," *Women in the Middle Ages and the Renaissance: Literary and Historical Perspectives*, ed. Mary Beth Rose (Syracuse: Syracuse University Press, 1986), and Laura Levine, "Men in Women's Clothing: Anti-theatricality and Effeminization from 1579 to 1642," *Criticism* 28: 2 (Spring 1986), see Catherine Belsey, "Disrupting Sexual Difference: Meaning

and Gender in the Comedies," *Alternative Shakespeares*, ed. John Drakakis (London: Methuen, 1985), pp. 166–90; Phyllis Rackin, "Androgyny, Mimesis, and the Marriage of the Boy Heroine on the English Renaissance Stage," *PMLA* 102 (1987), pp. 29–41; and Karen Newman, "Portia's Ring: Unruly Women and Structures of Exchange in *The Merchant of Venice*," *Shakespeare Quarterly* 38 (1987), pp. 19–33.

9 Orgel, "Nobody's Perfect," p. 13.

10 Sedgwick, *Between Men: English Literature and Male Homosocial Desire* (New York: Columbia University Press, 1985), p. 2.

11 Antonio's marginalization parallels that of Antonio in *The Merchant of Venice*, whose bond to Bassanio is initially honored and redeemed by Portia, but later displaced by her manipulations of the ring plot which, paradoxically, foster her subordination in a patriarchal heterosexual economy.

12 Montrose, " 'The Place of a Brother' in *As You Like It*: Social Process and Comic Form," *Shakespeare Quarterly* 32: 1 (1981), pp. 28–54.

13 Ibid., p. 51.

14 Howard, "Crossdressing," p. 434.

15 Ibid., p. 435. Terms can be confusing here, in part due to translation. In Luce Irigaray's formulation, *la mascarade* is "An alienated or false version of femininity arising from the woman's awareness of the man's desire for her to be his other, the masquerade permits woman to experience desire not in her own right but as the man's desire situates her." Masquerade is the role (playing) required by "femininity." Thus, Rosalind's improvisation is really closer to *mimetisme* (mimicry) which, in Irigaray's terms, is "An interim strategy for dealing with the realm of discourse (where the speaking subject is posited as masculine), in which the woman deliberately assumes the feminine style and posture assigned to her within this discourse in order to uncover the mechanisms by which it exploits her" (*This Sex Which Is Not One*, trans. Catherine Porter, Ithaca: Cornell University Press, 1985, p. 220).

16 Saslow, *Ganymede in the Renaissance: Homosexuality in Art and Society* (New Haven: Yale University Press, 1986), p. 2.

17 Orgel, "Nobody's Perfect," p. 22.

18 Barber, *Shakespeare's Festive Comedy*, p. 231. See also W. Thomas MacCary, *Friends and Lovers: The Phenomenology of Desire in Shakespearean Comedy* (New York: Columbia University Press, 1985).

19 Phyllis Rackin, "Historical Difference / Sexual Difference."

20 Peter Stallybrass helped me with this formulation.

21 Laurie Osborne, "The Texts of *Twelfth Night*," *ELH* (Spring, 1990), pp. 37–61. Osborne's excellent analysis of the manipulation of the placement of the Antonio scenes in eighteenth- and nineteenth-century performance editions suggests that the playtexts themselves indicate changing significations of homoeroticism.

22 The *Oxford English Dictionary*'s first entry for "anxiety," as in "The quality or state of being anxious; uneasiness or trouble of mind about some uncertain event; solicitude, concern," is 1525. The first entry for "jealous," as in "Vehement in feeling, as in wrath, desire, or devotion" is 1382; for "Ardently amorous; covetous of the love of another, fond, lustful" is 1430; and for "Zealous or solicitous for the preservation or well-being of something possessed or esteemed; vigilant or careful in guarding; suspiciously careful or watchful" is 1387.

23 I am indebted to Peter Stallybrass for reminding me of the difference between heterosexual and homoerotic phallic imagery.

24 *Romeo and Juliet* III.i.113–15; *Antony and Cleopatra*, I.iv.5–7; and *Coriolanus*, IV.v.111–23. I am indebted to Phyllis Rackin for reminding me of some of these instances, and her further amplification in her talk "Historical Difference / Sexual Difference."

25 Randolph Trumbach's historical analysis bears this out; see "The Birth of the Queen: Sodomy and the Emergence of Gender Equality in Modern Culture 1660–1750," *Hidden from History: Reclaiming the Gay and Lesbian Past*, ed. Martin Duberman *et al.* (New York: New American Library, 1989), p. 133.

26 For an analysis of triangular desire, see René Girard, *Deceit, Desire, and the Novel: Self and Other in Literary Structure*, trans. Yvonne Freccero (Baltimore: Johns Hopkins University Press, 1965).

27 Howard, "Crossdressing," p. 432.

28 *Henry IV, part 1*, i.iii.29–69; *Hamlet*, v.ii.82–193 and iii.ii.368–9; *King Lear*, ii.iv.271–8.

29 Trumbach, "Birth of the Queen," p. 134.

30 Joseph Pequigney, "The Two Antonios and Same-Sex Love in *Twelfth Night* and *The Merchant of Venice*," unpublished manuscript presented to the Shakespeare Association of America, 1989, p. 11.

31 I am following David Bevington's numbering of the sonnets; he follows Thomas Thorpe, the original publisher of the sequence. In "Making Love Out of Nothing At All: the Issue of Story in Shakespeare's Procreation Sonnets," *Shakespeare Quarterly* 41: 4 (Winter 1990), pp. 470–88, Robert Crosman takes up the issue of homoeroticism from a sympathetic if rather uninformed historical perspective. Whereas Pequigney argues that the first seventeen "procreation" sonnets record a gradual evolution of the poet's feelings for the young man, Crosman argues that Shakespeare first pretended to fall in love with his patron as a strategy of flattery, and then discovered he was no longer pretending.

32 For an explanation of the repetition compulsion, see Sigmund Freud, *Beyond the Pleasure Principle*, trans. James Strachey (New York: Norton, 1961).

33 Thomas Laqueur, *Making Sex: Body and Gender from the Greeks to Freud* (Cambridge: Harvard University Press, 1990).

34 Stephen Greenblatt, "Fiction and Friction," in *Shakespearean Negotiations: The Circulation of Social Energy in Renaissance England* (Oxford: Clarendon Press, 1988), p. 89.

35 Saslow makes a similar point about Michelangelo's status as a transitional figure; see "Homosexuality in the Renaissance: Behaviour, Identity, and Artistic Expression," in *Hidden From History: Reclaiming the Gay and Lesbian Past*, ed. Martin Duberman, Martha Vicinus, and George Chauncey Jr. (New York: New American Library, 1989), pp. 90–105.

36 See, for instance, Laura Mulvey, "Visual Pleasure and Narrative Cinema," and "Afterthoughts on 'Visual Pleasure and Narrative Cinema' inspired by *Duel in the Sun*," *Feminism and Film Theory*, ed. Constance Penley (London: Routledge, 1988), pp. 57–79; Janet Bergstrom and Mary Ann Doane, "The Female Spectator: Contexts and Directions," *Camera Obscura: A Journal of Feminism and Film Theory* 20 / 21 (May / Sept. 1989), pp. 5–27; and Irigaray, *This Sex Which Is Not One*, pp. 23–33.

37 Jean Howard alerted me to the fact that class differences are implicated in these erotic differences: as nostalgic pastoral, *As You Like It*'s class hierarchy is diffused and inclusive; *Twelfth Night*, on the other hand, is thoroughly aristocratic and, with the exception of Maria, marginalizes those figures below the rank of "gentleman."

38 Sedgwick, *Between Men*, p. 216.

39 Rackin has initiated such a comparative analysis of transvestism in "Androgyny, Mimesis, and the Marriage of the Boy Heroine on the English Renaissance Stage."

40 Robert Stoller, *Observing the Erotic Imagination* (New Haven: Yale University Press, 1985), p. 15.

Part XII

Performance Criticism

40 Shakespeare and the Blackfriars Theatre   732
    Gerald Eades Bentley
41 The Critical Revolution   745
    J. L. Styan
42 *William Shakespeare's Romeo + Juliet*: Everything's Nice in America?   750
    Barbara Hodgdon
43 Deeper Meanings and Theatrical Technique: The Rhetoric of
    Performance Criticism   762
    William B. Worthen

I n the last years of the twentieth century a group of like-minded critics began to seek out one another and to theorize the practice of studying dramatic texts as represented on the stage. In this critical category, as in new historicism and textual criticism, students of Shakespeare have led the way in thinking originally and rigorously about a new kind of critical practice. The word "new" is perhaps something of an exaggeration – or perhaps to some extent a form of advertisement – as it often is when emerging voices seek to extend a critical mode and put their distinctive stamp on it. Some form of performance study has been practiced since Aristotle, probably ever since actors began performing plays, and certainly one finds versions of it in the early modern period. In *A Midsummer Night's Dream* the mechanicals' fears about their terrific power over their audience – "a lion among ladies is a most dreadful thing" – attests to Shakespeare's own fascination with the conditions of representation and the theoretical relationships among text, actor, and audience.

From the Restoration to the present, dramatists, critics, poets, actors, and spectators have commented productively on the status and effects of Shakespearean performance:

a few well-known cases include the diary entries of Samuel Pepys in the seventeenth century; the reflections of such essayists as William Hazlitt and Charles Lamb (e.g., the latter's view that *King Lear* is more effective on the page than on the stage); newspaper reportage, some of it quite extensive, of productions starring the great nineteenth-century actors such as Kean and Irving; Ellen Terry's lectures on Shakespeare's characters, commentaries that in her old age she combined with recitations of major speeches on her tours of America; and Harley Granville-Barker's *Prefaces to Shakespeare*, in which the innovative modernist director and playwright articulates his insights about staging practices and interpretation gathered over a career in the theater. All these documents might be considered practical forms of performance criticism, although most of them would have been thought of as "stage history." Performance criticism, then, is a broad church, encompassing reviews and other forms of journalistic opinion, stage history, biography, autobiography, directors' notes, studies of physical spaces in which plays are performed, accounts of acting companies and their commercial dealings, and other such loosely related subcategories.

The mid-twentieth-century version of what we now call performance criticism was practiced by such learned and diligent scholars as Gerald Eades Bentley, Alfred Harbage, and other students of the early modern stage and its audience. E. K. Chambers's *The Elizabethan Stage* (1923; four volumes) and Bentley's *The Jacobean and Caroline Stage* (1941–68; seven volumes), for example, represent a combination of scholarship and criticism typical of the period. For the most part, these scholars were more interested in theater history than in performance. Other relevant mid-century studies include Harbage's *As They Liked It* (1947), an investigation of the Elizabethan audience; his *Shakespeare and the Rival Traditions* (1952); and Bernard Beckerman's *Shakespeare at the Globe, 1599–1609* (1962). All these scholarly books were helpful in grounding Shakespeare's theatrical practice in the material and commercial contexts of early modern London, thereby making possible more historically informed studies of Elizabethan and Jacobean performance. The recent archival and historical investigations of such scholars as Andrew Gurr, Roslyn Knutson, and William Ingram should be seen as continuations of such necessary work.

Bentley's essay included here offers a typical example of his important contribution and, by extension, the similar work of others. Published in 1949 in the first volume of *Shakespeare Survey* – then a new journal whose pedigree (the Shakespeare Institute in Stratford) and editorial board made it immediately prestigious and central to the discipline – the essay argues that physical space determines artistic direction. Specifically, Bentley believes that the success of the King's Men in converting the hall at Blackfriars into an indoor theater, a "private theater," encouraged their principal dramatist to exchange tragedy for the mode of romance. Plays such as *Cymbeline* and *The Winter's Tale* exemplify a theatrical form associated with magic and music and thus suited to the controlled, more intimate hall theater. Bentley may overstate his case slightly, and the position has been modified and complicated by more recent scholarship and criticism. If his argument seems almost self-evident at the beginning of the twenty-first century, our response attests to the success of such stage historians at articulating and documenting their views.

At about the same time, some other students of Shakespeare, exhibiting something of a theoretical bent, began to approach performance as a distinct mode of understanding the Shakespearean text. Chief among these was J. L. Styan, who presented his views in a series of thoughtful and respected critical studies, some devoted chiefly to Shakespeare and others to a range of dramatists and periods of world drama. The landmark study in the development of performance-based criticism is his *Shakespeare Revolution: Criticism and Performance in the Twentieth Century*, published in 1977. In it Styan surveys the achievements of influential twentieth-century stage directors, outlining the movement from the pictorial extravagance of Victorian Shakespeare, through William Poel's efforts at an Elizabethan revival, down to Peter Brook's radical conception of the theater as an empty space. Such a critical enterprise was not in itself new: eighteenth- and nineteenth-century writers left detailed accounts of production styles and delighted in comparative analysis, and twentieth-century scholars such as Arthur Colby Sprague contributed careful studies of actors and other features of theatrical history. But Styan surpassed his predecessors not only by extending his survey into the 1970s, but also by coordinating the analysis of performance with the treatment of texts as literature: in other words, he allowed performance criticism the same intellectual dignity as literary criticism.

What was genuinely new is Styan's stated purpose of making such archival information available to scholars and critics who could use it as evidence about the meaning of the Shakespearean text. According to this view, theatrical performance could help to solve scholarly problems with which it had thus far had nothing to do, particularly cases of textual obscurity. For example, early in *The Shakespeare Revolution* Styan cites Granville-Barker's response to a newly published scholarly study of Shakespearean punctuation:

> It is unwise to decide upon any disputed passage without seeing it in *action*, without canvassing all its dramatic possibilities. For a definitive text, we need first a Shakespeare Theatre in which a generation of scholars may be as used to seeing as to reading the play.[1]

Styan's account details a rapprochement between the enterprises of scholarship and theatrical performance. He demonstrates that directors such as Barry Jackson and Tyrone Guthrie were relying increasingly upon advances in scholarship, and conversely that scholars such as John Dover Wilson were becoming increasingly hospitable to the heuristic possibilities of the stage. Bolstering his position with support from such unassailable scholar-critics as Harry Levin, Stanley Wells, and Norman Rabkin, Styan established himself as an advocate – and an eloquent one – for the hermeneutic value of performance.

The indisputable success of his effort to encourage conversation between stage and study is visible in the burgeoning of books about performance in the 1980s and 1990s. The University of Manchester Press, for example, introduced a *Shakespeare in Performance* series: in each volume a well-known scholar looks critically at how a single Shakespeare play has been represented in major productions from the sixteenth century to the present. Similarly, Cambridge University Press created an equivalent series, *Shakespeare in Production*, in which the text is complemented with explanatory notes drawn from the theatrical history of the work. In most of such volumes the critic employs theatrical records, journalistic reports, interviews with actors and directors, production photographs, promptbooks, and other such instruments to illuminate the interpretive possibilities of familiar and unfamiliar plays. Not surprisingly, emphasis tends to fall on twentieth-century productions owing to the greater availability of archival information.

As the subdiscipline advanced, however, critics interested in performance began to raise questions about the fundamental nature of the endeavor, debating particularly the definition of terms and doing so with some theoretical sophistication. For example, Styan concludes his introductory chapter by claiming that "The search is on, for the theatrical effect and experience of the original performance, in the belief that the meaning is in the experience."[2] The grounds for controversy are easy to discern, and postmodernism raises a red flag. What is "the experience"? What is "the meaning"? What is "the original performance"? Can these questions ever be answered satisfactorily? Such problems of definition lead to further complexities: What is the epistemological status of performance? of *a* performance? of the text? of *a* text? What is textual authority? Clearly the study of Shakespearean performance had become engaged with the move toward theory in English studies at large during the 1980s and 1990s. As critics and scholars began to interrogate the nature of textual authority, to consider the problem of multiple texts, and to cope with the indeterminacy of meaning (see chapters 18 and 19, this volume), their questions had a profound impact upon the theory of theatrical representation.

The effect of that second revolution on the study of performance is summarized at the beginning of James Bulman's 1996 collection of essays, *Shakespeare, Theory, and Performance*:

> [Styan] subscribed to the notion that Shakespeare's texts are stable and authoritative, that meaning is immanent in them, and that actors and directors are therefore *interpreters* rather than *makers* of meaning. He believed, too, that audience responses to the plays are not historically particular, but universal. What *The Shakespeare Revolution* failed to take into account was the radical contingency of performance – the unpredictable, often playful intersection of history, material conditions, social contexts, and reception that destabilizes Shakespeare and makes theatrical meaning a participatory act. This volume marks how far we have come since the revolution.[3]

Bulman's volume contains essays by many significant contributors to performance study at the end of the twentieth century. Of these critics, William B. Worthen has probably written the most searching studies of how we might think about the competition between text and performance. His 1989 *Shakespeare Quarterly* essay reproduced here constitutes an early, succinct statement of the problems he would later develop in *Shakespeare and the Authority of Performance*.

The increasing respectability of performance studies in the academy did not delight everyone, however. While not going so far as to revive the Bradleyan idea of the "dramatic poem," some scholars have demurred at the theoretical and practical arguments of the performance critics. Concerned about the potential exclusivity of performance as a mode of representation, they argue that the theatrical origin of Shakespeare's dramatic texts does not warrant privileging the theatrical performance as somehow more "authentic" than reading. Harry Berger, Jr., in particular, has been vocal and witty in claiming that stage-centered criticism is "reductive."

The proponents of the New Histrionicism, as it may be called, argue that reading is irresponsible unless it imitates playgoing, and in its strongest form this argument establishes the empirical experience and psychology of playgoing as the exemplar whose privileges and constraints are to be reproduced in armchair interpretation.[4]

Such objections have provoked a number of side skirmishes between partisans of page and stage, but the complaints of Berger and others have also had the salutary effect of increasing self-consciousness and theoretical rigor in performance criticism. Recent students of performance have become more alert to such traps as generalizing audience response from limited accounts or accepting the notion that performance affords unmediated access to the playwright's intentions.[5] And, like almost every other category of criticism, performance studies seem to be progressing at a very rapid rate.

A final consideration is another kind of performance: film. When Styan was writing in the 1960s and 1970s, Shakespeare on film was relatively rare. Except for the few Olivier films, the brilliant if eccentric work of Orson Welles, and the unique adaptations of Kurosawa, filmed Shakespeare had not developed in the way cinematic pioneers had thought it would. But from about 1979, when the BBC and Time-Life presented their first televised plays in a series comprising the entire Shakespeare canon, film and video became more significant as cultural phenomena and thus more valuable as documents in an expanded field of study. A decade later Kenneth Branagh's films, especially *Henry V* (1989) and *Much Ado About Nothing* (1993), deliberately sought to increase Shakespeare's popular appeal. And all these efforts have generated others, both relatively straight filmed performances (Almereyda's *Hamlet*) and free adaptations (*10 Things I Hate About You*). One of the leaders in the cultural study of film is Barbara Hodgdon, whose lively style and breadth of reference have given her a prominent role in the new kind of performance study. Her essay on Baz Luhrmann's *William Shakespeare's Romeo + Juliet* exemplifies the verve and insight of her work generally. At the end of the twentieth century the territory on which the Shakespearean revolution was taking place suddenly widened.

Notes

1 *The Shakespeare Revolution: Criticism and Performance in the Twentieth Century* (Cambridge: Cambridge University Press, 1977), p. 2.
2 Ibid., p. 9.
3 *Shakespeare, Theory, and Performance*, ed. James C. Bulman (London: Routledge, 1996), p. 1.
4 *Imaginary Audition: Shakespeare on Stage and Page* (Berkeley: University of California Press, 1989), p. xii.
5 See Bulman, *Shakespeare, Theory, and Performance*, pp. 6–7.

40

Shakespeare and the Blackfriars Theatre

Gerald Eades Bentley

It is necessary at the outset in a discussion of this sort to place Shakespeare in what seems to me his proper context – a context which none but the Baconians and Oxfordians deny, but which most scholars and critics tend to ignore. That context is the London commercial theatre and the organized professional acting troupe.

Shakespeare was more completely and continuously involved with theatres and acting companies than any other Elizabethan dramatist whose life we know. Most Elizabethan dramatists had only their writing connection with the theatres, but Shakespeare belonged to the small group which both wrote and acted. In this small group of actor-dramatists, the best-known names are those of Heywood, Rowley, Field and Shakespeare. Of this thoroughly professionalized band, Shakespeare is the one most closely bound to his company and his theatre, for he is the only one of the four who did not shift about from company to company but maintained his close association with a single acting troupe for more than twenty years. Besides this, he was bound to theatres and actors in still another fashion which makes him unique among all Elizabethan dramatists: he is the only dramatist we know who owned stock in theatre buildings over an extended period. His income was derived from acting, from writing plays, from shares in dramatic enterprises, and from theatre rents. From the beginning to the end of his writing career we must see him in a theatrical context if we are not to do violence to the recorded facts. At the beginning is our first reference to him in Greene's allusion to the "Tygers hart wrapt in a Players hyde"; at the end are his own last words, so far as we know them, in his will. This will is mostly concerned with Stratford affairs, but when he does turn to the years of his London life and his many London associates, he singles out only three for a last remembrance. These men are John Heminges, Henry Condell, and Richard Burbage – all three actors, all three fellow-sharers in the acting company of the King's men, all three fellow-stockholders in the Globe and the Blackfriars. If Shakespeare's proper context is not the London commercial theatres and the professional troupes, then evidence has no meaning, and one man's irresponsible fancies are as good as another's.

Now in spite of all the evidence that Shakespeare's dominant preoccupation throughout his creative life was the theatre, most scholars and critics of the last 150 years have written of him as the professional poet and not as the professional playwright. For the most part he has been studied as Spenser and Milton and Keats are studied. For a century and a half the great majority of studies of Shakespeare's genius and development have been concerned with literary influences and biographical influences and not with theatrical influences.[1] We have studied his sources and his text, his indebtedness to Ovid and Holinshed and Montaigne and Plutarch. Even in biographical studies the preference has always been for the non-theatrical aspects of Shakespeare's life – his boyhood in the woods and fields about Stratford, his marriage and his wife, the death of his son Hamnet, his relations with Southampton and Essex, his supposed breakdown, his retirement to Stratford. Now any or all of these facts, or alleged facts, no doubt had an influence on the great creations of Shakespeare. I do not suggest that our study of them should be discontinued. But given the verified documentary evidence which we have, is it not dubious practice to devote a large part of our investigations to the more or less problematical influences in Shakespeare's career and to devote a very small part of our efforts to that enormously significant influence which dominated the majority of his waking hours for the twenty-odd years of his creative maturity? A dozen or more unquestioned documents show that Shakespeare's daily concern was the enterprise of the Lord Chamberlain-King's company. Shakespeare had obviously read Ovid and Holinshed and Lord North's *Plutarch*; surely he must have mourned for the untimely death of his only son; but none of these can have occupied his mind for so long as his daily association with the enterprise of the Lord Chamberlain-King's men. Of the factors in his life and development which we can now identify, this was surely the most important.

Now what are the events in his long and absorbing association with this troupe which we can expect to have influenced his work? One of the first must have been the protracted plague closings of 1593 and 1594, for out of this disaster to all London players the Lord Chamberlain's company apparently rose.[2] Another must have been the assembling of the players and the drawing up of the agreement for the formal organization of the Lord Chamberlain's company. The record suggests that Shakespeare was one of the leaders in this organization, for when the new company performed before the court in the Christmas season of 1594–5, payment was made to Richard Burbage, the principal actor, Will Kemp, the principal comedian, and William Shakespeare.[3] How did the great possibilities offered by this new troupe, destined to become the most famous and most successful in the history of the English theatre, affect the writing of its chief dramatist?

In the winter of 1598–9 occurred another event which must have been of absorbing interest for all members of the company. This was of course the building of the Globe on the Bankside. Here was a theatre built for the occupancy of a particular company, and six of the seven owners were actors in the company. Assuredly it was built, so far as available funds would allow, to the specific requirements of the productions of the Lord Chamberlain's men. What facilities did Shakespeare get which he had not had before? How did he alter his composition to take advantage of the new possibilities? Can there be any doubt that as a successful man of the theatre he did so? Yet I know of no study which attempts to assess this vital new factor in relation to Shakespeare's development.

The next event which must have been of great importance for Shakespeare's company was its involvement in the Essex rebellion. This exceptional case has received the full attention of critics and scholars because of its supposed relation to a performance of Shakespeare's *Richard II*. Actually, however, the Essex rebellion, much though it must have excited the company for a few months, was the least influential of all these factors affecting the company's activities and Shakespeare's development. Apparently the company's innocence was established without much difficulty.[4] There is no indication that their later performances or Shakespeare's later writing were affected by the experience. Though the events were sensational, and though they must have caused great anxiety for a time, they cannot be thought of as events of long-term significance in the history of this group of men who were so important and influential in Shakespeare's career and development.

Of much more importance in the affairs of the company was their attainment of the patronage of James I less than two months after the death of Elizabeth.[5] This patronage and the King's livery certainly became one of the important factors in creating the great prestige of the company. In the ten years before they became the King's company, their known performances at court average about three a year; in the ten years after they attained their new service their known performances at court average about thirteen a year, more than those of all other London companies combined.[6] They were officially the premier company in London; a good part of their time must have been devoted to the preparation of command performances. Surely this new status of the troupe must have been a steady and pervasive influence in the development of its principal dramatist, William Shakespeare.

The final event which I wish to mention in the affairs of the King's company was perhaps the most important of all. There is no doubt that it made a great change in the activities of the company, and I do not see how it can have failed to be a principal influence in Shakespeare's development as a dramatist. This event was the acquisition of the famous private theatre in Blackfriars. No adult company in London had ever before performed regularly in a private theatre. For thirty years the private theatres with their superior audiences, their concerts, their comfortable accommodations, their traffic in sophisticated drama and the latest literary fads, had been the exclusive homes of the boy companies, the pets of Society. Now for the first time a troupe of those rogues and vagabonds, the common players, had the temerity to present themselves to the sophisticates of London in a repertory at the town's most exclusive theatre. I suspect that this was one of the turning points in Tudor and Stuart dramatic history. Beaumont and Jonson and Fletcher had begun to make the craft of the playwright more socially respectable. The increasing patronage of the drama by the royal family, and the growing splendour and frequency of the court masques which were written by ordinary playwrights and performed in part by common players, were raising the prestige of the drama and the theatre from its Elizabethan to its Caroline state. The acquisition of the Blackfriars in 1608 by the King's company and the full exploitation of the new playhouse must have been the most conspicuous evidence to Londoners of the changing state of affairs. Surely it is impossible that the King's men and their principal dramatist, William Shakespeare, could have been unaware of this situation. Surely they must have bent all their efforts in the selection and performance of old plays and in the commissioning and writing of new ones to the full exploitation of this unprecedented opportunity. The new state of affairs must have been apparent in much that they did, and it must have influenced decidedly the dramatic compositions of Shakespeare.

So far, it has been my contention that all we know of William Shakespeare has shown him to be above all else a man of the theatre, that during the twenty years of his creative maturity most of his time was spent in closest association with members of the Lord Chamberlain-King's company and in thought about their needs and their interests, and that therefore in the affairs of this company we should seek one of the principal influences in his creative life. I have mentioned six events which (so far as we can tell through the mists of 350 years) seem to have been important in the affairs of that theatrical organization. These events are not all of equal importance, but each of them, except possibly the Essex rebellion, must have had a marked effect on the activities of Shakespeare's company and therefore on the dramatic creations of Shakespeare himself. Each one, it seems to me, deserves more study than it has received in its relation to the development of Shakespeare's work.

Let me invite your attention now to a fuller consideration of one of the most important of these events in the history of the Lord Chamberlain-King's company, namely the acquisition of the Blackfriars Theatre. What did this event mean in the history of the company, and how did it affect the writing of William Shakespeare?

Probably we should note first the time at which the Blackfriars would have begun to influence the company and the writing of Shakespeare. All the dramatic histories say that the King's men took over the Blackfriars Theatre in 1608, and this is true in a legal sense, for on 9 August 1608 leases were executed conveying the Blackfriars Playhouse to seven lessees: Cuthbert Burbage, Thomas Evans, and five members of the King's company – John Heminges, William Sly, Henry Condell, Richard Burbage, and William Shakespeare.[7] The few scholars who have examined in detail the history of the King's company have noted, however, that Shakespeare and his fellows probably did not begin to act at the Blackfriars in August of 1608. The plague was rife in London at that time; fifty plague deaths had been recorded for the week ending 28 July, and for a year and a half, or until December 1609, the bills of mortality show an abnormally high rate from the plague.[8] Though specific records about the closing of the theatres are not extant, we have definite statements that they were closed for part of this period, and comparison with other years suggests that there must have been very little if any public acting allowed in London between the first of August 1608 and the middle of December 1609. Therefore, it has occasionally been said, the Blackfriars was not used by the King's men much before 1610, and no influence on their plays and their productions can be sought before that year.

This conclusion of little or no influence before 1610 is, I think, a false one. It is based on the erroneous assumption that the actors and playwrights of the King's company would have known nothing about the peculiarities of the Blackfriars and that they would have had no plays prepared especially for that theatre until after they had begun performing in it. Actors are never so stupid or so insular as this in any time. The King's men, we may be sure, were well aware of the Blackfriars and the type of performance it required, or specialized in, long before they came to lease the theatre. There must be many evidences of this, but three in particular come readily to mind.

Seven years before, in 1601, the King's men had been involved in the War of the Theatres, which was in part a row between the public theatres and the private theatres. The chief attack on the public theatres and adult actors was made in Jonson's *Poetaster*, performed at the Blackfriars. Certain actors of the Lord Chamberlain's company, and possibly Shakespeare himself, were ridiculed in this Blackfriars play. The reply, *Satiromastix*, was written by Thomas Dekker and performed by Shakespeare's company at the Globe.[9] Certainly in 1601 at least, the company was well aware of the goings on at Blackfriars.

A second piece of evidence pointing to their knowledge of the peculiar requirements of the Blackfriars is the case of Marston's *Malcontent*. Marston wrote this play for the boys at the Blackfriars, who performed it in that theatre in 1604. The King's men stole the play, as they admitted, and performed it at the Globe; the third edition, also 1604, shows the alterations they commissioned John Webster to make in order to adapt a Blackfriars script to a Globe performance, and in the induction to the play Richard Burbage, speaking in his own person, points out one or two of the differences between Blackfriars requirements and Globe requirements.[10]

Finally, and most familiar of all evidence that the King's men were quite alive to what went on at Blackfriars, is the "little eyases" passage in *Hamlet* and Shakespeare's rueful admission that, for a time at any rate, the competition of the Blackfriars was too much for the company at the Globe.

Clearly the King's men did not have to wait until their performances of 1610 at the Blackfriars to know how their plays needed to be changed to fit them to that theatre and its select audience. They had known for several years what the general characteristics of Blackfriars performances were. Indeed, the leading member of the company, Richard Burbage, had a double reason for being familiar with all the peculiarities of the Blackfriars, for since his father's death in 1597 he had been the owner of the theatre and the landlord of the boy company that made it famous.[11] We can be perfectly sure, then, that from the day of the first proposal that the King's men take over the Blackfriars they had talked among themselves about what they would do with it and had discussed what kinds of plays they would have to have written to exploit it. It is all too often forgotten that in all such discussions among the members of the King's company William Shakespeare would have had an important part. He had more kinds of connections with the company than any other man: he was actor, shareholder, patented member, principal playwright, and one of the housekeepers of the Globe; even Burbage did not serve so many functions in the company. Few men in theatrical history have been so completely and inextricably bound up with the affairs of an acting troupe.

When would the King's men have begun planning for their performances at the Blackfriars? We cannot, of course, set the exact date, but we can approximate it. There is one faint suggestion that consideration of the project may have started very early indeed. Richard Burbage said that Henry Evans, who had leased the theatre from him for the Children of the Queen's Revels, began talking to him about the surrender of his lease in 1603 or 1604.[12] These early discussions evidently came to nothing, for we know that the boys continued in the theatre for three or four years longer. Burbage's statement about Evans does suggest the interesting possibility that the King's men may have dallied with the project of leasing the Blackfriars Theatre as early as 1603 or 1604. This, however, is only the faintest of possibilities. The Blackfriars was tentatively in the market then, but all we know is that Burbage had to consider for a short time the possibility of getting other tenants for his theatre. Whether the King's men came to his mind and theirs as possible tenants, we do not know.

We can be sure that active planning for performances at the Blackfriars did get under way when Burbage, who was both the leading actor of the King's men and owner of the Blackfriars Theatre, knew for certain that the boy actors would give up their lease and that arrangements for a syndicate of King's men to take over the theatre could be made. Conferences among these men – the Burbages, HemINGES, Condell, Shakespeare, and Sly – and probably preliminary financial arrangements would have been going on before a scrivener was called in to draw up a rough draft of the lease. Such preliminaries, which must come before a lease can be formally signed, often consume months. We know that the leases were formally executed on 9 August 1608;[13] therefore discussions in June and July or even in April and May are likely enough. We know that the Blackfriars Theatre was available as early as March 1608, for in a letter dated 11 March 1608 Sir Thomas Lake officially notified Lord Salisbury that the company of the Children of Blackfriars must be suppressed and that the King had vowed that they should never act again even if they had to beg their bread. General confirmation of this fact is found in a letter written two weeks later by the French ambassador.[14] Thus it is evident that in March of 1608 Richard Burbage knew his theatre was without a tenant. March to July 1608, then, are the months for discussions among the King's men of prospective performances at the Blackfriars.

What did this little group of Shakespeare and his intimate associates of the last fourteen years work out during their discussions in the months of March to July 1608? One of the things they must have considered was alterations of their style of acting. As Granville-Barker has pointed out,[15] the acting in the new Blackfriars before a sophisticated audience would have to be more quiet than in the large open-air Globe before the groundlings. It would be easier to emphasize points in the quiet candlelit surroundings, and "sentiment would become as telling as passion". There must also have been extended discussions of what to do about the repertory: which of the company's plays would be suitable for the elegant new theatre and which should be kept for the old audience at the Globe? Some of their decisions are fairly obvious. *Mucedorus*, which Rafe in *The Knight of the Burning Pestle* says he had played before the Wardens of his company and which went through fifteen editions before the Restoration, was clearly one of the Globe plays which might be laughed at by a Blackfriars audience. Similarly, *The Merry Devil of Edmonton* was not a good Blackfriars prospect. Certain other plays in the repertory might be expected to please at the Blackfriars; Marston's *Malcontent*, for instance, could easily be changed back to its original Blackfriars form, and Jonson's *Every Man in His Humour* and *Every Man out of His Humour*, though nine and ten years old, had been played by the company at court in the last three years and ought to be suitable for the Blackfriars.

These discussions of the old repertory, though no doubt important to the company then, are fruitless for us now. I know of no evidence as to their decisions. More important are the proposals for new plays for the Blackfriars, and I think we do have some evidence as to what these decisions were. The experienced members of the King's company were familiar with the fact so commonly recorded in the annals of the

Jacobean theatre that new plays were in constant demand. With the acquisition of the new theatre they had an opportunity to claim for their own the most profitable audience in London. We know from the later Jacobean and Caroline records that this is just what they did.[16] It seems likely that one of the foundations of their later unquestioned dominance of the audiences of the gentry was their decision about plays and playwrights made in their discussions of March to July 1608.

One of their decisions, I suggest, was to get Jonson to write Blackfriars plays for them. He was a likely choice for three reasons. First, because he was developing a following among the courtly audience (always prominent at the Blackfriars) by his great court masques. At this time he had already written his six early entertainments for King James – those at the Coronation, at the Opening of Parliament, at Althorp, at Highgate, and the two at Theobalds. He had written for performance at Whitehall *The Masque of Blackness, The Masque of Beauty, Hymenaei,* and the famous *Lord Hadding- ton's Masque.* The sensational success of these courtly entertainments made Jonson a most promising choice to write plays for the courtly audience which the King's men did succeed in attracting to Blackfriars.

A second reason which would have led the King's men to Jonson as a writer for their new theatre was his great reputation among the literati and critics. In this decade from 1601 to 1610 the literary allusions to him are numerous, more numerous than to Shakespeare himself. The poems to Jonson and the long prose passages about him in this time are far more frequent than to Shakespeare; quotations from his work occur oftener, and I find three times as many literary and social references to performances of his plays and masques as to Shakespeare's. Poems about him or references to his work are written in these years by John Donne, Sir John Roe, Sir Dudley Carleton, the Venetian ambassador, John Chamberlain, Sir Thomas Lake, Sir George Buc, Sir Thomas Salusbury.[17] This is just the kind of audience which might be attracted to the Blackfriars, and which, eventually, the King's men did attract there.

There was a third reason which would have made Jonson seem to the King's men a very likely bet for their new theatre: he had already had experience in writing plays for this theatre when it was occupied by boys. Before the conferences of the King's men about their new project he had already had performed at Blackfriars *Cynthia's Revels, The Poetaster, The Case Is Altered,* and *Eastward Ho.* Possibly just before the time of the conferences of the King's men he had been writing for the Blackfriars another play, *Epicoene,* for he says in the Folio of 1616 that the play was performed by the Children of Blackfriars, but the date he gives for performance comes after their expulsion from the Blackfriars Theatre. Not only had Jonson had the valuable experience of writing four or five plays for the Blackfriars, but the Induction to *Cynthia's Revels* and his personal statements about boys of the company, like Nathan Field and Salathiel, or Solomon, Pavy,[18] strongly suggest that he had directed them in their rehearsals. What valuable experience for the King's men planning their first performance in this new theatre!

Now all these qualifications of Jonson as a prospect for the King's men are, in sober fact, only speculations. Perhaps they simply show that if *I* had been participating in the conferences about the Blackfriars I should have argued long and lustily for Ben Jonson. Alas, I was not there! What evidence is there that they really did agree to secure his services for the company? The evidence is that before these conferences he had written only four plays for the Lord Chamberlain's or King's company – three, nine, and ten years before – nothing for the company in the years 1605–08. After these conferences, he wrote all his remaining plays for the company, with the exception of *Bartholomew Fair* six years later, a play which he gave to his good friend and protégé Nathan Field for the Lady Elizabeth's company at the Hope, and *A Tale of a Tub*, twenty-five years later, which he gave to Queen Henrietta's men. Jonson's first play after the reopening of Blackfriars was *The Alchemist*; it was written for the King's men, and numerous allusions show clearly that it was written for Blackfriars. So were *Catiline, The Devil Is an Ass, The Staple of News, The New Inn*, and *The Magnetic Lady*. Of course we lack the final proof of recorded reference to a definite agreement, but the evidence is such as to suggest that one of the decisions reached by the King's men in the reorganization of their enterprise to exploit the great advantages of their new theatre was to secure the services of Ben Jonson to write plays for the literate and courtly audience at Blackfriars.

Another decision, which I suggest the King's men made at these conferences, was to secure for their new theatre the services of the rising young collaborators, Francis Beaumont and John Fletcher. These gentlemen were younger than Jonson by about ten years, and as yet their reputations were distinctly inferior to his, but they had already displayed those talents which were to make their plays the stage favourites at Blackfriars for the next thirty-four years,[19] and were to cause Dryden to say sixty years later that "their plays are now the most pleasant and frequent entertainments of the stage".

One of the great assets of Beaumont and Fletcher was social. In the years immediately before and after 1608, the London theatre audience was developing the social cleavage which is such a marked characteristic of the Jacobean and Caroline drama and stage. In Elizabeth's time the London theatre was a universal one, in which a single audience at the Globe could embrace Lord Monteagle, Sir Charles Percy, city merchants, lawyers, Inns of Court students, apprentices, servants, beggars, pickpockets, and prostitutes. The later Jacobean and Caroline audience was a dual one. The gentry, the court, the professional classes, and the Inns of Court men went to the Blackfriars, the Phoenix, and later to the Salisbury Court; the London masses went to the larger and noisier Red Bull and Fortune and Globe. This new state of affairs was just developing when the King's men had their conferences about the Blackfriars in 1608. They evidently saw what was coming, however, for in the next few years they understood and exploited the situation more effectively than any other troupe in London. Indeed, the very acquisition of the Blackfriars and its operation in conjunction with the Globe was a device which had never been tried before in London and which is the clearest evidence that the King's men knew just what was happening.

Under these circumstances, then, the social status of Beaumont and Fletcher was an asset for the company in their new house. Francis Beaumont came of an ancient and distinguished Leicestershire family, with many connections among the nobility. John Fletcher was the son of a Lord Bishop of London and one-time favourite of Elizabeth. To a Blackfriars audience the social standing of these two young men would have been more acceptable than that of any other dramatist writing in London in 1608.

Another asset which made Beaumont and Fletcher valuable for the new enterprise of the King's men was their private theatre experience. So far as we can make out now, all their plays before this time had been written for private theatres and most of them for the Blackfriars. *The Woman Hater* had been prepared for the private theatre in St Paul's, but *The Knight of the Burning Pestle, The Scornful Lady*, and *The Faithful Shepherdess* were Blackfriars plays. I think we can add to this list *Cupid's Revenge*. This play has been variously dated, but two forthcoming articles by James Savage[20] seem to me to offer convincing evidence that the play was prepared for Blackfriars about 1607 and that it displays a crude preliminary working out of much of the material which made *Philaster* one of the great hits of its time and one of the most influential plays of the seventeenth century. In any event, Beaumont and Fletcher were among the most experienced Blackfriars playwrights available in 1608. It is true that in 1608 none of their plays had been a great success; indeed the two best, *The Knight of the Burning Pestle* and *The Faithful Shepherdess*, are known to have been unsuccessful at first. The King's men, however, were experienced in the ways of the theatre; it does not seem rash to assume that at least one of them knew enough about audiences and about dramatic talents to see that these young men were writers of brilliant promise – especially since that one was William Shakespeare.

Beaumont and Fletcher, then, because of their experience and social standing were very desirable dramatists for the King's men to acquire in 1608 for their new private theatre. What is the evidence that they did acquire them? The evidence is that all the Beaumont and Fletcher plays of the next few years are King's men's plays, several of them famous hits – *Philaster, The Maid's Tragedy, A King and No King, The Captain, The Two Noble Kinsmen, Bonduca, Monsieur Thomas, Valentinian*. The dating of many of the Beaumont and Fletcher plays is very uncertain because of their late publication, and it may be that two or three of the later plays were written for other companies, but at least forty-five plays by Beaumont and Fletcher were the property of the Jacobean and Caroline King's men.[21] None of their plays before 1608, when Blackfriars was acquired, was, so far as we can find, written for the King's men. It seems a reasonable assumption, therefore, that another of the policies agreed upon at the conferences of 1608 was to secure the services of Beaumont and Fletcher for the company in its new enterprise at the Blackfriars.

The third of these three important changes in policy which I think the King's men agreed upon at their conferences about the new Blackfriars enterprise in 1608, is the most interesting of all to us, but it was the easiest and most obvious for them. Indeed, it may well have been assumed almost without discussion. It was, of course, that William Shakespeare should write henceforth with the Blackfriars in mind and not the Globe.

Why was this decision an easy and obvious one? The company could assume, of course, that he would continue to write for them, since he was a shareholder and a patented member of the company and a housekeeper in both their theatres. Since the formation of the company, fourteen years before, all his plays had been written for performance by them, always, in the last ten years, for performance at the Globe. All his professional associations as well as his financial ones were with this company, and probably no one in the group even considered his defection. Burbage, Shakespeare, Heminges, and Condell were the real nucleus of the organization.

This new enterprise at the Blackfriars was a very risky business. As we have noted, no adult company had ever tried to run a private theatre before. The King's men not only proposed to make a heavy investment in this new departure, but they intended to continue running their old public theatre at the same time. Every possible precaution against failure needed to be taken. One such precaution would be the devotion of

Shakespeare's full-time energies to the Blackfriars instead of the Globe. They could trust Shakespeare; he knew their potentialities and their shortcomings as no other dramatist did – indeed, few dramatists in the history of the English theatre have ever had such a long and intimate association with an acting company as William Shakespeare had had with these men. If anybody knew what Burbage and Heminges and Condell and Robert Armyn and Richard Cowley could do on the stage and what they should not be asked to do, that man was William Shakespeare. He could make them a success at the Blackfriars as they had been at the Globe if any one could.

Another reason for the transfer of Shakespeare's efforts was the fact that the Globe could be left to take care of itself with an old repertory as the Blackfriars could not. For one thing, there was no old repertory for the Blackfriars, since the departing boys appear to have held on to their old plays. For another thing, it was the Blackfriars audience which showed the greater avidity for new plays; the public theatre audiences were much more faithful to old favourites. They were still playing *Friar Bacon and Friar Bungay* at the Fortune in 1630 and Marlowe's *Edward II* at the Red Bull in 1620 and *Dr Faustus* at the Fortune in 1621 and *Richard II* and *Pericles* at the Globe in 1631.[22] In the archives of the Globe at this time there must have been a repertory of more than a hundred plays, including at least twenty-five of Shakespeare's. Moreover, certain plays written for the Globe in the last few years, like Wilkins's *Miseries of Enforced Marriage* and the anonymous *Yorkshire Tragedy* and *The Fair Maid of Bristol* and *The London Prodigal*, had provided playwrights who might be expected to entertain a Globe audience with more of the same fare, but who could scarcely come up to the requirements of sophistication at Blackfriars. Altogether, then, the Globe repertory had much less need of Shakespeare's efforts in 1608 than did the Blackfriars repertory.

Why should Shakespeare have wanted to write for the Blackfriars, or at least have agreed to do so? The most compelling of the apparent reasons is that he had money invested in the project and stood to lose by its failure and gain by its success. He was one of the seven lessees of the new theatre; he had paid down an unknown sum and had agreed to pay £5. 14s. 4d. per year in rent.[23] He had at least a financial reason for doing everything he could to establish the success of the Blackfriars venture, and what Shakespeare could do most effectively was to write plays which would insure the company's popularity with the audience in its new private theatre.

A third reason for this postulated decision of the King's men in 1608 to have Shakespeare devote his entire attention to the Blackfriars and abandon the Globe was that the King's men saw that the real future of the theatrical profession in London lay with the court and the court party in the private theatres. Their receipts for performances at court showed them this very clearly. In the last nine years of Elizabeth, 1594–1602, they had received from court performances an average of £35 a year; in the first five years of the reign of the new king, 1603–7, they had averaged £131 per year in addition to their new allowances for liveries as servants of the King.[24] The Blackfriars and not the Globe was the theatre where they could entertain this courtly audience with commercial performances. There is no doubt that in the next few years after 1608 the Blackfriars did become the principal theatre of the company. In 1612 Edward Kirkham said they took £1,000 a winter more at the Blackfriars than they had formerly taken at the Globe.[25] When Sir Henry Herbert listed receipts from the two theatres early in the reign of King Charles, the receipts for single performances at the Globe averaged £6. 13s. 8d.; those for single performances at the Blackfriars averaged £15. 15s., or about two and one-half times as much.[26] In 1634 an Oxford don who wrote up the company simply called them the company of the Blackfriars and did not mention the Globe at all;[27] when the plays of the company were published in the Jacobean and Caroline period, the Blackfriars was mentioned as their theatre more than four times as often as the Globe was.[28] Such evidence proves that the Blackfriars certainly did become the principal theatre of the King's men. I am suggesting that in the conferences of 1608 the King's men had some intimation that it would, and accordingly they persuaded William Shakespeare to devote his attention to that theatre in the future instead of to the Globe.

So much for the reasons that Shakespeare might be expected to change the planning of his plays in 1608. What is the evidence that he did? The evidence, it seems to me, is to be seen in *Cymbeline, The Winter's Tale, The Tempest,* and *The Two Noble Kinsmen,* and probably it was to be seen also in the lost play, *Cardenio.* The variations which these plays show from the Shakespearean norm have long been a subject for critical comment. The first three of them in particular, since they are the only ones which have been universally accepted as part of the Shakespeare canon, have commonly been discussed as a distinct genre. Widely as critics and scholars have disagreed over the reasons for their peculiar characteristics, those peculiarities have generally been recognized, whether the plays are called Shakespeare's Romances, or Shakespeare's Tragi-Comedies, or his Romantic Tragi-Comedies, or simply the plays of the fourth period. No competent critic who has read carefully through the Shakespeare canon has failed to notice that there is something different about *Cymbeline, The Winter's Tale, The Tempest,* and *The Two Noble Kinsmen.*

When critics and scholars have tried to explain this difference between the plays of the last period and Shakespeare's earlier work, they have set up a variety of hypotheses. Most of these hypotheses have in common only the trait which I noted at the beginning of this paper – namely, they agree in considering Shakespeare as the professional poet and not the professional playwright. They turn to Shakespeare's sources, or to his inspiration, or to his personal affairs, or to the bucolic environment of his Stratford retirement, but not to the theatre which was his daily preoccupation for more than twenty years. Dowden called this late group in the Shakespeare canon "On the Heights", because he thought the plays reflected Shakespeare's new-found serenity. Such a fine optimism had, perhaps, something to recommend it to the imaginations of the Victorians, but to modern scholars it seems to throw more light on Dowden's mind than on Shakespeare's development. Dowden's explanation seemed utterly fatuous to Lytton Strachey, who thought that the plays of "Shakespeare's Final Period" were written by a Shakespeare far from serene, who was really "half enchanted by visions of beauty and loveliness and half bored to death". Violently as Dowden and Strachey differ, they agree in seeking subjective interpretations.

Best known of the old explanations of the peculiarities of the plays of this last period is probably Thorndike's:[29] the contention that the great success of *Philaster* caused Shakespeare to imitate it in *Cymbeline* and to a lesser extent in *The Winter's Tale* and *The Tempest.* In spite of the great horror of the Shakespeare idolaters at the thought of the master imitating superficial young whipper-snappers like Beaumont and Fletcher, no one can read the two plays together without noting the striking similarities between them. The difficulty is that although the approximate dates of the two plays are clear enough, their *precise* dates are so close together and so uncertain that neither Thorndike nor any subsequent scholar has been able to prove that *Philaster* came before *Cymbeline*, and the Shakespeare idolaters have been equally unable to prove that *Cymbeline* came before *Philaster*.

I suggest that the really important point is not the priority of either play. The significant and revealing facts are that both were written for the King's company; both were written, or at least completed, after the important decision made by the leaders of the troupe in the spring of 1608 to commission new plays for Blackfriars, and both were prepared to be acted in the private theatre in Blackfriars before the sophisticated audience attracted to that house. It is their common purpose and environment, not imitation of one by the other, which makes them similar. Both *Philaster* and *Cymbeline* are somewhat like Beaumont and Fletcher's earlier plays, especially *Cupid's Revenge*, because Beaumont and Fletcher's earlier plays had all been written for private theatres and all but one for Blackfriars. Both *Philaster* and *Cymbeline* are unlike Shakespeare's earlier plays because none of those plays had been written for private theatres. The subsequent plays of both Beaumont and Fletcher and Shakespeare resemble *Philaster* and *Cymbeline* because they too were written to be performed by the King's men before the sophisticated and courtly audience in the private theatre at Blackfriars.

So much I think we can say with some assurance. This explanation of the character of Shakespeare's last plays is in accord with the known facts of theatrical history; it accords with the biographical evidence of Shakespeare's long and close association with all the enterprises of the Lord Chamberlain's-King's men for twenty years; it is in accord with his fabulously acute sense of the theatre and the problems of the actor; and it does no violence to his artistic integrity or to his poetic genius.

May I add one further point much more in the realm of speculation? Since John Fletcher became a playwright for the King's men at this time and continued so for the remaining seventeen years of his life, and since the activities of the King's men had been one of Shakespeare's chief preoccupations for many years, is it not likely that the association between Fletcher and Shakespeare from 1608 to 1614 was closer than has usually been thought? Shakespeare was nearing retirement; after 1608 he wrote plays less frequently than before; Fletcher became his successor as chief dramatist for the King's company. In these years they collaborated in *The Two Noble Kinsmen, Henry VIII*, and probably in *Cardenio*. Is it too fantastic to suppose that Shakespeare was at least an adviser in the preparation of *Philaster, A King and No King*, and *The Maid's Tragedy* for his fellows? Is it even more fantastic to think that Shakespeare, the old public theatre playwright, preparing his first and crucial play for a private theatre, might have asked advice – or even taken it – from the two young dramatists who had written plays for this theatre and audience four or five times before?

Perhaps this is going too far. I do not wish to close on a note of speculation. My basic contention is that Shakespeare was, before all else, a man of the theatre and a devoted member of the King's company. One of the most important events in the history of that company was its acquisition of the Blackfriars Playhouse in 1608 and its subsequent brilliantly successful exploitation of its stage and audience. The company was experienced and theatre-wise; the most elementary theatrical foresight demanded that in 1608 they prepare new and different plays for a new and different theatre and audience. Shakespeare was their loved and trusted fellow. How could they fail to ask him for new

Blackfriars plays, and how could he fail them? All the facts at our command seem to me to demonstrate that he did not fail them. He turned from his old and tested methods and produced a new kind of play for the new theatre and audience. Somewhat unsurely at first he wrote *Cymbeline* for them, then, with greater dexterity in his new medium, *The Winter's Tale*, and finally, triumphant in his old mastery, *The Tempest*.

Notes

Since this paper was prepared as a lecture for the Shakespeare Conference at Stratford-upon-Avon, it lacks the fuller documentation it might have had if it had been originally written for publication.

1 *The Cambridge Bibliography of English Literature* will serve as an example. The bibliography of Shakespeare fills 136 columns, of which one half-column is devoted to "The Influence of Theatrical Conditions". This is not to say, of course, that there have been no proper studies of the theatres and acting companies of Shakespeare's time. There are many. But there are comparatively few books and articles devoted to the examination of Shakespeare's work in the light of this knowledge or to a consideration of the specific influence such matters had on his methods and development.

2 E. K. Chambers, *The Elizabethan Stage*, ii, 192–3 and iv, 348–9; *William Shakespeare*, i, 27–56.

3 *The Elizabethan Stage*, iv, 164.

4 *William Shakespeare*, i, 353–5; *The Elizabethan Stage*, ii, 204–7.

5 *The Elizabethan Stage*, ii, 208–9.

6 Ibid. iv, 108–30.

7 *The Elizabethan Stage*, ii, 509–10. Technically Richard Burbage leased one-seventh of the theatre to each of the other six.

8 Ibid. iv, 351.

9 See J. H. Penniman, *The War of the Theatres*, and R. A. Small, *The Stage Quarrel*.

10 F. L. Lucas, *The Works of John Webster*, iii, 294–309.

11 J. Q. Adams, *Shakespearean Playhouses*, pp. 199–223.

12 The Answers of Heminges and Burbage to Edward Kirkham, 1612, printed by F. G. Fleay, *A Chronicle History of the London Stage*, p. 235.

13 *William Shakespeare*, ii, 62–3.

14 *The Elizabethan Stage*, ii, 53–4.

15 *Prefaces to Shakespeare*, 2nd ser., pp. 249–50.

16 See Bentley, *The Jacobean and Caroline Stage*, vol. i, chap. i *passim*; ii, 673–81.

17 See Bentley, *Shakespeare and Jonson*, i, 38–41, 65–7, 73–9, 87–90, and Bradley and Adams, *The Jonson Allusion-Book, passim*.

18 See "A Good Name Lost", *Times Literary Supplement* (30 May 1942), p. 276.

19 *The Jacobean and Caroline Stage*, i, 29 and 109–14.

20 "The Date of Beaumont and Fletcher's *Cupid's Revenge*" and "Beaumont and Fletcher's *Philaster* and Sidney's *Arcadia*".

21 *The Jacobean and Caroline Stage*, i, 109–15.

22 Ibid. i, 156, 174, 157, 24, 129.

23 *Shakespearean Playhouses*, pp. 224–5.

24 *The Elizabethan Stage*, iv, 164–75.

25 C. W. Wallace, *University of Nebraska Studies*, viii (1908), 36–7, n. 6.

26 *The Jacobean and Caroline Stage*, i, 23–4.

27 Ibid. i, 26, n. 5.

28 Ibid. i, 30, n. 1.

29 Ashley H. Thorndike, *The Influence of Beaumont and Fletcher on Shakespeare*.

41

The Critical Revolution

J. L. Styan

I f in this survey there has been more emphasis on stage production than literary criticism, it could be judged that the initiative in recovering Shakespeare has shifted to the theatre, that the biggest single advances have been made there. In 1900 readers turned to the scholar to elucidate the plays: in 1970 scholarship seems suspect and the stage seems to be more in touch with their spirit. Nevertheless, it is the contention of this book that without the rediscovery of the Elizabethan stage, the achievement of Tyrone Guthrie in recapturing the mutuality of play and audience would not have been possible, and without the sense of Shakespeare as a dealer in visions, culminating in the kind of 'interpretation' associated with the name of G. Wilson Knight, Peter Brook would probably not have found the surprisingly wide acceptance from academic critics that he has. Knight's distinction between 'criticism' and 'interpretation' is worth recalling:

> The critic is, and should be, cool and urbane, seeing the poetry he discusses not with the eyes of a lover but as an object; whereas interpretation deliberately immerses itself in its theme and speaks less from the seats of judgement than from the creative centre.[1]

Accept that, and we can accept much that is unconventional and threatening in Brook.

The giant figure behind both Guthrie and Brook was Harley Granville-Barker, whose early work at the Savoy foreshadowed our notions of Shakespeare's stagecraft and thematic interpretation when neither had reached a satisfactory maturity. If all this seems tendentious – as indeed it must at this crucial point in the development of our response to the plays – what remains true is that the Shakespeare known to both critic and playgoer in late Victorian times has changed utterly after two or three generations. Criticism has shifted its position as radically as have Shakespearean acting and directing. Except in the cinema, the straining towards a psychological and pictorial realism for Shakespeare is all in the past. The half-apprehended mystery of a supremely non-illusory drama and theatre, that of Shakespeare and the Elizabethan stage, promised to open new worlds for discovery and conquest. The immense influence of Granville-Barker upon all major Shakespeareans in this century might be explained on these grounds alone: his was the promise.

It follows that histories and surveys of Shakespeare criticism, which appear with desperate regularity as contributions to Shakespeare periodicals as well as in book form, cannot hereafter ignore the events and developments that are usually collected separately in 'stage histories'. Our understanding of Shakespeare today is not divisible, and any unnatural separation of reader and playgoer implied by these publications will suggest a critical inadequacy, a failure to integrate current knowledge. The factors which contribute to our changes in Shakespearean taste and sensibility now seem infinitely wide; an article here, a performance there, an interview or a broadcast, an aesthetic theory, a trend in contemporary playwriting perhaps.

On this point, it may be thought that the development of Shakespeare production and criticism towards a fuller recognition of his non-illusory assumptions suggests in the last few years the direct influence of the work of Bertolt Brecht. It is true that Brecht's theories of epic theatre and his ideas about distancing an audience have had an incalculable impact on our thinking about the basis of communication in drama, especially since the formation of the Berliner Ensemble in 1949 with its subsequent visits to other capitals. Brecht's own 'adaptations' from periods of drama carefully selected for their highly conventional manner – those of Greek tragedy, Elizabethan tragedy and eighteenth-century comedy – made their contribution to our better understanding of the kind of theatre of imaginative release which preceded the realism of Ibsen and Strindberg.

But Brecht's practice served to accentuate and demonstrate what was becoming known about Shakespeare before. Poel and Granville-Barker would have concurred with Brecht's reiterated statement about the undesirability of a theatre of hypnosis and the need for an 'epic' theatre:

> The stage began to tell a story. The narrator was no longer missing, along with the fourth wall ... The actors too refrained from going over wholly into their role, remaining detached from the character they were playing and clearly inviting criticism of him.
>
> The spectator was no longer in any way allowed to submit to an experience uncritically (and without practical consequences) by means of simple empathy with the characters in a play. The production took the subject-matter and the incidents shown and put them through a process of alienation: the alienation that is necessary to all understanding. When something seems 'the most obvious thing in the world' it means that any attempt to understand the world has been given up.[2]

It is also worth remembering that Guthrie's fundamental work on Elizabethan open stagecraft was done before he knew much of Brecht. Now, whether the playgoer turns to a production like John Barton's ritualistic *Richard II* at Stratford, 1973, or to Joseph Papp's seasons of free-wheeling Shakespeare in New York, past traditions of realistic presentation are being stripped away and the spirit of Elizabethan ritual and role-playing reminds him of Shakespeare's essential theatricality in a way that Brecht would fully have endorsed.

It is a sign of the times that the previously unthinkable has happened in Britain: John Russell Brown, a professor of drama, was in 1974 appointed as an associate of the National Theatre in London, just prior to the opening of the National Theatre proper on the south bank of the Thames. This followed upon the slow but steady growth of a few university drama departments in the United Kingdom. The appointment is a matter for congratulation to both the profession and to academia. However, it is ironic that in the same year Brown should publish a polemic against directors of Shakespeare.[3] This is hardly a sign of the times, and may even seem to be an unwarranted regression, since the intermittent dissatisfaction of lovers of Shakespeare with his stage representation has been common for two hundred years. Brown's attack, however, is specifically against the power of a director to dictate the Shakespeare experience and to impose his interpretation upon an audience. This charge was sufficiently answered by Guthrie in 1960[4] on behalf of all directors and actors: both actor and director regard their responsibility as one of 'interpretation' to some degree – it is what they are paid for. The analogous activity is that of the literary critic who traces themes as if the plays were labyrinthine puzzles, except that by picking about in the text he appears to show proof that he is not falsifying the evidence. The critic also regards his responsibility as one of interpretation, though he may lack the power of the stage to *test* his thesis.

I submit that Brown's proposal to allow actors and audience to explore Shakespeare without the intervention of a director would produce no different result. Indeed, the tyranny of the actor has not been unknown in the past, and the tyranny of an audience is the worst of all worlds. But then tyrannous excess is not the mark of a good director either. Good drama, and Shakespeare in particular, expects all parties to the play to make their creative contribution, or else the dramatist would be a tyrant himself; and I cannot think of a playwright who is less of a tyrant in this way than Shakespeare.

Critical commentaries will inevitably continue to isolate themes in the plays: to recognize 'meaning' is the conceptual end-product of any reading or playgoing experience of Shakespeare. But John Russell Brown is right to insist that the play on the stage expanding before an audience is the source of all valid discovery. Shakespeare speaks, if anywhere, through his medium. The important development in Shakespeare studies in this generation had also been anticipated in Granville-Barker: the perception of the plays as blueprints for performance.[5] When Hamlet speaks his soliloquy, 'To be or not to be', it is nowadays proper to remember that this is no soliloquy at all, and that our audience's eyes will also be watching Ophelia at her orisons as well as Claudius and Polonius behind the arras: what we *perceive* is a suicide statement coloured by the piety of a religious girl and the politics of those in power in Denmark.

The text-as-score is of course only the basis and beginning of perceptual criticism. This approach also views Shakespeare as a self-conscious artist working out immediate structural problems of stage communication, in which 'each poem contains its own poetics'.[6] Each play is shaped by the need to make its statement dramatically workable as its author explores the farther reaches of his theme in the conventional terms of his art. In 1938, E. M. W. Tillyard groped for a concept to describe the operation of the symbolism in Shakespeare's last plays, plays in which he found the playwright trying to express more than ever before, and invented the slippery concept of 'planes of reality'. 'There are times', Tillyard argued, 'when in the realm of action even the simplest and most normal people find their scale of reality upset', and he went on to hail

Shakespeare as the outstanding author who was 'familiar with many planes of reality and gifted incomparably with the power of passing from one to another'.[7]

Conveying the experience of different levels of perception to an audience, urging their imaginative expansion, has also been lightly investigated by S. L. Bethell, Anne Righter and a handful of others. For Bethell, the 'multi-consciousness' of the Elizabethan audience explained how it might be at once involved with an illusion and detached by a sense of its own reality. Shakespeare's drama lay between 'the two extremes of absolute conventionalism and absolute naturalism': 'His characters are not merely personified abstractions, but, on the other hand, they are not precisely like real people.' In the course of a single play, the Elizabethan playwright slips up and down the scale between convention and realism, and 'this rapidity of adjustment is a principal component in Shakespeare's remarkable subtlety'. Bethell finds this a special characteristic of his unself-conscious art, and concludes,

> I believe I am justified in asserting that there *is* a popular dramatic tradition, and that its dominant characteristic is the audience's ability to respond spontaneously and unconsciously on more than one plane of attention at the same time.[8]

Shakespeare's freedom with time and place, the impersonation and presentation of character, the mixing of comedy and tragedy, and many other phenomena of the Elizabethan theatre, are now studies which await discussion and experiment. Anne Righter's seminal work on the theatrical metaphor,[9] and the degree of assumed illusion in the writing and reception of a play, must be seen in this context of conscious or unconscious stagecraft.

None of this work can now proceed far without the active assistance of the stage itself. In a recent conference on Shakespeare and the Theatre in New York, the customary controversy between traditionalists and modernists over the practising theatre's faithfulness to Shakespeare was heard again, and in a comment Louis Marder questioned whether recent eccentricities of production were helpful or harmful:

> Whether it is done for shock value, for clearer interpretation, or for making Shakespeare our contemporary, one cannot help wondering whether putting characters on trapeze bars (Brook's *MND*), on hobby horses and stilts (John Barton's *R2*), in shorts or nude, with comic warriors in *Tro.* (Lincoln Center N.Y. Festival production), making Goneril and Regan super-sensual (The [British] Actors Co. in Brooklyn, N.Y.), or Orlando's tickling Charles the Wrestler into surrender (The National Shakespeare [touring] Company), makes any improvement in Shakespeare.[10]

And he added, 'Only the text can tell us what Shakespeare intended'. The gist of this book has been to suggest that to stop short at the text is now a kind of surrender, for the text will not tell us much until it speaks in its own medium.

If I may dare to paraphrase a passage from E. H. Gombrich's *Art and Illusion*,[11] both actor and scholar can render only what their sense of the dramatic medium will allow, for they see what they interpret before they interpret what they see. Their Shakespeare originates in the mind, in their reactions to Shakespeare rather than in Shakespeare himself. But as the style and idiom of their interpretation gain currency in each other's eyes, so they must with audiences and readers. Actor and scholar will teach each other, not what Shakespeare 'means', but what his possibilities are beyond logic. Nor will these be exhausted. The scholar will modify the actor's illumination, the actor will modify the scholar's, a process of infinite adjustment. Shakespeare remains uncharted territory waiting to be explored and articulated. But the object of all this earnest endeavour, the experience in some degree of Shakespeare's greater vision, cannot be reached without the humble services of both parties.

Notes

1 Prefatory Note to the third edition, *The Imperial Theme*, London, 1951, p. vi.

2 'Theatre for Pleasure or Theatre for Instruction' in John Willett, *Brecht on Theatre*, London, 1964, p. 71. The original was written about 1936.

3 *Free Shakespeare.*

4 See Chapter 10, p. 180 above.

5 After Granville-Barker's *Prefaces to Shakespeare* (1927–1947), see especially Arthur Colby Sprague, *Shakespeare and the Actors: The Stage Business in His Plays, 1660–1905* (Cambridge, MA, 1944), Richard Flatter, *Shakespeare's Producing Hand* (London, 1948), Ronald Watkins, *On Producing Shakespeare* (London, 1950), Rudolf Stamm, *Shakespeare's Word Scenery* (Zürich and St Gallen, 1954), John Russell Brown, *Shakespeare's Plays in Performance* (London, 1967) and J. L. Styan, *Shakespeare's Stagecraft* (Cambridge, 1967). *Shakespeare's Plays Today* (London, 1970) by A. C. Sprague and J. C. Trewin and the series *In Shakespeare's Playhouse* (London, 1974) by Ronald Watkins and Jeremy Lemmon are of recent interest.

6 See James L. Calderwood, *Shakespearean Metadrama*, Minneapolis, 1971.

7 *Shakespeare's Last Plays*, London, 1938, pp. 61, 68.

8 *Shakespeare and the Popular Dramatic Tradition*, pp. 13, 17, 29.

9 *Shakespeare and the Idea of the Play.*

10 *The Shakespeare Newsletter*, vol., xxiv, no. 1, February 1974.

11 New York, 1960, pp. 63 ff. (the A. W. Mellon Lectures in the Fine Arts, 1956).

42

William Shakespeare's Romeo + Juliet:
Everything's Nice in America?

Barbara Hodgdon

I want to begin with an anecdote. When I proposed writing about Leonardo DiCaprio – and titling my essay, 'Was This The Face that Launched a Thousand Clips' – one colleague, taking me somewhat seriously, mentioned the best-selling Leo books, and another sent me a Hong Kong action comic in which 'Leon' single-handedly foils an evil gang and gets the girl. A third, addressing my penchant for reading Shakespearean and popular bodies, glanced at how the Shakespeare myth insists on the physical spectre of the Bard with the Forehead and at the delicious possibility that someone like DiCaprio might have played Cleopatra. A fourth was decidedly visceral: 'The most watery Romeo in film history? His acting is appalling, his affect minimal, and his intelligence – well, why go on? I can understand why teenage girls fall all over themselves for him. But you? Tell me it isn't so'![1] Such concerns about my 'low' taste and possible adolescent regression point to the lack of critical distance and loss of rational control associated with an intense engagement with the popular; but then, such over-involvement and over-identification, traits traditionally ascribed to women, do mark the popular (and especially its emphasis on the body) as a feminine realm.[2]

These fraught notions trope what I take to be the competing, contradictory horizons of reception surrounding Baz Luhrmann's 1996 *William Shakespeare's Romeo + Juliet*. How, I want to ask, does that film resonate within both 'Shakespeare-culture' and global popular culture? And how are those echoes linked to DiCaprio, the film's 'beautiful boy' star and 'modern-day Romeo', for whom Prince William has recently emerged as a royal twin?[3] Although I am especially interested in looking at how diverse audiences refunction Luhrmann's film and DiCaprio's presence to serve their own uses and pleasures,[4] I also want to look at the relations among text, image and music in the film itself and at how citations from those economies escape and are caught up in a cultural narrative that offers to renegotiate the fictions of and frictions between the academic study of filmed Shakespeare and the 'popular' – what Internet discourse calls DiCaprio ideology or, alternatively, DiCapriorgasm.

Among recent Shakespeare films, Luhrmann's not only most stridently advertises itself as a product of global capitalism but also knowingly flaunts how that culture consumes 'Shakespeare'. In an America where Wendy's Dave, wearing a silly floppy hat, holds up a burger and intones 'To be or not to be'; where 'Something wicked this way comes' promotes the newest black Lexus; and where a clip of Kenneth Branagh's St Crispin's Day speech, equated with a football coach's locker-room pep talk, climaxes a (1997) Superbowl pre-game show,[5] seeing Shakespeare's words appear on billboards for loans or massage parlours – The Merchant of Verona Beach, Mistress Quickly's – as product slogans for Phoenix gasoline or ammunition – 'Add more fuel to your fire', 'Shoot forth thunder' – and brand names – Romeo drives a silver Eclipse – comes as no surprise. The logical Madison Avenue descendants of Matthew Arnold's touchstones and of New Criticism's emphasis on language as glowing artifact, these sound bites sign Shakespeare in and on the film's surface in flashes, confirming that he is indeed the universal brand name and, as W. B. Worthen writes, extending beyond *Romeo + Juliet* to embrace Shakespeare the Author and cultural icon, marking how the film traces and re-places signs of its origins.[6]

The film's opening, where a grainy image of an African American TV anchorwoman speaking the prologue grounds Shakespeare's language in the familiar discourse of popular news-speak, stages that replacement: nearly half the speech turns into print headlines or graphic poster art, further fragmented through flash edits and slammed at viewers. Elsewhere, especially but not exclusively in the ball sequence, the film restyles textual culture as fashion or fetish and writes it onto actors' bodies or their props, as with Montague's 'Longsword' rifle, Tybalt's Madonna-engraved pistol, or Mantua's 'Post-post haste' dispatch van. At times, this traffic between verbal and visual imagery reads as hyped-up anti-Shakespeare-culture panache; at others, it appears curiously literal. Although *Romeo + Juliet* is clearly a film with an attitude, its tone ricochets between Wall-and-Moonshine tongue-in-cheekiness and playing it straight, between selling Shakespeare as one-off visual in-jokes and tying its scenography, almost over-explicitly, to the word. Voguing in a white Afro, silver bra and garter belt that evoke Mab's 'moonshine's wat'ry beams', Mercutio not only punningly embodies the fairy Queen but out-masquerades Lady Capulet's Cleopatra, marking the power of his own extravagant artifice in terms of her even more parodic bodily display. Juliet's white dress and wings literalize her as Romeo's 'bright angel'; he becomes her 'true knight', a Boy King Arthur in shining armour – guises that situate the lovers within medieval Christian romance even as they send up that myth. Although Dave Paris's astronaut get-up connects him metonymically to the heavenly Juliet, it just as clearly spaces him out to the story's margins, together with those like Capulet's gold-bespangled, purple toga-ed Nero / Antony, the Trimalchian host of this feast of poses and corruptions.[7] Equally saturated with signs, Tybalt's pointed face, neat moustache and black disco outfit, complemented by red-sequined devil's horns and vest, code him as a macho Prince of Cats whose two cronies dressed as white-faced skeletons foreshadow his violent end. And when, after the balcony-pool sequence, Romeo meets Mercutio, his shirt blazons a heart circled by a wreath of roses, capped with a 'very flame of love', and emanating rays of golden light – the Dante-esque symbol that, glossed by 'My only love sprung from my only hate', serves as the signature logo for the film, the CDs and the official web site.[8]

Sensing an obligation to speak for Shakespeare (especially given his perceived demotion within the American academy), most mainstream critics balked at such over-determined commodifications of his text. Mourning the cuts, they produced resistant readings tied to notions about verse-speaking protocols (singling out Pete Postlethwaite's properly British Friar and Miriam Margolyes's Latina Nurse for praise) and focused on those aspects of the film – notably, how the storm sequence following Mercutio's death mirrors 'the characters' ageless passions'[9] – which fit within traditional knowledge-making frames. This is hardly an unfamiliar story: critics once attacked Zeffirelli's *cinéma vérité* documentary of Renaissance Verona, now ensconced in the educational pantheon, on precisely these grounds. But rehearsing it seems curious, given *West Side Story* and, more recently, the Bologna–Taylor film, *Love Is All There Is*, and the Oscar-winning *Titanic*, or *Romeo and Juliet* with three hours of water (and a remodelled close). Certainly the slasher-porn *Tromeo and Juliet*, an evil twin poised between nineteenth-century burlesques and Luhrmann's film, where 'She hangs upon the cheek of night / Like some barbell in a thrasher's ear' describes a Shirley Temple-curled Juliet whose sleeping potion transforms her into a pig, offers a stronger case for devalued Shakespeare.[10] Still, even those who, like the *New Yorker's* Anthony Lane, preferred 'John Gielgud filling the aisles with noises',[11] acknowledged the appeal of Luhrmann's bizarre parallel universe comprised of twentieth-century icons and inventive raids on the cinematic canon, from *Rebel Without a Cause* to Busby Berkeley musicals, Clint Eastwood–Sergio Leone spaghetti westerns, and Ken Russell's or Fellini's surreal spectaculars. Freeze-frames identifying characters recall *Trainspotting*; in the high-voltage Capulet–Montague shoot-out, Shakespeare meets cultist John Woo (a Hong Kong action film director now working in Hollywood); John Leguizamo's Tybalt sailing through a frame and then appearing in slow motion quotes a device characteristic of contemporary action-spectacles, introduced in *Bonnie and Clyde*; and when, backed by chorus boys in purple sequins, Mercutio performs before a triptych of Madonnas, Shakespeare moves into music video by way of *To Wong Foo, With Love* and *Priscilla, Queen of the Desert*.[12]

If this be postmodernism, give me excess of it: that impulse seems to propel what might be dubbed a semiotician's dream or, as Peter Matthews writes, 'the most radical reinvention of a classic text since [Kurosawa's] *Throne of Blood*'.[13] To say that subscribes to a particular take on postmodernism as well as on viewing pleasure, one that derives a sense of identification from dissonance and disjuncture: from hearing early modern language through the flat affect of American speech (which at best works productively to remind spectators of the play's provenance at the same time as they see it made contemporary); and from seeing the story set in a decaying and decadent city over which, à *La Dolce Vita*, a colossal statue of Christ looms, separating the skyscrapers erected by warring corporate owners – a world that comments on our own and renders understandable the importance of 'filial duty, religious devotion, family honour, and the institution of marriage [and] emphasizes the ritual performance of ancient hates'.[14] That angle of vision aligns more with the film's target market, youth, than with the adult critical community, who constructed that audience as 'other' – attuned to a culture of cars, guns, fashion and music but not to Shakespeare – and, with few exceptions, either disassociated from or condescended to it. 'So enslaved by its worship of Energy that you want to slip it a Valium', wrote *Newsweek*; 'Watching it simulates having a teenager in the house,' said the *Los Angeles Times*.[15] Teenagers, however, embraced Luhrmann's move to drag High-Culture Will over to the neighbourhood: mounting a still-active Internet discourse (in January 1998 alone, some two years after the film's release, hits on the official web site reached 8 million),[16] they made *Romeo + Juliet* their cultural property and took into their own hands knowledge-making and its attendant power.

Michel de Certeau's distinction between *strategies* – interpretive modes performed from positions of strength and tradition and employing property and authority belonging to literary 'landowners' – and *tactics* – moves belonging to relatively dispossessed and powerless reader-spectators – offers a useful framework for placing the claims of both communities.[17] Whereas those who seek to monitor and manage youth culture and uphold the Shakespeare industry have access to an existing public forum, the young speak freely only in the marginal spaces they themselves create, absent of parental control and of educational protocols – circumstances which trope the power relations of the play.[18] Yet however socially peripheral, this conversation the young hold with themselves remains symbolically central to a wider conversation that implicates *Romeo + Juliet* within a network of cultural meanings by which and through which we – as agents in that culture – live.

Simultaneously commercial teaser and memory archive, the film's official web site invites viewers to look at image files and video clips from late-night star interviews, listen to sound bites, meet 'Bill' Shakespeare, download a *Romeo + Juliet* screensaver, play a 'Do You Bite Your Thumb at Me' game, and explore a Verona Beach Visitors' Guide: What to Wear, Getting There (glossed by 'Go forth with swift wheels'), Night Life (clubs called Midnite Hags, Pound of Flesh, and Shining Nights) and a list of Sponsors. The site's epigraph image – Romeo and Juliet kissing, framed by boys with guns, all pointing at the couple – perfectly condenses one of the film's central tropes: the desire for a private, utopian space within a threatening social world. The film also rehearses other aspects of this sub-cultural imaginary: a sense of adult indifference and betrayal, of loss, fragmentation, and despair. As one fan writer put it, 'Complete with death, hate, love, feuds and the hopelessness of the inner city, *William Shakespeare's Romeo + Juliet* is a true look at how we live and think today'.[19] In such a world, these viewers perceive Romeo and Juliet's love as an anchor – an 'image of something better' that teaches what utopia would *feel* like; writes one, 'I'm in love with a fictional tragic romance because I don't like tragic reality'.[20] Such longings find their fullest expression on 'Totally Decapitated: World Headquarters of the DiCaprio Cult', a web fanzine (similar to Shaksper) whose contributors 'share Leonardo DiCaprio as a common source of inspiration'; using film and star as experiential resources, they integrate the meanings attached to both into their lives.[21]

Unlike those devoted to 'flaming' or 'foaming' – 'the closest I've ever come to understanding the play ... the only thing missing is SUBTITLES'! or 'I'd die for Leo ... he is such a hot babe'! – this site offers a space for activity and agency where participants can immerse themselves in the film's world, scribble in its margins and create their own texts. A Palace Chat Room, for instance, 'takes you right inside the vibrant and dramatic world of *Romeo + Juliet*, where you can see yourself and others as graphical "heads" ', handle and even create props, move from room to room, and talk with other fans. Each issue prints poetry (in French as well as English): inspired by the film's images, some incorporate Shakespeare's lines; others, such as 'Révicide' and 'Génération virtuelle', link the play's themes to contemporary anomie; still others (future Oxfordians?) play out anagrams of Leonardo. Reproducing Shakespeare's balcony scene, one issue invites readers to compare text to film; in another, one can listen to a piano rendition of Tchaikovsky's fantasy-overture. All suggest fans who have moved beyond their pre-assigned roles as cult consumers to collaborate with Shakespeare, using his texts (much as scholar-critics do) to stage their own performances.

Yet if the 'zine forges an alternative community through Shakespeare, it concentrates primarily on his surrogate, DiCaprio's Romeo – the 'boy-poet [who] embodies the perfect lover'.[22] As Dennis Kennedy writes, the actor's body is not only the object of the most intense and profound gaze in the culture but, at times when notions of the body undergo change, it becomes a site where that cultural crisis is represented.[23] Appealing to the precarious liminality of early to late adolescents, DiCaprio functions as a tabula rasa on which fans project the romance of identity and, using tactics of personalization and emotional intensification, voice their desire for 'truth' instead of lies, for transparency instead of manipulation, for a 'real' hero in a world without them. As fanwriter Sonia Belasco says: 'When our president is cheating on his wife, when the mayor of the city I live in gets caught doing crack, when everything is about money and hate and violence ... [Leo] mirrors us ... what we want to be, what we are, what we'll never be'.[24] Taking on idealized – and ideological – contours on and off the web, DiCaprio's body morphs into other texts, especially *Titanic* – and especially for girls. My fifteen-year old niece, who disavows 'loving Leo', nonetheless has seen most of his films, including *Titanic*, three times – but only once with her boyfriend. What threatens him with loss tells her a different story, a 'romantic feminism' found only at the movies.[25]

In a culture fascinated by youth and in a subculture where one is most interesting if one's sexuality cannot be defined, DiCaprio's pale androgynous beauty – sharp Aryan looks and hint of exotic heritage, a quintessential Greek boy god – makes him a polysexual figure, equally attractive to young women and to gay and straight men. Just as *Romeo + Juliet* is not precisely a chick flick – one where more tears than blood are shed – but, given its coterie of boys who crash cars and carry big guns, can be 're-branded' within a masculine discursive space, DiCaprio's Romeo straddles several cultural masculinities. On the one hand, he figures the vulnerable 'new man' (romancing Juliet and spending the last half of the film in tears); on the other, by gunning down Tybalt, he conforms to contemporary fictions of violent masculinity and subscribes to its homosocial honour codes. Moreover, because he is embedded in a fiction that fetishizes his body as well as those of other men, one premised on a forbidden, secret love in which Juliet can substitute for Mercutio, his presence yields to a queer reading.[26] As Joshua Runner, author of regularly featured web diaries, puts it, 'Romeo, Romeo whyfore art thou Romeo? Tending to girls' fantasies, leaving nothing for the boys who exist. Juliet, divine perfection, you may be his sun, but the pale moon needs love too.'[27] Indeed, it is precisely because Leo disrupts dominant fictions of masculinity that his transitional, differently eroticized body can be read as exemplary, as providing a safe harbour for sexual awakening; and by offering fan writers opportunities to externalize and work through their anxieties about sexuality, the site serves a therapeutic function.[28]

Although mainstream critics read his body from a greater distance, even the most conservative found DiCaprio riveting; comparing him to James Dean, the cult figure of their generation, many decoded his affect in terms of intensity and authenticity, citing his 'passionate conviction', 'an ardour you can't buy in acting class', a performance that is 'all raw emotion'.[29] Favouring him with 'brooding rock-star closeups',[30] the film urges a near-oneiric encounter with Leo's face. Writes José Arroyo, 'He … bears the brunt of the feeling … It's his face in close-up … indicating how he wants, longs, feels, and suffers. [But] it's [also] the way he *moves* in the Mantuan desert when he hears of Juliet's death, not just that the camera lifts up suddenly to crush him that expresses his grief but the way he falls on his pigeon-toed heels. It's a superb performance'.[31] Or, more specifically, a superb *physical* performance, for even the friendly *Rolling Stone* was hearing echoes of another Romeo: '[Leo] doesn't round out vowels or enunciate in dulcet tones, but when he speaks, you believe him.'[32] In short, the idea that both DiCaprio and Claire Danes are 'doing Shakespeare' lends a kind of pseudo-Brechtian distantiation to their performances, marking off Danes's Valley-speak – 'I was about to do the famous balcony scene, and I was thinking, like, this is a joke, right? How am I going to do this in a fresh way'? – from iambic pentameter.[33] Yet because she handles the unfamiliar verse better than the more awkward DiCaprio, it feels culturally 'authentic' – at least in relation to gendered adolescent stereotypes about linguistic facility – especially when, in the balcony scene, as the pair seem to discover words and ways of thinking, viewers can *see* that happening: he learns from her how to talk the talk, she from him how to act like a natural born lover.[34]

A witty send-up of the play's hallmark scene, Luhrmann's balcony-pool sequence underscores the film's distinctions between the carnivalesque, associated with Verona Beach, where prostitutes solicit older men beneath a billboard advertising 'Shoot forth thunder', or with the Capulets' masquerade ball, and the natural world inhabited by the lovers. First seen silhouetted in pale orange light, Romeo gaze out to sea in a deliberately painterly 'still' that not only sets him apart from the frenzied pyrotechnics of the opening gang war but links him metonymically to Juliet, introduced as she surfaces, like a mermaid rising from the sea, from her bath. At the ball, when Romeo douses his face in water to clear his head, a cut from his face beneath the water to his mirrored reflection suggests a return to self and keys his glance at Juliet through a fishtank, as, in slow motion, to the opening strains of Des'ree's 'Kissing You', exotic tropical fish glide over their faces, already side by side even though separated. These images culminate in the pool where the pair appear first as bodiless heads floating on its surface, their desire condensed into an exchange of looks.[35] But once they take the plunge, the water joins them as one body, out of their depth in love and immersed in a private space, simultaneously enclosed within the social and remote from it. On the one hand, representing the lovers as at one with life-giving nature – and naturalized within it – situates their rebellion within heterosexual norms; on the other, it plays into a conventional opposition between *eros* and *thanatos* which confuses those assumptions. For another image chain – Romeo submerging in the pool to avoid the guard; Mercutio dying in the same space where Romeo was introduced; Tybalt falling backward into a fountain, a shot reprised as nightmare when Romeo wakes from his tryst with Juliet; and her last sight of Romeo, an extreme close-up of his face under the water – not only places both lovers in jeopardy but catches them up within a widening circle of homoerotic and homosocial relations.

Those relations are most clearly marked when an extended close-up of Romeo embracing the dead Mercutio, framed by the crumbling seaside proscenium arch, dissolves to a shot of Juliet on her bed, reframing her briefly with the fading image to link Mercutio's death and the possibility of her fulfilled desire. Yet meditating on gender is not the only way Luhrmann's film hits the hotspots of current conversations, both within Shakespeare studies and in the culture as a whole. Because it takes place, not in a Eurocentric culture, but in a multicultural borderland – a mythic geographical space open to variant readings (Miami, California, Mexico) – the film not only accentuates the performative possibilities for 'othering' but ties its representation of gender to somewhat slippery markers of ethnicity and class. Capulet figures the Mediterranean Old World and a nouveau-riche status which set him apart from the white Montague's tacit, if not precisely represented, affiliation with old money; though inflected with old-world codes, Tybalt and the Capulet boys inhabit a new-generation, New World Latino culture. In this multi-ethnic mix, Mercutio and Juliet are the two most liminal, most transgressive figures. As the white Romeo's 'double', Mercutio shares his gender-bent androgyny but is marked off from him by a flagrant racial 'exoticism'. From the outset, but especially during the Tybalt–Romeo fight, a series of triangulated shots consistently places Mercutio in the middle, a position he shares with the Chief of Police–Prince figure, also a black actor. Apart from the Friar (differently marked by his RSC-trained voice), coding blackness as the sign of mediation works, somewhat uncomfortably, to attribute the failures of mediation as much to skin colour as to the law's – or religion's – impotence and delay.

Yet by insisting on the significance of black voices – especially those of women (the African American news anchor, Des'ree's ballad, 'Kissing You' [the film's 'love theme'] and Leontyne Price's rendition of Wagner's *liebestod*) but also that of the choirboy who sings Prince's 'When Doves Cry' – to frame *Romeo + Juliet* and to articulate two crucial events in the lovers' story (their meeting and their death), the film not only gestures toward embracing African-American experience but also acknowledges the contributions of that culture to both popular- and high-culture art forms.[36] Moreover, although the film's overall narrating position differs substantively from that of the TV anchorwoman, that position can be read as a figure for Luhrmann's own marginal status as an Australian national who observes and anatomizes a 'foreign' American culture. Simultaneously, however, *Romeo + Juliet* seems unable to register most 'other' identities except in terms of stereotypes – Margolyes' highly exaggerated vocal performance – or drag – Diane Venora's non-Latina Lady Capulet staggering like an Egyptian; Harold Perrineau's Mercutio queening his role. That inability becomes especially slippery in terms of Claire Danes's Juliet, who, much like *West Side Story*'s Maria, does not need to pass to become a Montague: in spite of being a young Hispanic woman whose father is depicted as a 'minority', her white skin already 'places' her. Because of this, her ethnicity appears as a kind of drag impersonation which, in equating her with Mercutio, not only adds an erotic frisson to her attraction for Romeo but also makes his love a promise of integration into some idealized realm of 'whiteness' associated with purity, virginity and perfection.[37]

Even if these dislocations and slippages of ethnicity operate merely as another instance of the film's postmodern aesthetic, they nonetheless produce potential socio-political resonances. Yet *Romeo + Juliet* makes no overtly tactical alignment with melting-pot ideologies. In decoding it, however, mainstream critics called its ethnic politics into question and gestured toward restoring classical paradigms and privileging 'whiteness'. How, they wondered, could Governor Paris permit his son to woo a Mafia Don's daughter? How could the police chief banish a killer instead of locking him up? And how was it possible that 'the milky-skinned Juliet [could be] daughter to the thuggish Capulet, or that prep-school handsome Romeo's best friend was the black disco-diva Mercutio [and that he hung out] with a crew of boys from the hood via Mad Max'?[38] Coming from the right (*Commonweal*) as well as the left (*Village Voice*), such queries suggest critics who imagine they reside somewhere other than an America where such blurrings and crossings of ethnic, racial, gender and class boundaries occur daily. Yet even more troubling is how they attest to an ideological failure, offering evidence that the promise of an integrated social fabric ordained by public discourse about constructing nationality is just that – a conversation, not a cultural reality.

As the film negotiates its closing moves, these tropes of failed mediation and integration are remapped in terms of voices and bodies and pushed into a contemporary performative space ideally attuned to the play's imaginative repertoire, music video.[39] For just as the set speech and the soliloquy functioned as verbal icons of interiority for the early modern drama, music video, which expresses emotions and interior states of mind through lyrics and collaged images, represents a late twentieth-century equivalent. After all, it shares characteristic modes – stylistic jumbling, dependence on fragmentation and pastiche, rapid accumulation of images, blurring of internal and external realities – with Shakespeare's early verse, especially that of this play, which, as Anthony Lane notes, exhibits the ' "just-you-look-at-this" quality of a young playwright' who, like the film's young director, is simply showing off.[40] Heightening the film's strategy of putting text-as-image on commercial display and cutting it to the beat of a non-Shakespearean sound, several mini-music-video inserts refunction the play's ending, unmooring its traditional narrative designs and simultaneously preserving, though reinflecting, its meanings.

Two of these – one keyed by Romeo, the other by Juliet – map their desires onto the Friar, who envisions a happy ending. Interweaving his words with Prince's 'When Doves Cry', the first reprises the opening headline, 'Ancient Grudge', but adds a news photo of Montague and Capulet shaking hands; linked by flash cuts of flames, these yield to a grainy image of Juliet and Romeo kissing, across which a dove flies in slow motion, and then to the radiant heart. Yet, although this vision confirms the Friar's decision to marry the lovers, a cut to Mercutio's and Benvolio's parodic gun-play picks up a billboard ad for recliners – 'Such stuff as dreams are made on' – undermining his hopes of peace and union. Later, when Juliet seeks his advice, the Friar appears in left screen as a talking head, his narrative of the effects and consequences of the sleeping potion glossing an image chain that concludes with an extreme close-up of Juliet's eyes, which key shots of Romeo and her exchanging smiles and, then, of the fatally missent letter. On the videocassette, this segment is letter-boxed, not scanned, deliberately calling attention to its special status and to what its X-ray vision diagnoses: the most improbable gimmicks that mark the play's early modern heritage – the potion and the letter. Framed up within the Friar's imaginary, made hyper-real and morphed into MTV's contemporary gimmickry, those devices appear indeed the very stuff of dreams. Nonetheless, his visions construct two spaces of ending: one recirculates the religious iconography of divine union, the other anticipates a resolution for the lovers' dilemma. Cutting off the latter's more fully 'real-ized' space, the film draws on the former to generate another, even more breathtakingly surreal, dream space of ending.

That space condenses and intensifies the lovers' desire for a private universe, a utopian room of their own. Visually as well as metaphorically interior, it takes place inside the church but travels beyond Shakespeare's implied setting and his text into a knowing, aesthetically satisfying, cinematic plenitude addressed to and complicit with a spectatorial imaginary that idealizes and mystifies the lovers' experience as their own. After Romeo dies, an extreme close-up of the gun pointed at Juliet's temple articulates her own death; as the gun's report bleeds over the cut, a high-angle long shot reveals her body falling beside Romeo's onto the bier, flanked by hundreds of candles that illuminate the church aisle lined with banked flowers and blue neon crosses. The shot holds in silence until Leontyne Price's voice, singing the *liebestod* from *Tristan and Isolde*, keys a cut that shifts the perspective, so that the lovers float above the candles, transforming bier to altar.[41] Images reprising their shared moments – catching sight of one another through the fish tank; laughing together at the ball; the ring, inscribed 'I love thee' – link bier with wedding bed where, beneath a fluttering white sheet, they again exchange smiles across a cut. When the image of the bier returns, the camera angle further inverts and disorients point of view, so that instead of looking down at them, we seem to be looking up at a Tiepolo-like ceiling fresco, and the candle-flames have become radiant catherine-wheels that evoke the exploding fireworks at the ball, as if to visualize Juliet's fantasy of 'cut[ting Romeo] out in little stars'. At the centre of their own jewelled orrery, they appear as a treasured artifact, a pair of saintly pilgrims joined in eternal embrace. Exalting their love-death, the sequence offers a sensual experience in which subject identity is lost in the image: read by the body and through the body, its affect is further enhanced by a visual and aural saturation that makes it appear, not as a sign of absence but of an intensely pleasurable present.[42]

In locating the lovers' mythic union inside rather than outside the narrative design, the film offers to rewrite the traditional reading formations associated with the play, those which, as Jonathan Goldberg notes, not only privilege heterosexual love but, by giving value to the lovers' private experience, disconnect the personal from the political.[43] Although the thousand-candle tableau may suggest that love is all there is, its garish MTV excess also clearly marks it as an imported fantasy, something cooked up when an old play confronts a new medium. And that is precisely the point: highlighting the tension between the two, Luhrmann's film juxtaposes medium and message, has it both ways. As the candle-flames dissolve into bubbles to freeze frame the lovers' underwater kiss, a long fade to white, accompanied by the *liebestod*'s final strains, dissolves in turn to the 'social real' – a white-sheeted body on a hospital trolley. Chastizing Montague and Capulet – 'All are punished' – the Police Chief passes their silent figures, looking at the second white-sheeted body being loaded into an ambulance.[44] Glossed by the voice of the newswoman who spoke the opening prologue, these images then turn to grainy video; reframed within a TV monitor, that image fades, finally, to video snow.

Michael Bogdanov's 1986 RSC production, of course, anticipated this ending: there, the unveiling of the golden statues became a photo op that enhanced the Prince's public image, and it was Benvolio who, after all had left, rose from a nearby café table to mourn his friend's death.[45] Ten years later, Luhrmann's film denies, or suspends, any promise of securing the social through either the heterosexual or the homosocial. That points, all too knowingly, to how, in our present cultural moment – at least in America – there seem to be no answers, fictional or real, religious or legal, to gender, ethnic and class differences and conflicts, to generational strife, or boys with guns. If, as the web discourse on Leo tells us, chick flicks do matter, then *William Shakespeare's Romeo + Juliet* matters even more: it bears watching precisely because it has been watching us.

Notes

1   In order, these colleagues are Bill Worthen, Joseph Schneider, Peter Donaldson and Jim Bulman, whose e-mail communication I cite. The mass market DiCaprio books are Grace Catalano, *Leonardo: A Scrapbook in Words and Pictures* (New York, 1998); Catalano, *Leonardo DiCaprio: Modern-Day Romeo* (New York, 1997); and Brian J. Robb, *The Leonardo DiCaprio Album* (London, 1997). For the filmscript, see *William Shakespeare's Romeo + Juliet: The Contemporary Film, The Classic Play* (New York, 1996).

2   See, for instance, Mary Ann Doane, *The Desire to Desire: The Woman's Film of the 1940s* (Bloomington, 1987), pp. 2–16.

3   See *Life*, 'Special Royals Issue: A Guide to the 28 Monarchies of the World' (Summer 1998). The cover features 'The Boy who WILL be King'. Remarks Prince William: 'I think [DiCaprio will] find it easier being king of Hollywood than I shall being king of England', pp. 58–9.

4   My framework derives from Paul Smith, *Clint Eastwood: A Cultural Production* (Minneapolis, 1993). As I turn to reception, I am indebted to Janet Staiger, *Interpreting Films: Studies in the Historical Reception of American Cinema* (Princeton, 1992).

5   Dave is the owner and 'advertising star' of Wendy's (a chain restaurant) TV commercials; the Lexus is a luxury car; and the Superbowl is an annual US title football game – a media-constructed 'holiday' occasion.

6   W. B. Worthen, 'Drama, Performativity, and Performance', *PMLA* 113.5 (October 1998), 1103. My thanks to Worthen for providing me with a copy of his essay before publication and for comments on an earlier version of this essay entitled 'Totally DiCaptivated: Shakespeare's Boys Meet the Chick Flick'.

7   As in Luhrmann's debut film, *Strictly Ballroom* (1992), it is parents, not children, who are the 'unnatural' – or parodically perverse – gender performers.

8   As for Zeffirelli's film, two CDs were released, one with and one without dialogue. For the official web site, see http://geocities.com/MotorCity/4147/ romeo.html.

9   Janet Maslin, 'Soft! What light? It's flash, Romeo', *New York Times*, 1 November 1996.

10   See *Tromeo and Juliet*, dir. Lloyd Kaufman; Troma Video Entertainment, 1997; 107 minutes.

11   Anthony Lane, 'Tights! Camera! Action!' *New Yorker*, 25 November 1996, p. 66.

12   Most mainstream reviews cite several of these 'classic' filmtexts. I am indebted to seminar students for some of the references to cult films.

13   Peter Matthews, review of *William Shakespeare's Romeo + Juliet*, *Sight and Sound* (April 1997), 55.

14   Speaking of the team's search for a location, Catherine Martin, the film's designer, remarks on how Mexico had many of the elements necessary to make a contemporary version work. 'Religion still has a very strong presence there, culturally and visually; marriage is still big, and sex before marriage is frowned on. There are whole streets in Mexico City which are only bridal shops. And the social structure is closer to that of Elizabethan times than anywhere else in the modern world: a few very rich people with guns, and the vast majority poor'. See Jo Litson, '*Romeo and Juliet*', *TCI: The Business of Entertainment Technology and Design*, vol. 30 (November 1996), 46.

15 See David Ansen, 'It's the '90s, so the Bard is Back', *Newsweek*, 4 November 1996: 73; Kenneth Turan, 'A Full-Tilt Romeo', *Los Angeles Times*, 1 November 1996, F1.

16 Overall, forty web sites are devoted to the film; 500 to Leonardo DiCaprio. I am indebted to Erik Steven Fisk, 'Professor Shakespeare, Director Shakespeare: Examining the Role of the Bard on the Way into 2000 à la *Romeo + Juliet*', unpublished seminar paper.

17 Michel de Certeau, *The Practice of Everyday Life* (Berkeley: University of California Press, 1984); cited in Henry Jenkins, *Textual Poachers: Television Fans and Participatory Culture* (New York and London, 1992), pp. 44–5. These distinctions point to the boundaries separating elitist and popular texts, marking cultural space as a contested territory. The reviewers' comments also point to what Jenkins identifies as a frequent mistake: treating popular culture productions as though they were the materials of elite culture. See Jenkins, *Textual Poachers*, p. 60.

18 Zeffirelli's *Romeo and Juliet* had a similarly divided reception history. See, for example, Jill L. Levenson, *Shakespeare in Performance: 'Romeo and Juliet'* (Manchester, 1987), p. 123; and my 'Absent Bodies, Present Voices: Performance Work and the Close of *Romeo and Juliet's* Golden Story', *Theatre Journal* (October 1989), 341–59.

19 Comment from fan writer on http://www.Asu.edu.

20 From 'The Diaries of Joshua Runner', a regular feature of 'Totally Decapitated'; the cite is from Issue Four and is dated 25 November 1996. The web site address is http://www.com/leo/issuefour/html. For the idea of using stars as resources, see Richard Dyer, *Stars* (London, 1979), pp. 59–60.

21 Jenkins argues that, by blurring the boundaries between producers and consumers, spectators and participants, both web discourses and fanzines constitute a cultural and social network that spans the globe. See *Textual Poachers*, esp. pp. 45, 279.

22 Quote from 'The Diaries of Joshua Runner', 10 November, 1996.

23 See Dennis Kennedy, 'Shakespeare Played Small: Three Speculations About the Body', *Shakespeare Survey 47* (1994), p. 10.

24 Sonia Belasco, 'Totally Decapitated', Issue Ten: prose.

25 See Katha Pollitt, 'Women and Children First', *The Nation*, 30 March 1998, 9.

26 See, for instance, Jonathan Goldberg, '*Romeo and Juliet's* Open Rs', in *Queering the Renaissance*, ed. Jonathan Goldberg (Durham and London, 1994), pp. 218–35. See also Robert Appelbaum, ' "Standing to the Wall": The Pressures of Masculinity in *Romeo and Juliet*', *Shakespeare Quarterly*, 48.3 (1997), 251–72; and Paul Smith's notions of hysterical or wounded masculinity in Smith, *Clint Eastwood*. See also Ellen Goodman, 'Romancing a New Generation of Women', *Des Moines Register*, 12 May 1998, 7A; and Pollitt, 'Women and Children First'.

27 'The Diaries of Joshua Runner', 8 November 1996. Wolf, another frequent contributor, writes, 'He is the embodyment [sic] of what we need, someone like us to hide with ... someplace far away'; responding to a fan calling himself 'Like Minded' who had rented the film and found himself desiring Leo, Wolf urges him to read Shakespeare's sonnets addressed to the young man, saying that he himself had found comfort in them. 'Totally Decapitated', Issue Five: prose.

28 On fan writers, see Jenkins, *Textual Poachers*, pp. 152–84. On internet discourse and therapy, see Sherry Turkle, *Life on the Screen: Identity in the Age of the Internet* (New York, 1995). See also Janet H. Murray, *Hamlet on the Holodeck: The Future of Narrative in Cyberspace* (New York, 1997). Significantly, the fan writers cited do not represent all cultures: Joseph Schneider's students (women as well as men) at the University of Hong Kong, for instance, prefer Bruce Willis or Jet Li, the Hong Kong action film star, to Leo, who is 'too boyish' for their tastes – 'not a real man'. Harold Bloom puts such opportunities for meaning-making into a wider context. Shakespeare, he writes, 'teach[es] us how to overhear ourselves when we talk to ourselves'; the true use of Shakespeare, he goes on to say, is 'to augment one's own growing inner self', a process that will bring about 'the proper use of one's own solitude, that solitude whose final form is one's confrontation with one's own mortality'. See Harold Bloom, *The Western Canon* (New York and London, 1994), pp. 30–1.

29   In order, quotations are from David Horspool, 'Tabs and Traffic Jams', *Times Literary Supplement*, 11 April 1997, 19; Peter Travers, 'Just Two Kids in Love', *Rolling Stone*, 14 November 1996, 124; José Arroyo, 'Kiss Kiss Bang Bang', *Sight and Sound* (March 1997), 9.

30   Kuran, 'It's the '90s', F1.

31   Arroyo, 'Kiss Kiss', 9.

32   Travers, 'Just Two Kids', 124.

33   Claire Danes quoted in Christine Spines, 'I Would Die 4U', *Premiere*, v. 10 (October 1996): 137.

34   I appropriate 'natural born lovers' from Joe Morgenstern, 'Mod Bard; Muted Vonnegut', *Wall Street Journal*, 1 November 1996, A11. Morgenstern, however, in alluding to Quentin Tarantino's *Natural Born Killers*, gives the phrase a different sense from mine.

35   Just before they fall into the pool together, they are posed on either side of a statue of Pan, another marker of this 'natural' though man-made setting.

36   My thanks to Margo Hendricks for pointing out how the film works to situate black women's voices at its centre.

37   See Arroyo, 'Kiss Kiss', 8; and Richard Dyer, *White* (London and New York, 1997), esp. pp. 70–2.

38   These objections, as well as the citations, are from Richard Alleva, 'The Bard in America', *Commonweal*, 6 December 1996, 19; and Amy Taubin, 'Live Fast, Die Young', *Village Voice*, 12 November 1996, 80. The problematics of reading the film's multiculturalism also embraces how casting invites blending actors' performances in *Romeo + Juliet* with their most recent roles: for instance, American viewers might well connect Brian Dennehy (Montague) to his most recent appearances as a hawker of antacids on TV rather than to his film roles or to stage performances at New York's Public Theater.

39   *Romeo and Juliet*'s focus on adolescent rebellion and narcissistic love and its obsession with sexuality and violence pre-tailors it for MTV, which addresses the desires, fantasies and anxieties of the young. See E. Ann Kaplan, *Rocking Around the Clock: Music Television, Postmodernism, and Consumer Culture* (New York and London, 1987), esp. pp. 5–7, 31. On MTV, see also Jenkins, *Textual Poachers*, pp. 233–40; Richard Dyer, 'Entertainment and Utopia', in *Movies and Methods, Volume II*, ed. Bill Nichols (Berkeley, 1985); and John Fiske, 'MTV: Post-Structural Post-Modern', *Journal of Communication Inquiry* 10: 1 (Winter 1986), 74–9.

40   Lane, 'Tights!', 75.

41   Sung by a black soprano, this aria not only connects the lovers to the most famous of all love-deaths but also represents an instance of how the film's soundtrack, much like its casting (which blends stage and film traditions) mixes opera, classical music (phrases from Mozart's Symphony 25 introduce Romeo) and pop culture, especially music from groups that mix white, black and latino / latina or hispanic voices.

42   I adapt these terms from Fiske, 'MTV', pp. 74–9.

43   See Goldberg, '*Romeo and Juliet*'s Open Rs', esp. pp. 219–20.

44   Peter Holland suggests a pertinent analogue: the moment in Bob Fosse's 1979 film, *All That Jazz*, where a cut from Ben Vereen's final production number (celebrating the Fosse-character's death) yields to an image of a body bag being zipped shut.

45   See my 'Absent Bodies, Present Voices', especially p. 358, n. 47.

43

Deeper Meanings and Theatrical Technique: The Rhetoric of Performance Criticism

William B. Worthen

My own major interest has always been Shakespeare in the theatre; and to that my written work has been, in my own mind, subsidiary. But my experience as actor, producer and play-goer leaves me uncompromising in my assertion that the literary analysis of great drama in terms of theatrical technique accomplishes singularly little. Such technicalities should be confined to the theatre from which their terms are drawn. The proper thing to do about a play's dramatic quality is to produce it, to act in it, to attend performances; but the penetration of its deeper meanings is a different matter, and such a study, though the commentator should certainly be dramatically aware, and even wary, will not itself speak in theatrical terms.[1]

I would like to pause briefly over these remarks, taken from the preface to G. Wilson Knight's *The Wheel of Fire*, in order to raise the general question of the relation between "text" and "performance" in Shakespearean "performance criticism." An "actor, producer and playgoer," Knight candidly describes the difficulty of assimilating commentary on the dramatic text to the "dramatic quality" that can be seized only in performance. Yet while Knight finds this "dramatic quality" to be producible only in the language of the stage, he also finds that "theatrical technique" is incapable of penetrating to the "deeper meanings" available to "literary analysis." This is an arresting limitation. It seems that critical commentary can disclose the text's "deeper meanings" precisely because it is not coextensive with the text it represents. Performance, on the other hand, is naturalized to the drama, and so exhausts the play's "dramatic quality" at the moment the text is staged. Conceived not as a discourse for representing the text but as a "technique" for realizing the drama onstage, performance can only reiterate the text in its own technical terms. As a result, "performance criticism" – the "literary analysis of great drama in terms of theatrical technique" – fails to approach the play's "deeper meanings" because the "theatrical technique" it imitates is not itself seen to be critical, invasive, interpretive. "Performance criticism" becomes an expendable enterprise, offering neither the "meanings" of literary criticism nor insight into the truly "dramatic quality" provided by performance.

Knight trains our attention on a basic problem in dramatic criticism, one that has now preoccupied Shakespeare studies for decades: how to relate the signification of the dramatic text to the practices of performance. What is surprising, though, is that the extensive "tradition" of performance criticism – reaching, it has been argued, from Granville-Barker's *Prefaces to Shakespeare* and the early work of M. C. Bradbrook through the more recent work of John Russell Brown, J. L. Styan, Bernard Beckerman, Michael Goldman, and others – has been more successful in reifying Knight's polarity between text and performance than in suspending it.[2] The cultural authority of "Shakespeare" (which includes but exceeds Shakespeare's plays) has shaped the text / performance question in Shakespeare studies, marked as it is by the desire to identify and conserve the authority of the text in performance. Despite an impressive body of scholarship, in some respects performance criticism remains stalled at Knight's impasse, bound by an opposition between a "subsidiary" critical practice and a conception of performance – and so of performance criticism – natural to the "detextualized" practices of the theatre.[3] This covert, perhaps unrecognized, opposition has prevented performance criticism from developing an acknowledged complex of aims, methods, theoretical consequences, and principles of persuasion. The text / performance dichotomy, and the interpretive priorities and assumptions it governs, stands at the center of the disciplinary ambiguity that characterizes performance criticism *as* criticism. More important, it prevents performance criticism from pursuing what I take to be its justifying critical agenda: to locate the space and practice of criticism in relation to the practices of performance.

We need only recall Lamb's criticism of the role of Lear ("essentially impossible to be represented on a stage") and Hunt's remarks on Kean's Othello ("the masterpiece of the living stage"), Jonson's and Shakespeare's attitudes toward play publication, or Aristotle's discrimination between drama (plot, character, diction, thought) and spectacle, to be reminded that text and performance have long seemed to compete for legitimacy as means of representing the drama.[4] In our era the critical derogation of performance is usually, and somewhat unfairly, charged to the widespread influence of the New Criticism. New Criticism treated the drama in terms of its normative literary genre – the lyric – and so presented the dramatic text as a verbal icon. Applying its powerful interpretive technology to formal, verbal, thematic, and generic features taken to be determined by the text, New Criticism necessarily discredited stage performance – as well as criticism speaking "in theatrical terms" – as extrinsic to a play's literary design. While New Critical practice sharply discriminated against stage performance as a means of interpreting the dramatic text, performance did have an oddly important function in New Critical thinking. Despite its investment in the text as a closed, organically coherent system, the "heresy of paraphrase" implicit in much New Critical writing and pedagogy points to the reader's engaged performance of the poem as one that should exceed and enrich the formal, verbal, and thematic determinations of critical analysis. Of course, New Criticism placed strict limitations on the validity of interpretation generated by reading-as-performance. For as performance, reading was naturalized to the text's internal dynamics, seen as a mode of recovering meanings rather than as a means of producing the text in a different order of signification. Unlike reading, in this sense, stage performance enlarges on the text, forces it to speak in languages that often exceed the determinations of the words on the page. "In acted drama," Brooks and Heilman remind their readers, "we have costumes, settings, and 'properties'; but drama as literature has no such appurtenances."[5] To the New Critical temperament, theatrical performance and a criticism derived from it must seem ungrounded, a kind of interpretive free play.[6]

More recently, of course, literary criticism has tended to disperse "*the* text" of New Criticism, displacing "meaning" from within the verbal design that was said to contain it to the contingent relationship between *a* text and the contextualizing, even constitutive, practices that are seen to produce it: the interests and affiliations of its initial production, for instance; the practices of the interpretive communities that have transmitted it throughout history; the technologies that have reproduced it materially; the metaphysics of which it is a part; the pressures of politics, ideology, gender; and so on. Jean E. Howard and Marion F. O'Connor introduce their recent anthology, *Shakespeare Reproduced*, in just this way, remarking that "Far from distorting the 'true' meaning of an unchanging text … such constructions *are* the text."[7] This relocation of "meaning" from within the text to the ways in which a text can be made to perform has fundamentally altered both the practice and the consequences of literary criticism of the drama, especially in Renaissance studies. And yet the textualizing function of stage performance has remained largely isolated from this wider effort to place the text within the discourses of cultural life. The essays in *Shakespeare Reproduced* "collectively" place "the Shakespearean text in relationship to Elizabethan texts other than the text of nature; and they examine the ideological function of Renaissance theatrical practices and representations in light of a range of other cultural practices."[8] With a few important exceptions, however, stage acting is largely omitted from the catalogue of "discourses" that inform criticism of "theatrical practice" and the ideologies it represents. In part, this omission arises because acting is so fully identified with what Bakhtin calls the "closed individuality" of the "new bodily canon" that its discursive formalities seem invisible or nonexistent.[9] To this extent Robert Weimann is right to point out that ideological criticism of the drama currently finds in performance a troubling excess and indeterminacy not unlike those puzzling the New Criticism. Much as performance cannot be reduced to the verbal order of the text, so the "pleasure" of the theatre "cannot exclusively be defined in terms of ideological structures and categories, any more than other forms of corporeal activity, such as eating, laughing, smiling, and sneezing can be reduced to ideological gestures of subversion or rehearsal."[10] As a result of this exclusion, though, the entire spectrum of activity called "acting" remains inscribed within the text of nature. Whether by design or by default, literary criticism of the drama persists in assigning the performer's "text" to the subjective caprice of the actor's freedom.

"Performance criticism" seeks to replace "textual" interpretation with "performance" and its criticism as a means of representing the drama's truly "dramatic quality." But the persistence of the "text against performance" question points to an ongoing interdependence between "performance" and "literary" critical modes. Performance criticism can define a "sense of the authentic" precisely because it regards performance as preserving an authentic text; this "text" is, of course, the product of the "literary" critical practice it often claims to dislodge.[11] Many versions of performance criticism avowedly locate performance (and so "performance criticism") as supplemental to the designs of the text, mapping the text's meanings onto the histrionic and pictorial relationships of the stage. I am thinking here of most treatments of "subtext" in Shakespearean characterization, metadramatic and metatheatrical criticism, iconographical readings of stage imagery, and what might be called "directorial criticism" – the idealized description of how a Shakespeare play might orchestrate the conventions of the Elizabethan theatre on the modern stage in order to recover "the Shakespeare experience."[12] James H. Kavanagh rightly implies that the assumptions about both text and performance saturating this "ostensibly alternative 'stagecraft' commentary" tend "to produce a kind of para-literary ideological discourse," one that casts the stage in a lapsed relation to the authority of the "literary" text.[13] By displaying the privileged status of textual to performance signification, such criticism not only extends New Critical attitudes toward the drama but also sidesteps the definitive challenges that a performance criticism ought to address: how the text is traced and transgressed both by theatrical and by critical strategies for producing it as drama.

These versions of Shakespearean performance criticism have been, and should continue to be, deservedly influential in our thinking about text / performance relations; in many respects they represent the most scrupulous engagement with the problems of how texts operate in performance that we have available to us. But by grounding meaning – even performed meaning – in the text, such criticism itself runs the risk of being repudiated by the more polemical version of performance criticism that I wish to address here (and which forms the body of work I will refer to as "performance criticism" in the remainder of this essay). The kind of criticism I have in mind grounds itself in the drama's theatrical "origin" as a means of displacing textual interpretation, either by limiting interpretation to the presumed capacities of Elizabethan performance practice or, more often, by contextualizing the play within a universal definition of the purposes, forms, and meaning of enactment. This more insistent "performance criticism" also accepts the New Critical valuation of a "text against performance" but simply reverses the terms of the question, urging the priority of the lively and spontaneous performance over the "impractical" insights reached by criticism (even, many times, the insights of "iconographic" or "directorial" criticism). As Richard David has it, "It is for this reason that half (I sometimes think all) the subtleties exposed by commentators are not, as actors would say, 'practical' "; if "meaning" can't be played, it "cannot be integral to the drama as drama."[14] As an object of inquiry, "performance" is marked out as a special zone of individual expression, a kind of wild semiology set apart from the institutional practices that govern criticism and that inform signifying practices in the culture at large.

This brand of performance criticism has driven the wholesale adoption of the "theatrical dimension" in Shakespeare pedagogy and criticism. Yet despite the salutary effects of conceiving Shakespearean drama as theatre, in practice this mode of performance criticism has significant liabilities and limitations. Granted, John Russell Brown's complaint (of 1962) that "Critics, trained in literary disciplines, are apt to think that theatrical experience is coarse and vulgar" has been fully replaced by Richard

David's "commonplace of criticism" that "Shakespeare's plays were written for the theatre, and only in the theatre develop their full impact."[15] But has this "shift from page to stage, from analysis of the plays as literature to a new interest in the plays as performance,"[16] produced a substantive change in our thinking about text / performance? Writing in the 1984 *Shakespeare Quarterly* special issue devoted to teaching Shakespeare, Homer Swander takes a path-breaking position: "To read a script well is to discover what at each moment it tells the actor or actors to do"; "Shakespeare's words, deliberately designed by a theatrical genius for a thrust stage with live actors and an immediately responding audience, cannot be satisfactorily explored or experienced in any medium but his own."[17] In order to understand what the text "tells an actor or actors to do," however, we must regard "acting" as both an interpretive and a signifying practice, articulating a dialogic relationship between the text and the *mise-en-scène*, and between the *mise-en-scène* and the audience. How does acting reproduce a text? How does the actors' training enable them to conceive the text as *telling* them to *do* anything in particular? How does a range of perceived acting opportunities constitute a strategy for reading the play *as* actable, as representable to an audience in the theatre? A similar line of questioning might, of course, be trained on directors, designers, and so on, but that's not the point. As the history of theatre demonstrates, stage performance always requires a highly formalized body of activities: techniques for training and preparation; conventions of acting and staging style; habits of audience disposition, behavior, and interpretation. Richly diverse and historically localized, these practices articulate the text as "acting" within the wider range of signifying behavior specific to a given theatre and culture. Swander's view of "dramatic quality" appears to oppose the New Critical priority of text-to-performance but in fact duplicates it: while the text produced by criticism is irrelevant to the stage, the performance-text speaks directly to the actors through a privileged "technique," one that retains textual authority precisely by emptying "performance" of its interpretive, textualizing, ideological function.

John Russell Brown is more blunt about it: "Readers and critics have become increasingly aware that the plays were written for performance and reveal their true natures only in performance."[18] A shaping force in performance criticism, Brown is careful to recognize the historical specificity of acting, the difference between Shakespeare's actors and our own. Recently, for example, he reminds us that "modern actors are not those Elizabethan and Jacobean actors for whom Shakespeare wrote his plays and that they bring to rehearsals many prejudices and skills which Shakespeare could not have imagined and lack others that he took for granted"; indeed, he concludes that "the same argument can be leveled against any reading of the plays. No one person can reconstruct a historically accurate response, even if we could know what that might be."[19] Fair enough. But Brown's recognition leads not to an inspection of modern acting's historical and cultural contingency but to an effort to essentialize the relation between modern acting and the authority of Shakespeare. For, like Knight perhaps, Brown assigns the difference between Elizabethan and modern acting to the level of technique, a stylistic difference that only masks the fundamental identity between all modes of performance, governed as they are by the inherent qualities of Shakespeare's text:

> Perhaps Elizabethan actors were cruder or more eloquent, or more formalized and less lifelike, than their modern counterparts, but every actor who steps onto a stage has to

bring a whole self into play and must relate what is spoken to what is there, palpably, before the audience. No actor can cheat for very long; incomplete performances, or those which have some elements at odds with others, will be recognized for what they are by audiences and by fellow actors. *We need have little doubt that modern actors are responding to qualities inherent in Shakespeare's text*; if they did not, they would find acting in his plays a troublesome labor and not a great pleasure.[20]

Garrick, Irving, and Olivier each applied a different histrionic technology to their roles, methods of interpretation and of signification that not only required different acts of attention from their audiences but conveyed markedly different ideologies of action, character, and meaning. To preserve the unchanging "true natures" of Shakespeare's texts in performance, Brown must present the true nature of performance as equally inert, unaffected by alterations in the condition of the stage, in the social function of theatre and theatricality, in styles of acting on and offstage – regardless of how deeply acting may be implicated in local conceptions of the subject, the self, human identity and action: "His theatre was different from any we know today, but the essential act of performance was the same."[21]

Although it questions the adequacy of "literary" interpretation in order to advance stage-oriented readings, this sense of performance casts the *mise-en-scène* as a vehicle for reproducing the authority of the text, a text whose "dramatic quality" is both determined and recovered through a universal and transparent stage technique. To put it more generally, such "performance criticism" naturalizes the *mise-en-scène* as an ideal zone of realization, iterating meanings "written for" its operation, rather than conceiving it as a rhetoric for strategically producing the drama as theatre. Despite the claim that it legitimates performance as a mode of inquiry independent of both "literary" criticism and its "text," performance criticism of this kind represses the rhetorical character of performance and so conceals its relation to other, similarly institutional, means of producing textual significance.

Some consequences of this conception of "performance" – that actors "realize" the text rather than produce it – are dramatized by the highly regarded television series "Playing Shakespeare." The aim of the series is not, of course, to provide access to live Shakespearean theatre, to the kind of event that performance criticism should legitimately address. Indeed, rather than staging Shakespearean performance, "Playing Shakespeare" stages "performance criticism" itself and richly illustrates how the assumptions of performance criticism sustain critical, interpretive, and pedagogical practice. Playing the part of avuncular critic / director, John Barton repeatedly urges his actors to discover the "infinite" interpretive freedom at their disposal through a scrupulous reading of "the text" and its "ambiguities." And yet any viewer of the series must feel that the performances and Barton's direction are far from infinite in their variety. Indeed, Barton's illustration of the divergence between criticism and theatre provides an arresting instance of the ideological complicity between his directorial practice and the "literary" notions he repudiates. In the "Set Speeches and Soliloquies" episode Barton invites David Suchet to read a convoluted passage of criticism "from one of the world's leading theatrical magazines." The passage begins,

> This ambiguity is one of the significant aesthetic counterparts of the broad philosophic drift defining the modern age ... In theatre, *Hamlet* predicts this epistemologic tradition

> ... The execution of the deed steadily loses way to a search for the personal modality of the deed ...

and continues on for a few more heavily edited sentences.[22] The passage is hardly amusing; it is, of course, the manner in which it is produced in Barton's lecture / performance that makes it funny, that determines its performed meaning for us. In part the text's emphatically "academic" quality seems inflated, pretentious in contrast to Barton's ingratiatingly low-key style. But the passage becomes funnier in Suchet's delivery, for he not only hectors us, he speaks in what – to me at least – sounds like an oddly aggressive, distinctly American accent, one perhaps touched by a trace of Brooklynese – "duh leading uhsthetic problem." This is, in fact, a notable instance of the "textualizing" function of performance style. The choice of dialect here can hardly claim to arise solely from the text. Instead, the dialect suggests that this voice speaks in the wrong accents, accents that mark its critical perspective – its origin in America, and in "literary" study – as unspeakable in the powerful, legitimating sonorities of the RSC style. How the passage becomes textualized by performance largely determines how we will decode it, and so determines what we will take it to mean. Spoken in the wrong accent, it must be saying the wrong thing.

Barton then turns to Michael Pennington, about to deliver Hamlet's "To be, or not to be" soliloquy, and says, "Michael, come and follow that." Pennington first gives an underplayed, obviously "intellectualized" reading, one that seems to illustrate the unsatisfying results of following the dictates of an overabstract and literary conception of the part. Then Pennington gives the soliloquy a second try. Following Barton's direction to "share it with us," to "open himself to his audience," Pennington gives a lively reading, broadening his range of movement, and making explicit contact with the audience offstage. In other words, Pennington produces the speech through our contemporary conventions of Shakespearean stage characterization: a concentration on psychological motivation complicated by a degree of openness to the theatre audience, the post-Brechtian compromise between "realistic" and "theatrical" characterization typical of the RSC since the mid-1960s.[23] The results here are, however, confusing, despite Barton's enthusiasm and the elegance of Pennington's enactment. For Pennington's performance, oddly enough, seems to conform to the thematics of character described by the vulgar American. Both Pennington and his "Hamlet" seem engaged in a "search for the personal modality of the deed" in the public confines of the stage, a search typical of "the leading aesthetic problem of the actor in the modern theatre – the interpretation of action through characterologic nuance."[24] (This reading is actually emphasized by the "textualizing" work of the camera, which after showing Pennington full-length in front of an approving audience, shortly closes to a head shot, stressing the interiority of Pennington's performance.) The point here isn't that the critic is really in the right, or that Pennington's performance "illustrates" such critical conclusions about *Hamlet*. It's that theatrical practice – the production of "character" as an effect of "acting," in this case – is not an unconstrained means of realizing the text but a practice related to other modes of cultural transmission, signification, and interpretation. The acting that Barton praises as a matter of "common-sense rather than of interpretation" clearly owes its "common-sense" to its ideological redundancy, the degree to which the actor's rhetoric of characterization comports with practices for identifying "character" – as well as the "self" and "acting" – available in the culture at large.[25] By regarding his own direction and the actors' training as transparent techniques for the preservation of textual "ambiguity," Barton specifically represses acting and direction as *theory*, as a way of locating the theatre's production of meaning in relation to the signifying practices that the stage shares with film, television, sports, social behavior in general, or even with criticism.[26]

Performance criticism of this kind claims for "performance" an exclusive access to the "dramatic quality" of the text, while at the same time subverting its claims as signifying practice by insisting on the "freedom" of performance from the signifying formalities that make "meaning" possible and determinable. Yet, the "test question" of such criticism – "Can this be played?" – dramatizes the impasse we come to when we regard "playing" as the realization of an immanent textual significance.[27] For the idea that performance *can* test criticism risks the priority of the stage that performance criticism has worked so hard to claim. Such a test implies a kind of redundancy between critical and performed "meaning," as though writing and acting were able to render the same message through entirely different means of articulation. The "test" serves to confirm only those "meanings" already assimilable to the privileged presentation of the performer. This redundancy, however, seems more likely to threaten the priority of performance, since it suggests that the stage tests "meanings" already formulated elsewhere, either as a feature of its own technique or in an unstaged engagement with the play (such as reading, criticism). This belatedness creates the possibility that a test might work in both directions at once: it would subject the insights of criticism to the physical immediacy of the *mise-en-scène* and also subject the mute languages of the stage – acting, design, costume, direction – to rhetorical criteria of coherence, integration, and theoretical rigor, testing the production's retextualization of the drama as performance. One example of such a testing might be a scene in which a line of business establishes the stage referent of a line of speech, as in Donald Sinden's business with the sundial in John Barton's 1969 *Twelfth Night*. Sinden describes how he used a piece of business (adjusting the sundial to conform to the time on Malvolio's watch) to provide a referential context for a series of lines: " 'Why everything adheres together' (glance at sundial) 'that no dram of a scruple' (look at watch) 'no scruple of a scruple' (back to sundial) 'no obstacle' (look at watch). Check 'sunbeam' to sundial and adjust it until correct time is shown during – 'no incredulous or unsafe circumstance.' "[28] In her fine article "Re-viewing the Play," Miriam Gilbert notes "the way in which the 'business' actually fits the language, taking off from 'everything adheres together' and then finding a concrete example where things don't adhere together until the stone is shifted."[29] To "test" such a "fit," though, might well require us to develop a fuller and more specific account of the production's systematic means of relating the dramatic text to its physical milieu onstage. Is this a real "discovery" about the play or a funny gimmick unrelated to the production's engagement with the play as a whole? To answer such a question would be, so to speak, to subject performance choices to the "test of criticism."

Let me try to suggest what is at stake here. Regarding performance as realization represses the institutional practices already inscribed in the theatre, in gesture and intonation, in the body and its behaviors, the "textualizing" formalities that render theatre significant. In so doing, we disqualify the processes that produce meaning in the theatre as legitimate objects for our attention and scrutiny. Indeed, we dramatize the degree to which we are still firmly in the grip of the rhetoric of theatrical naturalism, with its characteristic erasure of the machinery of theatrical production from our view. Yet a variety of such discourses necessarily intervenes between the text and its stage production, much as it does between the text and its production as reading experience or as critical activity. Terry Eagleton has remarked that "text and production are distinct formations – different material modes of production, between which no homologous or 'reproductive' relationship can hold. They are not two aspects of the same discourse – the text, as it were, thought or silent speech and the production thought-in-action, articulate language; they constitute distinct kinds of discourse, between which no simple 'translation' is possible."[30] But to say that text and performance are incommensurable is, I think, again to miss the point that the text is "against performance" of all kinds, to the degree that it necessarily differs from *any* discourse that represents it – reading and criticism as well as acting. Text and performance are dialectically related through the labor of enactment, in which the instruments of representation – both literary and theatrical, critical and performative – "transform the 'raw materials' of the text into a specific product, which cannot be mechanically extrapolated from an inspection of the text."[31] The production of the text's "meanings" in the theatre requires the application of a complex machinery of interpretation and of signification, whose adequacy – like the machinery of criticism – cannot be "mechanically extrapolated" from the text because it is engaged in making the text, producing it as theatre. Where homology may be possible, then, is not between text and performance, nor between the results of "literary" interpretation and of stage production. Much as the effect of performance is not itself immediately assimilable to "criticism," so too our readerly "ideas" about the dramatic text are not illustrated in a direct manner in the theatre. Performance criticism should look instead to the relationship between the practices that we use to stage the text as "drama," both as criticism and as theatrical performance.

Our ability to read a text as "drama," then, is enabled by the practices that allow us to read it both as literature and as theatre.[32] Such a sense includes not only the strategies that allow us to read the text as instigating the behaviors we recognize as "acting," but also the interpretive habits that guide our performance as readers and critics. This contingency could be illustrated in a number of ways. One version of performance criticism might trace the relationship between textual criticism and stage performance as means of producing the dramatic "text." The extensive controversy surrounding contemporary Shakespearean editing can only be touched on here. Yet in an important sense, textual and performance criticism share – or might come to share – an interest in determining how "the text" has been produced as a cultural artifact, and how the process of production inscribes itself into – and perhaps constitutes – the "text" it represents. To regard the text at the moment of its insertion into social discourse doesn't, of course, imply that editorial choices can or should be limited to what is performable.[33] For as A. R. Braunmuller argues, while textual opacities often depend for their resolution on what the editor thinks is happening in the dramatic action and in its stage enactment, such decisions often rely on a romanticized, overly narrow, or simply outmoded understanding of stage practice.[34] A familiar framework of conventions defines what "works" in the theatre. Editors also produce a text in relation to interpretive and signifying conventions that legitimate certain versions of "the text" as authoritative, and so legitimate what such texts can say.[35] Like the *mise-en-scène*, the *mise-en-page* places the text and its production at issue; in this regard performance criticism might take Shakespearean textual criticism as a paradigm. For not only does this controversy locate the act of reading as a social behavior potentially related to other performances, it raises in a cogent and powerful manner the central issue still eluding performance criticism: the problematic relation between the text's origin, its initial production, and its reproduction throughout history.

J. C. Bulman and H. R. Coursen's *Shakespeare on Television*, a recent anthology of articles and reviews on televised Shakespeare, is also to the point.[36] The articles here repeatedly attend to the differences between the text in the theatre and the text on television. The lack of physical space, the loss of scale, the use of closeup to render characterization intimate, the shifting balance of intensity from public to private scenes, the need to cut the text to accommodate American broadcasting conventions, the placement of "high" art in the mass media: such concerns are all part of how television retextualizes the drama by producing it in its own rhetoric. "Dramatic quality," in this sense, is a function neither of dramatic criticism nor of theatrical productions but defines that intersection between the text and the cultural institutions that enable us to produce it meaningfully.

Finally, to raise a more directly theatrical example, performance criticism might ask how acting in a particular historical mode – the American Method, for instance – textualizes "character" as performance. Performance criticism might address the relation between criticism's production of "character" analyses, the reading / interpretive practice implied in Method actor-training and preparation, and the ways that Method signification articulates interpretive activities for its audience, enabling the spectators to read (and so to write) the script of "character." Method acting renders a certain kind of interpretation legitimate by qualifying the subjects of characterization – the "character" and the performing actor – in particular ways. It leads us to find "character" at the subtextual level, to view its most important activities as impulsive or reactive, to feel as though "character" is discovered only through indirection, and to privilege events that seem to have a certain degree of expressive immediacy as authentic and motivational. "Character," like the acting that produces it, is progressive, developing through the operation of desire toward a particular goal, a motivational "objective." This goal, like the fiction of continuous "character" itself, can only be recognized from a transcendental – or voyeuristic – perspective, by an audience who is itself not subject to such staging, such disclosure.

If I am right in thinking that Stanislavskian attitudes toward acting and character suffuse American acting, then there's little point in trying to repudiate the Method as a vehicle for Shakespearean drama: we can hardly imagine acting not imbued with these values of "truth," interior fidelity, subtextual vitality, character coherence, and so forth.[37] Yet the rhetoric of the Method is at once a mode of representation and a mode of suasion. In so far as the Method remains inscribed by the practices of the proscenium stage, it provides a strategy for constituting character "objectively," as an object overseen by an unacknowledged, absent audience. Stanislavsky's attention to "public solitude," and the Method's concentration on the actor's "private moments," are both, in this sense, means for training the actor to create character before – not with, not for, not among – a silent majority of disembodied spectators. These practices clearly textualize character in ways probably undesirable – even unimaginable – on Shakespeare's more open, public, and interactive stage. As epilogues, soliloquies, and various versions of direct address to the audience imply, enactment of "character" in the Renaissance may have been a more collaborative or even collusive activity, one in which the seam between actor and character may well have been visible ("indicated," in Method terms) for good effect – patronage, crowd management, and so on. In this sense, then, to naturalize the structure of dramatic roles to the practices of the Method obscures certain potentialities of Shakespearean characterization, the possibility of representing "character" as a strategy of mediation, one that transpires between stage and audience and so responds to the "given circumstances" both of the play and of the theatre that sustains it. Both requiring and reifying the absent audience, Method acting manifests the ideological terrain of the naturalistic theatre from which it is drawn, and so subjects actor, "character," and spectator to its relations of legitimate interpretation.

To describe how the theatre subjects texts and performers to its process is a daunting challenge, one that performance critics have pursued with energy and success. But to make such insight valuable, we need to locate its claims as criticism. The first move in such a venture would be to displace the enervating polarization of "criticism against performance" (the subtext, so to speak, of the "text against performance" controversy), in that our access to the text is always through its performance, a performance continually taking place offstage – as reading, education, advertising, criticism, and so on – before any stage performance is conceived. Shakespeare performance criticism seems inexplicably isolated from the theoretical and methodological inquiries that might help to direct it, isolated in many instances even from the new historicism's general interest in theatrical and cultural representation. Indeed, as James R. Siemon remarks, "Among the factors that make performance-oriented criticism of Elizabethan drama of such potential importance, none seems more promising than the evidence of Renaissance interest in those features that qualify all signifying activity as performance and thereby render it so much more complex than analyses of rhetorical strategy, poetic device, propositional content, or the 'character' of the speaker can suggest."[38] Performance criticism is defined by its attention to "signifying activity as performance"; for this reason it should more tenaciously undertake to expose what Kenneth Burke might have called the "lie" at the heart of theatre.[39] This would mean understanding the rhetoric implicit in our conceptions of performance and in performance practice throughout history, the "body of identifications" that sustains acting and directing, and that informs our critical, interpretive, and signifying practice outside the theatre as well.[40] Theatrical production writes the drama into stage practice. Performance criticism should reveal the affiliations between this writing and the very different acts of inscription that make the theatre readable. To understand the drama, we need to understand all the ways that we make it perform.

Notes

1   G. Wilson Knight, *The Wheel of Fire*, 4th ed. (London: Methuen, 1949), p. vi.
2   For a state-of-the-art gathering of performance criticism of Shakespeare, see Marvin and Ruth Thompson, eds., *Shakespeare and the Sense of Performance: Essays in the Tradition of Performance*

Criticism in Honor of Bernard Beckerman (Newark: University of Delaware Press; London and Toronto: Associated University Presses, 1989); I refer here to the Thompsons' essay "Performance Criticism From Granville-Barker to Bernard Beckerman and Beyond," pp. 13–23. The Thompsons also provide a useful appendix, "Suggested Readings in Performance Criticism," pp. 252–6.

3   On the "detextualization" of the body, "the transfer of meanings from language to nonhuman forces in 'nature,' " see Harry Berger, Jr., "Bodies and Texts," *Representations*, 17 (1987), 144–66.

4   Charles Lamb, "On the Tragedies of Shakespeare, Considered with Reference to Their Fitness for Stage Representation," in *The Works of Charles Lamb* (London: 1818); Leigh Hunt, *Theatrical Examiner*, No. 338 (4 October 1818). These essays are conveniently reprinted in *Prose of the Romantic Period*, ed. Carl R. Woodring (Boston: Houghton Mifflin, 1961), pp. 229–40, 383–4.

5   Cleanth Brooks and Robert Heilman, *Understanding Drama* (New York: Henry Holt, 1945), p. 25. That the lyric is the normative mode of *Understanding Drama* is perhaps suggested by the subordination of visual to verbal in the drama: "That is, if drama seems on the one hand to give up so many means of expression that it must become blunt and fumbling, it at the same time makes compensating adjustments. For it gains the precision and exactness essential in literature, first, by the very act of eliminating everything but a bare central theme and, second, by dealing with that theme in the most expressive but at the same time the most controlled kind of language. So, ironically, in considering the special symbols of drama we have inevitably come around to an earlier point, its sharing of the symbols of poetry. One cannot strictly compartmentalize drama, for at its height it combines two modes of concentration" (p. 26). For a brief history of the development of New Criticism's treatment of Shakespearean drama, see Charles H. Frey, "Teaching Shakespeare in America," in his *Experiencing Shakespeare: Essays on Text, Classroom, and Performance* (Columbia: University of Missouri Press, 1988), pp. 130–3.

6   I am much indebted to Dolora Wojciehowski for suggesting this qualification and for sharpening my thinking about the practice of criticism in general.

7   Jean E. Howard and Marion F. O'Connor, "Introduction," *Shakespeare Reproduced: The text in history and ideology*, Jean E. Howard and Marion F. O'Connor, eds. (New York and London: Methuen, 1987), pp. 1–17, esp. p. 4.

8   Howard and O'Connor, p. 12.

9   Mikhail Bakhtin, *Rabelais and His World*, trans. Hélène Iswolsky (Bloomington: Indiana University Press, 1984), p. 320.

10   Robert Weimann, "Towards a literary theory of ideology: mimesis, representation, authority," in *Shakespeare Reproduced: The text in history and ideology*, pp. 265–72, esp. p. 272.

11   See Marvin and Ruth Thompson, "Performance Criticism From Granville-Barker to Bernard Beckerman and Beyond," in *Shakespeare and the Sense of Performance*, p. 15.

12   For a gathering of recent examples, see the following essays from *Shakespeare and the Sense of Performance*: Marvin Rosenberg, "Subtext in Shakespeare," pp. 79–90; on stage imagery, Inga-Stina Ewbank, "From Narrative to Dramatic Language: *The Winter's Tale* and Its Source," pp. 29–47; on the recovery of Elizabethan staging, J. L. Styan, "Stage Space and the Shakespeare Experience," pp. 195–209. In other words, some of the standard approaches to performance criticism seem to operate in ways that frankly subordinate performance to designs said to be located in the text: most metadramatic and metatheatrical readings; generally phenomenological accounts of the plays' histrionic designs (Michael Goldman, *Shakespeare and the Energies of Drama* [Princeton: Princeton University Press, 1972] and *Acting and Action in Shakespearean Tragedy* [Princeton: Princeton University Press, 1985]); contextual accounts of performance ideology (William B. Worthen, *The Idea of the Actor: Drama and the Ethics of Performance* [Princeton: Princeton University Press, 1984]); studies of the symbolic function of stage position and gesture (Robert Weimann, *Shakespeare and the Popular Tradition in the Theater: Studies in the Social Dimension of Dramatic Form and Function*, ed. Robert Schwartz [Baltimore and London: The Johns Hopkins University Press, 1978]; David Bevington, *Action Is Eloquence: Shakespeare's Language of Gesture* [Cambridge, MA, and London: Harvard University Press, 1984]); and perhaps even deconstructive readings of text / performance,

such as Harry Berger, Jr., "Text Against Performance in Shakespeare: The Example of *Macbeth*," *Genre*, 15 (1982), 49–79. See also Richard Levin, "The New Refutation of Shakespeare," *Modern Philology*, 83 (1985–86), 123–41.

13   James H. Kavanagh, "Shakespeare in ideology," in *Alternative Shakespeares*, John Drakakis, ed. (London and New York: Methuen, 1985), p. 147. In the "directorial" mode of dramatic criticism, I would include studies by Bernard Beckerman, *Dynamics of Drama* (New York: Drama Book Specialists, 1979); Ralph Berry, *Shakespeare and the Awareness of the Audience* (New York: St. Martin's Press, 1985); Harley Granville-Barker, *Prefaces to Shakespeare*, 2 vols. (Princeton: Princeton University Press, 1978); Jean E. Howard, *Shakespeare's Art of Orchestration* (Urbana and Chicago: University of Illinois Press, 1984); Emrys Jones, *Scenic Form in Shakespeare* (Oxford: Clarendon Press, 1971); Ann Pasternak Slater, *Shakespeare the Director* (Totowa, NJ: Barnes and Noble, 1982); J. L. Styan, *Shakespeare's Stagecraft* (Cambridge: Cambridge University Press, 1967). Although such work has been extremely, and rightly, influential in opening the stage (in the abstract) as a site of signification, it tends to ask how staging can be made to contribute to or to articulate textual "meanings" without raising the intervening practices of acting or directing as a mediating discourse.

14   Richard David, *Shakespeare in the Theatre* (Cambridge: Cambridge University Press, 1978), pp. 16, 17. See also J. L. Styan, rev. of Ann Pasternak Slater's *Shakespeare the Director, Modern Philology*, 83 (1985–86), 71. A version of this attitude sustains much current thinking about Shakespeare-teaching practice; see Jay L. Halio, " 'This Wide and Universal Stage': Shakespeare's Plays as Plays," in *Teaching Shakespeare*, ed. Walter Edens, et al. (Princeton: Princeton University Press, 1977), pp. 273–89; and see *Shakespeare Quarterly*, 35 (1984), 515–656, a special issue devoted to "Teaching Shakespeare." Of course, as Richard Levin has remarked, the claim that "these plays can be really understood only in performance, or even that they really exist only in performance" leads to a subversion of textual authority not desired by even the most "extreme performance critics." To take performance criticism at its word, Levin argues, is to disseminate the play's authority over any and all performances of it, an assumption that reverses the New Critical tendency to conserve authority within the bounds of the text itself: "If a play really exists only in performance, then, since there would be no way to determine *which* performance (since that would bring us back to the author's text, and so confer 'reality' upon it as well), it would have to mean *any* performance. This would mean that any alterations made in the text during any performance, even including actors' errors, would become parts of the 'real' play. Then there would be no 'real' play, but only the aggregate of all the different performances, which would all be equally legitimate, since the author's text, and hence his meaning, could no longer be relevant, and the sole criterion for judging them would be whether each one 'worked' in its own terms. But then it would make no sense to say that a play can be really understood only in performance, because there would be no independent 'reality' apart from the performance that could be understood. Thus the assertion that a play can be understood only in performance would seem either tautological (if the play and the performance are identical) or self-contradictory (if they are not)." See "Performance-Critics *vs* Close Readers in the Study of English Renaissance Drama," *Modern Language Review*, 81 (1986), 545–59.

15   John Russell Brown, "Theatre Research and the Criticism of Shakespeare and His Contemporaries," *Shakespeare's Plays in Performance* (London: Edward Arnold, 1966), pp. 223–37, esp. p. 224. This essay was originally published in *SQ*, 13 (1962), 451–61. Richard David, p. 1.

16   Sherman Hawkins, "Teaching the Theatre of Imagination: The Example of *1 Henry IV*," *SQ*, 35 (1984), 517–27, esp. p. 519.

17   Homer Swander, "In Our Time: Such Audiences We Wish Him," *SQ*, 35 (1984), 528–40, esp. pp. 529, 540. A sense of how markedly the ideology of performance-based teaching has shifted in a decade may be gained from Jackson G. Barry's remark in the 1974 *Shakespeare Quarterly* teaching issue: "This essay attempts to show that the dramatic medium does not in itself distort a play" ("Shakespeare with Words: The Script and the Medium of Drama," *SQ*, 25 [1974], 161–71, esp. p. 161). A longer view of the institutionalization of Shakespeare is taken by Charles Frey in "Teaching Shakespeare in America" and by Alan Sinfield, "Give an account of Shakespeare

and Education, showing why you think they are effective and what you have appreciated about them. Support your comments with precise references" in *Political Shakespeare: New essays in cultural materialism*, eds. Jonathan Dollimore and Alan Sinfield (Ithaca, NY, and London: Cornell University Press, 1985), pp. 134–57. On the ideological significance of various Shakespearean performance institutions, see Sinfield, "Royal Shakespeare: theatre and the making of ideology" in *Political Shakespeare*, pp. 158–81; and Graham Holderness, "Radical potentiality and institutional closure: Shakespeare in film and television," in *Political Shakespeare*, pp. 182–201.

18 John Russell Brown, *Discovering Shakespeare: A New Guide to the Plays* (New York: Columbia University Press, 1981), p. 1.

19 John Russell Brown, "The Nature of Speech in Shakespeare's Plays," in *Shakespeare and the Sense of Performance*, pp. 48–59, esp. p. 57.

20 John Russell Brown, "The Nature of Speech in Shakespeare's Plays," p. 58, italics added.

21 John Russell Brown, *Discovering Shakespeare*, p. 8. In his fine examination of this "revolution" in our conception of Shakespearean drama, J. L. Styan similarly assigns the authority of "meaning" not to the constitutive acts of stage production but to the prior authority of the text and of its creator. Innovative directors like Playfair, Jackson, and Guthrie, for instance, "sought repeatedly to give their audiences what they took to be the stuff of the Shakespeare experience. As far as it could be reclaimed three centuries later, they tried to capture and translate the temper of the original. Each man's search was for an authentic balance between the freedom a Shakespearean script grants the actor and the responsibility of recharging the play's first meaning." See J. L. Styan, *The Shakespeare Revolution* (Cambridge: Cambridge University Press, 1977), p. 5.

22 John Barton, *Playing Shakespeare* (London and New York: Methuen, 1984), p. 101, Barton's ellipses. Indeed, Barton elides three passages which in the original occur in three separate paragraphs covering two pages of text; Barton's target is, in fact, much more directly interested in the relationship between text and performance than Barton's heavily-edited quotation would suggest to a listener or to a reader: "As for staging, the theatre of modern realism thrusts the actor into the very center of the theatrical event. Like Paganini, Shakespeare, in the writing of *Hamlet*, casts the performer as virtuoso, a role elusively part of, yet apart from, the play's central personage. *This* treachery plagues every staging of *Hamlet* and *exemplifies the leading aesthetic problem of the actor in modern theatre – the interpretation of action through characterologic nuance and rarefaction*" (italicized portions quoted by Barton and read by Suchet); see Donald M. Kaplan, "Character and Theatre: Psychoanalytic Notes on Modern Realism," *Tulane Drama Review*, 10 (1966), 93–108, esp. p. 103.

23 On the problems of a "radical" style in the RSC, see Walter Cohen, "Political criticism of Shakespeare," in *Shakespeare Reproduced: The text in history and ideology*, pp. 18–46, esp. p. 31.

24 Barton quotes Kaplan in *Playing Shakespeare*, p. 101.

25 On Barton's part in the politicization of RSC productions, see Sinfield, "Royal Shakespeare." For a discussion of "Common Sense as a Cultural System," see Clifford Geertz, *Local Knowledge* (New York: Basic Books, 1983), pp. 73–93.

26 Although I'm not concerned with the specific utility and limitations of actors' accounts of performance here, a good sense of their ways of approaching a text can be gained from Philip Brockbank, ed., *Players of Shakespeare: Essays in Shakespearean performance by twelve players with the Royal Shakespeare Company* (Cambridge: Cambridge University Press, 1985); and Russell Jackson and Robert Smallwood, eds., *Players of Shakespeare 2: Further essays in Shakespearean performance by players with the Royal Shakespeare Company* (Cambridge: Cambridge University Press, 1988). But as Charles Frey remarks in his generally sympathetic review of *Players of Shakespeare*, their training may tend to privilege a traditionally character-oriented sense of the drama: "They can provide few fresh observations about whole-play concerns, and they haven't much of a clue as to what advanced scholarship is suggesting about new historicist, materialist, feminist, or other challenging readings, readings that will in time trickle along – though in what theatrically imbibable forms remains to be seen"; see Frey's rev. of *Players of Shakespeare*, *SQ*, 38 (1987), 114–17, esp. p. 117.

27 David Samuelson, "Preface," in *Shakespeare: The Theatrical Dimension*, Philip C. McGuire and David A. Samuelson, eds. (New York: AMS Press, 1979), p. xv.

28 See Philip Brockbank, ed., *Players of Shakespeare*, p. 62.

29 See Miriam Gilbert, "Re-viewing the Play," *SQ*, 36 (1985), 609–17, esp. p. 612.

30 Terry Eagleton, *Criticism & Ideology* (London: Verso, 1978), p. 66.

31 See Eagleton, p. 65. In the passage I have quoted here, Eagleton assigns such transforming labor to "the theatrical instruments (staging, acting skills and so on)"; I am suggesting that comparable labor is undertaken in any act that produces the text, such as reading.

32 As Miriam Gilbert suggests, our ability to read texts and performances may require a commitment to re-reading performances in the way we habitually re-read texts; she describes the value of seeing Jonathan Miller's 1974 *Measure for Measure* for a second time: "The second viewing was a calmer, but also more interesting experience; the interpretation was the same, but my reaction was less defensive, less insistent on 'my' reading, more able to accept what the actors and director were showing me about the play" (p. 610).

33 In suggesting (as I will in what follows) that Shakespearean editing might provide a paradigm for conceiving some of the concerns of performance criticism, I don't mean to suggest that such a paradigm would in fact solve our problems. Indeed, much of the controversy surrounding the Wells and Taylor *Complete Works* has arisen not so much because the editors distinguish between "literary" and "theatrical" versions of the plays, but because they justify their choice of the "theatrical" version as copytext through the kind of rationale that is often found in performance criticism: "Nevertheless, it is in performance that the plays lived and had their being. Performance is the end to which they were created, and in this edition we have devoted our efforts to recovering and presenting texts of Shakespeare's plays as they were acted in the London playhouses which stood at the centre of his professional life." See Stanley Wells and Gary Taylor, eds., *William Shakespeare: The Complete Works* (Oxford: Clarendon Press, 1986), p. xxxviii.

34 See A. R. Braunmuller, "Editing the Staging / Staging the Editing" in *Shakespeare and the Sense of Performance*, pp. 139–49. For a frank, and provocative, discussion of the editor's role in the determination of stage directions, see Stanley Wells, *Re-Editing Shakespeare for the Modern Reader* (Oxford: Clarendon Press, 1984), chap. 3.

35 As Jerome J. McGann argues in his examination of manuscript and printed texts as indices to authorial intention, even the author's fair copy shows "that the concept of authorial intention only comes into force for criticism when (paradoxically) the artist's work begins to engage with social structures and functions. The fully authoritative text is therefore always one which has been socially produced; as a result, the critical standard for what constitutes authoritativeness cannot rest with the author and his intentions alone." See *A Critique of Modern Textual Criticism* (Chicago: University of Chicago Press, 1983), p. 75.

36 Bulman and Coursen, eds., *Shakespeare on Television: An Anthology of Essays and Reviews* (Hanover, NH, and London: University Press of New England, 1988).

37 In my view, the Method's assumptions and practices for the production of character continue to sustain American acting and actor training; it might certainly be argued, though, that as a formal body of work the Method's influence was confined to an historical era in the American theater that came to its close with the experimental theater of the late 1960s and early 1970s. In either event, marking the period and scope of the Method's influence seems to me an issue separate from the description of the general contours of its rhetoric.

38 James R. Siemon, rev. of R. Chris Hassel, Jr.'s *Songs of Death: Performance, Interpretation, and the Text of Richard III*, *SQ*, 40 (1989), 104–6, esp. p. 105.

39 Kenneth Burke, *A Rhetoric of Motives* (Berkeley, Los Angeles, London: University of California Press, 1969), p. 23. I am thinking of Burke's remark that "Rhetoric is concerned with the state of Babel after the Fall. Its contribution to the 'sociology of knowledge' must often carry us far into the lugubrious regions of malice and the lie."

40 Burke, p. 26.

Part XIII

Postcolonial Shakespeare

44   Nymphs and Reapers Heavily Vanish: The Discursive Con-texts
     of *The Tempest*   781
     Francis Barker and Peter Hulme
45   Sexuality and Racial Difference   794
     Ania Loomba
46   Discourse and the Individual: The Case of Colonialism in
     The Tempest   817
     Meredith Anne Skura

In 1945, at the beginning of the period covered by this book, the term "Postcolonial Shakespeare" would have been meaningless to most scholars; by 2000,
the end of the period covered by this book, it was understood by virtually
everyone. Whether or not the language was familiar, the phenomenon that it describes
was known to millions of readers. As one of the leading postcolonial critics points out,
"More students probably read *Othello* in the University of Delhi every year than in all
British universities combined."[1] That suggestion opens a window onto one feature of the
landscape that postcolonialists survey: the relation between the Shakespearean text and
readers outside North America and Europe. More specifically, such critics identify and
assess the ways that Shakespeare has been used to propagate the ideas, establish the
practices, and advance the goals of empire, particularly the British empire. And for many,
the postcolonial project is nothing less than "the task of 'provincializing Europe.'"[2]

Postcolonial critics of Shakespeare deliberately ally themselves with other, recently
emerged critical schools, particularly feminism and cultural materialism. An umbrella
term for the general approach (i.e., criticism not confined to Shakespeare) is subaltern
studies, and critics who work under such a rubric consider themselves students of

institutional oppression or marginalization, imperial ideology, literary appropriation, and other manifestations of power, especially on a global scale. Race, of course, is a crucial dimension of the subdiscipline, as are questions of nationalism, gender, and identity. Margo Hendricks and Patricia Parker have addressed themselves to the interpenetration of these topics in their collection entitled *Women, 'Race,' and Writing in the Early Modern Period:*

> "Race" as that term developed across several European languages was a highly unstable term in the early modern period, a period that saw the proliferation of rival European voyages of "discovery" as contacts with what from a Eurocentric perspective were "new" and different worlds, the drive toward imperial conquest and the subjugation of indigenous peoples, and the development (and increasingly "racial" defense) of slavery.[3]

As a means of unifying these various topics, postcolonial critics have set about to document and criticize the way early modern writing contributes to the production of "the Other," the fantasy of difference by which the West defines itself.

Like postcolonial criticism generally, which derives from the work of Frantz Fanon, Gayatri Chakravorty Spivak, Edward Said, and Homi Bhabha, to name only the most influential figures, postcolonial Shakespeare criticism has made much of the topic of "hybridity." Shakespeare's plays and poems, as probably the most canonical works in all Western writing, are seen as contributing to the creation of the hybrid colonial subject, the recently liberated victim of colonialism whose discourse derives from and cannot escape the language inherited from the oppressor.

> Colonial masters imposed their value system through Shakespeare, and in response colonized peoples often answered back in Shakespearean accents. The study of Shakespeare made them "hybrid" subjects, to use a term that has become central to postcolonial criticism and which is increasingly used to characterize the range of psychological as well as physiological mixings generated by colonial encounters.[4]

Such an argument is an application of the more general postcolonial approach, of course, but many Shakespeare critics further interrogate the notion of hybridity, applying it not only to subjects but also to texts. They point out that the performance of the Shakespearean text in the colonial and postcolonial theater – indeed, even the act of reading Shakespeare in India, for example – has produced a kind of hybrid Shakespeare. In the words of Dennis Kennedy, there are "other Shakespeares, Shakespeares not dependent upon English and often at odds with it."[5] Investigation of how "Shakespeare," Shakespeare as a cultural force, has been employed in the creation, maintenance, and undoing of empire represents an important branch of postcolonial inquiry.

A different kind of inquiry involves reading Shakespeare's plays in light of the principal themes of the postcolonial project. *The Tempest* is the most obviously available text for such analysis. Prospero's island, located in "the still-vexed Bermoothes," implies a Caribbean setting, but the court party is returning to Europe from North Africa, which would seem to place the action in the Mediterranean. In either case, the political concerns of the play are informed by this location on the margins between Europe and the realm of barbarism. The travelers have attended the wedding of Alonso's daughter to the King of Tunis, a marriage between a European woman and an African man that the bride's uncle explicitly deplores. And long before the emergence of subaltern studies the relationship between Prospero and Caliban had been taken as an analogue not only of slavery, but also of the domination of indigenous peoples by European intruders.

Othello, of course, is the other major object of scrutiny. A central topic of concern is Othello's origin: in the Folio title, *The Tragedy of Othello, the Moor of Venice*, the inconsistency in the appositional phrase forecasts the play's concern with the problem of the Other, the status of the African outsider in a closed, elite European community. And, of course, the racial slurs spoken by some of the characters raise historical questions about how original audiences understood the represented actions and ideas. The pervasive and subtle treatment of color in *Othello* has occasioned frequent, and sometimes passionate, comment about the obstacles that race poses to our readings of early modern texts. On this point, Michael Neill has written helpfully:

> Because *Othello* is a tragedy about "race" written before the terminology of "race" was even invented, we cannot (as some recent critics have attempted to do) read it as either "racist" or "anti-racist"; instead it is an essential document of the process by which we learned to think about such ideas at all – something that we need to come to terms with as part of the slow and painful process of thinking our way out of this pervasive and deeply destructive fiction.[6]

What *Hamlet* was to the nineteenth century and *King Lear* to the twentieth, *Othello* bids fair to become for the twenty-first, and its cultural centrality owes much to the energies and passion of the postcolonial critics.

Beyond *The Tempest* and *Othello*, a surprising number of texts respond to post-colonial analysis. *Titus Andronicus* receives attention owing to the African origins of Aaron, the principal villain. He is also, with Tamora and the other Goths – "barbarians" – an object of the Romans' xenophobic scorn. In *The Merchant of Venice* the princes of Morocco and Aragon and the reactions they arouse in Portia bear on the central theme of Jewishness and Christian responses to it. In *Antony and Cleopatra* the exoticism of the Egyptian setting has prompted fruitful discussion based on Said's ideas of Orientalism.

Similar questions of ethnicity and patriotism treated in plays such as *Henry VI, Part One* and *Henry V* have led postcolonialists to a profitable consideration of the histories. We may recall the scenes early in the *Henry VI* plays in which Joan of Arc is mocked for being a witch and, what is worse, for being French, concerns which reappear in the characterization of Margaret of Anjou. And the second tetralogy extends concerns of nationalism and power: in Richard II's contempt for the uncivilized Irish, in the depredations performed by the Welsh women upon the corpses in Mortimer's army, in the disputes among the Irish, Scots, Welsh, and English soldiers summarized in Captain MacMorris's "What ish my nation?"

The relative youth of postcolonial criticism makes a reading list more nearly manageable than for other critical subdisciplines, but it must be said that some of the critical language in postcolonial studies requires careful attention and sometimes repeated readings. Shakespearean versions of the method have been less prone to jargon and critical abstraction, and the essays presented below are eminently readable. Barker and Hulme's essay on *The Tempest* is typical of postcolonial studies in the 1980s, and during the 1990s Ania Loomba judiciously and persuasively joined the conversation. Postcolonial critics have not been without their critics, however, and an example of a measured rejoinder is represented by Meredith Skura's "Discourse and the Individual: The Case of Colonialism in *The Tempest*."

Notes

1   Ania Loomba, *Gender, Race, Renaissance Drama* (Manchester: Manchester University Press, 1989), p. 10
2   Ania Loomba and Martin Orkin, "Introduction" to *Post-colonial Shakespeares* (London: Routledge, 1998), p. 19.
3   *Women, 'Race,' and Writing in the Early Modern Period* (London: Routledge, 1994), p. 1.
4   Loomba and Orkin, *Post-colonial Shakespeares*, p. 7.
5   *Foreign Shakespeare* (Cambridge: Cambridge University Press, 1993), p. 2.
6   "Post-Colonial Shakespeare?: Writing Away from the Centre," in Loomba and Orkin, *Post-colonial Shakespeares*, p. 185.

44

Nymphs and Reapers Heavily Vanish: The Discursive Con-texts of *The Tempest*

Francis Barker and Peter Hulme

I

No one who has witnessed the phenomenon of midsummer tourism at Stratford-upon-Avon can fail to be aware of the way in which 'Shakespeare' functions today in the construction of an English past: a past which is picturesque, familiar and untroubled. Modern scholarly editions of Shakespeare, amongst which the Arden is probably the most influential, have seemed to take their distance from such mythologizing by carefully locating the plays against their historical background. Unfortunately such a move always serves, paradoxically, only to highlight in the foregrounded text preoccupations and values which turn out to be not historical at all, but eternal. History is thus recognized and abolished at one and the same time. One of the aims of this essay is to give a closer account of this mystificatory negotiation of 'history', along with an examination of the ways in which the relationship between text and historical context can be more adequately formulated. Particular reference will be made to the way in which, in recent years, traditional notions of the historical sources of the text have been challenged by newer analyses which employ such terms as 'inter-textuality' and 'discourse'. To illustrate these, a brief exemplary reading will be offered of *The Tempest*. But to begin with, the new analyses themselves need setting in context.

II

The dominant approach within literary study has conceived of the text as autotelic, 'an entity which always remains the same from one moment to the next' (Hirsch 1967,

p. 46); in other words a text that is fixed in history and, at the same time, curiously free of historical limitation. The text is acknowledged as having been produced at a certain moment in history; but that history itself is reduced to being no more than a background from which the single and irreducible meaning of the text is isolated. The text is designated as the legitimate object of literary criticism, *over against* its contexts, whether they be arrived at through the literary-historical account of the development of particular traditions and genres or, as more frequently happens with Shakespeare's plays, the study of 'sources'. In either case the text has been separated from a surrounding ambit of other texts over which it is given a special pre-eminence.

In recent years, however, an alternative criticism, often referred to as 'structuralist' and 'post-structuralist', has sought to displace radically the primacy of the autotelic text by arguing that a text indeed 'cannot be limited by or to … the originating moment of its production, anchored in the intentionality of its author'.[1] For these kinds of criticism exclusive study of the moment of production is defined as narrowly 'historicist' and replaced by attention to successive *inscriptions* of a text during the course of its history.[2] And the contextual background – which previously had served merely to highlight the profile of the individual text – gives way to the notion of *intertextuality*, according to which, in keeping with the Saussurean model of language, no text is intelligible except in its differential relations with other texts.[3]

The break with the moment of textual production can easily be presented as liberatory; certainly much work of importance has stemmed from the study of inscription. It has shown for example that texts can never simply be *encountered* but are, on the contrary, repeatedly constructed under definite conditions: *The Tempest* read by Sir Walter Raleigh in 1914 as the work of England's national poet is very different from *The Tempest* constructed with full textual apparatus by an editor / critic such as Frank Kermode, and from the 'same' text inscribed institutionally in that major formation of 'English Literature' which is the school or university syllabus and its supporting practices of teaching and examination.[4]

If the study of the inscription and reinscription of texts has led to important work of historical description, it has also led to the formulation of a political strategy in respect of literary texts, expressed here by Tony Bennett when he calls for texts to be 'articulated with new texts, socially and politically mobilized in different ways within different class practices' (Bennett 1982, p. 224). This strategy also depends, therefore, on a form of intertextuality which identifies in all texts a potential for new linkages to be made and thus for new political meanings to be constructed. Rather than attempting to derive the text's significance from the moment of its production, this politicized intertextuality emphasizes the present *use* to which texts can now be put. This approach undercuts itself, however, when, in the passage from historical description to contemporary rearticulation, it claims for itself a radicalism which it cannot then deliver. Despite speaking of texts as always being 'installed in a field of struggle' (Bennett 1982, p. 229), it denies to itself the very possibility of combating the dominant orthodoxies. For if, as the logic of Bennett's argument implies, 'the text' were wholly dissolved into an indeterminate miscellany of inscriptions, then how could any confrontation between different but contemporaneous inscriptions take place: what would be the ground of such a contestation?[5] While a genuine difficulty in theorizing 'the text' does exist, this should not lead inescapably to the point where the only option becomes the voluntaristic ascription to the text of meanings and articulations derived simply from one's own ideological preferences. This is a procedure only too vulnerable to pluralistic incorporation, a recipe for peaceful co-existence with the dominant readings, not for a contestation of those readings themselves. Struggle can only occur if two positions attempt to occupy the same space, to appropriate the 'same' text; 'alternative' readings condemn themselves to mere irrelevance.

Our criticism of this politicized intertextuality does not however seek to reinstate the autotelic text with its single fixed meaning. Texts are certainly not available for innocent, unhistorical readings. Any reading must be made *from* a particular position, but is not *reducible* to that position (not least because texts are not infinitely malleable or interpretable, but offer certain constraints and resistances to readings made of them). Rather, different readings struggle with each other on the site of the text, and all that can count, however provisionally, as knowledge of a text, is achieved through this discursive conflict. In other words, the onus on new readings, especially radical readings aware of their own theoretical and political positioning, should be to proceed by means of a *critique* of the dominant readings of a text.

We say critique rather than simply criticism, in reference to a powerful radical tradition which aims not merely to disagree with its rivals but to *read their readings*: that is, to identify their inadequacies and to explain why such readings come about and what ideological role they play.[6] Critique operates in a number of ways, adopting various strategies and lines of attack as it engages with the current ideological formations, but one aspect of its campaign is likely to have to remain constant. Capitalist societies have always presupposed the naturalness and universality of their own structures and modes of perception, so, at least for the foreseeable future, critiques will need to include an *historical* moment, countering capitalism's self-universalization by reasserting the rootedness of texts in the contingency of history. It is this particular ground that what we have been referring to as alternative criticism runs the risk of surrendering unnecessarily. As we emphasized earlier, the study of successive textual inscriptions continues to be genuinely important, but it must be recognized that attention to such inscriptions is not logically dependent on the frequent presupposition that *all* accounts of the moment of production are either crudely historicist or have recourse to claims concerning authorial intentionality. A *properly* political intertextuality would attend to successive inscriptions without abandoning that no longer privileged but still crucially important *first* inscription of the text. After all, only by maintaining our right to make statements that we can call 'historical' can we avoid handing over the very notion of history to those people who are only too willing to tell us 'what really happened'.

III

In order to speak of the Shakespearean text as an historical utterance, it is necessary to read it with and within series of *con-texts*.[7] These con-texts are the precondition of the plays' historical and political signification, although literary criticism has operated systematically to close down that signification by a continual process of occlusion. This may seem a strange thing to say about the most notoriously bloated of all critical enterprises, but in fact 'Shakespeare' has been force-fed behind a high wall called Literature, built out of the dismantled pieces of other seventeenth-century discourses. Two particular examples of the occlusive process might be noted here. First, the process of occlusion is accomplished in the production of critical meaning, as is well illustrated by the case of Caliban. The occlusion of his political claims – one of the subjects of the present essay – is achieved by installing him at the very centre of the play, but only as the ground of a nature / art confrontation, itself of undoubted importance for the Renaissance, but here, in Kermode's account, totally without the historical contextualization that would locate it among the early universalizing forms of incipient bourgeois hegemony (Shakespeare 1964, pp. xxxiv–lxiii). Secondly, source criticism, which might *seem* to militate against autotelic unity by relating the text in question to other texts, in fact only obscures such relationships. Kermode's paragraphs on 'The New World' embody the hesitancy with which Shakespearean scholarship has approached the problem. Resemblances between the *language* of the Bermuda pamphlets and that of *The Tempest* are brought forward as evidence that Shakespeare 'has these documents in mind' but, since this must remain 'inference' rather than 'fact', it can only have subsidiary importance, 'of the greatest interest and usefulness', while clearly not 'fundamental to [the play's] structure of ideas'. Such 'sources' are then reprinted in an appendix so 'the reader may judge of the verbal parallels for himself', and the matter closed (Shakespeare 1964, pp. xxvii–xxviii).

And yet such closure proves premature since, strangely, source criticism comes to play an interestingly crucial role in Kermode's production of a site for *The Tempest*'s meaning. In general, the fullness of the play's unity needs protecting from con-textual contamination, so 'sources' are kept at bay except for the odd verbal parallel. But occasionally, and on a strictly *singular* basis, that unity can only be protected by recourse to a notion of source as explanatory of a feature otherwise aberrant to that posited unity. One example of this would be Prospero's well-known irascibility, peculiarly at odds with Kermode's picture of a self-disciplined, reconciliatory white magician, and therefore to be 'in the last analysis, explained by the fact that [he] descend[s] from a bad-tempered giant-magician' (Shakespeare 1964, p. lxiii). Another would be Prospero's strange perturbation which brings the celebratory masque of Act IV to such an abrupt conclusion, in one reading (as we will demonstrate shortly) the most important scene in the play, but here explained as 'a point at which an oddly pedantic concern for classical structure causes it to force its way through the surface of the play (Shakespeare 1964, p. lxxv).' In other words the play's unity is constructed only by shearing off some of its 'surface' complexities and explaining them away as irrelevant survivals or unfortunate academicisms.

Intertextuality, or con-textualization, differs most importantly from source criticism when it establishes the necessity of reading *The Tempest* alongside congruent texts, irrespective of Shakespeare's putative knowledge of them, and when it holds that such congruency will become apparent from the constitution of discursive networks to be traced independently of authorial 'intentionality'.

IV

Essential to the historico-political critique which we are proposing here are the analytic strategies made possible by the concept of *discourse*. Intertextuality has usefully directed attention to the relationship *between* texts: discourse moves us towards a clarification of just what kinds of relationship are involved.[8]

Traditionally *The Tempest* has been related to other texts by reference to a variety of notions: *source*, as we have seen, holds that Shakespeare was influenced by his reading of the Bermuda pamphlets. But the play is also described as belonging to the *genre* of pastoral romance and is seen as occupying a particular place in the *canon* of Shakespeare's works. Intertextuality has sought to displace work done within this earlier paradigm, but has itself been unable to break out of the practice of connecting text with text, of assuming that single texts are the ultimate objects of study and the principal units of meaning.[9] Discourse, on the other hand, refers to the *field* in and through which texts are produced. As a concept wider than 'text' but narrower than language itself (Saussure's *langue*), it operates at the level of the enablement of texts. It is thus not an easy concept to grasp because discourses are never simply observable but only approachable through their effects just as, in a similar way, grammar can be said to be *at work* in particular sentences (even those that are ungrammatical), governing their construction but never fully present 'in' them. The operation of discourse is implicit in the regulation of what statements can and cannot be made and the forms that they can legitimately take. Attention to discourse therefore moves the focus from the interpretative problem of meaning to questions of instrumentality and function. Instead of *having* meaning, statements should be seen as *performative of* meaning; not as possessing some portable and 'universal' content but, rather, as instrumental in the organization and legitimation of power-relations – which of course involves, as one of its components, control over the constitution of meaning. As the author of one of the first modern grammars said, appropriately enough in 1492, 'language is the perfect instrument of empire'.[10] Yet, unlike grammar, discourse functions effectively precisely because the question of codifying its rules and protocols can never arise: the utterances it silently governs speak what appears to be the 'natural language of the age'. Therefore, from within a given discursive formation no general rules for its operation will be drawn up except against the ideological grain; so the constitution of the discursive fields of the past will, to some degree, need comprehending through the excavatory work of historical study.

To initiate such excavation is of course to confront massive problems. According to what we have said above, each individual text, rather than a meaningful unit in itself, lies at the intersection of different discourses which are related to each other in a complex but ultimately hierarchical way. Strictly speaking, then, it would be meaningless to talk about the unity of any given text – supposedly the intrinsic quality of all 'works of art'. And yet, because literary texts *are* presented to us as characterized precisely by their unity, the text must still be taken as a point of purchase on the discursive field – but in order to demonstrate that, athwart its alleged unity, the text is in fact marked and fissured by the interplay of the discourses that constitute it.

V

The ensemble of fictional and lived practices, which for convenience we will simply refer to here as 'English colonialism', provides *The Tempest*'s dominant discursive contexts.[11] We have chosen here to concentrate specifically on the figure of usurpation as the nodal point of the play's imbrication into this discourse of colonialism. We shall look at the variety of forms under which usurpation appears in the text, and indicate briefly how it is active in organizing the text's actual diversity.[12]

Of course conventional criticism has no difficulty in recognizing the importance of the themes of legitimacy and usurpation for *The Tempest*. Indeed, during the storm-scene with which the play opens, the issue of legitimate authority is brought immediately to the fore. The boatswain's peremptory dismissal of the nobles to their cabins, while not, according to the custom of the sea, strictly a mutinous act, none the less represents a disturbance in the normal hierarchy of power relations. The play then proceeds to recount or display a series of actual or attempted usurpations of authority: from Antonio's successful palace revolution against his brother, Prospero, and Caliban's attempted violation of the honour of Prospero's daughter – accounts of which we hear retrospectively; to the conspiracy of Antonio and Sebastian against the life of Alonso and, finally, Caliban's insurrection, with Stephano and Trinculo, against Prospero's domination of the island. In fact it could be argued that this series *is* the play, in so far as *The Tempest* is a dramatic action at all. However, these rebellions, treacheries, mutinies and conspiracies, referred to here collectively as usurpation, are not *simply* present in the text as extractable 'Themes of the Play'.[13] Rather, they are differentially embedded there, figural traces of the text's anxiety concerning the very matters of domination and resistance.

Take for example the play's famous *protasis*, Prospero's long exposition to Miranda of the significant events that predate the play. For Prospero, the real beginning of the story is his usurpation twelve years previously by Antonio, the opening scene of a drama which Prospero intends to play out during *The Tempest* as a comedy of restoration. Prospero's exposition seems unproblematically to take its place as the indispensable prologue to an understanding of the present moment of Act I, no more than a device for conveying essential information. But to see it simply as a neutral account of the play's prehistory would be to occlude the contestation that follows insistently throughout the rest of the first Act, of Prospero's version of true beginnings. In this narration the crucial early days of the relationship between the Europeans and the island's inhabitants are covered by Prospero's laconic 'Here in this island we arriv'd' (i.ii.171). And this is all we would have were it not for Ariel and Caliban. First Prospero is goaded by Ariel's demands for freedom into recounting at some length how his servitude began, when, at their first contact, Prospero freed him from the cloven pine in which he had earlier been confined by Sycorax. Caliban then offers his compelling and defiant counter to Prospero's single sentence when, in a powerful speech, he recalls the initial mutual trust which was broken by Prospero's assumption of the political control made possible by the power of his magic. Caliban, 'Which first was mine own King', now protests that 'here you sty me / In this hard rock, whiles you do keep from me / The rest o'th'island' (i.ii.344–6).

It is remarkable that these contestations of 'true beginnings' have been so commonly occluded by an uncritical willingness to identify Prospero's voice as direct and reliable authorial statement, and therefore to ignore the lengths to which the play goes to dramatize its problems with the proper beginning of its own story. Such identification hears, as it were, only Prospero's play, follows only his stage directions, not noticing that Prospero's play and *The Tempest* are not necessarily the same thing.[14]

But although different beginnings are offered by different voices in the play, Prospero has the effective power to impose his construction of events on the others. While Ariel gets a threatening but nevertheless expansive answer, Caliban provokes an entirely different reaction. Prospero's words refuse engagement with Caliban's claim to original sovereignty ('This island's mine, by Sycorax my mother, / Which thou tak'st from me', I.ii.333–4). Yet Prospero is clearly disconcerted. His sole – somewhat hysterical – response consists of an indirect denial ('Thou most lying slave', I.ii.346) and a counter accusation of attempted rape ('thou didst seek to violate / The honour of my child', I.ii.349–50), which together foreclose the exchange and serve in practice as Prospero's only justification for the arbitrary rule he exercises over the island and its inhabitants. At a stroke he erases from what we have called Prospero's play all trace of the moment of his reduction of Caliban to slavery and appropriation of his island. For, indeed, it could be argued that the series of usurpations listed earlier as constituting the dramatic action all belong to that play alone, which is systematically silent about Prospero's own act of usurpation: a silence which is curious, given his otherwise voluble preoccupation with the theme of legitimacy. But, despite his evasiveness, this moment ought to be of decisive *narrative* importance since it marks Prospero's self-installation as ruler, and his acquisition, through Caliban's enslavement, of the means of supplying the food and labour on which he and Miranda are completely dependent: 'We cannot miss him: he does make our fire, / Fetch in our wood, and serves in offices / That profit us' (I.ii.313–15). Through its very occlusion of Caliban's version of proper beginnings, Prospero's disavowal is itself performative of the discourse of colonialism, since this particular reticulation of denial of dispossession with retrospective justification for it, is the characteristic trope by which European colonial regimes articulated their authority over land to which they could have no conceivable legitimate claim.[15]

The success of this trope is, as so often in these cases, proved by its subsequent invisibility. Caliban's 'I'll show thee every fertile inch o'th'island' (II.ii.148) is for example glossed by Kermode with 'The colonists were frequently received with this kindness, though treachery might follow', as if this were simply a 'fact' whose relevance to *The Tempest* we might want to consider, without seeing that to speak of 'treachery' is already to interpret, from the position of colonizing power, through a purported 'description'. A discursive analysis would indeed be alive to the use of the word 'treachery' in a colonial context in the early seventeenth century, but would be aware of how it functioned for the English to explain to themselves the *change* in native behaviour (from friendliness to hostility) that was in fact a *reaction* to their increasingly disruptive presence. That this was an explanatory trope rather than a description of behaviour is nicely caught in Gabriel Archer's slightly bemused comment: 'They are naturally given to trechery, howbeit we could not finde it in our travell up the river, but rather a most kind and loving people' (Archer 1979). Kermode's use of the word is of course by no means obviously contentious: its power to shape readings of the play stems from its continuity with the grain of unspoken colonialist assumptions.

So it is not just a matter of the occlusion of the play's initial colonial moment. Colonialist legitimation has always had then to go on to tell its own story, inevitably one of native violence: Prospero's play performs this task within *The Tempest*. The burden of Prospero's play is already deeply concerned with producing legitimacy. The purpose of Prospero's main plot is to secure recognition of his claim to the usurped duchy of Milan, a recognition sealed in the blessing given by Alonso to the prospective marriage of his own son to Prospero's daughter. As part of this, Prospero reduces Caliban to a role in the supporting sub-plot, as instigator of a mutiny that is programmed to fail, thereby forging an equivalence between Antonio's initial *putsch* and Caliban's revolt. This allows Prospero to annul the memory of his failure to prevent his expulsion from the dukedom, by repeating it as a mutiny that he will, this time, forestall. But, in addition, the playing out of the colonialist narrative is thereby completed: Caliban's attempt – tarred with the brush of Antonio's supposedly self-evident viciousness – is produced as final and irrevocable confirmation of the natural treachery of savages.

Prospero can plausibly be seen as a playwright only because of the control over the other characters given him by his magic. He can freeze Ferdinand in mid-thrust, immobilize the court party at will, and conjure a pack of hounds to chase the conspirators. Through this physical control he seeks with considerable success to manipulate the mind of Alonso. Curiously though, while the main part of Prospero's play runs according to plan, the sub-plot provides the only real moment of drama when Prospero calls a sudden halt to the celebratory masque, explaining, aside:

> I had forgot that foul conspiracy
> Of the beast Caliban and his confederates
> Against my life: the minute of their plot
> Is almost come.
>
> (IV.i.139–42)

So while, on the face of it, Prospero has no difficulty in dealing with the various threats to his domination, Caliban's revolt proves uniquely disturbing to the smooth unfolding of Prospero's plot. The text is strangely emphatic about this moment of disturbance, insisting not only on Prospero's sudden vexation, but also on the 'strange hollow, and confused noise' with which the Nymphs and Reapers – two lines earlier gracefully dancing – now 'heavily vanish'; and the apprehension voiced by Ferdinand and Miranda:

> *Ferdinand:* This is strange: your father's in some passion
> That works him strongly.
> *Miranda:* Never till this day
> Saw I him touch'd with anger, so distemper'd.
> (IV.i.143–5)

For the first and last time Ferdinand and Miranda speak at a distance from Prospero and from his play. Although this disturbance is immediately glossed over, the hesitation, occasioned by the sudden remembering of Caliban's conspiracy, remains available as a site of potential fracture.

The interrupted masque has certainly troubled scholarship, introducing a jarring note into the harmony of this supposedly most highly structured of Shakespeare's late plays. Kermode speaks of the 'apparently inadequate motivation' for Prospero's perturbation (Shakespeare 1964, p. lxxv), since there is no obvious reason why he should so excite himself over an easily controllable insurrection.

What then is the meaning of this textual excess, this disproportion between apparent cause and effect? There are several possible answers, located at different levels of analysis. The excess obviously marks the recurrent difficulty that Caliban causes Prospero – a difficulty we have been concerned to trace in some detail. So, at the level of character, a psychoanalytic reading would want to suggest that Prospero's excessive reaction represents his disquiet at the irruption into consciousness of an unconscious anxiety concerning the grounding of his legitimacy, both as producer of his play and, *a fortiori*, as governor of the island. The by now urgent need for action forces upon Prospero the hitherto repressed contradiction between his dual roles as usurped and usurper. Of course the emergency is soon contained and the colonialist narrative quickly completed. But, none the less, if only for a moment, the effort invested in holding Prospero's play together as a unity is laid bare.

So, at the formal level, Prospero's difficulties in staging his play are themselves 'staged' by the play that we are watching, this moment presenting for the first time the possibility of distinguishing between Prospero's play and *The Tempest* itself.

Perhaps it could be said that what is staged here in *The Tempest* is Prospero's anxious determination to keep the sub-plot of his play in its place. One way of distinguishing Prospero's play from *The Tempest* might be to claim that Prospero's carefully established relationship between main and sub-plot is reversed in *The Tempest*, whose *main* plot concerns Prospero's anxiety over his *sub*-plot. A formal analysis would seem to bear this out. The climax of Prospero's play is his revelation to Alonso of Miranda and Ferdinand playing chess. This is certainly a true *anagnorisis* for Alonso, but for us a merely theatrical rather than truly dramatic moment. *The Tempest*'s dramatic climax, in a way its only dramatic moment at all, is, after all, this sudden and strange disturbance of Prospero.

But to speak of Prospero's anxiety being staged by *The Tempest* would be, on its own, a recuperative move, preserving the text's unity by the familiar strategy of introducing an ironic distance between author and protagonist. After all, although Prospero's anxiety over his sub-plot may point up the *crucial* nature of that 'sub' plot, a generic analysis would have no difficulty in showing that *The Tempest* is ultimately complicit with Prospero's play in treating Caliban's conspiracy in the fully comic mode. Even before it begins, Caliban's attempt to put his political claims into practice is arrested by its implication in the convention of clownish vulgarity represented by the 'low-life' characters of Stephano and Trinculo, his conspiracy framed in a grotesquerie that ends with the dubiously amusing sight of the conspirators being hunted by dogs, a fate, incidentally, not unknown to natives of the New World. The shakiness of Prospero's position is indeed staged, but in the end his version of history remains *authoritative*, the larger play acceding as it were to the containment of the conspirators in the safely comic mode, Caliban allowed only his poignant and ultimately vain protests against the venality of his co-conspirators.

That this comic closure is necessary to enable the European 'reconciliation' which follows hard on its heels – the patching up of a minor dynastic dispute within the Italian nobility – is, however, itself symptomatic of the text's own anxiety about the threat posed to its decorum by its New World materials. The lengths to which the play has to go to achieve a legitimate ending may then be read as the quelling of a fundamental disquiet concerning its own functions within the projects of colonialist discourse.

No adequate reading of the play could afford not to comprehend *both* the anxiety and the drive to closure it necessitates. Yet these aspects of the play's 'rich complexity' have been signally ignored by European and North American critics, who have tended to listen exclusively to Prospero's voice: after all, he speaks their language. It has been left to those who have suffered colonial usurpation to discover and map the traces of that complexity by reading in full measure Caliban's refractory place in both Prospero's play and *The Tempest*.[16]

VI

We have tried to show, within the limits of a brief textual analysis, how an approach via a theory of discourse can recognize *The Tempest* as, in a significant sense, a play imbricated within the discourse of colonialism; and can, at the same time, offer an explanation of features of the play either ignored or occluded by critical practices that have often been complicit, whether consciously or not, with a colonialist ideology.

Three points remain to be clarified. To identify dominant discursive networks and their mode of operation within particular texts should by no means be seen as the end of the story. A more exhaustive analysis would go on to establish the precise articulation of discourses within texts: we have argued for the discourse of colonialism as the articulatory *principle* of *The Tempest*'s diversity but have touched only briefly on what other discourses are articulated and where such linkages can be seen at work in the play.

Then again, each text is more than simply an *instance* of the operation of a discursive network. We have tried to show how much of *The Tempest*'s complexity comes from its *staging* of the distinctive moves and figures of colonialist discourse. Discourse is always performative, active rather than ever merely contemplative; and, of course, the mode of the theatre will also inflect it in particular ways, tending, for example, through the inevitable (because structural) absence of any direct authorial comment, to create an effect of distantiation, which exists in a complex relationship with the countervailing (and equally structural) tendency for audiences to identify with characters presented – through the language and conventions of theatre – as heroes and heroines. Much work remains to be done on the articulation between discursive performance and mode of presentation.

Finally, we have been concerned to show how *The Tempest* has been severed from its discursive con-texts through being produced by criticism as an autotelic unity, and we have tried therefore to exemplify an approach that would engage with the fully dialectical relationship between the detail of the text and the larger discursive forma-tions. But nor can theory and criticism be exempt from such relationships. Our essay too must engage in the discursive struggle that determines the history within which the Shakespearean texts will be located and read: it matters what kind of history that is.

Notes

1 Bennett 1982, p. 227; drawing on the argument of Derrida 1977.

2 For the theory behind the concept of inscription see Balibar 1974 and 1983; Macherey and Balibar 1978; and Davies 1978. For an accessible collection of essays which put this theory to work on the corpus of English literature, see Widdowson 1982.

3 Intertextuality is a term coined by Julia Kristeva 1970, from her reading of the seminal work of Mikhail Bakhtin, 1968, 1973, 1981.

4 For Raleigh's *Tempest* see Terence Hawkes, 'Swisser-Swatter: making a man of English letters,' in J. Drakakis (ed.), *Alternative Shakespeares* (Methuen, 1985), pp. 26–46; Kermode is editor of the Arden edition of *The Tempest* (Shakespeare 1964); on the formation of 'English' see Davies 1978.

5 Stanley Fish (1980, p. 165), whose general argument is similar to Bennett's, admits that in the last analysis he is unable to answer the question: what are his interpretative acts interpretations *of*?

6 Marx's work was developed out of his critique of the concepts of classical political economy that had dominated economic thought in the middle of the nineteenth century. We choose here to offer a critique of Kermode's introduction to the Arden *Tempest* (Shakespeare 1964) because of the *strengths* of his highly regarded and influential work.

7 Con-texts with a hyphen, to signify a break from the inequality of the usual text / context relationship. Con-texts are themselves *texts* and must be *read with*: they do not simply make up a background.

8 MacCabe 1979 offers a helpful guide through some of discourse's many usages. The concept of discourse at work in the present essay draws on Michel Foucault's investigation of the discursive realm. A useful introduction to his theorization of discourse is provided by Foucault's essays, 1978 and 1981. His most extended theoretical text is *The Archaeology of Knowledge*, 1972. However, a less formal and in many ways more suggestive treatment of discourse is practised and, to a certain extent theorized, in his early work on 'madness' and in more recent studies of the prison and of sexuality, where discourse is linked with both the institutional locations in which it circulates and the power functions it performs: see Foucault 1967, 1977, 1979a. For a cognate approach to discourse see the theory of 'utterance' developed by Valentin Vološinov, 1973.

9 On the weakness of Kristeva's own work in this respect see Culler 1981, pp. 105–7.

10 Antonio de Nebrija, quoted in Hanke 1959, p. 8.

11 In other words we would shift the emphasis from the futile search for the texts Shakespeare 'had in mind' to the establishment of significant patterns within the larger discursive networks of the period. The notion of 'English colonialism' can itself be focused in different ways. The widest focus would include present con-texts, the narrowest would concentrate on the con-texts associated with the initial period of English colonization of Virginia, say 1585 to 1622. In the first instance many of the relevant texts would be found in the contemporary collections of Hakluyt (1903–5) and Purchas (1905–7). For congruent approaches see Smith 1974; Frey 1979; Greenblatt 1980, chapter 4; and Hulme 1981.

12 See Macherey 1978. Macherey characterizes the literary text not as unified but as plural and diverse. Usurpation should then be regarded not as the centre of a unity but as the principle of a diversity.

13 Kermode's second heading (Shakespeare 1964, p. xxiv).

14 This is a weak form of the critical fallacy that, more chronically, reads Prospero as an autobiographical surrogate for Shakespeare himself. On some of the theoretical issues involved here see Foucault 1979b.

15 This trope is studied in more detail in Hulme 1986 chapters 3 and 4. See also Jennings 1976.

16 See for example Lamming 1960 and Fernández Retamar 1973. Aimé Césaire's rewriting of the play, *Une Tempête*, 1969, has Caliban as explicit hero. For an account of how Caliban remains refractory for contemporary productions of *The Tempest* see Griffiths 1983.

References

Archer, Gabriel (1979) 'The description of the new discovered river and county of Virginia ..., [1607], in Quinn, D. *et al* (eds) *New American World*, vol. 5. London: Macmillan.

Bakhtin, Mikhail (1968) *Rabelais and His World*. Cambridge, MA.: MIT Press.

—— (1973) *Problems of Dostoevsky's Poetics*. Ann Arbor, MI.: Ardis.

—— (1981) *The Dialogic Imagination*. Austin: University of Texas Press.

Balibar, Renée (1974) *Les Français fictifs: le rapport des styles littéraires au français national*. Paris: Hachette.

—— (1983) 'National language, education, literature', in Barker, F. *et al.* (eds.) *The Politics of Theory*. Colchester: University of Essex, 79–99.

Bennett, T. (1982) 'Text and history', in Widdowson, Peter (ed.) *Re-Reading English*. London: Methuen, 223–36.

Césaire, Aimé (1969) *Une Tempête*. Paris: Seuil.

Culler, J. (1981) *The Pursuit of Signs*. London: Routledge & Kegan Paul.

Davies, Tony (1978) 'Education, ideology and literature', *Red Letters*, 7, 4–15.

Derrida, J. (1977) 'Signature event context', *Glyph*, 1, 172–98.

Fernández Retamar, Roberto (1973) *Caliban: Apuntes sobre la Cultura de Nuestra América*. Buenos Aires: Editorial la Pleyade.

Fish, Stanley (1980) *Is There a Text in this Class?: The Authority of Interpretive Communities*. Cambridge, MA.: Harvard University Press.

Foucault, Michel (1967) *Madness and Civilization: A History of Insanity in the Age of Reason*. London: Tavistock Publications.

—— (1972) *The Archaeology of Knowledge*. London: Tavistock Publications.

—— (1977) *Discipline and Punish: the Birth of the Prison*. London: Allen Lane.

—— (1978) 'Politics and the study of discourse', *Ideology and Consciousness*, 3, 7–26

—— (1979a) *The History of Sexuality*, vol. 1. London: Allen Lane.

—— (1979b) 'What is an author?', in Harari, J. V. (ed.) *Textual Strategies: Perspectives in Post-structuralist Criticism*. London: Methuen, 141–60.

—— (1981) 'The order of discourse', in Young, Robert (ed.) *Untying the Text: A Post-structuralist Reader*. London: Routledge & Kegan Paul, 48–78.

Frey, Charles (1979) '*The Tempest* and the New World', *Shakespeare Quarterly*, 30, 29–41.

Greenblatt, Stephen (1980) *Renaissance Self-Fashioning from More to Shakespeare*. Chicago: University of Chicago Press.

Griffiths, Trevor R. (1983) ' "This island's mine": Caliban and colonialism', *The Yearbook of English Studies*, 13, 159–80.

Hakluyt, Richard (1903–5) *The Principle Navigations, Voyages Traffiques and Discoveries of the English Nation* [1589], 12 vols. Glasgow: James MacLehose and Sons.

Hanke, Lewis (1959) *Aristotle and the American Indians*. Bloomington, IN.: Indiana University Press.

Hirsch, E. D. (1967) *Validity in Interpretation*. New Haven: Yale University Press.

Hulme, Peter (1981) 'Hurricanes in the Caribbees: The constitution of the discourse of English colonialism', in Barker, F. *et al.* (eds) *1642: Literature and Power in the Seventeenth Century*. Colchester: University of Essex, 55–83.

—— (1986) "*Colonial Encounters*, Europe and The Native Caribbean, 1492–1797" London: Methuen.

Jennings, Francis (1976) *The Invasion of America: Indians, Colonialism and the Cant of Conquest*. New York: Norton.

Kristeva, Julia (1970) *Le Texte du roman*. The Hague: Mouton.

Lamming, George (1960) *The Pleasures of Exile*. London: Michael Joseph.

MacCabe, Colin (1979) 'On discourse', *Economy and Society*, 8, 4, 279–307.

Macherey, P. (1978) *A Theory of Literary Production*, trans. Geoffrey Wall. Reprinted London: Routledge & Kegan Paul, 1980.

—— and Balibar, E. (1978) 'On literature as an ideological form: Some Marxist propositions', *Oxford Literary Review*, 3, 4–12.

Purchas, Samuel (1905–7) *Purchas His Pilgrimes* [1625], 20 vols. Glasgow: James MacLehose.

Shakespeare, W. (1964) *The Tempest*, ed. Frank Kermode. London: Methuen.

Smith, James (1974) '*The Tempest*', in *Shakespearian and Other Essays*. Cambridge: Cambridge University Press, 159–261.

Vološinov, Valentin (1973) *Marxism and the Philosophy of Language*. New York: Seminar Press.

Widdowson, Peter (ed.) (1982) *Re-Reading English*. London: Methuen.

45

Sexuality and Racial Difference

Ania Loomba

Men's Power

In the context of its female Indian readers, the violence repeatedly committed on the female body in Renaissance (and especially Jacobean) tragedy takes on an urgent contemporaneity that challenges not only the self-enclosed and self-referential readings of traditional criticism but also a simplistic First World feminism which is in danger, as Spivak points out, of becoming complicit with imperialism ('Imperialism and sexual difference', pp. 225–6). It is true that the similarity between violence in the plays and that which is directed against women in India, is startling and, I shall suggest, an important factor in assessing how these plays can be received. Even the most sober and conservative estimates of the latter would have to acknowledge the following: wives are murdered for dowry (in Delhi alone, the reported figure is two such deaths daily) rapes and sexual exploitation of 'poor and *dalit* (lower-caste) women, and of nurses, office-workers, domestic servants, by landlords, employers and policemen, (are) part of their daily lives' (Kishwar and Vanita, p. 255) and are daily escalating; age-old and high-tech methods coexist as female infanticide continues and intrauterine chromosomal examination (amniocentesis) is used to abort female foetuses on an unprecedented scale (see Miller); the practice of widow immolation, sati, is vigorously defended in its sporadic revival, 169 years after being officially abolished and in the countryside, women are still harassed and even killed on the grounds that they are witches. These are but a few examples of a situation where the average woman is constantly vulnerable to patriarchal and class violence and the ideologies attaching to it. While recounting such facts we need always to bear in mind the long history of Western accounts of the pitiable condition of non-European women, a history which inevitably went on to suggest the barbarity and primitivism of such societies and the superiority of Western civilisation. As Indian feminists have stressed, however, the increasing oppression against women must be analysed in the context of modern Indian society and its contemporary contradictions, not as an unfortunate remnant of a feudal past.[1]

It is in this context too, that we need to see how institutionalised readings of Renaissance tragedy work. In this body of drama, female transgression, both real and imagined, is repeatedly and ruthlessly oppressed by the family, state, church and judiciary: Desdemona (*Othello*), the Duchess of Malfi, Vittoria (*The White Devil*), Bianca (*Women Beware Women*), Annabella (*'Tis Pity She's a Whore*) and Beatrice-Joanna (*The Changeling*) all break the rules of female conduct and are punished. Early modern Europe witnessed the mass-scale burning and torture of women as witches, and Renaissance drama makes it clear that 'witch' is a category flexible enough to cover any sort of female deviance and rebellion.

The much-vaunted theory of the spiritual chaos of Jacobean drama implicitly connected female disobedience with a degenerate social order, and thus contributed to silencing any notions of disobedience which actual women readers may harbour. In the Indian classroom, it commits another violence – that of imposing universalised models of human relationships upon subaltern readers; paradoxically, the points of intersection with our lives are carefully excluded. For example, as undergraduates at Miranda House, Delhi (the name is not insignificant) who were 'dissatisfied' with Desdemona's silence in the face of her husband's brutality, we were told that we did not 'understand' her because we had never been 'in love'. *Othello* thus became a sort of universal text of love, and love implied female passivity. It can be argued that in many ways we were 'prepared' for such readings by the popular Western romantic novels which flood the Indian market, and which are consumed by English-speaking urban schoolgirls in vast quantities. In these novels, as the English Studies Group point out, 'The subordination of the woman to the narrative-ideological syntax of home and children is strikingly visible in the progressive extinction of her powers of articulate speech'. They cite an instance from Barbara Cartland's *Lord Ravenscar's Revenge*: ' "That is ... what I ... felt", Romara said, "but I never ... thought, I never ... dreamt, that you would ... feel ... the ... same". "You seemed in so many ways to be like my mother", Lord Ravenscar said' (p. 261). 'High' and 'low' literature thus together reinforce common-sense assumptions about a woman in love.

Many college students in India occupy a very uneasy space where romantic love, 'free choice' and sexual passion can exist as ideals (nurtured also by popular cinema, where they become reconciled to common-sense notions of female obedience), but where the probable reality of their own marriages is entirely different. Desdemona's defiance of her father plays on and encourages such an ideal, but she then betrays it by her submissiveness. Discussions with my own students later located such a betrayal as the source of our uneasiness. By being murdered, Desdemona comes uncomfortably close to the battered wives that now crowd the Indian (especially urban) scene. A recent Indian feminist interpretation of several Shakespearean plays as spectacles of wife-murder can be seen as a response (though unacknowledged as such) to the similarities; it also implicitly addresses the discomfiture of readers told to accept rather than question Desdemona's silencing and locates this within the daily experience of Indian women (see Vanita, 'Men's power, pp. 32–9).

Such a view is both compelling and disturbing. But reading the play as a black woman immediately problematises the notion of men's power and therefore also any comparisons we may make. I found it difficult to accept that 'Othello's words could easily be interchanged with Claudio's' or that 'universal harmony' is at stake here (Vanita, p. 35). Western feminist interpretations have also claimed that 'the play's central theme is love – and especially marital love, its central conflict is between men and women' (Neely, p. 212). If Othello is treated as a prototype of universal man and his blackness is not even hinted at, we return to the paradigms of preferred readings: 'Othello, *like most men*, is a combination of the forces of love and hate, which are isolated in impossibly pure states in Desdemona and Iago' (Kernan, p. 80). If we probe deeper into how male violence is constructed in the plays, however, our critique of the silencing of women in literature and in the classroom can include an exposure of other sorts of violence and silences. A text like *Othello* can then be seen to have a more complex resonance in the Indian situation, and indeed in the Western classroom as well.

Christopher Norris has pointed out that, despite variations, *Othello* criticism from Johnson to Leavis can be seen as part of 'a certain dominant cultural formation in the history of Shakespeare studies. It is an effort of ideological containment, an attempt to harness the unruly energies of the text to a stable order of significance' (p. 66). I suggest that this stable order, could only be invoked by the simultaneous exclusion of both gender and race; therefore, firstly, as a recent feminist essay points out, both 'Othello critics' (who sentimentalise Othello) and 'Iago critics' (who emphasise Iago's realism and 'honesty') 'badly misunderstand and misrepresent the women in the play' (Neely, p. 212), and secondly, as Ruth Cowhig indicates, the question of race is 'largely ignored by critical commentaries' (p. 8).[2] In 1693, Thomas Rymer interpreted the play as 'a caution to all Maidens of Quality, how, without their parents' consent they run away with Blackamoors …' (p. 89). This combined a patriarchal view of female waywardness and the necessity of obedience, a racist warning against the rampant sexuality of black men, and a class consciousness which prioritises the submission of women 'of Quality'. Nearly 300 years later, Leslie Fiedler, among the first in recent times to acknowledge the connections between the racial and sexual themes, argues that Othello moves from being a stranger whose colour establishes his difference ('cultural' rather than ethnic) to becoming, towards the end of the play, '*colourless*: a provincial gentleman-warrior, a downright English soldier fallen among foreigners; which means that he no longer functions archetypally even as a stranger, much less a black' (p. 160). For this downfall of the inwardly white Othello, Desdemona the 'white witch' and Iago the true black are jointly held responsible. Emilia is 'first and last an untamed shrew' and generally, the women 'by their lives and functions … seem rather to sustain Iago's view of women' (p. 141).

It is a measure of the problem I want to highlight that although Carol Neely criticises Fiedler's misogyny, she both ignores his racism (which is less crude than Rymer's or Ridley's but there nevertheless) and makes no attempt to analyse the impact of Othello's blackness on the sexual relations in the play.[3] To address sexual difference at the expense of the racial is to produce what Newton and Rosenfelt have called 'a feminist version of "the" human condition' (p. xvii) which is especially invalid for women in the 'third world', who are at the juncture of both sorts of oppression. Although the question of race has been admirably discussed recently (see Cowhig and Orkin's essays), it is often ignored or underplayed even by those concerned with alternative and political criticism, and has not been fully inserted into discussions of gender difference.[4]

In a brief article, Ben Okri points out that 'to reduce the colour is to diminish the force of the sex. Working together they can be quite unbearable' (p. 563). Even though no simple mapping of racial difference on to the sexual is possible precisely because Othello's colour and gender make him occupy contradictory positions in relation to power, I shall suggest that firstly, Othello's blackness is central to any understanding of male or female sexuality or power structures in the play; secondly, the filtering of sexuality and race through each other's prism profoundly affects each of them, thus indicating more clearly what Lentricchia has called the 'multiplicity of histories' of both authority and resistance; and thirdly, such interweaving does not *dissolve* the tensions between different forms of oppression but acknowledges and addresses them, as well as placing the schisms and discontinuities of identity (which recent criticism has seen as foregrounded in Renaissance drama; see Dollimore, *Radical Tragedy,* and Belsey, *The Subject of Tragedy*) within the neglected context of racial difference.

Historicising Racism

It had been a major problem for critics of the play to reconcile Othello's blackness with his central position in the play. Therefore either his colour was ignored, or much critical effort was expended in trying to prove that Shakespeare did not intend him to be black at all (see Cowhig, p. 16). Both views are premised upon racist notions of black inferiority. The notion that 'all men are the same' includes the apparently conflicting one that 'blacks are inferior, and hardly men at all'. Ridley's efforts to prove Othello's non-negroid racial origins are notoriously and crudely racist: 'There are more colours than one in Africa, and that a man is black in colour is no reason why he should, even to European eyes, look sub-human' (p. li). Then we also hear that 'for Shakespeare, "black" does not describe an ethnic distinction.... "fair" has a primarily moral significance'; that there was no racism in Elizabethan England, that the kind of horror that contemporary audiences might feel at a black / white mating is therefore no part of the play; that since 'miscegenation had not yet been invented' we are to read the blackness of Othello as primarily symbolic' and finally, 'it is no real surprise, therefore, to discover that Othello was not ethnically "black at all" in the sources from which Cinthio drew his story' (Fiedler, pp. 143–5). It is no real surprise either to discover that Fiedler's moral categories quickly slide back to ethnic ones. How colours come to be invested with moral connotations is precisely the history of racism.

Evidence of such a history during Elizabethan times has been accumulating, and here I will only amplify aspects that crucially link it with the question of gender. G. K. Hunter identifies a 'powerful and ancient tradition associating black-faced men with wickedness ... (which) came right up to Shakespeare's own day' (p. 35). Part of this tradition derived from a Bible-centred conception of the world in which humanity was graded according to its geographical distance from the Holy Land – hence black people were devilish because they existed outside both the physical and the conceptual realm of Christianity. Blacks became identified with the descendants of Ham, and their colour a direct consequence of sexual excess. The devil and his associates, even in

Reginald Scott's fairly rationalist *The Discovery of Witchcraft*, were inextricably linked with blackness: 'a damned soul may and doth take the shape of a blackamoore' (Hunter, p. 34).

Hunter also includes a general cultural hostility to strangers as a factor influencing racial prejudice, but erroneously locates this to 'a response to the basic antinomy of day and night' which to him explains the presence of racism 'all over the world (even in darkest Africa) from the earliest to the latest times'. This dangerously universalises and naturalises white racism, whose various histories indicate interlinking situations of oppression rather than a trans-historical colour consciousness. Eldred Jones's pioneering study *Othello's Countrymen* established that Shakespeare did not depend on literary sources for his portraits of black people and that there was a growing black presence in England with evidence of its widening contact with white inhabitants. Hakluyt's *Principal Navigations* bears witness to the beginnings of slave trade: between 1562 and 1568, Hawkins brought 'blackamoors to England' and sold hundreds of black slaves to Spain; so there were 'several hundreds of black people living in the households of the aristocracy and the landed gentry' (Cowhig, p. 5).

Thus Hunter's arguments that Elizabethans had 'no continuous contact' with black people and 'no sense of economic threat from them' (p. 32) are historically disproved. But the crucial point is that the black presence was both perceived and constructed as a threat by the state. Royal proclamations and state papers nervously point to the 'great numbers of negroes and blackamoors in the country, of which kind of people there are already too manye'. Queen Elizabeth's correspondence with the Privy Council, seeking to deport eighty-nine black people, is significant. A warrant issued on 18 July 1596 contrasts black or 'those kinde of people' with her white subjects or 'Christian people' in a passage startlingly illustrative of the Orientalist split between a superior European culture, constituting 'us', and the inferior non-European peoples and cultures, constituting 'them'. This split, as Said has argued, is a crucial component in establishing the hegemony of the former (*Orientalism*, p. 7). But Elizabeth's communiqué also crucially puts forward the argument that blacks will create unemployment, 'want of service', for her white people. Here again she evokes the myth of a rampant black sexuality and their 'populous' numbers, seeking to limit and control black presence in the imperial country (quoted Cowhig, p. 6).[5]

Its echoes in today's immigration and deportation laws are not accidental but are ensured by a continuous reworking of past prejudices in later relations of dominance. Cedric Robinson speaks of the ways in which the ideologies of earlier feudal relations were both preserved and transformed in the new mercantile and colonial situation. He says that the identification of black with evil had not only been directed against strangers but had also sought to preserve the superiority of the upper classes, since the European nobility projected itself as drawn from different ethnic and cultural groups than the common people. Thus travelling merchants were regarded as foreigners. According to Robinson, racism was not simply a result of capitalism. Rather, capitalism itself was profoundly shaped by ideas of racial differentiation. Therefore, although the ideal of a unified greater Britain was encouraged, the 'tendency of European civilisation through capitalism … was not to homogenise but to differentiate – to exaggerate regional, subcultural, dialectical differences into "racial" ones' (Robinson, p. 27).

A similar tendency is traceable in the case of women; increasing restrictions upon their activities, inheritance and public participation accompanied the widening separation of the centres of production and consumption, even as the dominant ideology posited the notion of woman as a more equal companion of man. Women, and indeed other marginalised peoples, were excluded from the projected ideals of self-fulfilment and self-fashioning, of personal achievement and mobility; sexual difference became a central preoccupation of religious and secular authority. Irreconcilable contradictions with respect to women as well as 'those kinde of people' are opened up by such exclusions; in both cases, medieval differentiations were not simply adopted, but modified and altered in the new circumstances.

Therefore the definition of 'black' supplied by a pre-sixteenth century version of the Oxford English Dictionary as 'deeply stained with dirt ... having dark or deadly purposes, malignant' was useful beyond medieval religious and cultural chauvinism. Even this chauvinism has been attributed by Robinson to the failure of the project of a greater or unified Europe during the eleventh and twelfth centuries and to its transference 'from one of terrestrial social order to that of a spiritual kingdom, Christiandom' (p. 10). Both Hunter (p. 3) and Said (*Orientalism*, p. 63) note that the new knowledge about foreign peoples generated by Renaissance expeditions was filtered through and shaped by existing ideologies and prejudices. But 'a traditional religious outlook' which Hunter uses to explain why increasing factual information 'lay fallow' was itself adapted and pressed into colonial service. Winthrop D. Jordan says that the linkage between black and devil 'represented a projection onto the African of the bourgeoisie's own anxieties about their role as entrepreneurs in the burgeoning capitalist developments that threatened to disrupt the social order' (quoted Lawrence, pp. 61–2). It is true that racist ideologies are not solely constructed for the purposes of rationalising the economic aspects of colonial plunder, but this rationalisation is certainly a crucial component of them (see Lawrence, 'Just plain common-sense', p. 57).

Hence common-sense attitudes towards black people in *Othello* (which will be identified shortly) indicate both the older tradition of hatred towards blacks and a newer expediency, a more complex ideology of racism. The attitudes of modern audiences / readers may not be identical with those of Shakespeare's original audiences; moreover, the play's readership is not a unified category and Indians among them have experienced a different history of racism. Even so, contemporary colour prejudices are interlinked; they draw upon and rework this earlier history.

There is a historical dependency between patriarchalism and racism. In Europe, the increased emphasis on heterogeneity of peoples and groupings that Robinson mentions occurs alongside the escalation of patriarchal discourses on the separateness of female identity from masculine. As I have said, in the Indian subcontinent, the consolidation of power involved racial, sexual, and caste exclusions. In the colonies, racism specifically 'called out the basic sexist tendencies' in the colonised countries and cultures, 'calcified existing ones and introduced others' (see Ogundipe-Leslie). Helen Carr points out that 'colonialist, racist and sexist discourse have continually reinforced, naturalized and legitimized each other during the process of European colonization' (p. 46). Although the *specificity* of racism and patriarchy should not be blurred by this analogy, the connections are important. Both women and racial 'others' are posited as biological and natural inferiors and similar characteristics are attributed to them:

... in the language of colonialism, non-Europeans occupy the same symbolic space as women. Both are seen as part of nature, not culture, and with the same ambivalence: either they are ripe for government, passive, child-like, unsophisticated, needing leadership and guidance, described always in terms of lack – no initiative, no intellectual powers, no perseverance; or on the other hand, they are outside society, dangerous, treacherous, emotional, inconstant, wild, threatening, fickle, sexually aberrant, irrational, near animal, lascivious, disruptive, evil, unpredictable. (Carr, p. 50)

Thus the operations of patriarchalism seek to extend the control and authority of man as father over women, and white man as father over black men and women. Both black people and women are in need of guidance, yet both threaten to elude and disrupt it.

'Ravenous Tigers' and 'Inhuman Dogs'

Cowhig points out that 'only as we recognise the familiarity of the figure of the black man as villain in Elizabethan drama can we appreciate what must have been the startling impact on Shakespeare's audience of a black hero' (pp. 4–5). Shakespeare made significant departures from his source material, from other representations of blacks on the Renaissance stage, and from his own earlier portraits of Moors (as both Hunter and Cowhig have shown). The tradition of the black villain-hero in Elizabethan drama resulted in a series of negative portrayals of black men, such as Muly Mahomet in George Peele's *The Battle of Alcazar* or Eleazor in *Lust's Dominion*, written by Dekker and others. In Shakespeare's *Love's Labour's Lost*, 'Black is the badge of hell / The hue of dungeons and the school of night' (iv.iii.250–1). In Cinthio's version of the Othello story, his 'blackness already displeases' Desdemona, and Othello carefully plots how to murder her without being caught. Hunter points out that Shakespeare changes many features of Cinthio's tale, but not the colour of the hero. A brief look at Shakespeare's earlier fullest treatment of race in *Titus Andronicus* reveals the extent to which *Othello* departs from the usual linkage of black men with deviant white women.

In *Titus Andronicus* the 'siren' queen, Tamora (ii.i.23) and the 'inhuman dog, unhallowed slave', Aaron (v.iii.14) are not only lovers, not only accomplices in unleashing a tale of 'murders, rapes and massacres, / Acts of black night, abominable deeds, / Complots of mischief, treason, villainies' (v.i.63–5) but are almost interchangeable: each is separately referred to as a 'ravenous tiger' (v.iii.95 and v.iii.5). The recurrent horrors of the play are actually the result of a savage tussle for 'Roman empery', which has recently been consolidated by a victory over the 'barbarous Goths' (i.i.22, 28) but they are projected onto the 'others' of Roman imperial patriarchy.

Roman nobility claims to be both masculine and 'civilised'; Titus is its grand patriarch, deriving his status from his twenty-five sons, twenty-one of whom have been 'slain manfully in arms' (i.i.196), from the beauty and virtue of his daughter, 'gracious Lavinia', who is 'Rome's rich ornament' (i.i.52) and from his own military exploits. If Rome has become a 'wilderness of tigers' because of its rulers' disregard for the people, and because of their brutal traditions and scramble for power – Tamora points out: 'was never Scythia half so barbarous' (i.i.131) – what better scapegoats than a black man and a disorderly woman?

The play does not really acknowledge them as scapegoats, however, for blackness and deviant womanhood emerge as pathologically evil. Significantly, there has been no debate about the colour or ethnic origins of Aaron the Moor, no effort to prove that Shakespeare had not seen Moors, or that racial hatred and miscegenation had not been invented in Elizabethan times for, unlike Othello, Aaron is more easily reconciled to the stereotype of black wickedness, lust, and malignity. His unmitigated evil is repeatedly linked to his physical features, both by himself and by others. Thus he refers to:

> My fleece of woolly hair that now uncurls
> Even as an adder when she doth unroll
> To do some fatal execution.
>
> (II.iii.34–6)

Or again,

> Let fools do good, and fair men call for grace:
> Aaron will have his soul black like his face.
>
> (III.i.205–6)

Tamora, Aaron's lover, is white, but she is a Goth and therefore barbarous. She and Lavinia between them split the patriarchal stereotype of woman, for if Lavinia is civilised, 'gracious' (I.i.52), 'gentle' (II.v.16), passive, virtuous, chaste and obedient, Tamora is 'barbarous', 'most insatiate and luxurious woman' (v.i.88) and a 'siren' (II.i.23). Lavinia is enclosed by Roman patriarchy: king, father, brothers, husband, nephew; Tamora challenges it: militarily (by waging a war against Rome), sexually (by marrying and manipulating its ruler and maintaining a lover), and racially (because she and her lover are both 'barbarous'). Appropriately she becomes the agent of Lavinia's destruction, along with the 'irreligious Moor, / Chief architect and plotter of these woes' (v.iii.121–2). Tamora's sons are wicked because of their mother: 'O, do not learn her wrath – she taught it thee ... Even at her teat thou had'st her tyranny' (II.iii.143–5). But Tamora is no simple image of maternal destructiveness. She combines the attributes of the warrior woman – masculine prowess, military skill – and of the Amazon – usurping of male authority, sexual promiscuity (see Shepherd, *Amazons*). She is both the epitome of stereotypical female duplicity and the converse of stereotypical female subservience.

Both Tamora and Aaron become embodiments of pure evil; the supposedly uncontrollable sexuality of women and blacks motivates their liaison. Aaron's blackness makes her honour

> ... of his body's hue,
> Spotted, detested and abominable.
> Why are you sequest'red from all your train,
> Dismounted from your snow-white goodly steed,
> And wand'red hither to an obscure plot,
> Accompanied but with a barbarous Moor,
> If foul desire had not conducted you?
>
> (II.iii.73–9)

Their child is accordingly a 'devil', 'as loathsome as a toad / Amongst the fair-fac'd breeders of our clime' (IV.ii.67–8). At the end of the play, evil is exposed and purged through the literal expulsion of Aaron and Tamora. He is to be walled up and starved, while she must be thrown 'to beasts and birds of prey' (V.iii.198). Lavinia, the compliant woman is, by contrast, to be embraced in the bosom of the civilised world and 'closed in our household's monument' (V.iii.194). But passive as she is, her rape has made her too impure to live.

Thus evil is officially located outside Roman patriarchy. But we are reminded that Rome itself is 'a wilderness of tigers' (III.i.54); that Tamora's reign of terror is unleashed after she becomes 'incorporate in Rome, / A Roman now adopted happily' (I.i.462–3); that Titus himself 'threw the people's suffrages / On him that doth tyrannize o'er me' (IV.iii.19–20); that Tamora at one level merely revenged Titus for what he did to her son. Moreover, Aaron occasionally strains his stereotype. Whereas both Tamora and Titus are responsible for their children's deaths, the black man, stereotypically denied human emotions, barters his own life to ensure his son's safety. What is more important, it is while defending his child that Aaron 'momentarily becomes a representative of his race, protesting against prejudice' (Cowhig, p. 3). He claims to be better than his white adversaries: 'ye sanguine, shallow hearted boys! / Ye white lim'd walls! Ye alehouse painted signs' and asserts that 'coal black is better than another hue' (IV.ii.97–9). Thus even in this play the apparently secure stereotypes of black barbarity and female deviance are, although marginally, opened out. In *Othello*, I shall suggest, common-sense ideas about blacks are evoked but more clearly questioned, disclosed as misrepresentation. And, crucially, this disclosure is closely interwoven with the disturbance to patriarchal authority.

Racism / Patriarchalism

I will locate a movement which is precisely the opposite of the one seen by Fiedler and will trace Othello's passage from an honorary white to a total outsider, a movement that depends on the impact of both racial and sexual difference.[6] In other words, Othello moves from being a colonised subject existing on the terms of white Venetian society and trying to internalise its ideology, towards being marginalised, outcast and alienated from it in every way, until he occupies his 'true' position as its other. His precarious entry into the white world is ruptured by his relation with Desdemona, which was intended to secure it in the first place, and which only catalyses the contradictions in Othello's self-conception. So instead of the unified subject of humanist thought, we have a near schizophrenic hero whose last speech graphically portrays the split – he becomes simultaneously the Christian and the Infidel, the Venetian and the Turk, the keeper of the State and its opponent. At the same time, Desdemona passes from being his ally who would guarantee his white status to becoming his sexual and racial 'other'. As will be discussed later, she too is a split, inconsistent subject and occupies not one but various positions in the play, not only as Othello's 'other' but also that of the Venetian patriarchy.

The 'central conflict' of the play then, if we must locate one, is neither between white and black alone, nor merely between men and women – it is rather between the racism of a white patriarchy and the threat posed to it by both a black man and a white woman. But these two are not simply aligned against white patriarchy, since their own relation cannot be abstracted from sexual or racial tension. Othello is not merely a black man who is jealous, but a man whose jealousy and blackness are inseparable. Similarly, Desdemona's initial boldness and later submission are not discordant in the context of her positions as a *white* woman and a white *woman*. There is thus a tripartite and extremely complex relationship between black man, white woman and the state.

In the first 125 lines of the play, racist images of Othello's blackness abound – he is 'thick lips', 'old black ram', 'a Barbary horse', 'devil' and 'a lascivious Moor'. It is significant that, unlike Aaron's case, these images are evoked almost exclusively in the context of his contact with a white woman, which transforms the latent racism of Venetian society into Brabantio's virulent anger and Iago's disgust. From honoured guest to that of an inhuman Othello becomes 'such a thing as thou' (I.ii.71) whose liaison is 'against all rules of nature' (I.iii.101) (see Cowhig, p. 8). Brabantio's conviction that Othello has used magic to win her at once dislodges Othello to the status of a barbaric outsider, an animal whom he claims his daughter was afraid to look upon. Here Othello is associated with an activity with overwhelmingly female connotations i.e. witchcraft. Cleopatra too, it may be recalled, is accused of magically enchanting Antony. But Cleopatra's feminine wiles are specifically linked to her being an Egyptian and we are reminded that sorcery is repeatedly constructed as being an uncivilised and un-Christian activity as well; in themselves Othello and Cleopatra cannot be sexually attractive.

Constructing the Other

Othello is a Moor, but there is no real clarity as to his precise origins despite references to his being sold in slavery and to his unChristian past. Debates over whether Othello was black, brown or mulatto anxiously tried to recover the possibility of his whiteness from this ambiguity which, on the contrary, alerts us to the very construction of the 'other' in Orientalist and colonial discourses. While we must recognise that each non-white race or group has an individual identity, a uniformity is conferred upon them by their common differentiation from white civilisation. Robinson notes that 'prior to the eleventh or twelfth centuries the use of the collective sense of the term barbarian was primarily a function of exclusion rather than a reflection of any significant consolidation among these peoples' (p. 10). Thus, to consider Othello as a black man is not to gloss over the textual confusion but to concur with Fanon that colonial discourse itself erases differentiation between its various subjects and treats all outsiders as black; while locating its racism therefore, we need to stress the common exclusion of its 'others', whose political colour rather than precise shade of non-whiteness is what matters.

The conversion of the outsider to the service of dominant culture is a crucial feature of the European encounter with other peoples. Hence the alien must also be incorporated (Said, *Orientalism*, p. 71). Othello is valuable as a Christian warrior, or the exotic colonial subject in the service of the state. In the Senate scene, the Venetian patriarchy displays an amazing capacity to variously construct, co-opt and exclude its 'others'. Brabantio is certain that the Senate will back his opposition to Othello's marriage, and if it appears strange (or remarkably liberal) that they don't, we need only to recall their concern with the Turkish threat. Othello the warrior is strategically included as one of 'us' as opposed to the Turkish 'they': 'You must therefore be content to slubber the gloss of your new fortunes with this more stubborn and boisterous expedition' (I.iii.227–8).

Iago's famous 'motiveless malignity' (as Coleridge called it) according to Greenblatt still 'remains opaque' (*Renaissance Self-Fashioning*, p. 236). This is partly because many of Iago's statements are often regarded as irrational, and as evidence of his almost mythic, hardly human wickedness. The following passage is often cited as an example of such illogical behaviour:

> ... Now I do love her too;
> Not out of absolute lust, though peradventure
> I stand accountant for as great a sin
> But partly led to diet my revenge,
> For that I do suspect the lustful Moor
> Hath leap'd into my seat; the thought whereof
> Doth like a poisonous mineral gnaw my inwards;
> And nothing can, nor shall content my soul
> Till I am even'd with him, wife for wife ...
> (II.i.285–93)

In what sense does Iago love Desdemona? Does he really suspect Emilia with Othello? Rather than confusion of motive, the passage illustrates the way in which sexual desire is expressive of a power struggle, here in a specifically racist context. Iago 'loves' Desdemona in the same way as Ferdinand loves his sister, the Duchess of Malfi. In the latter case, erotic desire, brotherly possessiveness and male authoritarianism blend as expressions of aristocratic bonding, and of protection of state and family power. Similarly Iago's 'love' speaks of a racial and patriarchal bonding whereby he becomes the 'protector' of all white women from black men. More specifically, as a white woman, Desdemona belongs to him rather than to Othello. Such possessiveness over all white women is also reflected in the fear (rationalised as 'suspicion') of losing his wife to Othello.

As Cowhig indicates, Iago's disgust at Desdemona's choice reveals an almost phobic racist horror:

> Not to affect many proposed matches,
> Of her own clime, complexion and degree,
> Whereto we see in all things nature tends –
> Foh! one may smell in such a will most rank,
> Foul disproportion, *thoughts unnatural.*
> (III.iii.233–7; emphasis added)

This interchange between Iago and Othello allows us to see that the 'naturalness' which dominant ideologies invoke to legitimise themselves, and which is central to common-sense thinking generally, is a flexible category. For Othello, seeking to efface his own blackness through Desdemona's love, a patriarchal view of female constancy as 'natural' is necessary. Therefore for him Desdemona's supposed dishonesty becomes 'nature erring from itself' (III.iii.231). But Iago reinterprets erring nature to define Desdemona as a white woman, whose love for and constancy to Othello is 'unnatural'.

So he yokes together stereotypical notions of both 'black' as repulsive and 'female' as ever-capable of unnatural transgressions.

As Lawrence correctly points out, whereas the rapes of black women by white men were seen as a sort of favour to the black race, the mating of white women with black men was regarded as fatal. Whereas the first extended the power of the white man over all women, the latter eroded his own territory, and allowed for the possibility of its 'invasion'. In the Indian context, British (and other colonial) men indulged in widespread sexual liaisons with (including rapes of) Indian women as a matter of course. But the horrors of British women taking on Indian lovers are obsessively foregrounded in literature as diverse as Forster's *A Passage to India*, Paul Scott's *The Raj Quartet* and Jhabvala's *Heat and Dust*; they persist as a feature of contemporary racism: 'in Britain today, the question is never: would you allow your son to marry a black girl? It is always: would you allow your daughter to marry a black man?' (Lawrence, 'Just plain common-sense', p. 72). Such a nexus of the fears evoked by black and active female sexuality is responsible for engendering the extreme horrors of *Titus Andronicus*, where it results in racial pollution. From Elizabeth I's communiqué deporting blacks, referred to earlier, to today's British immigration laws, the 'preservation' of the white race is seen to be at stake. Fanon offered a psychoanalytical explanation for this fear, pointing out that racist phobia always reduces the black man to his sexual potential: 'the father revolts because in his opinion the Negro will introduce his daughter into a sexual universe for which the father does not have the key, the weapons, or the attributes' (p. 165).

So what is especially threatening for white patriarchy is the possibility of the *complicity* of white women; their desire for black lovers is feared, forbidden, but always imminent. The spectre of a combined black and female insubordination 'threatens to undermine white manhood and the Empire at a stroke' (Lawrence, p. 64). The effort then becomes to project the white woman's desire as provoked by the animalistic lust of the black man, a notion which is traceable as far back as the fifteenth century in Europe and much earlier in India. The myth of the black rapist is even more useful, for it perpetuates black animalism while obliterating female agency, and thus simultaneously 'erases' the two most problematic areas for patriarchal racism – the humanity of the alien race and the active sexuality of women.

Even if she is passive, however, the white woman's contact with the alien male pollutes her. In chapter 6, the black man's supposed rapacity will be further discussed in the context of *The Tempest*. But in *Othello* the problem arises precisely because Othello is not a rapist and Desdemona is not an unwilling victim of his sexual assault. Their desire cannot be contained within the myth of the black rapist. In spite of this, Iago's racism and his misogyny together make him confident that the 'relation between an erring barbarian and a super-subtle Venetian' can be easily disrupted (1.iii.356).

'Haply for I am black'

Othello is described in terms of the characteristics popularly attributed to blacks during the sixteenth century: sexual potency, courage, pride, guilelessness, credulity, easily aroused passions; these become central and persistent features of later colonial stereotyping as well. At the beginning of the play he is seemingly well entrenched in and accepted by Venetian society – an honorary white, whose hyperbolic speech is an attempt to speak better than any the language of his adoptive civilisation (see Serpieri, p. 142). The vulnerability of his entry prompts him to reiterate his intrinsic merits, his lineage and his achievements; he appears confident that these will match Brabantio's racism:

> My services which I have done the signiory
> Shall out-tongue his complaints ...
>
> (i.ii.18–19)

Othello needs to believe that 'my parts, my title and my perfect soul / Shall manifest me rightly' (i.ii.31–2). He is to discover that the dominant ideology encouraged by his adoptive society, especially the notion of the power and indestructible essence of the individual, is doubly illusory when your skin is black.

But if Othello is not archetypal man, neither is he simply *any* black man. The drama of racial difference is played out on spaces already occupied by divisions of class. He is involved in the process of social mobility and self-fashioning as are others around him, but on somewhat different terms. Brecht rightly pointed out that

> he doesn't only possess Desdemona, he also possesses a post as general, which he has not inherited as a feudal general would, but won by outstanding achievements, and presumably snatched from someone else; he must defend it or it will be snatched from him. He lives in a world of fighting for property and position, and his relationship with the woman he loves develops as a property relationship. (quoted Heinemann, p. 217)

Iago is jealous of Cassio's preferment, and also of Othello, who is more successful in their common pursuit of status. Iago gains considerable wealth from duping Roderigo: 'I have wasted myself out of my means. The jewels you have had from me to deliver to Desdemona would half have corrupted a votarist' (iv.ii.186–88).

However, class differences cannot be sealed off from others, as Stuart Hall has pointed out in the context of contemporary Britain: 'Race', he says, 'is the modality in which class relations are experienced' (quoted Gilroy, p. 276). Applied to *Othello*, this illuminates the profound invasion, intensification and alteration of class or gender relations by race. Iago's jealousy of Cassio's advancement does not become deflected into hatred for Othello, as is sometimes supposed. Rather, each breeds the other, for Othello is the racial inferior who is socially superior, the outsider who has become the means of Iago's own preferment. Greenblatt has persuasively and correctly argued that Iago's ability to improvise and control events and the lives of others should be located as an effect of colonial ideology which seeks to 'sustain indefinitely indirect enslavement' by moulding the psyche of the oppressed (Greenblatt, *Renaissance Self-Fashioning*, p. 229). But we need to add that such an ideology is not just generally imbibed but shaped and spurred by Iago's specific experience of racial hatred.

Desdemona is both her father's 'jewel' (i.iii.195) and her husband's 'purchase' (ii.iii.9). As the guarantee of her husband's upward mobility, she is similar to Bianca (*Women Beware Women*). But unlike the latter, Desdemona is also the gate to white humanity. Slowly his conception of his own worth comes to centre in the fact that she chose him over all the 'curl'd darlings' of Venice. Her desire for him – 'for she had eyes, and chose me' (III.iii.193) – replaces his heritage or exploits as proof and measure of his worth. It thus becomes the primary signifier of his identity; that is why 'my life upon her faith' (I.iii.294) and 'when I love thee not, / Chaos is come again' (III.iii.92–3). That is why if she loves him not, 'Farewell! Othello's occupation's gone' (III.iii.361). Frantz Fanon's description of the encounter between the black man and white woman, although somewhat reductive of female sexuality, illuminates this aspect of Othello's desire:

> Out of the blackest part of my soul, across the zebra striping of my mind, surges this desire to be suddenly white ... who but a white woman can do this for me? By loving me she proves that I am worthy of white love. I am loved like a white man.
>
> I am a white man ... I marry white culture, white beauty, white whiteness.
>
> When my restless hands caress those white breasts, they grasp white civilization and dignity and make them mine. (p. 63)[7]

At the same time, we must remember that Othello actually emphasises his difference in order to bridge it and win Desdemona. His 'magic' consists of invoking his exotic otherness, his cultural and religious differences as well as his heroic exploits, which involve strange peoples and territories. He oscillates between asserting his non-European glamour and denying his blackness, emphasising through speech and social position his assimilation into white culture. He is thus hopelessly split; as Homi Bhabha writes in relation to Fanon's split subject: 'black skins, white masks is not ... a neat division; it is a doubling, dissembling image of being in at least two places at once which makes it impossible for the devalued ... to accept the colonizer's invitation to identity' ('Introduction', p. xvi).

Desdemona's Disobedience

The erosion of Desdemona's power and assertiveness has already been presented as central to evaluations of the play. Fiedler characteristically calls it the power of the 'white witch'; Tennenhouse desribes it as 'the power to speak the language of the law, which in turn gives her the power to give her own body in marriage' (*Power on Display*, p. 125). Greenblatt, by contrast, locates it in her very submission to desire which arouses sexual tension in Othello (*Renaissance Self-Fashioning*, p. 250). I suggest that Desdemona's disobedience and later submission are both related to the shifting positions she occupies in relation to Othello, and to the contradictions that they impose upon her. Cowhig insightfully locates Desdemona's love in the context of a white woman's fantasies for the exotic male:

> ... is she not more attracted to the exotic myth of 'otherness' than to the real man? Given the enormous popularity of travel books among white women (the Earl of Shaftesbury in 1710 was to lament the fact that 'a thousand Desdemonas were so obsessed with stories of African men that they would readily abandon husbands, families and country itself to 'follow the fortunes of a hero of the black tribe'), can we not say that Desdemona was an early travel book 'fanatic'? (p. 13)

If we are not to subscribe to the usual myths about female propensity for 'romance', however, the susceptibility of Desdemona and her sisters (for example, later figures such as Hardy's Tess) to the proverbial outsider must be viewed in the additional context of the confinement of the woman and the increasing restriction of her mobility and freedom. If Iago's 'love' for Desdemona and Ferdinand's for the Duchess are emblematic of the desire to 'protect' race, property and power through the enclosure of the woman, Desdemona's fascination conversely indicates her desire to break the claustrophobic patriarchal confine. Travel, adventure, and freedom being male domains, she first wishes 'that heaven had made her such a man' and then begins to love Othello 'for the dangers I had pass'd' (i.iii.163, 167). Projected on to the outsider are all the fantasies of freedom and love, both of which are unable to be even visualised from within her world. It is true that Desdemona only invokes the right to owe duty to her husband and not her own autonomy. But in so doing she defies patriarchal control over her desires. Desdemona's eroticism is particularly disturbing in its explicit and frank avowal of the 'downright violence' of her passion and her claim to 'the rites for why I love him' (i.iii.248, 252; see also Greenblatt, *Renaissance Self-Fashioning*, p. 250).

Tennenhouse underlines the connections between sexual relations and the political body of Elizabethan and Jacobean England: 'Desdemona poses a specifically Jacobean assault on monarchy when she assumes authority over her body and persuades the senate to assert the priority of a contractual relationship over and against the will of the patriarch' (*Power on Display*, p. 127). The early modern state was not only increasingly misogynist but made explicit the usefulness of patriarchalism for tightening its authoritarian controls. State legislation strengthened the household as an instrument of social control, and laws against every category of potentially deviant people – the poor, vagrants, prostitutes, witches and even alternative religious orders – attempted to sweep the population within the boundaries of the household and strengthen the authority of the father (Hill, *Society and Puritanism*; Stone, *The Family*, Kelly, *Women, History, Theory*). The consolidation of the state involved a consolidation of the family as its primary unit: 'the word "father" is an epitome of the whole gospel' (Thomas, p. 319). Gordon Schochet has pointed out that social hierarchies were explained in terms of natural or divinely sanctioned status and political authority, understood in terms of the patriarchal theory of obligation. The parent–child relationship served the precise function of making governance intelligible and 'all that had to be done was to expand the experienced and comprehensible and therefore acceptable category of relationships subsumed under the parent–child rubric to include that between ruler and subject' (p. 439). Hence James I argued that 'By the Law of Nature the King becomes a naturall Father to all his Lieges at his Coronation' (p. 55).

Tennenhouse is therefore right in concluding that 'if Jacobean drama proves one thing ... it is that sexual relations are always political' and that Desdemona's desire is politically subversive. At the same time, I am uncomfortable with his intention to '*dissolve* the sexual theme into those (thematics) which ... determined the components of Jacobean drama and the nature of their relationship: Kingship versus kinship; natural versus metaphysical bodies of power; the signs and symbols of state versus the exercise of state power' (*Power on Display*, pp. 123–4). For if sexual relations are political only in the way that the non-sexual is, their very specificity is denied. As Gerda Lerner put it, 'all analogies – class, group, caste – approximate the position of women but fail to define it adequately. Women are a category unto themselves; an adequate analysis of their position in society demands new conceptual tools' (quoted Kelly, p. 6). The sexual theme can be contextualised but not dissolved, and the analogy of the wife–husband or child–father relation to that of subject and king cannot explain the entirety of Renaissance gender relations. Active female sexuality is disruptive of patriarchal control, not just because it is an emblem for, or analogous to, other sorts of rebellion, but because it directly threatens the power base of patriarchy which is dependent upon its regulation and control.

I will emphasise again that Desdemona's desire is especially transgressive because its object is black, which Tennenhouse ignores and Greenblatt underplays. If Desdemona is the most explicitly erotic and sensual of Shakespeare's heroines, it is precisely because her choice is seen as 'unnatural', not only by Iago and Brabantio (and even, naggingly, by Othello himself), but also, most probably, by the audience. Her expressions of love do not unambiguously confirm their suspicions about female response to black men because they also shatter the assumption that black men need to force their attentions on white women.

In the Senate scene, while Desdemona is surprisingly bold and explicit for a modest maiden facing the Venetian state, Othello finds it necessary to deny 'the palate of my appetite'. I would agree with Cowhig that 'these speeches relate directly to Othello's colour. Desdemona has made it clear that his "sooty bosom" is no obstacle to desire; while Othello must defend himself against the unspoken accusations, of the audience as well as of the senators, because of the association of sexual lust with blackness' (p. 10). At the end of the scene, Othello is exonerated from the sexual slur and accordingly pronounced an honorary white: 'your son in law is far more fair than black' (i.iii.290).

Consider also the meeting of the lovers at Cyprus after the storm. Othello would happily die in order to arrest the perfection of their meeting for 'not another comfort like to this / Succeeds in *unknown fate*' (ii.i.190–1; emphasis added). Desdemona's reply, on the contrary, optimistically looks forward: 'our loves and comforts should increase / Even as our days do grow'. For Neely, this is evidence of her greater realism, and more generally, of greater female maturity in sexual relationships. I prefer to see it, at least partly, as an indication of her greater confidence, which Othello, as a black man, cannot share. His words betray an insecurity which has already been catalysed by Brabantio's reaction; his present 'wonder' and 'joy' are partially compounded of disbelief at actually possessing her just as his desire to revel in the moment betrays uncertainty about the future.

Desdemona's power, then, is the confidence of both race and class – of an upper class Venetian beauty, secure in the attentions of men around her and in the advantages of her position. She shares something here with the confidence of Beatrice-Joanna in Middleton's *The Changeling*. Desdemona's persistence on Cassio's behalf, for example, reflects an upbringing where women are taught that their power lies in their ability to cajole and chide men into favouring them. Her initial confidence in her own persuasiveness and her methods, coquettishly insistent, owe something to the illusion of female power in the ethic of courtly love. This slowly gives way to the more sobering reality of the power of the husband over the wife, a power that Othello asserts despite his blackness, or is it because of it? Away from the world in which she has grown up,

Desdemona becomes less assured and confident. Her transformation from a woman who confronts both her father and the Venetian Senate to the wife who submits to her husband's insults is not a result of truly feminine love but a manifestation of the contradictions imposed upon her by a racist, patriarchal and bourgeois society.

It is important, of course, to guard against reading dramatic characters as real, three-dimensional people. But, as Alan Sinfield says, Desdemona seems even more discontinuous than Othello because she is 'less a developing consciousness than a series of positions that women are conventionally supposed to occupy ... (She) makes sense not as a continuous subjectivity ... but in terms of the stories about "woman" that were and are told in patriarchal ideology' ('*Othello*', pp. 20–2). Female inconsistency is a complex amalgam of being 'scripted by men' (the phrase is Sinfield's), not only literally, in the plays, but generally, in patriarchal society.

Desdemona's Obedience

Othello needs to encourage Desdemona's sexual freedom up to the point that it ensures his own mobility but also subsequently to curb it. He is proud of her speech in the beginning of the play, for it confers a power and a legitimacy on him. Later he smothers her voice, for she must speak and move on his behalf only and not when it is suspected that he is not the object of her passion – 'O curse of marriage, / That we can call these delicate creatures ours, / And not their appetites' (iii.iii.272–4). This is not a general male dilemma however: if we take into account the importance of Desdemona for Othello's entire existence in white society, then the power of the misogynist idea of the changeability, duplicity and frailty of women to rouse and disturb Othello and his vulnerability to Iago's tales of female inconstancy become clearer. He has begun to feel the limits of self-fashioning for a black man in a white world.

At each point that women's frailty is impressed upon Othello, it is in conjunction with his own blackness. Brabantio is the first to plant the possibility of Desdemona's duplicity in Othello's mind ('She has deceiv'd her father and may thee', i.iii.293) which is picked up by Iago later;

> She did deceive her father, marrying you;
> And when she seem'd to shake and fear your looks,
> She lov'd them most.
>
> (iii.iii.210–12)

The interweaving of misogyny and racism in Iago's later speeches cannot be missed. Women, in his opinion, are capable of the most unnatural acts, such as loving black men, and the greatest fickleness, such as ceasing to love them. By asking Othello to acknowledge this he both questions Othello's humanity and appeals to his manhood: 'Are you a man? Have you a soul or sense?' (iii.iii.378); 'Would you would bear your fortune like a man'; 'Good sir, be a man'; 'Marry, patience; / Or I shall say you are all in all in spleen / And nothing of a man' (iv.i.61, 65, 87–9). The more he questions Othello's humanity, the more he appeals to his masculine power over women. Promising to kill Cassio, he begs Othello to 'let her live', although Othello has up to that time never hinted at killing Desdemona. Just as Othello's white identity was dependent upon Desdemona's love, his destruction of her involves a belief in women's frailty which helps him 'rationalise' her supposed infidelity. Desdemona begins to embody the common patriarchal dichotomy of the white devil. For Othello, this is the only way to yoke together the otherwise contradictory experiences of being black and a man. Therefore Desdemona's schisms are deepened as Othello's are, even though one seeks to heal itself at the expense of the other.

Greenblatt accounts for Othello's vulnerability to Iago's narrative by referring to the guilt that Christian orthodoxy imposes upon all forms of passion or sexual pleasure and specifically excluding racial difference: 'Nothing *conflicts* openly with Christian orthodoxy, but the erotic intensity that informs every word is experienced in tension with it. The tension is *less a manifestation of some atavistic "blackness" specific to Othello than a manifestation of the colonial power of Christian doctrine over sexuality*' (pp. 241–2; emphasis added). Why should Christianity, an adoptive religion for Othello, inform his psyche more fundamentally than the blackness which pervades every aspect of his history and identity? On the contrary, sexual guilt (possibly including that conferred by Christianity) is rooted in and intensified by a colour consciousness. Thus Othello begins to subscribe to what we may see as a Christian patriarchal view of woman as deceiver and sinful, but because of, not over and above, his blackness.

Evident in the imagery of black and white is Othello's internalisation of his own inferiority as well as the wickedness of women. As his position as honorary white erodes, Desdemona becomes the honorary black; her duplicity makes her 'a subtle whore, / A closet-lock-and-key of villainous secrets' (IV.i.21–3) as well as 'begrim'd and black / As my own face' (III.iii.391–2). In the speech at Desdemona's bedside, the whiteness of her skin makes it both necessary and difficult to kill her – necessary because her beauty makes it possible that 'she'll betray more men' (V.ii.6) and therefore Othello must act on behalf of all men (including, ironically, Brabantio), thus 'transcending' his colour to become, in his view, a sort of everyman; difficult because it is still the signifier of all that is desirable to Othello, and all that he cannot have, reminding him that he cannot be everyman. Desdemona, or rather, what she represents and what she is made to represent by Iago, thus makes Othello alternate between two definitions of his own identity – he is a *man* in relation to her femininity and *black* in relation to her whiteness. The contradictions should be kept in mind when we view his necrophiliac fantasy to 'kill thee, / And love thee after' (V.i.17–8).

Alongside the sexual tension the play charts Othello's increasing racial isolation. As his precarious integration into white society vanishes he becomes more obviously the alien (critics have often noted the upsurge of his non-European past, his pagan history), and more alone and isolated; it becomes even more obvious that he is also the only black around. Compare the confident Othello of the Senate scene to the lonely figure of the last scene, desperately recalling his services to the state, and unlike Hamlet or Antony, delivering his own eulogy. As already noted, his last words graphically capture the split of his identity into Christian and infidel – he becomes the 'circum-cised dog' that he once killed. The Turk's crime was that he 'beat a Venetian and traduc'd the state' (V.ii.357). Thus even a last picture of the time when he could act on behalf of white society, as one of 'us' cannot be simply evoked but is slashed by his position as outsider. The flimsily put together zebra-striping of his mind disintegrates into its constituent polarity of black and white.

Lonely figure, yes, but he is also the murderer of his wife. An opposition of male to female, as feminist critics have pointed out, is most clearly articulated by Emilia:

> They are all but stomachs, and we all but food;
> They eat us hungerly, and when they are full,
> They belch us.
>
> (III.iv.105–7)

But to prioritise this, to set up an uncomplicated opposition between the world of men and the world of women, the former being 'political, loveless and undomesticated' (Neely, p. 215), would contribute to the rupture posited in patriarchal thought between private and public, political and domestic. The world of men is itself deeply divided, as indeed is the world of women. Moreover, racist innuendoes inform even the most casual moments of the play:

> If she be black, and thereto have a wit,
> She'll find a white that shall her blackness hit.
>
> (II.i.132–3)

Who is 'the patriarchy' or 'the authority' in the play – Iago, Othello, Brabantio, the Senate? If it is all of them, what do we make of the tensions between them? If Othello the patriarch triumphs, what of Othello the black man who disintegrates? *Othello* should neither be read as a patriarchal, authoritarian and racist spectacle, nor as a show of female or black superiority. Iago has often been seen as related to the Vice figure in a morality play. Unlike the morality Vice however, he does not simply challenge accepted morality but is also the spokesperson for racist and patriarchal platitudes. His position as a sort of mediator between audience and action and his oft-commented upon role as producer of the play within the play are crucial. He undoubtedly articulates many of the viewers' common-sense attitudes, and hence even while his plot offends them, it seeks their complicity. As Peter Stallybrass says, Iago's narrative is believed by others 'not because Iago is superhumanly ingenious but, to the contrary, because his is the voice of "common sense", the ceaseless repetition of the always-already "known", the culturally "given" ' ('Patriarchal Territories', p. 139). Jean E. Howard has made the same point in relation to Don John in *Much Ado about Nothing*, who, like Iago, is often seen to be constructing the plot and manipulating the characters of the play. His trick of substituting Margaret for Hero at the bedroom window 'silently assumes and further circulates the idea that women are universally prone to deception and impersonation ... Don John lies about Hero, but his lie works because it easily passes in Messina as a truthful reading of women' (Howard, 'Renaissance antitheatricality', pp. 174–5).

Therefore, not merely Iago's, or Brabantio's, but the audience's assumed responses are under scrutiny. At one level, the stereotypical is upheld, for Desdemona *is* duplicitous and Othello *is* barbarous. But the play is open to a radical and alternative reading precisely because it unravels and problematises these stereotypes by laying bare the process of their construction. We then get a view of duplicity and barbarity as ideological constructs rather than natural aspects of women or black people.

Ben Okri became painfully aware of Othello's colour during a production in London's Barbican:

> It was the first time I had seen it performed on stage. I was the only black person in the audience. The seats beside me were occupied by three white girls. They noisily crackled their packets of sweets and giggled a lot. I wanted to tell them to be quiet. But I suspected that if I spoke faces would turn towards me. After a while I couldn't bear it any longer. When I spoke what I feared happened. Faces turned, eyes lit up in recognition. My skin glowed. I felt myself illuminated, unable to hide.
>
> I used to agree with C. L. R. James that *Othello* is not a play about race ... If it did not begin as a play also about race, then its history has made it one. (pp. 562–3)

This history has been varied: Martin Orkin has recently shown how 'in South Africa, silence about the prevailing racist tendencies in *Othello* actually supports racist doctrine and practice' ('Othello and the plain face of racism', p. 166). Orkin places the continuing prescription, for South African students, of the Arden edition of the play, with Ridley's notoriously racist introduction, in the context of the apartheid state (*Shakespeare Against Apartheid*, p. 107). Surely the fact that it is also the standard text in India, as is Kermode's edition of *The Tempest* cannot be viewed as an accident. Nor is it inconsequential that African students are the butt of racist jokes in Delhi. In India, the assumption often is that we are outside racist structures, even while our own brands of colour prejudice, which are complexly intertwined with caste, regional and class differences, and which have been deepened by the colonial encounter, not only flourish but are being intensified. Many of the common-sense notions that have been identified in white racism would be closely echoed in the instance of an inter-caste marriage in India. Finally, the patriarchalism of Indian society does not stand outside its own history of colour consciousness.[8] Instead of allowing it to become a means of confirmation of these attitudes, Othello must be seized as a point from which we may examine and dismantle the racism and the sexism which both our own hegemonic ideologies and years of colonial education have persuaded us to adopt.

Notes

1 Kishwar and Vanita's *In Search of Answers* includes many accounts of contemporary violence against women in India. See also Mies, *Patriarchy and Accumulation* for an analysis of how older customs are given a modern revival and intersect with 'modern' practices. For a report on persecution of women as witches in Bihar see *Hindustan Times*, 11 October 1987. Recently, an eighteen-year-old Rajput girl was burnt on her husband's pyre in Deorala, Rajasthan, while thousands of people watched. Later many more collected for a festival at the site and money poured in to build a temple there. Fierce protests by women's organisations were countered by revivalist processions, meetings and publications. Hindu revivalists have been contending that abolition of sati amounts to a violation of an individual's rights and therefore also of a woman's freedom. Under the guise of sophisticated sociological analysis, there has also been the argument that sati is being opposed today only by a westernised section of the Indian intelligentsia who do not understand India, her customs or their spirit. Kishwar and Vanita's article, 'The burning of Roop Kanwar', shows how sati is not just a simple revival of an ancient practice, but ties in with dominant political and economic interests. It also discusses how, despite its promulgation

of new anti-sati legislation, the Indian government has failed to, and is not interested in, dealing with the issue.

2   I am indebted to Cowhig's essay; despite the fact that she concentrates on the neglect of race in *Othello* criticism, whenever she does mention gender relations she relates them to racial politics. I am also indebted to Errol Lawrence's analysis of common-sense racist assumptions, which, along with Fanon, illuminates several aspects of the play.

3   Both views, then – of Othello as an archetypal man and as a black man – are premised upon racist notions of black inferiority. We might assume that crudity such as Ridley's is somewhat passé, but its assumptions are traceable in more sophisticated accounts. Fiedler, for example, ends up asserting Othello's essential, moral whiteness and Iago's status as the true black. Ridley's arguments, although in other respects very different, similarly oscillate between rescuing Othello from the status of a black (he may be African but is he altogether negroid?), arguing for his inherent inferiority (he is somewhat deficient in reason and intellect though a warm, loving, instinctual creature), and thoroughly ignoring Desdemona (he evaluates her worth by the dignity with which she faces men who have seen her publicly struck).

4   Karen Newman's article, ' "And wash the Ethiop white" ' and Martin Orkin's book, *Shakespeare Against Apartheid* both make significant departures (in different directions) from previous criticism of the play. I saw them at a very late stage in the production of this project, so I am unable to comment on them fully. Newman's article is unique in beginning to interrelate racial and sexual difference, and Orkin brings together the contexts of production and reception – so both together discuss many of my own concerns here. I differ from Orkin's assessment of the Venetian Senate: 'no evidence emerges in the detail of the language to suggest that they share a hidden racist disapprobation of Othello (p. 65). I also think that to say that 'Othello, Desdemona and Cassio seek only love and honor in the play' (p. 88) is to gloss over the ways in which they are themselves 'flawed' by the racial structures: we need to guard against viewing any of them as simple oppositions to a racist Iago.

Even otherwise radical critics have not purged their language of the racist moral connotations commonly attached to colour: Greenblatt, for example, speaks of the 'dark essence of Iago's whole enterprise' or the 'unfathomable darkness of human motives' (*Renaissance Self-Fashioning*, pp. 233, 251). It should be noted that such 'slips' coexist with an explicit devaluation of race as a theoretical parameter, which I will discuss shortly. Eagleton's discussion of the play (*William Shakespeare*) takes almost no account of Othello's colour.

5   Elizabeth's communiqué (quoted by Cowhig, p. 6) reads:

> An open warrant to the Lord maiour of London and to all Vice-Admyralls, Maiours and other publicke officers whatsoever to whom yt may appertaine. Whereas Casper van Senden, a merchant of Lubeck, did by his labor and travell procure 89 of her Majesty's subjects that were detayned prisoners in Spaine and Portugall to be released, and brought them hither into this realme at his owne cost and charges, for the which his expenses and declaration of his honest minde towards those prisoners he only desireth to have lycense to take up so much blackamoores here in this realme and to transport them into Spaine and Portugall. Her Majesty in regard to the charitable affection the suppliant hath showed being a stranger, to worke the delivery of our countrymen that were there in great great misery and thraldom and to bring them home to their native country, and that the same could not be done without great expense, and also considering the reasonableness of his requestes to transport so many blackamoores from hence, doth thincke yt a very good exchange and that those kinde of people may well be spared in this realme, being so populous and numbers of hable persons the subjects of the land and Christian people that perishe for want of service, whereby through their labor they might be mayntained. They are therefore in their Lordship's name required to aide and assist him to take up suche blackamoores as he shall finde within this realme with the consent of their masters, who we doubt not, considering her Majesty's good pleasure to have those kinde of people sent out of her

lande and the good deserving of the stranger towardes her Majesty's subjectes, and that they shall doe charitably and like Christians rather to be served by their owne countrymen then with those kinde of people, will yielde those in their possession to him.

6   I use the term 'honorary black' following Alison Heisch's phrase 'honorary male' in relation to Elizabeth I. Heisch, in her essay, 'Queen Elizabeth I and the persistence of patriarchy', argues that Elizabeth strengthened patriarchal rule by emphasising her masculine attributes; I am suggesting that Othello stresses his usefulness to white society, his adoption of its rules of conduct, his achievements, which make him acceptable in order to efface the negative connotations of blackness, in the same way that Elizabeth needed to claim that she had a heart and stomach of a king even though she had the body of a woman.

7   I use this comment with some reservations; it needs to be carefully and selectively used for the idea that black men's inferiority has resulted in all of them lusting after any white woman [and] has been used to perpetuate the myth of the black rapist.

8   Some of the things I have been speaking of surface in the history of the Hindu epic *Ramayana*. This tells the story of the heir apparent to the throne of Ayodhya, Rama, who was exiled to the forest for fourteen years by his father on the direction of the latter's fourth wife. There, Rama's wife Sita was abducted by a demon king, Ravana. The battle which followed resulted in Rama's victory and his subsequent return to his kingdom. The development of the story over the centuries bears testimony to the grafting on of various episodes emphasising chastity, wifely devotion and obedience, demonising of female propensity for evil as well as idealisation of the stereotype of a passive wife on to an originally simple story. Uma Chakravarti has suggested that these additions were made to the *Ramayana* in accordance with increasing Aryan taboos on women and alongside the socio-economic development of feudal society, and later tied in with medieval consolidation, so that the depiction of Sita represents the codification of the stereotype of a passive Hindu woman (pp. 68–75).

But it still remains to be analysed how this process also reveals a deepening racial differentiation. The original geographical parameters of the story in North India subsequently expanded till Ravana's kingdom became popularly located in the South, and became identified with what is today Sri Lanka. Ravana's people are *rakshasas*; the term originally signified a lower caste and today is taken to mean 'demon'. Rama's originally dark colour has faded to a near-white representation on the stage and cinema, whereas Ravana becomes ever darker. In the story's current serialisation on the national television network, Ravana's court is depicted through South Indian dance and music forms. We need to locate how racial differentiation crept in and how it is connected to the theme of the passive wife, as well as to the depiction of the wicked woman. While Sita, the 'white' wife is chaste and obedient, the 'alien' woman is sexually licentious: Ravana's sister Swarupnakha propositions Rama's brother Lakshmana. Not only does he chop off her nose and ears, but this incident is the provocation for Ravana's abduction of Sita. Thus the wicked step-mother, the promiscuous alien woman and the non-Aryan male collectively constitute the evil forces of the story.

References

Belsey, Catherine, *The Subject of Tragedy* (London and New York, Methuen, 1985).

Bhabha, Homi, 'Introduction' to Fanon, 1986.

Carr, Helen, 'Woman / Indian: "the American" and his others' in Francis Barker *et al.* eds., 1985.

Cowhig, Ruth, 'Blacks in English Renaissance drama and the role of Shakespeare's Othello' in Dabydeen, ed., 1985, pp. 1–25.

Dabydeen, David, ed., *The Black Presence in English Literature* (Manchester University Press, 1985).

Dollimore, Jonathan, *Radical Tragedy; Religion and Ideology in the Drama of Shakespeare and his Contemporaries* (Brighton, Harvester, 1983).

Fanon, Frantz, *Black Skins, White Masks*, trans. Charles Lam Markmann (London and Sydney, Pluto Press, 1986).

Fiedler, Leslie A., *The Stranger in Shakespeare* (Hertfordshire, Paladin, 1974).

Gilroy, 'Police and thieves' in CCCS, 1982, pp. 143–82.

Greenblatt, Stephen, *Renaissance Self-Fashioning* (University of Chicago Press, 1980).

Heinemann, Margot, 'How Brecht read Shakespeare' in Dollimore and Sinfield eds., 1985, pp. 202–30.

Hill, Christopher, *Society and Puritanism in Pre-Revolutionary England* (London, Panther Books, 1969).

Howard, Jean E., 'Renaissance antitheatricality and the politics of gender in *Much Ado About Nothing*' in Howard and O'Connor eds., 1987, pp. 163–87.

Hunter, G.K., *Dramatic Identities and Cultural Tradition, Studies in Shakespeare and his Contemporaries* (Liverpool University Press, 1978).

Jones, Eldred, *Othello's Countrymen: the African in English Renaissance Drama* (Oxford University Press, 1965).

Kelly, Joan, *Women, History, Theory* (Chicago, University of Chicago Press, 1984).

Kishwar, Madhu and Vanita, Ruth, eds., *In Search of Answers: Indian Women's Voices from Manushi* (London, Zed Books, 1984).

Lawrence, Errol, 'Just plain common-sense: the "roots" of racism' in CCCS, 1982, pp. 47–94.

Miller, Barbara Diane, 'Prenatal and postnatal sex-selection in India: the patriarchal context, ethical questions and public policy' (Michigan State University working paper 107, December 1985).

Neely, Carol Thomas, 'Women and men in *Othello*: "What should such a fool / Do with so good a woman" ' in Lenz *et al.* eds., *The Woman's Part: Feminist Criticism of Shakespeare* (University of Illinois Press, 1980).

Newman, Karen, ' "And wash the Ethiop white" – femininity and the monstrous in *Othello*' in Howard and O'Connor eds., 1987, pp. 143–62.

Newton, Judith and Rosenfelt, Deborah, *Feminist Criticism and Social Change: Sex, Class and Race in Literature and Culture* (New York and London, Methuen, 1985).

Norris, Christopher, 'Post-structuralist Shakespeare: text and ideology' in Drakakis ed., 1985, pp. 47–66.

Ogundipe-Leslie, Molara, 'African women, culture and another development', *Journal of African Marxists* (February 1984).

Okri, Ben, 'Meditations on Othello', *West Africa*, (23 and 30 March 1987) pp. 562–4; 618–19).

Orkin, Martin, 'Othello and the "plain face" of racism', *Shakespeare Quarterly*, 38, no. 2, (summer 1987) pp. 166–88.

—— *Shakespeare Against Apartheid* (Craighall, AD. Donker, 1987).

Ridley, M.I. ed., *Othello* (London, Methuen, 1958).

Robinson, Cedric J., *Black Marxism: the Making of a Black Radical Tradition* (London, Zed Books, 1983).

Rymer, Thomas, *A Short View of Tragedy* (1693) (Yorkshire, A Scolar press Facsimile, 1970).

Said, Edward, *Orientalism* (London, Routledge, 1978).

Schochet, Gordon, 'Patriarchalism, politics and mass attitudes in Stuart England', *Historical Journal* 12, no. 3, (1969), pp. 413–41.

Serpieri, Alessandro, 'Reading the signs: towards a semiotics of Shakespearean drama' in Drakakis ed., 1985, pp. 119–43.

Shepherd, Simon, *Amazons and Warrior Women: Varieties of Feminism in Seventeenth Century Drama* (Brighton, Harvester, 1983).

Sinfield, Alan, '*Othello* and the politics of character' (paper given at the University of Santiago de Compostella, Nov. 1987; forthcoming publication).

Spivak, Gayatri Chakravorty, 'Imperialism and sexual difference' *Oxford Literary Review* 8, nos. 1 and 2 (1986).

Stallybrass, Peter, 'Patriarchal territories: the body enclosed' in Ferguson, Margaret Quilligan and Vickers, Nancy J. eds., *Rewriting the Renaissance* (Chicago University Press, 1986) pp. 123–42.

Stone, Lawrence, *The Family, Sex and Marriage in England, 1500–1800* (London, Weidenfeld and Nicolson, 1977).

Tennenhouse, Leonard, *Power on Display* (London, Methuen, 1986).

Thomas, Keith, 'Women and the civil war sects' in Trevor Aston ed., *Crisis in Europe 1560–1660* (London, Routledge, 1965).

Vanita, Ruth, 'Men's power and women's resistance – wife murder in *Much Ado, Othello, Cymbeline* and *Winter's Tale* in Chatterji ed., 1986, pp. 23–39.

46

Discourse and the Individual: The Case of Colonialism in *The Tempest*

Meredith Anne Skura

For many years idealist readings of *The Tempest* presented Prospero as an exemplar of timeless human values. They emphasized the way in which his hard-earned "magical" powers enable him to re-educate the shipwrecked Italians, to heal their civil war – and, even more important, to triumph over his own vengefulness by forgiving his enemies; they emphasized the way he achieves, if not a wholly "brave," at least a harmoniously reconciled new world. Within the last few years, however, numbers of critics have offered remarkably similar critiques of this reading. There is an essay on *The Tempest* in each of three recent anthologies of alternative, political, and reproduced Shakespeare criticism, and another in the volume on estranging Renaissance criticism; *The Tempest* was a focus for the 1988 SAA session on "Shakespeare and Colonialism" and was one of the masthead plays in the Folger Institute's 1988 seminar on new directions in Shakespeare studies.[1] Together, the revisionists call for a move to counteract some "deeply ahistorical readings" of *The Tempest*,[2] a play that is now seen to be not simply an allegory about "timeless"[3] or universal experience but rather a cultural phenomenon that has its origin in and effect on "historical" events, specifically in English colonialism. "New historicist" criticism in general, of which much recent work on *The Tempest* is a part, has itself begun to come under scrutiny, but the numerous historical reinterpretations of *The Tempest* deserve closer attention in their own right,[4] and they will be the subject of the rest of this essay.

In assessing the "new" historicist version of the play, it is important to realize that here, even more than in other new historical criticism, an historical emphasis in itself is not new. Since the early nineteenth century *The Tempest* has been seen in the historical context of the New World, and Frank Kermode, citing the early scholars, argued in the fifties that reports of a particular episode in British efforts to colonize North America had precipitated the play's major themes.[5] In 1609 nine ships had left England to settle the colony in Jamestown, Virginia, and the *Sea Venture*, carrying all of the colonial officers, had disappeared. But its passengers reappeared in Virginia one year later, miraculously saved; they had wrecked off the Bermudas, until then believed demonically dangerous but now found to be providentially mild and fruitful. These events, much in the news in the year just preceding *The Tempest*, have long been seen as a relevant context for the play by all but a very few critics.[6] These earlier historical interpretations generally placed the play and its immediate source in the context of voyaging discourse in general, which stressed the romance and exoticism of discoveries in the Old as well as the New World. Even the "factual" reports in this discourse, as Charles Frey notes, were themselves colored by the romance of the situation, for better and for worse; and the traditional view was that *The Tempest*'s stylized allegory abstracts the romance core of all voyagers' experience.[7]

Nor had traditional criticism entirely ignored either Prospero's flaws[8] or their relation to the dark side of Europe's confrontation with the Other. Kermode had identified Caliban as the "core" or "ground" of the play, insofar as confrontation with this strange representative of "uncivilized" man prompts the play's re-examination of "civilized" human nature. Harry Levin, Leslie Fiedler, Leo Marx, and others had suggested that in trying to understand the New World representatives of "uncivilized" human nature, Prospero, like other Europeans, had imposed Old (and New) World stereotypes of innocence and monstrosity on the Native Americans, distorting perception with hope and fear.[9] Fiedler's landmark book had indeed placed *The Tempest* suggestively in the context of a series of plays about the Other (or, as he called it in 1972, the "Stranger") in Shakespeare, showing Caliban's resemblance to the demonized women, Moors, and Jews in the canon. O. Manoni had added that, in this process, Prospero displayed the psychology of colonials who projected their disowned traits onto New World natives.[10]

Why, then, so many recent articles? In part they are simply shifting the emphasis. Revisionists claim that the New World material is not just present but is right at the center of the play, and that it demands far more attention than critics have been willing to grant it. They argue that the civil war in Milan that had ousted Prospero should be recognized as merely an episode in a minor dispute between Italian dynasties, of little import compared to the transatlantic action;[11] they show how the love story can be seen as a political maneuver by Prospero to ensure his return to power in Milan,[12] and how even Caliban's attempted rape of Miranda can be seen as an expression not merely of sexual but also of territorial lust, understandable in its context.[13]

These recent critics are not simply repeating the older ones, however; they are making important distinctions. First and most explicitly, they are not calling attention to history in general but rather to one aspect of history: to power relations and to the ideology in which power relations are encoded.[14] The revisionists look not at the New World material in the play but to the play's effect on power relations in the New World. What matters is not just the particular Bermuda pamphlets actually echoed in the play but rather the whole "ensemble of fictional and lived practices" known as "English colonialism," which, it is now being claimed, provides the "dominant discursive contexts"[15] for the play. (Though the term "colonialism" may allude to the entire spectrum of New World activity, in these articles it most often refers specifically to the use of power, to the Europeans' exploitative and self-justifying treatment of the New World and its inhabitants – and I shall use it in that sense.) If Caliban is the center of the play, it is not because of his role in the play's self-contained structure, and not even because of what he reveals about man's timeless tendency to demonize "strangers," but because Europeans were at that time exploiting the real Calibans of the world, and *The Tempest* was part of the process. It is no longer enough to suggest that Europeans were trying to make sense of the Indian; rather, the emphasis is now on the way Europeans subdued the Indian to "make sense / order / money – not of him, so much as out of him."[16] Revisionists argue that when the English talked about these New World inhabitants, they did not just innocently apply stereotypes or project their own fears: they did so to a particular effect, whether wittingly or unwittingly. The various distortions were discursive strategies that served the political purpose of making the New World fit into a schema justifying colonialism.[17] Revisionists therefore emphasize the discursive strategies that the play shares with all colonial discourse, and the ways in which *The Tempest* itself not only displays prejudice but fosters and even "enacts" colonialism by mystifying or justifying Prospero's power over Caliban.[18] The new point is that *The Tempest* is a political act.

Second, this shift in our attitude toward the object of interpretation entails a less explicit but extremely important move away from the psychological interpretation that had previously seemed appropriate for the play (even to its detractors) largely because of its central figure who, so like Shakespeare, runs the show. Where earlier criticism of Prospero talked about his "prejudice," the more recent revisionists talk about "power" and "euphemisation." Thus, a critic writing in 1980 argued that *The Tempest*'s "allegorical and Neoplatonic overlay masks some of the most damaging prejudices of Western civilization";[19] but by 1987 the formulation had changed: "*The Tempest* is ... fully implicated in the process of 'euphemisation', the effacement of power," in "operations [that] encode struggle and contradiction even as they, or *because* they, strive to insist on the legitimacy of colonialist narrative."[20]

Psychological criticism of the play is seen as distracting at best; one recent critic, for example, opens his argument by claiming that we need to conceive *The Tempest* in an historical context that is not "hamstrung by specious speculations concerning 'Shakespeare's mind'."[21] Even in less polemical examples the "political unconscious" often replaces, rather than supplements, any other unconscious; attention to culture and politics is associated with an implicit questioning of individuality and of subjective experience. Such a stance extends beyond an objection to wholesale projections of twentieth-century assumptions onto sixteenth-century subjects, or to psychological interpretations that totally ignore the cultural context in which psyches exist. As Frederick Jameson argued in a work that lies behind many of these specific studies, it derives from the desire to transcend personal psychology altogether, because Freud's psychology remains "locked into the category of the individual subject."[22] The emphasis now is on psychology as a product of culture, itself a political structure; the very concept of a psyche is seen to be a product of the cultural nexus evolved during the Renaissance, and indeed, psychoanalysis itself, rather than being a way of understanding the Renaissance psyche, is a marginal and belated creation of this same nexus.[23] Thus the revisionists, with Jameson, may look for a "political unconscious" and make use of Freud's insights into the "logic of dreams"[24] – the concepts of displacement, condensation, the management of desire[25] – but they do not accept Freud's assumptions about the mind – or the subject – creating that logic.[26] The agent who displaces or manages is not the individual but the "collective or associative" mind; at times it seems to be the text itself, seen as a "libidinal apparatus" or "desiring machine"[27] independent of any individual creator.

The revisionist impulse has been one of the most salutary in recent years in correcting New Critical "blindness" to history and ideology. In particular it has revealed the ways in which the play has been "reproduced" and drafted into the service of colonialist politics from the nineteenth century through G. Wilson Knight's twentieth-century celebration of Prospero as representative of England's "colonizing, especially her will to raise savage peoples from superstition and blood-sacrifice, taboos and witchcraft and the attendant fears and slaveries, to a more enlightened existence."[28] But here, as critics have been suggesting about new historicism in general, it is now in danger of fostering blindness of its own. Granted that something was wrong with a commentary that focused on *The Tempest* as a self-contained project of a self-contained individual and that ignored the political situation in 1611. But something seems wrong now also, something more than the rhetorical excesses characteristic of any innovative critical movement. The recent criticism not only flattens the text into the mold of colonialist discourse and eliminates what is characteristically "Shakespearean" in order to foreground what is "colonialist," but it is also – paradoxically – in danger of taking the play further from the particular historical situation in England in 1611 even as it brings it closer to what we mean by "colonialism" today.

It is difficult to extrapolate back from G. Wilson Knight's colonialist discourse to seventeenth-century colonialist discourse without knowing more about the particulars of that earlier discourse. What is missing from the recent articles is the connection between the new insights about cultural phenomena like "power" and "fields of discourse" and the traditional insights about the text, its immediate sources, its individual author – and his individual psychology. There is little sense of how discourse is related to the individual who was creating, even as he was participating in, that discourse. The following discussion will suggest how such a relation might be conceived. Sections I and II briefly elaborate on *The Tempest*'s versions of problems raised by new historicist treatment of the text and its relation to the historical context; sections III and IV go on to suggest that the recognition of the individuality of the play, and of Shakespeare, does not counter but rather enriches the understanding of that context. Perhaps by testing individual cases, we can avoid the circularity of a definition that assumes that "colonialism" was present in a given group of texts, and so "discovers" it there.

I

How do we know that *The Tempest* "enacts" colonialism rather than merely alluding to the New World? How do we know that Caliban is part of the "discourse of colonialism"? To ask such a question may seem perversely naive, but the play is notoriously slippery. There have been, for example, any number of interpretations of Caliban,[29] including not only contemporary post-colonial versions in which Caliban is a Virginian Indian but also others in which Caliban is played as a black slave or as "missing link" (in a costume "half monkey, half coco-nut"[30]), with the interpretation drawing on the issues that were being debated at the time – on the discursive contexts that were culturally operative – and articulated according to "changing Anglo-American attitudes toward primitive man."[31] Most recently one teacher has suggested that *The Tempest* is a good play to teach in junior colleges because students can identify with Caliban.

Interpretation is made even more problematic here because, despite the claims about the play's intervention in English colonialism,[32] we have no *external* evidence that seventeenth-century audiences thought the play referred to the New World. In an age when real voyages were read allegorically, the status of allegorical voyages like Prospero's can be doubly ambiguous, especially in a play like *The Tempest*, which provides an encyclopedic context for Prospero's experience, presenting it in terms of an extraordinary range of classical, biblical, and romantic exiles, discoveries, and confrontations.[33] Evidence for the play's original reception is of course extraordinarily difficult to find, but in the two nearly contemporary responses to Caliban that we do know about, the evidence for a colonialist response is at best ambiguous. In *Bartholomew Fair* (1614) Jonson refers scornfully to a "servant-monster," and the Folio identifies Caliban as a "salvage and deformed slave"[34] in the cast list. Both "monster" and "salvage" are firmly rooted in the discourse of Old World wild men, though the latter was of course also applied to the New World natives. In other words, these two seventeenth-century responses tend to invoke the universal and not the particular implications of Caliban's condition. A recent study of the play's history suggests that "if Shakespeare, however obliquely, meant Caliban to personify America's natives, his intention apparently miscarried almost completely."[35]

Despite this lack of contemporary testimony, the obvious reason for our feeling that the play "is" colonialist – more so than *The Winter's Tale* or *Henry VIII*, for example, which were written at roughly the same time – is, of course, the literal resemblance between its plot and certain events and attitudes in English colonial history: Europeans arrive in the New World and assume they can appropriate what properly belongs to the New World Other, who is then "erased." The similarities are clear and compelling – more so than in many cases of new historical readings; the problem, however, is that while there are also many literal differences between *The Tempest* and colonialist fictions and practice, the similarities are taken to be so compelling that the differences are ignored. Thus Caliban is taken to "be" a Native American despite the fact that a multitude of details differentiate Caliban from the Indian as he appeared in the travelers' reports from the New World.[36] Yet it does seem significant that, despite his closeness to nature, his naiveté, his devil worship, his susceptibility to European liquor, and, above all, his "treachery" – characteristics associated in writings of the time with the Indians – he nonetheless lacks almost all of the defining external traits in the many reports from the New World – no superhuman physique, no nakedness or animal skin (indeed, an English "gaberdine" instead), no decorative feathers,[37] no arrows, no pipe, no tobacco, no body paint, and – as Shakespeare takes pains to emphasize – no love of trinkets and trash. No one could mistake him for the stereotyped "Indian with a great tool," mentioned in passing in *Henry VIII*. Caliban in fact is more like the devils Strachey expected to find on the Bermuda island (but didn't) than like the Indians whom adventurers did find in Virginia, though he is not wholly a monster from the explorers' wild tales either.[38]

In other ways, too, it is assumed that the similarities matter but the differences do not: thus Prospero's magic occupies "the space *really inhabited in colonial history* by gunpowder"[39] (emphasis mine); or, when Prospero has Caliban pinched by the spirits, he shows a "similar sadism" to that of the Haitian masters who "roasted slaves or buried them alive";[40] or, when Prospero and Ariel hunt Caliban with spirit dogs, they are equated to the Spaniards who hunted Native Americans with dogs.[41] So long as there is a core of resemblance, the differences are irrelevant. The differences, in fact, are themselves taken to be evidence of the colonialist ideology at work, rationalizing and euphemizing power – or else inadvertent slips. Thus the case for colonialism becomes stronger in so far as Prospero *is* good and in so far as Caliban *is* in some ways bad – he did try to rape Miranda – or is *himself* now caught trying to falsify the past by occluding the rape and presenting himself as an innocent victim of Prospero's tyranny. Prospero's goodness and Caliban's badness are called rationalizations, justifications for Prospero's tyranny. Nor does it matter that the play seems *anti*-colonialist to the degree that it qualifies Prospero's scorn by showing Caliban's virtues, or that Prospero seems to achieve some kind of transcendence over his own colonialism when at the end of the play he says, "This thing of darkness I acknowledge mine."[42] Prospero's acknowledgement of Caliban is considered a mistake, a moment of inadvertent sympathy or truth, too brief to counter Prospero's underlying colonialism: in spite of the deceptively resonant poetry of his acknowledgement, Prospero actually does nothing to live up to the meaning which that poetry suggests;[43] it has even been argued that Prospero, in calling Caliban "mine," is simply claiming possession of him: "It is as though, after a public disturbance, a slaveowner said, 'Those two men are yours; this darkie's mine.' "[44]

Nonetheless, in addition to these differences that have been seen as rationalizations, there are many other differences as well that collectively raise questions about what count as "colonialist discourse" and about what, if anything, might count as a relevant "difference." Thus, for example, any attempt to cast Prospero and Caliban as actors in the typical colonial narrative (in which a European exploits a previously free – indeed a reigning – native of an unspoiled world) is complicated by two other characters, Sycorax and Ariel. Sycorax, Caliban's mother, through whom he claims possession of the island, was not only a witch and a criminal, but she came from the Old World herself, or at least from eastern-hemisphere Argier.[45] She is a reminder that Caliban is only half-native, that his claim to the island is less like the claim of the Native American than the claim of the second generation Spaniard in the New World.[46] Moreover, Caliban was not alone when Prospero arrived. Ariel either came to the island with Sycorax or was already living on the island – its true reigning lord[47] – when Sycorax arrived and promptly enslaved him, thus herself becoming the first colonialist, the one who established the habits of dominance and erasure before Prospero ever set foot on the island. Nearly all revisionists note some of these differences before disregarding them, though they are not agreed on their significance – on whether they are "symptoms" of ideological conflict in the discourse, for example, or whether Shakespeare's "insights exceeded his sympathies."[48] But however they are explained, the differences *are* discarded. For the critic interested only in counteracting earlier blindness to potentially racist and ideological elements in the play, such ignoring of differences is understandable; for his or her purposes, it *is* enough to point out that *The Tempest* has a "political unconscious" and is connected in *some* way to colonialist discourse without specifying further.

But if the object is, rather, to understand colonialism, instead of simply identifying it or condemning it, it is important to specify, to notice how the colonial elements are rationalized or integrated into the play's vision of the world. Otherwise, extracting the play's political unconscious leads to the same problems Freud faced at the beginning of his career when he treated the personal unconscious as an independent entity that should be almost surgically extracted from conscious discourse by hypnotizing away the "defenses." But, as is well known, Freud found that the conscious "defenses" were as essential – and problematic – as the supposedly prior unconscious "wish," and that they served purposes other than containment.[49] Indeed, in most psychoanalytic practice since Freud, the unconscious – or, rather, unconscious mentation – is assumed to exist in texts rather than existing as a reified "id," and interpretation must always return to the text.

As in the case of the personal unconscious, the political unconscious exists only in texts, whose "defenses" or rationalizations must be taken into account. Otherwise interpretation not only destroys the text – here *The Tempest* – as a unique work of art and flattens it into one more example of the master plot – or master ploy – in colonialist discourse; it also destroys the evidence of the play as a unique cultural artifact, a unique voice in that discourse. Colonialist discourse was varied enough to escape any simple formulation, even in a group of texts with apparent thematic links. It ranged from the lived Spanish colonialist practice of hunting New World natives with dogs to Bartholomew Las Casas's "factual" account lamenting and exposing the viciousness of that hunt,[50] to Shakespeare's possible allusion to it in *The Tempest*, when Prospero and Ariel set spirit dogs on Caliban, to a still earlier Shakespearean allusion – or possible allusion – in the otherwise non-colonialist *A Midsummer Night's Dream*, when Puck (who has come from India himself) chases Greek rude mechanicals with illusory animals in a scene evoking an entirely English conflict. The same "colonialist" hunt informs radically different fictions and practices, some of which enact colonialism, some of which subvert it, and some of which require other categories entirely to characterize its effect.

It is not easy to categorize the several links between *The Tempest* and colonialist discourse. Take the deceptively simple example of Caliban's name. Revisionists rightly emphasize the implications of the cannibal stereotype as automatic mark of Other in Western ethnocentric colonialist discourse,[51] and, since Shakespeare's name for "Caliban" is widely accepted as an anagram of "cannibal," many read the play as if he *were* a cannibal, with all that the term implies. But an anagram is not a cannibal, and Shakespeare's use of the stereotype is hardly automatic.[52] Caliban is no cannibal – he barely touches meat, confining himself more delicately to roots, berries, and an occasional fish; indeed, his symbiotic harmony with the island's natural food resources is one of his most attractive traits. His name seems more like a mockery of stereotypes than a mark of monstrosity, and in our haste to confirm the link between "cannibal" and "Indian" outside the text, we lose track of the way in which Caliban severs the link *within* the text.[53] While no one would deny *some* relation between Caliban and the New World natives to whom such terms as "cannibal" were applied, what that relation is remains unclear.

To enumerate differences between *The Tempest* and "colonialist discourse" is not to reduce discussion of the play to a counting contest, pitting similarities against differences. Rather, it is to suggest that inherent in any analysis of the play as colonialist discourse is a particular assumption about the relation between text and discourse – between one man's fiction and a collective fiction – or, perhaps, between one man's fiction and what we take for "reality." This relation matters not only to New Critics trying to isolate texts from contexts but to new historicists (or just plain historicists) trying to put them back together. The relation is also vital to lived practices like censorship and inquisitions – and there are differences of opinion about what counts in these cases. Such differences need to be acknowledged and examined, and the method for reading them needs to be made more explicit before the implications of *The Tempest* as colonialist discourse can be fully understood.

II

Similar problems beset the definition of the "discourse" itself, the means of identifying the fictional – and the "lived" – practices constituting "English colonialism" in 1611. Given the impact of English colonialism over the last 350 years, it may again seem perversely naive to ask what colonialist discourse was like in 1611, as opposed to colonialism in 1911 or even in 1625, the year when Samuel Purchas asked, alluding to the "treachery" of the Virginian Indians, "Can a Leopard change his spots? Can a Savage remayning a Savage be civill?" Purchas added this comment when he published the 1610 document that Shakespeare had used as his source for *The Tempest*, and Purchas has been cited as an example of "colonialist discourse."[54] Purchas does indeed display the particular combination of exploitative motives and self-justifying rhetoric – the "effacement of power"[55] – that revisionists identify as colonialist and which they find in *The Tempest*. But, one might reasonably ask, was the discursive context in 1611, when Shakespeare was writing, the same as it would be fourteen years later, when Purchas added his marginal comment?[56]

There seems, rather, to have been in 1611 a variety of what we might call "New World discourses" with multiple points of view, motives, and effects, among which such comments as Purchas's are not as common as the revisionist emphasis implies. These are "colonialist" only in the most general sense in which all ethnocentric cultures are always "colonialist": narcissistically pursuing their own ends, oblivious to the desires, needs, and even the existence of the Other. That is, if this New World discourse is colonialist, it is so primarily in that it *ignores* Indians, betraying its Eurocentric assumptions about the irrelevance of any people other than white, male, upper-class Europeans, preferably from England. It thus expresses not an historically specific but a *timeless* and universal attitude toward the "stranger," which Fiedler described in so many of Shakespeare's plays. We might see this discourse as a precondition[57] for colonialism proper, which was to follow with the literal rather than the figurative colonizing of New World natives. But to assume that colonialism was already encoded in the anomalous situation in 1611 is to undermine the revisionist effort to understand the historical specificity of the moment when Shakespeare wrote *The Tempest*.

It is not easy to characterize the situation in 1611. On the one hand, Spain had long been engaged in the sort of "colonialist discourse" that revisionists find in *The Tempest*; and even in England at the time there were examples of colonialist discourse (in the rhetoric, if not yet often in the lived practices) produced by those directly involved in the colonialist project and expecting to profit from it. The official advertisements in the first rush of enthusiasm about Virginia, as well as the stream of defenses when the Virginia project began to fail, often have a euphemistic ring and often do suggest a fundamental greed and implicit racism beneath claims to be securing the earthly and spiritual well-being of the Virginia natives.[58] ("[We] doe buy of them the pearles of earth, and sell to them the pearles of heauen.")[59] These documents efface not only power but most practical problems as well, and they were supplemented by sermons romanticizing hardships as divine tribulation.[60] Scattered throughout this discourse are righteous defenses of taking land from the Indians, much in the spirit – and tone – of Rabbi Zeal-of-the-Land Busy defending his need to eat pig. (This was also the tone familiar from the anti-theatrical critics – and, indeed, occasional colonialist sermons included snipes at the "Plaiers," along with the Devil and the papists, as particular enemies of the Virginia venture.)[61]

On the other hand, even in these documents not only is the emphasis elsewhere but often there are important contradictory movements. For example, "A True Declaration," the official record of the Bermuda wreck, refers once to the Indians as "humane beasts" and devotes one paragraph of its twenty-four pages to the "greedy Vulture" Powhattan and his ambush. It notes elsewhere, however, that some of the English settlers themselves had "created the *Indians* our implacable enemies by some violence they had offered," and it actually spends far more time attacking the lazy "scum of men" among the settlers, who had undermined the colony from within, than demonizing the less relevant Indians.[62]

And on the whole, the exploitative and self-justifying rhetoric is only one element in a complex New World discourse. For much of the time, in fact, the main conflict in the New World was not between whites and Native Americans but between Spain and England. Voyages like Drake's (1577–80) were motivated by this international conflict, as well as by the romance of discovery and the lure of treasure – but not by colonizing.[63] Even when Raleigh received the first patent to settle and trade with the New World (1584), necessitating more extended contact with Native Americans, the temporary settlements he started in the 1580s were largely tokens in his play for fame and wealth rather than attempts to take over sizable portions of land from the natives.[64]

Only when the war with Spain was over (1604) and ships were free again did colonization really begin; and then "America and Virginia were on everyone's lips."[65] But this New World discourse still reflects little interest in its inhabitants. Other issues are much more widely discussed. For example, what would the New World government be like? Would James try to extend his authoritarianism to America? *Could* he? This was the issue, for example, most energizing Henry Wriothesley, Shakespeare's Southampton, who led the "Patriot" faction on the London Virginia Council, pushing for more American independence.[66] (As for James's own "colonial discourse," it seems to have been devoted to worries about how it would all affect his relations with Spain,[67] and to requests for flying squirrels and other New World "toyes.")[68] Of more immediate interest, perhaps, to the mass of real or armchair adventurers were the reports of

New World wealth that at first made Virginia known as a haven for bankrupts and spendthrifts, as well as for wild dreamers – followed by the accounts of starvation, rebellion, and hardship brought back by those who had escaped from the reality of colonial existence. Now the issue became "Is it worth it?" The official propaganda, optimistic about future profits, was soon countered by a backlash from less optimistic scoffers challenging the value of the entire project, one which sent money, men, and ships to frequent destruction and brought back almost no profit.[69]

Even the settlers actually living with the natives in the New World itself were – for entirely non-altruistic reasons – not yet fully engaged in "colonialist" discourse as defined by revisionists. In 1611 they had not managed to establish enough power to euphemize; they had little to be defensive about. They were too busy fighting mutiny, disease, and the stupidities of the London Council to have much energy left over for Indians. It is true that no writer ever treated Native Americans as equals – any more than he treated Moors, Jews, Catholics, peasants, women, Irishmen, or even Frenchmen as equals; travellers complacently recorded kidnapping natives to exhibit in England, as if the natives had no rights at all.[70] And it is true that some of their descriptions are distorted by Old World stereotypes of wild men or cannibals – though these descriptions are often confined to earlier *pre*-colonial explorers' reports.[71] Or, far more insidiously, the descriptions were distorted by stereotypes of unfallen innocent noble savages – stereotypes that inevitably led to disillusionment when the settlers had to realize that the Indians, like the land itself, were not going to fulfill their dreams of a golden world made expressly to nurture Englishmen. The "noble savage" stereotype thus fueled the recurring accusation of Indian treachery, a response to betrayal of settlers' fantasies as well as to any real Indian betrayal,[72] and one to which I will return in discussing *The Tempest*.

But, given the universality of racial prejudice towards New World natives along with all "Others," in this early period the movement was to loosen, not to consolidate, the prejudices brought from the Old World. The descriptions of these extended face-to-face encounters with Native Americans were perhaps even more varied than contemporary responses to Moors and Jews, who were usually encountered on the white man's own territory, where exposure could be limited and controlled. The very terms imported from the Old World to name the natives – "savages" or "naturals" – began to lose their original connotations as the differing descriptions multiplied and even contradicted themselves. The reports range from Harriot's widely republished attempt at scientific, objective reporting (1588), which viewed natives with great respect, to Smith's less reliable adventure stories (1608–31), disputed even in his own time by Purchas. And although these do not by any means live up to our standards for non-colonialist discourse, their typical attitude is a wary, often patronizing, but live-and-let-live curiosity, rather than the exploitative erasure which would later become the mark of colonialist discourse. So long as the conflicts remained minimal, Native Americans were seen as beings like the writers;[73] further, tribes were distinguished from one another, and recognition was granted to their different forms of government, class structure, dress codes, religion, and language.[74] And when conflict did trigger the recurring accusation of "treachery," the writers never presented the Indians as laughable Calibans, but rather as capable, indeed formidable, enemies whose skill and intelligence challenged that of the settlers.

Horrors had already been perpetrated by the Spanish in the name of colonialism; not learning from these – or perhaps learning all too well – the English would soon begin perpetrating their own. But that lay in the future. When *The Tempest* was written, what the New World seems to have meant for the majority of Englishmen was a sense of possibility and a set of conflicting fantasies about the wonders to be found there; these were perhaps the preconditions for colonialism – as for much else – but not yet the thing itself.

To place colonialist discourse as precisely as possible within a given moment (like stressing the differences between *The Tempest* and colonialist discourse) is not to reduce the discussion to a numbers game. What is at stake here is not a quibble about chronology but an assumption about what we mean by the "relevant discursive context," about how we agree to determine it, and about how we decide to limit it. Here too there are differences of opinion about what counts, and these differences need to be acknowledged, examined, and accounted for.

III

My point in specifying Shakespeare's precise literal and temporal relation to colonialist discourse – in specifying the unique mind through which the discourse is mediated – is not to deny that the play has *any* relation to its context but to suggest that the relation is problematic. In the effort to identify Caliban as one more colonialist representation of the Other, we fail to notice how remarkable it is that such a Caliban should exist. In 1611 there were in England no literary portrayals of New World inhabitants and certainly no fictional examples of colonialist discourse.[75] In so far as *The Tempest* does in some way allude to an encounter with a New World native (and I will for the remainder of this essay accept this premise), it is the very first work of literature to do so. There may be Indians, more or less demonized, in the nonliterary discourse. Outside of Shakespeare, however, there would be none in literature until two years after *The Tempest*, when they began to appear – feathers and all – in masques.[76] And Shakespeare went out of his way to invent Caliban: Strachey's account of the wreck on the uninhabited Bermuda islands – Shakespeare's main New World source – contains, of course, no island natives.[77] For these Shakespeare had to turn elsewhere in Strachey and in others who described the mainland colony in Virginia. Shakespeare was the first to show one of *us* mistreating a native, the first to represent a native from the inside, the first to allow a native to complain onstage, and the first to make that New World encounter problematic enough to generate the current attention to the play.

To argue for Shakespeare's uniqueness is not to argue that as fiction *The Tempest* is above politics, or that as a writer of fiction Shakespeare transcended ideology. It does imply, however, that if the play is "colonialist," it must be seen as "prophetic" rather than descriptive.[78] As such, the play's status immediately raises important questions. Why was Shakespeare – a man who had no direct stake in colonization – the first writer of fiction to portray New World inhabitants? Why then? Shakespeare had shown no signs of interest in the New World until *The Tempest*, despite the fact that there had been some colonial activity and some colonialist rhetoric for several years among those who did have a stake in it. How did the colonialist phenomenon spread?

To hasten over Shakespeare's relation to colonialism as if it were not a question but a conclusion is to lose one of the most important bits of data we may ever have about how such things as colonialism – and discourse – work. Problematic as it may be to speculate about an individual mind, it is even more problematic to speculate about the discourse of an entire nation or an entire period. One way to give substance to such large generalizations is to trace, in as much detail as may be available, the particulars on which they are based. Here the particulars include the individuals who produced, as well as reproduced, the larger cultural discourse – especially individuals like Shakespeare, who, more than almost any other, both absorbed and shaped the various conflicting discourses of the period.

To do this, as I have been arguing, it is necessary to consider the entire play, without deciding prematurely what is "only a distortion" or "only an irrelevance." In addition, however, we must also look to a context for *The Tempest* that is as relevant as colonialist discourse and perhaps even more essential to the presence of colonialism in *The Tempest* in the first place – that is, to the context of Shakespeare's own earlier "discourse." Only then can we see how the two fields of discourse intersect. In making use of the New World vocabulary and imagery, Shakespeare was in part describing something much closer to home – as was Jonson when he called the London brothel district "the Bermudas,"[79] or as would Donne when he found his America, his "new founde land," in the arms of his mistress. Or as was Dudley Carleton in a gossipy letter from London about Lord Salisbury enduring a "tempest" of reproof from a lady; or Sir Ralph Winwood in trying to "begin a new world by setting himself and his wife here at home."[80]

Long before writing *The Tempest*, Shakespeare had written another play about a ruler who preferred his books to government. Navarre's academy in *Love's Labor's Lost* was no island, but, like an island, it was supposed to be isolated from territorial negotiations. And Navarre, oblivious to colonial issues, though certainly not exempt from timeless aristocratic prejudice, brought his own version of Ariel and Caliban by inviting Armado and Costard to join him. Like Prospero, he asked his "Ariel" to make a pageant for him, and he imprisoned his "Caliban" for trying to "do" a wench. His relation to the two is not a matter of colonization but rather of condescension and ironic recognition, as Navarre is forced to see something of himself in the conflict between fiery Armado's over-active imagination and earthy Costard's lust.[81] Only much later did this pattern come to be "colonial."

The Tempest is linked in many other ways not only to *Love's Labor's Lost* but also to the rest of the canon, as continued efforts of critics have shown,[82] and it is revealing to see how, in each case, the non-colonial structures become associated with colonialist discourse. Indeed, the very details of *The Tempest* that revisionists see as marking the "nodal point of the play's imbrication into this discourse of colonialism"[83] are reworkings of similar moments in earlier and seemingly precolonial plays. The moment I will focus on for the rest of this paper is the one that many revisionists take as the strongest evidence in the play for the falseness of Prospero's position – the moment when the hidden colonialist project emerges openly,[84] when the "political unconscious" is exposed.[85] It occurs when Caliban's plot interrupts the pageant Prospero is staging for Ferdinand and Miranda, and Prospero is so enraged that Miranda says she has never seen him so angry. The explanation, it has been suggested, is that if psychology matters at all, Prospero's anger here, like his anger earlier when Caliban tried to rape Miranda, derives from the politics of colonialism. It reveals Prospero's political "disquiet at the irruption into consciousness of an unconscious anxiety concerning the grounding of his legitimacy" on the island.[86]

But the dramatic context counters the assumption that politics is primary in this episode. Like Caliban, Prospero differs in significant ways from the stereotyped "real life" characters in colonial political drama. Unlike the single-minded colonial invader, Prospero is both an exile and a father; and the action of the play is initiated when both these roles are newly activated by the arrival of Prospero's old enemies, those who had exiled him as well as his daughter's husband-to-be. At the moment of Prospero's eruption into anger, he has just bestowed Miranda on his enemy's son Ferdinand[87] and is in the midst of presenting his pageant as a wedding gift, wrapped in a three-fold warning about chastity.[88] If Prospero is to pass on his heritage to the next generation, he must at this moment repress his desire for power and for revenge at home, as well as any sexual desire he feels toward Miranda.[89] Both desires are easily projected onto the fishily phallic Caliban, a walking version of Prospero's own "thing" of darkness. Not only has Caliban already tried to rape Miranda; he is now out to kill Prospero so that he can turn Miranda over to Stephano ("she will give thee brave brood"); and Caliban does not even feel guilty. Caliban's function as a walking screen for projection may help explain why Caliban's sin does not consist in cannibalism, to which, one assumes, Prospero was never tempted, but rather in Prospero's own repressed fantasies of omnipotence and lust.[90] Of course Prospero is also angry that Caliban is now threatening both his authority on the island and his justification of that authority; but the extraordinary intensity of Prospero's rage suggests a conjunction of psychological as well as political passion.

This conjunction of the psychological and the political not only appears here in *The Tempest* but also characterizes a surprising number of Prospero-like characters in Shakespeare's earlier plays who provide a suggestive context for *The Tempest*. All through the canon one finds characters who escape from active lives to some kind of pastoral retreat, who step aside from power and aggression – and usually from sexuality as well – and from all the forbidden fantasies in which these are enacted. But while each adopts a disinterested stance, as if having retired behind the scenes, each sees life as a play and manipulates others still on stage in a way that suggests a fascination with what he has rejected and assigned to the "Others." And each of these has his "Caliban" and his moment of sudden, irrational anger when his "Caliban" threatens to overstep the limits defining him as "other" and separating him from "Prospero." At this moment of confrontation, boundaries threaten to disappear and hierarchies are menaced. And in each of the earlier plays, this moment is indicative of inner conflict, as the earlier "Prospero" figure confronts someone who often has neither property nor power to colonize, and whose threat is largely symbolic. In all these plays Shakespeare is dealing not just with power relations but also with the psychology of domination, with the complicated ways in which personal psychology interacts with political power.

As early as the mid-1590s, two figures show some resemblance to Prospero. Antonio, the merchant of Venice, sees the world as "A stage where every man must play a part, / And mine a sad one" (I.i.78–9). Almost eagerly accepting his passive lot, he claims to renounce both profit and love. But, as Marianne Novy suggests, a repressed self-assertion is hinted at in the passive / aggressive claims he makes on Bassanio and comes out clearly when he lashes out at the greedy and self-assertive Shylock with a viciousness like Prospero's towards Caliban, a viciousness he shows nowhere else.[91] He admits calling the Jew a dog and says,

> I am as like to call thee so again,
> To spet on thee again ...
> (I.iii.130–1)[92]

A related and similarly problematic exchange occurs in the *Henry IV* plays, written a year or so later, where role-playing Prince Hal, during his temporary retreat from power, had found a version of pastoral in Falstaff's tavern. After reclaiming his throne, when he finds that Falstaff has also come from the tavern to claim a role in the new kingdom, Hal suddenly repudiates Falstaff with a cruelty as cold as Prospero's anger at Caliban – and equally excessive: "I know thee not, old man." In both these cases, though the resemblance to Prospero is clear, the relation to an historically specific colonialism is hard to establish.

Then in *As You Like It* (1599) and *Measure for Measure* (1604) come the two exiled or self-exiled Dukes who leave home – one to "usurp" the deer in the forest (II.i.21–8), the other to "usurp" the beggary in the Vienna streets (III.ii.93) – and who most resemble Prospero. Duke Senior in *As You Like It* is banished to the pastoral forest of Arden, where he professes himself utterly content to live a life notable for the absence of both power and women (a "woeful pageant," he calls it cheerfully [II.vii.138]). He is saved from having to fight for power when his evil brother (unlike the one in Shakespeare's source) conveniently repents and hands back the dukedom; but an ambivalence about sexuality is at least suggested when this mildest of men lashes out at Jaques, precisely when Jaques returns from melancholy withdrawal and claims the fool's license to satirize society's ills – to "cleanse the foul body of the infected world."[93] "Fie on thee!" says the Duke,

> ... thou thyself hast been a libertine,
> As sensual as the brutish sting itself,
> And all th' embossed sores, and headed evils,
> That thou with license of free foot hast caught,
> Wouldst thou disgorge into the general world.
> (II.vii.65–9)

Jaques seems to have touched a nerve. Elsewhere Jaques makes a claim on behalf of the deer in the forest rather like the claim Caliban makes for himself on the island, complaining that Duke Senior has "usurped" these "velvet friends"; he even makes it "most invectively," having, like Caliban, learned how to curse. Just as in the case of Caliban, we cannot laugh away the claim the way the Duke does. But Jaques's complaint seems intended more as an insight into the Duke than a comment on the deer – whom Jaques later kills anyway.

The touchiest of these precursors, Vincentio in *Measure for Measure* (1604), is the one who most closely resembles Prospero. He too prefers study to government, and he turns over his power to Angelo, claiming "[I] do not like to stage me to their eyes" (I.i.68) – but then he steps behind the scenes to manipulate the action. Like Prospero, Vincentio sees his manipulation as an altruistic means of educating his wayward subjects into chastity, repentance, and merciful mildness; but it seems to serve more private needs of self-definition as well. For it first allows him, as "ghostly father," to deny any aggressive or sexual motives of his own, and then allows him to return at the end to claim both power and sexual rewards as he resumes his dukedom and claims Isabel.[94] Vincentio's "Caliban" is the libidinous and loose-tongued Lucio, who not only indulges his own appetites but openly accuses the Duke of indulging his, so that it is unusually clear in this case that the "Caliban" figure is a representation of the Duke's own disowned passions. Lucio's slanders include the claim that the Duke has "usurp[ed] the beggary he was never born to," but, like Jaques speaking for the deer, he is more concerned with revealing the Duke's contradictory desires here than with defending beggars' rights. Goaded by Lucio's insubordination, the Duke lashes out at him as he does at no one else and threatens a punishment much worse than the one he assigned to the would-be rapist and murderer Angelo or to the actual murderer Barnardine.

In the case of all of these "Prosperos," it is hard to see the attack on "Caliban" as part of a specifically colonialist strategy, as a way of exploiting the Other or of rationalizing illegitimate power over him rather than over what he represents in "Prospero" himself. To a logical observer, the Prospero-attack seems at best gratuitous – and the more frightening for being so. It has no political rationale. The "political" attack always takes place outside the play's old world, after the characters' withdrawal to a second world that is not so much a new world as one that projects, exaggerates, turns upside down, or polarizes the conflicts that made the old world uninhabitable. In the case of each earlier "Prospero," the conflicts seem internal as well as external, so that when he moves out to meet his "Caliban," he is always meeting himself. Political exile is also presented as self-estrangement, a crisis of selfhood expressed in social and geographical divisions. And in each case, Shakespeare exposes the fragility of such arrangements, whether they take the form of the pastoralization of the forest of Arden, or of the scapegoating of Shylock in Venice, or of Falstaff's carnival misrule in the tavern, or of the theatricalizing of the prison in Vincentio's Vienna, or of Prospero's "colonizing" of a utopian island.

Whatever varying political role each earlier "Caliban" plays as inhabitant of his second – or second-class – world, each seems to embody a similar psychological quality. In each case he displays the overt self-assertion that the retired or retiring "Prospero" cannot – or wishes not to – muster for himself, and that for Shakespeare seems to be the mark of the Other. Each is an epitome of what Shakespeare (perhaps in his own punning ambivalence about acknowledging it as his own) elsewhere calls "will."[95] This "will" includes a range of forbidden desires and appetites often attributed to the Other and always associated with the "foul body," as Jaques calls it; or with the fat appetitive body, as in Hal's picture of Falstaff; or with the body as mere pounds of flesh and blood; perhaps with what we might call, after Bakhtin, the "grotesque" body. And it is defined in opposition to the ethereal, or ariel, virtues such as "mercy," "honor," and "chastity" characterizing the various "Prosperos."

The "will" of these "Calibans" can carry suggestions of primitive oral greed, as in Shylock's desire to "feed fat" his revenge with a pound of human flesh, in Falstaff's voracious appetite, or in Caliban's name. Or it emerges in a rampant sexual greed, as in Falstaff, in Jaques's past, in Lucio, perhaps even in Shylock's reproductive miracles with sheep, and of course in Caliban himself. But the most alien aspect of self-assertion or "will" in these plays emerges in a primitive vengefulness. This vengefulness is associated with an infantile need to control and dominate and with the scatological imagery of filth – with a disgust at the whole messy, physical world that always threatens to get out of control. Thus Shylock's drive for revenge is linked to his Jonsonian "anal" virtues ("fast bind, fast find"), to his fecal gold, and to his tightly locked orifices ("stop my house's ears, I mean my casements" [ii.v.34]). Thus, too, Duke Senior's description of Jaques "disgorging" his "embossed sores" suggests that he is projecting onto Jaques his disgust at the idea of "the foul body of the infected world" – and his fear that Jaques will "disgorge" and overflow his boundaries rather than cleanse; Jaques's very name associates him with this scatological vision. Caliban, very much concerned with revenge, also takes on a taint of anality through the words of Trinculo and Stephano. The latter sees Caliban hiding under his gabardine with Trinculo and takes Caliban for a monster whose first act is to "vent" a Trinculo – a Gargantuan act of defecation; Trinculo elsewhere complains that Caliban led them to a "foul lake" that o'erstunk their feet till they smelled "all horse-piss."[96]

Thus, although Caliban is like the New World natives in his "otherness," he is linked at least as closely to Shakespeare's earlier "Calibans." What is interesting in any attempt to understand *The Tempest*'s uniqueness in other aspects is that in Caliban for the first time Shakespeare shows "will," or narcissistic self-assertion, in its purest and simplest form as the original "grandiosity" or "megalomania" of a child;[97] for the first time he makes the representative of bodily existence a seeming child whose ego is a "body ego," as Freud said, a "subject" whose "self" is defined by the body. There is a childishly amoral – and almost asexual – glee in Caliban's sexuality ("O ho, O ho, would't had been done!" he says of the attempted rape [i.ii.349]) and a childish exaggeration in his dreams of revenge ("brain him / … or with a log / Batter his skull, or paunch him with a stake, / Or cut his wezand with thy knife" [iii.ii.88–91]).[98] Like a child he thinks often about his mother,[99] and now that she is gone, he dreams of riches dropping from heaven and cries to dream again; like a child he was taught language and shown the man in the moon.[100] And like an imperious child he is enraged when his pie in the sky does not appear. If he rebukes Prospero for first stroking and then disciplining him, if he objects to being made a subject when he was "mine own king" (i.ii.342), this is the rebuke made by every child, who begins life as "His Majesty the Baby," tended by his mother, and who is then subjected to the demands of the community,[101] represented by the father. Childhood is the period in which anyone – even the most powerful Elizabethan aristocrat – can experience the slave's side of the master / slave relation, its indignities, and the dreams of reversal and revenge it can imbue. Appropriate and acceptable in a baby, all these traits (like Caliban himself) "with age [grow] uglier" (iv.i.191) – and far more dangerous.

Caliban's childishness has been dismissed as a defense, another rationalization of Prospero's illegitimate power.[102] But if it is a defense, it is one which itself is revealing. Caliban's childishness is a dimension of the Other in which Shakespeare seems extremely interested.[103] It is a major (not peripheral) source both of Caliban's defining characteristics and of what makes his relation to Prospero so highly charged. Caliban's childish innocence seems to have been what first attracted Prospero, and now it is Caliban's childish lawlessness that enrages him. To a man like Prospero, whose life has been spent learning a self-discipline in which he is not yet totally adept, Caliban can seem like a child who must be controlled, and who, like a child, is murderously enraged at being controlled. Prospero treats Caliban as he would treat the willful child in himself.

The importance of childishness in defining Caliban is suggested by the final *Tempest* precedent to be cited here, one that lies behind Prospero's acknowledgement of Caliban as his own thing of darkness – and in which the Caliban figure is literally a child. This figure is found in *Titus Andronicus*, where a bastard child, called "devil" and "slave," is cast out by his mother but rescued by his father, who promises – in language foreshadowing Caliban's imagery in *The Tempest* – to raise him in a cave and feed him on berries and roots.[104] Here the father is black Aaron the Moor, and the childish thing of darkness, whom Aaron is at some pains to acknowledge his, is his own literally black son. What is remarkable about this portrait of a barbarian father and son is that Aaron's is the only uncomplicated parental love in a play-world where civilized white men like Titus kill their own children on principle. It is a world, by the way, which contains the only literal (if unwitting) cannibal in Shakespeare's plays, the child's white mother. Unlike Titus, Aaron can love his child because he can identify with him; as an "uncivilized" black man, he can accept the greedy, sensual, lawless child in himself: "This is myself, the vigor and the picture of my youth," he says (IV.ii.108). This love, which comes easily to Aaron in acknowledging his own flesh and blood, is transformed in *The Tempest* to Prospero's strained and difficult recognition of a tribal Other whose blackness nonetheless figures his own.

The echoes of Aaron not only suggest the family resemblance between Prospero and Caliban. They also suggest that here Shakespeare is changing his earlier vision of authority. In the earlier play it is white Titus who – like Prospero – gives away his power and is betrayed; but it is black Aaron who is stigmatized as the vengeful villain. And Titus maintains this black-and-white distinction even while savagely carrying out his own revenge. But distinctions in *The Tempest* have become less rigid. By merging his fantasy about a "white" (but exiled and neurotically puritanical) duke with his fantasy about a villainous (but loving) "black" father, Shakespeare for the first time shows, in Prospero, a paternal leader who comes back to power by admitting rather than denying the "blackness" in himself. Prospero may not, as several revisionists point out, physically *do* much for Caliban at the end; however, what he *says* matters a great deal indeed, for his original transgression, when he first defined Caliban as the Other, was intellectual as well as physical. When Prospero finally acknowledges Caliban, although he is a long way from recognizing the equality of racial "others," he comes closer than any of Shakespeare's other "Prosperos" to acknowledging the otherness within, which helps generate all racism – and he comes closer than anyone else in colonialist discourse. Prospero acknowledges the child-like Caliban as his own, and although he does not thus undo hierarchy, he moves for the first time towards accepting the child in himself rather than trying to dominate and erase that child (along with random vulnerable human beings outside himself) in order to establish his adult authority.

Thus, although Shakespeare may, as the revisionists claim, to some degree reproduce Prospero's colonialist vision of the island, the play's emphasis lies not so much in justifying as in analyzing that vision, just as Shakespeare had analyzed the origins of dominance in the earlier plays. The play insists that we see Prospero's current relation to Caliban in terms of Prospero's own past; it contains the "colonial" encounter firmly within the framing story of his own family history. And though that history does not extend backward to Prospero's own childhood, it does begin with family ties and Miranda's memory of "the dark backward and abysm of time" (I.ii.50), before either she or Prospero had known the Other. Prospero was then, he thought, in total harmony with his world and himself, happy in his regressive retreat to his library-Eden; he was buffered from reality, he thought, by a "lov'd" brother so linked to himself and his own desires that Prospero had in him a trust with no "limit, / A confidence sans bound" (I.ii.96–7), like the trust that Miranda must have had in the women who "tended" her then. Only when Antonio's betrayal shattered that trust and Prospero was ousted from Eden – newly aware of both the brother as Other and of himself as a willful self in opposition – did he "discover" the island and Caliban. In a sense, then, Caliban emerged from the rift between Prospero and Antonio,[105] just as Ariel emerged from Sycorax's riven pine. Once the brother has shown that he is not identical to the self, reflecting back its own narcissistic desire, then he becomes the Other – and simultaneously rouses the vengeful Other in the self. In *The Tempest* the distance that a "colonialist" Prospero imposes between self and Other originated in a recoil from the closest relation of all; it was a recoil that in fact *defined* both the "distant" and the "close," the public and the private – the political and the personal – as separate realms. When Prospero acknowledges Caliban, he thus partly defuses an entire dynamic that began long before he had ever seen the island.

IV

When Shakespeare created a childish "Caliban," he was himself rounding out a dynamic process that had begun as long ago as the writing of *Titus Andronicus*. We will never "know" why Shakespeare gave to this final version of his exile story a local habitation incorporating aspects of colonialist discourse. But the answer lies not only in that discourse but also in him and in what was on his mind. Some of the most "specious" speculations about Shakespeare's mind have been stimulated by his presumed resemblance to Prospero at the end of the play: past his zenith, on the way to retirement, every third thought turned to his grave. Without trying speciously to read minds, however, it seems safe to say that to some degree Shakespeare had been for several years concerned with the aging, loss, mortality, and death that recur in so much of what we know he was writing and reading at the time. To this degree, both the play and its context deal with the end of the individual self, the subject and the body in which it is located. It is the end of everything associated with the discovery of self in childhood, the end of everything Caliban represents – and thus the greatest threat to infantile narcissism since His Majesty the Baby was first de-throned. John Bender has noted that the occasion of the play's presumed court debut in 1611 was Hallowmas, the feast of winter and the time of seasonal celebrations figuring the more final endings and death associated with winter.[106] As part of the celebrations, Bender suggests, the play might have served to structure a communal response to the recurring "seasonal mentality" brought on by the reminder of mortality. Whether or not this is true, that which "recurs" in seasons and communities comes only once to individuals; and as the final stage in Shakespeare's own "seasonal" movement from *A Midsummer Night's Dream* to *The Winter's Tale*, the play can be seen as staging a final "crisis of selfhood" and of betrayal like those in the earlier exile plays – but this time a far more extreme one.[107] For those who rage against the dying of the light, it is a crisis that awakens the old infantile narcissistic demand for endless fulfillment and the narcissistic rage and vengefulness against a world that denies such satisfactions.[108]

To one on the threshold of retirement from the Old World, the New World is an appropriate stage on which to enact this last resurgence of the infantile self. We take for granted the historical conditions generating utopian visions in the voyagers' reports outside the play. What the example of Caliban's childish presence in the play suggests is that for Shakespeare the desire for such utopias – the golden worlds and fountains of youth – has roots in personal history as well as in "history." The desire has been shaped by the most local as well as by the largest, collective, material constraints: by being born small and weak in a world run by large, strong people with problems of their own; by being born in "a sexed and mortal body"[109] that must somehow become part of a social and linguistic community. Caliban's utopia of sweet voices and clouds dropping riches (iii.ii.137–43) draws most directly on the infantile substratum that colored Columbus's report when he returned from his third voyage convinced "that the newly discovered hemisphere was shaped like a woman's breast, and that the Earthly Paradise was located at a high point corresponding to the nipple."[110] But the play's other "utopias" draw on it too. Gonzalo's utopia is more socialized ("nature should bring forth, / ... all abundance, / To feed my innocent people" [ii.i.163–5]); Prospero's pageant utopia is more mythic (a world without winter, blessed by nurturing Ceres); but, like Caliban's, their utopias recreate a union with a bounteous Mother Nature. And, like every child's utopia, each is a fragile creation, easily destroyed by the rage and violence that constitute its defining alternative – a dystopia of murderous vengeance; the interruption of Prospero's pageant is only the last in a series of such interruptions.[111] Each is the creation of a childish mind that operates in binary divisions: good mother / bad mother, love / rage, brother / Other.

That Shakespeare was drawn to the utopian aspects of the New World is suggested by the particular fragment of New World discourse that most directly precipitated (Kermode's suggestive term) the play – the Bermuda pamphlets, which record what was "perhaps the most romantic incident associated with America's beginnings."[112] What attracted Shakespeare, that is, was the story in which a "merciful God," a loving and fatherly protector, rescued a whole shipload of people from certain death; it was a story that countered thoughts of winter with reports of magical bounty in the aptly named "Summer Islands."

The concerns that made Shakespeare's approach to colonialist discourse possible may have been operative later in other cases as well. In analyzing the colonialist discourse growing out of political motives, it is important not to lose touch with the utopian discourse growing out of a different set of motives. Without reducing colonialism to "the merely subjective and to the status of psychological projection,"[113] one can still take account of fantasies and motives that, though now regarded as secondary, or as irrelevant to politics, may interact with political motives in ways we have not yet begun to understand – and cannot understand so long as we are diverted by trying to reduce psychology to politics or politics to psychology. The binary dynamics of infantile utopian fantasies can, for example, help explain why frustrated settlers succumbed *so easily* to the twin stereotypes of the Native Americans as innocent primitives who would welcome and nurture the settlers, and as hopelessly treacherous Others. They can serve as a reminder that the desire for friendship and brotherhood can be as destructive as a desire to exploit. Reference to irrational, outdated infantile needs can help explain why the settlers, once they actually did begin colonizing, set out with such gratuitous thoroughness to "reduce" the savage to civility. As James Axtell describes the process, "In European eyes, no native characteristic was too small to reform, no habit too harmless to reduce."[114] Such behavior seems to go beyond any immediate political or material motive and seems rather to serve more general psychological needs stirred up by conflict with the natives. The recent emphasis on the colonists' obvious material greed and rational self-interest – or class-interest – has unnecessarily obscured the role of these less obvious irrational motives and fantasies that are potentially even more insidious.

Shakespeare's assimilation of elements from historical colonialist discourse was neither entirely isolated from other uses or innocent of their effects. Nonetheless, the "colonialism" in his play is linked not only to Shakespeare's indirect participation in an ideology of political exploitation and erasure but also to his direct participation in the psychological after-effects of having experienced the exploitation and erasure inevitable in being a child in an adult's world. He was not merely reproducing a pre-existent discourse; he was also crossing it with other discourses, changing, enlarging, skewing, and questioning it. Our sense of *The Tempest*'s participation in "colonialist discourse" should be flexible enough to take account of such crossings; indeed our notion of that in which such discourse consisted should be flexible enough to include the whole of the text that constitutes the first English example of fictional colonialist discourse.[115]

Notes

1 Two of the earliest of these critiques were actually written, although not published, by 1960: George Lamming, "A monster, a child, a slave" (1960) in *The Pleasures of Exile* (London: Allison and Busby, 1984); James Smith, "The Tempest" (1954) in *Shakespearian and Other Essays*, ed. E. M. Wilson (Cambridge: Cambridge University Press, 1974), pp. 159–261. Two more articles, less politicized, followed in the sixties: Philip Brockbank, "*The Tempest*: Conventions of Art and Empire" in *Later Shakespeare*, eds. J. R. Brown and B. Harris (London: Edward Arnold, 1966), pp. 183–201; and D. G. James, "The New World" in *The Dream of Prospero* (Oxford: Clarendon Press, 1967), pp. 72–123.

  The recent group, returning to the political perspective of the first two, includes: Stephen Greenblatt, "Learning to Curse: Aspects of Linguistic Colonialism in the Sixteenth Century" in *First Images of America*, ed. Fredi Chiappelli, 2 vols. (Los Angeles: University of California Press, 1976), Vol. 2, 561–80; Bruce Erlich, "Shakespeare's Colonial Metaphor: On the Social Function of Theatre in *The Tempest*," *Science and Society*, 41 (1977), 43–65; Lorie Leininger, "Cracking the Code of *The Tempest*," *Bucknell Review*, 25 (1980), 121–31; Peter Hulme, "Hurricanes in the Caribbees: The

Constitution of the Discourse of English Colonialism" in *1642: Literature and Power in the Seventeenth Century*, Proceedings of the Essex conference on the Sociology of Literature, eds. Francis Barker et al. (Colchester: University of Essex, 1981), pp. 55–83; Paul N. Siegel, "Historical Ironies in *The Tempest*," *Shakespeare Jahrbuch*, 119 (Weimar: 1983), 104–11; Francis Barker and Peter Hulme, "Nymphs and reapers heavily vanish: the discursive con-texts of *The Tempest*" in *Alternative Shakespeares*, ed. John Drakakis (London and New York: Methuen, 1985), pp. 191–205; Terence Hawkes, "Swisser-Swatter: making a man of English letters" in *Alternative Shakespeares*, pp. 26–46; Paul Brown, " 'This thing of darkness I acknowledge mine': *The Tempest* and the discourse of colonialism" in *Political Shakespeare: New essays in cultural materialism* (Ithaca, NY, and London: Cornell University Press, 1985), pp. 48–71; Peter Hulme, *Colonial Encounters: Europe and the native Caribbean, 1492–1797* (London and New York: Methuen, 1986), pp. 89–134; Thomas Cartelli, "Prospero in Africa: *The Tempest* as colonialist text and pretext" in *Shakespeare Reproduced: The text in history and ideology*, eds. Jean Howard and Marion O'Conner (New York: Methuen, 1987), pp. 99–115; I would include two essays by Stephen Orgel somewhat different in their focus but nonetheless related: "Prospero's Wife" in *Rewriting the Renaissance*, eds. Margaret Ferguson et al. (Chicago: University of Chicago Press, 1986), pp. 50–64, and "Shakespeare and the Cannibals" in *Cannibals, Witches, and Divorce: Estranging the Renaissance*, ed. Marjorie Garber (Baltimore and London: Johns Hopkins University Press, 1987), pp. 40–66.

2   Hulme, *Colonial Encounters*, p. 94.

3   See, for example, Paul Brown, "This thing of darkness," p. 48.

4   In fact Edward Pechter, in one of the earliest of such scrutinies, cited several of the recent *Tempest* articles as especially problematic. See "The New Historicism and Its Discontents: Politicizing Renaissance Drama," *PMLA*, 102 (1987), 292–303. See also Howard Felperin, "Making it 'neo': The new historicism and Renaissance literature," *Textual Practice*, 1 (1987), 262–77; Jean Howard, "The New Historicism in Renaissance Studies," *English Literary Renaissance*, 16 (1986), 13–43; and Anthony B. Dawson, "*Measure for Measure*, New Historicism, and Theatrical Power," *Shakespeare Quarterly*, 39 (1988), 328–41.

5   *The Tempest*, The Arden Shakespeare, ed. Frank Kermode (London: Methuen, 1954), p. xxv. For an account of the work of earlier scholars exploring the connection between the play and these documents, see Kermode, pp. xxv–xxxiv, and Charles Frey, "*The Tempest* and the New World," *SQ*, 30 (1979), 29–41.

6   E. E. Stoll and Northrop Frye are the only exceptions I have seen cited.

7   Recently there has been a renewed emphasis on the romance elements. See Gary Schmidgall, "*The Tempest* and *Primaleon*: A New Source," *SQ*, 37 (1986), 423–39, esp. p. 436; and Robert Wiltenberg, "The '*Aeneid*' in '*The Tempest*,' " *Shakespeare Survey*, 39 (1987), 159–68.

8   See, for example, Harry Berger's important essay, "Miraculous Harp: A Reading of Shakespeare's *Tempest*," *Shakespeare Studies*, 5 (1969), 253–83.

9   Harry Levin, *The Myth of the Golden Age in the Renaissance* (Bloomington: Indiana University Press, 1969); Leslie A. Fiedler, *The Stranger in Shakespeare* (New York: Stein and Day, 1972); Leo Marx, "Shakespeare's American Fable," *The Machine in the Garden* (London and New York: Oxford University Press, 1964), pp. 34–72.

10 O. Manoni, *Prospero and Caliban: The Psychology of Colonization*, trans. Pamela Powesland (1950; rpt. New York: Praeger, 1964).

11 Hulme, *Colonial Encounters*, p. 133.

12 Hulme, *Colonial Encounters*, p. 115; Barker and Hulme, p. 201; Orgel, "Prospero's Wife," pp. 62–3.

13 Orgel, "Shakespeare and the Cannibals," p. 55.

14 As Paul Werstine wrote in the brochure announcing the NEH Humanities Institute on "New Directions in Shakespeare Criticism" (The Folger Shakespeare Library, 1988), "To appreciate *The Tempest* ... today ... we must understand discourses of colonialism, power, legitimation."

15 Barker and Hulme, p. 198.

16 Hawkes, "Swisser-Swatter," p. 28.

17 Thus stereotypes, for example, served as part of a "discursive strategy ... to locate or 'fix' a colonial other in a position of inferiority ..." (Paul Brown, modifying Edward Said on orientalism, p. 58).

18 Actually, this point too is a matter of emphasis. R. R. Cawley ("Shakspere's Use of the Voyagers in *The Tempest*," *PMLA*, 41 [1926], 688–726) and Kermode, among others, had noted in passing some similarities between the play's view of Caliban and the distortions of colonialist self-serving rhetorical purposes; but revisionists take this to be the important point, not to be passed over.

19 Leininger, "Cracking the Code of *The Tempest*," p. 122.

20 Paul Brown, pp. 64, 66. Brown also contends that *The Tempest* "exemplifies ... a moment of *historical* crisis. This crisis is the struggle to produce a coherent discourse adequate to the complex requirements of British colonialism in its initial phase" (p. 48).

21 Hulme, *Colonial Encounters*, p. 93. Later he does grant a little ground to the psychological critics in allowing that their "totally spurious" identification of Prospero with Shakespeare yet "half grasps the crucial point that Prospero ... is a dramatist and creator of theatrical effects" (p. 115).

22 "From the point of view of a political hermeneutic, measured against the requirements of a 'political unconscious,' we must conclude that the conception of wish-fulfillment remains locked in a problematic of the individual subject ... which is only indirectly useful to us." The objection to wish-fulfillment is that it is "always outside of time, outside of narrative" and history; "what is more damaging, from the present perspective, is that desire ... remains locked into the category of the individual subject, even if the form taken by the individual in it is no longer the ego or the self, but the individual body ... *the need to transcend individualistic categories and modes of interpretation is in many ways the fundamental issue for any doctrine of the political unconscious*" (*The Political Unconscious: Narrative as a Socially Symbolic Act* [Ithaca, NY: Cornell University Press, 1981], pp. 66, 68, italics added).

23 Stephen Greenblatt, "Psychoanalysis and Renaissance Culture," *Literary Theory / Renaissance Texts*, eds. Patricia Parker and David Quint (Baltimore: Johns Hopkins University Press, 1986), 210–24.

24 Jameson, p. 12. So, too, Freud's "hermeneutic manual" can be of use to the political critic (p. 65).

25 "Norman Holland's suggestive term," Jameson, p. 49.

26 Jameson, p. 67. Cf. Paul Brown, "My use of Freudian terms does not mean that I endorse its ahistorical, Europocentric and sexist models of psychical development. However, a materialist criticism deprived of such concepts as displacement and condensation would be seriously impoverished ..." (p. 71, n. 35).

27 Jameson discussing Althusser (p. 30) and Greimas (p. 48).

28 *The Crown of Life* (1947; rpt. New York: Barnes & Noble, 1966), p. 255.

29 See Trevor R. Griffiths, " 'This Island's mine': Caliban and Colonialism," *Yearbook of English Studies*, 13 (1983), 159–80.

30 Griffiths, p. 166.

31 Virginia Mason Vaughan, " 'Something Rich and Strange': Caliban's Theatrical Metamorphoses," *SQ*, 36 (1985), 390–405, esp. p. 390.

32 Erlich, "Shakespeare's Colonial Metaphor," p. 49; Paul Brown, p. 48.

33 Even St. Paul in his travels (echoed in the play) met natives who – like Caliban – thought him a god.

34 Hulme produces as evidence against Shakespeare these four words from the cast list, which Shakespeare may or may not have written ("Hurricanes in the Caribbees," p. 72).

35 Alden T. Vaughan, "Shakespeare's Indian: The Americanization of Caliban," *SQ*, 39 (1988), 137–53. He argues that the intention miscarried not only at the time but also for the three centuries following. He adds, "Rather, from the Restoration until the late 1890s, Caliban appeared on stage and in critical literature as almost everything but an Indian" (p. 138).

36 Hulme, while noting Caliban's "anomalous nature," sees the anomaly as yet another colonialist strategy: "In ideological terms [Caliban is] a compromise formation and one achieved, like all such formations, only at the expense of distortion elsewhere" ("Hurricanes in the Caribbees," pp. 71, 72). This begs the question: Caliban can only be a "distortion" if he is intended to

represent someone. But that is precisely the question – *is* he meant to represent a Native American? Sidney Lee noted that Caliban's method of building dams for fish reproduces the Indians'; though he is often cited by later writers as an authority on the resemblance, the rest of his evidence is not convincing ("The Call of the West: America and Elizabethan England," *Elizabethan and Other Essays*, ed. Frederick S. Boas [Oxford: Clarendon Press, 1929], pp. 263–301). G. Wilson Knight has an impressionistic essay about the relationship between Caliban and Indians ("Caliban as Red Man" [1977] in *Shakespeare's Styles*, eds. Philip Edwards, Inga-Stina Ewbank, and G. K. Hunter [London: Cambridge University Press, 1980]). Hulme lists Caliban's resemblances to Caribs ("Hurricanes in the Caribbees"), and Kermode cites details taken from natives visited during both the Old and the New World voyages.

37 The Indians who would appear in Chapman's 1613 masque would be fully equipped with feathers. See R. R. Cawley, *The Voyagers and Elizabethan Drama* (Boston: D. C. Heath; London: Oxford University Press, 1938), p. 359, and Orgel, "Shakespeare and the Cannibals," pp. 44, 47.

38 Shakespeare had apparently read up on his monsters (R. R. Cawley, "Shakespeare's Use of the Voyagers," p. 723, and Frey, passim), but he picked up the stereotypes only to play with them ostentatiously (in Stephano's and Trinculo's many discredited guesses about Caliban's identity) or to leave them hanging (in Prospero's identification of Caliban as "devil").

39 Hulme, "Hurricanes in the Caribbees," p. 74.

40 Lamming (n. 1, above), pp. 98–9.

41 Lamming, p. 97; Erlich, p. 49.

42 The play also seems anti-colonialist because it includes the comic sections with Stephano and Trinculo, which show colonialism to be "nakedly avaricious, profiteering, perhaps even point-less"; but this too can be seen as a rationalization: "This low version of colonialism serves to displace possibly damaging charges … against properly-constituted civil authority on to the already excremental products of civility, the masterless" (Paul Brown, p. 65).

43 Greenblatt, "Learning to Curse," pp. 570–1; Leininger (n. 1, above), pp. 126–7.

44 Leininger, p. 127.

45 As Fiedler's book implies (n. 9, above), she is less like anything American than like the Frenchwoman Joan of Arc, who also tried to save herself from the law by claiming she was pregnant with a bastard; Joan simply wasn't as successful (see pp. 43–81, esp. p. 77).

46 See Brockbank, p. 193. Even these details can be discounted as rationalizations, of course. Paul Brown, for example, explains Sycorax's presence as a rationalization: by degrading her black magic, he argues, Shakespeare makes Prospero seem better than he is (pp. 60–1). Hulme notes that Sycorax may be Prospero's invention, pointing out that we never see any direct evidence that she was present (*Colonial Encounters*, p. 115). Orgel links Caliban's claims of legitimacy by birth to James I's claims ("Prospero's Wife," pp. 58–9).

47 See Fiedler, p. 205.

48 Erlich, "Shakespeare's Colonial Metaphor," p. 63.

49 The trend, moreover, is to move away from anthropomorphic terms like "repression" or "censorship," themselves inherited from the political terminology on which Freud drew for his own. Like the vocabulary of "scientific" hydraulics on which Freud also drew for his notions of libido flowing and damming up, the older terms are being replaced by contemporary terminologies more appropriate to describing a conflict among meanings or interpretations, rather than between anthropomorphized forces engaged in a simple struggle "for" and "against."

50 Spaniards, he writes, "taught their Hounds, fierce Dogs, to teare [the Indians] in peeces" (*A briefe Narration of the destruction of the Indies by the Spaniards* [1542 (?)], Samuel Purchas, *Purchas His Pilgrimes*, 20 vols. [Glasgow: Maclehose and Sons, 1905–1907], Vol. XVIII, 91). This was apparently a common topos, found also in Eden's translation of Peter Martyr's *Decades of the Newe Wordle* (1555), included in Eden's *Historie of Trauaile* (1577), which Shakespeare read for *The Tempest*. It was also used by Greene and Deloney (Cawley, *Voyagers and Elizabethan Drama*, pp. 383–4).

51 Hulme, "Hurricanes in the Caribbees," pp. 63–6; see also Orgel on this "New World topos" in "Shakespeare and the Cannibals," pp. 41–4.

52 Neither was Montaigne's in the essay that has been taken as a source for the play. Scholars are still debating about Montaigne's attitude toward cannibals, though all agree that his critical attitude toward *Europeans* was clear in the essay.

53 This blend of Old and New World characteristics, earlier seen as characteristic of New World discourse, is acknowledged in many of the revisionist studies but is seen as one of the rhetorical strategies used to control Indians.

54 William Strach[e]y, "A true reportorie ...," *Purchas*, Vol. XIX, p. 62. For the citation of Purchas as colonialist, see Hulme, "Hurricanes in the Caribbees," p. 78, n. 21.

55 Paul Brown, p. 64.

56 This is an entirely separate question from another that one might ask: How comparable were Purchas's remarks, taken from the collection of travelers' tales which he edited, censored, and used to support his colonialist ideal, on the one hand, and a play, on the other? In *Purchas*, Richard Marienstras argues, "the multiplicity of interpretations modulates and reinforces a single ideological system. The same can certainly not be said of ... *The Tempest*" (*New perspectives on the Shakespearean world*, trans. Janet Lloyd [Cambridge: Cambridge University Press, 1985], p. 169). This entire book, which devotes a chapter to *The Tempest*, is an excellent study of "certain aspects of Elizabethan ideology and ... the way these are used in Shakespeare" (p. 1).

57 See Pechter (n. 4, above). This kind of "condition," he argues, is really a precondition in the sense that it is assumed to be logically (if not chronologically) prior. It is assumed to have the kind of explanatory power that "the Elizabethan world view" was once accorded (p. 297).

58 See, for example, the following contemporary tracts reprinted in *Tracts and Other Papers Relating Principally to the Origin, Settlement, and Progress of ... North America*, ed. Peter Force, 4 vols. (1836–47; rpt. New York: Peter Smith, 1947): R. I., "*Nova Brittania*: OFFERING MOST Excellent fruites by Planting IN VIRGINIA. Exciting all such as be well affected to further the same" (1609), Vol. 1, No. 6; "Virginia richly valued" (1609), Vol. 4, No. 1; "A TRVE DECLARATION of the estate of the Colonie in Virginia, With a confutation of such scandalous reports as haue tended to the disgrace of so worthy an enterprise" (1610), Vol. 3, No. 1; Sil. Jourdan, "A PLAINE DESCRIPTION OF THE BARMVDAS, NOW CALLED SOMMER ILANDS" (1613), Vol. 3, No. 3.

In *The Genesis of the United States*, ed. Alexander Brown, 2 vols. (New York: Russell & Russell, 1964), see also: Robert Gray, "A GOOD SPEED to Virginia" (1609), Vol. 1, 293–302; "A True and Sincere declaration of the purpose and ends of the *Plantation* begun in *Virginia* of the degrees which it hath received; and meanes by *which it hath beene advanced*: and *the ... conclusion* of *His Majesties Councel* of that Colony ... untill by the mercies of GOD it shall *retribute a fruitful harvest to the Kingdome of heaven, and this Common-Wealth*" (1609), Vol. 1, 337–53; "A Publication by the Counsell of Virginea, touching the Plantation there" (1609), Vol. 1, 354–6; R. Rich, "NEWES FROM VIRGINIA. THE LOST FLOCKE TRIUMPHANT ..." (1610), Vol. 1, 420–6.

59 "A Trve Declaration," p. 6.

60 Alexander Brown, in *The Genesis of the United States*, reprints extracts from the following pertinent documents: William Symonds, "VIRGINIA: A SERMON PREACHED AT WHITE-CHAPPEL ..." (1609), Vol. 1, 282–91; Daniel Price, "SAVLES PROHIBITION STAIDE ... And to the Inditement of all that persecute Christ with a reproofe of those that traduce the Honourable Plantation of Virginia" (1609), Vol. 1, 312–16; and, most important, William Crashaw's sermon titled "A New-yeeres Gift to Virginea," and preached, as the title page announced, before "Lord La Warre Lord Governour and Captaine Generall of Virginia, and others of [the] Counsell ... At the said Lord Generall his ... departure for Virginea ... Wherein both the lawfulnesses of that action is maintained and the necessity there of is also demonstrated, not so much out of the grounds of Policie, as of Humanity, Equity and Christianity" (1610), Vol. 1, 360–75.

61 In Alexander Brown, see William Crashaw for two of these references (in "A New-yeeres Gift to Virginea" [1610], and "Epistle Dedicatory" to Alexander Whitaker's "*Good Newes from Virginia*" [1613], Vol. 2, 611–20); and see Ralphe Hamor in *A True Discourse of the Present Estate of Virginea* (1615), Virginia State Library Publications, No. 3 (Richmond: Virginia State Library, 1957).

62 Pp. 16, 17.

63 For the general history of the period, see David Beers Quinn, *England and the Discovery of America, 1481–1620* (New York: Alfred A. Knopf, 1974); Alexander Brown's *Genesis* identifies similar shifting motives in the history of colonization. Such voyages were made famous by often-reprinted accounts, especially in collections by Richard Eden and Richard Hakluyt, both of whose anthologies Shakespeare would consult for *The Tempest*. In the introductory material in these collections, as in the voyages themselves, the self-interest is obvious but so mixed with excitement and utopian hopes, and so focused on competition with Spain, that the issue of relation to Indians was dwarfed by comparison.

64 If he didn't succeed in establishing a settlement, he would lose his patent. His interest in the patent rather than the colony was shown by his apparent negligence in searching for his lost colony (Quinn, n. 63, above, p. 300). He could hold onto his patent only so long as there was hope that the colonists were still alive; clearly the hope was worth more to Raleigh than the colony.

65 Matthew P. Andrews, *The Soul of a Nation: The Founding of Virginia and the Projection of New England* (New York: Scribner's, 1943), p. 125. An entire popular literature developed, so much so that the Archbishop of York complained that "of Virginia there be so many tractates, divine, human, historical, political, or call them as you please, as no further intelligence I dare desire" (quoted in Andrews, p. 125).

66 It is this issue rather than colonialism that stimulated an earlier period of political commentary on the New World material in *The Tempest*: Charles M. Gayley, *Shakespeare and the Founders of Liberty in America* (New York: Macmillan, 1917); A. A. Ward, "Shakespeare and the makers of Virginia," *Proceedings of the British Academy*, 9 (1919); see also E. P. Kuhl, "Shakespeare and the founders of America: *The Tempest*," *Philological Quarterly*, 41 (1962), 123–46.

67 Contributing to the welter of contradictory discourses was the Spanish ambassador's flow of letters to Spain insisting, not irrationally, that the whole purpose of maintaining a profitless colony like Jamestown was to establish a base for pirate raids against Spanish colonies.

68 Letter from Southampton to the Earl of Salisbury, 15 December 1609, in Alexander Brown, Vol. 1, 356–7.

69 The quantity and quality of the objections, which have not on the whole survived, has been judged by the nature of the many defenses thought necessary to answer them. See notes 58, 60, 61.

70 A practice that Shakespeare did not admire if Stephano and Trinculo are any indication.

71 As are the two monsters cited as possible prototypes for Caliban by Geoffrey Bullough (*Narrative and Dramatic Sources of Shakespeare*, 8 vols. [New York: Columbia University Press, 1958], Vol. 8, 240). There were exceptions, of course, as in George Percy's *Observations ... of the Plantation of ... Virginia* (1606), in *Purchas*, Vol. XVIII, 403–19.

72 See Karen Ordahl Kupperman, *Settling With the Indians: The Meeting of English and Indian Cultures in America, 1580–1640* (Totowa, NJ: Rowman and Littlefield, 1980), pp. 127–9. The origins of this nearly universal belief in Indian treachery are of course multiple, ranging from the readiness of the English to project their fears onto any available victim, whether Indians or mariners (who were also regularly accused of treachery in these narratives), to the prevailing stereotypes of the Other, to specific English acts of provocation, to the general tensions inherent in the situation. Without arguing for any one of these, I merely wish to suggest that the notion of "colonialist discourse" simplifies a complex situation.

73 Even as proto-white men, their skin as tanned rather than naturally black, etc. See Kupperman, and Orgel, "Shakespeare and the Cannibals."

74 Greenblatt, in his study of the ways in which white men verbally "colonialized" Indians, emphasizes the degree to which whites assumed that the Indians had *no* language. Although he notes that there were exceptions, he makes it sound as if these exceptions were rare and were largely confined to the "rough, illiterate sea dog, bartering for gold trinkets on a faraway beach," rather than to the "captains or lieutenants whose accounts we read" ("Learning to Curse," pp. 564–5). On the contrary, even the earliest travelers had often included glossaries of Indian terms in their reports (e.g., the Glossary in the introductory material of Eden's translation of Martyr's *Decades*

[1555], as well as in various later English reports reprinted in *Purchas His Pilgrimes* [1625]); and in reading through Purchas's helter-skelter collection, one is struck by the number of writers who grant automatic respect to the Indians' language. A possibly figurative rather than literal force for comments on the Indians' "want of language" is suggested by Gabriel Archer's account of a 1602 voyage. Here it is the English, not the Indians, who are deficient in this respect: they "spake divers Christian words, and seemed to understand much *more then we, for Want of Language, could comprehend*" ("Relation of Captain Gosnold's voyage," *Purchas*, Vol. XVIII, 304, italics mine).

75 See R. R. Cawley, *Voyagers and Elizabethan Drama*, passim, and *Unpathed Waters: Studies in the Influence of the Voyagers of Elizabethan Literature* (Princeton, NJ: Princeton University Press, 1940), pp. 234–41. Neither of R. R. Cawley's two books about the voyagers' influence on contemporary English literature cites any pre-1611 passage of more than a few lines. It is true that in the 1580s Marlowe's plays took off from the general sense of vastness and possibility opened up by voyages to the New as well as to the Old World. In addition Drayton wrote an "Ode to the Virginia Voyage," perhaps expressly for the settlers leaving for Jamestown in 1606; and one line in Samuel Daniel's "Musophilis" has a colonialist ring: he speaks of "vent[ing] the treasure of our tongue ... T' inrich unknowing Nations with our stores." True, too, that in a quite different spirit Jonson, Marston, and Chapman collaborated in *Eastward Ho* (1605) to make fun of gallants flocking to Virginia with expectations as great as those bringing foolish victims to Face and Subtle's alchemical chimeras. But while Marlowe participates in the spirit of romantic adventure associated with voyaging and treasure-hunting, and *Eastward Ho* satirizes it, neither deals at all with the New World or with the New World natives.

76 The three brief exceptions are references to Spanish cruelty to Indians, all published before the truce with Spain. The Stationers' Register lists "The crueltie of ye Spaniardes toward th[e] Indians, a ballad" (1586) and "Spanishe cruelties" (1601), now lost. Robert Greene notes in passing that the Spaniards hunted Indians with dogs, while by contrast the English treated the natives with "such courtesie, as they thought the English Gods, and the Spaniardes both by rule and conscience halfe Devils" (*The Spanish Masquerado* [1589], *Life and ... Works*, ed. Alexander B. Grosart, 15 vols. [London and Aylesbury: privately printed, 1881–86], Vol. V, 282–3). See Cawley, *Voyagers and Elizabethan Drama*, pp. 385–6.

77 When Strachey finishes with his account of the Bermuda episode and turns to a description of Virginia, he does devote one sentence to the Indians' treachery.

78 See Frey, p. 31.

79 In his edition of *The Tempest*, Kermode notes this parallel with *Bartholomew Fair* (ii.vi.76–7), "Looke into any Angle o' the towne, (the Streights, or the Bermuda's) ..." (p. 24, n. 223).

80 Letter from Carleton to Chamberlain, August 1607, in Alexander Brown, Vol. 1, 111–13.

81 Many other similarities link *The Tempest* to the earlier play, including some which might have been taken to suggest *The Tempest*'s focus on the New World. Thus, for example, Stephano cries out when he first sees Caliban, "Do you put tricks upon's with salvages and men of Inde, ha?" (ii.ii.58–9). But Berowne, though rooted in the Old World, resorts to similarly exotic analogies to describe the passion which Rosaline should inspire in his colleagues. Who sees her, he says,

> That, (like a rude and savage man of Inde),
> At the first op'ning of the gorgeous east,
> Bows not his vassal head ...?
> (*Love's Labor's Lost*, iv.iii.218–20)

See Kermode's note on the line in *The Tempest*.

82 Specific resemblances between subplots here and the plots of other plays have been noted (between the plot to murder Alonso and *Macbeth*, between Ferdinand's courtship of Miranda and *Romeo and Juliet*, etc.). See Alvin B. Kernan, "The great fair of the world and the ocean island: *Bartholomew Fair* and *The Tempest*," in *The Revels History of Drama in English*, 8 vols., eds. J. Leeds Barroll, Alexander Leggatt, Richard Hosley, Alvin Kernan (London: Methuen, 1975), Vol. III,

456–74. G. Wilson Knight has described the place of *The Tempest* in Shakespeare's overarching myth of the tempest. Even more suggestive, Leslie Fiedler has traced the less obvious personal mythology that provides a context for the play. Drawing on marginal details, he shows the play's concern with themes that pervade the entire canon, such as the interracial marriage that here, not accidentally, initiates the action of the play. His work is the starting point for mine.

83   Barker and Hulme, p. 198.

84   Hulme, *Colonial Encounters*, p. 133.

85   Paul Brown, p. 69.

86   Barker and Hulme, p. 202.

87   The last time Prospero got so angry that Miranda had to apologize was when Ferdinand began to court Miranda.

88   See A. D. Nuttall's discussion of the blend of colonialist and sexual tensions in *The Tempest*, "Two Unassimilable Men," in *Shakespearian Comedy*, Stratford-upon-Avon Studies 14 (London: Edward Arnold, 1972), pp. 210–40, esp. p. 216.

89   The incestuous impulse implicit in the situation is even clearer in Shakespeare's own earlier romances; both Fiedler and Nuttall, among others, have explored these in the context of the vast literature of romance that lies behind the play. See also Mark Taylor, *Shakespeare's Darker Purpose: A Question of Incest* (New York: AMS Press, 1982).

90   Fiedler, p. 234.

91   Marianne Novy, *Love's Argument: Gender Relations in Shakespeare* (Chapel Hill and London: University of North Carolina Press, 1984), pp. 63–82.

92   All Shakespeare quotations are from *The Riverside Shakespeare*, ed. G. Blakemore Evans (Boston: Houghton Mifflin, 1974). The earlier group of critics who had pointed out the racist assumptions in Antonio's behavior made many of the same points recently made on Caliban's behalf. The two cases are indeed similar, and although both can be seen as examples of "colonialism" – with the word "colonialism" used very loosely as it is today for any exploitative appropriation – the more historically specific "colonialist discourse" does not seem to be the appropriate context for Shylock.

93   Nuttall (n. 88, above) notes the strangeness of the Duke's explosion and the fact that Jaques's request for a fool's license "has shaken Duke Senior" (p. 231).

94   See Richard P. Wheeler's analysis in *Shakespeare's Development and the Problem Comedies: Turn and Counter-turn* (Berkeley and Los Angeles: University of California Press, 1981).

95   Primarily of course in the sonnets, but in the plays as well. See Novy's discussion of self-assertiveness in Shylock.

96   Caliban later joins the two courtly servants in appropriately scatological double entendres.

97   Norman Holland, "Caliban's Dream," *The Design Within: Psychoanalytic Approaches to Shakespeare*, ed. M. D. Faber (New York: Science House, 1970), pp. 521–33.

98   Compare Antonio's cold calculations as he plans to kill Alonso.

99   Albeit in a "My mommy is going to get you" fashion.

100   Nuttall, p. 225.

101   So, too, any child might complain that he was taught to speak and now his "profit on 't" is to be trapped in the prison house of language.

102   See Leininger, p. 125, for the most effective presentation of this view; also Paul Brown, p. 63.

103   Here, too, Shakespeare seems unusual. Not until our child-centered, post-Freudian age do we find writers so directly representing the aliens on our galactic frontier as children – whether as innocents like Steven Spielberg's E. T. or as proto-savages like his Gremlins. Others had associated the primitive with metaphorical childhood: De Bry's 1590 edition of Harriot's *Briefe and true report* and, later, Purchas's version of Strachey associated the primitive Indians with the childhood of the English nation, and writers spoke of the Indians as "younger brethren" (Kupperman, n. 72, above, p. 170). What is unusual in Shakespeare is the emphasis and the detailed portrayal of emotional as well as cognitive childishness. Leah Marcus argues, in another context, that the English in the chaotic and disorienting intellectual context of the seventeenth

century were especially susceptible to dreams of the golden age – and to sympathetic portrayals of childhood wholeness (*Childhood and Cultural Despair* [Pittsburgh, PA: University of Pittsburgh Press, 1978]). Most of the instances of such portrayals did not appear until later in the century, however.

104 Edward A. Armstrong, *Shakespeare's Imagination* (Lincoln: University of Nebraska Press, 1963), p. 52.

105 Might the brothers' definition by opposition perhaps have influenced Shakespeare's choice of names: *Prospero* and *Antonio*?

106 John B. Bender, "The Day of *The Tempest*," *English Literary History*, 47 (1980), 235–58.

107 It also marks Shakespeare's return to the pattern of withdrawal from active life used in *Love's Labor's Lost* – but this time with a difference. The earlier play had shown young men hoping to conquer death by forswearing the body and all it represents. *The Tempest* shows an old man coming to terms with death by acknowledging the body and what it represents.

108 Elliot Jacques offers a related account, in Kleinian terms, of the role of infantile demands and emotions in the effort to come to terms with death in "Death and the Mid-life Crisis," *International Journal of Psychoanalysis*, 46 (1965), 502–14.

109 John Forrester, "Psychoanalysis or Literature?" *French Studies*, 35 (1981), 170–9, esp. p. 172.

110 Cited in Levin (n. 9, above), p. 183.

111 See Bender (n. 106, above) on the way dreams are always followed by violence in the play; the violence is not a cause of the problem on the island but rather an effect.

112 Andrews (n. 65, above), p. 126.

113 Jameson cites as being "very much in the spirit of [his] present work" the concern of Deleuze and Guattari "to reassert the specificity of the political content of everyday life and of individual fantasy-experience and to reclaim it from … reduction to the merely subjective and to the status of psychological projection" (*The Political Unconscious*, n. 22, above, p. 22).

114 *The Invasion Within: The Contest of Cultures in North America* (Oxford: Oxford University Press, 1985), p. 54.

115 The original version of this essay was presented at a session on "Psychoanalysis and Renaissance History," chaired by Richard Wheeler at the 1987 MLA annual meeting. The current version has greatly benefited from careful readings by Janet Adelman, Anne and Rob Goble, Carol Neely, Marianne Novy, Martin Wiener, and several anonymous readers.

Part XIV

Reading Closely

47 Shakespeare's Prose   848
   Jonas A. Barish
48 The Play of Phrase and Line   861
   George T. Wright
49 Transfigurations: Shakespeare and Rhetoric   880
   Patricia Parker

I f many of the sections in this volume might have had alternative titles, this last one might have had several – "Formal Criticism," "Close Reading," "Stylistic Analysis," "Reading," "Beyond New Criticism," "Exegesis," "Reading for Form," "Explication de Texte," or one of many other combinations. Such implicit flexibility attests to the difficulty of how to define close reading and to its uncertain status at the end of the twentieth century. Is it an approach, like new historicism? Does it have a political valence, like postcolonial criticism? Is it associated with particular themes and concerns, like psychoanalytic criticism? Is it ideologically neutral? Is it a method? Is it a practice? Are there rules or guidelines for performing it? Critics of different generations and opposing persuasions will answer these questions in different ways. As a consequence of such elasticity, I have declined to attempt a definition and will instead simply introduce the work of three brilliant close readers, each of whom examines a different formal feature of Shakespeare's language.

Critics attending closely to verbal particulars experienced a rough couple of decades at the end of the twentieth century. The startling expansion of Shakespeare studies beginning in the 1970s, a broadening of horizons evident in this volume's range of entries, was characterized above all by a commitment to context. History, political discourses, culture and ideology, subjectivity – these and other topics engaged the collective critical imagination, and the distance required for perceiving those vistas produced a corresponding diminution in the visibility of literary forms. Also, the smudging of the distinction between literature and other forms of writing began to cast doubt upon the value of what used to be called "literary criticism." It would be possible to adduce passages from dozens of critics declaring suspicion of or hostility to formal inquiry, but such complaints will already be familiar to many readers, and this brief introduction is not the place to rehearse debates between the opposing claims of text and context. One summary comment will serve. Scanning the field in the last year of the twentieth century, Heather Dubrow wittily observed: "in the current critical climate, many scholars are far more comfortable detailing their sexual histories in print than confessing to an interest in literary form."[1]

Jonas Barish, George T. Wright, and Patricia Parker all justify their attention to formal properties thanks to the value of their critical perceptions and the persuasive clarity with which they articulate those insights. Barish is perhaps better known for his later work, *The Anti-Theatrical Prejudice*, in which he vividly traverses centuries of religious, philosophical, and other forms of opposition to the stage from Plato to the present. His first book, however, *Ben Jonson and the Language of Prose Comedy*, from which the excerpt printed here is taken, ranks among the most impressive of all stylistic studies. To create a foil for his analysis of Jonson's asymmetrical prose style and its implications for Jonsonian comedy, Barish conducts a detailed examination of the structure of Shakespeare's prose, demonstrating especially its Lylyan affiliations, shapely antitheses, and gratifying balances. Brian Vickers's *The Artistry of Shakespeare's Prose* is also essential reading for anyone interested in Shakespearean language, but Barish got there first, and his own prose is a pleasure to read.

George T. Wright is our leading expert on Shakespeare's meter. The chapter included here was published first in the *Shakespeare Quarterly* and then included in his authoritative *Shakespeare's Metrical Art*, a wide-ranging study of Shakespearean poetry, including chapters on what blank verse was like before Shakespeare took it up and what happened to it after he stopped writing. Metrical analysis, it is probably fair to say, is not students' favorite critical activity, and in this prejudice they recapitulate the views of many of their teachers. One explanation is that the study of iambic pentameter can easily seem trivial, an evasion of more momentous questions raised by the text. But Wright keeps his ear attuned not only to the sound and shape of the line but also to the interpretive implications of such acoustic patterns.

Patricia Parker also possesses a sensitive ear, alert to the contribution of Shakespearean rhetoric and wordplay. Following the lead of scholar–critics such as (on the one hand) M. M. Mahood and Kenneth Muir to (on the other) Raymond Williams and Catherine Belsey, Parker argues that comic and non-comic puns "lead us to linkages operating not only within but between Shakespeare's plays" and that "the terms of this wordplay make possible glimpses into the relation between the plays and their contemporary culture."[2] The chapter included here, reprinted from her *Literary Fat Ladies: Rhetoric, Gender, Property*, illustrates the mutuality of figures and ideas, demonstrating especially that certain themes appear as they do because of their rhetorical articulation. And her ability to tease out etymological and acoustic affiliations among apparently unrelated words, an inquiry that always remains rigorously historical, can be dazzling.

The analysis of Shakespeare's style is one of our most powerful tools for knowing him, for understanding his distinctive achievement and differentiating it from those of other writers. The work of other great stylistic critics might have been added to this section: Kenneth Burke, Helen Vendler, Rosalie Colie, Richard Lanham, not to mention many who appear in this volume under other rubrics. I close with a defense of stylistic inquiry written by Marshall Brown in the mid-1990s, when close reading was enduring considerable neglect or abuse.

> Through their style, cultural expressions become literary by resisting the idealizing universals into which our ideologies otherwise slide ... The study of style is the study of the minute precisions that correct any and all generalizations. A writer's style is the way he or she continues to differ from anything you have yet said about her or him. Its resistance to our critical mastery ... forces ever-increasing precision.[3]

Notes

1 "Guess Who's Coming to Dinner? Reinterpreting Formalism and the Country House Poem," *Modern Language Quarterly*, 61 (2000), p. 59.
2 *Shakespeare From the Margins: Language, Culture, Context* (Chicago: University of Chicago Press, 1995), p. 1.
3 " 'Le style est l'homme même': The Action of Literature," *College English*, 59 (1997), pp. 806–7.

47

Shakespeare's Prose

Jonas A. Barish

S hakespeare starts with the highly specialized set of expressive devices worked out by Lyly, inflects them variously, fills them with nuance, widens their range, and so finally transcends them, but without departing from the structural principles on which they are based. One tends not to notice the logicality of Shakespeare's prose because it is managed with such virtuosity as to seem as natural as breathing. But by his constant invention of fresh logical formulas, his endless improvising of new patterns, Shakespeare, if anything, carries logical syntax even further than Lyly.

The term logicality, here, refers not merely to the use of syllogisms, and other formal schemes, though these are numerous enough,[1] but to a stylistic habit that includes these and goes deeper: the habit, first, of treating a piece of discourse as argument, of tracking effects back to causes, discovering consequences from antecedents, elucidating premises, proposing hypotheses, and the like; and second, more important, the habit of proceeding disjunctively, of splitting every idea into its component elements and then symmetrizing the elements so as to sharpen the sense of division between them.

Shakespeare's early plays tinker inventively, but perhaps also a bit facilely, with the kind of formal Euphuism in which pages pick apart each other's language and match wits with their masters. It is in the great middle comedies, as Bond has shown (I, 150–4), that Euphuism has been assimilated into the marrow of the language and reigns as the undisputed expressive principle. Somewhat less absolutely, it dominates the prose of the Lancastrian histories, and it continues to supply the chief structural basis for the prose of the tragedies and late romances, while gradually being absorbed and transformed into a style greater than itself.

A general discussion of Shakespeare's prose being clearly out of the question here,[2] the following pages will try to sketch out a glossary of some of his logical tactics in order to indicate their radical importance in his language. Examples from the tragedies and late romances will be included to support the contention that the logicality, though it evolves, remains an essential stylistic principle even in the final phase.

Like Lodge, Shakespeare makes a heavy-duty particle of the conjunction "for" – the "cause-renderer," as Jonson calls it in his *English Grammar* (Herford and Simpson, VIII, 550). Examples are legion, and citation would be useless. One point, however, seems worth noting: despite the frequency of the word in Shakespeare – he probably uses it oftener than any other playwright of the period, Lodge included – it never comes to sound like a nervous tic, because Shakespeare, unlike Lodge, is not enslaved to it. It forms only one of a variety of logical hinges that by their constant interchange maintain the syntactic sequence. A few specimens of the logical linchpin "therefore" may be given; the following are all from *Much Ado about Nothing*.

> There is no measure in the occasion that breeds, therefore the sadnesse is without limit.[3] (L.121; i.iii.3–4)

> I am trusted with a mussell, and enfranchised with a clog, therefore I haue decreed, not to sing in my cage. (L.122; i.iii.34–6)

> … marry once before he wonne it of mee, with false dice, therefore your Grace may well say I have lost it. (L.124; ii.i.289–91)

> I cannot be a man with wishing, therefore I will die a woman with grieuing. (L.134; iv.i.324–6)

> Foule words is but foule wind, and foule wind is but foule breath, and foule breath is noisome, therefore I will depart vnkist. (L.138; v.ii.52–4)

Instances of the numerous substitutes for "therefore" – "hence," "ergo," "thus," "so," and the like – may be omitted, as may the occasional "because" or "the reason is" that doubles for "for."[4]

It is well to remember, when discussing such humdrum phenomena as the use of "for," "therefore," and conjunctions and correlatives, that they are not mere inert forms just because they are common.

> The greatest obstacle to recognizing the expressive value of rhetorical devices is the fact that they recur. One notices that Cicero uses a *litotes* or a *praeteritio* several times in a few pages, or so many hundreds of balances are counted in the *Ramblers* of Johnson … The so-called "devices," really no more devices than a sentence is a device, express more special forms of meaning, not so common to thinking that they cannot be avoided, like the sentence, but common enough to reappear frequently in certain types of thinking and hence to characterize the thinking, or the style.[5]

What applies to "the so-called 'devices' " applies to sentence types and syntactic formulas. They are significant, indeed, in proportion to their frequency; if the following pages tax the patience of the reader, it is because one must demonstrate, if only in a limited fashion, that certain kinds of construction appear *often* in Shakespeare, often enough "to characterize the thinking, or the style."

The cause-and-effect relation that Shakespeare indicates rather formally with such conjunctions as "for" and "therefore" he may suggest more unobtrusively by such formulas as "so ... that," where "so" indicates the way a thing is done and "that" describes its effect.

> *O she did so course o're my exteriors with such a greedy intention that the appetite of her eye, did seeme to scorch me vp like a burning-glasse. (L.160; MW I.iii.72–5)*

> *Hee must fight singly to morrow with* Hector, *and is so prophetically proud of an heroicall cudgelling, that he raues in saying nothing. (L.604; Troil. III.iii.248–9)*

> *For the Nobles receyue so to heart, the Banishment of that worthy* Coriolanus, *that they are in a ripe aptnesse, to take al power from the people, and to plucke from them their Tribunes for euer. (L.637; Cor. IV.iii.20–6)*

A related strategy, suppressing the "so," foretells the effect one hopes will follow a given cause. The "that" here is roughly equivalent to "in order that":

> *Let vs sit and mocke the good housewife* Fortune *from her wheele, that her gifts may henceforth bee bestowed equally. (L.204; AYL I.ii.34–6)*

> *... therefore I shall craue of you your leaue, that I may beare my euils alone. (L.278; TN II.i.5–7)*

> *Why I haue often wisht my selfe poorer, that I might come neerer to you. (L.697; Tim. I.ii.103–5)*

> *Wee will giue you sleepie Drinkes, that your Sences (vn-intelligent of our insufficience) may, though they cannot prayse vs, as little accuse vs. (L.295; WT I.i.14–17)*

One may also reach a conclusion by way of a qualification, first stating some real or imagined difficulty in a "though" clause, then overriding it in the main clause.

> *... though honestie be no Puritan, yet it will doe no hurt ... (L.251; Alls W I.iii.97–8)*

> *... though you change your place, you neede not change your Trade. (L.80; MM I.ii.110–11)*

> *... though patience be a tyred [mare], yet shee will plodde ... (L.427; HV I.ii.25–6)*

> *Though this be madnesse, / Yet there is Method in't. (L.769; Ham. II.ii.208–9)*

> *... though the wisedome of Nature can reason it thus, and thus, yet Nature finds it selfe scourg'd by the sequent effects. (L.794; Lear I.ii.113–15)*

> *Though I am not bookish, yet I can reade Waiting-Gentlewoman in the scape. (L.306–7; WT III.iii.73–5)*

> *Though thou canst swim like a Ducke, thou art made like a Goose. (L.28; Temp. II.ii.134–5)*

There is no reason why the "though" clause must precede the main clause in such cases, but Shakespeare, with his penchant for strongly marked disjunctions, usually makes it do so, and by adding the antithetic particle "yet" at the head of the main clause, he fences the two halves of the statement even more rigidly off from each other.

One of the hallmarks, indeed, of a logical style is its taste for disjunction. Needless to say, all language depends on disjunction, on separating strips of words into intelligible units, and – to speak not very paradoxically – every conjunction occurs at a point of disjunction. "Sir Cranberry stalked his prey waited" does not become coherent discourse until some division is made between the two halves, either with a vocal pattern that we may represent by a semicolon ("Sir Cranberry stalked; his prey waited ..."), or a comma ("Sir Cranberry stalked his prey, waited ..."), or else with some word like "while," "but," or "and," which cuts apart the two elements at the same time that it establishes some kind of relation between them. What we find in Shakespeare and in writers like him is a tendency to insist on the points of disjunction, to hold up the two pieces of the sentence side by side, in full view, to symmetrize them and brandish them in their matched antagonism. "The dragon bellows if attacked" contains an unobtrusive disjunction marked by the "if." "If attacked, the dragon bellows" walls the two elements more firmly off from each other by making a heavier vocal suspension. A writer like Shakespeare will tend to prefer the second pattern, and in fact Shakespeare's prose is honeycombed with sentences of this type.

> ... if a Trassel sing, he fals straight a capring, he will fence with his own shadow. If I should marry him, I should marry twentie husbands: if hee would despise me, I would forgiue him, for if he loue me to madnesse, I should neuer requite him. (L.183; Merch. I.iii.65–70)

> If you head, and hang all that offend that way but for ten yeare together; you'll be glad to giue out a Commission for more heads: if this law hold in Vienna ten yeare, ile rent the fairest house in it after three pence a Bay: if you liue to see this come to passe, say Pompey told you so. (L.84; MM II.i.251–7)

By placing the dependent clause before the major clause, Shakespeare achieves the maximum effect of climax, balance, and strong demarcation between the two halves. When the simple "if" formation is expanded by being doubled with its own antithesis ("If attacked, the dragon bellows; if ignored, he preens his scales"), we move into the domain of the highly disjunctive style, which pits each element rigidly against its opposite and matches it fiercely with its partner, dividing and binding in the same moment. "If thou beest a man, shew thy selfe in thy likeness: If thou beest a diuell, take't as thou list" (L.30; Temp. III.ii.137–9); or, more elaborately:

> ... if you pricke vs doe we not bleede? If you tickle vs, doe we not laugh? if you poison vs doe we not die? and if you wrong vs shall we not reuenge? if we are like you in the rest, we will resemble you in that. If a Iew wrong a Christian, what is his humility, reuenge? If a Christian wrong a Iew, what should his sufferance be by Christian example, why reuenge? (L.191; Merch. III.i.67–74)

A related discoupling mechanism, highly characteristic of Shakespeare, is the "if ... if not" formula. This stakes out logical alternatives and specifies the possible consequences of each.

Ile go sleepe if I can: if I cannot, Ile raile against all the first borne of Egypt. (L.210; AYL
ii.v.62–3)

If it bee worth stooping for, there it lies, in your eye: if not, bee it his that findes it. (L.278; TN
ii.ii.15–17)

... if your Father will do me any Honor, so: if not, let him kill the next Percie *himselfe. (L.392;*
IHIV *v.iv.143–5)*

When thou has[t] leysure, say thy praiers: when thou hast none, remember thy Friends.
(L.249; Alls W *i.i.227–9)*

If it be now, 'tis not to come: if it bee not to come, it will bee now: if it be not now; yet it will
come ... (L.788; Ham. *v.ii.231–3)*

If she will returne me my Iewels, I will giue ouer my Suit, and repent my vnlawfull solicitation. If
not, assure your selfe, I will seeke satisfaction of you. (L.841; Oth. *iv.ii.200–2)*

... if you will take it on you to assist him, it shall redeeme you from your Gyues: if not, you
shall haue your full time of imprisonment ... (L.93; MM *iv.ii.10–13)*

It is worth noticing here, as with most of Shakespeare's logical schemes, that though the pattern itself is highly formulaic, the completion of it is anything but predictable. "Ile go sleepe if I can" may prompt us to suspect an antithesis; "if I cannot" confirms the suspicion. But who could have foreseen the bizarre outcome, "Ile raile against all the first borne of Egypt"? Unlike Lyly, Shakespeare is never rigid. He achieves the maximum amount of syntactic lucidity without sacrificing his privilege of surprising us; he lures us into unexpected marshes or drops us into brambles with comical thud, or else conforms to expectation so generously and graciously that even this comes as a surprise.

Another way of splitting things into antithetic alternatives is to group them under opposed headings like "the one ... the other." This frequently produces even more strict patterning than the "if ... if not" scheme.

... the one is too like an image and saies nothing, and the other too like my Ladies eldest
sonne, euermore tatling. (L.122; Much Ado *ii.i.9–11)*

– Who ambles Time withal?
– With a Priest that lacks Latine, and a rich man that hath not the Gowt: for the one sleepes
easily because he cannot study, and the other liues merrily, because he feels no paine: the one
lacking the burthen of leane and waistful Learning; the other knowing no burthen of heauie
tedious penurie. (L.215; AYL *iii.ii.337–43)*

Out upon thee knaue, doest thou put upon mee at once both the office of God and the diuel:
one brings thee in grace, and the other brings thee out. (L.269; Alls W *v.ii.51–4)*

Prethee peace: pay her the debt you owe her, and vnpay the villany you haue done her: the one you may do with sterling mony, & the other with currant repentance. (L.399; IIHIV II.i.129–32)

You are mistaken: the one may be solde or giuen, or if there were wealth enough for the purchases, or merite for the guift. The other is not a thing for sale, and onely the guift of the Gods. (L.880; Cymb. i.iv.89–93)

Shee had one Eye declin'd for the losse of her Husband, another eleuated, that the Oracle was fulfill'd. (L.319; WT v.ii.80–2)

Again one may notice the richness and variety that Shakespeare packs into his logical schemes, the colloquial sting of Beatrice's "euermore tatling" in contrast to the more matter-of-fact "like an image"; the complex crisscross between the ignorant priest and the gouty rich man in Rosalind's lecture, which ends by making them sound like twins; the concise pun on "sterling mony" and "currant repentance" with which the Lord Chief Justice concludes his judgment on Falstaff; the surprising and affecting Latinisms – "declin'd" and "eleuated" – that portray the mingle of feelings in Paulina. Far from lending itself to stiffness, as it does in Lyly's romances, logical syntax in Shakespeare produces the utmost freedom and flexibility, like a ground bass on which an infinite number of variations may be played.

Schematic pointers such as "the one ... the other" may of course be replaced by the nouns or pronouns to which they refer:

Yet it had not beene amisse the rod had beene made, and the garland too, for the garland he might haue worne himselfe, and the rod hee might haue bestowed on you, who (as I take it) haue stolne his birds nest. (L.124; Much Ado II.ii.235–8)

For the boxe of th'eare that the Prince gaue you, he gaue it like a rude Prince, and you tooke it like a sensible Lord. (L.397; IIHIV I.ii.217–19)

Now blesse thy selfe: thou met'st with things dying, I with things new borne. (L.307; WT III.iii.115–16)

Nor is there any reason why the two alternatives cannot be expanded to include a third:

I maruell what kin thou and thy daughters are, they'l haue me whipt for speaking true: thou'l haue me whipt for lying, and sometimes I am whipt for holding my peace. (L.796; Lear I.iv.200–3)

Less fully developed alternatives may be expressed by the formula "either X or Y":

... in the managing of quarrels you may see hee is wise, for either hee auoydes them with great discretion, or undertakes them with a Christian-like feare. (L.127; Much Ado II.iii.197–200)

If this vncouth Forrest yeeld any thing sauage, I wil either be food for it, or bring it for foode to thee. (L.210; AYL II.vi.6–8)

... there is eyther liquor in his pate, or mony in his purse, when hee lookes so merrily. (L.63; MW II.i.197–8)

... thou hauing made me Businesses, (which none (without thee) can sufficiently manage) must either stay to execute them thy selfe, or take away with thee the very seruices thou hast done. (L.307; WT IV.ii.15–19)

For he does neither affect companies, / Nor is he fit for't indeed. (L.697; Tim.I.ii.30–1)

And if one of the alternatives is asserted over the other, the pattern may run, "not X but Y":

... the commendation is not in his witte, but in his villanie ... (L.123; Much Ado II.i.146)

... the yong Lion repents: Marry not in ashes and sacke-cloath, but in new Silke, and old Sacke. (L.397; IIHIV I.ii.220–2)

For the Gods know, I speake this in hunger for Bread, not in thirst for Reuenge. (L.617; Cor. I.i.24–5)

Expressions of choice, where the speaker asserts a preference for one thing over another, lend themselves naturally to antithetic formulation. The commonest disjunctive strategy here is the arrangement "rather X than Y."

I had rather (forsooth) go before you like a man, then follow him like a dwarfe. (L.67; MW III.ii.5–6)

I had rather my brother die by the Law, then my sonne should be vnlawfullie borne. (L.90; MM III.i.194–5)

I had rather be a Ticke in a Sheepe, then such a valiant ignorance. (L.604; Troil. III.iii.313–15)

... I had rather had eleuen dye Nobly for their Countrey, then one voluptuously surfet out of Action. (L.620; Cor. I.iii.26–8)

You had rather be at a breakefast of Enemies, then a dinner of Friends. (L.697; Tim. I.ii.78–9)

The antithetic halves, obviously, follow a variety of patterns. They may observe strict parison ("breakefast of Enemies," "dinner of Friends"), or exact antithesis without parison ("by the Law," "vnlawfullie"), or they may have no relation whatever outside the pattern in which they are set ("a Ticke in a Sheepe," "such a valiant ignorance"). And the same is true of such expressions of preference, or comparative judgments, cast in the form "more X than Y":

You haue Witch-craft in your Lippes, Kate: there is more eloquence in a Sugar touch of them, then in the Tongues of the French Councell; and they should sooner perswade Harry of England, then a generall Petition of Monarchs. (L.448; HV v.ii.302–5)

I will no more trust him when hee leeres, then I will a Serpent when he hisses. (L.610; Troil. v.i.95–7)

The Swallow followes not Summer more willing, then we your Lordship. (L.705; Tim. iii.vi.33–4)

If my Sonne were my Husband, I should freelier reioyce in that absence wherein he wonne Honor, then in the embracements of his Bed, where he would shew most loue. (L.620; Cor. i.iii.2–6)

Kings are no lesse unhappy, their issue, not being gracious, then they are in loosing them, when they haue approued their Vertues. (L.308; WT iv.ii.30–2)

Preference may be expressed more modestly, or with a tinge of irony, by disposing the antithetic choices under the formula "as … as."

I had as liefe they would put Rats-bane in my mouth, as offer to stoppe it with Security. (L.396; IIHIV i.ii.47–9)

I had as lief haue the foppery of freedome, as the mortality of imprisonment. (L.81; MM i.ii.136–8)

I had as liue haue a Reede that will doe me no seruice, as a Partizan I could not heaue. (L.858; Ant. ii.vii.13–15)

But the "as … as" disjunction may serve to affirm any kind of equivalence, literal or metaphoric:

It is as easie to count Atomies as to resolue the propositions of a Louer. (L.214; AYL iii.ii.245–6)

… they are as sicke that surfet with too much, as they that starue with nothing. (L.182; Merch. i.ii.6–7)

… thou art as ful of enuy at his greatnes, as Cerberus is at Proserpina's beauty. (L.594; Troil. ii.i.36–7)

… it is as dangerous to be aged in any kinde of course, as it is vertuous to be constant in any vndertaking. (L.92; MM iii.ii.237–9)

A more emphatic equation results from the pattern "as X, so Y," where "so" not merely insists on the identity between the two elements, but insinuates as causal relation between them.

… as Alexander kild his friend Clytus, being in his Ales and his Cuppes; so also Harry Monmouth being in his right wittes, and his good iudgements, turn'd away the fat Knight with the great belly doublet. (L.443; HV iv.vii.47–51)

… but as all is mortall in nature, so is all nature in loue, mortall in folly. (L.209; AYL II.iv.55–6)

… but as she spit in his face, so she defide him. (L.83; MM II.i.86)

For, as it is a heart-breaking to see a handsome man loose-Wiu'd, so it is a deadly sorrow, to beholde a foule Knaue vncuckolded. (L.894; Ant. I.ii.74–7)

One may observe that in the first example here, Captain Fluellen's Welsh dialect does not obscure the logicality of his syntax, just as, in the last example, Egyptian disorder and promiscuous living are suggested in the highly logical analogy of Iras. And so with virtually all the extracts so far cited. They are, at the same time, precise logical mechanisms, and completely appropriate to their speakers. The logical mechanism itself is an instrument that can be used in limitless ways. And there is hence no special moment or purpose for which Shakespeare employs it; rather, there are special moments and special purposes for which he deliberately discards it.[6]

When the two matching elements are to be semantically compounded rather than disjoined, Shakespeare still often contrives to emphasize the juncture, and hence the opposition between them, by some such device as the scheme "not only … but also."

… I shall not onely receiue this villanous wrong, but stand vnder the adoption of abhominable termes, and by him that does mee this wrong. (L.65; MW II.ii.307–10)

… and the cure of it not onely saues your brother, but keepes you from dishonor in doing it. (L.90; MM III.i.244–6)

… then must we looke from his age, to receiue not alone the imperfections of long ingraffed condition, but therewithall the unruly way-wardnesse, that infirme and cholericke yeares bring with them. (L.793; Lear I.i.299–303)

There is not onely disgrace and dishonor in that Monster, but an infinite losse. (L.33; Temp. IV.i.209–10)

But Shakespeare's fertility in the invention and use of disjunctive devices is almost limitless, and it would be as pointless as it would be vain to try to classify them all. If the reader's patience is not quite exhausted, we may cite a few instances that do not conform exactly to any of the categories so far discussed, merely to illustrate the freedom with which he improvizes.

O powerfull Loue, that in some respects makes a Beast a Man: in som other, a Man a beast. (L.76; MW v.v.4–6)

… where they feared the death, they haue borne life away; and where they would bee safe, they perish. (L.438; HV IV.i.181–3)

What a merit were it in death to take this poore maid from the world? what corruption in this life, that it will let this man liue? (L.90; MM III.i.240–2)

The Food that to him now is as lushious as Locusts, shalbe to him shortly, as bitter as Coloquintida. (L.823; Oth. i.iii.354–6)

Not so young Sir to loue a woman for singing, nor so old to dote on her for any thing. (L.795; Lear i.iv.40–1)

– He's a Lambe indeed, that baes like a Beare.
– Hee's a Beare indeede, that liues like a Lambe. (L.624; Cor. ii.i.12–14)

The foregoing tabulation makes no claim to completeness; it is intended only to be suggestive. (No mention has been made, for example, of the parisonic series, a logical formation on which Shakespeare relies throughout his career.) The cited extracts have been chosen partly for their brevity, so as to isolate the figures in question. But it goes without saying that Shakespeare is as versatile in combining them as he is resourceful in unearthing them in the first place. As we proceed from the simple schemes described above, we encounter more complex sentence structures, much less easy to classify, but often clearly reducible to composites of the simple figures, and hence stamped with the same logical clarity.

2. *Off.* 'Faith, there hath beene many great men that haue flatter'd the people, who ne're loued them; and there be many that they haue loued, they know not wherefore: so that if they loue they know not why, they hate vpon no better a ground. Therefore, for *Coriolanus* neyther to care whether they loue, or hate him, manifests the true knowledge he ha's in their disposition, and out of his Noble carelesnesse lets them plainely see't.

1. *Off.* If he did not care whether he had their loue, or no, hee waued indifferently, 'twixt doing them neyther good, nor harme: but he seekes their hate with greater deuotion, then they can render it him; and leaues nothing vndone, that may fully discouer him their opposite. Now to seeme to affect the mallice and displeasure of the People, is as bad, as that which he dislikes, to flatter them for their loue. (L.626; *Cor.* ii.ii.7–26)

It needs no tedious explication to demonstrate that such a passage consists of an intricate interlocking of many of the rudimentary analytic schemes, and that despite its greater intricacy, it displays the same clean edges and precision grinding that characterize its inner parts. Nothing floats ambiguously or tangentially from its reference; every element is locked firmly in place by the logic of the syntax.

Shakespeare's prose, of course, encompasses enormous range and variety, and one neither hopes nor wishes to classify it under a single rubric. With his prodigious mimetic powers, he could virtually erase his own voice and become his own linguistic antiself. Nevertheless, he does have a voice, and that voice emerges in the kind of passage we have been discussing. When Shakespeare mimics the polysyndetic gabble of Pompey or Shallow, or the gasping phrases of Mistress Quickly, or the slovenly jawing of the carriers at Gadshill, his control of decorum is so absolute that incoherence itself never falters. But no tragic hero talks like Pompey; no romantic heroine sounds like Mistress Quickly; no villain reminds us of Shallow. Whereas the language of heroes, fools, and villains alike – of Hamlet and the gravedigger, Falstaff and the Lord Chief Justice, Rosalind and Touchstone, Don John and Dogberry, Edmund and Lear's Fool, Autolycus and Polixenes – if we track it back to its syntactic skeleton, shares the same basic analytic structure, the logicality that in turn is traceable to Euphuism. The logical style, in Shakespeare, represents a norm from which the special idioms of Pompey or Shallow are purposeful departures. In Jonson, to anticipate, and to speak even more roughly, it is the other way around.

To the question of how these stylistic habits correspond to other aspects of Shake-spearean drama, one can offer only hesitant answers. The argumentative character of the prose, its tendency to stick close to its syllogistic basis and to acknowledge this openly through the abundance of logical links – these one might relate to the network of causality that composes the intrigue plot. The intrigue plot depends on a multitude of chain reactions in which events spring out of other events and in their turn precipitate others. Lyly, who carries his own kind of logicality to extremes, tends to lay parallel or antithetic elements side by side without stressing the nexus between them. To speak more simply, he uses fewer connectives, and his plots display an analogous tendency to juxtapose scenes without binding them to each other in causal sequence. Shakespeare, in this respect, resembles more closely the popular playwrights with their "for's" and "therefore's," with the difference that he works with a fuller magazine of logical links; what in the plays of his contemporaries often reduces itself to a linear arrangement of "A leads to B leads to C," becomes in Shakespeare a dense tissue of inner relations, complexly interdependent on one another.

The symmetry and exact balance in Shakespeare's prose, on the other hand, form one aspect of the ceremoniousness of Shakespearean theater. In the prose as in the verse, we feel that we are never far from incantation or ritual. Even when the characters speak with the astounding lifelikeness that Shakespeare seems to command so effort-lessly, we rarely lose the sense that they are talking a language superior to ours, more incisively rhythmical, more spacious, and more ordered. With the balanced, analytic syntax constantly feeding this sense even in moments of low tension, it requires only a slight tightening of the screws to bring us into the great formal harmonies of Falstaff's praise of sack, or Henry V's meditation on kingship, or Edmund's rejection of astrology. At such moments, even when the speaker himself is a spokesman for disorder, the resonant symmetries in the language seem to be reflecting a larger concord on which the plays repose as on a quiet.

Shakespeare's logicality, in any case, contributes to a prose style that – far from being "ungrammatical, perplexed and obscure," as Dr. Johnson complained[7] – is close to a model of clarity. And its clarity probably accounts in part for the unique hold its author's plays have maintained in the theater. Jonson's dramatic prose, winding and knotty, probably did not disturb an Elizabethan audience, but is likely to baffle a contemporary ear, which cannot predict where a sentence will go until it has already reached its destination. But Shakespeare maintains a balance between suspense and resolution just sufficient to satisfy the ear without taxing it. When we hear that "A good Sherris-Sack hath a two-fold operation in it" (L.412; *IIHIV* iv.iii.103–4), we have an advance blueprint of the discourse to be unfolded, and if Falstaff lingers over the description of Operation Number One, we wait expectantly but without irritation for Operation Number Two. When we hear that of two things, "the one" does such and such, we expect shortly to learn that "the other" does thus and so. When we hear "either," we know we shall soon confront the antithetic "or"; when we discover that someone would "rather" do something, we await the inevitable "than." And so with the dozens of other ways in which Shakespeare carves out divisions of thought. They not only foster clarity of exposition, they affect gesture and delivery, dictating antithetic or contrasting motion, and suggesting the proper weight for pauses and accents, enabling a speech to be heard slowly without fatigue or swiftly without bewilderment.[8] They form the building blocks of a speech that even today compensates for changes in the language, and carries an audience securely through any involutions of thought or plot. If these stylistic virtues play only a secondary role in the continuous presence of Shakespeare in the theater, their opposite (which is not a vice), a more irregular and captious syntax, may be held partly responsible for the unjust neglect of Jonson's great comedies.

Notes

1   See Hardin Craig, "Shakespeare and Formal Logic," in *Studies in English Philology, A Miscellany in Honor of Frederick Klaeber*, ed. Kemp Malone and Martin B. Ruud (Minneapolis, 1929), pp. 380–96; Sister Miriam Joseph, *Shakespeare's Use of the Arts of Language* (New York, 1947), *passim*; and, for specimens of formal logic in the Elizabethan drama at large, Allan H. Gilbert, "Logic in the Elizabethan Drama," *Studies in Philology*, XXXII (1935), 527–45.

2   One approaches the subject with more than usual diffidence because of the beating it has taken at the hands of other critics. Setting aside the various attempts to discover a principle governing the shifts between verse and prose, for which (most of them absurd) see the critical bibliography in Milton Crane, *Shakespeare's Prose* (Chicago, 1951), pp. 214–16, one finds mainly a highly charged impressionism combined with a spurious classificationism, as in J. Churton Collins, "Shakespeare as a Prose Writer," *Studies in Shakespeare* (New York, 1904), or Henry W. Wells, "The Continuity of Shakesperian Prose," *Shakespeare Association Bulletin*, XV (July 1940), 175–83. For an up-to-date bibliography see M. C. Bradbrook, "Fifty Years of the Criticism of Shakespeare's Style: A Retrospect," *Shakespeare Survey*, VII (1954), 1–11. Miss Bradbrook's suspicion (p. 4) that the study of Euphuism and related traditional topics has by now exhausted its usefulness is perhaps a wholesome caution; nevertheless only Bond, it seems to me, has fully grasped the importance of Euphuism in Shakespeare, and his documentation remains to be interpreted.

3   Quotations will be from the Folio facsimile edited by Sir Sidney Lee (Oxford, 1902). Each extract is followed by the page number in Lee, then by the corresponding act, scene, and line number in the edition of George Lyman Kittredge (New York, 1936). The following abbreviations are used:

IHIV:	*Henry the Fourth, Part One*
IIHIV:	*Henry the Fourth, Part Two*
HV:	*Henry the Fifth*
Much Ado:	*Much Ado about Nothing*
Merch.:	*The Merchant of Venice*
TN:	*Twelfth Night*
AYL:	*As You Like It*
Alls W:	*All's Well that Ends Well*
MM:	*Measure for Measure*
Troil:	*Troilus and Cressida*
MW:	*The Merry Wives of Windsor*
Ham.:	*Hamlet*
Oth.:	*Othello*
Lear:	*King Lear*

Tim.:	Timon of Athens
Cor.:	Coriolanus
Ant.:	Antony and Cleopatra
Cymb.:	Cymbeline
WT:	The Winter's Tale
Temp.:	The Tempest

4 E. A. Abbott, *A Shakespearian Grammar*, 3d ed. (London, 1897), pp. 101–2, cites a few appearances of the conjunction "for," but without giving any inkling of its frequency. Abbott, interested primarily in irregularities, i.e., in points of difference between Elizabethan and modern grammar, also ignores causal connectives such as "hence" and "therefore" whose usage remains unchanged in the modern language. Wilhelm Franz's exhaustive and imposing *Die Sprache Shakespeares*, 4th edn. of *Shakespeare Grammatik* (Halle, 1939), tabulates many of the logical devices, the correlatives, etc., discussed below, especially in pp. 427–473 ("Die Konjunktion"), but, again, chiefly in order to define the limits of Shakespearean grammar, the range of its possibilities, without concerning himself with whether such-and-such a syntactic scheme occurs once or a hundred times in Shakespeare.

5 W. K. Wimsatt, Jr., *The Prose Style of Samuel Johnson* (New Haven, 1941), p. 12.

6 With the following observation of Kenneth Muir I naturally find myself in hearty accord: "Shakespeare was in no danger of becoming too colloquial in his dialogue. Even his apparently colloquial prose is a good deal further from actual Elizabethan speech than the dialogue of Middleton or Jonson; and when in his verse he uses language of extraordinary simplicity the powerful effect is obtained largely by contrast with the more complex language used elsewhere" ("Shakespeare and Rhetoric," *Shakespeare Jahrbuch*, XC [1954], 60).

7 *Johnson on Shakespeare*, ed. Walter Raleigh (London, 1908), p. 42 – speaking, evidently, of Shakespeare's prose and verse alike.

8 Surprisingly, something like the same point was made by Ralph Waldo Emerson, in "Shakespeare, or The Poet," *Complete Works*, ed. Edward Waldo Emerson, 12 vols. (Boston, 1903), IV, 214: "Though the speeches in the plays, and single lines, have a beauty which tempts the ear to pause on them for their euphuism, yet the sentence is so loaded with meaning and so linked with its foregoers and followers, that the logician is satisfied."

48

The Play of Phrase and Line

George T. Wright

The tunes that he writes to, the whole great art of his music-making, we can master.
(Harley Granville-Barker, I.14)

From Uniformity to Variety

We saw earlier that Tudor poetry treated the iambic pentameter line as the sum of two phrases, the first of four syllables, the second of six. To meet this structural requirement, poets from Surrey to Sidney understood that they needed to find English phrases that filled the measurements: phrases exact in length and sounding an iambic pattern. For such an art, the phrase is clearly subordinate to the line. Among all the English phrases that occur to the poet as suitable to his other-than-metrical purposes, the poet must search for those that fit not only the iambic mold but the four-six pattern as well. Even today, amateur poets who try their hand at iambic pentameter will start in much the same way – by fishing among the phrases that carry the right content for the ones that also have the right form.

This way of writing verse imposes a grim authority on the metrical line and a rigid subservience on English phrases. It leaves the poet unable to select freely from the immense range of possible English phrases. In time a practicing poet – Gascoigne, for example – learns to cope cheerfully with this system of limited choices. But its implacable metrical requirements inevitably hamper his freedom of movement. The verse becomes an arrangement of phrases-that-meet-the-requirement, not a form that makes full use of the rhythmic resources of the English language. It is only after the rigid structure of the line has been modified that iambic pentameter verse becomes capable of accommodating a full spectrum of English phrases. By the end of Shakespeare's career, partly through the work of his predecessors and contemporaries, and partly through his own tireless experimentation, the English dramatic blank-verse line has become hospitable to virtually any phrases the poet wants to use. The clumsy and formulaic Tudor pentameter is gradually transformed into the flexible, sinuous line of Shakespeare's later plays.

This change comes about as the result of several related changes in the perception of the iambic pentameter line. First, the poets become aware that, unlike the stress of Latin poetry, English verse stress may be of different degrees. The five stressed syllables in a line need not be equal in stress; neither must the unstressed syllables. All that is required to keep the meter is a sense of alternating stresses, and this can be maintained by a line that permits different levels of stress in the correspondingly placed syllables of successive feet. The line thus implicitly recognizes that in English speech the syllables that serve as successive peaks of intensity do not all possess the same degree or kind of prominence, and the same is true of successive minor syllables.

The poets also become aware that they can make the iambic pattern more deliberate and grave through spondees, more rapid through pyrrhics, or more urgent through trochees.[1] To admit these possible patterns into iambic pentameter verse with some frequency is to admit a great number of potential English phrases, phrases that show not only a pattern of

Thĕ níght ĭs dárk

and

Thĕ níght ĭs dárk ănd stíll,

but also

Dárk ĭs thĕ níght,

Iň thĕ dàrk níght,

Thĕ dárk, stìll níght,

Nów thĕ dàrk níght,

and so on, patterns that appear frequently in Sidney's *Astrophil and Stella.*

In addition, the poets come to see that the line need not pause after the fourth syllable; it may pause instead after the sixth, or after the fifth or seventh, or later, or earlier, or not at all. So long a line must frequently break somewhere; most phrases in English are not ten syllables long, and although phrases can often be combined into larger word-groups that require no pause, readers and actors are likely in most lines to hear or enact a pause somewhere. But the increased freedom in placing the line break means that poets may now write phrases of three, five, or seven syllables as readily as phrases of four or six syllables. Obviously, tens of thousands of potential phrases will now be available to the poet which would not earlier have fitted the meter easily, and in time lines may divide after any syllable, or not at all:

Love? His affections do not that way tend (*Hamlet*, III.i.162)

My thought, whose murther yet is but fantastical (*Macbeth*, I.iii.139)

Then trip him, that his heels may kick at heaven (*Hamlet*, III.iii.93)

If you have tears, prepare to shed them now (*Julius Caesar*, III.ii.169)

Her father lov'd me, oft invited me (*Othello*, I.iii.127)

Love looks not with the eyes, but with the mind (*A Midsummer Night's Dream*, I.i.234)

I come to bury Caesar, not to praise him (*Julius Caesar*, III.ii.74)

If music be the food of love, play on (*Twelfth Night*, I.i.1)

Why speaks my father so ungently? This (*The Tempest*, I.ii.445)

This supernatural soliciting (*Macbeth*, I.iii.130)

Finally, the poets come to see that even the end-line stop is not sacred, that if the sense of a phrase may run over the midline pause, the sense of a line may run over the line-ending. At first, the freedom to extend the phrase over the line is used with considerable restraint; later, Shakespeare and others enjamb their lines frequently and even use the line-ending to separate words that belong to the same phrase.

Clearly, if the phrase can run over the line, and if the midline break can come anywhere or nowhere, the poet is under virtually no restriction in choosing his English phrases and sentences. They may be long or short, compressed or expanded; all that is required is that they be iambic. But even this requirement is much easier to meet when pronunciation is as flexible as Shakespeare's was, when trochaic, pyrrhic, and spondaic variation is frequent, when phrasal rhythms are more deeply attended to, and when the line may have extra syllables at the midline break or at the line-ending, may omit syllables at the beginning or at the middle of a line, or, if it is important, may admit or omit syllables anywhere. When we consider further that the mature Shakespeare feels free to write short lines and long ones, we can see that, unlike the earlier strict Tudor verse, Shakespearean iambic pentameter in its fully developed form alters the meter in a dozen ways to accommodate the variety of English phrasing. Under Shakespeare's direction, the phrase becomes liberated from the severe stewardship of an autocratic meter; indeed, by the end of his career the phrase sometimes appears to have taken the line into its own hands.

The Odd-Syllable Phrasal Break

Ants Oras's extensive survey of pauses marked by punctuation in the verse of Shakespeare and other poets and playwrights showed with great clarity the readiness with which late Elizabethan writers learned to let their lines pause after other syllables than the fourth.[2] Oras called particular attention to two developments in Shakespeare's pausing practice: an increase in odd-syllable pauses, and an increase in late-line pauses. Both these changes have momentous consequences for Shakespeare's iambic pentameter and for that of later poets and playwrights.

Spenser's readiness to break the line frequently after the fifth (or another odd) syllable accounts in part for the easy, melodious movement of his verse, its occasional trochaic current, and its rhythmical variety. This change immediately transformed iambic pentameter; it broke the iambic lock on the verse phrase. Whereas Gascoigne and poets of his generation wrote a verse that sounded essentially the same in every line – a four-syllable phrase followed by a six-syllable phrase – the perception that a line could as conveniently break after an odd syllable as after an even one made it possible for poets to achieve great variety: to break the ten-syllable line early or late; after a stress or an unstress; decisively, faintly, or not at all. Like Spenser, Shakespeare learned to write successive lines with very different rhythmical contours that nevertheless remained metrically iambic:

> Why rather, Sleep, liest thou in smoky cribs,
> Upon uneasy pallets stretching thee,
> And hush'd with buzzing night-flies to thy slumber
> (2 *Henry IV*, iii.i.9–11)

The second and third lines follow a mainly trochaic inner rhythm, in contrast to the stronger iambic cast of the first, though "rather" and "smoky" foreshadow what will in the next lines become the dominant trochaic pattern. Shakespeare and his most capable contemporaries knew how various a passage can sound when, with or without punctuation, the phrasing in one line breaks after the fourth or sixth syllable and the phrasing in the next one breaks after the fifth syllable (or vice versa) – in effect, when the phrasing of one line is iambic and that of the next (or last) is trochaic:

> Nor Mars his sword nor war's quick fire shall burn
> The living record of your memory.
> (Sonnet 55: 7–8)

> Thus was I, sleeping, by a brother's hand
> Of life, of crown, of queen, at once dispatch'd
> (*Hamlet*, i.v.74–5)

The perception that an iambic line does not have to be composed entirely or even largely of iambic segments but may comprise as many as four trochaic words and phrases must have been liberating to the poets:

> Like strengthless hinges, buckle under life
> (2 *Henry IV*, i.i.141)

> And never trouble Peter for the matter
> (*Romeo and Juliet*, iv.iv.19)

> Malice domestic, foreign levy, nothing
> (*Macbeth*, iii.ii.25)

> Most mighty sovereign, on the western coast
> Rideth a puissant navy; to our shores
> Throng many doubtful hollow-hearted friends
> (*Richard III*, iv.iv.433–5)

From this point on, all competent writers of iambic pentameter verse will take it for granted that the inner rhythm of the line may – indeed, must – be varied, that iambic lines will assimilate trochaic (or amphibrachic, or sometimes even dactylic) phrases. Henceforth, the better poets will recognize that variety is the key to energy, and they will use feet as various as those that appear in the opening line of Sonnet 30:

Whén tŏ | the séslsiŏns of | swèet síllent thought

Such a line would probably have disconcerted Gascoigne. Its two trochaic words are painlessly absorbed into the iambic meter. A break in phrasing occurs after the fifth syllable, and the line uses a pyrrhic, a spondaic, and a trochaic foot. Only one *foot* is trochaic here, but it is not one that involves either of the trochaic *words*. Shakespeare's iambic pentameter characteristically creates such complex and contradictory relations between iambic and trochaic feet, iambic and trochaic phrasing. In doing so, it shows that the art of iambic pentameter consists very largely in keeping such relations various, interesting, and, in some sense, natural.

The fifth- (or seventh-) syllable break also makes it possible to write lines in which the stress and the beat hold to the even syllables while the phrase and some major words do not:

> His eyes saw *her* eyes *as* they had not seen them
> (*Venus and Adonis*, 357)

> As he takes *from* you, I engraft you new
> (Sonnet 15: 14)

> On this side *my* hand, *and* on *that* side *yours*
> (*Richard II*, iv.i.183)

In these lines the even (iambic) *beat* is kept, the major stresses falling on alternate syllables; but the even-syllable phrasing and the expectation that stress will fall on words that belong to the major grammatical categories are *not* kept; and still the phrasing sounds natural. In Gascoigne's metric, all these variables had to fall together: beat, ictus, stress, phrase, major words. This much more subtle metric permits some of them on occasion to run counter to others, as they do in actual English speech, and results in a richer, more engaging line. The variety and vitality of Shakespeare's verse and that of many of his contemporaries depend substantially on the readiness with which they embed trochaic phrases, with or without punctuation or pauses, in the iambic line.

To sum up: the odd-syllable pause enables the poet to make use of differently shaped metrical segments, deploy a trochaic inner rhythm, and yet still adhere to an iambic meter, the iambic nature of a line becoming its deep structure, though not necessarily its surface form. Feet, as feet, become less audible. We can still locate them by analysis, but since, in the feminine line, the phrases run over the foot-margins, the way such lines conform to the meter will be less obvious. In time, scholars and poets may even come to doubt whether such lines, or *any* lines, are really composed of feet. That is, they will come to think of feet as intrusive markers and not merely as any set of syllables that constitutes one of the recurrent and constituent rhythmic units in a line; and they will therefore think the analysis of lines by feet a tedious, academic, and insensitive business (as it certainly can be when it is done in a tedious, academic, and insensitive way). But it is also possible to see the development of the odd-syllable pause as leading, in conjunction with many of the other refinements we have been tracing, to a subtle metric that conceals its artifice, in which the phrasing veils the structure. The iambic body runs on, foot by foot, but its bones show less and less: its segments varied in length, its iambs varied in strength, its feet hidden in the phrase.

Counterpoint of Line and Sentence

The other notable shift in Shakespeare's line is from a strong reliance on pauses after the fourth (or fifth) syllable to a preference for pauses after the sixth (or seventh), or even later. As Oras demonstrates (15–16), the late break makes enjambment more likely.[3] The frequent extra-metrical syllables and feminine (or even triple) endings contribute further to our impression, strong for the later plays, that Shakespeare is saying more than even the most elliptical lines convey.[4] But once enjambment becomes the rule rather than the exception, once the phrase typically ends in midline and the line in midphrase, we can see that there are two different orders at work in this verse: the metrical order, which obliges us to sustain, by voice or ear, the approximate regularities and lengths of a rhythmic pattern; and the grammatical order, which obliges us to follow the emerging structural relationships among the elements of our common speech and to apprehend these passing structures as meaningful aggregates, formally coherent, semantically significant, and rhetorically compelling. Both these orders we may, as listeners, occasionally lose track of; but they run a dual course, and if we fail to hear how they carry and shed one another, we miss a significant dimension of the play.

In Shakespeare's poems and earlier plays the two orders usually work together, without tension, in highly patterned single and double lines:

Queen		
Elizabeth:	What stay had I but Edward? and he's gone.	
Children:	What stay had we but Clarence? and he's gone.	
Duchess:	What stays had I but they? and they are gone.	
Queen		
Elizabeth:	Was never widow had so dear a loss.	
Children:	Were never orphans had so dear a loss.	
Duchess.	Was never mother had so dear a loss.	

(Richard III, ii.ii.74–9)

For wisdom's sake, a word that all men love,
Or for love's sake, a word that loves all men,

> Or for men's sake, the authors of these women,
> Or women's sake, by whom we men are men,
> Let us once lose our oaths to find ourselves,
> Or else we lose ourselves to keep our oaths.
> It is religion to be thus forsworn:
> For charity itself fulfills the law,
> And who can sever love from charity?
> *(Love's Labor's Lost*, iv.iii.354–62)

Impressive longer periods can be built out of such smaller units:

> This royal throne of kings, this sceptred isle,
> This earth of majesty, this seat of Mars,
> This other Eden, demi-paradise,
> This fortress built by Nature for herself
> Against infection and the hand of war,
> This happy breed of men, this little world,
> This precious stone set in the silver sea,
> Which serves it in the office of a wall,
> Or as a moat defensive to a house,
> Against the envy of less happier lands;
> This blessed plot, this earth, this realm, this England,
> This nurse, this teeming womb of royal kings,
> Fear'd by their breed, and famous by their birth,
> Renowned for their deeds as far from home,
> For Christian service and true chivalry,
> As is the sepulchre in stubborn Jewry
> Of the world's ransom, blessed Mary's Son;
> This land of such dear souls, this dear dear land,
> Dear for her reputation through the world,
> Is now leas'd out – I die pronouncing it –
> Like to a tenement or pelting farm
> *(Richard II*, ii.i.40–60)

But the syntax gradually becomes more flexible and sinuous, and sentences flow through less line-bound rhetorical units. As we saw earlier, Lorenzo and Jessica share each other's lines in love, Brutus and Cassius in quarrel. Boundaries of line and phrase are less often congruent. In *As You Like It*, Jaques's speech on the seven ages begins in midline, and so does his evocation of all ages but the second. For twenty lines, line and sentence never end together until the last line arrives at the completeness of death:

> Sans teeth, sans eyes, sans taste, sans every thing. (ii.vii.166)

Most speeches of this period still include many sentences or clauses that match the lines in length, but Shakespeare is increasingly willing to break the pattern of congruence by free enjambment and sentences that end in midline. By the end of *Hamlet*, a new speech can be heard, at least briefly:

Hamlet:	Sir, in my heart there was a kind of fighting	
	That would not let me sleep. Methought I lay	5
	Worse than the mutines in the bilboes. Rashly –	
	And prais'd be rashness for it – let us know	
	Our indiscretion sometimes serves us well	
	When our deep plots do pall, and that should learn us	
	There's a divinity that shapes our ends,	10
	Rough-hew them how we will –	
Horatio:	That is most certain.	
Hamlet:	Up from my cabin,	
	My sea-gown scarf'd about me, in the dark	
	Grop'd I to find out them, had my desire,	
	Finger'd their packet, and in fine withdrew	15
	To mine own room again, making so bold,	
	My fears forgetting manners, to unseal	
	Their grand commission; where I found, Horatio –	
	Ah, royal knavery! – an exact command,	
	Larded with many several sorts of reasons,	20
	Importing Denmark's health and England's too,	
	With, ho, such bugs and goblins in my life,	
	That, on the supervise, no leisure bated,	
	No, not to stay the grinding of the axe,	
	My head should be struck off.	25

(v.ii.4–25)

The passage still includes lines that read as complete sense-units from beginning to end (8, 10, 20–22, 24). But the special authority of Hamlet's voice, which many readers have interpreted as signaling a new maturity, derives from the assurance with which these sentences negotiate the metrical boundaries. Hamlet's excitement ("That would not let me sleep") is conveyed by the enjambment of "lay / Worse" in lines 5–6, by the break after the ninth syllable in line 6, and by the extended self-interruption that follows. Strong punctuation divides these lines (5–7) into segments of very different lengths and into phrases severely disconnected from one another. This segmentation continues in Hamlet's next speech, whose first seven-and-a-half lines are entirely composed of short phrases.

This kind of arrangement, especially when it begins with a short line, jeopardizes the listener's sense of the meter. We are given every opportunity to go astray as we try to fit the phrasal segments together to form lines that satisfy the ear's demand for metrical completeness. We may even think, for a couple of lines, that Hamlet, like so many Shakespearean speakers, has slipped once more into prose. Even if we do not go wrong, even if the printed page or the audible iambic current keeps us on track, we may experience the lines in this passage as composed of oddly fitted segments and as very different in character from the lines that follow (20–4), masterly in their way but eccentric, perfectly suited to Hamlet the impresario but needing, like him, to be watched.

From at least this point on in Shakespeare's career, line and sentence appear to have achieved a comparable eminence, the sentence acknowledging the metrical authority of the line on its own ground but extending the flow of words beyond the single or double line, and doing so primarily by means of more frequent midline beginnings and endings. These now take three distinct forms, depending on whether they begin or end in midline.

Some run from midline to midline (*a*):

> No! to be once in doubt
> Is once to be resolv'd
> (*Othello*, iii.iii.179–80)

> O brave new world
> That has such people in't!
> (*The Tempest*, v.i.183–4)

Others run from midline to full line (*b*):

> What beast was't then
> That made you break this enterprise to me?
> (*Macbeth*, i.vii.47–8)

> Look with what courteous action
> It waves you to a more removed ground.
> (*Hamlet*, i.iv.60–1)[5]

Still others run from full line to midline (*c*):

> It was the lark, the herald of the morn,
> No nightingale.
> (*Romeo and Juliet*, iii.v.6–7)

> The dark and vicious place where thee he got
> Cost him his eyes.
> (*King Lear*, v.iii.173–4)

Any of these forms may be amplified by means of additional lines between the first and the last. (Subscripts after the letter indicate the number of intervening lines.)

(a_1)
> You seem to understand me,
> By each at once her choppy finger laying
> Upon her skinny lips.
> (*Macbeth*, i.iii.43–5)

(b_1)
> If she must teem,
> Create her child of spleen, that it may live
> And be a thwart disnatur'd torment to her.
> (*King Lear*, i.iv.281–3)

(*c₂*)   If thou didst ever hold me in thy heart,
    Absent thee from felicity a while,
    And in this harsh world draw thy breath in pain
    To tell my story.
                (*Hamlet*, v.ii.346–9)

In the later plays of Shakespeare, these are the principal components of the characters' metrical speeches, which combine them into a smooth and various union of line and sentence. The two rhythmical powers, metrical and syntactical, are clearly distinct, with neither subservient to the other; both are impressive, formidable, even majestic structures, but they remain separate, held by the now commanding poet not in resolution but in poise.

We can see this system actively at work in the great speech Shakespeare provides for Macbeth to debate the murder of Duncan. The whole speech alternates from one to another of the three modes outlined above, *a*, *b*, or *c*, and we can chart them easily in the speech, noting as well the way subordinate cola *within* the sentences and within each other also vary from one of these line-arrangements to another (see figure 1).

The only departures from these three basic line-movements come in one or two short phrases, shorter than their lines, which, though caught up in the measured flow, still stand in some sense on their own: certainly "He's here in double trust" (12), and conceivably "which o'erleaps itself" (27). Such short phrases, and phrases shorter still, will appear much more frequently in later plays and break up what is here, in spite of everything, the graceful forward movement of the passage. Here the midline pauses momentarily halt that flow, but the ubiquitous enjambment starts it going again, and the principal impression of the verse, on anyone who can maintain a steady sense of the counterpoint between line and phrase, line and sentence, is of a sequence of lines more disposed to interior than to final pauses. Insofar as we register the ends of the lines at all, they resemble those hesitations that occur in speech not at the expected junctures, or not there only, but within phrases and before important words. Halted in the middle, hurried or hesitant at the end, the lines nevertheless continue to sound like iambic pentameter, but they seem cracked and weathered – like Hermione, showing their wrinkles, their lines of stress.

The Segmented Line

This counterpoint style is far removed from that of the early plays, with their long, continuous lines and line-by-line accumulation of rhetorical segments. But Shakespeare was to go further still. In *Antony and Cleopatra*, *Coriolanus*, *Timon of Athens*, *Cymbeline*, and the first half of *The Winter's Tale*, he develops a yet more radical and jagged technique for posing antagonistic lengths of line and phrase against each other. Most of the previous plays, from *Richard II* to *Macbeth*, include numerous passages notable for their mellifluous phrasing and gracefully extended arguments. But, except for a few famous measures in *Antony and Cleopatra*, this later group of plays contains almost no set speeches likely to tempt the inveterate memorizer. Speech here tends to be abrupt and agitated, the rift between phrase and line a constant feature of the verse. Shakespeare seems to have noticed that although sentences of English speech are often

If it were done, when 'tis done, then 'twere well
It were done quickly. If th' assassination
Could trammel up the consequence, and catch
With his surcease, success; that but this blow
Might be the be-all and the end-all—here,
But here, upon this bank and shoal of time,
We'ld jump the life to come. But in these cases
We still have judgment here, that we but teach
Bloody instructions, which, being taught, return
To plague th' inventor. This even-handed justice
Commends th' ingredience of our poison'd chalice
To our own lips. He's here in double trust:
First, as I am his kinsman and his subject,
Strong both against the deed; then, as his host,
Who should against his murtherer shut the door,
Not bear the knife myself. Besides, this Duncan
Hath borne his faculties so meek, hath been
So clear in his great office, that his virtues
Will plead like angels, trumpet-tongu'd, against
The deep damnation of his taking-off;
And pity, like a naked new-born babe,
Striding the blast, or heaven's cherubin, hors'd
Upon the sightless couriers of the air,
Shall blow the horrid deed in every eye,
That tears shall drown the wind. I have no spur
To prick the sides of my intent, but only
Vaulting ambition, which o'erleaps itself,
And falls on th' other—

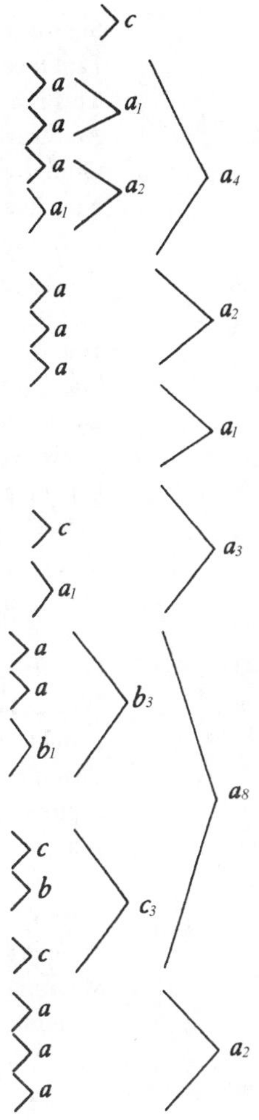

Figure 1 *Macbeth*, I.vii.1–28. Subscripts indicate the number of interior lines included in larger cola or sentences.

longer than a line, phrases are usually shorter, and that often a short phrase will constitute a short sentence. This perception results in a notable increase in short phrases that constitute whole sentences or cola, a tactic which sharply increases the number of breaks in some lines. Instead of the long, magisterially controlled sentences that stride through the flowing lines of the middle plays, Shakespeare now allows his characters to speak in short bursts much of the time. The phrases, syntactically disconnected, are at least as metrically regular as the verse of that earlier period (if anything, we find in these plays fewer medial trochees and proportionally fewer short lines and alexandrines). But the line is now capable of bearing almost any kind of phrasal freight; it can be broken into several segments, shaped and combined in a great variety of ways. In turn, it can break up the phrase into bits and pieces of any description. The strangeness of this verse increases with each play in the series, at least up to *Cymbeline* and the first half of *The Winter's Tale:*

So, so; come give me that: this way – well said.
Fare thee well, dame, what e'er becomes of me.
This is a soldier's kiss; rebukable
And worthy shameful check it were, to stand
On more mechanic compliment. I'll leave thee
Now like a man of steel. You that will fight,
Follow me close, I'll bring you to't. Adieu.
                    (*Antony and Cleopatra*, iv.iv.28–34)

Your voices? For your voices I have fought;
Watch'd for your voices; for your voices bear
Of wounds two dozen odd; battles thrice six
I have seen, and heard of; for your voices have
Done many things, some less, some more. Your voices?
Indeed I would be consul.
                    (*Coriolanus*, ii.iii.126–31)

           O Jove, I think
Foundations fly the wretched: such, I mean,
Where they should be reliev'd. Two beggars told me
I could not miss my way. Will poor folks lie,
That have afflictions on them, knowing 'tis
A punishment or trial? Yes; no wonder,
When rich ones scarce tell true. To lapse in fullness
Is sorer than to lie for need; and falsehood
Is worse in kings than beggars. My dear lord,
Thou art one o' th' false ones. Now I think on thee,
My hunger's gone; but even before, I was
At point to sink for food.
                    (*Cymbeline*, iii.vi.6–17)

As we can see from these passages, Shakespeare's later dramatic verse alters the classical line technique by adding other possibilities of line arrangement. These appear in earlier verse as well, but infrequently. Now they become characteristic.

1.   The segmented line may be divided more than once:

           How, dare not? do not? do you know, and dare not?
                    (*The Winter's Tale*, i.ii.377)

The laws, your curb and whip, in their rough power
Has uncheck'd theft. Love not yourselves, away,
Rob one another, there's more gold, cut throats
                    (*Timon of Athens*, iv.iii.443–5)

           Music; awake her: strike:
'Tis time: descend: be stone no more: approach
           (*The Winter's Tale*, v.iii.98–9)

2.   It may be divided into notably unequal segments:

> Hath borne his faculties so meek, hath been
>
>> (*Macbeth*, i.vii.17)

> Why speaks my father so ungently? This
>
>> (*The Tempest*, i.ii.445)

> Such, and such pictures: there the window, such
>
>> (*Cymbeline*, ii.ii.25)

3.   The sense runs over much more often into the next line, a tendency facilitated by Shakespeare's radically increased usage of weak and light line-endings. That is, Shakespeare ends many lines in his late plays with words we usually expect to *begin* phrases, word-groups, or clauses: *and, but; I, you, we,* and other nominative pronouns; *to, for, from, with, at, by,* and other prepositions; *which, that, who, whom, where, when, as if;* auxiliary verbs followed immediately by the main verb: *have / Done, would / Have, might / Be;* and *such / As, as / If, O,* and other introductory particles. Such endings lead us without pause over the line-ending. Along with Shakespeare's frequent fifth-foot pyrrhics, the weak or light ending (which is also pyrrhic) continues that diminution of emphasis with which Shakespeare frequently treats the line's last foot. That foot has already, in blank verse, lost its rhyme; now it loses its position as the foot most certain to receive strong stress and becomes, at least occasionally, as weak and transient as any other foot.

As we read or listen to this verse, as we are carried on the current of its sound, the end of the line is no longer our unambiguous destination. The phrase carves up the line, runs over the edges, comes to a stop where it pleases. Such at least is the impression it gives of having its own order to impose on the pliant line (which, as we have noted, is often remarkably regular). We have come a long way in a few years: from the line in which the component phrases followed to the end without demur the correct syllabic outline, to one in which a free and flexible sentence keeps the beat in its own highly individual way, the breaks coming anywhere – or, as one sometimes feels, anywhere but at the end of the line.

Such verse requires us to be equally attentive to the claims of the line and the claims of the sentence. We take for granted the syllable-and-stress requirements of the line, which are met here very complacently, but this verse has made us aware as well of the different kind of order to be found in the sentence, a grammatical order not easily described but known to every competent speaker of English. In Shakespeare's earlier verse, and in the verse of his older contemporaries, the order of the sentence is never so deeply insisted on. The usual problem for the poet, as we have seen, is to tame the phrase to the line, to look for phrasal combinations acquiescent enough in their rhythms not to rock the pentameter canoe. No doubt public conditions favorable to poets encouraged them to move quickly beyond this relatively primitive situation, and the enthusiastic response of a theater audience led a few poets to venture boldly toward grander conceptions of the relations between line and phrase. But it is Shakespeare, more even than Spenser or Donne or Jonson, who develops a style (or styles) capable of revealing in the most profound ways what the two orders mean, what different powers they stand for, and how both can be embodied at once, but differently, in identical sequences of words.

In the later plays especially, Shakespeare develops a tense verse art to which, in the English tradition, only those of Donne and Hopkins are comparable. Powerful prose passages compete with the verse for some of the sublimest material. The line is more and more cast into structural doubt by the techniques we have noticed: late-line pauses and free enjambment; a sentence that flows freely over the metrical margins; rashes of short-line exchanges that hover between verse and prose; brief and abrupt bursts of staccato phrases that in their jagged discourse seem almost, at times, to mock both line and phrase.

The style of these late plays (from *Antony and Cleopatra* to *Cymbeline*) bespeaks a distrust of sententious rhetoric, of the deceitful uses and users of language such as they all touch and turn on. Shakespeare is clearly rethinking the whole relationship of line and phrase. Both are in some sense treated as shams, as cheats, whatever their glories – like the grandiosities of Antony and Cleopatra, the honors of Coriolanus and the favors of the Roman people, the claims of friendship and patriotism in *Timon*, the flattery and empty vows of *Cymbeline*. *The Winter's Tale* and *The Tempest* quite obviously deal with the problem of extracting a gifted speaker from such disillusion. The enchanted worlds of the last full play and a half partake of that harmonious grace, that significant deliberateness, proceeds from Shakespeare's high command of the language theory of his time.

Equilibrium

The hallmark of the new verse is the autonomy of the phrase, no longer obedient to the line or the line-segment but with its own authority well established. In *The Winter's Tale*, the lines are still heavily punctuated; pauses are invited everywhere. But now, in the redemptive second half of the play, the tone has utterly changed, and techniques once used to halt the flow of speech serve only to divert it into the most graceful pools and eddies. (The punctuation, except for some apostrophes and hyphens, is that of the Folio.)

> *Perdita:*   Now (my fair'st friend),
> I would I had some flowers o'th' spring, that might
> Become your time of day: and yours, and yours,
> That wear upon your virgin-branches yet   115
> Your maidenheads growing: O Proserpina,
> For the flowers now, that (frighted) thou let'st fall
> From Dis's wagon: daffodils,
> That come before the swallow dares, and take
> The winds of March with beauty: violets (dim,   120
> But sweeter than the lids of Juno's eyes,
> Or Cytherea's breath) pale primroses,
> That die unmarried, ere they can behold
> Bright Phoebus in his strength (a malady
> Most incident to maids:) bold oxlips, and   125

The crown imperial: lilies of all kinds,
(The flower-de-luce being one.) O, these I lack,
To make you garlands of) and my sweet friend,
To strew him o'er, and o'er.

Florizel: What? like a corse?

Perdita: No, like a bank, for love to lie, and play on: 130
Not like a corse: or if: not to be buried,
But quick, and in mine arms. Come, take your flowers,
Methinks I play as I have seen them do
In Whitsun pastorals: Sure this robe of mine
Does change my disposition:

Florizel: What you do,   135
Still betters what is done. When you speak (sweet)
I'ld have you do it ever: when you sing,
I'ld have you buy, and sell so: so give alms,
Pray so: and for the ord'ring your affairs,
To sing them too. When you do dance, I wish you   140
A wave o'th' sea, that you might ever do
Nothing but that: move still, still so:
And own no other function. Each your doing,
(So singular, in each particular)
Crowns what you are doing, in the present deeds,   145
That all your acts, are queens.

                                 (iv.iv.112–46)

Now and then the periods open up for stretches as long as a line and a half (lines 113–14, 115–16, 119–20, 133–4), but never for longer than that, unless the last four lines are heard as providing a more ample climax to the rhetoric of flower and sea. Most of the phrases are closely guarded by commas or stronger punctuation. The marking is largely internal: twenty-two of the full lines have final punctuation, thirty interior; of these thirty, thirteen have more than one interior mark of punctuation. The strongest punctuation (periods, colons, question marks) is almost always interior (twenty-one to three); when it is not, it concludes very brief phrases (lines 129, 130, 142). But, despite the multitude of brief phrases, which constantly carve the line into short segments, the tone of the passage is unfailingly lyrical. Shakespeare has succeeded in adapting the staccato style to a legato technique; the mellifluous phrasing – marked by varied vowels, unclustered and largely liquid and nasal consonants, and graceful patterns of alliteration and assonance – gives to the passage (a survey of whose punctuation alone might lead us to expect it to be jagged and harsh) a smooth, unruffled flow. The almost entirely regular iambic character of that flow is disguised by the highly varied segmentation, which lends itself to pauses of different lengths and frequent minor shifts in tone. Indeed, this is justly one of the most admired lyrical passages in all of Shakespeare. But it achieves this eminence not through the swelling period and the resonant phrase. Each item in Perdita's cornucopia, or in Florizel's recitation of Perdita's graces, is struck off fresh, not weighted with grandiose phrasing. Even the classical references are to simple matters perfectly in harmony with the pastoral imagery – a far cry from the way Lear, Othello, and even Isabella grandly invoke nature and supernature to reinforce much more theatrically their much more melodramatic emotions:

And O you mortal engines, whose rude throats
Th'immortal Jove's dread clamors counterfeit,
Farewell! Othello's occupation's gone.
(Othello, iii.iii.355–7)

Blow winds, and crack your cheeks; rage, blow
You cataracts, and hurricanoes spout,
Till you have drench'd our steeples, drown'd the cocks.
(King Lear, iii.ii.1–3)

Could great men thunder
As Jove himself does, Jove would never be quiet,
For every pelting, petty officer
Would use his heaven for thunder,
Nothing but thunder!
(Measure for Measure, ii.ii.110–14)

The emotions are different, the people are different, the genres are different. But it is also the style that has changed, and characters in the last two plays are not so ready to invest in swollen rhetoric.

When Prospero then, in the highest-reaching speech of *The Tempest*, bids farewell to the magical powers he has grown old in exercising, his speech has a different relation to grandness from those we have been accustomed to hear from the commanding male protagonists of earlier plays. In many respects, the passage appears to return to the classical midline-to-midline arrangement of the great middle plays, from *As You Like It* to *Macbeth*. But the rhetoric is now more restrained than it has usually been. The references to supernatural forces are literal: Prospero, after all, has performed the acts he refers to, and specifically with the help of the powers he here invokes. To record this invocation, Shakespeare employs an iambic pentameter whose major variations come in the form of phrasal variety (the sense distributes emphasis to form pyrrhics, spondees, and trochees of different strengths, and even one straddling trochee), along with an unusually flexible management of the sentence-flow from midline to midline over line-endings that themselves may bear any degree of emphasis from slight to strong. Verse line and phrasal or clausal unit are rarely congruent. The sentences and the sentence parts run over the margins constantly and require different numbers of syllables in the succeeding lines to complete their sense. This passage perhaps most perfectly illustrates the concluding stage of Shakespeare's metrical artistry and exhibits the highest achievement of his art, attained precisely in the act of renouncing it:

Ye elves of hills, brooks, standing lakes, and groves,
And ye that on the sands with printless foot
Do chase the ebbing Neptune, and do fly him   35
When he comes back; you demi-puppets that
By moonshine do the green sour ringlets make,
Whereof the ewe not bites; and you whose pastime
Is to make midnight mushrumps, that rejoice
To hear the solemn curfew: by whose aid   40

(Weak masters though ye be) I have bedimm'd
The noontide sun, call'd forth the mutinous winds,
And 'twixt the green sea and the azur'd vault
Set roaring war; to the dread rattling thunder
Have I given fire, and rifted Jove's stout oak   45
With his own bolt; the strong-bas'd promontory
Have I made shake, and by the spurs pluck'd up
The pine and cedar. Graves at my command
Have wak'd their sleepers, op'd, and let 'em forth
By my so potent art. But this rough magic   50
I here abjure; and when I have requir'd
Some heavenly music (which even now I do)
To work mine end upon their senses that
This airy charm is for, I'll break my staff,
Bury it certain fathoms in the earth,   55
And deeper than did ever plummet sound
I'll drown my book.[6]

(v.i.33–57)

The rhetorical impulse to divide a subject into parts, and its parts into parts, an impulse often thwarted by the short-burst technique of the plays from *Antony and Cleopatra* through *Cymbeline*, recovers its energy here. Essentially, the passage says: (1) You minor natural and supernatural agents, (2) by whose aid I have exercised command over natural elements and processes, (3) I am now about to resign these powers. But each of these three cola is divided or developed differently, and with an impressive ease and force. Listening to the passage (even if we only read it from the page), we must attend at once to the strong rhythms of each individual line (the metrical measure) and to the imperious, complex sentences (the syntactical measure). But the measure counterpointed with the meter is more than syntactical: it is rhetorical as well. We find in such a speech not simply a succession of sentences but a rounded structure of assertions. The series of four invocations (lines 33–40); the recitation of Prospero's powers in four distinct cola, the first and fourth divided into three parts, the second and third into two ("given" and "rifted," "made shake" and "pluck'd up"); and, after the formal abjuration, the detailing of Prospero's three intended actions of renunciation: all these measure out stages in the procedure of imperial resignation. We follow, that is, all at once the metrical lines, the winding sentences, the tally of significant series, and the emotional curve of the entire rhetorical design.

It is this polyphony, this fourfold rhythm – of line, sentence, argumentative detail embodied in imagery, and accumulating rhetorical impact – that underlies most of Shakespeare's impressive dramatic poetry and is audibly present in this speech. The four are, of course, different in function and operation: the last two are carried forward on the first two – semantic content and emotional design ride on the meter and the syntax. But any account of the way a speech like Prospero's works must notice how all four proceed in time to achieve their collective design, which is complete only with the final word.

At the heart of this design is the meter, which has enabled the whole complex artifice to work so effectively. The midline-to-midline arrangement makes the metrical pattern less obtrusive, less evident, but it is still present to the ear and, in some sense, more deeply emphatic for its being less insistent. It helps the sentences and clauses to take their natural courses through the lines; it allows the rhetorical itemizing that goes on so prominently here; and, aided by euphonious sound devices (alliteration, assonance, and so on) and by metrical variations and segmentation that have emotional significance, it permits the passage to build and to resolve its syntactical and argumentative tension. Unhurried, magisterial, integral, this verse confirms the pact between phrase and line, phrase and sentence, at least as completely as any verse Shakespeare had previously written – evidence that his staff was not yet broken and buried, his book not yet drowned.

Notes

1 Poets, of course, do not compose poems by combining metrical formulas. As Paul Fussell sensibly reminds us (1974): "The fact that metrical variations … can be illustrated by scansion and analyzed dispassionately should not cause the reader to believe that, from the point of view of the poet (at least the good poet), they are anything but instinctual. Many poets whose work can be analyzed metrically according to the foot system would be astonished to be told that they have indulged in 'substitution'; the genuine poet composes according to the rhythms which his utterance supplies, and, although these rhythms frequently turn out to consist of 'normal' and 'substitute' feet, they do not necessarily begin that way" (500–1).

2 Oras's work is breathtakingly exhaustive. He treated poets from Chaucer to Davenant and, unlike most scholars who compile quantitative statistics on verse style (Tarlinskaja is another major exception), Oras did not choose representative passages of the works he surveyed; he counted *all* the interior punctuation in *all* the pentameter lines of a great many poems and plays – virtually the entire work of such prolific poets as Spenser, Shakespeare, and Jonson, along with extremely large portions of Chaucer, Marlowe, Donne, and many other writers. His results, presented in a formidable array of graphs and tables, show clearly where the poets who wrote in this period of about two hundred and seventy-five years preferred to place their marks of punctuation. To be sure, every such mark does not signal a perceptible pause in performance, nor does an absence of punctuation indicate a single, unbroken, line-long phrase. But a count of all the punctuation marks serves as a fairly accurate guide to where the phrase boundaries typically fall, and Oras's figures tell us much about the way Elizabethan and Jacobean poets and playwrights fitted the phrase to the line. The graphs as a group show a remarkable change from the old verse with its fourth-syllable pause in as much as 70 or 80 percent of its lines (74.1 in Henryson, 83.2 in Gascoigne, and figures approaching or exceeding 50 percent for most pre-Shakespearean nondramatic and dramatic verse) to a verse with more broadly distributed pauses, especially after the fourth, fifth, sixth, and seventh syllables.

3 Oras puts it this way (15–16):

> A strong pause after the sixth syllable still does not unbalance the pentameter line; the line keeps its self-contained symmetry. Enough space is left for a complete clause to be introduced, a substantial statement to be made, before the end of the line is reached. But when such a pause comes after the seventh, or even the eighth, syllable, the remaining space usually suffices only for a fragmentary statement which needs to be completed in the following line. In other words, very late pauses make for a run-on technique.

4 Oras (17):

> Some attention needs to be paid also to the growing frequency of extra-metrical syllables and feminine endings as Shakespeare's career progresses. Such additional

syllables make it possible to crowd more matter into a line, or any part of a line. In Shakespeare's late plays the metrical demand for three or four syllables may in fact be met by some five or six syllables, and more may be said in them than in the corresponding portion of a strictly regular line. Even the last third of a line thus expanded may accommodate as much matter as a full half-line or more. A pause theoretically close to the end of a line may thus actually be removed from it by a considerable number of syllables, all capable of communicating something.

5   When lines in this pattern are rhymed, they frequently end scenes or sections of scenes. Some examples: "O cursed spite, / That ever I was born to set it right" (*Hamlet*, i.v.188–9); "The play's the thing, / Wherein I'll catch the conscience of the King" (*Hamlet*, ii.ii.604–5); "Ever till now / When men were fond, I smil'd, and wonder'd how" (*Measure for Measure*, ii.ii.185–6).

6   The passage is perfectly regular – no short lines (until the last decisive one), no alexandrines, no extra syllables of any kind (except feminine endings and a few half-suppressed half-syllables, as in the monosyllabic pronunciation of "heaven-" and "even" in line 52). But the majestic sentences unroll their powerful parallelisms through midline pauses and line-endings of unusually various metrical character. Lines 36 and 53 finish on lightly stressed words ("that") that lead us gently over the line-boundaries; the end of line 35 races past its feminine ending to the light trochee or pyrrhic that begins the next line. Verbs at the end of some lines (41, 47, 51) reach over the line-ending to their object in the next; or objects at one line's end find their verb in the next (46–7, 50–1); and other incomplete forms must voyage past the line to be completed:

> whose pastime
> Is to make midnight mushrumps, that rejoice
> To hear …   by whose aid
>   …   I have bedimm'd
>
> Graves at my command
> Have wak'd their sleepers

As the punctuation makes clear, most of the lines (eighteen out of twenty-four) flow without stop into the next: commas (and a parenthesis) end only six of twenty-four lines; the stronger punctuation (five colons and semicolons, and two periods) places all the most decisive junctures at midline.

49

Transfigurations: Shakespeare and Rhetoric

Patricia Parker

Hysteron Proteron or the Preposterous

All his successors (gone before him) hath done't: and all his ancestors (that come after him) may. (*The Merry Wives of Windsor*)

In the final act of *The Winter's Tale*, the Clown, who is the Shepherd's son and foster-brother to the newly found Perdita, daughter to a king, remarks that he and his father are now in a "preposterous estate" (v.ii.148).[1] The phrase is routinely glossed as simply a comic malapropism, fitting enough for an untutored rustic to speak. What he means, goes the standard gloss, is that he and his father are now in a "prosperous estate," the correct phrase to describe their recent and dramatic rise from the lowly status of shepherds to the state of "gentlemen born" (v.ii.127). "Preposterous estate" is explained as a simple verbal error for the "prosperous estate" the Clown really means – an untutored slip of the lip, like Mistress Quickly's many similar malapropisms or like the repeated verbal slips of the "rude mechanicals" of *A Midsummer Night's Dream*. We are thus, it seems, within the familiar realm of Shakespeare's rustic wit, and the comedy here is a laugh restricted to a single line.

And yet there may be something more than a simple characterological slip in this "preposterous," and more involved than the comic effect of a single phrase. For "preposterous" itself is not only a term connoting the reversal of proper or natural order, a sense in which it appears frequently in Shakespeare, but also the name of a rhetorical figure or trope – *hysteron proteron*, routinely Englished in the Renaissance as "The Preposterous." Puttenham and others described it as a form of verbal reversal, one which sets "that before which should be behind" (Puttenham) or "that which ought to be in the first place ... in the second" (Angell Day), a reversal or exchange of place which is routinely linked with the proverbial putting of the "cart before the horse." Puttenham, like the other rhetorical authorities of the day, classes it under the general figure of disorder – "*Hyperbaton*, or the Trespasser" – and Peacham, also typically, links it to disruptions in other kinds of order and hierarchy as well. The author of *The Garden of Eloquence* classes it among the "Faults opposed to naturall & necessary order," immediately after a discussion of proper order, sequence, or placing "when the worthiest word is set first, which order is naturall, as when we say: God and man, men and women, Sun and Moone, life and death." *Hysteron proteron* is a preposterous placing, a trespass against "naturall" order insofar as proper syntactical sequence, or the order of the syntagm in Renaissance discourse, was to be the discursive counterpart of proper vertical hierarchy as well.[2]

The Clown's aberrant "preposterous" as a simple mistake for "prosperous" suggests echoes of precisely such a preposterous placing or reversal of natural order – as in the Italian *preposto*, which Florio's *Worlde of Wordes* informs us means "preferred, put before, made chiefe," or "advanced before others," and hence might easily be substituted for *prospero* as "prosperous, thriving ... luckie, fortunate." The Clown and his father have just, in this last Act's festive ending, been raised from low to high by good fortune, by an unlooked-for prosperity which might indeed be said to be "preposterous" even without having anything at all to do with its rhetorical counterpart. And yet there is more to say once we widen our lens beyond the focus of the single phrase. For only lines before the malapropped "preposterous estate" the same Clown remarks, "I was a gentleman born before my father" (v.ii.139), a line which produces rhetorically, by its ambiguous blurring of proper syntactical placement, a comic version of *hysteron proteron*. If the trope itself is understood – in its reversal of proper order – as "unnaturall," this particular comic line produces even further the unnatural or preposterous possibility of a son born before his father, a genealogical *hysteron proteron* not unlike the one Derrida remarks in his analysis of the Freud of *Beyond the Pleasure Principle*, observing a daughter who is in some sense his mother as well.[3]

What looked at first, then, like a simple malapropism on the Clown's part or a restricted verbal quibble on Shakespeare's already starts leading us farther afield, into the verbal reversals or syntactic ambiguities of other nearby lines. But it may also take us beyond this single scene to other preposterous placings in a play whose own ending depends upon a reversal, or to other Shakespeare plays which play with the idea of following and succession, of "naturall" or ordered sequence. Within *The Winter's Tale* itself, such a close juxtaposition of an apparently simply bumbling and mistaken "preposterous" with an actual syntactic analogue of "The Preposterous" or *hysteron proteron* would indeed lead us to other structures of reversal. For these same rustic shepherds are surrounded elsewhere in the play with echoes of Jacob and Esau,[4] the smooth man and hairy man who show up both by name and around the edges of other Shakespearean scenes of firsts and seconds, and their exchange. This particular biblical paradigm of reversal, in which Jacob – the second-born in the order of nature – is given priority over the first, is the model of the reversal of properly sequential or "naturall" order which gives us finally that great biblical *hysteron proteron* in which the second-born of brothers is spiritually first (Exodus 4:22), in which, in the curious riddling form of Matthew 22: 41–6, the Christ of the Gospels is both the "*son of David*" in the order of nature or genealogical line and David's Creator or "Lord," and in which a younger or second Testament is said to have priority over the elder or first.

If we begin to follow out the wider extensions of "The Preposterous" within *The Winter's Tale*, we are also inevitably led beyond the boundaries of this single play to other Shakespeare texts which play upon reversals which are simultaneously rhetorical and genealogical, which upset both the syntactic and the historical line – from Hamlet's ambiguous "that follows not" (ii.ii.413) in a play that has very much to do with causal and genealogical sequence, to Slender's pronouncement in *Merry Wives* that "all his successors (gone before him) hath done't; and all his ancestors (that come after him) may" (i.i.14–15). We would also be led to its implications for hierarchies of gender. Reversals in *King Lear*, for example, include not only that line in which it is by no means clear whether the "generation" that the barbarous Scythian is said to eat means his parents or his offspring (i.i.117) but also a plot in which the Lear who ironically in some sense *is* that Scythian is eaten or consumed by "daughters" whom he makes his "mothers," a preposterous reversal which the Fool explicitly allies with the familiar proverbial instancing of *hysteron proteron*, of putting the "cart" before the "horse" (i.iv.223–4).

Geminatio, or the Doublet

My jerkin is a doublet – Well, then, I'll double your folly. (*The Two Gentlemen of Verona*)

We might take a second rhetorical example, the case of the trope in which words are repeated with no intervening space between – *epizeuxis* in Greek, *geminatio* in Latin, or in English "the Doublet." *Geminatio verborum* (Cicero, *De oratore*, iii.liv.206) comes from *geminus* or "twin" and hence also from the verb *geminare*, "to double." Englished in Thomas Wilson's *Arte of Rhetorique* (1553), such "doublettes" make their appearance "when we rehearse one and the same word twice together," producing the "redoubling of a word" (Angell Day). Just as in Quintilian words may be doubled or twinned (*verba geminantur*) for the purpose of amplification as well as emphasis, so in the English rhetorics "doublettes" or the "oft repeatyng of one worde" not only engages the attention of the hearer but "makes the worde seeme greater," as Wilson puts it. It is a form of increasing *copia*, of making more copious by twinning or doubling.[5]

"Gemination" in English can also denote, however, as the *OED* reminds us, not just the "immediate repetition of a word or phrase … for the purpose of rhetorical effect" but, more generally, any kind of doubling, duplication, or repetition. Consequently, this trope easily attaches itself to other kinds of doubling – as, for example, when Fuller's *Pisgah* (1650 edition) explains Christ's putting forth not one but "both his hands" and saying not just "My God" but "My God, my God" as his "claiming by that gemination a double interest in God's fatherly affection" (iii.xii.345). Translated in the handbooks of rhetoric as "the Doublet," *geminatio verborum* not only provides a punning counterpart for that "doublet" which is a familiar article of clothing but becomes available as a figure for other kinds of twinning or doubling as well.

Shakespeare, as our epigraph suggests, puns on just this sartorial "doublet" in a play, *The Two Gentlemen of Verona*, which is itself full of various twosomes. He also employs the rhetorical trope of "the Doublet" with truly remarkable frequency, often in contexts which have to do with twins, with duplicates or seconds, or with doubling and duplicity of various kinds, in ways that link the tricks and turns of rhetoric at the local level of the line with the larger structures and plots of the plays themselves. In *The Comedy of Errors* – whose echoes of Jacob and Esau invoke the quintessential biblical *gemini* for its own doubling of rival twins – *geminatio verborum* has its counterpart in the whole play on doubling, twinning, or duplicity in which one twin is so to speak the repetition or "doublet" of the other. The play exploits the full range of verbal and other doublings – Luciana's speech to the wrong or duplicate twin with its "Ill deeds is doubled with an evil word" (iii.ii.20); the ironic playing on the citizen twin as "second to none" in the city (v.i.7); or the constant exploitation of amphibology, a form of speech which looks two ways at once. Its increase of *copia* by the further doubling of Plautus's twins is joined by the rhyming form of the couplet or "gemel" and by the multiple play on the double sense or doubling power of signs and words, their potential for "folded meaning" or "deceit" (iii.ii.36) and hence for reduplicating "error" as well, just as the duplicating or impostor twin is wrongly taken to be his double before the unrecognized doubling is exposed.

Such twinning is by no means restricted to comic play in Shakespeare: there are other, much darker structural analogues to this trope. Francis Bacon, in his discussion of the "coulers" of rhetoric, observes that "the sting and remorse of the mind accusing it selfe doubleth all adversitie … For if the evill bee in the sence and in the conscience both, there is a *gemination* of it."[6] Bacon goes on to speak of this "gemination" in tragedy in particular: "so the Poets in tragedies doe make the most passionate lamentations, and those that forerunne final dispaire, to be accusing, questioning and torturing of a mans self." Something very much like this "gemination" would seem to govern the whole last speech of Othello, where, after the evocation of the "Turk" who is in some sense his double there, the Venetian Moor, on "smote the Turk," kills not this narrativized other, but himself.

We might consider in an even more detailed way, moreover, the relation of such a verbal or rhetorical form to the problem of seconding or succession in the histories. In what is appropriately called the second part of *Henry IV,* that play's playing on its own doubling or seconding – as well as complementing and completing – relation to an original or first is full of suggestive linkages between the rhetorical "Doublet" or *geminatio verborum* and the larger problem of doubling, seconding, or repetition, including that involved in the genealogical and generational as in the rhetorical line. There would appear to be, that is to say, a link between rhetorical gemination, as a repetition with no intervening space between, and the whole problem of kingly succession which is the larger burden of the *Henriad,* as of the history plays as a whole.

Henry IV, Part 2 opens, in a self-reflexive way not uncommon in the Renaissance, with a play on the doubling or seconding involved in the very idea of a second part, as well as on the potentially treacherous *copia* or increase of the "body" of "Rumour." This second part – as might be expected of an extension which both doubles and completes its counterpart or textual other half – is also literally crammed with rhetorical Doublets, most spectacularly but by no means exclusively in Shallow's "Where's the roll? where's the roll? where's the roll? Let me see, let me see, let me see. So, so, so, so, so, so, so" (iii.ii.96–7) or his "Barren, barren, barren, beggars all, beggars all" (v.iii.7). Again, it joins rhetorically with a whole network of other kinds of doubling in a play which repeatedly reiterates the notion of the double. We have, for example, the description of the Archbishop of York as "a man / Who with a double surety binds his followers" (I.i.190–1), in lines which speak of the splitting in two of "body" and "soul" by the divisive power of rebellion, or the description of Falstaff as the "ill angel" (I.ii.164) or daemonic double of Hal, just after lines whose own exploitation of rhetorical *geminatio* ("gravy, gravy, gravy"; I.ii.162) summon up in the attendant doubleness of a pun the gravity of "gravy" and hence of his fat, the gravity which Falstaff as an elder so sorely lacks, and the grave he is headed for. We may remember, in this scene from *Part 2*, those lines in *Part 1* where fat Falstaff, who may be his own double or ghost, is punningly associated with "a double man" (v.iv.138).

Shakespeare's second Henry play, however, also calls attention to the other biblical *gemini* of Cain and Abel in its plot of a divided body politic (I.i.157). The problem of doubling in this second part, which both doubles and brings to an end its predecessor or first, includes the problem of how to put an end to the repetition which is civil war, the successive toppling of pretender kings by pretender kings. This fact brings together the play's political plot line, the threat to Henry IV's own stability ("For he hath found to end one doubt by death / Revives two greater in the heirs of life: / And therefore will he wipe his tables clean / And keep no tell-tale to his memory / That may repeat and history his loss / To new remembrance"; IV.i.197–202), with scenes which at first appear to have nothing to do with it. Act III, for example, opens with a scene whose ending recalls Richard II's prophecy that the Northumberland who helped Henry to his throne would one day challenge it – a doubling or repetition which Henry's very attempt to put down rebellion in this play would bring an end to. The scene concludes with lines on the "doubling" power of that Rumour who spoke the beginning of *Part 2* itself (III.i.97–8: "Rumour doth double, like the voice and echo, / The numbers of the feared"). This first scene, concerned with the repetition or doubling of pretenders, is then followed by a second, comic scene which begins with the rhetorical *epizeuxis* or *geminatio* of Justice Shallow ("Come on, come on, come on: give me your hand, sir, give me your hand, sir"; III.ii.1–2), and which treats of the death ("Jesu, Jesu, dead") of an otherwise utterly gratuitous character who just happens to be named – "old Double."

So much concentrated *geminatio* or wordy repetition occurs in the scene where Falstaff puts off his debt both to the Hostess and to the Law in the form of the Chief Justice ("do me, do me, do me ... Wilt thou, wilt thou ... Murder! Murder! ... with her, with her! Hook on, hook on") that it is hard not to come to the conclusion that this trope of amplification by doubling is the rhetorical counterpart of the copious extension produced by such putting off. For part of the death of "old Double," surely, has to do with this play's final repudiation of Falstaff: the first part had already, as we mentioned, linked him with a "double man," and his promise to Shallow that he can still make him "great," even in the very scene of his repudiation and casting out by Hal, is met by Shallow's doubting "I cannot perceive how, unless you give me your *doublet*, and stuff me out with straw" (v.v. 81–2).

The most telling use of the "doublet" in this play, however, links it, as a trope of seconding with no space between its identical repetitions, to the larger problem of Hal's own succession to kingship and his seconding of his father's name. The play's final Act gives us both together – rhetorical and generational doublet – in its version of the King's Two Bodies understood not vertically and simultaneously within a single person but successively within a single family line. "Not Amurath an Amurath succeeds, / But Harry Harry" (v.ii.48–9) is the formulation of this succeeding of father by son, king by king; and the former Prince Hal who is here described as having earlier mocked the workings of his father "in a second body" (v.ii.90), but who in his invocation of sleep (iv.v.20 ff.) had already seconded his father's own earlier ode to sleep (iii.i.4 ff.), now repeats or seconds his kingly father's functions, as he does his "father's words" (v.ii.107). This scene on the succession of this second "Harry" is then followed by one which gives us, yet again in the mouth of Shallow, a whole series of rhetorical "Doublets," including "Barren, barren, barren, beggars all, beggars all" and "A good varlet, a good varlet ... Now sit down, now sit down" (v.iii.7–15).

"Not Amurath an Amurath succeeds, / But Harry Harry" is itself, in its "Harry Harry," exactly a form of rhetorical *geminatio*, of repetition with no differentiating space between. And though the context of the line is the proclamation of a *difference* – this is not Amurath, our king, but English Harry – the immediate seconding of "Harry Harry" raises more subtly, at the microlevel of the incessantly reiterated trope, the larger question of what difference the whole two plays together at this point of succession may after all have made. *Geminatio*, as we have seen, is a trope of amplification or *copia*. But *copia* has its double in the phenomenon of mere "copy" or duplication made even more possible in the Renaissance by the duplicating power of print, a form of mechanical reproduction that Shakespeare elsewhere extends to the iterations of generation ("Although the print be little, the whole matter / And copy of the father"; "She did print your royal father off, / Conceiving you"; *The Winter's Tale*, ii.iii.99–100 and v.i.125–6).[7] The "Doublet" or immediate repetition is a form of such reproduction at the level of the line. One of the questions, then, this juxtaposition of "Harry" with "Harry" raises is whether this particular succession will mean a fruitful and copious development (as in "Harry's dead ... / But Harry lives, that shall convert those tears / By number into hours of happiness"; v.ii.59–61) or a simple copy, quotation, or repetition of his father or original. The rhetorical form in which one word or name immediately "succeeds" another in a scene whose whole context is kingly succession might lead, that is to say, to the question of precisely what difference has been made at this end by the whole Prodigal Son detour of Hal's adolescence, or in other words by the whole first and second parts of this doubled play. *Part 2*, in which the second Harry finally does follow the first by ending his period of truancy and becoming king, both continues on from *Part 1* and seconds or doubles it in succession; but its induction by "Rumour" recalls Virgil's Fama who starts the second part of the *Aeneid*, in which it is very much a question whether or not a second time will be a fruitful development over a first or simply a repetition or seconding of it in a "second Achilles" and "second Troy."

Sensus Germanus, or the German Sense

The phrase would be more germane [Q1, "more cosin-german"] to the matter if we could carry a cannon by our sides. (*Hamlet*)

In *The Merry Wives of Windsor*, whose involvement with two wives should authorize doubling much as the title of *The Two Gentlemen of Verona* does, the play on "double" and "doublet," as on doubles and *gemini* or twins, is extensive. One scene in fact directly links it to the duplication, or twinning, of a "copy" or "second edition" (*Merry Wives*, II.i.76), with a recall, once again, of the twins Jacob and Esau. The letter Falstaff sends to Mistress Page is exactly like, "letter for letter" (II.i.70), the one he sends to Mistress Ford. And the revelation of this twinning by the former of the two wives to the other is filled with figures of reduplication as well as specific invocation of the geminating power of print:

> here's the twin-brother of thy letter; but let thine inherit first, for I protest mine never shall. I warrant he hath a thousand of these letters, writ with blank space for different names (sure, more!), and these are of the second edition. He will print them, out of doubt; for he cares not what he puts into the press, when he would put us two. (II.i.72–9)

Other scenes of *Merry Wives*, such as the one between Shallow and Slender at the play's beginning, give us more comic versions of *geminatio* or the "Doublet" (as in Slender's "You'll not confess, you'll not confess," followed by Shallow's "'Tis your fault, 'tis your fault"; I.i.92–3). *Gemini* or twins appear directly in Falstaff's reference to Pistol and Nym as "a geminy of baboons" (II.ii.8). But perhaps most intriguing of all in this play is the way in which this "gemini" or *geminus* slides by sound as well as sense into a whole different complex, ultimately producing an involvement of mysterious "Germans" as well. The notorious boundary-crossing of sound here becomes the co-conspirator of Shakespeare's fatal Cleopatra, the pun. For, just as "gemman" was a vulgar sixteenth-century pronunciation of "German," and hence linked by sound to "geminate" or "twin," so in the play itself Doctor Caius, the French physician, pronounces "Germany" as "Jamany" (IV.v.87), not far indeed from that "geminy" of baboons.

Geminatio verborum is the rhetorical form of the "Doublet," as we have seen. "Double" in Shakespeare, however, can connote not just twofold or twinning but also treacherous or duplicitous – as *Henry VIII* makes clear in its "Say untruths, and be ever double / Both in his words and meaning" (IV.ii.38–9), as *Twelfth Night* reiterates in its repeated references to double-dealing in a play of twins (II.iv.74–5; III.ii.25; v.i.35), or as the double-meaning of the witches in *Macbeth* only belatedly reveals. Let us slide then from "geminy" to Germany, as *Merry Wives* does, and explore the slightly different case of what Erasmus famously called *sensus germanus*, a term which both he and his critics punningly dubbed "the German sense." *Germanus* in Latin can mean several things – a brother or close kin: an adjective meaning "genuine, real, or true," and the proper noun for a "German."[8] It also has this range of meaning in English, in ways which allow considerable Shakespearean punning and may even help to explain what those mysterious German thieves are doing in *Merry Wives*. The OED, for example, citing the *Towneley Mysteries* of 1460 (v.29: "Iacob, that is thyne owne germane brother"), makes it clear that the biblical pair of Jacob and Esau were not just *gemini* or twins but brothers "german." Germane "germans," or "cosin-germans," are everywhere in Shakespeare, as is the generalized sense of "german / germane" as closely related or kin. We have only to look at *Timon of Athens* (IV.iii.340: "Wert thou a leopard, thou wert germane to the lion") or *The Winter's Tale* (iv.iv.773–5: "Those that are germane to him ... shall all come under the hang man"), or at *Othello*, where "germans" is juxtaposed with "cousins" or kin (i.i.113: "you'll have coursers for cousins, and gennets for germans"). But the Shakespeare canon also plays insistently on the tension between the sense of "german" as "genuine" or "true" and the doubled meaning of "cozen" as both kin and cheating, or cozening.

Erasmus developed the specific sense of "german" or *germanus* as "genuine, faithful, or true" into the notion of the *sensus germanus* for the faithful paraphrase or duplication of an original text in his paraphrases of Scripture. We are told that the method was put forward as a reaction, and alternative, to modes of allegorical commentary which deviated far from – and hence betrayed – the great original or sacred text. For Erasmus, the *sensus germanus* was by contrast a mode of authenticity, and paraphrase a faithful "speaking alongside" the host text. But his opponents satirized him by taking the phrase as meaning "German sense" in reference to his nationality instead; and in a letter of 1523 Erasmus himself plays upon *germanus* in the doubled sense.[9]

This *sensus germanus* or kindred and genuine sense is opposed in Erasmus to the *sensus alienus* or distorted sense which deviates from, and thus betrays, the text's true meaning. As Terence Cave describes it, the "german sense" is a figure of authenticity "by means of which Erasmus attempts to close the fissure between the text and what it signifies, or – more problematically – between the discourse of Scripture and a new discourse seeking to reproduce its sense."[10] The *germanus* or "kindred" sense, then, like the *geminus* or twin, has as its function the faithful duplication of an original, as with the second "letter" described in *Merry Wives* as the "twin-brother" of the first. The "German sense," as "true sense," offers the ideal of an exact paraphrase or transparent translation, a genuine reproduction without distortion, in which the paraphrase or duplicating text would be both "german" and "germane," genuine or true and a faithful brother text, or kin. Yet, as Cave's critique of Erasmus makes clear, wherever there is two-ness rather than singularity, there is the possibility of duplicity. Paraphrase itself, inasmuch as even commentary which goes "alongside" a text also doubles and necessarily deviates from it, may also finally be not just a faithful "cozen-german" but involved in some kind of cozenage as well; its very otherness may involve it, as a process of translation, in the "alienating" or transporting such germaneness would seek to avoid.

Let us return, then, to those mysterious thieving Germans of *Merry Wives*. Shakespeare's own playing on "german" and "germane," in contexts which sometimes also evoke its closeness in sound to "gemmen" or "twin," conveys just such an awareness of the potentially treacherous or cozening "german." In *The Winter's Tale*, the Shepherd and his son are faced with the conflicting demand to be both "german" in the sense of "honest" and "true" and yet not "germane" in the sense of "kin" to Perdita, from whom they need to alienate themselves (iv.iv.773 ff.) when Autolycus reports the king's anger at his son's dalliance with a "shepherd's daughter." Hamlet remarks of Osric's extravagant, metaphorically transported terms that "The phrase would be more germane [or, as the first quarto has it, "more cosin-german"] to the matter if we could carry a cannon by our sides" (v.ii.158–9). And other Shakespearean instances exploit the potential cozenage or cheating of the "cozen-german" as cozening accompaniment or duplicitous duplicate.

The Merry Wives of Windsor itself combines play on "cozen-germans" with a host of verbal echoes which link German or *germanus* with *geminus* or twin, precisely in the context of cozenage of both kinds. Erasmus's much-punned-upon *sensus germanus* or "German sense" represented an attempt by a figure who was both a humanist and an interpreter of sacred text to claim the possibility of an interpretative glossing or translation which would be without error or duplicitous, alienating gap. In *The Merry Wives*, a figure called the "Host" similarly attempts to reconcile what he terms "the terrestrial" and "the celestial" – the warring Doctor and Parson of the play. Their revenge on him is to send those Germans whom he takes to be "honest men" (iv.v.72) but who cheat him and literally translate or alienate, in the sense of "steal," his property – "cozen-germans," as one character puts it, who finally "cozen" or cheat him by their duplicity:

Bard:	Out alas, sir, cozenage! mere cozenage.
Host:	Where be my horses? ...
Bard:	Run away with the cozeners ... three German devils, three Doctor Faustuses.
Host:	They are gone but to meet the Duke, villain, do not say they be fled. Germans are honest men.

Enter EVANS

Evans:	Where is mine host?
Host:	What is the matter, sir?
Evans:	Have a care of your entertainments. There is a friend of mine come to town, tells me there is three cozen-germans that has cozened all the hosts.

(iv.v.63–78)

It is immediately after these lines, as the Host, cozened by these honest-seeming but duplicitous Germans, finds himself "in perplexity and doubtful dilemma" (84–5) – terms which also suggest a difficult two-ness – that the Doctor pronounces his "Jamany" for "Germany" (87). The play as a whole repeatedly suggests a link between these cozening Germans and the idea of *gemini* or twins, from the description of Nym and Pistol (who may indeed *be* these same cozen-Germans) as a "geminy of baboons" to Falstaff's two love letters, the second of which is called the "twin-brother" of the first, in lines which once again recall the biblical paradigm of a cousining, but also cozening, twin. Divergent possibilities in Shakespeare rarely simply cancel each other out, and nothing in this association of sounds and puns removes the possibility that these Germans may also take us outside the text, to the much-debated contemporary reference to Germans in general or one Count Mömpelgard in particular.[11] But the very extent of its paronomastic cousining of Germans and twins suggests that there is plenty still to be done within the germane senses of the play itself.

Chiasmus, or the Crossing Scheme

Fixing our eyes on whom our care was fix'd (*The Comedy of Errors*)

An instance like the "german" from *germanus* might suggest ways in which wordplay in general in Shakespeare remains still, long after studies like Mahood's,[12] far from an equal partner in the business of interpretation with the continuing legacy of psychological and other models inherited from a certain reception of nineteenth-century narrative. Other instances would suggest, even more specifically, the comparative lack of critical investigation of Shakespeare's extensive play on the terms of language and discourse, on rhetoric as structure as well as trope. This lack affects everything, from the larger interpretation of particular scenes – in which it is often the logic of rhetoric, or of a particular rhetorical turn, rather than an anachronistic psychologic, which is being dramatized – to the minute particulars of editorial and textual scholarship. Iago's description of Cassio as "A fellow almost damn'd in a fair wife" (*Othello*, i.i.21), to cite just one instance, has given us at the level of a narrowly characterological criticism all of the speculation about a mysterious extratextual "wife" of Cassio or a lapse either on Shakespeare's part or in some aspect of the transmission of the text. Yet we might hear this line, uttered early in the play, not as a referential signal to the existence and subsequent textual effacing of a dramatizable person but rather as a particular verbal form, reminiscent of the proverbial jumping to conclusion that produces something like "Shee is a faire woman: Ergo, shee is unchaste." For in Blundeville's famous *Arte of Logike*, in the same era as the play, this is exactly the example, in the discussion "Of Probable Accidents, Conjectures, Presumptions, Signes, and Circumstances," of what was called an argument by "consequence," a form singularly appropriate to introduce a play in which precisely such jumping to conclusion from conjecture and circumstance is to become the plot of the tragedy itself.[13]

The next two examples, then, will be of interpretative or editorial cruxes and presuppositions in which a cul-de-sac of assumption might be circumvented by recourse to a rhetorical structure, or more widely to the whole discourse and lexicon of rhetoric which Shakespeare exploits so ubiquitously. First, chiasmus, that scheme of exchange or crossing produced, as Scaliger puts it, "when the first element and the fourth, and the second and the third are conjoined, giving a scissor formation in the sentence,"[14] or when some other, looser form of verbal crossing links the first and final word of a single line. In the opening scene of *The Comedy of Errors*, Egeon provides his extended narration of the shipwreck of his family, and of the stratagem employed by him and his wife to save themselves, their twin sons, and the corresponding servant twins from the threat of an "immediate death" (i.i.68) at sea:

> My wife, more careful for the latter-born,
> Had fast'ned him unto a small spare mast,
> Such as sea-faring men provide for storms;
> To him one of the other twins was bound,
> Whilst I had been like heedful of the other.
> The children thus dispos'd, my wife and I,
> *Fixing our eyes on whom our care was fix'd,*
> Fast'ned ourselves at either end the mast.
>   (i.i.78–85; my italics)

Henry Cuningham and R. A. Foakes, editors of the two Arden editions of the play, assume that there must be an inconsistency in these lines, a mistake or slip of memory on Shakespeare's part.[15] Egeon states here that it was the mother who was "more careful for the latter-born" (78), while he was responsible for the elder, when they bound the sets of twins to the "small spare mast" (79). The Arden editors therefore conclude that he can only be contradicting himself when he says only shortly after, in line 124, that he was subsequently left with the "youngest" rather than the eldest boy after the mast itself was "splitted in the midst" (i.i.103). The assumption comes from their visual construction of the placing of the children on the mast – that each child must have been placed on the same side as the parent "most careful" for him; for this leads to the conclusion that the mother should have been left with the "youngest" and the father with the elder twin when the mast was finally split in two. Hence the conclusion of a slip or mistake.

There is, however, another possibility, one which would not only reveal this relation of elder and younger to be anything but a "mistake" but would also lead us, via a particular rhetorical form, into the larger structures these lines adumbrate within the play as a whole. If we were to take a clue from the rhetorical crossing of a crucial line within this passage – "Fixing our eyes on whom our care was fix'd" – we might catch instead another possible visualization of the scene which would mirror the exchange and crossing this version of chiasmus rhetorically suggests. This would be a placing of the various family parts upon the mast in such a way that it is precisely a crossing which takes place: each parent bound to one end, gazing upon the twin most "cared" for not on the same but on the opposing half. The chiasmus as figure for a crossing both rhetorical and positional would, if taken seriously, elucidate what has been mistakenly assumed to be an oversight or memory slip on Shakespeare's part when Egeon tells his audience that he was left, after the splitting of the mast, with "My youngest boy, and yet my eldest care" (i.i.124), since the child bound by the mother would be on the father's half of the mast, and vice versa.

This chiasmic placing of the family parts, moreover, would not only remove any charge of a memory slip or error, which is only the projection of a particular visual construction of these lines, but would dramatically emblematize the sense of crossing or exchange which dominates the play right from this opening scene. For the repeated rhetorical sense of chiasmus or crossing in the continued phrasing of "youngest boy" and "eldest care" suggests that the very idea of crossing is being emphasized through-out Egeon's speech – an emphasis appropriate in any case to a scene where this father faces death precisely because he has crossed an absolute dividing line between two sides. Within the immediate context of these lines (i.i.78–103), the positioning, in this chiasmic sense, of the family members upon the mast would mean, as we saw, that in the splitting of the mast each parent is severed from the twin he or she had originally been most "careful" for. And the sense of an original crossing, missed if we assume that Shakespeare is simply nodding here, imparts an even greater dramatic tension to the subsequent seeking of one divided half for the other after their "unjust divorce" (i.i.104) at sea.

But there is also in the crossing of "elder" and "younger" here a further resonance, which would connect Egeon's extended and otherwise pointlessly detailed description of the placing on the mast with both the intervening "comedy of errors" and the reappearance of the question of "elder" and "younger" in the play's own closing lines. The detail of lines 78 and 82 ("My wife more careful for the latter-born ... Whilst I had been like heedful of the other") raises there a seemingly gratuitous echo once again of the biblical story of Jacob and Esau, the "younger" and "elder" twins on whose rivalry and birth order so much of subsequent Old Testament history depends. When the question of the birth order of twins resurfaces in the comedy's closing lines, it is between the two adopted twins, the Dromios:

Ephesian Dro:	Methinks you are my glass, and not my brother:
	I see by you I am a sweet-fac'd youth.
	Will you walk in to see their gossiping?
Syracusian Dro:	Not I, sir, you are my elder.
Ephesian Dro:	That's a question; how shall we try it?
Syracusian Dro:	We'll draw cuts for the senior, till then, lead thou first.
Ephesian Dro:	Nay then thus:
	We came into the world like brother and brother;
	And now let's go hand in hand, not one before another.
	(v.i.418–26)

There are many ways to play these final lines, from the two twins walking "hand in hand" through the door in a way appropriate to a sense of festive comic ending, to something less than the ideal reconciliation the words themselves suggest.[16] But the play's own setting – Ephesus, long linked by commentators to the Ephesus of Paul's New Testament journeys and the Epistle – as well as its two sets of twins, one "alien" and one citizen, recall the "wall of partition" between "stranger" or "alien" Gentile and citizen Jew from Ephesians 2, a division into sides as absolute as that between Syracusian and Ephesian in the *Comedy*'s opening scene. And hence the whole emphasis in the Epistle on the "Cross" (X) which reunites two divided sides, replacing the Old Law's division of Esau and Jacob, Gentile and Jew, by a reconciliation in which both become equally "adopted" sons (Ephesians 1:5). *The Comedy of Errors* begins with the "law" which sets a barrier between Syracuse and Ephesus and condemns Egeon, as the crosser of this dividing line, to "doom." In the intervening "comedy of errors," the exchange of place of "alien" and "citizen" twin is accompanied by more evocations of the smooth man and the hairy man (II.ii.64–109) from the archetypal biblical story of elder and younger twins, whose history, after the initial story in Genesis, does indeed go through various exchanges and crossings in which the elder or the younger is by turns the favored one. By the end of Egeon's one day's respite, and the whole complex comic set of changes and exchanges of place that ensue, the initial "doom" is converted into a "nativity" (v.i.400–6), in final scenes whose biblical echoes call to mind a "redemption" easily combined with the play's own commercial metaphors and the removal of barriers, walls, and partitions by that "Cross" which traditionally puts an end to "Error" itself.

The opening scene's recall of Jacob and Esau, "younger" and "elder" twin, evokes the Old Testament context of the Law and its divisions in the context of the "greater care" of each parent for each twin, just before that crossing on the mast which "Fixing our eyes on whom our care was fix'd" chiasmically suggests. But both the crossing over of sides and positions and the subsequent course of Egeon's narrative already attenuate the Jacob-and-Esau sense of parental preference:

> Our helpful ship was splitted in the midst;
> So that, in this unjust divorce of us,
> Fortune had left to both of us alike
> What to delight in, what to sorrow for.
>
> (1.i.103–6)

The rhetorical crossing of Egeon's lines, the ones the Arden editors take to reveal an error or slip ("My youngest boy, and yet my eldest care, / At eighteen years became inquisitive / After his brother"; 1.i.124–6), evokes a brotherly seeking more suggestive of the Joseph than the Jacob narrative, even as the crossing of the boundary by both Egeon and his "wandering" son already anticipates the play's ultimate reunion of divided sides. What a larger criticism of this play would make of its repeated recourse to biblical terms and structures is very much open to debate. But what had been perceived as a contradiction or mistake – the confusion of "elder" and "younger" in its opening scene – is not only not necessarily an oversight but a figure and a crossing crucial to the allusive movement of the play as a whole. The rhetorical crossing of "Fixing our eyes on whom our care was fix'd," if taken seriously within the lines in which it appears,[17] would lead us not just out of an unnecessary assumption of textual mistake or nodding but into something much broader than the single line. Rhetoric here is not just decoration but structural analogue and interpretive tool.

Dilation and Delation by "Circumstance"

The time When? about the sixt hour, when beasts most graze, birds best peck, and men sit down to that nourishment which is called supper: so much for the time When. Now for the ground Which? which, I mean, I walk'd upon: it is ycliped thy park. Then for the place Where? (*Love's Labour's Lost*)

A rhetorical structure or recourse to the language of rhetoric can, I would argue, very frequently offer clues to problems apparently opaque when approached from a different set of assumptions or editorial biases. Rhetoric and its lexicon can become interpretive tools even at the most basic levels of textual commentary and editing. Here, in relation not just to a trope like *hysteron proteron* or a structure like chiasmus, but rather to the whole tradition of rhetoric and its affiliations, we might take an even more important textual crux in Shakespeare than the one in *The Comedy of Errors*.

In the great Temptation Scene of *Othello*, Iago begins to put the Moor "on the rack" through those pauses, single words, and pregnant phrases which seem to suggest something secret or withheld, the possibility that his ensign "knows more, much more, than he unfolds" (III.iii.243). In the Folio version and all the authoritative texts of the play but one, Othello's response to Iago's technique refers to its "close dilations, working from the heart, / That passion cannot rule" (III.iii.123–4). Editors from Warburton onwards have puzzled over the meaning and import of "dilations" here – some citing one Renaissance meaning ("dilations" as "delays"), others, with Malone, the sense of "dilation" as rhetorical *dilatio* or amplification, and a few choosing to substitute for "close dilations" the single other possible text, "close denotements," found only in the earliest Quarto. Arden editor M. R. Ridley, confessing that, since the Folio phrase "can hardly have been due to a mere blunder," whoever put it there must have "meant something by it" but that he himself has "very little idea what that was," chooses to efface the Folio text altogether, substituting "close denotements" instead on the grounds that to this more neutral phrase at least "no reasonable objection can be made."[18] At this most basic level, a certain interpretive assumption affects even the text that readers of this edition of the play get to see.

But there is another possibility here, one which if followed out might lead us to see in the Folio's "close dilations" an overdetermined or portmanteau phrase which carries the burden of combinations particular to the plot and language of *Othello* as a whole. When Dr Johnson raised his eccentric but to subsequent editors fascinating suggestion – that the Folio's "close dilations" should be read instead as "close delations" or "occult and secret accusations" – it was frequently rejected and has been still, by Ridley himself, on the grounds that there is no evidence of "delations" in its Latin sense of "accusation" in Shakespeare's day. But in fact, as only a cursory glance at the *OED* or at contemporary texts would make clear, such instances abound. "Delate" or "accuse" in Renaissance English usage could not only be, in a variant spelling, identical in appearance and sound to "dilate" or amplify, but was even available for punning links with it (as in Bishop Hall's resonant "dilaters of errors, delators of your brethren," for instance). The Folio's "close dilations," that is to say, would not even need to be amended in its spelling to "close delations," as Johnson supposed, to be capable of suggesting both meanings, amplification and accusation, in the same phrase.[19]

This enigmatic phrase and textual crux, then, might not necessarily lead us to mere puzzlement or a throwing up of hands like Ridley's, nor to the necessity, and all too frequent editorial practice, of choosing one meaning *over* another – a process of elimination which so often presupposes a singularity of one definitive text or reduced authoritative meaning – but rather to the possibility of reading *Othello* more largely in relation to this semantic crossroads and all of the resonances it conjures. It would be just such a combination of amplification and accusation we would encounter in noticing, first of all, that rhetorical dilation is explicitly evoked within the play, and precisely within the context of a judicial accusation, in the central scene in Act I: Othello, accused of "witchcraft" in wooing Desdemona, is summoned before the judicial inquiry of the Venetian Senate and tells of her earlier entreaty ("That I would all my pilgrimage dilate, / Whereof by parcels she had something heard"; I.iii.153–4). His own narrative dilation before the Senate serves, in what has been called the "comic" context of this opening scene, to aquit him of the charge of which he is accused. But his description of Desdemona's "greedy ear" (I.iii.149), hungry to hear more of his discourse, ominously anticipates the play's later tragic turn, when Iago begins to "abuse" Othello's own increasingly insatiable "ear," and the "witching" effect of the ensign's eventual unfolding of what the "close dilations" of the great Temptation Scene have similarly only "in parcels" or in part revealed leads to the "delation" or accusation of Desdemona before *her* judge.

There is, however, even more to this link between rhetorical "dilation" and judicial "delation," a term which would lead us into the crossing of judicial and rhetorical not just in this play but in others as well. In the passage which provides our epigraph here, Armado's dilated or wordy accusation of Costard in *Love's Labour's Lost* proceeds by a detailing of what were known technically as "circumstances," the "who, what, where, why, when" we continue to learn in watered-down form in the continuation of ancient rhetoric into the techniques of modern composition. What we need to know for *Othello* and for the crossing of dilation and delation within it, is that these were the "circumstances" of a judicial accusation as well, part of what we still call "circumstantial evidence" offered to a judge when there is no direct or "ocular proof." Rhetorical dilation and judicial delation, that is to say, shared the same rhetorical form, detailing through the "circumstances," a combination which the bombast or verbal amplification of Armado's accusation exactly provides, but in a comic mode. *Othello* not only alludes self-consciously to the whole rhetorical tradition of "dilation" in Othello's description of his wooing, but increasingly brings to mind these "circumstances": in the Moor's angry demand to have an answer to his "What … How … who … ?" in the scene of the night brawl (II.iii.169–78); in Iago's "I will make him tell the tale anew: / Where, how, how oft, how long ago, and when / He hath, and is again to cope your wife" (IV.i.84–6); and in Emilia's "Why should he call her whore? Who keeps her company? / What place? what time? what form? what likelihood?" (IV.ii.137–8). Iago, we remember, promises "If imputation and strong *circumstances* / Which lead directly to the door of truth / Will give you satisfaction, you might have't" (III.iii.406–8; my italics), in the absence, precisely, of "ocular proof."

"Circumstances" both amplify and accuse, like the potentially crossed senses of the "close dilations" of the Temptation Scene. But they also contain a further link with the third sense evinced for the Folio's "dilations" – "delay." Minsheu's famous *Dictionary* of 1617 gives under "circumstance" not only "a qualitie that accompanieth a thing, as time, place, person, etc.," but also a "circuit of words, compasses, or going about the bush," a sense which it carries in *The Merchant of Venice* ("You … herein spend but time / To wind about my love with circumstance"; I.i.153–4). This sense too emerges in Iago's complaint, at the very beginning of *Othello*, against the wordy evasion of Othello's "bumbast circumstance / Horribly stuff'd with epithites of war" (I.i.13–14), and gives us elsewhere the Moor's own curiously amplified and even inflated "purple passage" of farewell to the "Pride, pomp, and circumstance of glorious war" (III.iii.354). The other appearance of dilation in this text is precisely in this sense of delay, in Iago's counsel to an impatient Roderigo that "wit depends on dilatory time" (II.iii.372). And, as Rymer complained, the play itself is full of delays occasioned by verbal amplitude. All three senses of "dilations" from that vexed Folio text, then – amplification, accusation, delay – combine with "circumstances" both verbal and judicial in ways that suggest the resonant contours of this portmanteau phrase within the entire play,[20] beyond those "close denotements" to which, as the more neutral and less textually justifiable phrase, "no reasonable objection can be made."

Rhetorical "circumstances," then, both dilate and indict, in that crossing of rhetorical and judicial which is so much at the heart of the whole tradition inherited from Cicero and Quintilian, and in a way rich with implications not just for the Folio text of those crucial lines from Act III but for the crossing of dilation and accusation within *Othello* as a whole. But the term also resonates elsewhere, in both comic and more tragic contexts. Autolycus questions the frightened rustics in a scene from *The Winter's Tale* whose detailing of the "circumstances" might have come straight out of descriptions of the form most "commonly requisite in presentments before Justices of peace":[21] "Your affairs there? what? with whom? the condition of that farthel? the place of your dwelling? your names? your ages? of what having? breeding? and any thing that is fitting to be known – discover" (IV.iv.717–20). The fact that this judicial form for ferreting out the truth should be used by a figure whose very name from the *Odyssey* links him with fables and lies is suggestive in a play which not only turns on the questionable verisimilitude of the fabrications of jealousy but also claims verisimilitude, precisely by "circumstances," for its own fabulous events ("Most true, if ever truth were pregnant by circumstance. That which you hear you'll swear you see, there is such unity in the proofs"; v.ii.30–2).[22] Rhetorical and judicial "circumstances" are linked as well in the accusation of Hero in *Much Ado About Nothing*, a play whose comic outcome depends on the interposition of an interval of delay: "circumstances short'ned (for she has been too long a-talking of), the lady is disloyal" (III.ii.102–4). And interrogation and potential "delation" form the subject of the tedious verbal amplifications of Polonius ("If circumstances lead me, I will find / Where truth is hid"; *Hamlet* II.ii.157–8), in a play which has to do not just with delay, but with the whole wider problem of ferreting out a mystery, of trying to find what, in the absence of ocular proof, would prove or disprove an accusation made from the play's very beginning.

The General and the Particular

> Where's our general? ... Here I am, thou particular fellow. (*Henry VI, Part 2*)

One of the principal organizing structures of argument and discourse is the disposition of the "general" into its "particulars." This is the tradition which Bottom mangles, along with so much else in *A Midsummer Night's Dream*, when, anxious to improve the level of organization, he responds to Quince's "Is all our company here?" (I.ii.1) with advice to "call them generally [that is "individually" or "particularly," says the gloss] man by man, according to the scrip (I.ii.2–3). Abraham Fraunce, in *The Lawiers Logike*, speaks of "Methode" in discourse as a disposition of "divers coherent axiomes" in which "the most general," as the head or "principall," is placed "first" and where the order then "descends" from the "generall" to the "special" or the "particular": "Therefore this method descendeth always from the generall to the specials, even to the most singular thing, which cannot be divided into any more parts."[23] He then goes on to treat of the "distribution" of the "general," making it clear that, in true Aristotelian fashion, discourse is to mirror the form of hierarchical descent from "general" to "particular."

Shakespeare plays constantly on this language of "general" and "particular," not just in more straightforward lines like the old Duchess of York's complaint in *Richard III* ("Alas! I am the mother of these griefs: / Their woes are parcell'd, mine is general"; II.ii.80–1), but also in paronomastic juxtaposition with the political "general" or head, as in *Henry VI, Part 2*, where Jack Cade – whose rebellion threatens hierarchy or proper order and descent in the body politic – answers his follower Michael's "Where's our general?" with "Here I am, thou particular fellow" (IV.ii.111–112).

Two plays in the canon recall with particular resonance, however, this discursive language of descent. In *Othello*, as we have seen, the tradition of the amplification of discourse is evoked in that speech in Act I where Othello reports on Desdemona's desire to hear the whole of what she had heard only "in parcels," or in some particulars. One way of opening out or parceling the "general" is by dividing it into its "circumstances," in the form we have already seen at work. But when we come to this play from the punning elsewhere in the canon on the "general" both as distinguished from the "particular" and as the military "general" or head, we may hear something more in its own multiple references to Othello as "our noble general" (ii.ii.11), and in what happens when the action descends into the particular and even the minute particulars of the domestic tragedy it becomes – in which Othello's "occupation" as general is "gone" (iii.iii.357) and in which the sign of descent into the particular becomes the handkerchief, that "trifle" of which Rymer so famously complained.

This descent into the domestic also bears implications for the question of gender in this play and the specifically domestic hierarchy of headship which at least one sixteenth-century discussion of descent from "general" to "particular" illustrated in combining a handbook of logic and rhetoric with a treatise on "household government."[24] The conclusion of Act III has puzzled commentators unsure of what Bianca means when she says "'Tis very good; I must be circumstanc'd" after Cassio has impatiently asked her to be gone because he waits upon more important things: "I do attend here on the general, / And think it no addition, nor my wish, / To have him see me woman'd" (iii.iv.193–5). Cassio "woman'd" in the homosocial world of war which dominates the male bondings of this tragedy recalls an earlier locution which similarly makes Desdemona an adjunct of the general ("But, good lieutenant, is your general wived?"; ii.i.60), or hintings that the doting and fondly "prating" (ii.i.224) general, wived, has already abandoned his proper station as "head" ("Our general cast us thus early for the love of his Desdemona"; ii.iii.14–15). For the "circumstancing" of Bianca not only involves the sense of her being put off or delayed in her suit, one of the possible resonances of "circumstanc'd" here, but makes her by implication an adjunct or "addition" to Cassio as he attends upon the "general." This resonance both catches the movement of the play from great things to small, general to particular, and, as feminist critics of the play have seen, ultimately also attaches to Desdemona, who, even as she is portrayed as having become the "general's general" – in a reversal Iago clearly contemptuously intends should invoke the familiar topos of woman on top – is in fact forced to become, as the play proceeds, simply and reductively an "adjunct," whose minute particulars increasingly preoccupy the "general" himself: "Our general's wife is now the general – I may say so in this respect, for that he hath devoted and given up himself to the contemplation, mark and denotement of her parts and graces" (ii.iii.314–18). When this language appears, then, in Iago's advice in the same scene to Cassio on how to "recover the general again" (ii.iii.272), the underlying resonances of the term pose the question of how – in the relentless linear logic in which the most minute particular, that "trifle," is pursued – this "general" might recover himself, and how far he will descend before the tragedy reaches its "bloody period."

It is in *Troilus and Cressida*, however, that this polarity of terms on which order and vertical hierarchy depend is most relentlessly, and most subversively, exploited.

Paronomastic play on the "general" and the "particular" is pervasive here, as is the simultaneously grammatical and political sense of "decline" (ii.iii.52).[25] Cressida mockingly remarks, of the few "three or four hairs" on Troilus' youthful chin, that "Indeed a tapster's arithmetic may soon bring his particulars therein to a total." Ulysses in the scene of the Greek council speaks of "Severals and generals of grace exact" (i.iii.180). But in one of the most striking and extended of these instances, the play that ensues when Cressida is kissed first by the Greek "general," Agamemnon, and then "in general" by a whole series of Greek particulars, makes clear the potential reversal which lurks within the apparently polar opposites:

> Agamemnon: Most dearly welcome to the Greeks, sweet lady.
> [*Kisses her.*]
> Nestor: Our general doth salute you with a kiss.
> Ulysses: Yet is the kindness but particular,
> 'Twere better she were kiss'd in general ...
> (iv.v.19–21)

"General" and "particular" here join in the promiscuous exchange, the "general" or "head" being only one "particular" in relation to the particulars which compose the generality. What Bottom seems simply to mangle in his confusion of "general" for "particular" in *A Midsummer Night's Dream* turns out to be a subversion of hierarchy potential within the exchangeability of the very terms of order – if the "general" is both the head *and* the commonality, and the "general" or single head here too "particular." The scene which makes most explicit the fact that women, including Cressida, function in the world of the play as mere objects of exchange itself turns on this exchange and reversibility of terms. If there is "language in her eye" (iv.v.55), as Ulysses remarks after proposing the kissing "in general," it is a language whose speculative instrument is the exchange in which she is only one form of declining.

The larger context for this reversibility and exchange is the play's relentless undermining of the language of order both in discourse and in the body politic, the logic as well as the rhetoric of "degree." It is the challenge to the authority of Agamemnon as "head and general" (i.iii.222) which prompts Ulysses' famous set piece on "degree, priority and place" (i.iii.86), all "in line of order" (88) down the "ladder" (102) from general to particular, and on the decline into which this order and, with it, the power of the "general," have fallen:

> The general's disdain'd
> By him one step below, he by the next,
> The next by him beneath; so every step,
> Exampled by the first pace that is sick
> Of his superior, grows to an envious fever
> Of pale and bloodless emulation.
> (i.iii.129–34)

This language dominates the scene in Act II where, as part of the plot to restore "degree" to the Greek camp and authority to Agamemnon, this general is counseled by Ulysses to "pass strangely by" Achilles (iii.iii.39–40), in a language of passing or "passage" which this bookish and wordy play elsewhere links subtly with discursive proceeding. This ploy causes the recalcitrant particular, Achilles, to seek the "general" in a reverse of the former suing of the "head and general" to him ("*Agamemnon.* What says Achilles? Would he aught with us? / *Nestor.* Would you, my lord, aught with the general?"; iii.iii.57–8). Given the use of "general" and "particular" elsewhere in the play to connote alternatively the common and the individual good, the question might connote both Agamemnon and the collective Greek cause from which this particular is in retreat.

It is, however, the exploding of this system of ordering, in politics as in discourse, which the play relentlessly pursues. Though Agamemnon himself speaks of "all the Greekish heads, which with one voice / Call Agamemnon head and general" (i.iii.221–2), Aeneas, arrived from the Trojan camp in this very scene, finds it impossible to distinguish the "general" from the particulars, as he fails to recognize this "head" ("How may / A stranger to those most imperial looks / Know them from eyes of other mortals?"; i.iii.222–4). Thersites will comment later that Ajax actually takes him for the "general" ("What think you of this man that takes me for the general?"; iii.iii.262). And Act II opens with Thersites' variations on the "general" as a "matter" for argument and discourse:

> Thersites: Agamemnon, how if he had biles – full, all over, generally?
> Ajax: Thersites!
> Thersites: And those biles did run – say so – did not the general run then? Were not that a botchy core?
> Ajax: Dog!
> Thersites: Then would come some matter from him; I see none now.
>
> (ii.i.2–9)

The "head and general," supposed to be a source of ordered and reasoned argument, the generation of "matter" for discourse as well as the hierarchical embodiment of order itself, is in this play only a "botchy core," the source of "matter" in an infected body politic.

Antimetabole, or The Counterchange

God send the companion a better prince! (*Henry IV, Part 2*)

We began with the form of reversal known as "the preposterous." We end this preliminary sketch of Shakespearean exploitation of the terms of rhetoric and discourse with another form of reversal, "antimetabole," in Latin *commutatio,* and Englished by Puttenham as "The Counterchange." This figure makes its appearance in the *Ad Herennium* (IV.39) as the effect produced "When two discrepant thoughts are so expressed by transposition that the latter follows from the former, although contradictory to it"; and in the Renaissance, in Susenbrotus, as that scheme in which a "sentence is inverted by becoming its contrary." Scaliger's treatment draws out the proximity of "antimetabole" (where "a sentence is changed to its contrary") to "antimetathesis," as "When we allow words to change places" and an "opposite meaning may be derived from the transposing of words."[26]

Quintilian gives the most frequently repeated example of the trope – *non ut edam vivo, sed ut vivam, edo* ("I do not live to eat, but eat to live") – as well as expressing the sense that such antithesis can add "a special elegance" to a speech. But further investigation of this antithesis, and a transposition effected such that "the latter follows from the former, although contradictory to it," reveals more at stake in Shakespeare's use of this scheme and trope than mere stylistic elegance or the pleasures of verbal antithesis.

Let us start with some of its Renaissance descriptions. Puttenham, in his discussion of "*Antimetabole*, or the Counterchange" in *The Arte of English Poesie* (1589), begins "Ye have a figure which takes a couple of words to play with in a verse, and by making them to chaunge and shift one into others place they do very prettily exchange and shift the sense, as thus:

> We dwell not here to build us boures,
> And halles for pleasure and good cheare:
> But halles we build for us and ours,
> To dwell in them whilest we are here.

Meaning that we dwell not here to build, but we build to dwel, as we live not to eate, but eate to live,"[27] in what had long become the familiar repetition of Quintilian's example. Antimetabole thus involves the question of what is the means and what the end, and of the subordination reflected in their proper ordering.

Descriptions of this scheme and trope, however, also raise the possibility within it of a reversed relation of ends and means, or even, as in the *Ad Herennium* definition, of a contradictory relation between what follows from, or follows what. John Hoskins, in the *Directions for Speech and Style* (1599), writes that "Antimetabole, or Commutatio, is a sentence inversed or turned back," and, in a way reminiscent of Quintilian's "elegant," remarks on its usefulness as "a sharp and witty figure."[28] But its affinity with reversal – or, even further, with what Scaliger glimpsed as its proximity to "antimetathesis," where not just a turn of phrase but an "opposite meaning" may be derived from "the transposing of words" – involves, at least potentially, something more.

Shakespeare's recourse to antimetabole is striking not just in its remarkable frequency but in its linking precisely with structures of reversal, in logical and in other senses. For antimetabole is never far from the question of logic and the linear ordering of ends and means it depends upon. It is, as Sister Miriam Joseph points out,[29] one of the figures used repeatedly by Shakespeare in relation to logical processes, since it turns a "sentence" around:

> Plainly as heaven sees earth and earth sees heaven.
> (*Winter's Tale*, i.ii.315)

> Grief joys, joy grieves, on slender accident.
> (*Hamlet*, iii.ii.199)

> For 'tis a question left us yet to prove,
> Whether love lead fortune, or else fortune love.
> (*Hamlet*, iii.ii.202–3)

And give to dust, that is a little gilt
More laud than gilt o'erdusted.
(*Troilus and Cressida*, iii.iii.178–9)

The fool doth think he is wise, but the wise man knows himself to be a fool. (*As You Like It*, v.i.31–2)

Shakespeare's use of and variations on this figure do serve the stylistic purpose of the highly wrought rhetorical turn, the comic or witty riposte, the neatly turned reply: the Duke's "And you, good brother father" to Elbow's "Bless you, good father friar" in *Measure for Measure* (iii.ii.11–12), for instance; Richard III's "There let him sink, and be the seas on him" to Stanley's "Richmond is on the seas" (*Richard III*, iv.iv.462–3); or Apemantus' turning of Timon's "What dost thou think 'tis worth?" into "Not worth my thinking" (*Timon of Athens*, i.i.213–14), to take just a few examples. But, if such uses were to be followed up and into the larger questions of particular plays, they would begin to adumbrate other important relations of reversal – reversals of direction, of cause and effect, of logical and ideological sequence.

Two of the examples above come from *Hamlet*. Another is that moment when, having killed Polonius by mistake, Hamlet summarizes the situation with "I do repent; but heaven hath pleas'd it so / To punish me with this and this with me" (iii.iv.173). All of Joseph's instances from this play – though cited merely as verbal or logical reversals without any larger interpretive reference – might take us into that *Hamlet*-in-reverse in which not just elements within the play but perhaps even more radically the play itself turn "tropically" (iii.ii.232) into their opposites.[30] They also, however, raise the question of the relation of such verbal instances of reversal to the sense in this play of tragic reciprocity as well as potential reversibility: not just the reversed pairing of Claudius's "Thanks, Rosencrantz and gentle Guildenstern" with Gertrude's immediately inverted "Thanks, Guildenstern and gentle Rosencrantz" (ii.ii.33–4), but also the "mighty opposites" ("To punish me with this and this with me") who compose the central pairing of the tragedy itself.

Such instances would also take us much farther afield, into the general question of "turning" involved in such tropic turns. After one scene of verbal sparring in *Twelfth Night*, in which the turn and reversal of antimetabole is exploited in a fashion that turns a meaning around, we have the following reply:

> Viola / Cesario: So thou mayst say the king lies by a beggar, if a beggar dwells near him; or the church stands by thy tabor, if thy tabor stand by the church.
> Feste: You have said, sir. To see this age! A sentence is but a chev'ril glove to a good wit. How quickly the wrong side may be turn'd outward!
> (iii.i.8–13)

Feste's comment seems apt enough as a commentary upon the uses of rhetoric – and of the newfangledness in which anything may be turned into its reverse. But the sense that things might indeed be capable of reversal has elsewhere in Shakespeare more than the sense of mere verbal turn, something like that "opposite meaning" which might, in Scaliger's phrase, obtain in such a verbal transposition, an "exchange" (Puttenham) which would indeed "shift the sense," including the sense, in antimetabole, of a proper relation or subordination of ends and means.

We need to note in particular, then, that several of the examples Puttenham gives of "*Antimetavole*, or the Counterchange" are political. For instance:

A wittie fellow in Rome wrate under the Image of Caesar the Dictator these two verses in Latine, which because they are spoken by this figure of Counterchaunge I have turned into a couple of English verses very well keeping the grace of the figure.
> *Brutus for casting out of kings, was first of Consuls past,*
> *Caesar for casting Consuls out, is of our kings the last.*

And then again:

Cato of any Senatour not onely the gravest but also the promptest and wittiest in any civill scoffe, misliking greatly the engrossing of offices in Rome that one man should have many at once, and a great number goe without that were as able men, said thus by Counterchaunge
> *It seemes your offices are very litle worth,*
> *Or very few of you worthy of offices.*[31]

One of the specifically political potentialities within this scheme or trope is the possibility not just of that verbal reversal, and subordination, in which, as the *Ad Herennium* puts it, "two discrepant thoughts are so expressed by transposition that the latter follows from the former, although contradictory to it," but also of its social counterpart, a *mundus inversus* or upside-down world, the sense given to it *in potentia* when a somewhat later text such as John Smith's *Mystery of Rhetoric Unveiled* (1657) speaks of it as "*Commutatio, Inversio*, a changing of words by contraries, or a turning of the words in a sentence upside down; derived from [*anti*] against, and [*metaballo*] *inverto*, to invert, or turn upside down." He goes on to speak of it as a "sentence inverst, or turn'd back," and remarks that it is "a form of speech which inverts a sentence by the contrary, and is used frequently to confute by such Inversion," that is, in logical argument.[32]

This aspect of antimetabole provides a perspective on at least one instance of its embedding in a text which has very much to do with political order and its temporary inversion – once again, *Henry IV, Part 2*. The linear movement of this play as it proceeds away from Falstaff and an only temporary prodigality to Law, Kingship, and Father has left more than one reader uneasy. We might note, then, that, within it, the potential alternative of reversal – which the play itself in its linear movement to ending and kingship makes only temporary, glimpsed in order to be cast out – is enacted rhetorically in a particular instance of antimetabole when the Chief Justice, representative of the Law which Falstaff evades and of the authority and state Hal will finally abandon him for, accosts the prodigal "companion" himself:

Chief Justice: Well, God send the Prince a better companion!
Falstaff: God send the companion a better prince! I cannot rid my hands of him.
(1.ii.199–201)

The same scene, just after this, gives us yet another reversal in Falstaff's "A pox of this gout! or a gout of this pox!" (1.ii.243–4).

The possibility of reversing the relation of "companion" and "prince" – a reversal unenactable as political reality or rewritten history – plays rhetorically, if only for a moment, with the sense of direction in which the plot is moving, as with the subordination of means or middles to their proper ends. Like revenge or succession in *Hamlet*, the teleological movement of drama is close to ritual, including the ritual of mock rule and its rerighting. Natalie Davis has argued that these moments of overturning have in themselves a kind of limited power, in spite of the foreclosure of the order which rehearses them.[33] What I am suggesting is that tropes of reversal, of insubordination or inversion, may ironize, precisely by performing, the very structure of a particular direction and process of deciding what is means and what is end – and, at least in figure, its alternative.

Preposterous Conclusions

Our natures would conduct us to most prepost'rous conclusions (*Othello*)

There are many more Shakespearean instances of rhetorical play involving a play on rhetoric and linked through the verbal economy of the pun to larger questions of interpretation and structure. Robert Weimann, in an essay on metaphor in Shakespeare, has characterized Elizabethan English as a language "which combined both a vast range of reference – social and natural – with a unique freedom of *epiphora*," a "liberty of transference" or translation.[34] The very term "translation," when it appears in Shakespeare – in the "translation" of Bottom in *A Midsummer Night's Dream* (III.i.119), the translating of "fortune" into "style" in *As You Like It* (II.i.19–20), the alienation of property in *Merry Wives*, or the transformation of "rivals" into "servants" in *Timon of Athens* (I.i.71–2) – recalls the trope of metaphor itself, Englished routinely as "Translation" or "The Figure of Transport." Beyond the literal resonances of the term, its transferences would take us, if pursued, into a network of sustained Shakespearean play on modes of transport, from the space of the stage in the French–English channel crossings of *Henry V* to the imaging of Pandarus the go-between as a ferry man or means of transportation in *Troilus and Cressida* (I.i.104; III.ii.11).

Many of the instances we have considered are examples where rhetorical structures operate as silent interpreters, straight-faced in their structural or their subversive force. *Geminatio* or the Doublet with no space of difference – in a play which generates not just the name but the entire existence of a character called "old Double" out of its own verbal twinnings – subverts through its obsessive repetitions the more official proclamations of progress from father to son. Falstaff's antimetaboles leave the trace of a whole unenacted countermovement within the teleology of the history he is cast out by. "Cozen-german" lurks within or sidles alongside the more innocent "German," translating and alienating its more simple reference. So pervasive, indeed, is the subversion of singularity by figure that to focus exclusively on questions of social and political context – as one form of reaction to decades of formalism now proposes to do – or to foreground the "political Shakespeare" without also taking seriously the linguistic one, is, for all its recontextualizing value, not just to work to the detriment of the kind of formal analysis that still so much needs to be done but unnecessarily to short-circuit or foreclose the process of moving from literary text to social text.

In the structures of these tropes, and in the larger discourse and structures of rhetoric, is embedded, I would argue, not only a language we need to be able to recognize in order to be better formalist readers or editors of Shakespeare, but one that would enable us to pose, in different ways from those so far pursued, questions of politics and gender, of social biography and ideology. In the case of the "general" and the "particular," order in discourse is already directly linked with order in the body politic through the existence of a common lexicon. But, in more indirect and subtle ways, even the other rhetorical tropes we have examined in this preliminary fashion point beyond the kind of analysis we have come to associate with a simple formalism. Forms of reproduction at the level of the line bring to mind the prevailing Elizabethan anxiety, of political succession. The genealogical *hysteron proteron* within the Clown's "I was a gentleman born before my father," in *The Winter's Tale*, mirrors not only one of the details known about its creator's biography but a common social practice as well – a son's retroactive creation of his father as a "gentleman" in an act which retrospect- ively created a line of descent for himself, the way that Shakespeare, like so many others of his social origin, rose suddenly (and not organically or "naturally") to the status of "gentleman born." At this level, the verbal reversal of *hysteron proteron* repeats a form and social practice of retroactively constructed lineages and preposterous descents which would make Slender's "ancestors (that come after him)" something more than a simple comic malapropism, just as Bottom's reversal of "general" and "particular" turns out to be not simply a mistake that reflects on his inability to get anything right. More incidentally, it would also reveal the preposterous genealogical reversals of fathers and sons in the critico-biographical musings of Joyce's *Ulysses* to be in this respect among our more perceptive rather than, disparagingly, our more eccentric Shakespeare criticism.[35]

Other rhetorical structures of reversal and exchange – crossings negotiated not just in *The Comedy of Errors* or the verbal turns of *Hamlet* or the *Henriad* – link the language of particular plays to the language of social ordering and political disposition, including constructions of gender. In *Love's Labour's Lost*, play on the logical, discur- sive and legal language of "in manner and form following" produces a man "following" a woman, a "prepost'rous event" (i.i.205–65) reflected in the play's own preposterous conclusion, in which the gender stereotypes of wordy women and silent men are reversed, and Berowne's punishment is, for a year, to "Visit the speechless sick" (v.ii.851, 888). In the passage of those enigmatic "close dilations" of *Othello's* great temptation scene, the description of Iago's pausing to "contract and purse" his brow, as if he had "shut up" in his "brain / Some horrible conceit" (iii.iii.114–15), "Some monster ... / Too hideous to be shown" (107–8), explicitly echoes the play's opening figure of a "purse" which can be opened and closed at will, in the context there too of something secret and concealed.[36] The "close dilations" of Iago's accusations of Desdemona – opening his verbal "show" (iii.iii.116) just wide enough to torment the outsider unfamiliar with an inside Iago understands better than he – similarly involve the controlled opening of something secret and concealed, like the births in the "womb of time" he promises "will be deliver'd" (i.iii.383). That minute particular or "thing" he has to "show" – a term elsewhere linked to the opening of a woman's secret place (*Hamlet*, iii.ii.144) – involves a hidden and offstage act, inaccessible to vision, which turns her from "A maiden never bold" (i.iii.94) into a whore, and her chaste "chamber" into the chamber of a "bawd" (iv.ii.20). When, then, we reflect that the closely guarded "chamber" of a woman's body was also something described as that "which may be dilated and shut together like a purse,"[37] we might begin to see how attention to the language of rhetorical opening in this play, in the context of the simultaneously fascinated and tormented jealous gaze of an outsider who is also, as husband, both owner and "general," would lead into the powerful gender politics as well as race politics of the tragedy.[38]

Antimetabole and its reversals, finally, are important not just to political contexts of undirectionality – including the line of succession and historical sequence in the *Henriad* – but to gendered questions of subordination and telos. Stephen Greenblatt cites the lines on the reversibility of the "chev'ril glove" from *Twelfth Night* ("How quickly the wrong side may be turn'd outward!") in order to underscore the relevance of this image of inversion to a contemporary anatomical as well as social construction of gender – in which the female was understood to be a reverse or inverted male, with the outside turned in ("Turn outward the woman's, turn inward, so to speak, and fold double the man's, and you will find them the same in both in every respect").[39] To note, however, that the rhetorical context of these Shakespearean lines on the "wrong side … turn'd outward" is the structure of exchange known as antimetabole would be to perceive a structure not just of simple reversal but of a specifically asymmetrical reversal. In the exchange, it remains paramount what stays subordinate and what principal – just as in the anatomical construction of gender in which male and female were understood as a reversible inside and outside it was clear what constituted a "wanton" (iii.i.20) turning of the wrong side outward in the sexual inversion of a woman's acting like a man.

The study of rhetoric in the plays, with some exceptions and with recent signs of real change in this regard, has for too long been viewed as the simple cataloging of tropes and devices or proof of Shakespeare's more than "small Latine & lesse Greeke." Such proof is helpful as a counter to what is still frequent resistance to a Shakespeare more versed, as a schoolboy, in the discourses he exploits than are his modern interpreters. Clearly the playwright who could use what the rhetoricians called *gradatio* at the same time as punning on the figure of "degrees" or "stairs" within it – as he does in *As You Like It*, say – as easily as could the learned Jonson in the "pretty gradation" of *Bartholomew Fair*, has suffered from the critical effacing of the linguistic by the simply psychological or by later versions of the Bard warbling his native woodnotes wild. To propose that we pay attention to the structural force of rhetorical figures is not in any way to propose the naive notion of a "master" or single revelatory trope, even when, as in the case of the "Doublet" in the *Henriad*, the figure appears so insistently. It is, however, to suggest that the impasse of a now apparently outworn formalism and a new competing emphasis on politics and history might be breached by questions which fall in between and hence remain unasked by both. It is also to propose, as Kenneth Burke somewhat differently did, the strategic and political resources of a technique that has too often been dismissed as merely formalistic and decorative, displayed prominently in early plays like *Love's Labour's Lost* and then outgrown. Rhetoric, too long the province of dusty scholarship, has returned in the different emphases of a more modern, formalistic theory. What is needed, however, is not just a return to the old-fashioned study of tropes, or a "rediscovery of rhetoric" by learning once again to use the names, or even the substitution of a more historically relevant lexicon for a predominant New Critical one in describing the movement of a soliloquy. Rather, we need to pay attention to the exploitation of the terms and structures of rhetoric, in ways which would lead into the figurative logic shaping both lines and scenes, and from the plays themselves into the order of discourse and discourse of order they both echo and turn on itself.

Notes

1   The edition of Shakespeare's plays used throughout is *The Riverside Shakespeare*, ed. G. Blakemore Evans (Boston, MA, 1974).
2   See respectively George Puttenham, *The Art of English Poesie* (1589), p. 181; Angell Day, *A Declaration of … Tropes, Figures or Schemes* (1599), p. 83; and Henry Peacham, *The Garden of Eloquence* (1593 edn.), pp. 118–19. Descriptions of the placing of "men" before "women" invoke an implicit gender politics.
3   See Jacques Derrida, "Coming into One's Own," in Geoffrey Hartman (ed.), *Psychoanalysis and the Question of the Text* (Baltimore, 1978), p. 144.
4   See, for example, *The Winter's Tale*, iv.iv.721 ff., and its play on "plain fellows" as opposed to "rough and hairy"; *The Merchant of Venice*, i.iii.66 ff., and the exchange between Launcelot Gobbo and his father in ii.ii; and the echoes of the Jacob and Esau figures in *The Comedy of Errors*, in the mother's preference for the younger and the father's for the elder twin in its opening scene, and in the comic play on "hairy men" and "plain dealers without wit" in the exchange on "bald" Time in ii.ii. The implication of this last is discussed below.
5   See Thomas Wilson, *The Arte of Rhetorique*, fol. 107; Angell Day, *Declaration*, p. 15; Quintilian, *Institutio oratoria*, ix.iii.28.
6   Bacon, "Of the Coulers of good and evill, a fragment" (1597), printed in his *Essays* (London, 1597; repr. New York and Amsterdam, 1968), p. 27.
7   On *copia* and "copy," see Terence Cave, *The Cornucopian Text: Problems of Writing in the French Renaissance* (Oxford, 1979), p. 4, and the translation of "to COPIE" as "Doubler, *duplicare*" in John Minsheu, *Ductor in Linguas* (*Guide into the Tongues*) (1617). The difference between a fruitful development, or difference, and mere imitation or copy might, in a larger reading of the Shakespearean canon, be seen to be raised frequently in generational form, specifically in the relation of fathers and sons.
8   See C. T. Lewis and C. Short, *A Latin Dictionary*, 1st edn (1879; repr. Oxford, 1962), under "germanus."
9   For a fuller discussion of this Erasmian term, see Cave, *Cornucopian Text*, pp. 88–91. Cave cites Erasmus's own play on the sense of the *sensus germanus* as the "German sense" in a letter of 1523.
10   Cave, *Cornucopian Text*, p. 90.
11   On the speculation surrounding these mysterious Germans, see H. J. Oliver's introduction to the Arden edition of *The Merry Wives of Windsor* (London, 1971), pp. xlvi–xlix.
12   M. M. Mahood, *Shakespeare's Wordplay* (London and New York, 1957).
13   See Thomas Blundeville, *The Arte of Logike* (1599; London, 1619), pp. 102–3. M. R. Ridley, editor of the Arden edition of *Othello* (London, 1958), p. 4, cites both some of the speculation about a possible wife and the kind of proverb form ("l'hai tolta bella? tuo danno") which would suggest a jumping to conclusion.
14   Julius Caesar Scaliger, *Poetices Libri Septem* (Lyon, 1561), iv, xxxviii.

15 For Cuningham's assumption of an "oversight" and Foakes's of a "conflict of details," see respectively *The Comedy of Errors*, 2nd edn., ed. Henry Cuningham (London, 1926), and *The Comedy of Errors*, ed. R. A. Foakes (London, 1962), on these lines. I have discussed this matter in greater detail in "Elder and Younger: The Opening Scene of *The Comedy of Errors*," *Shakespeare Quarterly*, 54, 3 (Autumn 1983), pp. 325–7.

16 I would argue, for example, that these biblical echoes and the typological nexus they form (which extends in this play well beyond the restricted verbal quibbles that Arden editor Foakes usefully points out) join the Plautine and other subtexts which make this comedy the densely allusive play it is, but not necessarily in the service of a conjunction rather than a disjunction of its various discourses.

17 As Kenneth Muir, in "The Uncomic Pun," *The Cambridge Journal*, 3, 8 (May 1950), pp. 472–85, proposes we take Shakespeare's puns more seriously, for instance.

18 See Ridley's extended gloss on *Othello* (London, 1958), iii.iii.127. *The Plays of William Shakespeare* (London, 1813), vol. 19, is a useful source of editorial glosses on the Folio's "close dilations," including Warburton's and Malone's and that of Samuel Johnson, below. I have dealt in more detail with the implications of this textual crux for a reading of the play as a whole in "Shakespeare and Rhetoric: 'Dilation' and 'Delation' in *Othello*," in Patricia Parker and Geoffrey Hartman (eds.), *Shakespeare and the Question of Theory* (New York and London, 1985), pp. 54–74.

19 See Bishop Joseph Hall, *Christian Moderation* (1640), ed. Ward, 38/1. The *OED* cites under "delate" three Renaissance uses of the term as "to accuse, bring a charge against, impeach, to inform against," including "dilatit of adultry," a phrase suggestive for *Othello* in particular; under the meaning of "to report, inform of (an offence, crime, fault)," Ben Jonson's *Volpone*, ii.vi ("They may delate / My slackness to my patron"); and under "delation," "delatory," and "delator" ("an informer, a secret or professional accuser") a good number of Renaissance examples. For the variant spelling "delate" for "dilate," as "to speak at large" or amplify, see, for example, the 1581 edition of Thomas Howell's *Devises* ("Some … with delayes the matter will delate") in the Clarendon Press edition (Oxford, 1906), p. 53, or Nashe's *Piers Penilesse* (London, 1592 edn.), p. 11, "Experience reproves me for a foole, for delating on so manifest a case." Norman Sanders, editor of the New Cambridge *Othello*, adopts the "close dilations" of the Folio text but in his supplementary note on it refers to adoption elsewhere of Johnson's "delations," "despite the facts that the evidence for such a usage in Shakespeare's time is non-existent, and that Iago's pauses could hardly be described accurately as accusations."

20 Rymer repeats the topos in his remark on Desdemona's continuing to talk even after she has been smothered: "We may learn here, that a Woman never loses her Tongue, even tho' after she is stifl'd." See *The Critical Works of Thomas Rymer*, ed. C. A. Zimansky (New Haven, 1956), p. 161.

21 Abraham Fraunce, *The Lawiers Logike* (1588; repr. Menston, 1969), p. 44.

22 In this sense as in so many others, *The Winter's Tale* seems a late romance version of *Othello*, particularly with regard to the potentially dangerous verisimilitude of this discourse of jealousy and its relation to the *enargeia* or "Counterfeit Representation" (Puttenham) essential to dramatic representation itself.

23 Abraham Fraunce, *The Lawiers Logike*, Book II, ch. 17, p. 113.

24 See Dudley Fenner, *The Artes of Logike and Rhetorike* (1584), Book II, ch. 6.

25 A fuller exploration of the language of rhetoric in this play would include Cressida's description of Troilus as a "minced man" (i.ii.256) when he is rhetorically divided into his "parts"; Achilles' perusal of the body of Hector "joint by joint" (iv.v.233); and its pervasive evocation of the tradition of *divisio, digestio*, and so forth. "Passage" and "passing by" in the combined sense of an extended discourse and an actual procession informs some of the more subterranean links within the scene in Act I (i.ii) which is taken up with the passing by, one by one, of the Trojan soldiers, and in the meantime involves an extended anecdote retailed by Pandarus, which Cressida describes as having been "a great while going by" (i.ii.170).

26 See Joannes Susenbrotus, *Epitome Troporum ac Schematum et Grammaticorum et Rhetorum* (Zurich, 1541), pp. 82 ff.; Scaliger, *Poetices Libri Septem*, III, xxxvii; Quintilian, *Institutio oratoria*, IX.iii.85.

27 Puttenham, *The Arte of English Poesie*, p. 217.

28 See John Hoskins, *Directions for Speech and Style* (1599), ed. Hoyt H. Hudson (Princeton, NJ, 1935), pp. 14–15.

29 For a description of antimetabole and the following instances from Shakespeare, see Sister Miriam Joseph, *Shakespeare's Use of the Arts of Language* (New York and London, 1966), p. 81.

30 For a reading of *Hamlet* in these terms, see Terence Hawkes's "*Telmah*," published in *Encounter*, 60, 4 (April 1983), pp. 50–60, and included in Parker and Hartman (eds.), *Shakespeare and the Question of Theory*, pp. 310–32.

31 Puttenham, *The Arte of English Poesie*, p. 218.

32 See John Smith, *The Mystery of Rhetoric Unveiled* (1657; repr. Menston, 1969), p. 116.

33 Natalie Davis, "Women on Top," *Society and Culture in Early Modern France* (Stanford, 1975), p. 130.

34 See Robert Weimann, "Shakespeare and the Study of Metaphor," *New Literary History*, 6 (1974), p. 166.

35 I refer, of course, to the Scylla and Charybdis episode in the library in *Ulysses*, which also contains much reference to Jacob and Esau.

36 For Shakespeare's association of the opening of a "matter" with the opening of a "purse," see *The Two Gentlemen of Verona*, I.i.129–30 ("Open your purse, that the money and the matter may be both at once deliver'd"), a line which also links both with the opening of a womb.

37 For the gynecological / obstetrical image of woman as a "purse" which can be "dilated and shut," see *The Works of Aristotle, the Famous Philosopher* (New York, 1974), pp. 81–2.

38 For a brilliant analysis of Othello's anomalous position as both outsider / Moor and insider / possessor of his wife, see Peter Stallybrass, "Patriarchal Territories: The Body Enclosed," in Margaret W. Ferguson *et al.* (eds.), *Rewriting the Renaissance: The Discourse of Sexual Difference in Early Modern Europe* (Chicago, 1986), pp. 135–42.

39 See both this passage from Galen and the analysis of the lines from *Twelfth Night* in relation to the reversibility of male and female in Stephen Greenblatt's "Fiction and Friction," in Thomas C. Heller *et al.* (eds.), *Reconstructing Individualism* (Stanford, 1986), pp. 39, 49.

Index

A Midsummer Night's Dream 481–94,
    499–510, 648, 671, 727, 823
  Amazonomachy 485, 486, 487–8
  celebration and neutralizing of royal
    power 502–3
  diachronic structure 486
  Elizabethan court culture 482, 499–501
  female sexuality 500, 509
  festive comedy 121–2, 501
  green world 97
  intertextual irony 493
  male disruption of female bonds 488,
    490–1
  metadrama 503–4
  metaphor 591–2
  misogyny 494
  nature imagery 54
  new historicist analysis 481–94, 499–510
  patriarchal ideology 489, 490, 493, 501
  production of Elizabethan culture 482
  rhetorical play 895, 897
  sexual and familial violence 493–4, 591–2,
    599
  sources 493, 507
  textual analysis 282–4, 285, 287–8, 297
  validation of marriage 489
  witchcraft 506
  see also individual characters

Aaron the Moor (*Titus Adronicus*) 779, 801,
    802, 833
Abbott, E. A. 860
Abbs, Peter 557–8, 560
the absolute 177, 178
acting companies
  cooperative organization 520
  performance receipts 741–2
  see also specific companies
actors
  actor–audience relationship 519–21, 523,
    527
  actor–dramatists 732
  actor–reporters 304, 306–8
  boy actors 306, 651, 674, 704–5
  female parts 642, 651
  objections to 194, 195
  pride 194
  transvestism 679–80, 681, 705, 706, 723–4
Adelman, Janet 321, 322, 323–37, 578, 588,
    612
Aeschylus 96
affective stylistics 221, 222
agency 377–8, 390, 419, 472–3
Aguecheek, Sir Andrew (*Twelfth Night*) 717,
    718
Albany (*King Lear*) 544
Alexander, Peter 579

Index

Allen, Percy 11

All's Well That Ends Well 6, 93, 197–8, 373
  disappearance and revival 98
  play metaphors 197, 198
  prose 850, 852

Althusser, Louis 467, 511

Amazonian mythology 485–6, 487, 494, 495

ambiguity 16, 17, 51–2

ambivalence 105–6, 107

anarchic will 147

Angelo (*Measure for Measure*) 198, 199, 201, 594

Anne (*Richard III*) 363

antitheses 17, 142, 168, 849–57

Antonio (*Merchant of Venice*) 191, 355, 356, 359, 361, 725, 829–30

Antonio (*Twelfth Night*) 708, 715, 716, 718–20, 722, 723

Antony (*Antony and Cleopatra*) 137, 142, 144, 205, 574, 576, 577, 578, 580, 581–2, 597–8, 716
  dominance anxieties 597–8
  madness 145
  protagonist thesis 578, 583

Antony and Cleopatra 125, 127, 128, 134–5, 137–8, 145, 570–90, 597–8
  anti-Cleopatra criticism 571–4, 575–7
  bawdy 574–5
  cosmography 53
  dependency 333
  Egyptian values 588
  emblematic entrances 139
  erotic play 722
  feminist reading 570–90
  fortune images 56
  generic unorthodoxy 583, 590
  the human predicament 134–5
  metaphor 53, 60, 205, 206, 597–8
  metrical analysis 871, 872
  mirroring 137–8, 140, 143–4
  performance history 516, 518
  play metaphors 205, 206
  postcolonial critique 779
  prose analysis 855, 856
  protagonist theses 578, 579, 583–4
  public, Roman values 577
  sexist criticism 570–85
  source 574, 580, 581–2
  tragic foil 129–30, 134–5

see also individual characters

Antony (*Julius Caesar*) 129

Apemantus (*Timon of Athens*) 521, 523, 526, 527

Archer, Gabriel 787, 841

Aristophanes 93, 95, 96, 97, 118, 121
  The Birds 95
  Ecclesiazusae 95

Aristotle 81, 94, 582, 676
  Nicomachean Ethics 687

As You Like It 120, 121, 191, 470–1, 642–4, 671, 708–13, 830
  class hierarchy 726
  cross-dressing 641, 705, 706, 708–9
  disruption of sexual difference 642–4
  festive comedy 120, 121
  green world 97, 98–9
  holiday humor 118, 709
  homoeroticism 708–13, 721, 722–3
  masquerade 709, 725
  primogeniture principle 470–1
  prose analysis 850, 852, 853, 855, 856
  scatalogical imagery 832
  source 644

see also individual characters

atheism 435, 436, 440

Auden, W. H. 166

authorship 1–3
  Oxfordian hypothesis 5–12

Axtell, James 836

Bacon, Francis 6, 8, 497, 501–2, 883
  Advancement 539–40
  "Of Adversity" 539

Bakhtin, Mikhail 468

Bamber, Linda 622

Banquo (*Macbeth*) 26, 27, 32

Barber, C. L. 91, 116–24, 371–2, 483, 611, 649, 698, 710, 724

Barish, Jonas 462, 679, 846, 848–60

Barker, Francis 781–91

Barnardine (*Measure for Measure*) 199–200

Barnfield, Richard 687, 688, 692

Barrell, Charles Wisner 9

Barton, John 767–9, 775

Bassanio (*Merchant of Venice*) 354, 355, 360

Bastard (*King John*) 112, 425

bastards 347, 350, 628

Bathurst, Charles 574

Beaumont, Francis 293, 734, 739–40
Beaumont and Fletcher
  A King and No King 740, 743
  Bonduca 740
  The Captain 740
  Cupid's Revenge 740, 743
  The Faithful Shepherdess 739, 740
  The Knight of the Burning Pestle 739, 740
  The Maid's Tragedy 740, 743
  Monsieur Thomas 740
  Philaster 740, 742–3
  The Scornful Lady 739
  The Two Noble Kinsmen 740
  Valentinian 740
  The Woman Hater 739
Beckerman, Bernard 728
Beckett, Samuel 176
  Endgame 178, 182, 187, 188–9
  Waiting for Godot 183, 184, 186–7, 190
Behrens, Ralph 589
Belsey, Catherine 374, 568, 623, 633–49
Bender, John 834–5
Benedick (*Much Ado About Nothing*) 594
Bénézet, Louis P. 8
Benjamin, Walter 479
Bennett, Tony 782
Benson, John 700–1
Bentley, Gerald Eades 728, 732–44
Benveniste, Emile 378
Benvolio (*Romeo and Juliet*) 165, 169
Berger, Harry, Jr. 322, 365–98, 730–1
Bermuda pamphlets 818, 825, 835
Berowne (*Love's Labour's Lost*) 21, 525–6
Bertram (*All's Well That Ends Well*) 197, 594
Bethell, S. L. 571, 578, 748
Bevington, David 91
Bianca (*Othello*) 35, 139, 659, 661–2, 664–5, 896
Bianca (*The Taming of the Shrew*) 406, 407
bisexuality 712, 721
Blackfriars theatre 728, 734–44
blank verse 846, 864
Blayney, Peter 300, 312
Blundeville, Thomas, Arte of Logike 895
Bobbitt, Philip 442
Bodkin, Maud 658, 659
Bogdanov, Michael 758
Boose, Lynda 568, 606–30
Booth, Stephen 91, 223, 225–44, 689

Bottom (*A Midsummer Night's Dream*) 485, 503
Bowen, Marjorie 8
Bowers, Fredson 266–7, 269–79, 294
boy actors 306, 651, 674, 704–5
Boy Bishops 97
Brabantio (*Othello*) 153, 660, 662, 803
Bradbrook, Muriel 150
Bradley, A. C. 44, 46–7, 48, 71, 90, 125, 132, 152, 320, 574, 583, 657
Branagh, Kenneth 731
Brandes, Georg 571, 578
Braunmuller, A. R. 770
Brecht, Bertolt 176, 216, 746, 806
Brockbank, Philip 536
Brook, Peter 150, 729, 745
Brooke, Nicholas 544
Brooks, Cleanth 16, 17, 19–34, 603, 773
Brooks, Harold 481–2
Brown, John Russell 747, 765, 766–7
Brown, Marshall 847
Browne, Sir Thomas 678
  Christian Morals 676–7
  Pseudodoxia Epidemica 677
Brutus (*Julius Caesar*) 129, 145, 210, 211–12, 214–15, 217, 218
Buc, Sir George 738
Buckingham, George Villiers, duke of 637–8
Bulman, James 730
Burbage, Cuthbert 735
Burbage, Richard 732, 733, 735, 736, 737
Burckhardt, Jacob 459, 460
Burckhardt, Sigurd 151, 209–19
Burke, Kenneth 776
Burton, Robert 679
Butler, Judith 653, 678

Calabresi, Guido 442
Calderwood, James 150
Caliban (*The Tempest*) 784, 787, 788, 789, 818–19, 820–21, 822, 823, 827, 829, 832
  childishness 832–3, 835
  Native American association 821, 838–39
  postcolonial interpretation 820–1
Callaghan, Dympna 568
Campbell, Lily Bess 90
Capel, Lord 639
Cardenio 742, 743
Carleton, Sir Dudley 738, 828

carnivalization 468
Carr, Helen 799
Cassandra 146
Cassio (*Othello*) 37, 38, 44, 48, 153, 659, 662, 896
Cassius (*Julius Caesar*) 51, 129
Catholicism 471, 670
Cave, Terence 887
Cavell, Stanley 322, 338–52
Cecil, Lord David 578
Cecil, Sir Robert 496
Cecil, Thomas 6
chain of being 428, 429, 430, 433
Chamberlain, John 738
Chambers, E. K. 58, 119, 305, 516, 728
Chapman, George 293
    Eastward Ho (Jonson, Chapman, and Marston) 738, 842
    Revenge of Bussy D'Ambois 192
Chaucer, Geoffrey 101
childhood 672, 678, 832
Children of Blackfriars 736, 737, 738
Chodorow, Nancy 479
chronicle plays 422
civic pageants 670
class system 513
Claudio (*Much Ado About Nothing*) 592, 665
Claudius (*Hamlet*) 230, 231, 232
Clemen, Wolfgang 17, 50–62, 130
Cleopatra (*Antony and Cleopatra*) 205, 206, 581, 597, 598, 803
    anti-Cleopatra criticism 571–4, 575–7
    feminine wiles 572, 584, 586, 803
    inconstant behavior 572, 583, 585, 586
    protagonist thesis 579, 583–4
    royalty 588–9
close reading 17, 612, 845–907
clowning 117, 122–3, 202
Cohen, Walter 568, 619, 620, 621, 625, 626
Coleridge, Samuel Taylor 47, 103, 109–10, 575
    Biographia 21–2
Colie, Rosalie 91, 667
colonialism 437–43, 824–827
    cannibal stereotype 823
    hybrid colonial subject 778
    infantile utopian fantasies 835, 836
    legitimation 787, 788
    Machiavellian anthropology 438
    missionary colonialism 437–41

New World discourses 824–6, 835, 836
    noble savage stereotype 826
    patriarchal discourse 799, 800
    power relations 441–3
    rape trope 495, 805
    sexist discourse 799
    Shakespeare's relation to 827–28, 836
Columbus, Christopher 835
comedy 91, 93–9
    assertion of the moral norm 95, 98
    Christian conception of commedia 96
    comic catharsis 95, 96, 118, 119
    death and revival 96, 98
    festive comedy 116–24
    folk ritual drama 97
    green world 97–9
    hyperbole 128
    New Comedy 93, 94, 96, 97, 99
    Oedipus situation 93, 94
    Old Comedy 93, 94, 116
    problem comedies 97
    resolution 94–5, 96, 98, 99
    ritual pattern 96
    romantic comedy 120, 261
    satirical comedy 119
    saturnalian pattern 98, 99, 116–20
    social integration 94
    symbiosis of art and social custom 117, 121, 123, 124
The Comedy of Errors 97, 637
    Plautine model 121
    rhetorical play 883, 889–92
Condell, Henry 289, 298, 732, 735
Congreve, William, *Love for Love* 93
consciousness 320, 321, 377–8
    discursive and practical 377, 378
    political unconscious 823
    practical unconsciousness 377–8
Cordelia (*King Lear*) 346, 350–1, 538, 541–2, 586
    psychoanalytic reading 338–41, 342, 343
Coriolanus 127, 128, 142, 145, 323–37, 717
    belly fable 324
    the crowd 323–4, 328, 332, 336
    denial of female values 34, 336
    feeding and dependence imagery 324–6, 328, 334
    language rigidity and distinctness 332, 337
    matricidal impulses 329, 331, 337

Index

Coriolanus (*cont'd*)
  metaphor 51, 60, 206–7, 323, 324–6, 328, 333, 334
  metonymy and synecdoche 337
  metrical analysis 871, 872
  mirroring 143
  mother–son relations 327, 330, 331, 332, 335, 369
  phallic aggression 324, 325, 326, 327, 328, 334
  play metaphor 206–7
  prose analysis 850, 854, 855, 857
  psychoanalytic readings 323–37, 369
  textual study 273
  vertical imagery 323, 324, 333
  see also individual characters
Coriolanus (*Coriolanus*) 42, 144
  abhorrence of praise 326, 334–5
  fantasy of self-sufficient manhood 325, 326, 327–8, 329, 331, 332, 333, 334, 336
  hatred of the populace 328, 329, 330, 336
  horror of showing his wounds 206, 328–9, 336–7
  isolation 332, 336
  phallic exhibitionism 328
Cornford, F. M. 118
Cornwallis, Sir William 695
cosmic order 423–4, 426, 431, 432
court masques 470, 734, 738
courtly love discourse 600–1, 693, 694–6, 698, 699
Cowhig, Ruth 796, 800, 807, 809, 814
Crane, Ralph 274
Cressida (*Troilus and Cressida*) 572, 586, 897
Crooke, Helkiah, *Mikrokosmographia* 675–6, 677, 678, 682
Crosman, Robert 726
cross-dressing 640–2, 641, 643, 644, 651, 674, 705, 708–9
The Crying Game (Neil Jordan) 674–5
Culler, Jonathan 222, 568
cultural materialism 511–14, 619, 777
  concerns 512, 513, 514
  historical context 512
  and ideological appropriations 513, 514
  and institutions 513
  and new historicism 514
  origins and evolution 511–12
  political commitment 512

power analysis 513
  and questions of class 513
  textual analysis 512
  theoretical method 512
Cymbeline 98, 728, 742–3, 874
  cross-dressing 643
  green world 98, 99
  metrical analysis 871, 872, 873
  prose analysis 853

Danby, John F. 545, 578
Dante 96
  La Vita Nuova 694
  The Divine Comedy 82–3
David, Richard 765–6
Davidson, Jaye 674–5
Davies, Sir John 427
  Microcosmos 427
  Orchestra 432
de Beauvoir, Simone 661, 667, 668
de Rougemont, Denis 601
de Saussure, Ferdinand 321, 633
de Sebonde, Raymond 425
  Natural Theology 431
deconstruction xii–xiii, 400, 459, 468, 477, 603
degree, doctrine of 428–9, 430, 433, 434
Dekker, Thomas 36, 293, 671
  Lust's Dominion 800
  Northwood Ho! (Webster and Dekker) 192
  Satiromastix 736
Delvecchio, Donna 302–3
Derrida, Jacques 400, 404, 406, 414, 415, 468, 640
Desdemona (*Othello*) 36, 41, 43, 134, 153, 154–5, 161, 656–7, 658, 659–60, 661, 662–4, 666, 795, 806–11
  disobedience and submission 656–7, 662, 663, 803, 807–11
  eroticism 808
  split subject 802
  vulnerability 657, 658, 665
di Gangi, Mario 653
DiCaprio, Leonardo 750, 751, 754–5
Dickinson, Emily 214
differentiation and undifferentiation 362–3
Dinnerstein, Dorothy 602
discourse analysis 365–98
  discourse of commonsense 374–5

discourse/story distinction 375–6
epigenetic/developmental paradigm 367,
   368, 371, 372
ethical discourses 379–81, 384
explicit and implicit discourses 375
father's discourse 382–4, 385
Freudian analysis 378
Lacanian paradigm 374, 390, 400
language ambiguity 366
language-game concept 376–7, 397
performative character of 367, 376, 390,
   394, 785, 790
positional discourses 378–9, 382–4
private-language argument 376
sinner's discourse 379–80, 384, 387, 388
   see also irony
Dodd, Alfred 11
Dollimore, Jonathan 459, 462, 467, 512,
   535–45, 568
Don John (Much Ado About Nothing) 812
Donne, John 17, 19, 20, 22, 24, 77, 158, 639,
   688–9, 738, 828, 874
Doran, Madeleine 150
Douglas, Montagu W. 8
Dowden, Edward 89, 572, 742
Dowden, Hester 11, 12
Dryden, John 423, 427–8, 739
Dubrow, Heather 699, 846
Duke (As You Like It) 830, 832
Duke (Measure for Measure) 198, 199–200
Duncan (Macbeth) 32–3
Dusinberre, Juliet 566–7, 613, 668
Duthie, G. I. 305–6

Eagleton, Terry 16, 479, 770, 776
Edgar (King Lear) 69, 137, 179, 180, 181–2,
   183, 189, 544
Edmund (King Lear) 67, 69, 137, 203, 344,
   348, 350, 380, 382, 541, 543, 544
education, English 547–64
   appeal to absolute values and qualities 550
   bourgeois ideology 551, 552, 553, 558
   class and gender inflection 548, 549, 554
   classical humanist approach 553–4, 556
   constructions of Shakespeare 548, 549–53,
      557, 558
   CSE examinations 556, 559, 562–3
   examination system 549, 550–3, 556, 559,
      561, 562–3

humanities programs 556, 559–60
   Leavisism 554, 555, 557
   literature curriculum 555
   problematization of education and
      culture 556–7
   progressivism 556, 557–8, 560
   student reading preferences 549
   and youth culture 555
Edwardes, Richard, Damon and Pithias 192
Edwards, Abraham 502
Edwards, Philip 307
effeminacy 38, 678–9, 680, 681, 716, 717–18
Egeus (A Midsummer Night's Dream) 489,
   501
Elam, Keir 374, 376, 397
Eliot, T. S. 20, 22, 128
Elizabeth, Queen 216, 482, 483–4
   Amazonian metaphor 494, 495, 496
   cult of virginity 498–9, 500
   martial maiden 496
   masculine attributes 496, 815
   maternal strategies 484, 496–7, 501
   Pelican Portrait 484, 505
   self-mastery and mastery of others 497–8
   sexual politics 501–2
   succession issue 498
   Tilbury speech 496
   two bodies doctrine 496, 508
Elizabeth (Richard III) 363
Elizabethan world picture 373, 418, 427–33,
   459, 618
emblematic entrances and exits 138–9
Emerson, Oliver 578
Emerson, Ralph Waldo 860
Emilia (Othello) 36, 42–3, 134, 153, 161, 655,
   661, 664, 670, 812
Empson, William 17, 35–49, 347, 348
enclosures 323
Enobarbus (Antony and Cleopatra) 129–30,
   137, 205, 577
Erasmus 634, 886, 887
Erickson, Peter 615, 616
Escalus (Romeo and Juliet) 169
essentialism 418, 459, 539
Essex rebellion 195, 216, 734, 735
Euripides 96
Evans, Bertrand 389
Evans, Henry 736
Evans, Thomas 735

Everett, Barbara 150–1, 152–63, 538
existentialism 538, 539

Falkiewicz, Andrzej 186
Falstaff 104, 832
  bogus repentances 105
  Henry IV Part I 108, 247, 248, 249
  Henry IV Part II 110–11, 249, 373, 451, 452,
    453
  Lord of Misrule 123
  The Merry Wives of Windsor 97–8, 886
  parody of knighthood 104
  rejection of 98, 112, 113, 248, 250, 453, 830
  senex and parasitus 98
family
  affective family 639
  dynastic relations 635–7
  feminist critique 606–21
  and gender privilege 612
  hierarchical gendering of family roles 609
  macrocosm–microcosm paradigm 608, 618
  methodological contestation 607–8
  new historicist analysis 621
  new and old meanings 634–10
  nuclear family ideal 609
  parent–child relationship 808
  patriarchal power 381, 609
  positional discourses 378–9
  psychoanalytic approach 321, 378–9,
    610–11, 614, 623
  in Shakespeare 673
  and state governance 808
  see also patriarchal ideology
Fanon, Frantz 805, 807
Farnham, Willard 578, 582
Felman, Shoshona 390, 604–5
Felperon, Howard 91
femininity 680
  conceived as castration 600, 601
  Freudian reading 599–600, 603–4
  phallocentric formulation 602
  and weakness 599–600
feminist criticism 321, 565–649, 777
  American feminism 607, 610, 611, 613,
    615, 617, 622, 624–6
  attacks on 622, 624
  concentration on power relations 566
  early feminist writing 566–7, 647
  editorial and textual studies 568

feminist–new historicist conflict 618–19,
    620–3, 626–7, 630
  and gender studies 568
  gynocritical stance 611, 629
  Indian feminist critique 794–5
  interdisciplinary work 568
  methodology debate 612–13, 629
  mid-movement survey 606–30
  pre-oedipal theory 369
  projects 566, 612
  and psychoanalytic criticism 321, 400, 568,
    591–2, 599, 610–11, 614, 623–4
  revisionism 611–12
  and social activism 625–6
  supposed ahistorical tendencies 623, 624
  tensions and conflicts 566–7
Fenichel, Otto 336
Ferdinand (*The Tempest*) 788
Ferguson, Margaret 628
festive comedy
  clowning 117, 122–3
  holiday parallels 121
  invocation and abuse 118–19
  kill-joys 119–20
  misrule 123
  release and clarification 119, 121, 123
  saturnalian comedy 119
  Shakespeare's construction of 121–4
  social origins 121, 123
Feuillerat, Albert 309
Fiedler, Leslie 660, 663, 667, 796, 797, 807,
    818, 843
Field, Nathan 732, 739
Figurenposition 521–32
film performance 731
film studies 617, 629–30
Fineman, Joel 322, 399–416, 701
First Folio 1, 89, 270, 289
  generic divisions 89
  setting and printing 271
Fish, Stanley 221, 222, 223, 479, 791
Fitch, Robert E. 575, 579
Fitz, L. T. (Linda Woodbridge) 567, 570–90,
    609, 628–9
Fitzgerald, James D. 315–16
Fletcher, John 114, 293, 734, 739–40, 743
  see also Beaumont and Fletcher
Florio, John, *Worlde of Wordes* 881
Fludd, Robert 408–11, 412

food riots 323

Fool (*King Lear*) 130, 135–6, 540

fops 717

Forde, Emanuel, *The Famous History of Parismus* 644–5

Forman, Simon 482–3, 484–5

Fortescue, Sir John 428, 429

Fortinbras (*Hamlet*) 138

Fortune theatre 517, 739, 741

Foucault, Michel 419, 463, 466, 474, 511, 652

foul papers 268, 274, 285, 288, 290, 293, 294, 298, 299, 301, 302–3, 308, 309, 310, 311, 312, 314–15

France (*King Lear*) 340, 341, 345

Frederyke of Jennen 641

free will and responsibility 154, 176

Freud, Sigmund 319, 320, 321, 378, 415–16, 599–600, 602, 603–4, 611, 666, 819, 823, 839

Friar Laurence (*Romeo and Juliet*) 169, 170

Frisbee, George 11

Frye, Northrop 90, 93–9, 488–9

Fussell, Paul 878

Galen 676

Galsworthy, John 7

Gardiner, Judith Kegan 611

Gardner, Helen 150, 162, 163

Garnier, Germain 675

Gascoigne, George 861, 864, 865

Geertz, Clifford 420, 455, 471

gender and sexuality 619–20, 651–726
    biological sex difference 619–20
    bisexuality 712, 721
    conception theory 675, 682, 721
    constructedness of gender 610, 612, 614, 712
    constructedness of sexuality 492
    disruption of sexual difference 642–7, 706
    effeminacy 38, 678–79, 680, 681, 716, 717–18
    female erasure 619, 620, 621
    female erotic pleasure 721
    femininity 599–600, 601, 603–4, 680
    gender anxiety 707
    gender hierarchy 411–12, 706
    gender and power 491
    gender reversal 615, 706
    homological sex thesis 652–3, 675, 676, 678

homosexuality 653, 680, 681, 698, 699, 700, 701–2, 722
    masculinity 653, 675, 681, 716–17
    maternal sexuality 322
    psychoanalytic approach 623
    Renaissance anatomical knowledge 491–2, 619–20, 652–3, 675–8, 682, 721
    sexual guilt and Christian orthodoxy 811
    subversive power of gender 706
    transvestism 679–80, 705, 706, 707
    see also homoeroticism

gender studies 568

genre criticism 89–91, 149, 468

Gertrude (*Hamlet*) 594

Giddens, Anthony 377, 378

Gilbert, Miriam 769, 776

Girard, René 322, 353–64

Globe theatre 516, 733, 736, 739, 741

Gloucester (*King Lear*) 67, 73, 137, 175–6, 179, 180, 181, 182–3, 184, 349, 350, 381, 382, 384, 537, 540–1, 542

Goddard, Harold C. 256–7, 571, 590

Goethe, Johann Wolfgang von 54

Gohlke Sprengnether, Madelon 321, 568, 591–605

Goldberg, Jonathan 621–2, 653, 681, 683, 758

Goldman, Michael 252

Gombrich, E. H. 246, 261–2

Goneril (*King Lear*) 69, 71

"good" quartos 296, 297, 298, 301, 303, 308, 310

Gosson, Stephen 194, 723, 724

Grafton, Richard, *Chronicle at Large* 426

Granville-Barker, Harley 45, 48, 175, 571–2, 574, 578, 579, 728, 729, 745, 746

Gratiano (*Merchant of Venice*) 354

Greek chorus 132

green world 97–9

Greenblatt, Stephen 223, 266, 321, 382, 396, 417–18, 419, 420–1, 435–40, 460, 469, 473–6, 620, 627, 705–6, 806, 807, 811, 814, 841, 904

Greene, Gayle 653, 655–68

Greene, Robert 8, 9, 97
    Friar Bacon and Friar Bungay 741

Greg, W. W. 268, 269, 285, 298, 301–2, 303–4, 305, 306, 312, 315

Greville, Sir Fulke 6, 502

the grotesque 176, 177, 178, 182–3
guild plays 670
Guthrie, Tyrone 729, 745, 746, 747

Hakluyt, Richard 440
  Principal Navigations 798
Hall, Stuart 806
Hamlet 125, 127, 133, 202, 215–16, 223,
    225–44, 370, 425, 529–30, 593–4, 674,
    887, 895
  appearance and reality theme 243
  audience responses, shifting 226–30, 231,
    232, 235, 236, 238, 244
  Christian context 233–4, 240
  editor-made text 225
  Figurenposition 526–8, 529–30
  free will and responsibility 154
  generic issues 233–4
  illogical coherence 242–3, 244
  language of prostitution 593
  metaphor 52, 53, 60, 593–4
  metrical analysis 231, 867–8, 869, 870
  mirroring 138, 139–40, 143
  motif recapitulation 139–40
  Oedipal conflict 371
  opposing voices 128, 129, 133–4, 141–2
  prose analysis 850, 852
  proverbial speech 531
  psychoanalytic reading 320, 371
  reader-oriented analysis 225–44
  rhetorical play 899, 900, 903–4
  suicide theme 240, 242, 243
  textual analysis 270, 273–4, 276, 277, 282,
    285–6, 291, 297
  see also individual characters
Hamlet (*Hamlet*) 138, 215–16, 231–2
  anger against women 593, 594
  fear of effeminacy 717
  madness 146, 235–6, 237, 238, 528
  "To be, or not to be" soliloquy 239–42,
    747
Hammond, Anthony 302–3
Haraway, Donna 682
Harbage, Alfred 520, 571, 728
Harding, D. W. 335
Harington, Sir John 497, 501
Harman, Thomas, *A Caveat for Common
    Cursitors* 449–51
Harriot, Thomas 435, 436, 438, 826

*A Brief and True Report of the New Found
    Land of Virginia* 436, 437–43, 449, 454,
    826
Harris, Jonathan Gil 513
Harrison, G. B. 271
Hawkes, Terence 657
Hawkins, Sherman 258, 259
Hayward, Sir John 429–30
Hazlitt, William 113, 728
Heilman, Robert B. 18, 63–85, 659, 665, 668,
    773
Helen (*Troilus and Cressida*) 593
Helena (*All's Well That Ends Well*) 197–8
Heminges, John 289, 298, 732, 735
Hendricks, Margo 778
Henry IV Part I 104, 105, 108, 128, 247–8,
    385–8, 390, 391–2, 444–7, 453
  comic parallelism 104, 105, 108, 109
  conflict of values 247
  crusade speech 385–7
  honor theme 108
  moral redemption 444
  new historicist reading 444–7
  power discourse 444, 446, 447
  prose analysis 852
  psychoanalytic reading 385–8, 391–2
  sinner's discourse 387, 388, 391
  spaciousness–claustrophobia balance 447
  unstable appearances 108, 110–11
  victim/revenger's discourse 387, 388, 391
Henry IV Part II 101, 108, 248–9, 249–50, 253,
    392–5, 448–9, 451–3
  anarchic potentialities of misrule 123
  donor's, victim's, and sinner's
    discourses 393–4, 395
  insomnia soliloquy 59, 366, 392–4, 452
  monarchical authority 452, 453
  new historicist reading 447–8, 451–3
  obsessive enumeration of details 451
  power discourse 447, 452
  predation and betrayal 447–8, 451, 452
  prose analysis 853, 854, 855
  psychoanalytic reading 392–5
  relation of comic and serious action 123
  rhetorical play 883–5, 901–2
  sickness and disease imagery 249, 250, 373,
    388, 392, 394, 448
  sleep imagery 58–9
  textual analysis 292

Henry V 98, 102, 103, 111, 245–62, 370, 371, 425, 453–5, 520
  Agincourt eve soliloquy 253
  celebrations of royal power 454
  colonialist discourse 453–4
  contemporary audience reception 246–7, 250–1
  Crispin's day speech 252
  doubleness of Shakespearean vision 254–61
  filmed performance 251, 252, 256, 257
  green world promise 251, 253–5
  Hal as master manipulator 259
  new historicist reading 453–5
  Oedipal conflict 371–2
  play metaphors 196–7, 199
  private/public conflict 262
  prose analysis 850, 854, 855, 856
  psychoanalytic reading 371–2
  reader-oriented analysis 245–6, 251–62
  Salic Law episode 256, 257
  shallow propaganda 260
  textual analysis 276
  wooing scene 253, 258
Henry VI Part I 272–3
Henry VI Part II 895
  clown episodes 123
  nature imagery 55
  textual analysis 276
Henry VIII 636, 637
Henry VIII 99, 100–1, 102, 114, 518, 519, 743, 821
Henslowe, Philip 517
Herbert, Sir Henry 741
Hermia (*A Midsummer Night's Dream*) 486–7, 488
Hermione (*The Winter's Tale*) 673
heteroglossia 468
Heywood, Thomas 193, 293, 310–11, 732
  A Woman Killed with Kindness 475, 637
  The Captives 302, 312, 315
  The Escapes of Jupiter 302
  The Golden Age 302
  The Silver Age 302
hierarchic cosmos 410–11
Higden, Ralph, *Polychronicon* 426, 429
Hill, Christopher 610
Hillman, James 600
Hinman, Charlton 266, 270, 273
Hinman Collator 266, 270

Hippolyta (*A Midsummer Night's Dream*) 648
histories 91, 100–5, 107–10, 422
  comic history 111–12
  curse of usurpation 103
  disorder, containment of 425, 426, 443
  doubleness of Shakespearean vision 101, 114, 254–61
  heavenly/cosmic order 423–4, 426
  King-enucleated state 103
  pre-oedipal theory and 368–9
  retributive reaction 102
  serio-comic dialectic 100–15
Hodgdon, Barbara 731, 750–61
Holbein, Hans, the Younger 634, 636, 637
Holbrook, David 558, 563
holidays 117–18, 120–1
Holinshed, Raphael 422
Holland, Norman 222, 479
homoeroticism 653, 704–26
  antitheatricalist paranoia 680, 681, 705, 706
  bisexual pattern 721
  boy actors 704–5, 706–7
  circulation of desire 705, 722
  comedies and 704–26
  and misogyny 722, 723
  phallic images 687, 690, 693, 716, 718
  reproductive anxieties 720–1, 722
  sodomitical theatrics 708
  sonnets and 686–702, 721, 722
  transvestism 679–80, 705, 706, 707
homophobia 722
homosexuality 653, 680, 681, 698, 699, 700, 701–2, 722
homosociality 670, 673, 687, 692–3, 700, 701–2, 722
Honigmann, E. A. J. 315
honor discourse 108, 381
Horatio (*Hamlet*) 128, 129
Hoskins, John, *Directions for Speech and Style* 899
Hotspur (*Henry IV Part I*) 247, 391
Howard, Jean E. 458–80, 625, 630, 709, 717, 764, 812
Howard-Hill, T. H. 302
Hulme, Peter 781–91
humanism 459
  classical 553–4
  ethical 538, 539
  existential 538, 539

Humphreys, Christmas 8
Hunter, G. K. 381, 384, 398, 536, 797, 798, 799
hyperbole 126–8
Iago (*Othello*) 44–5, 153, 155–6, 158, 161, 203, 217, 380, 594, 656, 804–5, 806, 810, 896
  clown aspect 40, 41, 42, 43
  dog symbolism 45
  motiveless malignity 47, 804
  psychology 46–9
  racism 804, 805, 810, 812
  slander on women 658, 660, 810
  tragic foil 130–1
  use of "honest" 35, 36, 37–41, 42
  Vice figure 812
iambic pentameter 846, 861, 862, 863, 864, 865
Ibsen, Henrik 94
  An Enemy of the People 95
identity formation 473
ideological function of literature 467–8
imagery *see* metaphor
individualism 159, 532, 559
Ionesco, Eugène 178
  Le Tueur sans gages 181, 184
Irigaray, Luce 321, 400, 412, 725
irony 16, 360, 361–2, 363, 389
  ambivalence 107
  dramatic 107, 389–90
  intentional 389
  rhetorical 389
  structural 389, 390
Isabella (*Measure for Measure*) 109, 199, 594
Iser, Wolfgang 222

Jackson, Barry 729
Jacques (*As You Like It*) 191, 830, 832
James I 734, 808, 824
James, Henry 45, 416
Jameson, Fredric 420, 504, 819
Jardine, Lisa 566, 706, 707
Jauss, Hans Robert 222, 479
Jessica (*Merchant of Venice*) 672
John of Gaunt (*Richard II*) 138, 372, 373, 394
John of Salisbury 193
Johnson, Cornelius 639
Johnson, Samuel 20, 258, 259, 260, 343, 423, 858, 893

Jones, Eldred 798
Jones, Ernest 320
Jones, Inigo 518
Jonson, Ben 94, 213, 293, 465, 521, 671, 734, 738–9, 828, 846
  attacks on the stage 194–5, 736
  courtly entertainments 738
  on Shakespeare 289, 291
  A Tale of a Tub 739
  The Alchemist 95, 465, 739
  Bartholomew Fair 465, 739, 821
  The Case Is Altered 738
  Catiline 213, 739
  Cynthia's Revels 738
  The Devil Is an Ass 739
  Eastward Ho! (Jonson, Marston, and Chapman) 738, 842
  Epicoene 738
  Every Man in His Humour 737
  Every Man out of His Humour 737
  The Magnetic Lady 739
  The New Inn 739
  The New Inne 191–2, 194
  The Poetaster 194, 736, 738
  Sejanus 213
  The Staple of News 739
  Volpone 95
Jordan, Winthrop D. 799
Julian calendar 211
Juliet (*Measure for Measure*) 199
Juliet (*Romeo and Juliet*) 164, 165, 166, 171–2, 593
Julius Caesar 127, 129, 209–15, 261
  creative tension 214
  doubleness of vision 261
  heroic foil 129
  imagery 51, 57
  orchard scene 210, 211–12
  political point 209, 213
  striking clock anachronism 210, 213
  theatrical metaphor 211, 212
  time references 210–11
  see also individual characters

Kahn, Coppélia 568, 603, 612, 618, 682
Kant, Immanuel 351
Kastan, David Scott 630
Kate (*The Taming of the Shrew*) 402, 406–8, 413, 416, 637

Kavanagh, James H. 765
Keast, William R. 17–18, 63–87
Kemp, Will 733
Kennedy, Dennis 778
Kent (*King Lear*) 83, 84, 130, 185, 351, 543
Kermode, Frank 784, 787–8, 789, 817, 818
Kierkegaard, Søren 351
King John 55, 112, 273, 425, 542
King Lear 8–9, 125, 127, 174–90, 198, 338–52,
    424, 431–2, 492, 535–45
  animal imagery 64
  avoidance of love 344, 345
  Christian metaphysic 83, 185, 186, 189,
    346–7, 535, 536, 538–9, 543
  clothes imagery 64, 76
  cosmography 53, 541
  cruelty 176
  dependency 333
  donor's discourse 379, 382, 383
  doubling 350
  downfall theme 184–6, 187
  emblematic exits 139
  fantasy of maternal betrayal 595–6
  father's discourse 382–4, 385
  first scene 338–42, 541–2
  fool metaphor 35
  gerontocratic emphasis 382
  the grotesque 176, 177, 178, 182–3, 184
  humanist reading 535–9
  inward action 135–6
  justice pattern 64, 77
  love/power trade 342, 343
  materialist analysis 539–45
  metaphor 35, 53, 61, 63–70, 73, 74, 76–7,
    79, 86, 202–4, 596
  metrical analysis 869, 876
  mirroring 138, 141, 143
  moral problems 78, 79, 82
  nature 79, 80, 86, 542–3
  New Critical reading 63–85
  new historical reading 475–6
  pantomime 180–3
  paradoxes 76, 77
  philosophy 75–6
  pity 536, 537, 538
  play metaphors 202–4
  power and property relations 542
  primary effect 81, 82, 83, 84
  prose analysis 850, 853, 856, 857
  proverbial speech 531
  psychoanalytic readings 338–52, 379,
    382–4
  redemption and endurance 64, 69, 83, 535,
    536–9
  refusal of closure 184, 543–5
  repudiation of stoicism 538, 540
  revisions 218
  rhetorical play 882
  scapegoating 347, 348, 349, 350, 352
  separation imagery 596
  sexual imagery 86
  sight and blindness imagery 64, 66–8, 73,
    74, 76
  suffering 179, 347, 536, 537, 540
  symbolic reading 84–5
  textual analysis 292, 305–6, 309
  theatrical history 174–5
  tragic foils 130
  two-text proposition 267
  see also individual characters
King's Men 312, 314, 728, 734, 735–40, 741–2,
    743
Kirkham, Edward 741
Kirsch, Arthur 666
Kirschbaum, Leo 305, 311
Klein, Melanie 321
Knight, Edward 301
Knight, G. Wilson 48, 337, 656, 745, 762–3,
    820
Knights, L. C. 512
Knyvet, Thomas 6
Kott, Jan 150, 174–90, 545
Kreeger, David Lloyd 10
Kris, Ernst 371
Kristeva, Julia 321, 400, 604, 648
Kuhn, Thomas 600
Kurosawa, Akira 731
Kyd, Thomas 121, 146, 437
    The Spanish Tragedy 168, 233, 314, 405

Lacan, Jacques 321, 322, 367, 368, 374, 390,
    398, 400, 414, 415, 473
LaCapra, Dominick 464, 468
Lady Macbeth (*Macbeth*) 26–7, 30–1, 32, 130,
    136
Laertes (*Hamlet*) 138
Lafew (*All's Well That Ends Well*) 373
Lake, Sir Thomas 738

Lamb, Charles 174, 730, 763
Las Casas, Bartholomew 823
Laurens, André du 677
Lavinia (*Titus Adronicus*) 801, 802
Lear (*King Lear*) 142, 144, 145, 175, 190,
    343–6
  experience of pity 537
  "Job's stage" 185, 188, 190
  madness 64, 70, 74, 146, 348, 539
  scapegoat 347, 348, 349, 350, 352
  suffering 175, 540
Leavis, F. R. 150–1, 152, 155, 156, 157, 158,
    159–60, 162, 554, 557
Leech, Clifford 535
Leontes (*The Winter's Tale*) 672, 673
Lerner, Gerda 808–09
Lever, J. W. 538, 575
Levin, Harry 151, 164–73
Levin, Richard 389, 774
Levine, Laura 679
Lewis, C. S. 698
Lewis, Wyndham 45
Lidz, Theodore 603
Lloyd, Michael 579
Lockey, Rowland 635–6
Lodge, Thomas, *Rosalynde* 644
The London Prodigal 741
Long, William B. 314
Loomba, Ania 780, 794–815
Looney, J. Thomas 4–12
Lord Chamberlain's Men (later, King's
    Men) 11, 520, 733, 735
Lorenzo (*Merchant of Venice*) 423
Love's Labour's Lost 6, 167, 405, 674, 800, 828
  aristocratic entertainment model 121
  clowning 122
  Figurenposition 524–6
  metaphor 20–1
  metrical analysis 867
  rhetorical play 894–5, 903
  textual analysis 280, 282
  winter–spring debate 97
Lowe, Lisa 369, 372
Lucentio (*The Taming of the Shrew*) 407
Lucio (*Measure for Measure*) 199, 200, 831,
    832
Luhrmann, Baz *see William Shakespeare's
    Romeo + Juliet*
Lyly, John 8, 97, 121, 848, 858

Macbeth 23–34, 61, 127, 142, 424, 444, 596–7,
    603, 674
  child imagery 23, 28–9, 30, 32, 33–4, 56
  clothes imagery 24–8, 33, 34
  cosmography 53, 61
  defense against femininity 596–7
  emblematic entrances 139
  inward action 136
  madness 145
  metaphor 17, 23–34, 52, 56–7, 58, 59, 61,
    193–4, 202
  metrical analysis 869, 870–71, 873
  mirroring 140, 143
  nature imagery 32–3, 54–5, 59
  New Critical reading 19–34
  paradox of power 596–7
  play metaphors 193–4, 202
  sleep imagery 58, 59
  sleep-walking scene 136
  tragic foil 130
  see also individual characters
Macbeth (*Macbeth*) 23, 25–6, 27, 28, 31–2, 33,
    34, 136, 142
  Macbeth–Satan parallel 25
  motivation 29–30
MacCabe, Colin 791
Macduff (*Macbeth*) 33
McFee, William 7
McGann, Jerome 267, 776
Machery, Pierre 467
Machiavelli, Niccolò 47, 342, 436, 438
  Discourses 437
  The Prince 437
Mack, Maynard 90–1, 125–48, 444
McKerrow, R. B. 299–301, 303
Maclean, Ian 678
McLuskie, Kathleen 614, 616–7
McManaway, James 309
madness 64, 70, 74, 145–6, 235–6, 237, 238,
    348, 528, 539
magic 471
Maguire, Laurie 568
Malcolm (*Macbeth*) 260
Malone, Edmund 265, 701
Malvolio (*Twelfth Night*) 119
Mamillius (*The Winter's Tale*) 138
Mann, Thomas, *Doktor Faustus* 113
Manningham, John 10–11
Manoni, O. 818

Marcus, Leah 570, 625, 843–44
Marder, Louis 748
Marian cult 483, 498
Markels, Julian 576, 578, 579
Marlowe, Christopher 8, 121, 435, 437, 438,
    842
  A Massacre at Paris 301
  Dr. Faustus 122, 741
  Edward II 194, 741
  Hero and Leander 706
  The Jew of Malta 531
  Tamburlaine 52, 426
marriage 697, 698
  aristocratic 498
  commodification 671
  companionate 637, 639
  economic impetus 466, 498
  Elizabethan 466
  feminist critique 613–14
  romantic 638–9
  in Shakespeare 673–4
  and sovereignty 637
Marshall, Cynthia 567
Marston, John 195
  Antonio and Mellida 192
  Antonio's Revenge 195, 538
  Eastward Ho! (Jonson, Chapman, and
    Marston) 738, 842
  The Insatiate Countess 195
  The Malcontent 313–14, 736, 737
  Sophonisba 195
  What You Will 195
Marxist criticism 466–7, 468, 471, 477, 607–8,
    610, 616, 617, 619, 623, 629
masculinity 653, 675, 681, 716–17
Massinger, Philip, Believe as You List 299
Masten, Jeffrey 653
materialist analysis 511–14
meaning
  and difference 640
  plurality of 633, 640
Measure for Measure 198–200, 369, 424, 444,
    465, 830–31, 900
  failure of comic resolutions 369
  metrical analysis 876
  play metaphors 198–200
  prose analysis 850, 851, 852, 854, 855, 856
  see also individual characters
Medwall, Henry, Fulgens and Lucres 642

memorial reconstruction 305, 306–7, 308,
    311, 316
Menander 93, 98
Menenius (Coriolanus) 51, 324, 325
The Merchant of Venice 95, 223, 353–62, 423,
    671
  anti-Semitism 353, 358, 779
  flesh and money symbolism 354–5, 356,
    359
  green world 97
  imagery 60
  mercy 359–60
  postcolonial reading 779
  prose analysis 851, 854, 855
  psychoanalytic reading 353–62
  revenge and retribution 354, 356–7, 832
  saint's discourse 380
  scapegoating 357–8, 359, 360, 361
  Shylock–Venetians symmetry 354, 355, 356
  textual analysis 270
  trial scene 357, 358, 359–61
  venality 354
Mercutio (Romeo and Juliet) 129, 170
Meres, Francis 5, 6
  Palladis Tamia 6
The Merry Devil of Edmonton (anon.) 737
The Merry Wives of Windsor 670, 673
  defeat of winter 97–8
  green world 97
  prose 850, 856
  textual analysis 274, 303–5, 307
  word play 882, 886, 887, 888
metaphor 16, 17, 19–34, 591–602
  abstractions 55–7
  and ambiguity 51–2
  anticipatory function 50
  and character elucidation 592
  Coleridge on 21–2
  cosmic 53–4
  cultural metaphors 600
  Donne tradition 19, 20, 22, 24
  and individual consciousness 592
  nature imagery 54–5, 59–60
  New Critical theory 72–3
  personifications 55–7
  play metaphors 191–208
  psychoanalytic interpretation 591–602
  structural function 592
  stylistic patterns of early plays 57

metaphor (*cont'd*)
  tragedies 50–61
  and unconscious awareness 592
metaphysical poetry 17
metatheatrical criticism 149–50
Method acting 771, 772, 776
metrical analysis 846, 861–79
  blank verse 846, 862
  counterpoint style 866–71
  enjambment 866
  equilibrium 874–8
  iambic pentameter 846, 861, 862, 863, 864, 865
  phrasal breaks 863–6
  segmented line 871–4
Middleton, Thomas 293, 671
  A Faire Quarrell 192
  A Game at Chess 192, 312
  The Changeling 795, 809
  The Roaring Girl 677–8
Mills, Laurens J. 574, 576, 578
Milton, John 17, 639
  Paradise Lost 147
mimetic desire 322
mimetic theory of literature 464, 466
miracle-play cycles 96, 112
Miranda (*The Tempest*) 572, 788
miscegenation 131, 797, 805
misogyny 567, 585, 609–10, 612, 628–9, 722, 723
Molière 94
Montaigne, Michel de 424–5, 540, 675, 840
Montrose, Louis 418–19, 420, 460, 469, 470–3, 480, 481–510, 623, 708–19
morality plays 112, 519
More, Sir Thomas 455, 634–5, 636
More, Thomas, II 635–6
Moseley, Humphrey 311
Moxon, Will 9–10
Mucedorus 737
Much Ado About Nothing 120, 128, 665, 895
  disappearance and revival 98
  holiday humor 118
  metaphor 592
  prose analysis 849, 852, 853, 854
Muir, Kenneth 650, 860
Mulvey, Laura 617
mummers' plays 97
Munday, Anthony 723

  Sir Thomas More 299, 301
Murry, John Middleton 56, 60, 579
music, inter-act 172, 173

Nashe, Thomas 9, 196
Native Americans 437–43, 463, 824–6, 836
nature imagery 54–5, 59–60
Navarre (*Love's Labour's Lost*) 828
Neely, Carol 630, 667–8, 796
Neill, Michael 779
New Bibliography 265–8
New Criticism 15–18, 19, 90, 149, 150, 221, 268, 458, 608, 763–4, 820
  close reading 17
  early proponents 16
  formalism 16, 17, 18
  innovations and controversies 16
  lyric as preferred text 90, 458
  privileging of text over performance 763–4, 765, 766, 774
new historicism 91, 223, 417–21, 568, 618–19, 625, 626, 627, 630, 820
  characteristics 420
  contextualization of Shakespearean drama 418, 419, 621
  criticisms of 420
  and cultural materialism 514
  family and 621
  feminist–new historicist conflict 618–19, 620–3, 626–7, 630
  gender and 620–1, 623
  history/literature binarism 467, 477
  and the ideological function of literature 467–8
  "newness" 460–1, 477
  privileging of male power 420, 460, 568, 627
  reaction against formalism 459
  in Renaissance studies 458–80
  representativeness problem 474, 477
  subversion/containment model 419, 420
  theoretical issues 419, 462–9
  see also cultural materialism
New World discourses 824–6, 835, 836
Newdigate, John, *Glausamond and Fidelia* 302
Newman, Karen 814
noble savage stereotype 826
Norris, Christopher 796

Nosworthy, J. M. 307
Numa Pompilius 437
Nurse (*Romeo and Juliet*) 170

Oberon (*A Midsummer Night's Dream*) 490,
    493, 499–501, 503
object-relations theory 322, 599
O'Connor, Marion F. 764
Octavia (*Antony and Cleopatra*) 574
Oedipus situation 93, 94, 368–9, 370, 371–2,
    396, 599, 602
Ogburn, Dorothy and Charlton 9–10
Okri, Ben 797, 813
Oliver (*As You Like It*) 712–13
Olivier, Laurence 251, 256, 257, 731, 767
Olson, Paul 482, 504
Ophelia (*Hamlet*) 146
Oras, Ants 863–4, 866, 878–79
Orgel, Stephen 91, 653, 669–83, 704, 707, 709
Orkin, Martin 813, 814
Orlando (*As You Like It*) 711, 723
Ornstein, Robert 91
Orsino (*Twelfth Night*) 717, 722
Orwell, George 352
Osborne, Laurie 706, 725
Othello 125, 127, 142, 152–63, 217, 260,
    594–5, 655–68, 671, 674
  ambivalent gender relationships 670
  characterization 153–5, 161
  class relations 36, 48, 806
  dog symbolism 45
  emblematic entrances 139
  free will and responsibility 154
  "honest" and "honesty" 35–49, 658
  masculine and feminine constructions 657,
    658–59, 661, 666
  metaphor 45, 52, 53, 55, 203, 594–5
  metrical analysis 869, 876
  mirroring 139, 140–1, 144
  moral world of the play 154–5
  nature imagery 55
  New Critical reading 35–49
  paradox of violence 595
  patriarchalism 802–3, 804, 812
  Petrarchan love 659
  play metaphors 203
  postcolonial critique 779, 795–7, 802–13
  prose analysis 852, 857
  protagonists' vulnerability 658

racial–sexual connections 796–7, 804, 812,
    813
  racism 779, 799, 802–3, 804, 810, 812
  rhetorical play 887, 892–93, 894, 896, 903
  sexual–social intersection 655–66
  sources 800
  textual analysis 292
  tragic foil 130–1, 134
  see also individual characters
Othello (*Othello*) 144, 153, 154, 594, 665–6
  ambivalence about sexuality 659, 660, 661
  blackness 666, 796, 797, 803, 804, 805–6,
    809, 811
  characterization 155–9, 161
  egotism 156–7, 158–9, 658–9, 661, 662
  fantasy of feminine betrayal 595, 660–1, 662
  and "honesty" 35, 37, 38, 40, 41–2, 43, 44
  honorary white 802, 803, 806, 811
  idea of honor 657, 666
  passion 155, 156
  racial isolation 811–12
  split subject 802, 807, 811
  vulnerability to Iago's narrative 657, 660,
    661, 810, 811
Ovid, *Metamorphoses* 162, 640
Oxford, Edward de Vere, earl of 3, 4, 5–12
  authorship hypothesis 5–12
  "Women" 5

Painter, William, *The Palace of Pleasure* 485,
    487
Palgrave, Francis Turner, *Golden Treasury* 5
Palladas 193
Paré, Ambroise 675
Paris (*Romeo and Juliet*) 165–6, 168
Parker, Patricia 778, 846, 880–907
Parolles (*All's Well That Ends Well*) 197
Parsons, Robert 437
Pasternak, Boris 167
pastoral literature 470, 471, 670–1
patriarchal ideology 381, 484, 567, 602,
    671–2, 704
  control of female sexuality 721
  familial 381, 609
  gender anxieties 707
  homosociality and homophobia 722
  matriarchal substratum 599
  multiplicity 672
  racism and 799–800, 802–3, 805

patriarchal ideology (*cont'd*)
  replication 672
  Shakespeare's reproduction of 614–17, 622
  and state governance 808
  threat of female sexuality 642, 809
  violence against women 599
Patroclus (*Troilus and Cressida*) 201–2
Peacham, Henry, *Complete Gentleman* 431
Pechter, Edward 626, 630
Peele, George 97
  Araygnment of Paris 499
  The Battle of Alcazar 800
Penn Warren, Robert 16
Pennington, Michael 768
Pepys, Samuel 728
Pequigney, Joseph 689, 698, 719, 726
performance criticism 150, 727–76
  actors' accounts 775
  comparative analysis 729–30
  film performance 731, 750–61
  hermeneutic value of performance 729
  historical modes of acting 771–2
  interrogation of textual authority 730
  objections to 730–31
  production styles 746, 747–9
  repertory 737–40, 741, 742–3
  scholarship 728
  stage histories 728, 746
  televised Shakespeare 771
  text-as-score 747
  text/performance dichotomy 762–72
  traditional/modernist controversy 748
Pericles 98, 307, 741
Perkins, William 679
personifications 55–6
Petrarchan sonnets 694
Petruchio (*The Taming of the Shrew*) 401–2,
  403, 404, 412–13
Phebe (*As You Like It*) 710, 711
Phèdre 342
Phoenix theatre 739
plague 733, 735
Plato 96
  The Republic 207, 423
Plautus 93, 96, 97, 121
play metaphors 191–208
Plutarch 211, 493, 507, 587–8
  Life of Marcus Antonius 580, 581, 582
  "Of Love" 687, 688

Poel, William 729
Polixenes (*The Winter's Tale*) 673
Pollard, A. W. 296, 297, 298–9, 313
Polonius (*Hamlet*) 176, 235–6, 237–8, 243
Portia (*Merchant of Venice*) 356, 360, 594,
  641, 671–2
postcolonialist criticism 777–843
postmodernism 730, 752
poststructuralism 476, 568, 633, 648, 782
power
  absolutist theatricality 455
  colonialism and 441–3
  cultural materialist analysis 513
  female/maternal 594, 595, 601, 615
  gender-based asymmetries 618
  monarchical 452, 454
  new historicist analysis 420, 460, 568, 627
  privileged visibility 455
  and property relations 542
primogeniture 470
Prince John (*Henry IV Part II*) 248, 258
problem comedies 97, 196
prompters and prompt-books 298, 299, 314,
  520
prose, Shakespearean 846, 848–60
  antithesis and balance 849–57, 858
  conjunctions and correlatives 849–50
  disjunction 851–56, 858–9
  euphemism 848
  logical syntax 853, 857, 858
  Lylyan affiliations 846, 848
Prospero (*The Tempest*) 784, 786, 788, 789,
  816, 817, 818, 819, 821, 827–8, 832, 833
proverbial speech 531
Prynne, William, *Histriomastix* 680, 681, 724
Psalm 63 408–10
psychoanalytic criticism 319–416
  discourse analysis 365–98
  familial relations 321
  feminism and 321, 401, 568, 591–2, 599,
  610–11, 614, 623–4
  and gender consciousness 321
  ideas of discourse 320–1, 322
  Lacanian model 321, 322, 368, 396, 400,
  414, 473
  metaphor and 591–602
  object-relations theory 322
  post-Freudian drift 374
  problem of consciousness 320, 321, 377–8

psychoanalytic theory, familial relations 614
Purchas, Samuel 824, 826, 840, 842
Puttenham, George 5, 6, 77
   Arte of English Poesie 469, 505, 702, 880,
      881, 898, 899, 901

queer theory 568, 653, 654
Quiller-Couch, Sir Arthur 554
Quilligan, Maureen 628
Quintilian 899
Quixote, Don 132

Rabkin, Norman 223, 245–63
racism
   black evil and lust stereotype 797–8, 799,
      801, 805, 809
   black men on the Renaissance stage 800
   black presence in England 798
   and capitalism 798
   constructing the Other 803–5
   historicizing 797–800
   miscegenation 131, 797, 805
   and patriarchalism 799–800, 801–3, 805
Rackin, Phyllis 567
Rainoldes, John, *Th'Overthrow of Stage
   Plays* 680, 683, 724
Raleigh, Sir Walter 109, 196, 435, 436, 437,
   636, 825
   Discoverie of Guiana 494–5
   History of the World 426
   "What Is Our Life?" 192
Ramayana 815
Ransom, John Crowe 16
The Rape of Lucrece 20, 22
reader-response criticism 221–62, 461, 463
Red Bull theatre 516, 739, 741
Regan (*King Lear*) 69
religious belief 435–7, 438
   Christian morality in the New World 443
   coercive belief 439, 440
   missionary colonialism 437–41
   orthodoxy and subversion 439, 440, 443
   political theology 443
Renaissance
   narratives of discontinuity and
      contradiction 460
   new historicist approach 458–80
   political theology 443
   as transitional period 460

Rendall, Gerald H. 8, 11
reputation 657, 667
revenge genre 233
revision 280–95
Reynolds, George F. 516
rhetoric and wordplay 846, 880–907
   antimetabole 898–902, 904
   chiasmus 888–92
   dilation and delation 892–5, 903
   doubling 882–5, 902
   geminatio 882–5, 886, 902
   hysteron proteron 880–1, 892, 903
   language of "general" and
      "particular" 895–8, 903
   reversal and exchange 903–4
   sensus germanus 885–8
   see also metaphor
Richard II 111, 216, 251, 370, 373, 391, 394,
   451, 734, 741
   conflict of values 247
   emblematic exits 138
   imagery 59–60
   metrical analysis 867
   mirror episode 112
   saint's discourse 380, 398
   textual analysis 292, 309
Richard III 57, 362–3, 895, 900
   metrical analysis 866
   scapegoating 362, 363
   technique of the curse 362, 363
   textual analysis 276
   villain's discourse 380
Richards, I. A. 16, 22
Ridley, M. R. 797, 814, 893
Riemer, A. P. 570, 575, 578, 584
Riffaterre, Michael 221
Righter, Anne 150, 191–208, 748
riots and rebellion 323, 434
   theatrical representation of 419
Robin Hood 98
Robinson, Cedric 798, 803
Roderigo (*Othello*) 45, 47, 153
Roe, Sir John 738
Romeo and Juliet 126, 129, 145, 164–70,
   592–3, 671, 674
   antitheses 168, 169
   authorial rewriting thesis 267–8
   bookish metaphor 166–7
   filmed performance 750–61

Romeo and Juliet (*cont'd*)
  form and formality 164–73
  masculine ethic 592, 593
  metrical analysis 167, 869
  nature imagery 54
  pairing and counterbalancing 168–9, 170
  performance history 518
  reduplication 169–70, 171
  sex–violence relation 592, 593, 602–3
  sphere of privacy 168
  textual analysis 267–8, 272, 274–5, 280,
    281, 282, 285, 298, 309
Romeo (*Romeo and Juliet*) 17, 145, 164–5,
  167, 168, 169, 170, 592–3, 678, 716
Rosalind (*As You Like It*) 120, 671–2, 708,
  709–11, 712
Rossiter, A. P. 91, 100–15, 150, 260
Rowe, Albert 557
Rowley, William 732
royal entertainments 498–9, 501
Rumour (*Henry IV Part II*) 110, 373, 393
Rymer, Thomas 36, 796

St. George plays 97, 124
St. John Chrysostom 193
St. Paul 697, 838
Salisbury Court 739
Salusbury, Sir Thomas 738
Sanders, Wilbur 535
Sartre, Jean-Paul 177, 539
Saslow, James 709
sati 794, 813–14
Saturnalia 98, 99, 116–20
scapegoating 347, 348, 349, 350, 352, 357–8,
  359, 360, 361
Schlegel, Augustus 572, 575
Schochet, Gordon 808
Schoenbaum, Samuel 2–3, 4–13
Schwartz, Murray 603
Sebastian (*Twelfth Night*) 715–16, 718, 719
The Second Part of the Return from
  Parnassus 192–3, 194
second tetralogy
  ethnicity and patriotism 779
  nationalism 779
  Oedipal triangle 371, 396
  parricidal impulses 370–1
  power discourse 447, 449, 455
  retributive reaction 102

  saint's discourse 380
  sinner's discourse 387, 388
  victim/revenger's discourse 387, 388
  see also Henry IV Part I; Henry IV Part II;
    Henry V; Richard II
Sedgwick, Eve 721, 722
self-dramatization 157–8, 161
Seneca 507, 538, 539
Sermon of Obedience 433–4
sexuality *see* gender and sexuality
Seymour, Jane 636–7
Shakespeare, William
  Ashbourne portrait 9
  attitude towards the stage 195, 196–7, 202
  biographies 1, 2, 733
  collaboration 743
  Grafton portrait 9
  habits of composition 290, 291
  intimate connection with theaters and acting
    companies 293–4, 732–5, 736, 740–2
  sexual politics 614–17, 622
  theatrical self-consciousness 150
Shakespeare Fellowship 8
Shirley, James, *The Court Secret* 301
Shylock (*Merchant of Venice*) 98, 119, 353–4,
  355–6, 357, 358, 359–60, 832
Sidney, Sir Philip 6, 122, 502, 702
  Astrophil and Stella 862
  The Lady of May 470
Siemon, James R. 772
signification 363–4, 367
Simpson, Lucie 579
Sinden, Donald 769
Sinfield, Alan 512, 513–14, 547–63, 810
Skura, Meredith 320, 780, 817–44
slave trade 798
Slowacki, Juliusz 179
  Kordian 179
Sly, Christopher (*The Taming of the*
  Shrew) 122, 405–6, 413, 416
Sly, William 735
Smidt, Kristian 309
Smith, Bruce R. 653, 684–703
Smith, John, *Mystery of Rhetoric Unveiled* 901
Snyder, Susan 91
sodomy 681, 683
sonnets 196, 684–703
  botanical and procreational images 684–5,
    687, 688

courtly love rhetoric 693, 694–6, 698, 699
dark lady sonnets 673, 692
editions 700–11
homoeroticism 686–702, 721, 722
homosexual desire 686, 692, 698, 699, 700, 701
language of Christian marriage 697, 698
language of erotic experience 698
love-as-jewel imagery 691
misogyny 720, 722, 723
power ideologies and structures 685, 688, 692, 695, 697–8, 699
reproductive anxiety 720–1
sexual desire 684, 685, 686, 687, 689, 692, 698, 699, 700, 701
sexual puns 687, 689–90, 693, 695, 720
textual analysis 292
to the young man 686, 689, 691, 693–5, 698
Southampton, Henry Wriothesley, earl of 9, 825
Spenser, Edmund 473, 698, 864
   Epithalamion 685, 688
   The Shepherd's Calendar 706
   The Faerie Queene 98, 160, 425–6, 486, 495–6, 497, 502, 640–1
Spivak, Gayatri 601, 602, 603, 605
Sprague, Arthur Colby 150, 729
Spurgeon, Caroline 17, 24–5, 28
stage conditions 515–34
   actor–audience relationship 519–21, 523, 527
   communal experience 520–1
   contemporary criticisms of 651–2
   Figurenposition 521–32
   front stage 517
   inner stage 516, 517
   male preserve 669–70
   picture–frame stage 518
   platform stage 517, 518
   tiring house 517
   upper stage 516–17
   yard 518
stage directions 269, 300, 518
Stallybrass, Peter 619, 724, 812
Steevens, George 687, 701
Stempel, Daniel 572, 576, 579, 585–6, 590
Stevenson, Robert Louis 45
Stone, Lawrence 466, 497
Strachey, Lytton 742

Strachey, William 827, 842
structuralism 378, 459
Stubbes, Philip, *The Anatomie of Abuses* 651–2, 679, 681, 724
Styan, J. L. 729, 730, 745–9, 775
stylistic analysis *see* metaphor; metrical analysis; prose, Shakespearean; rhetoric and wordplay
subaltern studies 777–8
subversion and contestation 472, 473, 474, 475, 476
Suchet, David 767, 768
Suleiman, Susan 222
Swander, Homer 766
Sycorax (*The Tempest*) 822, 839

tableaux vivants 515
The Taming of The Shrew 116, 202, 399–416
   discourse analysis 399
   discourse of subversion 399
   female language 399, 401–2, 402, 403, 406–7
   festive comedy–folk games parallel 122
   misogynistic gynecology
   patriarchal performance 400
   Petrarchan idealism
   psychoanalytic reading 399
   rhetorico-sexual indeterminacy 403–4, 406
   "rope-tricks" 402–3, 404, 416
   self-conscious literariness 401
   Sly framing plot 401, 416
   taming subplot 401–4
   verbal/visual opposition 407, 408
Tamora (*Titus Adronicus*) 800, 801, 802
Tarlton, Richard 519
Tate, Allen 16
Taylor, Gary 267–8, 280–95, 309
Taylor, Thomas 639
televised Shakespeare 771
The Tempest 7, 95, 139, 218, 443, 572, 742
   colonialist discourse 790, 817, 818, 819, 820–4, 828, 834, 835–836
   comedy of restoration 786, 790
   contemporary responses 821
   crisis of selfhood 834, 835
   earlier "Caliban" plays 829–32
   green world 97, 99
   incestuous impulse 829, 843
   interrupted masque 788–9

The Tempest (cont'd)
  intertextual criticism 784, 785
  legitimacy and usurpation 786, 787, 788
  metrical analysis 869, 873, 874, 876–7
  nature imagery 54
  new historicist criticism 817, 820
  postcolonial critique 778–9, 781–91,
    817–36
  prose analysis 850, 856
  Prospero–Caliban family relation 833–4
  psychoanalytic reading 789, 819, 829, 831
  revisionist critique 817, 818–20, 822, 823,
    828, 833
  scatalogical imagery 832
  sources 824, 840, 841
Tennenhouse 807, 808
Terence 93, 95, 97
Terry, Ellen 728
textual criticism 265–317
  authoritative version thesis 266–7, 268,
    294, 770–1, 776
  authorship 1–12
  compositorial analysis 269, 270–9, 282
  con-texts 783–4, 790, 791
  contemporary editing practices 770–1
  contextual background 781–2
  foul papers and bad quartos 268, 274, 276,
    285, 288, 290, 296–317
  intertextuality 782–3, 784, 785
  memorial reconstruction 305, 306–7, 308,
    311, 316
  multivocality emphasis 268
  New Bibliographical interpretation 265–8,
    269–79
  poststructuralist 782
  printer's errors 299
  psychological dimensions 366, 388
  reader-response criticism 221–3
  recovery and transmission problems 269,
    274
  source criticism 784
  spelling evidence 270, 272
  transmission history 266
  see also transmission history
theater
  attacks upon 680, 705
  audiences 739, 748
  closure 733, 735
  private theaters 734, 736, 739

  threat to masculinity and social
    stability 679, 681
  transvestism 679–80, 681, 705, 706, 723–4
  War of the Theatres 194, 736
  women playgoers 669
  see also actors; stage conditions
theater of the absurd 176–7
Thersites (*Troilus and Cressida*) 523, 524, 527,
  531
Theseus (*A Midsummer Night's Dream*) 481,
  487, 489, 493–4, 501, 503–4, 648
Thomas, Keith 471
Thomas, Sidney 309
Thompson, Ann 568
Tillyard, E. M. W. 418, 422–34, 459, 608,
  747–8
Timon of Athens 531, 874, 886–7, 900
  counterfeiting 204
  Figurenposition 521–3
  metrical analysis 871, 872
  play metaphors 204
  prose 850, 854, 855
  textual study 273
Titania (*A Midsummer Night's Dream*) 485,
  490, 491, 499, 500
Titus Andronicus 800–2, 833
  deviant womanhood 801, 802
  female stereotypes 567
  parental love 802, 833
  postcolonial critique 779, 800–2, 805
  racial pollution 805
  Roman values 800
  textual analysis 273
  xenophobia 779, 800
  see also individual characters
Todorov, Tzvetan 463
Touchstone (*As You Like It*) 712, 713
Traci, Philip J. 572, 574–5
tragedies
  ambiguity 51–2
  anarchic will 147
  Bradley's faults analysis 125–6
  Christian view of vengeance 233
  construction 125–48
  cosmography 53–4
  death and resurrection pattern 96
  emblematic entrances and exits 138–9
  the grotesque 176, 177, 178, 182–3
  imagery 50–61

indirections 135–41
inward structure 135–6
mirroring 137–41, 143
opposing voices 128–35
personifications 55–6
revenge genre 233
romantic tragedy 167
Shakespeare's accountability 216–18
tragic catharsis 95, 96, 177, 218
tragic hero 95, 96, 126–32, 158
antithesis 142, 143–4
cycle of change 141
downfall 177
foil 128–9
hyperbole 126–8
journeys 143–4
madness 145–6
regeneration 144–5
sacrificial ritual 96
Tranio (*The Taming of the Shrew*) 404
transhistorical human essence theory 462, 463
transition rites 471
transmission history 266, 269–79
authorial revision 267, 280–95
compositorial analysis 269, 270–9, 282
multiple versions 267
print production theories 298–303
printer's copy 298–301, 303, 311
printing-house characteristics 269
scribal transcripts 300–1
spelling evidence 270, 271, 272, 273
transvestism 679–80, 681, 705, 706, 707,
723–4
see also cross-dressing
Traub, Valerie 653, 682, 704–26
Traversi, Derek 115, 545, 570
Troilus and Cressida 200–2, 427
antifeminism 586
Figurenposition 523–4
honor and sexuality 593
imagery 57–8, 59, 200–2, 206
prose 850, 854, 855
rhetorical play 896–8, 900
textual analysis 276, 291
theatrical imagery 200–2, 206
time images 56
Tudor system of degree 112, 113
Turner Clark, Eva 8
Turner, Victor 471, 472

Twelfth Night 531, 573, 645, 646–7, 671, 674,
714–19
carnival society 97
class hierarchy 726
disruption of sexual difference 645, 646–7,
706, 724
holiday humor 118
homoeroticism 708, 714–19, 721, 722, 723
performance history 11
phallocentrism 716, 718, 722
prose 850, 852
psychic androgyny 719
rhetorical play 900, 904
transvestism 705, 706, 708, 719
see also individual characters
The Two Gentlemen of Verona 121, 167, 641,
645–6
cross-dressing 641
green world 97, 98
New Comedy 97
rhetorical play 882
The Two Noble Kinsmen 742, 743

Ulysses (*Troilus and Cressida*) 430, 432
unities 61, 423
Upton 444
Urkowitz, Steven 309
usurpation 103

Valeria (*Coriolanus*) 334, 336
Valiant Welshman (anon.) 192
Vendler, Helen 17
Venus and Adonis 20, 21, 22
Vickers, Nancy 628
Vincentio (*Measure for Measure*) 830–1
Viola (*Twelfth Night*) 645, 646–7, 714–15,
719, 723
Virginia colony 437–43, 817–18, 825–6, 827,
840
virginity, Protestant view of 487
Volumnia (*Coriolanus*) 207, 324, 325, 327,
330, 331, 332, 334, 335, 337, 369

Walker, Alice 270, 272, 306
War of the Theatres 194, 736
Ward, Bernard Mordaunt 8
Warren, Michael 267
Warren, Robert Penn 30
Warwick (*Henry IV Part II*) 448

Washington Shakespeare debate 10
Wayne, Don 465
Webster, John 140, 736
   Duchess of Malfi 193, 795, 804
   Northwood Ho! (Webster and Dekker) 192
   The White Devil 147, 795
Weimann, Robert 513, 515–34, 764, 902
Weird Sisters (*Macbeth*) 31–2, 33, 140
Welles, Orson 731
Wells, Stanley 309
Werstine, Paul 268, 296–317
Wheeler, Richard 91, 369–70, 698
Whitaker, Virgil 578
White, Allon 724
White, Hayden 397, 463, 464
Wilkins, George, *The Miseries of Enforced
   Marriage* 671, 741
William Shakespeare's Romeo + Juliet (Baz
   Luhrmann) 750–61
Williams, George 274, 275
Williams, Philip 270, 272, 273
Williams, Raymond 472, 512, 608
Wilson, E. C. 577
Wilson, John Dover 90, 104, 270, 275, 276,
   283, 297, 305, 729
Wilson, Thomas, *Arte of Rhetorique* 882
Wimsatt, William 16
Winnicott, D. W. 321, 322
The Winter's Tale 128, 492, 615, 637, 671,
   672–3, 728, 742, 887
   disappearance and revival 98
   emblematic exits 138
   homosociality 673

   metrical analysis 871, 872, 874–5
   pastoral world 97
   prose 850, 853, 854
   return to childhood 672–3, 855
   rhetorical play 880, 881, 887, 894–5, 899,
     902
   see also individual characters
Winwood, Sir Ralph 828
witchcraft 506, 803
Wittgenstein, Ludwig 376–7
women
   Christian patriarchal view of 811
   commodification 671, 706
   as Other 602, 670, 671, 799
   patriarchal and class violence 794–5, 796,
     813–14
   in public performance 670
   representation of 467, 468
   unruly women 495, 572, 680, 795, 800, 809
Woodbridge, Linda (L. T. Fitz) 567, 570–90,
   609, 628–9
Wordsworth, William 102, 105–7, 701
   "Tintern Abbey" 106
world as stage metaphor 150, 158, 191–208,
   520
Worthen, William B. 730, 762–76
Wright, Austin 578
Wright, George T. 846, 861–79
Wright, Thomas, *The Passions of the Mind in
   General* 678

Yeats, W. B. 32, 101, 102, 114–15, 257
Yorkshire Tragedy (anon.) 741

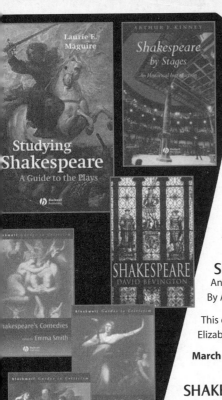